D0080765

ENCYCLOPEDIA OF TWENTIETH-CENTURY AFRICAN HISTORY

ENCYCLOPEDIA OF TWENTIETH-CENTURY AFRICAN HISTORY

Editor: Paul Tiyambe Zeleza

Deputy Editor: Dickson Eyoh

LONDON AND NEW YORK

First published 2003
by Routledge
11 New Fetter Lane, London EC4P 4EE

Simultaneously published in the USA and Canada
by Routledge
29 West 35th Street, New York, NY 10001

Routledge is an imprint of the Taylor & Francis Group

Typeset in Baskerville by Taylor & Francis Books Ltd
Indexed by Indexing Specialists (UK) Ltd
Printed and bound in Great Britain by TJ International Ltd,
Padstow, Cornwall

British Library Cataloguing in Publication Data
A catalogue record for this book is available from the British Library

Library of Congress Cataloging in Publication Data
Encyclopedia of twentieth-century African history /
edited by Paul Tiyambe Zeleza and Dickson Eyoh
Includes bibliographical references and index
1. Africa–History–20th century–Encyclopedias.
I. Zeleza, Tiyambe, 1955- II. Eyoh, Dickson, 1954-
DT29 .E53 2003
960.3'1'03–dc21
2002031682

ISBN 0–415–23479–4

Contents

Editorial team

List of contributors

Hamdi Abdulrahman
Cairo University, Egypt

Agbenyega Adedze
Illinois State University, USA

Oforiwaa Aduonum
Illinois State University, USA

Josephine Ahikire
Center for Basic Research and Makerere University, Uganda

Emmanuel Akyeampong
Harvard University, USA

Ousseina D. Alidou
Rutgers University, USA

Mark D. Alleyne
University of Illinois at Urbana-Champaign, USA

James Amanze
University of Botswana, Botswana

Nicole D. Anderson
University of Illinois at Urbana-Champaign, USA

Samuel Aryeetey-Attoh
University of Toledo, USA

Eric Aseka
Kenyatta University, Kenya

Sosina Asfaw
University of Illinois at Urbana-Champaign, USA

Lisa Aubrey
Ohio University, USA

Lamissa Bangali
University of Illinois at Urbana-Champaign, USA

Elabbas Benmamoun
University of Illinois at Urbana-Champaign, USA

Redie Bereketeab
Uppsala University, Sweden

Bruce J. Berman
Queen's University, Canada

Nemata Blyden
University of Texas at Dallas, USA

Eyamba Bokamba
University of Illinois at Urbana-Champaign, USA

Benn L. Bongang
Savannah State University, USA

Elias K. Bongmba
Rice University, USA

Richard A. Bradshaw
Center College, Danville, Kentucky, USA

Sheila Bunwaree
Council for the Development of Social Science Research in Africa (CODESRIA), Senegal

James Busumtwi-Sam
Simon Fraser University, Canada

Joseph S. Caruso
Columbia University, USA

Frederick Cooper
New York University, USA

Catherine Coquery-Vidrovitch
Université Paris VII, France

Jean-Philippe Dedieu
Ecole des Hautes Etudes en Sciences Sociales, France

LaRay Denzer
Northwestern University, USA

T.J. Desch-Obi
New York University, USA

Jan-Georg Deutsch
Center for Modern Oriental Studies, Germany

Momar Coumba Diop
Cheikh Anta Diop University, Senegal

Mamadou Diouf
University of Michigan, USA

Matthew B. Dwyer
Columbia University, USA

Romanus Ejiaga
University of Illinois at Urbana-Champaign, USA

M.A. El-Khawas
University of the District of Columbia, USA

Moha Ennaji
University of Fes, Morocco

Dickson Eyoh
University of Toronto, Canada

Laura Fair
University of Oregon, USA

Toyin Falola
University of Texas at Austin, USA

Sheila Finnie
Vancouver, Canada

Antonia Folarin-Schleicher
University of Wisconsin at Madison, USA

Richard A. Fredland
Indiana University, USA

John G. Galaty
McGill University, Canada

Olakunle George
University of Oregon, USA

Bakary Gibba
University of Toronto, Canada

Azzedine Haddour
University College London, UK

Eltigani Abdelgadir Hamid
Graduate School of Islamic and Social Sciences, USA

Nicole Hawkes
Boston University, USA

Sean Hawkins
University of Toronto, USA

Cheryl Hendricks
University of Rochester, USA

Fred Hendricks
Rhodes University, South Africa

Pablo Idahosa
York University, Canada

Amir H. Idris
Fordham University, USA

Uwem E. Ite
Lancaster University, UK

Lynette Jackson
University of Illinois at Chicago, USA

Michelle C. Johnson
Bucknell University, USA

Peter P. Jones
University of Illinois at Chicago, USA

Peter Kagwanja
University of Illinois at Urbana-Champaign, USA

Ezekiel Kalipeni
University of Illinois at Urbana-Champaign, USA

Ackson M. Kanduza
University of Swaziland, Swaziland

Tabitha Kanogo
University of California, Berkeley, USA

Riham Mahrous Khafagy
University of Illinois at Urbana-Champaign, USA

Martin Klein
University of Toronto, Canada

Kwaku Larbi Korang
University of Illinois at Urbana-Champaign, USA

Chima J. Korieh
University of Toronto, Canada

Bertin K. Kouadio
University of Missouri, USA

Benjamin Nicholas Lawrence
Stanford University, USA

Kafureeka Lawyer
Center for Basic Research, Uganda

Janet MacGaffey
Bucknell University, USA

Zine Magubane
University of Illinois at Urbana-Champaign, USA

Wunyabari Maloba
University of Delaware, USA

Tiyanjana Maluwa
United Nations Commission for Human Rights (UNCHR), Switzerland

Mahmood Mamdani
Columbia University, USA

Guy Martin
New York University, USA

Robert Maxon
West Virginia University, USA

Alamin M. Mazrui
Ohio State University, USA

Gertrude Mianda
York University, Canada

Judith Mitchell
McGill University, Canada

Thandika Mkandawire
United Nations Research Institute for Social Development (UNRISD), Switzerland

Alois Mlambo
University of Zimbabwe, Zimbabwe

Jama Mohamed
Wake Forest University, USA

Lupenga Mphande
Ohio State University, USA

Mustafa A. Mughazy
University of Illinois at Urbana-Champaign, USA

Godwin Murunga
Kenyatta University, Kenya

Abdul Raufu Mustapha
Oxford University, UK

Shadrack Wanjala Nasong'o
University of Nairobi, Kenya

Brent Never
Indiana University, USA

Abderrahmane N'Gaïde
Paris, France

Fallou Ngom
University of Illinois at Urbana-Champaign, USA

Sada Niang
University of Victoria, Canada

Tandeka Nkiwane
Smith College, USA

Francis B. Nyamnjoh
University of Botswana, Botswana

Nkiru Nzegwu
Binghamton University, USA

Cyril I. Obi
Nigerian Institute of International Affairs, Nigeria

Godson C. Obia
Eastern Illinois University, USA

Akin Ogundiran
Florida International University, USA

Philomina Okeke
University of Alberta, Canada

Akura Okong'o
Miami University, USA

Modupe Olaogun
York University, Canada

Adebayo O. Olukoshi
Council for the Development of Social Science Research in Africa (CODESRIA), Senegal

Joseph Ransford Oppong
University of North Texas, USA

William Y. Osei
Algoma University College, Canada

Tiffany Ruby Patterson
Binghamton University, USA

Neville W. Pule
University of Lesotho, Lesotho

John Rapley
University of the West Indies, Jamaica

Carina E. Ray
Cornell University, USA

Jeremy Rich
Corby College, USA

Mieka Ritsema
Yale University, USA

Stephen J. Rockel
University of Toronto at Scarborough, Canada

Mutuma Rutere
Kenya Human Rights Commission, Kenya

Ahmed Ali Salem
University of Illinois at Urbana-Champaign, USA

Zakia Salime
University of Fes, Morocco

Ebrima Sall
Nordiska Afrikainstitutet, Sweden

Gerhard Seibert
Instituto de Investigação Científica Tropical, Portugal

Robert W. Shenton
Queen's University, Canada

Ahmad Sikainga
Ohio State University, USA

Jacqueline S. Solway
Trent University, Canada

Charles Stewart
University of Illinois at Urbana-Champaign, USA

Wisdom J. Tettey
University of Calgary, Canada

Dominic Thomas
University of California, Los Angeles, USA

Tom Turino
University of Illinois at Urbana-Champaign, USA

Jane Turrittin
York University, Canada

Meredeth Turshen
Rutgers University, USA

Charles Ukeje
Obafemi Awolowo University, Nigeria

Cassandra Rachel Veney
Illinois State University, USA

Bjorn Westgard
University of Illinois at Urbana-Champaign, USA

Gavin Williams
Oxford University, UK

Alex Winter-Nelson
University of Illinois at Urbana-Champaign, USA

Stephen R. Wooten
University of Oregon, USA

A.B. Zack-Williams
Central Lancashire University, UK

Paul Tiyambe Zeleza
University of Illinois at Urbana-Champaign, USA

Bahru Zewde
Addis Ababa University, Ethiopia

Introduction

This encyclopedia explores the history of Africa in the twentieth century, during which the continent not only experienced profound transformations, but African history as a field of scholarly inquiry came into its own. Although the writing of African history goes back to the origins of the discipline of history itself, at the beginning of the twentieth century Africa was dismissed as a historical wasteland in the narratives of imperialist and Eurocentric historiography, which emphasized instead the civilizing impact of European activities on the continent, now reduced to a sub-Saharan contraption from which North Africa was severed. Critiques of imperialist historiography, combined with nationalist struggles against colonialism that led to decolonization and the emergence of new independent nations, culminated in the rise of a nationalist historiography that emphasized African activities. Later other historiographical traditions emerged, influenced by a motley array of intellectual, ideological, and social movements, especially Marxism, feminism, poststructuralism, development studies, cultural studies, and environmental studies, which emphasized the role of class, gender, identity, dependency, culture, and ecology, among many other things, in the historical evolution of African societies. By the end of the twentieth century, therefore, African history was truly a house of many mansions, a vast scholarly enterprise with its own specialized journals, presses, and discourses, a subject taught in schools and universities across the continent and in many other parts of the world. This encyclopedia seeks to capture this intellectual ferment in African historical studies by offering entries, especially the longer ones, that present critical interpretation which is placed in the context of the pertinent historiographical debates.

The twentieth century was one of the most tumultuous centuries in world history. Whether in culture and the arts, economy and society, science, medicine and technology, politics and ideology, relations of race, class and gender, demographic and spatial structures, environmental and epidemiological conditions, epistemological, theoretical and representational–expressive systems, the century was characterized by massive, complex, and contradictory transformations in all domains of human experience. It was a century of Janus-faced extremes. Globally the century saw the apogee of mass production and mass marketing, and their consummation in mass consumption and mass leisure; it inaugurated the age of mass communication and mass education; it ushered in the era of mass nationalisms and mass revolts driven by utopian ideals. But it was also a century of mass hysteria and mass murder, mass oppression and mass poverty, mass ignorance and mass disease. The century of unparalleled technological and scientific achievement, economic prosperity and population growth, progressive modernization and globalization, was also one marked by unprecedented global warfare and genocide, seemingly irreconcilable social and geopolitical divisions, major population dislocations, national and ethnic conflicts, racial, factional and religious chauvinisms, and various manifestations of colonialism, authoritarianism, and totalitarianism. For all the epic victories won by the movements for national liberation, for class and gender equality, and for civil and human rights, the twentieth century nevertheless closed with the gaps between rich and poor, both within and between nations, growing ever wider.

What was the nature of Africa's encounter with this most global of centuries – with its triumphs and tragedies, its accomplishments and failures, its passionate pronouncements and painful reversals, its uneven developments and complex demands? In what ways were the peoples and polities, the societies and states, the psychologies and cultures, the economies and ecologies, of the continent affected by – on the one hand – and themselves influenced – on the other – the changes and events that occurred during the century? This encyclopedia seeks to survey the constellation of global and local forces that interacted to shape political, economic, social, cultural, artistic, and environmental developments and relationships within Africa and between Africa and the rest of the world. Within this framework the entries examine patterns across the continent and within particular regions and countries. A major emphasis of the encyclopedia is on examining and capturing how ordinary people's lives changed as a result of the ways in which they responded to, mediated, and initiated the forces of change.

Coverage and contributors

In drawing up our list of entries we tried to balance breadth and depth of coverage with a number of other considerations. It was key to our conception of the encyclopedia that the entries should, unless clearly marked by temporal or spatial referents, cover the entire twentieth century; authors were therefore encouraged to trace the historical development of the process, phenomenon, or place being discussed from the beginning to the end of the century. Also, in the same vein, we wanted the encyclopedia to cover the entire continent, including North Africa, so authors were expected to draw examples from across the continent and make the pertinent interregional comparisons.

To help us arrive at a list of entries that was both comprehensive and manageable, we divided the entries into three broad groups of different lengths. The first group consisted of long (4,000-word) entries that would explore key topics and, as broad interpretive essays, would present the discussion of the phenomenon or process in question in its relevant historiographical context. Collectively these entries seek to examine the strengths and limitations of the epistemological and discursive frameworks that have informed analysis and debate about Africa's twentieth-century experience, and identify analytical challenges and visions for Africa, African history, and African studies more generally as we turn towards the twenty-first century. The second group, also covering specific topics, themes, or events, consist of shorter entries of 2,000 words each. In selecting the topics, we were guided by three considerations: first, that major events that had a profound impact on African societies were covered; second, that key thematic areas were covered (these included economic, political, social, cultural, demographic, and environmental transformations); and, third, that conventional and novel areas of African historical research and writing were covered. The third group of entries consisted of "area surveys" organized by region (geographical, environmental, and linguistic regions, and regional integration schemes), country, and major city, ranging from 3,000 words for some of the regional entries, through 1,000–1,500-word entries for the countries, to 600-word entries for the cities. These entries were designed to examine, respectively, the various ways in which regions and regional identities in Africa were formed and developed over the course of the twentieth century; the salient economic, political, social, and cultural histories of each of the continent's countries; and, finally, the histories of Africa's major cities.

Each entry also has a "Further reading" list, which varies according to the length of the entry. Entries are also internally cross-referenced (cross-references are marked with small capitals), and the longer ones sometimes list related entries under the heading "See also." All the entries aim to combine essential factual description with evaluation and analysis. The longer entries seek to outline and interrogate the theoretical frameworks and paradigms that have been used to analyze the topic in question. Overall the entries combine to make this an exceptionally rich collection of interdisciplinary analyses, firmly rooted in historical perspectives, of the major economic, political, social, cultural, demographic, and environmental changes that Africa underwent in the twentieth century.

The strengths of the encyclopedia lie in the team of editorial advisers and authors assembled. We were advised by a team of twenty distinguished historians and social scientists from Africa, Europe, and North America. The final list of entries was drawn up after extensive consultations with them. The advisers also suggested names of possible authors, and several volunteered to write some of the entries themselves. To ensure access to the widest possible pool of potential authors, we drew up extensive lists based on our personal contacts and suggestions from the editorial advisers, as well as advertising through many of the leading African history and African studies email discussion groups, such as H-Africa, and contacting several research networks, including the Council for the Development of Social Science Research in Africa (CODESRIA) and the US Association of African Studies Programs (AASP). In selecting authors we wanted to balance considerations of gender, nationality, career status (senior and junior scholars), location, and expertise. We believe we succeeded in assembling a team of authors whose vast knowledge is amply demonstrated in the text that lies before you. We acknowledge our indebtedness to them.

Paul Tiyambe Zeleza and Dickson Eyoh

Acknowledgments

Producing an encyclopedia requires the collaborative efforts of hundreds of people and many institutions. We would first like to thank Fiona Cairns at Routledge who suggested the project itself, and Dominic Shryane, also at Routledge, who oversaw its progress. Fiona and Dominic have the kind of cheerful qualities of skill, patience, and ability to offer good advice that authors only find occasionally among publishers. We are profoundly grateful to the friends and colleagues, too numerous to mention, who gave us advice, support, and sometimes contributions, often taking time from extremely busy schedules because they believed in this project. Above all we are deeply indebted to all the authors for being so generous with their time and expertise, and sometimes for being patient with our occasionally anxious deadline reminders. We would like to thank Fallou Ngom for translating four of the entries from French.

Each of us has more specific personal debts to acknowledge. Zeleza would like to thank the staff and colleagues at the Center for African Studies at the University of Illinois for all their assistance throughout the project, and to the university itself for granting him leave in the fall semester of the 2000–1 academic year and sabbatical during the 2001–2 academic year, during which he was able to concentrate on the encyclopedia. Also invaluable was the professional and personal support from Cassandra Rachel Veney. The amused inquiries from his daughter, Natasha Thandile, as to why the encyclopedia was taking so long, provided a reminder better than the official deadline from the publisher that the encyclopedia should not linger forever.

Eyoh would like to thank Cheryl Hendricks for intellectual and personal support over the time it has taken to complete the encyclopedia. Our daughter, Malaika, was but a few weeks old when we began working on it, and has grown to associate the word "encyclopedia" with things that too often kept daddy on the phone or computer at inconvenient times. Her impatience with such distractions was sufficient motivation to complete the project as soon was possible.

It is to our daughters, Natasha and Malaika, that we dedicate this encyclopedia, whose narratives of the past century will shape their future in the new century.

Paul Tiyambe Zeleza
Champaign, Illinois
Dickson Eyoh
Toronto, Ontario
28 January 2002

How to use this encyclopedia

This encyclopedia is intended to offer a relatively comprehensive outline and survey of African history in the twentieth century. Written by experts in their fields, the entries seek to offer brief but authoritative analyses of the main themes in twentieth-century African history. They have been structured and organized to facilitate easy reference and cross-reference. All the entries are accompanied by a "Further reading" section, which can be used for additional reading on the topic or area. Cross-references are provided both in the text (where they appear in **bold**) and in the "See also" sections that sometimes appear at the end of entries. The thematic entry list and comprehensive index also enable the reader to quickly locate other relevant entries in the encyclopedia.

There are five entry sizes:

- *600 word entries*: These are short entries offering basic information and trends in the twentieth-century history of some fifty-eight major cities.
- *1,000 word entries*: These offer historical overviews of the continent's fifty-three countries (the largest countries – such as **Algeria**, **Democratic Republic of Congo**, **Egypt**, **Ethiopia**, **Nigeria**, **Sudan**, and **South Africa** – are covered in 1,500 word entries), regional and international organizations (such as the **Organization of African Unity** and the **United Nations**), major languages and linguistic communities (such as **anglophone Africa** and **Arabic**), and major ecological zones (such as the **Niger Delta** and **tropical rain forest**).
- *2,000 word entries*: These offer more in-depth overviews and analysis of particular events (such as **First World War**), processes (such as **migrant labor** or **international trade**), topics (such as **genocides** or **sports**), and issues (such as **human rights** or **sex and sexuality**).
- *3,000 word entries*: These offer comprehensive overviews and in-depth analysis of the continent's five regions (**North Africa**, **West Africa**, **Central Africa**, **East Africa**, and **Southern Africa**), and a variety of important topics and themes (from the **Great Depression** and **law** to **race and ethnicity** and **telecommunications**).
- *4,000 word entries*: These article-length entries cover major topics and themes in twentieth-century African history, and offer original and extensive analysis of the topic, theme, process, or phenomenon concerned. These range from **African diasporas** and **agrarian change** to **visual arts** and **youth**. As interpretive essays these entries seek to interrogate the pertinent historiographical and theoretical debates and offer the reader fresh analytical insights.

Thematic entry list

Economic history

Environmental history

Demographic history

Intellectual history

Major cities

Maseru, Lesotho
Mbabane, Swaziland
Mogadishu, Somalia
Mombasa, Kenya
Monrovia, Liberia
Nairobi, Kenya
N'Djamena, Chad
Niamey, Niger
Nouakchott, Mauritania
Ouagadougou, Burkina Faso
Rabat, Morocco
Tripoli, Libya
Tunis, Tunisia
Windhoek, Namibia
Yaounde, Cameroon
Zanzibar, Tanzania

Major ecological zones

Great Lakes
Niger Delta
Rift Valley
Sahara
savanna
tropical rain forest

Major languages and linguistic communities

anglophone Africa
Arabic
francophone Africa
Fulani
Hausa
Lingala
lusophone Africa
Swahili
Yoruba
Zulu

Political history

civil society
colonial Africa
colonial conquest and resistance
decolonization
human rights
labor movements
law
nationalist movements
non-governmental organizations
peasant movements
refugees
socialisms and socialists
state: colonial
state: post-independence
women's movements

Regional histories

Central Africa
East Africa
North Africa
Southern Africa
West Africa

Regional integration

African Development Bank
Arab Maghreb Union
Central African Federation
Common Market for Eastern and Southern Africa
East African Community
Economic Community of West African States
French Equatorial Africa
French West Africa
Organization of African Unity
regional integration
Southern African Development Community

Religious history

African religions
Christian reform movements
Christianity
Islam
Islamic reform movements

Social history

alcohol and drugs
architecture
cinema
dance
education: colonial

Abidjan, Côte d'Ivoire

Abidjan is the principal city and economic capital of **Côte d'Ivoire**, with an estimated population of 3.5 million. The city is situated in the homeland of the Ebrie people. The birth and growth of Abidjan are closely related to the colonial history of Côte d'Ivoire. Grand Bassam was the first capital of the new colony (from 1895 to 1900), then Bingerville became the capital from 1900 to 1934. After that it moved once again, this time to Abidjan, which was chosen because the colonial authorities needed a location that was economically viable. With the construction in Abidjan of a port, a railway terminus that connected the coast with interior of the country and the Vridi Canal, major economic activity gradually came to an end in Grand Bassam. Abidjan was now economically and politically equipped to be the capital of modern Côte d'Ivoire. Another key factor in the choice of Abidjan as the capital was the yellow fever epidemic that killed a third of the white population of Grand Bassam in 1899. The survivors fled both from there and from Bingerville. From that time on, Abidjan attracted all types of people from Africa and other continents.

When the Crosson–Duplessis mission started railway construction in 1903, only six Europeans and 378 skilled African workers lived in what is now Abidjan. In 1912 the population increased to 1,400 and the workers moved farther north. There were 15,400 inhabitants by 1921, 17,000 when Abidjan became the capital in 1934, 45,000 by the end of the Second World War, 127,000 in 1955, 500,000 by the mid-1970s, and 2,000,000 in 1985. In 1970, that is ten years after independence, the port of Abidjan was one of the most dynamic in Africa. It contributed significantly to the growth of the city by attracting many migrant workers and their families. After the war Abidjan became the center of political activity in the colony, which was part of French West Africa.

By the late 1970s Abidjan was one of the most cosmopolitan cities in West Africa, famous for its shopping, for skyscrapers housing offices of national companies and international organizations, and burgeoning import substitution industries. It attracted migrants from rural areas and neighboring countries, not all of whom could find jobs, so the city faced increasing criminal activity, transportation problems, and unemployment. These reasons, the desire to diversify development, and the fact that Abidjan was the center of political discontent, especially among students and faculty at the University of Abidjan, led to the decision by President Houphouët-Boigny in 1983 to make Yamoussoukro, his native town, the country's new political capital. The transfer of political institutions and infrastructure from Abidjan to Yamoussoukro was still going on by 2000. Despite this, Abidjan remained the premier commercial and cultural center, and the preferred place of residence for most Ivoiriens, including government officials. In fact, Abidjan concentrated even more on its commercial role, notwithstanding the economic crisis and political instability that followed a military coup in the 1990s. Abidjan was home to the National University of Côte d'Ivoire where many of the first West African intellectuals were trained. A city noted for its vibrant cultural institutions and entertainment, Abidjan is full of contrasts, with ultra-modern residential areas (Cocody, Riviera, Les-Deux-Plateaux), over-crowded sections (Adjame, Trechville), and suburbs (Abobo-gare).

Further reading

Diabaté, H., Kodjo, L. and Bamba, S. (1991) *Notre Abidjan*, Abidjan: Mairie d'Abidjan, Ivoire Média.

LAMISSA BANGALI

Accra, Ghana

Accra is the capital city of **Ghana** with an estimated population of 2,000,000 people, located in the southeastern region of Ghana bordering the Atlantic Ocean. Although Accra today is a multi-ethnic and international city, it is also the home of the Ga peoples. The name Accra is believed to be a European corruption of *Nkran* (meaning "driver ants"), a name given to the Ga by their Fante neighbors to the west in remembrance of the Ga migration to their present home.

In the sixteenth century, Europeans changed the settlement pattern of the region forever. They built forts and castles from which they conducted their trade. By the end of the nineteenth century, the British had bought out the other Europeans and become the sole masters of the Gold Coast. In an effort to effectively extend their control over the protectorate, the British decided to move the seat of the colonial administration in 1877 from Cape Coast to Accra. From then on, Accra became the new seat of government and Ghana's leading commercial city.

As the center and symbol of colonial rule and oppression, any anti-British activities that were formerly aimed at Cape Coast were now redirected towards Accra. For the smooth running of the colony, the British took certain steps to spruce up the infrastructure of Accra by building roads, railways, an airstrip, utility services, hospitals, schools, and residential areas for British functionaries. Some of these institutions – such as the University College of Ghana (Legon), Achimota College and Korle Bu Hospital – are still famous landmarks in Accra today. Successive post-independence governments expanded the colonial infrastructure but, like most African capitals, Accra's exponential growth (from 388,000 people in 1960 to 1,000,000 in 1980 and 2,000,000 in 2000) was not matched by a corresponding improvement of the infrastructure. In the absence of planned development, home construction boomed without adequate road networks and utilities, leading to traffic jams and lack of efficient water, electricity, and telephone distribution.

Although Accra's economy was traditionally based on fishing and subsistence farming, the retail and small-scale manufacturing industries are now pre-eminent. The famous Makola market dominates the retail sector and the industrial base is made up of textile mills, salt production, chemical industries, wood and furniture industries, handicrafts, and so on. However, the government remains the single most important employer in the city, despite the fact that in accordance with the World Bank's structural adjustment program it has privatized several government industries leading to layoffs. Despite this setback, Accra is relatively better off than some of the other cities in West Africa and therefore attracts migrants from other regions of Ghana and neighboring countries.

Furthermore, after Ghana was declared independent on 6 March 1957, Accra became a major center of **Pan-Africanism**, an ideology fervently espoused by Kwame Nkrumah, Ghana's first president. Famous Pan-Africanists like George Padmore and W.E.B. DuBois spent their final days in Accra and were buried there. Nkrumah had vowed at independence that Ghana's independence would be meaningless unless all of Africa was liberated. Subsequently, Accra hosted in 1958 the All Africa People's Conference to support anti-colonial struggles. Nkrumah Mausoleum and the DuBois Center are major tourist attractions.

Besides its political significance, Accra is also famous for its cultural activities. While there are diverse modern forms of entertainment, the traditional annual Homowo (harvest festival) of the Ga people with its attendant rituals is a reminder of the pre-eminence of African customs over new cultural forms.

Further reading

Agbodeka, F. (1972) *Ghana in the Twentieth Century*, Accra: Ghana University Press.

Buah, F.K. (1998) *A History of Ghana*, London: Macmillan Education Ltd.

AGBENYEGA ADEDZE

Addis Ababa, Ethiopia

Addis Ababa ("New Flower" in Amharic) was founded in **Ethiopia** in 1886 by Empress Taytu, wife of Emperor Menilek II (reigned 1889–1913). The prime attraction of the site was its hot springs, which formed the nucleus for the urban settlement that soon developed. What assured its permanence was the influx and settlement of foreigners after the Ethiopian victory at Adwa (1896) and the importation of eucalyptus trees from Australia, which solved the country's perennial problem of providing enough wood and thereby averted the otherwise inevitable shift to another center.

In the early twentieth century, the city had two nodal points: the Imperial Palace (or Gebbi) and the religious-cum-commercial center Arada. Residences of members of the nobility served as smaller centers around which the settlements of their dependents and retainers sprouted. With the arrival of the Djibouti–Addis Ababa railway in 1917, another center was created in the southern outskirts of the town. This ultimately had the effect of pulling the town southwards. Before 1935 the dominant architectural tradition was Indian. The coronation of Emperor Haile Selassie I in 1930 gave the city international prominence, as representatives of foreign powers and the Western press flocked to attend the colorful event.

The short-lived Italian occupation of the country (1936–41) left its impact on the city. The Italians introduced their own distinctive architectural style, specimens of which survived to the end of the century. Following the colonial tradition, they also tried to set up a separate quarter for Ethiopians in the western part of the city. While this attempt was aborted by their expulsion in 1941, the westward extension endured and gave the city its major commercial center, Mercato, reputed to be the largest open-air market in Africa.

In the period after 1941, the southward expansion of the city continued. Two airports (the first built in the southwestern part of the city, the second in the southeast) became major residential centers for the affluent and for the growing expatriate community. The selection of Addis Ababa as headquarters of the Economic Commission for Africa in 1958 and the **Organization of African Unity** in 1963 elevated this hitherto largely insular city into an African metropolis. A construction boom in the 1960s gave it some of its major architectural landmarks – Africa Hall, the City Center, the Hilton, and, appropriately enough, its point of origin: the Hot Springs (*Fel Weha*).

Addis Ababa was also the seat of the national university, Haile Selassie I University, founded in 1961. Student agitation, spurred by growing social and economic ills, formed the background to the eruption of the Ethiopian Revolution in 1974. The major events of that revolution, leading to the overthrow of Emperor Haile Selassie I in September 1974, unfolded in the city. Following the nationalization of urban land and houses in July 1975, a new administrative structure was put in place. The city was divided into neighborhood associations (*Qabale*), which became the basic unit of administration for the rest of the century.

With the change of regime in 1991 and the ethos of decentralization that then prevailed, the national importance of Addis Ababa declined somewhat. The neglect or breakdown of services gave it a rather drab character. The expansion of its population, estimated to be about 3,000,000 in 2000, compounded the problem. The only positive notes were struck by the first-class Sheraton Hotel that graced downtown Addis and a ring road that was under construction but expected to revolutionize motorized traffic.

Further reading

Zekaria, A., Zewde, B. and Beyene, T. (eds) (1987) *Proceedings of the International Symposium on the*

Centenary of Addis Ababa, Addis Ababa: Institute of Ethiopian Studies.

BAHRU ZEWDE

African Development Bank

The African Development Bank (AfDB) was founded in August 1963 in the first wave of independence and began operations from its headquarters in **Abidjan**, Côte d'Ivoire, in July 1966. Its creation is deeply rooted in the ambition of the founding African states to have at their disposal the financial and political means for their own development, independently from former colonial powers and developed countries. Its very African character was and remains the main characteristic of this regional institution. The first president, Mamoun Beheiry, was Sudanese. Since then, the presidency has tended to reflect various linguistic affiliations and geographical equilibria, thereby avoiding potential divisions stemming from the considerable diversity of the continent. As the main guarantee of its independence, the African Development Bank asserted its pan-African intentions by denying membership and voting rights to countries outside the region, unlike its institutional peers that were founded at roughly the same period (the InterAmerican and the Asian Development Banks). Due to its apartheid policies, South Africa was the only African state to be excluded; this required a special resolution from the membership. It was only reintegrated in 1995, becoming the fifty-third regional member of the Bank. The Bank, as stated by the Article 1 of its charter, was dedicated "to contribut[ing] to the economic development and social progress of its members individually and jointly." Unlike the World Bank, the African Development Bank was controlled by its borrowers. Its capital basis was collectively and equally shared by its regional members, and its main target was the allocation of loans enabling the emerging nation-states to develop.

The African status of the Bank was, however, endangered and reduced by successive economic, financial and **debt crises** crippling the continent. Since its inception, several adjustments have been made to the original structure to tackle the scarcity of financial resources. Two facilities for concessionary loans were added: the African Development Fund in 1973 and the Nigeria Trust Fund in 1976. The African Development Fund admitted, for the first time in the AfDB Group's young history, non-regional participants. The Development Fund started to operate in 1974 with thirteen non-African states and the Bank. The Nigeria Trust Fund is a specific partnership between the Bank and the Nigerian government. The regional sovereignty of the Bank was most notably diminished by the adhesion of non-regional members in 1982, in spite of the strong opposition of Algeria, Libya, and Nigeria. Faced with unbearable macroeconomic pressure (oil shocks, falling commodity prices, drought), a rising number of countries were in arrears with their debt payments, threatening the financial stability and international stature of the Bank. The opening of capital and voting rights to non-regional members was the only solution if the Bank was to continue its activities, enabling it to raise extra funding from the international capital markets. This measure was accepted under strict conditions: The president of the Bank would have to be African and the headquarters would remain on the continent. In addition, non-regional participants were limited to only a third of the Bank's voting power. The Bank's authorized capital amounted to US$23.29 billion at the end of 1996. By 2000 the Bank's membership comprised fifty-three African countries and twenty-four non-African countries from the Americas, Asia, and Europe.

Despite these substantial modifications to the original spirit of the Bank, it has largely fulfilled its mandate. Since its creation, its staff have become increasingly professional. Trying to attract and train the best and brightest Africans, by December 2000 only 101 out of a total of 1,051 members of staff were from member countries outside Africa. The Bank has also tremendously strengthened its methods for appraising the financial and economic viability of projects financed and monitored loans. Through the implementation of internationally standard procedures, its legitimacy among multilateral organizations has been enhanced and this regional institution has been able to attract external resources from international capital markets, the Organization of Petroleum Exporting Countries (OPEC), and foreign governments. Since 1967 five general capital increases have been carried out. The international rating agencies granted the Bank their highest rating.

The Bank's operations cover the major sectors, with particular emphasis on agriculture, public utilities, transport, industry, health and education, as well as cross-sectoral concerns such as poverty reduction, environmental management, gender mainstreaming, and population activities. Between 1967 and 2000, 19.3 percent of the Bank's lending was devoted to the strategic agricultural sector. Most Bank financing is designed to support specific projects. However, the Bank also provides program-, sector-, and policy-based loans to enhance national economic management. The Bank also finances non-publicly guaranteed private-sector operations. The AfDB has granted an outstanding and increasing amount of credit, almost equally distributed over the continent but with a noticeable advantage given to northern Africa due to its advanced level of industrialization.

The AfDB has also coordinated its African capacity-building activities with regional organizations (including the **Organization of African Unity**), non-governmental organizations and other **international financial institutions** (IMF, World Bank). Although AfDB subscribes to the Structural Adjustment Programs' liberal orientation, AfDB's relationship with the World Bank is multi-faceted, being both collaborative through co-financed loans and competitive in lending activities. The World Bank is an extremely powerful and influential organization, gaining a large share of the lending market on the continent – sometimes to the detriment of the AfDB. However the symbolic African status of the Bank is an invaluable political asset, making it an intermediary between the African states and the developed countries. The AfDB Group is still voicing the social, economic, and financial concerns of the continent. At the beginning of the twenty-first century, it remains the continent's premier financial institution.

See also: Pan-Africanism

Further reading

English, E.P. and Mule, H.M. (1996) *The African Development Bank*, Boulder: Lynne Rienner.

Jerlstrom, B. (1990) *Banking on Africa: An Evaluation of the African Development Bank*, Stockholm: Swedish Ministry of Foreign Affairs.

Mingst, K.A. (1990) *Politics and the African Development Bank*, Lexington: University Press of Kentucky.

JEAN-PHILIPPE DEDIEU

African diasporas

African diasporas are communities of Africans and African-descended peoples who were dispersed outside the continent through forced and voluntary migrations. These communities are found around the globe – in Europe, the Americas and Asia. The formation of these communities began in ancient times but those found in modern times are the result of three historical forces:

1. forced migration and the slave trade, which scattered African peoples into Europe, across the Atlantic to the Americas, and through the Indian Ocean into Asia;
2. "voluntary" migrations, generally resulting from movements associated with European colonialism and world wars; and
3. labor migrations related to both colonialism and decolonization.

A conceptual difficulty in mapping the history of African diasporas is the very meaning and definition of the term "diaspora." Many definitions do not explain diasporas formed through voluntary migration with no thought of return, nor the development of a diasporic consciousness and identity that is sustained over many generations, even after the loss of a relationship with a homeland. The concept of "diaspora" originated in other historical and cultural contexts – namely Jewish and Greek history. "Diaspora" is the Greek word for "dispersal," though its most common usage has been in reference to the scattering of Jews throughout the West. For African-Americans, however, the Biblical roots of the concept of diaspora have particular meaning. Early activists, historians, and clergy frequently cited Psalm 68: 31, which says "Ethiopia shall soon stretch out her hands unto God," as a way of describing the black (world) condition and the source of liberation. Ethiopia has been a metaphor for a black worldwide movement against injustice, racism, and colonialism.

The modern usage of the term "African diaspora" is a product of the scholarship and political movements of the 1950s and 1960s. It served in the scholarly debates as both a political term with which to emphasize unifying experiences of African peoples dispersed by the slave trade and an analytical term that enabled scholars to talk about black communities across national boundaries. Much of this scholarship examined the dispersal of people of African descent, their role in the transformation and creation of new cultures, institutions, and ideas outside of Africa, and the problems of building Pan-African movements across the globe. Obviously, specific historical contexts determine the relative importance of each of these elements. A real or symbolic homeland is not necessary to articulate a relationship between diasporas. A shared history of displacement, suffering, adaptation, or resistance may be as important as a teleology of origin/return.

There are distinct differences between nations and diasporas. Diasporas are both of and beyond the nation. Diaspora is both a process and a condition. As a process it is constantly being re-made through movement, migration, and travel, as well as imagined through thought, cultural production, and political struggle. Yet, as a condition, it is directly tied to the process by which it is being made and re-made. In other words, the African diaspora itself exists within the context of global race and gender hierarchies that are formulated and reconstituted across national boundaries and along several lines. These include legal lines that curtail citizenship in polities that claim to be democratic and economic lines through the planned persistence of plantation/colonial economies and a world market that makes those economies untenable. It also includes cultural and social lines which ascribe negative cultural value to indigenous forms, while simultaneously appropriating these expressive cultures for political and commercial purposes and through systems that define and limit access based on race and gender. This occurs in both open and segregated societies. Finally, diaspora moves along imperial lines through the international development of "Jim Crowed" modes of industrial production. We must also pay attention to the ways in which differences in empire – the French, English and Spanish, or US for that matter – defined colonial/subordinate subjects and structured definitions of race/gender, citizenship, and national identity. In other words, the arrangements that this hierarchy assumes may vary from place to place but it remains a *gendered racial hierarchy*.

Overview of African diasporas

African diasporas in Europe date back to at least the eighth century, when Moors from North Africa entered Spain. They ruled there until the Reconquista in 1492. The role of Moorish Spain in launching the Renaissance in Europe has not been studied to a significant degree. Yet it was medieval universities, academies of music, and translation centers in Moorish Spain that facilitated cultural input to medieval Italy and Spain from Asia, the Middle East, and North and West Africa. Africans entered other European countries before the slave trade as well. But it was Europe's involvement in the slave trade that brought large numbers of Africans across to Europe. As Europe cemented its colonial rule over Africa at the end of the nineteenth century, more Africans were displaced for use as labor or in the military, to acquire a colonial education, and often to live in political exile.

The transatlantic trade scattered more than fifteen million Africans throughout the Americas from the end of the fifteenth to the middle of the nineteenth centuries. Slavery and freedom shaped the formation of the African diasporas in every country in North and South America. Though these societies were distinguished by language, national heritage, and cultural articulations, they were linked by the development of a new world Africanicity, plantation economies, racial identities, and cultural forms that transcended national formations.

As in Europe, the African presence in Asia dates back to the East African slave trade which began as early as AD 100, although its volume was then relatively small. Slaves were used in the pearl-diving industry, on date plantations, as soldiers throughout Arabia, Persia and India, and as dock workers on the Indian Ocean. They were also used as concubines and domestic servants in Muslim communities. The history of these communities is fragmentary – although new research is uncovering more information – and it is unclear to what extent these communities can be identified as diasporas.

By the end of the nineteenth century, African diasporas – communities with distinct African identities – were located around the globe. Colonialism, empire building, world wars, wars of liberation, and decolonization expanded these communities worldwide. By the beginning of the twentieth century, African diasporas were global.

Africans in Europe

At the beginning of the twentieth century, cities like London, Paris, and Lisbon had substantial pockets of African people. Though most were not citizens but members of the colonial world from Africa, the Caribbean, and even North America, they constituted part of the workforce and were becoming an integral part of the culture, despite the discrimination they faced, which created a common cause and consciousness among them. Algerians and Africans from French West Africa worked in port cities on the docks, in restaurants as waiters and janitors, and as servants in the homes of the elite in France. Racial bias and cultural difference set them apart from the larger society and they tended to cluster in separate neighborhoods. There were sources of division even within the diaspora communities. Class, religion, and national origin sometimes presented barriers to communication. Algerians, who were Islamic and North African, tended to cluster in their own communities within the larger diaspora community. Another source of division was generational. New arrivals often had to make a place for themselves among those that had been in Europe for several generations. Yet their identity as Africans was safeguarded by a European racism that never allowed complete assimilation, although distinctions were made by Europeans between North Africans and West Africans – in France, for example, North Africans were still characterized as "dirty Arabs." The Arabic identity at times trumped the African identity of North Africans but colonial realities reminded Algerians in France and the Sudanese in London that they were also African.

Africans, West Indians, and African-Americans established their own institutional structures in European cities which also became sites of cultural and political activity that had important implications for the homeland. Of particular significance in this period is the political activity in these communities. Though colonial rule was just becoming institutionalized in Africa, anti-colonial activity had already begun both on the continent, in the colonies in the Caribbean, and within Europe itself. The development of the Pan-African movement is one example of this activity. It began in Europe and was led by Africans from the Americas. The first Pan-African Congress was convened in London by Henry Sylvester Williams, a Trinidadian barrister. He was aided, and the conference was attended, by several prominent African-Americans, including W.E.B. DuBois, later known as the "father of **Pan-Africanism**," and representatives from the Caribbean and Africa.

This meeting was the first of seven such meetings through the 1920s, four of which took place in Europe. The next four meetings were convened by DuBois between 1919 and 1927 in Paris, London and Brussels, London and Lisbon, and New York. Within diaspora communities the fate of the race was always the foundation for political activity. What is significant about African diasporas is that national identities often become submerged within racial identities. The end of the First World War created many new problems in both the French and British empires. For African people in France the problem of assimilation and the representation of the colonies in the metropolitan parliament was elevated to serious debate. While most Africans in both Paris and London worked in menial jobs, for black French intellectuals the end of the war brought disillusionment and dissatisfaction. Political representation in the

French parliament by Blaise Diagne and Gratien Candace, which was accepted before the war, was not accepted any longer. Indeed, many who had fought in the war on the side of the French felt betrayed by these black deputies. These and many other issues spoke to feelings of alienation of Africans in European society.

By 1929 these issues of African identity, culture, and political representation expressed themselves in the literary protests of the Negritude movement. Students from the Caribbean and French colonies in Africa were led by Léopold Senghor from Senegal, Aimé Césaire from Martinique, and Léon Damas from French Guiana. At the heart of the debate for these "black Frenchmen" was the question of whether one was African or French.

But Africans from the Caribbean and West Africa were not the only ones to look to France for freedom from colonialism and racism. Many African-Americans had fought in France and returned there after the war, believing that they could escape the harsh racism of the United States in a country where they had been treated differently. Ironically, these Americans saw a racial paradise where many African workers from French West Africa and Algeria lived a hell. On the margins of European society, the Africans nonetheless created communities that were vibrant in their culture. The Americans too found a place in Europe, particularly in France where they built communities and businesses. They also became important producers of music, especially jazz, just as those from West Africa became artists and writers.

African communities in Europe expanded after the Second World War. Britain, like all other European countries, was desperate for labor. In 1948 the Nationality Act granted citizenship to citizens of Britain's colonies and former colonies. With citizenship and a British passport came the right of lifelong residence in Britain. Initially Africans from the Caribbean were slow in taking Britain up on its offer. Migration from West Africa was equally slow. But as unemployment skyrocketed on the islands, Caribbean migrants began to arrive to take jobs, especially in transport, hotels and restaurants, and nursing. They were young and took English citizenship.

In short order, they encountered considerable prejudice. Most Englishmen held negative views of African people from Africa and the Caribbean, and a fringe group were openly hostile. By 1962 racism had entered politics. In 1959 there was a move to set immigration controls by Tory MPs. In 1962 the first Commonwealth Immigrants Bill became law. Two years later, Peter Griffiths, a Tory candidate, defeated a Labour minister with the slogan, "If you want a nigger for a neighbour, vote Labour."

By the mid-1970s two out of every five black people in Britain were born in the country. In the key areas of employment, housing and education, they still faced substantial discrimination, and the issue of police racism became a major subject of debate. In response, a black resistance movement emerged. In 1981 the conflict between the police and black youth exploded in Brixton in south London and spread to other cities. These racial tensions were to shape the fabric of relations in England into the twenty-first century.

By the end of the century, the migration of Africans into European countries had exploded. Significant numbers of Senegalese and Somalis were migrating to Italy, Moroccans were flocking to Germany and the Netherlands, Algerians to France, Ethiopians to Sweden, Congolese to Belgium, and Nigerians and Ghanaians to Britain and all across Europe. In short, African migration in Europe spread from the United Kingdom, France, and Portugal, formerly dominant imperial powers in Africa, to the northern European countries, principally Germany and the Netherlands, as well as southern ones, including Italy and Spain, which had until the 1970s themselves been countries of emigration. This intense migration is the result of economic displacement in African countries and the desire of Africans from the continent and diasporas to carve out a better life for themselves. These Africans are forming new communities in hostile terrain. They foreshadow the continuing development of the globalization of African people and the economic and social tensions that these diasporas will generate. Their identity as Africans is becoming one that is transnational and global, as many must communicate with family scattered around the globe and all the while confront racial forms of discrimination.

Africans in the Americas

African diasporas in the Americas were originally a direct outgrowth of the transatlantic slave trade. Slave societies peppered the landscape bordering the North and South Atlantic and, when slavery ended, African peoples in the Americas shared the legacy of slavery as they entered the twentieth century. Labor exploitation, racial discrimination, struggle over citizenship rights, and the creation of vibrant cultural forms that defined and were rejected by the nation are the characteristics shared by African people in the Americas. The specific nature of these characteristics varied from society to society.

Labor exploitation continued to define African life experiences in the Americas long after slavery ended, and migration was one the major responses to this labor problem. In the United States, former slaves were relegated to the plantations or became menial labor in urban locales. After the turn of the century, racial violence and economic motives drove many to migrate to the urban south, then the western United States, and finally to northern industrial cities, such as Chicago, Pittsburgh, and New York, where African-Americans worked as domestics, maintenance workers, or in hotels and other service industries, or sought employment in industries such as steel and automobile manufacturing, or on the railroads.

In the Caribbean, well into the twentieth century, African peoples remained in rural agriculture and on sugar plantations. As industry spread, such as bauxite mining, many sought employment away from the agricultural sector. Economic depression forced thousands to migrate to other islands, seeking work in agriculture and creating new diasporas *within* older diasporas. For example, in the early twentieth century, workers from the British West Indies began migrating to Cuba to work on sugar plantations, to Costa Rica to work the coffee plantations, and finally to the Panama Canal zone to work for Americans. In the canal zone they encountered American forms of racial discrimination. From there many migrated to the cities on the Eastern seaboard of the United States, particularly New York City. Cubans migrated to Miami but many, particularly Afro-Cubans, migrated to Ybor City and Tampa to work in the tobacco industry. Few Afro-Cubans had been allowed to benefit from the lucrative employment in tobacco in Cuba, hence their desire to migrate. Most were relegated to the sugar plantations and rural agriculture or menial employment in the cities.

The United States had acquired Puerto Rico from Spain after the end of the Spanish–American–Cuban–Filipino War in 1898 and, as a result, Puerto Ricans began migrating to New York City in large numbers. Many of these Puerto Ricans were of African descent. By mid-century then, there was an African Caribbean diaspora in the United States.

Those in the French Antilles, particularly Martinique and Guadeloupe, and French Guiana were part of France's *départements et territoires d'outre-mer* and, therefore, French territory. Their economic situation was little different from the other islands but most did not migrate; when they did, they migrated to France or other French-speaking countries. Haitians, on the other hand, migrated to other islands, particularly the Dominican Republic, to work the sugar plantations, as well as to Jamaica and Cuba. They also began migrating to the United States in the early twentieth century, a migration that has continued into the twenty-first century. With growing nativism in the United States, many Haitians and other black migrants are encountering increased discrimination.

Though Brazil has been touted as a "racial paradise," the lived experience of Afro-Brazilians does not support this representation. After the end of slavery, Afro-Brazilians were well represented in the agricultural sectors where they continued to work on sugar and coffee plantations. But they were also firmly rooted in the urban sector. In Salvador, São Paulo, and Rio de Janeiro, despite official claims to the contrary, Afro-Brazilians – like their counterparts in other societies in the Americas – suffered from racial discrimination, albeit with a twist. Most Afro-Brazilians in these cities live in the *favelas* or slums which ring these cities and they are the targets of police violence and economic exploitation. This profile of Africans in Latin America is repeated in Colombia, Honduras, Peru, Chile, Nicaragua, and El Salvador.

Thus Africans in the Americas have continued to face racial discrimination. In the Unites States, until the Civil Rights movement of the 1960s, African-Americans lived in conditions similar to those created by apartheid. Though *de jure* and technically *de facto* segregation has disappeared, racial violence has continued into the twenty-first century. Many organizations were formed at the beginning of the century to fight this discrimination, including the National Association for the Advancement of Colored People (NAACP) and the Urban League. The Jamaican migrant Marcus Garvey formed the Universal Negro Improvement Association (UNIA), a black nationalist organization which spread throughout the Caribbean, Africa, and Europe. The African Blood Brotherhood (ABB), a Marxist–nationalist organization, was founded in the early twentieth century by radical West Indians. After its demise, many of its members joined the Communist Party in the United States. Also, as students from the continent learned of racism in the United States, they became active in the Pan-African movement. The most prominent of these was Kwame Nkrumah.

In Cuba, the struggle to end racial discrimination also took a political form. Africans in Cuba were not homogeneous, being divided by free ancestry, cultural, educational, class, sexual, and regional differences. Yet African cultural traditions were widespread and nurtured in the *cabildos de nación*, religious and mutual aid societies in urban areas. In urban centers, such as Havana and Matanzas, secret societies like the all-male Abakua flourished. Though not all black Cubans remained close to their African heritage, the number who did was nevertheless significant. But these identities were refined and redefined in the 1868 and 1898 wars for national liberation. Afro-Cuban participation was widespread in both, and the military leaders became leaders of the fight for political equality after the wars ended. Further, the military experience created networks that proved useful in organizing the black population for political struggle. Afro-Cubans fought for the right to be both Cuban and black, and this struggle led to the first black political organization in the Americas: the Partido de Independiente de Color. The determination to maintain their cultural and racial identity, coupled with an equal determination to be fully participating citizens of the nation, led to the so-called "race war" of 1912 in which thousands of the Partido members were massacred by the Cuban army. The outcome of this struggle limited the ability of Afro-Cubans to organize nationally along racial lines and curtailed their efforts to define their citizenship in such terms. But this struggle did not destroy the formation of an Afro-Cuban identity. That identity moved to cultural forms in music and religion.

Notions of race in Brazil were complicated and shaped by changing demographic and regional variation. Social convention established a distinction between mulattos and blacks, a distinction found in certain official records like the census. In the minds of all Brazilians, blackness was incompatible with social and economic advancement, so success was itself a source of whitening. In Salvador, social protest was couched in the fight for cultural autonomy for African-based cultural expressions like *candomblé* and *capoeira.* In São Paulo, a strong black press flourished in conjunction with political organizations such as the Frente Negra Brasileira. In each instance, Afro-Brazilians responded to the material and political reality that confronted them and found ways to struggle for equality in those locales.

As a protest against discrimination and a process of cultural creativity, Africans in the Americas have produced a rich cultural heritage that is now claimed by the nations that continue to marginalize African people. In the 1920s the Harlem Renaissance, in conjunction with the Negritude and Latin American Negrismo movements, produced literature and art that captured the colonial imagination. Writers such as Langston Hughes, Countee Cullen, Zora Neale Hurston, and the Jamaican writer Claude McKay were in contact with writers of the Negritude movement such as Senghor, Césaire, and Damas, as well as Jean Price-Mars and Jacques Roumain of Haiti, and Nicolás Guillén of Cuba.

At the end of the twentieth century, Africans from all over the continent were migrating to the United States for education and jobs. Many who came as students remained as workers in the transportation industry as cab drivers or at airports in major American cities such as New York, Los

Angeles, and Chicago. They also worked in hotels, in restaurants, and in construction. Many have become peddlers selling goods from Africa on city streets or in flea-markets in the southwest. North Africans find communities of Muslims in cities like Atlanta and Chicago, and establish businesses and mosques. Many also worked in American universities as professors, in the medical professions, and as engineers. Many encountered an American form of racism that for some was bewildering and for others part of the development of a diasporic identity.

As African people from all over the Americas continue to migrate back and forth across national boundaries, the discovery of a self-identity as a raced population is increasing. At the same time, African-Americans are succeeding economically in the United States. But this success is double-edged. A growing number of African-Americans are rejecting identification with other oppressed people and have become completely "Americanized." They are now helping to make the imperialistic policy that restricts the lives of many African peoples. Furthermore, the political realities in Africa, the Caribbean, and Latin America are such that many African rulers and leaders assist willingly in maintaining global racial hierarchies. It is even profitable for them to do so. The outcome of these experiences in a global world increasingly dominated by the United States and its imperialistic policies promises new formations that are just becoming apparent.

See also: non-African diasporas; Pan-Africanism

Further reading

Brock, L. and Fuertes, D.C. (eds.) (1998) *Between Race and Empire: African-Americans and Cubans Before the Cuban Revolution*, Philadelphia: Temple University Press.

Butler, K.D. (1998) *Freedoms Given, Freedoms Won: Afro-Brazilians in Post-Abolition São Paulo and Salvador*, New Brunswick: Rutgers University Press.

Carter, D.M. (1992) *States of Grace; Senegalese in Italy and the New European Immigration*, Minneapolis: University of Minnesota Press.

Gilroy, P. (1991) *Ain't No Black in the Union Jack: The Cultural Politics of Race and Nation*, Chicago: University of Chicago Press.

Ifekwunigwe, J.O. (1999) *Scattered Belongings*, London: Routledge.

James, W. (1998) *Holding Aloft the Banner of Ethiopia: Caribbean Radicalism in Early Twentieth-Century America*, London: Verso.

LeMelle, S. and Kelley, R.D.G. (eds.) (1994) *Imagining Home: Class, Culture, Nationalism in the African Diaspora*, London: Verso.

Stovall, T. (1996) *Paris Noir: African-Americans in the City of Light*, New York: Houghton Mifflin.

TIFFANY RUBY PATTERSON

African religions

Religious pluralism in Africa

There are a variety of religions in Africa. Indigenous religion, the focus of this entry, is practiced in different forms, although these practices may not always be called "religion." Religion is a way of life and an expression of what Paul Tillich has described as "ultimate concerns." Religious traditions have been documented all over Africa and it has become customary to refer to Yoruba religion, Zulu religion, Dinka religion, Nupe religion, Akan religion, and so on. These religions are distinctive, and have developed differently. However, there are common features that allow us to discuss them together. Scholars do not agree on what to call these religions. They are variously described as "traditional," "local," "indigenous," or even "classical" religions – or simply as "African" religions (the term used in this encyclopedia). This latter designation is not meant to imply that Christianity and Islam are any less African for their adherents, some of whose societies have been following these religions for many centuries, some even going back to the period immediately after the two religions were founded.

Thus Africa is home to many religious traditions, including the so-called "monotheistic religions." **Christianity** entered Africa in antiquity and colonial missionary expansion brought a European version of it to Africa. Modern Christianity arrived in Africa in a violent and divisive manner because it came in the form of denominations. **Islam** also has a long history in Africa, having entered North Africa not many years after the birth of the religion. Today nearly half of the people in Africa practice Islam. Judaism exists in Africa; it used to have a lot of followers in North Africa and has a large following in South Africa where a lot of Jews have settled. In addition to these three, Africa is also home to religions like Sikhism, Jainism, Buddhism, Baha'i, and Parsee and Chinese religions.

African indigenous religions in history

African indigenous religions have a long but often neglected history. Their genesis is rooted in the emergence of human settlements in Africa. African indigenous religions are historical religions because each society has developed with its sense of ultimacy, and we can have access to the symbols that make up their sense of ultimacy by studying their myths, rituals and moral ethos. The history of these religions is different because, in reconstructing one, scholars do not look for a towering founding figure but rather at the evolution of a historical community, its spirituality, and engagement with the symbols that provide access to extra-human power that can be used to organize and concretize life on earth. Participants at the 1971 Dar es Salaam conference on African religions were convinced that interrogating oral traditions and archival material would enable scholars to reconstruct histories of religion in Africa. One of the participants at the Dar es Salaam conference, Dr. Matthew Schoffeleers, later published his ground-breaking work *River of Blood: The Genesis of a Martyr Cult in Southern Malawi, c. AD 1600.* Schoffeleers' success in mapping out the development of the M'Bona cult in the Lower Shire Valley, and M.L. Daneel's study *The God of the Matopo Hills: An Essay on the Mwari Cult in Rhodesia* (1970), demonstrate that by studying the religious institutions of the community, language, and oral tradition, as well as the degree to which religious life is interwoven with political, symbolic, and ritual authority, one can reconstruct the history of these religions.

Colonial domination of Africa was violent in all forms and African religions became direct targets for attack by colonial authorities and by modern versions of Christianity and Islam. Ali Mazrui's (1986) notion of "triple heritage" involved in many ways a violent confrontation, because the proselytizing Christian and Islamic traditions uncompromisingly demanded the rejection of other religions by people who had converted to the new versions of Christianity and Islam, and in some cases even the forced resettlement of those people. Both religions brought social services and stronger evangelical marketing techniques – African religions could not compete with these innovations. Missionaries derided African gods as pagan, and preached against African traditions and belief in spiritual forces, magic, sorcery, sacrifices, and ancestor veneration. They made fun of African rituals and competed with local rainmakers in order to humiliate and discredit them. Missionaries' impatient desire for change led to assaults on rites, such as female circumcision among the Kikuyu in Kenya, and brought social upheaval. Even those sympathetic to African religiosity often considered it merely to be *preparatio evangelica.* The verbal and institutional violence thus perpetrated against African religion has been described by Bolaji Idowu in his classic work *African Traditional Religion: A Definition* (1973) and fictionalized by several African writers, including Chinua Achebe and Mongo Beti.

Colonial authorities on their part frequently engaged in the destruction of African religiosity. They passed judgment on witchcraft controversies when evidence – even from anthropologists with colonial ties – demonstrated that it was a complex system for dealing with misfortune. They destroyed shrines and executed priests. British colonial authorities suppressed the Cult of Katawere on the Gold Coast (Ghana), the Mau Mau uprising, and the Bamucapi regional cult in southeastern Africa.

The introduction of Western education and social services created ambiguity and confusion among many Africans about their religions. This opened up a new type of class distinction based on a capitalist economy and bureaucratic system. The so-called "modern" elites who benefited from colonial modernity and its new religions experienced what DuBois called "double consciousness." They tried to recover what was lost through the Negritude movement, a search for authenticity, and other forms of Africanization, but these did not necessarily include thoroughgoing attempts to recover suppressed religious values. Double consciousness at times was manifested in urban areas with people who had forgotten the rudiments of indigenous religions depending on others who claimed to practice traditional healing, but perverted traditional medical systems. However, it must be pointed out that, despite these assaults, indigenous religions survived.

African response to colonial violence

First, there were passive responses. Many Africans continued to practice their religion, rejecting conversion to new religions. Others practiced *bricolage*, becoming Christians without abandoning indigenous faith. For such people, Islam and Christianity were merely additional schemes by which to explain the human condition. Robin Horton (1993) argues that for these people new religions were merely a catalyst for change that would have come to African societies with time. For them, it was not merely the ability to manipulate symbolic practices, but an intellectual question dealing with how one could be Christian or Muslim and yet remain true to cherished African traditions.

Second, Africans used their religion to fight against colonial violence. The Nyabingi cult, which started in the late nineteenth century in East Africa, was a resistance cult that used medicines to protect itself from European weapons. The colonial authorities defeated them in 1928. Similarly, the Maji Maji movement of Kinjikitile organized resistance against the Germans in East Africa, believing that sacred water would protect them against European bullets. Elsewhere, the Mambo cult in Kenya, Mwari cult in Zimbabwe, and Poro cult in Sierra Leone were all used to fight against colonial power. The Kikuyu established independent schools and churches. Prophetic leaders emerged in different parts of the continent, rejecting colonial society and seeking ways of including African traditions in the search for a new social order.

Basic ideas about African religions

Indigenous religious life is locally specific, although different religions share common characteristics in their attempts to deal with the spiritual, social, cultural, and material dimensions of life, and the interaction between humanity and divinity. The components of these religions include mythology, divinity, spirits, rituals, spirit possession, human agency, morality, and a world beyond.

Mythology and cosmology

In each community, religious views draw from narratives that we generally call "myths" but, following Paul Ricoeur (1976), may call "primary language." Myths legitimize authority, space, social organization, a moral universe, and the practices that ensure its continued existence. These charter stories recall the past, engage the present, and shape the future. Myths inform people of the creation of the world and the separation between the abodes of divinity and human beings, assigning responsibility for this separation to human disobedience. For example, Susanne Blier (1987) has recorded myths from the Batammaliba elders, which indicate the Kuiye, the Batammaliba deity, created the world and humanity, and provided everything the first humans needed. However, humanity complained because Kuiye did everything for them and this forced divinity to withdraw into the sky. This resulted in the coming of death, and difficulties, but divinity also provided rain, and the materials and tools needed to survive under their new circumstances. Myths also present the beginning of social conflicts, marriage, the idea of a human family, and ways for humanity to remain in touch with divinity and seek wisdom for difficult decisions. According to Dogon myths, Amma, the supreme deity, created the world beginning with a primordial egg, which was divided into two placentas. Each placenta had a male and female twin. Ogo, the male twin, decided that he was going to create his own world and forced himself out of the egg. What he created was not pure. He later returned to recover his female pair, but she was no longer there. He returned to earth and started to populate it, but with beings who were imperfect because he had created them through incest. The result was chaos. Amma restored creation by killing the female twin and using her blood to cleanse the chaos created by her twin brother Ogo.

Divinity and spirits

African communities believe in divinity, lesser divinities, and spirits. Divinity created the world, is transcendent, provides for humanity, and knows everything. African gods have been erroneously described as *deus otiosus* and *deus remotus*, because it was believed they were removed from the people. African theologians John Mbiti from Kenya, E. Bolaji Idowu from Nigeria, and Gabriel Setiloane of South Africa have been critical of colonial officials and missionaries for belittling the African understanding of god. But they, in turn, have been accused by some scholars of Christianizing African gods or reducing the complexity of African religions to a monotheistic system. Beyond the controversy, the reality of God in African society cannot be denied. God's name is Olorun or Olodumare for the Yoruba, Inkosi Yezulu (Chief of the Sky) for the Zulu, Chukwu for the Igbo, Amma for the Dogon, and Kwoth for the Nuer.

The lesser divinities and spirits derive their authority from God, and people worship and offer sacrifices to them. African divinities represent, serve, and carry out the will of divinity. In the Dogon religious tradition, some of the spirits give and restore life. The 401 Yoruba divinities are called Orishas; these are people who had lived good lives and were deified on their deaths. The first two Orishas, Obatala and Oduduwa, were sent to earth by God to create people. Other divinities include Shango, the divinity of thunder, who is believed to have been the fourth King of Oyo. Shango is connected with healing and people always keep a pot of water in his sacred area from which people can drink and with which they can wash themselves. Esu is an important divinity because he opens the way. He is also an ambiguous character, rewarding people or punishing those who forget their duty to divinity and to Esu himself. Orunmila is the Orisha of wisdom who provides counsel and divination. He is associated with law, order, and harmony. Ogun is the Orisha of iron and war. There are also female divinities in the Yoruba pantheon, including Oshun, the goddess of living water, who is revered as the great mother. In the town of Oshogbo she is worshipped and petitioned with particular fervor, as it is believed that the town was blessed by her and this has made the townspeople wealthy. The Oshun festival in Oshogbo has become an important cultural as well as religious event for the entire community.

Other spirits include spirits of the dead who may come back to bother people who have ignored their responsibilities to them. People often offer sacrifices to ward off such spirits. Ancestral spirits come back and help people to conduct personal and communal business, and understand and follow moral precepts. Elders often consult them by pouring libations of food and wine. It is also believed that the ancestors and their spirits will punish members of the community who neglect them or forget to offer them a share of food and drink.

Religious authorities

Many indigenous religions have a simple structure in which heads of households provide vital services such as consultation with ancestors. Such a role is filled by many elders in Lugbara society in northern Uganda. Religious specialists include diviners, who serve as consultants and counselors. They help people make decisions in life and also determine the cause of misfortunes through divination. Divination sessions can be elaborate activities during which the diviner, in the case of Yoruba religion for example, uses a special divining tray and other instruments. The diviner, who is called *babalawo* (literally "father of secrets"), uses a tray and dice to produce a combination of numbers out of a possible 256 that speaks to one's problem. The resulting combination is then linked to verses, called *odu*, which can be interpreted to give guidance to a seeker. Other religious specialists include spirit mediums that receive messages and communicate to people.

Priests in African religions have specific functions to perform for the community. Evans-Pritchard (1956) indicates that the Nuer priest is a respected religious authority who has powers to assist people but can also inflict punishment through curses. The priest is expected to be an honest person, a peacemaker who provides sanctuary for fugitives and negotiates on behalf of criminals. He also assists people in time of sickness, performs rituals, controls rainmaking, and helps people succeed in hunting and in war.

Prophets call on their communities to act justly, speak on behalf of divinity, and inspire religious changes in society. Nuer prophets responded to social and economic dislocations in colonial society by performing rituals aimed at empowering people, healing diseases, and carrying out protests against the colonial government. These prophets sometimes even separated themselves from their communities as a means of empowering themselves in the service of those communities. Some well-known prophets were Ngundeng, a Nuer prophet who fought against British colonialism, and Kinjikitile, who led the Maji Maji revolt in Tanzania.

Sacred spaces

Africans worship God in different spaces, which include shrines that may be located in individual homes, at palaces, or in other specifically designated places. Sacred places may also be by water, or in forests, ancient ancestral settlements or sacred groves, or the burial places of kings as with the sacred shrines of Buganda. The Oshun festival takes place in the courtyard of the Oba and the sacred grove of Oshun. Liturgical life in Africa thus takes place in what Zahan called "elementary cathedrals," the elements being water, earth, air, and fire. Sacred places associated with water include streams, rivers, lakes, and springs; the ones associated with earth include the ground itself, rocks, crossroads, hollows, hills, and mountains; those associated with air include trees and groves; and those Zahan associates with fire include the hearth where food is prepared, the blacksmith's forge, and the fires of a volcano.

Rituals

Rituals and ceremonies can be defined as repetitive symbolic action used to communicate and institutionalize community values with the aim of effecting change in the life of the individual or society. Jean Comaroff (1985) demonstrates that rituals continue to reenact the historical and social practices of a community. Life-crisis rituals include birth rituals and development rituals, such as initiation, that are supposed to transform boys and girls into men and women. During these rituals, the adult members of the community pass on to the neophytes those values of importance to the community. Life-cycle rituals include funeral ceremonies to honor the dead. Among the Wimbum of Northwest Province in Cameroon, the funeral ceremonies of a chief last three weeks and there is generally no work in the village during these ceremonies.

Rituals of affliction are performed to rebuff a spirit that has come to afflict someone. Certain spirits often return to afflict those who have ignored them. Such affliction may include illness, failure in business, barrenness, and so on. The afflicted individual gets help from a ritual specialist, who performs healing rituals. It is not always the case, however, that affliction is negative. Sometimes afflictions are a sign that one has been called to become a healer or join a cult; the rituals performed in such as case would be initiation into a healing cult.

Spirit possession

Religious life involves the experience of possession, which affects individuals and members of a cult, and takes place among practitioners of indigenous religions, Christians and Muslims, and is not limited to one gender. Earlier literature suggested that spirit possession among women of the Sar cult in Somalia was a form of protest against their marginalization in society. However, Janice Boddy (1989) argues that possession in the Zar cult in Sudan demonstrates a multi-layered phenomenon and is not limited to life on the periphery. In general, someone who is possessed experiences the presence of a spirit that controls and influences their behavior. Possession can be sudden, and the one who is possessed speaks for the spirit. The relationship of the possessed to the spirit is described as a marriage. Some mediums induce possession by going to a sacred place to smoke the sacred pipe and wait till the spirit possesses them. Illness may also be an indication that someone is possessed. Possessed people seek treatment from those who have experienced possession themselves. Women who manage the crises of possession are referred to as Zar doctors. Spirit possession can also reflect discontent with the political situation or express nationalist ideologies, as was the case in Zimbabwe during the lead-up to revolution when political activity among the African population was still restricted by the white-minority regime.

It is difficult to map out all of the subtleties of spirit possession, but one important lesson that can be drawn from the phenomenon is that spirit possession offers an opportunity for understanding individuality, relations with the body, and how affected individuals continually reconceptualize the self. Islam and Christianity have not eliminated spirit possession, as the existence of the Nya cult of Mali demonstrates. In some other parts of Africa, adherents to Christianity have tried to adapt aspects of spirit possession into Christianity. In the literature, both men and women may be involved in spirit possession.

Personhood and morality

African religions recognize individual personhood as well as community identity, even though the idea of community has often been advanced at the expense of individuality. Yoruba religious ideas portray the creation of individual persons with distinct destinies. Individuals are also responsible for making sure that they fulfill their destinies or ask divinity to bless them and help them attain their destiny. Morality is not necessarily a set of rules, but rather the living of life in such a way as to fulfill one's destiny and contribute to the general good of the community. Evil is that which distorts personal relationships and causes social dis-ease. Evildoers can use evil magic and negative occult powers to bring misfortune to others and the community. Diviners help members of the community find out the causes of misfortune and the sacrifices they need to offer to restore healthy relationships and wholeness to the community.

Religion and art

Cameroonian theologian and historian Engelbert Mveng (1964) once described African art as "a cosmic liturgy and religious language." In affirming these spiritual dimensions in African art, we must insist that first and foremost African art reflects the creative and aesthetic endeavor of individual artists to reflect on their world. Rosalind Hackett (1996) demonstrates that African art focuses on and shapes understanding of humanity, destiny, death, procreation, secrecy, power, divinity, spirits, and healing. Susanne Blier (1987) has argued that art brings together the worldview of people and its use in architecture is very important in human settlements. William Bascom (1993) suggests that there is a close association between African sculpture and religion. Religious ideas were also brought out in votive figures, the design of initiation stools, divination materials, staffs used for various performances, and musical instruments. To that list can be added the masquerade figures of different associations, like the Gelede of the Yoruba or the Kwifon of the Kwifon Society of the northwest province of Cameroon, which claim spiritual as well as political power.

African religion in the post-colonial world

Indigenous religions remain alive in African communities, despite the attacks by people who have converted to other religions and see indigenous religion as a form of "paganism." Hackett (1996) argues that indigenous religions are being revitalized today precisely because of universalization, modernization, politicization, commercialization, and individualization. Their survival and appeal lies in the fact that they continue to inform and provide the basis for morality, culture, and authority at the local level. Royal authority, coronations, rituals, and community festivals are often linked to these religions. Moreover, healing and local knowledge of medicinal plants remains an important part of health care in many parts of Africa.

Political domination, economic crises, and the decline of the state have posed new questions for many Africans, who argue that the people are suffering because the ways of the ancestors have been ignored in the wake of modernity. There is a desire among some to recover the values that had yielded to other explanatory schemes. In addition, there are two things that hold out hope for indigenous religions. First, these religious ideas thrive in the African diaspora in a variety of forms of religious expression that scholars call "African-derived religions." As these religious traditions explore their African roots, they are likely to build new fires and rekindle dying flames back in Africa. Second, the academic study of African religions has developed and matured as a field of inquiry at leading universities in Africa, Europe, and the Americas. Institutional validation has come from the creation of the African Religions Group at the American Academy of Religion (AAR), the International Association of the History of Religions (IAHR) and regional associations for the study of religion in Africa. African religions have survived being disparaged by travelers, missionaries, and colonial anthropologists to become a critical discipline. While such study is not an evangelical activity, the respectability African religions are beginning to enjoy will certainly contribute to the growth of those religions.

Modernity, colonialism, post-colonialism, and postmodernism have radically altered certain religious practices. However, the magic and occult powers generally called "witchcraft" or "sorcery" continue to offer rival explanations and means of control of social reality. Although colonial authorities, the Christian tradition, and even leaders of indigenous religions have attacked occult practices, they remain an important part of the worldview of many people in Africa today. Scholars have begun to recognise the fluidity and complexity of this system of knowledge; others appreciate this, but raise ethical questions about its discourse and alleged practices, calling for the development of an ethical perspective that will enable people to deal with indigenous religions in more productive ways than excommunicating or executing people who are suspected of misusing occult power. The indigenous religious authorities who have to deal with such issues are faced with a difficulty, not least because these powers have now invaded the state and authority structures of many African countries.

See also: Christianity; Christian reform movements; Islam; Islamic reform movements

References and further reading

Bascom, W. (1973) "A Yoruba Master Carver: Duga Meko," in W. D'Azevedo (ed.), *The Traditional Artists in African Societies*, Bloomington: Indiana University Press.

Behrend, H. and Luig, U. (eds.) (1999) *Spirit Possession: Modernity and Power in Africa*, Madison: University of Wisconsin Press.

Blier, S. (1987) *The Anatomy of Architecture: Ontology and Metaphor in Batammaliba Architectural Expression*, Chicago: University of Chicago Press.

Boddy, J. (1989) *Wombs and Alien Spirits: Women and Men in the Zar Cult in Northern Sudan*, Madison: University of Wisconsin Press.

Comaroff, J. (1985) *Body of Power, Spirit of Resistance: The Culture and History of a South African People*, Chicago: University of Chicago Press.

Daneel, M.L. (1970) *The God of the Matopo Hills: An Essay on the Mwari Cult in Rhodesia*, Leiden: African Studies Center.

Evans-Pritchard, E.E. (1956) *Nuer Religion*, London: Oxford University Press.

Hackett, R.I.J. (1996) *Art and Religion in Africa*, London: Cassell.

Horton, R. (1993) *Patterns of Thought in Africa and the West: Essays on Magic, Religion and Science*, Cambridge: Cambridge University Press.

Idowu, E.B. (1973) *African Traditional Religion: A Definition*, Maryknoll: Orbis Books.

Mazrui, A. (1986) *The Africans: A Triple Heritage*, Boston: Little Brown.

Mveng, E. (1964) "Black African Arts as Cosmic Liturgy and Religious Language," in K. Appiah-Kubi and S. Torres (eds.), *African Theology En Route*, Maryknoll: Orbis Books.

Olupona, J.K. (ed.) (1991) *African Traditional Religions in Contemporary Society*, New York: Paragon House.

Ranger, T. and Kimambo, I.N. (eds.) (1972) *The Historical Study of African Religion*, Berkeley: University of California Press.

Ricoeur, P. (1976) *The Symbolism of Evil*, Boston: Beacon Press.

Schoffeleers, J.M. (1992) *River of Blood: The Genesis of a Martyr Cult in Southern Malawi, c. AD 1600*, Madison: University of Wisconsin Press.

Van Binsbergen, W.M. and Schoffeleers, M.J. (eds.)

(1985) *Theoretical Explorations in African Religion*, London: Kegan Paul International.

ELIAS K. BONGMBA

agrarian change

Agrarian change is a social and historical concept based on the changing relations between land, labor, markets, states, and ideologies in the process of agricultural production. These attributes take particular forms and appear in distinct combinations in various places at different times, giving rise to different agrarian structures and agrarian systems of production.

Agrarian change also connotes a number of distinct elements. First, it contains notions of systemic change, from one type of agrarian production to the other – for example, from subsistence to export production or from peasant to capitalist production. This may sometimes involve a change in the scale of operation. A systemic change at this level will affect the agrarian structure, changing the relative mix of small, medium and large farms within agriculture. Second, there may be changes in the agricultural produce, as in the shift from groundnuts to cereals in some parts of the Sahel in the 1970s. Third, there may be changes in the organization of the production process itself. Land is crucial to agriculture, and access to it is determined by social, ideological, and political factors. Land is necessary, but not sufficient, for agricultural production. People must use their tools to work the land. Access to, and command over, labor is therefore equally central to any system of agricultural production. Labor may be recruited through a variety of means, and the relative importance of the control of land, labor, and capital may change over time, giving rise to changes in labor regimes which then have systemic consequences. Different types of tenancy may ebb and flow, while the work and social conditions, and the political outlook, of different classes in the production process may change. Fourth, agrarian change may be driven by changes in the technologies and techniques of production. An example is the introduction of irrigation projects in many parts of Africa. Fifth, change may be driven by changing market conditions which may be tied to improved access, the emergence of new demands or the disappearance of previous markets. Sixth, changes may be driven by demographic and environmental pressures. Finally, change is often dictated by the colonial, settler, and post-colonial states; by their actions and inaction, their ambitions and prejudices. Access to land, to labor, and to markets depend on the actions of political authorities. States not only seek to control access to land, they also authorize, regulate, enforce, and tolerate the rights of husbands, fathers, employers, chiefs, and the state itself over the labor of others. They also define the rights of workers and their organizations. Landowners have often found it impossible to recruit, direct, and maintain a labor force through wage payments alone. They have used their access to national governments, and commonly their control over local government, to secure various measures to restrict the mobility of labor and to deny farm workers access to better jobs or to independent incomes. It is the totality of these structural, sociopolitical, and historical processes which amounts to agrarian change in any particular society. It is neither unilinear nor irreversible, but its effects are often long-lasting.

Agrarian change in twentieth-century Africa was a long and complex process. A key theme in this process is the role of the colonial state. In Africa, the colonial states facilitated the expansion of commodity production. They subjugated other political authorities – African, Arab, and Afrikaner – and brought economic transactions under the jurisdiction of the colonial courts and administration. They established common currencies, and invested in railways and, belatedly, roads. They defined the territorial boundaries within which, and the transport routes along which, trade would expand. They also secured supplies of labor for themselves, for settler farmers, and for mining companies, appropriated and allocated land, and defined people's different rights to land. Colonial governments not only promoted and constrained economic activities, but also directed their benefits to favored groups – indigenous, settler, and metropolitan. Pre-colonial Africa was characterized by a great variety of forms of political organization, agricultural production, allocation of livestock, religious practices, access to land, kinship, and inheritance systems. Rulers and other office-holders claimed a variety of payments in recognition of their authority and of the services they rendered. Colonial rule and the expansion of commerce and of capitalist production did not eliminate diversities, but it did lead to a restructuring and, in important respects, a certain homogenization of social arrangements. Where pre-colonial forms of political authority or land tenure were retained, they acquired new substance under changed circumstances.

A second theme in the process of agrarian change is the commercialization of agriculture which, even early in the century, undermined the all-embracing myth of subsistence production. This commercialization of not only the products of agriculture but also of land, labor, and the implements of agriculture intensified as the century wore on. A third theme is the intensified integration into the capitalist world economy leading, in many instances, to monocrop economies that can be characterized as "dessert and beverage economies." A fourth theme is developmentalism and its modernist pretensions. At the start of the twentieth century, colonial societies appeared to offer great opportunities for social engineering. Various colonial proconsuls sought to remake African societies in accordance with their own peculiar visions. Colonial "development" had an explicitly moral dimension. It would extend the benefits of "civilization" to Africa by promoting commerce, agriculture, and, with reservations, wage labor and Christianity. At the same time, the colonial state would protect the native "community" and the soil from the disruption attendant on the spread of commercial relations. Thus the colonial state gave rise to developmentalism and the emphasis on soil conservation, "betterment" planning, large irrigation schemes. More recently it has also given rise to the post-colonial state's emphasis on the green revolution and biotechnology.

A fifth theme, particularly in the final decades of the twentieth century, is the share of non-farm incomes in the total income of African farmers. Rural households usually combine farming with other ways of earning incomes, both craft production and, especially in the twentieth century, wage employment. Farm and non-farm, wage and non-wage incomes complement one another; most rural households increasingly depend on both to meet their needs and obligations. The twentieth century saw the increasing importance of the non-farm sector and Deborah Bryceson's theory of "de-agrarianization" (Bryceson and Jamal 1997) even suggests that non-farm incomes may have become dominant. Finally, diversity is an important theme of agrarian change in Africa. The colonial period saw the development of peasant and proletarian households, as well as many households that combined both statuses. The expansion of commodity production took different forms in different colonies, and within each colony. State policies varied in response both to different combinations of class interests and to states' own needs to secure the revenues to fund their activities. Hancock (1942) distinguished between the "trader's frontier" and the "settler's frontier" in Africa. In the former, colonial governments promoted peasant agriculture; colonial companies sought to profit from, and colonial governments to tax, trade in peasant produce. In the latter the requirements of settler farmers and mining companies for labor took precedence. In the "settler's frontier" of South Africa, for example, the "alliance" of gold and maize led to the development of an elaborate and extensive labor migrancy system, while in the "trader's frontier" of Nigeria, continued African control of land and the dominance of agriculture by peasant smallholders led to a peasant-based trajectory; the expansion of agricultural production has not always required, or followed from, the concentration of holdings into large-scale enterprises. This distinction can, however, be too heavily drawn. Several colonies accommodated both settler farmers and African peasant producers in an uneasy relationship. Colonial ideologies and policies concerning rural societies often transgressed territorial boundaries; they were freely imported into African colonies from other parts of Africa, from India, and from the metropolitan worlds of Britain and the United States. The diversity of processes and outcomes, for both the colonial and post-colonial periods, is best illustrated on a country-by-country basis. In the second part of this article, we explore the divergent trajectories of some of Africa's largest countries and economies: South Africa, Egypt, and Nigeria.

Agrarian change in South Africa, Egypt, and Nigeria

In South Africa, capitalism came to predominate in agricultural production, as in mining and manufacturing. White settlers appropriated most of the country's land. They used the military, administrative, and fiscal powers of the state to establish, subsidize, and sustain variants of capitalist agriculture, employing black farm workers and, in the later decades of the twentieth century, adopting advanced mechanical and chemical technologies. Mining wealth provided the revenues that allowed the state to subsidize the costs of capitalist farming in the twentieth century. Commodity production by African peasant farmers was marginalized. Capitalist agriculture in South Africa had its origins in many forms of recruitment and control of labor, including initially slave and indentured labor, and later tenant, forced, migrant, and wage labor. Restrictions on access to land and obligations on all adult males to pay taxes were used to get Africans to work for wages. Workers' freedom was constrained by passes and by vagrancy laws to restrict their mobility. Production was expanded to meet South African, African, and overseas markets. For maize, wheat, wine, sugar, milk, and vegetables – indeed most crops other than wool and some fruits – the most important markets were the mines and the expanding towns and cities of South Africa itself. White farmers were served by railway branch lines and low tariffs on crops, and by the Land Bank. Poorer farmers sought state intervention to secure their access to cheap land, cheap credit, cheap labor, and high prices. Agricultural marketing was dominated by state, cooperative, and corporate interests.

Rural blacks engaged in a long and bitter struggle to maintain their control of land, and some form of access to land where whites had excluded them from it, and to recover, retain, and build up their herds of cattle. Indigenous peoples sought to defend their polities from white conquest. Some migrated beyond the frontiers of white settlement. Others migrated to work in the mines and towns, initially to acquire money to buy guns or cattle, and later to secure their own subsistence needs and to contribute to the needs of their families and to the costs of farming in the reserves. Before 1913 some purchased land and others became squatters on white-owned land. Urbanization created opportunities for Africans with access to land and to markets to increase the production of maize, sorghum, wheat, wool, and meat for sale. Peasant commodity production developed particularly in areas where black farmers acquired title to their land, or on mission lands. Production also rose in the native reserves and black tenants extended peasant commodity production on to the land designated for white farming.

Black farmers competed with whites for the use of land, for labor, and in the markets for commodities. White farmers in turn competed for labor with mineowners and with commercial and industrial firms. "Native" policy, that is labor policy, was the outcome of a series of uneasy and unstable compromises between mining, agrarian, commercial, and industrial interests. Africans were to be confined to the native reserves, which provided a reservoir of migrant labor. Whereas mineowners looked to the reserves, and to neighboring territories, to supply their labor, farmers were generally more concerned to restrict blacks' access to land and the ability of black farm laborers to seek work elsewhere. Africans were neither to own nor to rent land in white areas. These principles were embodied in numerous laws, notably the Native Land Act of 1913, which reserved 7 percent of the country's land area as "native reserves," and the Natives Trust and Land Act of 1936, which increased the land to be available to Africans to 13.6 percent. The acts laid the legal foundations, combined with successive pass laws, for the separation of the supplies of labor for mining, agriculture and manufacturing, though without bringing an end to competition for labor and the political battles this brought about. Implementation of these laws would be a slow process, extending over many decades. Similarly, many of the consequences for agricultural producers in the reserves of these and other acts only became fully manifest over subsequent decades.

Farmers in the native reserves were increasingly constrained by insufficient land for cultivation and grazing, poor access to transport and markets, and the loss of males to migrant labor. Government sought to protect the soil and to raise agricultural productivity by "betterment" planning, by which land would be allocated to woodland, arable, grazing, and residential areas, and people relocated into concentrated villages. But "betterment" disrupted people's lives and reduced the land available to them for farming. It was used as part of a strategy of resettling even more people into the Bantustans (African reservations). It became a source and focus of local resistance to the chiefs through whom it was imposed. While peasant producers had been able to increase agricultural production and maintain livestock numbers in at least some of the native reserves during the first half of the century, over the last three decades of the twentieth century stagnating or even declining production was accompanied by rapidly increasing population and the massive movement of people into the impoverished Bantustans.

From the 1960s, the state carried out a concerted and continuing assault against African freehold rights, renting of land, and labor tenancy on white farms; this was a significant part of the massive relocation of black people in accordance with the plans of the apartheid state. Labor tenancy was formally abolished in 1980, though some farmers continued to employ people under tenancy agreements. The prohibition of tenancy ended in 1985. The prosperity of white farms depended on state pricing and support policies, and was vulnerable to an ever-rising weight of debts. In the 1980s capitalist farmers were squeezed between rising interest rates and costs of inputs and stagnant prices for their produce. The number of white farmers declined: in 1950 there were 117,000 farms, in 1980 there were about 69,000 farms and fewer farmers – some 59,000 in 1985, of whom 17,700 produced three-quarters the total gross farm income. The contribution of agriculture to South Africa's export earnings also declined sharply from the 1960s. In 1991 the legal reservation of land to whites was finally ended.

Agrarian change in South Africa appears as a story of the development of capitalist white farming and the elimination or marginalization of peasant African farming. When they were not left destitute, rural Africans were steadily transformed into proletarians, working for wages on farms, mines, and in towns. By the end of the century, peasant production appeared to have a past, but neither much of a present nor any sort of future. With the end of apartheid in 1994, land reform and land restitution were put on the political agenda, but this market-driven process has yet to deliver substantial changes.

The history of agrarian change in Egypt took a different trajectory. Boasting one of the oldest agricultural systems in the world, Egyptian agriculture underwent important changes from the nineteenth century, as the country embarked on modernization. New crops and irrigation systems were introduced, all of which transformed cultivation practices and land-ownership patterns. In the nineteenth century, Mohammed Ali and his successors built canals and dams that facilitated perennial irrigation, and they encouraged the cultivation of long-staple cotton for export as a way of earning foreign exchange. Over time, such policies led to the development of a land-owning rural oligarchy and an impoverished peasantry. Since time immemorial, Egypt depended on the waters of the Nile, so efficient water management was crucial. During the twentieth century more dams were built, culminating in the giant Aswan Dam built after the 1952 revolution. Improvements in the water and irrigation systems made it possible to expand the land under cultivation and increase the number of crops grown. For example, while one annual crop was grown after the Nile floods at the beginning of the nineteenth century, by the 1970s up to six different crops could be grown. But agricultural intensification required changes in fertilization, since it engendered declining soil fertility and mud from the Nile floods was no longer available as a result of the improvements in water distribution. Because of costs it took many decades for peasants to adopt the use of mineral fertilizer widely. Instead, they began to rely on dung from livestock, so that the close link between agriculture and livestock production, forged in the nineteenth century with the spread of *saqqiyas* for irrigation which required animals to operate, became even closer. The growing importance of livestock among peasants has also been associated with the spread of Alexandrian clover (*bersim*) production, and livestock's growing food and economic value. By the end of the century *bersim* production had eclipsed cotton, wheat, and even maize, which had become the main peasant staple earlier in the century.

If water availability and management set the physical parameters of agricultural production, peasant indebtedness and state policy set the social contexts. The debt problem became so severe that in 1913 the government passed a law forbidding the expropriation of peasants' land for debt non-payment. Under the law peasants could also not access agricultural credit without collateral, which did little to improve their conditions. The rural agrarian crisis deepened as population growth accelerated, and as extended family units gradually dissolved and land was subdivided into ever smaller individual family parcels. During the first half of the twentieth century the differentiation and inequities between the big landowners and the peasants became ever wider and more evident as a source of political conflict, despite the attainment of independence in 1922. The 1952 revolution sought to change that. In effect, however, it continued the long tradition of state intervention in agriculture. Nasser's radical government enacted a series of land-reform laws that broke the power of the landowning oligarchy. These reforms fixed maximum sizes for holdings of land, thus allowing the state to confiscate large estates. The rents paid by peasants were capped and evictions were made more difficult. Compulsory state cooperatives were set up. But the reforms were not targeted at all landowners, rather they mostly affected those associated with the previous regime. In any case, large estates constituted only 13 percent of the arable land, so that expropriation was not, in itself, a solution to the country's deepening land crisis. Indeed, whether intended or not, such measures and the state's subsequent interventions in the agrarian sector tended to benefit not tenant farmers but the so-called "rich peasantry" or "rural middle class" who were subsequently described as a key constituency of the post-1952 political order.

The reforms produced little food security. In fact, Egypt's dependence on food imports actually grew to one of the highest levels in the world, by 1980 it had risen to 70 percent of local consumption for wheat alone. Despite various efforts to liberalize the agrarian sector through the early 1990s, it remained heavily regulated, with peasant cultivators frequently required to grow cotton which was purchased by the state at below-market rates. Not surprisingly, this led to large-scale evasion of cropping requirements by the peasantry, resulting in some easing of state controls. In 1992 the state enacted a land-reform law that was aimed at reversing many of the protections given to peasants in the 1950s, and allowing landowners both to evict their tenants and to substantially increase rents. The impact of this law, implementation of which was delayed until 1997, is debatable. One the one hand, some observers see it as a further indication of the market-driven transformation of post-*infitah* Egyptian society and the abandonment of the "socialism" of the Nasser era. On the other hand, it is not entirely clear to what extent the law actually came into force. Rural violence in the lead-up to its implementation, and the involvement of radical urban activists on behalf of the peasantry, seems to have led the state to refrain from sanctioning any large-scale dispossession of peasant cultivators.

Of all the British colonies in Africa, Nigeria most clearly exemplified Hancock's "trader's frontier." Few plantations were set up, and they had little success. Nigerian agriculture thus remained more exclusively in peasant hands. The building of railways by the colonial government created conditions for the expansion of commercial production of bulky arable and tree crops, and of the trade in livestock. By the end of the colonial period, Nigeria was the world's largest exporter of palm produce, groundnuts, and, after Ghana, of cocoa. Nigeria also exported quantities of cotton, rubber, shea nut, and sesame seed. An oligopoly of foreign merchant companies dominated imports and exports. African and Levantine traders distributed and bulked these commodities to and from numerous local markets. The twentieth century also saw a sustained expansion of agricultural production for the Nigerian market, and the development of a complex and extensive network of trade in grains, roots, pulses, livestock, kola nut, and other crops, conducted by African traders. In Nigeria peasants demonstrated their ability to produce exports and secured the government's revenue base. The colonial government therefore resisted demands from some British businesses that they provide land, labor, and trading monopolies for plantations in southern Nigeria. The government itself assumed ownership of land in the north, and vested control of land in the chiefs to protect peasant land from alienation. In practice, Nigerians bought and sold land, though in most rural areas the availability of farmland kept prices relatively low. In southern Nigeria, "native strangers" gained access to land and crops through rent- and share-tenancy agreements.

Southern cocoa and palm produce generated more exports and revenues than northern groundnuts, cotton, and beniseed. Official policy was generally cautious about interfering with existing farming practices. Attempts were made in northern Nigeria to develop irrigation and to introduce ox-ploughing and manuring. Some communities from areas infected by tsetse fly, and others from densely populated districts, were resettled in villages. None of these policies made much impact on production. In the 1940s cocoa farmers opposed the compulsory cutting out of trees infected by swollen shoot. Office-holders and merchants used various institutions to try to secure labor from their subjects, clients or debtors, and to obtain irrigated land and contracts from the state. But they lacked the control of land necessary to subordinate producers to wage labor on their own terms. Throughout Nigeria, peasant households emerged as the predominant form of rural producers. In many communities, the management of different crops was divided between men and women. Among both Yoruba and Hausa farmers, men managed crop production and claimed the labor of their sons and of their wives. Economic opportunities outside the household enabled sons to contest these demands and to modify their terms and gave rise to conflicts, often covert, over men's capacity to command their wives' labor-time. Seasonal migrant workers were recruited from diverse areas to harvest crops. Nevertheless, family labor predominated and most wage labor was recruited from local farming families. In the absence of a landless class in the rural areas, agricultural wages remained relatively high.

The colonial government tried to regulate cotton markets and promoted cooperative marketing of cocoa. During the **Second World War**, the state took over the export and pricing, first of cocoa and then of palm produce, groundnuts, and cotton, using the merchant firms as its agents. After the war, the state marketing boards justified their licensing of produce traders by the need to regulate competition and thereby protect the producers from exploitation by "middlemen." From the Second World War until 1986, the state marketing boards used their monopoly over exports to impose very heavy taxation on rural producers. However, agricultural exports only began to decline sharply (in the cases of groundnuts and palm nuts to zero) after the Nigerian civil war and the rise of mineral oil exports. Imports of wheat, rice, maize, meat, milk, day-old chicks, and even vegetable oils then rose precipitately, accentuated by the overvaluation of the naira. The experience of the 1972–4 Sahel drought combined with the rise in food imports to justify enormous investments in gravity irrigation projects to produce wheat and rice in northern Nigeria. Increased demand for food encouraged farmers, particularly in the northern states, to shift production to, and expand production of, grain for urban and for rural markets in Nigeria and Niger. In 1986 the marketing boards were abolished, the naira was devalued, and the import of a wide range of agricultural commodities banned. This raised the prices of export and locally consumed crops. Rising producer prices encouraged an expansion of cocoa and cotton production, though not to the levels of 1970. Government initially welcomed rising food exports, but banned them when prices rose sharply after a poor harvest in 1987, thus raising the costs of cross-border food trade. Devaluation, combined with the ban of wheat imports, sharply increased the price of wheat bread, encouraged the illegal import of wheat flour, and justified massive subsidies for wheat production, now under tubewell irrigation.

State "modernization" of peasant agriculture is a recurring theme in agrarian change in Nigeria.

From the 1950s, Nigerian governments initiated various projects, some funded by international agencies, to modernize peasant agriculture and to promote large-scale farming, capitalist and state-run. They financed settlement schemes, established plantations for cultivated oil palms, rubber, and sugar, and set up state farms and ranches. Governments also subsidized and distributed credit, fertilizers, and tractors, promoted high-yielding cocoa trees and yellow maize, as well as spending enormous sums on grandiose irrigation projects. The 1979 Land Use Decree gave governments the capacity to control the disposition of land, but they faced political limits to their capacity to appropriate land for irrigation schemes, ranches and large-scale farming schemes. Governments' efforts to promote agricultural production were marked by an ignorance of the conditions under which peasants cultivated and of the demand for their crops, and by high costs and poor, generally negative, net returns. Irrigation project managers failed to make farmers conform with their choice of crops. The major contribution of governments in Nigeria to increasing agricultural production was in building and maintaining roads. The Nigerian state subsidized the entry of urban-based capitalist farmers into potentially lucrative but import-dependent niches. After the adoption of structural adjustment in 1986, the state gradually withdrew from involvement in agricultural production, leading to the collapse of many parastatals and state farms.

See also: capitalisms and capitalists; economy: colonial; economy: post-independence; pastoralism; peasants; plantation agriculture; structural adjustment programs

References and further reading

Beinart, W., Delius, P. and Trapido, S. (eds.) (1984) *Putting a Plough to the Ground*, London: Longmans.

Bryceson, D. and Jamal, V. (eds.) (1997) *Farewell to Farms: Agrarianization in Sub-Saharan Africa*, Ashgate: Aldershot.

Bundy, C. (1979) *The Rise and Fall of the South African Peasantry*, London: Heinemann.

Craig, G.M. (ed.) (1993) *The Agriculture of Egypt*, New York: Oxford University Press.

Faris, M.A. and Khan, M.H. (ed.) *Sustainable Agriculture in Egypt*, Boulder and London: Lynne Rienner.

Forrest, T. (1981) "Agricultural Policies in Nigeria, 1900–1978," in J. Heyer, P. Roberts and G. Williams (eds.), *Rural Development in Tropical Africa*, London: Macmillan.

Hancock, W.K. (1942) *Survey of British Commonwealth Affairs*, vol. 2, part II, London: Oxford University Press.

Helleiner, G. (1967) *Peasant Agriculture, Government and Economic Growth in Nigeria*, Homewood: Irwin.

ABDUL RAUFU MUSTAPHA
GAVIN WILLIAMS

alcohol and drugs

Alcohol has played a lengthy role in the history of Africa as a ritual artifact, an economic good, and a social marker. Indigenous beers were brewed from sorghum and millet in West Africa (*dolo* or *pito*) and in South Africa (*utshwala*), and banana beer was made in East Africa. Palm wine from the oil and raffia palms was an important ritual and social drink in West Africa, similar to the use of coconut wine in East Africa. The entry of European liquor dates from the opening of Atlantic trade from the fifteenth century, and reinforced the pre-existing ritual and social uses of alcohol. Significantly, European distilled liquor had a long shelf life, and this quality enhanced its value as an economic commodity, even facilitating the use of cases of European gin as currency in southern Nigeria in the nineteenth century. The introduction of Islam to North Africa from the seventh century AD, and its spread to the Western Sudan and the East African coast, lessened the importance of alcohol in these areas because of the Islamic prohibition of alcohol, although consumption of drugs such as khat persisted. In fact Muslims in northern Nigeria apparently use drugs much more than southern Nigerians.

Indigenous drugs also existed and cannabis appears to have grown wild in Ethiopia and Southern Africa for centuries. It was also incorporated into ritual, aiding monastic contemplation in Ethiopia, and healing therapy in Zimbabwe. The use of foreign hard drugs such as cocaine and heroin has been on the increase since the mid-1980s as a spillover effect of the utilization of West, East, and Southern Africa as transit points in the smuggling of heroin and cocaine to the European and North American markets. Today, while distilleries and breweries form an important component of formal industrialization projects in Africa, the clandestine market for and trafficking in hard drugs have become a crucial aspect of informal economies. Henry Bernstein (1998) describes the trafficking in marijuana, cocaine, and heroin as among the most dynamic and valuable of Africa's "non-traditional" exports and re-exports.

Pre-colonial Africa

In many pre-colonial societies, liquor played an important role in many aspects of life, from spirit possession, festivals, court protocol and judicial processes to rites of passage. Among the Akan of Ghana, the powerful sought to monopolize the ritual and social use of alcohol, and chiefs and elders systematically denied young men and women access to it. Alcohol marked social hierarchy and lubricated social relations, with young men and women involved in the production of alcoholic drinks, but not in the consumption of them. Drink, wealth, and power were intimately connected, and the advent of European liquor fed into this earlier demand and use. The ritual and social uses of alcohol provide an important entry into the religion, philosophy, and culture of several African societies. For the Kofyar of Nigeria, the beer-brewing cycle even determined the structure of the week, and the meaning and importance of beer were central to the Iteso of Uganda and Kenya.

An important irony in the social history of alcohol in Africa was that this most valuable fluid was one of the cheapest products manufactured in Europe. While African chiefs and elders sought to restrict access to alcohol, it was in the financial interest of European merchants to maximize their sales of liquor. And for commoners who sought to subvert the control of the traditional establishment, European liquor was an important symbol of protest and self-assertion. Indigenous temperance movements emerged in a bid to codify the elder's temperate and regulated use of alcohol. Chiefs and European missionaries would form an important alliance in their struggle against liquor use by commoners.

Indigenous drugs such as cannabis, khat, and iboga were in use in pre-colonial Africa in Ethiopia, Somalia, Kenya, Zimbabwe, Mozambique, South Africa, and Cameroon. But the absence of studies prevents a thorough examination of the use of these substances in the pre-colonial and colonial periods. Indeed, even in independent Africa, material on drug use remains scarce, with seizure statistics representing one of the key sources of evidence. The social use of khat in the Horn of Africa and East Africa is not of recent origin, and the use of the iboga plant by Mbwiti healing cults in Cameroon and Gabon certainly dates from before the colonial period. In the Binga area of Zimbabwe, consumption of cannabis has been described as traditional.

Colonial Africa

Financial self-sufficiency was a prime concern of all colonial governments. The demand for liquor, especially in West Africa with its long immersion in Atlantic trade, provided European governments with a tax base. Liquor policy and liquor revenues came to constitute major pillars in colonial rule. The absence of large groups of white settlers in West Africa minimized concerns about drink, social disorder, and the threat to colonial rule. Between 1892 and 1903 import duties on liquor provided over 55 percent of the total revenue of the colony of Lagos and 38 percent of the Gold Coast's revenue. Colonial concerns were different in East and Southern Africa, with their settler communities, and liquor legislation was only relaxed as colonial control became firmly established.

Threats to colonial dependence on liquor revenues were often external. European missionaries were disappointed that the rhetoric about ending the slave, gun, and liquor trade to Africa had proved empty when it came to liquor traffic. They agitated for temperance and prohibition in colonies such as the Gold Coast and southern Nigeria. International conventions on liquor were another important check on colonial liquor policy.

The Brussels Convention of 1890 banned European liquor across a wide belt of the African interior between latitudes 20° North and 22° South. The predominantly Muslim communities of northern Nigeria and the northern territories of the Gold Coast fell under this proscription. The St. Germain-en-Laye (France) conference of September 1919 banned "trade spirits" from the African market, defined as spirits manufactured specifically for trade to Africans and not normally consumed by Europeans. But the concession that each colonial government could define what was meant by "trade spirits" enabled many to circumvent the purpose of the convention.

However, it was internal pressure that led to the revision of colonial liquor policy in British West Africa from the late 1920s. The emergence of a popular culture revolving around European-style drinking bars, dance bands, popular music (like highlife), and comic opera ("concert") – and massively patronized by young men and women in towns and peri-urban villages – gave chiefs and the educated African elite cause for concern. The imposition of huge tariffs on imported liquor, and the plan to gradually ban the importation of Dutch geneva or gin into the Gold Coast, coincided with the economic depression of the 1930s. Colonial liquor revenues plummeted with the drop in liquor imports, and frustrated commoners switched to the patronage of illicitly distilled gin (*akpeteshie*). Colonial governments were forced to reduce duties on imported liquor to make them more competitive, though this was without much success. As nationalist forces gathered strength after the Second World War, *akpeteshie* entered the nationalist agenda, and politicians promised the legalization of this distinctly African drink on the assumption of independence. The situation was not very different in Southern Africa, where the denial of European liquor to Africans in Zambia and Zimbabwe made its acquisition a major demand for educated Africans as a sign of political parity. Thus the traditional symbolism of alcohol and its ties to power came to inform the nationalist struggle and discourse.

Independent Africa

The importance of the alcohol industry to government revenue has persisted into the post-colonial era, with breweries and distilleries playing a central role in industrialization and economic development. Indeed, with limited markets for manufactured goods, the alcohol industry was often the only profitable industry in the early years of independence. This continued the political, social, and economic importance of alcohol.

From the 1940s the use of cannabis extended to West Africa, and returning servicemen from Asia are credited with its introduction. The common use of the terms "Indian hemp" and *bhanga* (of Hindi derivation) are cited as evidence of this Asian provenance. Initially used by servicemen, and certain occupational groups associated with arduous and dangerous work, cannabis use fed into a class- and counter-culture that rationalized what were criminal activities.

Further continuities are suggested in the ties between cocoa farmers and *akpeteshie* distillation in the colonial period, and cocoa farmers and cannabis cultivation in the independent era. The intercropping of cocoa and oil palm made the distillation of *akpeteshie* from oil palm an important provider of cash in the period before the cocoa trees began to bear fruit. Since cocoa grows in deep forest areas, it was easy to conceal illicit distillation from the authorities. Likewise, high-quality cannabis grows in deep forests, again providing cash for cocoa farmers in the period between harvests. With the decline in the world market price for cocoa after 1958, cocoa farmers may have been encouraged to diversify into cannabis cultivation, especially as the market expanded to incorporate students, musicians, and others engaged in the elaboration of youth culture. A 2001 police report indicates that many farmers in the region now find the cultivation of Indian hemp or marijuana more lucrative than maize. Another report makes a similar observation for the cocoa- and coffee-growing areas of Cameroon.

Economic decline in Africa in the 1970s, together with increasing demand, may have reinforced the cultivation of cannabis as a cash crop. In Ethiopia and Kenya, khat cultivation is a legal enterprise with considerable economic benefits. Southern and western Africa now account for the bulk of Africa's supply of cannabis with South

Africa, Mozambique, Nigeria, and Ghana being the major sites of production. Reports by the United Nations Drug Control Program, though admittedly not comprehensive, provide increasing evidence about drug production, trafficking, and consumption in Africa. According to its 1996 report, African countries are responsible for a quarter of herbal cannabis and a tenth of cannabis resin seized worldwide.

Cannabis production, distribution, and consumption provided pathways for the incorporation of cocaine and heroin from the 1980s. The tightening of controls at European and North American airports encouraged heroin traffickers from Thailand and cocaine traffickers from Brazil and other Latin American countries to use Africa as a staging point in their activities, and Africans as couriers or "mules." For Africans involved, the financial rewards were highly enticing, irrespective of the risks. Today Africans are serving lengthy prison terms in Thailand, Europe, and North America. There is also growing evidence that consumption of heroin and cocaine in Africa is on the rise. Initially pioneered by "jet-setters" and those who had lived abroad, dealers who sell small quantities of cannabis in Ghanaian cities are also dealing in heroin and cocaine, indicating that cocaine (especially crack cocaine) and heroin are ceasing to be high-end drugs. Similar to cannabis use, cocaine and heroin are smoked instead of injected, and the injection of hard drugs is viewed by many as a habit not indulged in by Africans. The use of these hard drugs among street children in urban Ghana has been reported. A Ghanaian newspaper has warned that young people in general are switching from cannabis to cocaine and heroin. Further specific research will flesh out these sketched outlines, but it suffices to conclude – in line with the 1999 UN report on the drug nexus in Africa – that a drug crisis may lie in Africa's future if strong measures to deter current trends are not implemented.

See also: leisure; youth

References and further reading

Akyeampong, E. (1996) *Drink, Power, and Cultural Change: A Social History of Alcohol in Ghana, c.1800 to Recent Times*, Portsmouth: Heinemann.

Bernstein, H. (1998) *Ghana's Drug Economy: Some Preliminary Data*, London: SOAS CDPR.

Karp, I. and Bird, C.S. (eds.) (1980) *Explorations in African Systems of Thought*, Bloomington: Indiana University Press.

Pan, L. (1975) *Alcohol in Colonial Africa*, Uppsala: Scandinavian Institute of African Studies.

United Nations International Drug Control Program (1997) *World Drug Report*, Oxford: Oxford University Press.

United Nations Office for Drug Control and Crime Prevention (1999) *The Drug Nexus in Africa*, Vienna: United Nations Publication.

EMMANUEL AKYEAMPONG

Alexandria, Egypt

Alexandria is the major port and second largest city in **Egypt**. It is home to 40 percent of the country's industry, with a population of four million that increases to six million in the summer because of tourism. The city stretches over seventy kilometers along the coast, with urban areas extending over 100 square kilometers. During the first half of the twentieth century, Alexandria's socioeconomic situation enabled it to develop into an international metropolis that attracted people from various parts of the world. While Europe was suffering from economic depression, Alexandria bustled with business activity and was thus able to reduce taxes. At the same time, foreigners were made welcome, and tolerance of different cultures and beliefs was prevalent. Foreigners were allowed to own businesses, trade in the bourse, and were exempt from Egyptian law.

The result was continuous waves of European and Middle Eastern immigrants, some attracted by economic prosperity and some fleeing persecution or political unrest in their home countries. In 1917 the number of foreigners was 70,000 out of a population of 435,000, and by 1927 it reached 99,605. These numbers sky-rocketed in the wake of the Second World War, when thousands of Jews emigrated to Alexandria where the Jewish community was considered the world's most organized and the most prosperous. By 1952 a quarter of the population was Greek and, according to some estimates, only 30 percent of the residents were Egyptian.

The presence of such diversity encouraged the development of the cultural and intellectual life of the city, which Lawrence Durrell (author of *The Alexandria Quartet*) called "a melting pot." Among these foreigners were E.M. Forster, who moved to Alexandria where East and West meet, to write *A Passage to India*, and the Greek poet C.P. Cavafy. Other foreigners helped establish the **cinema** industry in Egypt, such as the Greek-born Omar Sharif and the Hungarian Stephan Rosti. Middle Eastern royalty and other members of the elite were attracted by the high standards of education provided at Alexandrian schools such as St. Mark's College and Victory College, which Jordan's late King Hussein attended.

Readers of Forster's guide to Alexandria or Lawrence's novels would be surprised to see it today. The end of the Second World War was the beginning of a series of dramatic socioeconomic changes. In 1947 the Egyptian government mandated that 90 percent of all workers and more than 50 percent of joint stock holders be Egyptians. The result was the lay-off of 60,000 foreign workers. The 1956 Suez War, in which Israel attacked Egypt with the backing of Britain and France, resulted in the expulsion of all British and French residents. The 1967 war precipitated the migration of Jews to Israel, resulting in the shrinking of the Jewish population of Alexandria from 14,860 in 1947 to less than 200 by the early 1980s.

These changes encouraged the migration to Alexandria of thousands from the rural lower classes, who within a couple of decades developed into an educated middle class. The 1970s brought an economic boom, with the shift from socialism to a capitalist free-market policy of unrestricted imports and exports. Soon Alexandria regained its popularity as a business center and beautiful summer resort, and its size doubled from the 1950s. International intellectual interest in the city has also been growing since the early 1980s with the establishment of Sangour University and an international francophone university, the discovery of parts of the ancient lighthouse, and the building of the Alexandria Library, second only to the US Library of Congress.

Further reading

Forster, E.M. (1961) *Alexandria: A History and Guide*, New York: Doubleday.

Jobbins, J. and Megalli, M. (1993) *The Egyptian Mediterranean*, Cairo: The American University in Cairo Press.

MUSTAFA A. MUGHAZY

Algeria

Algeria is located in northern Africa, bordering the Mediterranean Sea, **Morocco**, **Tunisia**, **Libya**, **Mali**, **Mauritania**, **Niger**, and Western Sahara, and has a total area of 2,381,741 square kilometers. Its population was estimated at 31.2 million in 2000, constituted primarily of Arabs and Amazighs. Algeria's name originates in the Arabic word *al-Djazair*, a plural noun for "island." The country was a colony of France from 1830 until 1962.

In order to understand the nature of the French colonial regime in Algeria, it is necessary to look at colonial laws, especially the *senatus-consultes* of 1863 and 1865, and their underlying ideological function. The 1863 *senatus-consulte* expropriated the land of the colonized on a massive scale and paved the way for colonial settlements. The Warnier Laws of 1873 "Frenchified" what remained of the land of the *fellahs* by handing it over to unscrupulous speculators. Settlers then established an economy that satisfied the needs of mainland France, transplanting vineyards and citrus groves onto lands that used to produce grain. The 1865 *senatus-consulte* stipulated that Arabs and Amazighs were French subjects; it allowed them to apply for French citizenship, with the proviso that they follow the French code and renounce their "personal status," namely their Muslim identity. In reality, the offer of citizenship amounted to nothing: the Muslims would not relinquish their cultural identity; moreover, the applications for citizenship met with an unfriendly reception from the colonial administrators. Thus the 1865 *senatus-*

consulte created a fracture at the core of the concept of French citizenship: it subjected the colonized to French laws, but denied them most of the civil rights pertaining to political citizenship. The *senatus-consultes* of 1863 and 1865 therefore worked in tandem to expropriate the colonized and deny them subject status. Subsequently the Jonnart Laws, passed in 1919, aimed to enfranchise the elite, but did nothing for the predominantly uneducated mass of colonized people. Furthermore, these reforms were couched in terms of segregation: the Jonnart Laws grouped the enfranchised elite in a separate electoral college that offered no rights to parliamentary representation. This very restricted program of reform baffled supporters of integration but, from the outset, settlers reacted against them. In May 1920 the Congress of Algerian Mayors urged the French government to return to its former policy of securing the interests and colonial future of the settlers. The government was not only compelled to respond with a law, passed August 1920, that repelled the Jonnart Laws, but also had to reinstate the previous *code algérien de l'indigénat.* This established an apartheid regime that was in complete contradiction with the practices of French civil institutions and common law which had been introduced into Kabylia after the Mokrani Rebellion in 1874 and extended to the rest of the country by further legislation in 1881.

From 1920 to 1945 political relations in Algeria took the shape of a pyramid, with the colonial administration at the top and three opposing political tendencies at the bottom: Jeunes Algériens, the Ulemas and the Parti Populaire Algérien (PPA). Jeunes Algériens (or the "lay" reformists) were in favor of assimilation. The Ulemas' "religious" reformism advocated a return to those very traditions that the colonizers had tried to obliterate. The PPA was radical in its political demands, having emerged from the Etoile Nord-Africaine – a shadow organization to the French Communist Party. In 1934 the French socialists and communists formed a coalition government under the premiership of Léon Blum. In his government, Minister of State Maurice Viollette, the former Governor-General of Algeria, drafted a bill for political reform which reintroduced the assimilationist proposals of the Jonnart Laws as the Blum–Viollette Bill of 1935. All the European mayors and deputies in Algeria boycotted it. The failure of the bill precipitated a political impasse in colonial Algeria. On 8 May 1945 the indigenous people in Sétif were allowed to parade and lay a wreath to commemorate those Algerians who fell serving under the French flag in the Second World War. Thousands appeared on that day carrying nationalistic and anti-colonialist banners. The demonstrations culminated in a clash between the French police and the nationalists. Over 45,000 civilians were massacred by French police in Guelma, Karata, and Sétif. The importance of the 1945 crisis as a landmark in the political history of Algeria cannot be overemphasized: not only did the crisis express the failure of the rhetoric of assimilation, but it announced the beginning of the end of French Algeria.

Almost a decade after this crisis, the Algerian War ignited. On 1 November 1954 the FLN (National Liberation Front) took arms to liberate Algeria from the shackles of colonialism. Its struggle would continue until 1962. In the summer of 1956 Algiers witnessed a brutal cycle of terrorism and counter-terrorism. In January 1957 Governor-General Lacoste put Algiers under the military control of General Massu. The latter instigated a campaign of torture and state terrorism, commonly known as the Battle of Algiers. In 1958 General Challe extended the state terrorism developed by Massu to the whole of Algeria. To restrict the movement of the FLN and cut the military supplies coming to it from Tunisia, the French army constructed the Morice Line along the Algerian–Tunisian border. On 8 February 1958 French planes bombed Sakhiet Sidi Youssef, a Tunisian village near the Algerian border. The hostilities claimed the lives of hundreds of thousands of civilians – eventually hostilities were to claim a million lives.

Fearful of a political settlement to the Algerian War, the generals in Algiers encouraged demonstrations led by the *ultras* (extremists among the French settlers). On 13 May 1958, under the threat of a *putsch*, General de Gaulle returned to power. The Algerian War had an impact on the political institutions of mainland France. It undermined the premises upon which French democracy was built, leading to the collapse of the Fourth Republic. General de Gaulle wrote the French constitution, set up the Fifth Republic, and presided over the decolonization of Algeria, a significant event for the liberationist movement that was sweeping Africa at the time. After the 1961 referendum, de Gaulle started to negotiate with the FLN. Two issues complicated negotiations: the discovery of vast reserves of natural gas and oil in the Sahara, and, more importantly, the prospect of having to repatriate almost a million French settlers (*pieds noirs*). Initially France proposed to keep the Sahara under its political control and only grant independence to part of Algeria, but the Algerians rejected this proposal. An agreement on independence was finally reached on 18 March 1962. Most of the settlers were repatriated.

Ben Bella set up the first government in 1963, staying in power until 1965 when he was removed in a coup staged by Colonel Haouri Boumediene. Boumediene's presidency lasted until 1978. The economy, health care, housing, education, and rapid population growth were immediate problems for Algeria in the aftermath of decolonization. Until 1962 the economy was primarily agricultural, complementing that of mainland France. In addition to wine, citrus fruits, and other agricultural products, Algeria provided the raw materials for French industry. The exploitation of natural gas and oil by French companies generated income for the newly independent state. In 1971 Boumediene nationalized this vital resource, enabling Algeria to take giant strides toward industrialization. Under his leadership, Algeria's foreign policy was characterized by non-alignment and anti-imperialism. Boumediene sought to Arabize the administration and attempted, albeit unsuccessfully, to bring about an agrarian revolution. However, clientelism weakened the socialist ideals of the Algerian revolution: a military dictatorship replaced the colonial state, and power was concentrated in the hands of the single-party FLN government. After Boumediene's death in December 1978, Colonel Chadli Ben Jadid was elected president. He carried out the same policies as his predecessor. During his presidency, the gap between the military ruling class and the rest of the populace became obvious. In the 1980s the drastic fall in the price of crude oil threatened the Algerian economy. The looming economic crisis precipitated uprisings in 1988, but Chadli had already introduced a program of economic and political reforms. In 1987 the Ministry of Planning was abolished and the Chamber of Commerce revived, with a view to encouraging private-sector development and opening the Algerian economy to foreign investment. In 1989 Chadli ratified a new constitution that put an end to one-party government. It is ironic that the democratization of Algeria's political system opened the floodgates of political turmoil. Disenchanted with the FLN, a disgruntled population rallied behind their opponents – namely, the Islamic Salvation Front (FIS) – in order to effect change. It was no surprise when the FIS secured a landslide victory in the first round of the 1990 election, but the decision by the military to suspend the election was to spark a civil war that raged throughout the 1990s.

Further reading

Behr, E. (1976) *The Algerian Problem*, London: Greenwood Press.

Haddour, A. (2000) *Colonial Myths, History and Narrative*, Manchester: Manchester University Press.

AZZEDINE HADDOUR

Algiers, Algeria

In Arabic the word *al-Djazair* refers both to the country **Algeria** and to its capital city, Algiers. Situated in the north, Algiers is both the largest seaport city and *wilaya* (province) in Algeria. The Spanish held the city for a short period in the sixteenth century, before the Turks annexed it to their empire. Prior to the colonization of Algeria by the French in 1830, Algiers was one of the major cities of the Ottoman Empire. It was, in fact, the capital of the Barbary Coast, whose fleet dominated the Mediterranean. Then, during the colonial period, Algiers was the administrative center for Algeria as a French *département*. During the **Second World War**, after the Allies landed in

North Africa in 1942, Algiers became the seat of the provisional government of Free France. In the 1950s, during the Algerian War, Algiers was a battlefield. In 1956 it witnessed a brutal cycle of terrorism and counter-terrorism, with Governor-General Lacoste putting Algiers under military control in January 1957 and instigating the campaign of torture and state terrorism that is commonly known as the Battle of Algiers. On 13 May 1958 the generals in Algiers encouraged demonstrations led by the *ultras* that precipitated the collapse of the beleaguered Fourth Republic: under the threat of a coup, General de Gaulle returned to power to preside over the decolonization of Algeria.

Algiers is made up of two parts: the old city, the Casbah, with its narrow and winding streets overlooking the bay of Algiers, was chiefly built by the Turks as a fortress in the sixteenth century; the modern section of the city, on the other hand, was built by the French to accommodate European settlers. After Algeria won its independence in 1962, most of those settlers left the city and returned to Europe. Independence had a major impact on the population of the city. The departure of the *pieds noirs* (French settlers) encouraged a rural exodus that brought masses of hitherto dispossessed *fellahs* into the city, hoping to improve their standard of living, as well as internal migration from other parts of the country. This galloping population growth meant that the city had expanded to accommodate over a million people by 1970; by 1987 its population had risen to 1.7 million, and by 2000 to 4.4 million. Overcrowding became one of the major problems for the city, whose main districts include Birmandreis, Bologhine, Bouzaréa, el-Biar, el-Harrach, Hussein Dey and Kouba.

The port of Algiers was of great strategic importance to France's colonization of Algeria and its neighbors Tunisia and Morocco, particularly for France's trade with its colony. Wine, citrus fruits, and raw materials for French industry such as iron ore and phosphates were exported from Algiers to mainland France. By the end of the century, the port was still a very important refueling station in the Mediterranean, and vital to the economic life of post-colonial Algeria. In addition, trade relies on the Dar-el-Beida airport, situated approximately eighteen kilometers from the city center, and on the rail network that connects Algiers to the rest of the country.

Culturally, the city has given its name to two major literary movements: Algérianisme, founded by Louis Bertrand, Robert Randau, Jean Pomier, and Louis Lecoq in 1921, and the Ecole d'Alger (Algerian School), founded by Audisio and Albert Camus in 1935. Camus himself achieved international acclaim for fiction and philosophical writings on the absurd, winning the 1957 Nobel Prize for Literature. Algeria's main cultural institutions include the University of Algiers (one of the major universities in Algeria), the National Library, and the mosques of Sidi Abel-Rahman and Ketchaoua.

Further reading

Çelik, Z. (1997) *Urban Forms and Colonial Confrontations: Algiers under French Rule*, Berkeley: University of California Press.

AZZEDINE HADDOUR

anglophone Africa

Anglophone Africa refers to those countries that were part of the British colonial empire and have continued to use the English language locally and internationally for official and popular communication. In the main, the African elites who took over from the colonists after independence maintained their commitment to English as an official language.

By the end of the **First World War**, Britain was in control of two territories in northern Africa (Egypt and Sudan), four in Eastern Africa (Kenya, Somalia, Uganda, and Tanzania), four in West Africa (Nigeria, Ghana, Gambia, and Sierra Leone), and six in **Southern Africa** (Malawi, Zambia, Zimbabwe, Botswana, Lesotho, and Swaziland). Some were administered as colonies, others as protectorates, and yet others by chartered companies. Despite the differences, the colonial mission was to control the colonies for the benefit of the imperial metropole using local administrative functionaries, whether traditional rulers or the new Western-educated elite. The role of the latter became important as they grew in numbers and political influence through the activities of the **nationalist movements**.

The interwar period witnessed more determined efforts by the colonial governments to expand education in the British colonies. Previously education had largely been left to the Christian missionaries. This was also a period that saw the growth of African nationalism, buoyed up by the ravages of the **Great Depression** and the **Second World War**. Britain emerged from the war much weaker than before and, soon after, the demise of its empire in Asia began with the independence of India and Pakistan in 1947. In the British African colonies, frustrated ex-servicemen played an important role in the gathering storms of anti-colonial struggle. They had shed much of their high regard for whiteness and European superiority during the war, and had expected to be generously compensated, as a group and for their colonies, economically and politically. The language of "self-determination" or the right to self-governance, fostered by the United Nations, gave the nationalists an international platform to air their demands. **Decolonization** began eleven years after the war, with the independence of Sudan in 1956, followed by Ghana a year later. The majority of British African colonies gained their independence in the early 1960s, except for the remaining settler colonies in Southern Africa which gained their independence later.

After independence, the shared colonial experiences of British Africa created a unique anglophone identity, despite the fact that many nations dissolved the Westminister parliamentary model in favor of one-party governments. Initially the new African governments maintained strong economic links with Britain, which remained a major market for their exports and source of imports, and whose companies dominated agricultural and industrial investment and production. Indeed, for many years the currencies of many British ex-colonies were linked to the British pound, although these monetary ties were severed much quicker than was the case in **francophone Africa**. An important institution in the maintenance of linkages between Britain and many of its former African colonies was the **Commonwealth**. Also, the educational systems in most of the newly independent countries retained their British character. Above all, English was retained as the official language, which gave these countries a sense of collective identity and distinguished them from francophone and **lusophone Africa**.

English, although the official language of fewer countries than French, became the most widely spoken language in Africa. It was the language spoken in some of Africa's largest countries, both those that had been British colonies – Nigeria, Sudan, Egypt, and South Africa – and those that had not – Ethiopia. English also spread to other countries that had not been part of the British empire: for example, lusophone Mozambique, which is surrounded by anglophone countries, or francophone Rwanda, which is tied to anglophone Uganda. The spread of English was linked to its international supremacy, enhanced by the processes of globalization, including structural adjustment programs, whose liberalization and privatization of education reinforced the exclusion of the poor and the empowerment of cosmopolitan middle-class elites. Despite its rapid spread, English encountered several obstacles. There were the indigenization efforts in countries like Tanzania, where emphasis was put on Swahili, and in Egypt and Sudan, which opted for Arabic. There was also the increased legitimization of pidgin and creole, especially in West Africa, which reduced the domains of standard English.

Ali Mazrui and Alamin Mazrui (1998) distinguish four categories of countries in relation to the use of English. In the first group, English is the language of both society and the state, as in the anglophone Caribbean countries. There were no such countries in Africa. The majority of anglophone African countries belonged to the second group, in which English was the language of the state but not of society. The third category is where English was neither the language of the state nor of society, but was used only for specialized purposes, as in Mozambique, or had been jettisoned in favor of local languages, such as in Sudan and Somalia. The final category consists of those countries that rely mainly on other world languages, such as French. The spread of English both enriched and undermined many indigenous languages, enriching them through loan words and undermining them by restricting the domains of their use, especially marginalizing them in public life and educational systems. In so far as English was restricted to the elite, the majority of the population were shut out from national discourse, which had grave consequences for democracy and development.

Besides English and the Commonwealth, anglophone countries also shared concerns about the nature of relations with the **European Union**, and, more importantly, the **international financial institutions** and the developmental challenges of **debt crises**, promoting **regional integration** and effective systems of governance. These problems were of course not confined to the anglophone countries, but there were institutions and discourses concerning them that had an anglophone accent.

References and further reading

Gifford, P. and Louis, W.R. (1988) *Decolonization and African Independence: The Transfers of Power, 1960–1980*, New Haven: Yale University Press.

Mazrui, A.A. and Mazrui, A.M. (1998) *The Power of Babel: Language and Governance in the African Experience*, Oxford: James Currey.

PETER P. JONES

Angola

Angola, named after the ancient Mbundu state of Ngola, is the seventh largest country in Africa, with a total area of 1,246,700 square kilometers. It is bordered by **Namibia**, **Zambia**, **Congo**, and **Democratic Republic of Congo**. By 2000 it had an estimated population of 13.1 million, divided into several ethnic groups, the most populous being the Ovimbundu (37 percent), Kimbundu (25 percent), and Bakongo (13 percent). Afro-Portuguese and Europeans respectively constituted roughly 2 and 1 percent of the population. The main livelihood for 85 percent of the population was still agriculture, which accounted for only 12 percent of the gross domestic product. The principal exports were petroleum and diamonds, while other exports included fish, timber, sugarcane, coffee, cotton, and sisal. Although rich in natural resources, Angola's economy was in disarray due the continuous warfare that has plagued the country from 1961.

Angola's history in the first half of the twentieth century was marked by the imposition of ever-increasing Portuguese military and economic control of the colony. In order to maintain its claims over the entire area, Portugal spent the first two decades conducting campaigns of military conquest and promoting white settlement in the interior. The Benguela Railway and some new towns followed in the wake of military colonization, but the Portuguese were never able sustain Angola with an adequate settler population or capital to develop its economy. In 1932 Portugal became a fascist dictatorship under António Salazar, who sought to integrate Angola into the Portuguese economy. Despite new financial policies, substantial economic growth in Angola did not occur until after the Second World War when higher coffee prices brought wealth to the colony's plantations. Salazar's racial politics legally divided the vast majority of indigenous Angolans (called *indíginas*) from *assimilados* (Africans or mixed-race Afro-Portuguese who spoke Portuguese and adopted Portuguese customs). Harsh laws forced *indíginas* to carry identification cards and subjected them to forced labor, while similar laws limited the economic advancement of *assimilados* in the colonial system.

Resentment of these policies became endemic and the period from 1961 to 1975 was marked by the liberation struggles of three competing nationalist movements. The first two movements were formed when a number of incipient liberation groups led by urban *assimilados* merged together to form the MPLA (Popular Movement for the Liberation of Angola) in 1956 and the FNLA (National Front for the Liberation of Angola) in 1962. The MPLA had its support base in the Kimbundu region near the capital of Luanda, but moved its headquarters to Conakry in Guinea after the arrest of many of its leaders in 1959. The FNLA drew its support from the Bakongo populations of both Angola and neighboring Zaire, where the organization based its operations. The first large-scale uprisings of the liberation struggle began in 1961 with localized attacks on Portuguese establishments. Despite the heavy-handed military response by Salazar and attempts to stave off future uprisings through an infrastructure development program, violence continued to escalate in the colony and to draw worldwide attention. The MPLA mounted guerrilla incursions from the Congo into the enclave of Cabinda and from Zambia into eastern Angola. In 1966 the former foreign minister of the FNLA, Jonas Savimbi, formed a third nationalist movement called UNITA (National Union for the Total Independence of Angola) based on the support of Angola's largest ethnic group, the Ovimbundu of the central highlands.

The Portuguese increased their army in Angola to 60,000 and resettled more than a million rural Africans into military-controlled villages in an attempt to prevent the spread of insurgency. Yet these resettlement villages caused a significant breakdown in the previously important agricultural sector, which never fully recovered. Military expenditure forced Portugal to open Angola to foreign investment by corporations such as the US-based Gulf Oil. The colonial wars also took a toll on Portugal itself where a military coup in 1974 instituted a new government that met with the nationalist movements and agreed to Angolan independence from 11 November 1975 under a transitional government with representatives from all three liberation movements.

Rather than bringing an end to the conflict, however, this transitional period ushered in a new stage of conflict pressured by **Cold War** politics. Fighting began even before independence and power was never handed over to the transitional government nor to any of the three movements. The United States first funded the pro-West FNLA and then UNITA after the Soviet Union supported MPLA. Realizing their tenuous position relative to the powerful MPLA, the FNLA and UNITA formed an alliance. Later, although the alliance had discredited UNITA in the eyes of many of its supporters, a joint UNITA and South African military force drove north from the South African colony of Namibia and advanced to within 100 kilometers of Luanda. The United States suspended support for UNITA, and 10,000–12,000 Cuban troops helped push them and the South African troops back, establishing the MPLA as the victor of the succession struggle.

Angola was admitted into the United Nations in December 1976, but its development plans were hampered by internal factional disputes and continued warfare against UNITA and South Africa. The MPLA, under its president Agostinho Neto, formally adopted Marxism–Leninism in 1976, which strengthened its ties to Cuba and the Soviet Union, but also undermined its attempts to revive the agricultural sector of the economy. Angola's communist stance, along with its support of the Namibian independence movement, caused South Africa to launch an undeclared war on Angola that would make conflict a constant part of life in Angola through to the end of the 1980s. South African military aggression began with attacks on a Namibian refugee camp in Angola in 1978 and the bombing of a provincial capital in 1979. Equally as threatening for Angola's hopes of peace, UNITA – with South African training and support – was transformed into a serious military threat and infiltrated the countryside, further disrupting the agricultural sector. President José Eduardo dos Santos, who succeeded Neto in 1979, sought to end the conflict with South Africa through international diplomacy. The United States, troubled by the Soviet and Cuban presence in Angola, entered into negotiations with Angola, Cuba, and South Africa. After a long series of talks, agreements were reached in 1988 that called for Namibian independence from South Africa in 1990, the withdrawal of Cuban troops from Angola, and a UNITA and MPLA peace accord.

Yet the process of national unification, essential for any real development in Angola, would not be achieved in the twentieth century. The government instituted a number of reforms and joined the International Monetary Fund in 1989, but this did not improve the situation of the average citizen. The MPLA voted in its Third Party Congress in December 1990 to institute economic liberalization and a multi-party system, opening the way for negotiations with UNITA. By the end of 1991, dos Santos and Savimbi had signed a peace agreement in Bicesse, Portugal, that was backed by the United States and the Soviet Union. In August 1992, a multi-party democracy was instituted, ushering in the Republic of Angola. Hopes for peace ran high, but after the multi-party elections resulted in a narrow victory for dos Santos in September of that year, Savimbi dismissed the election as a fraud and returned to war. By the following year, UNITA had expanded their territory significantly, although a major military loss at Kuito and sanctions against arms and fuel trade with UNITA by the United Nations would later put UNITA back on the defensive. The ongoing conflict, with its widespread use of land mines, continued to contribute to the deterioration of agricultural production. Moreover, the United Nations estimated that 1,000 people were dying each day, often from starvation and disease.

A second attempt at peace was initiated in 1994 with the signing of the Lusaka Protocol, which agreed to a ceasefire, the inclusion of UNITA in the national government, the demobilization of UNITA troops, and the establishment of UN peacekeeping forces. The implementation was far behind schedule in 1996, when Angola's oil reserves were expanded with the discovery of new offshore oilfields. In 1997 UNITA had joined a Government of Unity and National Reconciliation, but Savimbi avoided the capital and small-scale skirmishes continued. By 1998 the war had resumed, with both sides playing an active role in conflicts in the Democratic Republic of Congo. The MPLA suspended the coalition government, while a splinter group, UNITA Renovada, split off from Savimbi. Yet Savimbi's UNITA retained control over substantial production of diamonds and was able to reassert control of over much of the countryside. In 1999 the government made significant military advances, taking back Andulo and Bailundu, the main cities under UNITA control. The United Nations pulled out its mission in the same year and the twentieth century closed with warfare continuing to disrupt the hopes of prosperity for this potentially wealthy country. But following the death of Jonas Savimbi, the UNITA leader who was killed by government soldiers in February 2002, Angola appears to be heading for a new era of peace.

Further reading

Bender, G.J. (1980) *Angola Under the Portuguese: The Myth and the Reality*, Berkeley: California University Press.

Hodges, T. (1987) *Angola to the 1990s: The Potential for Recovery*, New York: Economist Publications.

T.J. DESCH-OBI

Antananarivo, Madagascar

At the beginning of the twentieth century, Antananarivo, the capital of **Madagascar** and its largest city, was occupied by the French. Its population was 75,000, which had increased to 95,000 by 1911. The city was built on a dozen steep slopes. The former residence of the Merina royal family (the Merina were the largest ethnic group in the capital) was located at the top of the slopes, below which were the administrative, financial, and commercial districts. During colonial rule, the dominance of the capital was evident in the concentration there of economic, educational, and administrative bureaucracies, as well as the country's transportation system. Railroads connected Antananarivo with the country's chief port, Toamasina. Antananarivo's economy, controlled by French firms and closely integrated with France's economy, concentrated on the export of agricultural products – vanilla, coffee, sugarcane, cloves, and cocoa.

The city's social and cultural institutions during the colonial period illustrated the influence of the French and the Catholic Church, and the emergence of new social classes. Those who had converted to Christianity, learned to speak French, attended Western missionary schools, and adopted French cultural habits were members of the elite, while those who had not were considered members of the urban lower class. However, the Malayo-Indonesian culture of the majority population was evident throughout the city in the forms of language and cultural tradition. Most Malagasy maintain close ties between the living and the dead, and ancestral tombs were integral to their daily lives.

During the struggle for independence following the Second World War, Antananarivo served as a base for the nationalist movement led by the Independence Congress Party of Madagascar whose members were largely recruited from the burgeoning middle class.

Following Madagascar's independence in 1960, the French presence remained glaringly obvious. In the 1960s and 1970s Antananarivo experienced rapid population growth as landless people fled the depressed rural areas and flocked to the capital in search of employment and other amenities. Since the city did not have the economic, social, and educational capacity to accommodate new arrivals, many of them were forced, along with the working poor, into slum areas where conditions were rough and difficult.

Antananarivo continued to be the center of political developments in the 1970s. Intellectuals and students intensified their criticism of the country's structure of government, economic disparities, and neo-colonial relationship with France, which was evident at the University of Madagascar itself where the bulk of the faculty was French, instruction was in French, and the students were awarded French, not Malagasy, degrees. Antananarivo and its educational institutions played a very influential role in the uprisings that resulted in President Tsiranana being ousted in 1972. The uprisings started as student strikes, but were supported by protests from workers, the unemployed, the churches, and even by some members of the ruling party.

During the 1970s and 1980s Antananarivo was the center of political activity under President Didier Ratsiraka who practiced his own version of Marxist socialism. Political and social unrest continued in the capital into the 1990s as multiparty democratic reforms were introduced and a structural adjustment program, demanded by the International Monetary Fund and World Bank, was instituted. Although Antananarivo was still suffering from many economic ills by the end of the twentieth century, it was the country's main industrial center: meat, beverages, textiles, and sugar were the main commodities produced there, along with petroleum refining. It also remained the country's main urban center, with a population of 1.5 million at the end of the century.

Further reading:

Covell, M. (1987) *Madagascar: Politics, Economics, and Society*, London: Frances Pinter.

CASSANDRA RACHEL VENEY

Arab Maghreb Union

Algeria, **Libya**, **Mauritania**, **Morocco**, and **Tunisia** established the Arab Maghreb Union (AMU) in 1989, bringing into existence the long-held dream of Maghreb integration. These North African countries extend over 4,800 kilometers from the Atlantic Ocean to Egypt, with a population over sixty million people. In 1989 their collective gross domestic product exceeded US$100 billion, not to mention US$40 billion in foreign trade. Although these states vary in terms of size, population, natural resources, and political regimes, they share a common heritage in terms of culture, language, religion, and history. They are all former colonies, predominantly Arabic-speaking and Muslim, and their populations are a mixture of Arab majority and Amazigh minority.

Several economic and political factors gave birth to the AMU. Economically, the five Maghreb states faced tremendous economic crises in the 1980s due to drought and sharp drops in prices for their prime export minerals. The results were sky-rocketing levels of unemployment and external debt in all of these states. Furthermore, they had to face the repercussions of the enlargement of the European Economic Community southwards to include Spain and Portugal, the two most important European trade partners of the Maghreb states. Politically, the AMU was meant to provide a framework to settle several inter-Maghreb conflicts, the foremost of which was over the Western Sahara. This particular dispute exploded in an open war in 1975–6 that engulfed three Maghreb states and had since become a determining factor in their bilateral relations. Indeed, the establishment of the AMU was a result of both Algeria's and Morocco's acceptance of the **United Nations** peace plan in the Western Sahara. Moreover, the AMU provided a counterbalance to **Egypt** returning to the Arab fold in the late 1980s and becoming involved in another Arab supraregional organization, the Arab Cooperation Council. Equally important was the rise of several Islamic movements in the Maghreb countries which posed a real political challenge to their regimes. The AMU was implicitly meant to facilitate security cooperation between these regimes.

Therefore, the heads of the Maghreb states formed the AMU by signing the Marrakesh Treaty. Its aims were to foster economic development and increase trade among their countries by allowing the free movement of goods, services, labor, and capital. The declared Sahrawi Arab Democratic Republic was excluded, thanks to King Hassan's efforts. The AMU permanent apparatuses were established at the fourth summit meeting in September 1991. They included the presidential council, which was to meet annually; the parliament or consultative council, which comprised twenty representatives of each state; the judicial organ, which was to interpret the treaty; the investment and foreign trade bank; the Maghreb University and Academy of Science; and the general secretariat, based in **Rabat**. By 2000 there had been only one secretary-general, the Tunisian Muhammad Amamou, who was charged with supervising the follow-up and specialized committees.

However, through the 1990s the AMU achieved few of its political and none of its economic goals. From a political perspective, each Maghreb state maintained its own foreign policy on the basis of national interest. Consequently, the five Maghreb states had five different positions during the 1990 Arab Summit that addressed the Iraqi invasion of Kuwait and American deployment of troops in Saudi Arabia. The 1992 UN sanctions imposed on Libya were another severe test of the AMU during its formative years. The four other AMU members supported Libya vocally, but preferred to abide by the Security Council resolution. Furthermore, the Western Sahara issue persisted as a stumbling block for inter-Maghreb cooperation, especially since Morocco delayed the UN-proposed referendum and Algeria renewed its support of the independent Sahrawi movement, POLISARIO. Perhaps the only political achievement of the AMU were the security arrangements to crack down on politically active Islamic movements. For instance, Algeria deported the leader of the major Tunisian Islamic movement and Morocco handed Algeria many of its militants. While the presidential council did not meet after 1994, the interior ministers met frequently and concluded several agreements. The result was a suppression of the Tunisian and, to lesser extent, Moroccan Islamic movements, and total collaboration with the military-backed Algerian regime that brought the 1991 democratic elections to a violent halt after the Islamic Salvation Front had won a decisive victory. However, when Algeria's internal political violence crossed the Moroccan border in 1994, relations between the two countries became very strained and the border was closed.

From an economic perspective, the AMU did very little to achieve the goal of economic integration. Although the 1990 Maghreb summit decided to implement a customs union by 1995, the union did not materialize due to the many political disagreements between the Maghreb states. Moreover, the AMU failed to provide a framework for foreign-policy coordination that ideally might have resulted in fair trans-Mediterranean relations. Instead, after a few European–Maghreb meetings, individual Maghreb states negotiated separately with their giant European counterpart, the **European Union**, thereafter concluding separate, arguably unfair, Mediterranean partnership agreements with Tunisia and Morocco in 1995. Libya had been excluded from the very start, but negotiations between the European Union and Algeria were still ongoing by 2000.

Thus the AMU was dormant from the mid-1990s and its members turned away from it, preferring other regional organizations or bilateral relations. Mauritania, Algeria, and Tunisia strengthened their relations for a while, but failed to implement the Treaty of Fraternity and Concord they had signed in 1983, with the establishment of full diplomatic relations between Mauritania and Israel in 1999 finally sinking these efforts. By contrast, Libya turned southwards, establishing the Community of Sahel-Saharan States (COMESSA) in 1998, which Tunisia and Morocco joined a year later. Ironically, it was Egypt that arranged a Maghreb summit in April 2000, during the first European–African summit, but the attempt to revive the AMU failed.

See also: Islamic reform movements; League of Arab States; regional integration

Further reading

Mezran, K. (1998) "Maghribi Foreign Policies and the Internal Security Dimension," *The Journal of North African Studies* 3, 1: 2–24.

Zoubir, Y.H. (2000) "Algerian–Moroccan Relations and their Impact on Maghribi Integration," *The Journal of North African Studies* 5, 3: 43–74.

RIHAM A. KHAFAGY

Arabic

The spread of Arabic in East and West Africa

After the Arab conquest of Egypt in AD 642, subsequent waves of Arab migrants, such as the Banu Hilal tribes in the eleventh century, moved from Egypt to North Africa under the pressure of the Fatimid rulers. From there, Arabic spread southward along the Atlantic coast from Morocco into Mauritania and Mali. As a result, the variety of Arabic spoken in Mali is the same as the Hassaniyya Arabic spoken in Mauritania. In areas where Arabs conducted trade, yet never settled in significant numbers, their language did not replace indigenous languages; instead Arabic-based pidgins and creoles evolved. For example, under the reign of Mohammed Ali in Egypt (at the turn of the nineteenth century) trade and military endeavors that involved recruiting indigenous people resulted in the emergence of Ki-Nubi, an Arabic-based pidgin that was later creolized. Ki-Nubi is now spoken in the Sudan, Kenya, and Uganda, and it was also spoken in Tanzania and Somalia. Under similar circumstances Juba Arabic emerged as a pidgin in the south of Sudan to become the lingua franca of the region. However, Juba Arabic was not only creolized, but also "normalized" as a dialect of Arabic because of its continuous contact with local dialects of Arabic in northern Sudan.

The strong commercial ties between eastern Arabia and **East Africa**, the establishment of the Omani Dynasty in Zanzibar, and the wide spread of the Islamic tradition enhanced the development of cultural and trade centers along the African coast between Somalia and Mozambique. As a result, Arabic spread widely in this region and its influence on indigenous languages, especially Swahili, was quite pronounced. In fact, a literary tradition of Swahili was developed using the Arabic script.

The spread of Arabic was not restricted to eastern Africa. It also moved westward across the continent along the savanna belt into Chad, Cameroon, Senegal, Niger, and Nigeria. For example, Turku was an Arabic-based pidgin that evolved in Chad and was later replaced by another variety of Arabic that is now spoken by 300,000 people. In fact, Arabic has become the lingua franca of today's Chad. Today, Africa is home to the largest Arabic-speaking population – far surpassing the Arabian Peninsula, the place where the language originated.

Diglossia

In the Arab countries of **North Africa**, where Arabs migrated and settled in significant numbers, there are two varieties of Arabic: standard or classical Arabic and colloquial or vernacular Arabic. The two varieties differ in their phonological, morphological, lexical, and syntactic systems. The former is written and is used in formal contexts such as education, religious services, and administration, as well as for official, legal, and business documents. It is learnt through formal education in schools. The latter, which varies from one country to another and from one locality to another within a single country, is the spoken variety. It is learnt at home and is considered the native language. While there is a codified script for writing standard Arabic, there is no standardized writing system for the spoken dialects. Music and literature can be in either variety, though the colloquial predominates in popular music and the standard in written literary works.

When Arabic was introduced into North Africa, there were two major languages in the area: Amazigh in the Maghreb (as well as parts of Egypt) and Coptic in Egypt, in addition to numerous languages in the Sudan. All these languages came under pressure as Arabic spread. Coptic eventually gave way to Arabic, and by the fourteenth century it had become a liturgical language for the Coptic community in Egypt. Amazigh, however, still survives, particularly in Morocco and Algeria.

However, it is rare now to find a monolingual Amazigh speaker: most Amazigh speakers also speak the local colloquial variety and have some proficiency in standard Arabic. The status of Amazigh, in particular, has been a source of tension in Algeria and Morocco. By 2000 Amazigh was not considered an official language and was not taught in schools, though there were plans to do so in both countries due to protests from the Amazigh-speaking communities. Amazigh speakers have long aspired to a more prominent role for Amazigh, but this aspiration has been frustrated by opposition from the Arabic nationalist camp, which views it as a threat to the Arab identity of the Maghreb, and also from the religious camp, which views it as a way to question the supremacy of the Arabic language – the language of Islam. Of course the proponents of Amazigh respond by saying that several other Muslim countries have other official languages (Iran, Senegal, Indonesia, Pakistan, and so on).

Arabic has also been in confrontation with the European languages brought by colonial powers such as French (in the Maghreb), Spanish (northern Morocco), and English (Egypt and Sudan). English did not diminish the status of Arabic in Egypt, mainly because education was limited to a bourgeois elite and because of the active role in maintaining Arabic that was played by al-Azhar religious university in Cairo and by religious schools (*kuttaab*) in most villages. On the other hand, the situation is acute in the Maghreb. France introduced new education and administrative systems entirely in French. Arabic was relegated to the religious and Islamic legal spheres. As the countries gained independence in the late 1950s and early 1960s, Arabization became one of the national goals. This has been a difficult process. While it has proved relatively easy to Arabize the administration, it has proven difficult to do so in the education system, particularly in the sciences where French still dominates. This situation has also been the source of tension between those who see the continuing presence of French as a challenge to Arab identity and a sign of dependence on the old colonial powers and those who see it as a necessary means for development and communication with the rest of the world, particularly the West.

Further reading

Owens, J. (2000) *Arabic as a Minority Language*, New York: Mouton de Gruyter.

Versteegh, K. (2001) *The Arabic Language*, Edinburgh: Edinburgh University Press.

ELABBAS BENMAMOUN
MUSTAFA A. MUGHAZY

architecture

The subject of African architecture has received very little scholarly attention in comparison with other forms of African art, such as sculpture, music, and dance. However, the design and construction of public buildings, homes, places of worship, towns, and cities play an important role in determining how people live and interact within their environment. More than simply providing shelter, architecture is a means of political, social, economic, and spiritual communication. African architecture eludes generalization, owing to the variety of climates, landscapes, settlement patterns, religions, and cultures that dictate how, where, and why structures are built in different parts of the continent. However complex the nature of twentieth-century African architecture, the resulting character of modern buildings and urban areas in Africa may be attributed to what Ali Mazrui (1986) calls the "triple heritage" of mixed techniques, motifs, and values influenced by Islamic, Western, and indigenous cultures.

At the start of the twentieth century, colonial urban planning policy set the course for architectural projects in Africa. Building styles and their arrangements, as well as the commitment to putting infrastructure into place, derived from the attitudes and objectives of the European colonial power in question. Though the colonial architecture first created by Europeans in Africa may have superficially taken into account the local climate, cultural practices, and indigenous building techniques in developing a practical style, most primarily sought to recreate the colonial cities in their own image.

From the fifteenth century, the Portuguese were active in the construction of forts and military outposts along the western coast from **Ghana** to

Angola, thereby facilitating their trade in gold and slaves, but they executed little in the way of urban planning and construction in the nineteenth and twentieth centuries. Though a few urban areas, such as Lobito in Angola (founded in 1913), were the focus of Portuguese industrialization and commercial activity, the resulting prosperous downtown areas were occupied primarily by Portuguese until independence in 1975. The outlying hill regions that surround Lobito and other cities were home to squatter camps and shantytowns that reflect the lack of provision made for residential housing and urban planning. The Portuguese were, however, active in the construction of churches in association with Christian, especially Jesuit, missions. These churches are marked by plain, unelaborated surfaces influenced by seventeenth-century Italian designs, which may be found in nearly every city along the Angolan coast. In the old port city of **Luanda**, the presence of towering historic churches constructed of masonry, such as the Jesuit Cathedral of Luanda (1628), stand in marked contrast to the traditional rectangular family dwellings of Angolan fishermen. These structures line the banks of the rivers and are constructed of palm-frond mats netted together, frequently with the roof reinforced by a sheet of aluminum, demonstrating the coexistence of both European and indigenous building traditions.

In contrast to the Portuguese, the English initially set up temporary residences, schools, and public buildings to serve their commercial ventures in colonies in Nigeria, Sierra Leone, and Ghana. These temporary structures recreated the Victorian houses and country villages with formal gardens that were familiar to the British. Concentrated efforts at infrastructural planning and **urbanization** by the British were focused on strategic regions, such as **Accra**. The British colonial government built public structures, such as the Post Office and the Parliament building, that used Classical influences and Renaissance styles based on English models. These buildings were constructed to assert the authority of the British colonial power, both to the indigenous population and to other colonial powers.

Unlike the planning that took place at Accra, the sprawling city of **Lagos**, one of the largest cities in all of Africa with an estimated population of 13.5 million in 2000, urbanized without formal British planning. The landscape of Lagos, which is surrounded by lagoons and marshes, made it difficult to develop; in addition the colonial administrators focused infrastructural projects on areas occupied by Europeans, making difficult the coordination of roads and drainage systems between various areas of the city at different stages of development. British building projects in Lagos during the early part of the twentieth century included gothic churches and Renaissance- and Elizabethan-style government structures. But during the oil boom of the 1970s, Lagos experienced rapid urbanization. Among the numerous building projects initiated by the independent Nigerian government were a national theater and high-rise office buildings for the newly created federal bureaucracy, mostly in the global modernist style. With little formal urban plan, the districts of Lagos are extremely disjointed and the swelling population has created severe traffic congestion, housing shortages, and the development of some of the worst slums on the continent.

In their more permanent settlements in South Africa, the English invested more resources and materials in the construction of commercial buildings, religious buildings, and parks. These Classical and Gothic designs remain architectural landmarks to this day. Dutch settlers also had a significant impact on South African architecture. The architecture of South Africa is thus particularly Western in style, albeit with that syncretism found in other areas of the continent. For example, the so-called "Cape Dutch" style of house that has become part of the South African architectural vernacular, originated in Europe. There it had been designed to fit European social and meteorological conditions, but it was slowly adapted to the different social and climatic conditions of South Africa. The thick walls and whitewashed plaster exterior were adapted over time to serve as protection against the heat, but the steeply pitched roof, originally designed to shed snow, was somewhat unnecessarily retained. The decorative gables, sometimes excessively exaggerated, became a method of expressing wealth and prosperity among Dutch settlers.

Despite the Cape Dutch and other vernacular styles, the unique architecture of South Africa in the twentieth century is defined by apartheid. During the course of the twentieth century, land was divided and distributed unevenly on the basis of race, and Africans were relegated and relocated to barren rural homelands based on traditional ethnic affiliations, as well as being subjected to urban housing relocation programs based on racial segregation. The racial zoning of urban spaces and residential communities had an enormous impact on urban growth, people's access to space, health and sanitation, social interaction, and the prevalence of crime and violence, demonstrating the depth to which the architectural use of space can shape political, economic, and social relationships.

The French policy of assimilation toward their colonies was manifest in their architecture and the urban development of cities such as **Dakar** and Casablanca. In an effort to make the colonies an extension of France, urban centers constructed by French architects and planners were fashioned in the image of Paris. Plans for the new African cities were even considered to be experimental testing grounds for strategies to address urban and social problems, such as overcrowding and pollution, that were being experienced in France. Many buildings constructed by the French in colonial cities retain essentially European plans and concepts, but employ motifs and stylistic elements derived from Islamic architecture. The application of such decorative elements and Islamic symbols, seen particularly on public buildings and most frequently in North Africa, is referred to as "Arabisance." French and Swiss architects were particularly active in North Africa. Among them was le Corbusier, who concentrated a number of his architectural activities in Algeria in an attempt to solve urban housing problems. A leader in architectural thinking, le Corbusier's ideas of the house as a machine and of a city for three million people were very influential in the growth and planning of twentieth-century cities in Africa, though he gave little thought to the regional traditions or cultural background of the people that he designed for.

The twentieth-century trend toward urbanism in Africa, initiated by colonialism and driven by industrialization, has vast implications for the division of space and for the style of buildings, as well as associated political, sociocultural, and economic effects. While the problematic relationship between architecture and industrialization may be considered universal, dominating trends in architectural thinking in both the West and the developing world, it has caused particular difficulties in Africa. Up until the **Second World War**, urban and infrastructure planning in the colonies had been managed by foreign architects and builders using primarily imported resources and materials from the industrialized colonial powers. In the postwar period of independence, leaders of many new African countries were confronted with the task of building new capitals, schools, and hospitals, sometimes with no skilled builders or architects to do the work. Some students from colonized countries who studied architecture in England or France returned to their countries after independence to help with the effort of nation building. However, they were schooled in a Western vocabulary and had difficulty stylistically connecting with their own traditions in such a way as to give architectural identity to the emerging nations. Moreover, they faced the additional obstacle of being unable to realize intended designs for modern building projects because of the lack of an industrial base that could produce the required manufactured building components.

Despite the financial and developmental challenges confronting African nations with regard to building projects, some of the most impressive and largest-scale feats of architecture in the world were accomplished in Africa in the latter part of the twentieth century. The King Hassan Mosque in Casablanca, Morocco, and Our Lady of Peace Basilica in Yamoussoukro, Côte d'Ivoire, are good examples. The King Hassan Mosque was completed in 1993 at a cost of US$1 billion. It occupies 22.5 acres of land, and accommodates 25,000 worshipers inside and a further 80,000 on the platform outside. Using 300,000 square meters of concrete, 40,000 tons of steel, 250,000 tons of Moroccan marble, and 30,000 square meters of plaster, the gigantic structure boasts the tallest minaret in the world, reaching 200 meters. Our Lady of Peace Basilica was built over three years and completed in 1990. It is the second largest church building in the world, after the Vatican. Though the official government cost for the basilica is US$200 million, unofficial estimates range from US$500–900 million. Planned by President Houphouët-Boigny as a gift to the Vatican, Our Lady of Peace measures 149 meters in height and can hold 7,000 seated people with enough room for 14,000 to stand. It contains 7,432 square meters of glass, the most ever used in a church, and the entire cathedral is air-conditioned, costing nearly US$10 million annually to maintain. The church has been seen as a symbol of excess and political mismanagement, as only 11 percent of Ivoiriens are Catholic; in fact, the majority are Muslim.

Though the skylines of international cities such as Nairobi, Lagos, Abidjan, Johannesburg, Accra, and Cairo are dominated by Western-style architecture, in the last three decades of the twentieth century attention has shifted to consider more traditional forms of African construction when undertaking building projects. Architects practicing in Africa have given more serious thought to so-called "tropical architecture," using materials and building techniques that allow for greater temperature control and better ventilation; many of these have been in use by Africans for centuries. These techniques include using an east–west layout for buildings, with the long side of the building facing south; creating transverse ventilation of rooms that are accessible from an outside space; using a double layer for roofs; and using light exterior colors to reduce heat absorption. Another successful trend in recent African building projects concerns the application of community planning initiatives. An example of such a project is the Yaama Mosque in Tahoua, Niger. Built over a twenty-year period from 1962, the mosque was a project undertaken by the whole village to which everyone made a contribution, from the landowner to the people who carried water, gathered wood, and made sun-dried mud bricks. Using traditional and adapted methods, the mosque was renovated and expanded so that it remained the architectural and spiritual center of the village.

The Yaama Mosque received the 1986 Aga Khan award for community building projects. Whereas many African architects have been trained in predominantly Western traditions, international recognition of architects and communities collaborating on buildings in regional vernacular style, sensitive to cultural and community needs, will ensure the preservation and application of valuable knowledge in both urban and rural environments.

References and further reading

Elleh, N. (1997) *African Architecture: Evolution and Transformation*, New York: McGraw Hill.

Mazrui, A. (1986) *The Africans: A Triple Heritage*, Boston: Little Brown.

NICOLE HAWKES

Asmara, Eritrea

Since 1993 Asmara has been the capital of independent **Eritrea**, with a population estimated at about 400,000 in 2000. It is located at the center of the Eritrean plateau, at an elevation of 2,325 meters. The name "Asmara" indicates the joining of four villages, an event that is supposed to have happened around 1500; the united village was then known as *arba'ete asmera*, meaning "four that united."

Asmara was a village with only a few thousand residents until the Italians, who had arrived in 1890, made it the capital of their new colony in 1900. Over the 1930s the population of the town grew by 30 percent per year, reaching 98,000 by the end of the decade; more than half of these inhabitants – 53,000 people – were Italian. When the Italians established their East Africa Empire, Asmara rapidly became the leading city in Italian East Africa. Several parts of Asmara were established as residential areas for different Italian military units, bearing the names of either the battalions who lived there or their commanders. Gradually, however, they became residences for the growing civilian and professional Italian population. Separate localities were also built for black soldiers, again with names that described their populations. When apartheid was introduced in the city in 1936, a strict separation was established between white and black residential areas, known respectively as *nazionali* and *indigeni*. The local population was prohibited from entering Campo Cintato, the part of the city where most Italians lived, and sexual relations between blacks and whites were declared illegal.

With the defeat of Italy in East Africa, the Italian population decreased considerably, but under British rule (1941–51) Asmara witnessed another phase of expansion. For the first couple of years the city's role as a point of departure for the Allied forces in their campaign against Nazi Germany and Fascist Italy led to hectic economic activity and thereby to further growth for the city. When Ethiopia annexed Eritrea in 1952, however, the growth of the city was reversed. Many firms, businesses, and industries were ordered to move to central Ethiopia. Investment slowly died down, no new infrastructure was built, and the existing infrastructure was no longer maintained. As the liberation struggle gained pace, Asmara suffered no actual physical damage, but it was further isolated and neglected. This not only held back development, but also meant that basic facilities were left to degenerate. From 1974 to 1991, when the city was ruled by the Dergue, the population of the city was halved.

By 2000 the city still contained some industries, most of which were from the Italian colonial period and in poor condition. These included food processing, dairy products, alcoholic beverages, textiles and clothing, matches, cement, and leather goods. Despite forty years of neglect, the city has kept an Italian flavor. The city's main buildings include the Roman Catholic cathedral (1922), the Grand Mosque (1937), St. Mary's (the main Orthodox Church), the former palace (now the seat of government), the legislative assembly, the municipal building, and Asmara University (founded in 1958, but only gaining university status in 1968). Now a clean and peaceful city, Asmara's beautiful buildings, coffee shops and palm trees still draw visitors.

Further reading

Bondestam, L. (1989) *Eritrea: Med Rätt till Självbestämmande* (Eritrea: With the Right for Self-determination), Uddevalla: Clavis Förlag.

Yosief, I. (1993) *Zanta Ketema Asmera* (History of the City of Asmara), Addis Ababa: Commercial Publishing.

REDIE BEREKETEAB

B

Bamako, Mali

Bamako was a major city during the time of the **Mali** empire. It underwent a transformation in the twentieth century from a walled town on a bank of the Niger River to a major administrative, commercial, and cultural center with a population of more than one million. Trans-Saharan trade gave impetus to the town's early development on the banks of the Niger River, where Moorish traders transferred goods brought by camel from the north to Soninke and Jula merchants who moved them south. In 1883 the French encountered a walled town with 6,000–8,000 inhabitants governed, along with thirty other villages, by the Niare clan. The names of Bamako's central neighborhoods reflect this history: Niarela (the founding Bambara-speaking clan), Touatila (later Tourela or Bagadadji), Dravela (Moorish clans) and Bozola (fisherpeople). By 2000 Bamako was contributing to the global economy, exporting agricultural (cotton and cattle) and cultural (music and film) products to the world at large.

After completion in 1905 of the railroad linking it to Saint-Louis (Senegal) and steamships on the Niger River at Koulikoro to the east, Bamako grew rapidly. The French chose Bamako as capital of the French Sudan in 1908, building an administrative complex. The city's earliest industry was a brickworks. Wolof laborers settled in Ouolofobougou and soldiers in Le Campement. Residents had access to a movie theater, running water and electricity before the First World War. An area settled by unskilled workers was called Kolikotogou ("the hoodlum's place"), yet Bamako remained safe, peaceful, and renowned for its hospitality. Muslim merchants lived in Dar Salam and Medina-Coura. After the First World War, the French added commercial establishments and administrative buildings, a central market, and tree-lined avenues. Innovations dating from the 1920s include Bamako's first radio station, highways linking Bamako to Guinea and Segou, a leprosy hospital, and a training center for crafts.

Conditions for Africans deteriorated during the Second World War, but Bamako's citizens benefited from development projects in the postwar era. The central mosque dates from the 1950s and the first bridge across the Niger, completed in 1957, led to the growth of Badalabougou on the Niger's right bank. The return of migrant workers from Senegal after the break-up of the Mali Federation swelled Bamako's population from 78,000 (1958) to 130,000 (1961). Annual population growth peaked at 10 percent in 1974 during the drought, stabilizing at 4.5 percent in the 1980s and 1990s.

Population growth coincided with degradation of economic conditions and increasing numbers of people living in poverty. Consumers experienced a 50 percent decline in buying power between 1962 and 1982. Imposition of **structural adjustment programs** contributed to the dominance of the informal sector, which absorbed 78 percent of all workers in 1989. Despite a new textile factory, Bamako's modern sector remained small with the government as the principal employer. Since unemployed young people had little alternative but to live at home and put off marriage, economic problems were bringing about changes in family and political life. Youth played a central role in the popular uprising which took place in Bamako in 1991, leading to the establishment of a democratically elected government. Urban amenities built in the 1990s included public monuments, the University of Mali, and a second bridge that eased access to the newer suburbs of Sogoninko, Daoudabougou, Faladie, Niamekor, and Senou (the airport). The influx of newcomers fleeing to Mali from war-torn West African countries contributed to the challenge of providing Bamako's burgeoning population with adequate housing and basic services, such as running water and electricity.

Further reading

Meillassoux, C. (1968) *Urbanization in an African Community. Voluntary Associations in Bamako*, Seattle: University of Washington.

JANE TURRITTIN

Bangui, Central African Republic

Bangui, the capital of the **Central African Republic**, is located on the northern bank of the Oubangui River, one of Africa's longest rivers and the largest tributary of the great Congo River. The city was founded in 1889 as a French military post and named Bangui after the local name for "rapids." Early resistance from the local population was eventually overcome and in 1894 the French declared Oubangui-Chari, the future Central African Republic, a French colony and part of **French Equatorial Africa**. A dozen years later, the picturesque but impoverished post became the administrative center of the new colony. As in much of French Equatorial Africa, the French relied on concession companies, which subjected the population to forced labor and provoked periodic rebellions. This economy of plunder was reflected in Bangui, which remained an urban backwater for much of the colonial period.

It was not until the Second World War that Bangui began to grow rapidly, buoyed up by economic growth fueled by the rise in the prices of the country's main exports – rubber, cotton, coffee, and diamonds – and postwar reforms that extended more rights to Africans and encouraged the colonial government to undertake infrastructural "development" projects to facilitate trade and quell growing African nationalism, dominated by the Union Oubanguienne and the Movement for the Social Evolution of Black Africa.

After independence in 1960, the growth of Bangui accelerated as rural–urban migration increased, the public sector expanded, and light manufacturing industries were established. By 1975 the city's population had increased to 279,800, and it more than doubled to 652,900 in 2001. The manufacturing industry included textiles, food products, beer, shoes, and soap. Perhaps even more vibrant was Bangui's role as a trading and transportation center. Its port handled most of the country's international trade, and the road network that connects the Central African Republic with Cameroon, Chad, and Sudan emanates from the city. Bangui's importance as a social and cultural center also increased, as new national institutions were established and located there, including the University of Bangui.

Despite its growth, Bangui suffered from the political turbulence that afflicted the country and from recurrent recessions hitting the economy from the 1970s due to declining commodity prices and corruption, exacerbated from the 1980s by **structural adjustment programs**. Symbolic of the deepening misfortunes of the country and city was the extravagant coronation in 1977 of Colonel Jean Bedel-Bokassa, who had come to power in a coup in December 1965, as emperor of the renamed Central African Empire. Yet, by the following year, the bankrupt government was unable to pay its civil servants. This and the reduction of school loans, combined with growing discontent against the venal Bokassa dictatorship in general, led to violent protests in the streets of Bangui, culminating in Bokassa being ousted. However, there was little relief either for the country as a whole or for Bangui itself. The city continued to be the site of political conflict and strife, whether in the form of recurrent coups d'etat, or violent protests by the increasingly impoverished residents of the city. For example, in 1996 and 1997 alone there were three army mutinies that ravaged the city. By 2000 much of Bangui's physical infrastructure was in a state of decay and its economy ravaged by unemployment, unpaid wages to civil servants, strikes, and an influx of refugees fleeing conflicts in neighboring countries.

Further reading

O'Toole, T. (1988) "Shantytowns in Bangui, Central African Republic: A Cause for Despair or Creative Possibility?," in R.A. Obudho and C.C. Mhlanga (eds.), *Slum and Squatter Settlements in Sub-Saharan Africa: Toward a Planning Strategy*, New York: Praeger, pp.123–32.

CASSANDRA RACHEL VENEY

Banjul, Gambia

Banjul, the capital of the **Gambia**, had an estimated population of 150,000 in 2000. The population of Banjul Island is composed of a majority of Wolof- and Aku-speaking peoples, although the island got its name from the Mande, who used to fetch a certain type of fiber used to manufacture ropes on the island (*banjul* is the Mande word for "fiber"). The Mande also form the majority of the inhabitants of the Greater Banjul Area.

Together with Serrekunda, Bakau, Fajara, and other parts of what is now known as the Greater Banjul Area, the city gradually absorbed the surrounding villages. By 2000, however, the authority of the Mayor of Banjul was restricted to the part of the city located on Banjul Island, whose population declined from 44,000 in 1983 to 42,000 in 1993 as people moved away from the original city to settle in the Greater Banjul Area. The island, once the seat of the colonial administration, remained the seat of the post-independence government, and boasted the only seaport and main commercial and banking centers in the country.

During the colonial period the city was called Bathurst, after an English lord of the same name. It was changed to Banjul in 1973. Because of its strategic location at the mouth of the River Gambia, European traders and colonial administrators found the city important for both trade and security purposes, especially for the control of traffic in and out of the River Gambia. Banjul Island was linked to the Greater Banjul Area and the western parts of the country by a bridge, and to the north bank of the river and the northern part of Senegal by a regular ferry service. The River Gambia runs through the entire length of the country, itself driving a wedge between the northern and southern parts of Senegal.

From colonial times the economy of Gambia was based on the cultivation of groundnuts for export, and rice and local cereals, as well as fishing and livestock production, for local consumption. After independence, trade and tourism also became important sources of foreign exchange for Gambia, with Banjul dominating both sectors. Most hotels, for example, were located in Banjul. By the 1990s up to 100,000 visitors arrived in good seasons, more than half of whom were from the United Kingdom. The tourist sector employed some 10,000 people, and provided an outlet for locally caught fish, locally grown fruit and vegetables, and local handicrafts. The liberal trade and foreign-exchange regimes of Gambia in the 1960s and 1970s, at a time when neighboring countries were quite protectionist, led to the existence of vibrant cross-border trade between Gambia and her neighbors, much of it departing from Banjul. As border controls were tightened and trade tariffs liberalized in the other countries in the late 1980s and 1990s, this trade lost some of its vigor.

Despite its relatively small size, Banjul remained a very lively city and the center of Gambian cultural life. It boasted one of the first private radio stations in West Africa, Radio Syd, started by a Swedish woman in the late 1960s, and by 2000 it had four other private radio stations broadcasting on the frequency modulation band, as well as government radio and TV stations. The city also had an international airport that handles several charter-flight routes during the tourist season (October to May), and maintained good connections with the cities of **Dakar**, **Freetown**, **Accra**, **Lagos** and London.

Further reading

Deschamps, H. (1975) *Le Sénégal et la Gambie*, Paris: Presses Universitaires de France.

EBRIMA SALL

Belgian Congo *see* Democratic Republic of Congo (known as Congo Free State from 1885 to 1908, the Belgian Congo from 1908 to 1960, Zaire from 1971 to 1997).

Benin

Benin, bordered by **Togo**, **Burkina Faso**, **Niger**, and **Nigeria**, and with a total area of 116,622 square kilometers, had an estimated population of 6.6 million in 2001. Its official capital is Porto Novo, but the *de facto* political and economic capital is **Cotonou**. Benin is almost entirely populated by Africans, comprising forty-two ethnic groups, of which the most populous and influential are the Fon, Adja, Yoruba, and Bariba. There are small minorities of Europeans (mostly expatriates), Lebanese and Indians engaged in the commercial sector. French is the official language, yet Fon and Yoruba are widely spoken in the south, and Nagot, Bariba, and Dendi in the north. By 2000 approximately 50 percent of the population practiced traditional African religion, primarily Vodun, while 30 percent practiced Christianity, and 20 percent practiced Islam. Syncretism was also widely embraced. Benin's literacy rate was approximately 38 percent (just over 50 percent for males and 23 percent for females).

Benin, then known as Dahomey, was colonized by France in the late nineteenth century. By the time the French encroachment began in the 1860s and 1870s, the once powerful kingdom of Dahomey was rent by internal leadership disputes that facilitated the French colonial conquest. Franco-Dahomian relations soured under King Gezo's successors, Glele and Behanzin, who refused to recognize French claims to the port of Cotonou. The French wanted to expand and control the port, and were attempting to send slave labor to Portuguese, Belgian, and German colonies. This had angered many Dahomians, who were already smarting from the effects of a drought. War between Dahomey and France erupted in 1890, and lasted until King Behanzin was captured in 1894 and exiled to Martinique. The French went on to conquer the rest of the country and, in 1904, incorporated Dahomey into French West Africa. But resistance to the French was by no means over. The imposition of taxation and forced labor, reinforced by military conscription during the First World War, led to the outbreak of revolts, beginning in the north before spreading to the south where French rule was more entrenched. In 1923 the protests spread to Porto Novo under the leadership of Islamic religious leaders and the burgeoning Western-educated elite, who complained about the repatriation of wealth from Dahomey to **Dakar**, the capital of French West Africa, as well as about the favoritism shown to French businesses at their expense. The French dominated the colonial export trade, which was based on palm oil and later maize, cotton, cocoa, and groundnuts.

Nationalist politics did not gather momentum until the Second World War. The Union Progressiste Dahoméene (UPD), dominated by the nationalist intelligentsia, attracted many returning ex-servicemen and urban workers. As a result of mounting nationalist pressure, in 1946 Dahomey was granted its own territorial council, as well as representation in the French National Assembly. But the franchise remained limited until ten years later, when the *loi-cadre* was passed, just prior to the territorial assembly elections. It was not until August 1960 that Dahomey gained its political independence from France under the leadership of the UPD, after nearly two years of self-government within the French community.

The first twelve years of independence were riddled with a sequence of military coups, and government changes and instability. The first president, Hubert Maga, was overthrown after only three years in office. In the sixth attempted coup, in 1972, Major Mathieu Kérékou came to power as head of a Marxist–Leninist regime. Kérékou effectively remained in power from 1972 to 1989. The regime consolidated its power around the so-called "revolutionary committees," which conducted disastrous anti-witchcraft campaigns against opponents and rural development programs built around cooperatives, collective farms, and state marketing agencies. But, by the 1980s, there was little to show for state socialism, as the majority of the population remained poor. Poor economic and financial performance, lack of accountability and responsiveness to Beninese and foreign donors, exacerbated by the expulsion of tens of thousands of Beninese from Nigeria and the closure of the Nigerian border led to the collapse of the one-party military authoritarian state machine. Beninese exiles in France, local Beninese civil society, and bilateral and multilateral donors demanded Kérékou abandon Marxist–Leninist principles and pluralize the political system to allow for opposition politics.

In February 1990 a National Conference was held, and a new and more democratic constitution drafted. In 1991 Kérékou lost the presidential elections to Nicephore Soglo, a former World Bank official. Soglo was to be the head of state for five years, but then lost the 1996 and 2001 presidential elections to Kérékou, who had abandoned socialism and now called himself a Christian Democrat. The election results were hotly contested in both 1996 and 2001, amidst allegations of fraud, vote rigging, irregularities, and the return of authoritarianism. In holding the National Conference, drafting a new constitution, and changing government leadership through the electoral process, Benin placed itself in the forefront of the democratization process in Africa, despite the challenges that remained. The 2001 elections even saw, for the first time, a Beninese woman, Marie Elise Gbeho, run for the presidency.

Benin is endowed with small offshore oil deposits, and unexploited high-quality marble, limestone, and timber. In 1982 the country began producing small quantities of oil, but by the close of the twentieth century production had halted. The basis of the economy remained agriculture, yet only 13 percent of Benin's land was arable. Its major crops included cotton, corn, sorghum, cassava, tapioca, yams, beans, rice, palm oil, cocoa, and groundnuts. Cotton brought in 80 percent of the official export receipts and accounted for 40 percent of the gross domestic product. In the 1990s Benin began trying to diversify its economy by developing tourism, expanding the manufacturing industry, and extending international trading relations away from France. The privatization of formerly government-owned commercial and industrial activities led to the expansion of the entrepreneurial class, but poverty was an enduring challenge.

Further reading

Decalo, S. (1995) *Historical Dictionary of Benin*, Lanham: Scarecrow Press.

Robinson, P. (1994) "Democratization: Understanding the Relationship between Regime Change and the Culture of Politics," *African Studies Review* 37, 1: 39–67.

LISA AUBREY

Bissau, Guinea-Bissau

The capital city and principal port of **Guinea-Bissau**, Bissau is located on the north shore of the Gêba River, where the river opens into the Gêba Channel. Bissau gained official status as a city in 1917. Because of its strategic location and natural harbor, it replaced Bolama as the capital of Portuguese Guinea in 1941. The 1991 census estimated Bissau's population to be 197,610, approximately 20 percent of the country's total population.

When Portuguese colonialism began, the area of Bissau was inhabited by the Pepel people, who, together with some neighbors, resisted conquest from 1880 to 1936. In 1908 the Pepel and Balanta nearly succeeded in expelling the Portuguese from the area, but the French navy blocked their efforts. During the colonial period, waves of migrants gradually transformed Bissau into an ethnic mosaic. By 1979 the Pepel constituted only 32 percent of the city's population. Although residents of Bissau speak many languages, Kriolu – a blend of Portuguese and indigenous languages – is most widely spoken. Kriolu's popularity increased during the war of liberation (1963–74), and in 1974 became the most widely spoken language of the newly independent nation of Guinea-Bissau.

Although the war of liberation was fought

almost entirely in the interior, Bissau was the official birthplace of the independence movement. In September 1956 Amilcar Cabral and five others held a clandestine meeting in Bissau at which they founded the Partido Africano da Independência do Guinée e Cabo Verde (African Party for the Independence of Guinea-Bissau and Cape Verde or PAIGC) and agreed to work peacefully toward independence. On 3 August 1959 the police intervened in a dockworkers' strike in Bissau, killing fifty and wounding over a hundred. One month after this event, which became known as the Pijiguiti Massacre, the approximately fifty members of the PAIGC – all of whom resided in Bissau – declared that independence must be achieved by any means possible, including armed struggle.

After independence, the PAIGC continued with plans to unify Guinea-Bissau and **Cape Verde**. Such plans ended abruptly in 1980, however, when Prime Minister João Bernardo "Niño" Vieira, frustrated in part by the overwhelming political power held by Cape Verdeans and *mestiços* (people of mixed African and European ancestry), staged a coup and overthrew President Luís Cabral, Amilcar Cabral's half-brother. Under Vieira's presidency (1980–99), Bissau witnessed the expansion of its commercial sector due to an increase in foreign investment and the liberalization of trade. Vieira has also been credited with transforming Guinea-Bissau from a single-party state into a multi-party democracy, although many dispute the legitimacy of his victories in subsequent elections.

Despite Vieira's reforms, Guinea-Bissau remained one of West Africa's poorest nations. The periodic devaluation of the Guinean peso in the 1980s and 1990s, and its eventual replacement by the CFA franc in 1997, led to an even deeper economic crisis, which was felt heavily by residents of the capital. In June 1998 a junta led by Ansumane Mané seized control of the Bra military barracks and the international airport in Bissau, demanding Vieira's resignation and a new round of elections. The armed conflict that ensued between the military junta and Vieira's supporters was fought almost exclusively in the capital, resulting in the evacuation of foreign nationals and the displacement of much of Bissau's population. Vieira was ousted in May 1999, and an interim government established until elections could be held. Kumba Yala was elected president in January 2000. As a result of extensive damage suffered during the fighting – including the destruction of the country's National Institute for Study and Research (INEP) – Bissau is still in the process of rebuilding.

Further reading

Forrest, J. (1992) *Guinea-Bissau: Power, Conflict, and Renewal in a West African Nation*, Boulder: Westview Press.

MICHELLE C. JOHNSON

Blantyre, Malawi

With a population of half a million people, Blantyre is the largest city in **Malawi**. It was founded by Scottish missionaries in 1876. The name Blantyre was given to this settlement in memory of the town where the Scottish explorer, Dr. David Livingstone, was born. The location of Blantyre in the agriculturally rich Shire Highlands and its temperate climate made it ideal for European settlement. It didn't take long before the missionaries were joined by European commercial settlers, pioneered by the African Lakes Company. As the numbers of European settlers increased, they began to grow coffee, tobacco, and tea in the valleys and plains of the highlands. From these humble beginnings, Blantyre experienced unprecedented growth. It was declared a municipality in 1895, distinguishing itself as the center of commerce and industry in the new British protectorate of Nyasaland, which was declared in 1891. In 1956 Blantyre was united with Limbe, a town some eleven kilometers to the east that had been founded in 1909 and had grown around the headquarters of the Malawi (then Nyasaland) Railways.

During the twentieth century, Blantyre distinguished itself as a center of political activism and agitation. African resistance to British colonial rule reached its peak in 1915 with the Chilembwe uprising near Blantyre. Chilembwe resented the poor treatment of African laborers by white settlers. Soon after the Chilembwe uprising,

Malawi began to see the formation of African pressure groups and associations, most of which were based in Blantyre. It was from these pressure groups that the Malawi Congress Party emerged, winning independence in 1964. Although not the designated capital, Blantyre continued to play a major political role. For example, although the capital was moved from Zomba to Lilongwe in central Malawi in the early 1970s, President Banda chose to build his palace in Blantyre, where he lived and ruled until he was ousted in 1994. Muluzi, who succeeded Banda, continues to live in Blantyre instead of Lilongwe. Blantyre is still seen by many as the center of political activity.

Blantyre has also been the center of cultural activity over the course of the twentieth century. The largest hospital in Malawi and two constituent colleges of the University of Malawi are located in the city. Blantyre also boasts some of the best secondary schools, established by missionaries during the colonial era. Other modern cultural amenities, such as cinemas and a major stadium, are also located in Blantyre. However, the provision of good housing for the majority of residents has been a major challenge during the twentieth century. In 2000 over 70 percent of the population lived in squatter settlements on the outskirts of the city. This was in part due to the rapidly expanding population. Estimated at 109,000 people in 1966, the population of Blantyre had expanded to 219,000 by 1977 and 332,000 by 1987. Such rapid demographic growth frustrated attempts to provide adequate facilities, such as housing and social services.

In spite of these difficulties, by the end the century Blantyre was the most important and vibrant commercial center in Malawi, with most of the country's industry and business located there. While Blantyre acts as the regional shopping and administrative center, Limbe is the center for wholesale commerce, conducted mainly by the Indian community. Limbe is also the headquarters for Malawi's tobacco auctions, one of Malawi's major exports.

Further reading

Garland, V. and Johnston, F. (1991) *Blantyre and the Southern Region of Malawi*, Blantyre: Central Africana.

Ross, A.C. (1996) *Blantyre Mission and the Making of Modern Malawi*, Blantyre: Christian Literature Association in Malawi.

EZEKIEL KALIPENI

Botswana

A landlocked, semi-arid country of approximately 1.5 million people in the heart of **Southern Africa**, Botswana entered the twentieth century as the Bechuanaland Protectorate. British rule was established in 1885 and affirmed in 1895. The frailty of the Protectorate was symbolized by the fact that its administrative center, Mafikeng, lay outside its borders. However, with the rise of apartheid after 1948, world opinion began to turn against **South Africa** and the threat of foreign incorporation declined substantially.

In 1900 Bechuanaland was a colonial backwater. The region had enjoyed a period of economic growth in the nineteenth century, but this was undermined by declining hunting stocks, by the displacement of local transport and trade opportunities after the completion in 1897 of the railroad connecting **Bulawayo** to South Africa, and by a series of ecological disasters in the 1890s that crippled the agro-pastoral economy. Declining economic opportunities in the Protectorate and the colonial hut tax, in place by 1901, contributed to the rising flow of oscillating male **migrant labor** to the South African mines, which continued until approximately 1980.

Political and economic developments in the nineteenth century contributed to the creation of powerful Tswana tributary chieftaincies in Bechuanaland. The chief was the center of the system; he presided over assemblies and rituals, allocated resources, directed the collective labor and military power of the age regiments (groups or associations formed around men of the same age range), and embodied the moral and political authority of the group. Chiefly power was affected in complex ways by the imposition of colonial rule. *Pax Britannica* and the fixing of formerly fluid and contested "tribal reserve" boundaries diminished the ability of subjects to dispute with their chief or splinter off and found new chiefdoms. Chiefs became the agents of indirect rule and were rewarded with 10 percent of the hut tax that they were forced to collect on behalf of the administration. They remained strong through the first half of the century, whereas the British administration was thin and had limited impact upon the fabric of local society. However, the effects of migrant labor and the commercialization of the rural economy eventually undermined the chiefs' ability to sustain order and function as economic patron.

In 1948 a key event crystallized diffuse patterns of change and signaled the decline of chiefly rule in favor of modern bureaucratic institutions and processes. While studying in England, Seretse Khama, heir to Ngwato chieftaincy (the largest and most powerful in the protectorate), married Ruth Williams, a white British woman. Powerful Tswana chiefs, the Protectorate administration, and the South African government were opposed to the marriage. A crisis ensued; Seretse was banished from the Protectorate and only allowed to return upon renouncing the chieftainship. After doing so, however, he helped establish the Botswana Democratic Party (BDP) and became, in 1966, Botswana's first elected president.

Botswana achieved independence without fighting or controversy; the political transition was smooth and did not follow a period of anti-colonial struggle. Thus no vanguard party or group emerged to consolidate power. The new ruling cadre represented a biracial elite, several of whom had worked together in the Legislative Council (LEGCO) that had been created by the colonial government to facilitate the transition to independence. The majority were large cattle ranchers, many had strong links with the rural peasantry, and they were interested in promoting a stable and profitable cattle industry. This elite, along with a small group of civil servants, was able to steer the country on a conservative, pragmatic, and disciplined path of capitalist growth through which the majority of the **peasants** have enjoyed some of the benefits of development. Levels of corruption, while on the rise in the 1990s, have remained low by international standards.

Multi-party, open, and peaceful elections have taken place every five years since independence. Support for opposition parties has fluctuated. Seen to be more radical than the BDP (many opposition leaders had links with liberation movements in South Africa), they have drawn most of their support from the urban areas where their pro-worker policies have resonance. As the rural economy declined and the links between the BDP and their rural base diminished in the final decades of the twentieth century, the opposition gained votes. Many believed that the opposition was poised to win the 1999 election, but a split in the party in 1998 secured the BDP's return to power.

In 1967, a year after independence, valuable diamond deposits were discovered beneath Botswana's Kalahari sands. By 1974 minerals had overtaken beef as Botswana's leading export and by the 1990s diamonds accounted for more than 80 percent of export earnings. Considered one of the world's twenty-five poorest countries at independence, by 1999 Botswana was ranked among the world's middle-income countries. Mineral wealth has enabled significant investment in infrastructure, health, and education, as well as permitting the creation of an expanding social safety net and encouraging the growth of the middle class.

At the end of the twentieth century, Botswana was widely celebrated as a model of peace, prosperity, and liberal democracy in Africa. However, current challenges to the state include continuing South African economic dominance, deep inequalities, increasing demands on the part of non-Tswana (for example, Kalanga, Kgalagadi) people for greater recognition, the internationalization of "Bushman" advocacy organizations, new tensions (especially over territory) with neighboring states such as Namibia, and above all the cataclysmic AIDS pandemic. Botswana had the world's fastest growing economy in the three decades preceding the millennium, but by 2000 also held the rather dubious distinction of having the highest prevalence of documented HIV cases in the world, with an estimated one in three adults testing HIV positive. The good prospects for Botswana's continued growth and development must therefore be tempered by the devastating consequences of AIDS.

See also: Southern African Development Community

Further reading

Edge, W. and Lekorwe, M.H. (eds.) (1998) *Botswana: Politics and Society*, Pretoria: van Schaik.
Samatar, A. (1999) *An African Miracle: State and Class Leadership and Colonial Legacy in Botswana Development*, Portsmouth: Heinemann.
Wylie, D. (1990) *A Little God: The Twilight of Patriarchy in a Southern African Chiefdom*, Hanover: Wesleyan University Press.

JACQUELINE S. SOLWAY

Brazzaville, Congo

The capital of **Congo** was named Brazzaville in 1883 after Pierre Savorgnan de Brazza (1852–1905), who headed several exploratory missions in Africa between 1875 and 1878 with support from France. With French control over the region secured, Brazzaville became the capital of French Congo as early as 1904, and then served as the capital of **French Equatorial Africa** from 1910 to 1960. Significantly, it was in Brazzaville that General de Gaulle staged the famous 1944 Brazzaville Conference that paved the way for debate on **decolonization** in French colonial Africa, culminating in Congo's inauguration as an independent nation-state in August 1960. Since then, even as the country has undergone the transition from Republic (1960–9) to People's Republic (1969–91) and back to Republic again (from 1991 onwards), Brazzaville has remained the capital.

Situated on the right bank of the expansive Malebo Pool on the Congo River, across the river from **Kinshasa**, Brazzaville is Congo's largest city, divided into eight densely populated neighborhoods and home to some 900,000 people by 2000, approximately a third of the country's total population. Brazzaville's ideal geographic location soon transformed the city into one of the most important colonial administrative and trading posts, facilitating the accumulation of raw materials and also the dissemination of colonial ideology along the river and into Central African territories that were otherwise difficult to penetrate. Access across Malebo Pool to the Belgian Congo and eventually, when the Congo–Ocean railway was completed (1921–34), to the Atlantic Ocean to the west formally secured Brazzaville's central economic and political role.

Congo's primary source of wealth is provided by rich offshore holdings in oil and the secondary industries associated with oil, such as refining and processing. Congo's rain forests have also generated considerable income from lumbering, while agricultural activity is essentially limited to cocoa, coffee, and palm oil. Other industrial activities include food processing, textiles, and beer bottling, while mining activities are restricted to zinc, copper, uranium, and natural gas.

Brazzaville has continued to occupy an important cultural, economic, and political role in the region, as well as in **francophone Africa**, while serving as Congo's administrative, educational (it is home to Marien Ngouabi University), and political center. The Marxist–Leninist authorities attempted to control cultural production, yet the capital nevertheless succeeded in gaining an international reputation for its art (the Poto-Poto School), music (Franco, Papa Wemba), theater (Rocado Zulu Theater Company), and literature (Emmanuel Dongala, Sony Labou Tansi). Phyllis Martin (1995) records the impressive growth of **leisure** activities enjoyed in colonial Brazzaville by Africans seeking to indigenize the city.

Congo declared its independence on 15 August 1960, and there have been considerable political changes since then. Fulbert Youlou, Alphonse Massemba-Debat, Marien Ngouabi, and Joachim Yhombi Opango were the first four presidents. Ngouabi inaugurated the shift towards Marxism–Leninism in 1969, an ideological model that survived throughout the legacy of Denis Sassou-Nguesso's presidency. The 1991 National Conference heralded the transition to democracy and multi-party rule, with the election of Pascal Lissouba, who remained in office until violent civil unrest broke out during 1997. The fighting resulted in thousands of deaths and such destructive violence that Brazzaville's architectural topography, characterized by wide boulevards and street cafes, was rendered unrecognizable. Following the civil war Sassou-Nguesso was returned to office, and the devastated city remained the Congo's most vibrant commercial, industrial, and cultural center.

References and further reading

Martin, P.M. (1995) *Leisure and Society in Colonial Brazzaville*, Cambridge: Cambridge University Press.

Obenga, T. (1998) *L'histoire sanglante du Congo-Brazzaville (1959–1997): Diagnostic d'une mentalité politique africaine*, Paris: Présence africaine.

DOMINIC THOMAS

Bujumbura, Burundi

In the nineteenth century, Usumbura (as Bujumbura was then known) was a small village. Following the incorporation of **Burundi** into German East African territory, modern Bujumbura was established as a German military outpost in 1899. It became the administrative center of the region when the League of Nations declared Ruanda-Urundi a Belgian mandate territory, following Germany's defeat during the First World War and the seizure of the German empire by the victorious powers. The growth of Bujumbura was facilitated by its location on the waterways of Lake Tanganyika, through which it was connected to traditional trade networks with the Belgian Congo and Tanzania. Besides, the lake supplied water to the growing urban population and sustained the nascent industrial sector. Bujumbura's hinterland, rich in maize, cotton, cassava, and bananas, provided food for the urban population.

In June 1962 the United Nations voted to grant Ruanda-Urundi independence as the separate states of Burundi and Rwanda, and Bujumbura became the capital of the new Burundian state. Lying in the western part of the country, Bujumbura became one of Burundi's sixteen provinces, its largest urban center, the hub of communications and commerce, and the seat of government. It became the country's main port and gateway, through which coffee, cotton, skins, and tin ore reached the world market via Lake Tanganyika, **Tanzania**, and the **Democratic Republic of Congo**. Light industry also developed, manufacturing consumer goods, such as textiles, paper, chemicals, blankets, shoes, and soap; assembling imported components; processing leather and agricultural products; and engaging in public works construction. Bujumbura constituted the lion's share of Burundi's 1.9 million labor force.

The city came to be served by a lake port, an international airport, and a road network. The airport was linked to three local airports, and the road network connected Bujumbura to other towns within Burundi, to Bukavu and Goma in the Democratic Republic of Congo, and to Kigali in Rwanda. A number of cultural and educational institutions, including the University of Burundi (founded in 1960), the Center of Burundi Civilization, an agricultural institute, a museum and numerous colleges transformed Bujumbura into a melting pot of cultures. It became the only region of Burundi where Swahili was spoken in addition to Kirundi and French. The city also hosted Burundi's four radio stations. In 1994 Bujumbura's population was estimated at 300,000.

The security, economic life, and stability of Bujumbura's population suffered from periodic eruptions of political violence involving Burundi's two main ethnic groups, the Tutsi and the Hutu. Residential segregation according to class, with the middle-class elite living in the better-off suburbs but the poor crowded into poor neighborhoods, while common in most cities, was complicated in Bujumbura by ethnic divisions and tensions. The level of violence escalated during the 1990s, when several suburbs of the city, especially Kamenge, were caught in the fighting between the Tutsi-dominated national army and Hutu rebel groups. For example, during some of the worst fighting in 1996, parts of the city went without water for a time after the electricity network was sabotaged, and for security reasons the International Committee of the Red Cross was forced to temporarily suspend all its activities in Burundi, except for emergency operations. In 2001, following another round of conflict in which armed militias attacked the city, international airlines suspended flights into Bujumbura. Despite these problems and challenges, Bujumbura has retained a certain vibrancy that comes from its position as Burundi's administrative, communications, economic, and cultural center.

Further reading

Lemarchand, R. (1996) *Burundi: Ethnic Conflict and Genocide*, Washington D.C.: Woodrow Wilson Center Press Series.

PETER KAGWANJA
MUTUMA RUTERE

Bulawayo, Zimbabwe

Lying along the Matsheumhlope River in southwestern **Zimbabwe**, Bulawayo is the country's second largest city, with a population of approximately a million people. It is the regional capital of Matebeleland, home of the country's largest minority ethno-linguistic group, the Ndebele, who are of Nguni origin and comprise 19 percent of the Zimbabwean population. Under King Mzilikazi, they migrated northward from Zululand in the nineteenth century and established a kingdom with its capital at Bulawayo. In 1893 they fought a spirited but unsuccessful war of resistance against British settler colonialism, following the occupation of Zimbabwe by Cecil Rhodes' British South Africa Company in 1890.

In 1896–7 the Ndebele and the Shona mounted another determined but also unsuccessful armed uprising against colonial rule in the first Chimurenga/Umvukela uprisings. Throughout the colonial period, Bulawayo was an important center of African nationalism and home to the veteran nationalist leader Joshua Nkomo, whose Zimbabwe African People's Union (ZAPU) party participated in the liberation war from the 1960s to 1980. After independence, Matebeleland was embroiled in a bitter civil war, as former ZAPU guerrillas fought government forces, following the dismissal of ZAPU ministers from the first independence government after arms were discovered on ZAPU properties. The conflict ended with the Unity Agreement of 1987, under which the ruling ZANU party and ZAPU merged into one party, renamed ZANU-PF.

In 1893 colonial settlers established present-day Bulawayo almost five kilometers south of Lobengula's pre-colonial court. Initially a small settlement of prospectors and farmers, Bulawayo grew to become a municipality (1897), a city (1943), and the second largest city in the **Central African Federation** (1953–63). It also became a major transportation hub in British Central Africa following the construction of rail links with South Africa (1897), Salisbury and the coast of Mozambique (1899), and Victoria Falls and Zambia (1905), and the introduction of a regular air service (1933). Until the Second World War, however, Bulawayo's economy grew slowly because of the country's small domestic market, although some secondary industries developed. Economic development quickened after the Second World War, as increased postwar European immigration stimulated industrial production: the town trebled in size between 1945 and 1956. Thereafter Bulawayo continued to witness spatial and demographic growth, while, economically, it became an important commercial and industrial center, manufacturing textiles, fertilizer, radios, food, metal products, cement, and other building materials. Bulawayo remains an important transportation hub and Zimbabwe's gateway to Botswana and South Africa through rail and road links to the border towns of (respectively) Plumtree and Beit Bridge.

With its unusually wide streets, designed when the town was founded to give turning room to a full span of wagon-pulling oxen, Bulawayo is also a cultural and tourist center. Apart from its many Victorian buildings, it hosts the country's Natural History Museum, with over 7,500 specimens, and the Mzilikazi Art and Craft Center, which produces various indigenous artifacts. Bulawayo also has the Bulawayo Art Gallery and a railway museum that displays steam engines, coaches, and other memorabilia from a bygone era, including the Pullman coach that carried Cecil Rhodes' body from Cape Town. Nearby are the Matopo National Park, containing Cecil Rhodes' burial place on World's View, the Khami Ruins (stone structures from the late Iron Age that are now a UNESCO Heritage Site), and the Chipangali Wildlife Orphanage and Research Center, a sanctuary for sick and orphaned domestic and wild animals. Bulawayo also boasts a number of higher education institutions, among which are the National University of Science and Technology and the Bulawayo Technical College.

Further reading

Hamilton, M. and Ndubiwa, M. (1994) *Bulawayo: A Century of Development 1894–1994*, Harare: Argosy Press.

ALOIS MLAMBO

Burkina Faso

Burkina Faso (formerly Upper Volta), with a total area of 274,200 square kilometers, is bordered by **Mali**, **Niger**, **Benin**, **Togo**, **Ghana**, and **Côte d'Ivoire**. It had an estimated population of 12.2 million in 2001. Colonization began in the late 1880s, culminating with the French occupation of Bobo-Dioulasso in 1895 and the defeat of Ouagadougou's Mossi army in 1896. In 1904 the territory became part of the colony of Haut-Sénégal–Niger, administered from **Bamako**.

The first quarter of the twentieth century was a period of extreme hardship for the peoples of Upper Volta. Tens of thousands of Voltaics were forced each year to labor in cotton fields and on construction sites, while others were conscripted into the military. Such policies, coupled with a punitive system of taxation, provoked popular revolts throughout the colony. In 1919 the French made Upper Volta a separate colony in order to better control its people and force them to cultivate cotton for export. In the late 1920s a series of droughts, coupled with plunging world prices for cotton, led to famine and eventual bankruptcy. As a result, in September 1932 the country was divided between the neighboring French colonies of Soudan and Côte d'Ivoire. Most of the territory went to Côte d'Ivoire, where Voltaic labor was needed for coffee and cocoa plantations, as well as for the construction of the Abidjan–Ouagadougou railway, which reached Bobo-Dioulasso in 1934.

Soon after the Second World War ended, the French government granted its colonies representation in the French National Assembly. Upper Volta was reconstituted as a separate territory in 1947, after intense pressure from the Mossi chiefs' conservative party, the Union Voltaïque (UV). The main nationalist, inter-territorial party, the Rassemblement Démocratique Africain (RDA) remained popular in the southwest, but in the north lost support to Mossi-dominated political parties such as the UV. Political factionalism during the 1950s, combined with the fact that Upper Volta was landlocked and poor in resources, boded ill for independence.

In March 1959 the RDA won an overwhelming victory in the legislative elections, bringing Maurice Yaméogo, a moderate, pro-French leader, to power – first as prime minister and then, after the country became independent from France on 5 August 1960, as president. Politics then became a series of power struggles between rival factions and leaders within the RDA, with the trade unions acting as power-brokers. Indeed, labor strikes contributed to the downfall of the corrupt Yaméogo regime, which was toppled in a military coup d'état led by General Sangoulé Lamizana in January 1966. Lamizana himself was overthrown in another coup, led by Colonel Sayé Zerbo in November 1980, which marked the end of the RDA dominance. Zerbo ruled through the Comité Militaire de Redressement pour le Progrès National (CMRPN). The CMRPN embarked on a program of economic and financial austerity, coupled with restrictions on civil liberties, which put it on a collision course with the trade unions. This conflict resulted in yet another military coup on 7 November 1982. This was led by a group of younger, more radical army officers. The new government, headed by Major Jean-Baptiste Ouédraogo, promised to reinstate political freedom and to promote social justice. In August 1983, however, yet another coup brought a left-wing faction, led by the popular and charismatic young captain Thomas Sankara, to power.

Aimed at empowering the disenfranchised rural masses, the Burkinabè revolution institutionalized new agencies of popular power: the Conseil National de la Révolution (CNR) and the Comités de Défense de la Révolution (CDRs). A basic needs-oriented economic and social development strategy was also initiated, as well as a non-aligned foreign policy. The various Marxist–Leninist political parties were absorbed into the new revolutionary structure, and the Union des Communistes Burkinabè (UCB) created. The CNR progressively cut itself off from the traditional social basis of previous regimes (the urban petty bourgeoisie), without gaining enough support among the peasantry, so it became increasingly isolated. Growing disagreement on ideology, strategy, and security issues culminated in a bloody coup on 15 October 1987, engineered by Sankara's closest ally Blaise Compaoré, which led to the violent death of Sankara and thirteen of his associates.

Soon after seizing power, the Compaoré regime initiated a "national rectification" process designed to redress the perceived excesses of the previous government. The Front Populaire (FP) replaced the CNR, and the Comités Révolutionnaires (CRs), with a somewhat reduced political role, replaced the CDRs. In June 1991 a new constitution was adopted by referendum. Meanwhile, growing opposition to Compaoré and his party led to the creation in September 1991 of a broad coalition of democratic forces, the Coordination des Forces Démocratiques (CFD). In October 1991 Compaoré resisted the CFD's call for a popular and sovereign national conference and created another support group, the Alliance pour le Respect et la Défense de la Constitution (ARDC). In presidential elections in 1991 and 1998, both boycotted by the opposition and with low turnouts, Campaoré was voted back into office. Economically, "socialism" was replaced by **structural adjustment programs**, and efforts were made to diversify exports by encouraging gold and vegetable production to complement the traditional exports of cotton, groundnuts, and livestock.

While appearing to play by the rules of multiparty democracy, and thus endearing itself to the international financial institutions, the Compaoré regime in fact persistently ignored the opposition's demands and consolidated authoritarian rule. The murder on 13 December 1998 of investigative journalist Norbert Zongo and three of his associates further exacerbated political tensions, becoming a political *cause célèbre.* Broad-based opposition to the regime by mass democratic movements (including student organizations and the powerful trade union Confédération générale du travail-Burkin) rallied around these murders. Ultimately, the undemocratic nature of the Campaoré regime, its frequent resort to political repression and abuse of human rights, and its involvement with rebel forces in Sierra Leone and Angola, threatened to lead to further social unrest and political violence.

Further reading

Englebert, P. (1996) *Burkina Faso: Unsteady Statehood in West Africa*, Boulder: Westview Press.

Meijenfeld, R. von, Santiso, C. and Otayek, R. (eds.) (1998) *La Démocratie au Burkina Faso*, Stockholm: International IDEA.

GUY MARTIN

Burundi

Burundi, with a total area of 27,834 square kilometers, borders **Rwanda**, **Tanzania** and **Democratic Republic of Congo**. In 2000 the country had an estimated population of 7.3 million. At the end of the nineteenth century, the population of Burundi largely consisted of Hutu farmers and Tutsi cattle-herders, with the latter having established a land- and cattle-owning aristocracy that imposed its power over the majority Hutu. Nonetheless, shared language and culture, and intermarriage, made social boundaries between the Hutu and the Tutsi relatively fluid. Unlike Rwanda, the Burundi Tutsi aristocracy did not develop into a highly centralized and militarized state bureaucracy. Instead it remained a loose unit, characterized by factional rivalries among royal princes (known as Ganwa).

Burundi became part of German East Africa in 1890 and was administered, together with Rwanda, as Ruanda-Urundi. In 1919 Ruanda-Urundi became a League of Nations' mandate territory, ruled by Belgium, after the defeated Germany was stripped of its African colonies; it then became a United Nations Trust Territory in 1946. Faced with a shortage of administrators, both Germans and Belgians established a system of indirect rule through the Tutsi aristocracy. They declared the Tutsi a Hamitic race, superior to the Hutu, and froze Hutu/Tutsi as racial categories by issuing identity cards that specified ethnic identity. They abolished the checks and balances of the feudal system, and replaced Hutu chiefs with Tutsi chiefs. The latter were given wide-ranging powers to enforce labor and raise taxes, often abusing these powers for their own benefit. The Tutsi were given a superior education to the Hutu, while the Hutu were only allowed to train for the Catholic priesthood.

Colonialism exacerbated intra-Tutsi aristocratic rivalries and Hutu/Tutsi social differences. Colonial economic policies, based on coffee production, were responsible for food shortages and famines such as the one that ravaged Burundi in 1928–9. Deprivation and tyranny fueled Hutu revolts, including one in 1934 that was suppressed by the Belgians, and stoked the embers of nationalism in Burundi. The anti-colonial struggle was itself an uneasy alliance between the monarchists, mostly Tutsi, and Hutu politicians. The fairly multi-ethnic Union du Progrès National (UPRONA) was officially registered in January 1960 under the leadership of Prince Louis Rwagasore, who was son of Mwambutsa IV, the Mwami (king). In the September 1961 pre-independence elections, UPRONA won fifty-eight out of sixty-four seats, half of which went to Hutu representatives. Burundi attained internal self-government in January 1962 and Rwagasore was elected prime minister. A month later, he was assassinated. In July 1962 Burundi became independent, retaining its monarchy with the Mwami as ceremonial head of a Tutsi-dominated state and André Muhirwa, a Tutsi Ganwa, as prime minister.

The Tutsi monopoly of power, and the execution in 1963 of five UPRONA opponents found guilty of assassinating Rwagasore, deepened Hutu/Tutsi hostility. In addition, Mwami Mwambutsa dismissed four Hutu cabinet ministers, precipitating political uncertainty and weakening the government. Wary of Tutsi/Hutu polarization, the Mwami invited Pierre Ngenendumwe, a Hutu, to form a new government in 1965. Ngenendumwe was assassinated by Tutsi militants, but succeeded by another Hutu, Joseph Bamina. In May 1965 the Hutu won a majority in the National Assembly, appointing Gervais Nyangoma as their leader. The Mwami, however, declined to make Nyangoma prime minister, instead appointing the Tutsi Leopold Biha. Hutu army officers staged a coup. Tutsi soldiers moved to suppress the coup, killing all the newly elected leaders, including Bamina and Nyangoma, and arresting thousands of Hutu policemen, army officers, intellectuals, and students. At the height of the crisis, the Mwami fled to Europe, delegating power to his son, Prince Charles Ndizeye. In July 1966 Ndizeye deposed his father and suspended the constitution. He was enthroned as the Mwami Ntare V, and made Captain Micombero prime minister. In November, Captain Micombero overthrew the Mwami and declared Burundi a republic, with himself as president.

In 1972 Hutu refugees invaded Burundi from neighboring countries, killing up to 2,000 Tutsi. Tutsi military reprisals killed between 80,000 and 300,000 Hutu civilians, generating thousands of refugees. In 1976, as Tutsi ethno-nationalism hardened, Jean-Baptiste Bagaza overthrew Micombero in a palace coup. Bagaza revitalized UPRONA and, in 1981, a new constitution declared UPRONA the sole party in Burundi. Bagaza was elected unopposed in August 1984, but was himself overthrown in 1987 by Major-General Pierre Buyoya, a more reform-oriented leader. Buyoya was still, however, reliant upon the Tutsi power-base. Although ruthless in dealing with Hutu opponents, Buyoya began to create an inclusive government, with a Hutu majority in his cabinet, taking Burundi on the road to democracy in the 1990s. In the 1993 multi-party elections, Buyoya lost to the Front for Democracy in Burundi (FRODEBU) candidate, Melchior Ndadaye, a Hutu. To allay Tutsi fears, Ndadaye formed a government of national unity with a Tutsi prime minister, but Ndadaye and six of his ministers were killed in an abortive coup in 1993. A wave of violence ensued, claiming between 50,000 and 200,000 lives, creating about 700,000 refugees and 250,000 internally displaced.

Ndadaye's successor, Cyprien Ntaryamira, was killed in a plane clash in April 1994, together with Rwanda's president. Although Burundi did not explode into violence like Rwanda, and despite Sylvestre Ntibantunganya's appointment as interim president, low-intensity inter-ethnic killings continued. Major-General Pierre Buyoya seized power for a second time in 1996. His regime was immediately ostracized by Burundi's neighbors, who imposed economic sanctions. Burundi's woes were aggravated by economic problems, including high population density – the second highest in Africa – monocultural production based on coffee, a narrow industrial base, poor infrastructure, external debt, and vulnerability to price fluctuations in the world market. The regime agreed to all-party talks, which culminated in the Arusha Peace Accord, signed in August 2000. Mediated by former South African president, Nelson Mandela, the Accord was nonetheless opposed by ethnic militants from small (predominantly Tutsi) parties and the internal wing of FRODEBU. Clearly, Burundi's future depends on reversing the colonial legacy of ethnic polarization, and instead nurturing respect for human rights and inclusive and democratic political institutions.

Further reading

Lemarchand, R. (1996) *Burundi: Ethnic Conflict and Genocide*, Washington D.C.: Woodrow Wilson Center Press Series.

Weinstein, W. (1976) *Historical Dictionary of Burundi*, London and Metuchen, New Jersey: Scarecrow Press.

PETER KAGWANJA
MUTUMA RUTERE

C

Cairo, Egypt

Cairo is the capital of **Egypt**, with an estimated population of 10.7 million in 2000. From the beginning of the last century, a map of the city would not have changed much in terms of its major streets and squares until the introduction of the tram, which connected Cairo's city quarters to the suburbs. This era witnessed the construction of bridges and a road network, the completion of the Egyptian railroad system, and work to protect the capital from river floods. In the meantime, the city's population increased from 681,000 in 1907 to 805,000 in 1917 as several new suburbs and satellite cities were built.

During the interwar period, population growth accelerated thanks to rapid industrial development, and to relative improvements in living conditions and health care. The latter attracted rural immigrants to the capital, a trend further encouraged by the railroad network which facilitated access to the capital from all over the country, although there was no physical expansion of the city. Cairo entered a new phase in 1952, attracting the country's largest share of social and economic development projects. Many industries were established – including iron and steel, textiles, cement, and several related specifically to the war – and the public sector expanded. The city increasingly became overpopulated from massive rural migration, and random residential areas proliferated in and on the outskirts of the city, despite efforts by successive governments to build new cities. By 2000 Cairo was one of the world's most densely populated cities.

Cairo was home to the Egyptian national movement that resisted British occupation, peaking with the 1919 revolution which resulted in Egypt's independence in 1922. Cairo was also center for a number of Egyptian and Arab scientific, literary, and cultural associations. It was also chosen in 1944 to become the headquarters for the **League of Arab States**. With the outbreak of the July 1952 revolution, Cairo became the center for many Arab and African nationalist movements, with Radio Cairo serving as platform from which to broadcast news of their struggles. Cairo also witnessed the assassinations of political and cultural leaders from Prime Minister Boutros-Ghali in 1915 to President Anwar Sadat in 1981, as well as the attempted assassination of the writer Naguib Mahfouz in 1994. It was also the center of outbreaks of political violence, sectarian clashes, and air raids during the Second World War and the Arab–Israeli wars of 1967 and 1973.

Cairo houses many educational institutions, including al-Azhar University, Cairo University, Ain Shams University, and Helwan University, as well as two private universities (6th October University and Misr International University). Among its most important tourist attractions are the Pyramids, the Sphinx, the ancient hanging church, and the citadel and mosque of Mohammed Ali, in addition to dozens of ancient mosques and churches. Cairo also houses the Egyptian Museum where ancient Egyptian artifacts are exhibited, as well as the Coptic Museum, the Islamic Museum, and a number of specialized and scientific museums, such as the Agricultural Museum, the

Railroad Museum, the Zoological Museum, the Military Museum, and the Post Museum. Cairo is famous for its historical quarters, each with its own distinct character. It is also home to a number of historic palaces, some of which have been turned into museums, while others serve as presidential headquarters or accommodation for foreign presidents and kings. As a cultural center, Cairo boasts numerous theaters and publishing houses, hundreds of daily newspapers and magazines, a relatively large movie production industry, and an opera house, and the city hosts scores of local, regional, and international arts festivals.

Further reading

Behrens-Abouseif, D. (2000) *The Cairo Heritage: Essays in Honor of Laila Ali Ibrahim*, Cairo: The American University in Cairo Press.

HAMDI ABDULRAHMAN

Cameroon

Cameroon, with a total area of 475,444 square kilometers, is located in coastal west central Africa and bordered by **Nigeria**, **Chad**, **Central African Republic**, **Congo**, **Gabon**, and **Equatorial Guinea**. With a population of 15,029,444 (1998 estimate), the country is often described as a microcosm of Africa itself. It is divided between a tropical forest region in the south, a savanna region in the center, and a semi-arid northern region. The population is composed of over 200 ethnic groups that speak twelve major African languages and countless dialects, and adheres to **Christianity**, **Islam**, and **African religions**. Reflecting its unique colonial heritage, French and English are the official languages. Primary economic activities include agriculture, which accounts for approximately 29 percent of gross domestic product and 75 percent of employment (1997 estimates), natural resource extraction and processing (especially lumber and petroleum), and light manufacturing (especially petroleum products, aluminum, textiles, food processing, and light consumer goods).

Cameroon's history in the twentieth century has been strongly defined by its triple colonial heritage. Germany initially colonized the country from 1884–1916, building a fair amount of the colonial-era infrastructure and introducing the production of agricultural exports in German-run plantations on the slopes of Mount Cameroon and by independent African farmers. After the First World War, Cameroon became a League of Nations mandate (redesignated United Nations Trust Territories at the end of the Second World War) and was divided between France and Britain. France received about 80 percent of the country, principally the eastern part (French Cameroons), and Britain received 20 percent, mainly in the west (British Cameroons). Britain abolished use of forced labor in former German-run plantations in 1916 and encouraged the production of export crops by independent African farmers. France continued using forced labor in plantations and for public works until the 1940s. Noticeable differences soon emerged in the levels of economic and social development of both territories. France invested significantly more in the development of basic infrastructure, education, and social services in its territory than did Britain, which governed British Cameroons as a marginal appendage to its larger and more valuable Nigerian colony.

The period after the Second World War witnessed the growth of nationalism, with the major nationalist parties professing as a goal the reunification of both territories. In the early 1950s, the nationalist movement in French Cameroons split into radical and moderate parties. The Union des Populations du Cameroun (UPC) was the main radical group; it drew most of its support for members of the Bamileke and Bassa ethnic groups in the south, and engaged in guerrilla warfare to press its demands for immediate independence and reunification of the territories. The French colonial administration responded to these strident demands for independence with brutal repression of UPC supporters and, after 1956, the devolution of political power to moderate elites who opposed the UPC. The Union Camerounais, led by Ahmadou Ahidjo, emerged as the dominant party of moderate politicians. Ahidjo became prime minister in 1958 and was founding president when the French Cameroons gained independence as the Republic of Cameroon on 1 January 1960. In

British Cameroons, the decolonization process involved a struggle between proponents of reunification with former French Cameroons and proponents of independent union with Nigeria. In a 1961 plebiscite, the northern section of British Cameroons voted to join Nigeria while the southern section chose reunification with Republic of Cameroon. This gave birth to a two-state (East and West) Federal Republic of Cameroon, with Ahidjo as the inaugural president.

Cameroon's post-independence leaders faced the challenge of building a new nation out of two colonies with different heritages in official language and political, administrative, and juridical traditions, as well as a myriad of other social and cultural divisions. The Ahidjo regime's nation-building strategy relied on the centralization of administrative and political power, repression of real or imagined political dissent, and the liberal use of patronage to ensure loyalty to the regime. In 1966 the Cameroon National Union was proclaimed the sole official party, and following a suspiciously lopsided referendum in May 1972, the Federal Republic was replaced with a unitary state. Ahidjo's regime carefully balanced the representation of regional groups in governmental and political institutions, and the distribution of patronage. Although marred by authoritarianism, the nation-building strategy was relatively successful, ensuring political stability and a growing sense of nationhood. Aided by a generally conservative policy-orientation, the economy grew at a steady enough pace for Cameroon to be ranked as a middle-income country by the early 1980s.

Ahidjo resigned as president in 1982 and was succeeded by Paul Biya. Two years into the transition, Cameroon's reputation for political stability was shaken by an attempted coup d'état. After the abortive coup, President Biya undertook a number of reforms, but did not alter the authoritarian cast of the state and political system. At the close of the 1980s, the economy began to stagnate and increased economic hardship fueled popular demands for political reform. After much resistance, the Biya regime conceded to demands for the legalization of political parties, and in 1992 Cameroon held its first multi-party election for twenty-five years. Political liberalization also created space for a proliferation of groups demanding greater political autonomy for regions, with the officially English-speaking Northwest and Southwest Provinces (carved out of former West Cameroon) the best organized and most vocal of such groups. Benefiting from the fragmentation of opposition parties, routine use of official violence to intimidate the opponents, and the manipulation of administrative rules, Biya's regime easily contained challenges to its incumbency and agitation for more substantive political reform. At the end of the twentieth century, Cameroon could be described as country where popular aspirations to democracy were far from being realized, where the economic future was uncertain, and where the citizenry still had to regain their badly jolted confidence in the future.

Further reading

Johnson, W. (1970) *The Cameroonian Federation: Political Integration in a Fragmented Society*, Princeton: Princeton University Press.

Takoungang, J. and Krieger, M. (1998) *African State and Society in the 1990s: Cameroon's Political Crossroads*, Boulder: Westview Press.

DICKSON EYOH

Cape Town, South Africa

Cape Town is situated in the Western Cape Province and is the legislative capital of **South Africa**. The town's historical development is intrinsically tied to Dutch and British colonialism. Cape Town, the first part of Africa to become a European settlement, was the administrative and commercial center of the Cape Colony. Dutch slavery gave rise to a large "mixed race" underclass, called "coloured." Coloureds still form the majority of Cape Town's populace (48 percent), followed by Africans (27 percent), whites (23 percent) and Indians (2 percent).

At the beginning of the twentieth century, Cape Town was undergoing rapid urbanization and industrialization. Construction, clothing, canning, and printing were the main industries. These industries were beset with racial tensions as white workers sought to limit competition from coloureds and Africans. The "Civilized Labour Policy," which contained the Apprenticeship Act of 1922, the Industrial Conciliation Act of 1924, and the Wage Act of 1925, secured white privilege and dominance in the labor market. In the 1960s the "Coloured Labour Preference Policy" placed coloureds in an advantageous position in relation to Africans. It also restricted African migration to the city. In the 1940s African women replaced coloured women as domestic servants. Coloured women began to work in the garment industry and service sector.

Residential segregation and political disenfranchisement accompanied workplace discrimination. "Race-based" urban planning began with the introduction of the Native Location Act in 1899. Africans were moved from District Six to the Ndabeni location. Langa, Nyanga, and Khayelitsha (all on the outskirts of Cape Town) formed the main African townships by the end of the century. Coloureds were removed from District Six and other white zoned suburbs in the 1960s. By the 1970s central Cape Town and the prime areas in its immediate vicinity were white spaces. Blacks were concentrated in state housing schemes on the sandy dunes of the Cape Flats. Cape Town, despite the construction of new houses under the Reconstruction and Development Program, still has an acute low-income housing shortage. This has led to sprawling squatter settlements.

Cape Town's liberal policy had initially granted blacks a qualified franchise (dependent on property-ownership and level of education). Africans were removed from the common voters roll in 1936, as were coloureds in 1956. Anti-segregation mobilization dominated black politics in Cape Town in the first half of the twentieth century. The African Political Organization (formed in 1902), the National Liberation League (1935), and the Non-European Unity Movement (1943) organized protests and spearheaded the Anti-Coloured Affairs Department campaign in the 1940s. This was also a period of radical trade unionism in Cape Town which saw the establishment of the Food and Canning Workers' Union in 1941. Leaders from this union formed the Coloured People's Congress in 1953. They became an affiliate of the African National Congress. State repression crippled political protests in the 1960s and 1970s. In the 1980s Cape Town's civic space was once again replete with student boycotts, rent boycotts, and labor strikes. The number of civic organizations mushroomed, including the United Democratic Front which was launched in the coloured suburb of Mitchells Plain in 1983. Notwithstanding the Cape Town populace's active anti-apartheid role, the majority of people in the Western Cape voted against the ANC in both the 1994 and 1999 provincial elections.

Cape Town is a prime tourist destination and hosts many historic sites: the castle, the slave lodge (which has become the South African Cultural Museum), and Robben Island. The city has two universities, the University of Cape Town (1918) and the University of the Western Cape (1966), as well as two technical institutions.

Further reading:

Bickford-Smith, V. (1999) *Cape Town in the Twentieth Century: An Illustrated Social History*, Cape Town: David Philip.

CHERYL HENDRICKS

Cape Verde

Cape Verde is an archipelago nation-state that consists of twenty-one islands and islets, located 620 kilometers west of **Senegal**. In 2000 it had an estimated population of 448,000. The nine inhabited islands are divided into a windward group called the Barlavento, consisting of Santo Antão, São Vicente (hosting the international port of Mindelo), São Nicolau, Sal (hosting the nation's international airport), and Boa Vista, and a leeward group called the Sotavento, consisting of Maio, Santiago (hosting the nation's capital of Praia), Fogo, and Brava. Cape Verde remained a Portuguese colonial possession from 1462 until it won its independence in 1975 through a collaborative liberation struggle with **Guinea-Bissau**.

The history of Cape Verde in the twentieth century was marked by environmental crises and emigration. Although its name literally means

"Green Cape," the archipelago is an extension of the Sahel wind belt in the Atlantic. In previous centuries droughts, which continued to plague the archipelago through the mid-twentieth century, had been marked by mortality rates of up to 50 percent. With Cape Verde's location at the crossroads of the Atlantic, its primary port of Mindelo provided an important service: supplying and repairing passing ships. This industry was often the island's primary source of income. Generations of Cape Verdeans sought relief through both maritime and whaling industries. Males participating in these activities emigrated to New England, as well as to South America (Argentina and Chile), during the previous century, creating their own economy of transportation which shipped women and families to New England to join male relatives. This long-standing emigration pattern was stifled by a series of US immigration laws between 1917 and 1922 that made literacy a condition for immigration. This was a significant barrier as few islands had schools that were open to the local people, making emigration from Cape Verde to the United States increasingly difficult for any but the privileged. Another barrier to emigration was the continued enforcement of contract labor laws that attempted to forcibly export Cape Verdean workers to Portuguese plantations in Portugal's other African colonies. To remedy having to participate in forced migration, many Cape Verdeans began emigrating to Senegal, where contracted wages were higher, and the threat of drought and potential famine greatly diminished. Other literate Cape Verdeans chose not to emigrate outside of the Portuguese Empire, but found employment in the colonial civil service throughout Portugal's African colonies.

Cape Verde's liberation struggle was linked with that of Guinea-Bissau. In 1951 a number of nationalists from the two colonies founded the Partido Africano da Independência do Guinée e Cabo Verde (PAIGC). The movement, under the dynamic leadership of Cape Verdean agronomy engineer Amilcar Cabral, sought the independence of both colonies with the aim of uniting them into a single nation. The PAIGC launched an armed liberation struggle against Portugal in 1961 from its headquarters in Conakry, Guinea. After more than a decade of fighting, Portugal – in response to UN pressure and its own revolution for democracy (1974) – was forced to liberate Guinea-Bissau (1973) and Cape Verde (1975). The PAIGC became the sole party of both nations, but plans for unification were derailed by a coup in Guinea-Bissau in 1980. The Cape Verdean branch of PAIGC was renamed Partido Africano da Independência de Cabo Verde (PAICV) and continued to rule as a one-party state until 1990. Responding to growing pressure, the PAICV then opened the country to political pluralism. Opposition groups united to form the Movimento para Democracia (MPD), which duly won fifty-six of the seventy-nine national assembly seats in the first multi-party elections in January 1991. In the following month's presidential election the MPD's Antonío Mascarenhas Monteiro defeated PAICV's long-serving incumbent Aristides Pereira. Monteiro and the MPD retained power in the elections of 1995 and 1996, although the PAICV would return to power shortly after the turn of the century, led by former PAIGC president Pedro Pires.

Since independence a number of programs have been implemented to overcome the legacy of colonial economic underdevelopment coupled with drought. Despite further droughts in the 1970s and 1980s, large-scale famine was avoided through the importation of food. Yet this resulted in the country running up a huge trade deficit that had to be financed by foreign aid. A more consistent threat than drought was the increasing fragility of the environment. Deforestation, overgrazing sheep and goats (damaging the delicate topsoil), and the cultivation of steep slopes (encouraging soil erosion) have created a series of environmental crises. In the 1980s programs to increase the island's capacity to retain water included dike construction and the planting of over three million drought-resistant trees. Other efforts took the form of terracing, irrigating, drilling for underground water, and the construction of desalination plants. Another important survival mechanism for Cape Verdeans was money sent back to the islands from the Cape Verdean diaspora. In 1968 the reopening of the United States to Cape Verdean immigrants led to massive migration. By the end of the twentieth century, the 500,000 people of Cape Verdean descent in the United States alone outnumbered the archipelago's population of nearly 400,000, with other sizable communities in Portugal, **Senegal**, **Angola**, **São Tomé and Príncipe**, France, Italy, Argentina, and the Netherlands. These diasporic communities send millions of dollars in regular remittances, amounting to nearly 20 percent of gross domestic product. The highest percentage of remittances came from Portugal.

The struggle for survival is still a way of life in the archipelago. At the end of the twentieth century, vocalist Cesaria Evora brought worldwide attention to the county through *morna*. This local musical genre reflects the stoic determination of Cape Verdeans to overcome both the physical separation caused by the diaspora and the hardship that characterizes their daily lives.

Further reading

Carreira, A. (1982) *The People of the Cape Verde Islands: Exploitation and Emigration*, Hamden: Archon Books.

Meintel, D. (1984) *Race, Culture and Portuguese Colonialism in Cabo Verde*, Syracuse: Syracuse University Press.

T.J. DESCH-OBI

capitalisms and capitalists

African history offers a useful antidote to universalizing conceptions of what capitalist expansion signifies. Africa has proved infertile ground for the implantation of capitalist relations of production. Rather than engaging the complexity of Africa's problematic relationship to capitalism, scholars have often followed two one-dimensional approaches. One is to assume that there is a normal pattern of capitalist expansion, but that Africa is an exception to it – an extreme case of cultural values, social structures, or political expediency impeding capitalist development. The second is to assume that Africa's non-transformation actually served world capitalism: Europe became capitalist and rich because it kept Africa backward and poor. Neither approach captures the dynamics of Afro-European history. Africa was never a blank slate of aboriginal poverty, primitive technology, and self-sufficiency. Nor was its history reducible to external domination and exploitation. Africa's diverse peoples, diverse geography, and connections within and beyond the continent provided both possibilities and limitations.

Africa has long experience with markets. But capitalism means something more than markets. Marx's treatment of it emphasizes both its historical specificity and its systemic quality: Capitalism was rooted in a process that turned everything produced and consumed into exchangeable commodities – including the most elusive commodity of all, human labor. Capitalism entailed free labor in a double sense: laborers were free from slavery or serfdom, but they were also "free" of access to land or other means of production, hence compelled to treat their labor as a commodity to be sold. The denial of access to productive resources depended on both coercion and cultural transformation, so that wage labor appeared "natural." The proliferation of trading organizations or of repressive systems of extraction – under colonial rule and otherwise – did not necessarily pry labor out of its place in local or personal arrangements and into the market.

The history of capitalism in twentieth-century Africa entailed much initiative – in cash-crop production and marketing – on the part of African entrepreneurs. Europeans invested in commerce, mining, and agriculture, and the building up of labor forces via coercion and wage incentives. But such actions – even when Africa became a major producer of minerals like diamonds, gold, or copper, or of crops like cocoa or palm oil – did not lead Africa to capitalist development. The closest one comes to an externally implanted capitalism was in South Africa, where the mineral revolution from the 1860s to the 1880s led to large European investment, the building up of vast mining enterprises, and the development of large wage-labor forces. But the key to the capitalist character of South African development was in agriculture: the earlier pattern of white settlement put in place a culturally, socially, and politically distinct land-owning class. Then, with the heightened incentives of mineral-based industrialization, white landowners tightened their grip on land, forcing tenants to become wage laborers and thereby bringing into being a landless African proletariat. Even then, the process was mediated by the skill of many Africans in using networks of personal dependence or familial self-reliance to keep the labor market at arm's length and by the state's creation of "reserves," where the largely unpaid labor of women supported families whose needs could not be covered by the remittances of largely male workers. Over the course of the twentieth century, the reserves became increasingly unable to provide even partial sustenance for African families; they became dumping grounds for Africans no longer "useful" to a racially articulated capitalist economy.

British and French officials in the 1890s and early 1900s also thought that they could harness African labor power to either African or European capitalists. In northern **Nigeria** or on the coast of east Africa, where Africans had developed large-scale commercial agriculture using slave labor, colonizers thought that they could maintain a land-owning class in a position of dominance while turning slave labor into wage labor. They learned that both ex-slaves and ex-masters could restructure forms of dependence and inequality without submitting themselves to the rigors of a market in labor. White settlers in **Algeria**, **Angola**, **Côte d'Ivoire**, or **Kenya** seemed to offer another route to capitalist development. But a combination of the settlers' own addiction to cheap, coerced labor supplies and the fact that African rural production outside the areas of European settlement remained an alternative meant that wage labor was rarely a lifelong experience. Africans, rather than becoming progressively enmeshed in wage labor, tried to combine farming, wage labor, and artisanal production.

African cocoa planters on the Gold Coast and later Nigeria, Côte d'Ivoire, and **Cameroon** found a niche in export markets, and developed an effective way of mobilizing labor and other resources without following the wage-labor script. Before the turn of the century, Gold Coast farmers migrated from the savanna edge to more favorable forest lands, obtained the right to use that land, and used their own kinship and other social relations to obtain labor and food as the cocoa trees matured. Later, they attracted migrants from more arid, northerly regions, who received remuneration in the form of crop shares and access to the patronage of the owner, as well as in cash. Some migrant laborers became planters in their own right. As good cocoa land was heavily taken up – by the 1930s in the Gold Coast, later elsewhere – relations between planters and labor tenants became more tense, but they did not polarize in the way they did in the classic case of agricultural capitalism in England. In fact, cocoa planters depended on good relations with the wider community to ensure recognition of their own claims to resources. What Sara Berry (1993) calls "accumulation without expropriation" characterized other crop systems as well.

Long-distance trade has a history much longer than colonization. In desert-edge West Africa, **trading diasporas** profited from lucrative trade. Colonial conquest often weakened such marketing systems without necessarily providing a more efficient alternative: frontiers and duties added to costs, and European firms often obtained monopolies. In coastal West Africa, many nineteenth-century African trading communities were marginalized in the colonial economy. In the worst zones of colonial extraction, such as the Belgian Congo, or in areas that served as labor-recruitment zones, colonial governments sometimes tried to suppress trade, for it provided alternatives to a low-wage labor market. But African traders found niches in connecting the few major axes (notably rail-roads) to the rural areas where most Africans lived.

In cities dominated by European businesses, African women often specialized in small-scale marketing, brewing beer, or providing housing for an impoverished, largely male working class. Female entrepreneurs faced even larger obstacles than males in converting the modest profits of trade into social or political capital that could allow them to expand their scale of operations. Trading businesses tended to grow in number rather than scale or internal integration. In some places, the most successful middlemen in colonial economies came from **non-African diasporas**, their success stemming from tight networks set apart from dependence on state support (characteristic of Europeans) and from too many community obligations (characteristic of African businesses).

For many centuries, entrepreneurs, indigenous or foreign, hoping to build large-scale productive systems found the obstacles to exploiting labor to be too large: African geography offered many places to take refuge from those exercising too close a form of power, and kinship offered collective strength to oppose efforts to capture labor power. Colonial rulers discovered that a measure of coercion, the need for cash income, and the feeble infrastructure provided for marketing cash crops might drive Africans into wage labor, but they would have possibilities for getting themselves out again. Some have argued that colonial capitalists wanted to preserve rural economies to make it possible to keep wages below the costs of supporting families, but short-term labor was all there was for sale in most of Africa, whether European capital wanted it that way or not.

During the **Great Depression**, colonial businesses and governments could slough off economic dislocation into a countryside where problems were not readily visible. But with the gradual economic upturn of the mid-1930s, colonial governments worried that peasants and small-scale traders, not European employers, would capture the fruits of recovery. Meanwhile, the islands of wage labor were both miserably endowed with infrastructure and services, and vulnerable to the collective action of African workers, which escalated after 1935.

This double bind was the impetus behind the new initiative in the 1940s of France and Britain to get serious about what they now called "development." This became the watchword of postwar colonialism, and on it rode the hopes of colonial regimes to exploit African resources more efficiently and to relegitimize colonial rule. Both objects proved elusive, but the most important point is that the very necessity for a state-run project of development reveals the limited extent to which either "economic" forces or colonial policy produced something that conformed to a capitalist economy. Developmentalist colonialism – the new wave of public investment by France, Britain, and, to an extent, Portugal and Belgium – did not produce a wave of private investment, except in the old areas of mining and commerce. Nationalist movements themselves faced an ambiguous situation: Could the end of colonial rule unleash the indigenous entrepreneurial spirit that had been bottled up by the monopolistic and discriminatory practices of colonial regimes, or were colonialism and capitalism an integrated, exploitative process which had to be overthrown in its entirety and replaced by some form of "African socialism"?

After independence, this distinction proved less decisive in practice than in theory. Socialist leaders could use the state to augment collective resources – or else for their own gain. Capitalists could use the state to foster private enterprise – or try to monopolize such resources for their own benefit and to prevent competition. Socialist and capitalist development did not necessarily imply distancing the independent state from privileged relations with multinational corporations or international financial organizations. Even in the late twentieth century, as international financial institutions preached the gospel of the market and forced African states to "privatize" state corporations and reduce economic regulation, privatization could still mean that the same people controlled the same resources.

If private landownership – and hence landless workers – appear to be the hallmark of capitalism worldwide, legally defining land titles as private has not itself pushed economies into capitalism. Rather than enhance security of land control, the registration of titles has more often generalized insecurity, as people mobilize political resources to make and counter claims to the ownership of each piece of property. A title can become yet another resource controlled by a "big man" – and kept out of the hands of other big men – rather than a means to obtain credit, hire labor, and set about the business of agricultural capitalism. Many African regimes, even those that claim to be "pro-market," are wary of the autonomy from the state that a property-owning, productive class might be able to exert, while capitalists are vulnerable from below in that their legal claims to land and their need to enforce property rights ultimately depend on court testimony and other forms of support from the very community they would otherwise turn into a landless, disciplined labor force.

Entering yet another century in which Africans are being told that their future lies in integration into markets, it is important to remember just how peculiar an institution capitalism is. Capitalism does not represent a replicable model so much as a particular historical experience of internalized exploitation, as well as strategic use of external resources. But Africa's economic experience in the twentieth century contains possibility as well as pain, and above all a variety of forms in which people, coming from particular social contexts but with wide connections, can organize production and commerce.

See also: economy: colonial; economy: post-independence; merchants; socialisms and socialists

References and further reading

Berry, S. (1993) *No Condition is Permanent: The Social Dynamics of Agrarian Change in Sub-Saharan Africa*, Madison: University of Wisconsin Press.

Cooper, F., Isaacman, A., Mallon, F., Roseberry, W. and Stern, S. (1993) *Confronting Historical Paradigms: Peasants, Labor, and the Capitalist World System in Africa and Latin America*, Madison: University of Wisconsin Press.

Peel, J.D.Y. (1983) *Ijeshas and Nigerians: The Incorporation of a Yoruba Kingdom, 1890s–1970s*, Cambridge: Cambridge University Press.

Rodney, W. (1972) *How Europe Underdeveloped Africa*, London: Bogle-l'Ouverture.

FREDERICK COOPER

Casablanca, Morocco

Casablanca is situated on the rich Atlantic plains of **Morocco**. It is the industrial and administrative capital of Morocco. It is known as a city of social contradictions and inequality, but also of hope and opportunity. The latter explains the city's expansion from two to five million inhabitants in the short period between 1985 and 2001. As early as 1907 the French began developing the port of Casablanca in order to exploit the export and fishing potential of the vast Atlantic sea. The port complex, which covers an area of 445 acres, is the heart of the modern Moroccan economy.

Post-independence Casablanca marked the history of its fierce and bloody resistance to French colonization by naming streets after its martyrs, but the depth of French colonial influence is still felt in the French names of other streets. Mosques, churches, and synagogues exhibit the cosmopolitanism and tolerance of the city. During the Second World War the name of Casablanca was associated with crucial world events. In 1942 American forces under the command of Lieutenant-General Eisenhower landed in Casablanca and a year later the Casablanca Conference – attended by President Roosevelt of United States, the British Prime Minister Churchill, and the French General De Gaulle – was organized to plan the defeat of the Nazis in Europe.

As the major industrial center in post-independence Morocco, Casablanca has the largest labor force of the country and was, unsurprisingly, at the center of large-scale riots against economic austerity in the 1980s and early 1990s. This labor force is employed in many different industries, including food processing and the manufacture of textiles, clothing, shoes, automobiles, electronics, and furniture. Women constituted more than 80 percent of the total labor force, especially in textiles and food processing. Foreign investment, mainly from European investors, was widely developed.

Casablanca's capital is essentially made up of three different elements of the wider Moroccan population: the old aristocracy from Fes, Moroccan Jews, and the southern Soussi. Some of these inhabitants migrated to Casablanca in the early 1960s to benefit from the colonial industrial legacy. The combination of these groups provides Casablanca with its cosmopolitan character – a cosmopolitanism that has fueled the desire of unemployed young people to cross the Mediterranean and cross the highly protected borders into Europe. Indeed, the problems of social inequality and poverty are more visible in Casablanca than in any other Moroccan city. Poverty is especially evident in the residential areas at the periphery of the city, where slums often surround rich residences, but Casablanca also faces serious problems with pollution, transportation, and insecurity.

To complicate the picture, Casablanca claims a modern cultural identity in addition to its historical identity. The presence of the large University Hassan II, the proliferation of private schools, and the existence of a cosmopolitan bourgeoisie favor the development of art and culture. Indeed, Casablanca al-Saoud library is one of the richest public libraries in Morocco. The Casablancan bourgeoisie also provide resources and support for the organization of many international, Arab, and Islamic governmental conferences.

Though Casablanca is little different from other Moroccan cities in terms of architectural diversity, it is the Hassan II Mosque that makes Casablanca one of the most attractive destinations for national and international tourism. The mosque, designed to stand on the shores of the Atlantic Ocean by a French architect, is the masterpiece of Moroccan arts and architecture. It is also the largest mosque outside Mecca, housing a library, a national museum, and large conference rooms.

Further reading

Oussman, S. (1994) *Picturing Casablanca: Portraits of Power in a Modern City*, Berkeley: University of California Press.

ZAKIA SALIME

Central Africa

More than anywhere else on the continent, Central Africa underwent incredible hardships in its relations with the colonial powers. On both sides of the Congo River, the French and the Belgians had the same goal: exploitation of the natural resources of their colonies at minimal cost. The French government refused to invest in **French Equatorial Africa**, which was nicknamed the "Cinderella" of the empire, instead giving total freedom to concessionary companies. The first of these companies, the Société du Haut-Ogoue, was granted the monopoly for commerce over half of eastern Gabon (some 11 million hectares). The system was enlarged in 1899 to involve forty other companies, all of which received thirty-year leases that covered all of the land around the Congo and south of Oubangui-Chari. These companies took advantage of their monopoly to keep prices at an absurdly low level. The French companies were primarily interested in trading ivory, the reserves of which quickly ran out. Companies in the Congo, however, specialized in rubber harvesting until the industry was ruined by the development of rubber plantations in Malaysia in early 1911. These companies were subsidized by their government, which provided all the necessary infrastructural investment – roads, bridges, and railways. Due to lack of money, especially during the two world wars, colonial administrators used forced labor. The construction of the railway (1922–34) resulted in 11,000 deaths.

The Congo was under the private control of King Leopold II, who sought to make the colony as profitable as possible. He turned it into one of the world centers of rubber production, a commodity that had been in great demand since 1896 with the development of the automobile industry. The colony proved invaluable to him personally, and also to the city of Brussels which he embellished with profits from the colony. Leopold's regime in the Congo was one of ruthless exploitation. The state was organized like a major production industry. The colonial staff were responsible for administration, recruiting workers, and for the production of rubber. Their promotion depended, among other things, on their economic and financial results. The colony was ravaged by forced labor used for porterage, the construction and maintenance of the railway, the collection of ivory, rubber, and wood, and the cultivation of cotton and palm-oil plantations, which came under the control of Unilever from 1928. Some estimates indicate that the population of the Congo dropped by at least a third, and probably by half, between 1880 and 1920. This demographic loss was matched in French Equatorial Africa where, by the end of first decade of the twentieth century, the inhabitants of once prosperous villages were infected with syphilis and sleeping sickness. In all, disease destroyed half of the population settled between Malabo Pool and the Atlantic Ocean.

Leopold's bloody regime of exploitation was so terrible that it became an international scandal in 1905. By 1907 he was forced to relinquish control of the so-called "red rubber" trade to the Belgian government, and the colony was renamed the Belgian Congo. A similar scandal emerged in French Equatorial Africa, where the level of exploitation was equally devastating. It was, however, less profitable because the necessary infrastructural investments had not been made. The major difference was that administrators and businessmen were supposed to be separate, with the former responsible for controlling the latter. In reality, colonial authority was very weak at the beginning of the colonial period, and numerous abuses were perpetrated by the private sector. The most serious of these were discovered not far from **Bangui** in 1904 and 1905, in the territory of the company of the M'Poko. There a young administrator uncovered the massacre of 750 Africans, as well as the murder of probably another 750 people who had refused to work the rubber plantations. The incident was suppressed for fear of another international scandal, but the need for reform was evident. In 1908 a federation was created, gathering together the territories of Gabon, Congo, Oubangui-Chari, and Chad. But it took another twenty years to bring the system of abuse and exploitation by the concession companies to an end. In 1911 the Forestry Company of Haut-Oubangui (which controlled 48 million hectares) united several old companies, but for many years it continued to terrorize local people. André Gide revealed the continuing scandal in 1927, in his work *Voyage au Congo*, but it was not until 1935 that the company finally agreed to give up its rights, bringing to an end its regime of economic terror.

The abuses continued in the Belgian Congo, but for a different reason. Rubber exploitation was soon superseded when mineral deposits were discovered. These were destined to become the country's wealth and misfortune. Anglo-Belgian investments prospered in the first decade of the century, profiting from the exploitation of the rich mineral resources in the south of the country, including copper in Katanga and diamonds in Kasai. Between the world wars, the colonial economy attracted enormous investment from international companies, including the Anglo-American Company of South Africa. Every able-bodied adult was considered a unit of production that could be put to work, and each year the regional governors agreed a maximum percentage of able-bodied adults that could be recruited without endangering the subsistence activities of the rural economy, which was necessary to provide food for the workers. The mining company of Haut-Katanga became a state within a state. It recruited cheap labor from all over the region, including Rwanda-Burundi, Nyasaland, and northern Rhodesia. The situation was so dreadful that in the mid-1920s an agreement was reached between the colonial government and Catholic missionaries to improve living conditions in the mining cities. Previously the mining companies had sought to control imported manpower by total subjugation. The workers were now given guaranteed salaries, advances on their wages to pay their dowries, a Christian education for their children, and the opportunity to organize leisure activities – but trade unions were still banned.

The economic situation in French Equatorial Africa had not improved at all, with the exception of Gabon. There major resources, such as *okoumé* wood, had begun to be exploited at about the same time as the copper in the Belgian Congo. From the First World War, Gabon – the only producer of *okoumé* wood – owed its rapid development to the introduction of plywood. The plywood industry, which consumed a lot of manpower, generated a class of overexploited workers, but eventually – during the 1950s – the private sector was forced to invest heavily in caterpillar tractors, power saws, and so on. Gabon itself, however, benefited little from the exploitation of its resources. In fact, accusations were made that Congo, whose capital Brazzaville was also the capital of the Federation, was being developed at Gabon's expense. From the 1940s many people migrated to French Equatorial Africa and the Congo for work. In French Equatorial Africa, the major source of work was forced labor on the Congo–Ocean railway. The railway took workers from everywhere except Gabon, which needed too many workers in its own forestry industry. Migrant workers in the Belgian Congo found work in the mines, cities, and harbors.

Political consciousness had begun to develop in Central African cities and workplaces from the 1920s. A branch of the League of Human Rights was formed in Libreville, while André Matsoua – a former Congolese volunteer in the Rif War (a repressive war against Morocco in 1925) –

attempted to create an Organization of the People of French West Africa in Paris. Matsoua was imprisoned by the colonial authorities on trumped up embezzlement charges and deported to Chad, where he died in 1942. His example inspired a messianic movement, known as "Matsouanism," in Lari, the Central African region from which he came. The ethnic mixture in rural areas and cities, and the cultural syncretism that resulted (much of it dating back to before colonial rule), made a mockery of colonial pseudo-tribal analysis, which inaccurately described French Equatorial Africa as being populated by backward, rural people and Congo as a gathering of "365 isolated tribes" in constant conflict with each other. Instead, the population showed its opposition to the vast colonial system of exploitation through revolts and religious movements. In eastern Gabon, there were two rebellions among the so-called "hostile Awanji people" in 1927–8, provoked by excessive taxation and the introduction of a compulsory market for supplies to the colonial administration. In Oubangui-Chari, the Mbaya people also rebelled, angered by a combination of obligatory porterage, forced recruitment for rubber production, and compulsory cultivation of cotton. The uprising (known as the Kongo-Warra War) was on a huge scale, despite the traditionally dispersed nature of power in the area, affecting more than 350,000 inhabitants and involving 60,000 warriors. The revolt, which began in 1927, extended up to eastern Cameroon and southern Chad, and did not come to an end until 1931. Estimates for the number of victims varied from 10,000 to 100,000. In the Belgian Congo, there were also massive uprisings against the Kivu National Company, first in the 1930s and then again in 1944 around Stanleyville (Kisangani). The uprising was triggered by the resuscitation of the savage rubber regime, coupled with the demands of the war effort. Popular protest also found expression in messianic movements, including the growing Matswanist movement in French Equatorial Africa and Kimbanguism in Zaire. Both of these movements were born in the interwar period and named after their founders; Kimbanguism, which was founded in the Belgian Congo, became the second most important religion in the country after Christianity.

Troops recruited from French Equatorial Africa at the beginning of the Second World War proved critical in the eventual French victory. Indeed, the very first soldiers to enter liberated Paris came from Brazzaville and Cameroon. This did not, however, immediately change the fate of the population of the colonies. Some of the hopes raised by the Brazzaville Conference in January 1944 that the colonial subjects would have more say in the running of their countries' affairs were quickly frustrated. In the economic domain, the 1950s were characterized by ambitious investment that yielded little by way of improvements to the lives of the colonized. In 1948, under the leadership of FIDES (the Investment Fund for Economic Development), French Equatorial Africa adopted a decennial plan with a budget of more than 50 million CFA francs: 75 percent was earmarked for infrastructure and production, the rest for social services. Priority was given to the improvement of water transportation and harbors. Industry was profitably involved in the exploitation of minerals (such as manganese and, after independence, petroleum and uranium in Gabon and diamonds in Oubangui), but the persistence of low salaries and low productivity showed the extent to which the economy was based on the old logic of extraction and exploitation. The situation in the Belgian Congo did not differ much: the profits made by big colonial enterprises were expatriated, rather than being invested in the welfare of the Congolese people themselves.

Further economic and social disruption was caused by the rapid increase of population in urban areas. Accelerated **urbanization** started in the 1930s and was unsuccessfully resisted by the government (except in the case of the mining compounds) until the late 1950s. Between 1940 and 1965, Brazzaville went from 25,000 inhabitants to more than 150,000, Libreville from 62,000 to 142,500, and Bangui from 24,000 to 72,000. In Congo and Gabon the balance between urban and rural populations began to tilt significantly toward the city as urbanization rates exploded. In Leopoldville, which already had a large population because of its mining industry, the city grew from 200,000 inhabitants in 1950 to 2 million in 1975. As centers of power, confrontation and transgression, the cities established themselves as crucial centres of colonial cultural creativity and contestation, where the administration was not able to control the emergence of an autonomous African culture.

On both sides of the Congo River, social investment was limited to small improvements to the health service and a limited development of the school system. In French Equatorial Africa, about 200,000 students attended elementary school out of a total population of about 4 million people in 1958, as compared to 22,000 in 1938. Secondary education remained inadequate, and no university was built in the region until the mid-1960s. In the Belgian Congo, by contrast, education was entirely in the hands of the missionaries. School education was essentially limited to primary or technical education, and the University of Lovanium (founded in 1948) remained the only institution of higher learning. While the colonial project was losing ground under the strain of an avaricious and backward colonial mentality that relied on sources of short-term economic gain that quickly dried out, a new and dynamic African culture was arising which was clearly beyond the control of the colonial political system. This culture was reflected by the explosion in Congo-Brazzaville of literature in French and by the inimitable Congolese music that soon became an essential part the national heritage of the Belgian Congo.

Independence happened everywhere the same year: 1960. Independence was preceded or immediately followed by violence in several parts of the region. In French Equatorial Africa there were riots in Brazzaville, during which rival groups massacred each other with the tacit support of the head of the government, Fulbert Youlou, who represented the interests of the south and was supported by France. In neighboring Congo, trouble occurred the year after independence, when the army mutinied. The mutiny was soon followed by a coup d'état and the assassination of Patrice Lumumba, hero of the independence struggle. For a short time after 1963 the entire eastern part of the country was controlled by Pierre Mulélé, the leader of an alliance between a small group of young revolutionary intellectuals and the rural population. Their goal was to fight for a "second independence" that would ensure social justice for all. A half decade of civil war ensued.

In the countries of what had been French Equatorial Africa, the brief outbreak of democracy that followed the introduction of the universal ballot in 1956 was brutally interrupted by two coups d'état. In Congo, the "three glorious riots" of unions and the lower classes from Brazzaville in 1963 led to the establishment of a scientific Marxist–Leninist autocratic regime, while in Gabon the dictatorship of Léon Mba established the one-party state in 1964. The trajectory of political events was the same in Congo/Zaire, with Mobutu coming to power in 1965 and establishing a single-party state in 1970 – his party survived into the mid-1990s. Mobutu's vicious dictatorship was sustained by major Western powers, headed by the United States and France, in the name of political stability and opposition to communism. Barthélémy Boganda's dreams of a "United States" of Central Africa were brought to an end by his accidental death in 1959. The country was in a state of disorder that came to a climax in 1975 with the tragic and comical dictatorship of the Emperor Bokassa, also supported by France. In 1973 Chad was also involved in both internal wars (between rival factions) and external wars (against Libyan and Sudanese territorial ambitions).

In Zaire the system of organized prebendalism and plunder under Mobutu created staggering inequalities between those who profited from the regime and the rest of the population. The gap between the rich and the poor grew rapidly in both cities and rural areas. By the 1980s the salaries of almost all wage-earners were less than the minimum for survival. Then, in 1990s, civil war erupted in the two Congos. In Brazzaville in 1995 there was a struggle for power between the rival armed supporters of Pascal Lissouba and Sassou Ngesso, which led to the destruction of almost the entire city. In Zaire, Laurent-Désiré Kabila came to power in 1997 but failed to bring stability. In fact, the country was soon torn apart once more, this time by warlords and local political factions fighting in support of the mining and territorial interests of neighboring countries (Uganda, Rwanda, Zimbabwe, Angola). After Kabila was killed in 2000, his son took over; initially he seemed to enjoying a greater degree of acceptance from the people than his father had.

By 2000 all the countries of Central Africa were in a state of crisis. They were confronted by two major obstacles. The first was internal: the need to overcome misery and despair that could lead to identity crises and ethnic prejudice, in turn provoking racism and even genocide. The second was external: the overweening power of transnational economic interest. In the Democratic Republic of Congo, in particular, armed groups had established themselves in mining areas so as to control the extraordinary wealth of diamonds, gold, cobalt, and so on; in Congo-Brazzaville and Angola, petroleum had the same effect. Thus adversaries were able to buy any kind of weaponry they felt was necessary to fight each other. These weapons came into Africa using formal and informal, both international and inter-African trade routes. This trade was supposedly illegal, but actually tolerated – if not encouraged. Despite this, there have been some positive social and political developments, particularly indications of a growing **civil society**. Against the backdrop of a century of almost uninterrupted savage colonial and post-colonial dictatorships, save the brief period of **decolonization** in the 1950s, this is a significant development.

See also: francophone Africa; state: colonial

References and further reading

Bernault, F. (1996) *Démocratie ambigues en Afrique Central Congo-Brazzaville, Gabon, 1940–1965*, Paris: Karthala.

Coquery-Vidrovitch, C. (2001) *Le Congo [AEF] au temps des grandes compagnies concessionaires, 1898–1930*, 2nd edn., Paris-Haye: Mouton.

Gide, A. (1927) *Voyage au Congo*, Paris: Gallimard.

Headrick, R. (1994) *Colonialism, Health and Illness in French Equatorial Africa, 1885–1935*, Atlanta: African Studies Association Press.

Hochschild, A. (1998) *King Leopold's Ghost: A Story of Greed, Terror, and Heroism in Colonial Africa*, Boston: Houghton Mifflin.

Martin, P.M. and Birmingham, D. (eds.) (1983) *History of Central Africa*, vol. 2, New York: Longman.

CATHERINE COQUERY-VIDROVITCH

Central African Federation

The Central African Federation (1953–63), also known as the Federation of Rhodesia and Nyasaland, comprised Southern Rhodesia (Zimbabwe), Northern Rhodesia (Zambia), and Nyasaland (Malawi). The Federation was established for both economic and political reasons. For its proponents, a federation would benefit member states considerably by providing a bigger and more attractive area of investment, widening the resource base, expanding the domestic market, generating employment, and promoting higher standards of living. Moreover, it was argued, the combined white settler colonies would be better placed to withstand the rising tide of African nationalism. The British government also supported the scheme because this would provide the necessary counterweight to growing Afrikaner power in South Africa, which had been demonstrated by the National Party's overwhelming victory in 1948, while at the same time creating auspicious conditions for the region's economic growth.

Within the region, support for the Federation idea mainly came from sections of the Southern Rhodesian white settler population, which stood to gain most from an expanded domestic market because Southern Rhodesia had a more developed and diversified agricultural and industrial economy than its neighbors. Opposition came from two sources: from white Southern Rhodesian right-wingers, who feared that the white population might be swamped by the enlarged combined African population, and from African nationalists (particularly in Northern Rhodesia and Nyasaland), who were suspicious that the Federation would entrench white supremacy in the region and extend to their territories Southern Rhodesia's obnoxious racially based sociopolitical and economic system. To woo African nationalists, architects of the Federation introduced the concept of a racial partnership between Africans and whites (albeit with Africans as junior partners until they had attained European standards – for the foreseeable future, in other words) in a united struggle to develop the region.

Administered from Salisbury in Southern Rhodesia, the Federation operated a two-tier system of government in which Federal administrative posts and structures, such as Governor and Parliament, were replicated at territorial level, with each country having its own Territorial Governor and Parliament, among other institutions. The constitution provided for a division of power and responsibility between the territorial and Federal governments, with territorial governments retaining autonomy over and responsibility for local matters, including African affairs, while the Federal government was responsible for pan-territorial issues like defence and foreign policy.

Economically, the Federation was a notable success, for the period 1953 to 1963 was one of such rapid economic development that the region soon became, outside South Africa, the most industrialized bloc in Southern Africa. Its agriculture, mining, and service industries also expanded and prospered. Similarly, levels of employment, wages, and savings rose considerably, while impressive infrastructural improvements were begun, such as the construction of the Kariba hydroelectric plant and the University College of Rhodesia and Nyasaland in 1957. Meanwhile, the Federation's cities and towns grew rapidly because of increasing rural-to-urban migration as Africans sought employment in the emerging industries. The numbers of white immigrants from Europe also rose to unprecedented levels.

Being the most industrialized part of the Federation and having the most diversified economy, Southern Rhodesia benefited the most from the Federation and at the expense of its partners. Nyasaland remained, essentially, a supplier of cheap labor to Southern Rhodesian farms and mines, while Northern Rhodesia contributed its copper export earnings, most of which were invested in Federal projects that largely benefited Southern Rhodesia. Southern Rhodesia also benefited from increased foreign investment and from the expanded local market. The inequalities of economic benefits created resentment against Southern Rhodesia in the other territories and fueled anti-Federation sentiment.

Similarly, African nationalists, particularly in the northern territories, grew increasingly antagonistic to the Federation. This was partly because, the policy of partnership notwithstanding, Africans remained politically marginalized, as shown by the fact that, although the African population was 3 million and the white population of the Federation only 300,000, Africans were allocated only six representatives (two representatives for each territory) in a Federal Legislative Assembly of thirty-five members. Moreover, racist policies and practices persisted, with African workers continuing to be paid lower wages than their white counterparts and Africans being forbidden to patronize hotels, restaurants, public toilets, and other service facilities used by whites. These and other grievances against colonial rule fueled militant African nationalism in all three territories, giving rise to the Malawi Congress Party under Kamuzu Banda and the United National Independence Party (UNIP) under Kenneth Kaunda in Northern Rhodesia. In Southern Rhodesia, nationalists founded several political parties in succession, beginning with the Southern Rhodesian African National Congress (SRANC) and, after that was banned in 1959, the National Democratic Party (NDP) and Zimbabwe African Peoples Union (ZAPU) in 1962, all under Joshua Nkomo. In December 1958, nationalist leaders from the three territories had met at the All-African People's Conference in Accra, Ghana, and resolved to campaign for the dissolution of the Federation and independence for their respective countries.

As anti-Federation pressure mounted, particularly in Northern Rhodesia and Nyasaland on the eve of their independence, right-wing elements among the Southern Rhodesian settlers also began to demand an end to the Federation, fearing that the Southern Rhodesian African population, infected by the feverish support for majority rule that had swept the continent since Ghana's independence in 1957, might prevail upon Britain to grant them independence under African majority rule – as it was about to do in Northern Rhodesia and Nyasaland. Under the banner of the

Rhodesia Front Party, these elements took power in Southern Rhodesia in 1962, thus bringing to power an anti-federalist party that was as committed to ending the Federation as its counterparts in Northern Rhodesia and Nyasaland, albeit for different reasons. Not surprisingly, the following year the Federation collapsed: Northern Rhodesia and Nyasaland became independent as, respectively, Zambia and Malawi, while Southern Rhodesia drifted irrevocably towards the Unilateral Declaration of Independence (UDI) under Ian Smith in 1965.

Further reading

Clegg, E. (1975) *Race and Politics: Partnership in the Federation of Rhodesia and Nyasaland*, Westport: Greenwood Press.

Franklin, H. (1963) *Unholy Wedlock: The Failure of the Central African Federation*, London: Allen & Unwin.

ALOIS MLAMBO

Central African Republic

The Central African Republic (CAR) covers an area of 622,436 square kilometers and is located in **Central Africa**, north of the **Democratic Republic of Congo** and bordered by six countries. It had an estimated population of 3.4 million in 1998. At the beginning of the twentieth century, the French granted huge concessions in their new colony of Ubangi-Shari (which became the Central African Republic) to private companies, whose brutal agents terrorized the local population into collecting wild rubber. During the 1910s, the French defeated or coopted the rulers of the region's slave-raiding states and attempted to reduce the power of the concessionary companies. Slave raiding was greatly reduced but the abusive activities of the private companies were not. During the 1920s, the French enforced the production of cash crops such as cotton and had roads built throughout the colony.

During the 1930s, critics of colonialism, including governor-generals of **French Equatorial Africa**, called for basic reforms, but local colonial administrators and company employees remained tyrants who could inflict physical punishment on Central Africans at will. Abuse of Central Africans increased during the Second World War because of pressure to produce more cash crops and collect more raw materials for the war effort. The war also forced France to redefine her relationship with her colonies, however, leading to local elections in Ubangi-Shari.

In 1947, Ubangi-Shari's first Catholic priest, Barthélémy Boganda, was elected to serve in the French National Assembly, where he became an outspoken critic of forced labor and arbitrary punishment in French Equatorial Africa. He formed his own political party, the Movement for the Social Evolution of Black Africa (MESAN), and eventually won such overwhelming electoral victories that by the mid-1950s one segment of the European business community formed an alliance with Boganda. The French administration also began to work with Boganda instead of against him.

In 1958, Ubangi-Shari obtained internal self-government and became the Central African Republic, a name which Boganda had initially chosen for the large federation of Central African states that he dreamt in vain of establishing. Then, on Easter Day in 1959, Boganda died in an airplane crash that appears to have been caused by the explosion of a bomb. A brief struggle for power between Abel Goumba and David Dacko, backed by the French, ended in a victory for Dacko. He became the CAR's first president at independence on 13 August 1960.

Dacko declared MESAN the only legal political party in 1962 and was reelected president in 1964 in a rigged election. Dacko promoted the growth of diamond exports but was unable to curtail a sharp fall in cotton production. The number of government employees increased dramatically during his term of office, which led to a problem that every Central African ruler has had to face: insufficient revenues to pay government salaries. This, in turn, led to dependence on the French to subsidize the CAR.

By late 1965 Dacko was ready to step down and let someone else deal with the nation's economic stagnation and financial crisis, and on 1 January 1966 General Jean-Bedel Bokassa led a coup that removed him from power. Bokassa soon abolished the constitution and dissolved the legislature. In 1972 he proclaimed himself president for life and in 1976 he became Emperor Bokassa I of the Central African Empire. Bokassa was initially somewhat successful in increasing the production of cotton, and he had a new central market and a national university built, but he soon focused on projects to enrich himself while government employees remained unpaid and students failed to receive their grants. Student riots broke out in early 1979, following the Emperor's order that they should wear uniforms produced at a factory owned by his family. In April 1979 hundreds of students were arrested, some of whom were beaten to death in prison. Concurrent revelations in the press about French President Giscard d'Estaing's receipt of diamonds as personal gifts from Bokassa proved very embarrassing to France. In September 1979, while Bokassa was visiting Libya, the French sent paratroopers to the CAR and returned David Dacko to power.

Fraudulent elections in 1981 confirmed Dacko's rule, but he again proved ineffective and resigned once more. He was replaced by General André Kolingba, who was strongly supported by the French. Kolingba used his office to place many individuals from his own ethnic group, the Yakoma, in privileged positions, thus reinforcing the influence in the CAR of those minority riverine peoples who had profited politically and commercially from their early collaboration with the French.

The end of the Cold War led to calls for multiparty democracy and the French pressured Kolingba to hold presidential elections in the early 1990s. These led to the victory of Ange-Felix Patasse in 1993. Patasse enjoyed the support of many "northern" ethnic groups: his father's Suma (Gbaya) people, his mother's Kare people, and the Kaba people he had lived among as a child, as well as other "northerners" also resented the power of the southern riverine and forest peoples (particularly the Ngbaka people who had been represented by Boganda, Dacko, and Bokassa). Once Patasse was in power, his patronage of "northerners" at the expense of "southerners," his failure to ensure that civil servants and soldiers were paid on time, and his alleged disregard of the new constitution resulted in a series of three unsuccessful but terribly destructive mutinies in 1996 and 1997, each led by military units composed mostly of "southerners."

Patasse was reelected president in 1999, but in May 2001 supporters of former president Kolingba made an unsuccessful coup attempt. Libyan soldiers came to Patasse's aid and many riverine inhabitants of the capital, Bangui, fled across the river to escape real or imagined retribution by Patasse's troops and supporters. Thus, at the beginning of the twenty-first century, French influence had waned and Libyan influence increased in the CAR.

Further reading

Coquery-Vidrovitch, C. (1972) *Le Congo [AEF] au temps des grandes compagnies concessionaires, 1898–1930*, 2nd edn., Paris-Haye: Mouton.

Titley, B. (1997) *Dark Age: The Political Odyssey of Emperor Bokassa*, Montreal and Kingston: McGill-Queen's University Press.

RICHARD A. BRADSHAW

Chad

Chad has an area of some 1,284,634 square kilometers. It is bordered by **Libya**, **Niger**, **Nigeria**, the **Central African Republic**, and **Cameroon**, and had a population of approximately 7.3 million in 2000. At the beginning of the twentieth century, Chad became a part of French Equatorial Africa and it was not until 1920 that it was considered a separate colony. However, the French had a difficult time imposing colonial rule over the entire territory: the central and northern regions had a significant power base and considerable wealth from their control of the trans-Saharan trade route. The southern part of the country was under direct colonial rule, and the Sara ethnic group in particular suffered under this rule. Many Sara men were conscripted to work on the railway in Congo Brazzaville. Many of them died there. Others were conscripted into the French military and served in both world wars.

Because of Chad's lack of resources, the colonial administration made very little investment in the colony. Furthermore, the limited amount of infrastructure they did build was in the south. For example, in Fort Lamy (renamed **N'Djamena** in 1973) there was only one school with one teacher in 1921. By 1933 there were only eighteen trained teachers in the entire country. The cultivation of cotton for export, including mandatory quotas, was forced upon the population in the south beginning in 1929. Income earned from the sale of cotton, remittances, and military pensions provided some southerners with a semblance of economic gain, and some southerners found employment in the colonial administration after attending mainly missionary schools. The rest of the population, especially the Muslims in the northern and central regions, had very little contact with the colonial administration. They continued to earn their living by herding, farming, and trading.

Following the Second World War, new political developments occurred in the colony, although change was relatively slow. Representative institutions were formed, along with the establishment of political parties. However, expansion and improvement of the colony's infrastructure remained virtually at a standstill. For example, the first high school was opened after the war ended, but as late as 1958 there were only three high schools in the colony.

Chad's political and economic prospects did not improve for its three million citizens following independence in 1960. François Tombalbaye, a Christian Sara from the south, became prime minister in 1959 and then president in 1960. It soon became apparent that Tombalbaye and other Sara politicians were neither committed to power sharing nor to the regional and national integration that was needed because ethnic, religious, regional, and economic divisions threatened the country's stability.

During Tombalbaye's presidential term (1960–75) political and economic conditions went from bad to worse, with scarce national revenue spent on the military. As his rule became more repressive, broad sectors of the population, including members of his own ethnic group, grew dissatisfied. The National Liberation Front (NLF) was formed out of armed groups based in the north. The French intervened on behalf of Tombalbaye, but Felix Malloum, a Sara and head of the military, overthrew him in 1975. Malloum's military regime was not able to curb the country's descent into political, economic, and social collapse, however, as the rebel groups in the north continued their armed struggle.

In the late 1970s Chad was plunged into civil war, ethnic conflict, and regional strife that lasted into the latter part of the twentieth century. The prolonged civil war and the ethnic and regional differences in the country changed as people adopted, shifted, and negotiated various allegiances and loyalties in their efforts to capture territory and power – or merely to survive. Furthermore, external intervention by Libya, France, the United States, and other countries only served to prop up one leader after another. Libya's intervention was the most significant. The Libyan army invaded Chad in 1980 and 1982, the Libyan government announced their intention to merge the two countries, and Libyans occupied the Aouzou Strip (located along Chad's northern border).

The prospects for peace began to improve following the collapse of the government headed by Hissene Habre in 1990. Idriss Deby took control of the government and called for a democratic, multi-party political system. Deby's government held a national conference in 1993, after disputes with political and military factions and Libya had been settled. Finally, a new democratic constitution was drafted: multi-party presidential elections were held in 1996 and national assembly elections in 1997.

The many years of civil unrest wreaked havoc on Chad's economy, leaving the country as one of Africa's poorest. The country's unexploited petroleum had the potential to improve the economy, however, especially after an agreement was signed with the government of Cameroon in 1995 for the construction of a pipeline to the Port of Kribi. The country's lack of transportation and communication facilities were further obstacles to development. In 1999 manufacturing accounted for 12 percent of the gross domestic product (GDP). The main industries, located in **N'Djamena** and Moundou, included cotton, textiles, meatpacking, beer brewing, natron (sodium carbonate), cigarettes, and construction materials.

Most of the country's population live in the fertile southern part of the country where the country's agricultural base is located. Disproportionately dependent on agriculture, droughts during the latter part of the twentieth century severely affected Chad's economy. The majority of the population was engaged in subsistence farming, livestock production, herding (sheep, goats, cattle), and fishing. The main agricultural product and export commodity was cotton, which accounted for 40 percent of GDP in 1999. Other principal crops included sorghum, wheat, millet, rice, manioc, and sugarcane. With the end of the civil war and the drought, with its accompanying food shortages, Chad finally has a chance of achieving growth and development.

Further reading

Azevedo, M.J. and Naadozie, E.U. (1998) *Chad: A Nation in Search of its Future*, Boulder: Westview Press.

Nolutshungu, S. (1996) *Limits of Anarchy: Intervention and State Formation in Chad*, Charlottesville and London: University of Virginia Press.

CASSANDRA RACHEL VENEY

Christian reform movements

From its very beginnings in Africa, **Christianity** has spawned numerous movements offering alternative religious agendas. Rather than isolating themselves from internal and global forces, these reform movements have articulated their agendas for change in a pluralistic context under the shadows of the colonial encounter, religious hegemony, and neo-colonial capitalist exploitation. They have also been affected by developments within the broader Christian tradition, such as the global missionary agenda, Vatican II (called by Pope John XXIII to address important issues such as the church in the modern world, ecumenism, religious liberty, and revelation), liberation/contextual theologies, and the rise of organizations like the All African Conference of Churches and the World Council of Churches.

Christian independency as a reform movement

Independent churches in Africa can be considered as reform movements because their *raison d'être* was to develop an alternative social agenda through the Christian tradition. These independent churches have also been variously called prophetic movements, new religious movements, African initiated churches, and African indigenous churches. These terms designate more than 8,000 Christian groups in Africa. Harold Turner (1967) categorized them as modern African religious movements to emphasize their connection with the colonial experience and the fact that these movements include churches, secessionist groups, prophetic movements, healing cults, and a variety of religious communities. He also distinguished them from neo-traditionalist movements that depended on African traditional religious ideas and Hebraist movements that emphasized monotheism and the teachings of the Bible. He made a further distinction between mission churches and separatist, independent, messianic, and prophetic movements. Today, scholars continue to use different designations. Key factors that determine the use of a particular name are independency, genesis, cultural grounding, complexity, and global linkages.

Historical development of the movements

Although our focus is limited to the modern period, it is instructive to note that Christian reform movements in Africa go back to the first four centuries of the church when the Donatist movement emerged in North Africa after persecution by Emperor Diocletian in *c.*303–5. During that persecution Christians were also asked to surrender sacred writings and register church property. The second reform movement that led to independency was the Antonian Movement started by Doña Beatriz Kimpa Vita who was born in 1684 in Kongo. In 1704 Doña Beatriz claimed that Saint Anthony came to her in a vision and gave a message to her about restoring the Kingdom of Kongo, now occupied by foreigners. She was critical of Capuchin missionaries for refusing to recognize black saints and claimed she was conceived by the power of the Holy Spirit. The Portuguese burned her at the stake in July 1706.

Several other movements burst on the African scene much later, in the wake of the colonial incursion into Africa. In 1894 Christian independency started in Johannesburg, South Africa, when former Methodists formed the first Ethiopian-type church. In 1898 Simungu Bafazini Shibe broke away from the American Zulu Mission to form the Zulu Congregational Church. In 1900 Malawi's John Chilembwe, who studied in the United States, set up his Providence Industrial Mission. Elliot Kamwana Chirwa, who had been introduced to the teachings of the Watchtower Movement by missionary Joseph Booth, started his own version of the movement in 1908 also in Malawi. In Liberia Prophet William Wade Harris received his call to preach in 1911. He moved to Côte d'Ivoire where he preached until he was expelled. In Nigeria, Christians were already thinking of establishing churches, which they called "African," and by 1919 there were probably twelve such churches in the city of Lagos alone.

During the second wave, charismatic and prophetic leaders started churches in different parts of the continent. In 1922 a movement started in Ibadan in Nigeria that was later linked with the Faith Tabernacle Movement from the United States. Due to doctrinal differences, the Nigerian group established its independence in 1928. The preaching of Evangelist Babalola helped spread the message of the movement and increased membership. The movement later cooperated with the British Apostolic Church and changed names several times, eventually adopting the name Christ Apostolic Church in 1943. Josiah O. Oshitelu founded the Aladura Churches in Nigeria after he received a vision from God in 1925. Central to his movement were faith, prayer, and fasting. In 1925 the Prophet Moses Orimolade Tunolase started a prayer group in Lagos that was to become the Cherubim and Seraphim Movement. Simon Kibangu received a call from the Holy Spirit during the epidemic of 1918, but his work as founder of a movement actually began in 1921 when he healed a sick woman. Other prophetic leaders who started movements during this period were Zakayo Kivuli of Kenya and John Maranke of Zimbabwe.

The third wave of independency came after independence. Some of the movements of this period include the Church of Christ of Africa, which broke away from the Anglican Church in 1963, the Mario Legio, Lumpa Church, the Eden Revival Church in Ghana, and the Alice Lakwena movement in Uganda. David Barrett (1986) reported that the number of independent churches had grown to 7,170 by 1985.

The motivations for independency

Several reasons have been given for the rise of these churches.

1 Some churches were started because of the desire to see Africans in positions of leadership within the church.
2 Some started because of nationalist sentiments, examples of which include movements in Nigeria and Ghana where several "Native" Churches were formed. The National Church of Nigeria (now called "Godianism") fits this profile.
3 Other movements started because of the rise of prophetic and charismatic leaders who initially did not intend to start new churches. Simon Kimbangu, whose movement grew into a large church, and William Wade Harris, the prophet whose preaching led to the establishment of the Harrist Church, originally did not intend to start new churches. However, other prophets had a definite vision for a new community and set themselves the task of establishing and building it. An example here is Isaiah Shembe, who started the Nazareth Church.
4 Christian independency was also established because Africans wanted to incorporate local beliefs and customs into the church. According to Fabian Ebousi Boulaga, they responded to a Christianity that was irrelevant to Africa because the mission churches had rejected the African worldview and culture. The Bitwi cult and the Nazareth Church of Shembe are good examples here. Leaders like Jordan Musamba of Malawi, who started the Last Church of God and His Christ, were convinced that Africans needed a church that would reflect the customs and manners that God gave to the African people.

5 Christian independency represented a rejection of colonial and foreign missionary praxis. In Kenya, colonialism and missionary Christianity were resisted because of the loss of land to Christian colonial settlers. The circumcision controversy, for instance, was instrumental in the creation of Kikuyu independent churches and schools. The Kenyan reformers, who also borrowed from Kikuyu ideology and religion, desired to practice *karing'a* (originally meaning "purity") on matters like initiation over which there was a struggle between the mission churches and the Kikuyu. Later on this term was used to refer to those who rejected missionary usurpation of land. These tensions also led to the formation of the African Orthodox Church of Kenya and the Agikuyu Spirit Churches whose leaders were considered prophets. Elijah Masinde (formerly part of the Quaker mission) was one of these prophets in western Kenya. He wanted to drive away colonial settlers and missionaries, and reinstate traditional religion. His movement was quashed and Masinde was put in a mental institution.
6 Christian independency expressed a desire for theological and liturgical freedom. Many of the new churches emphasized the importance of the Holy Spirit in life, as well as emphasizing church services, prayer, and a festive approach to worship.
7 Many churches were established to focus on physical and spiritual needs that were felt to have been neglected by the main churches.
8 The independent churches represented a commitment to and actualization of a philosophical orientation. For example, the now defunct Jamaa (Swahili for "family") was founded in the Democratic Republic of Congo by Placide Tempels to institutionalize ideas articulated in his *Bantu Philosophy*, linking human dignity to the three supposedly basic aspirations of the ancestors – life/force, fecundity/filiation, and union in love.
9 Many movements owe their beginnings to the general sociopolitical and cultural climate of discrimination, injustice, and economic marginalization that, in turn, encouraged the search for alternative spaces in which individuals and communities could grow spiritually, socially, economically, and emotionally.

These movements engaged and continue to engage critically with the Christian tradition and are determined to forge a praxis that reflects the ideological position of the founders, even if that results in rupture from older churches or in religious innovation. The older churches have not always been kind to these movements. They have derided them as sects or cults, and sometimes consider them non-Christian, but many of them have survived attacks from the mainstream churches and are still thriving today. Tshishiku Tshibangu (1993) has pointed out that they appeared as a result of "disappointment and enthusiasm." The leaders were disappointed with what the Christian tradition offered, but demonstrated great enthusiasm for the possibilities and potential of their new faith. It is in that light that one can see them as reform movements. A brief look at some of their beliefs and practices testifies to this reformist strain in the movements.

Researchers, following the work of Bengt Sundkler and Gerhardus Oosthuizen, have characterized the movements as either Ethiopian or Zionist churches in order to distinguish their practices. The designation "Ethiopian" stresses independence, because Ethiopia was never colonized. It is also one of the few African countries frequently referred to in the Hebrew Bible. These designations go back to the early days of the formation of these churches, particularly in South Africa where the Ethiopian churches were called *Ibandla lase Tiyopia*. Even those independent churches that did not see their work in political terms nonetheless worked for political reform by being active in the African National Congress.

The Zionist Churches, on the other hand, had their roots in the city of Zion in Illinois in the United States. One of the early leaders, John Alexander Dowie, stressed divine healing, baptism by immersion in the name of the Trinity, and the imminent return of Jesus. The growth of the movement in South Africa was marked by the creation of Zion cities. Zionists wear white robes, worship with bare feet, and carry holy staffs. Jean Comaroff (1985) points out that, in addition to these symbols following the Hebrew Bible, their use is a critique of the authority structures and praxis of the older churches. Well-known Zionist churches in South Africa include the ZCC of Engena Lekganyane and the Ama Nazaretha of Isaiah Shembe in Zululand. Shembe's movement has incorporated Zulu customs and the leader is called *inkosi*. Shembe wore Zulu clothing and shaped the liturgy of the movement by composing most of the hymns in use today. His followers believe in the gifts of the Spirit, who has replaced the role once filled by ancestral spirits. Healing is important to the movement. Christian independency was instrumental in the rise of the Black Consciousness Movement, the promotion of ethical living, self-restraint, and discipline, and it stressed liberation from evil powers, promoting physical and social well-being.

Christian independency and reform

Christian independency has been characterized by a number of attributes, such as baptism for believers, healing through prayer, revelation from a prophet, the gift of tongues and interpretation, African values in worship, sacred places, festivals, strict moral codes, and in some cases the prohibition of polygamy and the use of African sacred objects. Perhaps we can get a better sense of their desire for reform if we consider their outlook and praxis briefly and in broad terms.

First, the new churches introduced theological reforms. They incorporated African worldviews and ideas about God, sin, healing, and community into their theology. Their most distinct contribution lay in the reconciliation of the role of the Holy Spirit with African theology. In doing this they drew from African belief in spirits. The Shona people of Zimbabwe believe that the spirits of the deceased, called *mhondoro*, continue to affect the lives of the living. These churches emphasize the role of the Spirit in several areas:

1 Leaders like Kimbangu claimed they were called by the Spirit to preach. The founders of the Roho Religion in Western Kenya believe their movement was founded because their leaders received inspiration from the Spirit.
2 The Nazareth Church of Shembe has elevated the Holy Spirit in their confession of faith, leading to charges that they have neglected Jesus. Their statement of faith reads: "I believe in the Father, and in the Holy Spirit and in the Communion of the Saints of the Nazarites."
3 Leaders of Christian independency claim that they heal through the power of the Holy Spirit. Oosthuizen (1987) points out that in the Zionist churches, which believe in healing, such services are offered by the *abathandazi* (prayer leaders) and *abaprofeti* (prophets). They use different symbols, such as colors, vestments, cords, staves, and white candles. The color white represents the Holy Spirit. Although the Zionist churches heal through the power of the Holy Spirit, they also recognize that healing is a gift from the ancestral spirits.
4 Some of the leaders have also used the power of the Holy Spirit for political activism. Alice Auma started a Holy Spirit Movement in Northern Uganda with the belief that God had sent a prophet called Lakwena. Alice later organized a military wing, called the Holy Spirit Mobile Force, for an armed confrontation with the Ugandan government. The movement was defeated and Alice escaped into Kenya.

Second, Christian independency is concerned with reforms because they offer ecclesiological and liturgical innovation. The rise of these churches has brought with it alternative church structures and leadership, which is often based on traditional leadership models. Sheila Walker (1983) has demonstrated that members of the Harrist movement have always seen the Prophet as taking the same role as a traditional priest, even though they taught that he was a prophet who had pointed out that Christianity should be made meaningful to the people of Côte d'Ivoire. The prophet encouraged the use of Ivoirien instruments in worship. The Aladura churches emphasize prayer. Shembe introduced a liturgy that incorporated Zulu music, dance, and rituals. He set aside an *Ekuphakameni* (exalted place) on Mount Nhlangakhazi where Nazarites gather for worship and celebration. What is particularly distinctive about the worship services is that members wear colored gowns. These gowns do not merely indicate their separation from older missionary churches, but also symbolize the presence of the Holy Spirit. Worship services in the new churches include lively sermons and testimonies from members indicating the victories that the Holy Spirit has given them. The services are open to spirit possession and other manifestations of the Spirit.

Third, Christian independency has maintained a critical engagement with the social order and in some cases used such concerns as the basis from which to reform the Christian faith. The activities of religious movements in Africa offer a clear commentary on the social order, in ways similar to the Donatist Movement that had fought against *traditor* (lapsed) bishops during the persecution. Examples of social activism abound in Christian independency. The earliest prophetic movement to include a fervent nationalist element was the Antonian movement started by Doña Beatriz (mentioned above). Most East and Central African movements had sociopolitical concerns. In Malawi, John Chilembwe's Providence Industrial Mission was set up to provide social services for his people. Johane Masowe of Zimbabwe preached baptism by immersion at a time when heavy demands for money were being made by the colonial authorities and older churches. He healed people and encouraged them to work towards self-sufficiency. His movement organized its own schools and has now spread into nine different countries in the region. The Zionist Churches of South Africa offered hope and security for many urban dwellers who lived on the margins of apartheid society. Karen Field (1985) has also noted that, although the Watchtower Movement in Zambia was doctrinally apolitical, their engagement in social issues in Zambia was undeniable. The reform movements' concern for social welfare also contributed to utopian dreams and millenarian teachings. Among the Xhosa people, Prophets Nongqawuse and Nstikana combined their anti-colonial message with millenarian teachings, urging people to destroy their property in the hope their ancestors would return and the whites be destroyed. Millennial ideas led the Watchtower Movement to set a date for the end of the world: 14 October 1914. The Mwana Lesa movement, which started in Northern Rhodesia, combined millennial teaching with witchcraft cleansing. The deaths of members of the Movement for the Restoration of Ten Commandments in Uganda in the late 1990s indicates that radical commitment to millennial ideas continues among some groups.

Fourth, these movements demonstrate a remarkable commitment to the restoration of African religiosity and worldviews. In this respect, their most remarkable contribution is the restoration of healing in all its forms to the Christian agenda. In doing so, they have revived interest in traditional healing and, more importantly, kept alive a holistic attitude towards health and healing. Christian missionaries established hospitals, but their exclusive focus on biological explanations for illness and treatment did not always take into consideration the social dynamics of sickness and health. Christian independency revived holistic approaches and offered hope to many. However, they cannot heal all illnesses – as demonstrated by the fact that the scourge of HIV/AIDS continues to take its toll. The resources of healing found in the new churches may be lacking in this case, but the hope, comfort, and support they offer members who live with the disease testifies to the importance accorded to the idea of community among these churches.

Finally, Christian independency introduced reform by changing the role of women in the church. Women were founders of several independent churches and have held positions of leadership in many others, such as the Church of Christ Calabar, and the Cherubim and Seraphim in Nigeria. Women also function as prophetesses, receiving visions and dreams, and communicating them to the congregation. They preach and lead services. At the end of the twentieth century, some of the older churches in Africa still did not recognize women as leaders except in associations created mainly for women. The idea that women too receive the call of God through the Holy Spirit to start and lead churches has certainly given a new perspective to the place of women in the church.

Post-colonial developments

Christian independency remains a permanent feature of the African religious landscape. First, in the 1980s the Alice Lakwena movement led a rebellion in Uganda, indicating that religious independency continues to take a critical stance towards the established authorities and, if need be, will engage in conflict. Second, an important development in post-colonial Africa regarding Christian independency is a gradual "routinization of charisma." In Nigeria, Rosalind Hackett argues:

> the routinization of charisma is regarded as a necessary means to stability, survival and success, and several movements, such as the Brotherhood and the Celestial Church of Christ, have developed elaborate methods of disseminating spiritual power.
>
> (Hackett 1987a: 334)

Another example is the Kimbangu Movement, Eglise de Jésus Christ sur la Terre par le Prophète Simon Kimbangu, which continues to grow. Today it is one of the largest independent churches in Africa. Kimbangu was considered a prophet in the *ngunza* tradition in Kongo. He healed people, causing consternation because people would leave hospital and come to Nkamba, his home, to be healed. Some called him a messiah, destined to rule over Kongo. The colonial authorities arrested his followers and gave them life sentences. Kimbangu himself was arrested when he returned to Nkamba, tried for sedition and sentenced to death, but the Belgian king commuted the verdict to a life sentence. Kimbangu died in prison in 1951. On the eve of independence, the movement was recognized and Kimbangu's son Joseph Diangienda became the head of the church, unifying other groups into a single church with headquarters at Nkamba (which they consider the new Jerusalem). The movement has undergone what sociologists of religion call the "routinization of charisma": the leadership does not emphasize healing as Kimbangu did. They have established social services, such as schools, health centers, economic projects, and a seminary where leaders of the church are trained. The church is now a member of the World Council of Churches.

A third important post-colonial development is the commitment of some African-initiated churches in Zimbabwe to ecological and environmental restoration. M.L. Daneel (1999) has argued that an environmental and eco-theology has been born and is growing among the churches of Zimbabwe who see earth-keeping as a salvific enterprise covering the whole of creation. They collaborate with traditional leaders, spirit mediums, and political leaders in the attempt to resist ecological disaster. They have conceptualized environmental destruction as a sin that should be confessed so that the church can practice its healing and liberating mission – a mission that includes socioeconomic and environmental liberation. Their task is Christological because

> environmental abuse is sinful. It causes Christ to suffer and Mwari to judge, in retaliation, through drought. By its very nature the church in this context is or should be both protector and healer of the environment, ministering by implication to the wounded body of Christ.
>
> (Daneel 1999: 43)

They organize green rituals and liturgies to plant trees to restore the land in obedience to Mwari's commission to care for the earth. They draw inspiration from Zimbabwean traditions and the freedom struggle, arguing that Christ is the *muridzi venyika* (guardian of the land) and the believer's task is not *dominium terrae*, but healing and restoring the earth that is Christ's body. They espouse a Trinitarian ecological theology:

1. Mwari, the creator, is an insider and should not be seen as a distant remote god.
2. Christ is the earth-keeper and eucharistic services of planting reflect this view. Salvation covers all creation because Christ, as Nganga, is healer, savior, liberator, and restorer of creation.
3. The Holy Spirit is the spirit of creation, fountain of life, and the *murapi venyika* (healer of the land), who condemns destruction of the land.

The churches promote reforestation, the conservation of wildlife and water resources. Daneel (1999) states that this ministry has replaced fatalistic peasant attitudes with the conviction that they can use African religio-cultural values and Christian themes to end the destruction of the environment, thereby extending the *missio dei* to all creation through a self-governing, self-propagating, and self-supporting "existential people's theology."

Conclusion

Christian independency is part of the ongoing reformation of the African church. Today their emphasis on the role of the Holy Spirit brings them close to the Pentecostal movement that is moving across Africa in the wake of economic crisis. The renewal, if we might use Barrett's (1986) term, will continue to help these movements mature. They offer not only viable alternative religious perspectives, but also hope for many seeking meaning and fulfillment.

References and further reading

Barret, D.B. (1986) *Schism and Renewal in Africa: An Analysis of Six Thousand Contemporary Religious Movements*, London: Oxford University Press.

Comaroff, J. (1985) *Body of Power, Spirit of Resistance: The Culture and History of a South African People*, Chicago: University Of Chicago Press.

Daneel, M.L. (1999) *African Earthkeepers: Environmental Mission and Liberation in Christian Perspective*, Pretoria: UNISA Press.

Field, K. (1985) *Revival and Rebellion in Colonial Central Africa*, Princeton: Princeton University Press.

Hackett, R.I.J. (1987a) *Religion in Calabar: The Religious Life and History of a Nigerian Town*, Berlin: Mouton de Gruyter.

—— (1987b) *New Religious Movements in Nigeria*, Lewiston: Edwin Mellen.

Lan, D. (1985) *Guns and Guerrillas and Spirit Mediums in Zimbabwe*, London: James Currey.

Oosthuizen, G. (1987) *The Birth of Christian Zionism in South Africa*, South Africa: University of Zululand.

Ranger, T.O. (1986) "Religious Movements and Politics in Sub-Saharan Africa," *African Studies Review* 29, 2: 1–69.

Tshibangu, T. (1993) "Religions and Social Evolution," in A. Mazrui and C. Wondji (eds.), *UNESCO General History of Africa*, vol. VIII, *Africa Since 1935*, Berkeley: University of California Press, pp. 501–21.

Turner, H.W. (1967) *African Independent Church*, vol. 1, *History of an African Independent Church: The Church of the Lord (Aladura)*, Oxford: Clarendon Press.

Walker, S. (1983) *The Religious Revolution in the Ivory Coast: The Prophet Harris and the Harrist Church*, Chapel Hill: University of North Carolina Press.

ELIAS K. BONGMBA

Christianity

Introduction

Christianity is one of the most vibrant and dynamic religions in Africa. From the time of its inception to the present day it has brought tremendous changes in the social, economic, political, and religious life of African peoples. The beginning of Christianity on the continent goes back to the apostolic times – long before it was established in Europe. The first churches were established in Egypt. There is a general agreement among scholars that Christianity came to Egypt during the first century of our era. By AD 400 Christianity had spread across North Africa and become the religion of most of the population. This was to change following the rise and spread of **Islam** from the seventh century. During its heyday, Christian North Africa produced great thinkers, such as Origen, Tertullian, Cyprian, and Augustine, who influenced the development of Christian theology. In the fourth century Christianity spread to Ethiopia but failed to spread across the rest of the continent.

The missionary era in Africa is traced back to the nineteenth century, when Christianity began to grow more rapidly as European encroachment spread. In large measure, missionary expansion can be considered a result of imperial and commercial expansion, for in many instances European governments supported the missionaries. This was especially true in the field of education, which became a means of disseminating European and American cultures in Africa. There was also a theological factor, namely a spiritual revival in Europe and North America, characterized by an evangelical awakening. This impulse led to the formation of a number of missionary societies that were behind the spread of Christianity in various parts of Africa. In many cases the spread of Christianity was undertaken by African converts, as well as Christian missionaries from the **African diaspora**, especially from the United States.

The introduction or spread of Christianity in Africa in the nineteenth century was not an easy affair. Christianity had to contend with two other religions – traditional **African religions** and Islam – in the bid for converts. Other obstacles facing Christianity in the nineteenth century were the slave trade, local and colonial conflicts, and the early missionaries' lack of understanding of African cultures. Despite these obstacles Christianity spread far and wide and over the course of the twentieth century became one of the continent's leading religions, coming to play a vital role in the lives of large numbers of Africans. Elizabeth Isichei (1995) has estimated that there were 10 million African Christians in 1900 and 143 million in 1970, predicting that there would be 393 million in 2000. This means that by the end of the century one-fifth of all Christians in the world were Africans.

Christian denominations

All the major Christian denominations spread their tentacles in Africa during the twentieth century. They include the Catholic, Lutheran, Presbyterian, Anglican, Congregational, Methodist, Baptist, Moravian, Seventh Day Adventist, and Pentecostal Churches. The Catholic Church boasted the largest number of adherents. Various societies were involved in the spread of Catholicism in the nineteenth and twentieth centuries. The most notable included the Capuchin missionaries, the Jesuits, the Dominicans, the Augustinians, the Carmelites, the Lazarites, the Franciscans, White Fathers, the Holy Ghost Fathers, the Oblates of Mary Immaculate, and the Montfort Fathers.

The Lutheran Church was also introduced in Africa by a number of missionary societies. They included the Berlin Missionary Society (formed in 1824) and the Rhenish Missionary Society (established in 1828), which both sent missionaries to **South Africa** – in 1834 and 1829 respectively. By the 1850s Lutheran mission stations had been established in Cape Colony (1842), Orange Free State (1833), and Natal (1847). In the 1860s two societies spread to the Transvaal, and subsequently they expanded their evangelization in the sub-region, reaching South West Africa (**Namibia**) in 1857, Southern Rhodesia (**Zimbabwe**) in 1892, Tanganyika (**Tanzania**) and Lake Malawi in 1891. Another well-known society that spread the seeds of Lutheranism in Africa was the Hermannsburg Missionary Society, founded in 1849, which sent its first missionaries to East Africa in the 1850s but without much success. In 1854 the society established missionary work in Natal and thereafter in Transvaal and Bechuanaland Protectorate (**Botswana**) at the invitation of Chief Sechele of the Bakwena people.

Lutheranism was also introduced in Africa by missionary societies from the United States, such as the Board of Foreign Missions of the Lutheran Brethren in America, which launched missionary work in Cameroon and Chad in 1920 where it established schools, medical work, Bible colleges, and other missionary enterprises. Other US-based Lutheran societies included the Board of World Missions (Augustana Lutheran Church), founded in 1860, which started missionary work in Tanganyika (Tanzania) in 1922 on behalf of the German Lutheran Missions in Tanganyika, and the American Evangelical Lutheran Church, which had launched missionary work in **Liberia** in 1860. From Denmark came the Danish Lutheran Mission, founded in 1868, which started work in Tanzania from 1949.

Africa also saw the proliferation of Reformed Churches, sometimes known as Presbyterian Churches. The history of Presbyterian churches in Africa can be traced back to 1652, through the activities of the Dutch East India Company. In that year Jan Van Riebeeck arrived with a contingent of merchants at the Cape Colony to establish a station where vessels would be provided with fresh meat and vegetables. This marked the beginning of the Dutch Reformed Church in South Africa. The initial growth of the church among the indigenous people was quite slow. The church began to take shape with the arrival of slaves in 1658. From the Cape the church expanded to other parts of South Africa as the colonial frontiers expanded, eventually reaching Botswana, Zimbabwe, Northern Rhodesia (**Zambia**) and Nyasaland (**Malawi**). Presbyterianism was also introduced in Africa through the activities of British missionary societies, principally the Glasgow Missionary Society, the Scottish Missionary Society, and the London Missionary Society. The first overseas projects were in West Africa, but these were not successful. The Glasgow Missionary Society began mission work in South Africa in 1821. The death of David Livingstone raised concerns about the evangelization of Central Africa. To this effect an expedition to Nyasaland in 1875 led to the foundation of two missions, one at Livingstonia in the northern part of the country under the Free Church and another at **Blantyre** in the southern part of the country under the Church of Scotland. From Livingstonia, Presbyterianism spread over the Malawi border into Zambia in 1896. With the passing of time Presbyterianism was introduced in **Kenya** (1898), Gold Coast, **Togo**, and **Nigeria**.

The Anglican Church was also introduced in Africa by a number of missionary societies: namely, the Universities Mission to Central Africa (UMCA) and the Church Missionary Society (CMS). The UMCA was formed in 1858 as a result of David Livingstone's appeal to the Universities of Oxford and Cambridge to send out a mission to carry on the missionary work that he had began in Africa. The Universities of London and Durham, and for a time the University of Dublin, responded to the appeal. From the outset, the universities realized that in order to succeed they needed to work under the auspices of the Church of England. The first expedition of missionaries was sent to Malawi in 1860. It arrived the following year and set up a mission station at Magomero. Because of hardships, the mission withdrew to **Zanzibar** from where Anglican missionaries launched concerted missionary work to Pemba in Tanzania, northern **Mozambique**, Malawi, Zambia, and Zimbabwe. The Church Missionary Society, originally founded in 1799 under the name the Society for Missions in Africa and the East before changing its name in 1812, played a major role in the introduction of Anglicanism in several African countries, including South Africa, **Swaziland**, **Egypt**, **Sierra Leone**, Nigeria, Kenya, Tanzania, **Uganda**, and **Sudan**.

Africa also saw an upsurge of Congregational Churches. They were introduced through the missionary activities of the London Missionary Society, which was founded in London in 1795 by Congregationalists, Anglicans, Presbyterians, and Wesleyans. Stephen Neil (1964) has indicated that with the passing of time the London Missionary Society eventually became the missionary organ of the English Congregational body, which was contrary to its original intention. Congregationalism threw much of its missionary weight into Southern Africa and its early history is dominated by four great missionary figures: John Theodore Vanderkemp, John Philip, Robert Moffat, and David Livingstone. These missionaries left an indelible mark on the history of Congregationalism in Africa. The first missionaries landed at the Cape Colony in 1799. From there missionary ventures were launched into the interior and in due course Congregationalism spread to Natal, Orange Free State, and Transvaal in present-day South Africa, and beyond to the rest of Southern Africa, **Madagascar**, and other parts of the continent.

The Methodist Church also embarked on missionary work in Africa. Methodism was introduced in Africa from both Britain and the United States. From Britain Methodism was introduced through the activities of the Methodist Missionary Society, formed in 1813 for overseas evangelization. It was first brought to South Africa in 1833. Different Methodist groups in Britain, such as the Wesleyan Methodists, the Primitive Methodists, and the United Methodists, also planted the Methodist Church in Nigeria, Northern Rhodesia, Kenya, and Sierra Leone. From its humble beginnings Methodism spread to **Ghana**, the **Gambia**, Dahomey, the **Côte d'Ivoire**, Botswana, and many other parts of Africa. By 1932 many of these countries were Districts of the British Methodist Conference, but they eventually established their own conferences.

From America Methodism was introduced to Africa through the activities of the Missionary Society of the Methodist Church, which was founded in New York in 1819. It became an official agency of the Church of the General Conference Action in 1820. The first mission of this society was established in Liberia in 1833. Methodists launched missionary work in **Angola** (1885), the **Democratic Republic of Congo** (1886), and Mozambique (1893). Methodism penetrated Southern Rhodesia (Zimbabwe) in 1898 and was firmly established in Madeira, **Cape**

Verde, **Algeria**, and **Tunisia** by 1908. The Mozambique mission extended its work into South Africa in 1919, following the mineworkers who were exported from Mozambique.

Mention should also be made here of the Baptist Churches that undertook widespread mission work in Africa. The history of the Baptist Churches in Africa is associated with the formation of the Baptist Missionary Society, founded in England in 1792. It launched its missionary work in West Africa, beginning with Sierra Leone in 1795, followed by Fernando Po in 1841, Cameroon in 1844, and eventually the Belgian Congo, Angola, and other African countries. The Board of Foreign Missions of the Baptist General Conference, established in 1944, also undertook missionary work in Africa. This organization started medical evangelism in **Ethiopia** in 1950. Also notable is the Baptist Mid-Missions, an independent Baptist organization, whose missionary activities in Africa date back to the 1920s. Its intention was to start missionary work in French Equatorial Africa. Its efforts in the region were frustrated, but it succeeded in establishing Baptist missions in the French Congo (1921), **Central African Republic** (1920), **Chad**, Liberia (1938), Ghana (1946), as well as the Belgian Congo in 1953.

It is important to note that Africa has also been a mission field of Moravian Churches. It appears that when the Moravian Church embarked on its missionary enterprise, it was undertaken by the entire church rather than special missionary societies. The first efforts were made at the Cape of Good Hope, where a mission was established among the Khoi in 1737. George Schmidt, the missionary involved, was forced to abandon his work in 1744 because of a conflict with the Dutch Reformed Church. His work was only renewed half a century later in 1792. The Moravians also attempted to launch missionary work in Ethiopia. But several attempts between 1752 and 1768 failed dismally. A century later, in 1891 and 1897 respectively, they opened mission stations in the South Highlands of Tanzania and in western Tanzania, where work has continued to the present day.

It is worth noting that one of the churches that has had a tremendous impact in Africa is the Seventh Day Adventist Church. Seventh Day Adventists from the United States launched their missionary venture in South Africa in 1887. Their main agencies of missionary work were medical services, schools, evangelists, and the dissemination of Christian literature and personal work by lay members. By 1902 they had established their Conference and gradually gained converts among the indigenous people. From South Africa, the Seventh Day Adventists expanded their missionary work to **Lesotho** in 1899 and in 1894 they received a substantial grant of land from the British South African Company, which had colonized Zimbabwe, some fifty kilometers south-west of **Bulawayo**. There the Seventh Day Adventists started the Solusi Station. In 1902 they began missionary work in Malawi and by 1905 they had penetrated into Zambia. In 1907, under the patronage of the Empress, they embarked on missionary work in Ethiopia, where they started medical work especially at the Zaudi Memorial Hospital (opened in 1934). Before long, the Seventh Day Adventists established missions in Congo (1921), Botswana (1921), Uganda (1927), Sierra Leone, and many other countries.

The twentieth century also saw the proliferation of Pentecostal Churches in Africa. They comprise a group of Protestant Churches that trace their origin to the Holiness Movement that occurred in North America towards the end of the nineteenth century and at the beginning of the twentieth century. Among the earliest Holiness groups that began to operate as Pentecostal bodies were the Pentecostal Holiness Church, the Church of God, and the Church of God in Christ. Later other churches emerged as a result of mergers. These included the Assemblies of God, Churches of Christ, the International Church of the Four-Square Gospel, Pentecostal Assemblies of the World, the Church of God of Prophecy, Pentecostal Fire-Baptized Holiness Church, and the United Pentecostal Church.

The movement spread rapidly in the United States. Similar revivals took place in Europe, Asia, and Latin America. Eventually Pentecostalism spread to Africa. One of the bodies that were responsible for the spread of Pentecostalism in Africa was the Pentecostal Assemblies of Canada. This body sent its first missionaries to South Africa in 1905. Eventually churches were organized in all four provinces of the Union of South Africa. Subsequently, this same body sent missionaries to Liberia, Mozambique, and Zimbabwe, where missionaries started work in 1948. Zambia, especially the Copperbelt area, was opened to Pentecostalism by missionaries from Zimbabwe. Pentecostalism was also introduced in Kenya, Tanzania, and Uganda in 1913. The Pentecostal Holiness Church also introduced Pentecostalism in Liberia. This body sent two missionaries to South Africa – namely, Reverend and Mrs. K.E. Spooner – where they established sixty national churches. The Church of God Missionary Board concentrated its missionary efforts in Kenya, the Church of God in Christ launched missionary work in South Africa and Botswana, and the Church of God of Prophecy sent its missionaries to Sierra Leone, and South Africa, as well as Botswana. It is reckoned that in Africa the largest Pentecostal communities are in the Democratic Republic of Congo, Nigeria, and South Africa.

The impact of Christianity in Africa

Throughout its long history in Africa, Christianity has always been a dynamic and vibrant religion. The challenge it faced was to provide a theological interpretation of the world from both Christian and African perspectives. The imposition of colonial rule greatly facilitated the work of Christian missionaries. Not only did the colonial conquerors and missionaries often come from the same culture and share similar worldviews, they both saw the spread of Christianity as necessary for the expansion of Western civilization in Africa. Africans encountering the new religion for the first time responded in one of three ways: rejection, acceptance, or adaptation.

Many Africans rejected Christianity and stuck either to traditional African religions or to Islam. But significant numbers also converted. In many societies, the first to embrace the new religion were the less well-off members of society, such as ex-slaves, the destitute, social outcasts, and the poor. This was especially the case in East and Central Africa. In other areas, such as Botswana and Madagascar, missionaries sought to convert the rulers in the hope that their subjects would follow. In most places, Christianity spread rapidly after colonial conquest, which undermined many people's faith in traditional religion. As the religion of the conqueror, Christianity was regarded as containing some of the sources of European power. More concretely, many people converted to Christianity because it provided them with access to Western education, wage employment, influence, and power in the colonial world. Initially, the missionaries concentrated on converting adults, but from the 1920s and 1930s they put more emphasis on converting children. These children were enrolled in missionary schools where Christianity was part of the curriculum. Hence, the struggle over schools and education between adherents of Christianity, Islam, and traditional religions.

Many African Christians preferred to adapt their new religion by founding what have come to be known as independent or separatist churches. Some of these churches broke away from existing churches, usually because African clergy and their followers deeply resented European missionary control and the racism and contempt for African cultures that was rampant among missionaries. Others sprang up independently of any existing Christian denominations. These **Christian reform movements** represented attempts by Africans to assert their religious, cultural, and political independence. African initiative was not restricted to the founding of independent churches. From the beginning of colonial rule, African clergymen played a major role in the spread of the faiths of the established churches. In West Africa, for example, Krio missionaries from Sierra Leone greatly contributed to the establishment of Protestant missions, and the influence of the Catholic Church could not have spread as far as it did without the zealous work of African catechists. Over the course of the century, Christianity became increasingly Africanized in its clergy, liturgy, rituals, and beliefs.

Besides the Africanization of the churches, leaders of the various Christian denominations became increasingly aware of the need for cooperation in tackling the immense social, economic, and political changes and challenges facing the world. One of the distinctive characteristics of the modern church in Africa, therefore, has been a growing ecumenical movement. This awareness led to the formation of national Christian councils, regional ecumenical organizations, and finally the All Africa Conference of Churches in 1963, whose chief objective is to enhance ecumenical efforts among the Christian churches in Africa. African churches, therefore, have contributed significantly to the ecumenical movement worldwide, and have been deeply involved and committed to the work of the World Council of Churches since its inception in 1948.

Assessing the impact of Christianity in Africa during the century is not easy. At the social level, Christianity has both contributed to development and brought social division. Missionaries built churches, schools, teacher training colleges, universities, clinics, hospitals, and other social amenities that contributed to social and economic development. With the advantage of hindsight, it can be argued that Christianity was responsible for the creation of a new elite in Africa that spearheaded socioeconomic development in all walks of life. As a matter of fact, a number of African political leaders at independence were products of missionary schools, which continued to exist after independence. Apart from providing formal education in secular institutions, missionaries also provided theological training for the advancement of Christian missions in Africa. But Christianity also promoted social division, specifically between Christians and the followers of other faiths, and more generally through the processes of class formation that missionary-sponsored education helped foster: Christians acquired greater access to opportunities within the colonial state, society, and economy than either their Muslim compatriots or followers of traditional religions. The seeds of the Nigerian civil war, for example, were partly sown by the unequal regional opportunities that Christianity and colonialism engendered.

At the economic level, Christian churches were active in laying the foundations of a colonial economy (see **economy: colonial**). From the nineteenth century, they began to oppose the slave trade and to encourage the growth of "legitimate commerce," namely the production and trade of cash crops and other export commodities. In this regard there was a strong link between the spread of Christianity and export trade. This is evidenced by the fact that, in some instances, directors and other well-known home-based personalities of missionary societies were also directors of trading companies operating in the same area in Africa.

At the political level, Christianity in Africa took an active part both as a colonial factor and as an agent of liberation from colonial rule. It is a well-known fact that Christianity was a tool of colonial conquest, and used by colonial administrators to pacify Africans and take control of their land. As the popular saying goes: "Before Christianity came we had the land and the whites had the Bible. Now we have the Bible and the whites have the land." The history of Christianity in Africa is replete with examples of missionaries who acted as colonial agents. Although from time to time missionaries challenged colonial administrators on certain matters they quite often sought benefits from colonial governments and in turn worked to make converts docile and submissive to foreign rule. In some cases missionaries such as David Livingstone called on their home governments to establish colonial rule in their areas of missionary work. The role of Dutch Reformed Church in South Africa – the Afrikaner party at prayer – in providing theological justifications for racial segregation and apartheid, the official policy of the state from 1948 until the demise of National Party rule in the early 1990s, is well known.

But there were times when missionaries identified themselves with African interests and aspirations. This was the case with Joseph Booth, as seen in his slogan "Africa for the African." Christian churches were divided in their response to the emergence of **nationalist movements**. There were those who adopted the view that Christianity and politics should not mix, which in practice amounted to a tacit endorsement of the status quo. However, the question of political independence for the African people was such that the churches could not remain silent. In this regard, some openly supported and others opposed the movement for political emancipation. The supporters often held the view that the church should take an active part in the political and social emancipation of the people if it was to remain relevant to the new generation of politically conscious Africans. This became evident even in South Africa, where church leaders increasingly took sides with the poor and oppressed majority. In 1985 the Kairos document condemned the "state theology" of apartheid as "tyranny" and "idolatry." The South African Council of Churches, guided by liberation theology and working closely with the Catholic Bishop's Conference, became increasingly involved in the liberation struggle that eventually brought independence to South Africa in 1994. Elsewhere in Africa from the 1980s Christian churches were in the forefront of struggles for democratization.

The growth of liberation theology in parts of Christian Africa was part of the long search by African religious leaders and thinkers for a Christian theology relevant to Africa's realities and aspirations. From the 1960s a series of conferences were held to deliberate on models for the indigenization of the Christian church in Africa.

References and further reading

Amanze, J.N. (1998) *African Christianity in Botswana*, Gweru: Mambo Press.

—— (1999) *A History of the Ecumenical Movement in Africa*, Gaborone: Pula Press.

Baeta, C.G. (ed.) (1968) *Christianity in Tropical Africa*, London: Oxford University Press.

Elphick, R. and Davenport, R. (1997) *Christianity in South Africa*, Cape Town: David Philip.

Groves, C.P. (1955) *The Planting of Christianity in Africa 1878–1914*, London: Lutterworth Press.

Isichei, E. (1995) *A History of Christianity in Africa*, London: SPCK.

Neil, S. (1964) *A History of Christian Missions*, Harmondsworth: Penguin.

Parrinder, G. (1969) *Religion in Africa*, Oxford: Penguin.

Sundkler, B. and Steed, C. (2000) *A History of the Church in Africa*, Cambridge: Cambridge University Press

Weller, J. and Linden, J. (1984) *Mainstream Christianity to 1980 in Malawi, Zambia, and Zimbabwe*, Gweru: Mambo Press.

JAMES AMANZE

cinema

According to Mbye Cham (Cham and Bakari 1996), there are three categories of cinema that constitute significant forces in the history of African filmmaking. First there is "radical" cinema, in which film is considered not only as popular entertainment, but more importantly as socio-political and cultural discourse and praxis. Second is "imitative" or "escapist" cinema, which imitates the commercial films and melodrama of Hollywood (USA) and Bollywood (India). A good portion of the corpus of films from **Egypt** – perhaps the continent's largest film producer – are in this category (with the exception of the work of Yousef Chahine and Asma El Bakri), so are a large number of films from **Nigeria**. The third category is the hegemonic foreign (especially Hollywood) film. This consists of both those Hollywood films that tend to dominate African movie theaters and those Hollywood films set in Africa, such as *Out of Africa* (shot in **Kenya**) and *King Solomon's Mines* (shot in **Zimbabwe**), that revive or reinforce spurious stereotypes about Africa. This entry largely focuses on the first category of cinema and will focus on the defining moments of this cinema.

African cinema has been dominated by North Africa and francophone West Africa, which can partly be attributed to the relative availability of resources and equipment, including French financing in the case of West Africa, and colonial cultures that allowed the formation of intellectual and artistic elites earlier than in settler-dominated eastern and southern Africa. The situation in southern Africa began to change with the liberation of **Zimbabwe** and **South Africa**, two countries with relatively advanced filmmaking technical infrastructures, which seemed poised to join the ranks of major African cinema producers. In North Africa, Egyptian cinema tends to be largely commercial, while **Algeria** and **Tunisia** have led the production of more politically oriented films, followed distantly by **Morocco** and **Libya**.

African cinema advocates a re-presentation of the self free from "the language of derision" of colonial cinema (Mudimbe 1988: 51), ideologically positioning itself against various types of internal conflicts on the continent and invariably arguing for or against identity formation in an oppositional mode. African filmmaking has generally been marred by endemic financial difficulties, yet sustained by a rejection of political and cultural complacency. The films of this "last cinema" (Taylor 1987: 4) seek to voice the interests of the African masses, yet only marginally benefit from whatever distribution or exhibition channels exist on the continent. Finally, an increasing number of African filmmakers inhabit or maintain residences in Europe where they negotiate the funding of their projects with French, British, and Scandinavian agencies.

The invention of cinema was popularized on the African continent at about the same time as in European countries: films were being shown in Africa within five years of the creation of the art form. Frank Ukadike (1994) notes that in 1896 a vaudeville magician stole a telegraph from the Alhambra theater and used it to introduce motion pictures into South Africa. In 1905 mobile cinemas in Senegal started showing animated cartoons in Dakar and its suburbs. In the Maghreb the first experience of cinema dates back to 1896:

> Towards the end of the nineteenth century, the Algiers born Felix Mesguich had shot a number of street scenes in Algiers and Tlemecen for Louis Lumière and no doubt these formed part of the first Lumière screenings for settler audiences in Algiers and Oran in the autumn of 1896.
>
> (Armes 1996: 9)

In this early period, cinema was just another artifact of the imperial West. It was meant to represent Euro-American genius and instill a sense of pride in European expatriates. The films were shown primarily in urban centers that had large white European settler populations, in hastily set up theaters and in the presence of only a few native domestics, who would bar entry to other natives under the watchful eye of their white masters. For the majority of Africans, films were meant to mystify, dazzle, and awe – much like European clothes, European languages, cars, and table manners. In the early twentieth century, as the communicative features of the invention were revealed, measures were taken to control the content of films intended for the mass of unschooled Africans. In anglophone Africa, the Bantu Educational Project, led by L.A. Notcutt and funded by the Colonial Office,

> wanted ... to develop a different type of cinema for Africans because [it] considered the African mind too primitive to follow the sophisticated narrative techniques of mainstream cinema.
>
> (Diawara 1992: 4)

Diawara continues:

> In the Belgian Congo, the Belgian government passed a ... law forbidding the admittance to movie theaters, public or private, of people other than from the European and Asian races.

This was because the Europeans had "concluded that films were no good for Africans" (Diawara 1992: 12).

Notwithstanding these colonial strictures, North Africans opened up filmmaking, and were soon followed by West Africans. In Tunisia the end of the **First World War** coincided with the rise of the first local elites. All over the country, the Destour Party organized public debates on the issue of independence. In the ensuing atmosphere of indigenous self-examination, Chemama Chicly made the first African film: *Ein El Ghezal* (1924). Chicly's short film conjures up the nationalist political atmosphere of the day by locating its action in the historic city of Carthage. It features long descriptions of local places and its main protagonist is female. In West Africa, the first films appeared some twenty-five years later. In the 1950s **Guinea** was buzzing with debates on self-determination, cultural rejuvenation, and political independence. In 1955 the Guinean Mamadou Touré created *Mouramani*, which – much like Camara Laye's *L'enfant noir* – hardly dealt with the political issues that were gripping the elite. The film's nationalism lay in its portrayal of the land, the flora and fauna, and the peoples of Guinea. The same year, Paulin Soumanou Vieyra from **Senegal** produced *Afrique sur Seine*. However, Vieyra was living in France and subject to French regulations on filmmaking in the colonies. He was thus barred from filming in his native land by virtue of the law enacted in 1934 that is known to film critics and historians as the Laval Decree.

This decree gave the Ministry of the Colonies "the right to examine the scripts and people involved in the production [of films in the colonies] before [granting] authorization for filming" (Diawara 1992: 22). The Laval Decree was more effective as a threat than as a tool of indiscriminate repression. It was meant to inhibit creativity, and curb cultural protest. Given the high cost of filmmaking, it also served as a means of self-censorship. In this case, the country which had, a few years earlier, used film to encourage patriotism, goad young men into driving out German occupying forces, and extol the virtues of French indigenous traditions, worried that an unchecked, unregulated cinema in the hands of African nationalists could extend simmering anti-French sentiments to the illiterate peasant masses in its colonies. Diawara, quoting Vieyra, further argues that the development of sound movies in 1928 solidified the French position, as sound allowed African filmmakers to expose the abuses of the colonial system in languages spoken by an indigenous population that was unable to understand the French idiom. Vieyra and his associates were told they had to be content with filming in the streets of Paris, hence the title *Afrique sur Seine.* Only three other filmmakers faced censorship under the Laval Decree and all of them were of French nationality: Robert Vautier for a film secretly shot in **Côte d'Ivoire** in 1950 (*Afrique 50*), and Alain Resnais and Chris Marker for *Les Statues meurent aussi* (1955). In 1963, some five years after the independence of Senegal, Ousmane Sembene produced the founding film of African cinema: *Borom Sarret.*

Borom Sarret set the parameters of nationalist African filmmaking. It features actors Sembene trained on the spot: men, women, and children whose identities had been shaped both by traditional rule and the colonial experience, peasants recently granted official citizenship, and former colonials seeking to breathe life into the ideals promoted by nationalist leaders. *Borom Sarret* describes no fauna, flora, or picturesque coastline. Instead, it focuses on the pressures weighing down on an African man who is determined to earn a living by the strength of his own hands. The film shows traditional oral art forms and, in a gesture made memorable five years later by Djibril Diop Mambety in *Contras' City* (1968), subjects the camera to the slow hesitant pace of a horse-driven cart. Unlike its anthropological counterparts, the action of *Borom Sarret* takes place in a city still suffering from the violent exclusions of colonial rule. Hermetic divisions, silence, and human absence reign in the heart of the city, whereas its outskirts (the Medina, Colobane, and other poor suburbs) bustle with the noise, hopes, and tragedies of everyday life as soon as the muezzin utters his first call to prayer.

Borom Sarret "cast[s] away the mantle of mystery" of films like *King Solomon's Mines* (Vaughan 1960: 85), lifts the veil on the subtext of African bestiality found in other films like the Tarzan series, and acknowledges the existence of African laborers on the verge of political awareness. The film's protagonist, Modou, has a family, lives in humble dwellings, prays to Allah, and like many of his counterparts protects himself with amulets against the daily tribulations of city life. His wife gets up early in the morning to sweep the evil spirits energetically from the yard, and feed her husband and baby, and like many of her female counterparts divides the rest of her day between the kitchen, the local market, and her child. In the early morning light, most of Modou's passengers ride free on his horse-drawn cart: market women rushing to the food depot, out-of-work laborers, sick patients usually unable to get to the hospital, a woman in labor, and a father taking his dead baby to be buried. Coming just a few years after the removal of the French flag from the streets of Senegal, *Borom Sarret* exposes the betrayals of nationalist politics. It shows how the freedom fought for by the poor and illiterate had now been recuperated by a middle class that hides behind gates, police officers, maids, and sometimes even their children. *Borom Sarret* is also a founding film for African cinema in that it is a fictional film made with uncertain funds at a time when most budding filmmakers in Africa were forced to work making documentaries.

In the 1960s the African political class had discovered what the French and Algerian nationalists knew only too well: nothing could be more effective in image-building than a documentary, innocently presented to audiences cramped in a movie theater for a few hours of escapism. Most young African graduates of film schools in France, Germany, and the Soviet Union were offered positions in the national broadcasting companies of their countries as documentary filmmakers. The images they created were made all the more credible because the commercial features (be they westerns, Indian films, kung fu movies, or thrillers) preceding or following the documentaries in the local theaters had nothing to say about the nation and its people. In **Benin**, Pascal Abikanlou shot three documentaries between 1965 and 1969: *Escale au Dahomey* (1965), *Ganville, mon village* (1967), and *Premières offrandes de l'igname* (1969); in Côte d'Ivoire, Henri Duparc shot *La récolte du coton* (1967), *Achetez Ivorien* and *Profil ivoirien* (1968); in Senegal, Yves Badara Diagne featured athletes from all over the continent in *L'Afrique noire en piste* (1965), while Momar Thiam shot *Diabel le pêcheur* (1965) and *Les luttes casamançaises* (1968). The most prolific of the documentary filmmakers was to be Vieyra, who produced seventeen documentaries between 1957 and 1981.

These documentaries borrowed the alluring aesthetics of film in order to legitimize the governing elite. Newly elected presidents, ministers, and administrators were portrayed in the same buildings, wearing the same attire, seated on the same tribunals, boarding the same planes, riding in the same tinted cars as the former colonial administrators. They spoke a metropolitan variety of French, required translators like their white counterparts, and entertained lavishly. Other documentaries celebrated individual countries and their people's beliefs, daily activities, and popular entertainments. All showed countries as unified entities, led by men of international repute and composed of proud, industrious citizens – artists even. The documentaries played nightly in theaters, before or between two feature films. Features might include *High Noon*, starring Gary Cooper, Italian spaghetti westerns like *The Good, the Bad and the Ugly*, or French thrillers such as *A Bout de souffle*, starring Alain Delon. To migrant urban African audiences, the documentaries provided the first glimpse of a "self" that had been freed from the patronizing language of systematic denial that made up anthropological and colonial filmmaking. Shouts of acclamation would greet a familiar face on the screen, and collective boos rose at the image of a fallen sports hero or a government minister known for their bad French or English. To these audiences, the voice-over, articulated in varieties of French or English that signified power and deference to the old metropolis, mattered very little. They provided their own comments in languages as diverse as Wolof, Bambara, Fulani, and Sarakholé. In the midst of the unfamiliarity of the Euro-American feature films, these documentaries allowed the audience to commune with each other and the national elite, and perhaps temporarily align themselves with the broader propaganda objectives of the nation-state. Documentaries are still being made on the continent today, but in the vein of Laure Anne Folly's *Femmes aux yeux ouverts* (1994), Christiane Succab-Goldman's *A Bamako, les femmes sont belles* (1996), Flora Mbugu Schelling's *These Hands* (1992), Philip Brooks and Laurent Boccahut's *Woubi Chéri* (1998), Raoul Peck's personalized biography of Lumumba (1992), Salem Mekuria's *Deluge* (1995), David Achkar's fictionalized retelling of his father's ordeal at the hands of Guinea's secret police (*Allah Tantou*, 1991), Abderrahmane Sissako's poignant *La vie sur terre* (1998), and Jean Pierre Bekolo's *Aristotle's Plot* (1995). Such documentaries expand into dramatic retellings/descriptions of the limitations imposed by sexist constructions of gender, poor government, and devastating social problems that include women's health issues, child labor, and the effects of structural adjustment programs. The didacticism and propaganda of nationalist productions has given way to a relentless denunciation of internal conflict and the various other problems that continue to plague millions of Africans. Manthia Diawara's own documentary on Jean Rouch (*Rouch in Reverse*, 1995) should also be mentioned. In this film, he turns the anthropological gaze back onto one of its most important practitioners.

Sembene's second seminal film (*Mandabi*) ushers in an era of creativity and growth among the filmmakers of the African continent. The year 1968 had witnessed many student protests in the new nation-states of Africa. In campuses all over the continent, young people were holdings meetings about the conditions under which they had to study, on the future of the university, and inevitably on the future of the nation. *Mandabi*, itself produced in 1968, features no educational institution. Its characters do not mention, even in passing, any term associated with educational establishments. Yet the camera insistently lingers on idle school-age children. In town Dieng walks past adolescents in the market; at crossroads he sees them collecting fares on public transport; but he never sees them at school. *Mandabi* , just like *Borom Sarret*, exposes the total failure of the nation-state in the areas of education and social policy. Women turn out to be the sole active agents in this film, but they live at the margins of society and are active only in the effort to survive the nation-state's inefficiencies.

The filmic vocabulary of *Mandabi* informed the poetics of film that were adopted by the Pan-African Federation of Filmmakers (FEPACI). Orality is prominent in both, with characters featured in everyday cultural contexts, speaking African languages, engaged in the indigenous social semiotics of the ordinary life, and resolving conflicts on their own terms. Subsequently, in the films of Dikongue Pipa, Momar Thiam, Souleymane Cissé, and others, poor illiterate men and women attempt to redefine themselves in opposition to the reductionist gaze of the other. In Cheih Tidian Aw's *Pour ceux qui savent* (1971), Oumarou Ganda's *Le Wazzou polygame* (1970), Souleymane Cissé's *Finyé* (1982), and Mweze Ngangura's *Pièces d'identité* (1998), the reexamination of traditional values and practices in the light of new economic and political structures creates unfamiliar challenges. Filmmakers such as Gaston Kaboré (*Wend Kuuni*, 1982), Cheick Oumar Sissoko (*Guimba the Tyrant*, 1995), Dani Kouyaté (*Keita*, 1995), Souleymane Cissé (*Waati*, 1995), Kwah Ansah (*Heritage Africa*, 1988), and Haile Guerima (*Harvest 3000*, 1976) anchor their creations on the premise that no society can prosper that does not cultivate links between the present and the past. Children, teachers, and griots figure prominently in their films. Intergenerational and intercultural conflicts abound in Mansour Sora Wade's *Picc mi* (1994), Sembene's *Guelwaar* (1992), Jean Marie Teno's *Afrique, je te plumerai* (1992), and *Chef, la tête dans les nuages* (1994). When the characters are female, as in the case of *Wend Kuuni* (1982), the issues surrounding gender construction are forced out in the open. Cissé's *Baara* (1977) tells the story of the assassination of a plant supervisor by his corrupt employer, and the subsequent rioting of workers whose labor rights the deceased was trying to safeguard. However, among current filmmakers the Marxism that sustained the Manicheist film language of Sembene's early films is somewhat less prevalent.

Gender issues are a common concern in recent North African cinema: Tlali's *Les Silences du palais* (1993) conjured the slow pace of Assia Djebar's *La Nouba des femmes du mont Chenoua* (1979) and personalized the national historical perspective of Lakhdar Hamina's *Chronique des années de braise* (1975), portraying three generations of female servants among powerful and unscrupulous men. Nouri Bouzid's *Bent familia* (1992) dramatizes the anxiety of three educated women, trapped in their ancestral traditions, whereas Ali Ghalem's *A Wife for My Son* (1982) describes the sudden transformation of an eighteen-year-old girl into a wife. Finally, Merzak Allouache's *Omar Gatlato* (1976), *Bab el Oued* (1996), and *Salut Cousin!* (1996) scrutinize the construction of masculinity in Algerian society.

Women's filmmaking in Africa, like women's literary production on the continent, is ten years behind male filmmaking. Documentaries figure prominently in the various filmographies. Two pioneers stand out, however: Safi Faye and Sarah Maldoror. Faye's first film, *La passante*, was a fictional story that appeared in 1972. Three years later, she produced the film that established her status as a pioneer filmmaker: *Kaddu Beykat* (1975). Like most of its predecessors, it features characters who speak in their local languages, live outside the urban centers, and denounce the betrayal of ordinary people by their nationalist leaders. Unsurprisingly, *Kaddu Beykat* was censored by the Senegalese authorities. Faye's latest film (*Mossane*, 1991) builds on her preoccupation with women in society (also at the center of her earlier film: *Fadja'al*, 1979) to dramatize the way in which women's bodies are subjected to male control. In tone again evocative of Assia Djebar's work, the film features generations of women in conflict and partially absent men; like Mariama Bâ's *Une si longue lettre*, the film's resolution advocates giving women the freedom to determine their own destinies.

The second pioneer of African women's cinema is Guadeloupe-born Sarah Maldoror. In 1972, after making a few documentaries and two short fictional films, Maldoror created *Sambizanga*, a film shot in **Guinea-Bissau** that dramatizes the Angolan war of independence. Maldoror was among the founding members of the Federation Panafricaine des Cinéastes, and is the most vocal advocate of cinema as a tool for developing political awareness across Africa. Other women who have followed in her and Safi Faye's footsteps include Tsitsi Dangaremba from Zimbabwe (*Everyone's Child*, 1995), Flora Mbugu Schelling from **Tanzania** (*These Hands*, 1992), Anne Mungai from Kenya (*Saikati*, 1992), Fanta Nacro from **Burkina Faso** (*Le Truc de Konaté*, 1998), Onwurah Ngozi from Nigeria (*Monday's Girls*, 1993; *Why Men are Cracking Up*, 1994), and Moufida Tlali from Tunisia (*Les Silences du palais*, 1993).

At the end of the twentieth century, filmmaking in Africa is still plagued by lack of funding and poor distribution. Theater houses devoted to the promotion of African films are still scarce. National cinemas remain under heavy pressure from a global market which no longer suffers local creative ventures gladly. In a few African countries (Senegal, Côte d'Ivoire) popular cinema houses have recently been converted into commercial souks and leased to tailors and other artisans. Film schools are timidly appearing on the continent (Senegal, Burkina Faso, Zimbabwe, Mozambique) but, with no industry or local funding structures, filmmaking in Africa remains a highly individual, high-risk activity that can barely guarantee a living for the technicians graduating from these schools. Collaboration with national television companies has also proved awkward, as these organizations function under strict contracts with international conglomerates from Europe and America.

The failure to establish an African film industry, the scarcity of movie theaters, the difficulty of funding any project, coupled with the withdrawal of the nation-state from the cultural arena, have created various patterns of creative survival. Several filmmakers have elected to take up residence in Europe, drawing on a diverse and growing range of experiences and political agendas to articulate new images of Africa. For example, John Akomphrah argues that:

> There is the myth of African cinema and there is the reality of it. The myth is that it is largely made by people who live and work in Africa – but my sense is that the thing is much more fluid than that ... African cinema is a film world in search of both a constituency and a community, and it realizes that it is potentially a borderless cinema.
>
> (quoted in Petty 1999: 73)

The majority of African films still frame their messages within the range of signs afforded by the filmmakers' own cultures. However, stimulated by new and different necessities, a few filmmakers have broadened their scope to include other situations, cultures, and texts. A variety of religious myths inform Cheikh Oumar Sissoko's *La Génèse* (1999), French rather than Wolof is the principal language used in Sembène's *Faat Kine* (2000). Idrissa Ouédraogo's *Kini and Adams* (1997), filmed in Zimbabwe, was shot entirely in English with a cast from Zimbabwe and South Africa. In Cheikh Oumar Sissoko's *Guimba* (1995), one of the actresses utters an insult in Wolof to an usherette at the height of the action. Souleymane Cissé's *Waati* (1995) was shot in Zimbabwe with actors speaking different languages, and features these various idioms in the story. Finally, in the films of Djibril Diop Mambéty, horses, valleys, lonely heroes, and fragmented chase scenes involving uniformed police convey an atmosphere reminiscent of Euro-American thrillers or westerns. Filmmakers in Africa are embracing a greater diversity of stories, styles, techniques, and ideologies. Issues previously considered taboo or mentioned only in comic scenes (such as homosexuality in Sembène's *Xala*, 1974) are now considered legitimate subjects for the screen (as in Mohamed Camara's *Dakan*, 1997). Increasingly, a diverse and unfettered urban African popular culture is replacing the nationalist construct of the 1970s, prompting renewed debates about cinematic integrity.

Finally, the scholarly study of African cinema has developed considerably from the 1980s, with numerous articles, monographs, and reference books emerging, primarily from European and

North American academics, as well as numerous journals, websites, associations, and festivals taking the initiative and highlighting the achievements of filmmakers like Sembène, Med Hondo, and Ferid Boughédir. However, the criticism of African cinema still focuses on thematic issues, with little exploration of African film aesthetics. Studies focusing on film language, production, and issues relating to audience formation remain few and far between. Studies by scholars actually within Africa, where they are closest to the latest filmmaking developments, are also scarce.

See also: leisure; literature

References and further reading

Armes, R. (1987) *Third World Filmmaking and the West*, Berkeley: University of California Press.

—— (1996) *Dictionary of North African Film Makers*, Paris: Editions ATM, vol. 2.

Armes, R. and Malkmus, L. (1991) *Arab and African Filmmaking*, London: Zed Books.

Barlet, O. (2000) *African Cinemas: Decolonizing the Gaze*, trans. C. Turner, London: Zed Books.

Cham, M.B. and Bakari, I. (1996) *African Experiences of Cinema*, London: British Film Institute Publishing.

Diawara, M. (1992) *African Cinema: Politics and Culture*, Bloomington: Indiana University Press.

Mudimbe, V.Y. (1988) *The Invention of Africa: Gnosis, Philosophy, and the Order of Knowledge*, Bloomington and Indianapolis: Indiana University Press.

Petty, S. (1999) "The Archeology of Origin: Transnational Visions of Africa in a Borderless Cinema," *African Studies Review* 42, 2: 73–86.

Pfaff, F. (1988) *Twenty-Five Black African Filmmakers: A Critical Study with Filmography and Bio-Bibliography*, Westport: Greenwood Press.

Taylor, C. (1987) "Africa: The Last Cinema," in W. Luhr (ed.), *World Cinema Since 1945*, New York: The Ungar Publishing Company.

Ukadike, N.F. (1994) *Black African Cinema*, Berkeley: University of California Press.

Vaughan, J.K. (1960) "Africa and the Cinema," in L. Hughes (ed.), *An African Treasury*, New York: Crown Publishers.

SADA NIANG

civil society

Contemporary use of the concept of civil society is largely premised on the writings of eighteenth-century liberal political philosophers who were concerned about the concentration of power at the top of modern political systems. To these philosophers, civil society was a sphere of autonomous political activity between the family and the state, and its primary function was as a check against the abuse of power by political leaders. Rarely used in political analysis during most of the twentieth century, the concept acquired widespread currency in the analysis of democratic political participation and governance in the 1980s. In conventional use, networks of interest-based associations that are independent of the state are the foundation of vibrant civil societies. The popularity and conventional use of the concept has been much influenced in the closing decades of the twentieth century by the blossoming of the popular movements that overthrew Eastern European communist regimes and the pro-democracy movements across developing country regions. A common feature of the movements responsible for what has been termed the "third wave of democracy" was the significant role of civic and interest-based groups in mobilizing popular opposition to authoritarian rule.

African countries were caught in the third wave of democracy. In the 1980s only a handful – such as **Botswana**, **Mauritius**, and **Gambia** – had succeeded in maintaining multi-party electoral systems continuously since independence. Popular movements demanding an end to authoritarian rule resulted in the reestablishment of multi-party electoral politics in several African states in the early 1990s. The sudden mushrooming of pro-democracy movements in Africa surprised most observers. Many interpreted the important role played by independent urban-based associations in the development of these movements as evidence of the "emergence" or "resurgence" of civil society and its role as harbinger of democratization in Africa.

Pre-colonial African societies were rich in associations that provided frameworks for participation and community activities. The character of civil society in Africa in the twentieth century has been molded by social, political, and economic changes set in motion by colonialism. The establishment of new modes of economic activity and the introduction of Western education induced significant changes in social structures. These changes included the birth of working and professional middle classes and the growth of urban communities. Africans responded to the opportunities and challenges of colonial change by adopting familiar and creating new forms of associations that belonged to two broad types. First, functional or interest-group associations such as trade unions, professional associations, farmers' cooperatives, and religious, youth, and women's organizations. Membership in these types of association was multi-ethnic, as they were based on social and economic interests that cut across groups. Second, ascriptive-based associations, of which "home-town" associations remain ubiquitous. This type of association inclined towards ethnic homogeneity, as their members commonly shared kinship and communal ties.

Despite comprising the minority of the population, urban-based social groups led the growth of both types of association. In the early decades of the twentieth century, the working classes began to form trade unions. The smaller group of middle-class professionals started forming occupational associations, as exemplified by the founding in Sierra Leone of the Civil Servants Association (1907) and the Sierra Leone Bar Association (1919). Members of the educated middle classes also began establishing associations to articulate the interests of the African majority in colonial society. Examples of such groups included the Aborigines Rights Protection Society and the National Council of British West Africa, which were founded in Sierra Leone in 1909 and 1920 respectively. The growth of urban communities was fueled by the migration of men and women from rural areas in search of economic opportunities and new ways of living. Migrants relied on ascriptive-type associations as networks of support in polyglot cities. These associations organized recreational activities for their members and served as conduits of information about employment and housing. They also provided financial assistance to their members to help offset the costs of medical care, funerals, and weddings. Many became involved in the development of their members' ancestral regions by financing, for example, the construction of schools, clinics, roads, and water systems.

Although their primary objective was to promote their members' social and economic interests, both types of voluntary organization were easily drawn into the struggle for the rights of Africans to formal political participation and representation. Colonial states were, without exception, alien authoritarian systems of rule and colonial societies structured as race-based caste systems in which small numbers of whites monopolized power. The overwhelming majority of Africans were treated as subjects without citizenship rights and excluded from formal political participation. They faced systematic race-based discrimination in employment, access to bank credit, allocation of social services, and economic policies that were designed to prevent them from competing against European businesses. The racially motivated injustices experienced by Africans, regardless of social status, provided a basis for continuous widespread discontent with colonial rule.

The first half of the 1930s was a significant turning point in the evolution of civil society in African colonies. The collapse of international commodity prices during the **Great Depression** of the 1920s and 1930s, and its devastating effects on colonial economies, precipitated a wave of workers' strikes across Africa and colonized societies in the Caribbean and Asia during the first half of the 1930s. Farmers also engaged in various forms of organized protests. In **Ghana**, for instance, African farmers and commodity traders organized "cocoa hold-ups" – campaigns urging farmers not to sell cocoa to European-owned commercial firms, which were blamed for low producer prices and discrimination against African traders. Colonial authorities realized that the target of such mass protests was the colonial system as a whole and that dramatic reforms were therefore imperative for the continuation of colonial rule. In the second half of the 1930s, British and French colonial administrations in particular abandoned their laissez-faire approach to the management of colonial economies in favor of state-guided economic and social development. The new commitment to development resulted in more intense state regulation of economic activities and increased investment in education and other social services. Colonial administrations began to encourage the formation of functional interest-based groups as a means of channeling and controlling African participation. Typically, laws authorizing such groups placed them under the tight supervision of state agencies and proscribed their involvement in politics. The development initiatives of colonial states were elaborated at the end of the **Second World War** and lent further impetus to the patterns of social change that favored the growth of civil society. They also broadened and deepened resentment of colonial rule, as they intensified state intrusion into virtually all aspects of African life: from the production and marketing of agricultural commodities to the sexual habits of Africans.

The period between the end of the Second World War and the early 1960s represented the **decolonization** phase, during which African groups and imperial authorities negotiated the end of colonial rule. Decolonization processes were profoundly shaped by the increased politicization of civil society. Widespread economic hardship caused by war-related dislocations of international and domestic economic activity precipitated another major wave of mass protests by workers, cross-sections of urban groups, and farmers across African colonies during the final years of the war and after. This proved auspicious to the building of nationalist movements by the indigenous educated elite that were their vanguard. The indigenous elite relied mainly on functional and ascriptive-based associations to build territory-wide anti-colonial movements.

The decolonization phase terminated with the hurried creation by departing imperial authorities of liberal constitutional arrangements, including multi-party electoral systems, as the basis for the democratic governance of newly independent states. Shortly after independence, faced with the challenge of building nation-states, the ruling elite in most African countries abolished formal parliamentary opposition by adopting one-party rule, repressing the free press, and moving to erode the autonomy of functional interest-based associations. They tolerated, and in some instances encouraged, the growth of ascriptive-type associations, so long as they shied away from involvement in forms of politics not condoned by the government regime. By the mid-1960s authoritarian rule had become the norm and the military coup d'état the means of changing governments in most African countries. Authoritarian rule was combined with expansion of state control of economic activity. Economic changes, significant improvements in education, and the accelerated pace of urbanization, among other factors, drove the types of social change that have historically aided the widening and deepening of civil society, even as authoritarian regimes strove to stymie its political engagement.

The economies of most African nations began to stagnate in the mid-1970s, then went into steep decline through the 1980s and early 1990s. The erosion of the living standards of farmers, the urban working classes and the poor, and middle-class professional groups testified to the devastating effects of economic failure. To cross-sections of citizens of African countries, the primary root of economic failure was the twin evil of authoritarian rule and state domination of economies, so the democratization of political systems was imperative if their growing destitution was to be reversed. With the active involvement of long-established interest groups, political protests by mainly urban groups increased steadily in the 1980s. The 1980s also witnessed a proliferation of indigenous and international **non-governmental organizations** (NGOS). Many NGOs were engaged in humanitarian assistance to communities torn apart by political conflict and natural disasters, and in the provision of basic social services that states could no longer provide. Others were involved in human and civil rights advocacy and therefore more directly in agitation for the rule of law and multi-party democracy. External actors played an important role in this "resurgence" of civil society, and in the success of popular movements that compelled most authoritarian regimes to concede the reestablishment of multi-party political competition the early 1990s. From the late 1980s, international development agencies and Western governments became concerned with promoting democracy in African countries, mainly through support of multi-party electoral processes and the funding of NGOs.

Assessment of the state of civil society and its potential role in democratic nation-building processes in Africa at the close of the twentieth century leads to mixed conclusions. While many African political activists and political analysts celebrated its vibrancy, many others found little reason for such optimism. A fair description of civil society in the vast majority of African nations is that it is still incipient, poorly institutionalized, and riven by the characteristic divisions of class, gender, ethnicity, religion, and region. These circumstances reflected the continued and related weakness of market economies, and the small size of the working and middle classes, as well as the small number of private sector entrepreneurs. Despite some progress in economic liberalization, states remained the primary employers and leading private-sector groups depended heavily on them. The lack of economic autonomy meant that civil society groups and their organizations continued to be vulnerable to political pressure from ruling elites. External financial support for civil society groups helped to ameliorate the problem of resource scarcity, but this resulted in dependence on financial sources that could not be guaranteed beyond the short term. The heavy reliance on external funding sources raised the additional and troubling question of accountability, which is at the heart of democratic participation and governance: to what extent were civil society groups accountable to their foreign donors, as opposed to the local constituencies they purported to represent? To sum up, analysis of the past, present, and possible futures of civil society must necessarily be grounded in the dynamics of state formation and the socioeconomic transformations of particular African societies, and the complex ways in which these processes have been and will continue to be shaped by changing international contexts.

See also: capitalisms and capitalists; labor movements; nationalist movements; women's movements

Further reading

Ake, C. (1981) *A Political Economy of Africa*, Harlow: Longman.

Gyimah-Boadi, E. (1997) "Civil Society in Africa," in L. Diamond *et al.* (eds.), *Consolidating the Third Wave Democracies*, Baltimore and London: Johns Hopkins University Press.

Kasfir, N. (1998) "Civil Society, the State and Democracy in Africa," *Journal of Commonwealth and Comparative Politics* 36, 2: 1–20.

DICKSON EYOH

Cold War

The term "Cold War" normally refers to the sharp geopolitical conflict between the United States and the former Union of Soviet Socialist Republics (USSR) after the **Second World War**. The two superpowers were allies during the war, but their relationship deteriorated immediately after the war. Since the two had now become superpowers, their conflict affected all aspects of world politics, including Africa. So the Cold War became a major feature of postwar international relations.

Scholars differ on the origins or causes of the Cold War. Some blame the United States, others blame the Soviet Union or traditional "balance of power" politics. According to the first view, the USSR sought to expand its hegemony as part of a global strategy to spread communism throughout the world. The West, led by the United States, was forced to resist Soviet expansionism in order to protect democracy and capitalism. According to the second view, American imperialism provoked the Cold War. American capitalism, which had been greatly boosted by the war, was hungry for new markets and outlets for investment. The USSR did not accept the *pax Americana* and so the Cold War began. The third view maintains that, in the good old tradition of power politics, each side tended to assume – and see – the worst of motives in the other, justifying its own actions while denying any justification to the other side. Each approach has strong supporters, and can provide the facts to support their conclusions. Generally, the first approach was dominant up to the early 1960s, especially among conservative Western scholars, while the second was identified with radical or revisionist scholars or Soviet scholars. The third view appealed to students of *realpolitik*, and to social democrats in the North and nationalists in the South who were suspicious of unadulterated capitalism or communism as represented by the rival superpowers.

A series of events in the 1940s and 1950s strained relations between the two superpowers and fueled the Cold War. To the chagrin of the United States and its allies, there was the rise of new communist regimes in Eastern Europe. By 1945 communist parties were already quite strong in some of these countries. In Bulgaria communist ascendancy was achieved by 1944 and a People's Republic proclaimed two years later. In Yugoslavia and Albania communists who had led successful guerrilla wars against the Italians and Germans came to power. In Czechoslovakia and Hungary the communists came to power in 1948 following elections. But in East Germany, Poland, and Romania Soviet intervention was vital to the establishment of communist regimes. No less menacing to the Western alliance was the triumph of the communists in China in 1949, although this owed little to Soviet support.

For its part, the Soviet alliance was disconcerted by American policies of containment. The Truman Doctrine, first enunciated in 1947 in response to events in Greece and Turkey, offered sweeping promises of aid for "free peoples who are resisting attempted subjugation." Greece was involved in a civil war between the government and communist forces, while Turkey was under pressure to open up to the Soviet Union the strait that led into the Aegean Sea. Before long, the frontier of Soviet containment was extended to include the whole world. In 1948 the Marshall Plan was launched to revive the shattered economies of Western Europe. Initially the Soviet Union and Eastern Europe were included as potential recipients, but being suspicious of American intentions the Soviets declined and soon after announced their own plan for economic aid for Eastern Europe. In order to receive Marshall Aid, European governments were required to contain communist forces in their countries. Growing economic cooperation between the United States and Western Europe was soon translated into military and strategic cooperation, manifested in the formation of the North Atlantic Treaty Organization (NATO) in 1949. NATO's creation institutionalized the division of Europe into two camps, for six years later the Soviets created the Warsaw Pact.

The formation of NATO was partly stimulated by the Berlin crisis of 1948, triggered by the Soviet blockade of the city, which lay in the Soviet zone of a divided Germany. The Western powers responded with a massive airlift to supply their zone of the city. In late 1949 the Western powers turned their zone into the Federal Republic of Germany, while the Soviets turned theirs into the German Democratic Republic. An "iron curtain" had indeed descended upon both Germany and Europe. In that same year the Soviet Union tested a nuclear bomb, which ended the American nuclear monopoly and sent shock waves rippling through Western capitals. From that point on, the threat of nuclear conflict hung over the world. The Cold War turned into a shooting war with the Korean War of 1950–3, which pitted the two superpower blocs and their local allies against each other, at the cost of 4 million lives. It was the Korean War that finally drew the United States and Japan, bitter Second World War adversaries, into a strategic alliance, helping spread the Cold War into Asia.

After the Korean War there was a temporary thaw that was first shattered in 1956 by the Soviet invasion of Hungary and the Anglo-French invasion of the Suez, then again in 1958 by the Second Berlin Crisis, which led to the construction by the Soviets of the Berlin Wall in 1961. The 1960s had begun on a negative note with the shooting down of an American spy plane over the Soviet Union in 1960. This was followed two years later by the Cuban missile crisis, provoked by the Soviet installation of nuclear missiles in newly revolutionary Cuba and the US's refusal to countenance such a threat from its backyard. This was perhaps the moment of greatest tension in the whole Cold War period. It was resolved only when the Soviet Union backed down, agreeing to remove their missiles on condition the American government promised not to invade Cuba.

In the meantime, the United States became embroiled in an unwinnable war in Vietnam, which exposed the limits of American power. This helped create the conditions for detente between the bitter Cold War rivals in the 1970s. The fact that the USSR had reached nuclear parity with the United States also helped. The era of mutually assured destruction (MAD) had arrived. The loss of dominance by the superpowers over their allies further facilitated detente. In the American alliance, Western Europe and Japan had recovered economically, while China was asserting its autonomy within the Soviet alliance. Also, the reality of a divided Europe had become generally accepted and institutionalized. Western Europe had NATO and the European Economic Community, while Eastern Europe had the Warsaw Pact and Comecon. Finally, the development of the **Non-Aligned Movement** helped defuse the polarization of the world into two unyielding blocs. Symptomatic of the temporary thaw were the strategic arms limitation talks (SALT) and summit meetings between the leaders of the two superpowers.

But detente weakened from the late 1970s. In the United States powerful conservative forces emerged, crystallized around the Reagan administration that was established in 1980, bent on rolling back the welfare state at home and reasserting American power abroad. They pointed to successful liberation struggles in Africa and Asia as proof that detente had made the United States weak, opening "a window of vulnerability" (Wills 1987: 334) and encouraging Soviet expansionism. Two events in 1979 increased the American apprehension. One was the Iranian revolution, which led to the overthrow of the Shah, one of America's closest allies in the Middle East. The second was the Soviet intervention in Afghanistan. The first casualty of the new Cold War of the 1980s was the refusal by the US Congress to ratify the SALT2 Treaty that had been negotiated in 1979. The arms race intensified and Cold War rhetoric became increasingly bitter, with Reagan calling the Soviet Union an "evil empire." Cultural, trade, and other exchanges between the two countries declined to a minimum, and the United States increased its efforts to destabilize socialist regimes in the Third World, as exemplified by the US invasion of Grenada in 1983 and US support for both the "contras" who were fighting against the Sandinista government in Nicaragua and the rebels fighting against the government of Angola. At the same time, support was increased for rightwing dictatorships, including South Africa's apartheid regime.

However, there were moderating forces. The powerful peace movement in Western Europe helped temper some of the excesses of American foreign policy. A growing budget deficit and government debts also made it increasingly clear that the United States could not maintain a costly arms race indefinitely. More crucially, as evidence of economic stagnation mounted in the Soviet Union, pressure grew to reduce international tension. Mikhail Gorbachev, who assumed power in 1985, was determined to reform Soviet society and redirect its foreign policy, beginning a new era of *perestroika* (reform) and *glasnost* (openness). From the mid-1980s relations between the two superpowers thawed, as symbolized by the resumption of summit meetings and arms limitation talks, now renamed "strategic arms reduction talks." In 1987 they agreed to reduce their nuclear arsenals for the first time – by 4 percent. Preoccupied with its internal reforms, the Soviet Union watched as its client regimes in Eastern Europe faced emboldened reform movements. The mounting pressure culminated in the fall of the Berlin Wall in 1989. Two years later, the Soviet Union itself was no more, and with its demise came the end of the Cold War. As with its origins, how the Cold War was brought to an end has been hotly debated: it is variously attributed to American resolve, especially the military build-up under Reagan which the Soviet Union's stagnant economy was unable to match, or to Gorbachev's miscalculations and the failure of his reforms.

The Cold War's impact on Africa had both positive and negative aspects. On the positive side, it accelerated Africa's decolonization, providing a counter-hegemonic bloc against Western colonial power. The Soviet bloc offered much needed political, financial, military, and moral support to Africa's liberation movements. After independence, the Cold War gave African countries greater diplomatic influence than might have been the case otherwise. Also, the Soviet model proved attractive:

> socialism provided a powerful alternative paradigm of rapid, autonomous non-capitalist development, which profoundly influenced African

countries, socialist as well as non-socialist, and their intellectuals and planners.

(Hutchful 1991: 52–3)

But the Cold War had its costs, too. It sustained authoritarian regimes, which were bankrolled by foreign patrons and refused to reach the necessary accommodations with their national populations. Moreover, the Cold War led to the militarization of regional and national conflicts, from Southern Africa to the Horn of Africa, with ferocious wars festering endlessly because neither side was allowed to win a decisive military victory by the superpowers for whom the conflicts often served as wars by proxy.

The effects of the end of the Cold War were equally contradictory. Some of the wars that the Cold War had inspired or sustained came to an end, and democratization gained currency as Africa's dictators lost the protection of their godfathers in Washington and Moscow. But there were also fears that Africa would become more marginalized as it lost the geopolitical significance spawned by the Cold War. In particular some emphasized not only the dangers represented by the diversion of potential Western aid and investment from Africa to Eastern Europe, but also the fact that the removal of systemic alternatives to capitalism meant stricter neo-liberal conditionalities would be imposed on Western aid and investment in Africa. The extinction of Soviet socialism not only reduced the range of international alliances available to African nations, but also removed an alternative moral vision of development. Thus, after the Cold War, both dependent dictatorships and autonomous development became increasingly unsustainable in many parts of Africa.

References and further reading

Akinrinade, S. and Sesay, A. (1998) *Africa in the Post-Cold War International System*, London and Washington: Frances Pinter.

Garthoff, R.L. (1994) *The Great Transition: American–Soviet Relations and the End of the Cold War*, Washington, D.C.: Brookings Institution.

Hunter, A. (1998) *Rethinking the Cold War*, Philadelphia: Temple University Press.

Hutchful, E. (1991) "Eastern Europe: Consequences for Africa," *Review of African Political Economy* 50: 51–9.

Summy, R. and Salla, M.E. (1995) *Why the Cold War Ended: A Range of Interpretations*, Westport: Greenwood Press.

Wills, G. (1987) *Reagan's America: Innocents at Home*, New York: Doubleday.

PAUL TIYAMBE ZELEZA

colonial Africa

The Nigerian historian J. Ade Ajayi argued in the 1960s that the colonial period was an "episode" in African history – no more important than many others. He insisted that long-term historical processes followed indigenous dynamics, even under colonial overlordship, and that post-colonial government could build on pre-colonial heritages. Now that over thirty more years of post-colonial history has elapsed, Ajayi's argument seems harder to sustain. The colonial past still weighs heavily on the African present. Yet recent scholarship has made colonial history less colonial than it once was: European rulers could not make colonies into reflections of their desires and projects, even when they ruled. Colonial Africa was indeed the locus of fundamental and durable transformation, but the dynamic was one of struggle, adaptation, and reconfiguration.

Colonial rulers had contradictory visions of their venture. At one pole, colonizers treated people as objects to be used, and the fact that colonized people were "different" had to be continually reemphasized to ensure that all categories of people remained in their places. At the other pole, missionaries and social reformers sought to use political and cultural power to remake Africa in Europe's image. Colonial rule achieved a measure of stability only when it stayed somewhere in the middle of this spectrum. If it drew too close to the brutal pole, as in German Tanganyika and the Belgian Congo around 1900 or Portuguese colonies in the 1960s, the state risked rebellion by Africans and campaigns by humanitarian groups appealing to a European public that wished to repudiate their own undemocratic past. If the state drew too close to the universalistic, assimilative pole, as in French and British Africa in the 1950s, African political and social movements would see no reason why their demands should stop short of full equality. European rulers would then have to weigh the costs of resisting or acquiescing to such demands against an uncertainty as to whether colonial economies could do more than profit a narrow range of businesses.

What made colonial conquest possible made colonial rule difficult. European armies were effective because they had (thanks to the machine gun) concentrated firepower, the telegraph, and the ability to choose when and where to attack. But once a conquering army had swept through a region, killed warriors, burned homes, stolen cattle, and allowed African allies to share in the booty, it went somewhere else. It might return, but it left few people behind to turn conquest into order. Whatever the goals of a colonial state, it had to turn to indigenous hierarchies to extend its power to ground level. It needed the legitimacy and coercive capacity of local authority to collect taxes and round up labor, and it needed local knowledge. Under colonial administration the category "chief" included former kings, provincial leaders, heads of kinship groups, village elders, or sometimes people the colonial rulers mistakenly thought influential. Such people had to enforce colonial power – under threat of dismissal or worse – but could not be pushed too far or they would become too discredited to serve the regime. Translators and local police also became figures of local importance, the often arbitrary bottom level of the colonial hierarchy.

The colonial state, meanwhile, had to reconcile conflicting objectives: short-term revenue, long-term economic growth, responsiveness to different constituencies in the home country, and differing conceptions of the imperial polity (see **state: colonial**). The first approach was to grab what could be grabbed, and its most notorious instance was the Congo of Leopold II of Belgium. Treating the Congo as his personal fief, Leopold gave concessionary companies the right to exercise authority over particular zones of the Congo, profiting from whatever resources they could extract. World demand for rubber was then enormous. The companies – working through a hierarchy of agents and African mercenaries – used terror to make Africans collect quotas of rubber. But at the dawn of the twentieth century part of the European public wanted to distinguish a "modern," progressive colonialism from the colonialism of pillage, and a long campaign against Leopold's atrocities forced the reorganization of the Congo into a more conventional Belgian colony. The idea that a colonial regime could be held to certain standards would prove a two-edged sword: it underscored the normal, acceptable nature of regimes that avoided such visible inhumanity, while opening the door to further "humanitarian" critiques of the abuse and excess that was rarely far below the surface.

Respectable colonialism, as of 1900, took several forms. France stressed its "civilizing mission" in Africa, and countered republican criticism of colonization as opportunistic and anti-democratic by insisting that it would bring education, science, and enterprise to Africa. Furthermore, the French government argued that, as Africans acquired the necessary virtues, they would graduate from colonial subjects to French citizens. The project was belied by the minuscule resources actually devoted to education and health, and the minuscule numbers of Africans who were allowed to become citizens. But the republican discourse did create a measure of ambiguity that African political leaders, from the time of the **First World War**, were able to exploit, insisting that as Africans had learnt the French language and fought in French wars, their rights should be expanded as well.

Missionaries saw the African as a soul to be saved more than a body to be exploited, but the economic and the spiritual dimensions were not entirely distinct from each other. Many saw their own task as forging a different sort of African, an individual conscious of his or her relationship to God, acting as a rational being in economic interactions, becoming part of a routine of daily life conditioned by European norms. Commerce, civilization, and Christianity would go hand in hand, shaping Africa into a world of yeoman farmers and self-reliant artisans, unlike either the supposedly primitive past of Africa or the devastating industrialization that worried many people in

Europe itself. What was hardest for the missionary reformers to grasp was that Africans would take elements of the package they were being offered and reshape what they needed in their own ways.

All colonial governments, not just Leopold's, shared the impulse to treat Africa as a zone of extraction. But some governments, particularly in the early years of rule around 1900, were captivated by the possibility of transforming African society. They thought that they could free African labor from the bonds of African slave-owners or from the bonds of subsistence economies into a "free" labor market where their time would become useful. Perhaps some African elites could become capitalist employers, or else white settlers using African wage labor could open new vistas for mining and agriculture. What they had learned, roughly by 1914, was that the more ambitious projects – for reforming Africa or exploiting it more systematically – were inconsistent with the limitations of colonial rule.

Colonial governments could extract taxes – as long as they could get chiefs to do the dirty work – and impose labor obligations. It was harder for them to deny Africans access to land and force them to devote their lives to wage labor or to make African political elites into elements in a colonial bureaucracy, just as it was hard for missionaries or teachers to transform the values and social practices of African societies. The very local elites that might benefit from a colonial regime's support were the most likely to seek political supporters, clients, and other forms of personal, dependent relationships, rather than the impersonal and one-dimensional connection of employer to wage laborer or ruler to subject. So not only did the "bottom" of African societies seek alternatives to the roles that colonial social engineers had in mind for them, but so did the "top."

Colonial interventions had powerful but complex effects. Local elites tried to use colonial power even as the colonial governments were trying to use the local elites. Male elders and chiefs were often able to manipulate "tradition" so as to make many societies more patriarchal than they had been before colonization. But the complexity of social change in the twentieth century sometimes meant that young men or women had more opportunities to leave when rural life became too oppressive, so the elites had to tread carefully. White settler agriculture and large-scale mining could extract needed labor from large areas around them, but only if alternative modes of livelihood were systematically curtailed and labor sent through narrow, carefully policed channels – which demanded great expense and the forgoing of revenue from African peasant production. Parts of British Kenya and the Rhodesias, French Algeria and Côte d'Ivoire, Portuguese Angola and Mozambique, the Belgian Congo, and most systematically South Africa, experienced the ravages of settler colonialism; most of West Africa saw minimal white settlement, while mines and plantations functioned within complex regional economies. The very limitations of colonial transformations – social or physical – made colonial societies all the more lopsided, their economies heavily influenced by the railways and port facilities, and by the import–export companies that encouraged them to supply narrow ranges of cash crops in exchange for limited ranges of European manufactured goods.

By the First World War the most reformist of early colonial projects, notably in British and French Africa, had run out of steam. Both governments in the early 1920s debated using metropolitan funds for "development" programs to get colonial economies more innovative and active, but both decided that the money was better invested at home. Colonial ideologies in the 1920s turned inward: France and Britain made a virtue of their own limited power, arguing that responsible colonial policy meant change within the structure of existing cultures rather than change in a European image. Ethnographic knowledge was increasingly valued, both for its utility in manipulating indigenous authority and as a marker of a true Africa that had no reason to aspire to European culture or status. Colonial rule – which always had been "indirect" given that it was impossible without the complicity of African authorities – became even more self-consciously focused on indigenous political structures, which of course were reshaped by being subject to the overlordship of European authorities and by the strategies through which chiefs used their positions to their own advantage. The official effort in the

1920s at retraditionalizing Africa was, if anything, more urgent because of the fact that arguments in the name of "citizenship" had been made powerfully by African leaders in French Africa in the aftermath of the First World War – when many Africans served France – and that the growing number of mission-educated Africans in British Africa were claiming that their Western education entitled them to representation in local councils and the civil service.

The abuses perpetrated by British and French governments were subject to criticism from within, especially from a secular republican ideology in the case of France and a Christian, missionary-led lobby in Great Britain. In both cases, the non-communist left was more likely to favor reforming colonies than abandoning them, and reformers set themselves the task of bringing Africa out of backwardness as much as out of the clutches of white settlers, mining companies, and commercial houses. In Portugal – ruled by a dictatorship after 1926 – metropolitan society provided no reference point for critiques of colonial rule, and a willingness to use forced labor more blatantly than did other powers was attenuated mainly by a lack of capital to push productive investment. Scandals over forced labor erupted in Angola, while in Mozambique forced labor for sugar plantations, the port of Lourenço Marques, and other endeavors (often financed by British capital) drove many people to flee to neighboring British territory or to seek contracts for wage labor in the gold mines of South Africa. Belgian Africa, after the discovery of copper in Katanga, became a laboratory for the use of "stabilized" labor – pulled away from villages into permanent settlement in mine towns – under close supervision. What Belgians called the "Trinity" – the state, the Catholic church, and big business – left few niches open to Africans for entrepreneurship or participation in colonial institutions.

Germany's relation to its colonies took another turn. Its pro-settler policy in southwest Africa led to repression so severe it bordered on extermination after a rebellion by Herero in 1904, while in Tanganyika in 1905 another rebellion (whose catalyst was the forced cultivation of cotton) led Germany to retreat to a more conventional colonial policy of limiting plantations to certain areas and encouraging peasant cultivation elsewhere. But after Germany lost the "Great War" – during which East Africa became a battleground where Africans, conscripted by both sides, suffered greatly – its colonies became the mandates of victorious European powers. After 1919 Germany was a colonizing power without colonies, and Hitler drew on this sense of entitlement to rule others – no longer mediated by having to confront actual people – in building an ideology of racial entitlement and national grievance.

South Africa ceased, formally, to be "colonial" in 1910, when it became fully self-governing within the British commonwealth. But South African "native policy" shared much with that of its neighbors to the north, emphasizing not only the racial markers of distinctiveness but ethnic ones as well, locating Africans in "reserves" defined by "tribe" and using internal passports and residential controls – albeit pragmatically adjusted to suit the needs of the economy – to maintain a tightly segregated society. That South Africa had a 15 percent white population – compared to 5 percent in Rhodesia and a little over 1 percent in Kenya – was crucial in making possible a high level of bureaucratic control over Africans, the effective exclusion of Africans from rights to most of the arable land, and the close supervision by white landowners of African farm workers. The relationship of capitalism and colonialism, in short, took a different form in South Africa from anywhere else on the continent.

The **Great Depression** of 1929 pushed Africa more deeply into colonial mediocrity. The human effects of declining prices for African crops and declining production in European-run mines and farms could be concealed in the countryside. By then, Africans were so immersed in the cash nexus – for consumption as well as taxpaying purposes, and indeed in relation to aspirations for education for children – that they continued to produce export crops even when prices fell. The Depression lowered labor demand, but also incentives, so that forced cultivation and forced labor remained a feature. The claim of many officials that colonial regimes which used forced labor in the short term would teach lessons about the virtues of work were belied by the hatred most Africans had for it, the way it reduced incentives for employers to improve conditions or production techniques, the disruption of agriculture as families fled areas of intense round-ups, and the hypocrisy of the claim that African backwardness, a half century into the colonial era, still justified exceptions to the universal value attached to free labor.

Colonial Africa did not just consist of a series of territories. These territories were parts of empires, and each empire as a whole constituted a kind of political space. Officials thought in terms of imperial interests and of finding ways to justify unity while maintaining distinctions between different sorts of imperial subjects: the metropolitan Frenchman, at home or overseas, the "native," the displaced colonial subject (British Indians in British East Africa), and so on. Some non-Europeans might claim special rights in some cases, but not in others. For example, Senegalese born in the old parts of Senegal had the same rights as a French citizen, reinforced by their participation as French soldiers in the First World War, and (unlike Algerians) they did not have to renounce their right to have family matters handled under Islamic law in order to exercise citizenship. Meanwhile, Senegalese from outside these old colonial towns, as in most of French Africa, had no citizen rights at all, and were subject to the hated legal code, the *indigénat*, that gave local administrators arbitrary powers of punishment. But because France was an empire, Africans could see imperial citizenship as a privilege dangled before them that they could rarely take up. British Africans observed gradations of imperial affinity too: the Asian migrant suffered discrimination relative to white colonists, but were often in a more favorable economic position than Africans.

Opposition to colonial rule also took place on an imperial and sometimes even broader scale. The earliest activists in British Africa were from coastal, educated, Christian communities in West Africa, and their educational, trading, and professional interests connected Nigeria, the Gold Coast, Sierra Leone, and other British territories. Students from different colonies encountered one another in London. The National Congress of British West Africa, founded in 1920, was a pioneering political party whose focus was not the individual territory, but wider linkages between colonized people within the British empire. West African connections reached further than just this – via London, religious institutions, networks of sailors and other transnational workers, and such organizations as the Garvey Movement, which tied them to West Indians and African-Americans. The Pan-African Congresses expressed these linkages. Paris was a similar pole for French speakers, and that is where Léopold Senghor of Senegal, Aimé Césaire of Martinique, and other francophone Africans came together. Their politics focused on turning citizenship within the French system from something narrow, formal, and generally unavailable into something meaningful, while their cultural writing focused in contrast on a shared sense of African descent, which became known as Negritude. In the case of Algeria above all, many workers went to France, where they entered a milieu of leftist trade unions, including other colonized people. Opposition to colonialism was thus not initially focused on achieving self-government within territories, but on wider connections among oppressed people of color and on criticism of the demeaning racial ideologies and practices of colonial regimes. What kinds of political arrangements could come out of either pan-African mobilization or appeals to imperial citizenship were very much in question in the 1930s.

The crisis of the colonial system set in during the late 1930s. If political threats earlier in the decade could be diffused to diverse locations, the revival of commerce after 1935 put pressure on the narrow transportation routes and hubs of the neglected colonial infrastructure, bringing people back into miserable living conditions and rapidly rising prices for housing, food, and urban services. For the British – given the extent of economic integration – the crisis was indeed empire-wide, taking off from the wave of strikes and riots that swept the British West Indies between 1935 and 1938 even as an African strike wave began after 1935 in the copper-mining towns of Northern Rhodesia, spreading to the Gold Coast, Kenya, Tanganyika, and other nodes of the colonial economy. A smaller-scale strike wave hit parts of French West Africa in 1936–8, amplified in fact by the brief attempt of the Popular Front government to cooperate with budding trade unions. Then came the war, cutting off French Africa after France's defeat in June 1940, but putting escalating pressure on British Africans, as the need for tropical products mounted following Britain's loss of southeast Asian colonies and diminished ability to supply manufactured goods to Africa.

The prolonged pattern of strikes, shop boycotts, riots by urban Africans, and rural malaise profoundly shook the British Empire. Officials realized – at last – that their mediocre record of social and economic intervention over the past forty years left the Empire with weak tools for expanding needed production and even weaker means for responding to the challenges that were disrupting the few key sites on which a import–export economy depended. By 1939 officials in London realized that an imperial problem needed an imperial solution, and they looked to the concept of "development." For the first time, the metropole would pay the colonies rather than the reverse: funding would be directed not just to projects of immediate economic utility, but to improving infrastructure – including services for wage workers. The goal was both to give long-term production a boost, in the interest of Great Britain, and to ease the deprivations of the most dangerous element of the population – wage workers.

France, under German occupation between 1940 and 1944, faced the problem later, but in 1946 it too decided development would be the watchword of a new imperial era. Both powers looked to political as well as economic change, but both sought to strengthen and relegitimize imperial institutions. British governments reaffirmed what they claimed, unconvincingly, was an old British policy of slowly leading colonial territories to self-government – it was just that initially the timetable stretched into the distant future and African participation was directed toward local, rather than territorial, institutions. The French approach seemed, at first glance, the opposite: to emphasize the permanent unity of the French Empire, renamed the French Union, to give Africans representation (but not proportionate to population) in the Paris legislature, but to keep territorial governments (where Africans were of course the large majority) relatively weak. In April 1946 the French legislature – on a motion filed by African deputies – abolished forced labor. A month later the distinction between subject and citizen was also abolished, and with it the demeaning *indigénat*. But when opposition went beyond certain boundaries – as with rebellions in Madagascar in 1947 and Algeria in 1945 – they were repressed brutally.

The story of **decolonization** is told elsewhere in this encyclopedia. What is relevant here is what it reveals about colonial rule itself. Policies intended to reinvigorate and relegitimate colonial authority had the opposite effect: development initiatives unleashed numerous conflicts over resources, the openings to trade unions and political parties in British and French Africa encouraged the rapid escalation of claims on government, and the very insistence of colonial elites that the *empire* was a meaningful unit of political and moral authority meant that the validity of such claims could not simply be ignored – not without encouraging the kind of revolt that occurred in Algeria in 1954.

Meanwhile, colonial systems went from a normal part of the world order to something of doubtful legitimacy. Hitler gave racist ideologies a bad name and shook Europe's confidence in the power of its own civilization. It brought to the forefront of world politics two powers that identified themselves (whatever their practices) as non-colonial states: the USA and the USSR. Trying to respond to the profound crisis of political legitimacy – and the need to use colonial resources for economic recovery at the very same time – France and Britain argued ever more vehemently that their role was justified to bring backward people forward, to improve health facilities and schools, to incorporate Africans into democratic institutions, to advance their standard of living. Each of such claims opened the way to the counterclaims by African social and political movements that only Africans could determine African interests.

The crisis went to the core of the tension at the root of colonial systems: the tension between the need to incorporate people into an imperial polity and the need to differentiate. When policy leaned toward the latter in the 1920s and 1930s, colonial states faced challenges that they could contain and that did not shake their rulers' sense of their own authority. But in the post-war decade, Britain and France – pushed by African social and political movements – leaned decisively in the direction of assimilation, universality, and development. It was the most self-consciously developmentalist regimes that gave up first on retaining African colonies – Great Britain conceding self-rule to the Gold Coast in 1951 and independence in 1957, France devolving budgetary authority to elected territorial legislatures in 1956 and independence in 1960. Portugal, the weakest economically of the European colonial powers and the least affected by democratic scruples, held on until 1974. South Africa, and for a time Rhodesia, preserved white domination by claiming to act as a *national* power rather than an imperial one. The effects of the colonial idea in Africa lasted much longer than its legitimacy around the world.

See also: colonial conquest and resistance; economy: colonial; plantation agriculture; society: colonial; state: colonial; state: post-independence

Further reading

Césaire, A. (1972) *Discourse on Colonialism*, trans. J. Pinkham, New York: Monthly Review Press. (First published in 1955.)

Chanock, M. (1985) *Law, Custom and Social Order: The Colonial Experience in Malawi and Zambia*, Cambridge: Cambridge University Press.

Comaroff, J. and Comaroff, J. (1991, 1997) *Of Revelation and Revolution*, 2 vols, Chicago: University of Chicago Press.

Conklin, A. (1997) *A Mission to Civilize: The Republican Idea of Empire in France and West Africa, 1895–1930*, Stanford: Stanford University Press.

Cooper, F. (1996) *Decolonization and African Society: The Labor Question in French and British Africa*, Cambridge: Cambridge University Press.

Cooper, F. and Stoler, A. (eds.) (1997) *Tensions of Empire: Colonial Cultures in a Bourgeois World*, Berkeley: University of California Press.

Phillips, A. (1989) *The Enigma of Colonialism: British Policy in West Africa*, London: James Currey.

FREDERICK COOPER

colonial conquest and resistance

With the exception of **South Africa**, which was colonized in the sixteenth century by the Dutch, **Mozambique** and **Angola**, which were colonized in the sixteenth century by the Portuguese, and **Algeria**, which was colonized in the early nineteenth century by the French, the rest of the African continent came under European colonial rule only in the late nineteenth century. Colonies were acquired by Britain, France, Germany, Portugal, Italy, Belgium, and Spain through direct military conquest, trickery, treaties of protection, and other methods. This "scramble for Africa," which spanned the years 1870 to 1900 and necessitated the 1884/5 Berlin Conference to prevent possible European conflict over disputed claims in Africa, left the entire continent (apart from **Ethiopia** and **Liberia**) under European colonial rule. Conquest and colonialism were followed by repressive and exploitative regimes that led to the African people's loss of political and economic independence, the exploitation and appropriation of African land, labor, and other resources, and the marginalization and erosion of African culture and values, as well as knowledge and belief systems.

Liberia and Ethiopia escaped European colonization partly because they were both able to successfully play one European nation off against another. Liberia played Britain against France and Britain against Germany, benefiting from the fact that none of the European powers were prepared to allow other powers to gain a foothold in Liberia. Liberia also benefited from the protection of the United States, a country with which it had a special relationship that stemmed from the fact that Liberia's dominant population were descendants of freed slaves from the United States. When necessary, therefore, the United States flexed its muscles and made appropriate noises to scare off potential European invaders. American protection and European rivalry notwithstanding, Liberia did not escape partition entirely unscathed, losing some of its territory to the British and the French. In a similar way, Ethiopia was able to play Italy, Britain, and France off against each other to its own benefit. It also had a powerful army that inflicted a humiliating defeat on the Italians at the Battle of Adwa in 1896, thus gaining international respect and deterring further European incursions.

Various theories have been advanced to explain the conquest and partitioning of Africa at the end of the nineteenth century. For J.A. Hobson (1972 [1902]) and V.I. Lenin (1978 [1916]) economic developments in Europe prompted European imperialism at the end of the nineteenth century. The former argued that overproduction, under-consumption, and surplus capital in search of new fields of investment were the taproot of imperialism, while the latter contended that imperialism was the inevitable result of capitalism at its highest stage of development. For Joseph Schumpeter, imperialism was not fueled by economic considerations, but by the atavistic compulsion of human beings to dominate other human beings. For R. Robinson and J. Gallagher (1961) Africa was colonized not particularly for itself or the resources that could be exploited from it, but for strategic reasons: Britain was only concerned with protecting its sea route to India. Other scholars have emphasized either the missionary factor, European countries' quest for prestige, or local factors in Africa. These various theories notwithstanding, it is clear that the partition of Africa was fueled by many and complex factors, among which were the need among European countries for markets, sources of raw materials, new fields of investment, and outlets for their surplus population; the growth of competitive nationalism in Europe; the quest for national prestige; and strategic considerations. Underpinning economic and political factors was the pervasive influence of scientific racism, which preached that Europeans were not only superior to all others but also had a God-given mandate to spread "civilization" to the rest of the world (the idea of "the white man's burden"). In addition, missionaries sought to spread Christianity, and either preceded or accompanied European armies of conquest into Africa. Other influences were the activities of local factors in Africa, including individual European agents stationed there, such as Cecil John Rhodes in Southern and Central Africa.

As European nations competed to acquire territories in Africa, it became evident that, unless some ground rules governing the ways in which individual countries could claim territory in Africa were established, there was a real danger of European armed conflict over African territorial claims. It was to avoid such an eventuality that the Berlin Conference was convened in 1884–5. The various European powers gathered there agreed, among other things, that only when a country had achieved effective occupation through conquest and the establishment of an administration could its claim to a territory be recognized. Any disputes over claims were to be settled amicably. In addition, all countries undertook to end slavery and the slave trade in the territories they occupied. Significant was the fact that, although the conference met to decide the fate of the African continent, there was no African representation at all.

Before the Berlin Conference most European nations had relied on treaties with African rulers to further their interests in Africa. Thereafter, Europeans increasingly resorted to military conquest. The French, for instance, overran several west African states to establish a chain of colonies, while the British forcibly subdued **Ghana**, **Nigeria**, **Sudan**, **Uganda**, and **Kenya**, among many others. The Germans established their rule in southwest Africa (**Namibia**), **Togo**, **Cameroon**, and German East Africa (**Tanzania**), while the Portuguese consolidated their control of Mozambique, Angola, and **Guinea-Bissau**. Belgium acquired the Congo Free State, while Italy concentrated its conquest efforts in **Eritrea**, **Somalia**, and **Libya**. Its attempt to subdue Ethiopia failed dismally when the Italian army suffered a humiliating defeat at the Battle of Adwa. In the face of this European onslaught, most Africans put up stiff military resistance as will be shown below.

The nature and character of African resistance to European colonialism has been the subject of much heated debate among scholars of Africa's recent history. There are three schools of colonial history: the imperialist, nationalist/liberal, and radical/Marxist schools. In its efforts to justify European occupation and subjugation of African societies, the imperialist school argued that the occupation of Africa was necessary in order to "pacify" African societies that were hitherto ostensibly preoccupied with incessant, senseless wars and unnecessary bloodletting. Africans were thus expected to be grateful for European intervention, which brought "civilization" to the "Dark Continent." Confronted by the apparently paradoxical fact that most African societies challenged European rule, sometimes violently, early colonial commentators sought to explain such actions away by characterizing resistance as irrational, primitive, and backward-looking. They argued that those who resisted did so not as a result of well-considered rationally founded analyses of the threat of foreign rule, or from coherent and well-founded motives, but because such societies were naturally war-like and bloodthirsty. Conversely, those societies that did not overtly resist were labeled "peace-loving." Thus the myth of "collaborators" and "resisters" or "hostiles" and "friendlies," repeated through most imperial historiography, was born. It was also claimed that large-scale centralized and powerful African states were more likely to resist colonization than small-scale, decentralized, and weak states. The latter were likely to "collaborate" with European colonialists.

Recent scholarship has shown, however, that whether a society resisted or not depended not on its size or sociopolitical structures and organization, but on what the given society perceived to be the best way of safeguarding and promoting its interests and values under the given circumstances. It has also been conclusively demonstrated that stateless societies resisted colonialism with as much determination as centralized large-scale states. Similarly, the contention of imperialist historians that resistance was the irrational reaction of primitive superstitious societies who had been whipped into an orgy of anti-European violence by "witch doctors" and whose actions were backward-looking and resistant to "civilization" was strongly disputed by scholars of the nationalist/liberal school. Writing after the **Second World War**, they argued that armed resistance was fueled by, among other things, the determination of African communities to retain their sovereignty, preserve their culture, and protect their social, political, and economic interests. Thus, far from being irrational uprisings fed by superstitious beliefs peddled by "witch doctors," African resistance efforts were based on calculated and rational analyses, with religion often articulating the needs and interests of societies and helping to promote unity of purpose against a common enemy. Moreover, the assumption that religion was central to all struggles against European conquest was shown to be unjustified. In some cases, religious leaders played only a minimal role, while in others, rather than urging resistance, religious leaders in fact counseled acceptance of colonial rule. It is evident, therefore, that African societies responded to European colonialism in complex and different ways, depending on their informed assessment of the threat that confronted them, and that their responses were determined neither by the nature of existing political formations nor by any purported African predisposition to superstition.

Reacting to both the paternalistic Eurocentrism of imperialist history and the universalism and Romanticism of nationalist/liberal history, a radical/Marxist history emerged to disaggregate pre-conquest African societies and analyze prevailing material/social conditions and the various class interests they gave rise to. Thus scholars like Samir Amin (1974) and Immanuel Wallerstein (1974), among others, developed different explanations of the nature of African responses to conquest. Radical/Marxist scholars acknowledge that Africans resisted European domination, and that they had concrete and rational reasons for doing so, but unlike nationalist historians they view African resistance movements not as united African responses by classless societies to foreign intrusion, motivated only by religious and political considerations, but as the responses of certain economically privileged classes within African society whose economic interests were threatened by European colonialism. The radical school has also emphasized African resentment of European demands for cheap labor as the cause for African resistance, particularly with respect to uprisings in the early twentieth century and in those countries where Africans had, initially, acquiesced to European colonialism. While some cases of African resistance conform to the economic theory of African resistance, not all African uprisings can be explained simply by appeal to economic factors, as the following accounts will clearly show.

African concerns about the implications of colonialism for African sociopolitical and economic interests, and their role in fueling resistance, is clearly evident in the Maji Maji uprising of 1905 in Tanganyika (Tanzania). Here German conquest and colonization between 1895 and 1900 provoked a massive uprising. Contributing to the outbreak of armed resistance was the fact that colonialism brought with it taxes, forced labor, harsh working conditions on the plantations, and widespread physical abuse by plantation owners and by the *askaris* (African policemen) employed by the German government. The immediate cause of the uprising was the cotton scheme, which required Africans to work for twenty-eight days each year on cotton plantations with no obvious benefit for themselves – earnings from the sale of the cotton were appropriated by the settlers, while the African workers received meager wages. What the African workers opposed was not so much the growing of cotton, but the fact that they were having to grow this crop for the settlers' benefit at the expense of their own subsistence production.

Not surprisingly therefore, there were no less than ten armed uprisings between 1888 and 1900. They were all defeated. In 1905 Africans throughout southern Tanganyika took up arms once more in the Maji Maji uprising – people from across an area of more than 26,000 square kilometers participated. The uprising took its name from the protection that religious leaders (among whom Kinjikitile Ngwale was the most prominent) claimed could be provided against the European bullets by use of magic water. Using a very effective guerrilla strategy, Maji Maji fighters who called themselves *Askariyamungu* (soldiers of God) overran several German settlements and captured the German colonial capital at Kilosa. The uprising only collapsed in 1907, when the colonial settlers received reinforcements from Germany and embarked on a savage counter-offensive, burning crops and villages, and causing wide-scale starvation in the area. These genocidal strategies led to the loss of over 75,000 African lives through military action and famine. Although it failed to dislodge German colonialism, the Maji Maji mass uprising forced the German colonial authorities to reform their administration and practices. Kinjikitile's role shows that religion played a very important role in the Maji Maji uprising, as he used his position as a religious leader to foster unity and motivate anti-colonial fighters by reassuring them that theirs was a holy crusade, sanctioned by both the ancestors and by God, and that the holy water (*maji*) which he supplied would make them invincible.

Another example of armed resistance was the 1896–7 Chimurenga/Umvukela uprising in **Zimbabwe** (Southern Rhodesia). Through his British South Africa Chartered (BSAC) Company, which occupied the country and claimed it for Britain in 1890, Cecil John Rhodes spearheaded British colonialism in the country. After cheating King Lobengula of the Ndebele of southwestern Zimbabwe into signing away his land and authority to the British in the Rudd Concession, Rhodes dispatched a group of armed adventurers into Zimbabwe to claim the country for Britain. Known as the Pioneer Column, the group hoisted the Union Jack at Salisbury in 1890 and thus opened the way for British occupation. Wanting to destroy Ndebele power in the southwest, British settlers – under BSAC Administrator Leander Starr Jameson – provoked a war with them, leading to a short but bitter armed conflict in 1893. Facing defeat, Lobengula burnt his capital, **Bulawayo**, before retreating northwards towards the Zambezi River. A group of settler soldiers, led by Allan Wilson, pursued the fleeing Ndebele and were massacred to a man on the banks of the Shangani River.

In 1896 and 1897 both the Ndebele and the Shona took up arms against British colonial rule in the first Chimurenga/Umvukela war, which resulted in the deaths of 450 whites and 8,000 Africans before it was suppressed. The causes of the Chimurenga/Umvukela war were many and varied. British settlement had disrupted the Shona's long-standing and lucrative trade with the Portuguese on the Mozambican coast, while the settlers' land-grabbing had dispossessed many of the Africans. Moreover, in order to force Africans to work on white-owned farms and in white-owned mines, the colonial administration introduced head, hut, and dog taxes, as well as taxes on anyone with more than one wife, and used forced labor. Settlers also expropriated Ndebele cattle, thereby undermining African self-sufficiency. Working conditions were terrible, remuneration poor, and physical abuse by white bosses and foremen rampant. Politically, Africans resented the loss of their independence and the removal of their traditional political leaders, who had been replaced by hand-picked colonial surrogates.

The Chimurenga/Umvukela uprising was thus inspired by the Africans' dissatisfaction with colonial political and economic policies, and the deleterious effect of those policies on African people's way of life, as well as by the Africans' desire to regain their sovereignty and right to self-determination. As in the case of the Maji Maji resistance, religion played a role in the Chimurenga/Umvukela uprising, although there is controversy surrounding the degree to which religious leaders were involved in the uprising. According to historian Terence Ranger (1967), African religious leaders (spirit mediums) played a central role on coordinating, mobilizing, and inspiring the fighters; David Beach (1986), however, has argued that spirit mediums hardly featured in the uprising. What is indisputable is that there were some spirit mediums among the leaders of the Chimurenga/Umvukela uprising, including Mukwati, Kaguvi, and Nehanda, whose standing in African religious cosmology lent weight to the anti-colonial struggle and gave religious sanction to military campaigns. Imperialist historians considered the Chimurenga/Umvukela uprising to be an atavistic reaction that was inspired by witches and wizards, but those witches and wizards were in fact respected spirit mediums who played the role of revolutionary spiritual spokespersons, articulating the need to drive out intruders and giving spiritual meaning to the anti-colonial struggle in accordance with the age-old religious beliefs of the African people.

In the closing decades of the nineteenth century, Namibia also came under German rule. There, colonial rule also provoked armed resistance – this time from the Herero and the Nama, between 1904 and 1907 – having brought with it massive land alienation, loss of sovereignty, loss of cattle to incoming German settlers, numerous taxes, openly racist policies and practices that marginalized Africans, corporal punishment, and other ills. Not surprisingly, in January 1904 the Herero, under Samuel Maherero, rose up against German rule, asserting that for the Herero "it was better to die fighting than to die as a result of mistreatment, imprisonment or some other calamity." The Herero drove settlers from most of their territory, killing 100 of them and keeping the initiative until the settlers received military reinforcements from Germany in June. Under the ruthless leadership of General Lothar von Trotha, the German army embarked on a war of extermination, shooting Herero men, women, and children on sight, and driving thousands of them into the nearby Omaheke Desert to die of thirst and starvation. As the Herero uprising began to fall apart in late 1904, their neighbors – the Nama – embarked on an uprising of their own. For three years they waged an effective guerrilla campaign under Jacob Murenga, before his capture in 1907 led to the collapse of Nama resistance. By then the Nama–Herero wars had taken a heavy toll on the African population: by 1908 only 15,130 Hereros and 9,781 Namas were still alive, out of original populations of 80,000 and 20,000 respectively.

In northern Sudan, the Mahdiyya Islamic Movement or Mahdists – followers of Muhammad Ahmad al-Mahdi – spearheaded resistance. From 1881 to 1885 the Mahdists fought a successful *jihad*, eventually overthrowing the corrupt and oppressive Turco-Egyptian colonial government that had been violently imposed on Sudan in 1821. In 1886, however, they faced a new threat from British imperialism: a British army under Lord Kitchener invaded Sudan in an effort to impose British rule on the region. Under their new leader, Khalīfa 'Abdullah (who had taken over after the death of al-Mahdi in 1885), and his army commander Emir Mahmud Ahmad, the Sudanese fought several battles against the British invaders, the best known being the Battle of Atbara in April 1898 and the Battle of Omdurman in September 1898. Some 15,000 Sudanese died and 20,000 were wounded in the two battles. Mahdist resistance was finally crushed a year later at the Battle of Umm Diwaykrat, after which the British colonial rulers outlawed Mahdism and imprisoned or executed all of the Mahdist leaders. Although defeated and outlawed, Mahdists continued to resist British rule and were still fighting the British as late as 1914. Meanwhile, in Southern Sudan the Nuer and Azande peoples were equally resistant to the imposition of British rule. The Nuer maintained their armed resistance until the late 1920s, while the Azande, under the leadership of Chief Yambio, resisted both British and Belgian colonial forces until Yambio was captured and imprisoned in 1905. However, the Azande did not immediately give up their resistance. They were still opposing British rule as late as the First World War, when some of them made an unsuccessful last-ditch attempt to overthrow British colonial rule.

In West Africa, Africans vigorously resisted the French military invasions that threatened to undermine their way of life and destroy their sovereignty. For example, in Senegal, French imperial forces met determined resistance from fighters under Lat Dior Diop. From 1861, he fought French attempts to impose colonial rule on his society, before he finally died in battle at a place called Dekhle in October 1886. Similarly, between 1882 and 1892, the powerful African ruler Samori Touré, who had built a large empire and had a strong army of almost 38,000 men armed with modern guns, fought French imperialist forces bent on taking over his territory. In a major battle in 1892 between forces under his personal command and a French army, Samori's army was defeated and he was forced to retreat eastwards, setting up a new empire away from European interference. However, French imperialism followed him there, leading to several further battles between 1895 and 1897. Under increasing pressure of French aggression, he decided to withdraw to Liberia. Captured in 1898, he was deported to **Gabon**, where he died in 1900. Similarly, in what was to become British West Africa, some societies – among them the people of Benin, the Ijebu, the Asante, and the people of Itsekiri – put up stiff military resistance to British imperialism. Not all societies resisted, however. The majority of the Yoruba and Delta states chose not to contest British rule militarily. An important factor in their decision not to resist appears to have been the influence in their territories of European missionaries. These missionaries had resided among them for a long time and persuaded various Yoruba leaders to sign protection treaties with British representatives, paving the way for a relatively peaceful British takeover.

In Central and Southern Africa various communities, whether making up centralized powerful kingdoms or small, weaker political formations, resisted colonial rule and sought to maintain their independence. Thus the Nguni of Nyasaland, the Ovimbundu of Angola, the Ovambo of Namibia, the Makua and Lunda of southern Angola, and the Shangaan of southern Mozambique, among many others, engaged in military resistance to European rule. In addition to the examples given above, there were scores of other uprisings and resistance struggles across the African continent, timing and manifestations of which differed from society to society, although they all aimed at either keeping European colonialism at bay or dislodging colonial rule once it had already been established. All such resistance, however, ended in defeat. This raises the question of why African societies were unable to withstand the European onslaught.

Part of the answer is that Europeans had vastly superior weapons. African spears, bows and arrows, and old guns were no match for the devastating firepower of the newly invented European and American guns, particularly Gatling and Maxim machine guns. Moreover, Europeans were using highly trained and professional armies, while most African states had no standing armies. Furthermore, the economics of the European countries were more advanced, capable of marshaling vast amounts of wealth and resources, providing all the logistical support necessary to sustain protracted wars of conquest. In contrast, Africa's subsistence economies were weak and fragile, unable to support protracted military struggles against European aggression. Moreover, advances in medical technology (particularly the discovery of quinine) had removed the European fear of tropical diseases like malaria, and so made permanent European settlement possible. Lastly, Europeans benefited from the African people's lack of unity, with inter-ethnic as well as intra-ethnic disputes and armed conflicts preventing the formation of a stronger, more united and more effective anti-European front. Even where individual groups felt a common revulsion towards

European incursion, they were not always able to coordinate their responses. Thus the Europeans were easily able to crush one uprising, before turning their attention to the next. Such was the case of the Nama and Herero uprisings in Namibia. Given Europe's many advantages, therefore, Africa had little chance of successfully resisting European conquest at that point in history.

See also: colonial Africa; nationalist movements; state: colonial

References and further reading

Amin, S. (1974) *Accumulation on a World Scale*, New York: Monthly Review Press.

Beach, D. (1986) *War and Politics in Zimbabwe, 1840–1900*, Gweru: Mambo Press.

Betts, R.F. (1972) *The Scramble for Africa: Causes and Dimensions of Empire*, 2nd edn., London: D.C. Heath.

Boahen, A.A. (ed.) (1990) *UNESCO General History of Africa*, vol. VII, *Africa Under Colonial Domination 1880–1935*, London: James Currey.

Crowder, M. (ed.) (1971) *West African Resistance*, London: Hutchinson.

Fieldhouse, D.K. (1981) *Colonialism 1870–1945: An Introduction*, London: Weidenfield & Nicolson.

Hobson, J.A. (1972 [1902]) *Imperialism: A Study*, London: Allen & Unwin.

Isaacman, A. (1976) *The Tradition of Resistance in Mozambique: Anti-Colonial Activity in the Zambezi Valley, 1850–1921*, Berkeley: University of California Press.

Lenin, V.I. (1978 [1916]) *Imperialism: The Highest Stage of Capitalism*, Moscow: Progress Publishers.

Owen, R. and Sutcliffe, B. (eds.) (1972) *Studies in the Theory of Imperialism*, London: Longman.

Ranger, T.O. (1967) *Revolt in Southern Rhodesia, 1896–1897*, London: Heinemann.

Robinson, R. and Gallagher, J. (1961) *Africa and the Victorians: The Official Mind of Imperialism*, London: Macmillan.

Temu, A.J. and Swai, B. (1981) *Historians and Africanist History: A Critique*, London: Zed Books.

Wallerstein, I. (1974) *The Modern World System*, New York: Academic Press.

ALOIS MLAMBO

Common Market for Eastern and Southern Africa

The treaty that brought the Common Market for Eastern and Southern Africa (COMESA) into being was signed on 5 November 1993 in **Kampala** in **Uganda**, and ratified on 8 December 1994 in Lilongwe in **Malawi**. The establishment of COMESA marked a significant step in the process of the integration of the economies of Eastern and Southern Africa. Essentially, the formation of COMESA constituted a transformation of the Eastern and Southern African preferential trade area (PTA) into a common market.

Three main factors contributed to the establishment of the PTA. First was the need to address problems caused by the failure of attempts at federation in Eastern and Central Africa, which undermined political cooperation among states of the region. Second, there was an imperative need for subregional economic organization as a counterweight to apartheid South Africa's strategy of destabilization of the economies of southern African states. Third, the states of Eastern and Southern Africa recognized the need to adopt collective self-sustaining development as the only alternative to their traditional economic dependence on the industrialized countries of the North.

It was against this background that a meeting of Ministers of Trade, Finance and Planning was held in **Lusaka** in **Zambia** in March 1978. The meeting recommended the creation of a subregional economic community, beginning with a subregional trade area, which would be gradually upgraded over a ten-year period to a common market. Finally, an economic community would be established. Toward this end, the meeting adopted the Lusaka Declaration of Intent and Commitment to the Establishment of a Preferential Trade Area for Eastern and Southern Africa, creating an Inter-Governmental Negotiating Team to work out the terms of a treaty to that end. After three years of groundwork and negotiations, heads of government convened again in Lusaka on 21 December 1981 to sign the treaty establishing the PTA, which came into force on 30 September 1982 after ratification by the minimum requisite number of signatories. The treaty envisaged the PTA's later transformation into a common market, which emerged as COMESA in 1994.

COMESA was formed to enhance cooperation among member-states in the development of their natural and human resources for the benefit of all their people. A number of institutions were established to promote trade and development in COMESA. These include the COMESA Trade and Development Bank, and COMESA Re-Insurance Company, both based in **Nairobi** in **Kenya**; COMESA Clearinghouse and COMESA Association of Commercial Banks, both based in **Harare** in **Zimbabwe**; and the COMESA Leather Institute in **Addis Ababa** in **Ethiopia**. The principal decision-making organ is the COMESA Authority, which is composed of the heads of government for each of the twenty-one member-states. It is responsible for the general policy, direction, and control of the performance of the executive functions of COMESA, and for the achievement of its aims and objectives. Below the Authority is the Council of Ministers, which is responsible for ensuring the proper functioning of COMESA, and for taking policy decisions on COMESA programs and activities (such as monitoring and reviewing its financial and administrative management). Other decision-making organs include the Committee of Governors of Central Banks, the Inter-Governmental Committee, the Consultative Committee of the Business Community and Other Interests, and twelve Technical Committees. The COMESA Secretariat, based in Lusaka, is in charge of the daily operations and overall coordination of COMESA.

The establishment of COMESA aimed at deepening and broadening the integration process among member-states through the adoption of comprehensive trade liberalization measures, including the elimination of customs duties, and of tariff and non-tariff barriers to trade. It also sought to promote the free movement of capital, labor, and goods; and standardized technical specifications and quality control measures. It further aimed at standardizing taxation rates and conditions for industrial cooperation, intellectual property rights, and investment laws. In addition, COMESA sought the adoption of a single currency, the establishment of a monetary union, and the adoption of a common external tariff system. These measures, coupled with the harmonization of macro-economic and monetary policies throughout the region, were expected to result in the eventual formation of an economic community.

One of the factors that works against the success of COMESA is the fact that some of its member-states have multiple membership of other subregional economic groups, such as the **East African Community** and the **Southern African Development Community**. This divides the loyalty of member-states and spreads their commitment and resources too thinly, impinging upon COMESA. In addition, the concentration of decision-making powers in the hands of the heads of government of partner states, rather than in the hands of technocrats, poses potentials problems. Experience with regional integration schemes shows that such an arrangement creates conditions in which ideological and personal differences between individual political leaders impact on the operations of the scheme.

Nonetheless, COMESA offered great economic opportunities to Eastern and Southern Africa at the close of the twentieth century. These included greater industrial and agricultural productivity; better harmonized monetary, banking, and financial policies; and, with a population of over 400 million and an annual import bill of about US$35 billion, a broader and more competitive market for internal and external goods and services. Furthermore, the establishment of the COMESA Court of Justice, which became operational in 1998, enhanced the prospects for COMESA's success. The main functions of the Court are ensuring the proper interpretation and application of the provisions of the COMESA Treaty, and adjudicating matters referred to it under the terms of the Treaty. The Court is independent of both the Authority and the Council, and its decisions final and binding, and have precedence over decisions reached by national courts. This is indicative of the commitment of member-states to the integration process under the terms of the COMESA treaty.

Further reading

Carrim, Y. (1994) *The Preferential Trade Area for*

Eastern and Southern Africa, Bellville: Centre for Southern African Studies.

Musonda, F.M. (1997) *Intra-industry Trade Between Members of the PTA/COMESA Regional Trading Arrangement*, Nairobi: African Economic Research Consortium.

SHADRACK WANJALA NASONG'O

Commonwealth

The origins of the Commonwealth are rooted in the history of the British Empire. The term "British Commonwealth of Nations" was coined in 1914 by an Oxford scholar, Alfred Zimmern. The Commonwealth underwent three main phases. Between the **First** and **Second World Wars**, it was confined to Britain and its white settler dominions – Canada, Australia, New Zealand, **South Africa**, and the Irish Free State. The constitutional basis of this association, predicated on the four-fold doctrine of autonomy, equality, common allegiance, and free association, was defined through the 1931 Statute of Westminster. The second phase in the growth of the Commonwealth started after the Second World War, when a newly independent and republican India decided to stay in the Commonwealth, thereby establishing the principle of republican membership. The King (later the Queen) of England was recognised simply as "Head of the Commonwealth" rather than, as with the dominions, "Head of State." The transition to a post-imperial Commonwealth had began, and accelerated with the independence of African and Caribbean colonies from the late 1950s. By 1962 the Commonwealth had expanded to sixteen members from only eight in 1956, the year before landmark independence of **Ghana**. The Commonwealth witnessed another upsurge of rapid expansion in the 1970s and 1980s with the entry of several small island states from the Pacific and Caribbean, and of such countries as **Zimbabwe** (which achieved independence late) and Bangladesh (which had split from Pakistan). The Commonwealth had meanwhile entered its third phase, that of institutional consolidation. This came through the creation of the Commonwealth Secretariat in 1965, as proposed by Ghana's Kwame Nkrumah and Uganda's Milton Obote.

By 1990 Commonwealth membership stood at fifty states, representing a quarter of the world's population, and nearly a third of the membership of the United Nations. However, not all former British colonies joined or remained in the Commonwealth. The most glaring absence was that of the United States, which in the course of the twentieth century had come to surpass its former imperial master as a global superpower. In Africa, two countries declined to join: **Egypt** and **Sudan**. There, Arab nationalism had spawned deep distrust of continuing organizational links with a former imperial power that was seen as a supporter of Israel, the Arab world's sworn enemy. South Africa withdrew in 1961 following mounting criticism of its apartheid policies from the new African and Asian members. In Asia, Pakistan withdrew in 1972, but returned seventeen years later. In the 1990s some countries that had no formal ties as former British colonies, such as **Mozambique**, expressed interest in becoming members of the organization.

As the Commonwealth expanded, four trends became apparent. First, it became increasingly de-Briticized as the membership of formerly non-settler colonies became predominant. Second, it became more globalized as it began to operate like an ordinary international organization, with a permanent secretariat, specialized agencies, and leadership summits. Third, its members also became regionalized as they joined regional organizations (including Britain itself, which became a member of the European Community in 1973). Fourth, its popular and unofficial elements expanded with the growing importance of voluntary organizations, educational exchanges, and sporting and cultural endeavors in Commonwealth affairs. This expansion of functions led many critics to accuse the Commonwealth of having lost its mission. To some, the Commonwealth was a useless relic of empire. In Britain the Commonwealth was attacked on constitutional, ideological, and utilitarian grounds, respectively that it circumscribed British sovereignty, that it associated Britain with Third World despots who attacked Britain but wanted aid handouts, and that it was peripheral to

British interests, which were now tied more closely to Europe or the United States or both. Critics in Africa and Asia made the opposite arguments: that the Commonwealth was a sign of neo-colonialism, a sign of dependency, and used to inflate Britain's influence in the world.

Despite the criticisms, Commonwealth institutions and activities expanded, even if they were not always central to the global interests and alliances of the individual member states. The most visible public face of the Commonwealth became the biennial Heads of Government Meetings (CHOGMs). Held in different capitals of the "old" and "new" Commonwealth countries, the CHOGMs were dominated by issues concerning race, global inequality, the security of the small states, and regional cooperation and conflicts. From the 1960s to the 1980s Southern Africa remained the principal political issue. Initially, focus concentrated on Zimbabwe, where the settlers had unilaterally declared independence from Britain in 1965, then South Africa, whose apartheid policies and regional aggression against the frontline states in the **Southern African Development Community** provoked growing internal and international opposition. The issue of sanctions against the two countries pitted Britain against its African partners, and threatened the very survival of the organization. In the 1970s the issue of development and North–South dialogue also took center stage, in the context of debates about a new international economic order. From the 1980s environmental issues gained prominence, and in the 1990s greater attention was paid to democracy and human rights. Between 1965 and 2000 the secretariat was led, successively, by Arnold Smith of Canada, Shridath Ramphal of Trinidad, and Chief Emeka Anyaoku of **Nigeria**.

Less visible, but perhaps even more crucial, was the work done by the specialized agencies, including the Commonwealth Fund for Technical Cooperation (which provided technical assistance) and the Commonwealth Foundation (which facilitated linkages among professional associations and **non-governmental organizations**). All along, the Commonwealth has refined and elaborated its operations and principles to meet emerging challenges among its members and in the global community. In addition, there have been numerous programs intended to foster exchanges among ordinary people, through education, arts festivals, and (most popular of all) sports, especially cricket and the Commonwealth Games, which were started in 1930 and are held every four years. But the games were often boycotted by countries antagonistic to Britain's opposition to sanctions against South Africa's apartheid regime.

See also: anglophone Africa; European Union

Further reading

Kitchen, M. (1996) *The British Empire and Commonwealth: A Short History*, New York: St. Martin's Press.

McIntyre, W.D. (1991) *The Significance of the Commonwealth, 1965–90*, London: Macmillan.

PAUL TIYAMBE ZELEZA

Comoros

The Comoros islands are located in the **Mozambique** Channel, off the east coast of Africa. The capital city, Moroni, is on Grande Comore, which is the main island of the archipelago. The other islands are Moheli, Anjouan, and Mayotte. In 1998 the population of the Comoros was 548,000. The official languages are French and Arabic, while the indigenous languages of the Comoros are Bantu, which are closely related to **Swahili**.

The history of the Comoros in the twentieth century has been mainly characterized by political turmoil. Up to the late nineteenth century the Comoros were divided into seven sultanates. Sultan Saïd Ali of Grande Comore struck a deal with the French in the 1870s, and by 1886 the entire archipelago had become a French protectorate, administered from **Madagascar**. In the early twentieth century, French interest in the Comoros increased: the islands served as a counterweight to British influence in **East Africa**. In addition, many Comorians fought for France in the **Second World War**. Saïd Mohammed Cheik became the first popularly elected president in 1958. Between 1962 and 1964 Cheik moved the capital from Dzaoudzi, on Mayotte, to Moroni. A referendum on independence was held on 22 December 1974 and 94 percent of the total population voted for independence. Of those who voted on Mayotte, however, 64 percent wished to remain under French control – indeed, the history of Mayotte includes more Malagasy and European influence than the other islands. Nonetheless, on 6 July 1975 the Comoros were declared independent. The French maintained control over Mayotte, even though the independence referendum was supposed to be universally binding. A large French naval base is located on Mayotte, which allows them to control the strategic Mozambique Channel. Both the **Organization of African Unity** (OAU) and the **United Nations** (UN) support Comorian claims to Mayotte.

The first president of the independent Comoros, Ahmed Abdallah, was overthrown after only a few months in office by a socialist, Ali Soilih, who was assisted by European mercenaries led by Bob Denard. Soilih began a strict program of reform, increasing agricultural production and expanding educational opportunities. Soilih's austerity programs were unpopular, as was his increasing reliance on youth brigades to enforce the implementation of those programs. His foreign support also waned as he renounced both Islamic traditions and Western economic policies. In 1977 Abdallah overthrew Soilih, also with the aid of Denard's mercenaries, and led the country away from socialist economics. In the same year, two further events had a severe impact on Comorian society and economy. First, the volcano Karthala erupted on Grande Comore, destroying hundreds of homes and killing dozens of people. Second, anti-Comorian clashes in northwestern Madagascar forced several hundred settlers to evacuate and return to the archipelago. These events, combined with the general political turmoil, were to create an instability that continued to plague the country.

In November 1989 Abdallah was killed and Denard took control for several weeks, before being persuaded to leave by French and South African authorities. The head of the Supreme Court, Saïd Mohammed Djohar, was then elected president in March 1990. Then, in October 1995, Denard returned to Moroni to assist a military rebel group led by Combo. Denard and Combo held power in the capital until French paratroopers landed and forced Denard to leave. In 1996 another new president, Mohammed Taki, was elected. In 1997 the island of Anjouan declared its independence from the other Comoros, claiming that Taki had neglected the island's needs and denied Anjouanais influence in the republic's government. Anjouanais secessionists successfully repelled attacks by federal troops, initially calling on France to recolonize the island. This surprising demand arose from the frustration that many Comorians felt when witnessing the relative prosperity of French-held Mayotte. France refused to recolonize Anjouan, however, and soon an island president was named and local government took control of Anjouan's affairs.

Taki, who died in 1998, lost the support of the World Bank and IMF, and thereby of any other potential donors. His successor, Tadjidine Ben Saïd, was considered to have a much more conciliatory view towards the separatists, but by December 1998 the UN and OAU were still trying to piece together a peaceful solution to what was becoming an increasingly violent situation. In January 1999 **South Africa** hosted a regional ministerial meeting in an attempt to address the constitutional concerns of all parties, but achieved no concrete results. In April 1999 a peace agreement was drafted in Madagascar, but only Moheli and Grande Comore signed. Anjouan's resistance to the peace agreement led to an immediate outpouring of anti-Anjouanais sentiment on the main island. Many Anjouanais families resident on Grande Comore were harassed or beaten and ordered to leave the island. This unrest prompted Colonel Azali Hassounani to take military control of the government. In September 2000 Azali and the Anjouan separatist leader Lieutenant Colonel Saïd Abeid Abdereman signed an agreement to restructure the nation and restore the constitution. Then in December 2001 a group of gunmen attacked the island of Moheli and attempted to take control of the capital Fomboni. Comorian forces retook the island. The OAU and the Comorian authorities both believe a group of foreign mercenaries were trying to destabilize the nation before a referendum could be held on the new constitution. The referendum was nonetheless completed, and in December 2001 the constitution was approved with 70 percent of the vote.

A small percentage of the Comorian population are wage earners, most of whom are members of the civil service. The Comorian economy is based on the export of exotic spices, such as vanilla, cinnamon, and cloves. The Ylang-Ylang flower is also extremely important, as its oil is used in fine perfumes. The principal income for the majority of households is from agriculture. In May 2001 the World Bank approved US$11.4 million in credit to improve the country's infrastructure, especially on the outer islands. This type of foreign assistance, in combination with remittances from Comorians working abroad, makes up the largest part of the Comorian economy. The Comoros use the same CFA franc as many West African francophone countries (see **francophone Africa**).

Further reading

Ottenheimer, M. (1994) *Historical Dictionary of the Comoro Islands*, London and Metuchen, New Jersey: Scarecrow Press.

Guebourg, J.-L. (1994) *La Grande Comore: Des sultans aux mercenaires*, Paris: L'Harmattan.

MATTHEW B. DWYER

Conakry, Guinea

Conakry is the capital city of **Guinea**. It became the country's commercial and political capital in 1897. The decision to create a colonial center in Conakry led to the construction of both a major port and the Conakry–Niger railway in 1900. Increased economic activity shifted commercial routes to Conakry away from **Bamako** and **Freetown**. During the first decade of the century, colonial administrators focused on building the city's administrative and economic infrastructure. Senegalese and Sierra Leonean workers were brought in as construction labor. By 1910 the city had 8,000 inhabitants and had begun to welcome waves of merchants from **Libya** and Syria.

Until 1950 the perimeter of Conakry was limited to the northern tip of Tombo island. However, with the increased exploitation of bauxite and the opening of processing plants in 1952, rapid expansion began and Conakry grew to encompass more and more of the area south of the island. The population had reached 50,000 by 1953. During the 1950s Conakry became a thriving economic center due both to the influx of human, agricultural, and mineral resources into the city and to the emergence of trade unions, ethnic organizations, and anti-colonial activities. Guinea's rejection of de Gaulle's proposed French African Community in 1958 made Conakry one of the most celebrated African capitals. Under the leadership of President Sekou Toure, in the early 1960s Conakry was swept up in waves of national pride, international admiration, and increased communist support. The suburbs continued to expand as Conakry welcomed new arrivals from rural areas. New neighborhoods and routes to Kaporo and Donka were created to support increased traffic between the island and its expanding residential districts. However, as the suburbs grew, the colonial city began to decline: the Toure regime had no interest in restoring colonial edifices. After the death of Sekou Toure in 1984, the Second Republic declared an interest in the infrastructural development across the whole city.

Conakry expanded to meet the needs of its growing population, but not without costs. In 1958 the city covered 2,200 hectares and housed 78,388 inhabitants; in 1983 it encompassed 6,900 hectares and had 100,000 inhabitants; by 1993 the city sprawled across 10,000 hectares and was struggling to meet the demands of 1.5 million people, with the population predicted to reach 2 million by 2000. This sprawling urbanization, coupled with the chaotic construction of neighborhoods, led to severe traffic problems. The poorly built roads and sewage systems suffered further damage whenever there were heavy rains, and streets became impassable, homes and business would be flooded, and trade was often brought to a standstill, with employees kept away from their offices and merchants and customers unable to reach the city's markets.

Dominated by the Peul ethnic group, which controls enclaves of the city and dominates employment as academics, merchants and officials, Conakry is a city where neighborhoods and professions are determined largely by ethnicity.

There is little cross-cultural collaboration between Peuls, Malinkes, Soussous, and Forestiers in areas critical to social, political, and economic advancement. The exodus of farmers, fishermen, and livestock herders from rural areas to Conakry has also exacerbated the city's unemployment problems. Added to its employment woes, in the 1990s Conakry saw waves of refugees flee there from the civil wars in Liberia and Sierra Leone. All this taxed the resources of Conakry and its inhabitants. Nevertheless, the city remains Guinea's leading political, communications, and economic hub, centered around a modern port that is used to transport the country's chief exports – alumina and bananas. The industrial sector produces food products, automobiles, and beverages. Conakry was also the home of national cultural and educational institutions, including the Polytechnical Institute of Conakry.

Further reading

Niane, D.T. (1993) *La République de Guinée*, Conakry: Société Africaine d'Editions et de Communication.

NICOLE D. ANDERSON

Congo

The Congo has a population of little more than 2 million inhabitants (as opposed to almost 40 million in the **Democratic Republic of Congo**), and only covers a territorial space of 342,000 square kilometers, some seven times smaller than its neighbor. The country is divided into thirteen regions, and has six main ethnic groups. **Brazzaville** has been the country's capital since 1883.

Between 1875 and 1878 Pierre Savorgnan de Brazza (of Italian origin but a naturalized Frenchman) traveled in Africa on behalf of France, securing vast territorial possessions for his patrons and effectively giving France control over a large section of the Téké Kingdom. The southern and northern borders of the Congo were agreed with Portugal, Spain, Germany, and Belgium between 1884 and 1890. Finally, in 1903, a decree establishing the borders between Congo, **Gabon**, **Chad**, and the **Central African Republic** was signed. Brazza eventually served as Commissioner General of the French-Congo.

In the early 1920s the colonial authorities initiated the construction of the Congo–Ocean Railway, which was completed in 1934. Providing a link between Brazzaville and the Atlantic coastal town of Pointe-Noire, the network allowed for greater economic exploitation of inland areas. Today, the Congolese economy is essentially divided into three sectors: agriculture, lumbering, and petroleum. In terms of agriculture, limited amounts of cocoa, coffee, and palm oil are produced, but in insufficient quantities to meet local needs. The government is thereby forced to rely heavily on imports. Congo's rain forests have generated considerable lumbering activity, yielding significant exports. Yet it is the considerable offshore petroleum holdings that constitute the main source of income, with related industries – refineries and processing – leading the way in manufacturing, ahead of lumbering, textiles, beer bottling, and food processing, while mining activity is essentially restricted to zinc, copper, uranium, and natural gas.

Between 1946 and 1956 several nationalist parties were formed, including the Parti Progressiste Congolais (PPC), the Mouvement Socialiste Africain (MSA), and the Union Démocratique pour la Défense des Intérêts Africains (UDDIA). The first government, headed by Jacques Opangault of the MSA, was formed in March 1957, with Abbé Fulbert Youlou of UDDIA appointed prime minister in 1958. Following widespread ethnic conflict during February 1959 Youlou was named president, and the Congo declared its independence on 15 August 1960. The early years of autonomous rule were characterized by repeated political reform as the Congolese state negotiated its local, regional, and international status, all the while experimenting with various ideological models and influences at home.

Youlou remained in power until 1963 when, following widespread demonstrations and riots, and a general strike that came to a head between 13 and 15 August (events that are commemorated each year as the "Trois Glorieuses"), he was replaced by Alphonse Massemba-Debat. Massemba-Debat's presidency lasted until 1968, when Marien Ngouabi assumed power and adopted Marxism–Leninism as the ruling sociopolitical ideology. After Ngouabi's assassination in 1977, Joachim Yhombi Opango headed the administration until 1979. He was then voted out of office and succeeded by Denis Sassou-Nguesso, who would remain president until July 1990, when the Central Committee of the Congolese Worker's Party decided to abandon Marxism–Leninism. Instead they established a National Conference in order to implement pluralist democracy. The National Conference was held between 25 February and 10 June 1991 under the honorary leadership of Ernest Kombo.

The most significant political constituencies that emerged during this period were represented by Bernard Kolélas' Mouvement Congolais pour le Développement et la Démocratie Intégrale (MCDDI), Pascal Lissouba's Union Pan-Africaine pour la Démocratisation Sociale (UPADS), and of course the Parti Congolais du Travail (PCT) headed by Sassou-Nguesso. The spirit of reform culminated in Pascal Lissouba's ascendance to power, with the PCT's endorsement, during the second round of elections that followed presidential elections at the end of August 1992. Nevertheless, the electoral process had done little to eradicate ethnic loyalties and animosities, nor had it united the Congolese, and the violent civil unrest that accompanied the 1993 legislative elections lasted until February 1994. While the interim period was a time of relative calm in Congo, the presidential elections scheduled for July 1997 never took place. Civil war erupted on 5 June 1997, lasting until 17 October. During that time the country's infrastructure was destroyed, thousands of people were killed, and the capital Brazzaville was razed to the ground. Somewhat paradoxically, Sassou-Nguesso eventually regained power with French backing.

The region that encompassed pre-colonial Congo had a rich artistic legacy, but with colonialism and the introduction of print culture circumstances were radically altered. Yet Congo continues to enjoy a strong reputation for its various types of cultural expression. Shortly after independence, the Marxist–Leninist authorities began to exercise strict control and censorship over the media, transforming it into a tool for propagandists. The official newspapers – *Mwéti* and *Etumba* – were forced to follow the party line, and it was not until 1991 that legal reforms resulted in improved conditions for freedom of expression. Refusing to respect the tenets of socialist realist art, some writers established clandestine workshops and produced highly innovative texts in the tradition of resistance writing (they included Sylvain Bemba, Emmanuel Dongala, Henri Lopes, and Sony Labou Tansi). At the same time as Poto-Poto became famous for its art collective, the Rocado Zulu Theater Company achieved international fame. The musical fusions of some of Congo-Kinshasa's musicians, including Papa Wemba, Franco, Rochereau, and the Orchestre OK Jazz, also received international attention.

Congo's key strategic position in **francophone Africa** and Central Africa, along with its rich offshore holdings in oil, have attracted the continuing and unscrupulous attentions of the French authorities, who have refused to set aside their influence and relinquish their economic interest in the region. Entrenched political corruption has thereby been sustained, contributing to ongoing sociopolitical instability.

See also: French Equatorial Africa; socialisms and socialists

Further reading

Martin, P.M. (1995) *Leisure and Society in Colonial Brazzaville*, New York: Cambridge University Press.

Obenga, T. (1998) *L'histoire sanglante du Congo-Brazzaville (1959–1997): Diagnostic d'une mentalité politique africaine*, Paris: Présence Africaine.

Thomas, D. (2002) *Nation-Building, Propaganda, and Reconciliation: Literature in Francophone Africa*, Bloomington and Indianapolis: Indiana University Press.

DOMINIC THOMAS

Congo, Democratic Republic of *see* Democratic Republic of Congo

Côte d'Ivoire

Côte d'Ivoire covers an area of 322,460 square kilometers, and is bordered by **Ghana**, **Burkina Faso**, **Mali**, **Guinea**, and **Liberia**. The country had an estimated population of 16.4 million in 2000, including a large proportion of migrant laborers from neighboring countries. The country is divided between a tropical forest region in the south, and a savanna region in the north. It is also divided between a predominantly Muslim north, and a south where Christianity is more prevalent, albeit with a strong presence of African religions. Formerly one of the eight territories of the colony of French West Africa, Côte d'Ivoire has retained French as its official language. Despite the recent development of the petroleum sector, agriculture remains the primary activity, though manufacturing – in particular the processing of primary products – has been quite dynamic.

European contact dates back to the fifteenth century, when traders first began conducting business with coastal peoples. However, permanent settlement took place only in the late nineteenth century. Initially claimed by France, Côte d'Ivoire officially became a colony in 1893. Nevertheless, the French presence remained modest until after the **First World War**, at which time the colonial administration began encouraging the creation of settler farms in order to expand production of export crops. Influenced by the success of the French plantations, Africans – many of them former plantation laborers – began creating plantations of their own. With the profits generated by these farms, they began investing in the economies of the emerging towns. Both African and French farmers benefited from access to forced labor, an institution whereby any adults unable to pay for exemption had to give the government several days each year of essentially unpaid labor. Nominally used for public works, in Côte d'Ivoire forced labor was also employed to develop the plantation economy. By the **Second World War**, the African "planter bourgeoisie" had outstripped the French settler community in both numbers and output.

This set the stage for a fierce political struggle during the war. With the fall of France to the Germans and the creation of the Vichy regime, French West Africa's colonial governors opted to ally themselves with Vichy rather than with Charles de Gaulle's Free French government. Sympathetic to the settlers, the new colonial administration attempted to rein in the planters by, for example, denying them access to forced labor. In response, the planters organized politically, creating the Syndicat Agricole Africain (SAA). Félix Houphouët-Boigny, himself a large planter, became their leader. In 1944 the arrival of a Gaullist governor briefly tipped the political balance in the planters' favor. Eager to form alliances with local groups, and faced with the hostility of the Vichyist settlers, the new governor granted concessions to the planters. Shortly thereafter, Houphouët-Boigny went to France as a delegate to the new Constituent Assembly. While he was in France, he helped engineer the abolition of forced labor and thereby made himself into a nationalist hero back home. This cemented the hold of the planter elite on Ivoirien nationalist politics.

In 1946 the SAA gave rise to the Parti Démocratique de la Côte d'Ivoire (PDCI). Its political organization was so effective that within a decade it was the sole political party of note in the colony. Accordingly, it led the country to independence in 1960, at which time it thoroughly penetrated the state, creating a one-party regime. In contrast to the experiments of neighboring countries with variants of socialism, Côte d'Ivoire under the presidency of Houphouët-Boigny opted for a conservative and pragmatic course. The new government actually expanded the hiring of expatriate civil servants, and implemented pro-capitalist policies. At the heart of these lay a strategy of encouraging export agriculture in order to generate the revenues needed to develop urban industry. At the same time, government policies assisted the development of a local bourgeoisie by providing start-up capital and shares in state firms to local entrepreneurs, many of whom came from the planter class. Meanwhile, by nurturing networks of kinship ties and interlocking business interests within the country's political and economic elite, Houphouët-Boigny was able to bring a fair degree of inter-ethnic harmony to an otherwise fragmented country.

Côte d'Ivoire's initial two decades of independence were a time of prosperity and rapid growth. Output of its chief export crops – cocoa and coffee – expanded rapidly, while the country also developed other sectors of its agricultural economy. It also built up a large agro-industrial sector to process its primary exports. The country's growth rates were among the highest in Africa, leading observers to speak of the Ivoirien miracle.

However, problems had begun to emerge by the late 1970s. To fuel its development program, the country had built up a heavy burden of debt. When Northern governments began implementing monetarist policies to squeeze inflation out of their economies after the 1979 oil shock, demand for Ivoirien exports fell. At the same time, debt-servicing costs rose. The result was a prolonged recession in the 1980s. This, in turn, gave rise to dissatisfaction with the political regime.

Discontent broke into the open in 1990, when pro-democracy strikes and demonstrations spread throughout the country. In response, the government allowed a partial democratization that nonetheless left the PDCI in control. After the death of Houphouët-Boigny in 1993, the country's fragile ethnic balance became more strained. Houphouët's successor, Henri Konan Bedie, failed to maintain his mentor's practice of ethnic brokerage. The ruling party broke up and the government resorted to more naked repression. Matters came to a head in 1999, when General Robert Guei overthrew President Konan Bedie, breaking the Ivoirien military's tradition of non-interference in politics. Although the public initially welcomed the coup, Guei's authority was rapidly eroded when he tried to have himself elected president in a 2000 election that was widely decried as fraudulent. Street protests and violent demonstrations forced him to flee, and his opponent, Laurent Gbagbo, was declared president. Côte d'Ivoire's earlier stability, however, failed to return.

Further reading

Amin, S. (1973) *Neo-colonialism in West Africa*, trans. F. McDonagh, Harmondsworth: Penguin.

Rapley, J. (1993) *Ivoirien Capitalism*, Boulder and London: Lynne Rienner.

JOHN RAPLEY

Cotonou, Benin

Cotonou was founded as a trading post in the mid-nineteenth century by King Gezo of Dahomey Kingdom. Using the River Ouémé as a highway from the royal palm plantations to the sea, Cotonou assumed its unique position at the crossroads between the riches of the African interior and the thriving Atlantic trade. In 1890 the French sought to consolidate their hold on the Dahomean coast, and Cotonou in particular, by enforcing previous trade agreements. The Dahomean army, sent hurriedly by King Behanzin to expel the French landing party, was repeatedly defeated by the better equipped and better trained colonial force. The French colonizers turned Cotonou into the region's main port for agricultural products cultivated in the interior.

Once Dahomey was secured as part of French West Africa, the colonial authorities sought in 1900 to construct the Benin–Niger railway as a link between landlocked French Sahel and the sea. While situated on a sandy spit between the heavy Atlantic swell and the inland Lake Nokoué, the lack of a natural harbor greatly hampered Cotonou's ability to become a profitable commercial export center. The shipping industry relied on a wharf, constructed in 1891, that reached out into the Atlantic surf. With Dahomey's independence in 1960, the country's leaders sought to construct a permanent artificial harbor that would enable the city to compete with **Lagos**, **Lome**, and Tema for business from landlocked **Niger** and **Burkina Faso**. Finished in 1965, the harbor further changed the character of the once sleepy provincial town.

The people of Cotonou are drawn from the various ethnicities of southern Benin: the Fon, the Adja, and the Yoruba. Migrants returning from the African diaspora in Brazil formed the core of the educated elite in the city. The colonial administrators of French West Africa targeted the "Brazilians" as future civil servants for the entire region. Through concerted investment in African schooling and a steady stream of students to francophone universities, Cotonou became the "Latin Quarter of West Africa." With independence nigh and nationalism running high, educated Beninese civil servants returned from their posts abroad in the late 1950s. The influx of the educated elite marked the beginning of Cotonou as the *de facto* capital of the new Dahomean republic.

The colonial authorities limited the city's population by use of restrictive building permits. Not a total deterrent, Cotonou's population had slowly reached 160,000 residents by 1960. With independence, all the government ministries and the president himself moved to Cotonou, hiring the thousands of unemployed civil servants. The adoption of Marxism as the official government ideology in 1974 marked the expansion of the public sector to include dozens of government-owned industries, and Cotonou continued to grow in size and importance, spreading its boundaries through the construction of well-ordered neighborhoods. By the end of the twentieth century, Cotonou's population had reached 750,000.

The collapse of the Marxist regime left thousands of civil servants without work; government factories closed, salaries went unpaid for months, and banks failed. Massive unemployment forced the vast majority of Cotonou's residents into trading on the black market: an estimated 90 percent of all commerce is now in the informal sector. The sprawling Danktopa market, one of the most celebrated in West Africa, flourished as black-market trade with an increasingly destabilized Nigeria exploded. Benin's transition to democracy in 1990 made the country a trailblazer on the African continent and brought an influx of Western aid to the city. Paved avenues, resort hotels, and a new international conference center now stand intermixed with the thriving commercial life that once more defines the city.

Further reading

Cornevin, R. (1962) *Histoire du Dahomey*, Paris: Editions Berger-Levrault.

Ronen, D. (1975) *Dahomey: Between Tradition and Modernity*, Ithaca: Cornell University Press.

BRENT NEVER

D

Dakar, Senegal

Dakar, covering a surface area of 550 square kilometers, concentrates a substantial portion of the national population of **Senegal**: 14 percent at the time of independence and 21.6 percent in 1988. Senegal's capital city, Dakar had an estimated population of 2.4 million by 2000, of whom more than half were under twenty and over 90 percent were Muslims. Former capital of French West Africa, the city was taken over by the French in 1857, and its functions continued to expand after that. The first of many development plans dates from 1862. In 1901 it was decided to extend the town. A project covering the Plateau and the Médina was drawn up in 1914–15. A 1946 plan provided a basis for a broad program of infrastructural development. This plan was modified in 1957, following the creation of Dagoudane-Pikine, a zone destined for the *déguerpis* (displaced squatters) from the district of Rasmission. After independence, the state took important financial and institutional steps toward developing the city, but the gap between the real city and the official city remained a fundamental fact of Dakar's history.

The colonial and post-colonial authorities in Senegal equipped the city with a modern infrastructure (including railway, harbor, and airport facilities), and industrial investment was concentrated there – these factors made the city very attractive to the Senegalese population. Faced with this situation – and the possibility of tourist development – the state authorities organized the exclusion from the city of certain groups that were considered undesirable. The phrase *encombrements humains* (human clutter), used by the authorities at the time, was the justification for removing from central Dakar a mixed population of beggars, lepers, and street-peddlers. Between 1970 and 1980 particularly, this policy included the destruction and *déguerpissement* (removal of unplanned urban populations) of the slums closest to downtown Dakar. From 1985 onwards, the policy started to change; a program of rebuilding and legalizing squatter areas was implemented. The high price of building materials, the lack of centralized management and control of land reserves, the activities of land speculators, low household incomes, and the mobilization of financial resources in favor of social housing that benefited employees of the formal sector of the economy were the main obstacles to urban development policy. Basic public services (water, drainage, electric power, transportation, refuse collection) frequently broke down.

At the end of the twentieth century, Dakar's population was still growing, now through territorial expansion. The state authorities progressively tried to limit the proliferation of slums and squatter areas, and to support public housing programs in the old districts of Dakar and Dagoudane-Pikine. There was a wide gap, dating back to the colonial era, between Dakar and other regions. Dakar remained privileged in terms of both public and private investment. It was the main beneficiary of urban housing policy. Much of the health infrastructure was concentrated there, as well as import/export trade and the biggest manufacturers. Downtown Dakar, le Plateau, was host to the central state administration. While public transport companies suffered from structural deficiencies nationally, this concentration of facilities made transport problems in Dakar relatively simple to solve: an informal system of private minibuses, the *cars rapides*, consequently developed.

In the political sphere, ever since the colonial era Dakar has played a central part in national decision-making. Dakar hosted not only the headquarters of government ministries, but also those of trade unions and political parties. As a cosmopolitan city, Dakar also boasted a vibrant cultural and artistic life not found anywhere else in the country, and was the location for numerous national institutions, including Cheikh Anta Diop University (formerly the University of Dakar).

Further reading

Peterec, R.J. (1967) *Dakar and West African Economic Development*, New York: Columbia University Press.

MOMAR COUMBA DIOP

dance

Studies of African dance come from many perspectives. Some have taken an anthropological approach, giving descriptive analyses of dance forms that detail costumes, issues of gender, accompanying rituals, and the function of dance in society. Others have attempted a political approach, offering discussions of how political systems determine the creation and performance of different types of dance. Still others have studied how religion dictates the interpretation and performance of different forms of dance by examining how religion is used to prohibit or encourage the creation of and participation in dances. Emphasis on the form, style, and vocabulary of movements involved in dance is especially popular among scholars who analyze the semiotics of movement and posture, and of the different dance styles. A few scholars have taken a historical approach in their attempt to understand how past events influenced the creation and performance of African dance, or how dance movements reflect changes in society, while musicologists have examined the accompanying music or, at their best, considered how music and dance movements correlate.

Each of these different approaches has much to offer, but none can capture the essence of African dance. African dance is a complex interactive affair, involving movement, theater, sculpture, religion, music, the reenactment of past events, and gender issues. Further, over the past century Africans have merged new ideas from different cultures with their traditional dances in order to reflect the needs and realities of their own society. A thorough understanding of the development of African dance in the twentieth century requires a combined approach that looks at the anthropological and musical aspects, styles of movement, and religious overtones, as well as the historical events that inspired the creation and performance of particular dances. Such an approach contributes to our understanding of African dance, as both art form and cultural phenomenon, and of the role it plays in shaping identities. In order to understand it at this level of complexity, it is crucial to understand traditional African dance in its sociocultural context.

Traditional African dance is complex, multifaceted, and rich in tradition and form; it is a functional art that is inseparably linked with human existence and all the facets of daily life. For the most part, it is performed in open spaces by members of the same ethnic group to accompany work, to send the deceased off to the kingdom of the ancestors, to welcome the newborn into society, to summon the ancestors, or to initiate youths into adulthood. The symbolic gestures of the hips, hands, shoulders, legs, and head teach codes of conduct and transmit cultural values. Within the ritual context, African dance is an interactive affair that combines music, theater, visual display, and other artistic elements to create meaning.

One important component of African dance is the accompanying music. The combination of drums, bells, rattles, rhythm sticks, handclaps, flutes, and stringed instruments helps to create an atmosphere that stimulates the dancers' movements and enhances the expressive content of those movements. It also provides the rhythmic and melodic basis that is articulated in movement, regulating the scope, quality, speed, and dynamics of the movements through song texts and other sounds, and providing signals for the dancers that open up spaces for improvisation. In some pieces, the movement and the rhythms are so closely knit that changes in rhythm are accompanied by changes in the dancers' movements, so dancers rely on a specific kind of musical sophistication to enable them to identify and respond to the rhythmic shift. Special attire and visual display in the form of masks, facial and bodily decoration are used as additional media of communication to convey messages, and to enhance the execution of particular movements or the performance in general. Anklets, waist beads, and finger castanets add to the soundscape at the same time as emphasizing certain movements or extending particular parts of the body.

Traditional styles of and forms of organization for dances serve as metaphors for the structure of kinship and society, while also communicating aesthetic preferences, gender structures, and status through their marriage of movement, music, costumes, and the appreciative shouts of the audience. For the most part, newer dances continue this tradition but, at the same time, they have added dimensions to the performance and interpretation of dance.

Changes in African dance and the development of new styles occurred even in pre-colonial times, either when cultures on the continent exchanged ideas through trade or when newer dances were created in response to new needs in society. However, far-reaching transformation occurred as a result of contact with the non-African world, especially during the colonial and post-colonial periods. Many of the old dances died during the colonial period, but with independence many Africans revived those old skills and transformed them into new skills. The newer dances that were found on the continent in the twentieth century are as fascinating as they are diverse. They include older dances that, since the colonial period, have been recontextualized, formalized, and deprived of certain elements to make them suitable for performance on stage; they also include the popular social dances that accompany popular styles of music. The fact that these dances were created in response to colonialism makes them unique. They combine ideas from both traditional dance aesthetics and European styles. Generally speaking, most are performed for entertainment rather than having any specific religious or cultural value. For the most part, these dances are found in urban areas where people from different ethnic groups perform them, either indoors or outdoors, depending on the activity that the dance accompanies. Unlike the older dances, which were performed in a communal setting, these new adaptations are only performed by trained artists. These artists dance in enclosed spaces for audiences of ticketholders who applaud the agility and skill of each entertainer. In essence the older dances have assumed new meanings: they are now interpreted and consumed as works of art, devoid of cultural overtones. Inspired by traditional dance styles, these popular social dances combine local styles with foreign styles like the waltz, the rumba, the twist, or ballroom. There are further dances that are connected with Islamic or European military styles, but like the social dances they combine local musical and social practices with European and Arabic military, musical, movement, and symbolic resources.

The need for accompanying music is very strong, even with these new styles. For the most part, formalized dances are still accompanied by live music played on traditional instruments with traditional rhythmic patterns; the interaction between dancer and music is therefore intact. On the other hand, the live bands that accompany the dances associated with popular music styles combine traditional and Western instruments. Furthermore, in club settings the role of the master drummer has been replaced by the DJ; like the master drummer, the DJ determines the intensity, continuity, and style of the music through the choice of repertoire. Couple dancing is common in this context, with some degree of physical contact between the opposite sexes.

The different styles of African dance that existed on the continent in the twentieth century reflect Africa's history and creativity. The coexistence of old and new styles is a powerful manifestation of

Africa's flexibility and ability to move with the times, at the same time as holding on to the ancestral ways.

African dance during the colonial period

Syncretism and change in contemporary African dance are not determined by the colonial experience alone; they are parts of a multi-faceted historical process that involves a whole range of international political, social, and economic relationships between Africa and the non-African world, especially the West. Starting around the seventh century with the introduction of **Islam**, later followed by **Christianity**, Africa became colonized by two monotheistic religions that had no place for dance in their worship (Ajayi 1998). They waged war on the traditions of Africa, for not only did they see these traditions as contradicting what they preached, but they also saw them as a threat to the very survival of their ideology. Christian missionaries were perhaps the most relentless. The Christian moral ethic, which vacillates between perceiving the body, on one hand, as the site of soul/spirit and the Temple of God and, on the other, as "weak flesh," contrasted markedly with traditional African religion, which had been an inspiration for music, dance, and drama. So Christianity, which would later form the vanguard of modernity, imposed its ideas on Africa of what was good or bad, savage or civilized, and looked suspiciously at ritual uses of the body in dance. Making no attempt to understand the form, they condemned African dance as a savage practice – as "lewd" or "lascivious" – and preached against it while promoting Western cultural values and usage. Converts were forbidden from associating themselves with the traditional ways and those who were caught doing so were dealt with harshly. The converts, as they developed new tastes and beliefs, turned their backs on tradition and sometimes helped in the destruction of important ritual objects. This collaboration with the missionaries had deeply demoralizing effects on society as a whole. Many forms of dance were destroyed or went underground as a result of the persecution of practitioners who had been caught disobeying the missionaries' orders.

Another factor that helped undermine traditional African dance was colonization. Supported by their own bias and Christian ethics, the colonizing European countries showed no tolerance of traditional dances. In their attempt to "civilize" and control the minds and deeds of their "colonized subjects," they imposed stiff sanctions on the performance of these art forms. In addition, they introduced Western education with its weekly five-day timetables, which drastically reduced the number of days available for participation in initiation activities. Most rites-of-passage ceremonies became weekend events, thus decreasing the number of days available for imparting important cultural values through dance. In some societies, these activities and their accompanying dances were lost altogether. Others, such as the Swahili *chakacha*, which is now performed at wedding ceremonies, were reconfigured and recontextualized. The influence of Western thought through education and the media has also limited the function of dance in many African cities to mere audience reaction. At home and abroad, dances have moved from village square or shrine onto the concert stage or television screen, where dancers dressed in quasi-traditional or European costumes perform for a few hours in accordance with Western theatrical conventions.

The dances have shifted from outside events where everyone was once an active participant to indoor events for passive ticketholding audiences that applaud the skill of the dancers. Several dances have appeared on television programs or in movies. For example, the *tibol* dance, once performed by Bassari male initiates, was performed as part of the 1966 Dakar festival of African arts. The *enganda-za-higa*, a fierce Ugandan dance that was originally used to inspire warriors seeking revenge on rival clans, is now danced for pleasure. The purification rite of the Bini people of Nigeria now takes place on Nigerian television, not just in the villages. The Ewe *atsiagbekor*, which appeared in the early part of the century as a development out of traditional war dances, no longer prepares warriors for war. These dances, which were once tied to the sociocultural ideas of a particular society, are now stripped of their cultural meanings and performed as works of art – as art for art's sake. The audiences for dance in these new contexts are especially interesting and worthy of attention. They are of a particular class status, usually educated middle–upper class with newly acquired tastes. They can afford to pay the ticket price to be entertained by skilled and professional dancers, for whom they show appreciation by applauding politely at the end of each piece. Their role has shifted from participation in dances within a rural setting to the passive and urbanized consumption of art. Such formalized dance performances are popular with dance companies like the Ghana Dance Ensemble.

The idea of presenting these dances as formalized and sophisticated works of art became popular after many African countries gained independence. In 1950 there were only three independent African states – Egypt, Ethiopia, and Liberia – but from the late 1950s, as more countries gained their independence, many of them chose to reclaim their ancient names as a means of self-definition. In Senegal, the national ballet was founded in 1961 to present traditional dances on the basis of ideas drawn from the Negritude movement. In a similar attempt to upgrade the role of indigenous dance, many nations engaged in forms of cultural revival that showcased the traditional dances that had been denied them by colonialism. They organized dance competitions, festivals, and tours, featuring a range of dances from within their borders. Dance companies became particularly popular: every country has a national dance company, which is sponsored by its respective government or privately owed by individuals or institutions. Members of these companies include people of different ethnic groups. Having been grouped forcibly together within new national boundaries, the need to reinforce ethnic identity while developing a new national identity is served by these heterogeneous organizations at the same time as they ensure political solidarity and patriotism. Besides performing locally, these dance companies tour other countries, conduct workshops and classes for tourists, and perform at government functions. In 1963 Sierra Leone sent a national dance troupe to the New York World's Fair. The Ghana Dance Ensemble and the Ballets Africains of Guinea have made many trips abroad. In 1969 thirty-eight African countries sent representatives to Algiers for the First Pan-African Cultural Festival. The aim of this was to encourage dance troupes to travel outside their own countries to learn from other cultures, sharing knowledge and exchanging materials. Thus it is now common to find the Ghanaian dance troupe performing dances from other countries. In such cases not only do the contexts for performance change, but issues of gender and other factors that gave meaning to the original piece are compromised. For example, the *am-haraba*, a male war dance among the Sudanese Arabs, is performed for pleasure as a multi-gender dance by the Hemat-Arabs of neighboring Chad.

Another interesting recontextualization occurred in South Africa among black male migrant workers. Contract miners introduced their traditional music and dance styles into the townships where they were working long and painful shifts. The dances of these black South African miners were gradually formalized as expressions of both urbanization and apartheid. Originally associated with traditional customs, many of these stamping, striding, and acrobatic dances are now performed outside their original context in such as way as to provide a pressure valve that releases accumulated frustration and depression. The dances are also an important means of preserving the identity of migrant workers (Bender 1991).

New dance forms in the twentieth century

The new dances in Africa have been influenced by three major factors: occupation, importation, and colonization. Even before the partition of Africa and its occupation by foreigners, Africans were exposed to European dance styles. This was particularly true during and after the slavery period, as in the 1830s, for example, when Ghanaians learned how to play waltzes, fox-trots, and other ballroom dances on Western instruments to entertain colonial officers in their castles and forts. These Western styles slowly infiltrated the musicians' minds and inspired the creation of new styles of music and new forms of dance, including highlife with its accompanying brass orchestrations. In eastern Africa, the brass band music of the Sultan of Zanzibar and the military bands of colonial British and German armies inspired the creation of *beni ngoma*. *Beni ngoma*, which was performed initially by the Swahili elite of Lamu in the 1890s, is a syncretic dance that combines Western brass arrangements, costumes based on European military or civilian clothes, and a drill-style marching dance. The new dance became very popular in this part of the continent and was the first artistic expression to unite people in East Africa along class rather than ethnic lines. Inspiring regional variants, it went through many transformations. The popularity of this dance style exploded between the wars, with Africans seeming enthralled by the apparent invincibility and superiority of the Europeans. Later the dance lost popularity, when the weakness of Europe was revealed following the **Second World War**. Another new dance form, the *dansi*, emerged out of the experiences of freed slaves in Mombasa: like other popular social styles that emerged during the third decade of the century, this imitated European ballroom dancing.

Changes in styles of dance and the creation of new dances were hastened by the development of media technology, with cinema, radio, television, recorded sound, and dance bands and bars appearing in Africa. The rapid spread of the radio and gramophone in the 1920s exposed Africans to dance music of all genres. **Urbanization** also became a major factor of change. The growth and expansion of cities dissolved traditional ethnic ties, and new forms of entertainment crossed cultural and political boundaries. Pop music and dance are part and parcel of the large, all-embracing, heterogeneous, citified culture. These and other factors led to the development of regional styles such as highlife, *juju*, and *rumba*, which were fashioned after ballroom dancing and waltz, and came into their own after the Second World War. These newer styles were performed in dance bars, to accompaniments that combined Western and local instruments, becoming a medium for expressing the frustrations and uncertainties of urban life. These dances replaced traditional dances, and were very common in urban areas, especially at parties, in hotels, and in bars. This growth of popular music styles reflected social dislocation and modernization across the continent, and showed the influence of missionaries' choral hymns, military brass bands, and folk songs brought to Africa by merchant seamen.

Seamen were especially important to this new development; serving as cultural brokers, they brought ideas that they had learned in their travels back to the urban centers from which they had set sail. The Kru and Krios sailors of Liberia and Sierra Leone, especially, are credited with bringing back the new tunes and acoustic guitars that would later become staples for the early pop bands. These bands evolved during the 1920s as brass bands, guitar bands, and large urban dance bands playing waltzes, fox-trots, and twists. They became especially popular after independence spread across Africa in the 1960s and 1970s. These in turn inspired the creation of dances in traditional styles, such as the *kpanlogo* and *bóbóóbó* in Ghana. They both grew out of dance-band highlife and local drumming, but the latter was also influenced by Christian hymns and imagery. Another development in this area is more in line with the Western classical or art tradition. Subsumed under the term "folk opera," these other recent indigenous art forms combined dance, drama, costumes, music, and traditional imagery to create a new genre. Others, involved in dance more as an academic discipline, have created new dance styles that borrow heavily from American modern dance techniques. These are not popular dance styles, but rather creations by choreographers who have developed, by using stylized movement, individualized vocabularies to communicate and express their emotions and social messages. This style is evident in the dances of the Ballets Africains and the National Dance Theater of Ghana.

African traditions have had a great impact on the development of African-American and Latin American dance styles. When numerous Africans from different parts of the continent were taken to the New World as slaves, they carried in their memory dances that were later refashioned in the new context as *capoeira*, *calinda*, *samba*, break-dancing, or *juba*. Today, with the help of the mass media, many of these dances have found their way back to Africa, where they have undergone a second phase of refashioning and recontextualization. Such is the case with the Latin American *rumba*, an Afro-Cuban music and dance style that was created by Cuban slaves after their emancipation in the 1880s. This genre became very popular in the 1950s in many parts of French-speaking Africa, especially Central Africa. Initially, bands played cover versions of the original tunes in Spanish, but they then began to re-Africanize them by adding traditional rhythms and ideas, and using their own languages. In Zaire, especially, one *rumba*-style dance superseded another, from *kara-kara* to *boucher*, from *soukous*, *kiri-kiri*, *mombette* and *Apollo* to *ngwabin*. Characteristic of all these dances is the typical *rumba* movement: a hip motion that shifts the weight from one leg to another. In the late 1960s soul records by James Brown and Aretha Franklin inspired the *kiri-kiri*, while *Apollo* became popular when the Americans made their successful landing on the moon (the landing caused much excitement across Africa). Dancers in this latter style imitated the moonwalk of the astronauts (Bender 1991).

The expedition of the British West Indian Regiments in West Africa brought about the first contact between African-American and West African music. By the 1930s and 1940s African populations had heard jazz from the United States via the radio. In the 1950s jazz became the basis in South Africa for *kwela*, an imitation of ragtime and later swing that was played on pennywhistles. Accompanying this music was a style of dance called *pata pata*, a solo style in which two people touched each other's bodies to the rhythm of the accompanying music. In the late 1960s the abundance of cheap transistor receivers, powered by batteries or independent power supplies, fueled the mass dissemination across Africa of more jazz tunes, rock and roll, and soul music, even reaching rural areas. Besides the spread of radios, tours by Caribbean and African-American jazz bands and performers were important in this process of diffusion. Noteworthy among the tours of Africa that took place in the late 1950s and 1960s was that of Louis Armstrong. His tour further helped popularize the twist and big band orchestrations for pop bands. From about 1960, rock and roll, the twist, and other American social dances started becoming generally popular with the youth of Africa.

By the beginning of the twenty-first century, mass media had become a powerful force with far-reaching impact on traditional African arts. African-American popular music and dance styles are heard and seen every day, through commercials for Coca-Cola and high street fashion designers, while American music videos and awards shows transmit new fashions and aesthetic preferences in dance. African youth are drawn to the glamour of these new styles, and by tuning in they absorb the language, mannerisms, and movements of the pop stars. Hip-hop culture and rap music are especially popular. Break-dancing, the dance associated with the hip-hop, has not taken root, however. Instead, women "juke" or perform sensual gyrations of the buttocks, as some have put it: "celebrating their femininity with pride." Men, on the other hand, soulfully nod their heads on the music's strong down-beat, along with symbolic gestures of the hands and facial expressions, or perform rapid movements that fully articulate their arms and legs. The fashion codes and sampled and synthesized music of hip hop are occupying center stage in the pop scene among African youth, with creativity expressed through the lyrics as much as through the music. African youth have adopted and adapted African-American hip-hop dance styles to voice their own concerns as they struggle to survive in a world of unstable governments, unemployment, and harsh economic uncertainties. In this new context, the new styles continue the African tradition of imparting ideas about the realities in society through dance.

See also: leisure; music; youth

References and further reading

Ajayi, O.S. (1996) "In Contest: The Dynamics of African Religious Dances," in K.M. Asante (ed.), *African Dance: An Artistic, Historical, and Philosophical Inquiry*, Trenton: Africa World Press Inc., pp. 183–202.

—— (1998) *Yoruba Dance: The Semiotics of Movement and Body Attitude in Nigerian Culture*, Trenton: Africa World Press Inc.

Bender, W. (1991) *Sweet Mother: Modern African Music*, Chicago: University of Chicago Press.

Dagan, E.A. (1997) *The Spirits Dance in Africa:*

Evolution, Transformation, and Continuity in Sub-Sahara, Westmount: Galerie Amrad African Arts Publications.

Nketia, K.J.H. (1975) *The Music of Africa*, New York: W.W. Norton & Co.

Ranger, T.O. (1975) *Dance and Society in Eastern Africa 1890–1970: The Beni Ngoma*, Ibadan, London, Lusaka and Nairobi: Heinemann.

Tierou, A. (1992) *Dooplé: The Eternal Law of African Dance*, Switzerland: Harwood Academic Publishers.

Warren, L. (1972) *The Dance of Africa: An Introduction*, Englewood Cliffs: Prentice-Hall.

OFORIWAA ADUONUM

Dar es Salaam, Tanzania

Dar es Salaam, founded by Sultan Majid of Zanzibar in the mid-1860s, became the capital of German East Africa in 1891. Its main attractions were a deep-water harbor and its proximity to up-country caravan routes. At first the population was small, but a relatively advanced infrastructure was quickly established. The city's residential layout was racialized: colonial officials occupied the garden suburbs to the east, next to the commercial center, while Asians and Africans were situated to the west. In 1913 the total population was 22,500, including 1,000 Europeans and 2,500 Asians.

Construction of the Central Railway began in 1906. It reached Kigoma in 1914 and linked Dar es Salaam to the Great Lakes region. The city entered the British period as a major regional and national commercial center. Dar es Salaam was a Muslim town, although from the 1890s Christian missions there attracted followers. Early residents included Sudanese and Manyema soldiers employed by the Germans, but the largest group were Zaramo from the surrounding hinterland, who in 1956 still formed about 35 percent of the population. Other significant immigrant groups included Rufiji, Luguru, and Nyamwezi.

From early in the century, most urban communities had their associations, which were dominated by elders, and served as burial and welfare societies. They sometimes concentrated on development in the hinterland. Women and youths favored multi-ethnic dance societies (there were at least fifty-eight of these in 1954) that often served ritual exorcism purposes, while the popularity of occupation- and employment-based football clubs indicated the emergence of a new class structure in the city.

Times were hard during the depression years of the 1930s, although an African landlord class emerged during the interwar period. Of employed resident Africans some 60 percent earned less than fifteen shillings a month, a third of the men were unemployed, and malaria and tuberculosis were rife. Conditions worsened during the **Second World War** and immediately afterwards, as the African population doubled, largely due to rural–urban migration. These years also saw the beginnings of industrialization. Construction replaced domestic service as the main source of employment, and a large section of the population subsisted through casual and informal work. Squatter settlements proliferated, although some public housing had been constructed by 1950.

African frustration over their exclusion and powerlessness reached a peak during the 1950s. Leaders of the small African capitalist class of traders and landlords made important contributions to the nationalist movement, which was led by Julius Nyerere. The indefatigable Bibi Titi Mohamed mobilized thousands of women, and the radical newspaper *Kwetu* advanced African political thinking. Earlier, strikes had disrupted the port several times, most notably in 1947.

After independence in 1961, immigration to Dar es Salaam accelerated. In 1967 the population was 273,000; in 1997 it was at least 1.4 million. Urban services deteriorated in the 1980s because of the national economic crisis. Residents massively evaded state regulations, with consequent growth of the informal economy such that more than half of the urban population relied on it for survival, especially women. Poverty persisted through to the end of the twentieth century, worsened by high rates of malaria infection and other diseases, but it was offset to some degree by new investments in roads, telecommunications, and tourism.

Both unplanned and planned areas are dominated by Swahili-style housing. Numerous Omani and colonial buildings remain, particularly near the harbor. The Asian commercial zone has considerable architectural interest, with many early twentieth-century buildings. Notable additions since independence include the University of Dar es Salaam, and the giant concrete edifice that is the Kariakoo market.

Further reading

Illife, J. (1979) *A Modern History of Tanganyika*, Cambridge: Cambridge University Press.

STEPHEN J. ROCKEL

debt crises

Long-term economic prosperity often requires extensive public investment in roads, ports, schools, research facilities, and many other forms of infrastructure. Since countries lacking these resources usually also lack the finances to build them, it can be necessary for a government to borrow funds from abroad to pay for needed investment. However, just as some level of borrowing can enhance future prosperity, too much debt can become a drag on future economic growth. If the burden of debt repayment is greater than the gains provided by the investments, a country suffers from its borrowing. Whenever the debt burden becomes too great compared to the nation's income, the debt becomes a crisis both for the borrower, whose economy is smothered by the pressure to repay, and for the lender, who must ultimately accept that the debt cannot be repaid in full. By the 1980s many African countries found themselves in debt crises of this nature.

Roots of the debt crises

Africa's debt came on suddenly in the last quarter of the twentieth century. Through the colonial period, the continent was not the recipient of financial lending and most countries took on little debt from public sources or private banks in the first decade of independence. However, two changes occurred in the middle of the 1970s that made borrowing appear highly attractive. First, member-states of the Organization of Petroleum Exporting Countries (OPEC) made financial windfalls by restricting exports and driving petroleum prices to record heights. The profits these countries made were deposited in financial institutions that then sought to lend the money out to earn interest income. This great influx of funds to be lent led to lower interest rates and increasingly attractive terms for borrowers. Hence, the oil price shocks of the 1970s resulted in "petro-dollars" being lent on relatively good terms.

Just as loans suddenly became more available in the 1970s, many African countries suddenly appeared to have enhanced borrowing capacities. Weather-related crop failures in Latin America caused the prices for many African agricultural exports to shoot upward in the mid-1970s. Booms in the prices of coffee, cocoa, and tea (as well as petroleum) brought sudden infusions of income into many African economies. Projecting this higher income into the future, many lenders concluded that African countries could safely sustain higher levels of debt than they had been holding. Since loans meant access to funds that could be used to help develop their economies, countries borrowed heavily, expecting to repay with the revenues from continued export of primary products.

The assumption that high export prices for primary commodities would allow countries to repay their debts proved to be false. Through the 1980s prices for Africa's export commodities dropped steadily and the volume of exports also tended to fall. Rather than becoming a signal that price projections had been overly optimistic, the falling export revenues were treated as justification for increased borrowing to stabilize spending until prices bounced back. In fact, export prices did not return to the high levels of the previous decade. Even as export revenues fell, it became clear that few of the investments made with borrowed funds would generate a stream of profits sufficient to pay off the debts. Meanwhile, interest rates rose, increasing the costs of paying the debt in those countries, such as **Nigeria** and **Egypt**, where loans had been made largely at variable rather than fixed rates. A combination of temporarily cheap credit, unrealistically high expectations about countries' capacity to repay, and unproductive investments quickly moved African states from being relatively under-indebted to holding a crippling debt burden.

Size and scope of the debt crises

In 1971 the total external debt of Africa south of the Sahara was US$8,763,500,000. By 1980 the debt had grown to US$60,820,000,000, and in 1998 it exceeded US$230,000,000,000. This growing debt would not have been a concern if the capacity to service it were also rising. Because international debts must usually be paid in either US dollars or the currency of the lending country, the capacity to repay a loan is measured by comparing an economy's debt to the foreign currency it earns through exports. Financial institutions generally consider a debt of more than twice annual income to be unsustainable. Debts of this scale are likely to be beyond the immediate ability of the county to pay and efforts at repayment are likely to inhibit investments and growth in the economy. In 1998 twenty-one African countries held debts of more than twice their annual export earnings, ten of these countries had debts of over four times their annual export earnings and two countries (**Sudan** and **Guinea-Bissau**) had external debts of over twenty times their annual export earnings.

Another way to gauge the severity of a debt crisis is to compare the debt service, the amount which must be paid each year, with annual income from exports. In the 1970s only a handful of African countries spent more than 10 percent of their export earnings on debt servicing. By 1986 twenty-two African economies spent over a quarter of their annual export earnings on servicing old debts. At some point in the 1980s or 1990s, thirty different African countries experienced debt-service burdens of this magnitude. These heavily indebted countries included North African states like **Morocco** and Egypt, oil exporters like Nigeria, ostensibly market-oriented agricultural economies like **Kenya**, and states like **Tanzania** that were identified with socialist policies. In Guinea-Bissau, **Madagascar**, **Malawi**, **Mozambique**, and **Zambia**, over half of the annual export earnings for 1986 were diverted into servicing debt. **Ghana** and **Uganda** reached this threshold later in the 1980s. These debt-service payments crippled the ability of governments to provide basic services to their people and to make the investment that would allow them to generate the income to pay debts in the future.

Two aspects of Africa's debt set it apart from debt incurred in other developing regions. First, in contrast to debts incurred by middle-income countries like Mexico and Brazil, most of the African debt was from national governments or **international financial institutions** rather than from private banks. Second, unlike other low-income regions, debt in Africa was largely incurred on commercial terms rather than at concessionary rates. Concessionary aspects in the lending terms implied a grant element of about 15 percent of the debt in North Africa and 25 percent in Africa south of the Sahara. By comparison, loans to South Asia in the 1980s had a grant element amounting to 40 percent of their value. Whereas private lenders were financially threatened when Latin American countries appeared close to defaulting on their debts, the national governments that had lent to African states did not immediately feel the pressure to address the crises. Meanwhile, the non-concessional nature of the debt implied accumulating financial strain on the debtor governments.

Strategies for resolving the crises

Starting in the 1980s creditors did respond to the threat that African states might default on their debts. A series of agreements were reached that established a process of debt rescheduling under multilateral agreements such as the Paris Club. These programs initially focused on renegotiating loans so that they would be paid back over a longer period of time. In this way, the immediate debt-service burdens on a country could be reduced to a reasonable level, without actually canceling any debt. This process provided temporary relief for the finances of some African states, but it did not enhance their capacity to pay the debt itself. Rather, rescheduling moved the debt-servicing problem into the future.

In 1987 the World Bank launched a Special Program of Assistance (SPA) while the International

Monetary Fund (IMF) established the Enhanced Structural Adjustment Facility (ESAF) to help address the debt problem. These programs aimed to ensure that debtors could grow economically and gain the capacity to honor debts. The programs provided concessionary loans to low-income countries whose economic growth was inhibited by their debt burdens, on the condition that the borrowing government undertake policy reforms that the lenders considered necessary for restoring economic growth. The SPA and ESAF loans were to be used to pay down non-concessionary debts and future economic growth resulting from policy reforms was to cover the cost of the new concessionary credit. The Toronto Agreement of 1988 extended the trend towards improving the terms of existing debt by specifying mechanisms for lending governments to transform non-concessionary loans into concessionary ones. These systems reduced the total debt burden of African states, but their impact is hard to measure since creditor governments may have reduced their foreign assistance spending in Africa as they added grant elements to the debt. Furthermore, a large debate centered around whether the policy reforms that were tied to the World Bank and IMF loans actually contributed to better economic performance and whether they served to alleviate or exacerbate poverty in Africa. In any case, through the terms of the SPA and ESAF loans, international financial institutions exerted broad influence over the domestic policies of African governments.

In 1996 the international community, through the World Bank and the IMF, launched the Heavily Indebted Poor Countries (HIPC) initiative to provide relief in situations where old debts continued to hold countries in poverty. This program represented recognition that debt relief had to be more dramatic and that it needed to be structured to address poverty in the debtor states. Of the twenty-two countries identified by the program as warranting this intervention, twenty were in Africa. Although many creditors had resisted the idea of outright debt forgiveness, the severity of Africa's debt compelled a shift from debt renegotiation to debt cancellation. Under the HIPC initiative and the enhanced HIPC initiative of 1999, creditor governments and international financial institutions contributed to a trust fund to finance debt forgiveness. As in earlier programs, countries taking HIPC initiative support were required to implement specific policy measures. In addition, the program required governments to use funds that were diverted from debt repayment to support poverty reduction through strategies developed with **civil society** participation.

By 2001 over US$34 billion had been committed to debt relief under the HIPC initiative. Early results of the program appeared encouraging. Under the program, Mozambique, for example, received US$4.3 billion in debt relief, cutting the value of its debt by 72 percent. Over the period 1996 to 2000, the country's debt-service spending dropped from US$135 million to US$14 million, while spending on social services rose from US$78 million to US$178 million. Nineteen other African countries in the initiative were projected to increase their social spending by a third, while reducing debt-service costs to under 10 percent of export earnings by 2002.

The international response to Africa's debt crises evolved from rescheduling, merely delaying the inevitable, to debt consolidation with policy conditionality, before finally turning to debt forgiveness. By 2001 there were early signs of improvement, but the crisis had not been resolved. The African debt crisis was significant for many reasons. In one respect, it represented a lost opportunity. Had borrowing in the 1970s been more limited and investments better targeted, the debt could have enriched the future. Instead it left countries struggling with interest payments on debts that showed few benefits. Perhaps more significantly, the debt crises created a situation in which international financial institutions acquired unprecedented influence over the domestic policies of independent African states.

See also: economy: post-independence; structural adjustment programs; international trade

Further reading

Abbott, G. (1993) *Debt Relief and Sustainable Development in Sub-Saharan Africa*, Aldershot: Edward Elgar.

Abdulai, S.Y. (1990) *Africa's External Debt: An Obstacle to Economic Recovery*, Vienna: The OPEC Fund for International Development, Pamphlet Series No.27.

HIPC Unit, World Bank (2001) *Financial Impact of the HIPC Initiative: First 22 Country Cases*, Washington, D.C.: World Bank.

Kote-Nikoi, N. (1996) *Beyond the New Orthodoxy: Africa's Debt and Development Crisis in Retrospect*, Aldershot: Avebury Press.

World Bank (2000) *2000 World Development Indicators*, Washington, D.C.: World Bank.

ALEX WINTER-NELSON

decolonization

To many historians, the term "decolonization" refers to the end of formal European colonial empires in Africa, rather than to the termination of Africa's subordination to Europe (or the West more generally). Beginning with the restoration of the monarchy in **Egypt** in 1922 and ending with the demise of apartheid in **South Africa** in 1994, the process of decolonization was quite complex, involving both peaceful transitions and wars of liberation, both local accommodations and international conflict. In 1945 only three African countries enjoyed nominal independence: **Liberia**, the troubled republic established by freed American slaves in the nineteenth century; **Ethiopia**, the ancient kingdom recently liberated from the fascist Italian occupation of 1936–41; and Egypt, which had enjoyed internal self-government since 1922. In 1960 alone seventeen colonies achieved their independence, bringing the total of independent African states to twenty-seven, mostly concentrated in North, West, and Central Africa. In the early 1960s the winds of decolonization swept through East Africa, and from the mid-1970s the settler strongholds of Southern Africa began to fall.

What accounts for this remarkable historical process? As on every key question in African history, scholars are divided. Some argue that African nationalism was primarily responsible for the dismantling of the colonial empires. Among nationalist historians, then, decolonization is essentially seen as a heroic story of nationalist struggle and achievement. Others contend that decolonization was a product of imperial policy and planning. Thus to imperialist historians the metropoles held the initiative and nationalism was merely of nuisance value. These two approaches seek to tell the story of decolonization in the context of colonial–imperial relations, singling out either the demands of the colonies or the deliberations in imperial capitals. A third approach seeks to place decolonization in the context of changes in the system of international relations.

These approaches need not be mutually exclusive. Such a complex process as decolonization was undoubtedly a product of many factors. It involved complex interplay between the prevailing international situation, the policies of the colonial powers, and the nature and strength of the **nationalist movements**, which in turn reflected internal conditions in both the metropoles and the colonies, and also the ideologies and visions of the post-colonial world. There were clearly variations in the patterns of decolonization among regions and colonies conditioned by the way in which these factors coalesced and manifested themselves. Decolonization was also affected by the relative presence and power of European settlers and by each colony's perceived strategic importance.

Decolonization gathered momentum in the context of rising Pan-Africanism, emerging new international movements, and transformations in the global order. A movement launched towards the end of the nineteenth century and dedicated to the liberation and solidarity of African peoples on the continent and in the diaspora, **Pan-Africanism** emerged from the **Second World War** more militant than ever. From the Manchester Pan-African Congress of 1945, which was attended by some of Africa's first post-independence leaders, such as Kwame Nkrumah and Jomo Kenyatta, came demands for mass nationalism and independence. It was also in 1945 that the Arab League was formed. Pan-Arabism was destined to play a crucial role in nationalist mobilization in northern Africa, especially following the creation of Israel in 1948 and the shock of Arab defeat by the new state. The ideologies of Pan-Africanism and Pan-Arabism found fertile ground in the bustling

Egyptian capital of **Cairo** under Gamal Abdel Nasser, who saw Egypt as the center of three circles. These circles were Islam, the Arab world, and Africa – in short, Islamic resistance, Arab nationalism, and Pan-Africanism.

Meanwhile new international movements, which challenged European colonialism and bolstered African nationalism, were also emerging. From eastern Europe and eastern Asia came new sympathetic communist states. India gave the stirring example of massive non-violent resistance, inspired by Mahatma Gandhi whose philosophy and tactics had been honed in segregated South Africa. Boosting this nascent Afro-Asian solidarity was the Bandung Conference of 1955, which brought together newly independent African and Asian states. Soon the Afro-Asian and global anti-colonial movements grew into the **Non-Aligned Movement**, which provided an additional vehicle for African nationalists to mobilize international opinion against colonialism.

Other international developments before and after the Second World War also facilitated decolonization. The **Great Depression** of the late 1920s and early 1930s was particularly critical. It wreaked havoc on the world economy and the lives of millions of people, in the process stoking the fires of nationalism everywhere. Among the major powers it led to growing protectionism and imperial rivalry. Economic planning, state intervention, and social welfare also became acceptable as effective means of capitalist economic management. Among the colonial powers economic interventionism and protectionism were extended to the colonies, while desperate Germany turned to the Nazis and militaristic Japan sought salvation by invading China. As might be expected, given their underdeveloped and dependent status, colonial economies were hit hardest. People in the colonies blamed their falling commodity prices and wages, and deepening material hardships on colonialism, which lost any legitimacy it may have acquired.

Thus the Great Depression sowed the nationalist seeds that, on the one hand, germinated into the horrendous tragedies of the Holocaust and the Second World War and, on the other, into the emancipation of hundreds of millions of people from colonial subjugation in Africa and Asia. Further fueling African nationalism in the 1930s was the Italian invasion of Ethiopia in 1935. Prized for being the only African state to successfully repel the European colonial conquests of the late nineteenth century, the invasion of Ethiopia with the apparent connivance of the major powers enraged Pan-Africanists everywhere. Hardly had the dust settled from the Great Depression and the invasion of Ethiopia, when the thunderclouds of war broke out.

The Second World War brought death and destruction on a scale never before experienced in world history. Africa was not spared. North Africa became an important theater of war, and from across the continent millions were conscripted to fight on behalf of their respective colonial masters. Many millions more were commandeered to produce "strategic raw materials" for the war effort. Colonial political economies were profoundly shaken and transformed by the war. Besides the hardships, the war changed attitudes and expectations on both sides of the colonial divide. Forced labor and cultivation were reintroduced in some colonies, which resulted in food shortages. There were also widespread shortages of consumer goods, rising inflation, and falling real wages and commodity prices. The consequence was unprecedented urban unrest among workers and the fledgling nationalist elites. The wave of strikes experienced in the mid-1930s in response to the Great Depression resumed, and engulfed commercial centers in West Africa and the mining centers of Southern Africa, culminating in the general strikes that rocked railroads and harbors from **Mombasa** to **Dakar** between 1946 and 1948. Peasant resistance also spread. There were crop holdups and attacks on chiefs in **Ghana**, and squatter agitation on settler farms in **Kenya** that would soon explode into the liberation war known as Mau Mau.

The Second World War weakened the imperial powers both ideologically and materially. The Nazis gave racist ideologies, including colonialism, a bad name. The colonial powers could no longer explain why self-determination was permissible for states Hitler had conquered but not for the Africans who had fought against Hitler's forces. The mystique of the colonial powers was also irreparably shattered: France had been conquered by the Germans, and Britain had won only thanks to the United States and the Soviet Union. African soldiers returning from the war not only came back with diminished esteem for the colonial powers and Europeans in general, but with heightened expectations for a new postwar dispensation. In short the ex-servicemen, impatient for change, would be in the vanguard of the mounting nationalist struggles.

Also favorable to the African nationalists was the fact that the two new superpowers, the United States and the Soviet Union, were opposed to old-style European colonialism in their competitive bid to win hearts and minds and markets in the developing world. The Soviets were more prepared than the Americans to provide the nationalists with both moral and material support. The Cold War, in effect, enabled the nationalists to leverage their interests against the colonial powers. No less significant in the rhetorical stakes was the United Nations, where the developing countries soon predominated and which provided a critical platform for the nationalists to air their grievances and aspirations. The United Nations also directly affected the demise of colonialism by overseeing the decolonization of its trusteeship territories, beginning with **Libya** in 1951, followed by **Togo**, **Somalia**, **Burundi**, and **Rwanda** in 1960, and **Tanzania** in 1961. Once these territories achieved their independence, it was difficult to justify the subjugation of their often more developed neighbors. Less noticeable at the time, but important in the decolonization drama in the long run, was the growing importance of multilateral financial institutions and multinational corporations, which lessened the significance of formal colonialism as an instrument of imperial domination and exploitation. In 1944 three new international agencies were established: the World Bank, the International Monetary Fund (IMF), and the General Agreement on Tariffs and Trade (GATT), predecessor to the World Trade Organization. These were to alter the face of the global economy, and the fate of Africa. After the war, age-old foes Germany and France inaugurated the process towards European unification with the formation of the European Common Market, which provided the old colonial powers with a new geopolitical outlet for their global ambitions. This period also witnessed the growing importance of multinational corporations in international trade and investment. These corporations – many from the United States, Japan, and Germany – wanted to open up colonial markets, and their governments were only too keen to assist. For example, one of the provisions for recipients of Marshall Aid, which included Britain, was that US nationals would have unrestricted access to colonial raw materials. These developments may not have strengthened African nationalism, but they probably weakened European colonialism.

Clearly the colonial powers were increasingly on the defensive internationally and within the colonies themselves. More often than not they reacted to pressures they did not and could not control. Because of wartime devastation their hold over the colonies was less secure than before, even though they needed the colonies more than ever. This gave rise to the contradictory policies of what some historians call the "second colonial occupation": the introduction of reforms in the face of intensifying imperial interventions in colonial affairs. The reform imperative was demonstrated most visibly through new colonial development schemes and constitutional maneuvers. In 1945 the British established an expanded Colonial Development and Welfare (CD&W) program, while a year later the French created the Economic and Social Investment Development Fund (FIDES), both of which were used mainly for infrastructural development.

These schemes were presented as examples of British and French "aid" to the colonies. The reality was quite different. They were designed to assist in the recovery of metropolitan industries and camouflage the dynamics of colonial exploitation. Thus while the CD&W provided £140 million between 1946 and 1956, the sterling balances of the African colonies alone held by the British treasury stood at £1,446 million by 1955. This was more than half the total gold and dollar reserves of Britain and the Commonwealth, which then stood at £2,120 million. The colonial sterling balances were crucial for Britain, which had emerged from the war owing £6,000 million – making it the biggest debtor nation in the world – and with foreign reserves low and rapidly vanishing.

Also too little and increasingly too late were the constitutional reforms that were introduced by the colonial powers. At the Brazzaville Conference of 1944 Africans in the French Empire were promised participation in the management of their own affairs, as well as the abolition of forced labor and the hated *indigénat* system according to which colonial "subjects" were liable to penal sanctions. The French constitution of 1946, however, eliminated any possibility of evolution towards independence. It was in the context of France's attempts at colonial restoration – as evidenced by the constitution, the war of reconquest in Indochina, the repression of the nationalist movement in Madagascar, and so on – that protests by political parties and labor unions in the French colonies gathered momentum.

Unlike the federated French colonies, which were regarded as overseas provinces of France, British colonies were administered separately. This meant that constitutional reforms were often specifically tailored for each colony. In general the British would, goaded by nationalist agitation, introduce incremental expansion of African representation in the executive and legislative councils, sanctified at critical moments by commissions of inquiry or new constitutions. In Britain's settler colonies the situation was a lot more complicated. The exigencies of war had given the settlers an opportunity to increase their economic and political power at the expense of the African majority. The Kenyan settlers dreamt of turning Kenya into a white man's country, but what they got was Mau Mau. Their counterparts in Northern Rhodesia, Southern Rhodesia, and Nyasaland proceeded to create the Central African Federation in 1953 in the face of stiff African opposition. Further south, in the most powerful settler regime of them all, South Africa, the Nationalist Party assumed power in 1948 and codified age-old segregation into unyielding apartheid rule.

France had its settler laager in **Algeria**. As Algerian nationalism grew, some concessions were made. In 1944, for example, it was agreed that for the first time Muslims would be given French citizenship and could be elected to the national assembly without having to renounce their religion. The settlers were bitterly opposed to these token concessions and in the ensuing protests some 20,000 Algerians were killed. Tensions further mounted with the introduction of the "Algerian Statute" in 1947, which provided for the election of an Algerian Assembly under settler control and reaffirmed Algeria's status as a part of France. In response young Algerian radical nationalists formed the underground movement that would grow into the armed National Liberation Front (FLN) in the mid-1950s. It was led by Ahmed Ben Bella, who was destined to become Algeria's first president in 1962, after a bitter liberation war that claimed over a million lives.

Portugal, like France, considered its colonies as overseas provinces and was determined to hold on to this myth. Portugal's obduracy was underpinned by the fact that it was a relatively poor country under a fascist dictatorship whose imperial power, buttressed by the stronger powers, was central to its aspirations for national greatness. In the 1940s and 1950s Portugal encouraged massive settler migration to its African colonies. These colonies attracted half of all emigrants, twice as many as Brazil. The settler population of **Angola** nearly quadrupled from 44,083 in 1940 to 172,529 in 1960, and that of **Mozambique** more than trebled from 27,400 to 97,200. As the structures and spaces of settler colonialism expanded, demands for African land and labor increased, while prospects for African political, economic, and social advancement diminished. It was a fine recipe for fierce struggle, which duly erupted in the Angolan rising of February 1961 in **Luanda**, followed a month later by a massive rural insurrection in the northern coffee-growing regions of the country. The revolt was violently crushed. In its wake Angolan nationalists resorted to guerrilla warfare. Before long, wars of liberation also broke out in the other Portuguese colonies: in **Guinea-Bissau** in 1963 and Mozambique in 1964. For the next decade Portugal, with considerable support from its NATO allies, waged ferocious but unwinnable wars that ended with the independence of the colonies and the overthrow of the fascist state itself in 1974. Portugal earned the dubious distinction of being the first and last European colonial nation in Africa.

Portugal met its imperial demise almost entirely in Africa. For the larger imperial powers there were multiple graveyards. France's imperial ambitions in South Asia were buried in 1954 with the military catastrophe at Dien-Bien-Phu. Although it failed to learn from its defeat in Vietnam and immediately embarked on another disastrous war in Algeria, France's global status was diminished. France was further humiliated over Suez in 1956. The Suez debacle was also a turning point for Britain, which had been in imperial retreat for a decade, most notably with the independence of India, its imperial "jewel," in 1947. The Suez crisis pitted Arab nationalism against European imperialism, and Egypt against Israel. Following the revolution of 1952, which abolished the monarchy and ended residual British power, Nasser sought to turn Egypt into a bulwark against Israeli and European aggression. Frustrated by the refusal of the Western powers to provide military and financial aid, Egypt nationalized the Suez Canal in July 1956. In October, Israel, Britain, and France invaded Egypt in a desperate effort to overthrow Nasser's regime and return Egypt into a pliant semi-colony. The invasion failed, thanks to worldwide political outrage and concerted diplomatic pressure from the Soviet Union and the United States. Britain and France lost face and influence in the region and the developing world as a whole, while the star of Nasser's Egypt rose. But Britain failed to learn from the Suez crisis and did not fundamentally change its policies in what remained of its African colonial empire. It was left to the nationalists in each colony to bring that about.

The nature and dynamics of African nationalism were exceedingly complex. To begin with, the spatial and social locus of the "nation" imagined by the nationalists was fluid. It could entail the expansive visions of Pan-African liberation and integration, territorial nation-building, or the invocation of ethnic identities. Secular and religious visions also competed for ascendancy. Some nationalists wanted the future political kingdom to follow the edicts of Islam, others preferred capitalism stripped of its colonial associations, and yet others professed various socialisms – Marxist, African, or Arab. These visions were often inspired as much by internal discourses as by the need to make gestures to foreign ideological friends. The 1950s and 1960s were a period of great intellectual ferment, which saw a flowering of African thought and creativity in literature, the arts, and political philosophy. Thus decolonization was also a literary movement, a cognitive protest against the imperial scheme of things.

Articulated and fought on many fronts – political, economic, social, and cultural – nationalism embodied self-conscious struggle by African peoples to protect and promote their interests and identities through the assumption of colonial state power. The actual articulation of nationalism of course varied from colony to colony, even in colonies under the same imperial power, depending on such factors as the way the colony had been acquired and was administered, the presence or absence of settlers, the traditions of resistance, the social composition of the nationalist movement and its type of leadership. Anti-colonialism was expressed through political and civic organizations, including professional parties, youth organizations, welfare associations, ethnic unions, and trade unions, as well as cultural and religious organizations, such as independent churches, and **peasant movements**. Almost invariably the political and civic organizations were led by urban-based elites, although their members were drawn from both urban and rural areas, especially as mass political parties developed. The membership of cultural and religious organizations was similarly broad. The peasant movements were largely confined to the rural areas, although some of their leaders and ideas might be drawn from urban elites and workers. Campaigns, petitions, demonstrations, and boycotts were the weapons of choice for the political parties and civic associations. In addition to using some of these tactics, trade unions relied on strikes, while the independent churches encouraged their members to disobey colonial laws, boycott colonial institutions, and sabotage colonial infrastructure. Rural peasants engaged in both individual and collective acts of protest – including rebellions – to protect their land, livestock, and livelihoods.

It was often assumed in old histories of African nationalism that women were not as involved as men. Research conducted since the 1970s shows that this was clearly not the case. The nationalist movements contained many illustrious women leaders and activists. Women were to be found in the political parties, trade unions, independent churches, welfare associations, peasant movements, and as combatants in the liberation struggles of Algeria, Kenya, Angola, Mozambique, Guinea-Bissau, **Namibia**, and South Africa. There were also protests organized entirely by women. Renowned examples include the Aba Women's War of 1929 in Nigeria, and the 1958–9 Anlu Women's Uprising in **Cameroon**, as well as the spontaneous uprisings of South African women in the 1950s.

At critical moments the protests of the urban and rural crowds would erupt into riots, which were often brutally suppressed, often resulting in the further radicalization of the nationalist movement. Ghana's road to independence, for example, was shaped by events surrounding a demonstration in February 1948 during which two ex-servicemen were killed and many others injured. Immediately riots broke out in **Accra** and another twenty-nine people were killed. Before long, riots had spread throughout the country, fanned by local grievances. A state of emergency was declared and nationalist leaders detained. That only served to inflame nationalist fervor, and the militants (led by the charismatic Kwame Nkrumah) formed a more radical mass party, the Peoples' Convention Party, which launched a "Positive Action" campaign involving civil disobedience, strikes, and boycotts, demanding "Independence Now!" In 1951 Nkrumah was led from prison to the prime minister's office after his party won the bulk of the seats under a new constitution. Six years later Ghana achieved its independence.

Nkrumah's path was traversed by many other African leaders. But in the settler-dominated colonies neither mass parties and charismatic leaders nor "peaceful" protests were enough to bring about independence. Armed struggle became imperative. These struggles were often launched after long years of unsuccessful peaceful protest. Such was the case in South Africa, where there had been waves of protest, encompassing peasant resistance and periodic rebellions, defiance campaigns, boycotts, strikes and other forms of mass action. These were spearheaded by some of the continent's largest independent church and **labor movements**, as well as one of its oldest political parties, the African National Congress, which was formed in 1912. In the 1940s the country was rocked by strikes and other protests, and the ANC adopted a more militant strategy, especially following the establishment of the ruthless apartheid regime in 1948. In 1960 the ANC decided to embark on armed struggle after it was banned following the Sharpeville Massacre.

The armed struggle was complemented – in fact soon superseded, following the arrest of the nationalist leaders – by a new wave of protests in the 1970s, led by students, workers, consumers, and religious leaders, and culminating in the Soweto Uprising of 1976. By the 1980s the regime was on the defensive as the country increasingly became ungovernable and internationally isolated, and the economy stagnated. As with other beleaguered colonial regimes before, it responded with both the sticks of repression and the carrots of reform. However, it was clear that the system of racial capitalism had run its course. But the ANC and the other liberation forces were unable to win a decisive victory, so a negotiated settlement was hammered out. In May 1994 Nelson Mandela, the venerable nationalist icon, was inaugurated as the first president of a free South Africa, ending 342 years of European settler rule.

This marked the end of Africa's long road to decolonization. By then dozens of African countries had been independent for over thirty years, and the limits of decolonization had become quite apparent. For millions of Africans, self-determination, development, and democracy remained as elusive as ever. It was tempting – but misleading – under such circumstances to forget that the end of European colonial rule marked a significant moment in the annals of African history.

See also: intellectuals: colonial; state: colonial; women's movements

Further reading

Betts, R.F. (1998) *Decolonization*, New York: Routledge.
Birmingham, D. (1995) *The Decolonization of Africa*, Athens: Ohio University Press.
Cooper, F. (1996) *Decolonization and African Society*, New York: Cambridge University Press.
Hargreaves, J.D. (1988) *Decolonization in Africa*, Harlow: Longman.
Mazrui, A.A. (ed.) (1993) *General History of Africa: Africa Since 1935*, Oxford: Heinemann.
Wilson, H.S. (1994) *African Decolonization*, London: Hodder.

PAUL TIYAMBE ZELEZA

Democratic Republic of Congo

With an area of 2,345,000 square kilometers and a population of approximately 50 million divided into 250 ethnic groups, the Democratic Republic of Congo (DRC) covers a vast area of Central Africa. Administratively, the country is divided into ten provinces, and it shares borders with nine countries. French is the official language, although there are four other main languages: **Lingala**, Kikongo, Tshiluba, and **Swahili**.

The DRC is blessed with exceptional natural resources, from vast and fertile agricultural lands through plentiful mineral deposits to enormous water resources from the Congo river, which stretches 4,700 kilometers (the fifth longest river in the world) and whose hydroelectric power potential is impressive. Despite its immense natural wealth, by 2000 the DRC was still one of the poorest countries in the world. Colonization inaugurated a period of systematic plunder of the country's wealth, a process compounded by the Mobutu and Kabila regimes. In 1998 the DRC's per capita income of US$130 per year was one of the lowest in Africa.

The DRC was born out of the Berlin Conference of 1884–5. Then called the Independent Congo State, between 1885 and 1908 the territory was King Leopold II's personal property. During this period, the country's resources were systematically and violently exploited, as exemplified by the rubber plantations, causing millions of deaths. An international outcry forced the king to relinquish control and in November 1908 the territory became a Belgian colony.

Colonial control of the Belgian Congo was exercised by indirect rule through a strict collaboration between "the colonial trinity": government, corporations, and missions. In order to maximize profits in the economic domain, the colonial administration imposed obligatory production of cash crops, focusing on palm-oil and cotton production managed by large European companies. Companies such as Lever (1911) and Cotonco (the Belgian Congo's Cotton Company – 1920) were created to market and process agricultural products. Beginning in 1936 the colonial state promoted the so-called *Régime de paysannats* (peasants' regime), an agricultural policy intended to increase peasant production but that did not in fact bring about change, since agricultural production was already geared toward export production.

Industrial development began in 1906 with the creation of the Union Minière du Haut Katanga (UMHK), which began copper production in Kolwezi, and the Congolese Forestry and Mining Company (Fourminière). Beginning in 1920, the UMHK also produced cobalt, uranium, and radium. Congolese uranium was used to produce the first atomic bombs, dropped on the Japanese cities of Hiroshima and Nagasaki during the **Second World War**. The colonial economy was dominated by mineral production, whose enterprises functioned using a local labor recruited by force.

With respect to social life, the colonial state imposed European civilization as an aspirational goal and source of social values. One of the structures of cultural conversion was provided by the missionary-run schools, which were used to inculcate Christian morals and socialize auxiliaries to serve the white administration. Laws were enacted that supported the missionaries' work. In addition, legal categories were created that distinguished "natives" (*indigènes*) from the "civilized" (*civilisés*) resulting in several hierarchically opposed categories: non-indigenous residents of the center versus indigenous residents, detribalized individuals versus villagers, literate school graduates (*évolués*) versus *indigènes*, literate school leavers (*immatriculés*) versus *indigènes*. In terms of gender relations, the same categories applied: French-speaking educated man, husband or father (*évolué/musenji*) versus non-French speaking wife, "woman of the state" (*mwasi'ya état*) versus woman dependent on a man. Above all, the law provided support to the church by promoting the monogamous family, which conformed to Christian morality. The wife was expected to confine her activities to the domestic sphere. From the administration's point of view, this was the way to emancipate indigenous women: by educating them to be like wives in the metropole. Schools and *foyers sociaux* taught women domestic skills and Christian morality in local languages, distancing them from public life and salaried work, and making them subject to strict rules. These laws limited women's mobility, particularly in towns, where they were only permitted to establish themselves as the dependent of a man.

On 30 June 1960 the Belgian Congo was proclaimed independent, becoming the Democratic Republic of Congo (DRC). Independence was declared quickly because of the escalation of struggles by social reform movements that had broken out in 1959. The first government, under President Kasavubu and Prime Minister Lumumba, took control of a country in chaos. On 5 July, La Force Publique – the army inherited from the colonists – mutinied in Leopoldville. Six days later Katanga proclaimed its independence. Belgium sympathized with the Katangese cause. Kasavubu and Lumumba solicited direct military aid from the UN, and contacted the Soviet Union for support. In early August, South Kasai proclaimed its autonomy. In an effort to contain the separatists, Lumumba solicited without success the support of the USA and Canada. Because of his strong nationalist views, Lumumba was distrusted by the Belgians, Americans, and the Catholic Church, which considered him a communist. Matters deteriorated further with a split between Kasavubu and Lumumba. Lumumba was eventually arrested and murdered in January 1961, causing widespread protests in the Congo itself and all across Africa.

The next few years saw a succession of governments, until Mobutu took the presidency following a coup d'état in November 1965. In 1966 he installed himself as president at the head of a powerful and oppressive regime. The years between 1964 and 1968 witnessed rebellions in the east and west of the country. At the start of his rule, Mobutu won the sympathy of the university students because of his nationalist ideas. Then in 1969 the government turned against the students, violently suppressing a peaceful demonstration and killing hundreds of the demonstrators. In 1971 Mobutu cynically introduced the program of authenticity, in which people were supposed to reclaim their African values and names: the DRC was renamed Zaire, as were the Congo river and the country's currency.

The years 1977 and 1978 were marked by the two wars in Shaba, initiated by Katanganese military police who had taken refuge in **Angola**. They were crushed with the support of the Moroccans, Belgians, and French. Civilian protest began mounting in the 1980s. In January 1982 the Union pour la Démocratie et le Progrès Social (UDPS) was founded by Etienne Tshisekedi. It was not, however, until 24 April 1990 that democratic dialogue with Mobutu began. At a demonstration in May 1990, at a peak of excitement for the democratic movement, some 300 to 347 students from Lubumbashi University were massacred. A national conference on sovereignty opened on 7 August 1991 with the stated purpose of bringing about national conciliation. Representatives of 227 political parties attended and sessions continued through to 16 December 1991, but the conference made little progress.

With respect to the economy, the Mobutu regime's first years (1967–70) experienced relatively rapid growth, but the policy of Zaireanization put in place between 1971 and 1974 proved a costly failure. When the price of copper fell on the world market in 1975, the Congolese economy started reeling – copper accounted for 70 percent of state revenue. It never really recovered. Massive endemic corruption only made matters worse. Economic mismanagement led to growing dependency on external aid, whose contribution to the gross national product rose from 4 percent in 1980 to 11 percent in 1987.

In October 1996 Kabila and the "war chiefs" in

Kivu began an offensive to remove Mobutu from power. The campaign lasted for eight months with sustained aid from **Rwanda** and **Uganda**. On 17 May 1997 Kabila proclaimed himself head of state, granting himself all executive, legislative, and military power. Feeling that they had the right to control the territory they had conquered, Rwanda and Uganda deployed troops in the eastern provinces, massacring Hutu refugees suspected of having participated in the **genocide** in Rwanda in 1994.

Beginning in 1998 a second rebellion broke out, this time between Kabila and his allies, Rwanda and Uganda, whom he had accused of violating the territorial integrity of the DRC. **Civil society** in the country was no longer prepared to tolerate the foreign occupiers, and international opinion began to turn against Kabila because of his disregard for human rights and increasingly dictatorial rule. Armies from **Zambia**, **Angola**, and **Namibia** came to Kabila's assistance, however, confronting Rwandan and Ugandan troops on Congolese territory. By the end of 2000 the DRC was deeply fragmented: the territory west of **Kinshasa** was controlled by the Congolese armed forces, while Angolan soldiers held the land south of Kinshasa. In the Kivu region, there were Namibians and Zimbabweans, alongside the *mai' mai'* militias, the *interhamwe*, and former Rwandan troops. Opposed to these were Congolese rebel factions, aided by Rwanda and Uganda. These countries have all participated in the continuing plunder of the wealth of the eastern part of the country. On 16 January 2001 Kabila was assassinated. Nine days later his son Joseph became president, very quickly signaling that he was open to establishing democratic rule – a stance that was designed to appeal to the demands of the international community.

See also: Central Africa; Congo

Further reading

De Villers, G. (1995) *De Mobutu à Mobutu: Trente ans de Relations Belgique-Zaïre*, Brussels: De Boeck.

Lamotte, O., Roosens, C. and Clement, C. (eds.) (2000) *La Belgique et l'Afrique Central, de 1960 à nos jours*, Brussels: GRIP.

N'daywele Nziene, I. (1997) *Histoire du Zaïre: de l'héritage ancien à l'age contemporain*, Louvain-la-Neuve: duculot.

GERTRUDE MIANDA

development of African history

The roots of African historiographies

The writing of African history goes back to the origins of the discipline of history itself. Large parts of northern Africa were the focus of systematic study by historians of the Mediterranean and Islamic worlds from the very dawn of these civilizations, since the region was an integral part of both. North African scholars not only wrote on the histories of their own societies, but also commented on West and East Africa, as well as Europe – the great ones among them reflected on the philosophy of history itself. According to St. Augustine, the great North African theologian who perhaps articulated the first philosophy of history in *The City of God*, history is inevitably universal and metahistorical in that it entails movement towards divine providence.

The first serious challenge to providential history came in the fourteenth century in the works of Ibn Khaldun, another North African and one of the greatest historians of all time. He postulated a cyclical theory of history, and his work anticipated modern historical methodology and influenced interpretations of Maghreb history well into the twentieth century. It is to Khaldun that we owe one of the earliest surviving fragments of the history of the Mali empire. Besides trade commodities, the regular commerce between North and West Africa also carried cultural traffic, including Islam and scholarship. A host of North African scholars wrote on West African history and society, among them al-Mas'ūdī (*c.*950), al-Bakrī (1029–94), al-Idrīsī (1154), Yākūt (*c.*1200), Abu al-Fidā' (1273–1331), al-'Umarī (1301), and the legendary Ibn Battūta (1304–69), an Amazigh who traveled across West and East Africa, Arabia, India, China, and Turkey.

West Africans also produced their own written histories. The best include *Ta'rīkh al-Sūdān* and *Ta'rīkh al-Fattāsh*, both produced in Timbuctu in the seventeenth century. Among the famous historical chronicles published in the next two centuries are the Kano Chronicle and the Gonja Chronicle (*Kitab al-Ghunja*), produced in modern-day **Ghana** in the eighteenth century, a country that was far from being Islamized, which shows that Arabic, much like English or French today, was the language of intellectual discourse beyond the confines of Muslim and Arab territory. In east Africa the best known of the histories is the Kilwa Chronicle. In the nineteenth century writing in local languages (such as **Hausa** and **Swahili**) using Arabic script spread and local histories were produced. In **Ethiopia**, a country that boasts one of the world's longest literary traditions, historical works were being produced by the fourteenth century. These included the Chronicles of the Wars of Amda Sion.

African history, as both a process and a discipline, were to be profoundly transformed from the fifteenth century by European expansion. Many of the early European writers visiting African coastal regions – especially in western Africa, the linchpin of the Atlantic slave trade – did not set out to produce historical works as such, although their works were later used as historical sources. They were mostly interested in describing contemporary conditions. But several self-consciously historical works were produced, such as Oliveira de Cadornega's *History of the Angolan Wars* (1681), Job Ludolf's *Historia Aethiopia* (1681), Silva Correira's *History of Angola* (*c.*1792), Benezet's *Some Historical Account of Guinea* (1772), Norris's *Memoir of the Reign of Bossa Ahadee* (1789), and Dalzel's *History of Dahomey* (1793). From the late eighteenth century throughout the nineteenth, the volume of European travel literature grew rapidly. Some of this travel writing sought to incorporate historical accounts. Notable examples include James Bruce's *Travels to Discover the Source of the Nile* (1790), T.E. Bowdwich's *Mission from Cape Coast Castle to Ashantee* (1819), Joseph Dupuis' *Journal of a Residence in Ashantee* (1824), Heinrich Barth's *Travels and Discoveries in North and Central Africa* (1857–8), M. Guillain's *Documents sur l'histoire, la géographie et le commerce de l'Afrique orientale* (1856), and Gustav Nachtigal's *Sahara and Sudan* (1879–89).

Much of this work was unapologetically Eurocentric, especially as the Atlantic slave trade expanded and the need to justify it grew. Some scholars have stressed the fact that many Portuguese writings, for example, were based on unreliable sources, or were interpreted out of context, or were more interested in literary style and fantasy because Renaissance historiography put greater emphasis on telling a story well, in an erudite fashion, and with literary embellishments, than relating the facts or adopting a critical approach to sources. Africa was increasingly portrayed as "primitive," and as the drums of imperialism began beating, its salvation was seen to lie in European overlordship or outright conquest. Eurocentrism was given philosophical imprimatur in Friedrich Hegel's *Philosophy of History*. There he declared, categorically, that Africa "is not a historical continent; it shows neither change nor development." The portion that showed historical light in Hegel's judgment – namely, North Africa – was not really a part of this benighted continent. Thus was born the imperialist historiography that was to cast a permanent pall over African historiography in the twentieth century: the racist truncation of Africa into a sub-Saharan contraption.

In the meantime, North Africa itself was encapsulated into the orientalist paradigm, dissected so brilliantly in Edward Said's book, *Orientalism*. Orientalism, a discursive practice of constructing and consuming for imperialism other peoples and lands, combined cultural condescension towards Islam, paternalistic possessiveness towards ancient Egypt, and ulterior selectivity in ignoring the role of North Africans, especially the Moors who had ruled Spain for centuries, in the transmission of classical civilization and the establishment of modernity in Western Europe. Indeed, as Martin Bernal has argued in his controversial tome, *Black Athena*, not only was Egypt progressively divorced from the rest of Africa – only to be smuggled in occasionally, as with the Hamitic hypothesis, when the intention was to show that things like state formation or iron technology diffused from there to naturally backward "black" or "sub-Saharan" Africa – but it was also progressively demoted as the source of Greek civilization as maintained in the Ancient model. The emerging Aryan model could not countenance the idea that Greece, seen both as the epitome of Europe and its pure childhood, was the product of the mixture of native Europeans and colonizing Africans and Semites. The history of ancient Egypt became a special preserve of the arcane subdiscipline of Egyptology. For the rest, emphasis was placed upon permanence and continuity.

But there were countervailing historiographies, both modernist and traditional. The challenges of the West and modernity preoccupied many North African intellectuals, both those trained in the newly established Western tradition and those subscribing to the much older Islamic tradition. Both sought to explain the roots of the relative decline of their own societies vis-à-vis Europe. Western-educated scholars in West Africa and the **African diaspora** began producing histories that emphasized African civilizations and achievements. The vindicationist tradition found a powerful voice in Oluadah Equiano's *The Interesting Narrative of the Life of Oluadah Equiano* (1789), in which Equiano told the remarkable story of how he won freedom from slavery and recounted the history of his Igbo people. Even more scholarly and combative were the works of the great Liberian scholar, Edward Blyden, whose trilogy – *A Vindication of the African Race* (1857), *Christianity, Islam, and the Negro Race* (1869), and *The Negro in Ancient History* (1887) – set the tone for much twentieth-century nationalist and Pan-Africanist thought and historiography. Besides these large civilizational histories, national histories were also published by Krio and other intellectuals, such as A.B. Sithorpe's *History and Geography of Sierra Leone* (1868), J.B. Horton's *West African Countries and Peoples* (1868), C.C. Reindorf's *The History of the Gold Coast and Asante* (1895), as well as work by Samuel Johnson, the influential missionary, whose classic *History of the Yoruba* was completed in 1897. From the diaspora came the writings of Alexander Crummel, and in the early twentieth century those of W.E.B. DuBois, most memorably his *The World and Africa* (1946), and W.L. Hansberry's lifelong research on the image of Africa and Africans that was presented by classical writers. Incidentally, Afrocentricism – especially popular in the African diaspora, which has appropriated Bernal, is fixated on ancient Egypt, and has reactivated Greek texts – inadvertently reproduces Eurocentrism by regarding Egypt as Africa's civilizational fountainhead.

In addition to these, there were what we can call, for lack of a better term, the "traditional" historians, those who (like the famous griots of West Africa) chronicled the histories of their states and societies, mostly using the oral mode, although their narratives were sometimes appropriated by the literary historians. Thus, at the beginning of the twentieth century, most of the major historiographical traditions had already been established. We can distinguish four: the imperialist, nationalist, traditional, and Islamic historians. In the course of the twentieth century, new historical schools and perspectives would emerge, most notably Marxist and feminist historiographies.

Twentieth-century historiographies

With the exception of Ethiopia and **Liberia**, Africa entered the twentieth century under European colonial bondage. Not surprisingly, imperialist historiography held sway until the **Second World War**, when the forces of nationalism and **decolonization** gathered momentum. On the rare occasions when leading Western historians referred to African history, it was to deny its existence. In the notorious words of the Oxford historian, Hugh Trevor Roper, uttered as late as 1963:

> Perhaps, in the future, there will be some history to teach. But at present there is none: there is only the history of the Europeans in Africa. The rest is darkness . . . and darkness is not a subject of history.
>
> (Quoted in Fage 1981: 31)

Imperial historians mostly discussed, in positive light, the policies of colonial governments and the activities of colonial auxiliaries, from European merchants to missionaries. When Africans did appear in their narratives it was to condemn their societies and cultures, or to chronicle their modernization. Those who resisted colonial conquest or colonial rule were depicted as atavistic or ungrateful saboteurs, prey to "tribalism" or communism.

In fact, in-depth study of African societies was largely left to anthropology, which – with its functionalist–positivist paradigms and ethnographic present – exonerated, if not extolled, colonialism. The history syllabus at Makerere College in 1950, for example, hardly contained any African history courses. What passed for such history comprised, to quote the syllabus, "The Arab and American slave trades; Abolition; African explorers; Chartered Companies; Missions; Partition and Colonization; the First World War in Africa." By 1959 the Eurocentric syllabus had been modified slightly to accommodate "the History of Tropical Africa from 1750 to the present" and "the History of East Africa from 1850 to the present." A decade later, half of the history courses at Makerere and the two other East African universities, Nairobi and Dar es Salaam (then constituent colleges with Makerere of the University of East Africa), were in African history. The struggle for African history had been won. But that is to jump ahead of the story.

While imperialist historiography ignored North Africa as a part of African history, it found an auspicious home in racist South Africa. The English/Afrikaner divide among the ruling white minority found expression in the historiographical divide between largely liberal English historians and nationalist Afrikaner historians. From the 1920s, when liberal historiography became dominant in the English-speaking universities in South Africa, the country was seen through the prism of race and culture, and its history was interpreted as a series of racial and cultural interactions between the Afrikaners, Africans, and British in the context of a changing and modernizing economy. In this historiography, Afrikaners became the eternal villains behind the development of apartheid, while the English were portrayed as enlightened – ignoring the role of British capital in the construction of South Africa's racial capitalism. Africans, for their part, appeared generally innocent, or were portrayed with undisguised paternalism; their Herculean struggles against settler colonialism were left unacknowledged. In fact, until the late 1960s the history of Africans in South Africa was largely an adjunct of anthropology. In the meantime, nationalist Afrikaner historians concentrated on chronicling the travails and triumphs of the Afrikaner nation, pitted against the imperialist English and "primitive" Africans.

But the production of historical knowledge was not an imperial monopoly, even in the darkest days of colonialism. This is because colonialism and its various projects were always contested. The perennial struggles over the organization of the colonial economy, politics, and culture created spaces for the production of anti-imperialist historical knowledge by the "traditional" historians, Western-educated historians, and Islamic historians. In short, the griots did not die, nor did the Islamic schools disappear, and the children who went to the colonial schools later turned into anti-colonial historians. There were also colonial critics in the imperial metropoles themselves. The relationships between these groups were complex and contradictory, and they varied from place to place and changed over time. Their methods, audiences, and objectives also differed in some cases and overlapped in others. Their very existence was a challenge to imperial historiographical hegemony. More importantly, their work – in content, method and context – affirmed the historicity of Africa, the humanity of Africans, and the criminality and culpability of colonialism.

After the Second World War these critiques crystallized into nationalist historiography, whose development was a by-product of, and a significant factor in, the intensification of the national liberation movement. Nationalist historiography represented an ideological and methodological revolt and advance on imperialist historiography. Independence created favorable conditions for the production of nationalist historiography. National universities were established. The ranks of professional historians swelled. Research funds were provided by governments, private foundations, and other agencies keen to promote and exploit Africa's intellectual bloom. Historical associations were formed, journals launched, and publishers scrambled for the latest research findings. Famous schools emerged, most prominently the Ibadan school (which denounced the shortcomings of missionaries and colonial governments, and launched an influential series) and the Dar es Salaam school (which popularized dependency approaches). Nationalist historians painstakingly sought to unravel African activity, adaptations, choice, and initiative. They chronicled the rise and fall of Africa's ancient states and empires, long-distance trade, migrations, and the spread of religions, and critiqued colonial policies, celebrated the growth of nationalism, and reincorporated Egypt and North Africa into the mainstream of African history. They gave the fragile new states historical identity by writing national histories that stretched into the pre-colonial past. In this way continuity in national history was conjured up, national memories invented. Thus nationalist historiography provided the African nationalists and the new states with a legitimizing ideology.

The nationalist perspective influenced historical writing in Europe and North America, where African history was incorporated into university history syllabuses, and specialized African studies centers mushroomed. The first lectureship in African history at a British university, as distinct from either imperial or "oriental" history, was established at the University of London in 1948. Soon specialized institutes were established, such as the Centre for West African Studies in Birmingham and the Centre for Southern African Studies in York. In 1962 the *Journal of African History* was launched, and in 1964 the Association of African Studies of the United Kingdom created. In France, where the first chair in African history was created at the Sorbonne in 1958, Africanist historians remained far fewer than anthropologists. Progress was made elsewhere in Europe, especially in Germany and Scandinavia, where specialized institutes of African studies were also established. In the 1960s and 1970s African history expanded in Eastern Europe, particularly in the USSR, Poland, and Czechoslovakia. In North America interest in African history had a much longer history among African-Americans. Its expansion to the historically white universities was largely a post-Second World War development, facilitated by the establishment of African studies centers. The first of these was set up at Northwestern in 1948 as part of national security concerns, which led to the marginalization of the African-American tradition. By the time the African Studies Association was created in 1957, fewer than 70 doctoral theses on African history had been completed, but in the next decade more than 300 were produced. In Canada, African history also blossomed from the 1960s, with major centers at Dalhousie and McGill, to mention just two. The Caribbean and South America, despite their large African populations, joined the African studies bandwagon slowly. The first lectureship in African history at the University of the West Indies was only created in the late 1960s.

The methodological forte of nationalist historiography lay in its discovery of new methods of data collection. Oral traditions, historical linguistics, and historical anthropology joined written and archeological sources as valid areas for historical research. Oral methodology served as a link between "academic" and "traditional" historiography, although the relationship between "traditional" and "academic" historians was often an instrumental one, with the latter using the former solely as informants rather than as active collaborators.

From the 1970s the nationalist school began to face challenges. Critics charged that nationalist historiography focused on the "voices" of the ruling classes, rather than the "masses." It was accused of providing cultural heroes and validation for myths of African classlessness propagated by the elites in order to mask and legitimate their privileged interests. It was also charged that nationalist historiography was too preoccupied with showing that Africa had produced organized polities, monarchies, and cities, just like Europe, so that it wrote African history by analogy and thereby subsumed it to European history, failing to probe deeper into the historical realities of African material and social life before colonial rule. As for the colonial period, nationalism was such an "overdetermining" force that only feeble efforts were made to provide systematic analyses of imperialism, its changing forms, and their impact, not to mention the processes of local class formation and class struggle. Not all national histories were culpable. Economic issues, particularly blockages against industrialization and the history of the large landowning class, were important themes for some Egyptian historians from the 1950s.

Critiques of nationalist historiography coincided with growing disenchantment with the limited successes of independence in bringing about development, democracy, and self-determination, and lessening external dependency. It was in this context that Marxism became increasingly popular as a paradigm of social science research. Marxist influence grew with the triumph of radical liberation movements in the early 1970s, and the adoption of Marxism as a developmentalist ideology by several African political parties and states, as well as by Western intellectuals who were dissatisfied with bourgeois liberalism and Western imperialism in the **Third World**. The Marxist historians examined the processes of production, social formation, and class struggle, as well as the complex mediations and contradictory effects of imperialism in modern Africa.

Marxist historiography, broadly defined, came in different theoretical and national configurations. There were many Marxisms and Marxists, some labels were worn by choice and others by association, either in self-congratulation or derision. Some of the Marxist-inspired work was schematic, doctrinaire, and pretentious. Theoretically ambitious scholars tried desperately to fit Africa into linear Marxist modes of production, and when that did not work they invented their own tropicalized modes of production, or saw the encounter between Africa and Europe as an articulation of modes of production. Nonetheless, some of the work was rich and enlightening. Particularly impressive were studies on labor and workers, agriculture and peasants, and the changing structures of Africa's incorporation into the world economy. Hardcore Marxists often did not regard dependency theorists as fellow travelers – indeed there was much theoretical and ideological bloodletting between the two – but they shared more affinities than differences in their emphasis on exploitative economic structures and processes. The Marxists preferred to concentrate on the internal dynamics, while the *dependistas* were more interested in the external dynamics; many, of course, combined both. Before long, radical historiography had even broken into the settler laagers of southern Africa, where a new breed of radical historians challenged liberal historiography. They began to map out the growth of the South's racial capitalism (although some were more inclined to emphasize class than race) and to demystify the Portuguese myth of lusotropicalism and racial tolerance.

The apotheosis of the African historiographical revolution was the publication of two rival compendiums, each in eight volumes: the *UNESCO General History of Africa* and the *Cambridge History of Africa*. Jan Vansina calls the UNESCO project "a unique venture in twentieth-century historiography." It is, he continues,

> the most impressive venture of this century, not only because of its size or complexity, but because it involved authors from the most diverse origins belonging to all the schools of thought then active in international academic circles.
>
> (Vansina 1993: 350)

The *General History* brought together the largest group of historians ever assembled to work on a research project and generated, in addition to the volumes themselves, numerous symposia and invaluable archival guides that will have a lasting impact on African historiography. The project was born out of Pan-African nationalism, for it was at the founding meeting of the **Organization of African Unity** that UNESCO was asked to undertake the project. Launched in 1965, it was finally completed in 1993. The *Cambridge History* was launched soon after and completed earlier, some say to pre-empt the *General History*. It was dominated by British historians, unlike the *General History* whose volumes were edited by African historians.

Despite the immense achievements that they represented, both histories had some serious shortcomings. In particular, their coverage of gender and women's history was poor. For example, in the *General History*, women are only mentioned on 4 out of 861 pages of Volume 6 and 14 out of 865 pages of Volume 7. The same pattern can be seen in the *Cambridge History*, where women appear on 10 out of 956 pages in Volume 6, 30 out of 1,063 pages in Volume 7, and 9 out of 1,011 pages in Volume 8. The underrepresentation of women could be found in virtually all of the major historical texts written up to the 1980s. Feminist historians began to challenge women's marginalization in African historiography, a challenge buoyed up by the growth of the women's movement and the women-in-development project. From the 1980s there was an explosion of feminist-inspired histories, many of which simply sought to restore women to history, to record women's activities and experiences in relation to conventional themes of African historiography, while some sought to engender African historiography as a whole.

The 1980s and 1990s also saw the rise of new approaches and topics. Most fruitful was the emergence of environmental history. More controversial were studies inspired by poststructuralism, postmodernism, and post-colonialism, approaches that shared a distrust of the "metanarratives" of nation, class, and sometimes gender, and the positivism and dichotomies of modernist history. They insisted on hybridity, contingency, decenteredness, and ambivalence, and the centrality of discourse in historical experience. With the exception of some historians in post-apartheid South Africa and a few in **francophone Africa**, the "post-"s did not seem to find much favor among Africa's historians, either on the continent or outside it. But the advocates of postcolonial studies argue, to quote Ania Loomba, that:

> [they] intensify and sharpen debates about the social fabric, and make it imperative for us to weave the economic realities of colonialism with all that was hitherto excluded from "hard" social analysis – sexuality, subjectivity, psychology and language. They remind us that the "real" relations of society do not exist in isolation from its current ideological categories.
> (Loomba 1998: 37)

If nothing else, the "post-"s made historians more aware of the discursive practices and implications of their own discipline and forms of knowledge production.

See also: intellectuals: colonial; intellectuals: post-independence

References and further reading

Fage, J.D. (1981) "The Development of African Historiography," in J. Ki-Zerbo (ed.), *UNESCO General History of Africa. Methodology and African Prehistory*, London: Heinemann, pp. 25–42.

Gran, P. (1978) "Modern Trends in Egyptian Historiography: A Review Article," *Journal of Middle East Studies* 9: 367–71.

Jewswiecki, B. and Newbury, D. (1986) *African Historiographies: What History for Which Africa?*, Beverly Hills: Sage.

Loomba, A. (1998) *Colonialism/Postcolonialism*, London and New York: Routledge.

Ogot, A.B. (1978) "Three Decades of Historical Studies in East Africa, 1947–1977," *Kenya Historical Review* 6, 1–2: 23–33.

Temu, A.J. and Swai, B. (1981) *Historians and Africanist History: A Critique*, London: Zed Books.

Vansina, J. (1993) "UNESCO and African Historiography," *History in Africa* 20: 337–52.

Wright, H.M. (1977) *The Burden of the Present: Liberal–Radical Controversy Over Southern African History*, London: Rex Collins.

Zeleza, P.T. (1997) *Manufacturing African Studies and Crises*, Dakar: CODESRIA.

PAUL TIYAMBE ZELEZA

diasporas *see* African diasporas; non-African diasporas; trading diasporas

Djibouti

Djibouti is a small country in northeast Africa at the southern entrance to the Red Sea, covering an area of 23,000 square kilometers and bordering the Gulf of Aden to the east, **Eritrea** to the north, **Ethiopia** to the west and south, and **Somalia** to the southeast. Its population of 623,000 (1998 estimate) is divided into two main ethnic groups, the Afars (about 37 percent) and the Issa Somalis (about 50 percent). Over the course of the century, various "immigrant" groups have settled in the territory, including Issas and Gadaboursi Somalis from Somalia, Yemeni Arabs, Ethiopians, Indians, and a sizable European minority (about 10,000 in

1998). The Europeans are mostly French civilians and military personnel, who live in and around Djibouti city (many of them arrived in 1990 when France joined the multinational operation against Iraq in the Persian Gulf). Djibouti has also been a haven for significant numbers of **refugees** from areas of Eritrea, **Ethiopia**, and Somalia that have been affected by wars and drought.

Djibouti's modern history has been dominated by French colonial and commercial interests. The French founded the town of Djibouti in 1887 to secure a refueling port for ships traveling in the Indian Ocean, and to promote trade with Ethiopia. From 1896 to 1967 the territory was called *Côte Française des Somalis* or "French Somaliland." The establishment of colonial authority in the interior was accomplished in conjunction with the building of a railway from Djibouti to **Addis Ababa** between 1897 and 1917. During the twentieth century the port and railway provided a massive stimulus for exports of salt, coffee, hides and skins, cereals, and livestock, and imports of firewood, cotton cloth and other fabrics, cement, fossil fuels, and other industrial and consumer goods.

Alliances forged during the construction of the railway with local chiefs became the basis for local administration during the colonial era and afterwards. Some local rulers cooperated, others had to be removed. The opening of the railway and the port of Djibouti led to the economic decline of other towns along the Somali coast, a displacement of the camel caravan trade, the gradual curtailment of slave exports, and the expansion of French investment and speculation. From 1896 to 1955 the port was dominated by two companies, Compagnie de l'Afrique Orientale and Compagnie Maritime d'Afrique Orientale. From 1909 to 1977 the railroad was controlled by the chartered Compagnie du Chemin de Fer Franco-Ethiopien and financed through the Banque d'Indochine, later known as the Banque Indo-Suez.

The late 1940s and early 1950s were characterized by administrative reforms, greater French military presence, and nationalist activities. During the **Second World War** the colonial administration sided with the French Vichy government. Following the ouster of the Italians from Ethiopia and Eritrea, the British imposed a blockade on Djibouti until early 1942. After 1946 Djibouti became an important port of call for troops on their way to the French war in Indochina. These experiences coincided with political reforms in 1945 and 1950, including the creation of an advisory representative council, consisting of separate bodies for Europeans and "natives." By this time, each ethnic community had begun to form political youth "clubs," although between 1946 and 1949 Gadaboursi Somalis and Arabs tended to dominate "native" representation in Djibouti. The situation changed after riots in 1949, when Issa fought against Gadaboursi in Djibouti city and the French banned all "clubs." A few years later, Issa and Afar leaders began to play more prominent roles.

In 1956, when France granted local autonomy to its colonies, the representative council was replaced by a government council elected by a territorial assembly. The governor retained veto powers. In 1957 Mahmoud Farah Harbi, an Issa, became the first "native" elected to the French National Assembly and the first "native" vice president of the government council. In 1958 Harbi unsuccessfully called for independence from France in a referendum. He was replaced in 1959 by Hassan Gouled Aptidon, also an Issa, who had opposed independence. From 1959 to 1966 debate raged in the colony over the pace of **decolonization** as several political parties were formed; Gouled publicly supported those calling for union with France, which were led by Ali Aref Bourhan of Tadjourah. Then in 1967 Gouled resigned from government and joined a political party calling for independence. A second referendum was held in 1967, resulting in another victory for the pro-French side, more riots, and the country's name being changed to *Territoire Français des Afars et des Issas* ("French Territory of the Afars and Issas"). Thereafter the French continued to influence politics by supporting pro-French Afar leaders, like Ali Aref, while Gouled and others campaigned against them. In 1977 the "yes" vote finally triumphed in a third referendum under the leadership of Gouled and the Ligue Populaire Africaine pour l'Indépendence. Djibouti became an independent republic on 27 June 1977, with Hassan Gouled Aptidon as its first president.

Since independence Djibouti has seen a great deal of political turmoil. In 1981 the country held its first presidential elections and Gouled, the sole candidate, won. From 1981 to 1992 Gouled continued to preside over a one-party regime, in spite of the attempts by opposition movements to dislodge him and periods of civil unrest. Armed conflict ensued between the government and the Front pour la Restauration de l'Unité et de la Démocratie (FRUD) between 1991 and 1994. Djibouti adopted its first constitution in 1992, allowing for the creation of up to four political parties. In late 1994 a peace agreement was signed between the government and FRUD. For the rest of the decade, opposition to an alliance between FRUD and the Rassemblement Populaire pour le Progrès (RPP) remained divided and charges of human rights violations against the government continued. In the legislative elections of 1997 the RPP–FRUD won all of the seats. Then in 1998 Gouled decided to retire from politics. He was replaced by Ismael Omar Guelleh, Gouled's former secretary and security chief.

Further reading

Alwan, D.A. and Mibrathu, Y. (2000) *Historical Dictionary of Djibouti*, Lanham: Scarecrow Press.

Dubois, C. (1997) *Djibouti 1888–1967: Héritage ou frustration*, Paris: L'Harmattan.

JOSEPH S. CARUSO

Douala, Cameroon

Located twenty-four kilometers from the Atlantic Ocean, on the banks of the Wouri river, Douala is capital of the Littoral province, and the largest city and economic hub of the region and of **Cameroon** itself. It is thought to derive its name from Duala, the ethnic group indigenous to the area. The city is divided into seven *quartiers* (districts): Akwa, Bassa, Bonaberi, Bonapriso, Bonajo, Diedo, and New Bell.

The city's growth in the twentieth century has been imprinted by European imperialism and colonialism, starting with its role as a major station for the transatlantic slave trade. In 1884 Germany claimed Cameroon as a colony, and in 1907 renamed as Douala the three clan-based villages of Akwa, Bell, and Diedo. Buea, in the Southwest Province, served as the administrative capital, but Douala continued its role as the leading center for interior and overseas trade. The Germans drained the swamps, laid railway lines with the city as terminus, and built other infrastructure. After the **First World War**, France took over the section of Cameroon (French Cameroon) that included Douala. The French colonial administration reinforced the city's economic position, especially with the gradual development of light manufacturing of consumer goods and semi-processing of agricultural products in the last years of colonial rule. Douala was home to a sizable population of *colons* (French settlers) and a magnet for migrants from other regions in search of economic opportunities.

The colonial-era infrastructure was further developed after independence, as the city grew to handle over 95 percent of maritime traffic for the country and region. Manufacturing industries, most importantly aluminum products, petrochemicals, textiles, beverages, saw-milling, and processing of agricultural commodities, were concentrated there. It was where the headquarters were located for the transnational companies that dominated the country's manufacturing, financial, construction, and high-technology service sectors, as well as the preferred center of operations for a growing class of indigenous entrepreneurs. The population expanded rapidly from 380,000 in 1975 to 723,000 in 1985; it reached 1.3 million in 1995 and by 2000 was estimated at 1.7 million. The massive influx of people and continuous expansion of the city's boundaries surpassed the government's capacity to maintain adequate urban infrastructure and services, particularly health, housing, roads, and public security.

The Douala elite, who – because of long contact with the West – formed a substantial portion of the indigenous elite during colonial rule, and the city's budding working-class communities played a significant role in the nationalist struggle. Following the institutionalization of authoritarian rule by the Ahidjo regime after independence, political activity not sanctioned by the regime declined and the population seemed preoccupied with economic issues. This changed with the growth of the popular struggle for political liberalization in the late 1980s. Between May and December 1991 Douala became the epicenter of the ghost town (*ville morte*) operation. This was a civil disobedience campaign that sought to make Cameroonian cities ungovernable by shutting down all economic activities and thereby forcing the regime to concede the opposition's demand for a return to multi-party politics. At the end of the twentieth century, Douala was still unchallenged as both economic and cultural capital of Cameroon, but the strains of rapid growth and two decades of economic adversity were visible in its run-down infrastructure. It was a city whose central business district (Akwa), and administrative district (Bonapriso), as well as the residential neighborhoods of the elite, looked planned but in need of maintenance. These locations were surrounded by congested and rather squalid shantytowns that housed the majority of the city's population of long-settled and recent migrants.

Further reading

Seraphin, G. (2000) *Vivre à Douala: L'imaginaire et l'action dans une ville africaine en crise*, Paris: L'Harmattan.

DICKSON EYOH

Durban, South Africa

Durban is situated in the province of KwaZulu-Natal, which is home to the Zulu ethnic group. It is the fastest growing city in **South Africa**. Durban's growth is intimately tied to settler-colonial rule.

"Native reserves" were established in Durban in 1846. The close proximity of the Inanda and Umlazi reserves (which constitute KwaZulu) enabled the town's labor requirements to be met via a *togt* system (that is, short-term migratory labor). The port served as the economic catalyst for the growth of the town. Africans primarily worked at the docks or as rickshaw-pullers and washermen. Sugarcane farming was also instrumental to Durban's economic development. The labor requirements for this agricultural sector were met through indentured labor from India. After their contracts expired many Indians settled in the urban area. They set up a competitive trading market in the CBD (central business district). After complaints by white traders the council attempted to restrict the political and economic power of Indian traders through disenfranchisement, the levying of a poll tax, and limiting trading licenses. These measures ignited the "passive resistance" campaign in which Gandhi played a prominent role.

Manufacturing developed after the **First World War**, and underwent a growth spurt in the 1930s and 1940s. The industries were concentrated around metal and engineering, construction, chemicals, clothing, and textiles. After manufacturing, transport, commerce, and tourism are the main sectors of the economy. The informal economy accounts for 6.7 percent of Durban metropolitan's gross domestic product.

Industrialization and the decline of economic conditions on the reserves increased African migration. By 1951 Durban's Indian and African population were roughly equal at 170,000 each, with the white population reaching 149,000 plus a further 17,000 "Coloureds." Up until the 1950s residential patterns in Durban were relatively uncontrolled. Africans were predominantly housed in single-quarter barracks, or occupied backyard sheds and other informal dwellings. Indians tended to live on or near their trading premises in the CBD. Whites occupied the desirable residential areas, the old borough and suburbs in the inner periphery. It is only after the increase in the migratory patterns of African women following 1920s that African townships were established; these were primarily financed through the municipal sale of beer. Housing remained inadequate and large squatter settlements, such as Cato Manor, emerged in the 1940s. The passing of the Group Areas Act in 1950 changed residential patterns, creating racially segregated townships and suburbs. Africans were relocated to the outer periphery, where townships were established on the border of the reserves. Indians were moved to Chatsworth. Although the apartheid government tried to stem the flow of African migrants to the city, the proximity of the reserves to Durban made this impossible.

Durban's black labor force has a long history of protest, and the Durban strikes of 1973 were important in reactivating the black trade union movement in South Africa. Durban also experienced popular protests against removals, passes, and (as in the rest of South Africa in the 1980s) the growth of civic organizations and anti-apartheid demonstrations. In the late 1980s violence between Inkatha Freedom Party (IFP) supporters and African National Congress (ANC) supporters engulfed the African townships and rural areas. The IFP, which has a primarily Zulu-based constituency, has been the dominant political party in the region. It won both the 1994 and 1999 regional elections.

The University of Natal (founded in 1909) and the University of Durban-Westville (founded in 1960) are located in the city. Cultural sites of interest are the Durban Museum, Art Gallery and Local History Museum.

Further reading

Maylan, P. and Edwards, I. (1996) *The People's City: African Life in Twentieth-Century Durban*, Pietermaritzburg: University of Natal Press.

CHERYL HENDRICKS

E

East Africa

To many, East Africa consists of **Kenya**, **Tanzania**, and **Uganda**. The wider eastern African region extends beyond the three countries, of course, but this entry focuses on these countries. Twentieth-century East Africa experienced slightly more than sixty years of European colonial rule, and slightly less than forty years of independence. The region's peoples thus had much in common, but despite similarities (particularly in terms of the colonial heritage) East Africa's passage through the twentieth century was also marked by diversity.

At the start of the century, a smaller portion of the East African region was under colonial control than most other parts of Africa. Nevertheless, East Africa was in the midst of the first colonial occupation. This process, which lasted until roughly the start of the **First World War**, not only brought alien rule to the mainland in the form of violent conquest and the creation of colonial states (see **state: colonial**), but also was accompanied by significant **environmental change** in the form of droughts and epidemic diseases that affected humans and livestock. It also brought economic innovations and population diversity in the form of European and Asian migrants. German control over mainland Tanzania and what were later **Rwanda** and **Burundi** had only been attained in 1898, while British claims to Kenya and Uganda had yet to be made effective. These latter countries experienced a gradual **colonial conquest**; it was not until well after the First World War that most of the northern portion of Kenya, for example, was brought under British control. Similarly, the international boundaries setting off the East African region evolved as a result of changes over the first half of the century. The boundaries had their origin in the late nineteenth-century "scramble for Africa," which demarcated the region on the basis of criteria that often had little to do with African conditions. Twentieth-century alterations to these boundaries were similar. The wishes of the inhabitants were hardly taken into account in major transfers of territory to different jurisdictions that included the transfer in 1902 of Uganda's Eastern Province to the East Africa Protectorate (which became Kenya after 1920), the transfer of Rwanda and Burundi to Belgium in 1919, and the ceding of most of what was known as the Jubaland province of Kenya to Italy in 1924.

Nevertheless, the establishment of colonial rule by Germany and Britain, though different in many particulars, had much in common. Besides the gradual nature of the imposition of alien rule, the two European powers relied heavily upon local assistance in the establishment of a new authority structure. African intermediaries became an important linchpin for control of the colonial states created by Britain and Germany to govern East Africa. Nevertheless, the colonial states were characterized by authoritarian patterns of government, with selected local individuals coopted as beneficiaries on the basis of patronage relations that had been established right at the start of the century. While entrenching authoritarianism, colonial rule also created new divisions within the region, mostly based upon the often artificial construct of ethnicity (see **race and ethnicity**). Both the Germans and the British were concerned to base their administration on "tribes." This involved considerable political and social engineering, as pre-1900 East Africa had been characterized by political and social heterogeneity. Yet there had to be tribes, and the tribes had to have leaders. As the conquest of the region continued after 1900, the European rulers found it relatively easy to identify and to work with the authority structures and leaders of kingdoms such as Buganda or Zanzibar but – for the thousands of East Africans who had lived under different forms of government – the difficulty of determining who wielded political influence and which people exactly should be members of newly recognized ethnic groups were issues of significant concern for most of the colonial era.

In addition, the initial period of the twentieth century witnessed the establishment of an economic structure that had a lasting impact on East Africa. At first Germany and Britain wished their East African colonies to pay for themselves, making few demands on the imperial treasury. In practice, this meant that the colonial powers sought to exploit East Africa's human and natural resources on the cheap. State coercion played a powerful part in this, with the provision of forced labor for government and private employers continuing well into the 1920s. Although the colonial rulers invested in building railroads to open up the interior to trade, the development of export trade was largely left to private initiatives. For some portions of the region, notably southern Uganda, this meant stimulating peasant production – in this case of cotton. The Germans also fostered cotton as a crop for African peasants, though with less success. In Kenya and German East Africa (later known as Tanganyika), on the other hand, the settlement of European farmers came to be accepted early in the twentieth century as a means of generating profitable exports. Although the number of settlers taking farms in East Africa, developing mixed farms or plantation agriculture (for example, sisal), was not as numerous as in **South Africa** or **Zimbabwe**, the white farmers had a considerable impact on East Africa's economic, political, and social fabric prior to the mid-1960s. Their presence led not only to segregationist social practices, but also to land and labor problems, particularly in Kenya, together with largely uneconomic levels of state support for European agriculture.

Even more significant, however, was the fact that the production of both African peasants and European settlers was largely directed toward the export of agricultural commodities. No attempt was made to stimulate industrial production, and the East African economies became firmly extroverted with their role in the wider world economy changing little for most of the twentieth century. Uganda became a major exporter of cotton and coffee; German East Africa (Tanganyika) of cotton, sisal, and coffee; and Kenya of coffee and sisal. Later in the century, new export crops (such as tea in Kenya) became important, but the dependent, external orientation of East Africa's economies remained a constant. Within East Africa itself, another lasting impact of the colonial economy was the differentiation that came in its wake (see **economy: colonial**). As capitalism entrenched itself among the region's peoples (see **capitalisms and capitalists**), differences in wealth separated households and individuals. Just as significant, those portions of the region (such as the Lake Victoria basin) that were most heavily populated at the start of the century, and closest to the railway lines and new urban centers that followed colonial control, were more "developed" in terms of transportation infrastructure, export production, schools, and health-care facilities. Other areas, like the Lake Turkana basin, remained without viable exports or infrastructure.

As noted earlier, the first colonial occupation made East Africa part of a **non-African diaspora**. It brought Europeans to the region as farmers, colonial officials, and Christian missionaries. People from British India and Portuguese Goa also settled in East Africa after 1900. More numerous than the European residents of East Africa, those from South Asia (referred to as "Indians" prior to 1947 and Asians thereafter) came to East Africa as contract workers, servants of the colonial state, and primarily as retail (and later wholesale) **merchants**. In this role, the Asians acted largely as middlemen in the economies of the East African territories. Thus, while African people constituted the overwhelming majority of the population of East Africa, the region also played host to European, Asian, and Arab peoples (the bulk of the Arabs came to the Indian Ocean coast, Zanzibar, Pemba, and smaller islands during the nineteenth century).

In addition to the creation of tribes, population diversity, and social differentiation, other significant social changes marked the first colonial occupation. Significant social innovations followed from the spread of Christianity and Islam after 1900. While to a degree the adherence to these religions by increasing numbers of East Africans and the declining importance of traditional faiths represented a triumph of external ideas and influences, it is important to remember that, as with the creation of ethnic identities and the adoption of cash crops, African initiative and agency played a crucial role.

Not everyone within East Africa accepted the political, economic, and social innovations that accompanied and followed the first colonial occupation. The region thus produced varied forms of resistance to colonial rule. These included passive resistance, armed revolts, the formation of separatist churches, millennial movements, and political associations. Following the **Second World War**, **nationalist movements** emerged in each of the colonies, articulating a demand for majority rule and independence.

East Africa also experienced change as a result of involvement in the twentieth century's two world wars. As a result of the First World War, German East Africa – minus Rwanda and Burundi, which were placed under Belgian control – passed to Britain as Tanganyika Territory. With Tanganyika now under British control, the British authorities considered bringing the region under a single government. From the mid-1920s to 1943 officials in London pushed the idea, termed "Closer Union," but without success. Many in Tanganyika, Uganda, and Zanzibar saw such a union as providing a vehicle for domination by Kenya's European settlers. After the Second World War, an East African Common Services Organization was set up to administer on a regional basis the railways, post, telecommunications, and so on.

The end of the Second World War also witnessed other changes of significance for the region. The second colonial invasion of the region stretched from the late 1940s to the 1960s. It altered little the dependent nature of the region's economies, but the increase in the number of Europeans, the expanding scope of state activity, the spread of formal education, and attempts to force the pace of rural development produced discontent among the region's African population. This discontent gave considerable impetus to the emergence of mass nationalism, which was a major African initiative and had a profound effect on the region's future.

Faced with a rising tide of discontent and protest, articulated by nationalist political parties, and facing a lengthy insurgency in Kenya in the form of the Mau Mau Rebellion, Britain decided by 1960 to speed up **decolonization**. By December 1963 all of East Africa had attained political independence, forming four separate states: Tanganyika (1961), Uganda (1962), and Kenya and Zanzibar (both 1963).

The newly independent states quickly moved in different directions as far as ideology and political structure were concerned, but East African politics and government over the last portion of the century nonetheless had many elements in common. Following the violent overthrow of the Zanzibar government in January 1964, the island (and Pemba) were united with Tanganyika to form the republic of Tanzania. The East African states all quickly assumed the form of republics. For most of the period between independence and 1991, Kenya and Tanzania were – despite holding regular elections – one-party states. Uganda's political experience was marked by more substantial changes in the system of government, with military coups removing civilian governments on two occasions, a war of liberation eliminating the murderous regime of General Idi Amin (1971–9), and an insurgency leading to the triumph of the National Resistance Army in 1986. For the most part, the region's political systems were characterized by a powerful executive with weak legislative and judicial branches. In these systems, the legacy of the colonial era was powerfully represented: for example, such practices as detention without trial, the use of patronage, and state control of the media continued. After 1991 this pattern was altered, to some degree, by the reintroduction of multi-party politics in Kenya and Tanzania. This was the result of calls for a "second liberation" by opponents of the authoritarian systems and of international pressure for change that grew in strength following the end of the Cold War. Uganda, on the other hand, continued to reject multi-party politics in favor of the movement system (a no-party system). Yet, even in Kenya and Tanzania, the end of the century found the ruling parties of previous years still powerfully entrenched.

With political independence, on the other hand, the way was opened to new attempts to bring about the unification of the region under a federation. The **East African Community**, created in 1967, provided for greater regional cooperation than had the Common Services Organization, and it was intended to redress the balance of interterritorial trade that had operated in Kenya's favor during the colonial period. Nevertheless, the community lasted slightly less than a decade, collapsing in early 1977. The member-states had not followed common economic policies, and the interregional common market had continued to operate to the benefit of the Kenyan economy. Most serious of all, the 1971 military coup that brought Idi Amin to power in Uganda made it impossible to bring about community consensus: Tanzania, in particular, refused to participate in community decision-making with the Ugandan dictator.

The tension that marked Tanzanian–Ugandan relations during the 1970s escalated to become independent East Africa's second regional conflict. The first had followed Kenya's independence and involved an insurrection by Somalis, largely resident in Kenya's Northeastern Province, which aimed at secession and union with **Somalia**. Uganda gave support to the insurgents, and the resulting so-called *shifta* (bandit) war lasted until 1967. Far from being a guerrilla insurgency, the conflict between Uganda and Tanzania escalated into a full-scale war following Uganda's invasion of northwestern Tanzania in late 1978. With the assistance of Ugandan exiles, Tanzania launched a successful counter-invasion of Uganda, which culminated in the expulsion of the Amin regime in April 1979.

While these conflicts brought the destruction of lives and property, they did not result in any change in the region's boundaries, which remained as at the end of formal colonial control. Neither did armed conflict within the region's states produce boundary alterations. Uganda was deeply impacted by civil strife, however, particularly during the 1982–6 period, which led to the further changes in the country's government that have been noted above.

With interregional and internal conflict marking the post-1963 period as it had the colonial era, other continuities marked the independence era. This was most obvious in the economic sphere. Although in theory Kenya and Tanzania established different economic priorities and policies (capitalism as opposed to socialism), and Uganda moved from state control to economic collapse, all followed the statist path that had marked the last years of colonial rule in seeking to attain rapid economic development after independence. They all established state control over commerce and economic planning, and set up large numbers of parastatal enterprises. Exports were expanded and new sources of foreign exchange developed (for example, tourism); efforts were also made to develop industrial production. But the latter was import substitution industry which, as in the last portion of the colonial period, did little to alter the dependent position of East Africa. While European farmers were no longer a main source of exports and the region was not dependent on an imperial ruler, regional differentiation had changed little by the end of the twentieth century. The Lake Turkana basin, to take one example, lacked basic roads, schools, and profitable exports. This contrasted starkly with the economic and social conditions of the areas around Mount Kenya and Mount Kilimanjaro. East Africa's economies continued to be extroverted, and economic dependency reached its nadir at the end of the century with the East African nations heavily dependent on the World Bank and the International Monetary Fund (IMF). This was reflected in their adherence to **structural adjustment programs** imposed by those bodies, often to the detriment of the region and its inhabitants. At the same time, many economic indicators (for example, exchange rates and balance of payments) pointed to a worsening position in the world economy compared to earlier decades.

Socially also, East Africa presented a picture of change and continuity during the post-independence period. Following political independence, racial segregationist policies with regard to schools, hospitals, and public facilities disappeared. Most European settlers left the region, as did many Asians – the most striking instance being the expulsion of thousands of Asians from Uganda by Amin. Nevertheless, East Africa retained European, Asian, and Arab minorities through to the end of the century (for example, Kenya had more than 34,000 Europeans and 85,000 Asians). The African population of East Africa has experienced huge growth over the last four decades of the century. The result of improved health care, education, and food production, the region's population explosion put great pressure on social services. Nevertheless, the region witnessed significant improvement in many important social indicators up to the 1990s: these included expanded adult literacy, increasing average life expectancy, and reduced infant mortality. Access to formal education also expanded dramatically during the same period.

Yet the region's economic downturn, which began in the 1980s and intensified in the 1990s, caused difficulties for the region's citizens and governments as they sought to maintain progress in attacking what the governments identified as the significant enemies of development: poverty, ignorance, and disease. All over the region economic difficulties combined with the increasingly devastating impact of HIV/AIDS to shorten life expectancy and reduce the percentage of school-age children enrolled in schools in comparison to ten or fifteen years earlier. By the end of the twentieth century, all of East Africa faced the daunting prospect of attempting to meet a serious disease and health-care crisis with dwindling state resources.

Also in the social sphere, ethnicity continued to have a profound impact over the last decades of the century, particularly in Kenya and Uganda. The ethnic groups that had emerged from the colonial occupation continued to be recognized as socially and politically important entities. Ethnic rivalry and conflict was a common feature of the political scene in the two states.

It is thus apparent in looking over the history of twentieth-century East Africa that the different parts of the region, though marked by diversity, have much in common. Although East Africa's political systems were far different in 1999 from what they were in 1900, for example, the region's position in the world economy was not.

Further reading

Brett, E.A. (1973) *Colonialism and Underdevelopment in East Africa*, Nairobi: Heinemann.

Maxon, R.M. (1994) *East Africa: An Introductory History*, Morgantown: West Virginia University Press.

Oyugi, W.O. (ed.) (1994) *Politics and Administration in East Africa*, Nairobi: East African Educational Publishers.

ROBERT MAXON

East African Community

East African Community (EAC) institutions evolved during British rule in East Africa. They included the EA Court of Appeals, a university, the EA Common Services Organization, a customs union, and the EA Veterinary Research Organization (which extends back to 1919). The EAC was formally constituted in June 1967, with **Kenya**, **Uganda**, and **Tanzania** its only members. It collapsed in 1979, though recent efforts to create an Eastern and Southern African organization will likely reinvigorate its efforts. Because of independent funding, several constituent institutions continued to function, free of political intervention.

The impetus to create and sustain the colonial institutions of the EAC had both economic and political elements. The presumed purpose of common markets is free trade among the members, leading to economic equality. Surrounded by partners with little economic promise – the

Portuguese colony of **Mozambique**; Belgian-dominated Zaire (see **Democratic Republic of Congo**), **Rwanda**, and **Burundi**; and impoverished **Ethiopia**, **Sudan**, and **Somalia** – there was a need for these three states to control their economic fate. Politically, the members desired to free themselves from colonial domination, while nonetheless persisting with British law and language, and to enhance their influence in the emerging **Organization of African Unity** (OAU). Clear objectives for the EAC were lacking in the treaty.

Governance was through the "Authority" (comprising the three presidents) and a legislative assembly with limited powers, an institutionally weak structure that was unable to provide coordinated planning. Five overlapping councils were created, and some twenty-seven institutions created or allowed to continue, dealing with such varied areas as banking, harbors, medical research, income tax, and marine fisheries. Roughly half were located centrally in Kenya.

The economic disparities among the members proved to be irremediable. Kenya, relatively wealthy, accounted for half the community's trade. It was aggressively capitalist, benefiting from substantial foreign investment (59 percent of the total during the life of the EAC), tourism, and other economic inputs. Socialist Tanzania, shunned by the Cold War-wary West, received assistance primarily from a struggling China. The Chinese-assisted Tazara railway, which delivered Zambian copper to the port of **Dar es Salaam**, was excluded from the EAC umbrella. A pipeline from **Mombasa** to **Nairobi** provided Uganda's oil. Ideological differences exacerbated railway and highway disputes to the extent that the border between Kenya and Tanzania was closed for a period in 1974.

Inherently problematic was the triadic nature of decision-making. Decisions were either unanimous, or they necessarily represented two members "ganging up" against the third. This contributed to persistent unhappiness. The members had not developed their own sense of identity prior to submerging it in the Community. The degree of harmony required to conduct the EAC's business was such that most of the problems experienced would never have arisen had the requisite political will existed. This reasoning suggests that the existence of the community could not resolve problems that had not previously been settled.

The regime of Idi Amin obviated meaningful Ugandan participation in the EAC after Nyerere of Tanzania refused to countenance him, and the Authority did not meet after he had assumed power. Controlling 6 percent of EAC trade by 1974, Uganda flirted with Libya's pariah regime, while Tanzania was drawn into the Southern African Development Co-ordination Conference (SADCC), the grouping dedicated to eradicating apartheid from **South Africa**. This fissure presaged the collapse of the EAC. Hostility culminated in Tanzania's successful 1979 invasion of Uganda to unseat Amin. President Moi, however, withheld support for fear of finding socialist regimes on two sides of Kenya.

International affairs intruded into the community as well. It has been pointed out that, while China supported Tanzania (to the extent that its trade exceeded Britain's in 1974), the United States favored capitalist Kenya and the Soviet Union joined Arab states in bolstering the Amin regime. President Kwame Nkrumah of **Ghana**, the leading proponent of African unity, opposed such regionalism as an impediment to the preferable Pan-Africanism.

East African Airways (EAA) serves as a good metaphor for the problems of the EAC. Each member contributed two planes. Kenya saw profitable advantage in bringing tourists from Europe. Tanzania felt a need to supplement its deficient infrastructure by creating an unprofitable national commuter airline. Chaotic Uganda could not participate. These differences were exacerbated by Kenya's need to transport tourists to the Serengeti plains in northern Tanzania. Ultimately, the EAA collapsed.

Key elements in the operation of the EAC were the Transfer Tax and the Distributable Pool. The tax was designed to protect infant industries in Tanzania and Uganda by restricting exports from Kenyan enterprises. Its effect was to encourage duplication rather than innovation, contrary to the purposes of a common market. The Distributable Pool was funded by a percentage of customs and corporate taxes. Half remained with the Authority, while the other half was distributed equally, thus redistributing wealth from Kenya to the other two members – a modest effort that disappointed Tanzania and Uganda, with their agricultural economies. The East African Development Bank (EADB) was another redistributive mechanism, but it suffered from inadequate resources. The EADB was to receive funds equally from the three members, but its disbursements were to be according to a ratio: Kenya was to receive 22.5 percent, and the other two countries 38.75 percent each. Over the lifetime of the EAC, Kenyan and Tanzanian intra-community exports increased 74 percent and 110 percent respectively, while Uganda's dropped 130 percent. Each year Kenya enjoyed a sustained positive balance of trade with the other members, even though most of its trade was outside the community.

As the pre-eminent integration effort in the developing world, the EAC has been carefully scrutinized for lessons. Hazlewood (1975) identified twenty questions suggested for future integration efforts by the failure of the EAC. Political will is offered as the requisite for integration, and it was certainly lacking in the EAC. Uneven distribution of wealth and uncomplementary economies were further problems, as was the intrusive Cold War climate. The opportunity for new efforts remains, however. By the 1980s renewed cooperation was already under way, including a common East African passport.

Reference and further reading

Hazlewood, A. (1975) *Economic Integration: The East African Experience*, London: Heinemann.

Potholm, C.P. and Fredland, R.A. (eds.) (1980) *Integration and Disintegration in East Africa*, Lanham: University Press of America.

RICHARD A. FREDLAND

Economic Community of West African States

The heads of states and governments of the fifteen independent countries in **West Africa** signed the treaty establishing the Economic Community of West African States (ECOWAS) on 28 May 1975 in **Lagos** in **Nigeria**. This bold move brought together newly independent states of varying sizes and diverse historical, political, and economic backgrounds to give practical expression to several failed attempts at regional economic cooperation. For much of the period preceding the decade of independence, the metropolitan colonial powers, Britain and France, dictated the direction and degree of economic cooperation among their respective colonies in the region. Unfortunately, by the time most West African countries attained independence, beginning with **Ghana** in 1957, many of the cooperation agreements were either faltering or had collapsed. Yet this did not diminish the growing awareness that regional integration was critical for economic development and self-reliance in the region.

A series of bilateral and multilateral meetings were held to drum up support for the idea of West African integration, beginning with the call for a free trade zone in the subregion. It was spear-headed by President Tubman of **Liberia**, President Eyadema of **Togo**, and General Yakubu Gowon of **Nigeria**, who pledged support for the creation of an embryonic West African economic community between their respective states in diverse spheres such as trade, industry, currency, and the movement of people and goods. They were supported by private-sector leaders within the Federation of West African Chambers of Commerce. These efforts were, however, marred somewhat by the traditional enmity between **francophone** and **anglophone Africa**, especially when France instigated the Communauté Economique de l'Afrique de l'Ouest (CEAO) to serve as a countervailing bloc against the increasingly popular Nigeria-led ECOWAS project.

The treaty establishing ECOWAS aimed to "promote cooperation and development in all fields of economic activity." To achieve its ambitious objectives, the treaty – and the protocols annexed to it – provided for, among other things, a progressive elimination of custom duties and charges; the abolition of quantitative and administrative restrictions on trade among the member-states; the establishment of a common custom tariff and commercial policies toward third countries; the removal of obstacles to the free movement of people, services, and capital; the harmonization of agricultural policies and the promotion of common projects in the member-states; the harmonization of the economic and industrial policies of the member-states, and the elimination of disparities in the level of development; the harmonization of monetary policies; and the establishment of a fund for cooperation, compensation, and development. The major institutional frameworks included the Authority of the Heads of States and Governments, to serve as the highest decision-making organ; the Council of Ministers; the Tribunal of the Community; the External Auditor; the Technical and Specialized Commissions; and the Executive Secretariat. As a tribute to the francophone/anglophone undertone in West African politics, and of the significant roles played by Nigeria and Togo, the Executive Secretariat and the headquarters of the Fund for Cooperation, Compensation, and Development were sited respectively in **Lagos** (now Abuja) and **Lome**.

Three decades after its establishment, ECOWAS could boast of only limited successes and many failures. First, and most fundamentally, the Community was not able to effectively transcend the colonial divisions – and mistrusts – that characterized relationships between anglophone and francophone member-states. Second, the level of intra-regional trading and infrastructural development remained low. Indeed, the level of intra-regional trade never exceeded 10 percent, mostly limited to unrecorded and illicit informal-sector activities, particularly smuggling. Third, ECOWAS was unable to generate adequate funding, without external support, to prosecute important projects. At the same time, the celebrated ECOWAS Protocol on the Free Movement of Persons, Goods, and Capital was hamstrung by the imposition of different forms of barriers, accentuated by persistent xenophobia. The fourth problem concerned the poor administration of the institutions of ECOWAS, particularly the Executive Secretariat. On many occasions, the host country, Nigeria, had to subsidize or pick up its administrative and operational bills.

Although it failed woefully in the socioeconomic sphere, the Community was more successful in defining the broad parameters for political and security relations within the subregion, which was, for much of the 1990s, the theater of volatile armed civil insurrections and wars. With the outbreak of hostilities in Liberia and neighboring **Sierra Leone**, the Community raised a multinational peacekeeping force, the ECOWAS Monitoring Group (ECOMOG) to mediate between the warring rebel factions. Despite various constraints – and being the target of scathing criticism – general consensus favored the retention and improvement of ECOMOG's operational mandate.

By the turn of the century, ECOWAS was under pressure to redefine itself for the twenty-first century. There were strong concerns that economic integration was not enough. This prompted the Authority of the Heads of States and Governments to initiate a comprehensive evaluation of the treaty and institutions of ECOWAS with a view to ensuring that the Community effectively grappled with the enormous challenges imposed by globalization. In the aftermath of this internal self-assessment process, three new institutions were established for ECOWAS: the Community Parliament; the Economic and Social Council; and the Community Court of Justice. But it was feared that the new institutions would accentuate financial burdens on the organization. In fact, at the beginning of 2002 the 120-member Community Parliament, inaugurated in **Bamako** in **Mali** in November 2000, had not met due to lack of funding. Clearly, ECOWAS had a lot to learn if it was to begin setting incremental but achievable goals and objectives. It needed to abandon its failed top-down approach to regional integration for a more creative, people-oriented style since, in the final analysis, it is the peoples of West Africa, not the political and economic elites, that should be the ultimate beneficiaries of the enterprise.

See also: regional integration

Further reading

Okolo, J.E. and Wright, S. (eds.) (1990) *West African Regional Cooperation and Development*, Boulder: Westview Press.

Olowu, D., Williams, A. and Soremekun, K. (eds.) (1999) *Governance and Democratisation in West Africa*, Dakar: CODESRIA.

CHARLES UKEJE

economy: colonial

Until the end of the **Second World War**, the colonial economy operated on principle by valorizing African labor, land, produce, and resources with as little imperial expenditure as possible. The operation of this principle, however, was conditional in any particular colony on the level of the development of pre-colonial means and relations of production, previously established commodity production and commercial contacts, the timing of the establishment of rule and the level of resistance presented, the relative economic and political strength of the colonizer, and the resource endowments known or "discovered" by the colonial power.

The temporal division between the pre-colonial and colonial economy is indistinct. By the end of the nineteenth century, a settler economy was firmly established in both the northern and southern extremes of the continent in **Algeria** and the Cape, and rudiments of a colonial economy had been established at a number of points, especially along the coast of **West Africa**. Thus in many regions a colonial economy was established well in advance of the twentieth-century high tide of colonial rule. Conversely several decades after the partition, large areas of the continent that were formally under European rule remained either outside of or only marginally integrated into the colonial economy. These included much of **North Africa** south of the coastal littoral, large portions of the Sudanic zone, and much of a wide swathe running from the Congo River basin east through the Great Lakes region to the coast of **East Africa**.

This temporal and spatial unevenness was in part due to the nature of pre-colonial relations between Africans and Europeans. For the sole purpose of understanding these relations, the peoples of the African continent can be divided into a number of discrete zones of engagement. The first of these was the North African coast and **Egypt**. Here the direct exchange of peoples, ideas, and commodities between Africans and Europeans was millennia-old, forming the nexus of the "Mediterranean World." By contrast Afro-European relations along the west coast of the continent, from present-day **Senegal** to **Angola**, were the product of the supersession of the Mediterranean nexus. Here the trade in various commodities, most importantly in slaves destined for the New World, carried on by Western European states was of crucial moment in the creation of an "Atlantic World" of commerce, settlement, and political power. Further east, from the Cape of Good Hope to the Somali coast, there existed the ancient world of Indian Ocean commerce and politics into which first the Portuguese and later the Dutch appeared as violent interlopers attempting to gain control of the lucrative commerce there. However, until the nineteenth century, only rarely did Europeans penetrate more than a few kilometers from the coast. This unevenness of engagement with Europe was to prove an important element in the creation of various colonial economies.

Another determinant of the nature of the colonial economy is the issue of the level of development that had occurred by the time European rule was established. As befits a huge continent, a vast range of means and relations of production existed. If, on the one hand, the continent could in Egypt boast of an ancient society whose technological feats still baffle its contemporary students, it also contained in the San and Ituri of the dense Congolese forest in southern Africa, peoples whose technology was all but Neolithic. Similarly political organization ranged from the highly urbanized, stratified, and state-forming Hausa, Amhara, Yoruba, and Swahili (to name but a few) to those peoples including the Tiv, Mende, Masai, Dinka, and Nuer who managed their political affairs by means other than a formal pre-modern state structure. The presence or absence of recognizable and comprehensible (to their European conquerors) forms of political organization would also have an important impact on the establishment of the colonial economy.

Also important was the level of development of

the European conquerors themselves. This ranged from the world's pre-eminent industrial and commercial power – namely, Britain – to the politically weak and economically dependent state of Portugal. Along this range was to be found the burgeoning powerhouse of Germany, the established industrial economy of France, industrialized but politically weak Belgium, the aspirant economy of Italy, and a comparatively less significant Spain. The African interests of these powers in part corresponded to their relative positions. Thus for most of the nineteenth century Britain, which enjoyed a relatively unchallenged commercial and industrial dominance, was content with an informal African empire in which African produce was acquired through commercial relations with African brokers and rulers. The two important exceptions to this were Egypt where, especially after the building of the Suez Canal, global strategic concerns dictated a more active intervention and the Cape Coast of **South Africa**, which having been acquired from the Dutch in the post-Napoleonic settlement, held similar strategic interest. Other partial exceptions were **Lagos**, **Freetown**, Cape Coast, and other entrepôts that had been acquired in the process of suppressing the Atlantic trade in slaves.

Early nineteenth-century French interest in the conquest of African territory initially stemmed from an imperial post-Napoleonic hangover in which Algeria was to be made part of a greater imperial France through the settlement of a colonizing population. Other smaller possessions, such as the Four Communes of what is today Senegal, were acquired piecemeal as the result of French commercial interests. However, by the last decades of the nineteenth century, French interests sought to carve out formal territories of control to pre-empt or limit British occupation. While a colonial lobby of German commercial interests pressed for the establishment of a formal German Empire in Africa, the official German attitude was more ambiguous. Thus the acquisition of **Togo**, **Cameroon**, Tanganyika, Southwest Africa, and the kingdoms of **Rwanda** and **Burundi** had at least as much to do with their potential use in German diplomatic strategy as they did with any economic interests. Late nineteenth-century Portuguese claims to African Empire were in part held over from the long-gone mercantilist world, in part the stuff of dreams of a Portuguese Renaissance, and in part convenient for other European powers who could use Portugal as an acceptable surrogate for control by other more powerful countries, primarily Britain. Fantasies of empire were also initially at the heart the imperial drive of the Belgian King Leopold, who sought to establish a personal fiefdom in the **Congo**, while a combination of desire for the restoration of ancient Roman imperial glory and for the provision of an outlet for their impoverished peasantry motivated the Italians.

Despite the kaleidoscopic possibilities presented by the interweaving of the various factors noted above, all colonial powers initially faced the problem of making colonies pay for their conquest and administration. Initially this was achieved in part by the pillage and looting attendant on the conquest itself. However, this robber economy usually, but not always, gave way to the more settled problem of tax or tribute collection. Colonial administrations attempted to solve this problem in number of ways, dependent on the opportunities to hand. The path of least resistance, where conditions permitted, was the imposition of indirect taxes in the form of import and export duties. Such taxes had the virtue of being largely invisible to producers and consumers, and were already generally an accepted part of life. In some regions, notably southern **Nigeria**, such indirect taxation was to remain a mainstay of colonial revenue through to independence.

Where indirect taxation was not feasible or where it yielded less than was desired, colonial states had recourse to direct taxation. This took a wide variety of forms, only limited by the imagination of colonial administrators. Huts, farms, and wives were all taxed at some time by one colonial regime or another. Initially the form in which such taxes were collected gave rise to problems for both colonial authorities and their African subjects. Where there had existed, in the pre-colonial period, states to which Africans had paid taxes or tribute, the imposition of colonial taxation – though irksome in timing and amount – was not a complete innovation and could initially be collected through existing mechanisms. However, taxes collected in produce or local currencies were of little use to colonial administrations that had to meet their expenses in currencies negotiable in Europe. This reality gave rise to the problem of getting such currencies into circulation. In those large areas of the continent in which a regular codified system of tax collection had not previously existed, direct taxation was often strongly resisted. In such cases, recourse was routinely made to punitive raids that often saw the destruction and/or looting of African crops, livestock, and dwellings, as well as the levying of fines.

Not infrequently hostages were taken who were set to work. This kidnapping was itself part of a larger use of forced or – euphemistically – political labor that was common throughout much of the continent, especially in the early decades of colonial rule. Ironically, it had been the existence of slavery and slave-trading that had been one of the near-universal justifications for colonial conquest. However, given the high demand for labor for various colonial projects ranging from railroad construction to commodity production, the relative dearth of population, the low wages offered by employers, and the reluctance of at least some of the continent's peoples to engage in wage labor if alternatives were available, labor to meet colonial demands was often not forthcoming. Thus pre-existing forms of unfree or coerced labor, as well as new forms, were widely used to procure labor for porterage, the army, and a host of other uses. Often such forced labor was used as a form of taxation itself. One of the most heinous instances of such a use of unfree labor was in the Congo under King Leopold of Belgium's rapacious regime, during which the collection of wild rubber was enforced through the amputation of limbs of those who failed to meet their imposed obligations.

Given the harshness of the forced labor conditions, those who were capable of taking advantage of existing or new means of paying taxes through the production of agricultural commodities or through voluntary wage labor often did so. This was particularly true where, as in much of West and parts of East Africa, crops such as groundnuts, cocoa, coffee, and cotton could be grown under smallholder conditions. The incentives to produce such crops were high, in the latter nineteenth and early twentieth centuries, as prices were relatively good. In other areas, notably those marked off (such as **Kenya**) for European settlers, Africans were legally debarred from producing certain commodities so that they could not compete with settler farmers and would have to sell their labor and/or crops. In still other settings, including much of Portugal's colonies of Angola and **Mozambique**, as well as the French **Côte d'Ivoire**, labor for agricultural commodity production was forced and shortfalls physically punished.

The high level of the variability of economic demands and opportunities made and offered by the colonial economy generated many migrations, both large and small. In some regions – Mozambique and **Niger** to name two – Africans fled both high taxation and conscripted labor by moving to adjacent colonies – Nyasaland and Nigeria respectively. Although seasonal and other forms of migration had long been part of the African repertoire of survival, migrants now moved in order take up the economic possibilities offered by land capable of producing such lucrative crops as cocoa or coffee. Others, avoiding both harsh taxation and forced labor, took advantage of the opportunities offered for wage labor, no matter how difficult, in the mines of South Africa and the Gold Coast, or the tinfields of the Jos Plateau in Nigeria.

Enforced migration also occurred in those areas where settler populations forcibly removed African populations from their land. The most striking examples were at the northern and southern ends of the continent, in Algeria and South Africa respectively, but such expropriation also took place in, among other regions, German Tanganyika, Kenya, Southern Rhodesia, Nyasaland, Mozambique, Angola, Italian **Libya**, Algeria, and Côte d'Ivoire. In such regions migrants were often reduced to forced or wage labor, or became indebted "servants" on land they once called their own. Others were forced to migrate to overcrowded native "reserves" where they scratched out a pitiful existence.

While many of the horrors of forced labor continued, effective resistance was muted until the 1930s. During the intervening period, the problem for the colonial authorities changed from one of subduing the African population to one of effectively exploiting it. The achievement of this end was initially hampered mightily by the **First World War**, which disrupted the nascent colonial economies by reducing the shipping available for imports and exports. Recruitment, often forced, of soldiers and porters numbering in the hundreds of thousands withdrew labor from the colonial economy. The fighting itself, especially in East Africa, caused widespread economic dislocation. The shortfall of agricultural labor and the movement of population, fleeing the conflict and conscription, occasioned hunger and famine. The movement of troops spread disease to an already weakened population. The most spectacular instance of the latter was the immediate postwar influenza pandemic, a worldwide phenomenon that saw a large number of African deaths.

The First World War was immediately followed by a rapid boom–bust cycle in the years 1919–21. At the end of the war pent-up demand for African products drove prices up and fed into a global speculative frenzy. However, the shortage of shipping and reduced European purchasing power meant that the rise in prices was short-lived. This was followed in 1921–2 by a rapid collapse in the prices of export commodities as the true costs of the conflict were realized.

This boom and bust cycle, which was to be reproduced less dramatically throughout the 1920s, mightily aided a process of concentration and centralization of the European capital involved in the import–export trade, which gave rise to fewer but larger and more powerful European merchant companies. These commercial entities, which often linked commercial, shipping, and banking functions, severely tilted the balance of market power in their favor, leaving African export producers at the mercy of price-fixing "rings" made up of formerly competing companies.

In general the 1920s witnessed the regularization of the colonial economy, as more and more African workers and farmers were incorporated into its orbit. A key part of this process, where Africans retained control of their land, was what has been referred to as the "peasantization" of African rural producers. This process saw their production patterns become increasingly bound up with the production of commodities for export, not only as a means of paying taxes but also to satisfy the steadily increasing need for consumption goods necessary for their own social reproduction. As this process continued, these producers became steadily more vulnerable to crises of social and indeed physical reproduction, in which shortfalls in income generated from commodity and labor sales threatened their existence.

The 1920s also saw the increasing regularization of settler and plantation regimes. In the so-called "white highlands" of Kenya, for example, European colonials had initially survived by extracting rents in kind from the African producers who lived on settler estates. Over time, however, these rents gave way to the more regular employment of wage labor. Africans who were resident on settler farms – and whose agricultural production had once been considered an asset – were now seen as a liability and forcibly removed to overcrowded African "reserves." Plantations, relying on the coerced labor of agricultural producers (for example, in cotton in Mozambique), also became a steadily more regularized feature of the colonial economy. Here, in the face of produce prices that made voluntary production of export crops uneconomic, compulsion was used either to directly access labor or to force rural producers to grow particular crops.

Given the overall desiderata, as stated at the outset of this entry, of all colonial powers to spend as little as possible on their colonial possessions, little was spent (aside from in mining where capital investment was a necessity) on transforming the means of African commodity production. What was spent was largely confined to the provision of a minimal transportation infrastructure designed to facilitate the import–export economy. This was indeed minimal, however: facilities for internal communications remained at a remarkably low level.

Throughout the 1920s the broadly held fiction among colonial authorities was that Africans, be they export-crop producers or wage laborers, were mere sojourners in the market who, in the face of either low prices or unemployment, could simply retreat into a hypothesized subsistence economy.

The world depression of the late 1920s and 1930s gave the lie to this view, exposing the manifold weaknesses of the colonial economy. Central to these was the low level of expenditure on improving output performance. Even in commodities such as palm produce, where African producers held a historic advantage, they increasingly faced lower-cost competition from more heavily capitalized Asian producers. Nearly as important was the overcommitment of particular regions and colonies to the production of a limited number of export commodities. When markets for these shrunk, there was little in the way of diversification to ameliorate the resulting impoverishment. Fiscal policy was also a problem: despite the collapse in prices taxation levels remained high, exacerbating the loss of purchasing power.

In areas such as northern Rhodesia where wage labor in the mines had become important, the view that miners were only temporary wage laborers who could revert, at short notice, to being self-subsistent rural producers was exposed as a fantasy. Even if, as later research would show, there had been no smooth, irreversible trajectory of proletarianization, wage labor had become, for many, an indispensable part of the economic reproduction of many individuals and households. Unemployment or a catastrophic fall in wages created severe social dislocation for which, given the near complete absence of any official welfare measures, there was little remedy.

The result was, throughout the 1930s, a series of strikes, produce hold-ups, riots and rebellions that would shake the colonial polity to its foundations and force the beginnings of an economic restructuring through new forms of statist intervention. Initially such intervention was small in scale and, at best, ameliorative in intent. The formation of cooperative societies, the introduction of innovations such as "mixed farming," and the implementation of often ill-designed "anti-erosion" measures were all attempts to lower the cost of rural production or consumption in order to maintain the flow of agricultural exports in the face of low producer prices.

It was during the late 1930s that "development," a term that had hitherto been used as synonymous to "exploitation," came to acquire the new connotation of statist economic intervention intended to promote increased production through a variety of means, including a minimal attempt to increase in the welfare of commodity producers. Statism in itself was not new; indeed, the colonial economy itself was the outcome of direct state intervention in the form of the conquest itself. However, the statist intervention of late 1930s and after was different in significant ways. Perhaps the most important of these was the argument for direct regulation of commerce in those regions where African smallholder production of commodities predominated. Here the most important innovation was the creation of "marketing boards," officially designed to stabilize producer prices while simultaneously checking the power of oligopolistic European firms to artificially control prices of imports and exports. Marketing boards were, in fact, put into place during the Second World War, but not for the reasons initially stated. They were rather introduced as part of the overall state regulation of the economy required by the war effort itself. Ironically, given the exigency of war, they were controlled by the officers of the very firms whose activities they had been initially proposed to combat.

A second (though largely abortive) thrust of "development" was the direct intervention in commodity production through state-financed and -sponsored "settlement" schemes in which "modern" mechanized forms of production were to be introduced. Some state-sponsored schemes for the large-scale production of agricultural commodities pre-dated the 1940s by some distance. Among the earliest and, for a time, most successful was the Gezira scheme in **Sudan**, in which cotton was produced under tenant labor conditions. Most others, including the ambitious French cotton-producing scheme of the "inland delta" of the Niger River, were near disasters. The Belgians and the French had successfully produced a limited quantity of palm products under plantation conditions in their respective Congos; the Portuguese attempt to introduce regularized "plantations" in its colonies, however, was an economic failure.

The Second World War itself brought much economic hardship to most Africans. While fighting on the continent was largely limited to North

Africa and the Horn, substantial numbers of Africans served abroad. As in the First World War, shipping was limited, and exports and imports restricted. Official price controls generated the rampant inflation of a black market, while wages stagnated. Some areas suffered near famine conditions while the development and welfare plans of the late 1930s for the most part remained on the drawing board. The ensuing African discontent over these economic conditions did much to fuel the nascent postwar movements for independence.

By the late 1950s and early 1960s, when the bulk of the continent (save the Portuguese colonies, Southern Rhodesia, and South Africa) became independent, the means and relations of production of Africa's colonial economies continued to be of a low level and uneven in nature. The boom in primary commodities that followed the Second World War masked these basic weaknesses of the colonial economy. This permitted a transition to independence amid buoyant economic conditions, and the embarkation of various newly independent governments on ambitious development plans and schemes. Only later, when demand and prices for Africa's commodities fell and other more efficient producers of the same or substitutable commodities appeared on the world market, would the true legacy of the colonial economy become apparent.

As might be expected, historians use different approaches in analyzing colonial economies. Ralph Austen (1996) distinguishes between market (or liberal, classical/neoclassical) and structural (subdivided into substantivist, Marxist, and dependency) perspectives. The former focus on specific producers, whether individuals or firms, and how they negotiate various factors in the material and social environment to maximize returns on effort or minimize risks to security. The most famous neoclassical treatment of African economic history is provided by A.G. Hopkins (1973). According to Hopkins, colonialism inaugurated an "open economy" of increased market opportunities, which West Africa seized with alacrity. The structuralists tend to focus on the structural forces and hierarchies that determine the processes of economic development and underdevelopment. Walter Rodney's treatise on *How Europe Underdeveloped Africa* (1972) is representative of the dependency approach.

Well-known typologies of colonial economies include Samir Amin's (1972) tripartite division: Africa of the labor reserves (Algeria, Kenya, and much of southern Africa); Africa of trade (West Africa, **Uganda**, **Morocco**, and **Tunisia**); and Africa of concession companies (Central and Equatorial Africa, and Portuguese colonies). There is also Thandika Mkandawire's (1987) typology distinguishing between rentier and merchant economies, in which surpluses were extracted from respectively agriculture and mining. Far more common is the distinction often drawn between settler and peasant economies or modes of production. As useful as these approaches and typologies are, none can by itself fully explain the nature and dynamics of the colonial economy across the entire continent.

See also: colonial Africa; Great Depression; manufacturing: modern; peasants; plantation agriculture; state: colonial

References and further reading

Amin, S. (1972) "Underdevelopment and Dependence in Black Africa: Historical Origins," *Journal of Peace Research* 2: 105–20.

Austen, R. (1996) *African Economic History*, London: James Currey.

Hopkins, A.G. (1973) *An Economic History of West Africa*, London: Longman.

Issawi, C. (1982) *An Economic History of the Middle East and North Africa*, New York: Columbia University Press.

Konczacki, Z.A., Parpart, J.L. and Shaw, T.M. (1990) *Studies in the Economic History of Southern Africa*, London: Frank Cass.

Mkandawire, T. (1987) "The State and Agriculture in Africa: Introductory Remarks," in T. Mkandawire and N. Borenane (eds.), *The State and Agriculture in Africa*, Dakar: CODESRIA.

Munro, J.F. (1976) *Africa and the International Economy 1800–1960*, London: J.M. Dent & Sons.

Rodney, W. (1972) *How Europe Underdeveloped Africa*, London: Bogle-l'Ouverture.

Zeleza, P.T. (1993) *A Modern Economic History of*

Africa, vol. 1, *The Nineteenth Century*, Dakar: CODESRIA.

Zwanenberg, R.M.A. and King, A. (1975) *An Economic History of Kenya and Uganda*, London: Macmillan.

ROBERT W. SHENTON

economy: post-independence

Initial conditions

By 1960, the modal year of African independence, African economies were among the least developed in the world. The decade preceding independence had witnessed some development, partly due to efforts by the colonial powers following the **Second World War** to improve the welfare of the colonized people (if only to forestall growing nationalist pressures for independence) and partly due to the favorable terms of trade for a number of tropical products. However, the full effects of such favorable conditions were blunted by the colonial policies, which siphoned off the foreign earnings of the colonies to assist in covering the dollar shortage from which postwar Europe suffered. In the process, vast sterling reserves were accumulated in the United Kingdom.

It is perhaps not surprising that the nationalists viewed independence as a major instrument for addressing the problems of poverty and underdevelopment, problems they were acutely aware of. As in most parts of the colonized world, national independence was associated with what was known as the "right to industrialization." The flip side of the nationalist ideology of sovereignty and national unity was developmentalism, which embraced the ideologies of modernization and assumed that the state would play a central mobilizing role in the development process. For the nationalists, independence would end the enforced bilateralism that tied colonial trade to that of the erstwhile colonial power in essentially unequal trade relations. It would also allow diversification of sources of investment and technology.

For the colonial power, the issue was how to hand over political power to native elites while maintaining their economic foothold (or stranglehold). One should also recall here the importance of the ex-colonies in maintaining the Cold War power balance. Any attempt at radical economic transformation met with strong resistance from the colonial powers, and many of the African economies had to settle for what was then known as "the neo-colonial solution," in which nominal political independence was achieved without the benefit of economic autonomy.

The "golden years"

The period between the end of the Second World War and the oil crisis has been termed the "Golden Age of Capitalism." Most African countries achieved their independence during this period. It was an age characterized by a financial global order that gave considerable leverage to individual nation-states to purse their own welfare and development policies. Significantly, it permitted considerable space for "development planning." Virtually every new state immediately embarked on some kind of development plan. In some cases the plans, often written by ex-colonial officials seconded to the new states, were no more than a modified version of the "Colonial Welfare and Development" plans that colonial powers had introduced in the aftermath of the war in response to the clamor for national independence and social justice. The emphasis of most of these programs was on education, health, agricultural modernization, and the improvement of infrastructure.

Up until the second oil crisis, many African economies had performed relatively well. In the 1967–80 period, more than a dozen countries had a growth rate of 6 percent. These countries did not only include those rich in minerals, such as **Gabon**, **Congo**, **Nigeria**, and **Botswana** (which boasted the highest economic growth rate in the world for nearly three decades), but also such countries as **Egypt**, **Kenya**, and **Côte d'Ivoire**. It should also be pointed out that good performance was not only confined to the economics sector. Perhaps even more impressive was the progress in the social and the physical infrastructure of these countries.

There were significant attempts to mobilize savings. As a consequence, much of this growth was sustained by domestic savings, which increased significantly after independence, reaching on average 21.5 percent by 1980. Close to a third of the countries had savings rates that were higher than 25 percent by 1980. The rates of savings and investments of the high-performing African countries compared well with those of "developmental states" in East Asia. Significantly, during these phase of relatively high growth, a large share of financing involved domestic resources.

Industrialization

By the end of the twentieth century, Africa was the last frontier of "late, late industrialization." In no part of the world was the level of industrialization – as measured by share of industry in gross domestic product (GDP) or manufactured value added (MVA) per capita – so low, especially in sub-Saharan Africa. The levels of industrialization of African countries fell below the historical norms established by such economic historians as Chenery and Syrquin (1975). This was partly an outcome of colonial policy to prevent industrialization in the colonies. Colonial powers tended to view their colonies as outlets for their industrial products, and as sources of raw materials. Not surprisingly the "right to industrialization" became one of the rallying slogans of the **nationalist movements**.

It was during this phase that some steps towards industrialization were taken. Although much was said about processing raw materials for export, focus was directed towards policies that selectively supported industrial activities for the production of goods for the domestic markets. Great hope was placed on the role of the private sector, which would no longer be confined to that of the erstwhile colonial power. However, quite early in the process it occurred to virtually every African government, irrespective of its ideological predilections, that the state would have to play an important role by either acting as entrepreneur or by providing finance to the private sector. In the absence of a vibrant indigenous capitalist class, the state assumed the leading role. Investment banks were set to mobilize foreign and domestic resources to be channeled toward priority sectors. Protection was provided to industry through what was then a standard set of import substitution policies, which political independence had now made possible.

This point of departure prompted a spurt of industrialization that promised that African countries might catch up. The rates of growth of industry, averaging 7.3 percent in the period 1965–73 and 6.7 percent in the period 1974–9, compared well with those of high-performing economies. Wage labor increased significantly, although it often fell below the rates of urbanization. A new cadre of skilled workers emerged during this phase. Most of the industries were light manufacturing goods production. Few countries attempted the production of intermediate and capital goods.

By the mid-1970s there were growing concerns about the patterns and sustainability of the development model. Critics began to point to the unequalizing processes it was unleashing between urban and rural, and within each of these sectors. Some wrote about the emergence of a "labor aristocracy" attached to those transnational oligopolies or parastatals that were able to pay much higher salaries than the informal sector in which most of the new rural migrants found themselves. International organizations, such as the International Labor Organization, pointed out that the pattern of growth was not meeting the basic needs of the population. The World Bank also joined in this critique, calling for "growth with equity." Significantly, none of these new strategies called for the retreat of the state from interventionism, except perhaps in removing the constraints they imposed on the informal sector. Within Africa itself, voices were raised against the deepening dependence of economies on foreign financial institutions, on the social differentiation taking place, on the waste of economic surplus, and on the venality and lack of commitment to development of African leaderships.

Regional organizations such as the Economic Commission for Africa (ECA) pointed out that the narrowness of the GDP of individual African economics meant that import substitution could not proceed beyond the relatively easy phase of light consumer goods manufacture. In addition, the bargaining position of individual countries against transnational corporations (TNCs) was weak. There was no reciprocity to ensure that the rents earned through protective measures would be spent for further accumulation and not sent abroad through all kinds of mechanisms of transfer pricing. Industry, which was built under high protective walls and with state subsidies, failed to earn its own foreign exchange for the importation of both investment and intermediate goods. Consequently, the foreign exchange squeeze that followed the deterioration of trade led to serious capacity under-utilization.

A major weakness of the model of accumulation was its failure to transform agriculture. Instead many African governments treated agriculture very much as the colonialists had done: as a source of surplus without any substantial investment from the non-agricultural sector – which presumably served as a "vent for surplus" for the agricultural sector. To be sure, some countries (especially the mineral-rich states) did not rely on surpluses from agriculture, and indeed some made substantial transfers to agriculture through subsidies for inputs, infrastructure, pan-territorial pricing, and so on. However, even in these cases, state support to agriculture was less transformative than it was distributive. The point here is not merely that the pricing policies were wrong, as the international financial institutions have been wont to insist, rather it is the failure to outline the dynamic and mutually beneficial linkages that should be forged between agriculture and other sectors, and to ensure greater responsiveness of each sector to the demands of the other. This was one aspect of the disarticulation of African economies that leading African economists had inveighed against.

Finally, there was the fact that the development model was so weakly embedded in society. First, the authoritarianism adopted by virtually all African countries meant that economic policy never had much political anchorage, except perhaps when it was performing well with respect to growth. Second, although much was said about socialism, most countries remained within the mixed economy model that prevailed after the Second World War. They did little to encourage the emergence of a domestic capitalist class, preferring instead to attract foreign capital. Many governments were skeptical of the viability of a domestic capitalist class, while others were viscerally hostile towards the emergence of such a class – sometimes for ideological reasons, sometimes for ethnic or racial reasons. Still others doubted whether, in the prevailing world economic order of transnational capital, African capitalists would ever be more than compradors, buying and selling foreign goods, or "drone capitalists."

African governments were not happy with the levels of economic growth that, while historically unprecedented in Africa, were lower than those of the East Asian economies. Indeed, in 1977 they asked the World Bank to assist them in devising strategies that would enable them to raise their rates of growth from the then 5.1 percent to the Asian levels of 7–8 percent. They also asked ECA to draw up a continental plan that would accelerate the structural transformation of Africa, enhance collective self-reliance, and give Africa a new profile in the world. The results of these requests were the *Lagos Plan of Action* (LPA), published by the **Organization of African Unity** (OAU) in 1981, and the *Accelerated Development in Africa: An Agenda for Action*, published by the World Bank also in 1981 (this latter was popularly known as the "Berg Report"). The positions implicit in these documents were diametrically opposed to each other, although the Berg Report claimed that its proposals were the short- to medium-term counterpart of the LPA. The Berg Report was based on the Washington Consensus, which called for liberalization of markets, export orientation, and privatization within a fundamentally sound international order. Significantly, it assumed unilateral freeing of trade on a non-preferential basis. The LPA was based on the creation of a central decision-making authority, with a structure for coordinated and reciprocally preferential policies, and called for a "New International Economic Order." The aim was to deepen the process of industrialization by creating large enough markets of intermediate and capital goods. Although the LPA dominated the official discourse on regional cooperation, the subsequent unfolding of events decisively tipped the policy scales in favor of the Berg Report, which was to set the stage for the policies that steered African economies for the next two decades.

Crisis

By end of the 1970s African economies were plunged into what was to be known as the two "lost decades." The proximate cause of the crisis in Africa was the oil crisis – changes in policies in the advanced countries that eventually spilled over to African economies. The dramatic fall in terms of trade (especially for the non-oil-producing African countries), the deflationary policies pursued by major Organization for Economic Co-operation and Development (OECD) economies, the high interest rates, and eventually the freezing out of African economies from financial markets all contributed to the crisis. Initially African countries believed, and were advised, that they could finance their way out of the crisis without making major economic adjustment. However, the Mexican financial crisis of 1981 dried out the private sources of external financing for Africa. Individual countries were forced to resort to the Bretton Woods Institutions (BWIs) in Washington, whose own understanding of the African crisis had been codified by the Berg Report. This also meant that the LPA was no longer relevant, as member-states individually succumbed to the conditionalities of the BWIs.

The shift in the ideological climate in the developed countries and the rise of neoliberalism in key countries such as the United States, the United Kingdom, and Germany spilled over into the international financial institutions. According to the new thinking, all the structuralist concerns that had characterized development economics and some of the lending policies of the World Bank were deemed wrong. Markets allocate resources efficiently everywhere and the key distortions were not those of "market failure" but of "government failure." One-sided externalist interpretations of the African crisis were now replaced by equally one-sided internalist ones, which considered state policies as the sole culprit.

Following the crisis, there was new criticism of Africa's development model emanating from international financial institutions. One set of arguments focused on the rent-seeking activities of economic interest groups. It was argued that import substitution policies were favored by the urban capitalist class and by the workers in the protected sector who could benefit from protected industries. Others argued that the room for provision of favors opened by interventionist policies dovetailed with, and were fanned by, the patron–client politics of African countries. These two formulations of the origin of import substitution dominated much of the external analysis of the African predicament. These positions suffer from a number of weaknesses. The first is that most of the groups that were to eventually benefit from import substitution were in fact products of import substitution industrialization. The best that one can therefore say is that, once import substitution was in place, these groups defended or "captured" such policies to the detriment of the nation's economic development. However, even this argument has to deal with the puzzle that groups that presumably benefited from import substitution strategies have at times been at the forefront of the struggle for liberalization of the economy. As to the patron–client explanation, this suffers from the fact that regimes that had identical patron–client relationships pursued different policies – from the open, export-oriented strategies of **Malawi** and Côte d'Ivoire to the more inward-looking ones of **Guinea** and **Ghana**. Furthermore, within each country, the putatively patron–client relationship sustained a wide range of policies.

In light of the latter criticism, it is perhaps salient to point out that the policies pursued with respect to industrialization were the orthodoxy of the day. African governments were often advised by, and received loans from, international financial institutions and bilateral donors to pursue these policies.

Adjustment and the lost decades

By the 1990s there had been major changes in African economies towards more market-oriented economies and yet, by the end of the second decade, the "accelerated growth" promised by the World Bank in 1981 had not been achieved. GDP growth rates were generally lower than in the 1970s. In many African economies, the rates of growth of MVA had fallen continuously from the 1970s, with the consequence that there was deindustrialization as the share of manufacturing fell in two-thirds of the countries. As a result of the failure to raise domestic saving, reverse capital outflows, and attract foreign capital, investment ratios declined from 23 percent of GDP in 1975–84 to 18 percent in the 1999.

The new strategy, while paying perfunctory homage to the aspirations of industrialization, focused on agriculture. Here the message was "Get the Prices Right" by doing away with the monopsony of state-owned marketing boards and liberalizing the markets. By the 1990s dramatic changes had taken in policies towards agriculture. However, even in this sector, the record was dismal. The fluctuations in growth rates reflected climactic changes and changes in terms of trade rather than macro-economic policy reforms. There were at least two reasons for the policy failure. The first was that the policies had underestimated the supply response of an agriculture that was so severely technologically constrained. Second, there was a misreading of what the state's role had been in African agriculture. Few governments had really made their pricing policy stick, for the simple reason that they did not have good administrative reasons to suppress parallel markets. A government's relationship with agriculture was not always predatory, it also could involve the provision of subsidies, infrastructure, and social services. In the absence of industrial transformation and gains in agricultural productivity, African economies failed to significantly restructure their exports, despite trade reforms and massive currency devaluations. Most of the gains in the export of so-called "non-traditional" goods were of a one-off character, which resulted from a switch from domestic to external markets without much increase in total output.

By the end of the century it was clear that **structural adjustment programs** (SAPs) had failed as a strategy of development. There has been considerable controversy over many aspects of SAPs, their appropriateness as a policy instrument in developing countries, and their effectiveness as instruments of structural transformation. African critics have pointed out that the excessive emphasis on stabilization basically overwhelmed any developmental intentions the strategies may have had. Indeed, the strategies had undermined long-term growth process through neglect of both physical and human capital formation. From the advocates of SAPs, there have been three types of responses. One is that not enough time has elapsed to reap the gains of adjustment Second, that not enough has been done by way of reforms, largely due to the recidivism of Africa policy-makers. This was the view held up until 1995. The spurts of recovery in the 1996–7 period were hailed as evidence that finally enough reforms had taken place to be able to bear fruit. The recovery of those years led International Monetary Fund (IMF) economists to begin talking about a turning point. However, by 1997 the recovery had already began to evaporate. Interestingly, blame was placed on the Asian financial crisis, and the subsequent fall in terms of trade for African economies.

The recalcitrance of underdevelopment, even in the face of reform, has compelled the World Bank to move away from insistence on internal policy failures as the culprit and to embrace a whole range of explanations that only testify to loss of faith in the Washington consensus. In the spirit of the New Growth Theories that link economic growth to a wide range of determinants, the new explanations for the crisis include: financial depth; macro-economic policies; initial conditions like health, education, and fertility; ethnic fragmentation; political stability; geographical location; governance; social capital; colonial background; and even the international economy. Significantly, there is now greater recognition of external factors and Africa's vulnerability to them.

To take on board all these new concerns and move towards, in the words of its then Chief Economist Joseph Stiglitz (1998), a "post-Washington Consensus," the World Bank has proposed a "Comprehensive Policy Framework" that is reminiscent of the "development planning" it jettisoned. Paradoxically, the new broad agenda is being imposed on states whose bureaucratic authority has been severely eroded over the years during which planning units within various ministries were allowed to wilt under pressures from the BWIs. No surprise that institutional reform and "capacity building" are now on the agenda once again.

Within Africa itself there was considerable confusion as to what was to be done. On the one hand, the newly emerged political movements and civil societies expected democratization to bring substantive material and social gains. On the other hand, a new breed of technocrats, usually protected by international financial institutions and holding important positions in Ministries of Finance and Central Banks, were detached from these movements. The proliferation of **non-governmental organizations** (NGOs) also tended to overload the national agenda, as governments desperately sought to satisfy the diverse, often foreign-driven agendas of these movements. In those countries with democratically elected parties, the tendency among the new parties was towards more conservative economic policies, partly because they associated interventionist policies with their authoritarian predecessors and partly because of the constraints imposed by the conditionalities of the donors. There were initiatives for a new pan-African agenda adopted at the OAU Conference in **Lusaka** in 2001. Unlike the LPA, the new agenda was immediately linked to appeals for international support, with African leaders promising good governance and economic reforms in return for increased aid.

Aid, debt, and globalization

The way chosen to assist or force African countries to adopt a particular form of adjustment intensified African countries' aid dependence. Aid accounted for an average of 38 percent of central government expenditure, 48 percent of gross domestic investment, and 21 percent of imports of goods and services in 1978. By 1993 the figures were 63 percent for gross domestic investment and 38 percent for imports of goods and services, obviously unsustainable levels of dependency. Significantly, these ratios were declining in other developing countries, which relied more on private capital rather than official flows.

At the end of fifteen years of adjustment, African countries found themselves more heavily indebted than ever. One characteristic feature of the African debt was that it was with official rather than private institutions. Much has been said about debt relief, but little has happened. Indeed, if there is anything distinct about Africa's position in the global system, it is the way its debt has been lightly treated. The debt burden for individual countries is groundnuts by world standards, but the debt overhang it has produced for each country dims any prospect of recovery when 20 percent of those countries' exports are used to service debt. At the end of the 1990s there were new efforts at debt relief, such as the Highly Indebted Poor Countries (HIPC) initiative. Paradoxically, the access to such debt relief was predicated on adhesion to the policies that had contributed to indebtedness.

In addition to the conditionalities imposed by the BWIs, economic development in Africa had to respond to the exigencies of the trade regime spelled out by the World Trade Organization (WTO). There is considerable controversy over the effects of the WTO on African's development effort. The argument is over whether the trade regime imposed by the WTO allows individual countries to pursue development strategies. On the one hand, the insistence by the WTO on opening up all economies denies African countries the "learning by doing" that goes along with one phase of protected industrialization. Others argue that there were enough special provisions in the WTO protocols to allow African economies to pursue industrial policies favorable to infant industries. The debate may not be that important in light of the fact that the collapse of industrial policy in most African countries has not been due to the WTO. Rather it has been due to the conditionalities imposed by SAPs, which effectively deny individual countries the possibility of exploiting any favorable conditions in the WTO protocols.

See also: agrarian change; debt crises; food crises; manufacturing: modern; state: post-independence

References and further reading

Ake, C. (1981) *The Political Economy of Africa*, London: Longman.

Chenery, H. and Syrquin, M. (1975) *Patterns of Development, 1950–1970*, London: Oxford University Press.

Fransman, M. (ed.) (1982) *Industry and Accumulation in Africa*, London: Heinemann.

Mkandawire, T. and Soludo, C. (1999) *Our*

Continent, Our Future: African Perspectives on Structural Adjustment, Trenton: Africa World Press Inc.
Sender, J. (1999) "Africa's Economic Performance: Limitations of the Current Consensus," *Journal of Economic Perspectives* 13, 3: 89–114.
Stiglitz, J.E. (1998) "More Instruments and Broader Goals: Moving toward the Post-Washington Consensus," Helsinki: The United Nations University/WIDER (World Institute for Development Economics Research).

THANDIKA MKANDAWIRE

education: colonial

Colonial education was a European project that sought to provide the basis for the exploitation of African societies and perpetuation of European supremacy. Despite differences between Belgian, English, German, French, Italian, and Portuguese educational systems, goals, and policies, the overriding objective was to provide education that promoted the colonial project. Its practices were, therefore, largely divorced from local traditions and interests, except where these could be manipulated to serve colonialism. During the colonial period there were of course transformations in the colonial education policies and systems, as a result of not only the changing needs of the colonial political economy but also African responses and struggles. There was a general shift from the provision of education by missionaries in the early years to governments playing a more active role, and from an almost exclusive focus on primary and secondary education before the **Second World War** to a growing interest in higher education after the war.

Christian missionaries were a very powerful factor in the development of colonial education in most parts of Africa. All the evangelical missions – Anglicans, the Wesleyan Methodists, the Catholics, the Dutch Reformist Church, the United Methodist Missionary Society, the Lutheran Church, the Roman Catholic Mission, the Church Missionary Society, the Presbyterians, to mention just a few – were concerned about converting as many Africans as possible, and saw the school as a key instrument for doing so. Each denomination was anxious to produce its own pool of indigenous evangelists and preachers to help overcome the lack of knowledge most missionaries had of local languages, conditions, and customs, and the early African resistance to **Christianity**. In mission schools the Bible, catechism, and later special readers with moral themes, sometime translated into indigenous languages, were often used as textbooks. In later years, when the growing demands of the colonial state and economy for clerks and artisans heightened official interest in education, the general goal of that education remained virtually the same: schools were seen as instruments of Western civilization. For their part, Africans increasingly realized that education was an avenue for personal and community advancement in colonial society.

Colonial education policies

While the colonial schools were modeled on metropolitan schools, the intention and content of learning differed. In the colonies the aim was to produce and perpetuate underdevelopment and dependency. This was as true in French Africa, despite the French policy of "assimilation," as in British Africa, with its policy of "indirect rule." In virtually all the colonies a two-tier educational system was created, one for the indigenous population and another for the children of resident Europeans. In settler colonies there might also be a third tier for other immigrant races (mostly Asian) or mixed-race people. Colonial education policies were determined by many factors, including the nature of the colonial economy. In colonies dominated by concession companies and the extractive economies of plunder, as in French Equatorial Africa and Portuguese Africa, little education was provided beyond primary school. Similarly, the development of manufacturing, which required more skilled and stabilized labor, facilitated the expansion of colonial education.

The presence or absence of settlers also played a role, often meaning that the educational policies of the same colonial power could be different in different colonies. The presence or absence of Islam had a similar effect on educational policies. For example, British educational policy in **Nigeria** varied considerably from that in **Kenya**, because of the sizable presence of settlers in the latter, while there was unequal provision of education in the northern and southern parts of Nigeria because of the predominance in the north of believers in Islam – whose wrath the colonial state was anxious to avoid provoking. Likewise in **Egypt** the British tried to avoid direct interference with traditional Islamic education, only providing government schools to prepare the small local elite essential for government posts. Not only did the British explicitly view occupation as a period of tutelage during which they should not undertake to bring about basic changes in the local society, Lord Cromer – reflecting on the Indian experience – feared that extensive Western education would lead to the development of a large nationalist and anti-British elite.

As already mentioned, during the first decades of colonial rule missionaries dominated in the provision of education. This began to change after the **First World War** as colonialism became consolidated. In British Africa the policy shift began in 1925, when the British government summoned the governors of its African colonies to a conference in London. There it was agreed that the colonial governments would get more involved in colonial education. In French West Africa, where the colonial governments were already more involved in education, the role of primary education was expanded to include agriculture and vocational education. William Ponty, the Director of the Ecole Primaire Superieur, embarked on large-scale development of *écoles rurales* and vocational schools adapted to African conditions. This policy marked a retreat from assimilationist principles, and emerged at the same time as French teachers were agitating for curriculum reform in France. The Belgian colonial administration introduced the twin principles of "paternalism" and "gradualism" that, in practice, meant an almost exclusive focus on basic primary education to meet laboring needs. The policy made very little room for the provision of general education, and no room at all for the establishment of public secondary or higher education. Religious missions maintained a monopoly on colonial education in the Belgian colonies of **Congo**, **Burundi**, and **Rwanda**.

In the meantime, in the settler colonies, the Portuguese colonies of **Mozambique** and **Angola**, and the Italian colony of **Eritrea**, the dual education policy – a segregated approach to education for Africans and Europeans – became more entrenched. In Eritrea, separate schools were built for Italians and for different ethnic and religious groups – Eritrean Catholics, Muslims, and Coptic Christians. In Kenya and **Tanzania** different schools were also established for the different racial groups comprising Europeans, Asians, Arabs, and Africans. Similar policies were followed in the Portuguese colonies, and even more blatantly in **South Africa** and **Zimbabwe**, where for the longest while African education was left largely to the missionaries, leaving the government to concentrate on developing a modern academic and vocational education system for the European settlers. An interesting feature in the colonial education policies of all the colonial powers, however, was the emphasis placed on primary education, with little or no provision made for secondary and tertiary education.

Primary and secondary education

In the years immediately preceding the First World War, colonies throughout Africa began to witness the development of colonial education systems that were capable of providing perhaps 1–3 percent of their young citizens with two to four years of primary schooling, and a select few with some kind of secondary education. In French West Africa, the status as French citizens of the people of **Dakar**, Goree, Saint-Louis, and Rusfique stimulated the early development of schools. **Senegal** was an important French colony, and its capital, Dakar, not only served as the administrative headquarters for French West Africa but also was the starting point for colonial educational development. The first Western school was founded at Saint-Louis in Senegal in 1816 by a French missionary, Jean Dard, and by 1860 the French colonial government had established ten schools in major population centers. The total number of schools had increased to 536 by 1960. William Ponty School was the principal secondary school, training students from the eight territories of French West Africa in teaching, administration, law, and medicine. The levels of educational development were extremely uneven. By 1951 they ranged, for primary school enrollment, from 46 percent for Congo, 27 percent for **Gabon**, 18 percent for Senegal, 15 percent for Dahomey (now **Benin**), 10 percent for the **Central African Republic**, to 6 percent for **Côte d'Ivoire** and 2 percent each for Upper Volta (**Burkina Faso**) and **Chad**. French was the language of instruction, which implied the use of metropolitan educational materials.

The number of schools in British West Africa also increased as a result of initiatives by missionaries, Africans themselves, and later the colonial government. Education developed particularly rapidly among the Krios of **Sierra Leone**. By the mid-nineteenth century a higher percentage of children were going to school in **Freetown** than in Britain. Krios played an influential role in the spread of education in the region. For example, they introduced Western education to southern Nigeria, where in 1878 one of the early secondary schools to be established in the country, the Methodist Boys' High School, was founded by African merchants who wanted a secondary school for their sons. In contrast, it was not until 1909 that the first government secondary school, King's College, was established in **Lagos**. By 1912 there were 150 primary schools under government control, with a total enrollment of 16,000 pupils, while at the same time some 20,000 pupils were enrolled in unassisted mission and private schools. By 1926 the government had 126 primary schools and a secondary school, while the voluntary agencies had 3,827 primary schools, 17 secondary schools and 9 teacher-training colleges. Although the north and south were formally consolidated in 1914, disparity in the levels of education persisted. In the north, the British limited Christian missions and reinforced the role of Koranic schools, of which there were 25,000 in 1900 with an attendance of 143,312 pupils. By 1947 there were 564,431 pupils attending colonial primary schools in the south, while only 80,092 did so in the north. This gap created unequal access to employment and other economic opportunities, sowing the seeds of future conflict. Colonial education was also unequally provided for boys and girls: in 1947 the latter made up only 20 percent of primary school enrollments in the south and 24 percent in the north.

In most of central Africa, education was confined to elementary schooling until the 1920s. While primary schools were developed – enrollments rose from zero in 1879 to 46,000 in 1903 – secondary education was extremely limited. For example, by the time of independence there were, excluding priests, fewer than twenty Congolese who had graduated from a four-year college education. In the former Belgian Congo, and the small countries of Burundi and Rwanda, Roman Catholic seminaries offered limited secondary education that trained a select few for the priesthood. Equally limited were educational opportunities in East Africa, especially settler Kenya, where the first government primary school for Africans was not built until 1915. The first African secondary schools – the renowned Alliance High School, established by the Protestants, and St. John High School at Kabaa, established by the Catholics – only became full four-year secondary schools in 1938. Generally Africans resented the curricula of these schools, demanding reforms that would establish curricula similar to those in the settler schools. Dissatisfaction with colonial education led to the independence school movement, which complemented the movement for Christian religious independency. In **Uganda** missionaries were also responsible for establishing the famous Kings College, Budo, and Catholics and Protestants competed in setting up schools. Unencumbered by a settler population as in Kenya, the colonial government became more involved in African education immediately after the First World War. In **Ethiopia**, where education was pioneered by the Ethiopian Orthodox Church, a secular state system of education was introduced by Emperor Menilek in 1905 – teachers were recruited locally and from Egypt. The curriculum included French, English, Arabic, Italian, Amharic, Ge'ez, mathematics, science, physical training, and sports. The accession to the throne of the reform-minded Emperor Haile Selassie I in 1930 quickened the pace of educational development and coordination with the creation of the Ministry of Education. According to some estimates, by 1937 there were sixty-one schools with an enrollment of 5,057 pupils. During the reconstruction era (1941–51), the demand for educated and skilled manpower became urgent and more schools, including secondary schools like Haile Selassie I Secondary School (1943) and Wingate Secondary School (1946), were established.

In **North Africa** there was violent opposition to secularization as Western influence began to penetrate more deeply into the fiber of Islamic society. The challenges of the colonial education project were most pronounced in **Algeria** and **Tunisia** because of the presence of relatively large numbers of settlers. In Algeria the French supplanted Arab educational values and moved to effect and maintain Algerian subordination through Western education. Up to 1918 French efforts to educate Algerians were limited. Only 3 percent of Algerians were enrolled in public schools compared to more than 40 percent enrolled in Koranic schools, despite French efforts to control the expansion of these schools. The first public colonial school for Algerians and Europeans had been opened as early as 1833, and by 1870 more than forty Arab-French schools had been established in various cities. A new era dawned with the passage of the "Scholastic Law" in 1917, which made primary education compulsory for boys, particularly those children living within about ten kilometers of a regular "native" public school established for Algerians. This law – and the influence of returning migrant workers and soldiers, who had been to France and insisted on sending their children to colonial schools – led to a rise in school enrollments of 25 percent between 1920 and 1940. Nevertheless, only 15 percent of the total school-aged population got European or Arab education. In a new reform program adopted in 1944 the government announced its intention to enroll one million Muslim schoolchildren in primary school by 1964. Four years later the goal of colonial education was expanded to address gender and equity issues with an enrollment target of 2.5 million students by 1966. These ambitious goals were of course disrupted after 1954 by the Algerian war of independence. In Morocco active government participation in education started in 1912, when the colonial government set up a commission to study educational needs. In 1913 the Service de l'Enseignement was established. Five types of schools were founded, combining elements of the modern and traditional educational systems. The schools included *écoles des fils notables* (schools for the sons of important people), *écoles rurales* (rural schools), *écoles urbaines* (city schools), *écoles d'apprentissage* (schools for artisans), and *collèges musulmans*, post-primary institutions that admitted the best boys from the *écoles des fils notables* and really exceptional ones from the others. Few of these schools were established before 1934. For instance, only six *écoles des fils notables* were established between 1912 and 1934. By 1953, 6 percent of eligible Moroccans were in school.

In southern Africa several major factors affected the development of education, but none more so than race and its relationship to political power. For much of the nineteenth and early twentieth centuries the various missionary societies were primarily responsible for providing African education. Lovedale, destined to become the pre-eminent missionary education center in South Africa, was opened in 1824 with Reverend Govan as the first headmaster. Under Govan, the school worked hard to develop a curriculum, the content of which would be the same as the curriculum of the white schools, that was assimilationist in character. This seemed to blend well with the prevailing liberal ideology. The assimilationist ideal was aborted, however, under Lovedale's second principal, Dr. James Stewart. Stewart believed strongly in the superiority of the white race, and started to design a new curriculum that emphasized practical, industrial, and elementary education. These reforms were based on complaints he received from whites that there was too much bookwork and too little practical training taking place in mission schools. The new policy fitted nicely with the needs of an emerging industrial capitalism, in which increasingly disenfranchised Africans were required to provide skilled labor. From then on, segregation replaced liberalism and assimilation in educational policy. This reflected changes in the country's political order, changes that were themselves conditioned by the shift from a mercantilist to an industrialized economy. Cecil Rhodes, the mining magnate and prime minister of the Cape colony, even wanted to get rid of mission schools because they were producing people who constituted a threat to settlers' interests in the colony. Nonetheless the Lovedale model was to influence the development of secondary education for Africans throughout Southern, Central and East Africa, where it was replicated at various institutions, such as in Livingstonia in **Malawi**.

The apartheid laws of the 1950s, which included a series of educational provisions, further rigidified South Africa's racialized educational system. Four distinct educational systems existed, each with its own characteristics, to serve the four groups classified by apartheid: Africans, Coloureds, Indians, and Whites. There were glaring inequities in terms of standards, curricula, and resources allocated to the different groups. There were vast disparities in teacher/student ratios, the qualifications of teachers, the quality of buildings, and unit costs per student, which stunted the development of skills among Africans generally. This eventually hurt the economy, as it expanded way beyond the capacity of the white population alone to provide the required skilled labor. The introduction of "Bantu education" marked the beginning of a period of serious crisis in African education that was to last until the demise of apartheid in 1994, but whose effects were felt long after. The introduction of Bantu education was aimed at providing separate and unequal education for Africans that would inculcate in them a permanent sense of inferiority and subservience, intended to train them exclusively for employment in menial, low-wage positions in a racially structured economy. The Bantu Education Act placed all African schools under the jurisdiction of a separate Department of Native Affairs. Thus the missionaries and the community lost control over African schools. The medium of instruction included a change from English to the mother tongue, which was aimed at denying Africans full participation in a society where English and Afrikaans were the languages of power, public affairs, and public discourse. The South African pattern was reproduced in **Namibia** (under South African control after the First World War) and Zimbabwe.

Higher education

For most of the colonial period up to the Second World War, the educational priority of the different colonial powers was to provide lower- and middle-level personnel to aid the colonial administration and economy. Neither the church missions nor the colonial governments had plans for the expansion of education beyond the primary and secondary levels. The church feared that higher education would turn the new converts away from the spiritual faith they had already acquired, and colonial governments became worried that it would dislocate the supply of cheap labor that was urgently needed to maintain the colonial system. Higher education, it was believed, would lead to unemployment and subsequent socioeconomic problems, as well as to demands for racial equality in employment and other sectors of colonial society. Thus the educational policy was designed to consolidate colonial hegemony.

Africans who sought higher education were often forced to go to Europe and North America. Many of those who went to the United States attended Historically Black Colleges and Universities (HBCUs) because racial segregation was still the order of the day in American education. This helped strengthen the development of Pan-Africanist consciousness, as Africans met each other and fraternized with African-Americans. On their return, many of these Africans became leading nationalist figures. They included Nnamdi Azikiwe from Nigeria, Kwame Nkrumah from Ghana, Kamuzu Banda from Malawi, Ndabaningi Sithole from Zimbabwe, and Pixley Seme from South Africa, to mention just a few of them. Some of them returned to became influential educators, such as Ghana's J.E.K. Aggrey, who was appointed vice-principal of the newly founded Achimota College just before his death in 1927, or set up their own educational institutions modeled on the HBCUs, like South Africa's John Dube who founded an "indigenous Tuskegee" patterned after Booker T. Washington's Tuskegee Institute in the United States.

Nationalists demanded the establishment of higher education in the colonies. In West Africa they included people like James Horton, William Blyden, Casely-Hayford and Nnamdi Azikiwe, some of whom were associated with Liberia College (founded in 1862) or Fourah Bay College in Sierra Leone (founded in 1876). Equally significant were the contributions of parents and **non-governmental organizations** (NGOs). Private efforts dominated the scene until 1908, when the colonial governments started to provide some form of post-secondary education by establishing departmental training schemes aimed at producing high-level manpower to fill the civil service. African demands for higher educational institutions resulted in the establishment of Yaba College in Lagos in 1934, and the predecessor of Cheikh Anta Diop University in Dakar in 1918.

It was not until after the Second World War, however, that colonial governments accepted the need to provide university education. Commissions of inquiry, such as the Asquith and Elliott Commissions in British Africa, were launched to examine the feasibility of higher education. The mission of these universities was essentially seen as one of serving the colonial system. It was not until after independence that concerted efforts began to be made to redirect African universities to serve local needs. In 1948 the British government set up the universities of Ibadan in Nigeria and Legon in Ghana. In East Africa, Uganda's Makerere College, which had been founded in 1921 to train Africans in technical fields, was upgraded to a university college; so was Gordon Memorial College, which was combined with the Kitchener Medical School as Khartoum University College. In Ethiopia, the University College of Addis Ababa was founded in 1950. In francophone west and central Africa, old colleges were amalgamated and upgraded to university status, overseas branches of metropolitan universities were established, and entirely new universities were created, as in Dakar, Tananarive, Kinshasa, and Lubumbashi.

Initiatives taken in higher education in South Africa dated back to 1829, with the creation of the South African College at **Cape Town** (later renamed the University of Cape Town) and the Victoria College at Stellenbosch. This was followed by the establishment of the University of Cape of Good Hope in 1873 (later renamed the University of South Africa) and in 1916 the University College of Fort Hare for Africans. During the apartheid era further segregated universities and *technikons* (technical colleges) were established for each of the racial groups. The first university in Zimbabwe, Zambia, and Malawi (then under the **Central African Federation**) was established in 1955 as the University of Rhodesia and Nyasaland. In the rest of the region, university education awaited independence.

In North Africa, there already existed ancient Islamic universities, including al-Azhar in Cairo, which had been founded in 990. During the colonial period these universities expanded the range of disciplines they offered beyond the religious sciences. In the meantime, local rulers who were bent on modernization encouraged the establishment of Western-style universities, such as Cairo University (founded in 1906) and the American University in Cairo (founded in 1919). In Morocco the beginnings of modern higher education came with the founding in 1921 of the Institut des Hautes Etudes Marocaines and the Institut Scientifique Cherifien, both in Rabat.

See also: education: post-independence; colonial Africa; intellectuals: colonial; intellectuals: post-independence; professionals; society: colonial; society: post-independence

Further reading

Ajayi, J.A., Goma, L.K. and Johnson, G. (1996) *The African Experience with Higher Education*, Accra: AAU.

Altbach, P. and Kelly, G.P. (eds.) (1984) *Education and the Colonial Experience*, New Brunswick: Transaction Books.

Clignet, R. and Foster, P. (1964) "French and British Colonial Education in Africa," *Comparative Education Review* 8: 191–8.

Fafunwa, B. and Aisiku, J.U. (1982) *Education in Africa: A Comparative Survey*, London: Allen & Unwin.

Higgs, P., Vakalisa, N.C., Mda, T.V. and Assie-Lumumba, N.T. (2000) *African Voices in Education*, Landsdowne: Juta.

Mutua, R. (1975) *Development of Education in Kenya: Some Administrative Aspects (1846–1963)*, Nairobi: East African Literature Bureau.

Nkabinde, Z. (1997) *An Analysis of Educational*

Challenges in the New South Africa, New York: University Press of America.
Turin, Y. (1971) *Affrontements culturels dans l'Algérie coloniale: écoles, médecine, religion – 1830–1880*, Paris: Maspero.
Urch, G. (1992) *Education in Sub-Saharan Africa*, New York: Garland Publishing.
Waggaw, T. (1979) *Education in Ethiopia: Prospect and Retrospect*, Ann Arbor: University of Michigan Press.
Zvobgo, R. (1994) *Colonialism and Education in Zimbabwe*, Harare: SAPES.

ROMANUS EJIAGA

education: post-independence

Independence in the 1950s and 1960s generated new opportunities and challenges for national systems of education. The emerging African nation-states were forced by social demands, and the promises and hopes of nationalism as regards nation-building and development, to expand educational systems at all levels and to increase access. They were expected to eliminate racial inequality, expand schools and higher education, and transform curricula to better reflect local cognitive and social needs. They made considerable achievements, but faced serious challenges; indeed, from the "lost decade" of the 1980s the setbacks began to overwhelm the successes.

Post-independence education policies

The development of post-independence education in Africa was characterized by shifts in policies and priorities, which in large measure were influenced by changing national requirements and international conditions. Initially, these shifts were driven by efforts to rid Africa of the undesirable vestiges of colonial education and to develop truly national education systems. The initial challenge for post-independence education was to produce the cadres needed to replace the colonial administrators with indigenous administrators. Because only a small pool of trained local manpower was available in the period immediately following independence, and because there was pressure in the form of demand from both students and the labor market, the majority of African governments embarked on the rapid expansion of the educational system. The strategies adopted differed, however, because of variations in local conditions and colonial experience. For instance, the socialist-oriented states sought complete rupture with the educational systems and practices inherited from colonialism, emphasizing instead the provision of universal primary education, vocational education, and education for collective achievement and self-reliance. For their part, the capitalist-oriented countries made less effort to dismantle the inherited colonial education system, instead placing high value on the academic curriculum and maintaining educational systems that were differentiated in terms of facilities (private and public schools) and access (according to class, location, and other considerations).

Despite these variations, spawned by differences in wealth and political ideology, African governments were generally interested in making post-independence education more relevant to local needs. Education was recognized as a powerful engine for national development, whether in socialist **Tanzania**, with its policy of "Education for Self-Reliance"; in capitalist **Botswana**, whose national development plans emphasized universal access to primary education and general access to post-primary education; or in monarchist **Morocco**, where the National Commission of Educational Reform emphasized the right to education and equality of access to all citizens, regardless of sex and social origin. Innumerable national, regional, and international education conferences were organized to discuss how education could be made more relevant to African conditions and needs, and virtually every government issued national education policies and tried to introduce structural changes in the national education system in terms of quality, resources, levels and growth of enrollments, educational expenditures, access, and class size.

Primary and secondary education

In the early post-independence period the new nations embarked on an all-level development of education. Despite the different policy objectives, most countries witnessed phenomenal educational development. Particularly impressive was the exponential growth in primary school enrollment, especially following the introduction of universal primary education. Free and compulsory primary education was introduced as early as 1923 in **Egypt**, a year after the attainment of independence, but as late as 1996 in **Malawi**, twenty-two years after independence. In **Ghana** it was introduced in 1961, in **Nigeria** and **Algeria** in 1976, in **Senegal** in 1983, while in Kenya a partial free-education decree in 1971 abolished all fees in parts of the country that were considered disadvantaged.

Primary school enrollments rose from fewer than 12 million pupils in 1960 to more than 50 million in 1980, while the number of schools rose from 61,000 in 1960 to approximately 111,000 in 1980. Gross enrollment ratios at the primary school level for sub-Saharan Africa went from 45 percent in 1965 to 74 percent in 1995, and for **North Africa** and the Middle East from 62 percent to 94 percent. These figures of course hide wide divergence in performance among countries. In 1965, out of the forty-eight countries for which there was data, twenty-three had primary school enrollment ratios of less than 50 percent. In 1995, only eight did, ranging from a low of 9 percent for **Somalia** to 48 percent for **Gambia**. Only eight countries had enrollment ratios of 75 percent and above in 1965, ranging from 100 percent for **Zimbabwe**, **Gabon**, **Congo**, and **Mauritius** to 94 percent for **Cameroon** and **Lesotho**, 90 percent for **South Africa**, and 75 percent for Egypt; by 1995 there were twenty-four such countries, with eleven exceeding the 100 percent range, which reflected the huge backlog being absorbed. Thus by 2000 many countries had attained universal enrollment.

Secondary school enrollments also grew substantially, rising from 5 percent to 25 percent for sub-Saharan Africa and 20 percent to 62 percent for North Africa and the Middle East between 1965 and 1995. In 1965 secondary enrollment ratios averaged less than 10 percent in forty-one countries out of the forty-eight for which there was data. Egypt and Mauritius had the highest rates, at 26 percent, followed by **Tunisia** with 16 percent, South Africa with 15 percent, Ghana with 13 percent, Morocco and Gabon with 11 percent each, and Congo with 10 percent, while seven countries – **Guinea-Bissau**, Malawi, **Mauritania**, **Niger**, **Rwanda**, Somalia, and Tanzania – boasted a meager 1–2 percent. By 1995 only five countries had enrollment ratios of less than 10 percent – **Burundi**, **Mozambique**, and **Niger** (7 percent each), and Tanzania and Somalia (5 percent each) – while nineteen had ratios of over 25 percent, including ten with ratios of over 50 percent – **Libya** (102 percent (figure includes students outside that age group for that school level)), South Africa (84 percent), Egypt (74 percent), **Swaziland** (66 percent), **Botswana** (64 percent), Algeria, Mauritius, and **Namibia** (62 percent), Tunisia (61 percent), and Congo (53 percent).

Similarly, the number of primary school teachers swelled from 301,000 to almost 1.3 million between 1960 and 1980, although the pupil–teacher ratio remained roughly constant at 39:1. Similarly, over the same period the number of secondary school teachers increased from 45,000 to 366,000. It is interesting to note that the number of female teachers rose more quickly than male. By 1980 there were 60 percent of female teachers in pre-primary education, 40 percent at the primary level, and 30 percent at the secondary levels. The rise in the number of teachers, combined with the decline of their real incomes, greatly aggravated their economic situation and forced many of them to search for second jobs. Across the whole of Africa teachers' salaries consume between 40 percent and 87 percent of current public expenditure on education.

Impressive qualitative expansion of the educational system also took place, especially at the primary level, and increasingly at the secondary level, where curricula reflected increased African content and greater relevance to national circumstances. In a majority of African countries indigenous languages were increasingly used for instruction, especially in the early years of schooling. Significant progress was also made in the area of non-formal education. Adult literacy programs in Namibia, Tanzania, and **Kenya** demonstrated success through falling illiteracy rates. The adult literacy rate – for those aged fifteen and above –

rose from 29 percent in 1960 to 39 percent in 1990. By 1998 the adult literacy rate was 59.6 percent for sub-Saharan Africa and 59.7 percent for the Arab states, compared to the average for all developing countries of 72.7 percent.

In the face of this qualitative expansion, however, several factors affected post-independence educational developments and threatened future improvements. The population growth rate of 3.5 percent, compared to the global population annual growth rate of 1.9 percent, implied massive explosion in potential demand for educational services, especially at the primary level, to meet the goal of universal free primary education. The other challenge was diminishing financial resources, both in relative and absolute terms, partly as a result of recurrent economic recessions from the mid-1970s, and partly because of the imposition of ill-conceived structural adjustment programs that encouraged governments to divest "unproductive" social sectors, such as education and health.

In the early years after independence, education was accorded a very high priority. For example, in the 1970s budgetary allocations for education ranged from 18 percent in Zimbabwe, 21 percent in Nigeria, and 22 percent in **Côte d'Ivoire**, to 32 percent in Botswana, and 38 percent in Kenya. But from the 1980s, as African governments began facing serious economic problems and implementing structural adjustment programs, education expenditure began to fall in real terms, declining from 4.9 percent of gross national product (GNP) in 1970 to 4.4 percent in 1990, although it increased back to 4.9 percent in 1995. The ratio was below 3 percent in **Burkina Faso**, **Cape Verde**, **Central African Republic**, Guinea-Bissau, Nigeria, **Sierra Leone**, **Sudan**, **Uganda**, Zaire, and **Zambia**. In the period 1980–6, per capita expenditure on education fell from US$33 to US$15 and from US$42 to US$36 for the continent as a whole. Inadequate resources led to declining quality of education and low student performance, and in some countries (such as Angola, Guinea-Bissau, Mozambique, Somalia, and **Togo**) the growth in the primary enrollment rate fell to 4.3 percent in 1983 from 6.7 percent in 1970.

Although many continued to face unequal access to education, significant improvements were made after independence. At the primary level the male/female gap was narrowed considerably, but at the secondary level girls comprised only 34 percent of total enrollment, which worsened to 20 percent at the tertiary level. Female enrollment grew quite rapidly in some countries, however. For example, between 1960 and 1990 the three East African countries – Tanzania, Kenya, and Uganda – registered growth rates of 11.8 percent, 10 percent, and 7.5 percent respectively. By 1997 female enrollment rates were 85 percent of male enrollment rates at the primary level in the sub-Saharan region and 91 percent among the Arab states, and 76 percent and 66 percent respectively of the adult male literacy rate. In several countries, the rate of female enrollment equaled the male rate (Cape Verde, South Africa, Tunisia, Libya, and Mauritius) or exceeded it (Kenya, **Equatorial Guinea**, Lesotho, Botswana, Namibia, **Madagascar**, Tanzania, Malawi, and Rwanda). Countries and regions that achieved high overall participation rates naturally achieved improved rates for girls as well as boys, and rural as well as urban children. Many countries developed policies to bridge the gender and rural/urban gaps in education. For instance, Nigeria's National Policy on Access represented an attempt by the government to widen access in education. The policy objectives included, among others, better geographical distribution of schools.

These improvements were the result of massive government investment, as well as increased **urbanization**. But the problem of wastage and repetition of grades remained serious, especially for female students. Between 1960 and 1975 repeaters constituted about 15 percent of total enrollment in primary education in Africa. In the mid-1970s primary school repetition rates ranged from a high of 60 percent in the Sudan, 44 percent for Morocco, 41 percent for Tunisia, 39 percent for Burundi, 36 percent for **Benin**, Burkina Faso, Central African Republic, and Senegal, to 25 percent for Mauritius, 21 percent for Egypt, 13 percent for Malawi and Algeria, 7 percent for Kenya, and 1 percent for Ghana and Zambia. In terms of regional distribution, the repetition rates for **West Africa** were highest – 31 percent – followed by North Africa with 29 percent, and **East Africa** with 13 percent.

Dropout and repetition rates were especially high for females and rural students. In Uganda, for example, out of all girls that enrolled in Primary I in 1983, only 39 percent finished Primary VII in 1990. Some studies have stressed costs, cultural bias against women's education, and the value of girls' labor for households as reasons for the high dropout rate among girls. Teenage pregnancies and an evaluation system that stressed examinations also tended to eliminate girls, especially at the secondary school level. Dropping out and repetition also appeared to be most common among students from low socioeconomic backgrounds, and were more prevalent in rural than in urban areas. Causes included poverty, which gave rise to illness, malnutrition, and absenteeism; the high opportunity cost of schooling for poor families; inappropriate curricula and examinations, which were often excessively academic and designed to prepare a minority of pupils for upper secondary and higher education; badly trained teachers; lack of textbooks and materials; overcrowded schools; and a shortage of secondary school places, which led to repetition at the primary level. Some governments began to take steps to improve the flow of pupils through primary and secondary schools. Automatic or semi-automatic promotions were introduced, examination procedures were changed, or more resources were invested in primary education. To overcome girls' lack of confidence in countries where single-sex schools predominated at the primary and secondary levels, education in mixed schools was sometimes used as a means of enhancing self-confidence among girls by increasing their interaction and competition with boys.

Besides the above-mentioned problems, the HIV/AIDS pandemic brought new challenges to education. Children infected at birth did not live long enough to enroll in school; some of those enrolled dropped out in order to earn money for their families and for the care of ill relatives; large numbers of teachers fell ill and died; and because of the presence of HIV in the classroom and school, the process of teaching and learning itself became more difficult. The gains made in girls' education till then were partly reversed by the impact of AIDS. In larger extended families, when the principal wage-earner died, girls were likely to be taken out of school to save money or to take care of relatives or younger children. Thus HIV/AIDS threatened not only the vast economic and social capital invested in education, but also those gains that had already been made.

In terms of transfer rates from secondary to higher education, Africa's average of 10 percent was much lower than in developed countries. The reasons for this are quite obvious. The fact that there was a system of selection for admission to higher education was certainly one of the causes. Holders of the secondary school leaving certificates had to take fairly severe entrance examinations before being admitted to university education. More importantly, however, this simply reflected the limited number of tertiary institutions, notwithstanding the rapid expansion of higher education.

Higher education

Before the 1960s there were approximately forty-two universities in Africa, many of which were in North Africa and in South Africa. According to some estimates, after independence this number increased rapidly to approximately 90 in the 1970s, to 150 in the 1990s, and to more than 400 by the end of the twentieth century. Many of the new universities established in the 1990s were private, thanks to the climate of economic and political liberalization. Altogether, the number of tertiary students in Africa more than quadrupled from 782,503 in 1975 to 3,461,822 in 1995 – an average increase of 17 percent per annum, compared to an average world growth rate of 5 percent. The largest concentration of university students was in Egypt (850,051), followed by South Africa (617,897), Nigeria (404,969), Algeria (347,410), and Morocco (294,502). Between them the five countries accounted for nearly three-quarters of African students in tertiary institutions. In contrast there were twenty-three countries with fewer than 10,000 university students in 1995. Thus the size and scale of university systems varied enormously between African countries. Cairo University's 155,000 students and nearly 8,000 faculty members not only made it one of the largest universities in the world, but also meant it had more students and academics than many African countries combined.

The growth rates were quite spectacular in some countries. The number of universities in Nigeria, for example, increased from one at independence (Ibadan) to forty-three, thirty of them founded after 1978 during the oil boom years. In addition there were sixty-nine polytechnics or colleges of technology and of education. Enrollments rose from 44,964 in the 1960s to 404,969 in the 1990s. Similarly countries that had one national or regional university plus other institutions of higher education at independence had dozens by the mid-1990s. For example, Sudan had thirty-six universities, a third of them private; formerly socialist Tanzania had established nine universities, seven university colleges, and twelve other institutions of higher learning; Kenya had six public universities, eight private ones, four national polytechnics, and dozens of technological, professional, and educational institutions, as well as research institutes and centers; Uganda had fifteen universities (four public and eleven private), eleven national teachers' colleges, fourteen paramedical schools, six polytechnics and technical colleges, six colleges of commerce, and a handful of other colleges specializing in forestry, hotel management, and so on. There were, however, a few countries that experienced decline or stagnation in university enrollments between the 1960s and 1990s. These included Sierra Leone, **Mali**, Gabon, and **Guinea**.

There were also sharp gender differentials in terms of access to university education. While several countries had managed to attain gender parity at the primary and secondary levels by 2000, very few had managed to do so at the tertiary level. The exceptions were Botswana, Lesotho, Swaziland, Namibia, and South Africa. Across the continent as a whole, females made up 34 percent of primary, 22 percent of secondary, and 12 percent of tertiary level students. To be sure, gradual improvements were recorded in some countries. For example, at Makerere University in Uganda female admissions increased from 27 percent in 1990–1 to about 40 percent in 1999–2000, while at the University of Dar es Salaam, where an affirmative action program for female students was introduced, it increased from 13 percent to 16 percent between 1994 and 1997. The gender gap also manifested itself in fields of study and faculty distribution. Women were concentrated in the humanities and social sciences, while they were grossly under-represented in the sciences and most of the professional fields. Between 1994 and 1997 female enrollment in the sciences as a percentage of the total female enrollment in the tertiary sector ranged from 6.5 percent in **Chad**, 9.1 percent in Tanzania, 12.6 percent in Benin, 14 percent in Zimbabwe, and 16.7 percent in Uganda, to 32.4 percent in Tunisia, and 36.8 percent in South Africa. The percentage of female faculty was even lower than that of female students, even in countries which had achieved gender parity in enrollments. At the University of Dar es Salaam, for instance, women made up 11 percent of the faculty in 1999–2000 (down from 12.5 percent in 1997–8), while at Abdou Moumouni University in Niger they made up only 9.7 percent. Needless to say, the female academics were crowded in the lower ranks, as well as in the humanities and "soft" social science disciplines.

As multi-ethnic, sometimes multi-racial, and invariably classed societies, access to university education in African countries was further differentiated according to ethnicity, race, and class, as well as religious and cultural affiliation in some cases. Class became increasingly salient as the African middle classes grew after independence (in many cases thanks to the establishment or expansion of university education itself) and sought to reproduce themselves. Incidentally, the ravages of structural adjustment programs, which pauperized many sections of the middle classes, reinforced the chase for the middle-class credentials that university degrees provided. Thanks to massive currency devaluations these credentials could no longer be obtained easily from abroad, hence the intense pressure to expand university education at the same time as financial resources were diminishing. Expansion was also prompted by political action calculated to spread the fruits of *uhuru* (independence) across regions and ethnic groups. Thus much of the expansion noted above was based on a mismatch between enrollments and resources. The mix of gender, race, and class as differentiating and discriminatory markers of access to higher education was particularly potent in post-apartheid South Africa. Apartheid institutionalized racial hierarchies and inequalities at all levels of the educational system, and created an unwieldy and costly bureaucracy. Demands for educational reform and redress ranked high after 1994. Post-apartheid South Africa found itself with well-endowed white universities, which had little moral and political legitimacy, and poorly endowed black universities, which had little academic credibility.

Despite the efforts made by the African governments, the increasing provision did not keep pace with the increasing demands for access. With more than 750 million people in fifty-four countries, Africa's universities and other institutions of higher education fell far below prevailing needs. Their concentration in a few countries was also a cause for concern. By 1991 the continent's gross enrollment ratio in tertiary education was 3 percent, which compares with 7 percent for Asia, 17.6 percent for Latin America and the Caribbean, 29.5 percent for Europe, and 74 percent for North America. Africa's enrollment ratio per 100,000 inhabitants is the world's lowest. What these statistics illustrate is that higher education in Africa – at least in the number and regional distribution of institutions – compares poorly with higher education in other regions of the world. Among other problems, linguistic differences and poor transportation and communication systems on the continent severely restrict networking and collaboration. An entrenched culture of looking to the North for linkages also weakened intra-continental cooperation, although academic cooperation and exchange did expand in the 1990s, principally through research, computer, and library networks (some of them coordinated by the Association of African Universities); regional consortia; increased academic labor migration; and the proliferation of independent research centers.

With economic stagnation, structural adjustment, and the growing inability of the state to provide jobs, in some African countries serious doubts were raised about the sustainability of higher education. Indeed in the 1980s tendentious studies were produced questioning the cost-effectiveness of universities, arguing that higher education offered lower private and social returns than primary education, so that public interest in universities was substantially lower than in primary schools. So powerful did this misguided gospel become, that at least one country even considered closing its only university as a matter of policy. Many others maintained an ambivalent attitude towards the tertiary sector. In many African countries less than 2 percent of the gross national income was allocated to university education, in sharp contrast to the pattern in the developed countries, where resources devoted to university education constituted between 2 and 6 percent of GNP. In Nigeria, for example, the aggregate expenditure per student was less than US$1,000, as compared to about US$3,500 for a student in North America. While North American universities spent about 60 percent of their recurrent revenue on teaching and research, African universities spent less than 40 percent. The imbalance in functional resource allocation between instruction-related expenditure and expenditure on supportive services had a damaging effect on the efficiency and effectiveness of academic functions in African universities.

Thus from the 1980s began a period of declining public investment in the universities, which encouraged the growth of private universities, and the corporatization and commercialization of public university management and education. All this took a toll on the physical and pedagogical infrastructures: libraries and laboratories became outdated and under-equipped, research funds dried up, and salaries plummeted at the same time as student enrollments were rising. In the meantime, university–government relations deteriorated, as did relations between academic staff and university administrators keen on new market-driven models of university governance and financing, and students' dissatisfaction increased. The result was declining quality of teaching and morale among academics, who were increasingly forced to do consultancies or engage in informal-sector activities in order to survive. Some abandoned the academy altogether, or migrated to greener pastures abroad, both elsewhere in Africa and, increasingly, to the North.

See also: economy: post-independence; education: colonial; intellectuals: colonial; intellectuals: post-independence; professionals; state: post-independence; structural adjustment programs

Further reading

Abidi, S.A. (1988) *The Future of Education in Eastern Africa*, Kampala: Professors World Peace Academy.

Ajayi, J.A., Goma, L.K. and Johnson, G. (1996) *The African Experience with Higher Education*, Accra: AAU.

Chinapah, V. (1992) *Strategies and Modalities for Educational Financing in Africa*, Paris: UNESCO.

Fafunwa, B. and Aisiku, J.U. (1982) *Education in Africa: A Comparative Survey*, London: Allen & Unwin.

Higgs, P., Vakalisa, N.C., Mda, T.V. and Assie-Lumumba, N.T. (2000) *African Voices in Education*, Landsdowne: Juta.

Hinchliffe, K. (1987) *Higher Education in Sub-Saharan Africa*, London: Croom Helm.

UNESCO (1998) *Higher Education in Africa: Achievements, Challenges and Prospects*, Dakar: UNESCO.

Zeleza, P.T. (2002) *Rethinking Africa's Globalization*, vol. 1, *The Intellectual Challenges*, Trenton: Africa World Press Inc.

ROMANUS EJIAGA
PAUL TIYAMBE ZELEZA

Egypt

Egypt, which has an area of 1,001,449 square kilometers, is strategically located at the juncture of Asia and Africa, flanked to the north by the Mediterranean, to the south by **Sudan**, to the west by **Libya**, and to the east by Palestine, the Gulf of Akaba and the Red Sea. In 2000 it had an estimated population of 67 million.

The modern history of Egypt is marked by Egyptian attempts to achieve political independence, first from the Ottoman Empire and then from the British occupation that had started in 1882. The nationalist movement culminated in the 1919 revolution, which resulted in Egypt's attainment of partial independence in 1922. Economically the revolution revealed the growing national capitalist class, whose nationalism was manifested in the foundation of Misr Bank in 1920, which helped in establishing and fostering many national economic activities. Socially the revolution empowered a national Egyptian coalition between Muslims and Christians against the British strategy of divide and conquer. Moreover, the revolution brought women into the political field and allowed them to contribute to public activity, and facilitated the formation of various trade unions and national cooperative groups.

Partial independence proved inadequate and frustrating. Indeed, continued British interference in Egyptian affairs, and the desire of the Egyptian king to practice a political role, resulted in the decay of political life. Conflict was rife between the king and his supporters, the British representatives, and various national parties and forces from the extreme right to the extreme left. The most prominent of these nationalist forces from 1919 until 1952 was the Wafd Party, which largely expressed and reflected the interests of the landlord class, but won all fair and honest parliamentary elections. Official independence nevertheless permitted Egypt to join the League of Nations and sign international treaties.

The 1920s witnessed the birth of the communist movement in Egypt, first among Greek, Armenian, and Italian workers, for whom the communist organizations sometimes served as extensions of the communist parties in their native countries. The movement sought to bind the political struggle to the social struggle, and to the search for social justice and economic independence. Communist publications demanded the liberation and nationalization of the Egyptian economy, land reform, and obligatory military service. Although they articulated the demands of the people, the communist movement was dominated by foreigners, especially Jews, which limited its ability to recruit Egyptians and raised suspicions over its intentions once the Palestinian problem had arisen. The repressive measures of the Egyptian and British authorities further limited its scope of activity.

Opposed to the communist movement was the Muslim Brotherhood, established in 1928 by Hassan Elbana, who was eventually assassinated in 1949. The group was destined to play an important role in Egyptian politics. The 1920s also saw many other changes, including the transformation of the national university – established in 1908 and, from 1953, known as Cairo University – into a truly modern university, alongside al-Azhar University, which dates back to the year 990. The establishment of many other public and private universities followed.

Egypt was the scene of one of the most famous battles of the **Second World War** – the Battle of El Alamein in 1944, at which Montgomery defeated the famous German commander Rommel, a victory that was to be crucial to the German defeat. Egypt also participated in the Palestinian war in 1948. The Arab defeat, alongside deteriorating economic and social conditions, increased popular opposition to the political system in Egypt. This led to widespread instability, which manifested itself in frequent changes of governments, workers' and students' riots and demonstrations against the king and the occupation, and the assassination of government leaders and other symbolic figures. The fire of 26 January 1952, which devastated parts of **Cairo**, brought matters to a head. Political parties traded accusations, and the government clamped down on dissent, with the army quickly intervening.

The Free Officers, led by Lieutenant Colonel Gamal Abdel Nasser, took control of the government, removed King Faruk from power, abolished the monarchy, and declared the country a republic. From 1952 the political, economic, and social structures in Egypt were exposed to radical change. The new rulers sought to initiate reforms and establish a non-capitalist economy. The constitution was abolished, political parties banned and a one-party state instituted, the properties of many former members of the royal family and landlords were confiscated, many companies and banks nationalized, and some of the confiscated agricultural land was distributed to poor farmers. The system also began its transition towards a planned "socialist" economy by setting economic development plans that were to direct economic development in the country.

In the broader international sphere, Egypt contributed to the establishment of the **Non-Aligned Movement** (NAM). Quite critical to Egypt's emergence as the voice of **Third World** radicalism was the Suez War. The Egyptian takeover of the Suez Canal in 1956 led to a tripartite Anglo-French-Israeli invasion of Egypt. But intervention by the international community – particularly the two superpowers, the United States and the Soviet Union – prevented the accomplishment of the goals of the invaders. Egypt became an indefatigable supporter of national liberation struggles in Arabic and African regions, and also established a short-lived union with Syria from 1958 to 1961. Egypt was later involved in the anti-monarchical war in the Yemen, and was defeated in the 1967 war against Israel. This defeat had far-reaching political, economic, and social implications: economic plans were frozen and the resources of the country diverted into preparing for a new confrontation with Israel by which Egypt hoped to recover the occupied territories.

Anwar Sadat succeeded Nasser after the latter's death in September 1970. Sadat promised to follow Nasser's policies, but soon abandoned them. Experts from the Soviet Union were expelled in 1972, and central planning and the dependence on the public sector were forsaken in favor of the free-market capitalism. This led to the appearance of new classes, groups and interests, and massive social dislocation in Egyptian society. Migration to the Gulf countries grew. Tentative political liberalization followed, with the introduction of multi-party politics in 1976, including the establishment of political parties on other than a religious or sectarian basis. This did not, however, diminish the dominance of the ruling party. Closer relations were established with the West, especially the United States, culminating in US-sponsored negotiations and the 1979 peace treaty between Egypt and Israel that brought their long conflict to an end. Through the treaty Egypt recovered the territory occupied by Israel, but became regionally isolated as it was shunned by the rest of the Arab world. Economic liberalization, alongside increased external debt and the imposition of **structural adjustment programs** by the World Bank and the International Monetary Fund

(IMF), had negative effects and increased social tensions in the country.

The Sadat government failed to contain rising social anger, especially in the form of disputes and tension between Muslims and Christians. Ultimately Sadat himself was assassinated by a Muslim extremist group on 6 October 1981. President Mohamed Hosni Mubarak took over. Mubarak's rule demonstrated a commitment to the political system of his predecessor, although he wanted to build domestic consensus and show tolerance of the opposition. Although a state of emergency had been declared, many of those who had been detained at the end of Sadat's rule were now released. The ruling National Democratic Party remained dominant, however, despite an increase in the number of political parties to sixteen.

Regionally Mubarak was able to restore Egyptian–Arab relations in 1987, while maintaining good relations with the West. Egypt benefited from the second Gulf War in 1990; its participation in the international alliance for the liberation of Kuwait from Iraqi occupation resulted in the forgiveness of some of its external debt. But the war also resulted in the return of Egyptian laborers from the Gulf, which reduced remittances and affected Egyptian revenues. Revenues from tourism and the Suez Canal also plummeted. All this weakened the economy, creating a favorable atmosphere for the development of an armed Islamic opposition that began to oppose the authorities during the first half of the 1990s. The terrorists targeted symbols of the system, from the speaker of the Egyptian parliament and ministers to sensitive economic sectors like tourism. The level of terrorism abated in the second half of the 1990s, however.

On a more positive note, reforms were undertaken that benefited women, especially concerning issues of personal status (such as marriage). This was largely due to efforts by the First Lady, Suzan Mubarak; the National Council of Women; and the Council of Motherhood and Childhood. Egypt also hosted many international and regional conferences. Lastly many Egyptian personalities have gained international prominence and awards. These include Sadat, who won the Nobel Peace Prize in 1979; the novelist Naguib Mahfouz, who won the Nobel Prize for Literature in 1988; the scientist Ahmed Zowil, who won the Nobel Prize in Physics in 2000; and Boutros Boutros-Ghali, who served as Secretary General of the United Nations between 1990 and 1995.

Further reading

Sayyid-Marsot, A.L. (1985) *A Short History of Modern Egypt*, New York: Cambridge University Press.

Vatikiotis, P.J. (1991) *The History of Modern Egypt: From Muhammad Ali to Mubarak*, London: Weidenfeld & Nicolson.

HAMDI ABDULRAHMAN

environmental change

The concept of environmental change emerged as one of the major global issues of the twentieth century. In developing countries, especially those of Africa, rapid environmental change was deemed to be critical, as it paralleled such development issues as poverty and declining quality of human life. In particular, the twentieth century dramatized the cumulative effects of some aspects of environmental change with such key events as repetitive droughts, land degradation, deforestation, biodiversity loss, urban sprawl, and resource-based conflicts across the continent. Negative environmental events were not necessarily creations of the twentieth century but growing human populations and activities, mass poverty, improved information flows, and global environmental awareness sharpened perceptions and interests in environmental change. But African environments are varied and complex. In this regard, changes are not always readily discernible. Furthermore, perceived changes are far from uniform in type and nature across the continent, and causal factors of change also vary in place and time. Just as in other parts of the world, environmental change in Africa cannot always be viewed in a negative context.

The twin processes of desertification and deforestation, for example, epitomized perceived trends of environmental breakdown in Africa, particularly in the second half of the twentieth century. Associated with these perceptions was the general belief, especially from outside the continent, that escalating human population was a fundamental cause of rapid environmental change. Viewing population–resource relationships in a neo-Malthusian frame served to provide simple inference to potential environmental impacts in situations of resource-scarcity and population stress. However, such inferences ignore local human adaptations, innovations, changing human needs and relationships with local environments, and the dynamics of institutional and policy frameworks that respond to challenges of sustainable development. Admittedly, dramatic environmental events such as desertification provide pointers to environmental change but only as part of a context of multiple variables, processes, and outcomes with different magnitudes, time dimensions, and spatial effects. Some changes in the environment are cumulative and cyclical and, therefore, cannot be fully described in terms of one time frame of observance. Many early reports on African environments tended to be overly subjective and deterministic.

The twentieth century was a turning point in Africa's environmental history. The pace of socio-economic and political change was considerably rapid, during both the colonial and post-colonial periods, with widespread human development and biotic implications. Also environmental change could increasingly be monitored, isolated, and measured under the watchful eyes of local and international interests.

Factors behind environmental changes and approaches to environmental history

A basic characteristic of most environments is the fundamental concept of change. Any unit of the environment is made up of components that are dynamic in their relationships. At any given time, a component is likely to alter, increase or decrease in its functions within the unit, or respond poorly or above normal to the external environment. Any significant changes in the sum total of these parameters are likely to affect the average character of that unit. Character changes that are of low magnitude may be too subtle to be observed externally. On the other hand, changes that significantly affect component relationships are likely to be visible because the unit may take on different appearances and functions. Changes may be both physical and human-induced.

Changes in the environment are inevitable because of the different time and space functions on environmental parameters. Time permits functions and relationships to be established, while space offers the modifiers (natural or human) of the functions and relationships that help to create variations, usually perceived as change. In environmental change, variations in average or known system parameters become detectable over time as new conditions that are different from the original come to be established. Ideally, established reference baselines are crucial for measuring change. On the other hand, changes in the environment are not always linear, nor are they easily predicted.

Changes in the environment are not necessarily stress-induced. Within the natural context, environmental change is an integral part of the earth's physical and natural processes. Within a human context, however, some changes may be too abrupt or may lead to sudden departures from known normal life-sustaining functions. Changes of such magnitude may offer new challenges for adaptations. Other levels of change, however, are likely to offer potential opportunities for the betterment of human life and environmental renewal. Analysis of environmental change generally falls into the ambit of environmental history, as it generally involves information on human–environment interactions over time and space. What are the factors of environmental change in Africa? What are the approaches to environmental history?

African environmental history has been dominated by four interrelated areas of research and emphasis. First, there is considerable literature on the impact of colonialism on environmental change. There are three contrasting views. Early colonial writers celebrated European environmental knowledge, management, and policies, as well as the beneficial effects of those policies on what they assumed to be environmentally unsound African agrarian and pastoral practices. This perspective was replaced, after independence, by an apocalyptic interpretation of colonialism, which was accused of initiating Africa's environmental degradation and undermining Africans' capacity to deal with it. Helge Kjekshus (1977) laid out this thesis boldly in his study of environmental change in Tanzania, where he tried to demonstrate how colonial agrarian and environmental policies caused ecological disasters that decimated populations, and led to the expansion of the tsetse fly belt and the spread of trypanosomiasis. John MacKenzie (1988) told a similar story for southern Africa. Many others chronicled the motivations and effects of colonialism's highly intrusive conservationism at the level of policy, practice, and discourse, and the various factors underpinning it – from concerns about agricultural development, social control, and segregation, to tourism, science, and aesthetics. The third perspective, partly influenced by postcolonialist and postmodernist ideas, emphasizes the complexity and contradictions of environmental change, stressing the variability of outcomes, the fact that colonialism involved both negative and positive (though not always intended) environmental transformations, and that environmental change generated and was generated by both creative and failed adaptations.

The second area of concern has focused on indigenous or local knowledge. Research on the efficacy of indigenous environmental knowledge was popularized by Paul Richards (1985), who celebrated the vast ecological knowledge of African peasants and the soundness of their agricultural practices that were once derided by arrogant, but ignorant, European colonial officials and scientists. Later James Fairhead and Melissa Leach (1996) produced an influential monograph that challenged conventional views of deforestation, arguing that forests in savanna **West Africa** had not, in fact, disappeared because of human pressure, but were actually remnants of human settlement and cultivation – that deforestation was a myth. Other writers attacked the association between **pastoralism** and desertification, stressing the complexity and disequilibrium of **savanna** and sahel environments, and the multiple and environmentally sustainable strategies of pastoral production systems. In this regard, many questioned the neo-Malthusian association between **population** growth and environmental degradation by arguing, following Esther Boserup (1965), that population growth was actually a catalyst for both higher productivity and better environmental management. It was pointed out that rising hunger in Africa had less to do with environmental stress *per se* than the incorporation of African societies into the circuits of global capitalism that engendered a monocultural cash-crop economy and undermined strategies to cope with natural disasters, while intensifying the vulnerabilities of these societies to those disasters.

The third area of research interest has centered on African environmental ideologies and movements. Scholars working on this topic seek to unravel and analyze African environmental perceptions and representations as manifested in a wide repertoire of cultural constructions, from religious and cosmological ideas, fables and other creative narratives, to the aesthetics of space in the built environment. Also of great interest in this context is the history of **environmental movements** and ideas embodied in social and political conflicts and struggles. For their part, environmental feminists, or "eco-feminists" as they are sometimes called, seek to decipher the gendered perceptions and constructions of environmental changes and adaptations. Finally, there are environmental historians interested in tracing environmental changes, especially measuring climatic changes over long periods of time using the latest scientific methods and techniques. The work of Sheila Nicholson, for example, has done much to provide long-term reconstructions of climatic change in Africa over the past 20,000 years.

Environmental history enables historians to study the environment over time using multidisciplinary perspectives to understand the effects of past human interactions. Environmental history is particularly susceptible to powerful interpretative narratives because of the need to ascribe agency and order to human actions in the physical world. Quite often, environmental historians ground their environmental narratives on the ideological foundations that characterize African historiography in general. The variability of historical interpretations of environmental change is partly determined by the fact that there are many sources for environmental history, all of which are subject to different interpretations. Beinart (2000) identified several methods for gathering information about environmental history using cultural data. These include various cultural symbols, expressions, narratives, fables, and the changing built environment, whether in design or material make-up. All these hold a wealth of historical data on environments and environmental processes. Showers and Malahleha (1992) add the utility of oral environmental evidence in reconstructing the past because such evidence is derived from local ecological knowledge and observations. But local ecological views can be distorted or corrupted by other views because of the cross-fertilization of values and perceptions between cultures.

There are many other sources of past environmental information. Written records, such as diaries and reports by early travelers, missionaries, traders, and colonial government agents, have yielded rich environmental data. There are also instrumental measurements of meteorological phenomena and "proxy data" based on physical and biological data, which provide "fossil" evidence of the effects of past environmental change. Geological, archeological, and botanical evidence provides a rich source of information about climatic sequences. In all the African colonies, as well as after independence, survey agencies and cognate environmental agencies were established to collect baseline environment-related reference data that have proven useful for studying past environments. Recently, remote sensing technology and environmental monitoring devices with computer-assisted data storage, processing, and disseminating systems have revolutionized time-series environmental data. Modern methods of DNA analysis are also helping to pinpoint details of the ancestry of many of Africa's plants and animals, including their distribution in time and space.

Environmental changes and their effects during the colonial period

Colonialism established structures, functions, activities, and policy frameworks that directly or indirectly generated environmental change. New ways of relating to the environment and manipulating landscapes to satisfy new needs were established. Various agents of environmental change in twentieth-century Africa were spawned in the colonial era. Thus the colonial legacy has stretched its tentacles to negatively influence environment and development issues in independent Africa. But colonial rule also set the foundation for some positive environment and development processes. In a sense the inability of independent Africa to modify, add on to, and enhance these foundations has meant lost opportunities. Generally, the influence of the colonial factor on environmental change stemmed from its economic activities, principally agriculture, forestry, mining, and parks and game management. Also, some colonial socioeconomic planning policies affected future environmental processes.

A characterizing feature of colonial economic development strategies was the peripheral role allotted to indigenous people. African traditional knowledge and land-use systems were replaced wholesale by new Western technological systems. Colonial planning decisions also tended to disregard African interests and welfare. Kjekshus (1977) described the situation in colonial Tanganyika, where people were forcibly moved out of their settled and subsistence areas to make way for game and forest reserves. The Mbulu Game Reserve absorbed large areas of native grazing land, closed several settlements, and forced out about 10,000 people.

Ironically the colonial establishment that came to Africa with European scientists, experience, and perceptions was concerned with environmental degradation from the onset. The onus of degradation, however, was placed on the "wasteful" land-use practices of the natives. Several scholars have reported extensively on the efforts of early twentieth-century scientists and conservationists, such as Illtyd Pole Evans and John Philips in the 1920s and 1930s, at vegetation research and management in the southern African region. Pole Evans, for one, saw pastoralism as a major cause of environmental damage and was a major influence on the marginalization of traditional pastoral systems in favor of scientific grazing and land intensification. Philips extended the conservation activities of Pole Evans in the mid-1930s. In the long run, the work of such scientists led to the establishment of the park systems and rangelands in the southern and eastern regions of Africa to limit environmental degradation. With its European-centered values, however, these scientific resource-management efforts tended to neglect African interests, push local African populations into marginal areas, and concentrate land-use and poverty. The purpose of conservation was thus defeated, because environmental degradation was generated by the impact of scarce resources.

In **Kenya** several writers have discussed the experience of the Masai regarding colonial land-use policies and its effects on the environment. Through colonial expropriation, the Masai lost their high potential grazing lands to British settler farmers, and to national parks and game reserves such as Tsavo West, Amboseli, and Masai Mara. Colonial land-redistribution exercises (adjudication processes) further disadvantaged the Masai, as the rich and high government officials received those better areas that used to be dry-season grazing areas for the Masai. Overgrazing, soil erosion, and surface degradation became common and increased the threat of desertification. Drawing on the deep-seated Masai grievance, scholars have concluded that overstocking and drought did not cause environmental degradation, rather it was the colonial land-tenure system that did so by fragmenting Masai land and limiting traditional grazing opportunities. Others confirmed similar effects following the alienation of pastoral communities from their land in the Kenyan **Rift Valley** and the transformation of the area into the heart of the white highlands. Among the groups to suffer land expropriation in the Rift Valley, besides the Masai themselves, were the Samburu, Turkana, and subgroups of the Kalenjin, while the Kikuyu were restricted to "native" reserves and other areas too small to sustain families. Environmental degradation through soil erosion and overgrazing became common. Environmental regulation was sometimes used to limit African cash cropping, while at the same time allowing settler farmers to expand their use of cash crops.

Colonial French West Africa also experienced the colonizing mission of agriculture. French colonial intervention in African agriculture became direct after the 1920s. Efforts were made to remodel indigenous agriculture in line with French agrarian experience. European agriculture supplanted indigenous agriculture, which was considered primitive. A basic tenet of this new form of production was high rural population density, which would both promote and be promoted by intensive agriculture. Irrigation schemes provided by agencies, such as the Office du Niger, were central to these efforts, and the oxen-plow was introduced to enhance the productivity of farm labor. Under this policy, France transformed its African colonies into suppliers of raw materials. Initial efforts concentrated on groundnuts – later cotton was added. Groundnut production in **Senegal** had led to reduced grain production and increased dependency on food imports as early as the 1930s. The **Niger Delta** irrigation scheme, established to counterbalance shortfalls in local food production, was compromised by labor shortages, low soil productivity, and weed infestations.

French colonial agricultural policies led to deforestation of marginal lands, while intensive crop production and irrigation on marginal lands rendered the Sahelian soils vulnerable to desertification. Added to this was overgrazing, as nomadic pastoralists became hemmed in by new colonial borders and corridors of plantations. The introduction, in the name of agricultural modernization, of tractors and other heavy cultivation machinery only worsened the problem of soil erosion. Furthermore, by deliberately promoting high population densities, French colonial agriculture exposed the fragile areas of the Sahel to degradation. The extended droughts of the late 1960s and 1970s needed only these conditions of vulnerability to register their effects on people and livestock.

Logging, mining, **urbanization**, and urban-related infrastructural development added a further dimension to environmental change by increasing the rate of deforestation, species loss, and surface alterations. Those cash crops – such as cocoa, rubber, groundnuts, and cotton – that were introduced by the colonial system still dominated the cropping landscape of independent Africa. Maize, also a colonial introduction in some parts of the continent, became prominent in African landscapes and diets, with negative consequences during times of drought.

Environmental changes and their effects since independence

Post-independent African governments continued the policies of the colonial era. Debt servicing, economic restructuring programs, and other governmental obligations and initiatives to generate economic growth led to mass unemployment and urban poverty. The need for scarce foreign exchange to pay for imports and to service debt obligations led to new onslaughts on environmental resources.

Monocultural production, whether based on cash crops or minerals, remained central to many post-independence African economies. In the **Central African Republic**, for example, government promotion of state-owned coffee plantations to help modernize and expand the economy was intensified in the 1970s. International logging companies were actively canvassed. This intensified use of the environment led to increased deforestation. It took external pressure, spearheaded by the World Wide Fund for Nature, for the state to set up the strict Dzanga-Ndoki Ecological Park in 1990 and the subsequent Dzanga-Sangha Special Reserve – 3,400 square kilometers of buffer zone. Reminded of the colonial approach to forests and game reserves, the people of the Sangha Basin who lived close to those conservation reserves saw these new conservation efforts as a renewed threat to their economic livelihood.

The pastoralists continued to be marginalized economically and socially in independent Africa. The devastating droughts of the 1970s and 1980s in the Sudano-Sahelian belt worsened their vulnerability. Pastoralists in **East Africa** experienced similar economic marginalization, which was exacerbated by population dislocations due to wars and conflicts. Several scholars have concluded that the pastoralists, by and large, had lost the central position they held in the late nineteenth and early twentieth century and were now banished to the periphery of regional networks in the modern African state.

The introduction of new species – particularly aquatic species – led to significant changes in Africa's lake environments. Perrings has documented the devastating consequences of introducing fish species to African lakes during the colonial and post-colonial eras (Perrings, Williamson and Dalmazzone 2000). The Nile perch, a species introduced to Lake Victoria, was linked to the loss of more than 200 out of 300 endemic cichlid species. On the other hand, Perrings and Lovett have also recorded situations in which the introduction of exotic fish species has resulted in positive change. During the 1960s Tilapia fish were introduced into Lake Nakuru in Kenya as a biological control measure to combat mosquitoes. This enriched the biological diversity of the lake: where there were only flamingos and algae, there are now around thirty species of fish-eating birds.

Game and wildlife have suffered in armed conflicts in **Angola**, the Congolian rim, **Ethiopia**, **Liberia**, **Mozambique** and **Sierra Leone**. Refugees placed near vital parks, such as those on the border between **Congo**, **Uganda**, and **Rwanda**, have destroyed vital habitats of threatened primates. The waves of refugees created by conflicts had environmental consequences in themselves. The impact of vegetation loss and the conflicts that can generate were dramatized in eastern **Zimbabwe**. There Mozambican refugees, who intensively cut down young trees from the forests around their camps for fuel, encountered resistance from the local people. A violent conflict occurred in the eastern district of Nyanga North, where some hundred local inhabitants fought with the refugees, destroying property and leaving several people injured on both sides.

While negative environmental issues dominated the news in the twentieth century, there were concerted efforts at the national, regional, and international levels to promote environmental protection and minimize environmental degradation. International efforts were coordinated through the United Nations Environmental Program, with headquarters located in **Nairobi** in Kenya, while regional and national efforts have been coordinated by numerous inter-governmental agencies and **non-governmental organizations**, as well as through regional integration schemes such as the **Southern African Development Community**, the **Economic Community of West African States**, and the **Arab Maghreb Union**, each of which has developed environmental policies and agencies. Bilateral environmental agreements also became increasingly common. For example, in the late 1990s **South Africa** and **Botswana** established the Kgalagadi Transfrontier Park, amalgamating the Gemsbok National Park in Botswana and the Kalahari Gemsbok National Park of South Africa. The park developed a joint-management plan so that it could operate as a single ecological unit within which tourists would be free to move across what were previously boundaries between the two parks. This elimination of the barriers that marked national boundaries facilitated the free movement of wildlife. But the case of the Tembe Elephant Park illustrates the potential constraints of such transboundary initiatives. The Tembe Park in South Africa, established in 1983, closed its open fence with Mozambique in 1989 to prevent large-scale poaching from its then war-torn neighbour.

It is worth noting that independent Africa did not significantly increase the efforts at conservation begun during the colonial era. Indeed some forest and game reserves were released back to local populations as arable land. The pace of deforestation, species extinction, and arid land vulnerability increased in independent Africa. The West African forest subregion recorded the highest rate of forest loss in the world between 1981 and 1990. The Sudano-Sahelian belt remained quite vulnerable to drought-related impacts, due to weak institutional response mechanisms. Clearly the process of environmental change is complex. Change is a necessary part of all human and natural systems. Changes that are rapid and detrimental to long-term human and environmental welfare must be guided, but some changes actually reflect progress and are necessary. Furthermore, not all changes can be predicted. The colonial era set particular trajectories of environmental change in Africa, but weak economies and political problems in independent Africa have increased the vulnerabilities of African societies to negative environmental change.

See also: health and disease; population; Sahara

References and further reading

Anderson, D. and Broch-Due, V. (eds.) (1999) *The Poor Are Not Us*, Oxford: James Currey.

Anderson, D. and Grove, R. (eds.) (1987) *Conservation in Africa: People, Policies and Practice*, Cambridge: Cambridge University Press.

Beinart, W. (2000) "African History and Environmental History," *African Affairs* 99: 269–302.

Boserup, E. (1965) *The Conditions of Agricultural Growth*, London: Allen & Unwin.

Fairhead, J. and Leach, M. (1996) *Misreading the African Landscape: Society and Ecology in a Forest Mosaic*, Cambridge: Cambridge University Press.

Kjekshus, H. (1977) *Ecology Control and Economic Development in East African History*, London: Heinemann.

MacKenzie, J. (1988) *The Empire of Nature: Hunting, Conservation and British Imperialism*, Manchester: Manchester University Press.

Matampash, K. (1993) "The Masai of Kenya," in S.H. Davis (ed.), *Indigenous Views of Land and the Environment*, Washington, D.C.: The World Bank.

McCann, J.C. (1999) *Green Land, Brown Land, Black Land: An Environmental History of Africa, 1800–1990*, Portsmouth: Heinemann.

Mortimore, M. (1989) *Adapting to Drought*, New York: Cambridge University Press.

Perrings, C., Williamson, M. and Dalmazzone, S. (eds.) (2000) *The Economics of Biological Invasions*, Cheltenham: Edward Elgar.

Richards, P. (1985) *Indigenous Agricultural Revolution: Ecology and Food Production in West Africa*, London: Allen & Unwin.

Showers, K.B. and Malahleha, G. (1992) "Oral Evidence in Historical Impact Assessment: Soil Conservation in Lesotho," *Journal of Southern African Studies* 18, 2: 276–96.

WILLIAM Y. OSEI

environmental movements

The term "environmental movement" is commonly used to refer to the organized efforts of groups or individuals who share the desire to protect the environment from irreversible damage or degradation occasioned by natural or human-use systems. In the context of Africa, environmental movements can be seen as the organized groups, African and non-African, especially **non-governmental organizations** (NGOs), that have vociferously brought attention to the deleterious impact of colonialism, global economic change, and industrialization on the African environment. The common thread in such "movements" is that degradation rather than change has been a dominant factor. Within this frame of analysis such terms as "acid rain," "ozone depletion," "the greenhouse effect," "toxic waste," "deforestation," "desertification," "loss of biodiversity," and "industrial pollution" have suffused the literature and information provided by the media about African environmental degradation. The focus on the degradation of the environment has culminated in myriad solutions, both local and global, that seek to correct Africa's environmental damage by going back to a perceived "pristine" environment in which humans lived in harmony with their surroundings.

From this definition, environmental movements in Africa are a recent phenomenon, although concern for environmental issues dates back to a much earlier period. It was during the 1970s that international concern for environmental protection helped to create awareness of the need for environmental management in domestic and international policy. Although there is no clear, systematic documentation of environmental movements in Africa, some watershed events in the 1970s changed perceptions of the environment and established a model for dealing with environmental issues. First among these events was the intense global attention paid to the drought and desertification in the Sahel. Although the problem of drought was not new, the 1970s saw a concerted local, regional, and global effort to deal with it through reforestation programs and controlled grazing activities. The second event was the 1972 United Nations Conference on the Human Environment in Stockholm in Sweden, which created a new consciousness of and understanding about the management of the global environment. With the establishment of the United Nations Environment Program, symbolically located in **Nairobi** in **Kenya**, African environmental issues became global issues.

These contemporary approaches, which were born out of the attempt to redefine, understand, and thereby solve Africa's environmental crisis, could be interpreted as an African environmental movement. To some, this is merely a return to age-old practices that existed in pre-colonial Africa, when human land-use systems existed that created harmony between people and their natural environment. Yet, to others, proposing any cure for Africa's environmental problems is a grand obfuscation when the dominant factors creating such environmental degradation are still at play, often working at cross-purposes with intended solutions. These views represent only one small segment of the history of divergent opinions and responses to African **environmental change**. Current attempts to create and maintain Western-style environmental movements can therefore only be meaningful if couched in terms of the overall history of environmental change in Africa. The various shifts in viewpoint on human–environment relationships have driven policy initiatives and attitudes toward environmental use.

Pre-colonial period

The literature on environmental change in pre-colonial Africa either emphasizes the vulnerability of African societies to environmental stress, especially drought, and the destructiveness of African agricultural methods (simplistically reduced to "shifting" cultivation), or portrays the pre-colonial era as a Golden Age of harmonious relationships between humans and nature, blaming colonialism and underdevelopment for the environmental degradation of Africa. Neither approach satisfactorily explains the different ways in which African societies have dealt with environmental change and stress. To begin with, it is difficult to make generalizations for a whole continent that has employed so many different agricultural practices, land-use patterns, and socioeconomic and political systems. There is a continuum of land use, ranging all the way from discontinuous and extensive forms to continuous and intensive forms of cultivation. Seven major methods and techniques of cultivation and soil management have been identified: shifting cultivation, intercropping, agroforestry, terracing, wetland farming, irrigated farming, and mixed farming. This diversification in itself constituted an important dimension of environmental management. Over the centuries African societies had also developed adaptive strategies to minimize the impact of environmental stress caused by drought. These coping mechanisms were not only varied, encompassing the manipulation of production practices, social networks, and ecological reserves, but were often staggered to meet the different types or stages of subsistence crises.

In many societies these agricultural and environmental practices were buttressed by religious practices. In regions where **African religions** predominated, religious ideas provided environmental protection. Within each traditional religion were sacred locations to which access was prohibited. As a result of this religious reverence, certain environments were preserved virtually intact through their exclusion from deleterious human land-use activities. The respect for nature inherent in religious practice also encouraged the wise management of non-religious environments. This spillover effect occurred because of the important link between religious practice and land use. In many instances religion threatened punishment for acts of mismanagement that were deemed detrimental to the welfare of the community at large. In addition, traditional healers derived their herbs, spices, roots, barks, and leaves from the forests and other vegetation environments.

In short, historical accounts suggest that, while there was human degradation of the environment and environmental stress was not uncommon, African societies developed environmental protection practices and coping mechanisms that were often quite effective. Often the destructive impact of human activities on the environment was localized and limited.

Colonial period

The advent of colonialism changed not only the methods and magnitude of the procurement of raw materials from the environment, but also the perception of the relationship between humans and their environment. Some historians argue that, as colonialism increased the demand for African raw materials, the attendant production increases to meet this new demand led to the exploitation of environmental resources, and put pressure on the African environment. In effect what changed was not the African environment, but the redefinition of that environment to make it easy to exploit its rich natural resources. The changes to the African environment, although not deliberately organized, were facilitated by European conceptions of it as a virgin environment with unlimited potential for development, and exacerbated by the impact of population growth and accelerated commercial activity. McCann argues that:

> in each of these cases, however, the effect has been to set up a conflict between the global forces of conservation and those of local and international interests that are pushing for the exploitation of natural resources as an engine for development. Both sides of this struggle over Africa's rural resources have engaged in the manipulation of narratives of degradation either to blame local people's mismanagement or to see rural people as passive victims.
>
> (McCann 1999: 177)

Those who blamed local people for environmental degradation sought to open avenues of resource exploitation through technological development. Using Malthusian scare stories, colonial governments and development agencies took aim at the allegedly irresponsible land-use practices of African farmers, hunters, and herders, while portraying their own policies and programs as able to reverse and transform existing deleterious processes of land use, thereby saving the local people and the environment. As Leach and Mearns argue, with reference to similar post-colonial projects,

> the development policies and programmes that result commonly prove to be at best neutral and at worst deleterious in their consequences for rural people and for the natural-resource base on which their livelihoods often substantially depend.
>
> (Leach and Mearns 1996: 2)

As the wheels of development began to turn, natural-resource exploitation proceeded at a rapid pace in order to meet the heightened demand for tropical resources in European countries. In reality, protecting the environment was not a primary goal at this time; neither was the creation of development activities to sustain the livelihood of rural African populations.

Did these changes exacerbate or reverse environmental degradation? With the focus on development, environmental concerns seem to have taken a back seat. Increased demand for African agricultural and mineral raw materials created enabling conditions for the wasteful exploitation of the environment. New production systems were borrowed from European rather than African models of land-use management, thus monocultural practices replaced existing traditional and polycultural systems that were in harmony with the environment. As the colonial economy (see **economy: colonial**) became more entrenched, even less attention was paid to the environment. Deforestation, soil loss through erosion and leaching, overgrazing and desertification, and reductions in biodiversity became heightened problems in the wake of colonial economic development. The focus of rural agricultural production shifted from subsistence production of crops and livestock to the production of cash crops for export and plantation agriculture. Such monocultural farming methods left the environment vulnerable. At the same time as the best land was being taken for the production of export crops, rural peasant producers were targeted as cheap labor for this export-based production. Thus rural food production expanded into marginal lands, again increasing the level of environmental damage.

The post-colonial period

Has the post-colonial period seen a shift in the environmental attitudes of the colonial period? The evidence suggests not. Several significant factors have contributed to post-colonial policies and perceptions of the African environment. Post-colonial African countries embarked on rapid economic development strategies, which accelerated the pace of raw material extraction for export. This was seen as a necessary condition for generating funds for the expansion of infrastructure, agricultural mechanization, and industrialization. To the new leaders and their elite supporters the environment was merely a resource that could be exploited in order to meet development goals. Attempts at rapid development thus led to damaging incursions into hitherto preserved forest and other natural resources. The myopic focus on development, coupled with a lack of oversight about the exploitation of resources, meant that previously unused streams and rivers suddenly became dumping grounds for industrial effluent.

Post-colonial approaches to development tended to concentrate economic and political power in urban areas, which created a further dichotomy between urban and rural environmental interests. Anything rural was increasingly perceived as backward and needing transformation, which led to policies that promoted rural emancipation through massive rural resource exploitation. This twisted logic neither benefited the urban environments nor brought about any lasting improvement to rural livelihoods or the environment. Rural people embraced the development rhetoric and offered their labor and land to achieve economic development. Their disappointment was monumental when it became clear that the rural environment was being ravaged to feed parasitic urban areas, which functioned as little more than sites for the evacuation of African resources to the markets of developed countries. Forests were cut down systematically and at alarming rates for timber and urban fuel, while nutrient-rich soil was rapidly depleted through the production of cash crops to meet urban food demands.

In the 1960s many governments of newly independent African states saw calls for environmental conservation as a plot by the developed countries to deny Africa its rightful place in the comity of nations. True or not, this perception was fueled by the reality of Africa's technological inferiority in relation to the West. To gain access to technological and capital resources necessary for development, the hopes of African countries rested on extracting raw materials at an accelerated rate. Studies that expressed apprehension at the negative impact of unchecked population growth and the wanton loss of valued environments were quickly dismissed as calculated attempts by the West to stall economic progress and keep Africa and Africans underdeveloped. To the consternation of critics and observers, country after country embarked on giant government-sponsored construction projects – hydroelectric power plants, irrigation projects, commercial agricultural schemes, forestry development, and plantation agriculture – none of which had much in the way of safety mechanisms to control environmental damage. Indeed these projects were promoted as indicators of economic development, creating the illusion of fair competition with the North, but at great cost to the environment.

Given the cavalier attitude toward the environment that had been widespread up to this point, which factors or events brought environmental concerns to the forefront of local and international governmental policy, public awareness, and social consciousness? The 1960s and 1970s were the decades of high expectations that Africa would be able to reverse the real or perceived economic misfortunes inherited from the colonial era. The argument was simple: if the environment was to be sacrificed to build economic wealth, then some improvement in living conditions should be expected after two decades of raping the environment. But that was not the case. According to O'Connor (1991: 109), the decades of the 1960s and 1970s had brought very little change in material well-being. The disparity between haves and have-nots increased, and rural areas – where over 70 percent of the African population lived – saw increased poverty and hopelessness, leading increasing numbers of people to migrate to the cities. As massive rural–urban migration caused the rapid growth of city populations, the urban environment began to deteriorate at an equally rapid rate. These conditions mirrored the inadequacies and failures of extant development policies to live up to promised improvements in the living conditions for African populations.

The devastating droughts of the 1970s and 1980s, especially in the Sahelian zone, brought the debate on African environmental degradation to public attention. The interlocking problems of lack of rain, deforestation, overgrazing, overcultivation, water depletion, hunger, famine, and the resulting deaths of people and animals, coupled with massive emigration, brought environmental issues under the global microscope. Countries that once supported or condoned environmental degradation in the name of development became painfully aware of their vulnerability, and began to canvass intensely for the help of the international community. With the help of international donor agencies, philanthropic organizations, NGOs, and agencies of the United Nations, short-term relief became available. Long-term solutions, however, caused lending institutions and donor agencies to attach conditions to donations, such as making loans in return for certain conservation measures or poverty-alleviation programs.

The second factor that raised environmental awareness was the escalation of environmental pollution by mineral extracting companies, particularly those engaged in petroleum production. In **Nigeria**, **South Africa**, **Côte d'Ivoire**, and **Congo**, to name just a few, global environmental movements were beginning to expose the massive, sometimes irreversible, environmental damage caused by multinational companies (MNCs) and their affiliates. Through blind ambition or sheer greed, the ruling elites of such countries often colluded with the mining companies. Once again environmental degradation was being treated as a minor nuisance on the path of economic progress. As it became apparent that mineral wealth was not helping to transform the lives of the majority of rural people, and further that the environment that sustained the livelihoods of local people was being laid to waste, local groups and NGOs became vocal critics of the activities of MNCs.

The third factor that galvanized support for environmental protection was in actual fact an amalgamation of several indirect issues. Fluctuations in the price of African raw materials and agricultural products in the world market, and the replacement of some of those products with synthetic equivalents, exposed the vulnerability of African countries that raised funds for economic development through the wasteful exploitation of natural resources. This vulnerability was even more evident in the increased pace of environmental destruction that was occasioned by the need for an increased supply of industrial raw materials and minerals to compensate for the decline in global commodity prices. **Structural adjustment programs** (SAPs), initiated by the International Monetary Fund (IMF) and World Bank to deal with the world debt crisis in the 1980s, have been blamed for some environmental degradation. In some countries, SAPs were burdened with conditionalities that produced unintended and undesirable problems. By enabling timber companies to purchase new equipment, for example, the rate of deforestation increased: from 1983 to 1988, timber exports from **Ghana** increased from US$16 million to US$99 million, causing further depletion of the country's forest resources (Nyang'oro 2001: 224).

More than any other single issue, the deteriorating condition of wildlife gave impetus to concerns about African environmental problems. The wanton and rapid depletion of Africa's stock of wildlife and nature reserves encouraged international assistance, especially from the West, for the conservation of African wildlife. In Kenya, **Tanzania**, **Zimbabwe**, **Botswana**, and South Africa the wildlife-based tourism industry was in jeopardy. This was mainly due to poaching. Some experts estimate that Africa has lost more than 95 percent of its estimated 100,000 black rhino: by 2000 only 2,700 remained in the wild. The global passion for rhino horns, elephant tusks, and leopard skins, as well as for hunting as sport, made such unprecedented demands on wildlife that whole species became threatened or reached the brink of extinction. The movement to save Africa's wildlife was bolstered by the Convention on International Trade in Endangered Species (CITES), and by such organizations as the World Wildlife Fund (WWF) and Greenpeace.

From the 1970s until the end of the century, the redefinition of global environmental problems made the entire global community culpable stakeholders in the causes of environmental degradation. Moreover, nations of the world, under the auspices of the United Nations and environmental organizations, were coming to the realization that many environmental problems transcended national boundaries. As such their solution demanded the concerted efforts of the entire global community. It also became clear that short-termist reliance on environmental exploitation needed to be exchanged for wise and prudent use of resources in the present so as to safeguard them for the future. A new paradigm for environmental management began to emerge, as the nations of the **Third World**, including Africa, became vocal proponents of international aid in economic development, as well as in environmental management.

Several international conventions and treaties were critical in strengthening African environmental movements. By 2000 the movement to save Africa's environment had become a concerted international effort, geared toward dovetailing environmental protection with socioeconomic development. The 1987 World Commission on Environment and Development, commonly known as the Brundtland Commission, called for the development of new ways to measure and assess progress toward sustainable development. In tandem with efforts by UNEP, the World Bank, the IMF, and various NGOs, African governments increasingly realized the importance of links between environmental protection, alleviation of poverty, population-growth policies, and changes in land use for the attainment of sustainable development. The renewed concern among Africans about protecting the African environment was evident in the growing cooperation between NGOs and African governments in the fight to save the environment. A new spirit of international cooperation also emerged in the form of solidarity between UNEP, the **Organization of African Unity** (OAU), and the Economic Commission for Africa (ECA), which sponsored regular meetings of the African Ministerial Conference on the Environment.

Examples of movements

Although international and African conservation groups have focused attention on the threats to the African environment, "these issues ... are not necessarily the primary concerns of most environmental movements in Africa itself" (Fay 2000: 1). The movements have tended to be driven by the need to protect "local or regional natural resources" that are important in maintaining the health and livelihood of communities. It is such local or regional contexts that gave the movements relevance and allowed them to flourish. Environmental movements of this nature were nonetheless sustained by the work, dedication, and sheer courage of a few notable individuals, in collaboration with African and global NGOs, as well as the tenacity of local people who often provided necessary labor for the movements' activities. In this context, environmental movements have priorities that do not necessarily chime with the priorities of African national governments. According to Robert Fay,

> Africa's environmental movements have many different goals, but nearly all are demanding that citizens – particularly citizens whose voices have traditionally been marginalized – be granted greater control over the uses of national, regional, and local resources. In that sense, environmental movements in Africa are invariably political.
>
> (Fay 2000: 1)

Among the most notable environmental activists and organizations were Wangari Maathai and the Green Belt Movement in Kenya; Ken Saro-Wiwa and the Movement for the Survival of the Ogoni People (MOSOP) in Nigeria's **Niger Delta**; and the groups protesting against the Lesotho Highlands Water Project (LHWP) in southern Africa.

The Green Belt Movement was created by Kenyan biologist Wangari Maathai. Founded in 1977, it "has used tree-planting campaigns to empower women and to draw connections between environmental and economic impoverishment" (Fay 2000: 3). Maathai saw deforestation as a threat to soil quality, and a cause of rising fuel costs. Since its inception as a means of both protecting the environment and empowering the economically disadvantaged, the Green Belt Movement has employed more than 80,000 people, mostly women, and planted over 15 million trees. The women are given a financial reward for each tree they plant that survives longer than three months, and they derive the additional benefit of being able to use the fruit, leaves, and branches from the trees as food, fuel, or to meet other domestic needs. The movement has quickly grown beyond its initial boundaries: by the end of the 1990s it had offices and local participants in thirty African countries. Maathai's inspired vision was empowering women to take control of their environment in such a way as to also provide material benefits to participants in the scheme.

MOSOP typified another kind of marriage between environmental concerns and the struggle for self-determination. It also showed that national or global economic interests are often at odds with local economic and environmental needs. Although decades of oil drilling in the Niger Delta had produced enormous wealth for the country, oil spills, gas flares, and acid rain systematically destroyed the resource base and livelihood of the Ogoni. Farmland was left barren, drinking water was polluted, fish were few and far between in the rivers, and people's livelihoods, which depended on these resources, had vanished. Moreover, little of the wealth generated from oil production was reinvested in the area, either to promote alternative economic developments or curtail the severe ecological damage being done to the area. Founded in 1990 by Ken Saro-Wiwa, MOSOP's fight against economic and environmental injustice in Ogoniland was fiercely opposed by the oil companies and the Nigerian military government, which arrested and executed Saro-Wiwa and eight of his comrades in 1995.

The completion of LHWP in 1998 spurred a protest movement, formed from a coalition of environmental, religious, and civic groups in southern Africa. Although taxpayers had funded the US$1.1 billion project, the bulk of the water was being directed to the industrialized Gueteng Province in South Africa. The movement was established to protest against the project's adverse effects on poor communities, especially the flooding of thousands of scarce hectares of pastures and farmland, and the dislocation of thousands of rural dwellers. In recognition of the potent force of the LHWP movement, which grew into a multinational coalition, the World Bank approved a US$45 million loan for the construction of a second dam. This movement was a call for environmental justice in protecting both the environment and people's livelihoods.

Concerns about environmental degradation have metamorphosed all across Africa into powerful environmental movements whose common goal is to empower groups affected by environmental injustice and advocate remedies that recognise the linkage in affected areas between environmental degradation and people's livelihoods.

References and further reading

Fairhead, J. and Leach, M. (1996) *Misreading the African Landscapes*, Cambridge: Cambridge University Press.

Fay, R. (2000) *Africa: Environmental Movements in Africa*, http://www.africana.com/Articles/tt_453.htm.

Leach, M. and Mearns, R. (eds.) (1996) *The Lie of the Land: Challenging Received Wisdom on the African Environment*, Oxford: The International African Institute in Association with James Currey.

McCann, J.C. (1999) *Green Land, Brown Land, Black Land: An Environmental History of Africa, 1800–1990*, Portsmouth: Heinemann.

Nyang'oro, J.E. (2001) "Africa's Environmental Problems," in A.A. Gordon and D.L. Gordon (eds.), *Understanding Contemporary Africa*, Boulder: Lynne Rienner, pp. 217–43.

O'Connor, A. (1991) *Poverty in Africa: A Geographical Approach*, London: Belhaven Press.

GODSON C. OBIA

Equatorial Guinea

Equatorial Guinea, formerly known as Spanish Guinea, is a small country located in west central Africa, with a total area of 28,051 square kilometers and a population estimated at 486,060 in 2001. The country is made up of the mainland Mbini province (formerly Rio Muni), which borders on **Gabon** and **Cameroon**, and the island of Bioko (formerly Fernando Po). The mainland population is predominantly Fang, while the population of Bioko is primarily Bubi. Spanish and French are the official languages. The main economic activities are farming, forestry, fishing, and petroleum and natural gas exploitation. The impoverished majority of the population is engaged in farming, with cocoa and coffee as the main cash crops.

Equatorial Guinea's history in the twentieth century was strongly defined by its encounter with European imperialism and colonialism, beginning at the end of the fifteenth century with the establishment of Portuguese trading posts. Portugal traded both mainland and island territory to Spain in 1778, by which time their principal economic value had changed from supplying slaves and provisions to merchant ships to providing food and fruit to the ships enforcing the ban on the overseas slave trade. Spanish colonization of the territories was confirmed in the Treaty of Paris in 1900, but it took almost thirty years of brutal repression of the local population for colonial rule to be made secure. Spain confined its economic activities to cocoa, coffee, and palm-oil plantations on the mainland, continuing the neglect of the island, and invested very little in the development of infrastructure, education, and social services. The plantation economy was reliant on migrant labor imported from other colonies in **West Africa**, the southern African Portuguese colonies of **Angola** and **Mozambique**, and Asia. Britain unprofitably invested in palm-oil plantations on the island, with the use of migrant labor from eastern **Nigeria**. The prolonged European presence, and the steady inflow of imported labor from diverse regions, resulted in the creation of a strong creole culture: first on the mainland, and later on the island too, when freed slaves and repatriated former slaves from the Americas began to be resettled there in the mid-nineteenth century. In its African colonies Spain retained the Portuguese practice of dividing the indigenous population into assimilated and non-assimilated groups. The former were supposedly those who had, because of ownership of land and education, become culturally Spanish, and were thereby entitled to the rights and privileges of Spanish citizenship. The paucity of educational opportunities guaranteed that very few Africans made it into the ranks of the assimilated; even those who did never enjoyed the right to political representation.

The period after the **Second World War** witnessed the growth of anti-colonial agitation, which by the mid-1950s was dominated by two parties: the National Movement for the Liberation of Equatorial Guinea and the Popular Idea of Equatorial Guinea. Brutal repression of the **nationalist movement**, many of whose leaders were imprisoned or killed, sent both parties into exile. Again like Portugal, Spain's violent resistance to **decolonization** was because the country was governed by a fascist dictator. Compelled by United Nations policy, Spain began preparations to decolonize in the early 1960s. A referendum on self-rule was organized in 1963, and independence granted in October 1968. Francisco Macías Nguema, a Fang from the mainland, became the inaugural president.

Equatorial Guinea's post-independence history was defined by the mind-numbing tragic excesses of personal dictatorship. In 1969 Macías Nguema used as pretext what he claimed was an impending coup and protest by the large community of Nigerian migrant laborers to consolidate his power, which already was considerable because the country's Spanish-style independence constitution provided for an overbearing executive. He banned opposition parties, constrained the free press, and forced out most of the 7,000-strong Spanish community. Thus was initiated a regime whose brutality and megalomania rivaled that of Idi Amin in **Uganda** and Bokassa in the **Central African Republic**. Power was effectively controlled by Nguema, members of his immediate family, and kinfolk from his Esangui clan, and it was maintained through the officially sanctioned murder of thousands of suspected opponents. All schools were closed in 1975 and all churches in 1978. It was estimated that in ten years of terror more than a third of the population was murdered or forced into exile. The economy was devastated. The plantation sector, the primary source of foreign earnings, collapsed from lack of investment and the departure of migrant laborers. Foreign investors abandoned the country, shortages of basic goods became endemic, and a ban on private ownership and the operation of all sea-going vessels decimated the fishing industry.

In 1979 Macías Nguema was overthrown in a military coup led by his nephew, Army Commander Teodoro Obiang Nguema Mbasogo. Power remained firmly controlled by Obiang Nguema, his family, and clan members, however, and there was no reeducation in the casual violence visited on the population of Equatorial Guinea. Teodoro Nguema transformed himself into a civilian president, instituted single-party rule in 1982, and made membership of his Democratic Party of Equatorial Guinea mandatory. Under pressure from international donor agencies and Western governments, a multi-party constitution was promulgated in 1991 and opposition parties legalized in 1993. Nguema's party overwhelmed the opposition in the series of local and legislative elections that were organized soon after. These elections were universally condemned as fraudulent. Unfazed by international outrage, Nguema had himself elected for a further seven-year presidential term with 98 percent of the vote! In the last decade of the century, the economy of Equatorial Guinea was slowly reviving, having received a major boost from petroleum and natural gas production. But if a visitor had returned to the capital, Malabo, and rural areas after twenty years, they would have been dumbfounded by how little the new wealth had changed the material conditions of ordinary people by the end of the twentieth century. Instead avaricious personal and clan-based political rule prevailed amid the pretence of political liberalization.

Further reading

Klitgaard, R. (1990) *Tropical Gangsters*, New York: Basic Books.

Sundiata, I. (1990) *Equatorial Guinea: Colonialism, State Terror and the Search for Stability*, Boulder: Westview Press.

DICKSON EYOH

Eritrea

Eritrea, formerly an autonomous province of **Ethiopia**, is located in coastal northeast Africa. With a total area of 121,320 square kilometers, it is bordered by **Sudan**, Ethiopia, and **Djibouti**. Its population of 4.3 million (2001 estimate) is composed of four major ethnic groups: Tigrinya (50 percent), Tigre and Kunama (40 percent), Afar (4 percent), and Soha (3 percent). Islam and Coptic Christianity are the main religions, while a small minority belongs to the Roman Catholic and Protestant churches. English is the official language but most of the population speaks one or more of

Afar, Amharic, Arabic, Tigre and Kunama, and Tigrinya, or other Cushitic languages. Agriculture is the main economic activity, with 80 percent of the population engaged in farming and herding. Industrial activity is limited to light manufacturing with outmoded technology.

In 1890 Eritrea became Italy's first colony; "Eritrea" was the Greek name for the Red Sea. Resistance to Italian rule was mute, except for an uprising in 1894 that was provoked by excessive land expropriation. Italian rule brought about territorial, economic, political, and legal integration, making the country into a coherent geopolitical unit through both demarcation of its boundaries and socioeconomic transformation. Light industries – particularly construction, food processing, and mining – were established. The construction of railways and roads, coupled with the expansion of the postal system, telephone lines, and telegraphs created a communications network. This was followed by the rise of towns. All this contributed to the formation of Eritrea. By the end of Italian rule, the colonial political economy had stratified society. New social groups, which were to play a leading role in the political movement of the 1940s, emerged. On the negative side, low levels of education, harsh rule, and (particularly during the fascist regime) a system of apartheid characterized Italian rule.

Italian rule ended in 1941, when Eritrea was conquered by the British. The victorious Allied powers were initially entrusted with the task of settling territories formerly colonized by Italy, but the fate of the colonies was formally entrusted to the United Nations in 1949. In 1950 the UN General Assembly dispatched a five-nation commission to Eritrea to investigate the wishes of the people, after which the commission presented three proposals to the UN General Assembly. One of these was the federation of Eritrea with **Ethiopia** and, on 2 December 1950, the UN General Assembly passed a resolution to that end. This Federal Pact came into force on 11 September 1952, bringing British rule to an end and beginning the period of Ethiopian domination.

The British Military Administration, breaking with the restrictive practices of the Italian colonialists, had introduced political liberalization to Eritrea. By 1947, when the ban on the formation of political parties was lifted, several political parties had emerged, of which the Muslim League and the Unionist Party were the major ones, respectively representing the Muslim and Christian communities. In 1949 the Muslim League formed, with other smaller groups, an Independence Bloc that advocated independence; the Unionist Party favored union with Ethiopia.

The period between 1952 and 1962 is known as the "Federation Period." During that time, Eritrea constituted an autonomous unit of the Eritrea–Ethiopian Federation. According to the Federal Pact, Eritrea was to have its own constitution; government, including legislative, judicial and executive bodies; political parties; national symbols, such as a flag; national languages; stamps; administrative buildings; and so on. The constitution guaranteed freedom of speech, freedom of association, freedom to demonstrate, and labor rights. It also guaranteed the right to form trade unions and political parties. However, each of the provisions upholding the autonomous status of Eritrea were discarded, one by one, to the outrage of the Eritrean people. Eventually, on 14 November 1962, the Federation was formally abrogated.

A year before this, the armed struggle for Eritrean independence had been launched. Eritrean exiles, predominantly from the Muslim community, met in **Cairo** in 1960 to form the Eritrean Liberation Front (ELF). A year later, a dozen guerrillas proclaimed the start of the armed struggle for independence. This poorly armed guerrilla force grew into the formidable national liberation movement that was to engage the Ethiopian army for the next three decades. In 1970 the ELF split into rival fronts – the ELF and the Eritrean People's Liberation Forces (EPLF) – which led to the first civil war (1972–4). By the mid-1970s the liberation movement had grown considerably in size, resulting in the liberation of many villages and towns. By the end of 1977 only four towns in the whole of Eritrea remained out of the control of the liberation movement. However, with massive support from the Soviet bloc, the Dergue (rulers of Ethiopia from 1974 to 1987) were able to recapture most of the towns. Not long after, a second civil war broke out between the ELF and

EPLF. After raging from August 1980 to July 1981, the war ended with the defeat of the ELF. For the next ten years, the EPLF fought the Dergue with remarkable success, becoming the sole dominant organization in the eventual liberation of Eritrea.

A unique characteristic of the Eritrean liberation struggle was that it drew Eritreans from all social classes and every ethnic group, involving both men and women. Women constituted a third of the armed forces, with some even holding positions of leadership in the army. This representation has continued in peacetime, with 30 percent of parliamentary seats reserved for women, and undoubtedly marks considerable progress in the emancipation of women in the country.

The armed struggle came to an end in May 1991 after thirty bloody years with the military defeat of the Ethiopian forces. The EPLF then formed a government in **Asmara**. After two years of preparation, a referendum was held in which a resounding 99.8 percent voted for independence. Eritrea duly became a sovereign state in May 1993.

After enjoying a cordial relationship for five years, a war broke out between Eritrea and Ethiopia in May 1998. The war, which on the surface seemed to be a border conflict, is widely believed to have other motives. After raging for two-and-a-half years, a ceasefire was signed in **Algiers** in June 2000, establishing the borders between the two countries.

Further reading

Bereketeab, R. (2000) *Eritrea: The Making of a Nation, 1890–1991*, Ph.D. thesis, Department of Sociology, Uppsala University.

Iyob, R. (1995) *The Eritrean Struggle for Independence: Domination, Resistance, Nationalism 1941–1993*, Cambridge: Cambridge University Press.

REDIE BEREKETEAB

Ethiopia

Ethiopia, which covers an area of 1,130,00 square kilometers and borders **Eritrea**, **Djibouti**, **Somalia**, **Kenya** and **Sudan**, had an estimated population of 63.8 million in 2000. The twentieth-century history of Ethiopia effectively begins in 1896, when Ethiopian forces led by Emperor Menilek II (reigned 1889–1913) defeated the invading Italian army at the Battle of Adwa. That Ethiopian victory determined the country's international status and its political economy, as well as shaping the psychology of its people. While the rest of Africa (with the exception of **Liberia**) fell under colonial rule, Ethiopia remained free to determine the nature of her relationship with Europe and the rest of the world. But the independence that Ethiopia secured at Adwa was far from absolute. Landlocked and surrounded by European colonies, Ethiopia's freedom was curtailed by the colonial powers, who continued to strike deals affecting the country's destiny, sought to dominate its economy through a vigorous policy of commercial penetration and acquisition of concessions, and imposed an arms embargo that left Ethiopia at the mercy of fascist Italy forty odd years after Adwa.

The first decade of the twentieth century saw the beginnings of modernization. Menilek – his empire extended to unprecedented levels and foreign aggression thwarted – turned his attention to the introduction of some of the amenities of modern life: a bank, a school, a hotel, and a hospital, all built in the capital **Addis Ababa**. Work on a railway that linked the capital to the French-controlled port of Djibouti also began, reaching its Ethiopian destination in 1917. In 1907 Menilek instituted ministerial government, setting up the first cabinet in the country's history. But, particularly after 1908, the veteran warrior and diplomat, who had overpowered internal rivals and outmaneuvered external intruders, succumbed to illness. Although he did not die until 1913, his incapacitation unleashed a power struggle that was not fully resolved until the coronation of Emperor Haile Selassie I in 1930.

Although the ailing emperor had designated his grandson, Iyyasu, heir to the throne in 1909, this was not palatable to Menilek's formidable spouse, Empress Taytu, founder of Addis Ababa and the spiritual force behind the Ethiopian victory at Adwa. But her bid for power was quashed in 1910. The short-lived reign of Iyyasu, who assumed power at the age of fifteen, represented a contradictory amalgam of social purpose and personal desultoriness. While he introduced measures that promoted social justice and personal security, he engaged in campaigns that reduced some of his subjects to the worst form of servitude. Above all, his name is associated with a religious policy that tried to redress the overwhelmingly Christian bias in a country with a sizable Muslim population. But this measure was skillfully used against him by his opponents, who portrayed it as an attempt to convert the country to Islam. His domestic enemies struck an alliance with the neighboring colonial powers (Britain, France, and Italy), who had begun to view with alarm his flirtation with nationalist leaders in the region and his links with the Central Powers (Germany and Turkey) in the **First World War**. In 1916 Iyyasu was deposed and Menilek's daughter, Zawditu, ascended the throne. Ras Tafari Makonnen, the future Emperor Haile Selassie I, was Zawditu's heir.

The empress remained only a titular sovereign, with power steadily slipping into the hands of the ambitious and energetic Tafari. The steady erosion of her prerogatives was not taken lightly by her supporters. Through a series of plots and conspiracies – even one assassination attempt – they tried to stop Tafari's almost inexorable rise. But he proved too wily for their schemes. He enjoyed the support of the foreign legations, who regarded him as a reliable partner for their policy of economic penetration of the country. Tafari could also draw on the resources of a group of articulate and ardently patriotic intellectuals, whom he promoted and patronized. The entry into the League of Nations in 1923 was a major diplomatic triumph, although it did not save Ethiopia from fascist invasion in 1935. His famous tour of Europe in 1924, the first of its kind by an Ethiopian ruler, enhanced his international stature. Eliminating his opponents one after another, Tafari finally ascended the throne in November 1930, eight months after the death of Empress Zawditu and subsequent to the fall of her husband in the last battle of the struggle for power.

Haile Selassie was now free to lay the foundations of absolute rule, whose juridical basis was laid by the promulgation of the country's first constitution in 1931. Modern forms of military organization, including the creation of the Imperial Bodyguard in 1930 and the first military school in 1934, were coupled with fiscal and administrative centralization. But these moves toward consolidation were aborted by the invasion of the country by Mussolini, who used as a pretext a 1934 border clash in southeastern Ethiopia. The Italians launched a two-pronged attack from their adjacent colonies of Eritrea and Somaliland. The Ethiopian counter-offensives could delay but hardly stop the advance of fascist arms. Superiority in military hardware and logistics, the deployment of colonial troops from Eritrea, **Libya** and Somaliland – not to speak of the use of the prohibited mustard gas – secured for the Italians the victory that had eluded them in 1896. Triumphantly entering Addis Ababa on 5 May 1936, they proclaimed their empire of Italian East Africa, merging Ethiopia with their northeast African colonies.

But the fascist dream of empire soon turned into a nightmare, as resistance erupted all over the country. Although they lacked unity of command, the patriots corroded fascist authority, which was increasingly confined to the towns, and thwarted the Italians' ambitious program of agricultural colonization. Then in 1940 Mussolini made the biggest gamble of his life by aligning himself with Nazi Germany, and the armed struggle was internationalized. Britain, which now began to see Mussolini's empire as a menace at its colonial rear, launched a three-pronged invasion from the Sudan and Kenya. Already battered by the five-year guerrilla struggle, the fascist army collapsed and the emperor regained his throne on 5 May 1941 – five years to the day from the fall of Addis Ababa.

The restored emperor resumed his task of centralizing power and modernizing the country with redoubled energy. He employed his diplomatic skill to shed the shackles that his British allies had imposed on his prerogatives and strike a more enabling partnership with the new global power: the United States. This formed the international setting for the measures that Haile Selassie took to consolidate his power, and at the same time bring his country into the twentieth century. Pre-1935 measures of administrative and fiscal centralization were accelerated. A modern armed force – consisting of army, police, air force, and navy –

was instituted. Educational institutions were expanded up to university level. Further advances were made in strengthening infrastructure, including the setting up in 1946 of perhaps the most successful airline in Africa: Ethiopian Airlines.

Haile Selassie's regime failed in two crucial areas: political liberalization and the introduction of meaningful land reform. This failure generated opposition, which came from different directions. Concerned and enlightened members of the ruling establishment plotted to avert the catastrophe they saw coming. The emperor's own bodyguard staged an abortive coup d'état in 1960. In the years that followed, students agitated for fundamental social and economic change. In Eritrea protests that erupted following the termination of a UN-sponsored federation with Ethiopia soon evolved into an implacable armed struggle for independence. Finally, in February 1974, a popular upsurge shook the regime to its foundations. A military group known as the Dergue, riding on the wave of that popular movement, deposed the emperor in September 1974. Although it tried to introduce some measures of social and economic transformation, including the proclamation of a radical land-reform program, it proved arbitrary and dictatorial in its handling of both civilian opposition and dissent within its own ranks. Following the elimination of his main rivals, Mangestu Hayla-Maryam emerged as dictator in February 1977. Alliance with the Soviet Union gave Mangestu much needed support in repulsing Somali aggression and the advance of the Eritrean People's Liberation Front (EPLF), now the main group leading Eritrean insurgency. However, with the global changes of the late 1980s, Mangestu found himself abandoned by his superpower mentor. In the meantime, the EPLF and the Tegray People's Liberation Front (TPLF), which had emerged to the south, scored a series of military victories that toppled the regime in 1991. A TPLF-led coalition known as the Ethiopian People's Revolutionary Democratic Front (EPRDF) assumed power in Ethiopia. Eritrean independence was formalized in a referendum conducted in 1993. The two fronts led their respective countries in what to all appearances was exemplary harmony, until they fell out and between 1998 and 2000 engaged in one of the bloodiest and most bitter armed clashes the region had ever seen.

Further reading

Clapham, C. (1988) *Transformation and Continuity in Revolutionary Ethiopia*, Cambridge: Cambridge University Press.

Zewde, B. (2001) *A History of Modern Ethiopia 1855–1991*, Oxford: James Currey.

BAHRU ZEWDE

European Union

The European Union (EU) was established by the Treaty of Maastricht in 1992. At Maastricht, representatives of twelve European governments legally sealed the unification process begun in the 1950s. The treaty replaced and enlarged the scope of trade and economic relations among members of the European Community (EC) to include common monetary, defense, and citizenship policies, as well as a common currency: the euro. The EU retained the EC's institutions: the European Parliament, the Council of Europe, the European Commission, the Court of Justice, and the European Bank.

Following the destruction caused by the **Second World War**, Jean Monnet and Robert Schuman promoted the idea of an integrated Europe built on cooperation among nations in matters of common interest. The two Frenchmen believed that lasting peace would be achieved in Europe when the benefits of good trade and economic relations, for instance, were allowed to spill over into other areas such as security. Convinced by this idea, France, West Germany, Italy, Belgium, the Netherlands, and Luxembourg became the six core nations in a process of European unification, establishing the European Economic Community (EEC) by signing the Treaty of Rome in 1957. The EEC reduced tariffs and other trade barriers among its members, and set standards for trade with outsiders. By 1967 it had become the European Community (EC), expanding to incorporate the European Coal and Steel Community (ECSC) and the European Atomic Energy Agency (EURATOM). By the

Single European Act (SEA) of 1986, EC members pledged to work toward a borderless Europe, the details of which were stipulated in the Maastricht Treaty.

As EC members worked for unity in Europe, they established and gradually strengthened economic and diplomatic relations with their former colonies and territories overseas. These newly independent states had provided a steady supply of raw materials and primary products for European industry. To ensure continuity, the EC initialed a series of preferential trade agreements, beginning with two Yaounde Conventions in 1963 and 1969, the first of which principally brought together eighteen former French colonies and territories, the Associated African States and Madagascar (AASMs). With Great Britain's entry to the EC in 1973, its former colonies increased the membership of the new European partners to forty-six, linking the African, Caribbean, and Pacific (ACP) countries to the EC. In 1975 EC and ACP members launched trade negotiations in **Lome** in **Togo**, which were to be renegotiated every five years. ACP group membership increased in the 1980s, with Spain and Portugal joining the EU and bringing along their former colonies as well. Seventy-seven ACP and fifteen EU states replaced the Lome Conventions in 2000 with a new agreement, signed in **Cotonou** in **Benin**, which expanded the nature and scope of their relationship.

A key policy instrument throughout the Lome Conventions was an EC-financed compensatory scheme designed to remedy the harmful effects of instability of export earnings from specified agricultural products. The stabilization of exports (STABEX) policy provided funds to ACP farmers to make up for falling prices for sugar, wood, cocoa, coffee, and bananas; a similar facility (called SYSMIN) focused on mineral products, including petroleum and diamonds among others. STABEX and SYSMIN compensatory payments brought temporary relief to ACP farmers, but the slow disbursements of the funds and the limited number of agricultural products covered under the scheme were major drawbacks. The limited number of products covered under STABEX also discouraged diversification of agriculture within the ACP countries. STABEX's focus on primary products and raw materials limited domestic manufacture and stunted industrial development. Thus ACP countries lacked the capacity to compete effectively within the world economy. By 1999 ACP countries' share of world exports had fallen to 1.1 percent from 3.4 percent in 1976. Imports to the EU from ACP countries also decreased from 6.7 percent in 1976 to 2.8 percent in 1999. Despite a growing EU market, production and export levels fell in ACP countries, as did foreign exchange earnings.

By the end of the century, as the EU and ACP negotiated a new agreement, the brief initial vision in the 1960s of a co-managed partnership was nonexistent. So was the EU aid that had been considered an entitlement by ACP partners. Instead, the EC took over, formulated, and managed aid programs, laying down conditions for future aid. By the end of the Lome process, the debt crisis, the **structural adjustment programs** (SAPs) established by the Bretton Woods Institutions (BWIs), and domestic instability in some ACP states had further weakened their fragile economies.

The fifteen-member EU and the seventy-seven ACP countries did, however, sign a new agreement in June 2000 in Cotonou. Against the backdrop of mixed reviews of the Lome process, the reality of unequal relations between the North and the South was prominent in the new agreement. On the EU's terms, ACP states accepted the conditions for future aid, including good governance and respect for human rights. EU partners promised to provide resources to non-state actors, and integrate these in the policy process. The parties focused on poverty reduction and confirmed that development policy, which had not been a policy objective of the EC until the late 1980s, would to be central in their relationship. The new agreement reflected the broad scope of the dialogue begun in 1996 between the EU and ACP. Other aspects of the interdependent approach to development that were agreed upon included dialogue among parties to address peace-building, conflict-prevention and conflict-resolution policies; democratic principles and the rule of law; and the development of private sector initiatives and investment. The EU and ACP partnership ended the twentieth century with an ambitious set of ideals, and reflected their determination to correct the flaws of the Lome Conventions and build on their strengths, aware of complex coordination problems within the EU, and the political and economic limitations in ACP states.

Further reading

Brown, W. (2002) *The European Union and Africa: The Restructuring of North–South Relations*, London: Palgrave.

Kwarteng, C.O. (1997) *Africa and the European Challenge: Survival in a Changing World*, New York: Ashgate.

BENN L. BONGANG

F

families

The concept of "family" is difficult to define for Africa. The continent has a vast array of ethnic groups ranging in population from many millions to only a few thousand. Some groups (for example, the Abaluya or the Igbo) do not even have a word that readily translates as "family." Until recently, theoretical and empirical studies have tended to highlight kinship and descent rather than the family unit. Nevertheless, familial relations form the core of social life in Africa: marriage and procreation; economic production and social reproduction; ritual and religious association; and political participation.

Overview

A multitude of marriage systems have existed in Africa. In the twentieth century, marriage could be monogamous or polygamous, permanent or temporary; and involve almost total or just partial rights over a woman's procreative, productive, and sexual activities. Marriage arrangements usually entailed bridewealth transfers, differing widely in kind and extent from ethnic group to ethnic group, as well as within ethnic groups. Some groups required only token gifts to symbolize the new union between families, while others insisted on substantial amounts of money, specific commodities (often textiles, alcoholic drinks, or livestock), or labor service. Such exchanges could be a single transaction or repeated at different stages over the course of a contracting party's life.

In most African societies, polygamy (marriage to more than one spouse) was the ideal, although only a fraction of any population – royals, nobles, or wealthy individuals – formed such marital alliances. Except in a very few ethnic groups, polygamy usually involved polygyny (the marriage of a man to one or more wives); however, in the Plateau area of **Nigeria** and central **Congo**, polyandry (the marriage of a woman to one or more husbands) was common. Whether polygynous or polyandrous, marriage customs and practices were diverse, with huge variations among and within ethnic groups. Residence after marriage also varied. It could be virilocal (in the home of the husband) or uxorilocal (in the home of the wife) or each spouse could continue to live in the home of his or her parents. Likewise, arrangements for the upbringing of children were diverse, with a high preference for a relative other than the birth-parents taking over a child's upbringing. Although in some societies children could live with their parents until marriage, they might also at an early age or at puberty be sent to live with their paternal or maternal grandparents, maternal or paternal aunts or uncles, an older brother or sister, or a trusted cousin on either side. If marriage ended in separation or divorce, a woman, depending on her age, could join a new partner in an extramarital arrangement; return to the home of her parents or a sibling or an older son or daughter; or, more rarely, seek protection in a special residence for divorcees. Thus the panoply of family systems on the continent was remarkable for its diversity, a tribute to human ingenuity and innovation in creating and adapting social institutions to various environments, geography, organization of production, economic opportunities, ritual needs, war and peace, and political relations.

Because of the polygynous structure of most marriage systems, the smallest family unit usually consisted of a mother and her children, linked through co-residency with other co-wives, their children, and their husband. Each wife resided in her own room or domestic space in her husband's house or compound, possibly in association with other similar sets of family units. Besides having her own residential space, each wife enjoyed a range of rights to her husband's sexual attention, access to land use, ritual protection, and insurance of her children's rights to inheritance. A wife's status and rights within her husband's compound could be strictly circumscribed, and also depended on her rank in the hierarchy of wives; however, at the same time, she maintained independent status and a range of rights within her birth family in respect to legal and ritual protection, inheritance, leadership, and economic opportunities. Such rights in either the marital or the natal family differed greatly according to descent systems. Women often wielded great economic and political authority in matrilineal societies. In patrilineal societies, their comparative lack of economic and political importance in their husband's household could be counterpoised against the social and political importance they maintained in their parents' household.

Genealogical (descent) and marital relations comprise the nuclei of African family systems. Generational interaction between older and younger members of the family of different ethnic groups varies widely. That age commands respect and deference is embedded in social etiquette and in patron–client relations for economic and political activities. Thus elders possess and exercise considerable authority over junior family members, to the extent that they might coerce daughters and granddaughters into marriage alliances or divorce against their will; they might treat younger family members as servants and clients; or, in days gone by, they might even possess the power to sell certain categories of children into slavery. Shared descent also means that siblings are treated similarly. Kinship terms for father and mother might be the same as for uncle (father's brother) or aunt (mother's sister), inferring that lineal and collateral relatives possess the same moral rights and obligations.

How useful is the term "family"?

To scholars of Africa and government administrators, the term "family" has two distinct meanings. It might refer to the domestic unit comprising a man, his wife, and their children – that is, the elementary family – but more commonly this term refers to the extended family that in patrilineal societies embraces a man's brothers and sisters, and their children; his parents, their brothers and sisters, and their children; and extends beyond them into a network of similar extended families that comprise a lineage. In matrilineal societies the extended family proceeds in the same way but through the mother's side. During the colonial period, theories of kinship and descent were central to the evolution of anthropology as a discipline. They differentiated sharply between kinship and descent, as well as between jural, political, and familial spheres. Generally, when contemporary Western scholars used the term "family," they meant the small domestic unit of the elementary family.

From the early twentieth century, however, African intellectuals stressed the "extended family" as the core of indigenous social organization. Lawyers and local politicians, in particular on the coast of **West Africa**, wielded effectively their knowledge of specific ethnic lineage systems to curtail colonial incursions on control of land. In the 1930s intellectuals in **East Africa** adopted the same strategy in **Kenya** and other countries. With the growth of scholarship on Africa, the rise and fall of European colonialism, the rise of the African academy and intelligentsia, and the reassertion of African political independence, scholars and policymakers recognised that the term "family" covered a complex array of socioeconomic and political aggregates. While blood kinship could be a condition of membership to these aggregates, often there were various kinds of social and ritual contracts that allowed the core "family" group to incorporate outsiders within its arena of activities, often under fictitious kinship categories.

Further complicating discussion about the African family was the fluidity of gender roles. Gender roles were not clear-cut, with terms used for various identities translated as "female husband," "male daughter," and so on. In some societies, most notably the Igbo and Swazi (but also in other groups), women could assume the role of husband and marry a wife or wives. This had no homosexual connotation, rather constituting a socioeconomic relationship that was, and sometimes still is, recognised in customary law. Usually such female husbands were powerful and wealthy individuals, often childless, who employed marriage as a mechanism by which to form alliances with powerful men within and outside their families, to establish trade networks, and to acquire rights over children. Such a woman could, at the same time, be wife to a man, subject to the customary practices this required. Sometimes, if a man had no male children, he would select a daughter to remain in his compound. She was free to form liaisons with men, but the children she bore would be reared in her father's name. Male priests serving certain deities could dress in female attire, wear female hairstyles, and, in ritual contexts, be referred to as wives of a specific god.

Throughout the twentieth century, African conceptions of family focused on the large corporate group of the extended family as the pivot of social relations, economic production, and local governance. The institution of marriage itself was seen as an alliance between two families first and foremost, with the union of the specific couple being secondary. The ceremonial moment of the wedding did not necessarily require the actual presence of the bride and the groom. Unlike Europe and North America (and increasingly African cities too), the elementary family in rural Africa was not an autonomous unit of production, consumption, and property-holding. It participated with other persons and groups in herding or farming, food processing, craft production, trading, child-rearing, protecting the compound, and law enforcement. Associated groups varied widely across ethnic groups, but might include age groups, women's associations, men's associations, and youth groups. Membership of these groups included relatives, neighbors, and friends. The extended family controlled land rights, herds, and economic resources, often in conjunction with larger sociopolitical units: the lineage, the clan, the village or town council, or the ruler-in-council.

Customary rights of access to land, herds, and crops were well defined. In the case of divorce, wives in patrilineal families and husbands in matrilineal ones gave up the rights acquired through marriage, but still had rights to resources in their natal extended family. Practice differed concerning a wife's control and management of the income and wealth she generated. Among many ethnic groups, she surrendered control to her husband, but in others both wives and husbands retained control of their respective incomes, although they were expected to contribute to expenses connected with their children, family ceremonies, and emergencies. In the case of widowhood, women did not traditionally inherit their deceased husband's property, although they might expect to benefit from the inheritance of their children, especially sons. Indeed for much of the century widows were, in many places, themselves part of the husband's estate, to be inherited by his heirs, subject to certain prohibitions. For urban Christians and other elite families, civil marriage and new legislation permitted wives to inherit from their husbands, but this was unevenly enforced.

New ideas and indigenous inculturation

Contrary to the theories of the colonial anthropologists, it is doubtful that an "ethnographic present" ever existed. Rather, there was a process, a system of roles and relationships between a husband, his wife, and their children, alone or as part of a larger kin group. Kinship relations expanded and contracted: they absorbed and adapted according to the changing dynamics of the environment, social movements, new types of production and distribution, communal philosophy and religious belief, associational life, politics, state building or disintegration, and globalization. In the early twentieth century, colonial administrations, missionaries, and scholars recorded their impressions and collected data about social interaction and institutions at specific historical moments, with better or worse understanding of their meanings. They became imperfect tools for colonial administrators, because even as such ethnographies, amateur and professional, were being published, African social institutions were changing dramatically. It is debatable whether the pace and impact of such change in the twentieth century was more momentous or significant than that which occurred in the eighteenth and nineteenth centuries as the result of new forms of state building, the outflow of slaves across the continent and two oceans, intensifying conversion to **Islam** and **Christianity**, and increasing incorporation into the world capitalist system.

The twentieth century opened with most of the continent, except for **Liberia** and **Ethiopia**, under various forms of European colonial rule. It closed with all countries having regained their independence, but still struggling to forge viable systems of governance and cut new paths through the jungles of **structural adjustment programs** and globalization. The colonial situation involved the rapid expansion of a broad range of ideological and technological factors that had already been introduced in the nineteenth century: Western education, international trade, new agricultural technology and crops, new industries, and new forms of Christianity. Often the most effective agents of change were Africans themselves, especially groups like the Krios of **Sierra Leone** or progressive rulers like Mohammed Ali of **Egypt**, Jaja of Opobo (Nigeria), and Samori of **Guinea**. In the twentieth century, colonial policy reinforced and expanded trends already in motion, deeply affecting African family systems.

Both Islam and Christianity strengthened and spread under the protection of the colonial state, but conversion rates for both religions mushroomed after independence, especially during the era of economic crisis and structural adjustment. Before colonialism, Islam had already introduced different notions of the domestic roles of spouses, polygyny, concubinage, divorce, inheritance, education, child-rearing, and women's activity outside the home. Although its patriarchal structure often clashed with the norms of matrilineal societies, its acceptance of polygyny and concubinage fit in well with indigenous customs. Initially Christian attitudes about family relations and institutions proved less accommodating, often conflicting with indigenous kinship ideology, views of gender roles, and marriage customs, especially those involving polygyny, widowhood, and certain transgender traditions. In a number of countries, African Christians rejected wholesale acceptance of European teaching and reinterpreted Christianity in the light of indigenous institutions and philosophy, resulting in the foundation of a wide variety of African independent churches. One of the most important issues fueling this breakaway from established European denominations was polygyny. Besides incorporating the validity of polygyny in church doctrine, the new churches also became vehicles for reinterpreting women's roles as religious leaders and healers.

New laws and court systems established under colonialism also affected family systems, particularly the abolition of indigenous slavery and concubinage, child marriage, and woman-to-woman marriages. Equally important was the systematizing and codification of customary laws regarding marriage and divorce within ethnic groups. In those areas where divorce had been difficult or almost non-existent, the new ease of divorce led to an unprecedented rush by women to the colonial courts to sue for release from marriages imposed on them by their families. Moreover, the new transportation and communication systems aided women in expanding their economic opportunities, which in turn affected their families.

After independence, education and the mass media popularized new family values, reaching into the remotest villages. Newspapers and magazines, films and videos, the radio, television, and romance novels promoted ideas about the importance of love, the nuclear family, monogamy, women's empowerment, and a Western lifestyle. Particularly important were the simply written, popular advice manuals on engagement, marital relations, manners, and dress for both Christians and Muslims. The connection between ideology, new economic dynamics, and changing family patterns could be seen in the development of elite families in urban centers, especially among Christians. Muslims, too, were influenced by aspects of the ideology of love, ideas about child-rearing, and consumerism.

Configurations of twentieth-century family life

Coexistence of multiple family systems characterized twentieth-century social life. The colonial state established the geographic boundaries that formed the parameters of the independent states, encompassing multiple ethnic groups and necessitating tolerance, however imperfect, of competing cultural systems. Extended families and lineages often include adherents of different religions living in relative harmony. Among the Yoruba in southern Nigeria, for example, within a single extended family it was not uncommon to find couples or sets of spouses married according to customary law, others married according to Islamic custom, and still others married in a Christian church. Christians and Muslims might be monogamous or polygamous. Members of the larger family unit would have a clear understanding of the practices and beliefs of each type of marriage. Beyond the specifics of religion and marriage, however, they agreed on the importance of family unity, seniority, behavior codes, and inheritance. Among the Hausa and Fulani of northern Nigeria and **Niger**, non-Islamic forms of marriage still persisted in some areas, with a small Christian minority contracting church marriages. Among Muslim Hausas, there were three types of marriage: marriage involving complete seclusion (purdah), marriage involving partial seclusion, and marriage with no seclusion. Divorce was common, with women averaging three to four marriages in a lifetime. Moreover, individual women could experience two or more different forms of Islamic marriage.

Despite expectations that polygyny and the extended family system would decline with higher levels of Western education, urbanization, industrialization, and better child health, these systems remained popular and widespread throughout the continent. Efforts to place legal limitations on plural marriage in the Belgian Congo (1955; now **Democratic Republic of Congo**) and Guinea (1968) appear to have failed. A survey of polygyny in fifteen African countries from 1960 to 1977 showed the incidence of plural marriage ranged from a high of 36 percent in **Togo** to a low of 1.8 percent in **Algeria**. Eleven countries (including **Ghana**, Kenya, **Tanzania**, and **Senegal**) recorded that over 20 percent of their respective populations of married men had two or more wives. Such a clear preference for polygyny among a significant section of the population reflected the views shared by men and women, albeit for different reasons, about various features of "traditional" family systems and values.

Although Western-oriented middle-class urban elites in many countries opted for the nuclear family system promoted by Christian churches, the extended family system continued to offer many of the same advantages that it did in earlier times, but often redefined. Still important for agricultural production in rural areas, the extended family also functioned well in end-of-the-century urban settings, as a mechanism for mutual social security and economic cooperation. The young and more prosperous took care of the orphans, elderly, and infirm. Entire families formed unions and contributed money and manpower to support family industrialists or entrepreneurs in **Dakar**, **Brazzaville**, Leopoldville, Stanleyville, **Accra**, and other places. Later, many extended families extended their domains to include relatives in overseas diasporas. Home remittances from abroad sustained needy families through the difficulties brought about by structural adjustment and declining economies on the continent. Thus extended families were strengthened rather than diminished.

Instability and state intervention

At the end of the twentieth century, family systems across the African continent had to adapt to declining economies, deteriorating social services, and increasing turbulence in governance. The high mortality rates due to HIV/AIDS in parts of eastern and central Africa profoundly disrupted former family patterns. Famine, inter-ethnic conflict, and civil war caused large movements of refugees within countries and across borders. Many children were forcibly removed from their homes and coopted into military service by rebel armies. When peace was reestablished, many found themselves orphaned and homeless. These conditions resulted in the rise of child bread-winners, child-headed households, female-headed households, and an increase in street children. Affected groups had no choice but to adapt their beliefs and traditions to altered circumstances. New family types and new authority patterns emerged.

State policy-makers recognized the need to intervene, either in an attempt to restore former family values or to understand the structure of emergent systems. By the time that independence was restored to African states, family-planning centers and organizations were being set up in many places. Policy-makers and citizens slowly accepted the importance of the regulation of fertility and child spacing. By the beginning of the twenty-first century, some states had begun to encourage the idea that women should limit the number of children they bore. With the inauguration of the International Year of the Family in 1994 by the United Nations, many women's **non-governmental organizations** reaffirmed their earlier objectives of promoting family welfare issues. A number of First Ladies reinforced government policy interests by underwriting new national family-support programs. Indeed the impact of government policy from the 1980s and 1990s on family traditions and values promised to be an important problem in the new century.

See also: African religions; Christian reform movements; Islamic reform movements; law; sex and sexuality; society: colonial; society: post-independence

Further reading

Chilungu, S.W. (1989) "Marriage, Family and Kinship Ties in Africa," in S.W. Chilungu and S. Niang (eds.), *African Continuities/L'héritage africain*, Toronto: Terebi.

Fadipe, N.A. (1970) *The Sociology of the Yoruba*, Ibadan: Ibadan University Press.

Guyer, J.I. (1981) "Household and Community in African Studies," *African Studies Review* XXIV: 87–138.

Hansen, K.T. and Strobel, M. (1985) "Family History in Africa," *Trends in History* 3, 3/4: 127–49.

Lesthaeghe, R.J. (1989) *Reproduction and Social Organization in Sub-Saharan Africa*, Berkeley and London: University of California Press.

Marks, S. and Rathbone, R. (1983) "Introduction," special issue on the history of the family, *The Journal of African Studies* 24: 145–61.

Otite, O. (1993) "Marriage and Family Systems in Nigeria," in M.S. Das (ed.), *The Family in Africa*, New Delhi: M.D. Publications.

Radcliffe Brown, A.R. and Forde, D. (1950) *African Systems of Kinship and Marriage*, London: Oxford University Press.

Sono, T. (ed.) (1994) *African Family and Marriage under Stress*, Pretoria: Centre for Development Analysis.

Welch, C.E., III and Glick, P.C. (1981) "The Incidence of Polygamy in Contemporary Africa: A Research Note," *Journal of Marriage and the Family* 43: 191–3.

LARAY DENZER

First World War

The First World War broke out in Europe in 1914, which brought Britain, France, and Russia into open conflict with Germany and Austria-Hungary until 1918. Still in the early years of European rule, African countries were drawn into the war by their colonial masters, who required African resources of men, money, and raw materials. The struggle between the European powers over control in Africa was also one of the causes of the war, with rivalry over African possessions complicating long-standing conflicts in Europe.

Each Allied power took steps to protect its colonies, strengthening defenses against possible German attack. When victories over the Germans in their African colonies became certain, these security measures were relaxed. It then became necessary to ensure the loyalty of African subjects, if only to prevent them from supporting Germany, and by and large propaganda was used successfully to this end. Even so, troops had to be withdrawn from many areas for war service, opening the colonial authorities up to attack from many quarters. The Ottoman Caliph, for example, had called on all Muslims to revolt against the colonial powers. To meet these challenges, the colonial authorities either collaborated with or coerced local chiefs into serving as agents who would police their own people.

As might be expected, the European armies were reinforced by Africans, who were recruited to serve as soldiers, porters, and servants. Various methods of recruitment were used, including conscription. Many Africans were drawn into war service by the promise of wages and other benefits from the army, while a greater number were compelled to enlist by their chiefs – the chiefs having been ordered by the colonial authorities to supply men for the colonial armies. It soon became clear that the existing colonial armies were grossly inadequate, and the colonial powers resorted to draconian measures in conscripting Africans. The French recruited about 40,000 men from **Madagascar**, 270,000 from **North Africa**, and 211,000 from their equatorial and west African colonies. In **East Africa** the British likewise enlisted large numbers of Africans, including almost a million porters, as well as 30,000 troops and twice as many service personnel from West Africa alone. The German, Belgian, and Portuguese colonial authorities also conscripted tens of thousands of Africans.

Resistance to conscription became integral to the early history of African nationalism. Thousands went into hiding or relocated to avoid service. In many parts of **French West Africa**, where large numbers of people had crossed to British territories, resistance took the form of armed protest. There was a major call for jihad in the **Niger** and from the Tuareg in the **Sahara**. In areas where colonial control was still weak, as in the hinterlands of French West Africa, **Libya**, **Mauritania**, and **Morocco**, Africans were able to use the diversion created by the war as an opportunity for further anti-colonial resistance struggles. For a short time, the French lost power in a number of areas. Although fewer in number, there were also protests in British colonies, including unrest in northern **Ghana**, and rebellion among the Kwale Igbo in **Nigeria**. These resistance movements were not necessarily reacting to the war itself, but rather to the introduction of new or higher taxes and the imposition of new administrative systems.

The colonial governments embarked upon measures to obtain the loyalty of Africans, especially the chiefs who were needed for the successful recruitment or conscription of their people. The French paid some chiefs to recruit young men, and forced others to send their subjects into the army. Propaganda in support of the war effort was intense, and many among the African elite were convinced that the British and French were pursuing a just war against the Germans. African loyalty to and cooperation with the colonial powers, especially rulers and other members of the elite, was based on a number of factors. Where European powers had avoided excessively repressive rule, and indigenous chiefs been allowed to exercise power and even draw wages from the government, the war was not used as a rallying point for protests. This was the case, for example, with the British in Nigeria.

Africans saw service in different places, but the majority remained in Africa to confront the Germans in the colonies of Tanganyika, Kamerun, **Namibia**, and **Togo**. Africans who did not see active military service were also mobilized, but for war production of both established export crops and foodstuffs.

Consequences

Africa was affected by the war in many spheres: military, political, economic, and social. The results were not the same everywhere. In areas where there had been actual fighting, notably in the German colonies, the people suffered greatly. In the French colonies, where the burden of conscription had been heavy, there were anti-colonial protests and widespread resentment. Indeed, in many areas the colonial authorities' hold on power was weakened: their military were redirected to the war effort; markets and trade routes were disrupted; and the economic recession and growing unemployment that followed the war generated their own tensions.

Military recruitment had temporarily strengthened existing colonial armies, but many of the newly recruited troops perished. The actual number of casualties will never be known exactly, but it was undoubtedly large: of those recruited by the French almost 200,000 lost their lives, while nearly 100,000 lost their lives in the British campaign in East Africa. For the soldiers who survived the war, the experience broadened their view of both African affairs and world politics. They understood the causes of the war and the nature of imperialism, and could begin to consider the impact of colonialism on their own countries. Many acquired practical skills and a degree of technical education that they were able to put to good use after the war. For many the experience of Europeans in combat that they acquired during the war comprehensively undermined notions of white superiority.

African economies were affected in several ways. There was increased production of agricultural and mineral commodities for the war effort, but taxes were also increased and development expenditure cut. For example, Nigeria's expenditure increased by about £1,400,000; in 1915, despite reduced revenues, FF5,860,000 were sent to France from French West Africa. In addition, various colonies raised relief funds and local war subscriptions. The economic losses took other forms too, associated with political disturbances, wildcat revolts, the scarcity of essential commodities, abandonment of development projects, the conscription of able-bodied men, and general discontent and growing unemployment in a number of cities. The dislocation of populations, shortage of shipping, and high costs for freight led to panic and an aggressive search for alternative markets. In the early months of the war, the withdrawal of German traders from regions where they had been the primary buyers of export crops, led to a loss of income for many local traders and producers. Where army recruitment had been intense many villages and rural areas were devastated by the loss of productive labor, with the number of male farmers declining considerably. The war and immediate postwar years also witnessed widespread food shortages and epidemics, including the devastating influenza pandemic of 1918–19.

A major shift occurred in the organization of foreign trade, which created new tensions between Europe and Africa. During the war, many African export traders were displaced by foreign firms that manipulated war conditions to their advantage. French and British companies dominated the important export business, backed by their colonial governments. In addition, these firms took control of businesses deserted by the Germans, thereby controlling the import trade as well. Furthermore, foreign firms established combines that forced down producer prices, emerging after the war as large firms with enormous power over the market and prices in general – all at the expense of African producers.

Germany lost its African colonies, which were shared out as "mandated territories" by the newly created League of Nations. The Belgians took over Ruanda-Urundi, **South Africa** received **Namibia**, the British obtained Tanganyika and northern **Cameroon** (added to their Nigerian colony), the French took the rest of Cameroon, and the British and French divided **Togo**. The expectation was that the European powers would serve only as guardians; in practice, this meant little or nothing to the African population, who were still treated as colonial subjects. When the League of Nations was dissolved in 1940, the status of these mandated territories was left unclear. The expectation that these "guardians" would prepare the countries for self-government was largely ignored.

There were other notable changes to the pattern of colonial rule. In January 1914, for example, the British Protectorates of Southern and Northern Nigeria were amalgamated. In 1917 a large part of western **Egypt** was transferred to Italian Libya, and was then administered as three units (Tripolitania, Cyrenaica, and Fezzān). The triangle of land to the northwest of Anglo-Egyptian **Sudan** was transferred to Italy, also in 1917. In 1920 the French created the colony of Upper Volta from parts of the Niger, **Sudan**, and **Côte d'Ivoire**. Upper Volta was subsequently divided in 1932. Thus the modern map of Africa began to acquire its current shape.

Many of the economic and social changes affected politics, contributing to the emergence of African nationalism. Colonial conquests and the war had taken from Africans many of their businesses and administrative jobs. They began to realize that they would have to insist on – perhaps even fight for – reforms if they were ever to regain what they had lost. War propaganda had condemned Germany for wanting to dominate the world, and by 1919 the principle of self-determination had become widely known. Soon the right of all people to determine their own affairs had developed from being an anti-German slogan to one that the African elite could capitalize on – what was right for Europe was equally right for Africa. Even though independence was still distant, a spirit of national consciousness had begun to develop among Africans.

The colonial authorities by and large ignored this pressure from the African elites, and the expectation that the end of the war would bring power and prestige to Africans was not realized. Early leaders of the **nationalist movements** in Africa were anxious to see constitutional reforms that would give educated Africans a greater role in determining their own affairs, and political parties began to emerge: the National Congress of British West Africa, for example, was founded in 1920 to demand far-reaching political reform. Small concessions were granted in the 1920s, allowing a few people from the educated elite to sit on legislative councils in Nigeria and **Sierra Leone**. More significantly, in North Africa revolts in Egypt had led to its independence by 1922.

Another political outcome of the war was that it enabled the colonial governments to consolidate themselves. Even as African participants in the First World War began to expect remarkable changes in their lives, colonial governments were planning ways to make their control of Africa and its resources more permanent. The contribution of Africans to the war effort were simply ignored. Having won the war, the European powers in Africa felt even more confident of their ability to rule there: some officers expressed the opinion that they would remain in charge of the continent for ever. In some areas, such as the Belgian colonies and South Africa, colonial repression became more entrenched. Whether repressive or not, the victorious colonial powers shared one goal: the economic exploitation of Africa. In view of the devastation caused to their economies by the war, they saw the control of Africa as the best way of recouping their losses and rebuilding their economies.

See also: colonial Africa; Second World War; state: colonial

Further reading

Boahen, A.A. (1985) *UNESCO General History of Africa. Africa Under Colonial Domination 1880–1935*, London: Heinemann.

Digre, B.K. (1987) *The Repartition of Tropical Africa: British, French and Belgian Colonial Objectives During the First World War and the Paris Peace Conference*, Ph.D. thesis, George Washington University.

Lunn, J. (1999) *Memoirs of the Maelstrom: A Senegalese Oral History of the First World War*, Oxford: James Currey.

Page, M.E. (1987) *Africa and the First World War*, New York: St. Martin's Press.

Reigel, C.W. (1989) *The First World War in East Africa: A Reinterpretation*, Ed.D. thesis, Temple University.

TOYIN FALOLA

food crises

Food security refers to the continuous access by all people to adequate food supplies for leading an active, healthy life. All African governments set food security as a social goal, but poverty leaves a third or more of Africa's population facing hunger on a regular basis. In the last half of the twentieth century this chronic hunger repeatedly combined with political or natural disasters to explode into catastrophic famines. Declining food production per person, malnutrition, and famine represent three distinct, but related, food crises facing the African continent.

Food production trends

The failure of food and agricultural production to grow as rapidly as population sets Africa apart from all other world regions, and stands at the heart of the continent's multi-faceted food crises. According to the United Nations Food and Agriculture Organization (UNFAO), food production in Africa in the year 2000 was two times greater than it had been forty years earlier. Food production per person, however, was 10 percent lower in 2000 that it had been in the 1960s. Between 1970 and 1995, the share of African children who were underweight for their age dropped from 35 percent to 31 percent, but Africa's population grew so rapidly that the number of children who were undernourished rose from 24.5 million to 37.4 million over the same period.

At the end of the twentieth century, as at the beginning, most Africans lived in rural areas and earned much of their income as farmers or herders. Declining agricultural production per person has therefore meant declining income for many Africans. With this fall in income, food security has remained an unattainable goal in much of the continent. Ironically it is the more agricultural regions that suffer the greater poverty and, consequently, greater hunger. At the end of the 1990s the UNFAO estimated that over 40 percent of the population in **East**, **Central**, and **Southern Africa** was undernourished, but only 5 percent of the population in richer more industrial **North Africa**. In **West Africa** undernourishment was thought to affect about 20 percent of the population.

Chronic hunger

In any region, chronic and recurrent hunger are more prevalent among those with fewer resources. This means that in Africa hunger is more common in rural areas than in the cities. While urban poverty is a pressing problem for many people, incomes in rural areas tend to be lower and more variable than those in cities. At the same time, urban populations have historically benefited from more food programs and public services than rural dwellers. Rural food insecurity itself tends be seasonal. At harvest times there is relatively little hunger in rural areas. However, as grain stocks diminish, food becomes scarce and hunger becomes more common. As a result the period just before the harvest is often referred to as the "hungry season."

Following patterns of poverty, food insecurity is more prevalent among women than men. When women live in households with no adult males, they tend to have lower incomes than otherwise, leaving them more exposed to hunger. When women live in households with men, they often serve as "shock absorbers" in the households, going hungrier in times of shortage than do others, thereby protecting children and men to a limited degree. Women's greater tendency to suffer malnutrition is exacerbated by special nutritional needs during pregnancy and when nursing. Just as women suffer more hunger than men, so children tend to face greater malnutrition than adults. Again this is attributed to their relative powerlessness in society and to their special nutritional needs.

The poverty of a community can intensify problems of undernourishment. If the poor live in unsanitary environments with unreliable access to clean water, disease may limit people's ability to absorb what food they eat. Thus poor public health and sanitation services often magnify the negative effects of personal impoverishment on an individual's nutrition.

Chronic hunger leaves many marks on a population. It stunts children's growth, for example, which can be measured in the low height or low weight for age among populations that suffer malnutrition. Though it is more difficult to measure, hunger can also affect the mental development of young people. Inadequate nourishment leaves people weak and unable to work most effectively. It also leaves them susceptible to disease, thus contributing to morbidity and mortality in populations. Deficiencies in specific micronutrients, such as vitamin A, can have further detrimental effects on people's health, even if quantities of food are sufficient in caloric terms. Thus, through its detrimental impact on human development, health, and physical ability, hunger can be a cause as well as a consequence of poverty.

Famine

Poverty left many Africans food insecure in the twentieth century. When that poverty combined with environmental and political instability, famines erupted. Famine is a catastrophic food scarcity that results in widespread starvation and death. In the first half of the twentieth century, famines were a global phenomenon, striking in Europe (for example, Russia in 1913, 1920, and 1930) and Asia (for example, China in 1929 and 1946), as well as threatening Africa and the Americas. By the end of the twentieth century, famine had become a predominantly African tragedy. A partial listing of Africa's twentieth-century famines includes **Nigeria** (Biafra) in 1968–9; West African Sahel in 1969–74; **Ethiopia** in 1972–4, 1983–5, and 1989–90; **Angola** in 1974–6 and 1993–4; **Mozambique** in 1985–6; **Sudan** in 1984, 1988, 1993, and 1998; and **Somalia** in 1984, 1988, and 1992. The specific causes of each famine differed, but there are consistent factors that have made some countries especially susceptible to these horrible events. In most famines, impoverished populations who have been subjected to risky environments are faced with sudden political, military, or weather-related shocks. While the shocks are usually brief and occur with the famine, the conditions that gave rise to poverty and vulnerability were usually established long before the catastrophe.

It is common to associate Africa's famines with drought and crop failure. While drought has been the immediate cause of some famines, bad weather can only have this result if poverty has already made people vulnerable to starvation. Such vulnerability may arise when consecutive years of poor rainfall and crop failure impoverish a community (as was the case in the West African Sahel in 1969–74 and in Ethiopia in 1973), or when military conflict or gross economic mismanagement has the same effect. As the experience of **Zimbabwe** demonstrates, a single year of drought in an otherwise functional economy need not lead to famine. Zimbabwe's drought in 1990–1 reduced the crop harvest to 20 percent of the normal level, but timely imports of food and distribution of aid averted widespread starvation. In countries where there is relatively little abject poverty, there is no relationship between the weather and famine.

Most late twentieth-century famines in Africa were triggered by military conflicts. When food supplies are barely adequate under normal circumstances, the disruptions caused by wars almost inevitably result in famine. In the 1990s alone, war combined with chronic poverty generated famines in Angola, **Liberia**, **Sierra Leone**, Somalia, **Sudan**, and Zaire (now the **Democratic Republic of Congo**). Military conflict reduces food supplies by removing manpower from fields, by making land inaccessible or unsafe for farming, by destroying stocks, by diverting food harvests, and by thwarting the distribution of food aid. Destruction of infrastructure and restriction of transportation hinders the movement of food to areas where local production is insufficient, creating localized famines. Civil wars tend to erode solidarity and social safety nets that poor households often rely on in times of scarcity. In some cases, participants in civil conflicts use food as a weapon, actively creating famines to meet military goals. The use of land mines extends the effects of war long past the duration of the actual conflict. In 1999 Mozambique was thought to have 1–2 million unexploded anti-personnel mines, while 9–15 million such devices were thought to be in Angola. As with active warfare, the mines contribute to hunger by killing and maiming food providers, removing land from cultivation, and making the transportation of food costly or impossible.

Food policy

As the Biblical story of Joseph's service to the Pharaoh attests, food security has been an issue of consideration for African leaders and intellectuals for millennia. Much of the modern thinking about food security can be traced to the work of Thomas Malthus, who in 1798 argued that because there is only a fixed amount of land available for farming, population growth will tend to outpace growth in food production, resulting inevitably in hunger, famine, and dramatic increases in mortality. A Malthusian focus on the relationship between total population and total food production dominated thinking about food security through the 1970s, and motivated national food policies based on achievement of national food self-sufficiency – the capacity of a country to grow enough food to meet the needs of its population. Starting in the mid-1970s, the economist Amartya Sen began to argue that hunger and famine were a result of the inability of people to access food, not necessarily insufficient food production. Sen's "entitlements" framework stressed that the relationship between people's resources and the cost of buying or growing food determines their vulnerability to hunger. While declining agricultural production can result in reduced access to food by lowering the incomes of rural people and raising the prices of food, it is also possible for people's ability to access food to rise even as food production in their country declines, and it is equally possible for many people to become impoverished and food insecure even as food production per capita in their country rises to achieve food self-sufficiency.

After Sen's work, food policy began to focus more on households' and individuals' access to food, and less on national food-production trends. In Africa, however, food security and food self-sufficiency may be closely related. Because most people in Africa rely on their own farm production for both the food they consume and their livelihoods, declining food production implies reduced incomes. Furthermore, high transportation costs in much of Africa mean that when local food production is low, food can only be shipped in at high cost and with a high price. Consequently the crisis in food security in Africa is closely related to the decline in food and agricultural production per capita. Reversing the declining trend in food production per capita could address the food-security crisis, if the increased food production were achieved in a manner that raised the incomes of people who are vulnerable to hunger. However, increasing production while leaving the poorest in poverty will not solve the food crisis, whereas lifting the poor out of poverty without increasing food production could, in principle, free them from hunger.

Access to food is constrained by poverty. The rich very rarely suffer involuntary hunger, but the poor live in its shadow. Addressing Africa's food crises means addressing the complex problem of poverty alleviation in the continent. In some countries, reducing poverty might be achieved by increasing food production. In those places, national food self-sufficiency could be a route to food security for all. In other regions, production of non-food crops or industrial products could be the better way to reduce poverty and fight hunger. Finding the effective and appropriate paths to combat poverty is the challenge for the twenty-first century in each of the African states that now faces food crises.

See also: agrarian change; economy: post-independence; environmental change; health and disease; peasants; population

Further reading

Braun, J. von, Teklu, T. and Webb, P. (1999) *Famine in Africa: Causes, Responses and Prevention*, Baltimore: Johns Hopkins University Press.

Dreze, J., Sen, A. and Hussain, A. (eds.) (1995) *The Political Economy of Hunger: Selected Essays*, Oxford: Clarendon Press.

Foster, P. and Foster, H. (1999) *The World Food Problem*, 2nd edn., Boulder: Lynne Rienner.

Sen, A. (1981) *Poverty and Famines*, Oxford: Oxford University Press.

Smith, L. and Haddad, L. (2000) *Explaining Child Malnutrition in Developing Countries: A Cross Country Analysis*, International Food Policy Research Institute Research Report 111, Washington, D.C.: IFPRI.

UNFAO (1999) *The State of Food Insecurity in the World*, Rome: UNFAO.

ALEX WINTER-NELSON

francophone Africa

Africa provides historians with a particularly striking framework for the exploration of complex and complicated questions pertaining to colonialism, neo-colonialism, and **decolonization**. Following the now notorious "scramble for Africa," European language dissemination accelerated on the continent, and Africa continues to be described and demarcated according to the linguistic structures enacted through colonial contact with European powers.

France's most significant activity in Africa dates back to this historical juncture, although there were precursors to this revitalized imperial activity: explorers and travelers had long been active in Africa on France's behalf (most notably Pierre Savorgnan de Brazza), and **Algeria** had been a colony since 1830. Furthermore, any discussion of francophone Africa that focused exclusively on the activities of the French themselves would be inaccurate, since Belgium exercised considerable influence in the Belgian Congo under the leadership of King Leopold II (1865–1909) who had founded the International Association for the Exploration and Civilization of Africa in 1876.

Most commonly, francophone Africa is associated with the sub-Saharan region, although many other areas of Africa experienced – and continue to experience – significant French influence. In **North Africa**, in addition to the colony in Algeria, **Tunisia** and **Morocco** were French protectorates from (respectively) 1883 and 1912 until 1956 when they became independent nation-states. Countries in which French is today at least one of the official or administrative languages include **Benin**, **Burkina Faso**, **Central African Republic**, **Chad**, **Congo**, **Côte d'Ivoire**, **Democratic Republic of Congo**, **Djibouti**, **Gabon**, **Guinea**, **Madagascar**, **Mali**, **Mauritania**, Morocco, **Niger**, **Rwanda**, **Senegal**, **Togo**, and Tunisia. However, if one adheres to the more inclusive parameters outlined by the Intergovernmental Agency for the **Francophonie**, francophone Africa would also incorporate Algeria, **Burundi**, and **Egypt**. As far as Algeria is concerned, policies have been implemented designed to restrict expression in languages associated with European colonial histories, while in Egypt there are only a few French speakers.

The colonial enterprise included pedagogic (colonial education), religious (widespread missionary activity), political (the colonial state and administration), and of course economic (colonial economy) branches (see **economy: colonial**; **education: colonial**; **state: colonial**). These various mechanisms contributed towards the broader objective of achieving assimilation and generating cultural models based on a French prototype. To this end, France set up the conglomerate known as **French West Africa** (Afrique Occidentale Française) in 1895, with its capital in **Dakar**, which brought together as a federation regions that are today the independent nation-states of Benin, Burkina Faso, Côte d'Ivoire, Guinea, Mali, Mauritania, Niger, and Senegal. This was followed by the creation in 1910 of **French Equatorial Africa** (Afrique Equatoriale Française), with its capital **Brazzaville**, grouping the Central African Republic, Chad, Congo, and Gabon under the same jurisdiction. The Belgian Congo, meanwhile, remained under Belgian control.

A number of factors contributed to the gradual process of dismantling the empires of France and Belgium after the **Second World War**, foremost among which were anti-colonial resistance and insufficient resources to continue financing the colonies. Although General de Gaulle's famous speech in Brazzaville in 1944 did not offer independence from French rule, the *loi cadre* of 1956 allowed for precisely that: the gradual – and for the most part relatively peaceful (in sharp contrast to the bitter Franco-Algerian War of 1954–62) – transition from autonomous rule toward independence within the boundaries created by colonial partition of Africa, culminating in sovereignty for most countries during the early 1960s.

Newly independent countries experimented with and adopted many political systems: monarchy, military rule, Marxism–Leninism, African socialism, and so on. Naturally Africa was not immune to the various global realignments that characterized the period after the end of the Cold War and the fracturing of the Soviet Union during the late 1980s and early 1990s. In fact these events generated particular consequences for francophone Africa. Various experiments with democratic and electoral reform took place, and national conferences were held in a spirit of reconciliation between countries with political histories as diverse as Benin, Chad, Congo, Gabon, Niger, Madagascar, Mali, Togo, and Zaire (now the **Democratic Republic of Congo**). Furthermore, this period in history also coincided with the deaths of many of francophone Africa's long-time leaders, notably Ahmed Sékou Touré of Guinea in 1984, Félix Houphouët-Boigny of Côte d'Ivoire in 1993, and Joseph Désiré Mobutu (Mobutu Sese Seko) of Zaire in 1997. However, financial concerns, political corruption, and ethnic rivalry have jeopardized social equilibrium, and most countries enjoy at best only limited political stability, and at worst the constant threat of civil violence.

Nevertheless, francophone Africa continues to yield a plethora of extraordinarily vibrant and original cultural practitioners and intellectuals (see

intellectuals: post-independence), receiving international acclaim for its **cinema**, **literature**, and **music**, while the predominantly Christian and Muslim religious communities are thriving. Significantly, debates on the question of abandoning the European colonial linguistic heritage have not received the same degree of attention in sub-Saharan Africa as in **anglophone Africa**, where relinquishing English in favor of indigenous languages has gained considerable currency. Paradoxically then, francophone Africa appears to foster circumstances conducive to the elaboration of a collaborative network in French among those Africans who have navigated and traversed together the fragile landscape of the colonial experience.

It is also significant that, as francophone Africa enters the twenty-first century, individual member countries are now treated by the French Ministry for Foreign Affairs in the same manner as any other foreign country, rather than as one large separate *département*. This symbolic gesture allows individual member-states to maintain their link to the international francophone community, while simultaneously reinforcing francophone Africa's independence from imperializing and neo-colonial impulses.

See also: African religions; Arab Maghreb Union; colonial Africa; intellectuals: colonial; intellectuals: post-independence; nationalist movements; race and ethnicity; socialisms and socialists

Further reading

Clark, J.F. and Gardinier, D.E. (eds.) (1997) *Political Reform in Francophone Africa*, Boulder: Westview Press.

Kirk-Greene, A. and Bach, D. (eds.) (1995) *State and Society in Francophone Africa since Independence*, London: St. Martin's Press.

Manning, P. (1998) *Francophone Sub-Saharan Africa: 1880–1995*, Cambridge: Cambridge University Press.

DOMINIC THOMAS

Francophonie

Widely accepted as having been coined by the French nineteenth-century geographer Onésime Reclus (1837–1916) as a way of classifying communities according to their shared cultural characteristics, the term "Francophonie" means many things to many people. As a branch of a governmental body, under whose aegis former colonized and occupied communities sharing French as a communicative tool are gathered, Francophonie exhibits all the dangers and shortcomings inherent to any ideology. However, when the metamorphoses the French language has undergone to accommodate the remarkable cultural, political, and social circumstances of its speakers are accorded the recognition they deserve, the plural form – Francophonies – can be seen to be more valid than the paternalistic and hegemonic singular term Francophonie.

The Francophonie movement – if indeed one can refer to it in this manner – has historical roots in the violent and dehumanizing practices inherent to the objectives of the French civilizing mission and colonial education (see **education: colonial**). To think about Francophonie is thus also to confront the complicated history of French contact with other areas of the world. Depending on what criteria are employed in order to calculate the number of speakers of French – degree of proficiency, status as a mother-tongue, official national language, colonial legacy – figures vary up to a maximum of about 100 million worldwide. The French language can then be said to be present on every continent, in countries as diverse as **Congo**, **Madagascar**, Guadeloupe, Canada, **Mauritius**, Lebanon, India, Vietnam, and New Caledonia. No matter how one chooses to situate oneself with regard to Francophonie itself, the fact remains that more people speak French outside of France today than within its hexagonal borders.

The first summit of francophone heads of state was held in France in 1986, bringing together "those countries having in *common* the usage of French." Subsequent summits have been held at Quebec in Canada (1987), at **Dakar** in **Senegal** (1989), at Paris in France (1991), at Grand Baie in

Mauritius (1993; at this summit the defining criterion was altered to incorporate "countries *sharing* the usage of French"), at **Cotonou** in **Benin** (1995), at Hanoi in Vietnam (1997), and at Moncton in Canada (1999). There are now almost fifty member-states.

As early as 1970, on the initiative of twenty-one governments, the Agency for Cultural and Technical Cooperation (ACCT) was founded, a precursor to what is today the Intergovernmental Agency for Francophonie under the leadership of the former Secretary General of the United Nations, Boutros Boutros-Ghali. The organization's agenda includes cultural, economic, political, and social activities, and given its international membership is an increasingly respected and powerful body.

While the various frameworks invoked to describe international French-language communities have changed over time, transitions which have for the most part reflected concerns about Francophonie's hegemonic potential, emphasis has remained on developing adequate structures to foster the enriching possibilities available to such communities. Xavier Deniau, who has been an active proponent of Francophonie, underlined as early as 1975 the importance of promoting the respective cultures of francophone states, while nevertheless insisting on the communicative potential created by historical links. Léopold Sédar Senghor, a noted Negritude poet and president of Senegal from 1960 to 1980, also suggested ways in which Francophonie should be recontextualized, while foregrounding the dependence of France on its former colonies – but this time in a constructive, mutually constitutive relationship.

A somewhat paradoxical dynamic has been witnessed on a cultural level: International francophone writers and those residing in France's post-colonial communities have enjoyed increased exposure through France's efforts to promote the French language in the global linguistic community, while simultaneously being recuperated by France in a mutually symbiotic network of relations. Indeed, comments formulated by some of these cultural practitioners have much to reveal concerning the potential of Francophonie. For example, the Congolese novelist Henri Lopes has distinguished writing *French* from writing *in French*; his fellow countryman, Tchicaya U Tam'si, saw his own work as an opportunity to enrich his colonial linguistic heritage through cultural synthesis, arguing that while the French language had colonized him, he in turn now had the opportunity to colonize the French language. Perhaps the words of another Congolese writer, Sony Labou Tansi, exemplify a more cautious approach, through their emphasis on the imperializing tendencies of Francophonie's forefathers. For Tansi, writing in French is inseparable from originary colonial violence, a factor he fastens on in order to invoke the competitive and affirmative dimension of continued usage of French.

Clearly Francophonie must endeavor to accommodate the remarkable cultural, political, and social circumstances of its speakers, underlining points of intersection between cultures that have in common the French language. Once this has been achieved, interaction will move away from competition towards reciprocal dialogue, thereby no longer duplicating a relationship between dominant and subordinate cultures. Instead, it will stimulate the formulation of imaginative solutions to the demands and exigencies of such alternative configurations, enabling Francophonie to offer a productive framework for debates and various configurations of global discourse.

See also: francophone Africa; French West Africa; French Equatorial Africa; intellectuals: colonial; intellectuals: post-independence; literature

Further reading

Deniau, X. (1983) *La francophonie*, Paris: Presses Universitaires de France.

Judge, A. (1996) "The Institutional Framework of *la francophonie*," in L. Ibnlfassi and N. Hitchcott (eds.), *African Francophone Writing: A Critical Introduction*, Oxford and Washington, D.C.: Berg.

Le Marchand, V. (1999) *La francophonie*, Toulouse: Editions Milan.

Senghor, L.S. (1977) *Liberté III: Négritude et civilisation de l'universel*, Paris: Seuil.

Tétu, M. (1988) *La Francophonie: Histoire, problématique, perspectives*, Montréal: Guérin Littérature.

DOMINIC THOMAS

Freetown, Sierra Leone

Freetown was founded in 1787 by the Sierra Leone Company as a home for the Black Poor who had been promised manumission for fighting alongside the British in the American War of Independence. Other groups, such as the Maroons from Jamaica and the Nova Scotians, were also settled in the colony, and later joined by recaptives (captives bound for slavery) from slave boats on the High Seas who were subsequently freed in the colony by British naval vessels. In 1797 the Company was given a Royal Charter, and Freetown became a city with a mayor and aldermen – a tradition that lasted until local government was replaced by direct rule with the appointment of Sierra Leone's first president, Siaka Stevens, in the late 1970s.

The period from the 1830s to the 1870s was marked by pioneering intellectual activity, with a local Renaissance following the establishment of Fourah Bay College and a succession of post-primary schools after 1845. These educational institutions attracted students from all over the subregion, with the result that Freetown was described in the late nineteenth century as the "Athens of West Africa." From the mixed populations and influences that marked the period, a lingua franca emerged around the Westernized Africans. They soon became known as the Creoles, and their language became Krio. Not only did this group lead the British modernization of the region in terms of education, trade, and commerce, but they soon emerged as point of reference for other social groups and nationalities in the region. The Creoles boasted many Victorian luminaries, among them Sir Samuel Lewis, the first African knight; Dr. Africanus Horton, the first African to successfully own and run a commercial bank; and Bishop Samuel Ajayi Crowther, the first Anglican bishop. However, the bipolarity in the administration of Freetown, with Freetown itself administered as separate from the rest of the country, fostered a sense of division in the country, particularly after 1896, sowing the seeds of conflict that were to dog Sierra Leone in the late colonial and post-colonial periods.

When it gained its independence in 1961, Freetown was maintained as the capital of and remained the hub of commercial and administrative life in Sierra Leone. Freetown is surrounded by a series of mountain ranges, beautiful beaches, and one of the finest natural harbors in the world. Throughout the **Second World War** Freetown was an important station for the Royal Navy and, not surprisingly, provision was made in the independence agreement with Britain that when necessary facilities would continue to be provided for the Royal Navy. Prior to the disruption and displacement of much of the population by the civil war, which started in 1991, the spatial distribution of population reflected ethnic and religious settlements from the Victorian period: the eastern part of the city, including Foulah Town, Fourah Bay, Cline Town, and Magazine, was predominantly Muslim; the central and western parts, including Akemori, Portuguese Town, and Grassfield Kroo Town Road, remained predominantly Christian. By the end of the century Freetown was an overcrowded city, whose population consisted mainly of people displaced from the countryside, and with many buildings from the Victorian era destroyed during fighting between government troops and their allies and the rebels of the Revolutionary United Front and their one-time allies, the Armed Forces Revolutionary Council.

Further reading

Last, M. and Richards, P. (eds.) *Sierra Leone 1787–1987: Two Centuries of Intellectual Life*, Manchester: Manchester University Press.

A.B. ZACK-WILLIAMS

French Equatorial Africa

The first French colonists arrived in Equatorial Africa in 1839 and settled on the Gabon River. In 1849 they founded Libreville as the capital of the colony. French Equatorial Africa (originally called French Congo) was officially established in 1910. With its capital at **Brazzaville**, the federation was formed in large part through the efforts of Savorgnan de Brazza, who forged the link between French possessions in the Congo basin and those in **West Africa**. French Equatorial Africa comprised the present-day **Central African Republic**, **Chad**, **Congo**, and **Gabon**. The federation was ruled by a governor-general, resident in Brazzaville, with a deputy in each of the four territories. Until 1920 Chad and Ubangi-Shari were a single territory. About 259,000 square kilometers were ceded to Germany as a result of the Agadir crisis (1911), but were returned to France by the Treaty of Versailles.

In Equatorial Africa – except for the coastal areas of **Cameroon** and most of the Gabon and Central Congo rain forest, which contained natural products of interest to the European market (wild rubber, tropical timber, oil palms, and so forth) – the colonial administration systematically extracted the cost of administration from local peoples. In the short space of a few decades the population suffered great brutality and the region saw a significant level of depopulation as a result of this colonial encounter. The French granted about 70 percent of the territory to forty-one private concessionary companies, which survived until the 1920s. The allocation of land for plantations to European companies and individual settlers necessitated a much greater degree of forced labor. Company agents raided the forest people, seizing hostages and forcing villagers to hand over fixed quotas of ivory and rubber. In the Central Congo thousands of men were forced to work for very low wages as porters carrying supplies for the French army of conquest in Chad. Forced labor was also used in the building of railways from the coast at Pointe Noire to Brazzaville on the northern shores of Malebo Pool. The brutality and disease that confronted Africans in the labor camps led to the deaths of an estimated 16,000 in the railway projects alone, as well as to the decimation of villages. The brutal nature of colonial extraction of wild rubber, ivory, labor, and taxation led to armed rebellion during 1928–9. The situation in French Equatorial Africa thus became problematic both for colonial administrators and for the African population – even more so because for Africans the colonial situation threatened both their livelihood and their lives.

The depression of the 1930s and the political economy of the **Second World War** had profound political and economic consequences for the region. The conditions created by the depression and the war proved propitious for the growth of political movements. The failure to manage the territories through the private sector was also a major source of discontent. The failure of the concessionary system raised the political cost of local rule by provoking African resistance in the region. A new generation of administrators demanded reforms, with the support of the leftwing Popular Front government in France that had come into office in 1936. But the neo-mercantile stance, which aimed at integrating the colonies into the metropolitan economy, was incompatible with the liberal impulse to grant local populations greater self-determination.

As in other parts of Africa, the Second World War became a major catalyst for fundamental changes. It brought increased hardship to Africans and political turmoil at home, but also provided Equatorial Africa with an opportunity to chart a new course. During the Second World War, the federation supported the Free French and rallied against the Vichy regime. During the Fourth French Republic, French Equatorial Africa was given representation in the French parliament and in the assembly of the French Union.

Until the 1950s political organization in French Equatorial Africa was weak. French investment in the colonies in the 1950s led to the emergence of a new elite that became interested in political reform. In 1956 the French parliament passed the *loi cadre*, which granted full internal autonomy, but did not cede control over foreign policy, defense, or economic policy affecting the franc zone. The weakened economic and political position of France after the war provided the opportunity for the French government to incorporate their African colonies into a form of self-sufficient economic unit, and to experiment with the liberal ideology of the Gaullists and their left-wing allies. This led to the launch of a series of development projects within the African territories under the auspices of the Fonds d'investissement et de développement économique et social des Territoires d'Outre-Mer (FIDES).

The postwar development bears witness to increased African participation in the economy of the federation. But the increased participation of Africans in commerce brought them into conflict with Europeans. The period also witnessed the emergence of nationalist leadership. Nevertheless, the structure of the colonial state and the relationship of the African elite with the official bureaucracy influenced the **decolonization** process in Equatorial Africa, where African leaders had closer ties with Europeans and ethnic loyalty was more defined than elsewhere in Africa. French Equatorial Africa was very isolated from the external ideological influences that impacted European–African relations in the era of decolonization. But significant changes followed the end of the Second World War, with government support and the extension of French citizenship to Africa following the 1946 constitution. De Gaulle put the *loi cadre* into effect in 1958. The constituent territories voted to become autonomous republics. The federation was dissolved, and in 1959 the new republics formed a loose association called the Union of Central African Republics. In August 1960 they became fully independent republics within the French Community.

See also: economy: colonial; First World War

Further reading

Austen, R.A. and Headrick, R. (1983) "Equatorial Africa Under Colonial Rule," in D. Birmingham and P.M. Martin (eds.), *History of Central Africa*, vol. 2, London and New York: Longman.

Cooper, F. (1996) *Decolonization and African Society: The Labor Question in French and British Africa*, Cambridge: Cambridge University Press.

CHIMA J. KORIEH

French West Africa

A former federation of eight administrative groups, French West Africa was under French rule from 1895 until 1958. The constituent territories were **Senegal**, French **Guinea**, **Côte d'Ivoire**, and the French **Sudan**, to which Dahomey was added in 1899. Certain territories of the Sudan were grouped together under the name Senegambia and **Niger** (1903), which was to become Upper Senegal and Niger (1904). At the same time **Mauritania** was added to French West Africa. The colony of Upper Volta, founded in 1909 and attached in 1932 to Côte d'Ivoire, was reestablished as a territory of the federation in 1947. Upper Senegal and Niger was renamed the French Sudan in 1920. The federation was created in 1895 to consolidate French holdings in West Africa, and was definitively constituted in 1904. It was ruled by a governor-general, who resided first in Saint-Louis, then in Dakar.

French colonialism provoked stiff resistance from Africans in different parts of the territory. The most important leaders of resistance and anti-French feeling were Ahmadu, Sultan of Segu; Samori Toure of Kankan; Babemba of Sikasso; King Behanzin of Dahomey; Morgho Naba Boukari Koutou of Mossi; Rabeh of the **Chad** basin; King Agoliagbo of Abomey; and Mahmadu Lamine of Senegal. **Islam** and **slavery** were important in shaping French colonial rule in West Africa and the relationship between the French administrators and the local elite. By 1919 armed resistance and opposition had ceased. The political institutions of the region varied widely. But the French utilized local chiefs in administration and attempts were made to impose canton chiefs where chieftaincy institutions did not exist. Hostile chiefs were replaced and often states that were considered too large were dismantled. French policy stressed the development of assimilation, and later association, with the French awareness of cultural diversity leading to this change.

The crises of the **First** and **Second World Wars** and the **Great Depression** brought about fundamental changes. During the Great Depression the prices of African produce – groundnuts, coffee, and cocoa – declined drastically in the world market. The outbreak of the Second World War further disrupted the market for colonial produce that had previously been guaranteed by the metropole. The Second World War, in particular, also weakened the political and ideological foundation of French colonial rule in Africa, becoming a major catalyst for fundamental changes. French West Africa contributed 170,000 combatants to French war efforts, with the federation supporting the Free French and rallying against the Vichy regime. Free French recognition of this situation led to a government-sponsored conference in Brazzaville in January and February 1944, held to discuss colonial reforms. The war had exposed the poverty of Africans, especially within less endowed territories, but also provided French West Africa with an opportunity to seek political reforms. During what has been referred to as a "second colonization," this period witnessed greater infrastructural development, and the expansion of earlier forms of capital penetration in the territory. This was mainly carried out through the activities of the French Fonds d'investissement et de développement économique et social (FIDES).

The Second World War fostered a new relationship between France and her overseas territories in West and Equatorial Africa. The new relationship was institutionalized in the French Union of 1946. This policy affected the process of **decolonization**. Demands for secession or independence outside the assimilation framework were treated as treasonable and suppressed. In 1947 the railway workers of French West Africa – 20,000 of them – went on strike for five-and-a-half months in most parts of the territory. This was one of the great strikes that rocked postwar Africa, an epic event that has been immortalized in Ousmane Sembene's great novel *God's Bits of Wood*. Following on the heels of a successful strike by civil servants in 1946, the strikers demanded parity with French workers. The strike not only helped reshape relations between labor and capital, or more broadly between colonies and metropoles, it also exposed fissures between the working class and the nationalist elite, and within the labor movement itself. Colonial officials were anxious to prevent the labor force from turning into political pressure groups, but the strike nonetheless spilled over into a wider and longer term proletarian struggle and anti-colonial mobilization.

Mass parties developed under Sédar Senghor (the Bloc Démocratique Sénégalais) and Félix Houphouët-Boigny (the Parti Démocratique du Côte d'Ivoire). Political activity in the rest of the territory was weak. In 1958 the constituent territories, except for Guinea, became autonomous republics within the French Community. Guinea instead chose to become independent, earning it the ire of the French government. With Guinea's independence, the federation could no longer survive, and it was dissolved in 1959. By 1960 the former colonial territories had all become independent republics, with French Sudan changing its name to **Mali**. Upper Volta was renamed **Burkina Faso** in 1984. On achieving independence the new nations signed agreements with France on foreign aid and defense, which reinforced French dominance of the region well into the 1990s.

See also: economy: colonial; workers

Further reading

Cooper, F. (1996a) *Decolonization and African Society: The Labor Question in French and British Africa*, Cambridge: Cambridge University Press.

—— (1996b) " 'Our Strike': Equality, Anticolonial Politics and the 1947–48 Railway Strike in French West Africa," *The Journal of African History* 37, 1: 81–118.

Freund, B. (1998) *The Making of Contemporary Africa: The Development of African Society Since 1800*, 2nd edn., Boulder: Lynne Rienner.

Gifford, P. and Roger Louis, W.M. (1971) *France and Britain in Africa: Imperial Rivalry and Colonial Rule*, New Haven and London: Yale University Press.

Klein, M.A. (1998) *Slavery and Colonial Rule in French West Africa*, Cambridge: Cambridge University Press.

CHIMA J. KORIEH

Fulani

Fulani (also known as Pulaar, Pulo, Peul, Fula, and Fulbe/Fulfulde) is the language of a large group of people who are mostly located in the western African nations. Over the centuries, the language spread because the Fulani people were mostly pastoralists who traveled large distances to herd their livestock. By the end of the twentieth century, different varieties of Fulani were spoken across the region. Altogether the number of Fulani speakers was estimated at about 22 million people. Available sources indicate that 2.5 million people spoke the language in **Guinea**, 2,121,140 in **Senegal**, 178,000 in **Sierra Leone**, 175,000 in **Mali**, 150,000 in **Mauritania**, 217,800 in **Guinea-Bissau**, 233,300 in the **Gambia**, 450,000 in **Niger**, 668,700 in **Cameroon**, 8 million in **Nigeria**, 158,146 in **Chad**, 156,000 in **Central African Republic**, 750,000 in **Burkina Faso**, 48,200 in **Togo**, and 90,000 in **Sudan**. Thus Fulani is one of the most widely spoken languages in **West Africa**.

The most important dialects of the language are: Tukulor, primarily spoken in northern Senegal; Fulakunda, spoken in southeastern Senegal and Guinea-Bissau; Peul Jeeri, spoken in the region of Louga in Senegal; the Adamawa Fulani and Bororo Fulani of Cameroon; the Bagirmi Fula of Chad and the Central African Republic; the Bauchi Fulani and Toroobe Fulani of Nigeria; the Benin/Togo Fulani of Togo; the Gurma Fulani of Burkina Faso; the Krio Fula of Sierra Leone; the Fula Kita of Mali and Mauritania; the Sokoto Fulani of Niger and Nigeria; the Liptako Fula of Burkina Faso; and the Western Fulani of Niger. These varieties are generally mutually intelligible, despite differences in vocabulary.

Although the Bantu-like features of the language (consonant mutations) caused controversy among early scholars over its classification in the Atlantic language group, it was eventually accepted that the language belonged to the West-Atlantic branch of the Niger-Congo phylum. The major African languages related to Fulani are those of the West-Atlantic branch, especially Wolof and Seereer. These share more phonological, morphological, and lexical properties with Fulani than other languages in the Atlantic language group. Due to their long coexistence, these languages have been engaged with Fulani in a relationship of mutual influence and borrowing.

Historically the Fulani were mainly nomadic herders and traders. The routes they established in West Africa provided extensive links throughout the region, fostering economic and political ties between otherwise isolated ethnic groups. The Fulani were influential in West African politics, economics, and history for centuries. They played a significant role in the rise and fall of the Mossi states in Burkina Faso, contributed to the migratory movements of people southward through Niger and Nigeria into Cameroon, and were also responsible for introducing **Islam** and spreading the religion throughout western Africa.

Because of their early Islamization – dating to the thirteenth century – the Fulani people have long been influenced by Arabic, which allowed them to use the classical Arabic script of the Koran to write poems; then, during the twentieth century, the language came under the influence of French because of French colonization. The major sources of the spread and development of the Fulani language and culture throughout West Africa remained trade, Islam, and the nomadic nature of the Fulani lifestyle. Fulani dairy products were sold or traded to sedentary farmers for agricultural products and other luxury items. Fulani traders then traded these newly acquired items between various groups along their nomadic routes. Members of individual Fulani groups often settled among their sedentary neighbors, intermarrying and establishing trading contacts for future business transactions. Furthermore, Fulani speakers spread Islam in West Africa through trade, commerce, intermarriage, and sometimes jihad, such as those conducted by Fulani leaders Usman dan Fodio, Elhadji Omar Foutiyou Tall, or Maba Diakhou Ba. These factors contributed to the spread of Fulani people, their language, and their culture in twentieth-century West Africa.

Although linguists had been discussing the classification of West-Atlantic languages in Africa for decades, it was only from the 1970s that serious research was conducted on languages such as Fulani. The Center of Applied Linguistics of Dakar (Centre de Linguistique Appliquée de Dakar or CLAD) was commissioned by the Senegalese government to develop didactic materials for the promotion of Senegalese national languages alongside French. The CLAD subsequently developed writing systems for the six major spoken languages in Senegal: Wolof, Fulani (Pulaar), Mandinka, Soninke, Joola, and Seereer.

By the end of the twentieth century the study of African languages, especially Wolof and Fulani (Pulaar), was flourishing in Senegal: A ministry had been made responsible for the promotion of national languages, and several **non-governmental organizations** were involved in the teaching and promotion of local languages and cultures. In addition several Fulani speakers held doctoral degrees in linguistics and language-related areas, and were actively involved in research for the preservation, protection, and promotion of the Fulani language and culture. Guinea also had an extensive literature in Fulani, although the orthography was different from that used elsewhere. In Cameroon and Chad dictionaries and grammars of Fulani also existed. Unfortunately efforts to promote Fulani were more limited in the other countries. The overall development of literature in Fulani also remained less developed than it was for other major West African languages, such as **Hausa** and **Yoruba**. Nevertheless this seems likely to change, as a new generation of students in primary and some secondary schools in Fulani areas are being taught in Fulani.

Further reading

"Ethnologue: Areas: Africa – Fulani" (January 2002), http://www.ethnologue.com.

Ngom, F. (2001) "Pulaar," in J. Garry and C. Rubino (eds.), *Encyclopedia of the World's Major Languages: Past and Present*, New York: The H.W. Wilson Company.

Sylla, Y. (1982) *Grammaire Moderne du Pulaar*, Dakar: Les nouvelles éditions Africaines.

FALLOU NGOM

G

Gabon

Gabon, which covers an area of 267,677 square kilometers, is located on the Atlantic Coast in **Central Africa** and bordered by **Equatorial Guinea**, **Cameroon**, and **Congo**. The country had an estimated population of 1.5 million in 2000. Although dominated by rain forests, more than half of people in this sparsely populated country lived in the capital cities of Libreville and the economic hub of Port Gentil. The French government, which occupied parts of Gabon from 1843 onward, greatly influenced politics in the country after independence in 1960 by supporting the authoritarian regimes of Léon Mba and Omar Bongo. European companies – in the colonial period primarily exporting timber, but after 1960 also oil and mineral resources – dominated national politics and received strong support from the colonial and independent governments of Gabon. The end result of these policies was Gabon's reliance on foreign trade and its very high cost of living.

Gabon began as a small French post, Libreville, founded in 1843. Coastal clan chiefs surrendered their sovereignty in the Gabon Estuary, but the majority of Gabon was not conquered until 1900. Colonial invasion faced resistance from Fang clans in central Gabon and Punu, Nzebi, Obamba, and other groups in southern Gabon until the 1910s. Divisions between clans and the relative isolation of forest peoples hindered efforts at cooperation among resistance movements. The establishment of French concessionary companies in 1900, backed by French troops, led to violence and the destruction of older trade networks. Gabon became part of **French Equatorial Africa** in 1910.

The **First World War** devastated Gabon, as French and German forces clashed in northern Gabon and Cameroon. High taxes and state demands for soldiers and porters drew men out of villages and created widespread insecurity. The establishment of numerous timber camps in the Gabon Estuary and along the Ogooué River in Central Gabon brought many more men from villages in the Gabonese interior to the coast. Massive **food crises** struck most regions of Gabon between 1916 and 1926, killing over 60,000 people. Before the 1930s the French government exclusively supported timber camps, rather than building roads or creating an educational infrastructure.

French rule brought numerous cultural changes. Christian missionary efforts in the nineteenth century spread with colonial occupation (see **Christianity**). Their widely scattered missions offered Africans European-style education, as well as a foreign faith. Fang clans in the 1920s created a new religious movement, Bwiti, borrowing from Catholic and southern Gabonese religious traditions to criticize colonial rule. Mission-educated men adopted European clothes and language, but also led early efforts to challenge French colonial rule. A minority of mission-school graduates, such as Anchouey Laurent and Léon Mba, called for political reforms and increased African representation in the 1920s. The French government did little to give power to local chiefs or educated people before the **Second World War**.

Although officials briefly supported the pro-Axis Vichy government in France, Gabonese politics changed significantly after the war. De Gaulle gave new freedoms to Africans at the 1944 Brazzaville Conference, and African political parties formed after 1945. In the 1950s Léon Mba's Bloc Démocratique Gabonais (BDG) party faced opposition from the Union Démocratique et Sociale Gabonaise (UDSG) led by educated Fang French parliamentary representative Jean-Hilare Aubame. Fearful of Aubame, the French government and European timber entrepreneurs backed Mba and helped him win elections in 1957. Mba did not support full independence, but the collapse of the Franco-African Community envisioned by de Gaulle led to **decolonization** and independence in 1960.

Gabonese politics changed as a result of independence and the discovery of petroleum reserves in 1956. Léon Mba soon began to act as a dictator, imprisoning rivals and creating a one-party state in 1964. When military officers attempted to overthrow him in 1964, French soldiers invaded Gabon and reinstated Mba. French oil companies, particularly Elf, dominated oil exports and gave large sums of money to the Gabonese government. French mining firms exported uranium and manganese. Timber and cocoa cash-cropping became much less important. At Mba's death in 1967, a thirty-two-year-old former officer named Albert-Bernard Bongo (he changed his name to Omar Bongo on his conversion to Islam in 1973) took power with the active aid of the French government. Bongo profited greatly from the influx of revenue from mining and oil. Besides building up his wealth and instituting state patronage on a massive scale, Bongo banned opposition political parties and manipulated local fears of sorcery to maintain power.

Independence brought social changes as well. Though most state revenue remained in the hands of Bongo and a small cadre of officials, the development of public schools and ambitious transportation projects allowed more mobility for Africans. Large numbers of villagers moved to Libreville in search of work and educational opportunities. Many West African migrants moved to Libreville and they now dominate all forms of petty trade and numerous skilled labor positions. Poor urban planning and the lack of state support for agriculture led to heavy dependence on foreign food imports and high prices in the cities. Although Gabon continues to be a very patriarchal country, with most government benefits going to men, a number of women have received post-graduate degrees and government posts.

After the late 1970s Bongo's regime encountered opposition and obstacles. The Gabonese economy suffered due to the drop in oil prices and the decline of its existing crude reserves. The International Monetary Fund set up an austerity plan in 1986 that led to hardship. Mouvement de Redressement National (MORENA) and other opposition parties led by Mba Abessole and Joseph Renjambé called for democratic reforms. Labor unrest among oil workers and the mysterious assassination of Renjembé led to riots in 1990. Bongo agreed to democratic elections, and won in 1993 and 1998. Despite the development of a small wealthy class, most Gabonese touched little of the country's wealth. Although freedom of the press and opposition parties flourished, many Gabonese remained frustrated and hoped for radical change.

See also: colonial conquest and resistance

Further reading

Gardinier, D. (1992) *Gabon*, Santa Barbara: Clio Press.

Yates, D. (1996) *The Rentier State in Africa: Oil Rent Dependency and Neocolonialism in the Republic of Gabon*, Trenton: Africa World Press Inc.

JEREMY RICH

Gaborone, Botswana

Gaborone, the capital of **Botswana**, has been at the forefront of the country's remarkable demographic and socioeconomic transformation since independence in 1966. At that time Botswana was one of the world's poorest countries, largely dependent on mixed agriculture and remittances from its migrant laborers in South African mines. Between 1965 and 1990 Botswana had the fastest growing economy in the world, fueled primarily by the discovery and mining of diamonds. Concurrently Gaborone became one of the world's fastest growing cities.

When designing the capital in the 1960s, town planners expected Gaborone's population of 3,855 would grow to 20,000 over a period of twenty years. But by 1981 the population had reached 59,657, and 133,468 by 1991. The preliminary census results for 2001 indicate a population of 185,891, a slowing growth rate partly explained by the expansion of neighboring villages. From its inception, Gaborone was a magnet for people seeking employment, primarily in construction and the civil service, not only to the inhabitants of Botswana but increasingly for migrants from all over Africa, from Asia, and from elsewhere. The construction of numerous paved roads and a reliable public transportation system enabled people to commute from nearby villages, such as Gabane and Mogoditshane, whose populations doubled in the 1990s.

By the end of the 1990s Gaborone was the center for national government, which had been dominated by the Botswana Democratic Party from independence; the local city government, however, was largely in the hands of the opposition Botswana National Front. Gaborone was also developing into a regional hub, hosting the headquarters of the **Southern African Development Community** (SADC) and a proposed regional financial center.

The former Bechuanaland Protectorate had been administered by the British from across the border in Mafikeng in **South Africa**, until the seat of governance was relocated in 1965. The decision to build a new capital at a small settlement, then called "Gaberones," had been made by the Legislative Council in 1961. Located on government land, Gaberones had been a railway stop with a nearby government camp that included the district commissioner, a prison, police, and public works. Among the possible sites for the future capital, Gaberones was selected because of its central location and the ease of access it offered to six of the eight ethnic territories, because it was seen as a place lacking a significant history of European or African interest, and because of its proximity to the Notwane River.

Gaborone's original master plan in 1963 was based on a "garden city" model of low-density development with separate motor and pedestrian traffic. Socioeconomic groups were separated by the size of residential plots and *de facto* racial segregation, despite the intention of avoiding the discriminatory practices of neighboring South Africa. To the north of the Mall, with its government offices and shops, large residential plots were affordable only for elite Batswana and expatriates. Residential plots were smaller to the south of the Mall, but were still unaffordable for the thousands of construction workers who lived in a squatter settlement just south of the city they were employed to build. In the 1970s the squatter settlement, called "Naledi," was recognised by the government and provided with infrastructure. By the end of the century Gaborone's planners were attempting to reduce the city's socioeconomic segregation by integrating different plot sizes, while both the poor and the affluent were building communities beyond the city's boundaries. Among Gaborone's problems were the high cost of living, an increasing crime rate, and a high incidence of HIV/AIDS. Despite these problems, the government continued to invest in the construction of the city, providing infrastructure, employment, and schools for the growing population.

Further reading

Edge, W.A. and Lekorwe, M.H. (eds.) (1998) *Botswana: Politics and Society*, Pretoria: van Schaik.

MIEKA RITSEMA

Gambia

Gambia is totally surrounded by **Senegal** and has a total area of 11,295 square kilometers. It had an estimated population of 1.4 million in 2000. For a time the French in Senegal tried to persuade the British government to exchange Gambia for some of the territories in other parts of Africa or elsewhere, but the idea was opposed by a strong lobby of British merchants and by local chiefs.

Under British rule, the administration of the country was divided between a "colony," comprising Bathurst (**Banjul**), and the rest of the country – called the "protectorate." While the colony was administered directly by the colonial governor, the protectorate was ruled by non-resident commissioners through the local chiefs. Bathurst became the seat of the colonial administration, and an important commercial center. It was here that the local elites founded the first newspapers, political associations, and labor unions.

After the **Second World War**, a series of constitutional reforms led to gradual increases in the number of Gambians in the legislative council, and the extension of the franchise to the protectorate. The first political parties were then formed, and the balance of power began shifting in favor of elites originating in the protectorate. They formed the Protectorate Peoples Party in 1959, later renamed the Peoples' Progressive Party (PPP), which was led by David (later Dawda) Jawara, a veterinary doctor.

As **decolonization** gathered momentum, the country's size, peculiar geographical position, lack of resources, and low level of development became reasons for questioning the viability of Gambia as an independent state. The culture and history shared by Gambia and Senegal persuaded some of the Gambian elite to consider the unification of their country with Senegal (which had become independent in 1960), an idea that was also quite appealing to Senegalese leaders. A United Nations mission recommended three options: integration, federation, or confederation. Senegalese leaders favored the first option, while the Gambian elite preferred the third. In the end Gambia chose to become independent in February 1965, with Dawda Jawara as president, while maintaining close cooperative relations with Senegal.

Post-independence politics was for a long time largely dominated by the PPP. Regular relatively open electoral contests, the existence of private newspapers and radio stations, as well as trade unions, and the relative absence of violations of civil and political rights of individuals and groups earned Gambia the reputation of being one of the few liberal democracies in Africa at the time. The economy meanwhile remained largely similar to what it had been under British rule: monocultural agriculture based on the export of groundnuts and groundnut products. The external sector was later expanded to include tourism and the reexport of imported foods and consumer goods, thanks to a very liberal trade regime. In the process, while an urban-based class of merchants and politicians was developing, a large proportion of urban youth were unemployed, leading the Senegalese authorities to complain about the parallel trade that had developed in the subregion.

On the political front, from 1975 new opposition parties were formed, including the National Convention Party (NCP), the National Liberation Party (NLP), the Movement for Justice in Africa (Gambia) (MOJA-G), and the Gambia Socialist Revolutionary Party (GSRP). The more radical parties were, however, banned when in 1980 the government claimed it had uncovered a conspiracy against it. The country's first major political crisis occurred on the night of 29–30 July 1981. A group of civilians, in alliance with officers of the Field Force (Gambia's security service – the country had no army), tried to overthrow the government. The coup attempt was suppressed with the assistance of Senegalese troops. In November of the same year, the governments of Senegal and Gambia announced the signing of an accord to form a confederation of the two countries. The confederation was to be gradually transformed into a federation. But seven years later the institutions of the confederation were dissolved: the motivation for it had ceased to exist for the Gambian leadership, which had established an army for the country and a security service for the head of state. Gambia even sent troops to **Liberia** as part of ECOMOG, the ECOWAS Monitoring Group.

Jawara had meanwhile been reelected twice, in 1982 and in 1987, with comfortable majorities. New opposition parties were created in 1986: the People's Democratic Organization for Independence and Socialism and the Gambia People's Party. At a congress of the PPP in 1992, Jawara announced his intention to retire from politics, but was persuaded to stay on. However, in July 1994 Jawara and the PPP government were overthrown by the still relatively young army, led by Yaya A.J.J. Jammeh, who was then only twenty-nine years old.

The Armed Forces Provisional Ruling Council (AFPRC) called themselves "soldiers with a difference." Initially announcing their intention to stay in office for four years, they were later pressurized into reducing the transition period to two years. In October 1996 Jammeh, who had retired from the army and formed a civilian party called the Alliance for Patriotic Reorientation and Construction (APRC), won the election. He was reelected five years later. The APRC established political dominance, although opposition parties were allowed to operate and continued to be formed.

The economic recovery program introduced in August 1986 led to rapid liberalization of the economy. The Jammeh government embarked on a number of road-building, education, health, and other development projects, and the country's internal and external debts became heavy, even though annual growth rates averaged 5 percent. The economy was still fragile, with a heavy dependence on tourism and foreign aid. The human rights record of the government was also poor, with frequent violations of press freedom and other basic human rights. The question of Senegambian integration remained on the back burner.

Further reading

Gailey, H.A. (1964) *A History of The Gambia*, London: Routledge.

Touray, O.A. (2000) *The Gambia and the World. A History of Foreign Policy of Africa's Smallest State, 1965–1995*, Hamburg: Institute of African Affairs.

EBRIMA SALL

genocides

While it is accepted that genocides are as old as human civilization, the term was not coined until the middle of the twentieth century. A Polish lawyer, Raphael Lemkin, formulated the term in response to the Nazi Holocaust against European Jews, combining derivatives from the Greek word for race (*genos-*) and the Latin suffix *-cide* (to kill). The concept was given much firmer legislative expression when the United Nations adopted the Convention on the Prevention and Punishment of the Crime of Genocide in December 1948. The UN definition will be used in this entry, although in a rather loose manner so that instances of genocide claimed by the victims can also be included. The UN definition embodies the destruction of or the intention to destroy national, ethnic, racial, or religious groups. One of the abiding definitional problems for genocide concerns how genocide may be differentiated from civil war, war crimes, indiscriminate massacres, and other arbitrary killings. In Africa during the twentieth century colonization went hand in hand with many massacres of indigenous populations. In the process their culture, polities, and economies were disrupted, so much so that the French philosopher Jean-Paul Sartre concluded that colonization was intrinsically genocidal.

Genocides need to be differentiated from genocidal massacres or one-off killings, which are not driven by sustained attacks and a policy of extermination. While this differentiation may be worthwhile, it is also necessary to point out that there is no Chinese wall separating the two. Instead a genocidal massacre could give way to a more generalized policy of genocide. The crucial aspect of the definition concerns the intention to destroy a group of people and the choice of victims according to their identity in relation to such a group.

Colonial genocides in Africa had earlier occurred in a range of situations. For example, in **South Africa** the San people, who had refused to be subjugated to outside rule, were systematically exterminated. They were hunted down as if they were not human. Indeed Kipling's notorious poem, "Take Up the White Man's Burden," talks about them being half devil and half child. Genocides did not end with colonialism. The violence of the colonized against each other has also spilled over into genocide. There may be a variety of reasons for this continuing violence, but one of the longest-lasting explanations has been the manner in which colonialism carved Africa up into geographic spaces that could be called states on the basis of spheres of interest decided in Berlin, rather than what might reasonably have been in the interests of the indigenous populations. The conception of differences between settlers and indigenous peoples remains an abiding metaphor for the difficulties of constructing inclusive and legitimate states in Africa. It is thus useful to differentiate between genocides committed by colonists in the pursuit of their colonial objectives and genocides during the post-colonial era. It should be remembered, however, that foreign influence continued long after independence in every African state, and this added dimension has aggravated rather than alleviated conflict.

It is no coincidence that Germany was implicated in the first genocide to happen on African soil in the twentieth century. Their genocidal colonial policy against the Hereros, and their genocidal massacre of the Namas between 1904 and 1908, are brutally captured in the words of General Lothar von Trotha, commander-in-chief of German forces in **Namibia**:

> Throughout my period of duty here the eastern border of the colony will remain sealed off and terrorism will be employed against any Herero showing up. *That nation must vanish from the face of the earth.* Having failed to destroy them with guns, I will have to achieve my end in that way.
> (Cited in Drechsler 1980: 161; my emphasis)

About 80 percent of the Herero population were killed. The survivors were initially kept in concentration camps, then dispersed across the entire country as forced labor. The Herero – and later the Nama – were singled out for extermination precisely because they stood in the way of German colonialism and expropriation of land. They had attempted to defend their land and, while their initial attacks may have been successful, they very rapidly became unarmed civilians at the mercy of the German army.

While colonial genocides were clearly aimed at eliminating threats to external domination, post-colonial genocides were structured by a different set of internal and external forces. The context for many horrendous atrocities – some of which approach the severity of genocides in the colonial era – became the various attempts to forge and legitimate new independent states under conditions of continued metropolitan economic control, and political and military interference.

Some of the most notorious perpetrators of genocide in post-colonial Africa include Jean-Bedel Bokassa, Idi Amin Dada, and Francisco Macías Nguema. Bokassa appointed himself president-for-life of the **Central African Republic** in 1965, and by 1977 had crowned himself emperor. He was responsible for genocidal massacres, especially of schoolchildren who had had the audacity to stone his car. Although Bokassa was clearly responsible for committing gross violations of **human rights** against his political opponents, he did not develop a fully fledged policy of extermination. Like Bokassa, Amin installed himself as president-for-life in **Uganda** in 1977, after overthrowing Milton Obote in 1971. Shortly thereafter he purged the Ugandan army of troops from the Acholi community, which he had singled out as a major threat to his rule. A policy of genocide was then carried out against the Acholi. Thousands were killed, and hundreds of thousands were forced into exile. Nguema, president of **Equatorial Guinea** when it became independent in 1968, appointed himself president-for-life in 1972. He imposed extreme dictatorial and repressive policies, leading to the flight of an estimated 100,000 **refugees** to the neighboring countries of **Gabon** and **Cameroon**. At least 50,000 people were killed in an orgy of arbitrary violence against those perceived to be political opponents. Nguema's dictatorship was characterized by campaigns against intellectuals, and virtually the entire elite was accused of plotting against the state.

Other countries that have witnessed large-scale genocides include **Sudan**, **Ethiopia**, **Nigeria**, and **Rwanda**. In Sudan the villages of the people of the Nuba mountains have, since the late 1980s, been subjected to horrendous attacks through the policy of "combing" – or burning – entire villages suspected of harboring supporters of the Sudan People's Liberation Army (SPLA). There have also been regular abductions, especially targeting the educated elite. This genocide involves both direct murder and a range of measures designed to induce famine, so that there can be no viable support for SPLA soldiers. Human rights organizations have described in graphic detail some of the atrocities perpetrated by the government of Sudan on the Nuba people. The ethnic and religious diversity of Sudan makes it difficult to categorize the conflictual situation in simple terms. For example, the discord is often portrayed as a conflict between an Islamic north and a Christian south, yet the Nuba live in the central part of Sudan and many of them are Muslims. But the government of Sudan has called them an "ugly culture that must be removed," so their sustained program seems to fall neatly under the definition of genocide.

In Ethiopia, soon after the 1974 revolution that removed Emperor Haile Selassie from power, the Dergue, under Mengistu Haile Mariam, embarked on a campaign of violence against political opponents that is aptly called "The Red Terror." Tens of thousands of people accused of plotting to overthrow the new government were either killed or abducted, especially members of the Ethiopian People's Liberation Party. Mengistu recently defended these killings, arguing that "the so-called genocide was a war in defence of the revolution." He is in exile in Zimbabwe, wanted in Ethiopia on charges of genocide, but the Zimbabwean government has refused to extradite him.

In December 1999 the Odi Coalition Against Genocide was formed by forty organizations of **civil society** in the Niger Delta region of Nigeria. The aim was to draw attention to genocidal massacres perpetrated by the Nigerian army in their attempt to secure safe conditions for exploitation of oil reserves by multinational companies. Ken Saro-Wiwa, executed alongside eight Ogoni comrades by the Abacha regime in 1995, wrote a moving account entitled *Genocide in Nigeria: The Ogoni Tragedy* (1992), in which he detailed the effect on smaller ethnic groups of the division of Nigeria into distinct spheres of control by the dominant ethnic groups. Earlier, during the Nigerian civil war (1967–70), an estimated one million people had perished. While some argue that there was a systematic attempt to annihilate the Igbo population through forced starvation, the civil war was complicated by the way in which federal and central power were exercised. It is thus not easily reduced to simple formulas. It is worth noting, however, that the International Committee on the Investigation of Crimes of Genocide received a well-documented complaint from the government of Biafra that accused the Nigerian government of genocide.

The Rwandan massacres of 1994 have sparked a wide-ranging debate about whether or not they should be called genocide. If the UN definition is used, events in Rwanda clearly fit the bill. There was definitely a widespread intention to wipe out the Tutsi minority. But one thing remains unexplained: How was it possible for the main victims of the genocide, the Tutsis, to gain power in the post-genocidal state? The answer lies in the role of the Rwanda Patriotic Front (RPF), and more specifically the Rwanda Patriotic Army (RPA), in the battle for state power. It seems clear that there was a desperate attempt on the part of the ruling Hutu regime to hang on to power in the face of the military advance of the RPA. One of the unique features of the Rwanda genocide was the generalized nature of the perpetrators. Members of the Hutu majority became killers for a wide variety of reasons. Some had been forced into exile from their homes as result of the RPF advance in Rwanda, and others were refugees from Tutsi-inspired genocides in neighboring **Burundi**. But the overarching ideological reason for their participation rests with the fear propagated by Hutu leaders that the RPA would reinstate the Tutsi as colonial overlords and subjugators of the Hutu. Organized by the state and a splintered army that was on the verge of defeat, the mass of the Hutu population were swayed to participate in the killing of Tutsis (as well as of those Hutus who did not support Hutu supremacy in Rwanda).

The genocides and genocidal massacres in Africa have raised critical questions about the nature of the state and about the construction of a legitimate normative framework in post-conflict situations. In Rwanda and Ethiopia there are ongoing trials and prosecutions of people accused of genocide. The higher level perpetrators in the Rwanda genocide are being tried in the International Criminal Tribunal for Rwanda, which sits in Arusha in **Tanzania**. About 120,000 Hutu are currently facing charges of genocide in Rwanda.

In 1999 the self-appointed paramount chief of the Herero people in Namibia, Dr. Kuaima Riaruako, approached the International Court of Justice in the Hague to lay a charge of genocide against the German government. While in opposition, the current ruling party in Germany agreed that what had been done to the Herero was indeed genocide. Since taking power, however, they have remained silent on the issue. The claim for war reparations is clearly on the agenda for the people of the Africa, in the same way as are reparations for **slavery** and colonialism.

See also: colonial conquest and resistance; human rights

References and further reading

African Rights (1995) *Facing Genocide: The Nuba of Sudan*, London: African Rights.

Drechsler, H. (1980) *"Let Us Die Fighting." The Struggle of the Herero and Nama against German Imperialism (1884–1915)*, London: Zed Books.

Mamdani, M. (2001) *When Victims Become Killers: Colonialism, Nativism and the Genocide in Rwanda*, Kampala: Fountain Publishers.

Saro-Wiwa, K. (1992) *Genocide in Nigeria: The Ogoni Tragedy*, Lagos: Saros International Publishers.

FRED HENDRICKS

Ghana

Ghana, with an area of 240,000 square kilometers, is bordered by **Burkina Faso**, **Côte d'Ivoire**, and **Togo**. Its population was estimated at 20.2 million people in 2000. The modern nation of Ghana took shape as a British colony in about 1902, with the annexation of Asante and the Northern Territories, and after the **First World War** when the western third of German Togoland was added as a mandate. Ghana is generally flat, with some mountain ranges in the eastern part. It has many waterways – the most important is the Volta Lake, on which is built the Akosombo hydroelectric dam. There are three main vegetation zones: the savanna grassland of the north; the tropical forests of the central parts; and the coastal zone, where there are grasslands, lagoons, and estuaries.

Colonialism orchestrated a systematic exploitation of the country's agricultural and mineral resources. Cocoa, the most important export crop, was introduced in 1879, and Ghana became the world's leading producer. Although many farmers planted cocoa voluntarily, the colonial government determined the prices through European buying agencies. These were usually below the world market rate. Mining was equally important to the colonial economy. Ghana is rich in gold, manganese, bauxite, and diamonds. The mining sector since the colonial period has been dominated by European companies, which repatriate most of the profits.

Nationalist activities gathered momentum from the 1940s. In 1947 the United Gold Coast Convention (UGCC) was formed, inviting Kwame Nkrumah to become its general secretary. Disagreements over strategy led Nkrumah to found a more militant nationalist party, the Convention People's Party (CPP), in 1949. The CPP won the support of the masses with its popular demands for "Self-Government Now" and "Positive Action." Following the riots of 1948, Nkrumah was arrested, but unrest by workers and farmers continued. In 1951 the government decided to hold elections, which the CPP easily won, and Nkrumah was released from prison to head the new government. Independence came on 6 March 1957, after a difficult transition period. The country was renamed Ghana.

The new government initiated ambitious economic and social development programs. Educational achievements were particularly impressive: free and compulsory primary and secondary school education were introduced, with Ghana the first country to do so in the region, and polytechnics and universities were also established. Roads and hospitals were built, water and electricity provided to rural areas, and affordable housing was constructed in urban areas. Nkrumah's socialist-style economic policy also encouraged the development of state-owned industries, which he believed would lay the basis of Ghana's industrialization and development, to be sustained by the Akosombo hydroelectric dam.

On the political front Nkrumah's record was more mixed. Internationally he was hailed as the Pan-Africanist prophet of African unity and autonomy, but at home he faced growing opposition, including attempts on his life. Nkrumah tightened his hold on basic liberties, resulting in the enactment of a series of laws such as the

Preventive Detention Act, by which one could be arrested and detained for five years without due process. Several opposition leaders and imagined enemies within Nkrumah's own party were arrested. The situation was aggravated by worsening economic conditions due to a drop in cocoa prices, leading to a CIA-sponsored coup d'état of 24 February 1966. Thus began the era of political instability in Ghana.

The military government of the National Liberation Council had a new constitution drafted that led to elections in 1969. These were won by Kofi Busia, who had returned from exile to form the Progress Party. Busia's government quickly fell into the same malpractices as the CPP. In 1972 the soldiers carried out another coup, led by General Acheampong, who turned out to be corrupt and incompetent. In 1978 Acheampong was removed, due to growing popular opposition, but before new elections could be held Jerry Rawlings and a group of junior officers seized power for three months, purging the old corrupt militocracy before handing over power to the new elected civilian government led by Hilla Limann of the People's National Party (PNP).

Regrettably, the PNP failed to stem economic stagnation and decline, which was exacerbated by drought, indebtedness, and growing corruption. The government was overthrown by Rawlings on 31 December 1981. Rawlings' initially popular government promised radical reform and recovery, but his leftist policies and rhetoric were abandoned in the face of a **structural adjustment program** imposed by the World Bank. The subsequent privatization of state corporations led to massive layoffs, as well as reduction in subventions to social services such as health care and education. Growing domestic and international pressure forced the government to accept democratization. In 1992 elections were held and Rawlings' party, the National Democratic Congress (NDC), won; they won again four years later. Under term limits, Rawlings could not run for a third term. When elections were held in November 2000, John Kufour of the opposition National Patriotic Party (NPP) won.

Despite the various political setbacks, Ghana was ahead of many African countries in its economic, social, and cultural achievements. Textile mills, salt production, chemical industries, wood and furniture industries, and handicrafts dominated the country's industrial base. The Tema harbor handled cargo for many landlocked neighboring countries that took advantage of Ghana's good transnational highways to move their merchandise. Ghanaian universities produced some of Africa's best graduates, serving all over the world. In fact the Ghanaian diaspora was reputed to remit millions of dollars annually to bolster Ghana's economy. Kofi Annan, elected Secretary General of the United Nations in 1997, was one of the best-known members of the diaspora. Ghana was also a favorite destination for tourists, because of its beauty and cultural heritage, including traditional crafts (such as the manufacture of kente cloth), the unique pageantry of annual festivals, the ubiquitous highlife music, and historical monuments, including slave castles, which were a favorite destination for many African-Americans.

Further reading

Awoonor, K.N. (1990) *Ghana: A Political History*, Accra: Sedco Publishing.

Buah, F.K. (1998) *A History of Ghana*, London: Macmillan Education.

AGBENYEGA ADEDZE

globalization

From the 1980s the term "globalization" entered popular and academic discourse to refer to a wide range of complex and contradictory processes and phenomena that were seen as characterizing the late twentieth century. To some globalization was celebrated as inevitable and progressive, while critics of globalization pointed to the reinforcement of global economic inequalities, political disenfranchisement, and environmental degradation. There was no agreement about what globalization actually meant, except a sense that the world was somehow different from how it had been in the past: It was an increasingly interdependent, deterritorialized world, created by the emergence of new transnational information and computer technologies that tore asunder the spatial/temporal divides and distances of the past and shrank the world into a global village. In short, new economic, political, and cultural geographies were emerging that created a world of enhanced locational substitutability in which territorially based institutions, especially nation-states, were diminishing as barriers to the flows of goods, services, information, capital, technology, and people.

Globalization discourses

Discourse on globalization centered on its purported historical origins, and its technological, cultural, economic, and political dimensions. To the hyperglobalists, globalization was seen as a new phenomenon involving a fundamental restructuring of the global system, the emergence of a post-industrial, postmodern, or post-capitalist world, characterized by a new order of accumulation and social organization that was both inevitable and irreversible. They predicted the end of the nation-state and foresaw the emergence of global civilization. To the skeptics there was really nothing new about globalization. It was merely a polite way of saying imperialism – a world capitalist system for new neoliberal times – for the international economy was neither unprecedented nor was it truly global, since it continued to be dominated by the major economic powers of Europe, North America, and Japan. Indeed it was contingent and susceptible to interruptions and ruptures, as had happened during previous cycles of globalization. Finally, the so-called "transformationalists," who sought a middle ground between the hyperglobalists and skeptics, argued that late twentieth-century patterns of globalization surpassed those of earlier epochs in terms of the extensiveness of global networks, the intensity and impact of global interconnectedness, and the velocity of global flows. This era presented a historically unique confluence of patterns of globalization in all the dimensions of economic activity and in the domains of politics and culture.

The technological revolution was widely seen as the motor of globalization. It was argued that economically the spectacular advances in computing power and **telecommunications** made it easier to expand trade, enhanced the mobility of capital and the integration of financial markets, and turned information into an increasingly valuable asset and commodity. Culturally and politically the technological revolution strengthened transnational cultural communications and formations, facilitated networking among social movements, and helped to democratize the production and dissemination of information. But the privileges of the "network society" were still enjoyed by a global minority. Access to the new technologies and the information society was filtered through the unyielding hierarchies of location, class, gender, and generation. The divides between the technological haves and have nots, the information rich and information poor, between and within countries of the North and South, were huge and deepening.

Analyses of cultural globalization sought to map out the flows of information, ideas, imaginations, visions, values, and tastes. It was argued that these flows not only linked together previously separated cultures, forcing them to relativize themselves reflexively against each other, but also facilitated the development of new or syncretic transnational cultures. Globalization, it was claimed, restructured social identities constructed around religion, nationhood, ethnicity, and other social markers. These identities were often simultaneously reinvigorated and decoupled from locality. Debate centered on what characterized cultural globalization as process, policy, and product. As process, there were questions about the nature and direction of the cultural flows, as policy the issue was identifying the agents that drove it, and as product there was dispute on whether it led to cultural hegemonization, homogenization, heterogenization, or hybridization.

There were also heated debates about globalization's economic and political dimensions. The arguments were that world trade and investment had expanded rapidly; world financial markets had become more integrated and financial flows had exploded; world production was increasingly dominated by multinationals and flexible organizational practices; and a global consumer culture was emerging. But the empirical evidence for some of the economic trends remained quite mixed. The tendency was to extrapolate developments in the world of global finance to cover all forms of capital. Critics argued that national economies were still very much alive; that while trade had grown faster than world output since the **Second World War**, trade as a percentage of gross domestic product (GDP) remained small for most countries, and it was still lower as a share of global output in the 1990s than in 1913; that multinational corporations were neither truly global, nor did they control the bulk of global production; that despite the growing integration of financial markets, financial products continued to have a distinct spatial configuration because of persistent time–space distances between markets, systematic differences in countries' economic structures, and differences in regulatory regimes; and that the much-trumpeted capital flows did not consist largely of direct foreign investment, but rather of speculative capital that was often divorced from real economies. Perhaps more significant than the actual economic flows, according to the critics, was the imposition of global market discipline, the neoliberal ideology of economic deregulation and privatization, which entailed the erosion of long-standing social bargains embodied in social welfare programs, and deepened the inequality in bargaining power between labor and capital, forcing or facilitating governments' retreat from their social obligations.

Globalization debates also centered on the extent to which a new global political and military order had emerged. By the end of the 1990s few talked confidently of a "New World Order," or believed in Francis Fukuyama's "end of history" thesis. Indeed to some global disorder threatened, as depicted in the apocalyptic predictions of Samuel Huntington's "clash of civilizations," Benjamin Barber's "Jihad versus McWorld," and Robert Kaplan's "coming anarchy," in which he saw the apparent decay and self-destruction in West Africa as a harbinger of the future. For other observers, the late twentieth century would be remembered as the era of the "globalization of poverty," marked by the collapse of productive systems in the **Third World**, and the demise of national institutions and social sectors. Thus, instead of encouraging peace and security and international interdependence, some charged, globalization was reinforcing inequalities, polarizations, chauvinism, and conflicts within and among nations. It encouraged a widespread but uneven tendency towards the decomposition of **civil society** and traditional political formations, and a resurgent affirmation of primordial or sectarian identities. The world was experiencing "glocalization," in which the local and global were mutually constituted and reproduced. Political and economic processes involved rescaling both upward to the supranational or global and downward to smaller units, including communities and individuals.

The debate on political globalization specifically centered on the relationship between globalization and state power and globalization and democratization. The contention was that the national state was declining as transnational economic and cultural interactions grew, reducing the redistributive capacities and legitimacy of the state; as areas of traditional state responsibility became increasingly coordinated by or were ceded to international and regional political units and organizations; as a system of global governance emerged to deal with global problems, such as human rights abuse, environmental degradation, underdevelopment and inequality, war and disorder, and "globalizing panics," such as AIDS, which respected neither territorial boundaries nor the problem-solving capacity of any state; as world cities became increasingly and self-consciously transnational actors with their own agendas, world views, and networks; and as global civil society and reflexivity spread, thanks to the rapid expansion of international organizations and the tendency of politicians to blame national problems on global forces.

Pronouncements about the impending death of the state, however, appeared premature to many. They argued that states were not disappearing, but multiplying: There were more states in the 1990s than ever before in history. Also globalization appeared to lead to and require bigger rather than smaller government. In fact government receipts as a share of GDP rose from about 42 percent in 1990 to 44 percent in 2000 among the developed countries. States would still retain, it was predicted, roles as regulators to legitimate international economic regulations and give stability to financial markets; as orchestrators of social cohesion and economic cooperation between major social interests at the national level; and as guarantors of the rule of law, enabling plural communities to exist without excessive conflict.

The links between globalization and democratization appeared equally murky. The number of "democratic" states increased in the 1980s and 1990s, but so did the number of "illiberal democracies," even among Western countries where increasing numbers of people withdrew from the electoral process. Some even argued that insofar as globalization represented an increase in the power of capital over other social classes, it contributed to the shrinkage of democracy. As capitalism and neoliberal ideology became more dominant, and popular social classes and movements weakened, the sphere of private and unaccountable decision-making expanded, while that of public and accountable decision-making diminished. But the "Battle of Seattle" over the World Trade Organization (WTO) in 1999, and other subsequent anti-globalization protests, demonstrated that there was growing global resistance to capitalist globalization and a growth of globalization from below (i.e. the globalization of social protest movements), facilitated by the very technologies of globalization.

African perspectives

Discourses of globalization and Africa claimed, with various degrees of glee and gloom, that Africa was marginal and in crisis, that African polities, economies, societies, and studies were irrelevant to globalization. But many African leaders and scholars insisted that, understood as a historical process, the world had been globalizing for a long time, and that Africa had been an integral part of these processes, central to the construction of the modern world in all its ramifications – economic, political, cultural, and discursive – since the fifteenth century. This did not mean Africa's engagements with, and contributions to, globalization had necessarily been beneficial to its peoples. On the contrary, Africans had paid a high price in the construction of a more integrated world.

This point was made forcefully by Samir Amin (1997), the Egyptian scholar, who argued against the notion of Africa's marginalization, which implied on the one hand that the continent, or much of it, was out of the global system or integrated into it only superficially, and on the other that the poverty of African peoples was precisely the result of their not being sufficiently integrated into the global system. This was not borne out by the facts. For example, Africa's ratio of extra-regional trade to GDP was the highest in the world – in 1990 it was 45.6 percent, compared to 12.8 percent for Europe, 13.2 percent for North America, 15.2 percent for Asia, and 23.7 percent for Latin America. The question, therefore, was not about the degree to which Africa was integrated – for Africa was highly integrated – but the manner of its integration, why its integration had produced little autocentered development. His answer was that the slave trade and colonialism initiated Africa's integration into the world capitalist system in a most destructive way, while the devastating regime of structural adjustment during the 1980s and 1990s derailed the feeble attempts at autocentered development by some of Africa's more enlightened post-colonial states. Globalization via the market, he insisted, was a reactionary utopia that needed to be countered by developing an alternative humanistic project of globalization consistent with a socialist perspective based on a new global political system.

Amin's sweeping historical overview and impassioned critique of capitalist globalization was shared by many other African intellectuals. For example, the Ugandan scholar Dani Nabudere (2000) also argued that contemporary globalization was neither new nor a unilinear phenomenon. Unlike Amin, however, Nabudere saw globalization as first and foremost a cultural project – and then an economic and political one – driven by the West, which had supplanted the globalizations of other civilizations, including that of the Soviet-led communist movement. He traced its origins to the Christian universalism of the Crusades and the trading voyages of the European Middle Ages, through the scientific stage of the early modern period, to the subsequent eras of the industrial and capitalist revolutions, capitalist imperialism, and internationalization. The latter stage was first characterized by multilateralization and now by so-called globalization, which was marked by denationalization, deregulation, and the expansion of a post-Fordist economic system. For Africa, globalization meant **structural adjustment programs**, which derailed post-independence development efforts and led to what Nabudere called the "third colonial occupation," distinguished by the downsizing of the post-colonial state and downgrading of democracy. One of the consequences was the growth of traditionalism and neotraditionalism.

The disastrous consequences of contemporary capitalist globalization for Africa were outlined in graphic detail by Thandika Mkandawire, the Malawian scholar. He vigorously contested the neoclassical explanations of the African economic crisis of the 1980s and 1990s, which sought to absolve external factors, principally the international financial institutions, and blame the crisis on internal factors, such as poor natural conditions, lack of human resources, political conflicts, and especially policy failures. While conceding that African states had indeed made mistakes, Mkandawire was dismissive of the voluntaristic analyses of state policy offered by the World Bank and its academic friends. He put greater emphasis on the role of structural and external factors, specifically the global capitalist crisis of the 1970s and 1980s (which led to declining terms of trade for Africa and brought other external shocks) and the role of misguided policy advice, often offered by the same Western individuals and institutions who were now criticizing African states. Analyses of globalization and Africa were dismal, he believed, because most of the nuances that characterize the debate elsewhere disappear; as a result, the dominant view emphasized the hyperglobalists on the one hand, and the incomprehensible marginalization of the continent on the other. He insisted that Africans had to continue articulating their own agenda, rooted in the unfinished historical and humanistic tasks of progressive African nationalism: **decolonization**, development, democracy, nation-building, and regional integration, duly revised to reflect the changed times.

For many African intellectuals, therefore, globalization was seen as a destructive phenomenon and coercive ideology from the North which, despite some of its novelties, was little different from previous forms and phases of capitalist imperialism. As the renowned Nigerian scholar Claude Ake stressed, it was not an abstract universal that was magically emerging everywhere; it was concrete particulars that were being globalized. What was globalized was not Yoruba but English, not Turkish pop culture but American, not Senegalese technology but Japanese and German. It had always been the insufferable arrogance of the North, he observed, to conflate its own model of society with the ideal state of being. For Ake, then, uneven globalization was not only a process but also an ongoing structuration of power, the hierarchization of the world – economically, politically, and culturally – and the crystallizing of a domination, one constituted essentially by economic power. Contemporary globalization, he predicted, would not survive without solving the problem of uneven development and the poverty of much of the world's population.

Development of the world economy

The world economy underwent profound transformations during the course of the twentieth century. The manifestation of these changes in Africa, and the continent's participation in them, was quite uneven and varied. We can only point to broad trends in four critical areas. First, there was an enormous expansion of productive forces. Second, there were far-reaching institutional changes in the organization and regulation of the international economy. Third, the century experienced various cycles of economic disintegration and growth. Fourth, there were important shifts in the international division of labor.

An important factor in discussing the expansion of the forces of production is the growth in the world's population, which nearly quadrupled from 1.6 billion in 1900 to 6.2 billion in 2000. This demographic explosion was facilitated by declining death rates, especially in infant mortality, and characterized by rising life expectancy, urbanization, migrations, and shifts in global population distribution, whereby the relative share of Europe and North America declined while increasing for

Africa, Asia, and Latin America. By 2000, for example, Africa accounted for 13.5 percent of the world's population, up from 7.5 percent in 1900. Such exponential growth, as well rising standards of living, placed unprecedented demands upon the world's resources, from energy to food. In terms of energy, there was a gradual shift from dependence on coal to petroleum, which acquired great geopolitical significance and increased the role of Third World countries, including Africa, in global energy production. This became apparent with the rise of the Organization of Petroleum Exporting Countries (OPEC) and the oil crises of the 1970s. These countries also became major producers of minerals for the world's factories. As with oil, the mining industry was largely controlled by multinational corporations and did not always bring sustainable development to the producer countries. Regarding food production, despite the fact that Third World countries had large rural populations, the international food trade was dominated by the increasingly subsidized agriculture in European and North American countries, except for tropical products. In spite of the growth in food production, **food crises** and famines continued to manifest themselves periodically, especially in Africa and Asia. Finally, the expansion in the forces of production was facilitated by spectacular advances in technology. The key technologies ranged from electricity and new forms of transportation to telecommunications and computers, which enhanced productivity and global interconnectedness, and altered relations of production. Even if the resources for these technologies might come from the developing countries, the technologies were dominated by the developed countries, and their development became a contributory cause of the widening gap between wealth and poverty across the globe.

The institutional changes were also many and uneven. The ever-growing complexities of production, international trade, and national competition led to a greatly enlarged role for government in the economy. State intervention was *de rigueur* for the colonial economy, and became the basis of the socialist economies. Independent Third World states also adopted economic planning, with varying degrees of comprehensiveness, as an important tool of development. State intervention increased among the Western capitalist countries as well, as a result of the two world wars and the **Great Depression**. Keynesianism dominated economic policy until the late 1970s, when the neoliberals sought to overturn the welfare state, although the government's share of GDP continued to rise as indicated earlier. The twentieth century also saw the expansion of the corporate form of enterprise to ever wider spheres of activity, from production to distribution, and the spread of multinational corporations. These institutional changes were initially concentrated in the capitalist world, but quickly spread to the rest of the world following the collapse of socialism in the 1980s and 1990s. They were accompanied by the growth of working classes and powerful **labor movements**. During the second half of the century, however, labor movements were undermined by the growth of the welfare state in the Western countries, the socialist state in the communist countries, and the developmentalist state in the ex-colonial world, all of which used either material carrots or ideological sticks to coopt labor and tame its militancy.

As for economic disruptions, the most critical occurred during the two world wars, the Great Depression, and the global recession of the mid-1970s that ended the long postwar boom. The world wars led to massive destruction of investment and disruption of trade, and laid the basis for both prolonged global recession in the case of the first, and an unprecedented boom in the case of the second. These crises also facilitated shifts in global economic power: the **First World War** ended Britain's position as the leading industrial and trading nation, to be replaced by the United States. They also enabled the major independent countries in Africa (**Egypt** and **South Africa**), Asia (India, China, and Japan), and Latin America (Brazil and Argentina) to consolidate their drives towards industrialization. The **Second World War**, in particular, accelerated on the one hand the dismantling of the colonial empires, and on the other regional integration and global economic regulation, developments which altered the landscape of international economic relations. Decolonization contributed to Europe's hegemonic decline and regional integration, which culminated in the formation of the **European Union**. In the meantime, the newly independent countries embarked on development and mounted a concerted challenge against the operations of the global economic order, with varying degrees of seriousness and success. Efforts aimed at postwar reconstruction, primarily focused on Europe, led to the creation of the three Bretton Woods institutions: the World Bank, the International Monetary Fund, and the General Agreement on Tariffs and Trade, later succeeded by the WTO. These institutions played a major role in regulating the international economic system, and by the 1980s had come to be seen in the Third World as the policemen of exploitative global capitalism, responsible for imposing draconian structural adjustment programs.

These developments pointed to important shifts taking place in the international division of labor. After the Second World War, world trade grew faster than world production – by 200 percent and 123 percent respectively between 1963 and 1979. Manufactures assumed a greater share of world exports, eclipsing food and raw materials. The composition of manufactured exports themselves shifted away from consumer goods towards capital goods. The major beneficiaries were the industrialized countries, which accounted for 45 percent of world trade in both years. These trends, reinforced by uneven technical innovation and diversified demand patterns due to rising incomes, encouraged a change in the direction of total trade in favor of trade among the industrialized countries themselves against the exports of the developing countries. The pecking order among the developed countries shifted too, as Japan and Germany recovered and eclipsed Britain and France. The United States remained the leading world economy, although it enjoyed slower growth than its two wartime adversaries and by the mid-1980s had become the world's largest debtor nation.

In the meantime many Third World countries, including African nations, enjoyed rapid growth during the long postwar boom, although rapid population growth slowed average per capita growth rates. The highest rates were recorded among the oil-exporting countries and the newly industrialized countries. The prolonged global recession of the 1970s depressed Third World growth, although a few countries, such as China and **Botswana**, continued to grow rapidly. Relations between countries in the North and the South became strained as the latter pushed for a new international economic order in order to curtail the declining terms of trade for their primary products and redistribute global wealth. By the 1980s not only had foreign aid and direct investment from the North to the South declined, except for a few so-called "emerging markets," but there was also a net outflow of capital from the debt-ridden South to the North, which was also becoming more protectionist despite the rhetoric of free markets. By the end of the twentieth century, the South was more industrialized than ever, but global economic and political power still remained, as at the beginning of the century, in the hands of a handful of countries in North America, Europe, and Japan. Also, following the collapse of socialism, capitalism reigned supreme. Africa remained, despite regaining its independence, economically subordinated and relatively underdeveloped.

See also: capitalisms and capitalists; economy: colonial; economy: post-independence; socialisms and socialists

References and further reading

Ake, C. (1995) "The New World Order: A View from Africa," in H. Hans-Henik and G. Sørensen (eds.), *Whose World Order: Uneven Globalization and the End of the Cold War*, Boulder: Westview.

Amin, S. (1997) *Capitalism in the Age of Globalization*, London: Zed Books.

Barber, B. (1996) *Jihad vs. McWorld*, New York: Ballantine.

Beynon, J. and Dunkerley, D. (eds.) (2000) *Globalization: The Reader*, New York: Routledge.

Cameron, R. (1989) *A Concise Economic History of the World*, New York: Oxford University Press.

Holm, H.-H. and Sorenson, G. (ed.) (1995) *Whose World Order: Uneven Globalization and the End of the Cold War*, Boulder: Westview Press.

Huntington, S. (1996) *Clash of Civilizations*, New York: Simon & Schuster.

Kaplan, R. (1994) "The Coming Anarchy," *The Atlantic Monthly* 273, 2 (December): 44–76.

Kenwood, A.G. and Lougheed, A.L. (1983) *The Growth of the International Economy, 1820–1980*, London: Unwin Hyman.

Mkandawire, T. (1997) "Globalization and Africa's Unfinished Agenda," *MacAlaster International* 7: 71–107.

Nabudere, D. (ed.) (2000) *Globalization and the Post-Colonial African State*, Harare: Sapes Books.

O'Meara, P., Mehlinger, H.D. and Krain, M. (eds.) (2000) *Globalization and the Challenges of a New Century*, Indianapolis: Indiana University Press.

PAUL TIYAMBE ZELEZA

Great Depression

The Great Depression was arguably one of the most significant events of the twentieth century. For Africa, the Great Depression – like the **First World War** – served as an index of the continent's vulnerability due to its colonial status. However, it was also an indicator of Africa's centrality in global economic and geopolitical configurations. Even as export commodity prices tumbled, employment shrunk, commercial enterprises became bankrupt, state revenues plummeted, and scenes of abject poverty unfolded, the Depression was simultaneously a rude awakening regarding the fragile nature of colonial economies and their dependence on metropolitan economies, and a reminder that the fate of industrialized world was closely tied to Africa.

Previous studies of the Great Depression have concentrated on the industrialized countries. While there is little doubt that the Depression started in the West, it did not happen in isolation. The colonial empire was part of the global economy, and hence needs to be included in any comprehensive study of the period. Scholars are beginning to examine what impact the perpetual indebtedness of the colonies had on international trade prior to and during the Depression. Thus attention is increasingly turning to the **Third World**, not only in an effort to establish the economic impact of the Depression globally, but also to examine the nature of the links between the metropole and the periphery. There are also efforts to explore non-monetary causes of the Depression. More importantly, recent studies indicate the existence of connections between the Depression and political shifts and mobilization in Africa. In the economic realm some studies point towards situations in Africa in which the Depression spurred industrialization. This entry seeks to explore the multi-faceted impact of the Great Depression on Africa.

Economic historians are still debating the Great Depression, its underlying causes, where it originated, and why it was so widespread, so deep, and lasted for so long, as well as its impact on the international economy, politics, psychology, and economic thought. The roots of the Depression lie in dislocations in the structure of the international economy brought about by the First World War, and exacerbated in the 1920s in terms of international trade, which became more protectionist; of the international financial system, which became more unstable as countries abandoned the gold standard and international indebtedness rose; and of supply and demand as the production, especially of primary products, increasingly outstripped demand as indebted countries sought to raise their exports to pay their debts. The temporary boom of the mid-1920s, especially in the United States, did nothing to offset these problems. In fact many believe the Depression was triggered by the great crash in the New York stock market in 1929, which was itself spawned by problems in the US economy: the crisis in the agricultural sector; the slowdown of the construction industry, due to declining family sizes and the shortage of mortgage credit as speculative borrowing increased; and declining consumer spending on durable goods due to falls in agricultural income, rising personal and corporate debt, and increasingly unequal distribution of income.

Whatever the cause, the Depression had an immediate and far-reaching impact on Africa. Needless to say, this impact was complex and contradictory, with different countries, sectors, and social classes affected differently. The Depression sparked industrialization in some African countries. In **Egypt**, for example, the Great Depression fueled popular pressure for economic diversification. Egypt's attempts at industrialization in the nineteenth century had failed, partly frustrated by foreign intervention, especially following British colonization in 1882. Nationalist protests had forced Britain to grant Egypt internal self-government in 1922, so by the time of the Depression there was a new nationalist government determined to pursue industrialization behind tariff protection. Large-scale farmers who sought to escape the slump in cotton prices diversified their investments by financing industrial enterprises. Other local financiers, like Bank Misr, also boosted the industrial sector. This was a case of industrialization through import substitution, protected by tariff barriers. In the period between 1930 and 1940 industrial production in the textile, chemical, building materials, mineral, power, food, drink, and tobacco sectors doubled, and in some cases tripled.

A similar process took place in the other major semi-autonomous country on the continent: **South Africa**. In this case, settler economic nationalism was sustained by expansion in the value and production of gold. South Africa's national income increased by about 80 percent between 1932 and 1939, partly as a result of the rise in the price of gold. This unexpected windfall was channeled into extensive industrial investment, which served to strengthen white business and labor, and entrench segregation. In this context Africa's first modern steel plant was established in Pretoria in 1933. The prosperity in South Africa around the period of the Depression also enabled whites to buy more shares in the mining industry – up to a third by 1940 – which hitherto had been the monopoly of foreign capital. Elsewhere, in Southern Rhodesia (**Zimbabwe**) and the Gold Coast (**Ghana**) favorable gold prices cushioned the colonies against the extreme ravages of the Depression. Demand for copper from Northern Rhodesia and tin from Belgian Congo also rose during the Depression. By 1938 Africa was providing 16 percent of the world's copper output, and 12 percent of its tin. In **Sierra Leone** open-cast iron mining was established by the Baird Company of Glasgow. In short, the mining industry underwent a massive expansion at a time when other sectors of the economy were ailing.

Except for gold, the prices of almost all African commodities fell to a new low, most plunging to less than half their previous value. However, the Depression was also an opportune moment for peasant producers to demonstrate their resilience. Although badly bruised, they rallied to salvage badly ravaged household economies and human dignity. Africans mobilized diverse social and economic resources to expand production for internal and external trade, and to reduce the terrible effects of the Depression, which were borne by whole extended families. In their wake, colonial administrators also adopted novel ways of countering the unforeseen catastrophe. Ultimately expansion in the agricultural sector resulted in further decline in the prices of primary commodities. But the Depression did not spell doom at all times in all places in Africa.

As a producer of primary materials, Africa was worse affected by the Depression than industrialized nations. The prices of raw materials dropped more severely than those of manufactured commodities, sometimes by as much as 50 percent. For some commodities the fall was much larger, sometimes up to two-thirds or even more. For most African countries external trade fell by more than 40 percent, while the value of their international trade hovered at a third of its pre-1929 levels. For example, while coffee from **Kenya** fetched 86 shillings per 100 pounds of weight in 1929, by 1936 this had dropped to 46 shillings. For most commodities this downward spiral continued even after the Depression had peaked: by 1938 100 pounds of Kenyan coffee fetched a meager 23 shillings. By 1931 the value of Kenya's international trade had fallen to a third of its 1929 value. The price of cocoa from Abengourou in **Côte d'Ivoire** fell by 86 percent during the Depression, while the peasant farmers of the Gezira cotton scheme in **Sudan** received no net income whatsoever in 1930–1 and 1933. This resulted in sharp declines in gross national income. In **Nigeria**, for instance, it fell by about 66 percent between 1928 and 1934. Similar experiences were recorded in other African countries. That Africans continued to produce for the market amidst the plummeting prices is a clear indication of the extent to which they had become incorporated into the global capitalist economy. It was also an indication of their resilience. Unlike the white settler sector in Kenya, for example, of which close to 300 settlers became bankrupt, never to resume production in the agricultural sector, peasant producers soldiered on, albeit under very difficult conditions. Settlers in **Algeria** and **Madagascar** encountered the same uphill struggle. The Depression had exposed the vulnerabilities of the settler sector.

For the first time much of Africa experienced unemployment during the Depression. In **French West Africa** only 1.1 percent of the population was employed by 1932. Although by 1935 conditions had improved somewhat – the figure then stood at 1.6 percent – the impact of the Depression continued to be felt for a long time. As commodity prices fell and trade volume between the colonies and the imperial metropoles shrunk, employers – both corporate and individual – implemented massive retrenchments. For example, between 1930 and 1933 the Katanga copper mines laid off more than half of their workers, shrinking their workforce from 73,000 to 27,000 workers. Thousands of those workers returned to rural areas, swelling the numbers of **peasants** already reeling from falling prices for their crops. To a large extent rural areas bore the brunt of the Depression. In an unprecedented trend, all over Africa – both in the settler colonies and in regions where peasant cash-crop farming was predominant – labor migration was halted for the duration of the Depression. The layoffs precipitated untold suffering in societies whose lifestyles were becoming increasingly dependent on cash remittances from family members, mostly men. Everywhere images of extreme poverty and suffering were chronicled. In general the standard of living for most Africans fell, especially those who had become part of the colonial capitalist economy.

Despite widespread unemployment, there were no major labor disturbances during the Depression. However, once world economies began to stabilize, waves of labor unrest after 1936 were blamed on the Depression. In French West Africa and in **East Africa** this period was characterized by nascent trade union movements that sought to realize long overdue benefits for **workers**. These included decent living wages, better housing and working conditions, and bargaining power regarding their conditions of employment.

These bread-and-butter issues of the Depression period were at the core of most nationalist struggles in Africa. All over Africa the late 1930s saw the emergence of youth leagues, welfare associations, regional political parties, and trade unions that rallied around the grievances of workers and peasants. The growth of links between trade unions and the burgeoning **nationalist movements** in most of colonial Africa is well documented. Just as the First and **Second World War** precipitated political mobilization, the Great Depression sharpened the economic marginalization of Africans and created resistance against further financial exactions by colonial governments.

There was limited reprieve for those Africans who managed to keep their jobs during the Depression. Since the prices of consumer goods fell as much as wages did, workers' buying power was not always adversely affected. On the other hand, the employed had to bear the cost of supporting those of their kin who had fallen on hard times. This erased any advantage to be gained from the fall in the prices of consumer goods. There were, however, pockets of prosperity amidst extensive poverty. In **Senegal**, for example, the wages of agricultural workers in the groundnut-growing region witnessed an actual increase. For these workers, their buying power in the 1930s increased beyond the pre-Depression period. This buoyancy was unique in the 1930s, and remained so into the 1950s. These modest wage increases were also evident in **Dakar** in early 1930s.

The snowball effect of the Great Depression was extensive, affecting even the remotest parts of the continent. Rural areas were the source of actual laborers and provided a reservoir of prospective workers. Abject poverty increased migration to urban areas, thus swelling the number of "floating" job hunters. The rapid increase in unemployment skewed the market, making it difficult for job seekers to bargain for better terms of employment. This vulnerability of workers continued into the mid-1930s, keeping wages down even after prices of export commodities had began to rise.

While in general African countries were more adversely affected by the Depression than industrialized countries, within the colonies there were major differences between settler and peasant sectors. While settler production was largely geared for international markets and was therefore more vulnerable during the Depression, peasant producers targeted both the domestic and external markets. In the aftermath of the Depression, the internal market recovered much faster than the external, thus boosting peasant production. Even where the same commodity was traded in both markets, as in the case of maize in Kenya, the internal market for the cereal remained more buoyant during the Depression. Despite favorable government intervention by way of subsidies on inspection, storage, and freight for settler produce, the peasant sector proved to be the more resilient of the two sectors in Kenya.

The Depression served as a wake-up call for colonial powers to reevaluate their economic policies in Africa. More immediately the governments had to appraise the importance of Africa in the grand imperial design. Although the immediate concern was to keep colonial economies afloat, it was necessary to adopt both long-term and short-term measures. In general colonial governments shifted the burden of the Depression to Africans. For example, additional taxes were imposed on Africans in Kenya, Ghana, and Nigeria in an effort to bolster government revenues that were largely dependent on poll, hut, import, and export taxes. Where the poll tax existed it was increased. In Nigeria and Ghana these increases led to local protests, which symbolized and fed into the increased politicization of Africans.

Government intervention and protectionism became top priorities in the endeavor to salvage colonial economies. Austerity measures were immediately put in place. Governments were quick to implement the expansion of the production of primary commodities. Strict control of the varieties and quantities of crops grown for export were imposed; the government oversaw the pricing of export commodities, and at the same time controlled categories and quantities of manufactured imports. This was true of Britain and Belgium. These measures were largely implemented to safeguard industrial economies.

Trade between colonies and their respective imperial powers expanded rapidly during the Depression, thus strengthening the imperial hold over the colonies. The trade between France and its colonies in Africa rose from 10 percent to over 20 percent by 1935. Accounting for 12.5 percent of this rise, Algeria easily became France's major trading partner. During the same period trade between Britain and Africa expanded less rapidly, rising from 5.3 percent in 1930 to 7 percent by 1935, largely due to the gold trade in South Africa. Portugal focused on making its colonies major trading partners, in the hope of gaining a firmer control of the colonies' economic future while salvaging its own limping economy. Most governments curtailed expenditure on public projects, retrenched workers in government service, and implemented much-reduced wages. Although colonial governments were concerned about the recovery of local economies, they were careful to ensure that they did not jeopardize metropolitan manufacturing plants. Colonial importation policies failed to help colonial economies take advantage of the falling prices of manufactured goods. Additionally, foreign manufacturing houses in the colonies were given the monopoly in the processing of primary products.

Even as colonial powers prevailed on peasant farmers to increase their production of specific crops, in most colonies the subsequent massive increase in production was not accompanied by an increase in peasant income. In white settler colonies like Kenya, governments gave special attention to white settler production by subsidizing various aspects of their enterprise, including production, transportation, and marketing. Where peasant agriculture was given positive official attention, this was in recognition of the more vulnerable predicament of settler agriculture, and the need to bolster the more viable peasant option.

France tried to jump-start the economy of French West Africa by pumping loan money into the export sector. This way the colonies would command sufficient foreign exchange, and trade with the metropolitan manufacturers would be sustained. In some cases this effort to revamp colonial economies also took the form of ambitious construction projects in both urban and rural areas. In British Africa the Colonial Development

Act, which provided £1 million a year from 1929 to 1936, proved inadequate for the gigantic task of reconstructing the adversely affected economies. But the scheme launched the idea of "development" as a desirable and feasible state project, an idea that was to have a permanent effect on post-war and post-independence Africa. Although government intervention in peasant production managed to sustain government revenue, it had both positive and negative impacts on the finances of indigenous populations. Increased production did not always translate into increased income in a government freeze of wages, despite the rise in production. This situation lingered into the 1950s, when the agricultural producers realized better fortunes.

The onset of the Great Depression illustrated clearly the extent to which colonial states were dependent upon global economies, and the need for imperial powers to reevaluate their economic policies in Africa. It was also a period when Africans, despite the evident suffering unleashed by the Depression, displayed their tenacity by increasing production to unprecedented levels, sustaining colonial revenues, and emerging from the assault and indignities of the period more committed to economic expansion and political freedom. Almost overnight the Depression had turned colonial administrators into economic planners, forced to balance production and importation that were premised on a protectionist ethos that sought to ultimately safeguard metropolitan economies while ensuring the fiscal solvency of colonies. They also had to rise to the challenge of industrial action and political protest.

See also: economy: colonial

Further reading

Brown, I. (ed.) (1989) *The Economies of Africa and Asia in the Inter-War Depression*, London: Routledge.

Hopkins, A.G. (1973) *An Economic History of West Africa*, London: Longman.

Latham, A.J.H. (1981) *The Depression and the Developing World, 1914–1939*, London: Croom Helm.

Rothermund, D. (1996) *The Global Impact of the Great Depression, 1929–1939*, London and New York: Routledge.

Talbott, I.D. (1990) *Agricultural Innovation in Colonial Africa: Kenya and the Great Depression*, New York: Edwin Mellen Press.

TABITHA KANOGO

Great Lakes

The African Great Lakes are a prominent feature of the mosaic that constitutes Africa's physical landscape. Situated primarily in eastern Africa, the main Great Lakes are Lake Victoria, Lake Tanganyika, and Lake Malawi. The Great Lakes region, however, also includes smaller lakes such as Mobutu, Turkana, Kyoga, and Kivu. Tanganyika, Malawi and Victoria constitute part of three large international river basins in Africa. Lake Victoria is the headwater of the River Nile; Lake Tanganyika flows into the Congo River; and Lake Malawi feeds the Zambezi River.

The lakes share a common geological history having been associated with the tectonic forces that created the famous East African Rift Valley system over 1.5 million years ago. The lakes of the western branch of the Rift Valley are Lake Tanganyika (with an area of 33,000 square kilometers), Lake Malawi/Nyasa (30,000 square kilometers), Lake Mobutu (formerly Albert; 6,800 square kilometers), Lake Idi Amin (formerly Edward; 2,325 square kilometers), and Lake Kivu (2,700 square kilometers). Lake Turkana (formerly Rudolf; 7,200 square kilometers) is the only Great Lake of the eastern branch, although there are several small lakes in the region. Lake Victoria (68,000 square kilometers) and Lake Kyoga (2,700 square kilometers) lie between the two Rift Valleys. These two lakes are considerably younger than the Rift Valley lakes. Lake Victoria, the largest lake in Africa, occupies a shallow basin that reaches a maximum depth of only 80 meters, whereas Lake Tanganyika has an average depth of 20 meters and is the world's second deepest lake, reaching a maximum depth of 1,435 meters.

The three main lakes – Victoria, Tanganyika, and Malawi – are important sources of fresh water in their respective river systems. Several countries share the resources provided by some of these lakes: **Uganda**, **Kenya**, and **Tanzania** share Lake Victoria; the **Democratic Republic of Congo**, Tanzania, **Zambia**, and **Burundi** share Lake Tanganyika; and **Malawi**, **Mozambique**, and Tanzania share Lake Malawi. Tanzania is the only country that shares boundaries with all three lakes. The lakes of the Great Lakes region provide a variety of resources, including water reservoirs, an energy supply, transportation, fisheries, and tourism. They also contribute to the region's biodiversity, and are valuable subjects of scientific research. In addition to the riparian areas around Lake Victoria, both **Egypt** and **Sudan** owe much of their water supply to Lake Victoria, which supplies the River Nile.

The Great Lakes are important arteries of transportation for countries in the region, thus providing linkages for trade and development. For countries in the northern railway network – Kenya and Uganda – the only connection to the southern network in Tanzania is Lake Victoria. Lake Tanganyika has spurred development in Burundi by connecting the country to more developed parts of the lake. Hydroelectric power plants account for 78 percent of electricity in the Great Lakes region. Owen Falls Dam near Jinja, Lake Victoria, has been producing electricity since 1954. To reduce their vulnerability to fluctuations in world oil prices, most of the countries are searching for new sources of energy in the Great Lakes basins. Exploration for oil has taken place on Lake Tanganyika, Lake Mobutu, Lake Turkana, and the coastal plains.

There is a thriving fishing industry in the Great Lakes. The three major lakes – Victoria, Tanganyika, and Malawi – respectively produce 400,000 tonnes, 160,000 tonnes, and 40,000 tonnes of fish annually (Crul 1998: 22). With the supply of animal proteins in the region well below nutritional requirements, the fisheries are an important source of protein for people who live in the region, as well as constituting a good source of income. With the help of introduced species of fish, local fisheries in the Lake Victoria region have experienced increases in production. In some parts of the region, such as Kenya, a large-scale fishing industry has developed to produce fish for export to overseas markets.

The Great Lakes region also has enormous potential as a tourist destination, with its diversity of landscape, almost pristine coastal areas, plant and animal life, and wide range of riparian environments. At present the development of tourism is mostly limited to parks and nature reserves, mainly in Kenya, Tanzania, Malawi, and **Rwanda**. If ever developed to its full potential, tourism could be a major source of revenue for riparian countries in the region.

The human population of the Great Lakes has grown in response to increasing demands on the diverse resources of the region. In the mid-1990s the population of the Lake Victoria basin was about 28 million; the Lake Tanganyika basin had about 6 million; and the Lake Malawi basin had a population of about 6 million. While the population increase is a sign of the economic boom in the region, it raises serious questions about the impact of population on the natural resources and environment there. As resource use and population concentration intensify in the region, so does the threat of environmental degradation through water and land pollution, the destruction of biological diversity, and serious decline in water levels in the lakes through overuse.

The future of the Great Lakes rests on the collaboration of stakeholder countries in forging methods of holistic management for the lakes and their resources. Although economic conditions vary from country to country, nations of the Great Lakes region stand to benefit from instituting a management strategy that pursues long-term goals that integrate economic resource use and environmental protection. Unfortunately the region has witnessed some ferocious conflicts, including the **genocides** and massacres in Burundi and Rwanda, and wars between Tanzania and Uganda in the late 1970s, and in the Democratic Republic of Congo in the late 1990s.

References and further reading

Crul, R.C.M. (1998) *Management and Conservation of the African Great Lakes*, Paris: UNESCO.

Lehman, J.T. (ed.) (1998) *Environmental Change and Response in the East African Lakes*, Dordrecht: Kluwer Academic.

Ntakimazi, G. (1992) "Conservation of the Resources of the African Great Lakes: Why? An Overview," in R.H. Lowe-McConnel, R.C.M. Crul and F.C. Roest (eds.), *Symposium on Resource Use and Conservation of the Great Lakes, Bujumbura 1989*, Stuttgart: E. Schweizerbart'sche Verlagsbuchhandlung.

GODSON C. OBIA

Guinea

Guinea, which covers an area of 245,857 square kilometers, is located in **West Africa** and bordered by the Atlantic Ocean, **Guinea-Bissau**, **Senegal**, **Mali**, **Côte d'Ivoire**, **Liberia**, and **Sierra Leone**. It had an estimated population of 7.6 million in 2000, dominated by the Peuls (40 percent), Malinke (30 percent), Soussou (20 percent), with smaller ethnic groups making up the rest. It also hosted half a million refugees from the civil wars in Liberia and Sierra Leone. Some 85 percent of the population practiced Islam, 8 percent followed Christianity, and 7 percent indigenous religions. The primary natural resources of the country are bauxite, iron ore, diamonds, gold, uranium, hydropower, and fish. Over much of the twentieth century the primary agricultural products remained rice, coffee, pineapples, palm kernels, cassava, bananas, sweet potatoes, cattle, sheep, goats, and timber.

The colonization of Guinea began early in the nineteenth century when a French trading settlement was established, followed in 1849 by the declaration of a protectorate in the coastal region ruled from Senegal. A rudimentary colonial economy was established, first based on groundnut production, then followed by rubber. In 1880 **Conakry** was founded, and in 1891 the city became the capital of the new colony of French Guinea, established despite fierce resistance led by the legendary Samori Touré, whose forces were not defeated until his capture in 1899. Sporadic resistance continued well into the 1920s.

In 1900 major French, British, Swiss, and Belgian commercial houses begin to arrive, installing themselves in Conakry to set up import and export businesses in the colony. The production and extraction of agricultural and mineral resources, such as palm oil, rice, rubber, bananas, coffee, oranges, gold, bauxite, and diamonds, along with the construction of a major port in Conakry and of the Conakry–Niger railway, were the preoccupations of the French for the first forty years of the twentieth century. However, the 1940s marked a turning point in French colonial history, as France began to rethink its colonial policies and assess its losses from two world wars. At the 1944 Brazzaville Conference France decided to allow Africans to begin limited participation in the management of their affairs.

After the Brazzaville Conference political parties and trade unions began to garner increased power and support in Guinea with the help of a network of parties organizing and interfacing across the colonies of **French West Africa**. One of the most prominent was the Rassemblement Démocratique Africaine (RDA). In Guinea the RDA-affiliated Parti Démocratique de la Guinée (PDG) – led by Sékou Touré, a trade unionist and cofounder of the RDA – expanded its base by fighting against chieftaincy, which the party opposed because it had been coopted by the colonial administration. Under Touré's leadership the party also mobilized ethnic organizations and trade unions to unite Guineans in fighting against French rule. In 1958 de Gaulle submitted new proposals for a Franco-African confederation, but Guinea – alone among the French colonies – voted a resounding "no." Instead the country chose independence, which it gained later in the year. France abandoned Guinea, and Guinea's vote provoked bitter hostility from Senegal and Côte d'Ivoire. However, Sékou Touré was able to garner support from **Ghana** and Mali – the three eventually formed the short-lived Guinea–Ghana–Mali Union.

With his party in power Sékou Touré worked to insure that the PDG would be the sole party in Guinea, with the elimination of his adversaries his primary goal. Increasingly regarded as a dictator, Touré's tenure was marked by arrests, executions, and exile of many Guineans from their homeland. Ironically, while attaining infamy in his own country, Touré was regarded internationally as a brilliant nationalist politician and Pan-Africanist, loved by many, and regarded the world over as a leader who fought indefatigably for the liberty of the oppressed and downtrodden. Along with Senghor, Keita, Nkrumah, and Nyerere, he was considered one of the founding fathers of the **Organization of African Unity**. Touré courted the Eastern European countries in the search for foreign aid, helping to build up the country's bauxite mining industry. Parastatals were set up in the main sectors of the economy, but they became a drain because of corruption and inefficiency. By the late 1970s opposition to Touré's leadership was growing.

After his death in 1984 Touré was succeeded by Lansana Conte in a successful coup d'état. He reversed many of Touré's policies, and adopted a **structural adjustment program** that did little to alleviate the country's pressing poverty. In the multi-party elections of 1993 Conte transformed himself into a civilian president; he was still in power by the end of the decade, having won a second five-year term in 1998, although that election was marred by civil unrest, violence, voting irregularities, and the arrest of major opposition candidates. Modest economic growth occurred between 1996 and 1999 with the help of international financial institutions and donors. Thereafter the economy stagnated due to the reallocation of resources to the military to combat attacks from rebel forces in Liberia and Sierra Leone. Border skirmishes caused major economic disruption and violence, which decreased investor confidence, led companies to reduce expatriate staff, and provoked panic-buying that created food shortages in local markets. In 2000 alone over 1,000 Guinean civilians and members of the security forces were killed in cross-border raids involving Liberia and Sierra Leone. Corruption, limited government transparency, and blocked efforts at economic and fiscal reform exacerbated Guinea's economic downturn.

Under Conte's leadership Guinea's human rights record also remained poor, with widespread charges of killings, beatings, disappearances, torture, rape, and other atrocities leveled against the police and military personnel. The government was also accused of restricting freedom of speech, the press, assembly, movement and travel, as well as infringements of citizens' privacy, and manipulation of the electoral process. International attention and condemnation of Conte's government rose in 2000 in response to the arrest, trial, and conviction of Alpha Conde, an opposition presidential candidate in the 1998 elections.

Further reading

Devey, M. (1997) *La Guinée*, Paris: Editions Karthala.

Diawara, M. (2000) *In Search of Africa*, Cambridge: Harvard University Press.

NICOLE D. ANDERSON

Guinea-Bissau

Guinea-Bissau (formerly Portuguese Guinea) covers an area of 36,120 square kilometers, and is bordered by **Guinea** and **Senegal**. It had an estimated population of 1.2 million in 2000. It was declared a Portuguese colony in 1879, but conquest was not completed until the 1930s because of fierce resistance by the Balanta, Papel, Fellupe, Manjaco, Brame, Fula, and Mandinka ethnic groups, in response to which the Portuguese mounted protracted and bloody campaigns of retribution.

In conquered areas the colonial administration used Africans of local standing to collect taxes, recruit labor, and maintain law and order at the subregional and village levels. Bolama, strategic to the colony's groundnut trade, became the capital until 1941 when it was replaced by Bissau. Compulsory groundnut production was introduced to provide revenue, peaking and then falling in the 1880s, but reviving by 1910.

At the beginning of the 1900s Portugal consolidated its rule. Under António Salazar's "new state" – a fascist regime that came to power in Portugal in 1926 – colonial policies reflected the unmitigated police terror and brutal repression that took place in Portugal. Guineans were denied the most basic rights. Except for the very few who acquired "assimilated" Portuguese status, they were denied political representation, banned from trade union activities, rounded up for forced labor, and coerced into cash-crop production. They were also made to pay for their colonization in the form of taxes, and were subject to arbitrary beatings and imprisonment.

In an effort to strengthen colonial dependency Portugal closed Guinea-Bissau to foreign business and investment. Her trade monopoly continued well into the 1950s and 1960s. Without crop diversification the colony's agriculture deteriorated. Industrial development was forestalled. Only a few plants, workshops, factories, and sawmills were established in the 1950s and 1960s. Portugal's record in public education and health care was also appalling by any standard. Guinea-Bissau had virtually no infrastructure by the time of independence.

Consolidation of Portuguese rule continued through the 1950s with unbearable consequences for Guineans. Poverty-stricken itself, Portugal ignored calls for development, reform, and independence. Instead, on 11 June 1951, Portugal declared the colony an overseas province and intensified repression. Although a legislative assembly was established in 1972 after colonial reforms in 1961 and 1963, the move was merely designed to silence international critics.

In a bid to change the situation Amilcar Cabral and others formed the Partido Africano da Inedependência do Guiné e Cabo Verde (PAIGC) on 19 September 1956. Their initial support came from urban populations – the petty bourgeoisie, salaried workers, dockworkers, and craftsmen. Women also played a major role in the armed struggle. They participated at all levels of politics, health, education, jurisdiction, and military combat, and their own liberation became an integral part of the anti-colonial struggle. The PAIGC insisted that the struggle stretch beyond the battlefield, and lead to a new and just society free of all forms of exploitation.

A police attack on 3 August 1959 that killed fifty striking dockworkers and wounded more than a hundred led eventually to the launching of the armed struggle in 1963. With newly found political and social structures, and a full-time army comprised of 900 volunteers, the PAIGC began full-scale war in 1964. In 1967 it initiated guerrilla warfare, defeating the colonial army at many garrisons. By 1969 Portugal already knew that it could not win the war by military means. Its occupation of the colony had been reduced to the principal cities and a few fortified camps maintained only by aerial supply. By 1972 the PAIGC controlled most of the rural areas, and enjoyed strong underground support in Bissau and the other major towns that were still under Portuguese control. This was achieved against a colonial army of 35,000 soldiers, employing high explosives, napalm, and jet fighters.

In the early 1970s the PAIGC established an alternative administration, and tried to revive agricultural production in the liberated areas. A National People's Assembly was elected in liberated areas in 1973. Following Amilcar Cabral's assassination on 20 January 1973, independence was proclaimed and the colony became the Republic of Guinea-Bissau on 24 September 1973. Portugal did not, however, recognize the colony's independence until 10 September 1974, when the fascist regime in Lisbon fell and the Portuguese finally withdrew.

Under President Luís Cabral the PAIGC consolidated its power, winning the 1976 general elections by a landslide. By the late 1970s, however, signs of instability began to emerge, as Cabral's monopoly on power and misguided economic policies attracted dissent. Although the PAIGC ended coerced cash-crop production, it continued with colonial monopolistic economic policies. Peasants were again required to deliver their produce to state-appointed buyers. This renewed form of state monopoly, together with low producer prices, an overvalued peso, and an underdeveloped infrastructure, encouraged peasants to continue smuggling their products across the border or to emigrate. Despite Cabral's efforts to implement changes in the country, his regime could not completely break colonial economic patterns. Dissatisfied with the regime, João Bernado ("Niño") Vieira launched a successful coup on 14 November 1980, ousting Cabral and sending him into exile.

Vieira's regime also faced instability and numerous coup attempts. He nevertheless narrowly won the presidential election on 7 August 1994. Sociopolitical instability continued, and on 7 June 1998 General Ansumane Mane, the Gambian-born hero of the liberation war, launched a rebellion that finally removed Vieira on 8 May 1999. The Mane-led military junta formally handed the presidency to the speaker of the National Assembly, Malam Bacai Sanha, on 14 May 1999, but left a political vacuum. In the January 2000 presidential election Kumba Yalla, the leader of the opposition Partido de la Renovación Social (Party of Social Renewal or PRS), won by a landslide. His relations with General Mane remained tense, however, until the former military strongman was killed in a shoot-out with troops loyal to President Yalla on 23 November 2000.

Further reading

Galli, R. and Jones, J. (1987) *Guinea-Bissau: Politics, Economics and Society*, London: Frances Pinter and Boulder: Lynne Rienner.

Lopes, C. (1987) *Guinea-Bissau: From Liberation Struggle to Independent Statehood*, trans. M. Wolfers, Boulder: Westview Press.

BAKARY GIBBA

Guinea, Equatorial *see* Equatorial Guinea

Harare, Zimbabwe

Covering some 570 square kilometers, and situated in Mashonaland East Province in the north-central part of **Zimbabwe**, Harare is the country's capital city, home of successive colonial governments since British occupation, capital of the Federation of Rhodesia and Nyasaland (1953–63), and the seat of Zimbabwe's post-independence government. After its long march from **South Africa**, the Pioneer Column – funded by Cecil Rhodes' British South Africa Company (BSAC) – hoisted the Union Jack at Fort Salisbury (present-day Harare) in 1890. The country was named Rhodesia and claimed for Britain, with the fort named after the then British Prime Minister Gascoyne-Cecil, the third Marquess of Salisbury. Attaining municipal status in 1897, Salisbury was the home of the Shona until incoming settlers displaced the local communities. The town was renamed Harare in 1982, Harare being the name by which local inhabitants had known the small hill on the western edge of the original white settlement.

This modern city, whose streets were originally laid out in a grid-iron pattern and are lined with attractive jacaranda trees, developed from the beginning as a segregated city. Africans were confined to the so-called "townships," the first of which was Harare Township (now Mbare), built in 1897. Many African townships (now "high-density areas") were thereafter built on the southern rim of city. The farthest from the central business district is Chitungwiza, lying thirty kilometers southeast of Harare, which was built in the 1970s as a dormitory town for African workers servicing the white economy in Harare. Whites lived in the more spacious surroundings of the northern suburbs. After 1980 class, rather than race, determined residential patterns in the city.

With a population of approximately 2.5 million people, the majority of whom are Shona speakers, Harare is a major transport and communications hub, linked to the other Zimbabwean towns and the neighboring countries of **Botswana** (to the southwest), South Africa (south), **Mozambique** (east), and **Zambia** (north) by a network of railways and modern tarmac roads. The first railway line reached Harare from Beira in Mozambique in May 1899. In October 1902 a railway line connecting Salisbury to Botswana was completed, while in the period of the Unilateral Declaration of Independence (UDI) a line was added linking Beit Bridge on the South African border with the main Harare–Botswana railway. Harare is also serviced by numerous international airlines, boasting one of the world's longest runways.

Zimbabwe's major financial, commercial, and industrial center, Harare is home to the Reserve Bank of Zimbabwe, the Zimbabwe Stock Exchange, several local and international banks, and various international hotels (including the historic Meikles Hotel), retail outlets, and industrial establishments. Among its manufactures are textiles, clothing, beverages, tobacco products, cement and other construction materials, plastics, and various chemical products. At the center of Zimbabwe's most agriculturally productive region, Harare also hosts the food-processing industry and holds the largest tobacco auctions in the world. By 1985 its industries accounted for almost half of both manufacturing employment and net value of output of manufacturing in Zimbabwe.

Harare is an educational and cultural center. It is the home of the country's largest and oldest university, the University of Zimbabwe (1955); Harare Polytechnic (1927); Zimbabwe College of Music (1948); Gwebi College of Agriculture (1950); and the recently established Catholic University of Zimbabwe. It houses the National Archives, Library of Parliament, several teachers' colleges, the Queen Victoria Museum, and the National Gallery of Zimbabwe, featuring European paintings alongside traditional African art, including world-renowned Shona sculptures.

Further reading

Raftopoulos, B. and Yoshikuni, T. (1999) *Sites of Struggle: Essays in Zimbabwe's Urban History*, Harare: Weaver Press.

ALOIS MLAMBO

Hausa

Hausa is the most widely spoken West African language, and the most significant member of the Chadic branch of Afroasiatic languages. It is the first language of more than 40 million speakers in northern **Nigeria**, **Niger**, northern **Ghana**, northern **Cameroon**, and **Sudan**. It is also the second language of more than 10 million speakers throughout **West Africa** where, because of its links with trade and **Islam**, Hausa has become the most widely used lingua franca.

The native speakers of Hausa include the descendants of the original Hausa ethnolinguistic community, as well as the contact groups that have been culturally and linguistically assimilated to the Hausa as a result of trade, contact with Islam, historical conquest, and more contemporary interaction. While most Hausa speakers are Muslims, there is a minority of Hausa speakers who follow traditional religions or are Christian (see **African religions**; **Christianity**).

The introduction of Islam in Hausa-populated areas around the early thirteenth or fourteenth centuries led to the adoption of Arabic as the language of literacy. Literacy in Arabic served as a precursor to writing Hausa in Ajami – an indigenized version of the Arabic script. The dialogic interaction between the *'ulama* (scholars), who were fully conversant with Arabic, and the ordinary *mu'allim* (teachers), who had no more than basic literacy skills tied to their knowledge of the Koran, was foundational to the emergence of Ajami. This "mosque" factor was complemented by trade between the Hausa and merchants from the Arab world. Later the Islamic reformist movement of the early nineteenth century, which was initiated by Sheikh Usman dan Fodio, gave rise to an entire literary genre in the Hausa language: Jihad Ajami poetry. This, in turn, inspired a classical poetic tradition in Hausa that continues to this day.

The consolidation of Islam within Hausa society, however, transformed and deepened patriarchal structures and relations. The legacy of masculinist interpretations of Islamic doctrine meant that men were the most tutored in Islam in the institutional context of Islamic *madarassa* (Islamic schools). It was there that Arabic and Ajami literacy were taught. Unsurprisingly women were disadvantaged under this system, and the literature that arose from it was dominated by men. However, some women from *'ulama* households managed to become literate in both Arabic and Hausa, going on to produce important works of Jihad literature.

The different forms of European colonization of Hausa lands in the early 1900s affected the use of Hausa in those areas. In present-day Sudan, Hausa assumed an Islamic Arabized identity, resulting in the Hausa–Fulani Arabic literary tradition supplanting the Hausa Ajami tradition. In French-controlled territories, such as Niger and northern Cameroon, French policies of cultural and linguistic assimilation undermined the Ajami tradition by imposing French education as the sole type of formal education. This policy and its post-colonial legacy have hindered the development of formal education and literacy in Hausa, in both Ajami and Roman script. Thus Ajami literacy was broadly marginalized during the colonial period, and remains so, with its educational potential deliberately disregarded by the Western-trained post-colonial elite. In effect the French educational policy has led to the reinforcement of a primarily oral tradition of literary expression among a majority of Hausa-speaking peoples who do not have access to formal education.

The British, on the other hand, to some extent promoted literacy and formal education in local languages, as was the case in northern Nigeria where the majority of Hausa-speakers reside. However, the British were not keen to have their colonial subjects retain the use of Arabic script, nor to allow the continuation of Hausa literary creativity using Ajami. To the colonialists Ajami was a powerful repository of Hausa Islamic identity that threatened their hegemonic agenda. Consequently by the 1860s European missionaries had begun to use the Roman script for writing Hausa; by 1903 this new system was extended to the writing of Hausa educational texts. From the 1960s the Hausa language was used as a subject of and medium for instruction in the educational system in northern Nigeria. It also featured prominently in debates over what should become the country's national language. These debates were not repeated in Niger, where the French linguistic and cultural legacy was strong.

Overall Hausa continued to be one of the languages of Africa that drew the attention of numerous studies, by both Western and Hausa scholars. It was also studied in many Western institutions of higher learning, and became one of only three African languages into which UNESCO's eight-volume *General History of Africa* was translated. In print the Hausa language has fared well, with magazines, newspapers, books, pamphlets, and journals on religious, cultural, and others scholarly topics being produced, mostly by Nigerian publishers. While most of these Hausa publications were in Roman script, writing in Ajami began to gain popularity due to the rise of Islamic revivalism throughout Hausa territory and elsewhere in the Hausa diaspora. Pressures for democratization, along with cultural and religious revivalism, were creating new spaces for multimedia production of many and various discourses in Hausa, religious and secular, oral or written, in Ajami or Roman script or both. By the 1990s Hausa was featured on radio stations in Nigeria, Niger, Ghana, Cameroon, and **Egypt**. In addition to news programs on issues ranging from public health to party politics, there was an impressive output of popular culture (radio and TV drama, movies, comedy), attracting large audiences. Outside Africa there were special Hausa programs on the BBC, Voice of America, Radio Moscow, and Radio Beijing, as well as, by the end of the decade, on Voice and Vision, which is aired from the Islamic republic of Iran.

Further reading

Ahmed, U. and Bello, D. (1970) *An Introduction to Classical Hausa and the Major Dialects*, Zaria: Northern Nigeria Publishing Company.

Boyd, J. and Mack, B.B. (eds.) (1997) *Collected Works of Nana Asma'u, Daughter of Usman dan Fodiyo (1793–1864)*, East Lansing: Michigan State University Press.

Philips, E. (2000) *Spurious Arabic: Hausa and Colonial Nigeria*, Madison: University of Wisconsin African Studies Publications.

OUSSEINA D. ALIDOU

health and disease

At the beginning of the twentieth century, Europeans perceived Africa as a land of death, largely on the basis of their own experience; this perception persisted to the end of the century, with alarming predictions of soaring mortality rates due to Acquired Immune Deficiency Syndrome (AIDS). Africans had another perspective: They remembered a time when they could control familiar diseases, they were aware of how many new diseases Europeans brought to the continent, and they knew how many epidemics occurred as a result of colonial exploration, exploitation, and expropriation. A similar dichotomy of views exists about health care: Europeans take credit for bringing biomedicine to unattended sick populations, whereas Africans know they had recourse to many therapeutic systems and were cared for by a wide variety of healers (for example, bone-setters, herbalists, midwives). Indeed they continue to consult healers, especially for conditions like mental illnesses that biomedical practitioners are unable to treat successfully. This bipolar vision makes for interesting reading: On one side are the accounts of missionary and colonial medical services, and the autobiographies of European doctors who practiced in Africa; on the other are analyses of a holistic approach to care that appreciates the role of human or group interaction in the occurrence and treatment of ill health and disease, and descriptions of discoveries of the powerful pharmacological properties of local herbs. A third body of literature, mainly the writings of anthropologists and ethnologists, describes African therapeutic systems, but rarely with reference to the events of the twentieth century. Since the 1970s scholars have elaborated a theoretical framework to interpret African biosocial and cultural adaptation as part of a broad historical process in which colonization, capitalist agriculture, conflict, and increased population mobility, especially **urbanization**, have all played integral parts.

The defining impact of colonialism on African health and disease in the twentieth century is inescapable. In their decision to exploit African resources to their own advantage, the European powers challenged indigenous social and cultural organization, with endless repercussions for human and animal health, and for the disease ecology of Africa. This point can be illustrated in many ways. The colonists' often forced mobilization of labor – for war, transport (both porterage and the building of roads or railroads), mining, and plantation agriculture – deprived families, particularly the women left behind, of the most basic resource on which cultivation depends in the absence of mechanized technology. As food production suffered, so did nutrition, which is the basis of good health. In **East Africa** absent workers no longer controlled the environment, so diseases like trypanosomiasis (sleeping sickness, caused by the tsetse fly) overtook formerly protected areas, killing people and their livestock. In the parts of Africa where Europeans settled, planters and ranchers often claimed the best land, crowding Africans into arid, quickly eroded areas. This happened in **Zimbabwe**, for example, where the indigenous population were soon suffering from the common diseases of poverty. Malnutrition increased everywhere as the forced cultivation of certain foods resulted in the substitution of nutritionally poor cassava and maize for the traditional and nutritionally rich millets and sorghums; monoculture depleted the soil, making crops vulnerable to drought and infestation, and the cultivation of non-food crops for export exacerbated competition for arable land. European technologies brought new health risks: Mining exposed workers to injuries and to lung diseases like silicosis; irrigation produced chronic infestations of schistosome-bearing snails, which caused bilharzia, a disorder of the liver, bladder, lungs, and central nervous system; and guns made new kinds of wounds.

By 1900 Europeans had penetrated all parts of the continent, but the consolidation of control was an uneven process. Disruption and loss of life did not end with the slave trade; they continued with military campaigns to suppress African resistance – the 1905–7 Maji Maji revolt in German East Africa and the 1904–6 decimation of the Herero in **Namibia**, for instance – and with the crude extraction of resources – King Leopold II's brutal exploitation of the **Congo**, which resulted in millions of deaths, being the extreme example. Disease epidemics followed in the wake of the invaders: Scorched earth policies created famines and drove refugees into new disease environments for which they had no natural immunity. Smallpox spread rapidly in crowded markets and camps, and as traditional isolation and inoculation practices broke down. Endemic diseases like cerebrospinal meningitis and tick-borne relapsing fever spread epidemically as colonial companies and governments created or improved transportation networks. First the slave trade and then colonialism caused people to move on a scale not previously known, disrupting health care based on local knowledge of both diseases and cures, and depriving the sick of familiar nursing skills. Population numbers, already dropping in the nineteenth century, continued to fall. They did not begin to rise until after 1925, in some places not until after the **Second World War**. The involvement of many parts of Africa in the world wars itself permanently scarred society: The colonial powers recruited tens of thousands of men to fight in Africa and abroad, where they died of disease (notably malaria and dysentery) and their wounds; the influenza pandemic of 1918–19 claimed an estimated 2 million Africans; and the spread of sexually transmitted infections became a serious problem.

Because colonial powers established rule earlier in some parts of Africa than in others, they set up biomedical services at different dates. Their initial purpose, however, was everywhere the same: to protect Europeans (administrators, the military, and settlers) in the first instance, and to treat African employees in the second. Some of the largest employers maintained their own medical staff to screen job applicants and respond to emergencies; occupational health was an underdeveloped aspect of public health. Health services for the mass of rural Africans was left to the haphazard implementation of medical missions until after the Second World War when national liberation movements forced the expansion of education and health facilities. Segregated medical services, staffed almost exclusively by European men, were the norm almost everywhere, exacerbating scarcity by duplicating facilities. On the eve of independence colonial health care reached a mere 5–15 percent of the African population.

The structure of health care varied under different colonial regimes. A brief overview of the British and French services, which were the largest, will give an indication of their organization. The British instituted a decentralized, three-tier system based on reference hospitals in capital cities and provincial hospitals and satellite clinics (more often planned than realized) in rural areas. Public health – mainly sanitation and racial segregation – never accounted for more than 1 percent of the health budget, and maternal and child health services (normally a part of public health) were delegated to the missions. Provinces financed their own services from local taxes, so the poorest districts – some of which had a higher proportion of women than men – had the worst and least extensive services. In **French West Africa** from 1905 and **French Equatorial Africa** from 1910 the French military organized mobile medical units to conduct mass vaccination campaigns and bring other public health assistance to Africans. In addition to medical services for Europeans, the French opened several laboratories under the Pasteur Institute, a private body; some of them did useful work – for example, the production of anti-plague vaccines in **Madagascar** in 1935.

It should be remembered that biomedicine had little to offer in 1900. European researchers established the scientific basis of disease only in the last quarter of the nineteenth century. Practical medical applications lagged behind scientific advances. Tropical medicine was an infant specialty that lacked the thousand years of knowledge and experience that African societies had accumulated. Surgery and gynecology benefited from developments in antisepsis and anesthesia in the last half of the nineteenth century, but obstetricians disregarded millennia of midwifery. Nursing emerged from religious auspices to become a registered profession in England only in 1919. In 1900 public health was a new discipline riven by competing theories that pitted environmental reforms (for example, the draining of marshes to control the spread of malaria) against preventive medicine (the use of quinine to prevent and treat individual cases of malaria). Knowledge of nutrition was limited; for example, navy doctors had learned about scurvy and such on long sea voyages, but little was known about kwashiorkor, a protein and calorie deficiency that afflicted toddlers during weaning. Effective pharmaceutical remedies were not available until the Second World War, which prompted the development of antibiotics.

Colonialists' responses to the old diseases they found and the new illnesses they introduced were inappropriate, and did not touch the causes of sickness and death. Commercial, land, and labor policies impoverished Africans, undermined their health, spread and aggravated endemic diseases, and created many new health risks of which the most grave were chronic malnutrition and physical exhaustion. Undernourishment and fatigue increased susceptibility to all diseases (except smallpox), and raised death rates. In children malnutrition interacted synergistically with infections, turning banal childhood illnesses like measles into fatal conditions. Colonial medical services were blind to deficiency diseases and prescribed standard diets only to increase the work output of laborers in mines and on plantations. In general missionary and colonial medical services adopted an individual, curative, urban, and hospital-based approach to disease at a time when most Africans lived in rural areas and desperately needed relief from poverty.

Egyptian medicine dates back to Imhotep (*c*.2980 BC) and was a source of Greek medicine, which was eventually retransmitted to Europe and Africa through such institutions as the medical school founded in Alexandria in 322 BC and the many therapeutic systems associated with the world of **Islam**. Cairo's hospital and medical school were renowned in the eleventh century. In the tradition of prophetic medicine, marabouts addressed psychological problems: for example, in the sixteenth to eighteenth centuries they treated disruptions caused by the need to adjust to a market economy. Most other African therapeutic systems were loosely linked sets of practices, some more elaborated than others. Colonial rulers and missionaries condemned them as witchcraft, and the effect of proscribing their practice was to deprive African healers of new knowledge that they might have gleaned from cooperation with European physicians and scientists, as well as denying Africans a local source of accessible care.

The first Africans to receive training in biomedicine worked as orderlies for various army medical corps in the **First World War**. Afterwards colonial governments and missions offered training courses for auxiliary and paramedical personnel. Most training programs were for men, even nurses' training (elsewhere women predominate in nursing). Everywhere Africans seeking university-level medical education met barriers, and remarkably few of them succeeded in qualifying as physicians before independence. Despite colonial domination of African universities, medical schools, and laboratories, despite wars and a deteriorating political situation in many countries since independence, despite donor-driven fiscal austerity, **structural adjustment programs**, and other economic hardships, and despite the lack of all kinds of resources for research, African researchers have made remarkable advances in science and technology, creating a post-colonial literature of high caliber in the medical and social sciences.

The provision of biomedical care began to change after the Second World War under the twin impulses of **nationalist movements** for independence and the intervention of international organizations. In some countries **decolonization** was orderly, and independent governments inherited five-year development plans that included projections for the health sector. In others the transition was abrupt, as in the Congo where the **United Nations** intervened and brought in a corps of Haitian doctors (who were fleeing the Duvalier dictatorship) to provide medical care. Some independence movements, such as FRELIMO in **Mozambique** and the EPLF in **Eritrea**, made the provision of health care a priority in liberated areas. Other countries experimented with socialist models of health services after independence: for example, **Algeria**, **Tanzania**, and Zimbabwe made state provision of free care a goal of their social programs. In the 1970s Algeria, Mozambique, **Nigeria**, and Tanzania produced remarkable and creative innovations designed to spread health care under conditions of scarce technical and physical resources. Algeria required all specialists to work in the public sector, and opened the health professions by giving preferential admission to children of illiterate parents; Mozambique experimented with a public drug sector, consolidating all purchases in a central agency that bid for the lowest international prices; Nigeria invited local healers to work with psychiatrists in a village-based program for the mentally ill; and Tanzania mapped out geographical access, and then built facilities in the least-served areas.

The World Health Organization (WHO), believing that the proper response to health needs in the **Third World** was the transfer of biomedical technology, ignored African therapeutic systems. From 1949 it assisted colonial governments in organizing mass vaccination campaigns against diseases like tuberculosis. From the 1960s, as more countries won independence, WHO began to define the concept of national health programs, but assistance with single-disease campaigns prevailed over broad-based health systems. The efforts to combat smallpox and malaria illustrate these different approaches. In 1967, with staff and money from the United States, WHO launched a global campaign to eradicate smallpox, which is an acute, self-limiting disease preventable with cheap, low-level technology delivered by people with limited training. In 1979 WHO declared triumphantly that it had eradicated smallpox from the world. But the campaign had limited impact: It did not affect mortality rates, made no structural changes in national health systems, and did not require social or economic reorganization. A similar campaign could not eliminate malaria, which poses a much greater threat to Africans (nearly a million children die annually of the disease, which accounts for one-tenth of infant mortality in Africa). Malaria is a recurrent disease, dependent on an intermediate host (the anopheles mosquito), and there is still no effective vaccine. The eradication of malaria requires expensive, labor-intensive environmental engineering, an investment in window screens and bednets for every home, and a dense network of laboratories and health services; surveillance depends on a trained corps of medical and laboratory technicians. Instead of building the necessary health infrastructure to support the campaign, WHO abandoned malaria eradication in 1965. That decision would have catastrophic consequences as HIV, the virus that causes AIDS, spread through the continent in the 1980s.

African and other health ministers pressurized WHO to help them build national health services. After developing a plan to switch from curative services in urban hospitals to a primary health-care model that would serve the rural poor, WHO issued a challenge in 1978: "Health for All by the Year 2000." But in the 1980s the World Bank and the International Monetary Fund undermined this revolutionary strategy by imposing structural adjustment plans that called for budgetary austerity (which cut government health budgets), privatization (which encouraged private practice, further draining the public sector), currency devaluation (which reduced funds for imported drugs and equipment), and trade liberalization (which undercut local drug production). International and bilateral aid agencies began to fund a multiplicity of small projects run by private voluntary and **non-governmental organizations** (NGOs), further devaluing a public sector that donors dismissed as corrupt. This preference for NGOs accelerates the privatization of health-service delivery and represents a major shift in the health-care paradigm: Market values have replaced the state-welfare model and the postwar vision of humanitarian aid.

In competition with international charities for funding and personnel, **civil society** organizations began to flourish; in a number of countries these groups were especially concerned with health as a human right (see **human rights**). In **South Africa** many civics (as local NGOs are known) challenged the apartheid government: they argued for the elimination of racial discrimination in the health sector, and for the adoption of human rights standards for health professionals; they demanded medical documentation of torture, and condemned the mistreatment of the mentally ill, an issue Frantz Fanon had broached in Algeria in the 1950s. NGOs can be important advocates for issues like accountability and for neglected groups like the handicapped and mentally retarded. Estimates placed the number of disabled Africans by the end of the century at 50 million; excluded from education and employment, most lived in poverty. Inadequate transportation systems and architectural barriers immobilized the disabled at home, and the lack of health and rehabilitation services often condemned them to an early death. Their numbers were increasing as warfare and the planting of land mines continued.

War and armed conflict devastated many countries, causing civilian death rates and injury rates to rise. The health effects of wars were direct and indirect. They diverted resources from welfare to warfare; military strategies used starvation as a weapon of war; some armies deliberately targeted health services for destruction; and armed forces were vectors of disease, especially sexually transmitted infections. Light weapons were now found everywhere, recirculating from wars to crime waves; and tens of millions of land mines had yet to be removed, preventing people from farming or horribly injuring those who did. Wars also interrupted public health measures to control communicable diseases; destroyed housing, transport, and infrastructure; and disrupted food production and distribution, causing hunger and malnutrition that exacerbated the effects of most infections.

As a response to social conflict, many Africans joined cults of affliction, which had a long and in some cases continuous history: for instance, Equatorial Africans practiced some form of Lemba from the seventeenth to the early twentieth century. In the 1980s many Ugandans joined Alice Lakwena's Holy Spirit Movement, a cult of affliction centered on the healing of individual soldiers and infertile women. In 1986 Lakwena organized the Holy Spirit Movement Forces to wage war against the government, witches, and impure soldiers, using a complex initiation and purification ritual in which she freed the Holy Spirit soldiers from witchcraft and evil spirits. Although violations of health rights were perhaps most extreme in South Africa and Namibia, the need to treat the health consequences of torture, and the trauma of war and displacement, became critical in many countries. A center for victims of torture opened in **Cape Town** in South Africa, and NGOs were assisting projects in Eritrea, **Ghana**, **Guinea**, **Mali**, **Rwanda**, and **Sierra Leone**. The specifics of gendered methods of torture were only beginning to surface, as women's NGOs took up the issues of violence against women and rape in armed conflict.

The disruption and displacement that accompanied violence, falling living standards due to contracting labor markets, deteriorating health conditions tied to malnutrition and poor sanitation, and shrinking access to health care underlay African data on high rates of morbidity and mortality from all causes. Conditions of political and structural violence encircled high-risk settings for AIDS. The virus was spreading along the corridors of civil wars, the circuits of labor migrants, and the paths of fleeing refugees. Links between poverty and HIV infection were not widely investigated, but preliminary evidence suggested that the burden of AIDS fell more heavily on poor households. WHO described the transmission of AIDS in Africa as Pattern II (that is, the spread of HIV by heterosexual intercourse), in contrast to Pattern I industrial countries (where AIDS affected mainly homosexuals and intravenous drug-users). The number of HIV-infected women was far greater in Pattern II than in Pattern I countries; yet African women carried the additional responsibility of caring for relatives sick with AIDS, and for the orphans of relatives dead from AIDS. The assumed role of commercial sex work in the transmission of HIV in Pattern II countries added to the burdens of African women. The belief that women were the cause of sexually transmitted infections, including HIV, was widespread. As a result when a woman tested positive for HIV, her husband was likely to respond with violence, send her back to her relatives, or abandon her. The fact that AIDS was not a single disease but a syndrome of some twenty opportunistic infections that overtake weakened immune systems added to the problems of treatment. The diagnosis of these infections, the prescription of appropriate antibiotics, and the administration of anti-retrovirals required sophisticated medical facilities that rarely existed outside capital cities. The lack of a full range of public health services in provincial towns and villages complicated prevention, which required treatment of sexually transmitted infections and tuberculosis at the very least.

AIDS was present in many African workplaces, although its relation to working conditions was not known. Health risks on the job were not well studied in Africa. The burden of occupational illness and injury was unknown, beyond some data on mining enclaves. With only one in ten workers employed in the formal sector, and with trade union membership covering perhaps 3 percent of the workforce, **labor movements** pressed for investigation of poor working conditions in only a few countries, such as South Africa and Zimbabwe. The suspicion was that many jobs were hazardous to health and safety, and that fatalities among workers – for example, in the transport industry – were many times higher in Africa than in Europe. Even less was known about hazards in the unregulated informal economy. Although most African countries had factory and mine inspectorates, and some protective legislation covering workers' compensation, unemployment insurance, and pensions, injured workers in the informal sector had no recourse to disability pay.

Occupational health was yet another area in which policy-makers overlooked women. Women's heavy workloads, which were the combined result of macro-economic and patriarchal familial demands, took their toll on women's health, often resulting in higher death rates in childbirth. Death during pregnancy and the need for assistance in childbirth were just two of the many of the health issues of greatest concern to most African women by the end of the twentieth century. Others were the spread of the AIDS epidemic, especially among young women; mental illness and domestic violence, which appeared to be increasing alongside the dislocation of women and children that accompanied civil unrest and war; the persistence of harmful traditional practices such as female genital mutilation; and the impact of structural adjustment programs on health and access to health care. Many of these problems were tied to state policies. Whether apartheid, theocratic law, fiscal austerity, or structural adjustment, these policies imposed economic hardships that profoundly affected social organization. Not only were daily life and gender relations altered, but incremental shifts in how people responded to and participated in major cultural and religious institutions added up to fundamental social change. First among adversities was the lack of secure employment that would guarantee decent living standards. Without cash to purchase services, the decline of state provision for health, education, and other basic social needs made life that much more arduous, especially for women.

The future health challenges in Africa are many and daunting. Transboundary phenomena such as pollution, infectious diseases, and resource depletion were likely to assume increasing importance. The consequences of global warming, especially for arid and semi-arid regions, as well as for coastal areas and river deltas subject to flooding, were poorly understood and were potentially threatening to human and animal health. Climate change promised to exacerbate periodic and chronic shortfalls of water, in a continent where perhaps half the people did not have access to safe supplies of fresh water. And the study of emerging infectious diseases – by 2000 we knew of Ebola, Marburg, and AIDS, but in the future many others, equally deadly, could appear – required highly developed national research laboratories that had yet to be built and staffed.

See also: environmental change; population; professionals; socialisms and socialists; society: colonial; society: post-independence

Further reading

Du Toit, B. and Abdalla, I.H. (eds.) (1985) *African Healing Strategies*, Owerri, New York, and London: Trado-Medic Books.

Feierman, S. (1978) *Health Care in Africa: A Working Bibliography*, Waltham: Crossroads Press.

Feierman, S. and Janzen, J.M. (eds.) (1998) *The Social Basis of Health and Healing in Africa*, Collingdale: DIANE Publishing.

Georgis, B.W. (1986) *Selected and Annotated Bibliography on Women and Health in Africa*, Dakar: AAWORD.

Gran, P. (1978) "Medical Pluralism in Arab and Egyptian History: An Overview of Class Structures and Philosophies of the Main Phases," *Social Science & Medicine* 13B, 4: 339–48.

Patterson, K.D. (1978) "Bibliographic Essay," in G.W. Hartwig and K.D. Patterson (eds.), *Disease in African History: An Introductory Survey and Case Studies*, Durham: Duke University Press.

Stock, R. (1986) "Disease and Development or the Underdevelopment of Health: A Critical Review of Geographical Perspectives on African Health Problems," *Social Science & Medicine* 23: 689–700.

MEREDETH TURSHEN

historiography, African

see development of African history

human rights

At the beginning of the twentieth century the European invasion and almost total conquest of the African continent was complete. Colonialism subjected most Africans to various forms of human rights abuse, although Africans who lived under direct colonial rule in settler colonies suffered the most violations, examples including the colonizers of the Belgian **Congo**, **South Africa**, **Kenya**, southern Rhodesia (now **Zimbabwe**), and **French Equatorial Africa**. Africans in these colonies had their lands expropriated for European settlement, European farms, and European plantations. Many Africans were forced to work on the plantations and public works projects, others were forced to become migrant laborers in neighboring colonies, while many more were conscripted for various war efforts within and outside the continent. Village chiefs and elders who refused to cooperate in the forced recruitment of workers and soldiers were detained or forced into exile. Some colonial administrations forced Africans to produce cash crops that were then taxed to benefit the colonial economy. On the other hand, others were forbidden from producing particular cash crops that would have been in direct competition with those grown by Europeans. The most nefarious human rights violations surrounded the outlawing, debasement, and attempted destruction of African laws, customs, religions, languages, and dress.

During the first half of the twentieth century most Africans did not have the most basic political, social, or economic human rights: They did not have the right to vote, access to educational facilities and public accommodation, freedom of speech and movement, or due process under the law. Moreover many Africans throughout the continent were killed, injured, and raped with impunity by colonial officials and European settlers. These blatant human rights violations were often the catalyst for nationalist struggles for independence and liberation. The leaders of **nationalist movements** involved in the **decolonization** process, especially Kwame Nkrumah of **Ghana**, espoused the ideals of human rights. In addition the various organizations, associations, trade unions, and political parties that were crucial to the independence struggle saw the importance of and need for human rights.

Following the **Second World War** the international community, which excluded most of Africa because Africa was still under colonial rule, began to address human rights on what it called a "universal" level. The first legal instruments that claimed to address human rights internationally were the Universal Declaration of Human Rights, the Convention Against Torture, and the Genocide Convention, all signed in 1948. The Convention on the Elimination of All Forms of Racial Discrimination was signed in 1965, and the International Covenants on Civil and Political Rights and on Economic, Social, and Cultural Rights were signed in 1966, after most Africans were represented in the United Nations and other international bodies.

Other important international instruments included the Convention on the Political Rights of Women (1952), the Convention on the Elimination of All Forms of Discrimination Against Women (1979), and the International Convention on the Rights of the Child (1989). Most nations throughout the world – and African nations were no exception – were parties to these agreements; however, African nations (like many others) did not adhere to many provisions outlined in the agreements.

During the post-independence period Africans who represented various segments of society saw the need to institute their own human rights instruments. The International African Charter on Human and Peoples' Rights (the Banjul Charter) was adopted in 1981 by the **Organization of African Unity** (OAU), and promulgated in 1986. The Charter contained a number of important provisions that recognized the importance of African traditions and civilizations in human rights, along with the importance of individual rights and peoples' collective rights. The Charter extended human rights to include the right to development. Furthermore the Charter contended that civil and political rights were not separate from economic, social, and cultural rights. The Charter established the African Commission on Human and Peoples' Rights. The Commission was given a mandate to identify and investigate human rights abuses and to promote, through legislation and other measures, human rights throughout the continent. However it is important to note that the Commission had no enforcement power or machinery, and its inability to effectively address and curtail human rights violations was evident. In summary, the Charter, its mandate, and other international agreements provided first-generation rights (civil and political), second-generation rights (economic, social, and cultural), and third-generation rights (developmental and environmental) to all Africans, at least on paper.

The reality of the post-independence era matched the goals and missions of neither the international nor the African human rights documents. The continent experienced human rights violations on a massive scale, producing civil wars, **genocides**, **refugees**, internally displaced populations, military takeovers, political assassinations, and general unrest, although some democratic governments were eventually established. All of the underlying causes of human rights violations put individuals at greater risk of additional human rights abuses. For example, civil wars, ethnic strife, and genocide destroyed valuable, scarce infrastructure that included schools, hospitals, roads, bridges, and communications facilities, so that those individuals who were not directly affected by human rights abuses were indirectly affected by the loss of such facilities. Most African countries were not in the economic position to replace destroyed infrastructure. The result was millions of people who had their human rights to development violated, as well as their rights to a healthy and balanced environment and to information. In other words, people's rights to develop their personalities, to participate in the cultural life of a community, and to enjoy the arts were abused and violated when they were forced to flee, killed, injured, raped, detained, or denied access to those facilities that would have allowed them to develop culturally and participate in the community.

The factors and actors who produced human rights violations were numerous. Clearly the many years of autocratic rule in **Malawi**, Kenya, **Democratic Republic of Congo**, **Central African Republic**, **Uganda**, **Guinea**, and South Africa, to name a few, were the cause of many human rights violations. There were other losers in the struggle for human rights. The civil wars in **Nigeria**, **Liberia**, **Sierra Leone**, **Somalia**, **Ethiopia**, **Mozambique**, **Angola**, and **Sudan** subjected many individuals, including thousands of women and children, to human rights abuses by both government forces and rebel groups.

Military rule in various countries – from Nigeria and Liberia to Sudan and **Ghana** – also resulted in the abridgment of people's human rights, as freedom of the press, assembly, and speech were suspended, along with the detention, imprisonment, torture, and killing of many people. The many ethnic conflicts that culminated in civil war produced gross human rights violations, as illustrated in Somalia, Liberia, Sudan, and Ethiopia. However, the ethnic conflict between the Tutsis and Hutus in **Rwanda** produced levels of human rights violations that led to genocide in the early 1990s. With all the conventions, charters, and laws to protect human rights, the international community, including African governments, largely ignored this outrage. There were cases of modern slavery reported in Liberia in the early part of the twentieth century, and in Sudan and **Mauritania** in the latter part of the century. There were cases of female genital mutilation, spousal inheritance, and the inability of women to inherit property in some parts of the continent. It is important to point out that some Africans (supported by others throughout the world) argued that these practices and others were not human rights violations, but rather cultural practices protected by customary law.

During the second half of the twentieth century human rights became an important part of the political, economic, and social debates about the future of Africa. African intellectuals, students, politicians, journalists, leaders of grass-roots movements, ordinary citizens, and others discussed the importance and inclusion of human rights in national dialogue. In addition American and European intellectuals and policy-makers discussed, in particular, the role or lack thereof of human rights in traditional and contemporary African societies and cultures. At the end of the twentieth century questions were still being asked as to whether human rights were universal or culturally relative, and moreover whether they apply to Africa.

Although most African states were signatories to various international agreements on human rights, their applicability to Africa was not always certain. Part of the uncertainty was based on American and Western European contributions to and influence on early human rights documents. These documents were called "universal" and "international," but a broad representation of the world's population had very little input in drafting and ratifying them. In essence a few governments developed a set of absolute human rights principles that they attempted to impose on the rest of the world, while they themselves often ignored that same set of human rights standards. For example, when the Universal Declaration for Human Rights was developed in 1948, racial segregation was not merely a cultural practice in the United States: it was codified into law and had been ruled to be constitutional.

Those who supported the universal view of human rights argued that the international community was capable of developing a single set of human rights that applied across the globe. In other words human rights developed by the international community were applicable to all societies, and governments had the responsibility of devising and implementing laws and practices that were in accordance with international guidelines. This argument was supported by the belief that all societies respected human rights on some level, because people everywhere were accorded human dignity based on accepted norms of behavior. Others argued that human rights were not the same as human dignity. Human rights involved rights that the individual had in relation to the state. These were rights that individuals were entitled to exercise without interference by the state.

The relativist position on human rights in Africa supported the position that human rights principles had to take into consideration the culture and traditions of various African societies at different times throughout history. Those who supported cultural relativism asserted that human rights standards developed in the West did not automatically apply to Africa for a number of reasons. The cultural relativist position supported the belief that the community and not the individual was the most important component in pre-modern societies, and thus individuals derived rights from the community, through duties and obligations, and not from the state. Others maintained that the individual as a human being was not relevant to human rights because people were not identified as individual human beings, but rather as a part of a group (by age, gender, social status, family ties). There thus existed no opportunity for the individual to claim rights against the state.

There is another school of thought in the discussions and debates that did not support the universal or relativist position on human rights in Africa. There were writers, intellectuals, and scholars – mainly Africanists – who contended that human rights were not strictly the invention of European and American philosophers, nor were human rights absent in Africa before 1948. Furthermore some within this school of thought believed that some human rights were universal, while other rights were relevant only to particular societies during certain periods of history. In other words human rights were universal and culturally relative at the same time, and Africans had always recognized and protected human rights. Thus discussions on human rights in Africa at the end of the twentieth century recognized the past and contemporary importance of African traditions, cultures, and institutions, as well as how they had evolved over time.

See also: law; state: colonial; state: post-independence

Further reading

Abayomi, T. (ed.) (1993) *Human Rights and Democracy in Africa*, Lagos: Human Rights Africa.

McCarthy-Arnolds, E. (ed.) (1994) *Africa, Human Rights, and the Global System: The Political Economy of Human Rights in a Changing World*, Westport: Greenwood Press.

Welch, C.E., Jr. (1995) *Protecting Human Rights in Africa: Strategies and Roles of Non-Governmental Organizations*, Philadelphia: University of Pennsylvania Press.

Zeleza, P.T. and McConnaughay, P. (eds.) (2002) *Human Rights and the Rule of Law in Africa*, Philadelphia: University of Pennsylvania Press.

CASSANDRA RACHEL VENEY

I

Ibadan, Nigeria

Located in southwestern **Nigeria**, Ibadan is Nigeria's second largest city after **Lagos**, with an estimated population of 1.7 million people in 2000. From a theoretical perspective, the emergence of Ibadan as a city can be explained using the functional specialization theory of urbanization. However, from an empirical perspective, the historical origin of the city of Ibadan is far from clear. Some accounts suggest that the earliest group of settlers were fugitives from the nearby villages, others claim that it was founded either in the late 1820s or early 1830s as a military camp during the Yoruba civil wars and developed into the most powerful Yoruba city-state. In spite of these debates, Ibadan is a city of relatively recent origin, as well as the pinnacle of pre-European urbanism in Nigeria.

The heterogeneity of its population was a marked feature of Ibadan from its very beginning up to 1850. The economic growth of Ibadan between 1851 and 1900 relied heavily on slaves, while its political eminence throughout the second half of the nineteenth century made it an emporium for trade in the region. The assumption of control of the city in 1893 by British colonial government created the conditions of peace and security that were necessary for Ibadan to derive further advantages from its favorable location for commerce. The railway arrived in Ibadan from Lagos in 1901, and the line was extended northwards to Kano in 1912, thus ensuring the city's continuing economic importance. It is pertinent that the period 1901–51 saw increased economic activity between Ibadan and the outside world, especially European firms. The rise in the economic importance of Ibadan also attracted a number of people into the city, encouraging further diversification in the ethnic character of the population in terms of ethnic origin, education, and level of income. Migrants came from the east (the Ibo, the Ibibios, the Efiks, and the Ijaws), from the midwest (the Edos, the Ishans, and the Urhobos), and from the north (the Hausa, the Nupes, and the Igbirras). Data from the 1931 census showed a preponderance of females over males in Ibadan. This reflected changing economic conditions that had made it necessary for men to look for better opportunities elsewhere, including Lagos.

Historically Ibadan has been a center of education and research. The University College, Ibadan, was founded in 1948 as a college of the University of London, later becoming the autonomous and independent University of Ibadan in 1962. Ibadan is also the site of the International Institute of Tropical Agriculture, the Cocoa Research Institute of Nigeria, and the Federal Agricultural Research Institute. With an estimated population of nearly 2 million people in 2000 (up from about 850,000 in 1975), Ibadan is a traditional city, characterized by pre-industrial urban development in core areas and modern urban land-use in the outer parts of the city. It is a city where different planning paradigms and types of infrastructure have been adopted at different points in history.

Since 1950 the spatial size of the city has quadrupled as a result of urban sprawl and the migration of residents from inner-city areas to the suburbs. This has implications for effective provision of infrastructure and management in the city. The Sustainable Ibadan Project (SIP), an initiative of the United Nations Center for Human Settlements, commenced in 1994 with a view to enhancing the environmental planning and management capacities of local agencies and departments responsible for the city.

Further reading

Mabojunje, A.L. (1968) *Urbanization in Nigeria*, London: University of London Press.

UWEM E. ITE

integration, regional *see* regional integration

indigenous religions *see* African religions

intellectuals: colonial

Both a professional and a social entity, the African intellectual has a complex history. Intellectual traditions exist in indigenous languages and cultures, including Arabic. They also exist under the umbrella of **Islam**, which antedated European colonial rule, connecting with intellectual life and contesting it in ways that differ from African intellectual trajectories more directly spawned by the European–African encounters. These encounters forced virtually all African societies and their thinkers, regardless of their discursive tradition or expressive medium, to reckon with the state of their own economic, technological, and social development, making issues of modernity in an African context both practical and intellectual. The themes of "African regeneration" or "African renaissance," as well as of Islamic, Christian, or traditionalist reform, began to seriously engage African intellectuals in debate during the nineteenth century. In such a short entry as this, charting the trajectories of the different strands of African intellection during the colonial period is no easy task; what is modestly proposed here, then, is a genealogical interpretation of those intellectuals who were originally created as objects of the colonial/modern civilizing mission of Europe, but subsequently came through notions of African nationalism to represent themselves as subjects of an African modernity.

The cultural and cognitive formation of colonial intellectuals

Colonial intellectuals were part of the "middle class" that emerged in African societies following the continent's encounter with Europe. The result of European social engineering – the so-called "civilizing mission" – this middle class, as it had been dubbed by those who engineered it, was marked off from other "natives" by a qualitative cultural "outsiderness," albeit complicated by the fact that its members continued to retain their indigenous affiliations. This middle stratum is what Ray Jenkins, analyzing the evidence from coastal **Ghana**, has called "Euro-African society" – a sociocultural postulate rather than the strictly sociological one implied by the term "middle class." In Jenkins' assessment, this middle stratum was nothing less than a new ethnicity, a distinct "ethnocultural formation," with a "complex symbiosis" "rather than a clear merger" between itself and local ethnic communities (Jenkins 1985: 9).

The problem with Jenkins' sociocultural reading is that it does away with the vertical differentiation of the social field implied in the use of "class." Euro-African society was not a society unto itself; nor did it, through a horizontal differentiation, simply sit side by side with the collectivities within colonial sociality that he designates as "African" and "European." In the wider colonial social formation Euro-African society was articulated in a hierarchical relationship to African society and European society. A sociocultural reading informed by the notion of the hierarchy that was articulated by colonialism cannot but conclude, therefore, that what Europe's civilizing mission intruded into the various African societies of encounter was a modern caste system. So the "middle caste" was privileged as such by its cultural nearness to an "upper caste" – Europeans – and positioned relative to a "lower caste" (Jenkins' local Africans) in a shared enjoyment of prestige-value with the Europeans. The use of the notion of "caste" has its own special problems, however, as its ideal type is associated with the inherited and traditionally more or less hermetic and immutable hierarchies associated with religious notions of degrees of purity and pollution. The sociocultural phenomenon being described here was not the same: One was not necessarily born into this middle stratum; the admission ticket was acquisition of Western cultural traits through a European education. Again, if traditional castes are internally self-reproducing in terms of culture and occupation, with identities endogenous to the caste itself, in the case of the Euro-Africans an external input – the civilizing mission and its heritage – guaranteed their reproduction. This made them "castes" with a difference: as the identity of members of these modern "castes" was of exogenous derivation, it was a dependent identity – and vulnerably so – thereby creating its own problems.

In a 1914 talk called "The Future of West Africa," delivered on his behalf before a group of Euro-African students in **Lagos**, we find Casely Hayford (1866–1930), a prominent West African nationalist from the Gold Coast, looking back on the untranscendable and inherited contradiction constitutive of the Euro-African middle-class fraction to which he belonged. "The fathers have eaten sour grapes and the children's teeth are set on edge," Hayford lamented, referring to the fractured formation of middle-class consciousness (Hayford 1971: 100). What Hayford pointed out to his audience has recently been captured in Ghanaian critic Kwame Anthony Appiah's term "post-coloniality." Under the various forms of the African colonial order and its post-independence aftermath, an indigenous intelligentsia invariably finds itself in a conditions of "post-coloniality." To inhabit this post-encounter African condition, Appiah implies, is to occupy an ontological rift; it is to inhabit a cultural and cognitive space that is not and cannot be purely African. For it is to be set apart as a member of a "Western-trained group of writers and thinkers," a group that has been imposed upon to conduct its thinking and writing in a "Western style" – in accordance, that is, with intellectual and representational protocols that are disproportionately *not* of indigenous African provenance. At the Afro-Western interface, "post-coloniality" is therefore, Appiah writes, "the condition of what we might ungenerously call a comprador intelligentsia" (Appiah 1992: 149). V.Y. Mudimbe, the Congolese philosopher, notes in connection with this that the thought of most African leaders and thinkers who have received a Western education stood "at the crossroads of Western epistemological filiation and African ethnocentrism." "African ethnocentrism" is itself a near-impossible proposition, since "the concepts and categories underpinning [it] are inventions of the West." Overall, he concludes, "[m]odern African thought seems somehow to be basically a product of the West" (Mudimbe 1988: 185).

In the conception of "Africa" as a cognitive and ontological problem of post-coloniality, Casely Hayford anticipated these post-independence African intellectuals in his 1914 essay. His mode of dealing with the problem then was to proselytize, warning his youthful audience: "we miss the high mark of our national calling when we elect to be puppets in soul at the bidding of alien formulae." In other words, a choice – and one of great existential importance – confronted the nationalist writer-intellectuals within this conception of the problem. On the one hand, they and their middle-class kind could elect simply to be the compradors of a European narrative hegemonically projected onto Africa. On the other hand, middle-class intellectuals could, from their place of Afro-Western compromise, elect to project their intermediary selves that stood at the beginning, as progenitor and generator, of an African narrative of renewal, a narrative of African modernity. They might not have recourse to a pure outside that existed beyond the colonialist modernity they inhabited, but it was nevertheless an article of faith with them that they could not afford *not* to imagine the possibility of such an outside.

Africa: Between purity and parity

Compromised cultural and cognitive formation, with an existential resolve to transcend these conditions: Under these circumstances of being impossibly "inside" the West, but wanting equally impossibly to be "outside" of it, what was the middle-class colonial intellectual's modernist production and projection of Africa? On the one hand, we find them proposing a notion of Africa that is – that indeed must be – defined in terms of *difference*, an Africa thus centered in its own autonomy and authenticity. But this tugged against another desire in them, which we see in their advocacy of African modernity in terms of acquiring tools and instituting techniques from Europe that would enable African societies to improve their conditions. Even though colonial encounters had revealed to African societies how their deficiencies in science and technology and rationalist social organization made them candidates for European conquest, the intellectual's dream of African modernity never simply related to this. Africa's modern regeneration was consistently envisioned in terms of Africa rising to power. Modernizing development, in other words, was inscribed in an African desire for parity: It was about how (conquered) Africa was to be like – to be on a par with – (conqueror) Europe.

In this connection the pre-eminent Sierra Leonean radical nationalist figure, James Africanus Horton (1835–83), should be mentioned. Horton's meditations and prognostications in *West African Countries and Peoples* (1868) took as their theme independent nation-state formation as a practical West African necessity, and they came accompanied by a rational program for achieving this end. Horton's goal was an ultimately self-sustaining African power, and his concern is to be understood in terms of the African-American Martin Delaney's observation, made in 1859 to Egba chiefs in Yorubaland, that "The claims of no people are respected until they are presented in national capacity" (quoted in Horton 1969 [1868]: xiv). In order for a West Africa severally fragmented into ethnic groups – often in conflict with each other – to attain this national capacity, Horton argued, was a matter of enlightened Africans seizing on behalf of Africa the instruments of nationalist self-definition, including the institution of the modern state, from European civilization.

Horton's Liberian contemporary, E.W. Blyden (1832–1912), saw the modern in terms of a grave moral and existential problem of African alienation. Horton welcomed this alienation insofar as its rationalist fruits, redirected into the building of national capacity, portended an exponential rise in African power. An acquisition of modern power *qua* the nation-state was necessary to confer, as in Delaney's terms, worldly recognition on African countries and peoples. The modern as an African theme was, for Horton, a project for middle-class intellectuals who should seize the universalizing means already to hand in order to begin the empowering reconstruction of Africa.

But Horton's program begged these difficult questions: Could Africa be like Europe – that, is could Africa absorb European rationality into itself – without ceasing to be Africa? If so, how? Could Africa be similar without being assimilated? It is in this tension that the question of African modernity ceased to be a mere practical matter of modernizing along European lines, raising the question of African difference as a philosophical and ideological proposition for Euro-African intellectuals. This conundrum of African modernity was of course not unique to the Euro-African intellectuals: It also preoccupied African leaders and intellectuals rooted in the old Islamic scholarly traditions and states of north, west, and coastal east Africa.

This difficult philosophical problem is negotiated with great acuity in the seminal nationalist thinking of Blyden, the man widely regarded as the doyen of African nationalism. Appiah has noted of post-independence African intellectuals that they are to be known "through the Africa they offer ... through the Africa they have invented for the world, for each other, and for Africa" (Appiah 1992: 149). Blyden was the colonial pioneer of this threefold project of "worlding" Africa, of selving the middle class in an African image, and of going native with – "nativizing" – Africa. He was to lay these out in a comprehensive philosophy that set the tone and agenda for much that followed in Pan-African nationalist thought.

In his work Blyden offered a sustained critique of Western modernity, especially as it was expressed in the humanitarian civilizing mission in Africa. This critique was directed against what he conceived as this alien modernity's not-to-be-underestimated potential to rob Africa of an

"African personality." Those standing in the first line of attack of an "insurgent [Western] civilization," in Blyden's assessment, were the middle-class, educated Africans (quoted Wilson 1969: 252). They stood in danger of losing their African soul-essence in exchange for gaining the world meretriciously offered them by Europe. The solution for Blyden, however, was not for African societies to turn away from the modern, which was impossible since the historical clock could not be turned back to completely reverse the psychocultural and material effects of modernity on Africa. Rather Blyden was preoccupied with the difficult philosophical question of how the alienating element in the modern might be lived down – the modern, then, as it might be reformulated in a self-serving "African" image. The solution Blyden proposed was a return by Africans everywhere, in a mode of racial self-retrieval, to the authentic sources of their selfhood. He located this authentic self in an African nativity, a nativity which their education and/or Western acculturation had taught middle-class Africans to either forget or reject. Blyden stands, then, as the founder of an African tradition of conservative nationalism or "nativism."

Blyden's influence on nationalist thought was mediated through numerous protégés and their descendants, whose thinking inherited the paradoxes of Blyden's own thinking. For instance, Casely Hayford vigorously protested, as so many other colonial intellectuals would do, the inequality of the European–African colonial encounter, and the insidious destructiveness of Europe's self-appointment to "civilizing" Africa. Yet both Blyden and Hayford, products of European civilization, could also embrace this exogenous phenomenon, despite their fear of its powerfully alienating effect on, as they saw it, a racial and native integrity. Hayford, summing up the essence of the thought of his mentor, attributed to the latter the question: "What shall it profit a race if it shall gain the whole world and lose its own soul?" (Hayford 1969: 160). In spite of this, it was Blyden's conviction also that: "The African at home needs to be surrounded by influences from abroad" (Blyden 1967 [1887]: 277). Its colonialist implications notwithstanding, therefore, an alien and alienating modernity was a necessity to be embraced because it held within itself the promise, as Casely Hayford affirmed in 1903, of "the practical upliftment of the native tribes in the scale of civilization" (Hayford 1970: 8). In Horton's case, the nationalist urge to affirm something differently African – reflected in Horton's choosing to give himself the name "Africanus" – did not preclude his affirmation of "the English element ... unquestionably the best civilizing agency" (Horton 1970: iii).

Confronting the colonial intellectuals, therefore, was an imagining of the "African" in some self-consistent way as a different order of being, and in some self-centered way as an autonomous order of being. Yet this could not exclude from their search for the self-centered difference that they had imagined a consistency or consonance with the standards, norms, and rationality derived from an alien culture. In the one impossible Africa they dreamed of, the desire for purity (or an Africa "outside") sat cheek-by-jowl with a desire for parity (an Africa "inside") on the same terms as were enjoyed by others.

Africa in humanist and post-ancillary representation

These intellectuals also felt the pressing need to rehabilitate an African humanity that had been indifferently done down by the colonial imperial order. As registered in 1928 in J.W. de Graft Johnson's nationalist polemic *Towards Nationhood in West Africa*, the pressure on the colonial writer-intellectual was to rehabilitate African humanity towards a (modernist) conception of "African nationality" such that the entity so rehabilitated would garner "world recognition." As others of his nationalist ilk had done before him and were to do again after, Johnson entertained in this mode:

> great hopes, that the future will see the African better understood and appreciated, and given his due right of recognition in the Comity of Nations.
>
> (Johnson 1971 [1928]: v)

Nation and its consummation appeared in a projection of Africa's "worlding," of Africa's attainment, that is, of world recognition. Therefore, insofar as Africa was seen as occupying a place "below" the rest of the world, "worlding" was inscribed in a nationalist imaginary as an agenda for Africa's vertical integration within the human family.

But this, too, had its paradoxes. For the humanistic need to bring Africa into worldly representation meant that the nationalist writer-intellectuals had to insert the entity they imagined and appropriated in contrast into a complementary – or similar-making – domain of identification. "Ethiopia shall stretch forth her hands unto God": so went the humanistic rallying cry of African nationalist polemic. Yet, for colonial writer-intellectuals like de Graft Johnson to warrant the misrecognised humanity or "nationality" of "Ethiopia," world recognition meant that they were obliged to bring this construct into consistency or consonance with the norms of an exogenous – that is, colonialist and modern European – derivation. In another difficult proposition, the Africa of the self-centered nationalist imagining had somehow to be taken out of itself and reconciled with what, relative to itself, was ex-centric. On the one hand, for the Africa of the nationalist intellectuals to attain similarity in a worldly modernity, this construct had to capitulate to standards not of its own direct making. But this world-bound construct had, on the other hand, to be different too – otherwise it could hardly maintain the claim of being "African."

For an illustration of how the problem was registered and negotiated by colonial intellectuals, we may turn to a work by one of their post-independence "heirs": Wole Soyinka's *Myth, Literature and the African World* (1976). As captured in the title, the Nigerian writer-intellectual contracts to renegotiate a modernistic basis for the imagining of a self-consistent and self-centered "African world." Soyinka's post-independence African literary nationalism and its precursor in the pre-independence era are to be seen navigating a common philosophical terrain: how to figure out "Africa" in a worldly modernity – and vice versa. Soyinka addresses the problem through the writer's "secular vision," a projection that "combines a re-creation of a pre-colonial African world-view with eliciting its transposable elements into modern potential" (Soyinka 1976: 115). The demand placed on the writer of this secular vision appears to be one of restoring "Africa" to itself in the integrity and authenticity of a pre-colonial past: difference remains a desired option. Yet this restoration has also to come from a place, and in terms, other than the purely pre-colonial. The writer's desired return to the past, it turns out, is a desire to "re-turn" this past forward. Pre-colonial myth must negotiate a middle passage through what was instituted by European colonialism, and has survived in the aftermath of that colonialism, as a legacy of African possibility. As the writer steers old-world African "myth" through the middle passage of secular translation, the aboriginal being of this myth is renovated into becoming "literature." The "African" – as myth-become-literature – doubled its nature in being so rehabilitated; presumably, it also did so without forgoing its originality in the secular re-creation.

Yet the secular vision remains a paradoxical one, for its proponent imagines a structure that can be itself at the same time as it somehow supersedes and becomes other than itself. The writer was enjoined, in Soyinka's projection, to do the impossible: to retrieve "Africa" in its intact selfhood at the very moment that this "Africa" had to leave its intact self behind. What is more, the African modernity imagined in the secular vision was structured in compromise. Its agenda of thrusting a pre-colonial world forward, towards modern potential, also appeared to leave a desired African difference captive to standards and norms of an alien imposition. Hidden in Soyinka's modernizing solution of transposing (pre-colonial) myth into (post-colonial) literature – and it was the same story for his colonial predecessors – is the play of a residually colonial, alienating power. Modern potential for Africa – a would-be African modernity – came double-edged, inscribed at once with possibility and liability, and apparently without the option of the excluded middle.

Before 1870 and the rise of the New Imperialism, Euro-Africans had been more or less content to be imperial ancillaries, middle-class products and agents of the civilizing mission. The advent of colonial rule imposed social and existential disfranchisement upon the middle class by excluding its members from the apex of colonial society, which was reserved for white power, and by denying them meaningful political access to a social base comprising the mass of colonized natives. A perplexed Casely Hayford would be left wondering whether "the 'native' ceases to be a 'native' the moment he is educated" (Hayford 1969: 118). Colonial developments did not only, as it were, deny a middle class its political humanity; the problem was compounded by another denial. This one, operating as a racist principle of cultural exclusion, devalued the "cosmopolitan" humanity of the middle class that came with their Western education, and thereby dented their "worldly" self-image.

Out of middle-class disillusionment and the crisis of identity brought on by the New Imperial order, we see what might be called a "post-ancillary consciousness" taking shape. Following Blyden's lead, this new (self-)consciousness affirmed the existence of African personality, the same affirmation that francophone writer-intellectuals would later come to label "Negritude." In both instances, colonial intellectuals would preach to educated Africans that this Negritude or personality urgently required existential validation from among their ranks lest it disappear. As recommended by Blyden, and later Césaire and Senghor, the post-ancillary reconstruction of middle-class self-consciousness therefore mandated, for Euro-Africans, a return to an "Africa" variously imagined and constructed in the interplay between the native and the racial. This necessary return imposed on the colonial writer-intellectuals the task of articulating the beginning of a new, post-imperial narrative of Africa. This was to be a post-imperial narrative through which the intellectual in "Africa" would say "no" to the imperial; but it was a narrative still hatched in the imperial womb. Its "no" was also "yes" to the extent that its enabling categories – "race," "native," "nation," "Africa" – came from, or by way of, the cultural discourse of the imperial. What this demanded of the writer-intellectuals was that they inhabit the *inside* of the terms operating to define African racial demerit – as furnished by colonial/imperialist representation – if they were to imagine and effect a politics that could get to the *outside* of it. The native intellectual had to contest empire within the terms of its own representational hegemony. This is the necessity we find elaborated in Jean-Paul Sartre's paradoxical assessment of the Negritude of the francophone intellectuals as an "anti-racist racism." For Negritude to step outside racism as racism's "anti," Sartre implied, it had to be inside racism, working from within to alter the balance of power represented by its terms. The message of Negritude was effective and its politics effectual, as Sartre saw, in being (differently) articulated in accordance with the protocols of race, a representational *a priori* which, as representation, was no mere metaphor but rather had lived, material consequences. For race was furnished in that scene where imperial anthropology and imperial politics, colonialist knowledge and power, fed off and bolstered each other in marking off human differences while assigning relative human merit and social desert based on those differences.

In search of a new African narrative, colonial writer-intellectuals would come opportunistically to recover a nationalist politics and the codes of its discursive representation, within and in spite of their impossible situation, in conjunctural terms.

> And so, it is not I who make a meaning for myself, but it is the meaning that was already there, pre-existing, waiting for me.
>
> (Fanon 1967: 114)

Frantz Fanon's francophone lament in the 1950s reiterates the self-critical portion of anglophone Hayford's 1914 commentary in "The Future of West Africa." For these colonial intellectuals the challenge of making history and new meaning under circumstances, and within terms, not of their own direct choosing, came down to a creative rearticulation of the *a priori*. They had to swerve racial Africanicity, on the inside of imperial representation, from its coding as a fixed designation that imposed on the race attributes of incapacity/inferiority and produced Africa as a metaphysical vacuum, an anthropological nullity. The writer-intellectuals, in overturning imperial versions of Africa as a Hegelian "blank darkness," were charging themselves with post-imperially turning this Africa over, renewing the African image – for Africa itself and for the world at large.

See also: Christian reform movements; education: colonial; education: post-independence; intellectuals: post-independence; Islamic reform movements; Pan-Africanism; professionals

References and further reading

Appiah, K.A. (1992) *In My Father's House: Africa in the Philosophy of Culture*, New York and Oxford: Oxford University Press.

Blyden, E.W. (1967 [1887]) *Christianity, Islam and the Negro Race*, Edinburgh: Edinburgh University Press.

Fanon, F. (1967) *Black Skin, White Masks*, New York: Grove Press.

Hayford, C. (1969) *Ethiopia Unbound: Studies in Race Emancipation*, London: Frank Cass.

——, (1970) *Gold Coast Native Instructions*, London: Frank Cass.

——, (1971) "The Future of West Africa," *The Truth about the West African Land Question*, London: Frank Cass.

Horton, J.A. (1969) *West African Countries and Peoples*, intro. G. Shepperson, Edinburgh: Edinburgh University Press.

——, (1970) *Letters on the Political Condition of the Gold Coast*, London: Frank Cass.

Jenkins, R. (1985) "Gold Coasters Overseas, 1880–1919," *Immigrants and Minorities* 4, 3: 9

Johnson, J.W. de G. (1971 [1928]) *Towards Nationalism in West Africa*, London: Frank Cass.

July, R. (1967) *The Origins of Modern African Thought*, New York: Praeger.

Mudimbe, V.Y. (1988) *The Invention of Africa: Gnosis, Philosophy, and the Order of Knowledge*, Bloomington and Indianapolis: Indiana University Press.

Peterson, B. (2000) *Missionaries, Monarchs and African Intellectuals*, Trenton and Asmara: Africa World Press Inc.

Sartre, J.-P. (1988) "Black Orpheus," in S. Ungar (ed.), *"What is Literature?" and Other Essays*, Cambridge: Harvard University Press.

Soyinka, W. (1976) *Myth, Literature and the African World*, Cambridge: Cambridge University Press.

Wilson, H. (1969) *The Origins of West African Nationalism*, London: Macmillan.

Zachernuk, P. (2000) *Colonial Subjects: An African Intelligentsia and Atlantic Ideas*, Charlottesville: University of Virginia Press.

KWAKU LARBI KORANG

intellectuals: post-independence

As during the colonial period, post-independence African intellectuals were preoccupied with the questions of nationalism and modernity, and their implications for African cultural identity, economic development, and political autonomy. The way these questions were constructed – and engaged with – naturally varied among Africa's intellectual communities, which can be categorized into three groups (following Mazrui's "triple heritage" thesis): those immersed in Western, indigenous, and Islamic idioms and traditions (Mazrui 1986). This entry largely deals with the first group.

In the post-independence period the relationship between nationalism and intellectuals became a fraught and turbulent one. After the heady days of **decolonization**, the mantle of nationalism was worn by such a tantalizing range of dictators, and dragged through so much mud and blood, that it became difficult to imagine that it had ever enjoyed popular reverence or that intellectuals had anything to do with it. Yet in the early post-independence years the relationship between African intellectuals and leaders was characterized by euphoria and mutual respect, based on a shared vision of national sovereignty, nation-building, and development. This was a period when the views of intellectuals were solicited by the nationalists newly ascended to power, while the former readily obliged and often took pride in contributing to the crafting of national policies, relishing the exposure and prestige that came along with public presence. African intellectuals were willing to submit themselves to the demands of the nationalist and developmental state, which they viewed as the custodian of the development process. The nationalists, in their turn, needed the intelligentsia to provide the necessary technocratic skills, and to give credence and ideological coherence to the project of nation-building and development. The new governments demonstrated their faith in knowledge by the dramatic expansion in university education that was to produce the human resources for development.

Two central issues preoccupied both the nationalists and the intellectuals in the post-independence period. The first was the question of poverty and underdevelopment, along with the strongly felt imperative of "catching up." What would be the appropriate strategies for achieving development and eradicating the "scourges" of ignorance, poverty, and disease? The second preoccupation was that of "nation-building" and unity. How did one govern societies in which ethnic identities were strong and tended to glide easily into "tribalism"? Related to this was the need for consolidation of the newly attained sovereignty against the "neo-colonial" machinations of the erstwhile colonial powers that sought to maintain their economic and political presence and primacy. And closely related to this question was: What structures of state governance were appropriate for "development"? The intellectual correlate to the nationalist quest for political and economic independence was intellectual independence – an aspiration that was quite broadly shared in African intellectual circles and across the entire ideological spectrum. The independence sought by intellectuals ranged from the simple right to set their own research agenda or identify problems specific to their circumstances to a fundamental questioning of the basis on which the "West" had captured the epistemological ground and how the West had come to "know" Africans or, in the extreme, to "invent" Africans. This was part of what Mudimbe called the "search for the epistemological foundation of an African discourse" (Mudimbe 1988: 9).

Responses to the first question varied widely, ranging from those that sought to build on the inherited colonial development model in close relationship with erstwhile colonial powers (the "neo-colonial" path) to those that sought economic "delinking" from the capitalist system through collective self-reliance (the "radical nationalist" path). The conventional understanding within and outside Africa was that development needed a strong government that would be able to override the myopic "revolution of rising expectation" of the population and was willing to impose tasks that would only bear fruit in the long run. Consequently, regardless of the option chosen and ideological predilections of individual leaders, all the strategies of development privileged the state as a main actor in the development process and gave prominent positions to what were then considered as "modernizing elites."

The almost universal response to the second question was one-party rule. In its most idealized form, one-party rule would provide a common forum through which all groups would be heard while avoiding the fissiparous consequences of multi-party politics. The nationalist movements saw recognition of pluralism as opening oneself to the "divide and rule" machinations of the neo-colonialist forces that were bent on undermining African independence by nursing the fissiparous potential that social pluralism always harbored. Development presupposed a strong state running a coherent nation. Ethnicity was seen as inimical to both. It weakened the state by the conflicts it engendered, and the multiplicity of its claims simply denied the new countries their "national image." This image of the nation was essentially "European" in its mystified forms – one race, one language, one culture. Alternative images of nation-states – multi-ethnic, multicultural or multi-racial – were never seriously considered, and if considered had been so tarnished by apartheid's claims as to be of no lasting or sympathetic interest. So nationalism saw itself as up in arms against imperialism and the retrograde forces of tribalism.

The nationalists were egged on by the "modernization" school, which considered primordial identities and social pluralism as "barriers to development" and dominated studies of developing countries. If nationalist leaders could somehow inculcate in the minds of those mired in their tribal worldview a more cosmopolitan ("nationalist") worldview, modernization would begin. The leaders could, in a Weberian way, use their "charisma" to symbolize the new nations. The new myths that such charisma nurtured would gradually replace the retrograde and antidevelopmental myths of "tribe." In the process something else happened: in combating "tribalism," nationalism denied ethnic identity and considered any political – or worse – economic claims based on these identities to be as diabolic as imperialism. This position eventually tripped on the inherent contradictions of "one-party participatory democracy" by its failure to reconcile what were obviously socially pluralistic arrangements in terms of class and ethnicity, with political and economic arrangements that were monolithic and highly centralized.

There was considerable sympathy towards this view of the institutional and political exigencies of the nationalist project in intellectual circles, and indeed many scholars – both African and non-African – provided the theoretical armor for this position. One should emphasize, however, that although there were cases of intellectual opportunism in the support of the nationalist project, most intellectuals' self-perception was that they were engaged in offering critical support to the project. Since most of them shared the nationalist objectives, and since they in some way were skeptical of the appropriateness of foreign institutions, they were at pains to discover or highlight the democratic or "popular" kernel in the many variants of "one-party" democracy, while at the same doubting the commitments of individual leaders to use the apparatus and institutions in a democratic manner.

The era of disenchantment

By the 1970s the relationship between the nationalists in power and intellectuals had begun to sour as a number of sources of conflict asserted themselves. Intellectuals now inveighed against the stultifying nationalist ideology, in the extreme going as far as rejecting the nationalist "nation-building" and "development" project. There were a number of reasons for this turn of events. First was the conflict over the relationship between excellence and relevance of African universities. Initially governments bent over backwards to show that their standards of education and administration were as good as those of similar institutions in the erstwhile colonial metropolises. Soon the "relevance" issue spilled over into questions of the quality of the education process, with academics insisting on standards and governments insisting, in a populist manner, on relevance. The nationalists sometimes read this ambivalence as "colonial mentality" or "elitism." They often argued that the research conducted in the new African institutions was "irrelevant," by which they meant that it was not immediately usable in policy matters. Governments tended to reduce relevance to the provision of uncritical technical support and affirmations of the ideology of the ruling party. They denigrated basic research in favor of what was called "applied research." In this they were strongly supported by donors – both governmental and non-governmental.

Second, the relatively cozy relationship between the state and the intelligentsia was undermined by the end of the lucrative employment opportunities that indigenization and the expansion of the public sector had created. Increasingly governments felt less in need of human resources from the universities. This decline in the demand for local expertise and intellectual input in the development process was partly the result of the conceptualization of the African university as something to simply produce the "manpower" to indigenize the civil service. Once indigenization was achieved, most governments had little incentive for continued support of the universities. The World Bank, which had assumed an intellectual leadership among aid donors and other funding institutions through its **structural adjustment programs**, provided theoretical armor to this position by arguing that the rates of return on tertiary education were much lower than those on lower levels of education. The result of all this was a scandalous neglect of higher education for much of the 1980s and 1990s. As a consequence the "brain drain," especially to the United States, that had been a trickle turned into a veritable flood.

Third, African intellectuals had grown increasingly critical of their governments and had become more strident in their assertion of their academic rights. The abuse of authority by the political leadership, the obvious positive correlation between authoritarianism and poor economic performance, the demystification of nationalism, the growing political protests, and the explosion of conflicts that had hitherto been covered up by repression – all this emboldened African academics to begin to speak out and insist on both academic freedom and democratization The oppositional stance of most of them and their unwillingness to be "usable" by some of the unsavory regimes in Africa did not help much in cementing the relationship between the state and the local intelligentsia, who resented demands that they serve as mere mouthpieces of the state. There were, of course, some who played the role of sycophants and court jesters, but these remained quite few.

The repressive politics that became the norm simply left no room for the growth of intellectuals occupying public space. The putatively consensus-building functions of the one-party state had been overwhelmed by the authoritarian exigencies of uniformity. Many spaces that were open (at least theoretically) to intellectuals elsewhere were either erased, infested by informants, or occupied – sometimes physically – so that neither "ivory towers" nor "Olympian detachment" were meaningful options. In addition most of the spaces over which academics could exercise their autonomy were funded by outsiders, who also sought to delimit the intellectual spheres by insisting on their own priorities. Such were the constraints that in most cases the choice was between exile, sullen self-effacement and invisibility, or sycophantic and fawning adulation of power. There were, of course, those who heroically gave themselves the option of standing up and fighting – ending up in jail or dead. One should also bear in mind that as "national" intellectual spaces were squeezed by the state, African intellectuals actively sought to create new regional or continental spaces through which they could find a voice.

Fourth, African governments relied heavily on foreign mentors, admirers or sycophants for intellectual inspiration or affirmation. Thus Nyerere had a band of foreign "Fabian socialists" who had easy access to him; Kaunda had John Hatch as a close intellectual associate, whom he invited to be the first director of the Institute for Humanism; Nkrumah had surrounded himself with Pan-Africanists, such as George Padmore and W.E.B. DuBois. In later years there were European and American "radicals" who were later to appear as peripatetic advisers to a whole range of "progressive" regimes in Africa. While the reliance on foreign expertise and inspiration was voluntary in the early years of independence, with most expatriates sympathetic to the nationalist cause, the situation toward the end of the twentieth century was entirely different. Reliance on foreign expertise was the result of the collapse of the "national project" and the assumption by foreign financial institutions and donors of greater functions in the elaboration of policy. This further marginalized local intellectuals, often pauperizing them or reducing them to "local consultants," which produced new wave of African professions closely linked with the need for greater control of development by the aid establishment and its insatiable quest for feasibility studies, evaluations, and "rapid assessment" results. Professionalization of intellectual life was thus not due to the munificence of African states, but to the contracts from foreign governments and **non-governmental organizations** (NGOs). The full impact of the "consultancy syndrome" on intellectual activities was to turn large numbers of the intelligentsia into paid "native informants" for the foreign aid and consultancy industry. African governments could only access their own intellectuals through donor-contracted reports. This should not be interpreted as suggesting that African intellectuals were close to the foreign projects. Donors themselves usually exhibited ill-disguised contempt for local intellectuals whom they treated as mercenary, or felt criticized them without offering alternatives, or considered to be part of the rent-seeking or clientelist cliques that had benefited from past policies so that their opposition to donor-imposed "reform" was self-serving. With such a view of local capacities, donors were to embark on the unending task of "capacity-building," always under the tutelage of technical assistants.

Fifth, was the penchant of African leaders to assume the role of "philosopher king," and reduce intellectual work to the level of incantation of the thoughts of the leader. Leaders sought to acquire intellectual hegemony by themselves or through advisers constructing intellectual frameworks that would guide national debates. Nkrumah's Pan-Africanism and Nkrumahism, Nyerere with his Ujamaa, Senghor with Negritude, and Kaunda's Humanism are some well-known ideological constructs. In many cases the ideological schemas propounded by African leaders were highly idiosyncratic, and often so incoherent as to be beyond the comprehension of the propagators themselves. Mobutu's "authenticity" immediately comes to mind. Adhesion to these ideas was not merely difficult; it was also hazardous to those sycophants who diligently sought to follow the leader through infinite twists and turns as the leader sought to bridge the cavernous gap between the rhetoric of national goals and the reality of predatory self-aggrandizement.

Finally, there was the complete misunderstanding of the task that lay ahead. African leaders either overestimated the power and capacity of the "political kingdom" that Nkrumah had enjoined them to seek, or underestimated the intellectual and political complexity of the processes of development and nation-building. The task that lay before them demanded innovative institutional arrangements, creative management of state–society relations, and strategic thinking about Africa's position in the world system. None of these could be achieved by *ex cathedra* pronouncements from the state house or military camp whence power increasingly emanated. They required profound reflection and dialogue, and an engaged intellectual and scientific community.

The conflict between the state and the intellectuals would not obscure the many debates and considerable self-criticism emanating from intellectual circles. Part of the self-criticism among African intellectuals was that these were "extroverted," or too attentive to intellectual fads from abroad. There were many debates on the relevance of African research, especially on whether the basic research carried out in African institutions really addressed the key issues and whether, when it borrowed concepts, that research was sufficiently sensitive to the specificities of Africa's own conditions. Some critics went as far as to suggest that African intellectuals were no more than informed native guides, compradors in trafficking cultural commodities. The second criticism was that African intellectuals had accepted the statist project of "development," pointing as evidence to their tendency to view the state as the motive force of social change and development or to define themselves only in relationship to the state. The focus by African intellectuals was not on the criticism of development *per se*, but on examining what went wrong in achieving what they generally viewed as desirable. Few Africans engaged in the existentialist preoccupation with the self, still less in angst-ridden vituperations of material progress. Those of a postmodern temperament criticized African intellectuals for advocating the "enlightenment project" of development and nation-building that had constituted some of the "metanarratives" that brought so much suffering to African people. African intellectuals were criticized for "developmentalism" because they merely criticized governments for abandoning the developmental vision that was so central to nationalism, and succumbing instead to policies imposed by external financial institutions.

There were heated exchanges on the integrity of African intellectuals and their relationship with the state. Some impugned the intellectual integrity of African intellectuals. The sight of intellectuals placing their services at the disposal of dictators or foreign funders was cited as an example of lack of moral fiber. Linked to this was the failure to create the instruments of a genuine autonomy that might have ensured a participatory involvement with society commensurate with the stature of those intellectuals. The absence of independent publishing or distribution endowed with financial resources from non-governmental sources, and the lack of research outfits with independent financial backing, also contributed to the atomization of the intelligentsia. The lack of autonomous institutions for self-expression gave an impression that African scholars had succumbed to the injunction "Silence: Development in Progress" peddled by African governments. This is not a fair characterization. By any standard African intellectuals were not silent, submissive, or subservient. Indeed some have suggested that the likelihood is that they talked too much and too soon, on the assumption that they were part of the dominant African elite. Finally, African academics were constantly reminded that they were part of the privileged class and "bourgeoisie of the diploma" to boot. They were accused of being the Trojan Horse of Western culture, disseminating ideas that undermined or denigrated their own cultures. These attacks came not only from governments, but also from foreign observers and colleagues. Given the visceral populism of African intellectuals, this attack probably hurt the most, and a number of governments were able to mobilize sections of the population to attack universities using such arguments. Compounding matters was the question of the language of scholarship and expression. The case for the use of a national or regional lingua franca was often made in the literary world, Ngũgi wa Thiong'o being probably one of the most outspoken on the issue. The fact that much of intellectual output and debate was in the language of the former colonial masters undercut the ability of African intellectuals to communicate with the broad public.

While engaged in confrontations with the state and self-critical debates, African intellectuals had to address the unequaled preponderance of the study of their continent by foreigners for whom Africans constituted the "other" against whose invention African intellectuals inveighed. African scholars were, like scholars elsewhere, torn between the quest for universalistic understanding of society, on the one hand, and the need to bring out the specificities of their societies, on the other. The African intellectual community had to simultaneously confront the "Afropessimism" and cynicism that increasingly characterized the study of Africa, while at the same not being seen to be defensive of a political and social order against which they themselves were harshly critical. The issues of who should study Africa and how were brought to the forefront by the dramatic increase of Africans studying and writing about Africa from the diaspora. Besides their own anguished reflection on their social responsibility to Africa, many of these scholars found themselves engaged in the many debates about "area studies" and multiculturalism in their host countries.

The era of democratization

By the 1980s both nationalism and its main projects had fallen on hard times – betrayed by some of its heroes, undercut by international institutions and forces of **globalization**, reviled and caricatured by academics, and alien to a whole new generation of Africans born after independence. The increasing demands for democratization further focused the attention of intellectuals away from the state as the agent of change toward the (re)emergent **civil society**. In addition the democratization process opened up new spaces. African intellectuals became much freer than they had been at any point since independence. The sullen silence of the 1980s was broken by the emergence of the movement for democratization. Among intellectuals it also marked a growing consciousness of themselves as a social group, with rights and responsibilities. Once again African intellectuals adapted a self-consciously public position on national issues. But they worked under incredible conditions. They emerged from the debacle of authoritarian rule much less tarnished by involvement with the oppressor than, say, the Japanese intellectuals were with the fascist regime. They thus had the opportunity of moving away from a focus on the state to engage other social actors that had been unleashed by both political and economic liberalization.

Concurrent with the process of democratization was that of globalization, whose most direct expression in Africa was the policy conditionality of the Bretton Woods Institutions, which insisted on liberalization of the economy. Globalization refers both to the actual processes driven by trade, finance, and technology, and to the ideological expressions of such processes. Perhaps the most insidious effect of globalization was at the ideological level, where it was given a twist that tended to denigrate national ideologies of social change, and to underrate local initiatives and ideas. In addition the need to attract the attention of foreign capital further re-enforced the persuasiveness of this ideological posture. Keen to gain an international reputation, many political leaders were much less inclined to appeal to their own people – let alone listen to local intellectuals.

In the era of globalization and postmodernism, African scholars were accused of being insular and provincial, and ultimately doomed to fail due to the ineluctable forces of globalization. The quest for "endogenous" or "self-reliant" or "autocentric" intellectual development was dismissed as either chauvinistic "nativism" or unrealistic sloganeering. A new generation of scholars, who were completely alienated from the nationalist discourse, sought escape into cosmopolitanism that further alienated them from the concerns of their societies. Compounding matters was the fact that significant amounts of African scholarship were now placed outside Africa as a result of the "brain drain."

By the end of the century a striking result was that few African leaders sought to cultivate an indigenous "intellectuariat" that was, in the Gramscian sense, "organic." The kind of rapport that the Indian nationalist sustained with the intellectual in the post-colonial period or the links that Jewish intellectuals had to the Israeli state were rarely seen in Africa. There was nowhere like that in Africa, except perhaps **Algeria**, where the intellectuals were organic to the FLN movement and government, and **South Africa**, where Afrikaner intellectuals were close to the apartheid regime. One consequence is that the African nationalist post-colonial project had no organic intellectuals, and the few that sought to assume that role were reduced to purveyors of apologetics. The debates on the reconstitution of state–society relations, on democratization, and on Africa in the world revived interest in the role of intellectuals in African societies. Such debates promised to lead to a repositioning of the African intellectual in society – not as merely a tolerated excrescence of the West, but as a critical ingredient in societies that were self-reflexive.

See also: Christian reform movements; education: colonial; education: post-independence; state: post-independence; Islamic reform movements

Further reading

Ajayi, J.F.A., Goma, L.K.H. and Johnson, G.A. (1996) *The African Experience with Higher Education*, London: James Currey.

Appiah, K.A. (1992) *In My Father's House: Africa in the Philosophy of Culture*, London: Methuen.

Diouf, M. and Mamdani, M. (eds.) (1994) *Academic Freedom in Africa*, Dakar: CODESRIA.

Falola, T. (2001) *Nationalism and African Intellectuals*, Rochester: University of Rochester Press.

Hountondji, P. (ed.) (1997) *Endogenous Knowledge: Research Trails*, Dakar: CODESRIA.

Mazrui, A.A. (1986) *The Africans: A Triple Heritage*, Boston: Little Brown.

Mkandawire, T. (1998) "The Social Sciences in Africa: Breaking Local Barriers and Negotiating International Presence – The M.K.O. Abiola Distinguished Lecture Presented to the 1996 African Studies Association Annual Meeting," *African Studies Review* 40, 2: 15–36.

Mudimbe, V.Y. (1988) *The Invention of Africa: Gnosis, Philosophy, and the Order of Knowledge*, London: James Currey.

Ngũgi wa Thiong'o (1986) *Decolonising the Mind: The Politics of Language in African Literature*, Nairobi: Heinemann Kenya.

Zeleza, P.T. (1997) *Manufacturing African Studies and Crises*, Dakar: CODESRIA.

THANDIKA MKANDAWIRE

international financial institutions

In July 1944 a United Nations Conference held at Bretton Woods in the United States conceived two of the most powerful international financial institutions, whose influence increasingly affected Africa over the next half century. This conference was meant to provide the postwar world with organizations that could undertake the reconstruction of Europe, and prevent repetition of the 1930s economic crisis. To this end the representatives of forty-four nations present at the conference emphasized the necessity of founding institutions designed to structure international monetary relations and creating the framework for a liberal world system that would ensure free trade and financial flows. Both headquartered in Washington, D.C., the International Monetary Fund (IMF) and the International Bank for Reconstruction and Development (IBRD, the original structure of the future World Bank Group) came into existence at the end of the **Second World War**, each with its own specific mandate.

Since its inception in 1945 the IMF has been more strictly focused on monetary and financial issues, with a macro-economic perspective based on the stabilization of balance of payments and currency exchange rates, as well as international reserves. This institution provides its members with many services, ranging from technical support in its areas of expertise to loans in support of reform policies or for crisis resolution. In operation since 1946, the IBRD is dedicated to reducing poverty and promoting long-term development, and has a more sector- or project-tailored approach than the IMF. To better comply with its mandate, it has included several new affiliates to its original structure, thereby forming the World Bank Group. The best known of these affiliates are the International Finance Corporation (IFC), established in 1956 to enhance private investment, and the International Development Association (IDA), founded in 1960 to provide donor-funded concessionary loans to low-income member-countries. As of December 2000 these two leading international financial institutions were governed by slightly more than 180 member-countries, whose voting power is related to their respective share in the world economy. At that date the United States had a leading position with 17 percent of the votes.

At the beginning of the 1970s the IMF and the World Bank took into consideration dramatic growth in the discrepancy between Western countries and states from the South (or the **Third World**). Of alarming relevance to this inequality was the continuing degradation of the African continent, plagued with drought, famine, and **food crises**, and severely hit by the two 1970s oil shocks, inflationary pressures, and large debt arrears. Several World Bank studies have paid closer attention to the plight of low-income countries and paved the way for a stronger commitment to remedying this considerable imbalance of prosperity. According to an influential report called *Accelerated Development in Sub-Saharan Africa* (World Bank 1981), an inefficient public sector, overvalued currencies, undue protectionism, the overexpansion of governmental services, and the slow growth in agricultural production were mainly responsible for the African economic decline. In order to tackle this deep crisis, and correct these apparent causes, the IMF and the World Bank Group jointly agreed on a policy basis for lending. Strict conditions were attached to debt rescheduling and the disbursement of new loans to persuade borrowing countries to change their governmental policies. Loan conditionalities were a means of exerting considerable pressure on those African states that were in search of new financial resources for development, such that they embraced market-oriented reforms and gave up the nationalist economics of central planning that had prevailed since independence.

In the early 1980s various **structural adjustment programs** (SAPs) were implemented. The World Bank Group set up the first structural adjustment loans (SALs) in 1980, and sectoral adjustment loans (SECALs) in 1983, while in 1986 the IMF devised a new credit facility: the structural adjustment facility (SAF). The liberal principles of these programs were widely endorsed by the international donor community, which included multilateral agencies, private investors, and Western governments (notably the former colonial powers), but also by the **African Development Bank**. This institutional consensus, often referred as the "Washington Consensus," made it almost impossible for African states to access financial resources from any source without strictly observing this neoliberal orthodoxy.

In this context most of the currencies of the continent were devalued to make African exports more competitive in international markets. Public services and state-owned enterprises were partially privatized, and foreign direct investment encouraged. Government spending was severely reduced to restore budgetary equilibrium. A partial disengagement of state from social sectors was introduced (notably in the higher education system). Agriculture received the main share of this new capital allocation, at industry's expense, with a special emphasis on export production and smallholder farming. The infrastructure sector was also prioritized through development projects of transportation systems (highways, ports, railways).

The implementation of these structural adjustment programs was widely criticized in Africa, and also in Europe and North America. Considered by numerous economic analysts as a radical misconception of African economic realities, these programs were harshly denounced for having caused considerable social and political damage in young African nations, and an unprecedented pauperization of the lower and middle classes. Despised by

African public opinion, the international financial institutions as a whole were accused of undertaking the recolonization of the African continent by increasing its dependency on industrialized countries. Social unrest, urban riots, demonstrations led by students on campuses, and hostile parliamentary debates spread across Africa in protest against the imposition of these measures. The IMF and the World Bank Group may have begun to integrate sounder social policies into the general framework of their actions by the end of the 1990s, but the modalities necessary for an equitable and lasting development of Africa were still to be found.

See also: debt crises; economy: post-independence

References and further reading

Alidou, O., Caffentzis, G. and Federici, S. (eds.) (1999) *A Thousand Flowers: Social Struggles against Structural Adjustment in African Countries*, Trenton: Africa World Press Inc.

Mosley, P., Harrigan, J. and Toye, J. (1991) *Aid and Power: The World Bank and Policy-based Lending*, London: Routledge.

Onimode, B. (ed.) (1989) *The IMF, the World Bank and the African Debt*, London: Zed Books.

World Bank (1981) *Accelerated Development in Sub-Saharan Africa: An Agenda for Action*, Washington, D.C.: World Bank.

JEAN-PHILIPPE DEDIEU

international trade

In principle free trade among nations can provide opportunities for economic growth that are absent when economies remain closed to one another. The theory of comparative advantage suggests that if a country exports the goods that it produces at relatively low cost, and imports the goods that it could produce only at great expense, its people will be able to consume more than would be possible without international trade. Moreover if revenues from exports are invested in public goods, such as schools and transportation infrastructure, trade will help a country become increasingly productive and prosperous over time. In the face of these theoretical gains from trade, Africa's experience reveals that a concentration on exports can coexist with economic stagnation and decline. Rather than disproving the theory of comparative advantage, this outcome reflects the problematic history of Africa's relations with the global economy. The patterns of international trade that persisted through the twentieth century were not established through bargaining among independent entities, but were imposed as part of a colonial strategy to benefit European states. The particular form of export orientation that was established in the colonial period was never intended to maximize Africa's economic potential, and the preservation of that trade structure did not serve the continent well.

From the end of the nineteenth century the colonial enterprise in Africa aimed to extend a trading system in which Africa served as a source of primary products for European industries and consumers. European manufacturers could then export processed consumer goods to African markets. In this way African economies were "developed" to play a limited role in a larger, colonial system. While the colonial strategy integrated Africa into a global commodity market, it did so in a manner that was not ideal from the perspective of an independent economy.

The colonial trading system could not develop under conditions of free trade. From the early decades of the twentieth century, firms such as the British East Africa Company operated in colonies with charters from the government that gave them protection from competition. The profitability of these firms was aided by a pattern of public investment that concentrated on infrastructure designed to serve the nascent export sector. Moreover the power of the state was used to compel Africans to produce crops or provide labor to support business enterprises. The charter companies and the forms of public investment ensured that trade was oriented toward the colonial center. In the 1930s and 1940s controls on foreign exchange and imports reinforced a tendency to import from the colonial metropole.

In the colonial scheme there was little imperative to invest the profits from trade in order to develop African economies in new, sustainable directions. Instead profits were spent in Europe. The drive to extract the maximum value from the continent probably reached a peak during the **Second World War**, when colonial powers sought to control African economies in support of the war effort. To the extent that profits were reinvested in Africa, investments were in activities that generated profits for the international firms doing business there, not in infrastructure to serve a public good. Thus development tended to be concentrated around mining sites, ports, and areas of European settlement.

The colonial regime succeeded in creating export-oriented economies in Africa. Between 1938 and 1949 the value of exports from Africa (excluding **South Africa** and **Egypt**) rose from US$788 million to US$2,632 million; by 1960 exports reached US$5,220 million, amounting to almost 20 percent of the total domestic product of the region. In a number of newly independent countries exports amounted to half of the national income. These exports were almost entirely in the form of unprocessed agricultural, forestry, or mining products, and they were almost entirely directed to Europe. This pattern of trade left the African colonies economically dependent on the ability and willingness of consumers in Europe to buy their products. That an economic downturn in Europe could be transmitted through trade contraction into an economic crisis in Africa was not a major concern to colonial administrators, but it was a problem for leaders of independent African states.

Not only were colonial African economies highly dependent on exports, their exports also tended to be concentrated on a very small number of commodities. In 1950 a single product accounted for more than 70 percent of exports from **Gambia**, Egypt, **Liberia**, **Mauritius**, **São Tomé and Príncipe**, Reunion, Northern Rhodesia (**Zambia**), **Uganda**, Gold Coast (**Ghana**), and **Sudan**. In each of these economies the top three exports made up more than 90 percent of total export revenues. A number of economies, including **Angola**, **Morocco**, **Nigeria**, and **Tunisia**, were considerably more diversified in their range of exports, but their exports were also primary products. Seven products (copper, cotton, coffee, cocoa, groundnuts, petroleum, and wood) accounted for 45 percent of the continent's exports in 1960, and over half of its exports in 1965. Other products that were critical in particular countries included palm oil, rubber, and tobacco. Concentration on a narrow commodity-base placed independent states in an exceedingly vulnerable position in the world market. Small changes in the prices of a single commodity could have a tremendous impact on the domestic economy. While this vulnerability was a small concern when these economies were conceived as components of a larger colonial whole, it became critical in the post-colonial period.

Early post-colonial leaders were well aware of the dependent economic relationships that persisted after political independence. To break these ties, many African states adopted trade policies that aimed to develop domestic industrial capacities, reducing the need for imports and thereby reducing the need to export. In the name of "import substitution industrialization" countries established or attracted industries to produce the finished products that, under the colonial system, had been imported. This typically implied relatively little investment in the existing export sectors (agriculture or mining), and taxation of those sectors to support the new industries.

It soon became apparent that the goods African consumers desired were not necessarily those that could be produced domestically at a low cost. In many cases the industries that were established to reduce the need to import finished products could only operate by importing large amounts of capital equipment and intermediate inputs. In other cases industries required such costly inputs or inappropriate technologies that they could not be sustained at all.

Reliance on imported inputs to support industrial production meant that African states remained dependent on commodity trade with Europe. Thus the continent faced the continued need to export primary products to pay for imports. Because relatively little investment had been made in the export sector, exports remained highly concentrated, and the pattern of trade with Europe was not altered. Moreover, since industries had not thrived after an initial period of rapid growth, the export sector remained a large share of African economies. In 1965 exports accounted for 21 percent of the continent's total domestic product. In four countries – Liberia, **Libya**, **Swaziland**, and Zambia – exports were over half of gross domestic product (GDP). By 1980 exports accounted for 31 percent of Africa's total domestic product, with ten countries (**Botswana**, **Democratic Republic of Congo**, **Gabon**, Liberia, Libya, Mauritius, **Namibia**, **Seychelles**, Swaziland, and **Togo**) receiving over half their national income from exports. In terms of concentration there was a similar intensification of the colonial pattern. In 1965, for example, the top three exports from **Kenya** accounted for 31 percent of the country's total exports; in 1980 Kenya's top three exports accounted for over 60 percent of the total. For **East Africa** as a whole, 32 percent of exports came from the top three commodities in 1970, 45 percent in 1980, and 60 percent in 1990. In **West Africa** the concentration on the top three export products rose from 39 percent in 1970 to 70 percent in 1980 and 81 percent in 1990.

In 1980, after some twenty years of independent rule, African economies remained dependent on a narrow base of exports sent to a small number of countries. The implications of this vulnerability were made dramatically clear in the 1980s when Africa experienced declines in the prices and quantities of exports from across the continent. Between 1980 and 1990 the terms of trade (the price of exports compared to the price of imports) fell by over 50 percent for the continent as a whole. Export revenues dropped substantially in all regions of the continent over this period. As a result of declining export revenues, foreign exchange was not available for importing the inputs required in many of Africa's industries. Consequently industry declined in much of the continent. Faced with simultaneous drops in industrial production, per capita food production, and export revenue, many countries in Africa turned to international lenders to finance imports. These countries eventually found themselves in **debt crises** that drove them into **structural adjustment programs** at the behest of the **international financial institutions** that financed their borrowing.

Economic dependence on the export of a small number of primary products left African economies vulnerable to price shocks resulting from factors such as demand changes in Europe, the entry of other suppliers, and the development of synthetic substitutes. The continent was also vulnerable to declines in revenue if output fell due to weather shocks, decaying infrastructure, or farmers' disinclination to grow or sell crops that were subjected to heavy taxation. To make international trade work well for Africa, most observers agree that diversification of exports is needed. This diversification could take the form of expanding both the range of commodities exported and the range of trading partners.

Diversifying products exported would open new areas to development, and would protect countries from declining terms of trade. Developing new trading partners would reduce the tendency for negative economic trends in Europe to be transmitted to Africa, and might also lead to further diversification of export products. To achieve diversification of exports to Europe and North America, African states will have to invest in the development of new sectors. In some cases, exports of new products will also require negotiation to gain access to developed economy markets that are protected from imports.

Diversifying trading partners is another mechanism whereby African economies may get more from international trade in the future. Whereas most countries of the world trade most heavily with their near neighbors, African states persist in the colonial pattern of trading more with Europe than with each other. In 1960 70 percent of African exports went to Western Europe, and a similar share of imports came from Western Europe. At the same time less than 7 percent of the goods exported from African states or colonies were traded within the continent. Intra-African trade remained less than 7 percent of the exports of African countries in 1997, while exports to Europe remained over 50 percent of their trade. While increased trade among African states seems to hold potential, obstacles to such trade include:

1 the orientation of much of the continent's infrastructure, which was built to facilitate the

movement of products out of Africa rather than across it,

2 the tendency for many countries to have similar resources, and thus similar production options, and
3 the small size of the African market.

While obstacles to diversification remain great, the potential for constructive international trade can only be realized if African economies develop new patterns of engagement in the global economy.

See also: economy: colonial; economy: post-independence; regional integration

Further reading

Frimpong-Ansah, J., Kanbur, R. and Svedberg, P. (eds.) (1991) *Trade and Development in Sub-Saharan Africa*, Manchester: Manchester University Press.

United Nations (1959) *Economic Survey of Africa Since 1950*, New York: United Nations.

World Bank (2001) *African Development Indicators, 2001*, Washington, D.C.: World Bank.

ALEX WINTER-NELSON

Islam

By the end of the twentieth century Islam was the dominant faith in Africa, with up to 60 percent of the population calling themselves Muslims. Over the course of the century the spread of Islam through Africa not only swamped other religions, but outstripped the rate of Islamic expansion in other regions of the Muslim world. Most of the rich mosaic of rites and schisms that make up the Muslim world at large are found in Islamic Africa, from North and East African coastal communities that can trace their origins to the years immediately after the Prophet's death to late twentieth-century Islamicist movements imported from the East. Adherents range from seventh-century Arab migrants and Arabized Amazighs in **North Africa** to twentieth-century Pakistani missionaries in **East** and **West Africa**. Around Cape Coast in **Ghana** there are Muslim communities that trace their conversion to ancestors conscripted into service by the Dutch East Indies Company in today's Indonesia in the early nineteenth century, and Hausa militia imported by the British soon after. South Asian Muslim populations in Natal were first brought there as indentured labor for sugar plantations in the mid-nineteenth century; Muslim clans stretching down the East African coast have family ties around the Indian Ocean that date back centuries. Where commerce provided opportunities, Muslim merchants settled, married, and brought Islam to communities as dispersed as **Malawi** and Ghana, **Uganda** and **Liberia**, the eastern **Congo** and northern **Côte d'Ivoire**.

During the twentieth century, colonial occupation and demands for labor in the colonial economies contributed to a new mobility for populations across the continent, new degrees of social dislocation, and new opportunities for the dissemination of Islam. The century opened with the pre-colonial Islamic states on the defensive, and colonial authorities providing surveillance of Muslim influence to contain Islam, which was viewed by the Europeans as a potentially subversive threat to their occupation. That very surveillance led to enhanced standing for some Muslim clerics, and a corresponding increase in their influence, particularly evident in the expansion of the Sufi (mystic) brotherhoods. The twentieth century closed with descendants of pre-colonial Muslim authorities still very much a part of national and political life, but it also brought a new style of Islamic leadership that had sprung up from a population now thoroughly integrated into the main currents of North Africa and the Middle East as a result of their study and travel in the Holy Lands, as well as through the internet and other electronic media.

The thirteenth century after the Prophet Muhammad's *hijra* or forced removal from Mecca (in AD 622, the beginning of the Islamic calendar) began in 1881. It was a moment at which prophetic literature in much of the Islamic world anticipated an "awaited deliverer" (a *mahdi*) who would prepare for the end of time. Several mahdis did, in fact, materialize during the ensuing forty years, perhaps the most famous of whom was the Sudanese Muhammad Ahmad b. 'Abdallah who launched his movement in 1881. This general and popular expectation of renewal and religious resurgence within Muslim communities across the continent was coterminous with the contemporary political partition of Africa by European powers that brought infidel rule over Muslim lands at the close of the nineteenth century. This may explain why Islam was so widely embraced in the early twentieth century as a way of insulating individuals and communities against the full force of European occupying forces by providing an alternative worldview to colonial **Christianity**. As if to reinforce this perception, French and British colonial administrations each, in different ways, attempted to manipulate Islamic authority, legal systems, and networks to benefit the colonial state. In so doing the colonial regimes effectively acknowledged and sanctioned a degree of Islamic influence over the lives of Africans that may not have always been present in 1900, but which soon did become a reality.

Across North Africa pan-Islamic ideas took root in the early years of the century that effectively tied Muslim intellectuals into the main Middle Eastern currents and resulted in a distinctly reformist, Islamic slant to anti-colonial movements throughout the first half of the century. In sub-Saharan Africa the dominant theme was the growing spiritual and political influence of the Sufi (mystic) brotherhoods (*tariqas*) as they became popular expressions of local and community values in an increasingly mobile and urbanized population. In West Africa the expanding Muslim population was confronted by Christian mission efforts south of the savanna lands, and Muslim (Koranic) schools and Western education competed with each other for the attention of the minds of African **youth**. It was Western, largely Christian, education that came to be the foundation of the secular, anti-colonial movements and the post-colonial state in most regions. But political mobilization within important Muslim populations across the continent, like **Senegal** and **Tanzania**, was heavily beholden to Islamic cultures in the late nineteenth and early twentieth century. Once independence was achieved and most colonial barriers to easy communication between African communities and the Holy Lands of Islam were erased, Muslim communities experienced something of a recrudescence. The appropriate place of Islamic law in secular states became a political issue, and the appeal of a modernized Islam within the fertile crescent was felt across Islamic Africa.

The period of European conquest of the Muslim populations in Africa may be dated as concluding only in 1934, with the last French expedition against a descendent of the southern Moroccan holy man, Ma'al-Aynayn, in the **Sahara**, but by the mid-1920s the dangers of holy war (*jihad*) being mounted against the occupying European forces was essentially over. The militant movements that fought European intrusion in the name of Islam were widespread, mainly in the northern tier of the continent. In the east, Muhammad 'Abdallah Hassan's wars against the British in the Horn of Africa lasted into the 1920s, and the Sudanese Mahdi's legacy in Darfur was upheld by Ali Dinar, who was killed by the British in 1916. In Libya the Sanusiyya, a Sufi *tariqa*, fought both Italian and French forces, and their prolonged conflict with Italy was rekindled in the Italo-Sanussi war between 1923 and 1932. Ma'al-Aynayn's *jihad* against French intruders in southern **Morocco** concluded at the end of the second decade of the century, only a few years before an Islamic Republic was carved out in the Riff, northern Morocco, in 1922, only to be defeated by combined Spanish and French forces two years later. In West Africa *mahdist* movements were reported, and quickly repressed, by French and British authorities in **Guinea**, and across the northern regions of Côte d'Ivoire, Ghana, and **Nigeria**. Down the East African coast the major militant reaction to European occupation, the Maji Maji uprising in southern Tanzania (1905–7), was by no means an Islamic movement, although Muslim clerics did take part. In its aftermath the faith expanded dramatically.

Widespread as these instances of militant resistance were, they did not engage most Muslims across the continent. However, with increasingly effective communications systems in the twentieth century, popular knowledge of these efforts became widespread, and no doubt had an influence on the next waves of Islamization in **colonial Africa** that were associated with pan-Islamic ideas and the Sufi *tariqas*. The debates that raged in **Cairo** at the turn of the century over the cultural price of modernization and the importance of a return to Islamic fundamentals in order to preserve the essence of the faith (known as the *salafiyya* movement) quickly spread across North Africa. *Salafi* cells were soon instrumental in the political maturation of anti-colonial thinking in Morocco and Tunisia, just as other pan-Arab and pan-Islamic associations had tied religious activists – mainly in North Africa, but also along the East African coast – into networks across the Muslim world in the early years of the century. Elsewhere in Africa a similar kind of networking was emerging in the name of the Sufi brotherhoods, where believers using the same prayer litany came together and formed informal associations that served to substitute for family ties in new urban environments and among new migrant laborers.

Pan-Islam in the early years of the century was part of a global phenomenon of irredentist movements that sought to identify and build on commonalities between geographically dispersed populations with shared language and culture. Within Africa the *mahdist* movement was itself one expression of pan-Islam. At the turn of the century the Ottoman Turks attempted to assert their influence across African communities, and at the outbreak of the **First World War** called on Muslims from Morocco to **Mozambique** to wage *jihad* against the colonial occupying powers. But it was the Sufi brotherhoods and the networks they represented that were the most pervasive influence tying together African's Muslim communities. Although there were dozens of brotherhoods to be found in most communities, certain dominant ones came to be associated with individual regions. Thus the Sanusiyya (mentioned above) held sway through much of the eastern half of the Sahara, while in Morocco the Hamadsha and Issawa emerged as popular expressions of Sufism, although the major brotherhoods were the Wazzaniyya, Tijaniyya, and Darqawa (Qadiriyya). Followers of the Moroccan holy man Ahmad al-Tijani (d.1815) dominated most of West Africa, although an offshoot of the Qadiriyya retained their historic influence. In **Sudan** followers of the Mahdi's legacy, who identified themselves as the Mahdiyya, became as influential as any of the other Sufi brotherhoods, which included the Khatmiyya and Salihiyya, and continued to be a presence in Sudanese politics right to the end of the twentieth century. On the East African coast the Qadiriyya and Shadhaliyya dominated. As regional holy men emerged to become the spiritual leaders of local communities, branches of these orders multiplied, taking the name of the local saint. Some, like the followers of the Wolof cleric Ahmadu Bamba (d.1927) in Senegal, gave rise to new brotherhoods altogether (the Muridiyya). By the middle of the twentieth century the Muridiyya, to which about 20 percent of the population in that country adhered, had emerged as a major economic and political influence. More typically local branches of the brotherhoods became focal points for displaced, urban workers, drawn to the prospect of wage labor in the colonial economies (see **economy: colonial**). In many of these communities affiliation with a brotherhood was nearly synonymous with being a Muslim, and mosques likewise became associated with particular Sufi affiliations. In Senegal (noted above), cities in northern Nigeria, and urban settings in East Africa the Sufi brotherhoods took on a political role, but in the countryside they were generally simple confessional paths that tied individual believers into the wider Muslim community that stretched across the continent and beyond.

The colonial powers, on occasion, themselves served as unwitting catalysts for the expansion of Islam. Apart from their very presence in Muslim lands, which led to the acts of resistance discussed above, some European authorities utilized the authority structures within Muslim communities and regions to rule through traditional systems, thus sanctioning the local Islamic authority. Most famous of these was the British administration and enhancement of the Sokoto Caliphate in northern Nigeria. Well after the departure of the British, the amirate system through which they had ruled the north remained solidly in place, forming the bedrock for political maneuvering in the region. The French-administered portions of Morocco emulated the British experience in Nigeria by working through the office of the Sultan, and in hundreds of local situations across Muslim Africa European administrators effectively sanctioned Islamic leadership by using local clerics as intermediaries. Even where effective colonial administration was not at issue, the period of colonial occupation led to a broad variety of accommodations between Muslim Africans and the colonial state. Some holy men simply withdrew from contact with the state; some actively pursued obstructionist tactics that were intended to set them apart through their non-compliance with infidel rule. Others collaborated with the Europeans, either in the hope of better protecting their communities from the full weight of colonial occupation or occasionally to simply further their own careers. On balance, the net effect of colonial administration was favorable to the expansion of Muslim communities and Islamic influence, although the full effect of this would not be evident until the last half of the twentieth century.

The colonial *pax* had its greatest impact in Muslim communities through the relative security (if not ease) of travel, **Arabic** and **Swahili** presses, schools catering to Muslim populations, and immigrant Muslim populations arriving from outside the continent. There was an increase in numbers traveling to perform the pilgrimage to Mecca. Out of reach for most Muslims in 1900, by the third quarter of the century provisions for the Hajj had become a major (and lucrative) industry in the population centers of Islamic Africa. Those who, by undertaking the pilgrimage, had acquired the title of Hajji(m)/Hajjia'(f) also brought home ideas and knowledge from the Holy Lands in the Hijaz, introducing reformist Wahhabi ideas from the Saudis after 1925, and later enabling *salafi* ideas to filter into diverse communities. They also brought home knowledge of an Islamic world that stretched to Central Asia and the Far East. This was the experience that, during the 1920s, shifted the spiritual center of the Islamic world for most Africans from the capital of the former Turkish Empire, Istanbul, to the Holy Lands of Arabia, located in the Hijaz.

Another development that owes partial debt to the colonial period was the use of the Arabic script (and generally the Arabic and Swahili languages) for communication between European authorities and Muslim communities. At one level the very use of a writing system that carried profoundly religious overtones served to reinforce the importance of the faith. This was not nearly as significant as the mainly religious texts that were produced in Arabic and Arabic script during the interwar years by local presses, not only across North Africa but also at sites down the East African coast, in **Kano** and Abeokuta (Nigeria), and in **Cape Town**. These "Islamic" presses may have produced a very limited number of editions by comparison to the flood of print material arriving from Europe, but they did reinforce a vibrant tradition of Islamic learning that competed with Western education. After independence this tradition of Islamic learning was reinvigorated and even came to challenge state-sponsored education in some post-colonial African governments. Colonial authorities also sanctioned Islamic education in many of their policies (sometimes even restricting Christian mission schools in Muslim communities like those of northern Nigeria) and in government schools, which made a place for Islamic teaching in their curricula, but they remained wary of the possibly subversive influence of the students who returned from North Africa, especially Cairo.

A final arena in which the colonial era introduced ideas to African communities from elsewhere in the Islamic world was in the incorporation into the colonies of Muslims from elsewhere in the European empires, mainly from India in British colonies but also Algerian teachers hired into **French West Africa**. The early immigration of Muslims from India to East Africa predated British conquest by fifty years, but laborers brought to build the railroad there or to grow sugar in Natal, and Muslims of Malay descent at the Cape, had a major impact on those regions; by 1915 perhaps a third of the Cape Coloured population adhered to Islam. But the most dramatic Islamic influence from the subcontinent came from the work of the missionaries of the Punjab holy man Ghulam Ahmad (d.1908), whose Ahmadi educators and proselytizers worked on the West African coast, as well as East Africa, during the interwar period, and provoked a violent reaction from some local Muslim clerics. Other external influences from Muslim populations elsewhere within the colonial empires, in addition to the Algerian schoolteachers who were brought to colonial-sponsored *madarassa* (schools) in territories across **francophone Africa**, were the Sudanese instructors who staffed colleges and the colonial bureaucracy in northern Nigeria. Movements like the Ahmadis, new communications and the easy dissemination of Arabic print media, and new opportunities for mobility all contributed to the ability of the Muslim leadership to find parity with other indigenous authorities in colonial communities. This is a status that evolved largely independently of the colonial system. One indication of this was the growth of regional Muslim political organizations and cultural associations during the 1920s and 1930s, organizations and associations that provided a fertile ground both for training new leadership and for the reception of ideas arriving from the heartland of Islam. Indeed in much of the continent a popular Islamic cultural revival can be seen over the first half of the twentieth century, most visible in the increasingly widespread adoption of the flowing Middle Eastern *jallabiya* among men and of forms of head covering or even veiling among women, dress that came to distinguish Muslims from non-Muslims across the continent.

The independence movements of the 1960s had the effect of unleashing a range of expectations and opportunities. They had been developing for a long time, but held in check by the colonial authorities. Just as a new mobility had been part of the colonial occupation, the post-colonial era brought a flood of new travel, by road and by air, to and from the Holy Lands. Communication with the heartland of Islam now also included print material on a dramatically increased scale, as well as radio, then television, and by the end of the century internet transmissions, all of which served to bring African Muslim communities into ever closer proximity with their coreligionists in the Hijaz and the East. The progression of popular engagement and political relevance of the wider Muslim world for Africans is illustrated by local reaction to successive international conflicts in distant Muslim lands. The Arab–Israeli conflict in 1967 provoked little reaction across the continent; twelve years later the revolution in Iran that brought Ayatollah Khomeini to power symbolized a resurgent Islam to which believers across the continent could relate. Khomeini's sermons could be purchased on tape in African markets. At the dawn of the new millennium, the American-led attack on Afghanistan led to riots and casualties in the streets of Nigerian cities and in **Nairobi**, and local recruitment drives in **South Africa** for young men to join the Taliban ranks against the infidel aggressor. These progressive degrees of African engagement with the wider Muslim world point to an emerging Islamic consciousness in the post-colonial era that is reflected in state-sponsored efforts to be sensitive to the aspirations of Muslim communities, and a strong emerging voice that is critical of "traditional" Islamic leadership and practices in African communities. Whether the cause is orthodox (*sunni*) or *shi'a* Islam, whether the crisis is Palestinian, Iraqi, or Afghani, their immediacy at a popular level marks a dramatic shift of worldview within African communities – an internationalization of Islam – during the closing decades of the century.

Independent African states have pursued a number of strategies to incorporate their Muslim populations into national agendas, perhaps the most visible and controversial of which have been joining international Islamic organizations and conventions. North African states had long been active in the Arab League (see **League of Arab States**), but for sub-Saharan Africa these memberships have become controversial when their sponsors propose agendas contrary to the interests of major national Muslim communities within independent states. The first of these was the Saudi-sponsored World Muslim League in 1962, which appealed to a membership of notables whose interests and influence contrasted sharply with the Islamic Call that was founded ten years later in Libya. In 1969 the **Organization of the Islamic Conference** was founded after the Six Day War to promote solidarity across Muslim communities, and it has taken on a United Nations-type role across the Islamic world.

The most dramatic development in the internationalization of Islam took place during the closing decades of the twentieth century: a flowering of movements seeking a revival of basic Islamic values and the reassertion of a progressive, networked, modern Islam that would link African believers to global networks of coreligionists. The engines of these "Islamist" movements, as they are called, and the ideas they are associated with were a reinvigoration of both long-standing Wahhabi influence from Saudi Arabia and the inspiration of the 1979 Iranian revolution. Among the most visible symbols of these influences was the construction of subsidized mosques across the continent (other countries like Morocco, Iraq, and some of the Gulf states also offered their largesse for mosque construction in Africa and around the world). But if these symbols were beholden to external resources, the Islamist movements were largely the voice of local youth and urban-dwellers. It was a voice that was sometimes strident in its attacks on establishment Islam, insofar as the Sufi *tariqas* and government affiliations with pan-Islamic coalitions were seen as "traditional" – even colonial – ways of containing and channeling Muslim activity in the state. Another feature of the Islamist activity was the introduction and enhancement of Arabized lifestyles, from language to dress and from popular culture to use of the mass media. Among their ambivalent roles were their efforts, at one level, to promote women to a new position of visibility within the Muslim community and, at another, to challenge the traditional role that women played in many societies as custodians and educators of Islamic values. By promoting cultural values that reaffirmed a modernization of Islam, Islamist groups also sought distance from subversive influences of Western culture. By adopting this stance they shared common ground with religious fundamentalists, although few would want to be confused with these more conservative movements. The public arena in which the Islamist groups frequently took positions included Arabic-language instruction in the schools, and state affiliation with international organizations within the Muslim world. But it was their efforts to champion appropriate applications of Islamic law (*shari'a*) in the lives of believers that was generally the most explosive issue, one fraught with tension as it pitted religion against the fragile state structures of many countries, and something that neatly demarcated "establishment" Islam from its Islamist challenge.

Islamist organizations gained real momentum in the 1980s and 1990s, and by the end of the century they could be found throughout the continent, in most every Muslim community. Where they attempted to form political parties, or to insert themselves in national political debates, they met fierce opposition from governments and were largely unsuccessful, although the National Islamic Front in Sudan and the Front Islamique du Salut in Algeria are notable exceptions. More typical are organizations like the Warsha ya Waandishi was Kiislam (Islamic Writers' Workshop), begun in 1975 in Tanzania; the Izala, begun in 1978 in Nigeria; and the Muslim Youth Movement, begun in 1970 in South Africa. All of these, like dozens of other local and national Islamist groups, have linked cultural revival to mosque-centered social networks, and even economic self-help projects. During this period, when some African states have lost ground in their ability to deliver social services, Islamist groups have stepped into the breach; in some countries they have taken their place alongside Western **non-governmental organizations** in providing basic social services. In local communities they have become highly visible through their attention to education, through their use of modern media, and in some quarters through their efforts to discredit the Sufi leadership.

At the close of the twentieth century Islamic Africa was ever more closely linked to the wider Muslim world, not simply through traditional Sufi *tariqas* and pilgrimages to the Holy Lands as was the case in the middle of the century, but as a result of new international networks and groups that are seeking to Islamize modernity, competing with traditional proselytizers of the faith.

See also: colonial conquest and resistance; Islamic reform movements; state: colonial

Further reading

Hodgkin, E. (1990) "Islam and Islamic Research in Africa," *Islam et sociétés au sud du Sahara* 4: 73–130.

Levtzion, N. and Pouwels, R.L. (eds.) (2000) *The History of Islam in Africa*, Athens: Ohio University Press.

Mazrui, A. (1988) "African Islam and Competitive Religion: Between Revivalism and Expansion," *Third World Quarterly* X, 2: 499–518.

Rosander, E.E. and Westerlund, D. (eds.) (1997) *African Islam and Islam in Africa*, Athens: Ohio University Press.

Stewart, C. (1990) "Islam," in A. Roberts (ed.), *The Colonial Moment in Africa: 1905–1940*, Cambridge: Cambridge University Press.

Stewart, C. and Peel, J. (1986) *Popular Islam in Twentieth-Century Africa*, Manchester: Manchester University Press.

CHARLES STEWART

Islamic reform movements

Derived from the Arabic *islah*, the term "reform" was originally used in the Koran (16:19) to denote a perennial concern for self-purification that every believer has to develop in order to resist spiritual and intellectual decay, as well as moral corruption. Accordingly the call for reform and the emergence of sporadic reform movements have become a recurrent phenomenon among Muslim communities. Some of these reform movements have evolved within the context of the struggle against colonial conquest, and they are often traced back to the teachings and works of prominent nineteenth-century Islamic personalities. African reform movements have been part of that historico-cultural movement, but they have also been an outcome of their own inner growth with indigenous sources of inspiration. From **Egypt** to **Morocco** and across the **Sudan** belt, a remarkable community of reform-scholars have emerged since the nineteenth century. Some of them stimulated religious revival, others ignited and developed fully fledged revolutions that resisted colonial forces or overthrew traditional dynasties, while a few of them took the reins of power and established new social orders. These legacies remained an inspiration through the struggles for independence and beyond.

Such a vibrant and complex phenomenon has brought to the fore several theoretical concerns among students of **Islam** and politics. Some scholars see reform as a step in a long and continuing process of conversion to Islam. The first stage of conversion, they argue, is necessarily a stage of "mixing," where traditional rituals coexist with new Islamic practices, but this is supposed to be followed by a second stage of "reform" through which ancient pre-Islamic practices are abandoned, allowing the converts to peacefully and gradually integrate into mainstream Islamic culture. In this view reform would ultimately win by its own intrinsic momentum. Other studies, however, suggest that the relationship between the aboriginal culture and the Islamic norms is not simply a relation of cohabitation – it is a relation of acculturation through which elements from the aboriginal African culture are identified with their counterparts in Islamic teachings. In this view, conversion to Islam is a decisive step by which many elements of Islamic doctrine are suppressed (due to their interpretation by indigenous literary elite), and many aspects of original pre-Islamic beliefs are retained and incorporated in the new emerging synthesis. The African masses living in remote rural areas – and who have contact only with less educated Muslims – would readily accept the version of Islam presented by their indigenous elites. Hence the view that Islamization begins with the borrowing into the African culture of Islamic features, and continues with even a greater substitution of Islamic elements for African ones, must not be accepted without qualification. What is under discussion is a continuing process of acculturation in which a literate indigenous elite plays a major role. This may help to explain why reform has also become an unceasing, reactive counter-process. What still needs to be explained is the nature of the religious actions that the reformers perform, how these actions become political, and when they become political how they do (or do not) become revolutionary.

Islamic reform movements are not a single monolithic phenomenon. Viewed broadly in terms of their regional distribution, ideological character, and social background, three complex reform movements can be identified. The first consists of the nineteenth-century movements founded by Sufi reform-minded scholars in **North**, **West**, and **East Africa**, and in the Sudan belt. These were based on the Bedouin people, whose contacts with towns and central governments was negligible, although some of them held strong defensive positions on important caravan routes. With their tradition of fighting and revolutionary tendencies, those movements remained a constant source of inspiration for the nationalist and post-nationalist reformers. In contrast, the second grouping consists of movements founded by urban scholars who – far from adopting or advocating a Sufi-style mystical approach to religious experience – were exposed in varying degrees to the full tide of European ideas and influence; for that very reason they could never strike a deep root into broad strata of society. Developed during the colonial and post-colonial era, the position of these movements vis-à-vis the colonial regime and nation-state was one of oscillation between cooperation and opposition. Their focus was mainly on education, and gradual, peaceful, institutional social change. The third group consists of the post-nationalist elite-centered reformers who took possession of whatever the second group had achieved, and began jockeying for political power and developing aspirations toward the establishment of an "Islamic state." A line must be drawn, however, between this last group and the younger generation of the 1970s whose point of departure was the rejection of the status quo – be it in terms of the secular nation-state, Western domination, the religious establishment, or the Sufi orders. The main idea of the radicals of the 1970s was to "get back to pure Islam." These were generally members of those militant organizations that came to be known in the English-speaking media as "fundamentalists," and who can hardly be fitted into the movements of reform.

In order to understand this diverse set of movements and tendencies of thought, a brief review of the basic philosophical foundations of reform, and of the conception of the ideal society that evolved in the minds of reformers, is required. Since earlier centuries of Islam, the prevailing maxim among scholars was that the success of the next generation of the Muslim community can only be ensured through the very factors that created its initial success and gave the religion its *raison d'être* fourteen centuries ago. What is implied here is that the Muslim community is susceptible, like all other communities, to corruption and decline. The remedy is twofold. First a reformer – being an individual or a group of scholars – has to stand up and call for a return to the principles upon which the community was initially based: that is, Koranic principles, the tradition of the Prophet, and the example of his companions. These are the "authentic" foundations of Islam, which naturally form the moral and legal criterion against which a Muslim's private and public behavior (whether he is a ruler or subject) should be judged. These foundations can be revitalized to become newly significant for addressing contemporary problems. Second the reformer has to seek ways of reinforcing the adherence of individuals and groups to these principles by way of commanding the good and forbidding the reprehensible. In the first process of developing the group's beliefs, the reformer's intellectual capacities are needed; the second process, however, needs his educational and organizational skills. In most cases a successful reformer provides both.

To be sure, this return to the first principles does not imply restoration. It is rather meant to revitalize the original beliefs by freeing the text of revelation from scholastic interpretation and historical particularities. Here a conceptual difference is drawn between the pure Koranic commands, and the law derived from them by the human intellect. But given the fact that the Koran does not regulate everything, and that the opinions of the schools of law are not binding, the reformers are implicitly resorting to a sort of limited rationalism – allowing human intellect to regulate a wide range of activities. In order to solve modern problems the Koranic text has to be the basis of the reformer's reflection, with the reformer's task always being to look for subtle concordances between Koranic principles and present-day occurrences. This is a process of free inquiry (*ijtihad*), which is necessarily associated with the process of reform. Free inquiry entails revisiting the tradition, criticizing and reassessing parts of it, and arriving at new conclusions. Free inquiry also entails a critical approach towards modernity, through which Western science and technology (seen as products of human reason) can be disentangled from their cultural underpinnings, and a new synthesis thereby developed – a synthesis that bypasses both Islamic traditionalism and Western secularism.

This new synthesis is a rather revolutionary and hazardous one. But, obviously enough, it is the consequence of the history through which it has passed, and it would be intelligible only in the light of that history. Since at least the nineteenth century there have evolved two major intellectual centers – Egypt and the Maghreb – where ideas of reform flowered. Each of them has accommodated a principal articulator of reform, a loosely structured community of scholars, a university college, and a periodical. Not surprisingly both of them focused on institutional change by means of education. The champions of the Egyptian center were Jamal al-Din al-Afghani and Mohammad Abdu, whereas Khair al-Din al-Tunusi, ibn Badis, ibn 'Ashur, and Malik Bennabi were the tireless exponents of reform in the Maghreb region.

Acting under the overwhelming pressure of events, Afghani (d.1897) and Abdu (d.1905) tried to forge a broad pan-Islamic alliance that might counterbalance European imperialism. In this regard they were keen to communicate with – and seek the support of – their coreligionists, the Sanusiyya of **Libya** and the Sudanese Mahdiyya, who were resisting British and French rule in their own countries. Neither the Afghani's pan-Islamism nor the Sanusi–Mahdi's revolution were able to achieve their final objectives. Subsequently Afghani and Abdu differed on aims and methods of Islamic reform. Ironically Afghani ended up in the Sultan's prison, whereas Abdu returned to Egypt to resume the reform project single-handed and through different channels. Abandoning the pan-Islamic strategy, he shifted his attention and energies from politics to education, and from revolution to gradual social and institutional change. It was this shift in strategy that drew attention to Abdu's works, popularizing his blend of Islamic "reformism," and earning him the admiration of the Muslim elites in various countries, as well as the sympathy of some European liberal scholars.

At certain junctures in its historical development Abdu's reformism came to be blended with the reformulation of his disciple Rashid Rida, who trimmed off Abdu's liberalism and brought him closer to the Wahhabism – a bundle of ideas came to be vaguely labeled as the *Salafiyya*. In Egypt itself the teachings of Abdu and Rida were adopted, with slight modifications, by Hassan al-Bana (1906–49), the founder of the Muslim Brothers. In **Algeria**, **Tunisia**, and Morocco Abdu's ideas were reproduced and developed successively by Abd al-Hamid ibn Badis (1889–1940), Mohammad Tahir ibn 'Ashur (d.1973), and Abd al-Karim al-Khattabi (1882–1963). This, however, should not obscure the fact that seeds of reform in the Maghreb region had already been sown by Khair al-Din al-Tunusi (d.1890), whose influence was probably more enduring than that of Afghani and Abdu.

The most important intellectual heritage left by Khair al-Din was the *Sadiqiyya* college he established, where the Islamic traditional sciences were merged with "modern" Western ones. Basing himself on that heritage, it was Mohammad Tahir ibn 'Ashur (1879–1973) who carried over the reform efforts to the realms of Islamic jurisprudence, Islamic social order, the **Arabic** language, and Koranic exegesis. In their footsteps, ibn Badis founded the *ulam* association, published an important periodical, and brought the reform ideals to the hearts and minds of Algerian intellectuals. Foremost among those was Malik Bennabi (d.1973), who related the concept of reform to **decolonization**, giving reform a new philosophical and sociological dimension. Muslim communities were colonized, he contended, because they were *colonizable*. To bring them back to life a decolonization process was needed, but it had to be a deep spiritual and psychological transformation rather than a mere political one.

It is interesting to note that during the runup to independence, most of these reformers joined forces with the anti-colonial liberation movements, with Islam interwoven into nationalism. But when independence was achieved, most of the African countries adopted a Soviet-type state socialism with a one-party system (see **socialisms and socialists**). Muslim reformers and scholars were sidelined, and looked on as being out of touch with the material needs of the masses, or as detrimental to social and political development. The reaction to that oppressive wave of secular nationalism and socialism was the emergence in the 1970s of a third type of reformer with a different strategy of reform. Hassan al-Turabi of Sudan, Rashid Ghanushi of Tunisia, and a few like-minded Islamists in Algeria and Morocco were compelled, in the heat of political competition, to change the strategy of reform from the educational field to the direct control of government machinery.

It is noteworthy that the majority of these reformers were not just slightly exposed to Western civilization, like Abdu and Rida: they had firsthand experience of it. Most of them were prolific writers, too, but all of them, surprisingly, were men. Women in leading positions were very few, though recent research indicates that there might have been some women in reform movements who played important roles within their own societies. Nana Asma'u (1793–1864), the daughter of Usman dan Fodio, was a legendary figure in the history of nineteenth-century reform. She was a multilingual, accomplished scholar who contributed significantly to the Islamic reform process in northern **Nigeria** by being a role model for Hausa–Fulani women (see **Fulani; Hausa**). She was involved in politics, female education, and social reform. She witnessed and reported on battles, and organized literacy training for rural women, bringing them into the main educational network. Asma'u translated some of her father's work into Hausa, which was the language of the masses, and in doing so popularized and reinforced his message. A mention could also be made of Fatima Zuhra al-Najjar, a member of the Algerian reformist movement in the late 1940s. She was an advocate of female education, a public speaker, and a grass-roots organizer. Another outstanding figure in this respect was the Egyptian writer 'Aisha Abd al-Rahman Bint al-Shati (d.1998). She was an original scholar whose works ranged from literary criticism, to Koranic exegesis, to politics and education. Like earlier itinerant Muslim scholars, she taught in Egypt, Sudan, Saudi Arabia, and Morocco, forming circles of students in all these places. A less popular but equally important political activist was Zeinab al-Ghazali, who was subjected by the Nasser regime to harassment and detention. Under the leadership of al-Turabi, the Sudanese Muslim Brotherhood included female politicians in the consultative assembly, and some of them held ministerial positions in the government. Thus it could be argued that female activists and scholars were able, if only in a bridging role as leaders, to make their presence felt in most of the reform movements. Some of them were engaged in extending and amplifying the message of the movements to potential recruits, and thus getting involved in grass-roots mobilization.

Like all complex processes reform can generate its own internal dynamics. Reformers may differ in their diagnosis of the decline of Muslim communities. Their programs of reform may also differ according to the different situations they face, the different regions they live in, the personalities of their leaders, tribal traditions of resistance, and the type of government under which they function. Some reformers find no option but to shift from reform to revolution, while others feel able to collaborate peacefully with the government of the day.

Among reformers there are the Sufi-oriented scholars who advocate the mystical approach to religious experience: Muslims are expected to wage *jihad* against their own worldly desires in order to conquer egotism and submit to God's will. This is a line of thinking that almost all Sufis follow; it is this line of thought that helped the Sufi orders to easily adapt themselves to existing African beliefs. That adaptation had, however, prompted some Sufi scholars of the nineteenth century to call for reform within the order, as well as within the larger Muslim community. The best known of the Sufi scholars that displayed such a revivalist spirit were al-Sanusi (1787–1859), Usman dan Fodio (1754–1817), and al-Haj Umar of the Tijaniyya order (d.1864). To them the adaptation of Islam to "African tradition" was repugnant. They saw all forms of "pagan" heritage – embodied in indigenous spirit-possession cults, sacred animals and trees, local shrines and symbols of veneration, the cults of saints, and prostration before kings – as symptoms of serious spiritual and doctrinal decay. It was al-Magili (d.1503/4), the renowned Amazigh scholar, who judged that both Sonni Ali and his people were "mixers" – irrespective of their profession of faith. That was so because Sonni and his people continued to venerate pagan shrines. In al-Magili's view, the "mixers" were dangerous because they led ignorant Muslims astray. But if these views were to be carried to their practical conclusion, reform would eventually lead to internal tensions within the Muslim community, or to conflicts between the reformers themselves. A cleavage between the legalist and mystical traditions, the idealists and the political activists, would always be a possibility, since these different characters would not always be perfectly blended. In the case cited above, al-Magili did not condemn the "mixers" alone; he also condemned the "venal *'ulama*" who approved the desires and actions of the king. Usman dan Fodio used to attack the "venal *'ulama*" on similar lines, and sixty-five years later the Mahdi of the Sudan followed suit – under the rule of the Mahdi's successor a number of official religious men were branded as "venal *'ulama*," and some of them were sent to prison. In another context reform does not appear to be an internal process within the Sufi tradition, but a detached legalistic and external effort directed against unorthodox customs and practices. Hence it necessarily appears to be an anti-Sufi process – similar to the Wahhabi reform. Such was the case with Abd al-Karim al-Khattabi (1882–1963), the Moroccan leader of the Rif rebellion against the Spanish (1921–6). Following the ideas of the Salafiyya movement, he opposed the Sufi brotherhoods, seeing them as a source of internal divisions. The association of the Algerian reformers in the late 1940s was similarly torn between a Wahhabi wing that was preoccupied with unorthodox funeral practices and moderates who were focusing on education and the colonial presence in their country. In another situation reform may manifest itself in a militant movement of protest directed against a foreign enemy, a "corrupt" state, or an autocratic Muslim leader. Under the general heading of "corruption of the state" stand a great number of charges. In the post-independence era, for instance, reformers attacked some nationalist leaders on the grounds of their having been subservient to colonial rule. In 1977 a group of students in Paris established their own Mouride association, distancing themselves from the brotherhood's traditional leadership in **Senegal**, and beginning to question the claims of leadership from Amadu Bamba's family.

As the targets of reform changed, so did its tactics and types of organization. To organize the followers around a knowledgeable charismatic leader was the conventional wisdom of the Sufis, but institutional-oriented reformers of the twentieth century shifted, for a variety of reasons, to formal committees and voluntary associations. These latter organizations would seek the support of the general public for specific projects, like building private schools and mosques, or financing publications. One obvious example of this shift can be seen in the Association of the Reformist 'Ulama, founded in 1931 in Algeria by Abd al-Hamid ibn Badis. The association's aim was to organize educational and cultural activities at the local community level. But with the relative relaxation of central control, the association's activities grew in scope and importance. Through informal connections, networking, and fundraising, leaders of the association were able to maintain lively grass-roots participation, publish a respected periodical, preside over a number of endowments, and build well-structured voluntary organizations that were later to become an important training ground for political tasks. The Egyptian Muslim Brotherhood, which itself developed out of voluntary benevolent societies, used to offer many educational and medical services. Evening courses on literature and the Koran were arranged by them in different neighborhoods, with some of them intended to attract rural migrants. Similar activities were also established in Sudan and many other African countries – especially Senegal, **Niger**, Nigeria, and **South Africa**.

But with the changing circumstances of the post-independence era, a new strategy of reform emerged, and it naturally dictated a new type of organization. Unlike the earlier loosely structured cultural and educational societies, the new movements began to depend largely on the effectiveness of their organizational skills. These included formal organization; establishing local and regional units; developing internal, quasi-military discipline; ensuring solidarity and cohesion of group personnel; and constructing a clear hierarchy of authority, as well as leadership cadres. Men and women from different social, economic, and ethnic backgrounds were brought into primary membership units, which were connected with larger clusters of units (or families) that mirrored the envisaged Islamic *umma* (Muslim community). The importance of teamwork and mutual trust were deeply appreciated and given an Islamic justification. Organizations of course served to discipline the members, mobilize them, and make the movement politically significant. There is no wonder, then, that most of the earlier voluntary organizations and fundraising committees developed over the 1970s and 1980s into Islamic banks and other important economic institutions (in Egypt and Sudan), while the schools and colleges developed into Islamic universities (in Sudan, Algeria, Niger, and **Uganda**); all of them were expected to contribute to the regeneration of the *umma*'s moral order, its efficacy, and its new dignity – this has been, admittedly, one of the most remarkable achievements of the reformers.

One final theme that has been well covered in contemporary research is the radicalization that most of the Islamic reform movements went through. Most of the researchers have tried to explain the rise of fundamentalism and militancy in the 1970s in terms of the socioeconomic hardship and shocks that were experienced by rural–urban migrants. What ought to be examined as well is the broader political system, and the underlying historico-cultural component. From the "scramble for Africa" in the late nineteenth century until the mid-1960s, most Muslim African communities were under colonial rule. Colonial rule was conceived by self-conscious Muslims as domination by "infidels," and they regarded resistance to it as a religious duty. The Sanusiyya of Libya, Amir Abd al-Qadir of Algeria, Mohammad al-Tishti Hamalla in **Mali**, the Mahdiyya of Sudan, and Mohammad Hassan of **Somalia** were venerated because of their anti-colonial *jihad* (struggle). *Jihad* did not only radicalize those earlier reform movements and accentuate their political function, but remained a live history for the succeeding generations. In cases where those radicals were militarily defeated (as most of them were) their followers were marginalized, pushed to remote rural regions, and left totally outside the mainstream of political and economic life. With rising educational standards, improvements in transport and communications, and greater amounts of printed material, it was only to be expected that contact between cities and countryside would be intensified. That is how the urban-based reform movements attempted to link up with these "floating" masses, but it also became an area of conflict and confrontation between the emerging Islamic forces and the incumbent military–socialist regimes. We may need here to recall the military coups that plagued most of the African Muslim countries, the widespread use of violence they resorted to, and the complete ruling out of the electoral process as a peaceful means of transferring political power. In many cases when these Islamic movements attempted to reach out for public support, their efforts were conceived as a threat and consequently nipped in the bud, with their leaders executed, driven underground, or forced to flee the country, as happened in Egypt, Sudan, Libya, **Tunisia**, Algeria, Somalia, and to a lesser degree Morocco and **Mauritania**. This type of violent politics became an institutionalized means of gaining power or sustaining it in such countries, and a society that has such a high capacity for violence has much more scope for revolution than for reform.

See also: African religions; colonial Africa; education: colonial; education: post-independence; Islam

Further reading

Christelow, A. (1987) "Ritual, Culture and Politics of Islamic Reformism in Algeria," *Middle Eastern Studies* 23, 3: 255–73.

Merad, A. (1979) "Islam," in E. Donzeil, B. Lewis and C. Pellat (eds.), *The Encyclopedia of Islam*, Leiden: E.J. Brill.

O'Brien, D.B.C. and Coulon, C. (eds.) (1988) *Charisma and Brotherhood in African Islam*, Oxford: Clarendon Press.

ELTIGANI ABDELGADIR HAMID

Ivory Coast *see* Côte d'Ivoire

J

Johannesburg, South Africa

Johannesburg is situated in the Gauteng Province, and is colloquially known as "Egoli" (place of gold). Greater Johannesburg comprises an area of 483 square kilometers, with an estimated population of 2.2 million. The town emerged with the discovery of gold in 1886. At the turn of the twentieth century it was the largest city in **South Africa**, and the economic hub of the country. Johannesburg currently accounts for more than 35 percent of South Africa's gross domestic product. The city's development has been permeated by "race-based" practices of "bleaching" the city, while maintaining a supply of cheap labor. But Johannesburg is also the city in which apartheid experienced its most rapid breakdown: the city is presently the most desegregated city in South Africa.

Mining has been central to the evolution of Johannesburg's economy. It induced the growth of both the manufacturing and commercial sectors. Most financial institutions and industrial corporations had headquarters in Johannesburg's CBD (central business district), but since the 1980s the CBD has been in decline, with many companies seeking safer and more aesthetically pleasing environments in the outer white suburbs.

Racial segregation and discrimination were present from the outset of the city's development. Africans were denied the franchise, prevented from owning land, and their entry into the city was highly regulated. The need for cheap labor in the mines, in industry, and as domestic servants attracted (or forced) many blacks into the area. They were expected to live in Klipspruit (present-day Soweto), which is a distance of nearly thirty kilometers from the city center, but most preferred to live nearer to the city, so mining companies erected large single-sex compounds around the town to house their labor force. Domestics (both male and female) tended to live in the backyards of their employers, while Sophiatown, Alexandra, and Pageview (the Indian area) became the other places where blacks settled.

Prior to the 1950s the city council had made many attempts to force blacks out of "mixed-race" slum areas in the city center and into dormitory residential areas like Orlando and the Western Native Township. The most violent forced removals came in the 1950s, when Sophiatown was bulldozed and 58,000 Africans forced out to Meadowlands and Diepkloof. Pageview was "cleansed" in the 1960s, and the Indian population relocated to Lenasia. Coloureds were moved to Coronationville, Riverlea, and Westbury (a new name for Western Native Township). Soweto is the largest African township. In 1983 government introduced a large-scale subsidized sale of houses in black townships, enabling an emerging black middle-class to purchase and renovate homes there. From the late 1970s there was also a steady stream of blacks back into residential areas in the city center, such as Hillbrow, Joubert Park, and Berea. By the end of 1980 the central city had largely been reclaimed.

Johannesburg was a center of resistance to apartheid: the Defiance Campaigns of the 1950s were strongest there; the Black Consciousness Movement established many civic organizations in the 1970s; and the Soweto student revolt of 1976 served as a catalyst for student revolts across the whole of South Africa. In the 1980s the city was besieged by labor strikes, rent strikes, and student boycotts, while street committees took over the day-to-day governance of the black townships.

There are two universities located in Johannesburg: the University of the Witwatersrand (founded in 1922) and the Rand Afrikaans University (1966). The city has a mix of modern skyscrapers, and old buildings: the Carlton Center, Brixton and Hillbrow Towers, and the old Johannesburg Fort and post office. The Johannesburg Civic Theater, Market Theater, and Art Gallery are a few of the many places of cultural interest in the city.

Further reading

Mandy, N. (1984) *A City Divided: Johannesburg and Soweto*, Braamfontein: Macmillan.

CHERYL HENDRICKS

Juba, Sudan

Juba became the capital of the British Equatorial Province when the colonial administration decided to move it from Mongalla in 1930. It subsequently developed into a colonial city with offices, schools, military barracks, and civil-service training centers. From then up to the present day, Juba has played a critical role in southern Sudanese politics. In 1947 the British held the Juba Conference, which imposed the unification of north and south **Sudan**. However, in 1955 the first phase of Sudan's civil war began – on the eve of independence. As in many other southern cities, Juba's inhabitants suffered various forms of violence and brutality after the outbreak of the war. When the Addis Ababa Agreement was signed between the Southern Sudan Liberation Movement (SSLM) and the government in 1972, the south became one region, with Juba serving the its capital. As a result Juba hosted the High Executive Council (HEC), which was responsible for internal security and local administration. By the mid-1970s Juba was receiving large number of refugees who had been repatriated from neighboring countries like **Uganda** and **Kenya**. Between 1972 and 1983 the new regional government transformed Juba into the commercial and political center of the south; in 1981 the first class graduated from the University of Juba, which had been established in 1977.

After a second civil war broke out in 1983, Juba was affected economically, socially, and militarily. In 1985, for instance, the Mundari (a pastoralist group) were attacked by the Sudan People's Liberation Army (SPLA) and forced out of their homeland, fleeing with their remaining cattle to Juba. About 17,000 Mundari were relocated into camps around Juba. In mid-1992 the Torit faction of the SPLA mounted a major attack on Juba, nearly capturing the city. Since then Juba has been completely transformed into a military garrison: It contains the headquarters of the internal security agency, military intelligence, and the Popular Defense Forces (PDF). In the immediate aftermath of the 1992 attacks, government forces responded with the summary execution of civilians and captured SPLA soldiers, with anyone who tried to resist or who was suspected of belonging to the SPLA being taken away and killed. Although the SPLA controls the surrounding countryside, Juba is still held by the government. It is also home to an enormous population of displaced people, many of whom have to be fed by horrendously expensive airlifts.

The total population of Juba was estimated in 1990 as 500,000, the majority of whom had been displaced from rural areas. This process of rural migration into the city for food and security had a serious negative impact on the environment and the economy. As a result of the SPLA siege and the lack of efficient transportation services, civil servants' salaries were only paid irregularly. Important facilities, such as hospitals and schools, were not repaired or maintained. With few educational facilities in Juba, large numbers of children were unable to go to school – some of the schools that did exist were occupied by refugees. Not only had the war destroyed the economic foundations of the city, but basic social services were suffered serious damage. It was left to the civilian women of Juba to develop different strategies to sustain daily life in the midst of civil war.

Further reading

Collins, R.O. (1983) *Shadows in the Grass: Britain in the Southern Sudan, 1918–1956*, New Haven: Yale University Press.

Lako, G.T. (1993) *South Sudan: The Foundation of a War Economy*, Frankfurt am Main: Lang.

AMIR H. IDRIS

K

Kampala, Uganda

Kampala, the capital of **Uganda**, had a population of 1.5 million in 2000. The city was originally the capital of the Buganda Kingdom, and known as Mengo. In 1890 Lugard, the British conqueror, chose one of the rolling hills near Mengo, and fortified it against Kabaka Mwanga's wishes. That hill was called Kampala. From these two hills, the city expanded to others, including Rubaga and Namirembe, which were occupied respectively by Catholic and Protestant missions. The four hills represented the structural features that were to characterize Ugandan politics.

From 1906 Kampala was officially designated a township and began to overshadow Mengo. The arrival of the **Kenya**–Uganda railway and the opening of Lake Steamers further enhanced its growth. Although Kampala came to be accepted as the commercial and administrative capital, for strategic purposes nearby Entebbe, a port on Lake Victoria, was made the political capital.

Kampala developed as a city of racial divisions. Kampala municipality was the preserve of European and Asian settlers, from which – until independence – local Africans were excluded by strict building rules and high rents. Consequently many Africans became urban squatters, resulting in the creation of extensive peri-urban slums around the municipality, close enough to sources of employment without venturing inside the expensive municipal boundaries. Other Africans lived in Mengo-Kibuga, which continued to grow, despite the ineffectiveness of the governing Buganda Town board.

The growth of Kampala City was bolstered by the economic boom that followed the **Second World War**, especially the establishment of import substitution industries, which further extended the boundaries of the city. Commercial activity also increased as a result of the higher wages that resulted from a wave of strikes – another characteristic of the postwar period.

Further impetus was given to the rapid growth of Kampala by the "Africanization" policy that was developed after Uganda's independence in 1962. The city continued to grow through industrial and commercial investment, mainly from joint ventures between the Indian business community and the Uganda Development Corporation. The 1960s also saw the establishment of Uganda Central Bank and the first commercial banks that were prepared to lend to Africans (apart from the Cooperative Bank that had been established in 1955).

The city's fortunes declined under Idi Amin's tyrannical regime (1971–8), during which there was widespread state-sponsored terror. The Asians – who dominated the commercial sector of Kampala – were expelled, and their businesses were expropriated, often to people with little business experience. While the city's population continued to grow, ageing buildings and infrastructural decay contributed to Kampala's visible dilapidation. The collapse of the formal sector led to the rapid growth of the informal sector, accelerating the growth of the city's slums in the 1970s. A rare phenomenon of urban to rural migration began to occur between 1975 and 1979. In fact Kampala's collapse could be read in the rapid growth of the border towns – centers for the main movers in the *magendo* (smuggling) economy.

In 1981 the government adopted a **structural adjustment program** that increased business activity once more. However, levels of investment remained low, because of continuing insecurity and the city's poor physical infrastructure. The situation changed after the establishment of a new government by the National Resistance Movement, which improved security and embarked on an aggressive program aiming at economic recovery. The informal sector continued to expand, enabling several social groups, including women, to operate small businesses; as business confidence was restored, investments – especially in real estate – grew. By 2000 the city had expanded from its original four hills to cover more than twenty hills – and it was still expanding.

Further reading

Nnaabalamba, A.J. (1988) *The Planning Process in Uganda: The Case of Kampala, 1962–1987*, M.A. thesis, University of California, Los Angeles.

JOSEPHINE AHIKIRE
KAFUREEKA LAWYER

Kano, Nigeria

Kano was founded around AD 999 as the center of a pre-Islamic **Hausa** state that reached its territorial and institutional height around 1500. It became a prominent trading center and the southern terminus of the trans-Saharan trade. It was also a major center for the production of indigo cloth, leather goods, and iron- and silverware. The pre-Islamic Habe Dynasty was removed by the Islamic *jihad* of 1806, to be replaced by the **Fulani**, and Kano Emirate became a subordinate part of the Sokoto Caliphate. Because of its commercial clout, Kano became a major cultural and ethnic melting pot. This intensified after the *jihad*, with immigrants arriving from as far afield as the coast of **North Africa** and the forest-belt of southern **Nigeria**. A common "Kanawa" identity developed out of this process.

The British occupied Kano in 1903, establishing a system of indirect rule through the Fulani aristocracy. Colonial rule led to major administrative changes in Kano. First, attempts were made to rationalize and systematize the city administration. Second, health and educational systems were introduced, based on Western models. Finally, colonialism transformed Kano into the hub of a major groundnut growing economy, a dynamic center of colonial commerce, an emerging industrial center, and a major focus for immigration. Kano became the northern terminus of the railways, and towering pyramids of groundnuts became the city's symbol.

During the process of **decolonization** in the 1950s, Kano emerged as the center of class-based populist politics in northern Nigeria. Some radical members of the Western-educated elite made common cause with traders and rich farmers in challenging aristocratic prerogatives and colonial rule. However, Kano was also noted for regionalist politics: in 1953 southern Nigerians, particularly Igbos, had been attacked by mobs of northern Nigerians. In 1964 such Kanawa sentiments came to the fore when the Sokoto prince and regional premier, Ahmadu Bello, dethroned Emir Sanusi.

A military coup in 1966 led to the creation of Kano state out of the northern region in 1967, with Kano as the state capital. The period between 1967 and 1979 was marked by massive infrastructural development, fueled by the oil boom and the enhanced administrative status of the city. Industrial production accelerated in tandem with increased **urbanization**, with textiles, plastics, oil, flour milling, and confectionery production the major industries, and the power of the Emir in urban governance was curtailed.

With the end of military rule in 1979, a radical populist party took over the government of the state, and Kano became the hub of radical anti-establishment politics in Nigeria. Between 1979 and 1983 there was further populist investment in infrastructure and social welfare. However, the effects of the oil crisis were becoming apparent, leading to major socioeconomic dislocation that culminated in the intra-Muslim Maitatsine religious riots in Kano in 1980. The military coup of 1983, and the adoption of **structural adjustment programs** in Nigeria in 1986, significantly worsened the economic and political situation in Kano: the municipal administration was increasingly fragmented into different local government areas; the corrupt practices of the military became entrenched in municipal governance; and industrial and economic development were reversed, leading to massive unemployment, urban decay, and environmental pollution.

Kano remained a major cultural, political, industrial, and commercial center in northern Nigeria, and its influence was felt in neighboring **Niger**, **Chad**, and northern **Cameroon**. However, there were clear signs of increased ethnic and religious tension in the face of political and economic crises, with several riots in Kano from 1991. The estimated population of the metropolitan area of Kano in the 1990s was 2.2 million.

Further reading

Abba, M.J. (1999) *Kano City and Fagge: A Historical Perspective*, Kano: Triumph Publishing.

ABDUL RAUFU MUSTAPHA

Kenya

Kenya, which covers an area of 582,646 square kilometers and is bordered by **Somalia**, **Ethiopia**, **Sudan**, and **Tanzania**, had an estimated population of 32.6 million in 2000. Although it was declared a British colony in 1895, conquest was not completed until 1908, with the British facing considerable resistance – especially from the Mazrui and Giriama along the coast, the Masai and Kikuyu in central Kenya, and the Nandi and Gusii in western Kenya. Conquest was facilitated, however, by prevailing ecological disasters and lack of unity among the colonists' opponents. Afterwards a colonial administration was established, and African chiefs were incorporated at the divisional and village levels to collect taxes, recruit labor, and maintain law and order. Accompanying the conquest was the construction of the Kenya–Uganda railway, which operated at a loss because neither Kenya nor **Uganda** were producing enough by way of exports. The governor of Kenya was convinced that only European settlers could establish a vibrant export economy, so settlers were given large tracts of fertile land in central Kenya and the Rift Valley, and later received preferential treatment in the allocation of infrastructural services, opportunities to cultivate lucrative cash crops (such as coffee), and marketing.

During the first two decades of the twentieth century, Kenya witnessed the consolidation of the colonial administration, the unsteady beginnings of settler agriculture, and the spasmodic development and underdevelopment of Kenya's peasantry. A coercive labor system was instituted, involving forced labor, migrant labor, and low wages, and colonial patterns of racialized class formation began to take root. The effects of incorporation into the British Empire also began to be felt, most brutally through the pulverizations of the **First World War**, and more subtly through the agents of colonial socialization: the mission church and school, the colonial town and market. In the meantime, working-class, peasant and petty-bourgeois nationalist struggles began to emerge.

In the 1920s the struggles for supremacy between the settlers and Africans were exacerbated by increased settler migration, the introduction of the stringent pass-system known as *kipande*, currency fluctuations and the Depression of 1919–22, and the debate over the Indian Question. Kenyan Asians felt discriminated against, to which the Colonial Office responded by proclaiming that African paramountcy (interests) would govern policy in Kenya. But what Africans experienced was colonial exploitation and the lack of development opportunities. The emerging educated elite formed new ethnic and national associations, such as the East African Association and the Kikuyu Central Association, and workers resorted to desertion, strikes, and the formation of trade unions. There was also the rise of religious and millennial protest, best represented by the cult of Mumbo, which rejected European ways and urged a return to African traditions.

The Depression of the 1930s exposed the weaknesses of the settler economy, and the importance of peasant production came to be appreciated even by the colonial state. The settlers began to diversify into stock raising and increase labor demands on their squatters, who resisted in various ways. Land and other economic grievances preoccupied leaders of the new political associations, many of whom were budding entrepreneurs. In the meantime, conditions in the towns were changing as import substitution industries grew, leading to the expansion and stabilization of the working class, which increasingly comprised women. Besides the formal sector, women also worked in the informal sector as petty traders, while the huge gender imbalance in urban areas led some to resort to prostitution. The educated class was also expanding, as the number of secondary schools increased. From 1936 Kenyan students could go to Makerere College in Uganda. Since the provision of education and health services was segregated, Africans often built their own schools.

Kenya's political economy was profoundly transformed by the **Second World War**. The settlers increased both their political and economic power as they adopted mixed farming on an unprecedented scale. Meanwhile 98,000 Africans were drafted into the army, and many more conscripted for private employers. Peasant cash-crop production also expanded, and rural differentiation increased. All this contributed to the widespread food shortages of 1942–3. Also during the war more manufacturing industries were established, thus accelerating the rates of **urbanization** and labor stabilization, although working conditions deteriorated. Not surprisingly the war years witnessed unparalleled labor unrest. Conditions also proved propitious for the growth of religious and political protest movements, among them the Kenya African Union (KAU), initially formed as a support group for Eliud Mathu, the first African to be nominated to the Legislative Council in 1944.

These processes accelerated after the war. New investment consolidated Kenya's position as the industrial and commercial capital of **East Africa**. The educated elite, led by the KAU, wanted to curtail settler power and agitated for greater African development and representation. The trade unions, first led by the African Workers Federation, then by the East African Trade Union Congress and the Kenya Federation of Labor, flexed their muscles through various strikes, including general strikes in **Mombasa** in 1947 and **Nairobi** in 1950. The number of rural protests was also rising, especially among the increasingly impoverished squatters and others opposed to government interventions over land-use and conservation. Violence increased and in October 1952 the government declared a state of emergency, arresting nationalist leaders, including Jomo Kenyatta.

The militants took to the forest, forming the Land Freedom Army (LFA), which waged a bitter guerrilla war commonly known as Mau Mau. Britain mobilized over 50,000 troops against the LFA, who found themselves fighting not only the British but also loyalists from their own communities. The LFA was dominated by the Kikuyu, because anti-colonial grievances were most concentrated in Kikuyu areas, but many more ethnic groups were involved in the Mau Mau movement than is usually acknowledged. By 1956 Mau Mau had been militarily defeated, with a death toll of 12,000 Africans and 100 Europeans, but the war ruptured the colonial order by burying the political dreams of the settlers and making constitutional and structural reforms imperative.

Political and economic reforms were undertaken in earnest from 1954, and accelerated after the first direct African elections of 1957. In the next few years, more constitutional changes were made in response to political agitation led by newly formed political parties: the Kenya African National Union (KANU) and the Kenya African Democratic Union (KADU), both founded in 1960. KANU was based on a Kikuyu–Luo alliance, and favored unitary government, while KADU was dominated by coastal and Rift Valley ethnic minorities who preferred federalism. In the general elections of May 1963, KANU won an overwhelming number of seats. On 12 December 1963 Kenya officially regained its independence. A year later it became a republic, with Kenyatta as president.

The Kenyatta era, lasting from 1963 to 1978, was characterized by steady economic growth, social development, and a drift into political authoritarianism. The economy grew at an average annual rate of 6.8 percent between 1965 and 1980, led by manufacturing, followed by services and agriculture (which remained the backbone of the economy). There was rapid growth of smallholdings and agricultural cooperatives, and the large farm sector was Africanized. The expansion of African businesses and tourism was also notable. There was massive investment in social services too, so that educational enrollment, literacy levels, population growth, and life-expectancy rates rose sharply. But the fruits of independence were unevenly distributed between regions, classes, and genders. Rural landlessness and urban unemployment increased, and women lagged behind men in every sphere. Politically the country became a *de facto* one-party state. In 1964 KADU members voluntarily joined KANU, while the radical Kenya Peoples Union, formed by former vice-president Odinga in 1966, was violently suppressed. Potential challengers to Kenyatta were eliminated: Charismatic Tom Mboya was assassinated in 1969, and the fiery J.M. Kariuki in 1975. As ideological expression was stifled, politics increasingly became personalized and tribalized, centering on intra-KANU intrigues about Kenyatta's successor.

Kenyatta died in 1978, and was succeeded by his vice-president, Daniel Arap Moi. Moi promised to follow in his predecessor's footsteps, but he soon tried to shift power from the Kikuyu to his own Kalenjin people, who were allied with previously marginalized groups. His rule coincided with an economic slowdown and the imposition from 1980 of **structural adjustment programs** at the behest of the World Bank and International Monetary Fund. Economic growth fell to an average of 4.2 percent in the 1980s, and even less in the 1990s. Economic difficulties soon led to political challenges to Moi's regime. In 1982 the failure of an attempted coup by air-force officers was followed by a crackdown on real and imagined dissidents. But as **civil society** became more restive, and the winds of democratic change began to blow from abroad, Moi was eventually forced to accept political liberalization. He won the 1992 and 1997 elections, but only because the opposition was badly splintered: he won less than half the votes cast each time. Tainted by corruption, human rights abuses, and a sluggish economy, Kenya's image as a model for the region is badly tarnished, but its struggle for a better future continues.

Further reading

Ochieng, W.R. (ed.) (1989) *A Modern History of Kenya, 1895–1980*, Nairobi: Evans Brothers.

Ogot, B.A. and Ochieng, W.R. (eds.) (1995) *Decolonization and Independence in Kenya*, London: James Currey.

PAUL TIYAMBE ZELEZA

Khartoum, Sudan

Khartoum is the capital of **Sudan** and of Khartoum province, and is located just south of the confluence of the Blue Nile and the White Nile, in the east-central part of the country. The name Khartoum is also used loosely to refer to the Greater Khartoum area, which includes the cities of Khartoum, Omdurman, and Khartoum North. The name is also used to refer to Khartoum province, which includes, in addition to Greater Khartoum, a rural area that was inhabited by about 460,000 people in 1983. Khartoum was founded in 1821 as a military garrison for Sudanese territory that had been captured by **Egypt**. By the 1880s it had grown rapidly into a flourishing commercial and trade center. In 1884–5, during a revolt against Turko-Egyptian rule, the city was besieged for ten months by the forces of Mohammed Ahmed el-Mahdi. The city was recaptured in 1898 by the British under Lord Kitchener, who subsequently directed its reconstruction. One result of this policy was the opening in 1903 of Gordon Memorial College (renamed the University of Khartoum in 1956). In 1909 a railway bridge was built across the Blue Nile, giving the capital city a convenient link to Port Sudan on the Red Sea coast. In subsequent years the city grew, expanding to the south, east, and west. In the context of the colonial economy, in which agriculture in general and cash-crop production in particular were highly valued, Khartoum functioned as a labor reservoir. Large numbers of people who had come to the city from rural areas to escape the slavery, famines, and other disasters inflicted on them by the Mahdist state, found themselves redeployed in the rural areas as laborers.

During the twentieth century Khartoum's population changed rapidly. After the **Second World War** migration to Khartoum intensified and became more permanent. The creation of an administrative and industrial center in Khartoum attracted many people. Consequently a large manufacturing and industrial sector developed, including printing, food processing, textiles, and glass manufacturing. By 1930 the population of this British colonial capital had reached 50,000 people; this had grown to 96,000 by the time independence was declared in 1956. Rural to urban migration has resulted in even greater growth since then: The 1973 census stated that there were 334,000 people in the city.

Between 1983 and 2000 Khartoum received an estimated 1.3 million displaced southerners as a result of the civil war, famine, and drought. Large numbers of the displaced, however, lived on the margins of the city. Khartoum's population almost doubled between 1983 and 1990 from 1.8 million people to 3.4 million. The presence of southern Sudanese in the north in general and in Khartoum in particular was not a new phenomenon, however. The displaced southerners had been preceded by migrant workers earlier in the twentieth century, and by slaves and soldiers in the nineteenth century. A number of factors attracted people to Khartoum in the post-colonial period. Key among these were the search for economic opportunities, improved public services, and a better life. To a lesser extent there were also political factors. The displacement of population that took place in the Sudan from the mid-1980s had an important social impact on Khartoum. The exodus from the south and southwest changed the ethnic and religious composition of Khartoum from one dominated by Arabized Muslim groups to a more diversified population with many more non-Muslim and non-Arab groups.

Further reading

Hamid, G.M. (1996) *Population Displacement in the Sudan: Patterns, Responses, Coping Strategies*, New York: Center for Migration Studies.

Sikainga, A.A. (1996) *Slaves into Workers: Emancipation and Labor in Colonial Sudan*, Austin: University of Texas Press.

AMIR H. IDRIS

Kigali, Rwanda

Kigali, the capital of **Rwanda**, had a population of more than 370,000 by the end of the twentieth century. Prior to colonization, Kigali was a major trading site for caravans in the Tutsi kingdom of Rwanda that were going to the East African coast. Modern Kigali was founded in 1907 by the Germans. It developed into a trading center under German colonial rule, which lasted from 1890 to 1919, and into a regional center during the Belgian colonial administration from 1919 to 1962. Kigali's location on Ruganwa River ensured a constant a supply of water to the burgeoning urban population of administrators, **workers**, and traders. Situated at the center of the country, the town could offer effective administration throughout. It was built on a plateau some 1,500 meters above sea level, with a climate that was attractive to European colonial administrators. A road network developed, connecting the city to all corners of the country, and later an international airport was added, linking the city to neighboring countries and the rest of the world.

Kigali became the capital and largest city of Rwanda, when on 20 June 1962 the United Nations voted to allow Ruanda-Urundi to become the two independent states of Rwanda and **Burundi**. Kigali became Rwanda's economic hub and main commercial center, attracting traders from various parts of the country. It also emerged as an industrial center, manufacturing cement, beverages, soap, furniture, shoes, plastic goods, textiles, cigarettes, paint and varnish, and radios, as well as having factories for tanning and for agricultural products. Cassiterite (iron ore) mining companies emerged, while a smelting plant was built in the city in the 1980s. The bulk of Rwanda's 3.6 million wage workers are employed and live in Kigali. Modern residential houses, office complexes housing government officers, embassies, and domestic and international trading interests also developed.

Kigali's regional status grew with the increasing integration of Rwanda into the East African economic bloc. In 1977 the city became the headquarters of an organization promoting the joint development of Kagera River, which brought together Rwanda, Burundi, and **Tanzania**. A cosmopolitan city containing a mix of cultures, including the Muslim quarter which is spread over the city's four hills, Kigali also became a center of learning, with a university and several technical colleges. It was also home to Rwanda's four radio stations. But the city suffered from the problems that usually accompany **urbanization** in developing countries. Economic problems, lack of employment opportunities, and increasing population in Kigali led to widespread poverty, growing slums, and escalating levels of insecurity and crime.

The city's growth and image were adversely affected by the country's political turmoil, especially the 1994 **genocide** in which between 10,000 and 50,000 Hutu and between 500,000 and 1 million Tutsi were killed – over 12 percent of the population. Kigali was partially destroyed by fierce fighting between Hutu militias and the army, and fighters from the Tutsi-dominated Rwanda Patriotic Front (RPF). The new RPF government had the difficult task of reconciliation and reconstruction, and for the country as a whole, not just Kigali – although the country's capital naturally became the focal point of reconstruction efforts. During the rest of the 1990s these efforts were frustrated by continuing political tension between Hutu and Tutsi political leaders, and some of their followers. Continuing problems included the repatriation of refugees from neighboring countries, the poor state of the economy, the inordinate delays in bringing the suspected perpetrators of the genocide to justice, and the country's involvement in the war in the **Democratic Republic of Congo**, which sparked a dispute with **Uganda** – Rwanda's erstwhile ally.

Further reading

Dorsey, L. (1994) *Historical Dictionary of Rwanda*, London: Scarecrow Press.

PETER KAGWANJA
MUTUMA RUTERE

Kinshasa, Democratic Republic of Congo

Kinshasa, capital of the Congo since 1923, is located on the south bank of the Congo River at the Malebo Pool. Kinshasa is thus the point of convergence for all of the territory to the east that is drained by the Congo River, as well as providing the connection point for river and land transport between the country's interior and the ocean. Kinshasa was founded in 1881 on the territory of two villages: Nshasa and Kintambo (or Ntamo). Since colonial times it has been the principal administrative, industrial, commercial, and cultural center of the **Democratic Republic of Congo** (DRC).

The city's rapid growth began during the colonial period. Its population grew from 14,000 in 1919 to 400,000 in 1960, the year of the country's independence. By 1990 the city's population had exploded to 3.2 million, and to an estimated 7.3 million by 2000. The city extended over 6.5 square kilometers in 1991, by 1960 in took up 55 square kilometers, and by 2000 occupied 584 square kilometers.

In the 1970s 25 percent of the Congo's wage **workers** lived in Kinshasa, and the city generated 50 percent of the country's wages, but unemployment was high and conditions hard for many of them: It was estimated that only a fifth had stable employment in 1980, with an average salary accounting for scarcely 20 percent of the workers' daily needs. The situation got worse in the 1980s, as real wages fell drastically, so that by 1990 hardly anyone could live on their salaries. Many relied on the thriving informal sector, including urban farming, in which women played a major role. These hardships were a direct result of economic decline during the Mobutu regime. In 1997 the inhabitants of the city welcomed Kabila's new regime, hoping for improvements that had still yet to materialize by the end of the decade.

In spite of these difficulties Kinshasa remains a vibrant cultural center. The city drew its cultural vitality from the ethnic mix of its inhabitants, and from their youthfulness. By the mid-1970s almost half the population of Kinshasa (known as "Kinois") were Kinshasa-born. As this young local-born population increased, cohabiting with diverse Kinois ethnic groups, the complex social dynamic gave birth to a distinctive urban culture and consciousness, manifested in (among other things) particular ways of understanding, expressing, and sharing the realities of daily life. Kinois identify themselves as *bana ya kin* ("children of Kinshasa") in contrast to *les bawuta* ("newcomers"). The city's inhabitants share a common Kinois culture, expressed in Congolese songs, in theater, in cartoons, in popular dance. Kinshasa is the heart of Zairean music. The city's inhabitants never stop singing of its beauty and, above all, how joyful life is there: in Congolese songs a period of *kin-la-belle* ("beautiful kinfolk") has been replaced by *kin-kiésse kin-la-joie*; that is, "joyful kinfolk". The city has itself become increasingly less beautiful; by the 1990s it was almost an open garbage dump. Local roads were impassable, with only the main Boulevard du 30 Juin staying open to traffic along its entire length. Under such conditions *kin-kiésse* expresses well what is still attractive in the city, which remains jovial, inventive, and frenetic. As Koffi Olomide sang: *toza na systeme ya lifelo moto ekopela kasi tozo zika te* ("We are in hell. The fire is burning, but we don't burn", capturing the indomitable spirit of the inhabitants of this great city.

Further reading

Gossens, F., Minten, B. and Tollens, E. (1994) *Nourir Kinshasa*, Paris: L'Harmattan.

Houyoux, J. and Niwembo, K. (1986) *Kinshasa 1975*, Brussels: ICHEC.

GERTRUDE MIANDA

Kiswahili *see* Swahili

Kumasi, Ghana

Kumasi (which may also be spelt "Kumase") is the second largest city in **Ghana**, with a population of over a million in 2000. It is also the capital of the Asante region and people. Due to its lush, green forest vegetation Kumasi is sometimes referred to as the "Garden City." The city is famous for its gold, kola nuts, and timber, and for trade. The history of Kumasi is intimately linked to the history of the Asante. The first Asantehene, Osei Tutu (*c.*1685–1777), was believed to have founded the town around 1680 as the capital of all Asante. It was where the Golden Stool was located, and people of the kingdom were expected to meet annually there to celebrate the Odwira festival and show their allegiance to the Asantehene. The festival is still observed.

Initially the Asante had good trade and diplomatic relations with European traders along the coast, but as they tried to maintain control over the coastal peoples who served as middlemen in the trade, conflict between the Asante and the Europeans became inevitable. From 1824 Asante fought several wars against the British, until in 1874 British troops sacked Kumasi, burnt the royal palace, and effectively brought the town and its people under imperial control. The final assault came in 1901, and the Asantehene Prempe I was captured and sent into exile in the **Seychelles** with his family, provoking widespread resistance. To curb any further rebellion by the Asante, the British appointed a resident commissioner for Kumasi, supported by a regiment of the West African Frontier Force.

By the time the British reinstated the Asantehene in 1935, Kumasi had lost its pre-colonial power and influence. Nonetheless the city was to become an important center of the colonial economy, being located in southern Ghana, where the cocoa and gold-mining on which the colonial economy depended were largely produced. Consequently some of the leading commercial and financial companies were established in Kumasi, beginning with the British Bank of West Africa in 1908. Kumasi also benefited from being the main point of intersection for the country's two railway systems, one from **Accra** and the other from Sekondi–Takoradi, as well as the road network that linked east to west and north to south. By 1948 Kumasi's population had risen to 80,000, from 24,000 in 1924. Kumasi also played an important role in the struggle for independence. It was home to the National Liberation Movement (NLM), led by Kofi Busia and supported by the Asante chiefs, which opposed Kwame Nkrumah's Convention Peoples Party; Kumasi later became a center of opposition to the government.

After independence Kumasi, recognised as capital of the Asante region, experienced considerable economic and population growth. It also continued as a cultural center, where both old and new were celebrated. The old was reflected in many cultural events at which participants adorned themselves in gold jewelry and beautiful handwoven *kente* cloth. Vestiges were also visible in the Manhyia Palace (home to the Asantehene) and its museum. The University of Science and Technology is based in Kumasi, and the city also boasts Kejetia Market, one of the biggest markets in **West Africa**. Above all, Kumasi has maintained its reputation as the epicenter of Asante identity and culture.

Further reading

Buah, F.K. (1998) *A History of Ghana*, London: Macmillan Education.

AGBENYEGA ADEDZE

L

labor movements

Although the development of the organized labor movement in Africa can be traced to the period following the **Second World War**, strikes and various forms of labor resistance had been appearing in many parts of the continent since the early days of European colonial rule and the introduction of wage employment. From the mining towns of **South Africa**, Rhodesia, and **Nigeria** to the port cities of **Mombasa** and **Dakar**, African **workers** engaged in various forms of protest against capital and the state. Some of these protests took covert forms, such as desertion, slacking, or the destruction of tools – all of which were disguised forms of resistance.

However it was in South Africa, where large-scale industrialization had begun in the second half of the nineteenth century, that a much more organized labor movement developed. The discovery of gold in the 1860s and diamonds in the 1880s transformed the South African economy, and led to the emergence of a large class of wage earners that included thousands of African and European skilled workers. The latter group brought with them the idea of trade unions. However, for obvious reasons, the South African working class remained divided along racial, occupational, and gender lines. Following the miners' strike of 1922, sometimes referred to as "the Rand Revolt," and the rise to power of the Labor Party, white workers gained significant privileges, and became increasingly differentiated from their black counterparts. One of the most important trade unions that emerged during this early stage was the Industrial and Commercial Workers Union (ICU), which claimed a membership of 100,000 workers. But owing to internal strife and tactical mistakes, the ICU was defunct by the late 1920s. A number of unions rose and declined during subsequent decades, including the Congress of Non-European Trade Unions (CNETU), which was dissolved after the defeat of the miners' strike in 1946, and the South African Congress of Trade Unions (SACTU), which developed a close alliance with the ANC and the Communist Party. However, SACTU was effectively crushed, and many of its organizers were exiled. One of the most powerful unions that emerged during the height of anti-apartheid struggle was the Congress Of South African Trade Unions (COSATU), a federation that represented about 565,000 workers. COSATU played a critical role not only in the demise of the apartheid regime, but also in the electoral success of the ANC in 1994.

Early development of the labor movement also took place in northern Africa, although there were different patterns and trajectories. In Tunisia there was a long struggle, from 1924 to 1946, to set up a labor movement. The first attempt was opposed by French trade unions and political parties, while the second attempt in 1936 was sabotaged by the nationalist party, Neo-Destour. Thus, when it was eventually established, the Union Générale des Travailleurs Tunisiens (UGTT) retained critical autonomy and distance from the nationalist party, a tradition that enabled it to fight for broader democratic reforms after independence, especially when struggles for democratization resurfaced in the 1980s. Elsewhere in the Maghreb, trade unions were largely founded "from the top," either by intellectuals – as was the Union Moroccaine des Travailleurs (UMT) – or by the leaders of political parties – the Union Générale des Travailleurs Algérienes (UGTA). Consequently these movements were susceptible to being coopted by the state in the wake of independence. In the case of **Algeria**, for instance, incorporation of trade unions into the populist state deprived the working class of the ability to articulate a social vision distinct from the failing modernist and developmentalist project of the state. Thus despite a proliferation of strikes and protests from 1975 to 1980, and again from the late 1980s, against a regime increasingly bankrupt politically and economically, political space was seized by Islamists who had their own alternative – anti-secular and intolerant – ideological agenda.

In other parts of Africa organized labor began to play an effective role in the period after the Second World War. As many historians have noted, the war era represented a watershed in the history of the labor movement in Africa. Before the war European colonial powers were mainly concerned about how many African workers they could obtain and how much labor they could extract from them. Now these powers were suddenly confronted with the existence of an African working class, with its own aspirations and agendas. This realization was prompted by the wave of strikes and labor uprisings that occurred in different parts of the continent between the late 1930s and the late 1940s. Strikes took place in the copper mines of Northern Rhodesia in 1935, and spread throughout the mines through religious organizations, dance societies, personal networks, and mass gatherings. A second bloody strike took place in the same region in 1940.

The intensification of strike action during the period after the war was a direct result of the harsh economic conditions that faced many African workers. During the war years, colonial powers, particularly Britain and France, became heavily dependent on African resources. As demands for food and cash crops increased, colonial powers imposed conscripted labor on African rural producers once more, prompting many to migrate to the cities. Rapid urban growth put serious strains on living conditions. At the same time growing inflation made wages inadequate. These conditions produced large-scale labor uprisings and riots that posed a serious threat to the colonial authorities. In this regard transportation workers, particularly on the docks and railways, took the lead in organizing labor protest. In view of their numerical strength, their strategic position in the colonial economy, and their skill level, transport workers were able to organize the most effective, militant, and dynamic labor movements. For instance, in **East Africa** the port city of Mombasa was the scene of intense labor uprisings in 1934, 1939, 1942, and 1945. Similar labor uprisings occurred in Nigeria in 1942, 1945, and 1949, on the Gold Coast in 1947 and 1948, in Tanganyika in 1947, in **Sudan** in 1947 and 1948, and in Zanzibar in 1948. In **French West Africa** the railway workers of Dakar, the leading port in the region, launched a two-month long strike that shut down the harbor, and crippled the transportation system across the whole region.

The postwar strikes represented major urban upheaval, and showed the ability of African workers to act collectively and articulate their grievances. The strikes took place at the peak of the nationalist struggle for independence, forcing European colonial powers to recognize the existence of an African working class and rethink their labor policies. Great Britain and France began to introduce new labor policies that were based on metropolitan models. These policies aimed at creating a stable, productive, and docile African working class, through the provision of family wages, decent housing and social services, and the legalization of trade unions and other institutions of collective bargaining. In this regard, the British Trade Union Congress (TUC) sent organizers to the African colonies to create what they described as "non-political unions."

African workers used their success in achieving legal recognition for the trade unions to press on with further demands. In addition to wage increases, colonial powers introduced a series of labor laws in the late 1940s and early 1950s. Moreover African labor movements provided an important social base for the **nationalist movement**. In many parts of Africa the labor movement was closely linked with radical leftist parties, such as the Sudanese Communist Party and Nkrumah's Convention Peoples Party. In Kenya Tom Mboya, a sanitary inspector, emerged as the leader of the Kenya Local Government Workers' Union, and helped structure an urban and labor policy that transformed the Kenyan labor movement into an effective force. In French West Africa, the most effective leader was Ahmed Sékou Touré, who began his career as a post-office clerk after his expulsion from technical college.

Labor movements in the post-colonial period

Two important factors had a great impact on the labor movement in post-colonial Africa: the nature of the post-colonial African state, and deteriorating economic conditions. It is a commonplace that, for the most part, the nationalist movements across Africa brought to power authoritarian regimes that vigorously sought greater control over social institutions and independent organizations. These regimes were particularly threatened by the militancy and tenacity of the trade unions. Those in charge of such regimes tried to present themselves as patrons of the working class, by promoting family wages and controlling the activities of the unions. In single-party states like **Ghana**, Nigeria, **Tanzania**, and **Zimbabwe**, trade unions became mere power-brokers between the state and the working class. Moreover, African states raised the slogan of "economic development," demanding that workers sacrifice their occupational demands for the sake of nation-building and economic progress. In countries like **Botswana**, where private enterprise was stressed and foreign investment encouraged, the government was prepared to put its full weight behind foreign corporations and squash workers' demands.

African labor movements had also been affected by the politics of the Cold War. Conservative regimes of the 1950s, particularly in Sudan and **Kenya**, exhibited great hostility towards radical, leftist trade unions and persecuted many labor activists. At the same time Western trade unions, such as the American AFL-CIO and the British TUC, tried to establish links with African trade unions and steer them away from the communist block. In the Sudan, where the trade union movement was dominated by communist elements, the Sudanese Workers' Trade Union Federation (SWTUF) established close links with the World Federation of Trade Unions (WFTU), which represented labor organizations in communist countries. In the 1950s al-Shafi' Ahmad al-Shaykh, the secretary-general of the SWTUF, held the same post in the WFTU.

Despite growing repression the labor movement in Africa continued to combat authoritarian regimes. In the post-independence period labor unions and other civic associations endeavored to play a greater role in the political and economic life of their respective countries. During periods of military rule African trade unions formed the core of popular resistance. For instance, between 1958 and 1964, Sudan was ruled by a military regime that prohibited political activities, banned trade unions, and detained many union leaders. Despite the regime's repression trade unions were able to carry out clandestine activities, forming a broad front with other political organizations, as well as organizing a massive campaign of civil disobedience and a general strike that forced the junta to step down in 1964. In Nigeria, a country that pursued a policy of free enterprise, the government tried to bring the union movement under its control. But state efforts to act as a patron by setting a standard wage backfired, producing a wave of strikes that culminated in the general strike of 1964.

The position of African labor unions was particularly precarious in those states that adopted the single-party system. The case of Ghana amply illustrates this point. The close link between Nkrumah's Convention Peoples Party and the trade union movement in the early 1950s dramatically changed in the post-independence period, as the CPP became increasingly authoritarian. One of the major confrontations between the government and the labor movement occurred in 1961, when the railway workers of Sekondi-Takoradi led a large-scale strike that received widespread support from the community. But the level of workers' opposition decreased as the government increased the level of repression. Following the downfall of Nkrumah, Ghana vacillated between military and civilian rule. The restoration of civilian rule in 1969 gave labor unions an opportunity to reorganize and resume their activities, but deteriorating economic conditions led to an unprecedented degree of worker resistance, characterized by great ferocity and destructive power. Workers attacked those union leaders who associated themselves with the government. These crises culminated in the government's decisions to abolish the Ghana TUC in 1971, and to impose a series of laws aimed at restricting union activities. However, the advent of the military regime of Acheampong, and the continuing deterioration of the economy, sparked off a more militant labor uprising and further violent strikes in 1977–8.

In Tanzania a close alliance developed between Tanganyika African National Union (TANU), the main nationalist party, and the Tanganyika Federation of Labor (TFL), which had been founded in 1955. Soon after independence, however, the Tanzanian government began to act vigorously to bring TFL under its control. It tried to implicate the TFL in a failed coup attempt in 1964, and eventually abolished the union. Under Nyerere's regime legal strikes became virtually impossible, and workers were further marginalized after the 1967 Arusha Declaration and government effort to introduce self-management. In **Zambia**, on the other hand, even though a one-party system had been successfully instituted, trade unions (particularly the copper miners' union) retained their autonomy and continued to mount strong resistance to the government. But this was largely due to the critical role of the copper industry in the country's economy.

The increasing authoritarianism of African states and deteriorating economic conditions in the 1980s had a crippling effect on the labor movement. In the 1990s, however, the growing trend of democratization has encouraged the hope that the African labor movement will regain the status it once enjoyed.

See also: civil society; urbanization

Further reading

Cooper, F. (1996) *Decolonization and African Society: The Labor Question in French and British Africa*, New York: Cambridge University Press.

Davies, I. (1966) *African Trade Unions*, Baltimore: Penguin.

Freund, B. (1988) *The African Worker*, New York: Cambridge University Press.

Gutkind, P., Cohen, R. and Copans, J. (eds.) (1979) *African Labor History*, London: Sage.

Mamdani, M. and Wamba-dia-Wamba, E. (eds.) (1995) *African Studies in Social Movements and Democracy*, Dakar: CODESRIA.

AHMAD SIKAINGA

Lagos, Nigeria

Lagos is located on the southwest coast of **Nigeria**, and is the country's largest city, chief port, and principal economic and cultural center. In 2000 it had an estimated population of 13.5 million. It served as the seat of the Nigerian federal government until December 1991, when Abuja became the official capital, but it remained the capital of Lagos state, one of the thirty-six states of Nigeria. The exact date of human settlement in Lagos is unknown, but historical evidence suggests it was a some point between the fifteenth and seventeenth centuries.

As the site of an old Yoruba settlement named Eko, Lagos served as a trading post for the Portuguese who developed Lagos as a major center for the trade of goods and slaves. Lagos had been involved in the slave trade since the eighteenth century, and it became an important slaving port for **West Africa** after 1821. In 1861 the British, who were by now vigorously opposed to slavery, proceeded to annex Lagos and govern it as a crown colony. British rule was opposed by several local Yoruba states, and it was not until the late 1880s and early 1890s that the British finally conquered them and were able to extend the territory of the colony. Overall the first fifty years of British influence in Lagos were geared towards consolidation rather than growth.

One of the most important factors in the development of the port of Lagos after 1901 was a series of constitutional changes. These gradually raised the status of the town until it became Capital Colony and Protectorate of Nigeria in 1914. The development of commerce, port functions, and industrialization between 1901 and 1950 led to a phenomenal increase in the population of Lagos. For example, the annual rate of growth was 3.4 percent between 1901 and 1950, but 18.6 percent between 1951 and 1963. The most important factor stimulating immigration into Lagos during 1901–50 was the widening gap between Lagos and the rest of the country in terms of employment opportunities.

In 1960 the city became the capital of the newly independent country of Nigeria. As Nigeria's oil industry boomed in the early 1970s, Lagos began to develop rapidly, with migrants from all over Nigeria and from neighboring countries flocking to the city. The ever-increasing population of this geographically disjointed city had significant implications for the provision of basic urban services, including energy, water, sewage, transportation, and housing. From 1985 urban renewal schemes for Lagos concentrated on upgrading slum communities, with active cooperation from their inhabitants. For example, in 1993 the World Bank provided funding for the Lagos Drainage and Sanitation Project, the primary objective of which was to improve health standards and living conditions in areas of Lagos that were subject to regular flooding. The United Nations has predicted that the population of the city's metropolitan area, which was only about 290,000 in 1950, will exceed 20 million by 2010, making Lagos one of the world's five largest cities.

By the end of the twentieth century Lagos was still an important center of intellectual and cultural life for Nigeria. This was evident from the number of important educational and cultural establishments located in the city, including the University of Lagos (founded in 1962), Yaba College of Technology (1948), Lagos State University (1983), and Lagos State Polytechnic (1977). Others were the National Library of Nigeria (1964) and the National Museum (1957), which has collections of archeology, ethnography, and traditional art. The National Theater (1976) stages plays, dance performances, and music concerts, and also houses collections of contemporary Nigerian art.

Further reading

Mabojunje, A.L. (1968) *Urbanization in Nigeria*, London: University of London Press.

UWEM E. ITE

law

Law may be defined as a body of norms or normative rules, aimed at governing human societies by regulating the conduct or behavior of the members of those societies in their interrelationships with each other, and with the community as a whole. Every human society or community of people is presumed to have its own laws, the totality of which constitutes that society's or community's legal system. African societies, like societies everywhere, have always had their own laws, which evolved over time and are recognized as providing a normative order on which the individual and collective behavior of the members of a given society is – or ought to be – based.

Three preliminary observations should be recorded at the outset. First, it is important to note that the very basic question of what is implied in the term "law" has been a subject of long-standing debate by anthropologists, philosophers, legal scholars, and other social scientists. The question becomes pressing when we attempt to arrive at an objective definition of law as distinct from custom and other forms of social practice, especially in the context of cross-cultural discourses and analyses. Second, it is important to draw necessary distinctions, particularly in discussions of law and legal systems in Africa, between custom and law, and to bear in mind that not all custom has the form and, therefore, the force of law. Finally, it should be recognised in these discussions that the terms "African law," "African customary law," and "African traditional law" are neither static nor uniform, but rather subject to significant variations in relation to time as well as location.

Any attempt at a concise definition of law is bound to encounter the difficulty of providing a description that is broad and universal enough to satisfy the different perspectives of those who view law as an institution that is intended, or must be employed, to advance some political movement, program or cause in a particular society or country at a particular time. Such a definition cannot as such address, as part of the task of elucidating the meaning of law, such important issues as what the notions of equality, democracy, **human rights**, legitimacy, or other ideals require in society.

In this entry, the term "law" is used in the narrow or limited sense to signify or denote the ensemble of rules that make up the normative system known as a legal system. The focus in such descriptive accounts is not on the meaning of the law (in a broad conceptual or philosophical sense), but on the identification of the body of laws that operate in and regulate the affairs of the members of the societies that live within particular territorial entities. The principal sources of this law may be customary rules that have evolved from the customary practices of the communities over a period of time, perhaps over centuries ("customary law"), enactments passed by parliaments or other legislative bodies in the colonial and post-colonial periods ("legislation" or "statutes"), legal rules that have evolved from the decisions handed down by judges in the process of settling disputes in concrete cases ("case law," comprising what in some systems is termed "common law" and principles of equity) and, in some Islamic societies, legal precepts based on the *Shari'a*.

Law under colonial rule

The colonial powers, with Britain and France as the major players, introduced in their respective colonies legal systems based on the legal philosophy, culture and laws of the metropolitan countries, supplanting or suppressing the indigenous legal systems that they found in place. The two principal foreign legal traditions imposed on the colonized territories were represented by the English common law – mainly developed through the decisions of judges in English common-law courts, and incorporating the doctrines of equity and statutes of general application in force in England at the time when the newly acquired colony was constituted – and the continental European civil law – based on the Napoleonic civil code. In addition the African territories colonized by Belgium, Germany, Italy, and Portugal also had legal systems largely based on the civil code, while in a few other colonies the legal systems were based on a mixture of the imported European law and Islamic law, based on the *Shari'a*. Islamic law was already well established in some parts of Africa, especially **West** and **North Africa**. Both the British and French, through their respective policies of so-called "indirect rule" and "assimilation," respected or (more to the point) tolerated both indigenous African customary or traditional law and Islamic law, wherever they were firmly established. In this setting, the indigenous customary law of the colonized populace – formulated not as a single set of native laws, but as so many sets of "tribal" laws – as well as Islamic law – where it applied – continued to exist and operate as parallel legal systems, principally in respect of matters that were regarded as being essentially or exclusively of concern to the indigenous or native populations. These were matters relating to family, land tenure, marriage and divorce, inheritance, succession, chieftaincy, settlement of disputes, and so on. However, the application of this indigenous law, both customary and Islamic, was in all cases subject to the so-called "doctrine of repugnance": it was not to be applied where it had been declared by the colonial authority as being "repugnant to civilized practice," often a controversial designation.

The African legal landscape in the colonial period was thus one based on a mosaic of legal cultures and traditions, combining as it did elements drawn from indigenous African law, colonial European law and Islamic law. However, it has been noted by most Africanist legal commentators and historians that this legal pluralism in the colonial era was more an expression of power relations in colonial society than a recognition and tolerance of any multicultural diversity. This legal pluralism itself reflected the bipolar, or bifurcated, nature of the colonial state in Africa. The colonial state was characterized by the division of society into two categories. On the one side were citizens, who belonged to the settler races (European or Asian), were accorded civil rights, and enjoyed a separation of powers under the rule of law; on the other side were subjects, who belonged to "tribes," were under customary law, with a chief who operated as mediating agent between the colonial state power and the colonized native populace and was the exemplar of localized despotism. Membership of this latter group depended not on where you lived (residence), but on which "tribe" you supposedly belonged to (ethnicity, indigeneity). Generally speaking, this group had no civil rights recognized by either the colonial state or the state's legal institutions (the law, the courts, and other attendant administrative machinery), although a limited category of urban-based, educated or middle- and working-class natives were gradually accorded a limited recognition of some of these rights.

It has been argued that this dualism in legal theory was actually a description of two distinct, though related, forms of power: the centrally located modern state (represented by the white colonial officials: commissioners, commanders, magistrates, and so on), and the locally organized native authority (represented by the tribal chiefs, headmen, and an assortment of colonially designated white and black officials). This dualism was, then, used to justify and reinforce the racial divide and bifurcation that were the hallmark of the colonial state. The key distinction lay in the fact that only those with citizen status enjoyed the benefits and protection of the civil law; the rest were subjected to the operation of customary law, which was not concerned with guaranteeing rights but enforcing custom. Race was the defining factor in this distinction. It can thus be seen that the law as an institution, and the attendant philosophy and practice of legal pluralism, were deployed as critical instruments in the design and definition of colonial power, and in the entrenchment of racism and the racialization of African societies in the colonial era.

Law after independence

One of the most difficult problems faced by African states following the collapse of colonialism and emergence of new independent states from the early 1960s, was that of identifying and fashioning national legal systems based on a specific body of law constituting the "national law" of each particular nation. An attendant challenge was that of reforming the law and legal systems inherited from the colonial state so as to cleanse them of the inbuilt bifurcation of state power and institutionalized racism that marked the apparatus and operation of the law and legal machinery of the colonial state. Conversely there was also a felt need to transform the law and legal institutions into instruments to facilitate the developmental and nation-building agenda of the newly independent states. This impulse for legal reform must be seen as part and parcel of the nationalist struggle against colonialism, and in some cases formed an explicit part of the anti-colonial platform adopted by most nationalists in the colonies from the late 1940s.

The impulse for reform took several trajectories. First, there was a call for the creation of a unified legal system, involving a blending of African customary law and the modern (that is, imported European) law, and the establishment of a single hierarchy of courts open to all as citizens. Several trends within this trajectory can be identified: codification and unification of the customary law to blunt its arbitrary edge, professionalization of its legal personnel (through appropriate legal training), and unification and alignment of its appeal procedure with the modern court system (represented by the various types of magistrates and high courts) to soften its administrative edge. This reform process resulted, for example, in the ambitious project of the "restatement" of African law, launched in 1959, aimed at restating and codifying the core substantive aspects of customary law: the law of persons and family, marriage and divorce, property (including land), and succession. By the mid-1960s attempts at presenting a single unified body of substantive customary law across ethnic or tribal boundaries had been undertaken in such countries as **Botswana**, **Gambia**, **Kenya**, **Malawi**, and **Tanzania**. On the other hand, **Ghana** and **Senegal**, for example, proceeded by way of attempts to arrive at a single body of law (combining both customary and European-derived law) enforced by a single system of courts, but with rather mixed results. Later, more radical attempts were made by the Marxist–Leninist regimes in **Ethiopia** and **Mozambique** – the group of so-called "radical modernizers" – to overhaul the colonial legacy altogether: in the case of Ethiopia by abolishing the customary law and replacing it with a modern civil code, again a process that met with only limited success.

The second trajectory of legal reform related to moves to change the court structure by building linkages between the customary courts and the modern courts. Two lines of reform have been identified in this respect: a minimalist tendency, which was inclined to maintain the dual structure (adopted by, among others, **Chad**, **Central African Republic**, **Nigeria**, and **Togo**), and a maximalist approach, which aimed at unifying the court system, in some cases by abolishing the customary courts altogether (for example, in **Côte d'Ivoire**, Ghana, **Mali**, **Niger**, Senegal, and Tanzania). In some cases, for example in Tanzania, these reforms were subsequently reversed or modified.

Perhaps the most far-reaching attempts at legal reform occurred within the post-independence framework of the "law and development" or "law and social change" debates. These debates were centered on the need to reform the law – not only in its administrative, procedural, and substantive senses, but also in terms of its wider institutional orientation – as one of the tools for facilitating post-independence development and nation-building. Here the focus was especially on the need to reform the land law (in particular the colonially constructed land-tenure systems) and the family law. Both radical states, such as Tanzania, and the more conservative ones, such as Kenya and Malawi, embarked on this type of reform.

Post-colonial African legal systems have also had to grapple with another set of problems relating to the issues of democracy, constitutionalism, and legitimacy of the post-colonial state. These issues are concerned with the question of the specific implementation of law in the form of constitutionalism and democracy, and their relevance to the African context. Constitutionalism in this respect can briefly be described, in a non-traditional sense, as fidelity to the principle that the exercise of state power must seek to advance the ends of society. Democracy, understood in the Western liberal paradigm, implies respect for the twin pillars of limited government and individual rights, around which all the other aspects (such as separation of powers, periodic elections, legitimacy, and rule of law) are built. Such a concept was embedded in most post-independence African constitutions, despite the fact that this was never part of the erstwhile colonial political or legal order, which was essentially despotic. However, for a variety of reasons, the first attempts at instituting a Western liberal democratic political order failed in almost all the newly emancipated states within the first decade or so of their existence. This failure remains the principal challenge facing the new African political leadership that has emerged as part of the contemporary independence movement in the post-1990 wave of democratization that is sweeping across the African continent.

Debates about the limited democratic reform that Africa went through in the post-independence era were linked to the debate about human rights and the legitimacy of the post-colonial state. In fact they were linked to debates about the possible existence of a distinct African concept of human rights. The weakness in most of these debates was an inability to distinguish between form and essence. Those who looked from a European perspective for a traditional conception of human rights and legitimacy, for a legally enforceable individual rights-oriented concept, quickly discovered that this was found only in very few traditional societies in Africa. If, on the other hand, they looked to the essence – the spirit, so to speak – and the end result or desired outcome of the concept of human rights, rather than to the process or form through which it presents itself, they discovered that African traditional societies actually catered to the well-being and social balance of the group, as well as its individual members, and that these structures and approaches often fulfilled similar functions to those attributed to various human rights institutions usually associated with the Western European human rights regimes. This approach naturally rejects the argument that comparing the two, form and essence, would be to confuse human rights with human dignity.

A proper understanding of the arguments in favor of an African conception – or any other conception for that matter – of human rights must surely begin with an acknowledgment of the centrality of the concept of human dignity, which ordinary people in all societies recognize (albeit with different names and configurations in different places), together with the desire for respect from their fellow human beings, which they believe they merit unless they have committed evil. This notion, drawn from these varied traditions, forms the metaphysical foundation (if any were needed) on which to ground human rights. To the extent that African societies share this notion (encapsulated in such concepts as *ubuntu* in various Southern African languages and traditions, and *animuonyam* in the Akan language of the Asante of Ghana, for example), this is an adequate basis on which to locate the existence of human rights in African societies and legal traditions today.

It has been argued that the outcome of post-independence legal reform in Africa was not so much a democratization of the legal system inherited from the colonial state as its deracialization. According to this view, while racial barriers which determined formal access to the law were removed, and a formal equality between citizens instituted, yet in essence for most countries all that was achieved was a formal, but substantively limited, modification of the social boundaries between the modern and the customary legal regimes. In theory the former was declared open to all citizens in the post-colonial state – natives and indigenes, as well as non-natives and non-indigenes – but, in reality, the latter continued to govern almost exclusively the lives of the natives – mainly the rural peasant communities – whose lives were always beyond the ordinary reach of the European-derived law. Despite the nationalist rhetoric of transformation and reform, in large measure the arrival of independence in the early 1960s saw the retention of the legal institutions and framework of the former colonial entities, while at the same time perfunctory attempts were made to contend with the traditional legal rules and institutions of the multiple ethnic groups that made up the populations of the new nations. By the end of the twentieth century the law and legal systems of almost every African country continued to be organized around a plurality of legal systems. While Africa was not the only continent to experience such legal pluralism, the phenomenon was particularly discernible in Africa due to the colonial and migratory imposition of European laws and legal cultures, over and above the spread of Islamic law in the previous centuries (as noted above). Indeed attempts to institute or extend Islamic law became a major political issue in several countries, from **Algeria** to Nigeria. Thus the law and legal systems of Africa today remain eclectic, derived as they are from a multiplicity of legal traditions.

See also: Islamic reform movements; race and ethnicity; state: colonial; state: post-independence

Further reading

Appiah, K.A. (2001) “Comment: Grounding Human Rights,” in M. Ignatieff (ed.), *Human Rights as Politics and Idolatry*, Princeton: Princeton University Press.

Elias, T.O. (1956) *The Nature of African Law*, Manchester: Manchester University Press.

Katz, A.N. (ed.) (1986) *Legal Traditions and Systems: An International Handbook*, New York/London: Greenwood Press.

Lindholt, L. (1997) *Questioning the Universality of Human Rights: The African Charter on Human and Peoples' Rights in Botswana, Malawi and Mozambique*, Aldershot: Ashgate Publishing.

Mamdani, M. (1996) *Citizen and Subject: Contemporary Africa and the Legacy of Late Colonialism*, Princeton: Princeton University Press.

Mann, K. and Roberts, R. (1991) *Law in Colonial Africa*, Portsmouth: Heinemann.

TIYANJANA MALUWA

League of Arab States

Established in 1945, the League of Arab States (commonly known as “the Arab League”) is a relatively old international governmental organization. The League is a culturally defined, regional organization, aiming at including all countries that identify themselves as Arab, regardless of whether they do so on ethnic, linguistic, or general cultural grounds. At a time of rising Arab nationalism, the League defined its functions as covering every aspect of the life of the Arabs, and of their relations with the rest of the world. The League structure to a large extent resembles that of the **United**

Nations: it has a General Secretariat, and numerous departments. According to the charter, the League Council (which is composed of ministers of member-states or their representatives) is the supreme authority of the League. With the success of the Arab Summit in January 1964, however, the summit became institutionalized and began to serve as a kind of unofficial super-council.

The historical experience of the League can be categorized into phases according to a mixture of normative and *realpolitik* criteria. The first phase started with the establishment of the League and ended with the emergence of ideological conflicts between member-states. Throughout most of this period the Arab countries were strongly influenced by colonial powers – or even still occupied by them. The prevailing ideology was a mixture of local and Arab nationalism, and none of the member-states was a hegemonic power. The norms governing the relations between these semi-independent states were generally conservative, because Arab states were sensitive to sovereignty issues. At the same time the strong and independent personality of the first Secretary-General of the League, Abdur-Rahman 'Azzam, played a balancing and active role in the organization. During this phase the League helped liberate countries in **North Africa** from the colonists (**Libya**, **Tunisia**, and **Morocco**), and supported freedom fighters in **Algeria**. The Arab defeat in the Palestine War in 1948 was an early shock for the League, but did not dramatically change its course of action.

In 1955 Iraq joined the British-controlled Baghdad Pact, and **Egypt** concluded an arms treaty with Czechoslovakia, inaugurating a phase of conflict among the League member-states. Revolutionary and conservative Arab camps had been established, and inter-Arab disagreements were internationalized. Moreover Egypt, which was aspiring to play a hegemonic role in the Arab world, had started advocating an Arab nationalism that many conservative Arab regimes found threatening. This might have truly been a golden age for Arab nationalism, but it was certainly not so for the Arab League, which found itself almost paralyzed in the circumstances. The revolutionary camp denounced the League for falling short of the nationalist aspirations of Arab peoples, while the conservative camp accused the revolutionaries of becoming tools of the Arab nationalists. The second Secretary-General, Abdul-Khaliq Hassonah, was a successful administrator rather than a political leader. Only on the few matters on which the member-states agreed was the League able to act with any degree of effectiveness.

The second phase ended dramatically with the Arab defeat in the 1967 Six Days War, but the third phase was an era of real Arab cooperation. In the 1967 Arab Summit in **Khartoum** in **Sudan**, the Arab countries had to put their ideological differences aside and work together to achieve common goals. The abundant monetary resources of the oil-rich states obviously helped in this regard. In addition the third Secretary-General of the League, Mahmoud Riyad, was an experienced diplomat who added impetus to the organization. Among the achievements of the League during this period were the establishment of several inter-Arab specialized organizations and economic projects, and a successful reaching out towards both the **Organization of African Unity** and individual countries (in Europe and the **Third World**). Egypt's unilateral decision to make peace with Israel marked the beginning of the end of this phase. At the 1978 Arab Summit, leaders condemned Egypt's decision, later severing diplomatic relations with the country. Although Egypt was not a hegemonic power in the League, no single Arab country could make up for Egypt's absence from the organization, and the Arab regional order entered an era of chaos.

During the 1980s the only Arab taboo was any kind of acknowledgment of Israel. Other than that, each Arab country had its own foreign policy, which rarely matched the foreign policy of any other Arab country. The League, whose headquarters moved from **Cairo** to **Tunis** in 1979, was again paralyzed. It was evident that the traditional norms and decision-making procedures of the League no longer worked. The fourth Secretary-General, al-Shazli al-Qulaybi, therefore suggested several amendments to the charter, but none was realized. By the late 1980s, however, rapprochement began to seem possible. Egypt returned to the League, and the League's headquarters returned to Cairo in 1990. Arab subregional organizations were also established, including the **Arab Maghreb Union**, and the League found common cause in their unanimous and vehement support of the Palestinian *intifada* (uprising). Then, shortly after this relaxation of inter-Arab tensions, Iraq invaded Kuwait in 1990, fragmenting the Arab world once more.

The fundamental international changes that followed the end of the **Cold War**, along with a questioning of the dominant norms of Arab politics after the Gulf crisis, had a damaging effect on the Arab League. Arab countries simply avoided interacting through the League, and the biennial meeting of its Council became a forum for disagreement. The League was so fragmented that disagreements on major issues could not be resolved. Over a whole decade only one Arab Summit was held. In these circumstances, the fifth Secretary-General, Ismat Abdul-Majeed, could do little to achieve his goal of Arab reconciliation. Moreover alternative Middle Eastern and Mediterranean regional groupings emerged. If any of these developed into a regional organization, it would inevitably exclude Arab countries and include non-Arab countries. In all cases Arab countries south of the **Sahara** would be excluded, and the League would thus become a cultural more than a political organization. By the end of the twentieth century, observers of the Arab scene were generally pessimistic about the League's prospects; nonetheless new developments over the course of the twenty-first century may prove the pessimists wrong, with the League embarking on a new bright phase of its development.

See also: decolonization; Organization of the Islamic Conference; regional integration

Further reading

Hilal, A. (ed.) (1993) *Jami'at ad-duwal al-'arabiya: al-khibra al-tarikiya wa mashro'at at-tatweer* (The League of Arab States: Historical Experience and Projects for Progress), Cairo: Cairo University Center for Political Research and Studies.

Shihab, M. (ed.) (1978) *Jami'at ad-duwal al-'arabiya: methaquha wa injazatuha* (The League of Arab States: Its Charter and Achievements), Cairo: The Arab League Institute of Arab Research and Studies.

AHMED ALI SALEM

leisure

Despite the central position of games and sports in Africa, the issue of leisure is not easy to explore, a problem exacerbated by the fact that, until the last few decades of the twentieth century, there was little research on the notion of and practices associated with leisure, particularly from historians. The social science literature that attempts to deal with games and sports, and the political, cultural, and educational attributes associated with them, tended to be poorer than the literature devoted to, for example, the relationships between games and the psychological development of children. Despite such negligence, the existing literature has helped identify some of the essential elements in the constitution of the space and the ideology of leisure. Yet the relationship of games, sport, and other leisure activities with, on the one hand, work, residence, wealth, health, education, and nationalism, and, on the other hand, patriotism, professionalism, and amateurism are critical to understanding the social history of African societies. Issues of identity, cohesion, educational and moral values, control, and belonging are manifested in studies of leisure activities as much as they are in studies of economic history, religious history, or anthropology.

One of the main challenges in writing histories of leisure is determining the activities that can be characterized as leisure. Can one construe activities described by ethnologists, travelers, and other historians or anthropologists – plays, games, pastimes, physical training, entertainments, dancing, going to bars, visiting friends and family – as ludic activity? Should one think of certain activities that, while related to aesthetic activities or playing, have a precise function in the socialization mechanism as leisure? In fact, in certain African societies, the integration of the aesthetic, playing, and the scientific, on the one hand, and ritual and performative domains, on the other, is constitutive of the modes of production that distinguish a homogenous society from any other. If that is the case, the question arises: Can human behavior only be regarded as play activity if it is separated from the expressive and constitutive procedures of traditional culture, and appears instead as a manifestation of the flexible and changing creativity of members of the given society? For example, should one consider hunting as conducted by initiated hunters, with its rituals and esoteric practices, as leisure in the same way as fox hunting for English aristocrats? How does one account for differences in rules and context between various traditional styles of African wrestling, their colonial and urban versions, and the Olympic Freestyle or Greco-Roman forms of wrestling? How does one identify **dance**, which is obviously more than an entertainment activity because it has a crucial role in the establishment and assertion of group solidarity and cohesion? How does one distinguish dances that are simply for entertainment from those that are physical expressions of religious devotion?

Similarly, can one consider games and sports outside their sociocultural context, outside the worldview of a group and the socialization processes in which they take place? Do we in fact have different models of leisure in Africa, which serve specific ends beyond the dichotomy between entertainment activities and useful activities that is used to circumscribe the space of leisure in the West? Is it a domain in which sources and resources are gathered for individual and collective emotional satisfaction, for cultural creativity, differentiation, and continual reimagination? These questions are particularly challenging when one attempts to find answers by using models proposed by Western literature on the theme of leisure. To most Western social scientists, the time for leisure remains interconnected with the time for work. Such a strong link defines leisure as a concrete activity, which is grounded in both time and space. Thus, in addition to work, leisure involves more than simple play and encompasses games, entertainment (artistic and musical), and sports.

The interesting aspect of studying games and sports in Africa is that the identification of activities that may belong to the domain of leisure, both for those who participate directly in them and for the spectators, seems to be easier to grasp in certain time periods. With respect to the pre-colonial era, which presents the most difficult challenges to those trying to establish what can be defined as ludic activity, the following are considered leisure activities: games, sports, dance, art, and **music**. More precisely, in the category of games are included archery or shooting contests, and social games (for example, *mancala/wuri*), and in the sport category there are non-ritual dances (such as the stick-fighting found among the Sotho and Xhosa peoples), swimming and wrestling (which are the most popular sports in **West Africa**, particularly among the Wolof and Igbo peoples), as well as the beer-drinking and hemp-smoking associated with the spitting contests of the Shanga Tsonga people in **Mozambique**, to name only a few examples. Most of these activities follow gender divisions. Thus even where dance is not exclusively a female activity, it is largely dominated by women, whereas swimming remains very expressive of masculinity. Discussing the history of the Tio Kingdom, Jan Vansina (1973) made a useful distinction between play activities that are prescribed by society (such as the obligations of members of an association or a secret society, the ceremonies involved in certain rituals, and familial visits) and non-compulsory play activities – "entertainment," in the Western sense of the word – whose only goal is personal satisfaction.

The difficulty of differentiating domains of African leisure is evident for the pre-colonial period, but it seems easier to locate leisure during the colonial era because metropolitan governments and the colonial administration often made successful attempts to use a statutory temporal domain to deal with leisure – both their own and traditional African practices. They marked out spaces for leisure practices, based on a strong belief in the need to separate leisure from work. The great motivation behind such colonial interventions was the desire to impose a European timeframe on colonized societies in Africa.

Leisure and colonial domination

In analyzing the question of leisure during the colonial era, the dominant approach insists on a strong correlation between leisure and the colonial project, more precisely between the time allotted to work and the time allotted to leisure. Terence Ranger indicates that during preparations for the 9th Imperial Congress of the British Social Hygiene Council Inc., the Southern Rhodesian Chief Native Commissioner and Secretary of Native Affairs, Charles Bullock, was asked to present a contribution to the session on "Labor and Leisure Overseas," in order to "promote leisure occupations and recreation in Native Locations and in organized bodies of native labor" (Ranger 1987: 196). Ranger suggests that this exemplifies attempts to reconcile colonial hygiene policies and social control. This double preoccupation produced a tension (relative to the time devoted to leisure and to the sites where such concerns were exercised) such that it became a ground for confrontation and permanent conflict between and within African and European communities. The Europeans tried to impose capitalistic and colonial structures on Africa that would establish a temporal and spatial order compatible with their project of economic exploitation by means of a process of cultural assimilation, and above all control of Africans' leisure activities.

Ironically, in British Africa the colonial administration initiated a process of introducing European games and sports, while removing the prestige that athletics and sports had always held in Britain. This paradox was reflected in **Southern Africa** by the limitation of cricket (for the British) and rugby (for the Boers), which became symbolic of racial and national characteristics, and more specifically the rituals *par excellence* of white supremacy. The Africans, on the other hand, redoubled their efforts to create an environment that satisfied their needs, while removing them from colonial social control and the colonial timeframe. In fact, as indicated by Belinda Bozzoli (1983), the Africans often turned these practices to their advantage.

The African appropriation of European-inspired leisure (particularly sports) by the multiple processes of reusing and integrating it in various ways into their own cultural grammar and into the political economy of colonization was quite complex. In fact the actors who confronted one another, in their diversity, were responsible for the mechanisms used in selecting the games and sports, traditional or colonial, that were present in the public space. Such choices were all part of the processes of mediation and contest that were unleashed by the colonial encounter. They were manifestations of the behavior and position of both Africans and Europeans in the very complex political and economic culture of colonial domination, under which social relations of control were exercised or endured, security was obtained or denied, and identities were displayed or dissimulated.

Entertainment activities became important in urban areas where the colonial work ethic required a strict control of the urban African population. The debate over defining and implementing mechanisms that would obtain the best results prevailed for several decades within administrative and scientific colonial circles. From the 1920s "educated Africans" participated in that debate. Two questions dominated colonial African controversies over leisure. The first concerned organizational modes. Some colonial officials supported an approach that privileged the introduction of European entertainment and sport activities, rigorously planned, with centralized organization and training activities, in order to help Africans living in urban areas to adjust better to city life. It was thought that in dispensing colonial activities, inappropriate "tribal" and African cultural activities could be kept out of cities and colonial areas. The opposite view argued for a more classical approach, based on command and control, that would define, first and foremost, the entertainment activities that were prohibited by the colonial administration. The second question was related to those sport and entertainment activities that were adopted by the state to serve its purposes. Some believed that the introduction of European leisure and sport activities was an indispensable precondition for the pursuit of the "civilizing mission." They believed that Western physical activities were a particularly useful antidote for the savage and "primitive" nature of Africans. They were seen as powerful instruments for conveying those moral qualities that were otherwise absent from African leisure. They were not therefore designed for relaxation or as games, but essentially for moral education, particularly under the British imperial system of education. Their purpose was to uproot the urban African, cutting him off from his ethnic milieu in order to root him in the urban landscape and culture by simultaneously teaching him discipline and team spirit. In this respect the creation of recreation areas contributed to the construction of moral discipline and a sense of duty (civic duty), which was indispensable to the achievement of the colonial project and the submission of the indigenous people.

In terms of the sports, games, and recreation areas that were under the supervision of the colonial administrative training department, a particular emphasis was put on promoting discipline and moral purity through leisure. The aim was to prevent indigenous people from succumbing to particular vices, involving young people in more profitable and healthy activities in order to fight against the alleged sexual excesses of both men and women, men's violence, alcohol consumption, obscene and immoral dances, criminal activity, and general disorder. Sport and European games would serve to forge an aesthetic and grammar of restriction that could then be used against those who got out of hand. Such behavioral excesses were part of African exuberance as constructed by the ethnology of the colonial administrators. Their principal goal was to involve Africans in a European-type use of time, with its institutional organization and ideology granting the central place to work.

Partisans of the civilizing mission of sport and entertainment used the public education system and Christian missions to promote their views. Their most renowned spokesman, Sir Frederick Lugard, insisted on the crucial importance in elementary education of entertainment activities that would build the character of African students. According to him, the playing field was a central site for the moral indoctrination of the African. The diffusion of European leisure activities through education had to serve, for both the colonial administration and the missionaries, as a fusion of morality and masculinity. Physical education was thus an essential element of the education system for both the British Empire and the British metropole.

Other European colonial powers, such as France, Portugal, and Germany, remained indifferent to the potential of moral instruction inherent in team games, turning away from the opportunity to create an ethical hegemony that was presented on the playing fields. Those who opposed sport's civilizing mission were divided in two groups. The first group believed that it was more efficient to keep Africans under the authority of traditional "tribal" governance. They were in favor of a simultaneous reorganization and reformulation of games and traditional African arts, music, and dances, in particular against such European proletarian sports as boxing, which was very popular. The second group – whose opposition was based on what they perceived as the extremely negative effects of boxing, but extended to other sports – focused on three disruptive problems. The first was that Africans adopted European sports by reconfiguring them to their own needs, particularly the promotion of individual initiative. Second, sport was used for the establishment of multi-ethnic organizations that could be used for purposes other than sport. Third, fights and clashes over sporting events could trigger wider conflicts that would be more dangerous to the colonial order.

The controversies about the consequences of introducing European leisure activities into the African context provide a general perspective on the Africans' logic of appropriation. In following the arguments of those who opposed the introduction of European entertainment activities, it can be seen how indigenous peoples adopted contact sports (boxing), as well as team sports (soccer), matching their modes of organization, structure, and participation to ethnic characteristics and loyalties, or to membership of regional and religious groups. In return, such sports variously influenced the nature, function, and mode of expression of ethnicity.

In short – whether it was boxing or soccer, entertainment or clothing, visiting bars and dancehalls or some other activity – the ways in which Africans appropriated such leisure activities were exceptionally creative. They illustrated the difficulties facing the colonial administration in their attempt to achieve total social control over African societies, particularly the urban sector. Is it logical to consider these processes as a manifestation of resistance in African societies or simply as diverse mechanisms for connecting with the colonial project, which was thereby subverted and reshaped by the very individual and collective actors it was attempting to train and control? The process of Africans remaking games and sports was very similar to the way that urban women became involved in producing and selling alcohol in clandestine bars, considered by Fred Cooper to have made them:

> shapers of an urban culture that was antithetical to hard work, that accepted forms of conduct that the state defined as criminal, and whose very cultural separateness made it at least a potential base for political organization.
>
> (Cooper 1983: 7–8)

Leisure and national construction

During the struggle for independence, sport and leisure activities played a crucial role in mobilization processes, centered on citizenship and social demands, carried out by the political parties, trade union organizations, and ethnic and religious groups which attempted to preserve the traditional forms of social networking. The structure of national coalitions and the heterogeneity of their political agenda (social and cultural) allowed room for the expression of both modern and traditional sport and leisure activities. Tension remained, however, between supporters of a return to African forms and those who had accepted Western concepts and practices of sport and leisure.

The tension between attempting to organize truly indigenous leisure activities, on the one hand, and participation in international competitions as sovereign nations on the other hand, created new situations in Africa. Sports, particularly soccer, took an active role in both the formation of the national imaginary and the expression of local identities (violent clashes between African states often occur during soccer matches). In return, the attempt to introduce play activities to the educational system that were based on African traditions did not have the results anticipated. On the contrary, entertainment and sport activities in post-colonial Africa followed social-class patterns. The African upper classes adopted sports like tennis, golf, and sometimes cricket as a sign of difference and marker of their elite status, while the popular masses turned to soccer. The ethnic, political, and class identities strongly associated with involvement in particular sporting activities were preserved.

The playing field thus became a territory of identity display – national, racial, regional, ethnic, and religious – but it was also potentially a site for successes beyond the limits of education and social background. Professional sport opened an important route for successful migration to Western countries, becoming a cosmopolitan answer to the many crises faced by Africans.

What remained of the attempts to reinvent truly African leisure activities? They were increasingly removed from schools and the formal education system, and relocated in community organizations and informal educational practices. As a result a culture of leisure that borrowed from both reimagined Western resources and reinvented African traditions (in which sport, music, dance, and clothing prevailed) took shape.

See also: cinema; dance; society: colonial; society: post-independence; music; sports; youth

References and further reading

Baker, W.J. and Mangan, J.A. (eds.) (1987) *Sport in Africa. Essays in Social History*, London: Africana Publishing.

Bozzoli, B. (ed.) (1983) *Town and Countryside in the Transvaal*, Johannesburg: Witwatersrand University Press.

Cooper, F. (ed.) (1983) *Struggle for the City. Migrant Labor, Capital and the State in Urban Africa*, London: Sage.

Giddens, A. (1964) "Notes on the Concepts of Play and Leisure," *Sociological Review* 12, 1: 73–89.

Martin, P. (1985) *Leisure and Society in Colonial Brazzaville*, Cambridge: Cambridge University Press.

Ranger, T. (1987) "Pugilism and Pathology: African Boxing and the Black Urban Experience in Southern Rhodesia," in W.J. Barker and J.A. Mangan (eds.), *Sport in Africa: Essays in Social History*, London: Africa Publishing Company.

Vansina, J. (1973) *The Tio Kingdom of the Middle*

Congo, 1880–1892, London: Oxford University Press.

Zeleza, P.T. and Veney, C.R. (eds.) (2002) *Leisure in Urban Africa*, Trenton: Africa World Press Inc.

MAMADOU DIOUF

Lesotho

Lesotho, which covers an area of 30,350 square kilometers and had an estimated population of 2.3 million in 2001, is completely surrounded by **South Africa**. It was colonized by Britain in 1868. Later, in 1871, Lesotho was annexed to the Cape Colony, before reverting to British rule in 1884. In addition to bringing the population under British control, and incorporating local authority structures such as chiefs into colonial administration, the British were also faced with the task of creating a pool of labor to work in the gold mines and on various colonial projects in the republics of **Southern Africa**. This was accomplished through an authoritarian regime of laws and taxation, and facilitated by an outbreak of rinderpest that decimated local livestock in the 1890s. Further, a combination of population growth and unsound colonial soil conservation policies led to a severe soil erosion that reduced available arable land. By 1936 over 100,000 Basotho men were, out of necessity, participating in **migrant labor**.

The first two decades of the twentieth century saw the emergence of organized reaction to colonial rule. In 1907 the Basutoland Progressive Association was formed, followed in 1919 by Lekhotla la Bafo (Council of Commons). These organizations differed significantly in their social composition and programs, but by demanding the involvement of commoners in the Basutoland National Council (BNC), which had been established in 1903 as a purely advisory body with a membership limited to senior chiefs; by criticizing the role of chiefs within the colonial system; by resisting attempts to incorporate Lesotho into the Union of South Africa; and by agitating for a bigger role for Basotho traders in colonial trade, these organizations laid the basis for the emergence of the independence movement during the second half of the twentieth century.

The formation of the Basutoland African Congress (BAC) by Ntsu Mokhehle and his contemporaries in 1952 marked the advent of agitation for independence. The BAC was short-lived, however, as disagreements over its program led to the formation of rival political parties. By 1965, when the first parliamentary elections were held, no less than four political parties contested them. Those elections were won by the Basotho National Party (BNP), defeating the older and relatively more established Basutoland Congress Party (BCP) – formerly the BAC.

On 4 October 1966 Lesotho regained its independence from Britain. The country's economy was characterized by dependence on migrant labor, revenue from the Southern African Customs Union (SACU), and aid from Britain. Foreign traders dominated the few existing commercial concerns, and there was no industry at all. What little infrastructure did exist in the form of roads and communications networks was limited to the capital, **Maseru**.

In the aftermath of the second general election in 1970, Prime Minister Leabua Jonathan declared a state of emergency, suspended the constitution, and declared the election results null and void. There followed a period of severe repression that resulted in the exile of the BCP leadership and the formation of the Lesotho Liberation Army (LLA) in the years between 1974 and 1979. The LLA conducted an armed struggle aimed at toppling the BNP.

Initially the BNP government pursued a policy friendly to **South Africa**, but by the mid-1970s it was clear that this policy had failed to yield any results. In the late 1970s government instead adopted a hostile policy towards the country. Lesotho joined the Southern African Development Coordinating Conference (SADCC), and together with eight other regional states dedicated itself to reducing dependence on South Africa. The government developed friendly relations with the African National Congress (ANC), and established diplomatic relations with the Soviet Union, Eastern European countries, China, North Korea, and Cuba. All these gave Lesotho a much higher profile internationally, and enabled it to receive unprecedented amounts of foreign aid, mainly from Scandinavian countries, thereby facilitating government intervention in different sectors of the economy. Yet structurally the economy remained unchanged: There was little industry, agriculture remained underdeveloped, and migrant labor persisted. Clashes within the ruling party, its Youth League, and the army, as well as South Africa's concerns about the presence in Lesotho of embassies from socialist countries, led to a military coup in 1986.

Lesotho returned to constitutional rule in 1993 after twenty-two years of civilian and military dictatorships. The BCP won the general election of that year, taking all sixty-five seats in the national assembly. Far from solving the country's political problems the new democratic dispensation was plagued by chronic instability. In 1994 King Letsie III toppled the elected government, and following the 1998 elections an alliance of political parties that had lost the elections – BNP, BCP, and Marematlou Freedom Party (MFP) – would have succeeded in seizing power by force but for an armed intervention by **Southern African Development Community** (SADC) forces, comprising troops from **Botswana** and South Africa.

The liberation of South Africa in 1994 ushered in a period of fresh challenges for Lesotho. The bulk of foreign aid disappeared, and for the first time this century the South African mines ceased to be a reliable source of employment for Basotho men. Insufficient numbers of jobs were created internally to absorb the thousands of jobseekers who entered the job market every year, partly because **structural adjustment programs** left the government without the means to create new jobs and partly because foreign companies remained reluctant to invest in Lesotho. The country also continued to lose skilled manpower to South Africa.

Malaise is not, however, limited to Lesotho's economic future. The politicians' inability to operate within a constitutional framework continues to plague the political system. Incessant and debilitating power struggles within the country's major political parties have adversely affected Lesotho's chances of creating homegrown options and solutions to economic problems. These struggles for power and persistent economic adversity have made Lesotho a very unstable country politically. As a result the last decade of the twentieth century saw Lesotho's sovereignty compromised by the role taken by South Africa, Botswana, **Zimbabwe**, and **Mozambique** as guarantors of the country's political dispensation.

See also: Common Market for Eastern and Southern Africa

Further reading

Bardill, J.E. and Cobbe, J.H. (1985) *Lesotho: Dilemmas of Dependence in Southern Africa*, London: Gower.

Gill, S.J. (1993) *A Short History of Lesotho*, Morija: Morija Museum and Archives.

NEVILLE W. PULE

Liberia

Liberia, with an area of 99,067 square kilometers, borders **Côte d'Ivoire** and **Sierra Leone**. It had an estimated population of 3.6 million in 2000. Liberia was established in 1847 by former slaves from the United States and the Caribbean, and by slaves recaptured from ships on their way to the Americas. They called themselves "Americo-Liberians," and proceeded to establish political institutions modeled on those in the United States. The True Whig Party (TWP) was founded in 1870, and maintained a monopoly on the political system until 1980.

At the beginning of the twentieth century, Liberia faced external threats, surrounded as it was by British and French colonial powers that wanted to annex some of the territory that made up the country's interior. To secure Liberia's sovereignty, government officials moved forward with plans to extend authority over the hinterland. The plan called for the incorporation of the indigenous population into the state through indirect rule. Few indigenous people were assimilated into the state, because only those Africans who were willing to accept the values and customs of the Americo-Liberians were granted citizenship.

By the 1920s the government's control over the hinterland was basically complete, and the system of indirect rule had been transformed into one of direct rule. The indigenous population was left in a precarious situation. This was manifested in abusive labor practices that forced children to work for Americo-Liberians without pay under the guise of apprenticeship programs. Both men and women were often conscripted by chiefs to work on public and private projects. The introduction of the Firestone Rubber Company to Liberia in 1926 witnessed the increased recruitment of involuntary labor. These labor violations brought Liberia to international attention, as the state was charged with condoning such labor practices.

The reign of President William Tubman (1944–71) changed the relationship between the Americo-Liberians and the indigenous population. Tubman established the "Open Door policy" that allowed foreign investors access to the hinterland to exploit reserves of timber, iron ore, gold, and diamonds, and establish cocoa and coffee plantations. As companies took advantage of this policy, people were needed to work in the mines and on plantations. Jobs in the government and legal profession were now open to indigenous people, which raised the demand for urban workers.

With revenues from foreign investment, the Tubman administration embarked on an economic development program. Infrastructure was built, giving the population of the hinterland access to teachers, doctors, and agricultural specialists. Men and women were also granted the right to vote, although the property requirement remained, effectively disenfranchising many citizens. At the end of Tubman's rule, the economy had begun to collapse, and political opposition was rising. Tubman was succeeded by his vice-president, William Tolbert. At first it appeared that Tolbert was committed to transforming the political system, calling for reforms in the civil service. Tolbert believed that the economy was too dependent on exports, and that larger investment in agriculture and other sectors was needed. He lowered the voting age, but the property requirement remained.

These proposals were taken by many people to indicate that the old system was being abolished. They gave rise to the People's Awakening Movement (PAM), the Movement for Justice in Africa (MOJA), and the Progressive Alliance of Liberia (PAL). PAM had support among the academic, labor, and grass-roots organizations, and its goal was to provide all Liberians with a voice in national politics. Moreover the men and women who had been enlisted into the Armed Forces of Liberia were favorable to PAM's causes. MOJA's goals were to raise awareness among students, farmers, and workers through demonstrations and strikes. PAL began among indigenous Liberians and expatriates living in the United States. Its goal was to involve the urban masses in direct action against the ruling class. Segments of the population began to express their anger over corruption and the widening economic gap between the Americo-Liberians and the masses.

Tolbert's political strength was tested in April 1979. Several things contributed to the military takeover in 1980: the government's wasteful spending on the **Organization of African Unity** (OAU) summit meeting at a time when inflation and unemployment were high; the rise in the price of rice; Tolbert ordering the police to open fire on protesters; bringing troops in from Guinea to quell riots; and the injury or death of many protesters. All of these took place in the context of an army that was frustrated with its own conditions: low pay, substandard housing, and lack of uniforms. Eventually the TWP was overthrown, and its leaders were charged with corruption, misuse of public office, violation of **human rights**, and neglect of the needs of the masses. Although the military takeover was bloody, Samuel Doe enjoyed the support of many people. He promised to return the country to civilian rule, and kept his promise. He did not hold elections, however, until he had changed his birth date to meet the presidential age requirement, and decided to form the National Democratic Party of Liberia (NDPL) and run in the October 1985 election.

By all accounts the NDPL lost the presidential race to the opposition Liberian Action Party (LAP), but a special commission appointed by Doe later announced that the NDPL had won the presidency. The new administration did not give the impression that civilian government would transform the political situation: Military decrees were not lifted, and some opposition parties and other leading organizations remained banned. The last two decades of the twentieth century witnessed Liberia's descent into the political abyss, as militias, factions, and rebel movements formed along ethnic lines. The end result was the overthrow of the Doe regime in 1989, and the disintegration of the state into a civil war that lasted until 1996. After many failed peace accords, national elections were held in 1997. Charles Taylor of the National Patriotic Front was elected president.

Further reading

Dolo, E.D. (1996) *Democracy Versus Dictatorship*, Lanham: University Press of America.

Huband, M. (1998) *The Liberian Civil War*, London: Frank Cass.

CASSANDRA RACHEL VENEY

Libya

Libya is the fourth largest country in Africa, with an area of 1,760,000 square kilometers, but in 2000 it had an estimated population of only 6.4 million. Its gross domestic product per capita (on a purchasing power parity basis) was US$6,697 in 1998, giving it one of the highest income levels on the continent. During the twentieth century Libya experienced several dramatic economic and political changes. It was an Ottoman province, then an Italian colony, a constitutional monarchy, and finally an Arab republic. It has also moved from being a poor country to a relatively rich one, thanks to its huge oil reserves.

By the beginning of the twentieth century the two Libyan provinces of Tripolitania and Cyrenaica had been part of the Ottoman Empire for five centuries. In 1911 Italy claimed that Europeans were abused in Libya, and attacked its coastal cities. There was widespread but short-lived resistance, before the Ottoman government ceded control to the Italians under the 1912 treaty of Ouchy. The two provinces were then strictly separated and made self-governing under Italian colonial authority. During the **First World War**, the Italians and British recognized Idris al-Sunnusi as Emir of Cyrenaica.

After the war, a republic of Tripolitania was declared and negotiated with the Italians "the Fundamental Law," which established a Libyan–Italian citizenship. This was also applied in Cyrenaica. But the colonial authority refused either to unite the two provinces or to hold the promised regional elections. Between 1923 and 1931 the Italians were forcibly resisted by guerrillas in Cyrenaica, and responded brutally: around 750,000 people – almost half of the population – were executed, forced into concentration camps, starved, or made to flee the country. The capture and execution of Sheikh Omar al-Mukhtar in 1931 severely weakened the resistance movement, paving the way for an Italian program of demographic colonization. Thousands of arable acres were confiscated, and almost 100,000 Italian villagers were settled there. In 1939 Libya was declared an integral part of Italy.

The Libyan desert was a major battlefield during the **Second World War**, and the fighting made a major impact on Libya. First, Italian colonialism was replaced by the British occupation of Tripolitania and Cyrenaica, and the French occupation of Fezzān. Second, exiled Libyans (particularly in **Egypt**) organized and called for an independent state. Thanks to the efforts of the Arab–Asian bloc, in 1951 the United Nations declared Libya an independent, federal constitutional monarchy.

The reign of King Idris al-Sunnusi (1951–69) witnessed three milestones. First, the royal regime signed agreements with Britain in 1953 and the United States in 1954 that allowed them to establish military bases in Libya, in return for annual financial and military aid. The regime was severely criticized for this by its Arab neighbors. Second, in the 1960s a huge reserve of oil was discovered – Libya rapidly became the second largest producer of oil among Arab countries, and sixth largest in the world. Although the average annual per capita income dramatically increased from US$35 in the 1950s to US$4,400 by the beginning of the 1970s, Libyans benefited from this national resource far less than the many international corporations that were involved. Moreover, in order to facilitate the work of these companies, King Idris abandoned the federal system and declared Libya a united state in 1963 – the third milestone of his rule.

In 1969 the army, led by a pan-Arab nationalist group called "The Free Officers," overthrew the monarchy and declared Libya an Arab republic. For the rest of the twentieth century Libya was ruled by Muammar al-Qaddafi, becoming a controversial model for revolutionary regimes.

In domestic terms the revolution had dramatic economic and political effects. Economically, the government negotiated successfully with the oil companies to raise oil prices and reduce production, and it confiscated all Italian property. The economy consequently bloomed: Oil revenues were invested in agriculture and construction, and used to import consumer goods. Politically, Qaddafi banned all political parties, favoring "the people's authority." The implementation of this system was criticized because the range of political candidates was restricted. The regime recognized no political opposition, although such opposition did become active in exile. This opposition was nonetheless fragmented and remained weak because of Qaddafi's charismatic leadership and combination of redistributive and coercive policies.

Qaddafi pursued an active foreign policy. First, shortly after the revolution, British and American military bases in Libya were evacuated, and Libya increasingly supported liberation and resistance movements around the world, including the Irish Republican Army, Palestinian groups, and the Japanese Red Army. Second, Qaddafi was eager to make the slogans of pan-Arab unity a reality, making several unsuccessful attempts to unite Libya with other Arab countries, including Egypt, **Sudan**, Syria, **Tunisia**, and **Morocco**, and establishing the Union of Magharibi States in 1989 (which effectively collapsed a few years later). Third, although Libya was perceived as threatening its African neighbors during the 1980s – it became involved in the civil war in **Chad**, laid claim to the Chad-controlled Aouzou Strip, and attempted to export the revolution to Sudan – its foreign policy had turned to Pan-Africanism by the 1990s. In return for this shift in policy, the **Organization of African Unity** supported Libya in its dispute with the United States and Britain, openly violating UN sanctions on Libya by resuming air flights and commercial relations in 1998. Libya's African foreign policy resulted in the establishment of the Sahel and Sahara States Grouping in 1999, and counterbalanced the failure of its pan-Arab foreign policy in the late 1980s.

As a result of this radical foreign policy, Libya was accused of supporting terrorism, and suffered the consequences. First, the United States attacked **Tripoli** and Benghazi in 1986, unilaterally imposing economic sanctions on the country. Then the United Nations imposed economic sanctions on Libya in 1992, when Qaddafi refused to give up two citizens accused of planning the bombing of a PanAm flight over Scotland in 1988. These sanctions were only lifted when the two accused were sent to face trial in the Netherlands in 2000.

See also: colonial conquest and resistance; regional integration

Further reading

al-Aqad, S. (1970) *Libya al-Mu'asirah* (Modern Libya), Cairo: The Arab League.

Simons, G. (1996) *Libya: The Struggle for Survival*, New York: St. Martin's Press.

RIHAM MAHROUS KHAFAGY

Lingala

Lingala is a Central Bantu language that belongs to the largest African language phylum: the Niger–Congo. It is spoken primarily in **Democratic Republic of Congo** (DRC) and **Congo** (Congo-Brazzaville), as well as in parts of five neighboring central African states: northwestern **Angola**, eastern **Gabon**, southern **Central African Republic**, and southwestern **Sudan**. There are no reliable statistics on the number of speakers of Lingala in the region by the end of the twentieth century, but estimates range from 20–25 million.

The origins of Lingala and the date on which it emerged remain a matter of continuing debate among scholars of Congolese languages. One hypothesis is that Lingala arose as a trade language in the early nineteenth century, but scholars disagree as to whether this took place first among inhabitants of communities along the Ubangi River, the Congo River, or the Mongala River. Another theory maintains that the rise of Lingala occurred as result of the colonization of Central Africa in the late nineteenth century, which by increasing the level of interaction between people of different ethnic groups may have facilitated the emergence of new lingua francas. Whatever its genesis may have been, Lingala is recognized as the most important of the four national languages of DRC and Congo-Brazzaville, and also arguably the most important lingua franca of Central Africa, both in demographic terms and in terms of prestige. Its importance grew in response to several sociohistorical developments that occurred before, during, and after colonization.

Specifically the rapid expansion of Lingala was facilitated by the usual agents of language-spread: trade, colonization, education, and **urbanization**; it also gained prestige through its privileged use for religious and administrative purposes, in the armed forces, and for music. As a result Lingala saw itself allocated several *de jure* or *de facto* functions in key public domains over the years. These included its adoption as the trade language along the Congo River and its tributaries from around the mid-1800s, and its subsequent imposition by the colonial government as the official language of the Equator Province (*c.*1890–1900). These policies received further impetus in 1929, when **Kinshasa** was established as the capital of the Belgian Congo and Lingala adopted as its official language in recognition of its strength as a lingua franca in an area that was otherwise known as Kikongo home territory. In 1930 Lingala was granted one of its best vehicles of expansion by being imposed as the official language of the colonial army, replacing the **Hausa** and **Swahili** that had been used by the colonial militia. The Lingalization policy was necessitated by the large number of Bangala recruits in the newly established colonial army; that the army was stationed in the provinces guaranteed the expansion of the language.

This expansion took a quantum-leap forward as Lingala, along with Kikongo, gradually emerged as the key language of Congolese popular music between 1940 and 1943. By 1960 Lingala accounted for 90 percent of the popular songs produced for broadcast across Central Africa. In the late 1950s Lingala began to emerge as the dominant language of the marketplace and of travel in both Congos, as both countries engaged their liberation struggles. The advent of political independence on 30 June 1960, under the leadership of a Lingala-speaking elite that included Prime Minister Patrice Lumumba, President Kasavubu, Minister of State Jean Bolikango, and General Joseph Mobutu, offered Lingala a third pillar of strength and means of diffusion. Lingala served as the default link language for mass rallies and political discourse. By 1961 its use as the official language of the armed forces was extended to other security forces: the national police, national guard, and air force. The adoption in 1966 of Lingala as the official language of the Catholic Diocese of Kinshasa – the largest parish of the largest denomination in DRC – provided a fourth base from which stable and rapid expansion of the language was practically guaranteed. These factors were complemented by the use of Lingala for advertisements on national radio and television in both Congos (from *c.*1968), and in DRC's most popular soap opera (which was called *Maboke*) at around the same time, as well as its utilization from the 1960s through to the 1970s as the language of the Central African liberation movements that were headquartered in Kinshasa. Finally, as emigration to other African countries and Western Europe increased over the 1980s as growing numbers of Congolese fled Mobutu's oppressive regime, musicians from DRC established "colonies" of Congolese music abroad, giving further impetus to the expansion of the language.

These developments, on top of those already occurring for the other national Congolese languages, greatly facilitated the expansion of Lingala within Central Africa and beyond it. Regular radio broadcasts of Congolese music to numerous countries within and outside of Africa were a direct outcome of such prior functional developments of Lingala, with the expansion and reputation of the language destined to increase once the DRC's economic and political situation stabilizes, and its immense resources are developed.

By 2000 Lingala was poised to become one of the most important languages in Central Africa. It was already viewed as the *de facto* "national language" of the DRC, being spoken (or at least heard) by a larger proportion of the country's estimated 50 million inhabitants than French, which served as the official language. For Lingala to assume a role as both *de facto* and *de jure* official national language, it needs to develop a significant body of literature to complement its supranational role in music. This seems likely to occur once the policy of limiting the use of Lingala and other national languages (Kikongo, Swahili, and Tshiluba) in primary education is changed, so that the use of these languages at all levels of education can be promoted. It was widely recognized that only through such a change of policy would the development of a Lingala literature, including reference tools of all sorts, become a possibility.

Further reading

Samarin, W.J. (1990–1) "The Origins of Kituba and Lingala," *Journal of African Languages and Linguistics* 12: 47–77.

Sesep, N.B. (1986) "L'expansion du Lingala," *Linguistique et Sciences Humaines* 271: 19–48.

EYAMBA BOKAMBA

literature

A properly illuminating discussion of the phenomenon of literature on the African continent should begin with an acknowledgment of its peculiar complexity. The primary reason for this complexity is the immense diversity of cultural traditions, racial and ethnic configurations, languages, and historical trajectories within the continent. We may follow convention and broadly classify the continent into sub-Saharan Africa, on the one hand, and Arab North Africa, on the other. Within this broad classification, there is a wide range of further delineations that can be made. For instance, the strong cultural influence of Islamic civilization on the northern parts of many West African countries, or in parts of Eastern Africa and the Horn of Africa, implies the presence of a long tradition of Koranic learning and the Arabic script, whereas most sub-Saharan societies were predominantly oral cultures until relatively recently – that is, until the nineteenth century. Likewise, significant differences between the colonial policies of the European nations regarding Africa have had major repercussions for the post-colonial political and cultural formations that resulted from colonial rule. This in turn has contributed to the diversity of literary creativity in Africa.

Related to this is the large number of languages used by Africans in their daily lives, in official business, and in leisure. This fact implies that multiple domains of expression exist, or have emerged from the continent over the course of the twentieth century, that can legitimately be classified as literary. The general practice in the scholarship of African literature is to introduce some measure of coherence into its vast heterogeneity by means of various subclassifications. Thus it is conventional to classify the literature in terms of region (**North Africa**, **East Africa**, **West Africa**, **Southern Africa**); language (**anglophone Africa**, **lusophone Africa**, **Swahili**, Amharic); or genre and medium (drama, poetry, fiction, and what has come to be called "orature"). Each of these classifications is useful, but it is important to stress that literature on the African continent is too diverse and vibrant to fit into neat taxonomic categories. The term "African literature" is meaningful and coherent, then, in much the same sense that terms like "European" or "Asian" literature are coherent. What these categories designate is not a tidily bounded body of literary productions, but rather a vast field of inherited, contemporary, and constantly growing output, unified principally by a common geographical space of origin. We should use the term "African literatures" – advisedly in the plural – to conceptualize and study the creative activity, rooted in language, of Africans over the course of their history and in the modern age. The account that follows will be informed by the conventional subcategorizations indicated above, but our approach is to proceed by following a broad historical trajectory. This will allow us to plot developments in African literatures with due stress on heterogeneity, and due recognition of the implications of this heterogeneity for widespread preconceptions about the continent.

Orality and performance

The oral tradition and formations of performance constitute the inherited as well as coeval dimension of what we call modern African literature. In parts of Africa where literacy and the culture of print arrived in the nineteenth and twentieth centuries, they met an already well-established tradition of oral expressiveness. In such societies, festivals, masquerade performances, and related oral forms provided avenues for artistic expression, and art forms – including the literary – existed as part of an ensemble of practices, an integrated system of seeing and doing, that was at once aesthetic and socially instrumental. This instrumentality could, and can, take various forms. Elaborate mythologies explained the mysteries of the world, and also served to socialize successive generations into the ways of seeing that enabled the community to preserve its way of life, while also coping with historical flux. For the pantheistic societies, multiple gods needed to be ritually placated so that the community itself could be revivified. Various forms of poetic and dramatic genres derived from this religious impulse.

Social hierarchies were also reproduced and encoded in poetic forms. The tradition of praise-singers is one way in which social hierarchy was encoded and celebrated. Many African societies had court poets, linguists, or chroniclers who served a number of functions, all of them having to do with cultural preservation and memorialization through language. The praise-singer or court poet was the one who preserved the history of the group, the lineage of kings, and the exploits of ancestors. Among the Mandinka of Western Africa, the exploits of Sundiata continue to be narrated in epic performances by griots. Epic traditions exist also in commemoration of figures like King Chaka and Askia Mohammed. The work of Africanist scholars like Karin Barber, Thomas A. Hale, Gordon Innes, Daniel P. Kunene, or Isidore Okpewho (himself an accomplished novelist) has helped to make this tradition known beyond their specific linguistic and ethnic contexts, thereby enriching our knowledge of this manifestation of Africans' creative imagination.

Griots and other practitioners of oral expressive forms continue to survive even in contemporary times. Of course, with the ascendancy of literacy and the culture of print, orature does not command the same authority as in former times. But such is the creativity and adaptive genius of African artists that performers have turned to such media as television, film, and compact discs to disseminate their work. Thus popular **music** on the African continent often provides an avenue for traditional storytellers and court poets to practice their craft. At the inauguration of Nelson Mandela as the first black president of **South Africa** in 1994, an oral artist performed to commemorate the event. The popularity of Senegalese pop-artist Youssou N'Dour is a related example: He comes from a lineage of griots, but has branched out onto the world-music industry by blending Wolof musical forms with Western commercial music. He thereby extends and transforms the image and domain of the traditional court poet.

The medium of print: Pioneers

That there is a tradition of literature in the European languages in Africa is the consequence of the continent's experience of colonialism. Compared to the Indian subcontinent, for example, Africa's experience of formal European colonial rule is shorter in terms of duration. Nonetheless, it has had a major impact on the continent's intellectual history in general, and the shapes and directions of literary creativity in particular. From the mid-nineteenth century onwards, the nature of interaction between the major European powers and Africa underwent a gradual but significant change. With the decline in, and subsequent abolition of, the slave trade, European attention shifted to developing what was called "legitimate trade" concerns in Africa. This was accompanied by the interest of various Christian missionary organizations in establishing stations in the interior of Africa as a way of converting Africans to **Christianity**. The establishment of Christian mission schools in Africa helped to further the missionaries' agenda of creating a class of educated and Christianized Africans who would help to convert and "enlighten" their brethren. This process accorded well with the plans of colonial administrators who were also interested in cultivating a class of educated Africans, in their case to serve in the colonial bureaucracy.

If the "scramble for Africa" and the Berlin Conference mark the entrenchment of formal colonial rule in Africa, the late 1950s and early 1960s witnessed the era of nationalist agitation and **decolonization**. The consequences of European colonialism in Africa include the transformation of rural village life by the advent of modern urban centers, the migration of youths from their home communities to Western schools and cities, the creation of an elite Westernized class, and the emergence of a lower cadre of literate Africans who had primary or secondary education. Members of this median class were integrated into sectors of the workforce and state bureaucracy at levels below the elite class, who generally possessed higher education. The transformations, then, exist at the level of social organization as well as of modes of life and individuals' identities. The emergence and development of written African literature in European and indigenous languages is inseparable from the complex cultural ferment generated by this historical process.

Historians have shown that the class of educated, mission-trained, Africans played a significant role in the nationalist movements in their respective societies. Likewise, members of the class were responsible for the development of literary creativity in the European as well as indigenous languages. These figures generally believed in the policy of modernization for Africa. They were also, by and large, believers in the ideas of Western liberal humanism. But they were also often cultural-nationalist in their sympathies. They respected traditional African cultures and wanted to present them in a positive light so as to persuade European racists to respect their integrity. As writers and cultural workers, they sought to celebrate the identity of colonized groups and contest uncharitable representation in Western colonial writings and intellectual traditions. Many of these writers and cultural workers were also active in the political arena. They used their writing as a weapon to serve the cause of colonial reform or nationalist agitation. They often used journalism and political pamphleteering to further the struggle for independence. This period can be dated from the late nineteenth century to the onset of decolonization in the mid-twentieth century. A lot of the literary writing of this period was in the genre of poetry, but plays and novels also came from the pens of this pioneering generation. Belonging in this group would be the work of figures like D.O. Fagunwa (**Nigeria**), who wrote fiction in Yoruba; Thomas Mofolo (South Africa) and Sol T. Plaatje (South Africa), who wrote in English; as well as Tswana, and Ham Mukassa, whose *Uganda's Katikiro in England* (1904), a travelogue of a 1902 visit to England (originally written in Luganda) that was annotated and republished by Simon Gikandi in 1998. J.E. Casely Hayford (**Ghana**) and Nnamdi Azikiwe (Nigeria) wrote non-fiction with a cultural-nationalist agenda. A similar dynamic is illustrated by Jomo Kenyatta, whose *Facing Mount Kenya* (1938) uses the rhetoric of academic ethnography to defend the rational social order of the Kikuyu people of central **Kenya**.

The fact that these writings cover a range of genres – from poetry to journalism to academic discourse – even within the corpus of specific individuals, indicates that the political and institutional context within which the writers worked was less suited to the compartmentalization of domains of address than nominal independence would later make possible. It also suggests that the achievement of these writers should not be narrowly sought in the specifically *literary* merits of their contributions. Technically this period can, with some validity, be said to represent the formative phase (to use a progressivist metaphor) of what we read and study today as modern African literature. But for all this, their achievement is no less important. The concerns they express, the problems of rhetorical choices and self-identity they had to confront, are precisely the issues that continue to preoccupy subsequent generations of African writers and cultural workers.

The medium of print: Continuators

From the 1930s many Africans, fresh from periods of higher education in Europe, began returning to their home countries. This period witnessed a new self-confidence on the part of black people in Africa, Europe, and the Americas. This was contemporaneous with cultural and intellectual developments like the idea of "the New Negro" and the Harlem Renaissance in the United States, and the Negritude movement in **francophone Africa** and the Caribbean. The publication that heralded and codified the Negritude movement in the francophone world was *Anthologie de la nouvelle poésie nègre et malgache* (Anthology of New Black and Malagasy Poetry), published in 1948 by Léopold Sédar Senghor, poet and later president of independent **Senegal**. In fiction, the Guinean novelist Camara Laye is also associated with the ideological tendencies of the "Negritude School." In anglophone Africa, the Nigerian writer Chinua Achebe is generally positioned as the founding father, so to speak, of African literature in the European languages. This is because of the unprecedented worldwide success of his first novel, *Things Fall Apart* (1958). This novel has been translated into several languages all over the world, and is possibly the most widely read piece of literature by an African author.

The achievement of Senghor, Achebe, and the other writers of the mid-twentieth century generation is that they drew on their traditional African oral heritage to create a literary idiom that refashioned Western poetic, dramatic, or novelistic traditions. In so doing they came up with new and interesting ways of giving voice to African realities and aspirations. They thus invented a fresh literary idiom for exploring the human drama of Africans confronting the vicissitudes of life, of modernity, and of self-understanding. The thematic preoccupations of the writers of this phase was varied. As may be expected, there was a concern with the conflict between Western values and the traditional culture of pre-colonial Africa. The writers sought to articulate the dilemma of their class – that is, the educated African, located between Western civilization and the persistence of traditional values. They also addressed broader themes having to do with the meaning of historical change itself. In all cases an overriding impulse was to accent the humanity of Africans past and present. The Egyptian novelist and short-story writer Naguib Mahfouz represents a similar achievement in North Africa. His works, originally published in Arabic, address the processes and consequences of change as the rich traditions of **Egypt** confront Western modernity.

In various ways, the most influential writers draw on indigenous resources – mythological systems, proverbs, and other oral rhetorical modes – to give their work a flavor of "African-ness." The Ghanaian novelist Ayi Kwei Armah, for instance, invokes ancestral raconteurs in the epic mode at pivotal moments of his novel *The Healers* (1978). In *Petals of Blood* (1977), Ngũgi wa Thiong'o from Kenya blends the third-person narrative voice with a collective one that recalls the rhetoric of a griot telling the panoramic story of an entire society's adventure in history. Nigeria's Gabriel Okara uses a kind of English that strives to reproduce the speech-patterns of his native Ijaw language in *The Voice* (1964). And Ahmadou Kourouma's *Les Soleils des indépendances* (1968; translated as *The Suns of Independence*) is written in French that bears the creolized trace of the writer's native language, Malinke. In *Season of Migration to the North* (1969), originally written in Arabic, Sudanese Tayib Salih creates a novel that exploits a form shared by the European novels and the Arabic narrative traditions. This form is called the "frame story" or "the-story-within-a-story." Using it enables Salih to comment on Joseph Conrad's *Heart of Darkness* – a novella that is well-known for its own use of a framing device – by rewriting features of Conrad's text from an African's perspective.

There are countless other examples. What they generally indicate is the attempt by the writers to create literary texts that speak to contemporary concerns in ways that carry signs of African settings and priorities. An ongoing debate in the study of African literatures is the extent to which the formal experimentation we have been outlining is indeed "African," if by that one means some unique quality to be found *only* in works by people who happen to be African by birth. The hard-wired determinism (referred to by critics as "essentialism") that such a notion of African-ness implies has been rejected by some critics, and others have criticized it as being empirically unfounded. These critiques have been necessary and valuable. For our purposes, what needs to be stressed is that the writers *claim* this uniqueness principally because they seek to celebrate African cultural traditions by recognizing it in and through language. Looked at this way, the notion of something called "authentic African-ness" is actually part of the rhetorical strategy the writers are using to announce their respect for African cultures.

Beginning from the mid-1960s many newly independent African countries started experiencing political problems, which subsequently intensified – bloody military coups d'état, civil wars, eruptions of sectarian violence, civilian and military dictatorships. These developments were accompanied by serious economic challenges, leading in some cases to stagnation. Many nominally independent African states maintain neo-colonial relations with Western powers, often to the benefit of the ruling classes. One consequence of these failures was widespread corruption and cynicism at all levels of society. Indeed, in some countries the state virtually collapsed in everything but name and superficial appearances.

African literature kept pace with these painful developments. Chinua Achebe's writing shifts from the optimism of the immediate independence era of the 1950s and 1960s, when the impulse was to affirm and defend things African from Western condescension, to the moment of disillusionment, when the politics of Nigeria turned sour. Achebe addressed the disillusionment in *A Man of the People*, *The Trouble With Nigeria* (an extended essay) and, in the 1980s, *Anthills of the Savannah*. Ngũgi's *Weep Not, Child* deals with the struggle for independence, and the state of emergency imposed on Kenya due to the armed rebellion of the Kenya Land and Freedom Army (usually referred to as the Mau Mau insurrection). By the time he wrote *A Grain of Wheat*, some critical anxiety about politicians in power surfaces. But Ngũgi still presents a measured optimistic vision for the future: an allusion to pregnancy in the novel's final moments points to the novelist's guarded optimism at this point. In *Petals of Blood*, *Devil on the Cross*, and *Matigari* the mood has completely changed, and what the novels give us are impassioned critiques of the rulers of Kenya and their complicity with imperialist interests. Most influential African writers show similar concerns with the political situations in their societies. Sony Labou Tansi (**Congo**), Wole Soyinka (Nigeria), Kofi Awoonor (Ghana), Jack Mapanje (**Malawi**), Mongo Béti (**Cameroon**), and Ousmane Sembene (Senegal) all wrote poetry, drama, or fiction against the societal ills that surrounded them. Many African writers were jailed, tortured, or forced into exile for speaking out against their governments.

The first generation of African writers and their immediate successors were predominantly male. Because of restricted access to education and prejudices about gender roles, it took longer for women to gain acceptance into the public sphere and begin to fully participate in defining political and intellectual directions for post-colonial Africa. Despite this formidable obstacle, African women have always contributed significantly to the traditions of writing on the continent. The work of female writers compels a reassessment of the assumptions of many male writers about the role of women in society and culture. Female writers direct attention to the subtle ways in which notions of cultural wholeness or resistance to political oppression often take a gendered form. Thanks to this gendered way of thinking about or representing culture, women are posited as embodiments of society's health and regeneration. Evidence of this representational ideology can be seen in the figure – common in male-authored texts – of the biologically and ontologically pre-programmed "mother"; of earthy, fecund Africa threatened by colonialist rape; or of the wife whose conformity to religiously sanctioned decorum is effected by her self-effacement. Female writers contest these figurations of femininity, rejecting the tendency to present male concerns as if these translated into the concerns of a universal "African" self. Instead the female writers place at center-stage the specific issues confronting women in colonial and contemporary Africa. For them, colonialism often colludes with the patriarchal oppression internal to many traditional African cultures. Thus the Senegalese novelist Mariama Bâ writes in *So Long a Letter* (1981) of the ways in which Islamic tenets, traditional Wolof caste-hierarchies, and European notions of modernization and bourgeois success interact to constrain women. In Zimbabwean Tsitsi

Dangarembga's first novel, entitled *Nervous Conditions* (1988), she pointedly locates two young girls and their mothers at the center of the narrative. In so doing the novel redresses the tendency to use female characters only as appendages or abstract symbols in male-authored texts about cultural progress or muscular nationalist struggles. Writers like Flora Nwapa (Nigeria), Ama Ata Aidoo (Ghana), Grace Ogot (Kenya), Ken Bugul (Senegal) and Bessie Head (Botswana) have thus added to the harvest of literary production in black Africa. In North Africa one can also cite the work of Algerian Assia Djebar and Nawal El-Saadawi of Egypt. Using different languages – the former French and the latter Arabic – both have focused on the plight and resilience of Arab women within the ferment of decolonization and modernization.

Literatures on the move

The second half of the twentieth century brought the intellectual current known as postmodernism. In Western literatures this was translated into highly experimental writing in the different genres. Many African writers participate in this trend. The works of J.M. Coetzee of South Africa bear the trace of postmodernism, as do the writings of Abdelkebir Khatibi of **Morocco**. The iconoclastic sensibility and fervid prose style of the late Dambudzo Marechera are often characterized as postmodernist, but it is useful to set his work against the background of black disempowerment in **Zimbabwe**. African writers based in European countries continue to make their mark: Nigeria's Ben Okri won the Booker Prize in 1991, and Moroccan Tahar Ben Jelloun's *La Nuit sacrée* (1987; *The Sacred Night*, 1989) won the prestigious Prix Goncourt in France in 1987. The anti-apartheid literature of South Africans Ezekiel Mphaphlele, Lewis Nkosi, Alex La Guma, André Brink, Nadine Gordimer, and Mongane Serote testifies to literature's capacity to educate the literate world against evil. The post-apartheid era has already yielded some reflective thinking from writers, as is evidenced in novels like *The House Gun* (1998) by Gordimer, who won the Nobel Prize for Literature in 1991. She was the third African to do so, after Soyinka in 1986 and Mahfouz in 1988. Beyond the decolonization era, after the heroic wars to rid lusophone Africa of Portuguese colonialism, and after the defeat of apartheid, literature remains on the move, and African writers on the watch.

Any panoramic discussion of African literature inevitably has to make broad sweeps, thereby leaving out some vectors and stressing others. In the academic study of African literatures the stress tends to be on literature written in the European languages. It is also the case that, because of the global influence of English and French, as opposed to Portuguese, the best-known writers are those who write in English and, less so, French. Likewise, because of the racism of nineteenth-century European scholarship – the intellectual tradition that dominates knowledge-production in the humanities and sciences – the tendency to bifurcate Africa into "North Africa," associated with Islamic/Arabic civilization, and "sub-Saharan Africa," associated with the black race, persists. We need to guard against this in principle, but also seek alternatives to it in critical practice.

Academic alternatives to deal with this situation cannot come easily. One step in the right direction is to see African literatures as, first and foremost, an activity of human minds grounded in concrete social contexts. Artists and their productions are always in motion, often ahead of academic discourses about them. For this reason scholarly criticism needs to keep reassessing its tools in order to keep up with the vibrancy of the literature. For now, because of the diversity of linguistic traditions on the continent and even within specific countries, research on particular linguistic traditions can be disseminated to a broader audience if the research is communicated in the dominant European languages. Clearly we need more research and greater cross-fertilization of information between scholars of the various languages and regional literatures. Developing or strengthening scholarly discourses in the various languages, indigenous and foreign, is also crucial. For this will contribute to the ideal of sustaining literature and criticism in the various languages, and making the fruits of this enterprise available across languages and regions.

See also: intellectuals: colonial; theater; visual arts

Further reading

Davies, C.B. and Graves, A.A. (eds.) (1990) *Ngambika: Studies of Women in African Literature*, Trenton: Africa World Press Inc.

Irele, A. (1991) "African Letters: The Making of a Tradition," *The Yale Journal of Criticism* 5, 1: 69–100.

Julien, E. (1995) "African Literature," in P.M. Martin and P. O'Meara (eds.), *Africa*, 3rd edn., Bloomington and Indianapolis: Indiana University Press.

Owomoyela, O. (ed.) *A History of Twentieth-Century African Literatures*, Lincoln and London: University of Nebraska Press.

Said, E.W. (1993) *Culture and Imperialism*, New York: Alfred A. Knopf.

OLAKUNLE GEORGE

Lome, Togo

Lome is the capital city of the small West African country **Togo**. Located in the southwestern corner of the country, Lome lies on the Atlantic coast immediately east of the border between Togo and **Ghana**. While the city's ethnic diversity has increased throughout the twentieth century, the Ewe continue to be Lome's most populous ethnic group. Estimations of the city's population for the 1990s vary widely, from 366,476 to 750,000, out of Togo's total population of 5 million. The discrepancy in Lome's population statistics may be partially explained by the exodus of approximately one-third of the capital's inhabitants to neighboring Ghana in 1993, after political violence and social unrest erupted as a result of Togo's severe economic collapse. Many of those who fled gradually returned in the years that followed, which meant Lome's population has been in constant flux through the 1990s.

The Germans selected Lome as the colonial capital of German Togoland just prior to the beginning of the twentieth century. During the period of German colonial rule Lome's infrastructure was significantly developed. By 1904 the colony's only major port was built in Lome, and construction of an extensive railway system linking the capital to various points in the hinterland followed shortly thereafter, along with communication networks, including postal, telegraph, and telephone services. As a result, Lome's commercial importance continued to eclipse that of other trading centers along Togo's coast.

In 1914 the French and British, who were subsequently to partition the colony, invaded German Togoland. After the conclusion of the **First World War** the partition's legitimacy was confirmed during the Paris Peace Conference of 1919: The French took possession of Lome, which remained the colonial capital of French Togoland. Lome's importance as the colony's pre-eminent commercial center continued under French rule. In the years following the **Second World War** the rapid growth of the export economy led to a quick rise in the city's population, as migrants from other regions in southern Togo flocked to Lome.

In April 1960, when Togo won its independence from France, Lome became the national capital. By the late 1960s Lome's commercial expansion had been given a powerful boost by growing limestone and phosphate exports, which funded the modernization of Lome's port and the development of the city's infrastructure to an unprecedented level. Within a span of five years (1967–72) Lome witnessed the development of new governmental, business, and industrial facilities; a central market; and Togo's first university. While Togo's main exports (cocoa, palm nuts, cotton, and coffee) all passed through Lome's port, processed foods and textiles were the primary products manufactured in Lome. Lome's industrious market women controlled the wholesale textile trade, and also formed a powerful constituency in national politics.

From the 1980s Lome became the site of ongoing conflict surrounding the presidency of General Etienne Gnassingbe Eyadema, who came to power in 1963 after leading a successful coup that resulted in the assassination of Togo's first president, Sylvanus Olympio. Tensions escalated during the 1980s when Togo's economy collapsed, and were further exacerbated by the **structural adjustment program** implemented by the Eyadema government in the early 1990s. Widespread dissatisfaction with the Eyadema regime and its policies led to a series of crippling strikes and riots in Lome. At the close of the twentieth century sociopolitical unrest continued to surface in Lome as a direct consequence of Eyadema's unwillingness to relinquish the presidency.

Further reading

Decalo, S. (1996) *Historical Dictionary of Togo*, Lanham: Scarecrow Press.

CARINA E. RAY

Luanda, Angola

Luanda is the capital of **Angola**, a country located in the western region of **Southern Africa**. It is the country's largest city, with a population of over 2 million. Luanda is also an industrial and commercial hub, as well as being the second most important port in Angola.

It was founded by Paulo Dias de Novais, who arrived on the island of Loanda in February 1575 with seven ships, carrying 4000 soldiers and 100 families. His arrival marked the beginning of the Portuguese colonization of Angola. In the following year they moved across to the mainland and established a settlement, São Paulo, which later became Luanda. The Portuguese were soon involved in the slave trade, using the city as an assembly and departure point for slave ships heading to Brazil, their main trading partner. Luanda was the first city to be founded by Europeans on the west coast of sub-Saharan Africa; twenty-two years later it became the administrative center of the colony.

At the beginning Luanda was not attractive to the Portuguese. The climate was harsh, and the city had little to offer. It had no paved roads until 1779, and no running water until a century after that. The population of the city was small. Four years after the abolition of the slave trade in 1836, the colonial authority opened Luanda to foreign shipping and promoted the export of raw materials. By 1850 there were many trading companies, exporting palm and groundnut oil, ivory, cotton, and coffee.

During the first seventy years of the twentieth century Luanda was a magnet to Portuguese and Africans alike. Africans left rural areas and went to the city to improve their standard of living, residing with other Africans who had been evicted from the city center to make room for the ever-increasing Portuguese population. Portuguese citizens, fleeing poverty in Portugal itself, came to Angola to make their fortunes, setting up their own business ventures or simply seeking employment.

Between the 1950s and 1970s the city grew rapidly, with its population reaching 200,000. With the increased population, new neighborhoods (such as Vila Clotilde, Vila Alice, Praia de Bispo, Mimar, and Quinaxixi) sprung up. Rising coffee prices on the world market generated more revenue for urban development. More than 1,000 new industrial companies were established, and most of the hotels in Luanda were built during this period. The increased revenue enabled the colonial government to settle more Portuguese in the colony. By 1970 there were two Europeans to every five Africans in Luanda, making the community unique in its blend of races, customs, and cultures.

Following independence in 1975 Luanda experienced severe economic hardship because of two factors: the exodus of Portuguese settlers, who had controlled the economy, and the insurgency by the National Union for the Total Independence of Angola (UNITA), which threw the country into a civil war. During the conflict the capital experienced sporadic blackouts and water shortages caused by rebel attacks. Many rural people, dislocated by the fighting, came to Luanda, causing a rise in unemployment and crime.

The end of the fighting in 1990 raised hopes that peace would be restored in the country, putting Luanda on the road to recovery. UNITA's Jonas Savimbi refused, however, to accept the results of the first democratic elections in 1992, and took the country back to war. His failure to fully implement the Lusaka Protocol (1994) led to the collapse of the peace process in 1998, and again placed Luanda on a collision course with UNITA. Savimbi was killed by government soldiers in February 2002.

Further reading

Palanque, L. (1997) *Angola: A Fabulous Country*, Luanda: LPE International.

M.A. EL-KHAWAS

Lubumbashi, Democratic Republic of Congo

After **Kinshasa**, Lubumbashi is the largest industrial and commercial city in the **Democratic Republic of Congo** (DRC). It is also the principal administrative center of the DRC's southeastern province of Katanga. Most importantly Lubumbashi is the copper capital, with Gécamines – formerly the Union Minière de Haut Katanga (UMHK), which was created in 1906 – the city's most important economic venture. Indeed Lubumbashi used to be called the "African Ruhr." The city is currently estimated to have more than a million inhabitants.

Lubumbashi was founded in 1910 under the name Elisabethville. Within a year the population had grown from 360 to 1,000 inhabitants. To develop mining the UMHK aggressively recruited labor from Katanga and Kasai, and from neighboring territories, especially **Zambia**. With mining development on the Zambian Copperbelt, the number of Zambian workers began to decrease so that, as early as 1898, an effort was being made to recruit labor from Ruanda-Urundi (see **Burundi**; **Rwanda**), and even as far afield as **Malawi** and **West Africa**.

Of the approximately 8,000 people who lived in Elisabethville after the **First World War**, 12 percent were white and 88 percent African. In 1920 management of the Union Minière was transferred from the British to the Belgians. This affected the regions from which labor was recruited, with the Belgians favoring the regions of Lomami and Lubilash. Completion of the Katanga–Port-Francqui railroad in 1928 consolidated this tendency. At the end of the 1920s two separate social environments coexisted in Elisabethville: The black population was segregated from whites, living either in the city or in Union Minière mining camps. Camp inhabitants lived in relatively better conditions, but were subject to hard work and heavy social controls. Benedictine missionaries provided social and educational services. Between 1945 and 1957 the European population grew from 5,000 to 13,000, while the black population grew from 70,000 to 170,000.

During the Katangese secession after independence, Elisabethville was the secessionist capital. The antagonism between the city's two largest ethnic groups was underlined by their political stance: Those from Kasai favored intervention from the United Nations, while those from Katanga sided with the secessionists. Many Kasaians returned to Kasai, fleeing ethnic cleansing. With the end of hostilities, between 1964 and 1975 the city's population grew from 250,000 to 400,000. Meanwhile in 1971, under the Mobutist policy of authenticity (sometimes referred to as "Zaireanization"), Elisabethville became Lubumbashi.

Though mining continued to be Lubumbashi's most important economic activity, the Lushois increasingly owed their survival to the informal economy, which was dominated by petty commerce in basic foodstuffs. According to the International Bureau of Trade (IBT), as early as 1986 14,945 petty traders supported 120,000 households. This represented 2.2 percent of the IBT's sample, which also included artisans who handled malachite, ironworkers, welders, weavers, and copperworkers.

Katangese in origin, Laurent Kabila resided in Lubumbashi during his so-called "war of liberation." From this city he signed agreements on mining rights with foreign companies, even though the rebellion had not taken control of the DRC. While in power Kabila wanted to give Lubumbashi a political status that would rival that of Kinshasa, which is why he installed the transitionary parliament's constitutive and legislative assembly (ACL-PT) in Lubumbashi in August 2000.

Lubumbashi is part of the historic "copperbelt" that nourished the colonists and sustained the railroad to South Africa. Given its history, resources, and geographic location, the city will continue in the future, as in the past, to be an object of greed throughout the region – and indeed the world.

Further reading

Fetter, B. (1976) *The Creation of Elizabethville*, Stanford: Hoover Institution Press, Stanford University.

Ndaywel è Nziem (1997) *Histoire de Zaire: de l'héritage*

ancien à l'âge contemporaine, Louvain-la-Neuve: Duculot.

GERTRUDE MIANDA

Lusaka, Zambia

Lusaka, the capital city of **Zambia** and regional capital of Lusaka province, had an estimated population of 1.7 million people in 2000. The city was founded in the 1890s in the center of the new colony of Northern Rhodesia, which was established by the British South African Company, and it was named after the area's village headman: Lusakas. The town's rapid growth began after the capital was moved from Livingstone to Lusaka in 1935. Lusaka was chosen because of its central location in the colony: It was connected by rail to both Southern Rhodesia and the mines of the Copperbelt. Its flat terrain and abundant underground rivers also made it ideal. The colonial government appointed a professor of town and country planning from the University of London to plan the layout and expansion of the city, although the city experienced haphazard growth as rural migration accelerated and peri-urban settlements were incorporated.

Lusaka's importance as an administrative, political, economic, and cultural center grew during the last two decades of colonial rule. The city benefited from the booming copper-driven economy. Moreover the **nationalist movement** centered their activities in Lusaka, along with the Copperbelt towns where Zambia's strong **labor movements** were based. Lusaka experienced its fastest growth after Zambia achieved independence in 1964, and controls on the influx of people were lifted. The early post-independence years were also marked by rapid economic development, some of which found its way into Lusaka in the form of construction of new housing, offices, and hotels, as well import substitution manufacturing industries. The city's population doubled within five years. It had previously (from the 1930s to the 1950s) been the main Copperbelt towns of Ndola, Kitwe, Mufulira, and Luanshya that had attracted massive migration from rural areas.

The city became increasingly cosmopolitan as it attracted residents from various parts of Zambia and the neighboring countries, as well as Europe and Asia. Lusaka's regional significance grew as liberation movements from **Angola**, **Mozambique**, **Namibia**, **South Africa**, and **Zimbabwe** set up their headquarters or regional offices in the city. It was there, for example, that consultations between the African National Congress and representatives of the South African apartheid state were held, which eventually led to the negotiations within South Africa itself that resulted in the demise of apartheid. It was also in Lusaka that the crucial 1979 **Commonwealth** summit was held, at which a settlement for Rhodesia's independence was negotiated. Cairo Road, Lusaka's main street, was a daily reminder of Cecil Rhodes' imperial legacy; especially his dream of building a railway from the Cape to **Cairo**, but it also represented Pan-Africanism and an appreciation of contribution by **Egypt** to **decolonization** in Zambia.

The fortunes of Lusaka declined as the economy went into a prolonged slump following the collapse of copper prices in the mid-1970s, and the imposition of **structural adjustment programs** in the 1980s. Despite this the city's population continued to grow rapidly, which resulted in acute shortages of employment, housing, and other social amenities. By the 1990s over half of Lusaka's residents lived in informal or irregular housing, while at the same time new shopping malls were sprouting in city. Not surprisingly Lusaka was at the center of the protest movement that led to the introduction of multiparty politics in the 1990s. In the meantime the city continued to play an important regional role, becoming the headquarters of the **Common Market for Eastern and Southern Africa**. Lusaka was also home to the University of Zambia, and other important national cultural institutions.

Further reading

Hansen, K.T. (1997) *Keeping House in Lusaka*, New York: Columbia University Press.

ACKSON M. KANDUZA

lusophone Africa

Lusophone Africa consists of five African nations that are grouped together by shared linguistic and historical experience: **Angola**, **Cape Verde**, **Guinea-Bissau**, **Mozambique**, and **São Tomé and Príncipe**. They share the common colonial experience of Portuguese rule, against which they fought to gain independence. Portuguese is the official language of Angola and Mozambique, the only language spoken in São Tomé and Príncipe, and the common language in Cape Verde and Guinea-Bissau.

In the late 1950s African nationalists in Angola and Guinea-Bissau talked about cooperating to free their countries from colonialism. In Paris in 1957 they formed the Anti-Colonialist Movement, which evolved into the Frente Revolucionaria Africana para a Independência Nacional (African Front for National Independence or FRAIN) in 1960. They later founded the Conference des Organisations Nationalistes des Colonies Portugaises (Conference of the Nationalist Organizations of the Portuguese Colonies or CONCP) in Algiers. This organization functioned as a coordinating body across the colonies, especially after the outbreak of armed struggle in Angola in 1961, in Guinea-Bissau in 1963, and in Mozambique in 1964. Although the liberation struggle in each colony stemmed from local circumstances and largely remained national, the members influenced each other's thinking and the timing for initiating armed struggle. In 1965 their leaders held the first conference of CONCP in **Dar es Salaam**. They exchanged information about the struggle, and planned to work together against the common enemy, Portugal, which was determined to maintain its colonies.

The Popular Movement for the Liberation of Angola (MPLA), the Partido Africano da Independência do Guinée e Cabo Verde (African Party for the Independence of Guinea and Cape Verde or PAIGC) and the Frente de Libertação de Moçambique (Front for the Liberation of Mozambique or FRELIMO) were revolutionary movements with similar ideologies. They advocated the use of Marxism, with some adaptations for African conditions, as a development strategy in the post-colonial period. They were supported by the Soviet bloc, but unsuccessful in attracting financial and material assistance from the West, which sided with Portugal – a NATO member.

During the 1960s and 1970s each colony fought its own war of liberation at its own pace, forcing the Portuguese to fight three wars simultaneously. These wars were costly, leading to growing opposition among Portugal's civilian population and the military. In April 1974 the Portuguese army overthrew their government, and proceeded to dismantle the empire.

The last meeting of CONCP was held in the capital of Mozambique in November 1974. Their final act was to support the MPLA, which was now fighting against a pro-Western faction backed by forces from **South Africa** and Zaire (now **Democratic Republic of Congo**). In a show of solidarity Mozambique and Guinea-Bissau sent troops to defend **Luanda**. Once the Portuguese colonies gained independence, the CONCP ceased to exist.

Between 1975 and 1978 the newly independent countries were busy getting their affairs in order and meeting the challenges of national reconstruction. Although the transition to independence went smoothly in Guinea-Bissau, Cape Verde, Mozambique, and São Tomé, it was turbulent in Angola. The MPLA had to fight insurgency supported by South Africa and the United States. Shortly afterwards Mozambique also found itself fighting rebels, armed by Rhodesia and again by South Africa.

There was an attempt to revive the CONCP or a similar organization in 1978. It was spearheaded by Guinea-Bissau's President Luís Cabral, who believed that cooperation was essential for development and a safeguard against external domination. Opposition came from Mozambique's President Samora Machel, who saw no reason for an association based on a language. But Cabral convinced Angola's President Agostinho Neto to host a meeting in Luanda in June 1979. They agreed to adopt identical development plans, to support African liberation struggles, and to set up a ministerial committee.

In March 1980 the group, including Angola's new president, José Eduardo dos Santos, met in **Maputo**. They agreed to meet annually, and scheduled the next meeting in Guinea-Bissau. Their plan was interrupted when Cabral was overthrown by a coup in November 1980. This was a major loss, because he had been the force that brought the group back together. With the situation getting worse in Guinea-Bissau and Cape Verde, a meeting was held in Luanda in December 1980. Guinea-Bissau did not attend. The other leaders sent a delegation to **Bissau** to ensure the safety and release of Cabral and other detainees. They also reaffirmed the necessity of preserving the cohesion that had been forged during the years of struggle. Machel was able to bring about a reconciliation between Guinea- Bissau and Cape Verde, which paved the way for the heads of state to meet in Praia, Cape Verde, in September 1982.

The group's most important meeting was held in Bissau in December 1983, where they discussed specific steps to institutionalize cooperation. They agreed to create a common bank, joint arrangements for air and sea traffic, joint training of personnel in various sectors, and common political positions at the international level. They also rejected a Portuguese proposal to institutionalize cooperation between the five African states, Brazil, and Portugal.

In April 1984 the group met in Maputo to discuss the non-aggression pact (the N'Komati Accords) between Mozambique and South Africa, and US efforts to get South Africa to pull troops out of southern Angola. As a result of this meeting there was better coordination between Luanda and Maputo. Both faced similar problems, stemming from external support for rebel groups in their countries.

The group kept meeting and adopting joint stances on issues of concern, including the criticism of Portugal for giving Angolan and Mozambican rebels access to the media, but in 1986 there was another setback, with the untimely death of Machel, who had dominated the group's work in the 1980s. Although the member-countries still wanted to cooperate, there was not much they could do to help each other because of their physical separation, differences in size and resources, and internal conflicts. With the collapse of the Soviet Union, aid from Moscow came to an end, forcing the governments of the lusophone countries to reconsider their socialist ideology. So, with the demise of communism, they began to introduce political and economic reforms in order to receive foreign aid from the West to fix their ailing economies.

Further reading

Cabral, A. (1969) *Revolution in Guinea*, New York: Monthly Review Press.

M.A. EL-KHAWAS

Madagascar

Madagascar has a total land area of 587,040 square kilometers, making it Africa's largest island. It is located in the Indian Ocean, east of **Mozambique**, and had an estimated population of 17.3 million in 2000. At the beginning of the twentieth century Madagascar was under French colonial rule, although resistance persisted until after the **First World War**. French officials held all political power, but they depended on Malagasies, who were only permitted to hold low-level government positions, to uphold colonial rule. The economy was based on export crops such as cotton, coffee, tobacco, rice, vanilla, cloves, and cocoa. Those Malagasies who accepted French culture and pledged their loyalty to France were considered assimilated, and education and social services were provided for them. However, they constituted a very small percentage of the population (only 8,000 in 1939) and the majority of people lived under harsh conditions. During the **Second World War** anti-colonial resistance was rekindled. The war caused a deepening of rural poverty, forcing many people to seek economic opportunities in urban areas. France's defeat in 1940 left the island under the control of the Vichy regime, which further fueled anti-colonial sentiments. In an effort to prevent Japan from using the harbor at Diego Suarez, Great Britain invaded Madagascar in 1942, but returned the island to the Free French government in 1943.

Nationalist agitation against French rule continued after the end of the Second World War, with ex-servicemen playing a leading role. The 1946 French constitution designated Madagascar an overseas territory, with limited powers for provincial assemblies and the representation of Malagasies in the French parliament. These concessions were not enough to quell the push for independence by the Democratic Movement for the Reconstruction of Madagascar, a new party that had the support of the Merina ethnic group that constituted 27 percent of the population. The colonial government conducted a campaign to destroy the party. An armed revolt broke out in the eastern part of the colony that later spread throughout the country, but it was crushed by a combination of military force and starvation brought about by a blockade of rebel-held areas in August 1947. Some 80,000 people were killed, and many more were imprisoned.

By the end of the 1950s, however, independence was on the horizon. In 1956 the French ended military rule, permitting people to engage in political activities, and a new party was established, called the Parti Social Démocrate (Social Democratic Party or PSD). This party was formed by progressive members of the Parti des déshérités de Madagascar (PADESM) – a party of coastal peoples, known as *côtiers* – who were opposed to immediate independence in the 1940s. In 1957 the remaining prisoners from the 1947 revolt were released. The following year Madagascar was voted into the French Community, and granted self-government. Philibert Tsiranana, the leader of PSD, was elected president in 1959. In 1960 indirect French rule was brought to an end, full independence granted, and the Malagasy Republic came into existence. Independence from France did not bring political stability, however, as ethnicity continued to define political parties: the PSD represented members of non-Merina ethnic groups, while Richard Andriamanjato, a Merina and mayor of **Antananarivo**, led the leftist Congress Party for the Independence of Madagascar.

In 1975 the economy suffered after the government nationalized the shipping, oil-refining, and mineral sectors, along with a leading French-owned trading company. In addition natural disasters, poor rural roads, the attempt to force peasants onto cooperatives and state farms, and a lack of investment in the rural sector adversely affected the economy. The production of food and export crops declined after 1975, with the exception of cotton. A severe drought in the late 1970s and early 1980s also exacerbated problems in the economy, crippling the main source of export earnings. Many people migrated to urban areas in search of economic opportunities, resulting in an increase in urban unemployment, unrest, and violence.

In the 1980s the economy grew slowly, rural areas experienced further unrest, and students protested against various government actions. As the government tried to suppress these protests, other opposition groups were formed, including the National Movement for the Independence of Madagascar, led by Monja Jaona. At first the group's main supporters were farmers from the southwestern part of the country, where the unrest had started; however, it began to gain the support of students and others in urban areas. Tsiranana was reelected in January 1972, but the violence did not stop and he relinquished power in May 1972. His successor was General Gabriel Ramanantsoa, who adopted nationalist foreign and economic policies, but his military rule solved neither the country's economic problems nor ethnic discord in the government (including the armed forces). In the 1970s and 1980s Madagascar had witnessed political leaders come and go through coups, the transfer of power, or political assassinations. The Supreme Revolutionary Council (SRC) was formed in 1975 under the leadership of Lieutenant-Commander Didier Ratsiraka, a *côtier* who nationalized various sectors of the economy.

During the final decade of the twentieth century Madagascar experienced severe environmental, political, and economic problems, but reforms were implemented in the wake of civil unrest. In 1990 democratic reforms were instituted. The government agreed to hold multi-party elections, which took place in 1992 and 1993. Madagascar also came under pressure from the International Monetary Fund to liberalize its economy. The Democratic Republic of Madagascar was still experiencing political instability at the end of the twentieth century, and was one of the world's poorest countries, with the vast majority of its population residing in rural areas. The economy was disproportionately dependent on export revenues from the agricultural sector, constituting 78 percent of gross domestic product. There was an abundance of minerals (topaz, garnet, chromite, mica, and graphite), but they were not economically exploited. With the discovery of natural gas and petroleum, an expansion in the fishing, forestry, and mining sectors, and one of Africa's highest literacy rates, the future of Madagascar is, however, promising.

Further reading

Covell, M. (1987) *Madagascar: Politics, Economics and Society*, London: Frances Pinter.

Feeley-Harnik, G.A. (1991) *Green Estate: Restoring Independence in Madagascar*, Washington, D.C.: Smithsonian Press.

CASSANDRA RACHEL VENEY

Maghreb *see* Algeria; Libya; Morocco; North Africa; Tunisia

Malawi

Malawi covers an area of 118,840 square kilometers, and is bordered by **Mozambique**, **Tanzania**, and **Zambia**. It had an estimated population of 12 million in 2000. Becoming a British protectorate in 1891, it was called Nyasaland from 1907, but was renamed Malawi – the name of an ancient kingdom there – after independence in 1964. The establishment of colonialism was preceded by the arrival of Christian missionaries, including David Livingstone, who called for colonization to facilitate evangelization. Cecil Rhodes' British South African Company also expressed interest in the territory, and had in fact been granted a charter in 1889. The establishment of colonial rule met with considerable resistance, especially from the Yao, Chewa, and Ngoni.

As British colonization of Malawi intensified in the early 1900s, and the number of European settlers increased, African resistance resumed. Much of the resistance was centered in the southern highlands, where settlers had seized African lands. In 1915 the Reverend John Chilembwe, who had received a college education in the United States, organized an uprising against the British, leading an attack on a large estate that resulted in the death of some whites. Chilembwe resented the poor treatment of African laborers on settler estates. In the following year, when Africans began to be conscripted into British army service in the **First World War**, Chilembwe's protests became more vocal, culminating in an uprising that was quickly crushed by the colonial authorities. Chilembwe fled, but was soon killed by colonial officers.

The 1920s and 1930s saw the consolidation of colonial rule throughout Malawi. A colonial economy and a rudimentary infrastructure were established. Most importantly the number of European agricultural plantations grew quickly, centered on coffee, tea, and tobacco production. To force Africans to work on these plantations, a form of forced labor known as *thangata* and various taxes were introduced, including the "hut tax." Due to harsh working conditions and low wages on the plantations many Malawians chose to migrate to more prosperous countries in the region, especially Southern Rhodesia (**Zimbabwe**) and **South Africa**. In fact there were soon as many Malawian migrant workers as there were Malawians working at home. In the meantime Malawi attracted Lomwe migrants, who were fleeing harsh Portuguese rule in neighboring Mozambique.

Between the 1920s and 1940s modern nationalism began to emerge, as elite Africans formed pressure groups called "native associations" whose aim was improvements in social and economic conditions. However, after the **Second World War** the nationalists began to talk openly of independence. The Nyasaland African Congress (NAC) was formed in 1944. It demanded colonial reforms and African representation on the Legislative Council. In the late 1940s and early 1950s the NAC was also vehemently opposed to the proposed federation of Rhodesia and Nyasaland, which was nonetheless established in 1953. Real power in the **Central African Federation**, as the nationalists had feared, lay with the settlers of Southern Rhodesia and, to a lesser extent, Northern Rhodesia (Zambia). These settlers were keen to strengthen their power against both apartheid South Africa to the south and potentially African-dominated states to the north.

The NAC was boosted by the return in 1958, after more than forty years abroad, of the charismatic Hastings Banda, who assumed leadership and quickly transformed the Congress into a mass movement. In 1959 riots broke out; Dr. Banda was arrested and jailed, together with some of his lieutenants, and a state of emergency declared. But it soon became clear to the British government that the federation could not be maintained. Forced to begin negotiating the end of colonial rule with Dr. Banda, they released him from jail in 1960. Banda became prime minister at independence in 1964, and the country's first president in 1966. In 1971 Dr. Banda proclaimed himself president-for-life, and he ruled Malawi as a dictator with the Malawi Congress Party (the NAC's successor) the country's sole political party. Unlike many of his neighbors Banda was a firm advocate of capitalist development, encouraging foreign capital investment, especially from Britain, Taiwan, the United States, and South Africa. Malawi established diplomatic relations with South Africa too, which isolated the country in African circles. Banda supported the plantation sector, even encouraging his ministers to acquire them, forcing peasants off the land. Facilities such as education and health were low priorities, while roads and railways serving plantations received the bulk of capital investment.

The end of Dr. Banda's dictatorship came in 1992 when Catholic bishops released a pastoral letter condemning Banda, touching off demonstrations throughout the country. Donor countries also cut off all non-humanitarian aid until Banda agreed to democratize the political system. A referendum on the introduction of multi-party politics was conducted throughout the country in 1993 in which over 67 percent of the votes were cast in favor of a new democratic system of government. Banda was subsequently voted out of power in the first multi-party elections in 1994. He died in 1997, at ninety-nine years of age, having ruled Malawi for thirty years.

The general election of 1994 brought the end of dictatorship, and the introduction of a democratic government led by Bakili Muluzi of the United Democratic Party. Muluzi immediately freed prisoners and reestablished freedom of speech and association, and the freedom of the press. Despite the country's ongoing economic and social problems, Muluzi won over 50 percent of the vote in the second presidential elections in 1999. Although multi-party democracy had been introduced, Malawi still faced many challenges, including out-of-control inflation, a severe economic crisis, soaring unemployment, malnutrition, HIV/AIDS, and rising crime. Running a multi-party democratic system under these dire circumstances did not prove easy: By 2000 some factions in the United Democratic Front were openly campaigning for return to one-party rule, and for Muluzi to be allowed to stand for a third presidential term when the constitution permitted only two terms.

Further reading

McDonald, R. (ed.) (1975) *From Nyasaland to Malawi: Studies in Colonial History*, Nairobi: East African Publishing House.

Phiri, K.M. and Ross, K.R. (eds.) (1998) *Democratization in Malawi: A Stock Taking*, Blantyre: Christian Literature Association in Malawi.

EZEKIEL KALIPENI

Mali

Mali covers an area of 1.24 million square kilometers, and is bordered by **Algeria**, **Niger**, **Burkina Faso**, **Côte d'Ivoire**, **Guinea**, **Senegal**, and **Mauritania**. It had an estimated population of 12.6 million in 2000. Malians are proud descendants of a series of ancient states, including the empires of Songhai and Mali, and the Bamana kingdoms of Segou and Kaarta. The famous Malian city of Timbuctoo played an important role during centuries of trans-Saharan trade, and served as a crossroads for cultural exchange between **North Africa** and **West Africa**. In the late nineteenth century, inspired in part by the allure of Timbuctoo, French military forces invaded the area and established a colonial presence. In 1894 they built a fort at **Bamako**, at that time a small trading community of several hundred people living on the banks of the Niger River. A century later Bamako had a population of close to a million.

Regional leaders, such as Samori Touré, proved to be formidable obstacles to French expansion. However, through a combination of treaties and treachery, the French proceeded to annex a vast inland territory. By 1920 the bulk of contemporary Mali was constituted as a discrete colony: the French Soudan. Through taxation, forced labor, and production quotas the French compelled agricultural commercialization in the hope of generating revenues for the metropole. They focused on cotton, groundnuts, and rice crops. Overall they had limited success. While farmers integrated cash-crop production into their well-established production systems, they typically only did so to a minimal extent. Despite an initial "civilizing" rhetoric there was relatively little activity on the Western side of the colonial ledger: few schools were built, few clinics or hospitals were established, and few local people were integrated into the French administrative structure or national culture. However, several thousand Soudanese did fight on the side of their colonial rulers in the **First** and **Second World Wars**. By mid-century the colonial state was on unsteady ground: The French dream of a lucrative inland empire was largely unrealized, and local political figures (such as Mamadou Konaté and Modibo Keita) had begun promoting a nationalist agenda in the French National Assembly.

In 1958 the semi-independent Soudanese Republic emerged, and in 1959 joined with Senegal in the short-lived Mali Federation. On 22 September 1960 the independent Republic of Mali was established. Modibo Keita became president of the first republic, adopting a socialist program and establishing close contacts with the Soviet Union and China. Keita's centralized economic programs and parastatal industries failed to foster the kind of growth many newly independent citizens had hoped for, and his rigid focus on a collectivist social and cultural agenda gained him few allies. On 19 November 1968, on a rising tide of popular and elite dissatisfaction, army lieutenant Moussa Traoré overthrew Keita in a coup d'état. Traoré moved quickly to consolidate power, installing himself as president – a position he held until 1992. Throughout his tenure Traoré forbade any oppositional political presence. Indeed it was not until 1976 that he allowed the formation of the second republic's first and only political party, his Union Démocratique du Peuple Malien.

Traoré followed a rather opportunistic development agenda. He rekindled relations with France, and opened relations with the United States and Canada, all the while maintaining his connections with the Soviets and Chinese. He continued to look to state-run enterprises for economic development, encouraging expansion of cotton and groundnut production, and promoting new livestock programs. However, economic conditions failed to improve, and the standard of living for most citizens remained low. Meanwhile the country's international debt burden swelled. In the 1980s, to the dissatisfaction of thousands of government employees, Traoré implemented the **structural adjustment programs** put forward by the World Bank and International Monetary Fund. He chose, however, not to implement the political side of their liberalization agenda.

In the late 1980s students, trade unionists, and opposition political leaders ratcheted up their long-standing criticism of the regime. Traoré responded to pro-democracy protests and union strikes with militarization and violence. In March 1991 over 100 student protesters lost their lives at the hands of government forces, and protesters killed the Minister of Education and several other officials. A military coup on 26 March 1991 forcibly removed Traoré from power, and a transitional government announced a plan for prompt transition to multi-party democracy. By mid-June 1991 twenty-two political parties were registered, and spirited political dialogue ensued. On 26 April 1992 Alpha Omar Konaré, leader of the Alliance pour la Démocratie au Mali, was elected to a five-year term as president of the third republic. Konaré, a publisher and cultural affairs leader, embarked on a program to build regional and international connections, working to support diversified economic development and supporting the growth of **civil society**. In 1997 Malians reelected him to a second term.

With an annual per capita gross national product of approximately US$250 in 1998, Mali was one of the poorest countries in the world. At the end of the twentieth century pastoralist populations in the north were still struggling to make a living, with the ebb and flow of separatist violence having hindered growth in the region for decades. Agriculture was the primary economic activity, with cotton and groundnuts remaining the principle cash crops. However, commercial agriculture was still intertwined with cultivation of sorghum and millet for household consumption. A minor industrial sector existed, but it was largely limited to Bamako. Infant mortality rates were high, and life expectancy low. Only about one-fifth of children actually attended school. Clearly Mali faced significant hurdles in the future. However, the Malian people entered the new millennium with a pragmatic understanding of the difficult terrain ahead of them. They were actively engaged in the creation of their new democracy, in the formulation of novel economic activities, and in negotiating the demanding relationships that comprised their multi-ethnic world. In attempting to construct a promising future in this challenging time, the citizens of the Republic of Mali continually drew inspiration from the great achievements of their ancestors.

Further reading

Imperato, P.J. (1996) *Historical Dictionary of Mali*, Lanham: Scarecrow Press.

STEPHEN R. WOOTEN

manufacturing: indigenous

Indigenous manufacturing in Africa involves the use of local knowledge and techniques for the mechanical and chemical transformation of agricultural and environmental resources (including forests and minerals) into consumable products. These products usually range from processed foods and other agricultural materials to mining, buildings, utilitarian tools, and luxury goods. African indigenous manufacturing is, for the most part, based on low-impact technology and locally sourced skills, and the recruitment into a particular manufacturing venture is often based on the family/inherited traditions, aided by division of labor based on age, sex, and the kinship system. Indigenous manufacturers often operate within the micro-enterprises of the informal economic sector, and their businesses are usually launched with capital from private savings and/or relatives, with further capital for expansion coming mainly from reinvested profits. The historical trajectories of indigenous manufacturing in Africa during the twentieth century were impacted by the associated sociocultural transformations of colonial and post-colonial rule and political economy.

Before the colonial era indigenous artisans maintained small-scale industries that supplied and sustained the needs of their societies in processed-food products and beverages, soap, cloth, footwear, jewelry, domestic utensils, furniture, arts and crafts, and so on. The distribution of specific types of manufacturing activity and products associated with each region of Africa was largely determined by ecological conditions and the local availability of raw materials, the degree of interregional exchange of commodities, and cultural innovation. For example, leatherworks and tannery industries were generally found in savanna and sahelian areas that were favorable to animal husbandry, and were generally not seen in the rain-forest belt where environmental conditions were not favorable to raising animals on a large scale.

Transformations and continuity

The first decade of the twentieth century marked the unprecedented integration of African commerce with that of the European colonial powers. In the consequent encounter between capital-intensive European manufacturing ventures and the labor-intensive indigenous African manufacturing techniques, artisans (technicians) were trained in the use of European technology for performing the same tasks as the pre-colonial indigenous craftsmen and artisans. Rigid distinctions were thereby created between the modern artisans, who made iron products for house construction, and traditional blacksmiths, who made hoes and other farming implements; between traditional woodcarvers and modern carpenters; between traditional builders in laterite soils and modern builders in brick and cement.

The landscape of African indigenous manufacturing was profoundly affected by colonial policies that sought to transform the continent into an importer of foreign manufactures, and exporter of raw materials in the form of semi-processed agricultural and mining products. In the face of large quantities of imported manufactures that flooded the African markets in the first quarter of the century, indigenous manufacturing began to collapse or was reduced to the informal sector, operating outside the purview of the new states. Among the earliest casualties were the iron industries: The availability of scrap metals from imported machinery destroyed local iron-smelting technology, as blacksmiths began to recycle the metals for local manufacture of iron products. Likewise cloth-dyeing and weaving began to rely on imported dyes and threads, thereby destroying or curtailing the ginning and dye-making industries.

The negative impacts of the colonial political economy notwithstanding, indigenous manufactures also underwent innovations and enjoyed some continuity. Blacksmithing is a good example. Although scrap metal from imported machinery, railway lines, and car wrecks, rather than smelted iron, became the source of blacksmiths' raw materials in the early years of the twentieth century, the range of iron products that were manufactured continued to build upon the pre-colonial repertoire. These varied from domestic implements (such as knives, plates, and trays) to farming implements (such as hoes, axes, machetes, and sickles), as well as from hunting tools (like guns, swords, and spears) to jewelry. Despite the fact that the imported counterparts of these objects were to be found in markets in every African city, the local blacksmithing products continued to thrive, especially in the rural areas, because of their competitively low prices and vital importance to agricultural production. Blacksmithing was particularly crucial to the agricultural economy because most farmers depended on local blacksmiths for the implements, chiefly cutlasses and hoes, needed for agricultural production.

Another area of innovation was cloth manufacture. Although the use of locally made fabrics was supplanted in many parts of Africa by Western modes of dress and imported factory-made fabrics, cultural norms, ethnic identity, and religious beliefs sustained indigenous cloth manufacture, with the possible exceptions of **Southern Africa** and parts of **East Africa**. Raffia and cotton were the two primary types of raw material for weaving. Raffia cloth was found largely among the Kuba peoples of **Central Africa**, where men exclusively cultivated raffia palm and wove raffia cloth. Cotton was, however, the dominant raw material for cloth manufacture across the continent, ranging from the plain *shama* cloth in **Ethiopia** to the multicolored *aso-oke* cloth of southwest **Nigeria** and the *kente* cloth of **Ghana**. Imported Headle's wire (an accessory on a loom that facilitates the weaving of threads into cloth strips) and the use of a longer reed were adopted in different parts of Africa to make cloth strips that were broader and longer than those woven on traditional looms. Looms using Headle's wire could also weave towels, napkins, and trousers, products that were not easily made on traditional looms.

The dyeing and weaving industries witnessed drastic changes, especially in terms of sourcing of raw materials. Although indigo dying was an ancient tradition in **West Africa**, the adoption of tie-and-dye and starch-resistant methods of making patterns on dyed cloth took place in the early twentieth century, when finer, evenly structured factory-produced cotton shirting became widely available and affordable. The fine texture of the cloth allowed women to experiment with stitching and tying before dyeing. Another major innovation in textile production was the adoption of dye-resistant starch for making patterns on dyed cloth, either by freehand painting or by stenciling. There is also evidence that, by the second quarter of the twentieth century, imported caustic soda and synthetic dye were being adopted to replace cassava starch-paste and locally produced dyes. Likewise threads from local spinning of cotton were largely replaced by imported threads and silk. In a sense, therefore, local cloth industries came to depend on imported and factory-made raw materials. The resilience of indigenous textile industries was proven by the weavers' and dyers' continuous innovations in the face of persistent shifts in taste, competition from factory-made textiles, changing technologies, dwindling local supplies of raw materials, and shortage of labor. The adoption by modern designers in West Africa of locally made cloth as a basis for modern African fashion designs also increased the demand for these products, both at home and abroad.

Ceramic production was another enduring indigenous craft. The choice of pottery over metal and plastic was often a function of cultural preference, and mostly found in rural areas. It is also, however, true that there is less bacterial activity in ceramic pots than in aluminum ones, that ceramic pots preserve food better than their aluminum counterparts, and that local pots have superior heat-retaining qualities that made them suitable for use on open fires. The repertoire of locally produced ceramics increased throughout the twentieth century. Ceramic products were no longer restricted to domestic cookware and ritual pots, with decorative ceramics and flowerpots also locally manufactured to cater to an urban clientele. Local innovations in ceramic technology, based on an understanding of the mechanism of evaporative cooling and the structure of clay, led to the creation of a new type of pottery that was used for food storage instead of expensive refrigeration or mechanized canning methods.

Rejuvenating indigenous manufacture

The economic crisis faced by many African countries in the early 1980s made imported and factory-made commodities less accessible to the urban middle class, and further reduced the purchasing powers of the rural populace and urban poor. There was thus an increased demand for consumer goods from indigenous manufacturers, including locally processed foods, cloth, soap, and pottery. These economic conditions stimulated policies aimed at using micro- and small-scale indigenous manufacture as the essential engine of sustainable economic development in different African countries. The revitalization of indigenous manufacturing thereby became a critical component of **structural adjustment programs**. In the new back-to-basics spirit, states were more willing to recognise the economic and cultural role of crafts in national development, prescribing procedures that were relevant to the preservation and development of craft skills, encouraging the adaptation of such skills to the needs and requirements of modern times, and proclaiming national responsibility for the marketing of local crafts at home and abroad. To achieve this goal the Nigerian government, for example, provided loans under its "Better Life for Women" program (1986–93) to female potters and other cottage-industry manufacturers, organizing them into cooperatives to facilitate access to resources for production, and made facilities (including land, kilns, and water boreholes) available for their use.

Non-governmental organizations, such as the United Nations Economic Commission for Africa (ECA), also initiated programs, renting out tools and training artisans in design, production, marketing, and business management in order to enhance the capacity of small-scale indigenous manufacturing enterprises to produce goods and services needed by other producers. An important dimension to these programs was the quest to incorporate women into rural and urban manufacturing projects. Noting the versatility of blacksmiths in Africa, the close relationship between blacksmiths and the rural populace, and the fact that blacksmithing is a male-dominated craft – even though women are responsible for about 80 percent of agricultural production in Africa – a 1997 IFAD/FAO/Japanese Government study suggested, among other things, that development planners should work in concert with local blacksmiths to design efficient, suitable, and cost-effective tools specifically for women farmers.

Thus, in conclusion, although the core of skills in indigenous manufacture were acquired from inherited traditions, there were innovations that broke traditional barriers. These innovations were readily seen in the food-processing, cloth, potting, and blacksmithing industries. Indigenous manufacture increasingly made use of imported raw materials or semi-finished products. Despite any innovations, however, the basic technology remained the same in many respects. In the case of pottery, for example, the pots were still made by hand, and the use of a potter's wheel for commercial production was generally shunned, partly because imported wheels were usually small, expensive, and incapable of producing the different sizes of pot that the potters liked to make.

Research suggests that the labor force marginalized by the formal sector remained in the indigenous manufacturing sector, which was dominated by the non-literate, women, and the poor. Although indigenous manufacturing remained the second most dominant economic activity after farming, it was subjected to the predations of foreign imports. Its potential contribution to economic growth was also undermined by lack of government support, and the failure to integrate indigenous crafts into mainstream technical education, especially at the elementary- and secondary-school levels. Clearly there was a need to bridge the artificial divide between science/technology and arts/culture, and between so-called "modern" Western technology and indigenous "traditional" crafts in government policies and public attitudes. Indigenous manufacturers also needed training in marketing strategies and cost-effective production, and assistance with access to raw materials and equipment.

See also: manufacturing: modern

Reference and further reading

Alemayehu, M. (2000) *Industrializing Africa: Development Options and Challenges for the Twenty-first Century*, Trenton: African World Press Inc.

IFAD/FAO (1997) *Agricultural Implements used by Women Farmers in Africa*, Rome: International

Fund for Agricultural Development/Food and Agricultural Organization.
International Bank for Reconstruction and Development (1984) *Towards Sustained Development in Sub-Saharan Africa*, Washington, D.C.: World Bank.
—— (1991) *World Development Report: The Challenge of Development*, Washington, D.C.: World Bank.
Kaplinsky, R. (1990) *The Economies of Small: Appropriate Technology in a Changing World*, London: IT Publications and Appropriate Technology International.
Karsten, D. (1972) *The Economics of Handicrafts in Traditional Societies*, Munich: Weltforum Verlag.
Stamp, P. (1989) *Technology, Gender and Power in Africa*, Ottawa: International Development Research Council.

AKIN OGUNDIRAN

manufacturing: modern

Modern manufacturing, the large-scale conversion of raw materials – by use of machinery – into products for the market, played a pivotal role in global economic development in the twentieth century. Modern manufacturing enterprises provided important sources of employment and incomes in many regions of the world. Many African governments, upon attaining political independence in the 1960s, enacted policies that aimed at expanding their economies by nurturing and deepening their manufacturing sectors. Yet Africa's manufacturing potential failed to blossom, and the envisaged manufacture-driven economic takeoff remained a pipedream in many countries. Africa's manufacturing sector lagged behind other regions of the world, and the continent remained a net producer and exporter of unfinished raw materials such as cocoa, tea, coffee, oil, gold, and diamonds.

The pace and nature of development of the manufacturing sector was not uniform across the continent, given differences in colonial experiences, post-colonial ideological paths, and the regional and geographical locations of the various African countries. The ways in which these sociopolitical factors interacted, together with an analysis of the growth rates of manufacturing value added (MVA) and the share of MVA in gross domestic product (GDP), have been used to assess and analyze the performance of modern manufacturing in Africa.

A complex array of both internal and external factors affected the development of modern manufacturing in Africa during the twentieth century. The failures and difficulties that beset the sector can be attributed to the colonial legacy; political ideologies; the effects of the **Cold War** era; poor policies; lack of markets, resources and infrastructure; and the constraints of the liberalization requirements and **structural adjustment programs** espoused by the World Bank and the International Monetary Fund.

Colonial manufacturing

In the early decades of the twentieth century there were just a handful of manufacturing enterprises in Africa. Manufacturing activities in many regions involved small cottage ventures, typically run by traditional craftsmen. These involved the production of artifacts including simple agricultural tools and implements, fishing boats, and so forth. These informal manufacturing enterprises were well developed across the African continent. **Egypt**, for example, had numerous small-scale textile mills that produced cotton and woolen fabrics.

Although most of Africa was still under colonial rule in the first half of the century, its manufacturing base did not develop at par with those of imperial economies. The policy of the colonial governments was to keep the colonies as sources of cheap raw materials and markets for their own manufacturing industries. In Egypt, for example, the enormous indigenous manufacturing potential was suppressed by the British government's policy of encouraging cotton exports – accounting for 90 percent of all exports in 1914 – at the same time as keeping the country open as a market for British manufactured goods. In **Liberia** the American company Firestone held large concessions of rubber plantations, and the exported rubber was used to develop the tire industry in the United States. Exports of agricultural products therefore produced the bulk of growth of GDP of most African countries. **Nigeria**, for instance, registered an annual 5 percent growth with exports of cocoa, palm oil, and groundnuts. Only 7 percent of the GDP of Africa could be attributed to manufacturing during the colonial period.

Unlike the experiences of most other countries in Africa, **Kenya**, **Zimbabwe**, **Zambia**, **South Africa**, and **Algeria** had quite significant modern manufacturing sectors during the colonial period. Zambia and South Africa needed heavy investments of capital in the mining industries that were already producing sizable exports of copper and gold. In addition South Africa, together with Zimbabwe, Algeria, and Kenya, had large white settler populations, which either themselves developed or facilitated, through economic nationalism, the development of significant manufacturing enterprises, including agricultural processing enterprises. South Africa developed the most extensive industrial base on the continent, involving the production of consumer, intermediate, and capital goods, while in Kenya a more modest industrial sector emerged involving cotton, wattle, sisal, tobacco, corn, and sugar processing, together with breweries, cement, and soda production.

The nascent manufacturing industries that were established in Africa during the first decades of the century were to expand further during and after the **Second World War**. The British government, for example, had a change in policy that encouraged manufacturing investments in the colonies. This change of heart was due to the disruption of transportation, which made it necessary for the colonies to be self-sufficient in essential imports. Semi-autonomous countries like Egypt and South Africa made even greater strides during and after the war. Egypt's industrial output increased more than 60 percent between 1946 and 1951. During this time the growth of urban areas became significant throughout the world, not only in industrialized countries but also in Africa. **Urbanization** created pools of labor for the emergent manufactures. After the war, there was the so-called "second colonization" of Africa, through which colonial empires attempted to legitimize their colonial control by continuing the minimal reforms enacted during the war years.

Modern manufacturing after independence

The pace of **decolonization**, however, seems to have overtaken these piecemeal reforms. With the attainment of independence, new African governments inherited economies with weak manufacturing bases. The dawn of political independence ushered in an era of rapid growth. The **North African** countries of **Libya**, **Morocco**, Egypt, and Algeria, together with Nigeria in **West Africa**, accounted for the bulk of manufactures. Manufacturing industries that became important in these countries included pharmaceutical, engineering, chemical, electrical, and textile industries, as well as agro-based industries like sugar refining, rice milling, and soft-drink production.

The state took an active role in promoting industrialization efforts. Import substitution and manufacturing for export were the main vehicles through which industrialization was to be attained. There were, however, widespread differences in the manner in which various African governments undertook these efforts. Each country's political ideology and orientation determined the pace and nature of progress. Most countries, irrespective of their political orientation, sought to develop their infrastructures with a view to attracting private investment. State-controlled parastatals and partnership with transnational corporations were promoted, and tariff walls erected to protect the new industries. Most governments resorted to heavy borrowing from overseas funding sources. In Algeria, for instance, the government established the National Company for Mechanical Construction (NCMC), which produced machine tools and agricultural equipment. In **Ghana** the government of Kwame Nkrumah embarked on an ambitious industrialization program that saw the construction of the Akosombo Hydroelectric Power Plant, the building of the Volta Aluminum Company (VALCO), and the setting up of agro-processing enterprises. The majority of ventures that were established in countries across the continent, however, eventually suffered from lack of capital. The expected funding from foreign sources was not always forthcoming. Some countries, such as Egypt and **Tanzania**, eventually nationalized all their major manufacturing enterprises.

During the post-independence period, Kenya, **Côte d'Ivoire**, and Zimbabwe emerged as important regional centers for manufacturing, with all of them pursuing policies influenced by the Western model of development. These countries were financed by both foreign investments and local capital. The Kenyan government (with the help of the World Bank) established financial institutions that supported manufacturing entrepreneurship. These included the Industrial Development Bank (IDB) and the Kenya Industrial Estates (KIE), established to develop small-scale enterprises. In the meantime commercial capital from Kenyan Asians and some African entrepreneurs was also diverted into the manufacturing sector.

In Côte d'Ivoire, capital from governmental, private, and foreign sources – mainly from France – drove the expansion and development of extensive manufacturing ventures, including motor-vehicle assembly plants, textiles, furniture, tobacco, plastic, and various food-processing enterprises. The government of Côte d'Ivoire increasingly became an important player in industrial development, and resorted to borrowing heavily from overseas. The effects of this policy were to be felt later in Côte d'Ivoire, as in other African countries, when its government was called upon by **international financial institutions** to reform and divest itself from direct involvement in industry.

Zimbabwe, on the other hand, presented a unique experience. The white settlers in Zimbabwe (then known as Rhodesia) declared independence from Britain in 1965. The period of the Unilateral Declaration of Independence (UDI), which ran from 1965 to 1979, saw the country register a steady expansion in its manufacturing sector. The country's isolation resulted in the extensive development and expansion of its manufacturing sector, which contributed about 26 percent of Zimbabwe's GDP. This growth was sustained until well after independence in 1980. Zimbabwe's manufacturing performance, however, faltered in the 1980s and 1990s as the country adopted **structural adjustment programs**, and faced charges of economic mismanagement and government corruption.

In the 1960s and 1970s other African countries that registered significant growth in their import substitution-driven manufacturing included Nigeria, **Botswana**, and Zambia. Although these countries showed increased growth rates in MVA, not much was gained in the form of overall economic growth. The lack of growth was attributed to the fact that African governments promoted manufacturing concerns within their own territories, without coordinating their efforts with those of their neighbors. There was therefore unnecessary duplication. Regional organizations such as the **Southern African Development Community** and the **Common Market for Eastern and Southern Africa** were later established to streamline and coordinate trade relations among member-countries. Expansion in the modern manufacturing sector was further hindered by lack of both local and overseas markets, poor government policies, inadequate skills, inefficiency, stifling bureaucracy, unreliable power, unreliable supply of inputs, paucity of infrastructure, and lack of those institutions needed to guide and nurture growth. Nigeria, for example, experienced inadequate high-level manpower and overdependence on oil revenue. **Mauritania**, **Congo**, **Gabon**, and Libya were other countries that depended almost exclusively on oil revenues for development.

Amid the general economic crisis engulfing much of the continent, Botswana, **Mauritius**, and South Africa proved to be exceptions. Mauritius developed and expanded its manufacturing base, with textiles and electronic equipment being important exports. Botswana managed to expand its manufacturing, using capital from exported diamonds, to move from an economy that at independence depended entirely on the export of beef products to an economy driven by textile mills, food processing, and breweries, as well as processing nickel and copper. Fiscal responsibility, stable government, a working democratic tradition, and the absence of loss-making state enterprises all led to the steady development seen in Botswana, which was the world's fastest growing economy from the late 1960s to the early 1990s. In South Africa the regional economic dominance that the country developed during the apartheid era was maintained even during the struggles against apartheid. The most important manufactured products from South Africa were textiles, chemicals, pharmaceuticals, beer, and soft drinks. Although the liberalization of trade and the end of apartheid enabled South Africa to explore markets that were not available to it during the period of economic sanctions and political isolation, investment in and exports from its manufacturing sector remained relatively low and uncompetitive in international terms.

In the 1980s and 1990s structural adjustment appears to have helped countries like **Uganda** and Ghana to arrest and even reverse industrial decline. From 1990 to 2000 Uganda's economy turned in a solid performance, reaping benefits from the policies started in 1986 under President Yoweri Museveni. The country embarked on a program of infrastructural rehabilitation, enticing exiled Ugandan entrepreneurs to return and reclaim their once profitable manufacturing enterprises in sugar processing and textiles. But for many other countries structural adjustment led to deindustrialization, as trade liberalization flooded local markets with cheaper imports or previously state-owned manufacturing enterprises were sold off to private interests that subsequently closed them down, as happened to the textile industry in Tanzania.

Collective attempts by African countries to promote industrialization, through programs like the Lagos Plan of Action (adopted in 1980) or through **regional integration**, largely proved ineffective in the face of an international policy environment that favored free markets, growing protectionism in the North that restricted markets for manufactured exports, and stiff competition for investment from the newly industrializing countries of Southeast Asia. Indeed the 1980s and 1990s saw African countries, with a few exceptions, experience a decline in their manufacturing sectors. By the close of the twentieth century, therefore, Africa's hoped-for economic takeoff, driven by import substitution and manufacturing for export, had not yet materialized.

See also: economy: colonial; economy: post-independence; manufacturing: indigenous

Further reading

Fransman, M. (ed.) (1982) *Industry and Accumulation in Africa*, London: Heinemann.

Khennas, S. (ed.) (1992) *Industrialization Mineral Resources and Energy in Africa*, Dakar: CODESRIA.

Nyong'o, P.A. and Coughlin, P. (eds.) (1991) *Industrialization at Bay: African Experiences*, Nairobi: African Academy of Sciences.

Riddell, R. (1990) *Manufacturing Africa: Performance and Prospects of Seven Countries in Sub-Saharan Africa*, London: James Currey.

AKURA OKONG'O

Maputo, Mozambique

Maputo is the capital of **Mozambique**, a country located on the southeastern coast of Africa. It is Mozambique's largest city, with an estimated population of 3.1 million in 2000. It is located in the southern part of the country on Maputo (Delagoa) Bay, an inlet of the Indian Ocean. It has served as an important gateway port for shipping on the east African coast, with railway services to **South Africa**, **Zimbabwe**, and **Swaziland**. Maputo houses the country's leading financial and commercial institutions, as well as major industries such as textiles, cement, and food processing.

During the colonial period the city was known as Lourenço Marques, after the Portuguese navigator and trader who explored the Delagoa Bay region in the 1540s. The Portuguese established a trading post there, and by 1787 had built a fort. The settlement grew slowly around the fort, becoming a town a century later. In 1907 Lourenço Marques became the administrative center of Portuguese East Africa.

The colonial administration developed Lourenço Marques into a major transportation hub in the Southern African region, giving several countries an outlet for shipping their minerals abroad. In 1895 a railroad was built, linking Lourenço Marques with the Transvaal in South Africa, and in 1909 South Africa agreed to ship at least 47.5 percent of its imports through the port. To promote the use of the port by other countries, railroads were also built connecting it with Swaziland and Rhodesia.

The growing economic importance of the city attracted many Africans and Portuguese over the first seventy years of the twentieth century, making it the major employment center in the region. Africans from the surrounding areas also came to Lourenço Marques looking for work. They provided the core labor force in the port, as well as on the railroads, in construction, and for domestic service. Portuguese immigrants also came to the city seeking employment or wishing to set up business ventures. They were given preferential treatment, with regulations instituted that favored them over Africans. Mozambique's economic growth in the postwar period resulted in Lourenço Marques' population tripling between 1945 and 1970.

In February 1976, after Mozambique gained its independence, President Samora Machel changed the name of the city from Lourenço Marques to Maputo. The city's economy deteriorated in the years after independence. Most Portuguese settlers, who had controlled every sector of the economy, left Maputo and Mozambique, and the port suffered from the loss of business with Rhodesia and South Africa. In March 1976 the government closed the border with Rhodesia, in compliance with United Nations sanctions, while South Africa's campaign to destabilize Mozambique, including an air raid on Maputo in May 1983, led to a sharp decline in South African traffic through the port.

The insurgency by the Resistencia National Moçambicana (Mozambican National Resistance or Renamo) in the 1980s forced some Mozambicans to flee their fields and homes to the capital, putting an even greater financial burden on the government. The fighting created instability and undermined tourism, which had been important to the economy: South African and Rhodesian tourists had frequently come to Maputo's beaches during the colonial period, generating a huge amount of revenue for the government that was now lost to the new regime. The end of tourism naturally damaged the hotel and restaurant business, and all other aspects of the tourist industry.

However, political and economic liberalization in the early 1990s paved the way for a cease-fire in 1992, putting Maputo and Mozambique on the road to economic recovery. It seemed likely that this process would take some time, however, with success depending on massive economic assistance from abroad.

Further reading

Kaplan, I. (1977) *Area Handbook of Mozambique*, Washington, D.C.: US Government Printing Office.

M.A. EL-KHAWAS

Maseru, Lesotho

Maseru, the capital of **Lesotho**, was founded in 1869, shortly after the country was colonized by Britain. From 1871 to 1883 Lesotho was governed from the Cape Colony, but Maseru's status was restored in 1884 when the country reverted to British rule. The settlement also survived being burnt down by forces from the Cape Colony during the Gun War (1880–1). By 1900 Maseru was a small settlement that comprised a handful of colonial administrative buildings, the odd trading store, and a number of peripheral villages, with a total population of well below 1,000. In the twentieth century, Maseru has become both the capital city and headquarters of the Maseru district.

With time Maseru developed into a town that boasted a chamber of commerce founded in 1890 by the trader George Hobson. Two newspapers served the growing community: *Mochochonono* ("The Comet"), founded in 1911, and *Basutoland News*, founded in 1927. In terms of services, streetlights were erected in 1933, and an improved water-supply system was put in place in 1949. Along with such developments, the class structure of colonial society in Maseru became more varied, consisting of colonial officials; white traders and professionals; African professionals, clerks and interpreters; and a small service class of domestic workers and shop assistants. Together these classes coexisted uneasily under British colonial tutelage.

With the formation of the Basutoland African Congress (BAC) in 1952, Lesotho began its march to independence. Maseru experienced its first general strike in March 1961 as the African population came together to protest against unfair labor practices, discriminatory legislation, unequal access to public amenities, and other features of late colonial society. In 1963 neighboring **South Africa** imposed border controls, and citizens of Lesotho who crossed Maseru Bridge into South Africa were required to show travel documents for the first time.

At independence in 1966 the population of Maseru was 36,688; ten years later it had risen to 62,312, and in 1986 it was 121,644. By the end of the twentieth century Maseru's population was estimated to be in excess of 200,000, about 10 percent of the total population of Lesotho. Independence undoubtedly ushered in a period of unprecedented and continuous – if unplanned – growth, for which there are a number of reasons. Government rapidly became the largest employer and, because most government work was centered in Maseru, especially with the abolition of local government after 1968, Maseru grew disproportionately in comparison to other district centers. Increasing landlessness and diminishing returns from agriculture in rural Lesotho meant that thousands made their way to Maseru in search of employment. Many younger families, dependent on earnings from **migrant labor**, tended to relocate to lowland areas – among these Maseru was one of the preferred locations. In the 1980s, as Lesotho acquired increasing amounts of aid, employment opportunities increased. Also in the 1980s employment opportunities in South African mines began to steadily decline, leading to an influx of people for whom agriculture had ceased to be a viable source of livelihood long before.

In many ways Maseru is the vulnerable capital of a vulnerable country. The city was the part of Lesotho that most often felt the pressure of apartheid South Africa's aggression through the 1980s. The city often also formed a battleground for competing political interests, culminating in the destruction of most of its Central Business District in 1998. It had been under siege from marauding opposition supporters who disputed the 1998 election results.

Further reading

Ambrose, D. (1993) *Maseru: An Illustrated History*, Morija: Morija Museum and Archives.

NEVILLE W. PULE

Mauritania

Mauritania, which has an area of 1,030,700 square kilometers, borders the north Atlantic Ocean, **Senegal**, **Mali**, **Algeria**, and the Western **Sahara**. In 2000 it had an estimated population of 2.6 million. The territory is composed of Arabs (both of Amazigh origins and Harridans with an Arab culture but black origins) and West African black ethnic groups (Barbara, Haalpulaar, Soninke, and Wolof). The Islamic Republic of Mauritania, as the country is officially known, is the result of French attempts to create a sort of "buffer state" between so-called "black" Africa south of the Sahara and "white" Africa north of the Sahara. Mauritania was colonized in 1899, a process that was met with such considerable resistance that conquest was not completed until 1912.

The northern and southern parts of the colony were governed separately until 1946 when the country was unified. Before then much of the colonial presence was concentrated in the south, which was governed as part of Senegal; the sparsely populated north was largely ignored. Thus the French presence did not have the same consequences for the different populations. For the sedentary peoples, France reproduced the same type of administration as elsewhere in **French West Africa**, whereas the social structures of wandering Arabs were largely left undisturbed. In the terms of colonial logic the south had to be "governed," while the north had to be "convinced." The colony was so poor that in 1926 revenue represented only 50 percent of expenditure. Besides paying taxes, the Mauritanians' cattle were also requisitioned and they were expected to provide free labor for public works. Until the end of the **Second World War** hardly any economic development took place in the country, but it was during the war that food shortages and other hardships, compounded by drought, encouraged the first stirrings of modern nationalist protest among the small educated elite of the country.

After the Second World War the economy was transformed by the discovery of iron-ore deposits in the north of Mauritania. In 1952 the Société des Mines de Fer de Mauritanie (Iron Mining Company of Mauritania or MIFERMA) was created with state capital, and it quickly became an important part of the economy – iron accounted for a growing share of the gross national product, rising to 15 percent by the 1990s. Political changes were also in the offing. Since 1920 Mauritania had been attached to French West Africa and the Senegalese politician, Léopold Senghor, represented both Senegal and Mauritania in the Constituent Assembly in Paris. But from 1946 Mauritania got its own representation. Horma Ould Babana of the newly formed socialist-leaning Entente Mauritanienne won the elections to become the country's first representative. Before long a new (more conservative) party emerged: the Union Progressiste Mauritanienne (Progressive Mauritanian Union party or UPM). Founded in 1947, one the new party's members, Sidi El-Mokhtar N'diaye, won the 1951 legislative elections, and was reelected in 1956. After the Aleg Congress in 1958, the Parti du Peuple Mauritanien (Mauritanian People's Party or PPM) was created to represent a broad spectrum of national opinion. Mokhtar Ould Daddah, a lawyer, became the party's secretary-general.

In November 1960 Mauritania became independent, with Daddah as president. The new country was soon confronted with internal racial and regional political tensions. Internally there were attempts to "Arabize" the country, partly designed to win support from **Morocco**, which was not to grant Mauritania diplomatic recognition until 1969. In 1966 a crisis shook the Mauritanian school system, when a law was passed imposing compulsory **Arabic** language teaching. Black intellectuals reacted by publishing a proclamation of protest. This and other policies damaged the process of nation-building. The government also soon established a one-party state, and embarked on a program of nationalization of the main industries, including mining.

From 1975, when Spain decided to leave after years of fighting against the Algerian-backed liberation movement known as the Polisario Front, Mauritania became embroiled in the regional conflict over the Spanish colony of Western Sahara. Morocco and Mauritania agreed to divide the territory between them, against not only the wishes of Polisario but also of much of Africa. Polisario turned its rage on the two countries, with war wreaking havoc on the Mauritanian economy and eventually triggering political protests. In July 1978 the government was overthrown. The Comité Militaire de Redressement National (Military Committee for National Recovery) took power, signing a peace treaty with Polisario in 1979.

Hardly had the external conflict disappeared, when another crisis erupted in the Mauritanian school system, leading to a long strike in the southern colleges. New movements, such as El-Hor and the Forces de Libération Africaines de Mauritanie (African Liberation Forces of Mauritania), emerged to protest against **slavery** and racial discrimination in the country. The state made some changes, creating the Institut des Langues Nationales (National Languages Institute) and proclaiming the abolition of slavery in 1981, but the country's elite did not show much enthusiasm for these reforms. The land reform of 1983–4 was even more fiercely contested, while black intellectuals continued to protest against their marginalization. In 1989, using a conflict between Mauritania and Senegal that sparked riots in both countries as a pretext, the state began to order the imprisonment and summary execution of black Mauritanians.

In 1991, responding to political pressure, a referendum was held over the establishment of a new democratic constitution. Maawiya Ould Taya, the military ruler from 1984, won the elections in 1992, a victory that he repeated in the 1997 elections, which were held despite a boycott by the opposition parties. In October 2000 the government dissolved the largest opposition party, and put the leader of another opposition party in jail. Taya's government tried to improve its image by appointing black Mauritanians to the cabinet; it pointed with pride to the economy's growth rate of 5.5 percent, inflation rate of 3 percent, and high rates of school attendance (90 percent) and sanitary coverage (70 percent). But to its critics Mauritania remained a divided country, where slavery, racism, and other violations of **human rights** were still common.

Further reading

Chassey, F. de (1985) *Mauritanie 1900–1975. Facteurs économiques, politiques, idéologiques et éducatifs dans la formation d'une société sous-développée*, Paris: L'Harmattan.

N'gaïde, A. (2000) "L'odyssée des déportés mauritaniens au Sénégal," paper presented at the Governance Institute, CODESRIA, Dakar.

ABDERRAHMANE N'GAÏDE

Mauritius

Mauritius, with an estimated population of 1.2 million in 2000, is located in the southwestern Indian Ocean. It had no indigenous population when it was first discovered by the Portuguese in the sixteenth century. The island was controlled by a succession of European powers: the Dutch (from 1638), then the French (from 1715), and the British (from 1810). Three main developments dominated Mauritian history during the nineteenth century: the abolition of slavery, the bringing of indentured labor from India, and the transformation of the Mauritian economy from one based on maritime activities to one based on the production of sugar for export. Mauritius achieved independence in 1968, under the leadership of Seewoosagur Ramgoolam's Hindu-dominated Labor Party

The beginning of the twentieth century saw various efforts being made by the different ethnic groups to organize politically. During the 1930s and 1940s lower classes on the island faced severe economic hardships, and the beginning of an organized class struggle made itself felt. The country experienced riots, violence, and industrial unrest. Heated political struggles between the dominant minority – Franco-Mauritians who represented the French sugar oligarchy – and the oppressed majority took place.

However, Mauritian political life changed significantly after 1948. Class solidarity waned considerably, giving way to communal groupings. The two decades preceding independence in 1968 were marked by different ethno-religious groups expressing deep concerns about the maintenance of their communal power, security, and privileges. In May 1965 riots broke out between Creoles and Hindus, resulting in several deaths. In order to reduce tension and dampen the fears of different communal parties the British scrapped single-member constituencies (on the grounds that they tended to overrepresent the Hindu community) and replaced them with twenty constituencies of three members each. In addition eight seats were to be allocated after the election to the "best losers," namely those representing communities that would otherwise be underrepresented in the main election. This system contributed to social cohesion, but politically divisive community loyalties persisted. (As late as February 1999 there was a new round of riots by the Creoles, who were still disproportionately represented among the poor.) In the 1970s the ruling party faced a growing challenge from a newly formed socialist opposition party called the Mouvement Militant Mauricien (MMM), which won nearly half the seats in the 1976 elections. In the 1982 elections they won a landslide victory, and the MMM's leader, Anerood Jugnauth, became prime minister. Despite internal splits, the MMM remained in power until 1995.

Over the course of the century Mauritius underwent notable economic changes. Poor sugar prices at the beginning of twentieth century, as well as the perennial problems of disease and infestation, led to the *grand morcellement* in which white landowners started selling their land. Indians bought small plots, which contributed to the rise of a small Indian planter class. The Indians also very quickly seized on expanding educational opportunities, and began to fill important positions in the colonial bureaucracy. The fear of Hindu hegemony led a substantial proportion of the Creole community, who had previously formed part of that bureaucracy, to migrate to Australia, **South Africa**, and Europe. The diversification of the Mauritian economy in the post-independence period – reflected in the establishment of an export-processing zone (EPZ) in 1972, and the expansion of the tourism and (towards the end of the century) offshore finance sectors – contributed to the growth of a Mauritian middle class. But economic power still remained in the hands of the Franco-Mauritians. Unlike EPZs in many other parts of the world, which attracted a large degree of foreign investment, the Mauritian EPZ saw local sugar capital channeled into the sector. Foreign direct investment from Hong Kong and South Africa also formed a substantial part of the capital available to different economic sectors. Despite efforts at economic diversification, sugar remained critical – bringing in about a third of foreign exchange – and the Creoles remained invisible in the new sectors as the experienced an economic boom.

As Mauritius stepped into the twenty-first century, its "success" story seemed threatened by several new challenges. The globalization and liberalization of trade under the aegis of the World Trade Organization threatened to adversely affect many of the semi-protectionist advantages enjoyed by Mauritius under the outgoing global trade regime. Particularly ominous was the dismantling of the Multifiber Agreement. The protected markets that Mauritius had enjoyed appeared destined to disappear. The initial spurt of foreign direct investment inflows that had fueled the boom in the 1980s and 1990s was also tapering off. The emergence of cheap labor in countries like **Madagascar**, Sri Lanka, and Vietnam contributed to the relocation of industries from Mauritius. Unemployment was on the rise, and sustaining a livelihood (particularly for those who were already on the fringes of an ethnicized and segmented labor market) was increasingly difficult. At the same time, however, Mauritius was confronted with a severe lack of skilled and qualified human capital, thwarting the country's aspirations to become an information-based economy.

Trapped in a "dependent development" model, and having to confront the exigencies of the global economy, Mauritius had to juggle various policies in an attempt to maintain its competitive edge: As economic difficulties increased and windows of opportunity became narrower, social cohesion was threatened.

The social and economic history of twentieth-century Mauritius highlights the fact that trickle-down development models privilege some and marginalize many. The marginalized often remain jobless, voiceless, rootless, and without a future. When minority communities are disproportionately visible in this category, interculturality and peace come under threat. By the end of the 1990s there was increasing talk of the need for an "equal opportunities act" in Mauritius, but it is not certain whether the mere passing of such an act would bring redress. Unless efforts are made to address entrenched inequalities, however, it is a distinct possibility that Mauritius' development will be derailed.

Further reading

Brown, L.W. (1991) *Mauritius: Democracy and Development in the Indian Ocean*, Boulder: Westview Press.

Storey, W.K. (1997) *Science and Power in Colonial Mauritius*, Rochester: University of Rochester Press.

SHEILA BUNWAREE

Mbabane, Swaziland

In 1903, following the end of the South African (Anglo-Boer) War, Mbabane became the administrative capital of **Swaziland**. Like many African urban areas at the beginning of the twentieth century, Mbabane was a small town that consisted of a few churches, schools, and shops established for the Europeans who settled there. There were a few Swazis employed by the colonial administration. Because Africans were not permitted to live in the town, they resided on the outskirts of the city; because their numbers were low and racism restricted their mobility, few leisure activities were available for Swazis. Mbabane was officially declared an urban area in 1912, but its population increased slowly.

By the 1920s the city had electricity and a few more stores; by the 1930s it had acquired more schools and churches, along with a hospital, running water, and telephones, and more people had access to electricity. A large percentage of the Swazi population was either engaged in **migrant labor** in **South Africa**, or worked in tin and asbestos mines owned by European companies.

Some Swazis farmed and raised cattle on their own land, while others worked on European-owned farms and plantations. In other words, the majority of Swaziland's population either worked outside the country for most of the year or resided in rural areas. In addition the infrastructure needed to support an industrial economy was not developed in terms of communications, roads, railways, or bridges. The city failed to attract many Swazis because it merely served as an administrative center, not as an economic center. Two important educational developments occurred in the 1940s that attracted people to the city, however: the Mbabane Central School was founded in 1940, and the Mbabane Trade School was started in 1945.

Foreign capital investment in forestry, iron ore, sugar, coal, and citrus fruits following the **Second World War** resulted in an increase in economic growth in Mbabane. The city's population increased in response to the demand for new workers. It became the commercial hub for the surrounding agricultural and mining regions. Due to its important location, Mbabane became the transportation center for the railroad that connected Mbabane with the nearby mines and the important Indian Ocean port of **Maputo** in **Mozambique**. Furthermore, as more people gained access to education, they migrated to the capital in search of economic and social opportunities. The semi-educated also sought economic opportunities in the capital as it became more difficult to earn a living in rural areas. By 1956 the city's population was 3,428; by 1975 it had increased to 24,000.

As major developments began to occur during the 1970s and 1980s, the capital experienced a population increase. Many residential areas were built in the suburbs, shopping centers were constructed that also contained office space, and several new office buildings were erected. By 1986 Mbabane's population had increased to 38,290, and by 1999 to 58,063. At the end of the twentieth century Mbabane was Swaziland's largest city and it served as the administrative, judicial, and commercial center of the country, with banks, hotels, theaters, shops, and malls. The city also contained light industry (publishing, plant assembly, motor mechanics, and warehousing) and transportation services. The residents of the city enjoyed a wide variety of leisure activities, including sports (soccer, golf, and rugby) and various cultural activities, including theater.

Further reading

Booth, A.R. (1983) *Swaziland: Tradition and Change in a Southern African Kingdom*, Boulder: Westview Press.

Forster, P. and Nisbande, B.S. (eds.) (2000) *Swaziland: Contemporary Social and Economic Issues*, Burlington: Aldershot.

CASSANDRA RACHEL VENEY

merchants

Analysis of merchants in Africa has often divided them into formal and European enterprises, on the one hand, and African trading diasporas and the "informal sector," on the other. Indigenous merchants have been seen as nascent African capitalists or as part of informal and culturally embedded forms of African sociality and survival. Buying and selling goods for profit, merchants included both those in wholesale trade with locals/foreigners and those selling goods locally at retail, such as storekeepers and shopkeepers, whether these individuals were "self-employed" or part of larger social or institutional networks and corporate bodies. While they have often been viewed separately, capitalistic and "informal" entrepreneurs and merchants in Africa developed in a much more related way than dominant approaches suggest. While many merchants in Africa in the twentieth century remained petty traders, others became part of a genuine commercial and industrial bourgeoisie. Yet the two groups relied on each other for material and social capital throughout the century.

Merchants in pre-colonial Africa used well-established trade routes, notably across the **Sahara**, in mercantile activity that linked Africa and Europe in substantial trade relations. While mercantile relations linked regions of Africa where production was oriented towards local needs, regional ties and strong networks were necessary to provide insurance, security, and credit. During the nineteenth century the **Fulani** were prominent merchants in **West Africa** because of their near monopoly on livestock trading for cocoa, coffee, textiles, and palm kernels – and later for diamonds and rice. Originally kinship (both real and fictive) or religious ties created tight corporate networks that helped to link communities and assist in competition with other merchants. Yet, as colonial power increased competition and ruptured networks during the early twentieth century, Fulani merchants developed ties and competitive relationships with the Lebanese and Indians. Similarly, for several centuries **Swahili** hegemony existed over eastern African trade with Europe and Asia. As commercial middlemen and cultural mediators, the Swahili linked the purchasers and producers of cloth, ivory, and gold, a role they reprised in their involvement with colonial powers along the caravan routes or the path of colonial administrative posts. However, around the turn of the century, British and German rule, as well as the start of the Uganda railway, allowed Indian finance houses to compete with local merchants and Swahili commercial relations began to lose importance in **East Africa**. The British also brought colonial coinage into widespread use, which devalued local currencies, as well as Swahili bonds of clientship with non-Swahili food growers, coconut tappers, fishermen and other producers. To maintain their activities, Swahili merchants had to rely on innovative commercial strategies.

During the early twentieth century, as European colonial power was instituted in Africa, taxation and alienation of land increased the pressure on local peoples to earn cash. Many Africans tried to sell crops, but they were often forced into **migrant labor**, whereas many merchants were able to pay taxes without disrupting their social standing. Yet colonial taxation and increased demand for and supply of foreign manufactured goods brought about a monetarization of aspects of social life that had previously been associated with more reciprocal social systems of prestation (coercion). In addition, new colonial currencies impoverished merchants holding traditional currencies.

The ties that African and colonial merchants created across geographic areas sometimes worked to unify those territories, as did colonial attempts to control the monetary systems of exchange used in mercantile activity. For example, the introduction of copper and silver coins around the turn of the century in the Gold Coast colony, Ashanti, and the Northern Territories made trade in the region easier to carry out, regulate, and exploit. At the time merchants traveled from **Kumasi** to **Accra**, **Lome** or **Cotonou**, trading cows for cotton and kola. Such trade worked to expand commercial unification of the region and produce vast fortunes for prominent African merchants. Similarly credits given to African merchants by colonial enterprises allowed Europeans to unify their axes of exchange with distant regions.

In order to guarantee the success of their endeavors, colonialists sought to add duties and enforce frontiers in order to eliminate the alternatives to wage labor offered by merchant activity. They also stabilized colonial merchant relations by buying goods, appointing buying agents, fixing prices for export, fixing producer prices, and setting quality standards for certain goods produced on the continent. Yet wage labor was resisted both by the men who could sell their labor and by those with whom they maintained social obligations. Social systems of labor, as well as established interests in the regional trade of peasant produce, meant that enterprises such as plantation agriculture, for example, were relatively unfruitful. Thus labor was never completely alienated from local systems of social value, however unequal.

Such embeddedness also contributed to the nature of merchant activity in Africa. Because profit is contingent on differences in regional prices, productivity was dependent on regular transport and exchange relationships to balance the risks of credit shortages, transportation costs, unskilled management, fluctuating selling prices, and competition from other merchants. Though they often siphoned off profit from local exchanges, merchant networks were involved in inter-ethnic and inter-community solidarity where reciprocity created mutual trust and obligation, perpetuating exchange. During the colonial and post-colonial eras, such networks continually allowed the poor and socially marginal to work outside of or against constraints imposed by the government or the rich. Thus ethnic, religious, and kin relations helped to stabilize relations across ethnic and national divides.

The **First World War** effectively ended the dominance of most prominent African merchants. Many could not mobilize the credit needed to withstand price swings in African produce and raw material commodities. European firms, however, could access substantial capital to manufacture, ship, distribute, and sell large quantities of goods at lower prices than their African competitors. Many Europeans were still forced to shift their merchandise and prices, however. Where companies competed with African merchants, the elimination of credits was often a way of limiting their power. As they saw their mercantile activity curtailed, some prosperous merchants entered their children into the European system of colonial education and the bureaucracy, while others diversified their wealth through investment in real estate and, later, in large-scale enterprises.

During the interwar period raw-material enterprises and exports increasingly drove many colonial investments in most colonies. Nevertheless most local economies until the Second World War were still driven by mercantile activity. Exceptions existed in **Southern Africa** where mineral exploitation offered an early entry for European enterprises. African merchants alternated in their cooperation or competition with companies like the Société Commerciale de l'Ouest Africain or the imperial British East Africa Company, precursors to multinational corporations, that were mainly involved in wholesaling produce, provisions, and manufactured goods. The Africans associated with them were primarily involved in the retail sale of provisions, but some European companies, like the Union Trading Company, had their own general stores to compete with African retailers. European companies relied on colonial governments to improve the local sociopolitical terrain, establish controls on prices and conditions of commerce, and guarantee their monopolies of importation when they became more porous with improvements in African means and advances in transportation.

With those changes colonial powers shifted their dealings to other prominent non-African merchants. The French, for example, shifted their support and confidence to Lebanese-Syrian merchants in much of West Africa, as the Fulani had done. Many of these Lebanese had tried to emigrate to Europe before or during the First World War, but were rerouted to West Africa. Strong patrilineal descent and a lack of women encouraged men to create large ethnic corporate units involved in merchant activities, and they soon replaced Africans in the kola and rice trade. Between the world wars this competition led to ethnic hostility, sometimes erupting into riots and violence. Other non-Africans occupied similar positions throughout Africa, including Jewish merchants in the Maghreb, Portuguese merchants in the **Congo**, or Asian merchants in **East Africa**, though in places like **Morocco** privileged business licenses were granted to African army veterans.

After independence Africans were more likely to obtain concessions that colonial enterprises once held, particularly in countries that nationalized foreign enterprises. Through reinvestment in real estate and business, these merchants strengthened their capitalist activities. For less successful merchants, much of their business entered the informal sector. Thus throughout Africa mainstay merchant work, including trade in fresh produce and manufactured goods like clothing and cosmetics, began to be encompassed within the "informal economy."

The "informal" sector of mercantile activity was a direct result of other changes. In many parts of Africa, changes in land tenure and land reform made subsistence activity and even crop-marketing increasingly difficult endeavors. In addition poor environmental conditions pushed women without much work experience and men who had lost their jobs into informal sector trading to survive. However, "informal" activities always overlapped with the formal economy. For example, by establishing accounts with banks or wholesalers, small merchants could often secure their relations with powerful institutions and decent terms of trade with foreign and "legitimate" businesses. In countries where investment had been concentrated during the colonial and early post-independence periods on the provision of public infrastructure, it was not until the 1970s that development efforts began to focus on private enterprise.

Yet while men were primarily involved in formal commerce and industry, it was predominantly women who worked in the informal sector of merchant activity. One of women's most prominent public domains of identity became bound up with merchant activity, even though limited to certain products. In trading surplus grains, meat, and vegetables, women's involvement was related to their own surplus production, blurring the conventionally understood domains of women's domestic and public activity. In **Zimbabwe** women's agricultural production at home helped maintain the system of African labor reserves, while males were involved in wage labor in towns, mines, and commercial farms. Though they competed with African men's businesses and white merchants, women's merchant activity continued.

In the 1980s "informal" merchant activity among women across Africa was supported by international lenders and **non-governmental organizations**. Business, accounting, and English-language training, as well as access to micro-credit, became a focus for development projects. However, these projects focused on semi-skilled, labor-intensive projects that could only be short-term activities for obtaining cash for basic needs. In addition, though women's market involvement in Africa had been ongoing and substantial, women's businesses were not accorded a legitimacy equal to that of other male-dominated or formal-sector businesses. Nonetheless women's merchant endeavors were more than auxiliary activities, as they constituted significant percentages of both the informal economy and of women's activities in general. Women's involvement in such enterprises allowed them to handle difficult economic conditions. In some areas of West Africa economic support was central to the experience of mothering, unifying both child-rearing and breadwinning, thereby building solidarity among women. In other parts of Africa, such as in Morocco, women's post-independence presence in merchant activity opened new domains of language, culture, and gender relations.

In rural areas of Africa merchant activity was limited by tight links between productive and consumptive spheres, and a lack of institutional support for merchant activity led to a tendency for them to be in a process of either waxing or waning. In spite of the ongoing complementarity between informal- and formal-sector mercantile activities in many areas, there continued to be no unity of production, commerce, or capitalist relations. Yet throughout the twentieth century merchant activity had been instrumental for Africans' survival through economic, social, and political changes.

See also: capitalisms and capitalists; economy: colonial; economy: post-independence; non-African diasporas

Further reading

Amselle, J.L. and Grégoire, E. (1988) *état et capitalisme en Afrique de l'Ouest*, Paris: Centre d'Etudes Africaines, Ecole des Hautes Etudes en Sciences Sociales.

Barry, B. and Harding, L. (eds.) (1992) *Commerce et commerçants en Afrique de l'Ouest: le Sénégal*, Paris: L'Harmattan.

Horn, N.E. (1994) *Cultivating Customers: Market Women in Harare, Zimbabwe*, Boulder: Lynne Rienner.

Laboratory (1983) "Connaissance du tiers-monde," in C. Coquery-Vidrovitch and A. Forest (eds.), *Entreprises et entrepreneurs en Afrique: XIXe et XXe siecles*, vol. 1, Paris: L'Harmattan.

White, E.F. (1987) *Sierra Leone's Settler Women Traders: Women on the Afro-European Frontier*, Ann Arbor: University of Michigan Press.

BJORN WESTGARD

migrant labor

Although there were significant earlier movements of people in search of livelihoods in Africa, the roots of migrant labor as a specific form of temporary wage employment are to be found in colonialism. Colonists required a ready supply of cheap labor for work on railways, plantations, estates and commercial farms, ranches, mines, and later in the factories as well. They faced a host of problems in their quest to secure an adequate supply of labor, not least of which was the self-sufficiency of the indigenous communities. State intervention in taxation and other levies constituted an extra-economic mechanism for the generation of labor. Importing indentured labor from India to work on the sugarcane plantations in **South Africa** and the railways in **Kenya**, as well as Chinese workers for the mines in South Africa, bears adequate testimony to the shortage of labor. Forced labor was necessary, especially during the early period of colonialism, to close the huge gap between supply and demand. Yet the demand for labor could not be satisfied in this manner.

The impact of migrant labor varied considerably from region to region, but generally out-migration from rural areas was lowest from places with a dynamic local economy and highest from those that were struggling to create employment and livelihood opportunities. The extent of the dissolution of rural societies depended on the nature and urgency of the labor demand, and coincided roughly with the proportion of land expropriated by European settlers. Thus in South Africa, where more land was appropriated by white settlers than in any other African country, the mass of the population was effectively denied the wherewithal to undertake independent farming as a means of creating livelihoods. The diminishing returns on tiny arable allotments compelled inhabitants of the reserves to seek wage employment elsewhere. The colonial authorities controlled the process through a complex web of parastatal recruiting agencies and later, under apartheid, with a four-tier system of labor bureaus that channeled labor to exactly where it was required. The South African case approximates a system of migrant labor more than any other, but migrancy was also vitally important in the reproduction of families across **Southern Africa**. Samir Amin (1972) has aptly named this situation – where a migrant workforce was immediately required – the "Africa of the Labor Reserves." Instead of a one-way movement from rural to urban areas, migration tended to be oscillating and circular, with a net outflow from rural areas over a number of decades.

Despite limited settler land alienation in **West Africa**, the colonial economy nonetheless generated extensive labor migration in regions of cash-crop production. In **Ghana**, for example, there was a long-term out-migration from the north to the south, where people moved to cultivate cocoa or to work in the mines. A complex sharecropping system emerged called *abusa*, which had been developed in the cocoa-growing regions and was later also used to very good effect in **Côte d'Ivoire**. In the 1930s groundnut cultivation for export in **Senegal** and **Gambia** attracted labor from neighboring **Guinea** and **Burkina Faso**. Similarly, in **East Africa** migrant labor was not restricted to settler-controlled **Kenya**, but also developed in **Tanzania** and **Uganda**. In Kenya the number of male labor migrants increased from 5,000 in 1903 to 120,000 in 1923. There were three main reasons for this conversion of independent producers to an ever greater dependence upon wage labor in Kenya, but these can easily be generalized to the whole of Amin's "Africa of the Labor Reserves": Insistence that taxes be paid in cash, alienation of land to prevent independent production, and colonial coercion through forced labor combined to create a steady supply of labor. In colonial Tanzania sisal, coffee, and wheat plantations relied very heavily on migrant labor from the central part of the country. The cotton and coffee plantations of Uganda attracted many migrants from **Rwanda** and **Burundi**. The cotton cultivation of Gezira in **Sudan** also required migrants from neighboring countries.

The story of migrant labor from **North Africa** is intimately linked to military, economic, and political developments in Europe. This link has gone through phases punctuated by the two world wars. In the early part of the twentieth century there were few Maghrebian workers in Europe, but that changed quite dramatically during the world wars, as unemployment in North Africa started to encourage citizens to seek work in Europe. When France was occupied during the **Second World War**, there were about 100,000 North Africans living and working there. The occupation obviously cut off this emigrant labor flow. Indeed in **Algeria**, for example, many of these migrants returned home during the war, only to be re-recruited by the German consulates in North Africa. The German forces of occupation expelled many French workers from industries and filled these positions with migrant North Africans. After the war many Algerian workers were recruited to work in the reconstruction of French industry and agriculture. From about the mid-1960s **Libya** started to attract labor from neighboring countries in the Maghreb, especially **Tunisia**. In contrast to Algeria, which exported mainly unskilled labor, many highly skilled Tunisians became migrant laborers. Even later in the century Tunisians still regularly crossed the border looking for work in Libya, despite the expulsion of foreign workers from Libya in the mid-1990s.

Migrant labor was the dominant form of wage labor in colonial Africa until about the Second World War. The movement towards permanent **urbanization** started to set in as fewer migrants returned to the rural areas, or, in the case of international migrants, to their places of origin. The focus of scholarly attention also shifted in this period to an appreciation of the special conditions confronting an urban African proletariat.

When forced labor ended in Côte d'Ivoire in 1946, there was a major reorganization of labor recruiting and migrancy. The colonial government suspended the subsidies it paid for the transport of migrant workers in 1950. In response the employers formed their very own Interprofessional Syndicate for the Conveyance of Labor (Syndicat interprofessional d'acheminement de la main d'oeuvre, SIAMO), which continued to offer these subsidies for transport of workers by rail or road. In Southern Africa international migrant labor was used extensively in the development of the South African mining industry. By 1973, in the mines affiliated to the South African Chamber of Mines, foreign migrants made up 80 percent of the labor force, with South African migrants accounting for only 20 percent. The foreign workers came from the following countries: **Angola**, Tanzania, **Zambia**, **Malawi**, **Lesotho**, **Botswana**, **Mozambique**, **Zimbabwe**, and **Namibia**. Due to a variety of political and economic reasons the relative proportions were 45 percent and 55 percent by 1978. For example, under the Mozambique convention the mining houses had agreed to pay part of the migrants' wages in gold to the Portuguese colonial government. But when FRELIMO took power in Mozambique in 1974 the mining industry started to reduce the number of migrants because of perceived political uncertainties.

Despite pronouncements about ending the migrant labor system, by the end of the twentieth century it remained vitally important as a source of labor in the mines. In 1971 the intolerable conditions for migrants in mining compounds – the huge concentration camps provided as residences for miners – in Namibia led to a massive strike that was a forerunner to the crucial Durban strikes of 1973, precipitating the emergence of an independent trade union movement in South Africa (see **labor movements**).

Besides the direct action of migrant workers, they were also engaged in a range of resistance activities that demonstrate they did not passively accept their lot. For example, the migrant workers in colonial Zimbabwe's gold fields regularly deserted, stole, destroyed tools, and managed to play employers off against each other. These hidden forms of resistance contributed in uneven ways towards the formation of workers' consciousness and its spread as the migrants returned to their rural homes.

African responses to migrant labor differed vastly from region to region, and during different periods of the twentieth century. During the initial phase there was some cooperation between traditional authorities in the recruitment of members of a particular community, but there was also direct resistance to foreign incursions on their land. The development of class-based responses to migrant wage labor emerged very early on as well, but this new form of consciousness did not neatly replace old allegiances and belongings. Instead a multiplicity of identities was forged, based on the wide variety of experiences that migrants encountered.

Migrant labor and low wages are virtually synonymous. Many African workers received a wage that permitted neither subsistence and the material support of whole families, nor retirement on the basis of urban employment. Oscillating migration became the only viable option for reproducing livelihoods under these conditions. Migrant labor should be seen in the context of the growing dependence upon wage income, and as the nexus between urban and rural lives. Migrant labor persists, but it could also give way to permanent urban residence as more and more laborers cut off their ties with rural areas and become fully settled in the urban areas. This has increased in South Africa since the demise of apartheid and the repeal of restrictions placed on African urbanization.

Not only the poor are migrants. In fact it is estimated that Africa as a whole loses about 20,000 professionals every year. Since this has been happening from about 1985 the drain on economies where there are serious shortages of skilled labor can well be imagined. For example, there are more than 21,000 doctors from **Nigeria** practicing in the United States alone, while there is a scarcity of medical practitioners in Nigeria's own healthcare system. Similarly 60 percent of all Ghanaian doctors trained locally in the 1980s left the country, according to the UNDP's 1992 Human Development Report, while in **Sudan** 17 percent of doctors and dentists, 20 percent of university lecturers, 30 percent of engineers, and 45 percent of surveyors went to work elsewhere. These migrants responded to being away from home in a wide variety of ways. Some retained strong links, sent regular remittances to their families, and routinely returned home on an annual basis. Others severed their links completely. If the latter happens, then migrant labor changes into immigrant labor.

There is agreement that migrant labor was the initial form taken by wage employment in Africa. However, there is much debate on how it should be explained. Some have argued that migrant labor was a preferred option for capital because it could save on the costs of reproducing families by expecting a wage subsidy from the rural sector. In contrast others have suggested that migrant labor was determined by the dynamics of precolonial African society itself. The debate is ongoing, but it has given way to a more all-encompassing emphasis on livelihoods in Africa.

There are a range of factors that are important in developing a paradigm for analyzing migrant labor and why people are willing to move. In the first instance, moving in search of work elsewhere could imply the pursuit of a better life for the workers and their families. This could be structured by income disparities between different regions, and by the labor migration policies in different countries. Political conflict is an important factor, especially when it has a direct impact on the prospects for livelihoods. Migrant labor is obviously different in different regions, reflecting political and economic diversity across Africa in both regional and temporal terms.

See also: economy: colonial; peasants; workers

References and further reading

Amin, S. (1972) "Underdevelopment and Dependence in Black Africa: Historical Origins," *Journal of Peace Research* 2: 105–20.

Crush, J. *et al.* (1991) *South Africa's Labor Empire: A History of Black Migrancy to the Gold Mines*, Oxford: Westview Press.

Kowet, D. (1978) *Land, Labor Migration and Politics in Southern Africa: Botswana, Lesotho and Swaziland*, Uppsala: Scandinavian Institute of African Studies.

Murray, C. (1981) *Families Divided: The Impact of Migrant Labor in Lesotho*, Cambridge: Cambridge University Press.

Ressaissi, R. (1984) *Settlement Colonization and Transnational Labor Emigrations in the Maghreb: A Comparative Study of Algeria and Tunisia*, Lund: Skrifter av Ekonoisk-Historiska Föreningen.

Stichter, S. (1982) *Migrant Labor in Kenya: Capitalism and African Response, 1895–1975*, Harlow: Longman.

UNDP (1992) *Human Development Report 1992*, New York: Oxford University Press.

FRED HENDRICKS

Mogadishu, Somalia

Mogadishu, founded in the tenth century, was by the end of the twentieth century a city of 1.2 million, reeling from more than a decade of civil war. The war had wrecked much of this once prosperous port city, which for centuries had participated in the trade between **East Africa**, the Arabian peninsula, and South and East Asia across the Indian Ocean. At the end of the nineteenth century, Mogadishu had a population of about 5,000, and consisted of three sectors: Xamar Weyne, Xamar Jajab, and Shangani. During the Fascist era, Xamar Jajab was completely destroyed in order to make way for Mogadishu International airport.

At the end of the nineteenth century the Italians settled in the smallest sector of the town, Shangani, because the population of Xamar Weyne was hostile to European settlement. Shangani became an exclusively European area. As the Italian population of the city increased, particularly during the Fascist era, the built environment of Shangani expanded, as all Italian buildings were located there. These included the famous Catholic church, hotels, bars, restaurants, and houses. Somalis meanwhile established other sectors in the city in addition to Xamar Weyne, building houses and establishing communities east of Shangani along the Lido beach, north of Shangani (Bakaara and War-dhiigley), and northwest of Xamar Weyne (Hodon). The growth of the city during the colonial era was due mainly to administrative rather than economic functions: It was the administrative center of Italian **Somalia**, and by 1935 had become the headquarters of the Italian East African Empire. Nevertheless, Mogadishu did host some commercial enterprises. More importantly it became the center of nationalist activities. The Liga dei Giovani Somali (Somali Youth League or LGS) was founded in the city in 1943. The LGS organized demonstrations and campaigned for Somalia's independence.

In the post-colonial period the political and economic power of the city was further entrenched when the city became capital of Somalia, overcoming efforts by some to locate the capital in Hargeysa in the north of the country. Mogadishu expanded rapidly in the 1960s and 1970s as the Somali government concentrated its investments on the city in a determined bid to establish a centralized and modern state. Light manufacturing industries were established. As the population of the city grew – to more than half a million by the late 1980s – so did its built environment, expanding further north of Hodon, War-dhiigley, and Bakaara; west towards the airport; and further northwest of the airport, where wealthy bureaucrats built their own suburb, christened *Booli Qaran* ("the Stolen Nation") by the general public. By the late 1980s Mogadishu was a cosmopolitan city with different architectural traditions (medieval, colonial, and post-colonial).

But the city's fortunes entered a period of perilous decline from the latter years of Siad Barre's dictatorship. In 1989, two years before the ouster of the regime, Barre's beleaguered troops bombarded the city for four weeks, destroying much of the city and killing 50,000 people. The forces of the United Somali Congress, which had overthrown Barre's regime, split into factions led by Mohammed Farah Aidid and Ali Mahdi Mohamed. These factions fought it out in the already devastated capital, killing tens of thousands of people, while many more fled the city. Still others moved into the city from a countryside ravaged by drought. The destruction of Mogadishu by competing warlords became a symbol of the decline and fall of the Somali state itself.

Further reading

Puzo, W.D. (1972) *Mogadishu, Somalia: Geographic Aspects of its Evolution, Population, Functions and Morphology*, Ph.D. thesis, University of California, Los Angeles.

Tripodi, P. (1999) *The Colonial Legacy in Somalia: Rome and Mogadishu*, Basingstoke: Macmillan.

JAMA MOHAMED

Mombasa, Kenya

Mombasa is the fourth largest city in **East Africa**, with a history going back more than a thousand years. It is largely a Muslim city, with a negligible non-Muslim population until the twentieth century. The building of the Uganda railway transformed the city's socioeconomic status, particularly its function in Kenya's network of plantations, while the nature of its commercial shipping changed with the advent of British colonialism. The volume of trade and the size of its population increased Mombasa's range of commercial activity and encouraged a more Swahili cultural outlook, but it retained the atmosphere of an ancient capital.

In 1888 the imperial British East Africa Company established itself in Mombasa, and embarked on the planning and building of the railway to Lake Victoria. Plans to build the railway in the early 1890s generated colonial politics of control and management, which led to Mombasa and the sixteen-kilometer strip then under the control of the Sultan of Zanzibar being transferred to the British government in 1895. As part of the British East African Protectorate, different cultures and races continued to mix in the city. There were numerous Islamic mosques, Sikh and Jain temples, as well as the Portuguese-built Fort Jesus, and an intricate network of narrow streets. The wealthy Arab and Swahili population was concentrated in the old town in the Kibokoni area. Mombasa's rich cultural heritage and ancient civilization made the city a major tourist attraction, and several hotels and beach resorts were constructed to serve an international clientele.

The city's central business district comprised a railway terminus, an industrial area, and the deep harbor of Kilindini, while large European commercial houses – set up between 1895 and 1914 – captured the lion's share of Mombasa's trade. Public and private schools were key elements of the town by the end of the twentieth century, serving a population of about a million people by the year 2000. From the beginning of the twentieth century, the modern city had been spreading out from the island-based central business district to neighboring Likoni, Kisauni, and Changamwe on the mainland to the south, north and west respectively. With the railway and Kilindini harbor, which was capable of servicing modern freighters, industrialization was encouraged and an increasingly cosmopolitan and non-Muslim immigrant population began to arrive, with Indians especially prominent in commerce. Hindus and Sikhs were initially involved in small- and medium-scale commercial enterprises, but gradually entered into large-scale commercial activity in competition with Europeans.

The colonial era brought with it sharpened social differentiation. The poor, who lived in sprawling low-class Swahili-style slum housing in Majengo, were increasingly involved in industrial unrest and strikes, of which the most outstanding were the general strikes of 1939 and 1947. Mombasa also became the seat of separatist racial politics in the 1950s, when its Arab inhabitants formed the Mwambao United Front to demand coastal autonomy. After **Kenya** won its independence Mombasa became the center of the tourist industry, which had become the country's major foreign exchange earner by the 1980s. The city continued to play an important role in the country's economic, cultural, and political life, but the restoration of multi-party politics in the 1990s resulted in a resurgence of separatist politics. Increasingly connected with religious interests, political activists continued to argue for a better deal for Mombasa and the whole coastal region.

Further reading

Kindy, H. (1972) *Life and Politics in Mombasa*, Nairobi: East African Publishing.

ERIC ASEKA

Monrovia, Liberia

Monrovia, the capital of **Liberia**, is a port city on the Atlantic Ocean. At the beginning of the twentieth century, Monrovia was divided into two sections: one section became known as Monrovia proper, where Americo-Liberians lived, while the other was Krutown. Although many members of the Kru ethnic group resided in this section of the capital, other ethnic groups (including the Bassa and Grebo) lived there too. Monrovia's population at the beginning of the twentieth century was only 4,000, of whom 2,500 were Americo-Liberians. By 1926 the Americo-Liberian population had doubled to 5,000, while other ethnic groups from the interior of the country had begun to migrate to the city in search of economic opportunities. The Americo-Liberians attempted to construct a capital similar to Washington, D.C., complete with a congress and senate, while the wealthy among them built houses in the antebellum style, reflecting their roots in the American South.

Until the 1930s the government would only employ educated Americo-Liberians, those who passed as Americo-Liberians, and those who were absorbed into the community through marriage, adoption, or patronage. Everyone else had to find employment with foreign commercial or construction companies as ship-loaders, deckhands, clerks, and domestics.

Monrovia's population increased slowly, which may be attributable to poor living conditions. Monrovians were poverty-stricken, without electricity, telephones, decent sanitation, hospitals, or any other amenities. The **Second World War** would change Monrovia significantly, however, because of Liberia's strategic location and rubber-producing capacity. The US government built Monrovia Free Port, which allowed supplies for the war and other raw materials to be shipped out more easily. A highway was constructed that linked Monrovia to Ganta, located on the border with **Guinea**. The port and highway increased the volume of Liberia's principal exports: rubber and iron ore. The establishment of the port, industrial growth on nearby Bushrod Island, and the increase in the numbers of educated people moving to the city from the interior brought about a population explosion. In 1956 the population was 41,000; in 1962 it was 80,000; by 1978 it had increased to 208,000.

From 1979 Monrovia was the site of considerable violence, as the country entered a period of civil unrest with demonstrations against the government's proposed increase in the price of rice. Several people were killed and injured. The violence continued following the assassination of President William Tolbert in 1980 by the People's Redemption Council (PRC), headed by Master-Sergeant Samuel Doe. A civil war broke out in 1989, spreading to Monrovia as troops from the National Patriotic Front of Liberia (NPFL), led by Charles Taylor, and the Independent National Patriotic Front of Liberia (INPFL), led by Prince Yormie Johnson, tried to oust Doe. As these two factions advanced toward Monrovia, the Armed Forces of Liberia (AFL) committed various **human rights** violations. The **Economic Community of West African States** (ECOWAS) deployed a peacekeeping force, the Economic Community Monitoring Group (ECOMOG), in Monrovia in August 1990. A month later Doe was assassinated by the INPFL. Fighting continued throughout the city, with many more people killed or forced to flee. By 1996 Monrovia had plunged into anarchy and much of the city's infrastructure had been destroyed.

At the end of the twentieth century Monrovia was beginning to recover following national elections in 1997. However, fighting erupted again in 1998, and the government began to force the internally displaced out of government-owned buildings and displacement centers. The situation did improve, however, and Monrovia's airport and port were re-opened. Nonetheless much of the infrastructure that had been destroyed during the fighting in Monrovia has yet to be rebuilt.

Further reading

Saha, S.C. (1998) *Culture in Liberia*, Lewiston: Edwin Mellen Press.

CASSANDRA RACHEL VENEY

Morocco

Morocco, with an area of 710,850 square kilometers and an estimated population of 28.1 million in 2000, borders **Algeria** to the east and **Mauritania** to the southwest, and links Africa to Europe through the Mediterranean Sea. Morocco's official language is **Arabic** and its religion is **Islam**. The Amazighs remain the main component of the population, and their language is widely spoken. The Atlas mountain range runs through the middle of the country, leading to extensive fertile plains and then the 1,400 kilometers of Atlantic coast. To the south and east lie dry steppes, which merge with oases and the **Sahara**. Agriculture forms the country's major economic sector, employing approximately 40 percent of the labor force and contributing 35 percent of exports. Phosphates, clothes, and fish are Morocco's major exports. Its geographic position explains Morocco's multi-ethnic and multicultural background, with the mosaic of architectural styles, types of music and art, and beliefs testifying to the country's hybrid identity.

In 1912 Morocco became a French protectorate, but with the Spanish occupying the northern part and the Western Sahara. Under General Lyautey, France adopted a dual structure of governance and policy of division, which consisted of isolating the Amazighs and creating modern institutions alongside the existing ones. The Berber Dahir (1934) excluded the Amazighs from Islamic legislation and education, while the modernization of agriculture and industry to meet the needs of French exports went along with the expropriation of rural populations, the introduction of waged labor, and the creation of a class of clients through education and privilege. During the **Second World War** the French conscripted 30,000 Moroccans to the fight against the Nazis and on the Asian Front.

From the 1920s the colonial authorities in the north faced armed resistance from the Amazigh leader Abdelkrim al-Khattabi. Other revolts broke out in the Atlas mountains and the desert. The Moroccan elite, formed at Quaraouine University in Fes and informed by the religious Salafi School and pan-Arabism, led riots in the cities. They organized a mass movement under the Istiqlal party, which had been created in 1943. The struggles against occupation took many forms, but with two principal areas of attack. The first was opposition to the Berber Dahir, and renewed emphasis on Islam as the unique source of identity and legislation. The second was the boycott of French schools and the establishment of schools controlled by the nationalists that would emphasize respect for both *authenticity* and *modernity*. In 1953 resistance culminated in King Mohamed V's exile to **Madagascar**, but three years later Morocco regained its independence. Spanish occupation of the Western Sahara ended in 1975, when King Hassan II organized a march of 350,000 people. But the Polisario Front disputed Moroccan sovereignty over the region.

In 1961 Hassan II became King of Morocco and established the first constitution. He had to address the colonial legacy of legal pluralism, a dual system of education, a vanishing handicraft sector, the collapse of traditional or existing forms of work and solidarity and systems of work, and a dependency on French cooperation. Hassan II also had to address the problems of a nation built on a combination of resistance and democracy. The king emphasized both the authenticity of tradition and necessity of building modern institutions. In 1963 the first elections were organized. The leading nationalist parties, Istiqlal, and the socialist Union National des Forces Populaires lost the elections to two newly created parties. In 1965 riots broke out in Casablanca led by the leftists, unions, and other political parties to protest government policy. A state of emergency was declared, and the constitution and parliament were suspended until 1970.

During the 1980s the implementation of **structural adjustment programs** caused other problems. This economic and social crisis was exacerbated by long periods of drought that caused massive migration to the cities, compounded by collapsing prices for phosphates and diminishing remittances from abroad. During this period growing Islamist groups provided the needed social services in the expanding poor suburbs. From the early 1990s the government responded with measures to encourage foreign investment and provide loans to young entrepreneurs. A zone of free trade with the **European Union** was also created, and a vague privatization program initiated. Neoliberalism was also associated with the introduction of political pluralism. The referendum of 1996 adopted a two-chamber system to reinforce the autonomy of the sixteen administrative regions.

The state of **human rights** was also on the agenda, with human rights violations used to justify the rejection of Morocco's formal application to join the European Union. At the beginning of the 1990s King Hassan created the consultative Council for Human Rights, followed by the Ministry in Charge of Human Rights. Women's massive mobilization to reform family law during the 1990s was acknowledged by the appointment of four women to the Secretariat of State in 1997, among them Nawal el-Moutawakil, holder of the 400-meters gold medal from the 1984 Los Angeles Olympics. This opening to **civil society** actors facilitated the emergence of a vast sector of voluntary organizations and services. The 30,000 **non-governmental organizations** that emerged operated across a wide range of development, health, education, and human rights issues. After King Hassan's death in July 1999, his son Mohamed VI continued to follow his father's policy. The appointment of a committee to compensate the families of the disappeared, and victims of torture or detention underlined the new commitment to democracy.

By the end of the twentieth century 35 percent of Morocco's population was under fourteen years of age. Unemployment was a major concern for those under twenty-five years old, for whom the unemployment rate was estimated at 22 percent in 1999. Some 65 percent of the population was illiterate, the majority of them women. This young and underprivileged population became increasingly disenchanted with the traditional political parties, and showed growing interest in further democratic reform, with **Islam** was becoming a major political force. The Arabic face of Morocco was revealed in the huge demonstrations during the Gulf War of 1991 and ongoing deep concerns over the Palestinian question. It was thus with a multiplicity of identities, hopes, and struggles that Morocco entered the twenty-first century.

Further reading

Boukia, R. and Miller, S.G. (eds.) (1999) *In the Shadow of the Sultan: Culture, Power and Politics in Morocco*, Cambridge: Harvard University Press.

Pennell, C.R. (2000). *Morocco since 1830: A History*, New York: New York University Press.

ZAKIA SALIME

Mozambique

Mozambique, with an area of 799,380 square kilometers, is bordered by **Tanzania**, **Malawi**, **Zambia**, **Zimbabwe**, **South Africa**, and **Swaziland**. It had an estimated population of 19 million in 2000. It was colonized by Portugal in the sixteenth century, but African resistance continued until 1919. During the first two decades of the twentieth century the Portuguese conducted military campaigns and developed administrative structures, while at the same time exploiting the colony's agricultural resources by granting concessions to companies involved in sugar and cotton plantations. Because the colonial authority had little or no administrative control over the areas where these companies operated, the colony was not ruled as a single political entity. Consequently different regions were subjected to different colonial experiences. Traditional chiefs and clan leaders were used to enforce exploitative labor policies.

Mozambicans felt the heavy weight of colonial administration. They were forced to use their land and family labor to grow crops for the state, and were not allowed to look after their own fields, which produced their food, until the work for the district was completed. In some areas taxes pushed male adults into forced labor that took them away from home. In southern Mozambique Africans were forced to choose between working for almost nothing in the colony itself or for slightly higher wages in neighboring countries. In exchange for contracting Mozambican labor to South Africa and Rhodesia, South Africa and Rhodesia agreed to use Mozambique's transit facilities for shipping.

Between 1928 and 1968 António Salazar, as minister and later premier, influenced events in Mozambique. He extended Lisbon's control over all aspects of the colony's administration and exploited the colony's resources for the benefit of Portugal. During the depression of the 1930s he used Mozambique as a supplier of raw materials. Mozambicans were forced to grow cotton for the state, as it was the most valuable cash crop and much needed in Portugal's textile industry, which could not afford to buy it on the world market. Production was tightly controlled, and Africans received very low fixed prices for cotton.

During the **Second World War** Mozambique benefited from Portugal's neutrality. Its revenues doubled because of huge demand from the warring nations for raw materials, although half of Mozambique's foreign trade was still with Portugal. With the new wealth, Portuguese companies took over foreign enterprises in Mozambique, leading to further exploitation of the colony's natural and manpower resources.

After the war Lisbon's continued insistence that Mozambique produce commercial crops ignited anti-colonial feelings, and led to protests in the Makonde cottonbelt. In 1960 police opened fire on a demonstration in Mueda, killing about 500 cotton laborers. Increased Portuguese repression and violence led exiled Africans to form three movements, each with a different geographic and ethnic base. In June 1962 their leaders put differences aside to form a single national movement: the Frente de Libertação de Moçambique (Front for the Liberation of Mozambique or FRELIMO).

In September 1964 FRELIMO began armed struggle in Cabo Delgado. After the PIDE (secret police) destroyed its infrastructure in the south, FRELIMO concentrated on the northern and central provinces, establishing cooperative farming and social services in the liberated areas. By the early 1970s FRELIMO's campaign had moved south and begun attacking economic targets and the Beira railway. Their successful campaign forced the Portuguese to relocate villagers into fenced compounds, and to Africanize the security forces.

In April 1974 there was a successful coup in Lisbon. In September the junta signed a ceasefire and transferred power to FRELIMO. In June 1975 Mozambique became independent. President Samora Machel established a one-party system, using Marxist ideology to guide nation-building. Although FRELIMO's leadership was multi-racial, most Portuguese settlers (who had controlled every sector of the economy) left within a year, leaving the country with few technicians, administrators, or professionals.

Machel inherited an economy that was closely tied to the white-minority regimes in **Southern Africa**. Despite his opposition to apartheid, he maintained economic ties with South Africa and continued to supply labor because he needed the foreign exchange earnings these workers brought home. However, South Africa moved to reduce its dependence on migrant labor, which negatively impacted the Mozambican economy.

FRELIMO also ran into problems with Rhodesia because of Mozambique's compliance with UN sanctions and support for the liberation struggle there. In retaliation Rhodesia trained and financed the Resistencia National Moçambicana (Mozambican National Resistance or Renamo), which sought to rally support among the discontented rural population who had been forced to work on state-run farms. By 1980 Renamo had lost Rhodesia's support, with the former colony becoming **Zimbabwe**. Renamo then moved to South Africa. With new arms and supplies it expanded its subversive campaign, killing civilians, destroying crops, and burning health clinics and schools. Many people left their homes or fled the country to escape the fighting. By the mid-1980s rebel activity had ruined the economy, forcing FRELIMO to alter their socialist policy. In 1989 the party dropped Marxism as the official state ideology.

The shift in policy did not stop the fighting, but Mozambicans were weary of war and critical of the government. In 1990 President Joaquim Chicano proposed a new constitution, stressing individual rights and guaranteeing universal adult suffrage by secret ballot. He established a multi-party system, an independent judiciary, and a free market economy. With these reforms in place, he sought a non-military solution to the internal conflict. After two years of talks, with the help of foreign mediation, the government and rebels signed the Rome Accords in October 1992, bringing the sixteen years of civil war to an end. Two democratic elections were held in the 1990s. Although there were many parties on the ballot, the contest was really between FRELIMO and Renamo. The ruling party won most of the legislative seats and the presidency, but Renamo had substantial support in the north and center of Mozambique. By 2000 democracy seemed to have taken root in the country, and the free market economy was holding steady.

See also: lusophone Africa

Further reading

Birmingham, D. (1992) *Frontline Nationalism in Angola and Mozambique*, Trenton: Africa World Press Inc.

Serapiao, L.B. and El-Khawas, M.A. (1979) *Mozambique in the Twentieth Century*, Washington, D.C.: University Press of America.

M.A. EL-KHAWAS

music

There was an explosion of creative energy and innovation in all types of African music during the twentieth century. In part this represents a continuation of indigenous musical dynamism within, and new musical influences among, different African societies before the mid-nineteenth century. With the increasing incursion of colonial regimes between the end of the nineteenth and the mid-twentieth centuries, modernist aesthetic ideologies and a vast array of new musical resources were introduced to the continent, generating myriad new local creations. With the rise of **nationalist movements** in the mid-twentieth century, music, **dance**, and other local cultural practices were drawn upon, fashioned, and "reformed" in light of modernist aesthetics for new political purposes. During the last twenty years of the twentieth century certain styles of African music entered transnational music markets in ways more pronounced than ever before, as part of a commercial phenomenon known alternatively as "worldbeat" or "world music." By this period relatively abundant scholarly and popular writing about African musics also helped raise the awareness and popularity of certain African styles within cosmopolitan circles in Europe, the Americas, and parts of Asia. At a detailed level of analysis musicians' responses to colonialism, nationalism, and the lure of transnational markets are as varied as the multitude of indigenous musical styles across the continent.

Thinking about indigenous African music-making

One tendency in Africanist musicology has been to treat "African music" as one thing. Sometimes detailed studies of one or two societies in a given country have been used to generalize about African music writ large. Thus, in John Chernoff's classic and otherwise excellent book (1979), the author uses his research primarily among the Ewe, and to a lesser extent the Dagbamba, of **Ghana** to make major pronouncements about "African music" and aesthetics. Other scholars have written with more specificity (see Waterman 1991 on the "Africa general versus Africa specific" debate). As in much Africanist scholarship, reference to "African" music is generally restricted to sub-Saharan Africa, excluding **North Africa**.

In regard to musical meaning, and the specifics of style and practice that are probably most important to the members of different African societies, description must proceed on a case-by-case basis. At the same time there are some general features of African musical performance that pertain to many societies, much like the European tonal harmonic system serves as a baseline for thinking about many styles of "Western music." Briefly these general African musical features include:

1. cyclical, open-ended forms;
2. dense, overlapping, polyphonic textures;
3. buzzy timbres;
4. the interlocking of musical parts (call-and-response being the most obvious example);
5. beat groupings dividable by twos and threes (for example, quick pulses), which allow for the interplay of duple/triple rhythms and rhythmic complexity;
6. musical ensembles organized around some players providing repetitive *core* parts and others providing *elaboration* parts;
7. *intensive* development and elaboration (within the cyclical form) rather than *extensive* elaboration (extending the form);
8. "music" and "dance" considered part of the same art form, rather than being conceptualized as separate arts; and
9. music-dance conceptualized as a social process rather than a set item or product.

These same features turn up in all types of African societies, ranging from Baka vocal music in **Central Africa** to Ewe drumming in Ghana and Shona *mbira* (lamellophone or "thumb piano") performance in **Zimbabwe**. Thus, in an Ewe drum ensemble, two or three smaller drums each play their own cyclical pattern. The patterns are designed to *interlock* with the other supporting drum parts (the accented strokes of one drum part fit within the spaces of other drum parts) to create a single dense gestalt. Ewe ensembles also use a double bell to create the overall guiding time-cycle (usually comprising twelve quick beats), and shakers are used to create a dense buzzy aura around the music. Together these instruments produce the *core* for the musical performance to accompany singing and dancing; the composed songs are often performed in call-and-response fashion. A lead drummer produces the *elaboration* part. He improvises rhythmic patterns that interlock with the *core* drum parts, or plays vocal phrases, or plays specific patterns that guide or fit with dancers' movements.

Across the continent, the same principles can be seen operating in a Shona *mbira* performance. The *mbira* is a *lamellophone*, an instrument-type indigenous to and common in most parts of Africa. Lamellophones have metal or reed keys resting on a bridge fastened to a sound board that is usually played within or fastened to a resonating gourd or box. In the region comprising **Zambia**, Zimbabwe, **Mozambique**, and parts of **South Africa** there are many different types of lamellophones. The twenty-two-key Zezuru (Shona subgroup) *mbira* became the most popular type in Zimbabwe by the end of the twentieth century (Turino 2000). Shona *mbira* is performed primarily for collective religious ceremonies for the ancestors. *Mbira* have shells or bottle-caps attached to the sound board and resonator to produce a buzzy timbre. Usually two or more *mbira* players perform together. The music comprises a lead part played by one musician and a second accompanying part that interlocks with the lead. The basic cycle of *mbira* music consists of four twelve-beat phrases, and gourd rattles accent the 12/8 meter, as well as producing a buzzy aura around the performance and creating the rhythmic drive for dancing. Although *mbira* players may add elaboration within the basic melodic-harmonic cycle (forty-eight beats) of the piece, the *mbira* and rattles produce the basic *core* of the performance, with singing and dancing being elaboration parts. While call-and-response singing is typical in other Shona song and drumming traditions, in *mbira* music vocal parts are often improvised to fit with the *mbira* melodies and to interlock more loosely with other singers' parts.

Participatory ethics are key to musical/dance performance in a majority of African societies and indigenous performance contexts. Value is placed on encouraging active musical and dance participation among all present, in contrast to *presentational* traditions where one group performs for an audience that sits still and silent. African participatory traditions allow for people to enter into the performance at a variety of levels of specialization. Most ensembles include highly specialized roles that require training and practice, such as lead drumming and *mbira* playing, as well as roles for neophyte performers, for example simple hand-clapping, shaker parts, vocal parts, and basic dancing.

There are exceptions to this participatory pattern. The drumming and trumpet performance that accompanies formal royal court events, for example among the **Hausa** of **Nigeria**, tend to be restricted to musical specialists. Before being overthrown in 1966, the *kabaka* (ruler) of Buganda maintained a number of specialist musicians, including a private harpist, a flute ensemble, a xylophone ensemble, a drum-chime (*entenga*), trumpeters, and royal drummers. In Mande societies (**Mali** and surrounding regions) there is a hereditary group of professional musicians–verbal artists known as *jelilu* who accompany praise singing and historical narratives with *kora* (twenty-one-string harp-lute), xylophones, or plucked lutes. Although typically not in a stage setting, these musicians often perform for wealthy patrons in a presentational manner.

The older notion that indigenous African musics remained static until brought into contact with Europeans is no longer tenable. There are numerous reports of changes in styles and musical fashions within African societies generated by inner dynamics. For example, there was a waxing and waning in the popularity of different Shona lamellophone types and repertories during the twentieth century, a process not influenced by Europeans. Stephen Hill describes how it was typical for the popularity of given dances to change from one generation to the next among the Wamatengo of **Tanzania**. Others have studied the diffusion of instruments between African societies in the pre-colonial period. Robert Kauffman (1975) has shown that even the incorporation of a European instrument such as the guitar does not necessarily signal "Westernization" or "modernization." He argues that the Shona of Zimbabwe simply incorporated a new instrument for playing music that was organized and conceptualized along indigenous lines (that is, with the traits outlined above). Similar cases of the guitar being incorporated to play what was essentially indigenous lamellophone, bow, or lute music are widespread for **West**, Central, **East**, and **Southern Africa**. In spite of the effects of colonialism and nationalism, indigenous musical/dance traditions remain vital in societies throughout the continent, and they continue to be performed alongside other spheres of music-making, especially that of urban-popular music.

Effects of European colonialism on musical life

The church and the military were the two colonial institutions that initially had the most direct effect on music-making in African societies. Missionaries taught European tonal harmony and European or American hymns, spirituals, and popular songs. Mission schools were particularly powerful institutions for teaching European music to African peoples. Since the schools were also important sites for the diffusion of the ideology of modernity, and for creating local cosmopolitan middle-class groups, European music became associated with "progress," social mobility, and higher status within black populations and the colonial order. Along with religious hymns, white mission-school teachers sometimes taught popular and "folk" songs associated with African-Americans that they felt to be appropriate for black children – including minstrel-like material such as "Shortened Bread" (1899). In addition to European harmony and particular musical repertories African children learned European aesthetics through school singing: Tightly arranged phrasing and transparent textures replaced the dense overlapping style of participatory performance, particularly among performers aspiring to middle-class status or people who had grown up on mission-station lands.

There are reports from different parts of the continent that missionaries discouraged indigenous music and dancing, but the impact of missionaries varied widely from one location to another (even within a single colony) and from one Christian sect to another. Moreover, even in heavily missionized regions religious beliefs comprised a whole range of syncretic responses, and the same is true for musical responses. Thus in Zimbabwe school singing led to a tightly arranged urban-popular vocal style, modeled after the Mills Brothers and the Inkspots, among urban middle-class performers in the 1940s and 1950s, and to a more syncretic rural style known locally as *makwaya*, which combined European harmonies with call-and-response organization and the dense overlapping textures of Shona performance.

In German and British colonies Africans learned to read music, perform European wind instruments, and play a cosmopolitan repertoire through training in the military. The black musicians who worked in military and police bands would often go on to careers in African jazz bands, or to create new urban-popular styles such as *highlife* in Ghana and Nigeria. Highlife was a blend of local rhythms, with jazz-band instrumentation and arrangements, and repertoire from the United States, England, and especially the Caribbean (for example, Cuban *son* and Trinidadian *calypso*), as well as from local composers. By the 1940s in Johannesburg ballroom dance orchestras and swing bands modeled on North American big bands were popular. In East Africa military bands served as a model for a syncretic style of dance known as *beni* (as well as other local names). In *beni* the dancers wear military-style costumes, and are accompanied by drums and kazoos in imitation of military bands.

By the 1920s transnational culture industries began affecting African music-making. North American and Caribbean 78rpm records of a variety of musical styles were diffused to urban and mining centers, as were inexpensive instruments such as production-line guitars, banjos, accordions, concertinas, and pennywhistles. American country music and jazz records provided models for African guitarists. As late as the 1960s South African and Zimbabwean guitarists were imitating American country star Jimmie Rodgers (d. 1933), and using stage names such as "Zulu Cowboy." Urban working-class musicians in the south were also influenced by jazz, using guitars and pennywhistles to create a new local "swing" style known as *kwela*.

In the rural areas of southern Africa guitars, concertinas, autoharps, and accordions were used to play indigenous music. In South Africa, for example, a guitar-style emerged that was modeled on Nguni musical bow performance, while in Zimbabwe musicians played *mbira* and drum songs using the acoustic guitar. In the 1950s itinerant Zimbabwean acoustic guitarists created a new style, later called *jit*, that was modeled on South African urban-popular genres such as *marabi* and *tsaba-tsaba*, combined with the local Shona 12/8 rhythmic feel. The creation of *jit* as a new genre illustrates the importance of intra-regional influences and borrowing, in the context of labor migration and the impact of regional cosmopolitan centers such as Johannesburg. In the south, solo performers sometimes used accordions and concertinas as a substitute for vocal choruses in songs in indigenous call-and-response form, or to play the cyclical core part to accompany vocal elaboration (in **Lesotho**, for example). That is, these foreign instruments were incorporated and adapted within local indigenous practices and aesthetic systems.

On the west coast, from **Freetown** to **Lagos**, sailors were also a source for emerging African guitar genres such as *palmwine*, an acoustic guitar-style using two-finger picking and melodies played over repeating chord progressions (for example, I, IV, II, I, V, I) for songs in local languages and with local indigenous or highlife rhythms. Among the **Yoruba** in Nigeria acoustic guitars or banjos with local and cosmopolitan percussion instruments were used to perform topical and praise songs in a style known as *juju*. In **Congo** acoustic guitars were used in mining centers to play new forms of syncretic recreational music that was formerly performed on indigenous lamellophones with percussion accompaniment. During the 1950s in Congo, Cuban music (especially the *son*, known internationally as *rumba* or *rhumba*) became the basis for the music played by electric guitar bands. Franco and his group OK Jazz was a leading exponent of this style, which diffused to cities throughout Central, East, and Southern Africa. From this imitative basis, a unique style of Congolese guitar-band music emerged in the 1960s, later known internationally as *soukous*. Similar developments, combining Cuban music, cosmopolitan instruments (guitars, bass, traps, horns), and local musical styles, were taking place in the Mande region.

Nationalism and music

The same types of syncretic musical processes set in motion during the colonial period were continued (and in some ways intensified) by **nationalist movements**, although the stylistic results acquired new political meaning. Nationalist movements across Africa had similar relationships to and impact on music and dance for a variety of structural reasons. As elsewhere in the colonial world, members of the indigenous middle class or elite formed the political vanguard to confront the twin requirements of forging a nation and taking control of the state. Music and dance were key tools for the process of nation-building. To link the political vanguard to "the masses," and to indicate the uniqueness of the imagined nation, indigenous music and dances were used as prominent public emblems and activities.

A particularly rich example of the complex fusion of music and nationalism, indigenous and modern musical traditions, can be seen in the career of Umm Kulthūm, Egypt's most celebrated singer and cultural icon of the twentieth century, whose career spanned from the 1910s to the 1970s. During Kulthūm's remarkable career there were transformations in musical aesthetics, technique and values, entertainment technology, and society, which she mastered and shaped. Her songs and performances, based on perfect Koranic diction, deep concern for textual meaning, attentiveness to her audiences, and emphasis on the significance of the listener, all valued in Egyptian religious song (*mashayik*), combined with classical Arabic and modern aesthetics and technical facilities, became anthems for the nation trying to rediscover and redefine itself.

Because of the modernist-cosmopolitan cultural position of the nationalist party leaderships, however, cultural nationalist projects were often designed to "reform" indigenous arts to bring them in line with the arts of other "modern" nation-states. Participatory music/dance traditions were transformed into presentational forms codified and arranged for stage performance. National dance troupes and ensembles were formed to represent the newly established nation-states, fashioning local indigenous arts according to cosmopolitan ethics and aesthetics for *international* tours and festivals, and for foreign visitors to the home country. Depending on the political situation within a given country national repertories and styles were codified, either representing all the diverse "ethnic" groups within the territory (creating the image of "unity in diversity") or favoring the emblems of politically dominant groups.

With the rise of nation-states a number of African kingdoms lost their sovereignty, leading to the decline of royal court music. In East Africa specialist ensembles formerly linked to royal courts were sometimes recruited to serve new political leaders. In Ghana Akan rulers continued to use the royal *fontomfrom* drumming tradition while, simultaneously, it was incorporated within Ghanaian state cultural institutions as a marker of Akan ethnicity alongside the arts of other groups to project "unity in diversity." In Mali the post-independence state became the new patron for professional musicians previously attached to former rulers. Modeled in part on European orchestras, the Malian state created a large official ensemble consisting of the instruments used by the *jelilu*, thus combining local and cosmopolitan aspects.

The typical ideological position of cultural nationalism held that "the best of local culture should be combined with the best of foreign influences" to create a unique yet "modern" (that is, modular cosmopolitan) nation-state. Thus the processes of cultural-musical syncretism instigated by various forces during the colonial period were given official sanction and institutional support during the nationalist and post-independence phases. The new "national" styles of indigenous music and dance, and their cosmopolitan aesthetic-ethical bases, are now a part of socialization through their inclusion in schools and other educational institutions. This official impetus for blending the "the local and the foreign" has been added to, and works in conjunction with, previously existing forces such as the influence of the capitalist music, film, and tourist industries.

African music and transnational markets

Increasing numbers of African artists gained international experience and exposure performing abroad in the context of official national dance companies, ensembles, and orchestras. Pre-existing urban-popular styles that blended local musical features with cosmopolitan instrumentation and styles were sometimes brought within the nationalist arena because they fitted the same syncretic mold advocated by cultural nationalism. Thus the addition of the hour-glass shaped *dundun* ("talking drum") to electrified *juju* bands in the period after the **Second World War** had a nationalist significance for the Yoruba in Nigeria (Waterman 1990). The Malian government supported *orchestras* with electric guitar, saxophones, and Latin percussion, and required the groups to play in a style that blended indigenous *jeli* traditions with Caribbean and other cosmopolitan influences. In Zimbabwe electric guitar bands such as Thomas Mapfumo and the Blacks Unlimited, the Green Arrows, and others performed *jit*, as well as indigenous Shona drumming and *mbira* music with political lyrics during the War of Liberation of the 1970s.

By the mid-1980s a new market category for selling music from **Third World** countries was emerging – "worldbeat" and, later, "world music" – in the context of a rising demand for such music in cosmopolitan centers in Europe, the Americas, and Japan. Jamaican reggae artist Bob Marley was the first worldbeat superstar marketed transnationally. Chris Blackwell of Island Records emphasized the importance of certain images, as well as the danceable beat, in connection with Marley's popularity. Marley's music combined the themes of black political liberation, the spirituality of Rastafarianism, and an exotic roots-music sound within a style that had already been heavily influenced by North American soul music and rhythm and blues. Marley's sound was thus simultaneously familiar and foreign-sounding to young cosmopolitan audiences in the United States, England, and Europe.

British and North American rock and pop artists, such as Peter Gabriel, David Byrne, Sting, and Paul Simon, helped to introduce worldbeat audiences to African music – much like folk-revival musicians had done for rural music among middle-class audiences in the United States and Europe beginning in the 1950s. For example, Sting's hit "Desert Rose" offered European and American audiences a brief introduction to Algeria's *rai* music through his collaboration with the renowned Algerian singer Cheb Mami. *Rai*, which literally means "opinion" in Arabic, was invented in western **Algeria** in the 1960s, spreading to

Morocco, as music of the impoverished and marginalized, whose deceptively simple and eloquent lyrics wrestle with poverty, political oppression, corruption, love, and sex. An even better-known case of African musical appropriation or export is Paul Simon's phenomenally successful worldbeat recording, *Graceland* (1986). In the liner notes Simon explained his choice of the South African artists and styles used on the album: the *mbube* music of Ladysmith Black Mambazo and *township jive* were both "familiar and foreign-sounding at the same time." The reason for this is that, like reggae, these South African styles were, at their inception, heavily modeled on North American music.

Similarly the *juju* music of Nigerian King Sunny Ade and the Zimbabwean *chimurenga* music of Thomas Mapfumo (both marketed by Island Records) contained "familiar" cosmopolitan features, blended with distinctive local "roots" components. In keeping with themes associated with Marley, Mapfumo was marketed on the basis of the political content of his music (the 1970s Zimbabwean political struggle) and the spiritual connection of the *mbira* (an instrument he included in his band only after he entered the transnational market). Thus, while marketed on the basis of cultural difference and exotic appeal, the African styles chosen for worldbeat marketing – *mbube*, township jive, Congolese *soukous*, *chimurenga*, *juju*, and Mande guitar bands, among others – were precisely those that were cosmopolitan in their inception, and thus well suited to the worldbeat audiences outside of Africa.

Bands playing these styles, and other touring African groups, also performed for the growing numbers of Africans living outside the continent; the dynamics of diasporic audiences were distinct from those of the rather fickle worldbeat market, and need to be considered separately. While Britain and the United States attracted music from anglophone Africa, France – with its large West and North African diaspora – was the center of musical exports from francophone Africa. Some musicians crossed these divides, such as the widely popular Senegalese singer Youssou N'Dour. In the meantime musical exchange from the African diaspora in the United States found its way to all of Africa, including North Africa. In Algeria, for example, hip hop spread rapidly among middle-class youth, then among the urban poor. By 2000 there were about a hundred hip-hop groups in the country, up from forty in 1990. They were mostly concentrated in Oran, where *rai* was invented, rapping or singing lyrics in French, Arabic, or Amazigh.

As is often the case, the popularity of given African styles abroad sometimes helped raise their popularity and viability at home. For example, Mapfumo's use of the *mbira*, in conjunction with his celebrated popularity abroad, raised the interest in this indigenous instrument among urban youth in Zimbabwe, who dreamt of starting bands and touring internationally. Meanwhile, at the end of the twentieth century, indigenous musical styles continued to be performed in indigenous contexts throughout the continent. While not isolated from cosmopolitan influences in the mass media and national cultural institutions, indigenous performers continued to operate from a basis of distinctive local ethical and aesthetic conceptions of music, dance, and performance. Within most regions the musical results of the different historical trends described in this entry coexisted and intersected, and will continue to generate new creative trends and styles.

References and further reading

Charry, E. (2000) *Mande Music: Traditional and Modern Music of the Maninka and Mandinka of Western Africa*, Chicago: University of Chicago Press.

Chernoff, J. (1979) *African Rhythm and African Sensibility*, Chicago: University of Chicago Press.

Cooke, P. (1998) "East Africa: An Introduction," in R. Stone (ed.), *Africa: The Garland Encyclopedia of World Music*, vol. 1, New York: Garland Publishing Inc.

Danielson, V. (1997) *The Voice of Egypt: Umm Kulthūm, Arabic Song, and Egyptian Society in the Twentieth Century*, Chicago: University of Chicago Press.

Hill, S. "Don't Live Primitive Lives Anymore: Nationalist Discourse and Modernity among Matengo Dancers," paper presented at the 44th

Annual Meeting of the Society for Ethnomusicology, Austin, Texas, 18-21 November.
Kauffman, R. (1975) "Shona Urban Music: A Process Which Maintains Traditional Values," in C. Kileff and W.C. Pendleton (eds.), *Urban Man in Southern Africa*, Gweru: Mambo Press.
Turino, T. (2000) *Nationalists, Cosmopolitans, and Popular Music in Zimbabwe*, Chicago: University of Chicago Press.
Waterman, C. (1990) *Juju: A Social History and Ethnography of an African Popular Music*, Chicago: University of Chicago Press.
—— (1991) "The Uneven Development of Africanist Ethnomusicology: Three Issues and a Critique," in B. Nettl and P. Bohlman (eds.), *Comparative Musicology and Anthropology of Music*, Chicago: University of Chicago Press.

TOM TURINO

N

N'Djamena, Chad

N'Djamena, the capital and largest city of **Chad**, is located in the southwest of the country at the intersection of the Chari and Logone rivers. In 1900 French troops captured Fort Lamy and made it the colonial capital. It was renamed N'Djamena in 1973. Because of its strategic location, N'Djamena served as an important transit center on the east–west pilgrimage route to Mecca during the twentieth century. During the **Second World War** the French relied heavily on the airport in N'Djamena for the transport of troops and supplies – at that time it ranked as the third busiest airport in the entire French Union.

Urbanization proceeded at a slow pace in Chad, and N'Djamena did not experience economic expansion or great population growth until after independence in 1960. In 1958 the city had a population of only 53,000; by 1960 it had grown to 90,000, however, and people continued to flock there, resulting in a population of 130,000 by 1972. The National School of Administration was built in 1963, followed by the University of Chad in 1971.

N'Djamena has served as the principal administrative, economic, military, and cultural center of the country, maintaining its significance and importance throughout the century, despite the protracted civil war. Beginning in the late 1970s, the war had devastating consequences for the city. Thousands of people began to pour into the city in search of physical and economic security, and this growth in population – in addition to damage caused by the war itself – took a toll on an infrastructure that had been fragile before the war began. At the same time thousands of people left the city after the overthrow of various governments. For example, when former defense minister Hissene Habre captured N'Djamena in 1982, many civilians fled under threats of murder, looting, and torture. Again in 1990 many people left N'Djamena following the overthrow of Habre by his former aide Idriss Deby. Even then peace and stability were still a long way down the road for the capital, as opposition groups staged various coup attempts against Deby.

In sum thousands of Chadians either left the capital or moved there as a result of the civil war and the accompanying **human rights** violations perpetrated by government and military troops, and various rebel groups. Finally, during the latter part of the twentieth century, the civil war and drought produced food shortages that forced people to flee into N'Djamena once more. Between 1993 and 2000 the city's population grew from 531,000 to 728,000.

Although the civil war persisted into the 1990s, N'Djamena continued to serve as the industrial and commercial hub of the country, with most of Chad's economic activity based there. The major industries in the capital were meat-, fish-, and cotton-processing, all of which benefited from good connections with the international airport. This was particularly important given that Chad had no railroad system and roads were often impassable during the rainy season.

As the capital became more stable at the end of the twentieth century, infrastructure was repaired or rebuilt. The Great Mosque and ruins of the ancient Sao civilization served as popular attractions for both citizens, 95 percent of whom were Muslim, and visitors. The city once again had restaurants, international hotels, and a busy market. N'Djamena was finally getting a chance to rebuild its reputation as one of the most attractive cities in the region.

Further reading

Decalo, S. (1977) *Historical Dictionary of Chad*, Metuchen: Scarecrow Press.

Kelley, M. (1986) *A State in Disarray: Conditions of Chad's Survival*, Boulder: Westview Press.

CASSANDRA RACHEL VENEY

Nairobi, Kenya

Nairobi is the capital of **Kenya**, and had an estimated population of 2.7 million in 2000. The city was founded in 1899 as a depot for the Kenya–Uganda railway, and named after the Masai term *enkare nairobi* ("place of cold water"). Also in 1899 the provincial capital moved from Machakos to Nairobi. Soon Nairobi attracted Indian traders, who established shops there. In 1908 the colony's capital was moved to Nairobi from **Mombasa**. To make the railway profitable the colonial administration invited white settlers to the country to develop commercial farming. They decided to make Nairobi a white-settler town, to which Africans only came as temporary laborers, adopting a policy of racial segregation that prevented non-Europeans from owning freehold property. In 1919 the Nairobi Municipal Council was established, and the first mayor was elected in 1923.

Although Africans were in the majority in Nairobi, making up over 60 percent of the population in 1926 (compared to 10 percent for Europeans and 30 percent for Indians), they had no representation and received the least both in economic terms and in terms of social services. Housing for Africans was the most critical problem, since they were bundled into congested and neglected "native locations" like Pumwani, Pangani, Shauri Moyo, Ziwani, and so on. In 1946 the African District Councils were established, by which elite Africans were coopted into leadership of the town. By 1950, when Nairobi was designated as a city, class divisions had began to replace racial segregation, and after 1962 this became the major challenge facing the first African mayor, Charles Rubia. During the 1950s Nairobi was at the center of the **labor movement** and nationalist struggles for independence.

After independence the challenges created by an independent, largely African city were most evident in the population increases: from 65,000 in 1948, population grew to 160,000 in 1960, 266,794 in 1962, 509,286 in 1969, 1.2 million in 1987, and an estimated 2.7 million in 2000. Such rapid growth intensified problems of overcrowding, inadequate housing, poverty and slum development, pollution, poor infrastructure, unemployment, and general anarchy. However, between 1962 and 1984 there was general economic prosperity for Kenya, and Nairobi became the leading city in **East Africa** described as "the Green City in the Sun." It attracted many people and numerous international organizations, providing headquarters for the United Nations Environmental Program, for example. It was home to the University of Nairobi and Kenyatta University, and the center of a booming tourism industry.

Periodically Nairobi faced problems due to a clash of interests between central government and the Nairobi City Council (NCC). In 1984 the Local Government Act was enacted, allowing the Minister for Local Government to dissolve any local authority suspected of mismanagement and replace it with a nominated commission. In 1985 Nairobi City Commission replaced Nairobi City Council. But a culture of impunity had begun in Nairobi that combined with overpopulation, inadequate infrastructure, unemployment, lack of amenities, and malfeasance to cause general urban decay. Site and service schemes failed to alleviate the problem of housing. Overcrowding, traffic jams, and crime became indicators of another phase of Nairobi's history. Occasionally the administration resorted to slum demolition and evictions, but these were hardly a solution. By 1990 poor governance and the demand for political pluralism ushered a new era for Nairobi.

In the 1990s Nairobi became the center of national pro-democracy movements. Social movements also sprang up, demanding improved services in the city itself. Though delivery of services remained poor, alternative solutions (like neighborhood groups and associations) began to be applied to cleaning and security in the city. Despite this, issues like the number of street children, traffic problems, insanitary conditions, and disease persisted.

Further reading

Werlin, H.H. (1974) *Governing an African City: A Study of Nairobi*, New York: Africana Publishing.

GODWIN MURUNGA

Namibia

Namibia, with an area of 824,268 square kilometers, borders **Angola**, **Zambia**, **Botswana**, and **South Africa**. By 2000 it had an estimated population of 1.8 million, of whom 87.5 percent were black, 6 percent white, and 6.5 percent mixed. Although English is the official language, the majority of Namibians speak Afrikaans, German, and/or indigenous languages (including Oshivambo, Herero, and Nama). Economically Namibia is heavily dependent on agriculture and mining. Officially known as South-West Africa, Namibia first became a German colony in 1884. The German conquerors faced heavy resistance from the indigenous people until 1908, during which period they committed wanton acts of destruction. The 1904 Herero uprising against colonial exploitation and oppression was soon followed by the Nama uprising, but both were crushed. In the ensuing **genocide** 80 percent of the Herero and 52 percent of the Nama were annihilated. Some of the survivors were sent into the Kalahari Desert where they inevitably perished. This bloody dawn of colonial rule led to labor shortages, and was followed by the creation of reserves, rigid segregation, and a system of pass laws, with the colony soon resembling its southern neighbor, South Africa.

In fact South Africa soon took control in 1915 when its troops overran the territory as part of the Allied war effort against Germany. In 1920 South African power was confirmed through a League of Nations' mandate, which would later be revoked by the United Nations when South Africa refused to prepare the trust territory for independence. It was hoped, in vain, that South Africa would promote the material and social progress of the inhabitants of the territory. Instead South Africa extended its segregationist and, from 1948, apartheid policies to Namibia. The colony's whites were given considerable democratic rights, while the indigenous people were further dispossessed of their economic and political rights, being herded into reserves that were later turned into homelands. They were left with only 40 percent of land in the country, while the European settlers – who accounted for only 7 percent of the population – controlled 60 percent of the land, and usually the most productive areas. It was clear that South Africa's colonial government wanted to turn Africans into a source of cheap labor for the colonial economy, which was based on commercial agriculture, fisheries, and mining run by white settlers. The South Africans expanded Namibia's infrastructure, linking it to their own country. For instance, the railway system was extended to Walvis Bay, on the border with South Africa, and to Cape Town, so that the flow of goods and people between South Africa and its new colony could be maintained.

These policies elicited resistance in various parts of the colony. From the 1920s new forms of protest began to emerge with the rise of trade unions and other political associations. But the blossoming of African nationalism came after the **Second World War**, and followed the imposition of apartheid in South Africa itself in 1948. Even before that at the first session of the United Nations General Assembly in 1946, South Africa requested that Namibia be incorporated into its Union. The UN refused, and thus began the battle between the world body and South Africa over the future of Namibia. In 1950 the International Court of justice (ICJ) ruled that South Africa could not unilaterally alter the legal status of the territory. Sixteen years later the UN General Assembly voted to terminate South Africa's mandate and to assume responsibility for the territory. In 1967 a Council for South-West Africa was appointed, and in 1968 the UN resolved that South-West Africa should be renamed Namibia. This was followed in 1971 by the ICJ declaring the South African occupation of Namibia illegal, ordering their withdrawal under threat of international sanctions. South Africa chose to stay, but faced increasing nationalist resistance, under the aegis of the war of liberation that had been declared in 1966.

By 1959 there were three movements in the colony: the Ovamboland People's Organization (OPO), the South-West African National Union (SWANU), and the Herero Council. In 1960 efforts were made by leaders of OPO to form a united national movement through the creation of the South-West African People's Organization (SWAPO), which soon won international recognition as the sole representative of the Namibian people, despite the continued existence of smaller political groups. SWAPO's most influential members included Sam Nujoma and Herman Toive Ja Toivo. Armed struggle in Namibia intensified following the independence of Angola, with the pro-SWAPO MPLA (Popular Movement for the Liberation of Angola) taking power. Half-hearted attempts by South Africa to reach an "internal settlement" through the Turnhalle Conference satisfied neither SWAPO nor the international community, and both international pressure and the liberation war intensified.

A series of conferences in the 1980s produced few results, until South Africa's defeat in 1987 at the Battle of Cuito Cuanavale, when the apartheid state (now facing its own escalating struggle for liberation at home) was forced to enter serious negotiations over Namibia's independence. The negotiations, involving the so-called "Contact Group" of five Western powers, agreed that South Africa would withdraw from Namibia and Cuban troops from Angola. A UN monitor group (UNTAG) was sent into the country to oversee elections and South Africa's effective withdrawal. SWAPO won the elections, defeating the conservative Democratic Turnhalle Alliance that had been favored by South Africa, and Namibia became independent in March 1990. Nujoma became the Namibia's president.

Despite the political changes, Namibia's economy remained dominated by settler-owned mining and agriculture. SWAPO abandoned its pre-independence socialist rhetoric and avoided undertaking major economic reform – over land, for example – although it embarked on various development projects and sought to build new national institutions, including the University of Namibia. Nujoma's democratic credentials were seriously damaged when his government decided to change the constitution, which forbade anyone from serving a third presidential term, in time for Nujoma to be reelected for a third time in 2000. In the meantime Namibia had become embroiled in regional disputes, most significantly in a war with the **Democratic Republic of Congo**. On the whole, however, the country appeared to have made a successful transition to independence.

Further reading

Kerina, M. (1981) *Namibia: The Making of a Nation*, New York: Book in Focus.

Leys, C. and Saul, J.S. (1995) *Namibia's Liberation Struggle*, London: James Currey.

BERTIN K. KOUADIO

nationalist movements

The rise and development of nationalist movements forms one of the most controversial periods in the study of twentieth-century African history. Part of this controversy revolves around some of the following key issues: the integrity of African nationalism; the definition of nationalist movements; and the inescapable complexity and controversy that surround the study of the "national question."

The study of African nationalism has often suffered from the claim that its core ideas, and even strategies, did not derive from Africa. To those who make such claims African nationalism has been depicted as an artificial, almost inappropriate, creation imposed by the African elite on unwilling or otherwise ignorant masses. These claims are mistaken on several accounts. Although it is true that many African elites, who later became nationalist leaders, read European treatises on nationalism, these were not the only source of their ideas and inspiration. Further, there is no evidence that all African nationalist leaders resolved to launch nationalist movements after their intellectual encounter with European nationalist writings. Available evidence indicates that African nationalism was woven out of many strands, which included overseas and foreign examples, Pan-African influences, local and specific grievances against colonial oppression and exploitation, defense of the integrity of African culture and traditions against European racial arrogance, desire to expand the material and social welfare of Africans, and desire for personal emancipation. Above all, however, African nationalism must be seen as a "revolt against the West."

The multi-ethnic composition of African countries has sometimes been used to point to the artificiality of these countries, and also to the impossibility of creating national unity and purpose out of them. This charge presumes that there are some "natural countries" with "natural boundaries." But historical evidence does not provide any examples in the modern period of such "natural countries." The "nation as an unchanging entity," with fixed boundaries and ethnic composition, is a theoretical construct that does little to enhance the study of the complex phenomenon of African nationalism. It is useful to recall here that in the modern period most countries have been, and still are, multi-ethnic and also multi-lingual. Multi-ethnicity cannot, therefore, be justifiably used to discredit the legitimacy or integrity of African nationalism.

Some of the criticisms leveled against African nationalism reflect the very bad name that nationalism acquired during the era of Nazism and Fascism in Europe, when nationalism came to be associated with unyielding intolerance and genocidal racism. This is in contrast with the role that it played in Europe in the nineteenth century, when nationalism was the highly valued route to freedom and dignity for Italians and the peoples of the Balkan peninsula, who had previously been oppressed by the Austrian, Ottoman, and French empires.

African nationalism, championed by the nationalist movements, was clearly forward-looking. Its basic thrust was to build new societies and not to re-create the social, political and economic structures that had prevailed in the pre-colonial period. It would have been impossible to undertake such institutional re-creation given the disruptive and fairly traumatic impact of colonialism on African societies. To be forward-looking, however, was a general principle; it did not provide a universal pattern of initiatives to be undertaken in pursuit of social and economic regeneration. Also not resolved by this principle was the complex problem of the interrelationship between the values and even structures of pre-colonial Africa, and the new values and structures introduced by colonialism.

The complexity of nationalist movements cannot be overemphasized. They had many social bases and objectives – ethnic, national, and international – and they operated and fought on many fronts – political, economic, social, and cultural. The growth of nationalist movements also varied, since colonies were acquired in different ways and at different times by different colonial powers that pursued different ideologies and administrative policies. The number and significance of European settlers and local traditions of resistance also affected the nature of nationalist expression. In organizational terms nationalist struggles articulated themselves through different organs as well: there were political and civic organizations, **labor movements**, cultural and religious movements, and **peasant** movements, just to mention the critical ones. Each of these movements, in turn, had its own locations of operation. The political and civic organizations were mainly urban-based, and led by the elite. The workers movements were also largely urban, but led by workers, while the religious movements straddled both urban and rural areas. The **peasant movements** were, of course, predominantly rural. Equally varied were the tactics used by these movements. The political and civic organizations used campaigns, petitions, the media, and demonstrations, while the chief weapons for the labor movements were strikes and consumer boycotts. The independent churches often urged their members to disobey colonial laws and shun colonial institutions. Peasants deployed both individual and collective acts of protest, involving flight, tax evasion, violation of agricultural regulations, attacks on loyalist chiefs and the police, boycotts of rural traders, holdups of produce, and rebellions. The gender dynamics of these movements were no less varied, depending on the relative presence of men and women. For example, women participated more fully as members of peasant movements than they did in labor movements, as the colonial working classes included far fewer women than men. Women were also more likely to be among the leaders of cultural and religious movements than among those of political and civic organizations, where leadership was a monopoly of the educated elite, which was predominantly male.

Phases of African nationalism

The development of nationalist movements in most of Africa under colonial rule followed a general pattern. First, there were associations and even churches formed as part of cultural nationalism. Second, there were several associations formed by the new elite to protest against specific localized grievances, which were predominantly economic. The first trade unions were also formed at this time. Third, there was mass nationalism. For most countries, this occurred after the **Second World War**. Last, there was the attainment of political independence. This rough pattern applied to almost all of the countries that attained their political independence before 1975. This constitutes what can be characterized as the first and dominant phase of African nationalism.

The second phase applies to the former Portuguese colonies of **Guinea-Bissau**, **Angola**, and **Mozambique**. Also included in this second phase are **Zimbabwe**, **South Africa**, and **Namibia**. During the second phase, and especially in the former Portuguese colonies, the struggle for independence was characterized by protracted guerrilla warfare. The triumphant nationalist movements in the former Portuguese colonies became more precise in their goals for societal development and national regeneration. These movements also adopted a Marxist ideology in a much more deliberate and consistent form than had been the case with the majority of the nationalist movements involved in the first phase. It should be quickly noted that not all of the countries included in the second phase pursued identical policies. Nonetheless, most of these nationalist movements undertook a far more detailed socio-economic analysis of colonial domination than those movements involved in the first phase. The distinction drawn here between these two phases of African nationalism is not absolute, for indeed there were several linkages between them. The distinction has been drawn in order to provide analytical clarity.

The first phase of African nationalism

How did the first phase proceed? After the brutal suppression of African resistance to the imposition of colonial rule, there emerged new strategies of resistance and accommodation to colonialism. One of the most pervasive of these strategies was what came to be called "cultural nationalism." On an institutional level it entailed the formation of breakaway independent African-led churches throughout most of Africa – resistance through religion and religious practices. Examples of these **Christian reform movements** included the Tembu Church, formed in 1884 by Nehemiah Tile in South Africa, and the South African Ethiopian Church, founded by Willie J. Mokalapa in 1892. In **West Africa** there was, for example, the Native Baptist Church in **Nigeria**, founded in 1888. In **East Africa** John Owalo founded the Nomiya Luo Church in **Kenya** in 1910. One of the most famous examples of resistance through religion in this period is John Chilembwe's rebellion in **Malawi** in 1915. Chilembwe, an African ordained minister, had used religion to condemn the brutality, exploitation, and inhumanity of colonial rule. In the Belgian **Congo**, among the Bakongo, Simon Kimbangu founded a Kimbanguist Church that was quite radical in its interpretation of the scriptures. Kimbangu "declared himself an emissary of God sent to deliver Africans from colonial rule" (Boahen 1989: 88). Alarmed by the appeal and power of his message, the Belgian colonial authorities held Kimbangu in jail from 1921. He died there after thirty years. Among radical religious sects, Dini ya Msambwa, founded by Elijah Masinde in western Kenya, should be mentioned. These breakaway churches and religious sects were an effort by Africans to resist the overwhelmingly Western cultural content of Christianity. It was an attempt to localize Christianity by making it compatible with core traditional values. But it also demonstrated a deliberate effort by Africans to be their own chief spiritual messengers. These churches also served a political role by sometimes rallying opposition to the excesses of colonial rule.

Beyond churches and religious sects, there were also educated Africans who formed political organizations to protest specific colonial policies. Almost every colony had one or more of these organizations. In Kenya there were, for example, the Young Kavirondo Association, the Young Kikuyu Association, and the Kikuyu Central Association. In **Uganda** there was the Young Baganda Association; in Tanganyika (**Tanzania**) there was the Tanganyika Territory African Civil Service Association. British West Africa, especially **Ghana** and Nigeria, had more of these associations, owing to a longer tradition of literacy and higher education. It would be fair to state that these organizations had minimal mass appeal; indeed, they were not expected to have a national constituency. Furthermore they did not directly demand political independence. They were reformist in intent, and moderate in their strategies. They limited themselves to making spirited appeals to local (or overseas) colonial authorities for redress over specific colonial policies. Some prominent people in these organizations were later to play crucial roles in the next stage of mass nationalism. These include Nnamdi Azikiwe and Obafemi Awolowo in Nigeria, and Jomo Kenyatta in Kenya.

To what extent are these organizations (and even the breakaway churches) nationalist movements? These initial organizations, although reformist and with limited constituency, represent what in retrospect might be considered the gestation period, leading to more widespread national awareness. They provided a legacy of revolt, resistance, and organization. The failure to achieve their limited objectives exposed the intransigence of the colonial rulers. In the subsequent stage of mass nationalism, nationalist leaders sought to improve on the strategies and objectives of these earlier organizations. It should also be remembered that the issues and grievances raised by these initial organizations were, on the whole, embraced by mass nationalism. These issues included working conditions and wages; land alienation; prices paid to cash-crop producers; forced labor; living conditions in expanding urban centers; expansion of educational facilities; racism and discrimination, especially in the provision of social services; and respect for Africans and their cultural traditions. This does not mean that every organization formed by Africans during colonial rule constituted a nationalist movement. What is clear is that the initial organizations formed to protest against colonial rule and its specific policies provided examples of resistance that were later emulated and improved upon during the stage of mass nationalism. It would be unfair to dismiss these initial organizations as being non-nationalist on account of having not demanded political independence. We should remember that nationalist struggles are essentially evolutionary: one stage builds on a preceding one.

What were the characteristics of mass nationalism? The rise of mass nationalism in colonial Africa was facilitated by several factors. These were a significant expansion of the educated population; the rise and expansion of mass communication outlets for Africans, especially newspapers and the radio; rapid migration to increasingly congested urban centers; unemployment; intransigence of the colonial governments; the excessive labor demands on the African population as a result of the Second World War; inflation and poverty in the immediate postwar period; the rise of trade unions; the **Cold War**; international pressure toward **decolonization**, especially through the newly formed United Nations; the example of India; the international pressure exerted on imperial powers to liquidate their empires; the rise of "professional politicians" among the African elite who were devoted to the organization of nationalist struggles; and a readiness on the part of the majority of Africans to respond positively and with enthusiasm to the nationalist message and its challenges.

By 1945 Western education had produced in many of the colonies a sizable number of highly educated Africans. There were many others who had acquired minimal or rudimentary education. For the highly educated ones (according to the standards and realities of the period) there was a marked shift away from accommodating colonialism toward active advocacy of its demise. Many were shut out from the better jobs, which were largely reserved for Europeans, and unable to find employment in positions commensurate to their qualifications. They came to a realization that colonialism could not be reformed to satisfy the material, cultural, and political aspirations of Africans. These elites were the new leaders of African societies, better able to represent the new pattern of social forces. There is no doubt that there was an element of personal ambition on the part of these professional politicians, yet it was also clear that they could not hope to be able to dislodge colonial rule without the active and enthusiastic support of the masses.

Although drastically weakened by the Second World War, neither Britain nor France (the major imperial powers in Africa) were anxious to liquidate their African empires in the immediate postwar period. France was eager to reassert its imperial authority, even after its own myth of imperial invincibility had been destroyed when the country fell so quickly to the German army. Between 1946 and 1962 France fought destructive colonial wars in a bid to reassert its imperial position in Indochina and **Algeria**. France had multiple complex economic, moral, strategic, and psychological ties to Algeria, not least the fact that Algeria was France's largest colonial trading partner. It is therefore not surprising that the political independence of Algeria was only won after a punishing guerrilla war in which over a million Algerians died. The guerrilla war was led and coordinated by the Front de Libération Nationale (FLN), the principal nationalist movement.

The launching of the guerrilla war under the direction of the FLN was, in many ways, a response to the grossly inadequate so-called "reforms" that France introduced in Algeria after the war. The FLN's political strategy was, to a very large degree, formulated to counteract the arrogant and racist cultural presumptions of French colonialism. The French had not only disparaged and disrupted the country's Islamic traditions, but also denied the very existence of a distinct Algerian culture. The FLN fashioned its operative ideological positions around cultural restoration, wrapped in the mantle of radical nationalism. While these ideological positions were successful in mobilizing the majority of the Algerians in support of the guerrilla war, they later became a source of significant social and political conflict in the post-colonial era.

In **French West Africa** France was equally determined to maintain its imperial control. Africa had provided Charles de Gaulle's Free French with an invaluable territorial base. In 1944 the Brazzaville Conference was convened to discuss, among other issues, the future of the French colonies. The resolutions adopted at this conference categorically ruled out the possibility of political independence for any of the colonies from the French imperial bloc. As international pressure mounted in support of decolonization, however, coupled with the rise of nationalist movements in its colonies, France moved to strategically adjust to these changing realities. There was also the example of nationalist movements in neighboring British colonies. The solution came via the 1958 constitution, referred to as "de Gaulle's constitution" in nationalist politics. De Gaulle's aim was to offer French African colonies a non-consequential change of status. There would be the new "French Community," under which France would retain the "essential powers." This would ensure that the countries in the French Community remained dependent on France for the foreseeable future. These constitutional proposals were submitted to a referendum in all the French West African colonies in 1958. Only **Guinea**, under the leadership of Ahmed Sékou Touré, voted to reject de Gaulle's constitution, instead opting for full political independence from the French Community. Following this vote, de Gaulle petulantly withdrew all French assistance from the new government of Guinea. In the subsequent period it became increasingly evident that the idea of the French Community as formulated in 1958 could not survive. So in 1960 de Gaulle agreed to the political independence of these African countries.

In the British colonies the road to political independence was led by Ghana under Kwame Nkrumah. Educated at Lincoln University, perhaps the oldest black university in the United States, Nkrumah returned to Ghana as a confirmed nationalist and Pan-Africanist. In 1945 he helped in the organization of the now famous Pan-African Congress in Manchester, England, which called for Africa's independence. When Nkrumah broke away from the United Gold Coast Convention and formed the Convention Peoples Party, he altered the pace of Africa's nationalist activism. The era of polite civil petitions was over. Through a well-organized and disciplined political party led by professional politicians, Nkrumah was able to spread his call for independence to the youth, market women, **peasants**, **workers**, and young professionals.

Particularly important for other African nationalists were the strategies employed by Nkrumah in Ghana, which many hoped to adapt to their own nationalist struggles. There was also the general applicability of Nkrumah's messages about Pan-African solidarity, unity, radical anti-imperialism, and racial pride, as well as his ambitions for the industrialization of Africa, which he believed would open the gate to economic prosperity and independence. In the years immediately after Ghana's independence in 1957 Nkrumah hoped to lead by example. He declared that Ghana's independence would remain meaningless unless it was "linked up with the total liberation of the African continent" (quoted in Esedebe 1994: 6). He provided aid to many nationalist movements, and in the process came to be identified as a "troublemaker" by the Western imperial powers.

Nkrumah called on his fellow African nationalists to pay attention to the contents of political independence, and also to be willing to shoulder some Pan-African obligations. It is here that many of the nationalists, and their movements, began to distance themselves from Nkrumah and his vision. Many of his old comrades in the Pan-African movement proceeded to pursue policies that were notably silent or evasive on Pan-African issues. Many avoided radical anti-imperialism. These included Hastings Banda of Malawi, Nnamdi Azikiwe of Nigeria, and Jomo Kenyatta of Kenya.

Several conclusions can be drawn about the nationalist movements during this first phase of African nationalism. They accepted the integrity of colonial boundaries and consequently the reality that Africans would belong to new, individual nation-states. Pan-African consciousness was not seen as being resolutely incompatible with national consciousness and allegiance to nation-states. On balance it is fair to conclude that internal factors (in separate countries) proved to be the chief determinant in the attainment of political independence. Regional developments also played a role. In Malawi and Zambia, for example, the rise of militant nationalism was linked directly to the tragic decision by the British government to impose the **Central African Federation** in 1953. The Federation was loathed by both Zambia and Malawi, as both countries feared it would lead to the imposition of Southern Rhodesia's virulent settler colonialism.

The first phase nationalist movements developed at a very specific period in recent world history: during the Cold War. Ideological tensions between the West and the Soviet Union had a critical impact on the nature and texture of decolonization that the imperial countries were willing to entertain. In the 1960s Britain, France, and the United States were very concerned about the ideological orientation of the rising tide of African nationalism. As far as possible very radical nationalists or those suspected of having communist tendencies were isolated and dislodged from positions of leadership, and power was handed to leaders perceived as amenable to imperial economic interests. This development – unfortunate and in some cases disastrous – immensely complicated the task of nation-building that the nationalist movements were expected to spearhead in the post-colonial era. It is in this period of waning enthusiasm by the masses for the results of political independence that the second phase of African nationalism was born.

The second phase of African nationalism

The triumphant nationalist movements in the second phase were the PAIGC (Guinea-Bissau and **Cape Verde**), FRELIMO (Mozambique),

MPLA (Angola), ZANU-FU (Zimbabwe), SWAPO (Namibia), and the ANC (South Africa). These movements were connected to some of the now-independent African countries, on whom they relied to varying degrees for bases and diplomatic support. Specifically Tanzania under Mwalimu Nyerere came to play a very significant role in the liberation struggles against racist colonial regimes in **Southern Africa**. This central role was largely facilitated by the reinvention of Tanzania's nationalism after the country attained independence. In the 1967 policy document known as the Arusha Declaration, Nyerere adopted radical socialist policies as the new guide for the country's development. The principal objective was to remake Tanzania as a self-reliant African socialist country. This new ideological orientation, which was socialist and Pan-African, both justified and celebrated Tanzania's support for other liberation movements. Nyerere remained one of the most important facilitators of the second phase of African nationalism. But as Nyerere himself realized, there were significant differences between these two phases on questions about the content of independence struggles, strategies for mass mobilization, and the nature of the social relations that would be pursued after liberation.

These questions received particularly elaborate consideration in the former Portuguese colonies. These countries were poor and underdeveloped, having been colonized by Portugal, which was a poor and brutal minor European power. In order to overcome this backwardness, safeguard national independence, and create egalitarian societies, these movements embarked on bold experiments in creating "an alternative civilization in Africa." They were eager to avoid the trap of neo-colonialism and exploitation, which were part of the unfortunate legacy of the first phase of nationalism. This process of deep analysis and thorough reflection on the meaning and value of independence produced in these movements some of Africa's most original and courageous thinkers of the post-Second World War period, including Amilcar Cabral, Agostinho Neto, Eduardo Mondlane, and Samora Machel.

One of the most admirable characteristics of the PAIGC, FRELIMO, and MPLA was their forthright and consistent advocacy of women's liberation. Against all odds, internal and external, these nationalist movements pursued the goal of women's liberation and gender equity. They came to identify women's liberation as an integral part of national liberation. Samora Machel was later to remark that: "The liberation of women is the fundamental necessity for the revolution, a guarantee of its continuity and a precondition for victory" (quoted in Urdang 1983: 9). Women were actively recruited by these nationalist movements, and they played indispensable roles as guerrillas, members of the mobilized non-combatant militia, recruiters, administrators, educators, and so on.

It is outside the scope of this entry to consider the complex course, history, and fate of these movements in the post-liberation period, or to consider why, by the end of the twentieth century, they had failed to safeguard the survival of the "alternative civilization" that they had won through so much pain, courage, determination, and sacrifice. But the speculation remains: Is another phase of African nationalism yet to come?

See also: colonial conquest and resistance; intellectuals: colonial; intellectuals: post-independence; socialisms and socialists

References and further reading

Anderson, B. (1991) *Imagined Communities*, New York: Verso.

Barraclough, G. (1964) *An Introduction to Contemporary History*, New York: Basic Books.

Boahen, A.A. (1989) *African Perspectives on Colonialism*, Baltimore: Johns Hopkins University Press.

Davidson, B. (1994) *The Search for Africa*, New York: Times Books/Random House.

Esedebe, O.P. (1994) *Pan-Africanism*, Washington, D.C.: Howard University Press.

Falola, T. (2001) *Nationalism and African Intellectuals*, Rochester: University of Rochester Press.

Hargreaves, J.D. (1988) *Decolonization in Africa*, London: Longman.

Hobsbawm, E.J. (1990) *Nations and Nationalism since 1780*, Cambridge: Cambridge University Press.

Mazrui, A.A. (ed.) (1993) *UNESCO General History of Africa: Africa since 1935*, Oxford: Heinemann.

Urdang, S. (1983) "The Last Transition? Women

and Development in Mozambique," *Review of African Political Economy* 27–8: 9.

WUNYABARI MALOBA

Niamey, Niger

Niamey is the capital city of **Niger**, the largest nation in **West Africa** in terms of physical size. Situated in the southwest of the country, along the left bank of the Niger River, Niamey is the country's largest and most populated city. Niger came under French colonial rule in the late 1890s, and shortly thereafter the French were motivated by the strategic location of Niamey, then a small town, to build a military post there.

It was not until 1926, however, that the French decided to relocate the colonial capital from Zinder to Niamey. The town's location along the Niger, which was the colony's only waterway, allowed the French to more easily conduct trade with their other West African possessions. From the colonial era Niamey also served as an important overland nexus for agricultural products, especially groundnuts, but also other trade goods, that originated in outlying regions of Niger and were transported to domestic and international markets, especially the cities of **Abidjan** and **Lagos**. However, trade with the neighboring countries was hampered by the lack of railway connections through nearby **Burkina Faso**, and by the poor quality of the region's road system.

In 1960 Niger won its independence from France, and Niamey became the nation's capital. During the 1970s Niger's valuable uranium reserves were successfully exploited. The profits from uranium exports, which accounted for 80 percent of Niger's total exports and 50 percent of the gross national product, financed the development of Niamey's modern infrastructure. A light industrial base emerged, consisting of small factories producing bricks, food products, beverages, ceramic goods, cement, shoes, and textiles. But the economic and political fortunes of the city suffered after 1980, when uranium prices fell drastically and Niger's economy virtually collapsed.

The country's economic problems generated significant sociopolitical tension. Major-General Seyni Kountche, who occupied the presidency at the time, attempted to restore the economy by implementing austerity measures designed to conserve state resources. Kountche's policies provoked widespread protest, however, most of which centered on Niamey. The rapid succession of presidents after the Kountche's death from natural causes in 1987 created an atmosphere of political and economic instability. As a result labor strikes and ongoing protests by students from the University of Niamey periodically crippled the city. Still unable to generate enough revenue to maintain many of the facilities constructed during the 1970s, Niamey's appearance at the close of the twentieth century conveyed a sense of promise yet to be fulfilled.

Despite its economic difficulties, Niamey's population continued to grow through the 1980s and 1990s, reaching an estimated 700,000 by the end of the century. The city's two largest groups of pre-colonial inhabitants, the Hausa and the Djerma-Songhai, continued to form the largest proportion of Niamey's population, and **Islam** was the capital's most widely practiced religion. Niamey functioned not only as Niger's governmental headquarters, but also its commercial and cultural center, and it was host to the University of Niamey and the National School of Administration. Other main attractions in the city included the Grand Mosque, and the outdoor National Museum, which displayed local artifacts, cultural exhibits, and even animals, and also housed an artisans' cooperative. The city's stadium, the Stade du 29 Juillet, was the center for sporting events, including soccer – the country's most popular sport. Another important venue was the Franco-Niger cultural center, which was used for theatrical productions, performance art, and film screenings.

Further reading

Decalo, S. (1997) *Historical Dictionary of Niger*, Lanham: Scarecrow Press.

CARINA E. RAY

Niger

Located in western Africa, Niger has an area of 1,267,000 square kilometers. The country is surrounded by **Algeria**, **Libya**, **Mali**, **Burkina Faso**, **Benin**, **Nigeria**, and **Chad**. With an estimated population of 10.4 million in 2000, Niger is inhabited by the Hausa, Fula Tuareg, Beri Beri, Arab, Toubou, and Gourmantche peoples, as well as by French expatriates. Muslims made up 80 percent of the population, while indigenous African religions and Christianity account for the remaining 20 percent. Although French was chosen as the official language at independence, the majority of the people speak Hausa and Djerma. In economic terms Niger faced serious difficulties due to a hot climate, overgrazing, soil erosion, and desertification, as well as poor infrastructure. By the end of the twentieth century 90 percent of the labor force was engaged in agriculture, 6 percent in industry and commerce, and 4 percent in government, while the agricultural sector accounted for 40 percent of the gross domestic product, industry producing 18 percent, and services 42 percent. Overall Niger relied on subsistence agriculture, livestock farming, cotton production, and foreign aid.

The Berlin Conference (1884–5) set the tone for Niger's history in the twentieth century. It was during that conference that Niger was placed under French control. The indigenous populations, particularly the Tuareg from the north, resisted invasion (1916–19) but were eventually defeated. In 1922 Niger, formerly part of **French West Africa**, became a separate colony administered by a Governor-General (based in **Dakar** in **Senegal**) and a Territorial Governor (based in Niger). The French Constitution of 1946 authorized limited political participation by local assemblies. This allowed the Parti Progressiste Nigerien (PPN) to be established as the country's first nationalist party. At the end of the **Second World War**, the Sawaba Party of Bakari Dibo became popular, threatening the very existence of Hamani Diori's PPN. Unfortunately Sawaba were unsuccessful in a referendum over independence, held in 1958 under the auspices of the Fifth French Republic. The PPN thereby regained power, which they still held at independence.

Niger became independent on 3 August 1960, with Hamani Diori the country's first president. Diori maintained a close relationship with France, but a weak economy (based largely on groundnut and uranium exports), ethnic warfare, and the tumultuous political climate brought little development to Niger and its people. The severe droughts of 1968 and 1979 worsened matters, forcing retrenchment for development projects and the public sector. This provoked widespread protests against the government, culminating in a military coup in April 1974. The new government launched relief measures and established a rural development program, called Samariya, through which aid was provided to peasants who had been regrouped on collectivized farms. A temporary rise in uranium prices in the 1970s brought some economic and political respite for the regime, but instability and protests returned when uranium prices fell. There was a temporary economic recovery from the mid-1980s, following the end of drought and inflow of foreign aid, but Niger nonetheless experienced a number of coups before it returned to civilian government in 1999. Seyni Kountche, who had just overthrown Diori, was faced with the task of salvaging the country's deteriorating economy.

After Kountche's death in 1987, Ali Saibou became president. Saibou encouraged the return of exiles to Niger, and released political prisoners, but repression continued. In fact in 1988 the range of political parties was reduced to one new party: the Mouvement National pour une Société de Développement; in the following year Saibou was elected president in controversial elections. In the meantime the country was forced to undertake a **structural adjustment program**, which only worsened the political and economic situation, with job cuts in the public sector and the removal of government subsidies leading to rising unemployment and other hardships. Matters came to a head in 1990, during which there was a confrontation between the security forces and university students. There were also demonstrations by workers' unions.

Niger was paralyzed. This forced the authorities to amend the constitution, legalize the registration of several political parties in April 1991, and set up a National Conference in July 1991. Twenty-four political organizations attended, along with several other organizations. The conference appointed Amadou Cheiffou as head of a transitional government. Mutinying soldiers took control of the media in February 1992, but civilians and political organizations joined together to protest against the military action. In February the following year a contested presidential election was held. Victory went to Mahamane Ousmane of the Convention Démocratique et Social–Rahama. Ousmane became the president of the third republic, and Souley Abdoulaye was appointed the new prime minister. But the challenge still remained of how to bring an end to the prolonged economic and social crisis. The state was virtually bankrupt. Unable to pay civil servants' salaries, it was in no position to undertake meaningful economic development projects. Promises made by the new government did not stop a wave of protest: The people of Niger had had enough.

In January 1996 another military coup, led by Ibrahim Bare Mainassara, overthrew the Abdoulaye government. At this point Niger's future became more uncertain. All major institutions were dissolved, and political parties were suspended again. Like his predecessors, Mainassara promised to improve government, combat corruption and injustice, and raise morale in the public services. But few were fooled, either at home or abroad. Amnesty International, which was monitoring the new government closely, revealed serious **human rights** violations, including summary detention, deportations, harassment of journalists, and imprisonment without trial. Mainassara's regime ended with his assassination in April 1999. A military government then ruled, until Mamadou Tandja was elected President of Niger several months later.

At independence Niger had dreamed of becoming a developed nation, but political instability – manifested in the numerous coups and socio-economic crises faced by the country, often compounded by drought and fluctuating prices for its principal export commodities – frustrated those ambitions. By the end of the twentieth century, this vast country was still groping for an effective way forward to a more prosperous future.

Further reading

Fuglestad, F. (1983) *A History of Niger, 1850–1960*, Cambridge: Cambridge University Press.

Le Vine, V.T. (1967) *Political Leadership in Africa: Post-Independence Generational Conflict in Upper Volta, Senegal, Niger, Dahomey, and the Central African Republic*, Stanford: Hoover Institution on War, Revolution and Peace.

BERTIN K. KOUADIO

Niger Delta

The Niger Delta is one of the largest wetlands in the world, spanning an area of between 20,000 and 40,000 square kilometers. Fed by heavy rains, it is made up of silt deposited mainly by the River Niger and its major tributary, the Benue. The terrain of the Delta is a swampy mixture of rivers, lakes, streams, and mud plains. The Delta comprises four ecological zones: coastal barrier islands, mangrove (salt water) swamps, freshwater swamps, and lowland forests. Each of these supports a high degree of biodiversity, as well as many different human activities.

The Niger Delta has a history dating back thousands of years. It is inhabited by ethnic minority groups such as the Ijaw (Izon), Etche, Ikwere, Andoni, Itsekiri, Urhobo, Isoko, Edo, Efik, Ibibio, and Ogoni, many of whom migrated to their present settlements from other parts of **West** and **Central Africa**. At the peak of the trans-Atlantic trade between the seventeenth and nineteenth centuries these peoples established trading houses, city states, and kingdoms along the Atlantic coast to maximize the gains made through their position as middlemen in the trade between the forest hinterland and European merchants on the coast. Since colonial times these groups have been marginalized, however, and subjected to the hegemonic designs of the dominant ethnic groups in **Nigeria**. As a melting pot of cultures and peoples, the Niger Delta has a rich cultural heritage that reflects the people's spiritual links with land and water, as well as transatlantic influences and culture. Yet within this apparent unity-from-diversity can be found some dichotomies. Intra-ethnic, inter-ethnic, inter-generational, intra-communal, and inter-communal conflicts have, for instance, arisen between the people of the low forest and those of the riverine areas, coming to the fore in struggles over access to and the sharing of scarce resources.

While the Niger Delta in its original form is vastly endowed with natural resources, this has been tampered with, and in most cases undermined by a host of human and economic activities over the centuries. Integrated into the global market as far back as the fifteenth century, the Niger Delta has been a melting pot of trans-global and local cultures, politics and economics. Farming, trading, and fishing have been the main economic activities at the community level. Others include the collection of non-timber forest products, hunting, net weaving, gin distillation, and canoe-building. However, the fragile ecosystem increasingly came under immense pressure from commercial fishing and logging interests, but more significantly from the operations of oil multinationals after Shell-BP struck oil in Oloibiri in 1956 and started exports in 1958, resulting in the depletion of forest resources and fish stocks, environmental degradation, and widespread poverty. This became more significant with the oil boom at the end of the Nigerian civil war in 1970, given that oil accounted for 80 percent of Nigeria's total revenues and 95 percent of its foreign-exchange earnings.

By the end of the century the Niger Delta was a living paradox. Environmental change in the oil-rich region created poverty, oil pollution, and degradation, which in turn fueled conflicts as a result of the push and pull between the multinationals that were extracting oil and the ethnic groups of the Niger Delta who were resisting the forces of global expropriation. Official records indicate that between 1976 and 1996, a total of 4,835 incidents resulted in the spillage of about 2,446,322 barrels, of which an estimated 1,896,930 barrels were lost to the environment. Company equipment, centralization, and exploration and transportation activities also undermined the fragile ecosystem. Even worse, statistics show that Nigeria flared more gas than any other country in the world. The result of all these factors was that people's survival was put at grave risk. Oil pollution destroyed the basis of their livelihoods: farming and fishing were damaged by the destruction of biodiversity and by soil becoming barren, with direct implications for people's nutritional and health status. This was in addition to the fact that people had already lost some of their land to the oil companies, with little or no compensation, and few could find jobs in the capital-intensive and high-skill oil industry.

After peaceful demands for equity and restitution were ignored, the minorities of the Niger Delta began organizing themselves into protest, resistance, and **human rights** movements to mobilize against the perceived predatory and polluting alliance between state and oil multinationals. Such protests were internationalized from the early 1990s by groups such as the Movement for the Survival of Ogoni People (MOSOP), and later by groups such as the Ijaw Youth Congress, Environmental Rights Action (ERA) and the pan-Delta resistance movement known as Chikoko.

As a result of these struggles, and the militarization of the struggles by the state in the 1990s, the political climate of the Delta was marked by tension: at one level, this existed between the people and the oil multinationals, at another between the people and the Nigerian federal government – partner of the multinationals. The inhabitants of the region accused the Nigerian government of destroying their environment through exploitation and neglect.

The links between politics and ecology in the Niger Delta reinforced the area's historical and geographical significance, even in the age of globalization. The resolution of the crisis in which the Niger Delta is immersed, and for which people like Ken Saro-Wiwa have died, will only come about both through the genuine democratization of state and society in Nigeria, and through global support for sustainable environmental practices, compensatory corporate responsibility, and respect for the rights of the oil-producing minorities whose lives are tied to their lands and waters.

See also: environmental movements

Further reading

Ashton-Jones, N., Arnott, S. and Douglas, O.

(1998) *The Human Ecosystems of the Niger Delta*, Benin City: Environmental Rights Action.

Human Rights Watch (1999) *The Price of Oil: Corporate Responsibility and Human Rights Violations in Nigeria's Oil Producing Communities*, New York: Human Rights Watch.

Obi, C.I. (2001) *The Changing Forms of Identity Politics in Nigeria under Economic Adjustment: The Case of the Oil Minorities Movement of the Niger Delta*, Uppsala: NAI Research Report No.119.

CYRIL I. OBI

Nigeria

Nigeria has an area of 923,768 square kilometers, and is bounded to the east by **Cameroon**, to the west by **Benin**, and to the north by **Niger**. The country had an estimated population of 126.6 million in 2001, making it the most populous in Africa. Nigeria is often said to have between 250 and 400 ethnic groups. In numerical terms the major ethnic groups are the Hausa-Fulani, Yoruba, Igbo, Ijaw, Kanuri, Edo, Ibibio, and Tiv. The country is almost evenly divided between Muslims and Christians, with a residual minority following indigenous religions. Nigeria was created by British imperialism in the late nineteenth century, starting with the establishment of the colony of **Lagos** in 1861. Subsequently the Oil Rivers Protectorate was created in southeastern Nigeria and the Royal Niger Company was given a charter to control northern Nigeria. By 1900 there were the Colony and Protectorate of Southern Nigeria and the Protectorate of Northern Nigeria, which were amalgamated in 1914 to create modern Nigeria.

Despite the amalgamation the British continued to run the two halves of the country as separate political, administrative, and legal entities. The governance of Lagos colony was also different from that of the rest of southern Nigeria. The inward-looking administrative ethos and practices in both north and south ensured that the two halves of the country developed as separate entities. This structural and psychological divide remained ingrained in Nigerian political life for the rest of the century. Indirect rule, conducted through local chiefs, accentuated localism. The 1922 Clifford Constitution sought to integrate the two provinces and the colony of Lagos, and to create more scope for the participation of the Western-educated elite in government. A Legislative Council was established and, for the first time, direct elections were extended beyond Lagos. Though only four of the forty-six members of this Council were elected, the new Council stimulated nationalist sentiments and the beginning of party politics.

The early colonial period also witnessed major economic, social, and demographic changes. Cocoa cultivation, started through indigenous economic initiatives at the close of the nineteenth century, flourished. This formed the basis for economic prosperity in western Nigeria. In the north the extension of the railway to **Kano** in 1914 led to a revolution in groundnut production. In the east palm production developed. Rubber, cattle, and cotton were other important sources of income. **Urbanization** intensified, increasing the size of old and new cities. Public utilities and transport infrastructure were constructed. In Jos tin mining developed, while Enugu saw the establishment of a coal mining industry. Forced labor was often used in the construction of infrastructure and in mining. Nevertheless a small working class emerged in the public utilities, the colonial bureaucracy, and in the European commercial companies through which economic activity in the colony was linked to the global capitalist system. **Peasant** cultivators and artisans constituted the bulk of the population.

By 1938 the National Youth Movement, representing the new educated and commercial elite, had superseded the Nigerian National Democratic Party, which was formed in response to the Clifford Constitution. The impact of the **Second World War** was to increase the tempo of social and political change, with ex-servicemen, organized labor, and students joining the fray. An umbrella nationalist movement, the National Council of Nigeria and the Cameroons (NCNC), was formed in 1944. Two constitutions – the Richards Constitution of 1946 and the MacPherson Constitution of 1951 – sought to respond to postwar pressures and nationalist criticism. Nigeria developed a bifurcated nationalist movement with a modern nationalism in the south, based on a Westernized elite, and a more traditional nationalism in the north, based on Islamic traditionalism and aristocratic symbolism. There was the Hausa-Fulani-dominated Northern Peoples Congress (NPC) in the north, the Yoruba-dominated Action Group (AG) in the west, and the increasingly Igbo-dominated NCNC in the east. In each region ethnic minorities were increasingly discriminated against. Independence was granted on 1 October 1960 on the basis of a federal constitution. Nigeria became a republic in 1963.

There was a major structural imbalance in the federation; in terms of both landmass and population, the north was bigger than the west and east combined. Furthermore, the regions were economically and constitutionally strong, whereas the center was weak. Ethnic and regional competition, manifested through a series of conflicts and crises, penetrated into the military establishment and led to the overthrow of the First Republic in January 1966. Denounced in parts of the country as an Igbo coup, in July 1966 this prompted another coup led by lower-ranking northern officers. Many Igbos were subsequently killed in pogroms in some northern cities. General Yakub Gowon broke the four existing regions into twelve states in 1967. Shortly thereafter, the military governor of the east, Chukwuemeka Ojukwu, declared the breakaway Republic of Biafra. The resulting civil war lasted until January 1970.

The creation of states in 1967 set the stage for curtailing the powers of traditional rulers in the north and west of Nigeria. The federal center also grew stronger under the military, with the emergence in 1970 of petroleum revenue as a major source of state funds, replacing dependence on agricultural exports. The political and administrative centralization of power was now matched by a fiscal centralization. The center increasingly dominated the states. Oil windfalls fueled nation-building ambitions: capitalist transformation of agriculture, promotion of state-led industrialization, and the construction of national infrastructure. Escalating corruption undermined the projects. Gowon was overthrown in 1975, due to widespread corruption and because he reneged on an earlier commitment to hand over power to an elected government.

The successor military regime, headed by Murtala Mohammad, purged the bureaucracy of Gowon's cronies and further intensified the centralization of the Nigerian state. Regional universities and television stations were nationalized, and even the trade unions were restructured to fit into the new all-embracing nation-building drive. A new local government structure and uniform land legislation were adopted across the country. An additional seven states were created in 1976, and a decision was taken to shift the capital to Abuja in the center of the country (although this did not immediately take place). On 1 October 1979 the regime was set to hand over power to an elected government. After Murtala was killed in an abortive coup in February 1976, his deputy, Olusegun Obasanjo, completed the regime's term of office. The drafting of the new constitution was marred by disputes over *shari'a* law.

The Second Republic was inaugurated in 1979 with an American-style presidential constitution under the leadership of Shehu Shagari and the National Party of Nigeria (NPN). Despite rules aimed at blocking ethnic and regional tendencies in the party political system, the old sectarian alignments resurfaced, with the rebirth of the NPC as the NPN, the AG as the Unity Party of Nigeria (UPN), and the NCNC as the Nigerian People's Party (NPP). Even the populist Northern Elements Progressive Union was reborn as the People's Redemption Party. The decline in oil revenue, which started around 1978, had reached crisis proportions by 1982. Continued ethno-regional conflict, economic mismanagement, widespread corruption, and electoral malfeasance in 1983 eroded the remnants of credibility for civilian rule. Military rule was restored in December 1983 under the stern and ultra-nationalist Buhari/Idiagbon regime, which was characterized by economic nationalism, intolerance and arbitrary rule, and failure to contain the economic crisis. Ibrahim Babangida seized upon the resulting popular disaffection, carrying out a palace coup in 1985.

Babangida's rule (1985–93) was characterized by elephantine corruption, divide-and-rule politics, the personalization of the state, and the displacement of collegiate military processes by purely personal ones. Religious tension increased when he single-handedly made Nigeria a full member of the **Organization of the Islamic Conference**. He created additional states in 1987 and 1991, bringing the total to thirty, and moved the capital from Lagos to Abuja. Babangida's rule saw the introduction of a failed **structural adjustment program**. His regime was also noted for the purported promotion of women's "empowerment" through jamborees organized by his wife. His repeated promises to hand over to an elected civilian government were cynically betrayed, culminating in his annulment of the 12 June 1993 presidential election. Under Babangida, the economic and social crises grew to unparalleled proportions. He was forced out of office in 1993 in the wake of the 12 June crisis. His unelected chosen successor, Shonekan, was overthrown in late 1993 by Sani Abacha.

Abacha's rule (1993–8) was the most brutal in Nigeria's history; it was also very corrupt. He sought to perpetuate himself in office through a fraudulent democratization process. Ethnic and social tensions heightened, and civil war was only avoided when he died suddenly in 1998. The regime created six additional states. Abacha's death led to the establishment of the Abdusalami regime, which conducted a hurried and troubled transition to civil rule in May 1999. The former military leader, Obasanjo, became a civilian president, but his rule was marked by further civil and religious disturbances, political and constitutional instability, insecurity of life and property, severe economic and social crises, and increasing loss of confidence.

Further reading

Achebe, C. (1984) *The Trouble with Nigeria*, London: Heinemann.

Coleman, J.S. (1958) *Nigeria: Background to Nationalism*, Berkeley: University of California Press.

ABDUL RAUFU MUSTAPHA

non-African diasporas

It is common to think of diasporas in the context of the Jewish or **African diasporas**. In terms of African history, non-African diasporas are rarely considered, yet there have always been diaspora groups resident on the continent who were not of African descent. The Lebanese, Indians, and Chinese are three of the largest groups of non-African settlers, outside of Europeans. These groups came to Africa, for the most part, under the auspices of one colonial power or another. Those who settled in Africa later entered the economic sphere in the various African countries, becoming successful traders and businessmen, while maintaining links to their homelands. Although it is arguable whether these three communities are diasporic communities in the strictest sense, lacking certain elements that have characterized other diasporas, they nevertheless share certain characteristics with other diaspora communities. Unlike some diasporic communities, members of these three diaspora communities were often voluntary migrants, and had the option of returning to their original homelands. However, like other diaspora communities, these three groups created diasporic identities. Though they relocated physically from one geographic locale to another, either voluntarily or involuntarily, for the most part they maintained ties and obligations to the homelands they left behind. They held on to many of their cultural practices, religion, language, and other social and cultural norms, never fully assimilating into their host societies.

Despite their individual differences, there are certain commonalities among these three non-African diaspora groups in the twentieth century. The roles they took on in the various countries they settled were comparable, and their mode of interaction and assimilation within these communities was also similar. They all faced initial non-acceptance by Africans, maintained a sense of superiority over the African populations, retained their cultural and social practices, and (with some exceptions) were generally unwilling to mingle with Africans, shying away from intermarriage or social intercourse with them.

Lebanese

The Lebanese, who first migrated to Africa in the late nineteenth century, had by the twentieth century become a significant part of many African countries, particularly in **West Africa**. Substantial Lebanese populations can be found in **Senegal**, **Côte d'Ivoire**, **Sierra Leone**, **Liberia**, and other countries. The Lebanese diaspora is made up of both Christians and Muslims: Before 1920 the immigrants were mostly Christians, but more and more Muslims began to migrate, particularly in the period after 1975 following the beginning of the civil war in Lebanon. Though their homeland is a distant memory for most, many maintain family, religious, and clan ties in Lebanon, and many of them return to their country of origin when they retire.

In the period between the two world wars, a large number of Lebanese emigrated to Africa, mainly to French colonies. Many of them engaged in trade and commerce, becoming middlemen between European import–export companies and African farmers. In the early part of the century they settled in the interior, learned local languages, and served as moneylenders to African populations. They soon edged out local African businessmen, undercutting their profits in trade. They established relationships with African producers, extended credit to farmers, and created other social ties. Though they maintained ethnic and family solidarity, a certain amount of exclusivity, and a condescending attitude toward the local African populations, some Lebanese men intermarried or cohabited with African women, producing children who served as a link between the two communities. Though some could be found in the professions, they were mostly shopkeepers and businessmen.

In the earlier part of the century Europeans were at the top of the trading hierarchy, controlling trade and production. The Lebanese and other Asians could be found in intermediate roles, serving as agents of European import firms, while Africans were relegated to the bottom of the trading hierarchy. By the 1920s and 1930s the Lebanese were buying agricultural produce and selling manufactured goods. Lebanese traders were favored by commercial firms, by banks, and by colonial states and administrations (see **state: colonial**), soon coming to dominate many aspects of the trade. For example, in **Sierra Leone** during the 1920s the Lebanese invested heavily in real estate and dominated the "lorry traffic" into the Protectorate. As a result of their success they faced hostility from the local African populations: In 1919 when railway workers protested and staged riots to demand better working conditions and wages, the Lebanese community was the main target of the riots. By the 1930s the Lebanese in Sierra Leone had moved into gold mining, and later they expanded into diamond mining. Local African populations regarded this with suspicion, seeing it as another means of Lebanese dominance over African economies. In the period after 1940 the Lebanese continued their supremacy in trade, as well as in mining enterprises. The Lebanese continue to have an ambivalent relationship with their African hosts, holding on to their status of wealth and political influence, while still reluctant to fully integrate with their host nations. This has led to ongoing negative perceptions. In the 1980s and 1990s Lebanese traders in West Africa were associated with terrorist activities. A 1989 explosion on a French airplane, originating in Africa and on its way to Paris, led to the hypothesis that a Shia Muslim terrorist network existed among Lebanese traders in Africa.

Indians

Like the Lebanese, their business success, their unwillingness to integrate, and the continuing presence of separate communities characterize the Indian diaspora in Africa. Though there are small communities of Indians in West Africa, the bulk of Indian diaspora communities can be found in **East** and **Southern Africa**.

In the early twentieth century a wave of Indian traders arrived in East Africa. In addition, at the turn of the century many Indians were brought to Africa by the British colonial administration as indentured laborers to build railways in Africa. Though many returned to India, others stayed, creating an Indian diaspora on the continent. They were by no means a monolithic group, coming from diverse cultural backgrounds, various professions, and different social classes. Some of the Indians soon established merchant firms, and became predominantly engaged in trade. During the 1920s Indians were employed in the colonial establishment as clerks, and were treated as British subjects. Nonetheless they were not given the same status as white settlers. In **Kenya** Indians were excluded from the White Highlands. Indians could be found actively involved in politics, and there was rivalry between Indians and British settlers. In **Tanzania** and Kenya during the 1920s Indians could be found in the legislative councils of the colonies. By the 1930s the number of Indians had grown significantly. As their numbers grew and they became politically active a certain amount of rivalry ensued between Indians and Africans, with each group vying for civil-service positions and clerkships within the various colonial administrations. In Kenya the African population often accused Indians of being "junior partners" to the colonial administration, particularly in the commercial sphere, and they were accused of siding with the British against Africans. Nonetheless, some members of the Indian community allied themselves with Africans, as was the case of Isher Dass, who affiliated himself with Jomo Kenyatta. Others were involved with trade unions and helped organize strikes among African workers, as did Makhan Singh. For the most part, however, the Indians continued to have separate communities, setting up their own social organizations, and often establishing their own schools.

In **South Africa** the position and status of Indians was somewhat different from that of their counterparts in East Africa. Originally brought in during the late nineteenth century to work on the sugar plantations of Natal, the Indians, like Africans, were subject to the laws of the apartheid system. The 1949 Mixed Marriage Act, which prohibited marriage between Europeans and non-Europeans, applied equally to Indians and Africans, as did the 1950 Group Areas Act, which put restrictions on their settlement and residence patterns.

It is as businessmen that Indians have made a mark. Like the Lebanese they engaged in all types of trade – import, wholesale, retail, and manufacturing. They maintained homogeneity and cooperation, working hard, and creating a favorable business atmosphere. This enabled them to expand their businesses. As they emerged as a small but prosperous group, hostility towards them grew. The most blatant manifestation of this hostility was the expulsion of Indians from **Uganda** in 1972. Though many returned to India, there were large numbers who had created lives for themselves in Africa, become citizens, and had few ties to India. Forced to leave the only place they considered a home, they ended up as expatriates in Europe, the United States, and other places. Their expulsion also led to a shortage of skilled manpower and to disruptions in Uganda's economy. Although the number of Indians has dwindled in places like Uganda, Indian communities continue to thrive in many African countries. South Africa and Kenya still have significant Indian populations. Though many have maintained ties with their homeland, continuing to visit relatives, and sending their children back to India to visit or for schooling, others have made the various African nations their home.

Chinese

A lesser-known non-African diaspora society on the continent is the Chinese. Though their numbers are small in contrast to the Lebanese and Indian diasporas, Chinese communities continue to be a part of many African countries. They can be found in West Africa in **Nigeria** and **Ghana**, but their numbers are larger in East and Southern Africa, in **Mauritius**, South Africa, **Madagascar**, **Zimbabwe**, and **Mozambique**. Though a small number of Chinese could be found in Africa before the twentieth century, it was during this century that a large number of Chinese immigrants arrived on the continent, brought to Africa for labor purposes or arriving as traders and entrepreneurs. In the early twentieth century, to counter the widespread withdrawal of African workers from the South African mines, Chinese laborers were transported by the British to the Transvaal area to labor in the mines. As their numbers grew, however, European settlers began to fear a Chinese takeover, particularly in the areas of trade and agriculture. For that reason the Chinese were segregated, and eventually recruitment of Chinese labor stopped. Similarly, in the late 1920s, French colonials in **Congo** brought Chinese workers to labor on the railways. Here the Chinese had an opportunity to influence their African counterparts as they engaged in a series of strikes, encouraging Africans to do the same.

Like the Lebanese and Indian diasporas, the Chinese maintain a certain separateness from their African hosts, establishing their own institutions like schools, temples, and other associations. Though some Chinese men intermarried or cohabited with African women, it is not a common practice. When they did produce children with Africans, the children were accepted and often sent to China to learn the customs and language of their fathers. Though most Chinese are involved in the commercial sphere as traders, businessmen, and restaurateurs, increasingly they can be found in the professions or even in politics. Since the 1950s the Chinese have been active as businessmen in places like Ghana and Nigeria, and since the 1970s as entrepreneurs in South Africa, **Lesotho**, and **Swaziland**. They have often been criticized for exploiting labor and maintaining separateness.

Though set apart from the populations in which they live, either by their physical difference or by their cultural norms, it is likely that future generations of these three non-African diaspora groups will become more easily assimilated into the cultures of the African nations where they live.

Further reading

Anshan, L. (2000) *A History of Chinese Overseas in Africa*, Beijing: Chinese Overseas Publishing.

Chattopadhyaya, H. (1970) *Indians in Africa: A Socio-economic Study*, Calcutta: Brookland Private.

Gecewicz, K.C. (1996) *Between a Rock and a Hard Place: Host Hostility and a West African, Lebanese Middleman Minority Community*, Ph.D. thesis, University of Southern Mississippi.

Snow, P. (1988) *The Star Raft*, New York: Weidenfeld & Nicolson.

William, S. and Skinner, E. (eds.) (1979) *Strangers in African Society*, Berkeley: University of California Press.

NEMATA BLYDEN

Non-Aligned Movement

The Non-Aligned Movement (NAM) was forged in the crucible of **Cold War** rivalry and the ambitious arms race that accompanied it, which replaced the alliance of the Allied Powers during the **Second World War**. The philosophy of the NAM in its formative years was to maintain an equal distance between the two Cold War superpower blocs, led respectively by the United States and the Soviet Union. The hope was that the Movement would:

1 become a reliable and impartial arbiter between the two blocs;
2 enable member-countries to pursue independent, "home-grown" domestic and foreign policies asserting their newly won independence; and
3 enable member-countries to attract development assistance from both blocs.

The intellectual desire for formation of the Movement was consummated at an informal meeting in Bandung on the Indonesian island of Java in 1955, sponsored by President Tito, along with President Nehru of India and President Nasser of Egypt. The first summit was held in Belgrade, Yugoslavia, in September 1961, with twenty-five countries from Africa, Asia, and the Middle East participating. Criteria for membership of the NAM are flexible. Prospective member-states are enjoined to:

1 adopt independent policies on coexistence with other states,
2 be consistent in supporting struggles for national independence, and
3 desist from cultivating and/or participating in bilateral and multilateral military alliances involving the Great Powers.

Although preoccupied with the political and security challenges posed by the Cold War, there remained a consensus that "colonialism in all its manifestations" constituted a major affront to the fundamental **human rights** of colonial peoples. It is a tribute to the NAM that its support for **decolonization** yielded the independence of many **Third World** countries. By 2000, African members of the Movement accounted for 49 out of a total membership of 133. Since the first meeting, at least twelve other Summit Conferences were held, at approximately three-year intervals, five of which took place in African capitals: **Cairo**, **Lusaka**, **Algiers**, **Harare**, and **Durban**. With the relaxation of Cold War tensions between the two superpowers in the mid-1960s, the priorities of the Movement shifted in favor of development-related issues and problems facing member-countries.

The founding fathers of the NAM made a conscious effort to de-emphasize rigid administrative structures and institution-building, preferring instead a Movement with flexible structures that could accommodate the disparate domestic- and foreign-policy interests of members, while also creating a strong basis for consensus- and solidarity-building. The chairmanship of the NAM passes from one host head of state or government to another. The highest authority of the NAM is the Summit Conference of Heads of States or Government, which holds its summit every three years. Two major committees service the summit: one on political issues, and another on economic and social issues. Next is the Coordinating Bureau, comprising Ministers of Foreign Affairs and Permanent Representatives to the United Nations. The bureau serves as the focal point for coordinating the affairs of the NAM between summits, most of which take place at the UN headquarters in New York. The Movement also works in concert with existing groups within the UN, such as the Group of 77 or the South–South Forum, using specialized working groups, contact groups, task forces, and committees.

The NAM was dogged by several criticisms from its inception. The most persistent was its inability to accurately define and defend its mission. It proved difficult, if not impossible, for it to give a politically acceptable definition of "non-alignment," precisely because the concept was arbitrary, fluid, and emotive. Another setback was that the Movement began to flounder in the aftermath of the death of its charismatic founders. One of the earliest manifestations of this decline was the inability of the Movement to use its voting preponderance at the UN General Assembly to ensure the adoption in 1972 of the New International Economic Order – a comprehensive blueprint highlighting the social and economic predicament facing Third World countries. Another shortcoming of the Movement was the obsolescence of its strategies, which traditionally relied on moral suasion. At the same time, the heterogeneity of the interests and concerns of its members often prevented the NAM from either speaking with one voice or reaching firm consensus on important global issues.

All these factors led critics to ridicule the Movement as an alliance of strange bedfellows. Critics also argued that the NAM had become anachronistic and dysfunctional in a post-Cold War global order. What is certain, however, is that the end of the Cold War left a big question mark hanging over the role and future prospects of the Movement. The major concern was its capacity to cope with the myriad new challenges posed by end of the Cold War and the advent of the twenty-first century, in an environment devoid of the ideological rivalry and tension that had given birth to the NAM in the first instance. The XII Summit Conference of the NAM, held in Durban, South Africa, in 1998, tried to articulate new priorities for the Movement in the new millennium. These included working tirelessly for the eradication of poverty and underdevelopment, controlling the spread of deadly diseases (including the dreaded HIV/AIDS), the emancipation of women, respect for the rights of children, **youth** development, social integration of the disabled, provision of jobs, and expansion of access to education and health services. Other issues related to the liberalization of the political system, and the pursuit of good governance, transparency, and accountability in the management of public offices and resources. Fortunately the prevailing global order provides a congenial environment for NAM to address these fundamental imperatives. The Movement must therefore abandon its obsolete assertiveness in favor of realistic advocacy, dialogue, and cooperation between members – as well as with non-member countries – in order to keep these burning issues on the global agenda.

See also: Organization of African Unity

Further reading

Arora, K.C. (1998) *Imperialism and the Non-Aligned Movement*, New Delhi: Sanchar Publishing.

Jackson, R.L. (1987) *The Non-Aligned, the UN, and the Superpowers*, New York: Praeger.

CHARLES UKEJE

non-governmental organizations

Non-governmental organizations (NGOs) are organizations that are supposed to have the following characteristics:

1 they are not arms of the state;
2 they do not receive a "substantial" portion of their operating budgets from government;
3 membership of such groups is voluntary, and their operating funds come from voluntary contributions and fundraising;
4 they are not beholden to the state in the pursuance of their organizational objectives;
5 they are autonomous, especially in the formulations of their organizational objectives;
6 they are non-profit-making; and
7 their earnings are put back into the organization for the continuation of their activities.

A further distinction may be drawn between organizations that are run by nationals of the country in which they operate – national NGOs (NNGOs) or local NGOs (LNGOs) – and organizations that are run by an international staff – international NGOs (INGOs). Some examples of local, national, and international NGOs are (respectively) Vindo Cooperative Society (VCS) in Voi, **Kenya**; Ghana Women's Initiative Foundation (GAWIF) in **Ghana**; and CARE International. By the 1990s there were thousands of NGOs in some countries: Morocco, for example, boasted more than 30,000 of them.

The discourse on NGOs in Africa in not a new one, although the term "NGO" is fairly recent. During the 1980s scholars began discussing the NGO phenomenon in the course of their attempts to unravel the relationship between state and society. In this context NGOs were defined as a stratum of **civil society**. Discussions about NGOs also emerged as a consequence of questions, from both African scholars and **international financial institutions** (especially the World Bank), about the role of the state in the development quagmire in Africa. Both groups, for different reasons, vested more hope, at least rhetorically, in people and their organizations – hence in NGOs – than in governments for meeting society's basic needs, and for enhancing their potential for making progress. As the state in Africa failed to deliver needed social services to the people, NGOs stepped in to fill the gap, especially as loans extended by multilateral institutions, specifically the World Bank and the International Monetary Fund (IMF), through **structural adjustment programs** (SAPs) did little, if anything, to improve the situation in Africa. Examples of these NGOs include associations of nurses and other health professionals, parents' associations, ethnic associations, religious associations, and even law and order associations such as the Resistance Councils (RCs) in **Uganda** and Sungusungu Defense Groups (SDGs) in **Tanzania**. These are among the organizations that were hailed by many as potentially bringing development, as well as democracy, to Africa from the bottom up. NGOs played a major role in alleviating social and economic stress in Africa. Increasingly some NGOs also put political pressure on governments to deepen democracy.

Although the term "NGO" is relatively new, and many of their activities were engineered to provide services that post-colonial governments did not – perhaps could not – provide, the NGO phenomenon was not itself new. Many earlier organizations could, in hindsight, have been called NGOs. These include the self-help and self-reliance organizations that sprang up in the 1970s to assist the state with nation-building; the Harambee organizations in Kenya are a good example, as is Maendeleo Ya Wanawake Organization (MYWO), which in 1987 was officially affiliated to the ruling Kenya African National Union (KANU) party. (MYWO was disaffiliated from KANU in 1992, reclaiming its status as an NGO.)

The history of NGOs and their activities date back even further. African indigenous organizations sprang up in the 1920s, 1930s, 1940s, 1950s, and 1960s – officially, as well as underground – to challenge colonialism. Many of these organizations became the catalysts for the political parties that emerged just prior to and after political independence. One example is the Youth Conference Movement (YCM) in Ghana, which emerged in 1929. The YCM was an amalgam of existing indigenous societies, clubs, and organizations (which also may be considered NGOs). Many liken the YCM to the Aborigines' Rights Protection Society (ARPS), founded in 1897 as the main Ghanaian organization for protesting the expropriation of land and other British colonial abuses. The YCM was the predecessor of the United Gold Coast Convention (UGCC), formed in 1947 to regain independence for Ghanaian people from British colonial rule. The UGCC also served as a precursor to the Convention Peoples Party (CPP), which led Ghana to independence. Similarly, in countries like **Malawi** in **Southern Africa**, the "welfare associations" of the early colonial period evolved into nationalist parties during the struggle for independence.

Other organizations had an even older history. These included burial societies, ethnic voluntary associations, and *nnoboa* groups to name but a few. *Nnoboa* refers to those traditions and traditional organizations in Ghana by which villagers came together to help each other with private farming and building projects. *Nnoboa* assistance was a kind of merry-go-round concept, in that it rotated around households and throughout villages, offering economic, psychological, and developmental support. The spirit of *nnoboa* remained very much alive in the NGO sector of the late twentieth century, and was the backdrop against which many NGOs – such as the Voluntary Workcamps Association of Ghana (VOLU) – formulated, implemented, and evaluated their activities. Schools, clinics, health services, and clean water were all provided through *nnoboa*.

The discourse surrounding NGOs has an imprecise and convoluted lexicon that sometimes confuses debate. NGOs focused on many issues including – but not exclusively – development, the environment, children, women, education, widows, single parents, the media, sports, water, family planning, research, democratization, and **human rights**. Some development NGOs were specifically called non-governmental development organizations (NGDOs). Other NGOs, including development NGOs, might be called people's organizations (POs), voluntary organizations (VOs), community-based organizations (CBOs), or people's voluntary organizations (PVOs). Some NGOs are local, some national, some regional, some continental, and some international. Some small local or national NGOs might have indigenous origins, or they might be branches of larger international NGOs. GAWIF had indigenous roots, while the Lion's Club Kenya (LC-K) was a branch of an international NGO. There were also NGOs that originated in the global South (**Third World**) – in Africa itself, for example – in addition to those from the global North – North America, perhaps. NGOs in the global South could have independent origins, or be extensions of NGOs in the global North; they might also have extensions in the global North that remitted financial and other resources to them. One example of this was the London Chapter of the 31st December Women's Movement (DWM). In addition NGOs in the global North might support NGOs in the global South without establishing local organizational extensions. One example of this was Marttalitto of Finland supporting one of MYWO's nutrition programs, rather than establishing a Marttalitto extension organization in Kenya.

NGOs could also be gender-specific. During the 1980s in particular, NGOs were viewed as almost synonymous with women's organizations. This was because women dominated the membership of NGOs in Africa, especially NGDOs, even when women did not lead such organizations. The 1980s was also a time of global organization and mobilization of women, supported primarily by the United Nations (UN) and Western governments. This decade of growing awareness and of women-in-development (WID) programs further fueled the proliferation of women's organizations, many of which received assistance for their projects and programs. An additional reason for the numerical dominance of women in the NGO sector is that men had maintained the governmental sector almost exclusively for themselves. Across the world, with few exceptions, men dominated government. By the mid-1990s only two women had been elected head of state, and only fifteen head of government. The state remained a masculine institution, and by design and default much of the NGO sector remained feminized. The exceptions were those NGO strata that dealt more directly with politics and public life. These were dominated by men, and included many of the think-tanks focusing on democracy and human rights.

There exists a great deal of controversy as to the function and effectiveness of NGOs in Africa. The crux of the question is whether or not NGOs brought about development and democracy. There are several schools of thought that present divergent answers to this question.

As many African NGOs functioned to fill gaps in the provision of essential services to relatively large populations, they most times did not function independently of other support organizations. Most African NGOs, either aggressively or less obviously, sought external support, as they were resource-poor organizations – reflecting the poverty of their countries and people. The phenomenon that thus emerged in many instances was an inter-organizational arrangement between African NGOs, African states, and foreign donors, an arrangement in which African NGOs were the central linchpin organizations. The way in which this inter-organizational relationship panned out was that African NGOs relied on the state and foreign donors for the financial and technical assistance necessary for the implementation of projects and programs, and on the state for permission to operate within any particular country. Many governments, like that of Kenya after the passage of the NGO Coordination Act of 1990, required NGOs to register with the government. Through registration the government minimized the risk of project and program duplication. The government also ensured that the organizations would abide by the rule of law. In some instances, by registering with the government, NGOs earned tax-exempt status. Many NGOs were suspicious of government registration, perceiving it as a form of regulation and control.

The optimistic school of thought on NGOs argues that African NGOs would bring about successful and more extensive self-reliant development in Africa. It argued that NGOs can prioritize the interests and needs of the people, and make space for ordinary citizens to define their own direction and development path. This school situated African NGOs at the center of the development policy process, leading the state and foreign donors despite their resource dependence. Such thinkers were optimistic about the success of NGO involvement in the development process, arguing that they brought to the fore innovative approaches that actually reached people at the grass-roots level, without the usual governmental and bureaucratic hassles. This school of thought also highlighted the development potential for women, given that women represented the bulk of NGO members. In sum it was believed that the trilateral partnership of African NGOs, the state, and foreign donors would be able to bring about successful development.

The school of NGO pessimism represented a diametrically opposite viewpoint. It argued that the inter-organizational relationships required for the development process made African NGOs vulnerable to foreign donors and the state, because such huge power differentials existed between the different "partners." Members of this school argued that African NGOs could be used – perhaps could even be created by foreign governments and/or foreign NGOs with the express purpose – of again colonizing Africa, this time from the bottom up: the trilateral inter-organizational arrangement, which such theorists did not consider a "partnership" at all, could likely bring about a new form of colonialism heretofore unseen – grass-roots colonialism. This school also argued that African governments could manipulate NGOs – perhaps create NGOs with this purpose too – so as to solidify their own power-base through patronage. That is, African governments might court, coopt, and/or coerce NGOs into supporting whichever government was in power, thereby undermining the democratic potential of both the organization and the people. Some pessimists pointed out that African governments might perceive NGOs as serious contenders for political power within the state, especially if they had access to finance from foreign donors, and hence fear and repress those NGOs. These pessimists further argued that African governments would use any means necessary to disempower NGOs. This school of thought did not believe that development was possible through tripartite inter-organizational relations.

The activities of African NGOs following the fall of the Berlin Wall in 1989 and during the period of what has been called "Afrostroika" – the call for political and economic change in Africa that followed the changes in Eastern Europe – fed the schools both of NGO optimism and of NGO pessimism. NGOs joined with other strata of civil society in either calling for an end to authoritarianism or blocking changes that would undermine the authoritarian governments already in power. Through the latter NGOs demonstrated that they were not by nature inherently pluralizing or democratizing, nor were they necessarily gender-sensitive. As the history of this third wave of democratization in particular demonstrated, NGOs were both part of pro-democratic civil society and resistant to the return to civil society. In other words some NGOs had, at one point or another in their lifespans, political agendas that intended to change the authoritarian nature of the state, while other NGOs did not because they personally benefited from the continuance of an anti-democratic state. Some NGOs swung back and forth between pro-democracy and anti-democracy, depending on what was at stake for them at any given time. Some called these "opportunist" or "chameleon NGOs."

Women's NGOs are particularly interesting in this regard, as many of them were created by the state. Many were led by wives or relatives of heads of states and/or governments, and functioned to support the state and the personalized rule of their husbands or relatives. Such organizations include the 31st December Women's Movement (DWM) in Ghana and Maendeleo Ya Wanawake (MYWO) in Kenya, as well as the Better Life Program (BLP) in Nigeria, which is led by former First Lady Mrs. Babangida, and the Family Support Program (FSP), under former First Lady Mrs. Abacha. There were also pro-democracy women's organizations that opposed anti-democratic women's organizations. These included the various national chapters of the Association Internales des Femmes Juristes (International Federation of Women Lawyers or FIDA), Women in Law and Development in Africa (WILDAF), the Ghana Women's Initiative Foundation (GAWIF), the Green Belt Movement (GBM) in Kenya, the banned Sudanese Women's Union (SWU), and Women in Nigeria (WIN). Other women's organizations either did not have overt political agendas, or changed position whenever it was beneficial to do so. These organizations included Accra Market Association (AMA), Registered Nurses Association (RNA), and Hairdressers Association (HA), all from Ghana. Some NGOs, such as Women Earnestly Ask for Abacha (WEAA), openly supported authoritarian governments.

These all raise serious questions about the legitimacy of NGOs. Some tread a fine line between being non-governmental and governmental. As the boundaries of interest for some NGOs are coterminous with those of the state, they may espouse the same agenda as the government, raising questions not only about their autonomy but also about which sector they belong to: non-governmental or governmental? In addition some NGOs receive an overwhelming amount of support from foreign donors, and are thus likely to implement their agendas. To what extent can these organizations be considered NGOs? The not-for-profit requirement for NGOs also presents obstacles to any attempt by NGOs to exist independent of "partnerships" with the state and foreign donors. Questions about how such NGOs are able to pay their staff and sustain their activities abound. Perhaps development and democratization activities that will continue over the coming decades will give us more conceptual clarity about the role of NGOs.

See also: globalization; nationalist movements; state: colonial; state: post-independence; women's movements

Further reading

Aubrey, L. (1997) *The Politics of Development Cooperation: NGOs, Gender and Partnership in Kenya*, London: Routledge.

Mama, A. (1999) "Dissenting Daughters: Gender Politics and Civil Society in a Militarized State," *CODESRIA Bulletin*, Dakar: CODESRIA.

Ndegwa, S. (1996) *The Two Faces of Civil Society:*

NGOs and Politics in Africa, West Hartfort: Kumarian.
—— (ed.) (2001) *Journal of Asian and African Studies*, special issue on democracy in Africa, XXXVI, 1.
Ninsin, K. (1998) *Ghana: Transition to Democracy*, Accra: Freedom Publications.

LISA AUBREY

North Africa

The long history of North Africa (**Algeria**, **Morocco**, **Tunisia**, **Libya**, **Egypt**, and **Mauritania**) pushed many contemporary Westerners to think wrongly that this region was old and unchanging. But people and politics in the region changed immensely, and many changes occurred at the levels of history, population, culture, politics, and economy. All six countries of North Africa experienced colonial rule. Algeria, Morocco, and Mauritania were under French occupation; Libya was under Italian rule; and Egypt was colonized by Britain. Colonization lasted longer in Algeria under the French (a total of 132 years) than in any other country of the region. In return for permission to colonize Egypt, Great Britain recognized Morocco as a French territory in 1904. France and Spain divided the country into zones of influence, with Spain receiving the northern and southern parts, and France establishing control over the more useful central part of Morocco. Despite sharing the same religion (**Islam**), language (**Arabic**), culture, and history, North Africa's journey through the twentieth century was characterized by diversity. The population included Amazighs, Arabs, people of mixed Arab–Amazigh stock, and Copts. The rural population, which represented about 70 percent of the population in the 1950s, fell to half of the population in the 1990s due to a rural exodus caused by several droughts.

At the beginning of the century North Africa was already under colonial control; the colonization process, which lasted until the 1930s, brought an alien administration and the creation of colonial states. This period was also characterized by continuous droughts and epidemics affecting people and cattle. Colonization also brought new techniques of farming, introduced dams, and created diversity in the population as more European settlers came to live the region. Later on Algeria, Morocco, and Mauritania became overseas *départements* of France (*l'Algérie française*), ruled by a privileged elite of European colonists (*colons*). They developed a modern economy, with new industries, banks, schools, shops, and services similar to those at home. Agriculture was geared to the French economy: Large estates produced wines and citrus fruit for export to France. The different colonial regimes established by France, Britain, and Italy had much in common. Although the form of government in each case was basically monarchy (Morocco, Tunisia, Libya, Egypt), the three European powers had to rely on local tribal leaders in order to establish their authority. Indeed European rulers had much influence and control on the monarchs and leaders in the region. The colonial states were heavily authoritarian, and they created new divisions in the region mostly based on ethnicity. Following a policy of divide-and-rule, the colonial governments attempted, for example, to divide Arabs from Amazighs in Morocco and Algeria, and Muslims from Copts in Egypt. Economically the colonial powers sought to exploit the natural and human resources of the region – all the while arguing that they had a "mission" to "civilize" indigenous people. Their economic infrastructure had a great impact on North Africa. Investment in building roads, railroads, ports, and airports increased trade with the region, and made the transfer of raw materials to the metropoles easier. The colonial powers resorted to state coercion in their attempts to develop industry, with both government and private companies using forced labor, and confiscated the land of indigenous farmers, which had a remarkable impact on North Africa's economic and social structures. The presence of colonizers on North African land caused conflict and led to labor problems, especially because of the states' great support for European agriculture. Colonial settlers did not encourage industrial production, but rather confined their efforts to exporting agricultural commodities. At the beginning of the twentieth century Egyptian agriculture was so completely dominated by cotton grown to feed the textile mills of

Lancashire, England, that grain had to be imported to feed the rural population. Irrigation projects were carried out to increase the amount of arable land.

North Africa became home to many European settlers, who came to the region as soldiers, military officers, missionaries, farmers, administrators, and teachers. Although North African people formed the majority of the population, in comparison to the white settlers they had no rights or privileges. The presence of settlers led to social changes among the population: European languages and culture were introduced, and new values and lifestyles were established. As a result significant cultural variation marked the region. Western influence began to predominate as increasing numbers of North Africans, especially the educated elite, became Westernized, adopting external ideas and Western ways of life. However, many people in the region resisted Western influence and colonial occupation. Colonial rule caused fierce resistance from tribes and their leaders, but the Muslim population remained a disadvantaged majority, subject to many restrictions. For instance, they could not hold public meetings or travel without the colonizer's authorization. A strong nationalist movement was established, starting from the 1930s, and manifested itself in different forms of resistance to colonization: nationalist parties and armies of liberation were constituted; violent attacks were made on the colonizers; and revolts were organized across the region, both armed and peaceful. After the **Second World War** nationalist feelings increased among groups of Muslims who had at first only wanted equality with the Europeans. The **nationalist movements** began demanding structural reforms of government. Faced with the rejection of these demands by the colonial forces, the nationalists began to demand independence. The fact that the colonial powers refused to grant even the smallest reforms or most minor rights to the peoples of the region gave major impetus to the emergence of mass nationalism and the armed struggle for independence.

In 1944 Moroccan nationalists formed the Istiqlal ("independence") party, which soon won the support of King Mohammed V and the majority of Arabs. Because of his full support for nationalist resistance, the sultan was deposed by the French rulers in August 1953, although he was returned to his throne by the French in October 1955. Abdelkrim al-Khattabi and Allal al-Fassi in Morocco, Ferhat Abbas in Algeria, Lahbib Bourguiba in Tunisia, Omar el-Mukhtar in Libya, and Saad Zaghlul in Egypt were among the most prominent nationalist leaders in the region. In Algeria alone the material and human costs of the war against France were huge. French casualties were about 100,000, Algerian more than 1 million. The increasing number of protests and intensifying battle for independence, fully supported by nationalist political leaders, as well as a serious guerrilla war in Algeria, persuaded France to speed up **decolonization**. Elsewhere the British army's occupation of Egypt ended in 1954, while Libya obtained its independence in December 1951. In March 1956 Morocco and Tunisia were proclaimed independent, and later Mauritania (1960) and Algeria (1962) followed suit.

As most European settlers – especially the wealthiest, best educated and most skilled – left the region after independence, social services suffered and several public facilities disappeared, forcing North African countries to hire professionals and experts from the former colonial powers so as to improve their economic and social structures. After independence all the North African countries joined the Arab League, but apart from that they quickly moved in different directions over their systems of government, policies, ideologies, and alliances. Egypt became a republic following a military coup of 1952 that ousted King Faruk. Similarly the liberation army in Tunisia, led by Lahbib Bourguiba, turned against the *bey* (monarch), who had no aptitude for government and showed a blatant disregard for public well-being. On 1 September 1969 Muammar al-Qaddafi also carried out a successful coup, declaring Libya a republic. Furthermore, while Morocco adopted a capitalistic system at independence, the other countries instituted Arab socialism as a means of reforming social and political life. In the 1960s foreign capital investments in Algeria, Libya, and Egypt were nationalized, as were public utilities and local industries. North African economies started to develop and to modernize as their role in the world economy changed over the years. Thus Morocco became the first North African exporter of phosphates; Algeria and Libya became great producers of oil and natural gas; and Morocco, Mauritania, and Tunisia developed their fishing industries. Later in the century these countries (particularly Egypt, Tunisia, and Morocco) developed tourism and exported new products, including clothing, carpets, handicrafts, and various agricultural products. With the introduction of capitalism among North African peoples, mentalities began to change and the gap between rich and poor became wider. Big cities (**Casablanca** and **Rabat** in Morocco, **Nouakchott** in Mauritania, **Cairo** and **Alexandria** in Egypt, **Tunis** in Tunisia, and **Tripoli** in Libya) were visibly more economically advanced in terms of people's revenues and social services like schools and hospitals, but also in terms of infrastructure and industrial production. Small towns and rural areas remained poor, on the other hand, with hardly any social services or infrastructure.

Morocco was the only country that adopted a multi-party system; other North African countries insisted on a single-party system. After many political reforms in the region, only Libya continued to reject the multi-party government. The Algerian political experience was marked by drastic changes in the system of government, with many military coups. The ruling party there – Front de Libération National (FLN) – failed to bring prosperity to Algerians, despite three decades in power: The country suffered from inflation and poverty, and the **youth** became disillusioned with the FLN. Similarly in Egypt the Wafd party brought people much hardship, unemployment, and social decline. As a result fundamentalist religious organizations, such as the Muslim Brotherhood in Egypt and the Front Islamic du Salut (FIS) in Algeria, gained support. The Algerian civil war (1990–2000), initiated by the Groupe Islamique Armé (GIA), led to the loss of thousands of lives and a considerable amount of property. Furthermore Egypt and several other Arab states went to war with Israel in 1948, 1967, and 1973. Although Egypt did not win the war, it regained control of the Suez Canal. A peace treaty between Egypt and Israel, based on the Camp David accords, was signed in Washington, D.C., on 26 March 1979.

In general, the political systems of the region were marked by authoritarianism, characterized by a powerful executive with firm control over the media and a weak judiciary. In this regard, the impact of colonial rule was evident, as most North African states adopted colonial patterns of authoritarian government, denying civilians civil rights to the extent that detention without trial was normal governmental behavior. Faced with a rising tide of globalization and democratization, North African states began changing their patterns of government in the early 1990s with the introduction of multiparty politics. This was the consequence of appeals made by Western powers, and the result of international pressure for democratic change following the end of the **Cold War**. Western countries agreed to provide economic aid and trade with North African countries, on condition they adopt the rule of law and protect **human rights**. Despite the adoption of multi-party government, most North African countries saw the pre-democratic ruling parties strengthen their hold on power. Yet the region also witnessed the impact of ethnicity over the 1990s, specifically in Algeria, Morocco, and Egypt. Amazigh populations (about 25 percent of the overall North African population) emerged as a strong political and cultural force. The demonstrations of Amazighs in the Algerian Kabylie region, which took place repeatedly over the 1980s and the 1990s, led to recognition of the sociopolitical importance of Amazigh cultural identity. Ethnic rivalry was also a common feature of the political arena in Egypt, which came to recognize the cultural rights of the Copts, who had great influence in Egyptian politics.

Following the constitution of blocs and unions around the world, North Africa also experienced a change as new attempts were made by the governments to unify the region under some sort of a federation. Pursuing his dream of Arab unity, Gamal Abdel Nasser of Egypt in 1958 effected a union between Egypt and Syria under the name of the United Arab Republic; however, this union lasted only three years before the Syrians rebelled and reaffirmed their independence. In 1980 King

Hassan II of Morocco and the Libyan leader signed a treaty forming the Union Africaine, which lasted barely a year. The Union du Maghreb Arabe, which was created in 1989, provided for greater regional cooperation and exchange – it was intended to redress the balance of trade that had been always to the advantage of the European Community. However, the tension that has marked Moroccan–Algerian relations over the Sahara since the 1970s prevented the federation from seeing daylight. Morocco recovered its territory in the Sahara (previously occupied by Spain) in 1975, but the Algerian government provided support to the Polisario Front, which was fighting for Saharan independence. In the 1980s and 1990s North African states implemented different economic policies aimed at creating greater social equity and economic growth. Algeria, Libya, and Egypt slowly moved from socialism to a market economy, and from state control to free trade, so as to avoid economic collapse. This move encouraged free enterprise, introducing new laws to encourage internal and external investment in the region. Thus exports increased, and new activities like tourism and remittances from emigrants (especially from Egypt and Morocco) grew in importance as sources of foreign currency. After Egypt took part in the US-led coalition that defeated Iraq in the Persian Gulf War of 1991, about half of its debt to the allies of US$20.2 billion was forgiven, and the rest was rescheduled.

Despite efforts to develop the economy and improve the well-being of the population, North African economies, in general, became increasingly dependent on the Western economies by the end of the twentieth century; most of the North African states still dependent on the World Bank and the International Monetary Fund (IMF) following their adoption of **structural adjustment programs**, which were disadvantageous to the overwhelming majority of their populations. Additionally, at the social level all indicators pointed to a remarkable increase of poverty and unemployment, especially in rural areas, and among the young and women. Nonetheless the population of North Africa experienced a huge rise over the last four decades of the twentieth century, as a consequence of improved health services, the expansion of education, and increased food production. In the 1990s the overall population of North Africa totaled more than 130,581,000. This demographic explosion put great pressure on the social welfare provision. Despite great economic efforts the region faced significant barriers to progress, chiefly the continuing problems of unemployment, poverty, and illiteracy. Government leaders acknowledged population growth as the principal cause of the region's economic problems, but the economy was also burdened by foreign debt, which in the early 1990s was more than twice the size of region's annual budget. In the early 1990s North African states began putting into place economic reforms that were recommended by the IMF and World Bank, relaxing price controls, reducing subsidies, and liberalizing trade and investment. On the whole the region made considerable progress in many fields, including agriculture, industry, technology, education, and health care. As a result average life expectancy increased, infant mortality rates decreased, and levels of adult literacy – as well as access to higher education – improved significantly.

All in all, as a region North Africa witnessed many changes over the twentieth century. Significant changes occurred in the fields of economy, society, politics, and culture. Various peoples and civilizations interacted across North Africa, where the mixing of people and ideas was greater than in many other regions. North Africa's political systems and social structure evolved over the twentieth century, along with changes and improvements to its economies. However, at the end of the century North African economies remained rather fragile; they were still too dependent on the West, and at the mercy of **international financial institutions**.

Further reading

Abun-Nasar, J.M. (1987) *A History of the Maghrib in the Islamic Period*, Cambridge: Cambridge University Press.

Amin, S. (1971) *The Maghreb in the Modern World*, Harmondsworth: Penguin.

Cooper, M.N. (1982) *The Transformation of Egypt*, London: Croom Helm.

Le Tourneau, R. (1962) *Evolution Politique de l'Afrique du Nord Musulman*, Paris: Armand Colin.
Vanderwalle, D. (ed.) (1996) *North Africa: Development and Reform in a Changing Global Economy*, New York: St. Martin's Press.
Vatikiotis, P.J. (1980) *A Modern History of Egypt*, rev. edn., New York: Praeger.
Waterbury, J. (1982) *The Egypt of Nasser and Sadat: The Political Economy of Two Regimes*, Princeton: Princeton University Press.

MOHA ENNAJI

Northern Rhodesia *see* Zambia

Nouakchott, Mauritania

Nouakchott, with a population of over 700,000, lies on a plateau approximately twelve kilometers from the North Atlantic coast of northwest Africa. It was a village until it was chosen to be capital of the Islamic Republic of **Mauritania** in 1956. Nomads had long frequented wells in the area, but the only inhabitants were Imraguen fishermen. During the French conquest of Mauritania in the early 1900s, the military hero Xavier Coppolani constructed a base thirty kilometers to the north. This was later abandoned and a new fort constructed in 1923, adjacent to what is now Nouakchott. In the 1950s discussions between North African leaders aimed at Saharan unification motivated France to grant Mauritania independence in an effort to block the creation of a potentially powerful "Greater Morocco." The task of choosing a capital city was controversial, mirroring tensions between Saharan nomads and Sahelian cultivators (northerners and southerners) that had been exacerbated over the colonial period. The capital would have to act as a fulcrum for these social divisions, and Nouakchott filled some of the criteria. In 1956 the new government, with supplementary financing from France, set about building a capital city. The project was completed in two phases. In the first phase (1957–9) government buildings and the infrastructure necessary to support government were completed. The second phase (completed in the early 1960s) established Nouakchott as a business and administrative center.

In the 1970s environmental disasters further destabilized nomadic society. Various social and ethnic groups – *haratine* (freed slaves); nomads caught between drought, political instability, and armed conflict; immigrants from **Senegal** and **Guinea** – sought refuge in Nouakchott. Most of these people moved into shantytowns (*bidonvilles* or *kébés*) outside the city limits. The elites, whose power had been weakened by the colonial administration's policy of ignoring traditional rules of succession and instead electing their allies as clan leaders, were unaccustomed to providing support for displaced people in the unfamiliar urban context. Widows and divorcées were left to fend for themselves. The city tried to limit the formation of illegal *bidonvilles* around Nouakchott by providing little more than a basic supply of electricity and water. The city also suffered from its own unique set of environmental problems. The flatlands near the sea had a high saline content, making the soil unproductive, and this section of the city was prone to flooding. In addition the process of sahelization continued, causing droughts and severe windstorms.

In 1989 tensions between Mauritania and Senegal came close to war. In Nouakchott more than 200 Senegalese were killed; the people of Senegal responded with the expulsion of more than 200,000 white Mauritanians, many of them *haratine*. Mauritania then expelled 100,000 Senegalese, together with 50,000 black Mauritanians. The market was emptied of Senegalese and Peul workers, and the face of Nouakchott changed, along with the dynamics of inter-ethnic politics there. Later some of these workers returned to the city, but ethnic conflict continued.

While Nouakchott continued to experience problems caused by an infrastructure inadequate to the demands placed on it, some positive signs existed. In the *bidonvilles*, where women were the head of up to 40 percent of the households, cooperatives were granted financial credit and training, allowing women to become self-supporting. A women's fishing cooperative flourished. Other groups made rugs, clothing, and jewelry. The city was also the center of active pro-democratic movements. A complex and fascinating city, by the end of the century Nouakchott had begun to experience economic growth in the construction, information technology, and telecommunications sectors.

Further reading

Désire-Vuillemin, G. (1997) *Histoire de la Mauritanie: des origines à l'indépendance*, Karthala: Collège des hommes et sociétés.

SHEILA FINNIE

O

Organization of African Unity

The Organization of African Unity (OAU) was founded on 25 May 1963 in **Addis Ababa** in **Ethiopia**. In 2000 it was transformed into the African Union. A product of pan-African ideals of continental liberation, unification, and development, the formation of the OAU represented a compromise between two groups: the so-called "Casablanca" and "Monrovia" countries. The latter were opposed to socialism, favored a loose association, and took a pro-Western stance in world affairs, while the former held the opposite viewpoint. The OAU Charter pledged to promote cooperation among independent African states, and eradicate colonialism in the rest of the continent. Among its key principles was non-interference in the internal affairs of member-states. Three governing bodies were established. The Assembly of Heads of State and Government, meeting once a year, discussed policy and considered recommendations from the Council of Ministers, while the General Secretariat, headed by a secretary general, ran the day-to-day affairs of the organization. Several specialized commissions were also established.

The OAU quickly expanded both its membership and range of functions. By 2000 it had fifty-two member-states, making it the largest regional organization in the world. Its newest member was **South Africa**, which the OAU had fought very hard to liberate from apartheid. South Africa brought to the organization considerable political and economic resources. From the start the OAU sought to accelerate the process of **decolonization** by giving support to **nationalist movements** still fighting for independence. It applied moral and political pressure against the colonial powers and regimes through the United Nations and other international forums. It specifically encouraged its members and the international community in general to isolate and apply sanctions against recalcitrant colonial regimes. Also, through its Liberation Committee, the OAU supported armed liberation movements, particularly in **Southern Africa**, although the funds made available to such movements were never large because many members defaulted on their contributions to the Committee and the OAU budget.

The OAU's record in mediating and resolving conflicts within and among African states was not very successful. Between 1963 and 1993 there were about twenty full-fledged civil wars in Africa. The OAU responded to these conflicts through the mediation of the secretary general, or by appointing eminent special envoys and ad hoc committees, or by endorsing the mediation efforts of individual leaders and subregional and international organizations. In December 1981, during the protracted civil war in **Chad**, the OAU sent a poorly financed and coordinated peacekeeping force to monitor a ceasefire between government and rebel forces. After this mission's failure the OAU avoided establishing regional peacekeeping on a similar scale, leaving that role to the United Nations and subregional organizations, and seeking instead to concentrate its efforts on peacemaking through conflict prevention and mediation. In 1993 the Division of Conflict Management was established, replacing the moribund Commission on Mediation, Conciliation, and Arbitration. Despite the adoption of a more activist agenda, partly forced by the reluctance of the major powers to intervene in the continent's conflicts after the end of the **Cold War** and by the inability of the overstretched UN to intervene effectively, the OAU's peacemaking capacities remained weak, as demonstrated during the **Rwanda** genocide of 1994 and the war in the **Democratic Republic of Congo** from 1998. The OAU's mediation efforts in African conflicts were undermined by the organization's lack of financial resources, the unwillingness of member-states to cooperate, and the tendency of the major global powers to disregard it.

Also mixed was the OAU's record in promoting economic development. During its early years the OAU concentrated on political issues and virtually ignored economic matters, which it left to the better organized and technically more capable United Nations Economic Commission for Africa (ECA). For example, the OAU's Economic and Social Commission only met twice between 1963 and 1973. This changed following the onset of recurrent economic recessions in many African countries from the mid-1970s. In 1976 a special OAU session was devoted exclusively to economic issues; it recommended the creation of an African economic community. Four years later, at another OAU summit, African leaders adopted the Lagos Plan of Action, which outlined a process of economic integration and development up to the year 2000. As Africa's economic crisis deepened in the 1980s, the OAU worked closely with the ECA, and issued a series of reform programs, such as the African Priority Program for Economic Recovery that was presented to the UN in 1986. Five years later fifty-one African states signed the Abuja Treaty, establishing the African Economic Community to promote economic, social, and cultural development and the integration of African economies over a thirty-four-year period. In 2001 the African Union was established. Some observers were skeptical about whether the ambitious objectives of the Union would be achieved, given the different stages of development among African countries, poor communications, divergent post-colonial ties, the strength of other global trading blocs, and the historic lack of political commitment among member-states to previous OAU projects.

On the question of **human rights**, to which the OAU Charter made little reference, there has been considerable progress. Tolerance of dictatorships and human rights abuses began to wane from late the 1970s as internal and external pressures grew on some of Africa's notorious tyrants. At the 1979 OAU Summit President Nyerere of **Tanzania** was supported for having helped in the ouster of Idi Amin from **Uganda**. The summit also ordered the preparation of an OAU Charter on Human and Peoples' Rights. The Charter was adopted in 1981, and an African Commission on Human and Peoples' Rights was created in 1986 to monitor human rights practices in member-nations. At the 1999 OAU Summit African leaders agreed that they would no longer accept coups d'état and would shun leaders who came to power through them, another clear indication of the OAU's growing commitment to human rights and democracy.

Further reading

El-Ayouty, Y. (ed.) (1994) *The Organization of African Unity After Thirty Years*, London: Praeger.

Naldi, G.J. (1999) *The OAU: An Analysis of its Role*, New York: Mansell.

PAUL TIYAMBE ZELEZA

Organization of the Islamic Conference

In the wake of an alleged Israeli attempt to burn down al-Aqsa Mosque in Jerusalem (in August 1969) a summit conference of Islamic states was held in **Rabat**, **Morocco**, with twenty-five heads of state and government attending. Pursuing the resolutions of that conference, the foreign ministers of these countries met again in Saudi Arabia (March 1970), where they set up the Secretariat General of the Organization of the Islamic Conference (OIC) and issued its charter. Therein the organization's objectives were specified as

1 the promotion of Islamic solidarity;
2 the consolidation of cooperation among members in economic, social, cultural, and scientific activities;
3 the elimination of racial discrimination and colonialism;
4 the safeguarding of Islamic holy places; and
5 support for the struggle of the Palestinians.

The following principles were also adopted:

1 total equality between member-states;
2 respect for the right to self-determination;
3 non-interference in the domestic affairs of other member-states;
4 respect for the sovereignty of member-states;
5 settlement of conflict by peaceful means; and
6 abstention from the use of force against any member-state.

Three governing bodies were established: the Conference of Heads of State and Government, the Conference of Foreign Ministers, and the General Secretariat.

In addition to the incident at the al-Aqsa Mosque, the organization had other historical roots. These could be traced back to the ideals of pan-Islamism developed by Afghani and Abdul in the late nineteenth century, and adopted in varying degrees by Asian and African peoples. For centuries Africans and Asians traveled annually to Mecca for Hajj (pilgrimage), interacting with Arab nations, exchanging ideas and commodities, and developing multi-racial Sufi brotherhoods. As a result barriers relaxed, and a new sense of an extra-territorial Islamic *umma* evolved. When Arab–Israeli relations deteriorated in the 1960s and a call for Islamic solidarity in defense of the holy lands of Islam was made, it was well received in most of the Muslim world. Thirteen of the twenty-five heads of state who attended the Rabat conference represented African countries; these were **Algeria**, **Chad**, **Egypt**, **Guinea**, **Libya**, **Mali**, **Mauritania**, Morocco, **Niger**, **Senegal**, **Somalia**, **Sudan**, and **Tunisia**.

But pan-Islamic sentiment was not enough by itself. From its very inception the OIC was envisaged as a political organ, and was indeed a product of uneasy ideological and political compromises between conservative monarchies (Saudi Arabia, Morocco, and Iran), revolutionary Arab nationalists (led by President Nasser of Egypt), and non-Arab African and Asian countries (who formed the majority of moderate members). The Saudis, whose kingdom embraces Islam's two holiest cities, aspired under their shrewd and ascetic King Faisal to lead the Muslim world. Faisal was a staunch opponent of both Israel and the former Soviet Union, and – disenchanted with Arab nationalism – campaigned tirelessly for pan-Islamism as a counter-ideology. Nasser, on the other hand, was engaged in a deadly war against Israel, and was desperate for military, economic, and moral support. In theory the organization was based both on Islamic principles and on a common opposition to Israel. In reality these came into conflict with each other. Many of OIC members considered themselves to be secular states, not bound by any religious principles. Furthermore some of the non-Arab Muslim countries (Iran, Senegal, Turkey) had diplomatic relations with Israel before and after the establishment of the OIC. Others, like Egypt, negotiated an agreement with Israel and resumed diplomatic relations, irrespective of the position of the organization.

Not surprisingly the organization faced a range of problems. Some of them were associated with the immense diversity of the member-states, extending from Morocco in northwestern Africa to Malaysia in Southeast Asia and Pakistan in central Asia. Other problems were associated with the political systems of the member-states, which ranged from conservative monarchies and military dictatorships through to republics and democratic socialist governments. A third set of problems stemmed from internal conflicts, over either territory or natural resources. Engulfed in ideological differences, conflicts of interest, and personal rivalries, delegates sometimes had trouble entering into dialogue with each other. The organization's constant concern was to minimize these differences between member-states.

In the wake of the Egyptian–Israeli war (1973) the organization reached its peak of importance, both nationally and internationally. In response to President Nixon's announcement that he was sending Israel US$2.2 billion-worth of arms, Faisal exploded with rage and shut off all oil to the

United States. Following the initiative of the Saudi king, the other oil-producing Arab states followed suit. Other non-Arab, non-oil Muslim countries severed their relations with Israel. From then onwards Faisal began to command special respect among the world's 600 million Muslims, and the organization began to attract more members. **Uganda**, for instance, was admitted to the organization in 1974, and **Nigeria** was accepted as an observer.

The oil blockade brought to the OIC's attention the viability and importance of economic cooperation among its members. Consequently the Islamic Development Bank (IDB) and Islamic Educational, Scientific, and Cultural Organization (IESCO) were established to foster the economic and social development of the less-advantaged members, namely the Asian and African countries. The performance of these institutions was relatively good. Nevertheless African countries were not satisfied, and some of them started to patch up their differences with Israel and the United States, or to establish alternative regional organizations. With the erosion of support, and increasing internal and external calls for democratization, some members of the organization made gestures toward political change. They called for a special conference on **human rights** and issued the Cairo Declaration (1990), but no one was convinced that major changes would be forthcoming. The organization, in fact, became a forum for the airing of grievances, rather than a serious consultative body. Nevertheless one should not conclude that the strong desire among Muslims for an indivisible *umma*, and the rich cultural heritage they share, cannot be translated into action – should an opportunity and good leadership present themselves.

See also: Islam; Islamic reform movements; League of Arab States

Further reading

al-Ahsan, A. (1988) *The Organization of the Islamic Conference*, Herndon: International Institute of Islamic Thought.

ELTIGANI ABDELGADIR HAMID

Ouagadougou, Burkina Faso

Ouagadougou is the capital and largest city of **Burkina Faso** (formerly Upper Volta). The city started as the residence of one of the powerful Mossi chiefs in the fourteenth century. Before long it became the imperial capital of the king of the Mossi people, the Mogho Naaba ("king of the world"). In 1896 French invaders set the city on fire when the Mogho Naaba refused to turn his kingdom into a French protectorate, part of the larger French colony of Haut-Sénégal–Niger. The colony of Upper Volta was created in 1919, dissolved in 1932, and re-created in 1947. Throughout this period Ouagadougou remained its capital. With the presence of colonial administrators and military personnel, Ouagadougou grew not only as an administrative center, but also as an attractive commercial center in the heart of the savannas of **West Africa**, connected to the Atlantic Ocean through the Abidjan–Niger railway, which had been built to speed up the flow of goods between the landlocked savanna regions and the sea. The construction of the railway, also known as the "economic lung" of Burkina Faso, began from **Abidjan** in 1903, reaching Ouagadougou in 1954.

Ouagadougou's population grew steadily during the colonial period, then exploded after independence, as people flocked to the city looking for waged employment in the burgeoning new industries, with textile factories, a brewery, and processing plants for agricultural products springing up. The city's early population included a few Europeans, local civil servants, security guards, and military personnel. In 1914, out of 19,344 residents, only 12 were European; at independence in 1960 there were 1,347 Europeans and 50,000 Africans out of a total population of 51,500. As the capital, Ougadougou was at the center of the country's political developments, including political protests and coups. In the 1980s the revolutionary regime of Captain Sankara, with its bold construction and social programs, attracted large numbers of people to Ouagadougou. Jobs were created, new movie theaters were built, and housing was made a priority. By 2000 the population of the city had reached 1.2 million.

This rapid growth led to problems including unemployment, traffic jams, and pollution from fumes, dust, and trash. However, the city boasted of several attractions, including historic sites and monuments, an age-old park, and three interconnected water reservoirs. By hosting FESPACO (Festival Panafricain du Cinéma de Ouagadougou – the Ougadougou Pan-African Film Festival) and SIAO (Salon Internationale de l'Artisanat de Ouagadougou – the International Arts and Crafts Trade Show), Ouagadougou became known as the capital of African cinema and the crossroads for arts and crafts. FESPACO started in 1969 with only five African and two European countries participating. By 1985 it had become the biggest cultural event in Africa, with about forty countries competing every two years for the prestigious Etalon de Yennega and several other prizes. For its part, SIAO became a major biannual market for African arts and crafts, which attracted exhibitors and traders from all across Africa and overseas. Both events contributed to the growth of tourism. For example, between 1988 and 2000 SIAO attracted more than 2 million participants and visitors.

By the end of the twentieth century Ougadougou was a modern and attractive city that was a source of pride for its citizens and the migrant workers drawn there from the neighboring countries. The city was also home to the national university and the Mogho Naaba, now a ceremonial king. The crime rate was very low, and the city's numerous bars and discos are always packed, especially on weekends.

Further reading

Madiéga, Y.G. and Nao, O. (1999) *Burkina Faso, cent ans d'histoire, 1895–1995*, 2 vols., Paris: Editions Karthala.

LAMISSA BANGALI

P

Pan-Africanism

Ideologies and forms of Pan-Africanism

Pan-Africanism was inspired by the desire to instil racial pride among African peoples on the continent and in the diaspora, to achieve their self-determination from European domination, to promote solidarity among them, and to foster their social and economic regeneration. Thus Pan-Africanism had two main objectives. First, to liberate Africans and the **African diaspora** from racial degradation, political oppression, and economic exploitation. Second, to encourage unity or integration among African peoples in political, cultural, and economic matters. Pan-Africanist ideas were derived from the experiences of – and struggles against – slavery, colonialism, and racism, as well as from European ideas of democracy, Marxism and socialism, and nationalist ideas from other parts of the colonized world, such as Gandhian philosophy. So Pan-Africanism was a complex movement, which had diverse origins, contexts, objectives, ideologies, and forms of organization.

At least six versions of Pan-Africanism emerged: transatlantic, black Atlantic, continental, sub-Saharan, Pan-Arab, and global. Proponents of the first imagined a Pan-African world linking continental Africa and its diaspora in the Americas. The second version confined itself to the African diasporic communities in the Americas and Europe, excluding continental Africa. This is articulated in Paul Gilroy's book *The Black Atlantic* (1993), in which the cultural creativity and connections of the African diaspora in the United States and Britain are celebrated, while continental Africa is largely ignored. The third focused primarily on the unification of continental Africa. The fourth and fifth restricted themselves to the peoples of the continent north and south of the Sahara, and in the case of Pan-Arabism extended itself to western Asia or the so-called Middle East. (Gamal Abdel Nasser proudly saw **Egypt** at the center of three concentric circles linking the African, Arab, and Islamic worlds.) The sixth sought to reclaim African peoples dispersed to all corners of the globe.

Each version developed at a different time and in a different way. For example, while transatlantic Pan-Africanism developed as a movement of ideas, with little formal organization apart from periodic conferences, and predated (indeed spawned) continental Pan-Africanism, it was the latter that first found institutional fulfillment with the formation of the **Organization of African Unity** (OAU). The connections and reverberations between these Pan-Africanisms were, and continue to be, intricate, complex, and contradictory, spawning both narrow territorial nationalisms and broad transnational movements, including dozens of **regional integration** schemes. Pan-African movements were often complemented and constrained by other transnational movements, those organized around religion, for example, or colonial linguistic affiliations.

The nationalists who led the movements for independence almost invariably subscribed to some form of Pan-Africanism, to the notion of a shared, collective African identity that was in opposition to European identity. There were several reasons for this. First, it reflected the overdetermination of race in the colonial world – the fact that globally colonialism imposed the subordination of the "darker" to the "lighter" races – and Africans everywhere seemed to be under some form of European oppression and exploitation. Second, the nationalists were linked through intricate institutional and ideological networks, for example, through education in regional and metropolitan universities, through participation in regional and international political organizations and social movements, and through the cultural intersections and traffic between Africa and the diaspora. Third, the project of nation-building was seen as both confined to and transcending colonial borders, as a forging of coherent post-colonial nation-states around the territorial space drawn up by the colonialists, states that would eventually be integrated together. But the internal demands of nation-building proved more pressing and enduring than those of Pan-African integration. As nationalism intensified in each colony, indeed, as independence was achieved, the struggles and visions of the future were increasingly anchored on the interests of the nation at the expense of Pan-Africanism.

Origins and development of transatlantic Pan-Africanism

Transatlantic Pan-Africanism had its roots in the dispersal to the Americas and Europe of African peoples through the dehumanizing Atlantic slave trade. The centers of this triangular trade – which connected western Europe, western Africa, and the Americas – became centers for the development of Pan-Africanism. As an ideology and a movement it first emerged among the enslaved Africans in the diaspora, because they were the earliest to bear the full brunt of European racism, oppression, and exploitation. Regardless of where they came from in Africa or what social position they had held in African society or now held in the Americas, they were all lumped together as racially "inferior." So they were more inclined to see Africa and Africans as a unit than were the Africans on the continent itself, who remained isolated or attached to their ethnic groups or nations. The lead taken by the African diaspora in the Caribbean and the United States in organizing Pan-Africanism can be attributed to the fact that racial ideologies there were more severe there than in Latin America. Also Britain was a colonial superpower, and later the United States became a global superpower.

Africans in the diaspora were constantly being reminded of Africa by their European masters, who tried to impress upon them that Africa was primitive. Repudiating this thinly veiled justification of slavery required diaspora intellectuals to focus on Africa and demonstrate that it had made major contributions to world civilization. Consciousness of Africa was also sustained by the continuous flow of people, ideas, values, visions, practices, and expressive forms of culture from Africa to the Americas and vice versa. After slavery was abolished there were waves of African students. From the Americas came the "Back to Africa" movements. Beginning at the turn of the nineteenth century, groups of free Africans from the Caribbean, Canada, the United States, and Britain moved to **Sierra Leone** and **Liberia**. There were also migrations from Brazil to **West Africa**. The new communities, called Krio in Sierra Leone or Saro in the **Niger Delta**, played a crucial role in the spread of Western modernity and in the development of Pan-Africanism. Among the most renowned Pan-African intellectuals was Edward Blyden, who migrated from St. Thomas at a young age and settled in Liberia. He saw Africa as a product of a triple heritage – the indigenous, Islamic, and Christian traditions – a concept that was further developed by Kwame Nkrumah, the first president of **Ghana**, and Ali Mazrui, the Kenyan intellectual.

Analysis of transatlantic Pan-Africanism tends to focus on the development of **nationalist movements** and ideologies. Pride of place has gone to the Pan-African Congresses associated with the great African-American scholar-activist W.E.B. DuBois, who famously declared that the "problem of the twentieth century is the problem of the color line" (DuBois 1990 [1903]: 24). Between 1900 and 1945 five Pan-African Congresses were held in Europe, attended by delegates from the continent and the diaspora, mostly from the English-speaking countries. The early Congresses called for increasingly substantial colonial reforms, while the 1945 Manchester Congress, the last to be held outside Africa, categorically demanded independence for African and Caribbean colonies. Delegates from the Congress, including Nkrumah and Jomo Kenyatta of **Kenya**, returned to their respective countries to lead nationalist movements to independence, which was largely achieved in the next three decades.

There were of course other movements besides the Pan-African Congresses. The Caribbean – a region that experienced both slavery and colonial rule, and was thus uniquely placed to connect the experiences of slavery in the Americas with those of colonialism in Africa – produced many of the leading Pan-African thinkers and organizers, such as Marcus Garvey from Jamaica and the illustrious revolutionary thinkers George Padmore and C.L.R. James from Trinidad. Garvey was the founder of the Universal Negro Improvement Association (UNIA) in 1914 in Kingston, which was relocated to the United States in 1915 and quickly became the largest African-American mass movement the country had ever seen. The UNIA established its own journal (*Negro World*) and a shipping line, and the flamboyant Garvey preached fervently for "Back to Africa" and the creation of a United States of Africa, one largely founded on capitalist principles. The annual UNIA Conventions were attended by delegates from more than twenty-five countries. The movement eventually collapsed, thanks to state machinations, aided by opposition to Garvey from other civil rights activists, including DuBois who had more scholarly and socialist inclinations.

During the 1930s both DuBois's Congresses and Garvey's Conventions were moribund. In their place emerged a series of Pan-African organizations, such as the League of Colored Peoples and the International African Service Bureau, both formed in England, which vociferously protested the Italian invasion of **Ethiopia** in 1935, an invasion that shook Africans everywhere. In the United States Paul Robeson, the famous singer and activist, founded the Council on African Affairs, while African students formed the African Students Association, both of which organized meetings and called for African development and independence. In Africa itself Pan-African sentiments were expressed through the lively African **press** and emerging political associations. In West Africa there was the National Congress of British West Africa (formed in 1920) and the West African Students Union (formed 1925), while in **South Africa** the African National Congress was formed in 1911. All of these organizations highlighted the abuses of colonialism, calling for African solidarity in the struggle for emancipation. In **francophone Africa** the Ligue pour la Défense de la Race Nègre (Universal League for the Defense of the Black Race) was founded in 1924, and called for the formation of a unitary black state embracing sub-Saharan Africa and the West Indies.

From the 1950s – as African and Caribbean colonies gained their independence – transatlantic Pan-Africanism waned, with nationalists concentrated on national development and regional integration. The Pan-African conferences hosted in Ghana in 1958 – the Conference of Independent African States and the All African Peoples Conference – were, for example, largely confined to continental Africans and state actors or leaders of nationalist movements. The attention of African and Caribbean leaders increasingly turned inwards to the OAU and the Caribbean Common Market respectively. No wonder the sixth Pan-African Congress of 1974, held in **Tanzania**, attracted relatively little interest. In the meantime, the struggle for civil rights in the United States was gathering momentum and scoring some legislative victories. In Latin America, where the politics of racial identity had historically undermined Pan-Africanism, there was rising African racial consciousness, as manifested in the four Congresses of Black Culture in the Americas that took place between 1977 and 1984. There were connections between these processes: The nationalist achievements in Africa and the Caribbean inspired civil rights struggles in the United States, while civil rights activists in the United States provided crucial support to liberation movements fighting against recalcitrant settler regimes in **Southern Africa** by applying pressure on the American government and companies.

The traffic between Africa and the Americas that facilitated and sustained transatlantic Pan-Africanism also involved periodic and cumulative cultural exchanges. For example, in the nineteenth and early twentieth centuries African-American missionaries played a critical role in the spread of **Christianity** in several parts of the continent, especially in West and Southern Africa. The influence of the cultural practices of the African diaspora on African expressive culture has also been remarkable. Many forms of popular **music** in twentieth-century Africa – from rhumba and jazz to reggae and rap – were imported from the African diaspora. The celebrated rhumba of the **Congo** was heavily affected by Cuban music; South African jazz reflected strong American influences; reggae in **Senegal** was borrowed from Jamaican reggae, and so on. In the realm of **literature** there were close connections between the literary movements of Africa and the diaspora, most significantly the Harlem Renaissance and the Negritude movement in the 1920s and 1930s. In the arts, more broadly, there were Pan-African festivals, such as the Colloquium of the World Festival of Black Civilization (FESTAC) held in **Nigeria** in 1977.

References and further reading

Blyden, N. (2000) *West Indians in West Africa, 1808–1880: The African Diaspora in Reverse*, Rochester: University of Rochester Press.

DuBois, W.E.B. (1990 [1903]) *The Souls of Black Folk*, New York: Vintage Books.

Geiss, I. (1974) *The Pan-African Movement*, Methuen: London.

Gilroy, P. (1993) *The Black Atlantic: Modernity and Double Consciousness*, Cambridge: Harvard University Press.

Harris, J.E. (ed.) (1982) *Global Dimensions of the African Diaspora*, Washington, D.C.: Howard University Press.

Lemelle, S. and Kelley, R.D.G. (eds.) (1994) *Imagining Home: Class, Culture and Nationalism in the African Diaspora*, London: Verso.

Magubane, B. (1987) *The Ties That Bind: African-American Consciousness of Africa*, Trenton: Africa World Press Inc.

PAUL TIYAMBE ZELEZA

pastoralism

Two-thirds of Africa's land is classified as arid or semi-arid, much of which is only habitable due to the practice of pastoralism or agropastoralism. Pastoralism is an economic system, practiced alone or in combination with agriculture, in which domestic livestock are raised on natural pastures by communities that substantially depend on their herds for their own subsistence. The type of stock raised by herders depends largely on climate: camels and goats predominate in areas where there is than 250 mm annual rainfall, cattle and sheep where that amount is exceeded. Since extensive herding tends to influence all aspects of culture, pastoralism also represents a form of society and a way of life. In the twentieth century, under both colonial and post-colonial administration, pastoralists have lost political autonomy and their near monopoly on the drylands as the state has gained sway. Faced with diverse currents of social change, periodic drought, and episodic conflict, most have seen distinctive aspects of their societies transformed and their economic security undermined.

About half of the world's pastoralists live in Africa – approximately 22 million people. With the exception of **Somalia** (where 60 percent are herders), pastoralists are minorities (averaging 12 percent of the population), even in the countries where they are most prevalent. Yet they occupy extensive lands, which is necessary for any herding economy, and hold or manage most of the nearly 60 percent of Africa's domestic livestock that are to be found in the arid and semi-arid lands. This apparent disequilibrium between a proportionally small pastoral population holding disproportionately extensive herds and grazing lands highlights one cause of their political decline in the twentieth century – the expansion of other communities into their land and the increase of state influence at their expense – and one cause for hope in the twenty-first century – that they retain grassland resources that are especially productive for extensive animal husbandry at a time when the demand for livestock and meat is growing.

Before the end of the nineteenth century and the onset of colonialism, pastoralists such as the Masai,

Turkana, Karamojong, Pokot (Suk), Somali, Oromo (Borana, Gabra, Orma), Rendille, and Barabaig of **East Africa**, the Baydan Moors, Fulbe, Kel Tamasheq (Tuareg), Shuwa Arabs, Dazagada (Tubu), and Zaghawa of **West Africa**, and the Sahel, Nuer, Dinka, Hadendowa, Kababish, Baggara, and Shukriya Arabs of **Sudan**, and the Zulu, Tswana, Herero, and Ndebele of **Southern Africa** exercised considerable political and military influence over extensive areas of grassland and savanna. Generally herding populations also held considerable power over their sedentary neighbors through social and political ties that involved both conflict and reciprocity, mutual livestock raiding and warfare combined with social exchange, intermarriage, and trade. Whether in the form of the Fulbe-engendered *jihad* states of the West African Sahel, Tuareg and Moorish predominance in the **Sahara**, the establishment of Somali hegemony over lowland areas of the Horn of Africa, the remarkable expansion of Nuer, Oromo, and Masai pastoralists in Eastern Africa, or the establishment of interlacustrine systems of kingship that symbolically highlighted the pre-eminence of herder elites, pre-colonial African history was strongly marked by the political and cultural prominence of societies characterized by the pastoral arts.

Gradually during the colonial period, and accelerating during the post-colonial epoch, the political position of pastoralists weakened. The twentieth century produced dramatic changes for pastoralists across Africa – changes that included their conquest, political division, and incorporation into states, the imposition of administration, introduction to market relations, loss of land, and subjection to voluntary and involuntary settlement.

Pastoralism under the colonial state

The establishment and consolidation of the colonial state struck pastoral societies precisely where they had previously enjoyed considerable advantage. First, military defeat for some diminished their regional position and undermined their sense of confident superiority. Second, a new lattice of external and internal boundaries often cut across the flexible spatial structures of pastoralists and attenuated or severed their social and economic ties with neighbors. Third, bureaucratic systems of political office and administration were established by colonial states on the basis of territorial rather than social or institutional ties, often in favor of sedentarists and centered in or near new towns and administrative and trading centers where pastoral presence was weak. Fourth, monetization established commercial relations where livestock, which had represented a multi-functional economic object of reference and preference, became one commodity among many, the value of which shifted with terms of trade that often favored grains and thus the larger interests of farmers and urban dwellers.

The establishment of national borders during the first phase of colonialism up to 1914 was especially onerous for pastoralists whose societies were often transected by new frontiers. Colonial states were most often fashioned around highland sites favorable for intensive agriculture (**South Africa**, **Zimbabwe**, **Kenya**, **Ethiopia**); rivers or lakes that provided fresh water, inland transport, and fisheries (**Mali**, Haut Volta, **Congo**, **Chad**, **Uganda**, **Malawi**); or coastal ports (Tanganyika, **Ghana**, **Côte d'Ivoire**). Halfway between or at the periphery of the geographical spaces favored for state-building, borders between British, French, Italian, German, and Portuguese colonial states were often drawn through dry, hot lowlands primarily inhabited by herding societies unique in being able to thrive in often marginal grasslands exploited through rapid, flexible seasonal movements. Given their mobility and their constant negotiation of borders, pastoralists came to be seen as "problems" for colonial (and post-colonial) governments due to the ambiguity of their affiliations, the ecological necessity of their continued (albeit wary) movements across frontiers, illegal transport of goods, black-market trade, and cross-border conflicts and raids.

In the second colonial phase, states established the right to appropriate native lands in order to commoditize the extraction of natural resources in West Africa, promote settler agriculture and ranching in East Africa, or establish mining enterprises in Southern Africa. As African farmers were confined to native reserves, pastoral groups were allocated fixed units of grazing territory. Among groups such as the Masai, the delimiting of reserves was followed by the demarcation of sectional boundaries, intended to establish a fixed association between social units and territories, and to diminish friction between pastoral groups. Yet rangelands often represented domains of shared use and overlapping rights, so the demarcation process often exacerbated rather than alleviated inter- or intra-group conflicts and undermined ties of cooperation, economic exchange, and reciprocity, eroding complex marketing networks between herding and agricultural communities. In both East and West Africa closed districts were designated for pastoralists, reducing their contact with settler and indigenous agrarian communities and further marginalizing them vis-à-vis the operations of colonial and then post-colonial states.

Colonial attempts to create a pool of laborers for the mining or settler agricultural sectors, by imposing poll or hut taxes payable only in monetary form, were relatively ineffective among pastoralists, who often disdained agricultural labor and had the means to generate money for taxes through livestock sales. Cattle taxes were also implemented to pressurize pastoralists into participating in livestock marketing. In their continuing social autonomy, resistance to wage labor, and determination to participate in markets only on favorable terms, pastoralists distinguished themselves from **peasants** and set themselves against the interests of the state. A body of colonial stereotypes and critical discourse arose that described pastoralists as "traditionalists" and "conservatives," "resistant" to change, and characterized by "irrational" attitudes towards livestock. Pastoralists were generally reluctant to sell domestic stock at the relatively low, fixed prices offered on colonial markets due to the multiple functions served by livestock – as objects valued for subsistence, economic and social exchange, bride-wealth, investment, insurance, rites of sacrifice, and as an idiom of symbolic expression. They pursued strategies of diversifying and accumulating herds under favorable climatic conditions as insurance against dry periods, and traded, loaned, gave, exchanged, and sacrificed livestock, in forms of circulation that defined the social and economic relations that made up a herding community.

Aiming to enhance economic self-sufficiency across Africa, colonial officials introduced grazing and resettlement schemes designed to promote African agricultural and livestock intensification. Administrators focused on problems of soil erosion and rangeland degradation, using the need for environmental conservation as a rhetorical bludgeon to discredit traditional methods of husbandry and demand changes in land-use practices through the pursuit of more sedentary ranching, with strict limitations on stocking rates.

Attempts at rangeland development began with the establishment of limited veterinary services and the installation of wells, boreholes, and mechanized pumping stations in West, Southern, and East Africa. Following the misplaced assumption that environmental degradation resulted from "irrational" practices of herd accumulation and overstocking, greater colonial effort was placed on preventing land deterioration by mandating limits on herd size, discouraging herd mobility, and in some cases initiating forced destocking. At the very least the colonial state sought to "maintain order" in pastoral regions, but even the pursuit of "progress" brought the state into conflict with pastoralists by attacking time-tried strategies of arid-land husbandry, thus threatening the pastoralists' economic security.

Post-colonial development, land tenure, and conservation

At independence in the early 1960s African governments inherited policies and perspectives that presupposed that rangeland degradation and non-commercial herd accumulation were facts, and pastoral strategies were at fault, ignoring the actual facts that desiccation of grasslands was highly cyclical and largely climate-driven, and that herd sizes were influenced by subsistence needs and market opportunities. Basically two approaches were taken. In the first the state sought to sedentarize pastoralists and appropriate rangelands for other purposes, creating large-scale commercial ranches, industries of mineral extraction, settlement schemes, irrigated plantations, nature reserves, and wildlife refuges.

In the second approach the state recognized pastoral rights to the land they occupied and used, and conceived of programs of "pastoral development" that would in principle strengthen the contribution of herders to national economies by creating more modern, commercially oriented forms of livestock production. The international development community supported these programs on the basis that customary pastoral units were not well suited to serve as custodians of development, given their large scale and reliance on traditional leadership, and that customary tenure systems (in theory characterized by insecurity, ambiguity of rights, and the drawbacks of common property) served to discourage investment and technological change, thereby constraining growth in the productivity of local agricultural and pastoral systems. Evidence, however, suggests that undermining customary systems often increases insecurity of land-holding, flexible systems of rights are more efficient, access to credit and rates of investment do not depend on formal title, and "modernized" land-use systems are often less productive than peasant or pastoral systems.

A pastoral development industry arose in the late 1960s aimed at creating ranching organizations on pastoral lands that would variously serve as units of ownership, coordinated land-use, management of water and grazing resources, development administration, residence, and political order. Examples are ranching or pastoral associations in **Mauritania**, **Niger**, and Tanzania; ranching "villages" in Tanzania; grazing blocks in more arid lands of Kenya and **Somalia**; "tribal" grazing lands in **Botswana**; and group ranches in Kenya. Entitling some, land reform often dispossessed others, with landlessness disproportionately affecting poorer pastoralists and women.

The group ranch program developed in Kenya in the 1970s was theoretically aimed at attaining increased productivity and enhanced prosperity in the pastoral domain; "groups" would be recipients of interventions in improved animal husbandry, receiving titles expected both to strengthen the security of community land-holding and to provide its members with access to credit that could be invested locally. In fact the creation of groups tended to undermine pre-existing forms of pastoral organization, and over time significantly diminished local security of land-holding. Corrupt practices, favoritism, and subdivision of group land into parcels under private title, many sold to outsiders, resulted in dramatic loss of land to the pastoral community. Furthermore governments and development projects were unable to sustain delivery of extension services intended to enhance livestock production. In some areas water development did open up pastures to more intensive use and market innovations did stimulate greater commercial sale of livestock, but land that had been sold was often turned to marginal cultivation or, if purchased for speculation, was left fallow.

Wildlife conservation began to impinge on the life of pastoralists in Africa with the declaration of the Serengeti–Ngorongoro in northern Tanganyika as a Closed Reserve in 1928–30 and as a National Park in 1940. In 1959 the area was divided into the Serengeti National Park in the west, from which Masai herders and diverse hunting communities were ejected, and the multi-purpose Ngorongoro Conservation Area in the east, where rights of pastoral residents have remained an issue of contention with government. Since then, pastoralists have lost some of their richest grazing and water resources as conservation areas have been declared in eastern and southern Africa that either exclude or limit access for local inhabitants. In Kenya alone, National Parks and Reserves occupied almost 30,000 square kilometers taken from former pastoral territories, which through the mid-1980s led pastoralists to tolerate poaching. However, in the 1990s community conservation programs began to proliferate, in which pastoralists accepted trusteeship over local wildlife and provided sites for tourism and service as guides. Coupled with severe anti-poaching campaigns, this policy lent new hope to conservationists by renewing the historical link between pastoralists and wildlife.

Tenure reforms were occurring at a time when many pastoralists were moving from mobile livestock herding to agropastoralism or town life due to poverty emanating from conditions of drought. Sedentarization near towns and market centers enabled some pastoral women to participate in the informal economy, selling dairy and vegetable produce, but sedentarization and privatization often rendered them economically vulnerable. Within the realm of pastoral property, women usually shared in "inclusive" systems of rights held by family members in key resources, obtaining usufruct rights in livestock and land through their relationships with fathers, husbands, sons, or brothers. Where tenure was privatized and land titles issued, women generally were marginalized since "exclusive" rights were most often allocated to males, who thereby gained undisputed control of land, cash crops, and larger-scale milk production. With increasing commercialization, women relied less on home-supplied milk and subsistence crops for household provisioning, and more on income from the petty sale of crops or dairy products to provide family food. Once in a position of relative self-sufficiency, many pastoral women became more dependent on male kin who, as herd- and land-owners, increased their control over female labor and incomes.

Sedentarization and economic diversification resulted in a decline in the emphasis on domestic pastoralism for some, resulting in increased out-migration of males seeking wage labor and an increase in destitute women left in rural areas raising families alone. In regions where pastoral households settled around famine relief and mission centers, women's workloads rose dramatically, since they often traveled long distances to sell milk and buy grain in markets, to find wood-fuel and building materials, or to seek access to wild plants and fruits used in food or local medicines. Out-migration of pastoralists from rural areas into small towns, trading centers, and cities in search of income-generating activities, coupled with the growth of towns, was accompanied by socio-economic differentiation, with patron–client relations evolving between wealthier "absentee" stockowners and the poorer pastoralists who tended their herds.

Responses to calamity and conflict

Pastoralists were considerably weakened at two key moments of political transition: at the onset of colonialism when pastoral populations and livestock were decimated by cholera, smallpox, rinderpest, and drought, and at independence when they were struck by drought and the threat of famine. From 1969 through the mid-1970s severe and prolonged drought occurred from the Sahel to the Horn of Africa, striking some of the poorest countries of the region: Mali, Chad, and Niger in the West African Sahel, and Ethiopia, Sudan, and Somalia in East Africa. Media attention resulted in an outpouring of international aid and famine relief. With the rise in environmental consciousness, human misery was linked with images of desertification, which helped mold world opinion that the cause of famine and degradation was misuse of resources by pastoral overgrazing, thus creating a consensus that herders should settle. More careful analysis, however, has demonstrated that desiccation is more often an outcome of low rainfall than grazing pressure. Rangeland vegetation shifts cyclically as a function of rain, and does not undergo long-term, irreversible decline through desertification. Local degradation is directly correlated with inappropriate spread of cultivation in lands too dry to support it over time, and nomadic settlement is most often a cause of pastoral dislocation and environmental decline, not its solution.

Missions were implanted in pastoral regions during the colonial period, and spread rapidly throughout the early post-colonial period, providing rural areas with schools, clinics, and places of worship, concomitantly stimulating sedentarization. Medical services served to undermine local practitioners and traditional medicine, as **Christianity**, **Islam**, and education undermined other customary practices, reflecting and stimulating social change. Upheavals in institutional beliefs and practices, however, were mitigated by a strong tendency towards syncretism between customary institutions and those associated with global forces and modernization.

Formal education was the most significant force for social change in pastoral areas, creating shifts in economic and cultural outlook towards individualism, commercial life, and **urbanization**. But increased school attendance by pastoral children created shortages in labor needed for livestock and agricultural production. Also social stratification based on education, political influence, and control of land and livestock emerged, distinguishing between townspeople, a commercial pastoral "elite," smallholding pastoral and agrarian "peasants," and semi-impoverished herders increasingly working for others in wage labor.

In brief, pastoralists reacted variously to political marginalization, land loss, threats of dispossession, and growing poverty through sedentarizing, diversifying their economic pursuits, and migrating to towns and cities. Alternatively, some renewed their commitment to the herding economy, opposing further land loss or subjugation to forces of state and market by engaging in political resistance in national and international arenas, or by armed conflict and violence.

Pastoralists engaged in conflict by competing with other herders for livestock, pasture, and water, struggling with cultivators over land (herders invade fields, farmers encroach on pastures), seeking greater autonomy within the state or secession from it as discontented or suppressed minorities, or striving to seize control of the state or to resist losing power by subduing subjected majorities or minorities. Parties clashed over both resources and views of the world; witness conflicting claims of sovereignty by states and pastoral polities, and divergent concepts of how land is valued, occupied, transacted, and used by herders and farmers.

Although they were minorities and politically marginalized in most states, communities of pastoral origin were majorities in Somalia, Mauritania, and the Western Sahara, dominant minorities in **Burundi** and (during colonialism and after 1994) in **Rwanda**. In Somalia and Western Sahara struggles occurred over control of the state. Arabic-speaking Sahrawi pastoralists formed the Polisario liberation movement in 1973 to oppose Spanish colonial rule, and continued to resist after 1975 when, despite their claims, the Western Sahara was ceded to Mauritania and **Morocco**. Supported by **Algeria** the Polisario fought a desert war of long-distance raids using Land Rovers, Kalashnikovs, and missiles, but – despite gaining recognition by the OAU and seventy countries for a "Saharan Arab Democratic Republic" – the Polisario were isolated in southern Algeria by Morocco, futilely awaiting a long-promised UN referendum that the Moroccans refused to hold. In Somalia civil war was stimulated by discontent among Somali refugees who fled Ethiopia during the irredentist Ogaden War. Conflict broke out in 1988 between the Darood and Isaaq clan families, ultimately bringing down the government of Siad Barre, as multi-sided warfare spread at the expense of central government. In 1989 a UN humanitarian relief and peacekeeping force successfully halted violence and provided aid, but withdrew after a disastrous attempt to intervene in factional fighting. Somalia was left without a central government during the 1990s.

Conflict between herders and farmers was dramatized in dry Mauritania, when Moorish and Fulani nomads moved to the wetter conditions along the Senegal River during the drought of the early 1970s. Dams built along the Senegal River in the 1980s created upheaval in land-holding among Arabic-speaking Moors, Fulani, and Soninke and Wolof of Senegalese origin, and intensified competition along the riverine border. Escalation of a grazing dispute in 1989 led to 200 people being killed in Mauritania, 50–60 in **Senegal**, and 200,000 black Mauritanians being deported to Senegal – most of them sedentarists of Senegalese origin, but also some Fulbe with herds coveted by the dominant Moors.

With pastoralists often being marginalized citizens, Somalis in the Ethiopian Ogaden, Tuareg in northern Mali and Niger, and Nilotic-speakers in southern Sudan sought regional autonomy or secession. When the French subjugated the camel-keeping Tuareg aristocracy in the central Sahara, they outlawed slavery; severed relations of nobles, cultivators, and tributaries; and pressurized nomads to settle. After rebelling at independence when their request for a Saharan state was ignored, the Tuareg rebelled again after the drought of 1984–5 due to resentment of Niger and Mali's inadequate response, and their perception that the police and military was like an occupying force. Special status was granted to northern regions in 1992, along with democratic control over local matters. The rebellion was variously seen as aimed at secession, the preservation of aristocratic privilege, or the establishment of democratic regimes. Clearly conflict rose due to the political and economic marginalization of pastoralists, and the inadequate balance struck between regional autonomy and state sovereignty, especially when expectations have risen due to modernization and democratization, and attention has been focused on rights held by minority groups, especially by "indigenous peoples," a status increasingly claimed by pastoral societies.

Conclusion

The creation of highly resilient polities in the continent's driest regions, surely one of the continent's finest achievements, is owed to pastoral communities practicing extensive, opportunistic, and highly mobile animal husbandry. The virtues of social autonomy, economic tenacity, spatial mobility, and cultural pride that have enabled herding societies to survive have, however, not been easily accommodated by colonial and post-colonial states. At a theoretical level, pastoralists and the state have clashed over the question of who holds sovereign rights over the vast drylands; at the practical level, pastoralists have exercised little influence or power within the context of the state, feeling themselves to be at the political periphery of nations and at the margins of global modernity. Pastoral lands and resources have increasingly become objects of competition and contention with expanding neighbors and with governments pursuing agrarian and livestock development, forest and wildlife conservation, tourism, or the extraction of minerals and other natural resources. Programs of livestock and rangeland development often failed to enlist the commitment of local communities, attempting as they did to replace time-tried land-use and production practices with untried techniques or forms of organization.

Yet, despite a twentieth-century history of alienation, individuals from pastoral communities have been assimilated into wider national societies through education or as part of a regional labor market, and now represent an important specialist group that uses sparsely populated arid and semi-arid lands to raise livestock, feeding growing populations across Africa. Pastoralists are deeply apprehensive of being controlled by states, are often resistant to sedentarist institutions, and have shown willingness to engage in multi-faceted struggles to secure and retain the resources they need. Given their rural base at the peripheries of power and competition for their land, dryland societies may experience displacement, social eclipse, and assimilation as an underclass within the national mainstream. But if they attain greater security of land-holding, increased regional autonomy, active development of a more diversified but livestock-dominated economy, and social justice, pastoralists may thrive as mobile ranchers providing meat to a continent, thus making optimal use of the unique arid and semi-arid grasslands that stretch across Africa.

See also: agrarian change; state: colonial; state: post-independence; economy: colonial; economy: post-independence

Further reading

Anderson, D. and Broch-Due, V. (eds.) (1999) *The Poor are Not Us: Poverty and Pastoralism*, Oxford: James Currey.

Bonfiglioli, A.-M. (1992) *Pastoralists at a Crossroads: Survival and Development Issues in African Pastoralism*, Nairobi: UNICEF/UNSO Project for Nomadic Pastoralists in Africa.

Fratkin, E., Galvin, K. and Roth, E. (eds.) (1994) *African Pastoralist Systems: An Integrated Approach*, Boulder: Lynne Rienner.

Galaty, J.G. and Bonte, P. (eds.) (1991) *Herders, Warriors and Traders: Pastoralism in Africa*, Boulder: Westview Press.

Joekes, S. and Pointing, J. (1991) *Women in Pastoral Societies in East and West Africa*, Issues Paper No. 28, London: Dryland Networks Programme.

Kurimoto, E. and Simonse, S. (eds.) (1998) *Conflict, Age and Power in North East Africa: Age Systems in Transition*, Oxford: James Currey.

Sanford, S. (1983) *Management of Pastoral Development in the Third World*, Chicester: ODI.

Scoones, I. (ed.) (1994) *Living with Uncertainty: New Directions in Pastoral Development in Africa*, London: Intermediate Technology Publications.

JOHN G. GALATY
JUDITH MITCHELL

peasant movements

Peasants are agriculturalists who control most of the land they work as either tenants or smallholders, who produce for the market and have obligations to other social classes. They pay either rent to landlords or taxes to the state, and sometimes both. In order to meet their obligations, they must produce for market. This means that they are vulnerable to natural disasters, to fluctuations in the prices of goods they market and inputs they need, and to the demands of their rulers. They usually have a sense of their common interests, though they often lack the organization necessary to protect those interests.

During the nineteenth century cash-crop production expanded dramatically in many parts of Africa, as Europeans gradually shifted from buying slaves to buying such commodities as palm oil, groundnuts, cloves, coffee, and cocoa. The market frontier moved well ahead of colonization until the 1880s. As colonial taxation policies forced Africans to seek incomes and the extension of rail and road networks facilitated the marketing of agricultural surpluses, the process of peasantization sped up. By the 1920s peasantization had extended into all but the most remote corners of Africa. It was blocked or skewed only in areas of white settlement, where settler regimes preferred that Africans work on white farms rather than cultivate for themselves. The expropriation of the best land and increasing population densities left Africans, particularly in South Africa, with barely enough land and, as population rose, not enough to feed themselves. In these areas able-bodied men became increasingly dependent on **migrant labor**, leaving women to feed their families, and often to produce enough of a surplus to market some of it, which was an important kind of resistance to colonial policy.

Though European conquest was often bloody, the most effective revolts came after the introduction of policies designed to coerce peasants into producing larger surpluses for market. The Rhodesian revolt of 1896, more broad-based and effective than resistance to the original conquest three years earlier, was a response to taxation and expropriation policies. The Maji Maji revolt, which between 1905 and 1907 wrested control of a large part of German **East Africa** from the colonizers, began with a revolt against forced cultivation. Forced cultivation and the imposition of taxation provoked much early peasant resistance. Revolts in **French Equatorial Africa** in 1897 and 1903 were a response to forced labor as porters. The Bambata revolt of 1906 was a response to imposition of a poll tax. In southern **Nigeria** the rumor that women were to be taxed led to a series of anti-tax riots, of which the best known is the Women's War, which took place at Aba in 1929. As later happened in **South Africa**, it was believed that soldiers would not fire on women – but fifty women were killed when troops panicked.

Maji Maji was the last of the great revolts of the early colonial period. More revolts did take place, especially during the **First World War** when the number of European personnel in Africa was reduced, but few of these revolts involved a military challenge to the colonial presence. The interwar period saw the development of peasant capitalism, as Africans opened up new lands and found ways to mobilize capital and labor to develop cash crops. John Iliffe (1969) speaks of this period as the "age of improvement." The process was important, but always limited by what Jack Wayne (1975) has called the "geography of opportunity." Peasant capitalists were mostly involved in crops that had a large cash return – like cocoa, coffee, and, to a lesser degree, groundnuts – and they thrived only in areas that had good transportation and easy access to markets. In most of Africa, peasants were more concerned with feeding themselves and producing enough of a surplus to pay their taxes and buy consumer goods.

In interwar revolts, peasants rioted, attacked chiefs, or burned down colonial offices, but a more common response was migration. Some simply left to earn money elsewhere, but military recruitment, forced labor, high taxes, and low prices often pushed people to move to avoid colonial authority. Colonial borders were porous, ethnic groups often straddled boundaries, and free land was generally available. Some people near borders moved back and forth depending on the political and economic situation. There was also more short-term movement. People would hide to avoid the census-taker, the tax collector, and the military recruiter.

Colonial censuses were notoriously inaccurate, largely because they were used to define tax obligations. As regimes during the late colonial and independent period moved to control the prices paid for cash crops, smuggling also became a form of resistance, with both peasants and merchants moving commodities from low-price to high-price areas. In the early years in South Africa peasants successfully played white farmers off against each other, moving from farm to farm to seek better terms. That option was, however, gradually closed off. As capital investment increased and the demand for labor decreased, African squatters found themselves with fewer and fewer options.

Peasants often resisted improvement policies, largely because colonial regimes often were ignorant of the consequences of policies that seemed to be scientifically correct. Anti-erosion policies often pitted women and poorer men against chiefs, rich peasants, and colonial administrators because they removed from cultivation the marginal lands these people depended on. In other cases shifting the field patterns threatened cooperative work systems. In **Kenya** women boycotted an anti-erosion scheme for two years. In **Tanzania** a group of women showed up for work carrying tiny hoes suitable only for weeding. In **Southern Africa** peasants opposed dipping to prevent disease because they objected to the fees and because the long treks to the dipping tank enfeebled their cattle. Often the problem was inadequate communication. Colonial governments rarely consulted peasants about when, where, or how. In **Ghana**, when peasants refused to kill healthy cocoa trees to stop the spread of swollen shoot disease, they were supported by Kwame Nkrumah's Convention Peoples Party; but, once in power, the CPP continued the program.

Peasant movements often failed because they were local, spontaneous, and lacked scale or adequate organization. Peasants growing cocoa and groundnuts organized "hold-ups" when sharp price fluctuations threatened their well-being, but these hold-ups were generally too local to have much effect. Peasants were most effective when linked to other social groups. In **West Africa** the interests of prosperous farmers converged with those of merchants, as both struggled against the monopoly position of European export–import houses. Efforts were made to organize African-controlled banks, cooperatives, and a shipping company. These generally failed, both because of the hostility of colonial interests and the limited resources of the organizers. Religious groups were often more effective, though on a smaller scale. In nineteenth-century **Nigeria** African independent churches taught people to grow cocoa and provided marketing networks for it. In Southern Africa churches like John Chilembwe's Providence Industrial Mission organized education and cooperation. Mission churches were also often important. The Basle Mission in Ghana played a major role in the spread of cocoa growing. Millenarian movements, like those led by Wellington Buthelezi in South Africa and Simon Kimbangu in **Congo**, opposed taxation and tried to set up schools and other institutions beyond the control of the colonial state.

Muslims also often played a major role. The Mourides in **Senegal** were responsible for a massive movement of landless peasants, most of them former slaves, to frontier areas where they could cultivate groundnuts and achieve a modicum of economic autonomy. Later the Mourides also became spokesmen for Senegalese peasants. In other areas Muslims – like the Hamallists of **Mali** or their Yakubist offshoot in **Côte d'Ivoire** – pushed an egalitarian agenda, and tried to limit the exploitation of the poor and of former slaves. Traditional religious leaders also played a major role in many revolts. The Rhodesian revolt of 1896 was led by shrine priests and spirit mediums. With Maji Maji, it was a shrine that provided the coordination. The Kongo-Warra revolt was led by a prophet. In the rebellion in the eastern Congo in 1964–5 traditional healers again played an influential role.

After the **Second World War**, **nationalist movements** developed rapidly and tried to unite different social classes. In most of Africa these movements moved toward independence with relatively little violence, but in areas of settler agriculture nationalists faced resolute opposition. At the same time the more militant nationalists found fertile ground in the simmering resentment of disenfranchised peasants. In Kenya the more radical nationalists found support among squatters and those expelled from lands expropriated by white settlers. In 1952 the British declared a state of emergency, forcing many hostile elements to seek refuge in the forests. Though isolated and poorly armed, the Mau Mau fighters resisted for four years and, in the process, forced the pace of **decolonization**. The French were similarly able to isolate a peasant-based guerrilla movement in southern **Cameroon** through brutal military campaigns directed at rural populations.

In **Guinea-Bissau**, **Mozambique**, **Angola**, and **Zimbabwe** more sophisticated rebel movements inspired by revolutionary ideologies – and often with training in guerrilla warfare – were able to take root among the alienated peasantry, with the peasants providing bases, logistical support, and recruits for the guerrillas. Guerrillas sometimes used force, but generally tried to win the support of peasants. In South Africa the control of the state was too effective to permit the development of liberated areas, but impoverishment, expulsion of Africans from so-called "black spots," and the increasingly harsh restraints of apartheid led to rural conflict, much of it directed at chiefs, other collaborators, and the state infrastructure.

The support peasants gave nationalist political parties and guerrilla movements generally won them few benefits after the struggle was over. The newly independent states were urban-based and generally anxious to keep city-dwellers happy. The more radical of the newly independent governments tried to force peasants into state-controlled units of production, which usually had disastrous results. All over, governments set up marketing boards, which purchased major crops, generally at a fraction of the world market price. Governments used these boards to extract revenue from peasants, but in the process limited the incentive for peasants to increase production or modernize methods. At the same time there was a long-term decline in world market prices. When the international banking community forced many countries to disband their marketing boards and agricultural development bureaucracies, the benefits to peasants were still limited. Governments have often tried to make peasants pay for inputs like improved equipment, fertilizer, and pesticides. Peasants have often responded simply by withdrawing from the market, or at least withdrawing from government-sponsored programs that offered them little. The *malaise paysanne* of 1968 in Senegal, for example, saw a sharp drop in marketing activity. Though peasants have given support to some post-colonial revolutionary movements, like that of Yoweri Museveni in **Uganda** or the opposition to the military dictatorship in **Ethiopia**, many of the guerrilla movements of the 1990s were brutal and dependent on force. Resistencia National Moçambicana (Renamo) in Mozambique, the Revolutionary United Front (RUF) in **Sierra Leone**, and the warlords in **Liberia** and **Somalia** all extracted what they wanted from the peasants with the barrel of a gun. Peasants still find themselves vulnerable to the harsh forces of the larger world.

See also: agrarian change; economy: colonial

References and further reading

Beinart, W. and Bundy, C. (1987) *Hidden Struggles in Rural South Africa*, London: James Currey.

Berry, S. (1993) *No Condition is Permanent: The Social Dynamics of Agrarian Change in Sub-Saharan Africa*, Madison: University of Wisconsin Press.

Bunker, S. (1987) *Peasants Against the State: The Politics of Market Control in Bugisu, Uganda, 1900–1983*, Urbana: University of Illinois Press.

Crummey, D. (ed.) (1986) *Banditry, Rebellion and Social Protest in Africa*, London: James Currey.

Iliffe, J. (1969) *Tanganyika under German Rule 1905–1912*, Cambridge: Cambridge University Press.

Isaacman, A. (1990) "Peasants and Rural Social Protest in Africa," *African Studies Review* 33: 1–120.

Isaacman, A. and Roberts, R. (eds.) (1995) *Cotton, Colonialism and Social History in Sub-Saharan Africa*, Portsmouth: Heinemann.

Kanogo, T. (1987) *Squatters and the Roots of Mau Mau*, Athens: Ohio University Press.

Klein, M.A. (ed.) (1980) *Peasants in Africa: Historical and Contemporary Perspectives*, Beverly Hills: Sage.

Ranger, T. (1985) *Peasant Consciousness and Guerrilla War in Zimbabwe*, Berkeley: University of California Press.

Watts, M. (1983) *Silent Violence: Food, Famine and*

Peasantry in Northern Nigeria, Berkeley: University of California Press.

Wayne, J. (1975) "Colonialism and Underdevelopment in Kigoma Region, Tanzania: A Social Structural View," *Canadian Review of Sociology and Anthropology* 12, 3: 316–32.

MARTIN KLEIN

peasants

Peasants are unmistakably rural-dwellers, and in much of Africa the overwhelming proportion of the population remains domiciled in areas outside the towns and major cities. While the rural character of the peasant remains an important distinguishing feature, the huge variation of other features – great diversities in sources of subsistence, systems of colonial rule, population density, ecology, forms of agricultural production, levels of integration into markets, and degrees of subordination to the state – makes a clear characterization of a typical African peasant impossible.

The application of the concept of peasants in Africa has been controversial and much debated. There are a variety of reasons for this, but the usefulness of comparing contemporary African cultivators and pastoralists with peasants in Asia, Latin America, and Europe remains the crucial factor. Some have argued that the basis for peasant existence is the family farm; others have suggested that it rests in the low level of mechanization in production methods used in agriculture; still others assert that it lies in the nature of subordination to political authorities and the manner in which farmers are integrated into regional and international markets, and in how their surpluses are appropriated. In contrast there is a view that peasants may be producing only for consumption, rather than for exchange, and that the unit of production (usually a family or household) doubles up as the unit of consumption. Finally, the nature of land tenure has been an important factor in the controversy surrounding peasants in Africa.

In much of the literature the land-tenure system is understood in terms of a dichotomy between private and communal systems; in fact pre-colonial Africa supported a far wider range of tenurial arrangements. The low level of development in African agriculture is often attributed to the lack of private ownership of land – the assumption being that private ownership would confer security of tenure, which would act as a spur for investment and saving, hence contributing to economic growth more generally. There is, however, mounting evidence that land-titling has not led to increased production and productivity, as in the cases of **Uganda**, **Somalia**, and **Kenya**. The form of tenure does not by itself either guarantee or hinder productive efficiency. In fact there is little evidence of insecurity in the usufruct rights that the so-called "communal system" conferred on communities, except in **Southern Africa** where the system was fundamentally distorted by the creation of confined labor reserves.

The history of African peasants in the twentieth century

Throughout the nineteenth and twentieth centuries African cultivators were integrated to different degrees into markets through exchange and the appropriation of surpluses. In some instances the integration was merely partial; in others the marketing and exchange of commodities formed an integral part of the existence of the community; in still others the market was merely marginal to the overwhelming dependence on subsistence farming. There were also various levels of utilization of non-family labor, a variety of dependencies on off-farm income, divergent technologies and methods of production, and a whole host of crop-types and ecological conditions. Finally the subjection of peasants to higher political authorities varied considerably, and their willingness to revolt against this subjection was dependent on an even wider range of factors. Under conditions of such complexity it is hazardous to generalize, and to compound matters the rate of change in agrarian social relations was remarkably different from region to region.

Depending on the definition of "peasant" employed by various authors, there is some debate about whether peasants emerged in pre-colonial Africa or as a result of the colonization of the continent. If we take some of the above characteristics together, then there is evidence that peasants emerged prior to colonization in much of **North Africa**, **Sudan**, **Ethiopia**, and many parts of **West Africa**, given the long tradition of commerce, trade, and **urbanization** in these areas. However, colonization integrated Africans far more firmly into the international capitalist market and local state structures.

The twentieth century in Africa is indelibly marked by colonization. Both the overall nature of African rural production and the peasantry themselves were profoundly shaped by the colonial presence. There are a whole variety of different forms by which political control of vast areas was assumed, often through very few colonial administrators and settlers. In some cases (**Senegal**, for example) colonialism did little to alter the production processes of African farmers, but merely sought to extract whatever surpluses were being produced. In contrast there was a rapid introduction of new technologies and new ways of organizing production and marketing after independence in Senegal. Colonization was successfully resisted in Ethiopia, largely because of the availability to the Ethiopian army of peasant conscripts bequeathed by a long history of peasant agriculture. In **Algeria** there were both Turkish and indigenous landowners prior to colonization, the former having access to the best lands and subordinating the latter to their interests. Colonization gave large estates and private enterprises land concessions at the expense of the peasants, thus transforming a substantial proportion of the latter into agricultural workers. In Sudan too a large indigenous landowning class emerged, giving rise to labor tenancy and even slavery. While land concessions were also granted to companies in colonial **Mozambique**, the indigenous population retained access to substantial portions of land, though many were forced to grow particular crops (such as cotton) expressly for the export market. Similarly in Uganda colonial policies were designed to maintain the existing organization of peasant production, but the peasants were taxed.

The extent of land alienation varied considerably. While in **South Africa** peasant production was systematically undermined by colonialism and territorial segregation, the land area under *de facto* indigenous control remained virtually intact in **Tanzania**. It seems possible to discern a correlation between the extent of white settler expropriation of land and the survival of indigenous agricultural production. Since the ultimate security for peasants rests in their ability to maintain access and control over rights in land and the availability of family labor, settler colonization necessarily clashed directly with African peasantization. In **Tunisia** peasants are still only partially integrated into markets. In fact it appears that peasants may choose non-marketable outputs for survival because of the unequal power relations of the market. Family labor remained of vital importance in Tunisia at the end of the twentieth century, constituting more than 80 percent of the active labor force. As with other North African countries, Tunisia displays an extremely skewed distribution of land ownership and access. The bottom 46 percent of the population possess only 8 percent of the land, while the top 3 percent owns 35 percent.

There are a whole host of reasons why peasants may mistrust the state. Taxes, duties, levies, commodity production, new crops, cash, and markets were all much more rigorously introduced during the colonial period. These measures were supposed to have the effect of either incorporating an existing peasantry or disturbing a pre-colonial redistributive economy and entangling its subsistence cultivators into wider markets, state control, and the provision of labor. There was no uniform way in which peasants and cultivators responded to the colonial encounter, and their responses also differed over time as colonial policies changed. Colonial policies depended on a whole variety of factors, the most important being the availability of resources. In 1900, for example, the French government decreed that the colonies would have to pay for themselves. In this regard coercion and subjugation of the indigenous population were the invariable outcomes, since the revenue to float the colonial state had to come almost exclusively from African producers.

Colonization of Southern Africa by white settlers followed a different trajectory. With few exceptions the land grabbed by whites in Southern Africa was held under freehold title, but Africans held the land under various versions of communal tenure. The white-claimed land became their private property. While there were few possibilities for Africans to own land by individual title deed, the overwhelming reality for Africans in Southern Africa was confinement to a distorted type of communal tenure in the reserves with restricted agricultural potential. Colonialism led to the modernization and commercialization of agriculture only in regions where there was a substantial proportion of white settlers who benefited from state assistance through tax rebates, transport concessions, marketing subsidies, low-interest credit, and so on. While white settlers could commercialize their farming because of this direct state intervention in their favor, African farmers were effectively denied the wherewithal to undertake proper farming. The extraction of agricultural produce from the indigenous population was significant in South Africa prior to the mineral discoveries of the late nineteenth century, but it gave way to the necessity of generating an adequate supply of labor for the incipient industries. It may be suggested then that the process of peasantization was replaced by proletarianization as more and more rural-dwellers were compelled into wage labor by the loss of access to adequate land for the reproduction of families. Of course this did not happen all at once or in a simplistic unilinear fashion, but the overall historical trajectory has very clearly been towards greater dependence on wage labor for the survival of families. Agricultural production, of course, did not disappear, and those who had access to multiple sources of subsistence and income invariably ended up being better off than the marginalized single-income families. At the same time it is important to point out that even episodic changes in urban work may have a major impact on the reliance on agricultural production. For example, with the decline of the copper industry in **Zambia**, peasant production assumed far more importance in the lives and livelihoods of rural-dwellers.

The situation in post-independence **Zimbabwe** mirrors that of Senegal in respect of production by the indigenous population. Before independence the so-called "peasant sector" produced only 6 percent of marketed output. After hardly a decade as an independent country the Zimbabwean peasants were producing 55 percent of marketed maize, 70 percent of the total national production in maize, and about 20 percent of total agricultural marketed output. Yet this undoubted peasant success must be seen in the context of differentiation in natural regions: The better endowed communal areas produce and market the bulk of the crop, whereas about 40 percent of the rural population market nothing at all. It should also be considered that the predominantly white commercial agricultural sector (made up of only 1 percent of the population) still contributes 80 percent of total marketed output, and most of the agricultural exports.

The post-colonial Mozambican situation was even more dramatic. Obviously haunted by the lack of security and the civil war, the state proceeded to abandon the model of large-scale state farms and attempted instead to encourage the growth of smallholder peasant farmers. Peasant success in Mozambique was abruptly disrupted by the natural disasters in the last few years of the twentieth century. In **Nigeria**, the most populous country in Africa, the oil boom of the early 1970s had the effect of increasing the urban population relative to the rural. In the process the dependence of many households on peasant agriculture for their susbistence and commodity production declined.

While colonialism clearly dominated the bulk of Africa's history over the twentieth century, the end of the century was marked by the implementation of **structural adjustment programs** in agriculture. Enforced from the 1980s onwards these programs had devastating effects on peasant production of agricultural commodities for domestic consumption and for international markets. In the main the programs led to cutbacks in agricultural subsidies; simultaneously the state-driven marketing boards were replaced by private merchants. The combined effect was a significant shrinkage in the peasant commercial sector in those countries that adopted such programs. Peasants engage in production that does not fit neatly into the rhythms of the just-in-time production, standardization, and uniformity that emerging control of international markets by agribusiness is making necessary. Yet, despite the dominant picture of African agricultural backwardness and peasant decline, there are some examples of spectacular success – such as the revolution in cotton production in **Côte d'Ivoire**.

The historiography of peasants

The historiography of peasant studies in Africa has its origins in various debates from the 1970s onwards, although there are also a number of earlier works (usually by British and American anthropologists). An article by Lloyd Fallers, interrogatively entitled "Are African Cultivators to be called 'Peasants'?" (1961), became particularly influential. It defined peasants in relation to the existence of markets and in respect of their subjection to external political authorities. Fallers arrived at the conclusion that the self-perception of African rural-dwellers was not characterized at all by a feeling of inferiority towards the authorities, unlike their Asian, Latin American, and European counterparts. Despite the fact that this massive generalization obviously failed to pay any heed to the variations and diversity of rural Africa, its direct question set the tone for more detailed discussions of the nature of rural relations in Africa.

Polly Hill's *Studies in Rural Capitalism in West Africa* (1970), which uses anthropological methods to study the economic activities of small groups of people in minute detail, is one of the finest examples in this tradition. Focusing on the rural agents themselves, Hill penetrated the intricate manner in which rural producers managed their economic lives, and in the process debunked many of the beliefs about African conditions that were held by her American and British counterparts. She made a passionate appeal for an "indigenous economics," firmly rooted in an understanding of the lives of rural producers in Africa and committed to rejecting popular myths. Two examples should suffice in this regard. First, she provides a textured analysis of how enterprising individual cocoa farmers are not unduly hindered by supposed communal exigencies and expectations from their kin, but instead manage to negotiate their way through such customs by accumulating capital and land that are regarded as their own for at least some of the time. She goes on to make the vital point that these very farmers insist on the individual initiative of the young men as a key to the prosperity of the entire lineage. Second, she discovered (to her surprise) that northern Ghanaian cattle-owners were not at all reluctant to sell off parts of their herds. In fact she found the opposite to be a problem – namely, the premature sale of immature animals.

There was clearly a place for capital accumulation in rural Africa, even under conditions of communal land-tenure, and it undoubtedly gave rise to substantial agrarian differentiation. It was a colonial myth that a lack of individualism among Africans explained their technological "backwardness" and cultural/economic uniformity. Hill wrote from a position of such obvious empirical substance and richness that her approach represented a full-frontal challenge to mainstream economists and government policy-makers who had not taken the trouble to study the local conditions in the same detail. This is a generous reading of their reluctance to acknowledge the emergence of an enterprising African capitalist class. A more pointed reading would suggest that her analysis contradicted a mythology of the uneconomic African that is based on the racism of colonial administrators. Hill's analysis was defined by an unambiguous micro-focus that made it very powerful. However, the strength of her work was also its weakness. Her sample was simply too small, in a situation of such extreme diversity and involving such vast geographic space, so that her findings are applicable to only a limited area.

It was left to Ken Post (1972) to attempt a more generalized account of peasantization in West Africa. He drew a distinction between two models (the communal cultivator/the peasant farmer), between two processes (the change from communal cultivator to peasant farmer/the incorporation of both into global capitalism), and between three relationships (the producer and the land/the producer and the market/the producer and the state). While at pains to indicate that these distinctions were ideal types, Post went on to describe each in the following terms: The communal cultivator was characterized by communal access to land, with group or individual usage, division of labor based on kinship, the absence of markets, political authority corresponding to kinship ties, and a largely homogenous culture. In contrast the peasant was characterized by individual land ownership, a separation between the division of labor and kinship, the presence of markets, detachment of political authority from kinship ties, and a distinction between various cultures. While comfortably analyzing the details of the relationship between the producer and the state, as well as between the producer and the market, he provides only perfunctory statements about the nature of land tenure and usufruct land rights. In this regard, Mafeje's (1985) contribution has been most useful. He argued that ownership, in the sense of exclusive freehold title, did not matter quite as much as effective control and security over land rights and access. He goes on to suggest that Post's treatment of the problem may have unnecessarily opposed these concepts to each other, since in practice it remains common in Africa for clans to regard land as their own and to reserve the rights to its use (and even disposal) without discarding the communal system. Viewed in this manner, the communal system may accommodate private appropriation and even capital accumulation.

Unlike the earlier work of academic scholars the debates of the 1970s were either an explicit response to the challenges posed by independence in **East Africa**, specifically in Tanzania and Kenya, or an ongoing analysis of the complexities faced in the remaining colonial regimes of the South. In Tanzania the great **Dar es Salaam** debates are an enduringly rich source of inspiration to young students of Africa. Here a group of committed scholars grappled with the realities of underdevelopment in a vibrant environment of debate and discussion. A veritable "Who's Who" of African studies participated: Archie Mafeje, John Saul, Goran Hyden, Mahmood Mamdani, Lionel Cliffe, Issa Shivji, Walter Rodney, and Henry Bernstein. A substantial body of knowledge emerged out of these interchanges, largely in reaction to the implementation of the *ujamaa* policies in Tanzania. While the debates considered a whole range of issues, peasant studies in Tanzania were significant for the whole of East Africa. The debates ranged from a consideration of the structural position of peasants in relation to agrarian and national questions, to discussions of the differentiation within rural populations, of which sections of the peasantry were likely to respond in a revolutionary way, of the role of international capital in a neo-colonial situation, of the responses of various strata of peasants to state intervention in the organization of rural production, and so on. For example, Bernstein and Hyden developed entirely different positions in relation to the manner in which peasants respond to state intervention. Bernstein argued that the state had caused immeasurable damage to independent peasant production, even through legal coercion. Far from being subjected to the state, Hyden (1980) argued (using Barrington Moore's classic study of development) that the reason for the backwardness of Africa was the fact that the peasantry remained uncaptured, unsqueezed – with sufficient independence over their own means of production to have a profound influence over the manner in which the society evolved.

Following hot on the heels of these peasant studies in Tanzania came the **Nairobi** discussion of the peasant question. This caused the epicenter of the historiographical discourse on peasants to shift from Tanzania to Kenya. Contrary to the Tanzanian focus on forced villagization and state intervention, the Nairobi-based discussion revolved around the nature of peasant differentiation and the possibilities for the emergence of an indigenous rural capitalist class, the nature of surplus appropriation, and the prospects of political alliances flowing from the interests of different sections of the rural population. The Kenyan discussion was premised on the reality of land concentration. As white settlement in the fertile highlands had the effect of debasing the Kenyan peasantry, by the time of independence the social processes leading to dependence on wage labor were deeply entrenched. Archie Mafeje (1977) argues in this regard that it is spurious to separate the peasant from the proletarian, since the two are so closely intertwined in a mediated situation of social change. Peasants are almost invariably also migrant workers, and their dual or even multiple dependencies render a singular identity quite inappropriate. Others – Colin Leys (1975), for example –

focused on the absence of a landlord class in Kenya and, by implication, much of sub-Saharan Africa. The extraction or transfer of surpluses from a differentiated mosaic of peasants in rural areas is thus not a simple and direct exchange between an exploited peasantry and rich landlords. Instead it is a complex interplay, involving a whole range of actors and structures in rural and urban areas. As racial barriers were removed by independence, the differentiation between black commercial farmers and rich peasants, on the one hand, and on the other the mass of poor peasants eking out an existence on the basis of multiple sources of subsistence has become entrenched. The expansion of agricultural production after independence had the consequence of deepening the levels of inequality in rural Kenya.

Discussions on the South African peasant question had two quite distinct sources. First, the debates in the liberation movements about the class character of the rural population informed particular strategies and struggles from the 1930s through to the 1970s. The agrarian question served as a vital, if neglected, aspect of these debates. The fact that white settlement had seized virtually 90 percent of the land in South Africa and 50 percent in Zimbabwe meant that the indigenous population had been squeezed into inadequate reserves, effectively constraining the development of an independent peasantry. While some argued that this constituted a displaced proletarian class, others suggested that the peasant character of the rural population remained a crucial factor in the politics of the country. (Archie Mafeje's insights concerning East Africa are also relevant in this regard.) The second source for engagement with the peasant question were usually white South African exiles and scholars living in Britain. This was part of a materialist broadside in South African historiography that was designed to challenge the liberal hegemony. There were a whole host of intra-materialist controversies, but it is perhaps worthwhile to divide these in a very rough manner into two broad approaches: the structuralists and the social historians. While the former were concerned about the manner in which sub-subsistence agricultural production acted as a wage subsidy, enabling the super-exploitation of the migrant laborer, the latter were interested in the manner in which African producers acted not merely as passive recipients of colonial and apartheid policy, but instead were active agents in the making of history.

As a body of knowledge directed toward the understanding of peasants as agents in agrarian structures, it is fair to say that these debates in East, West, and Southern Africa were crucial. They have certainly enhanced our understanding of agrarian relations in these broad areas. Precisely because of the diversity in local conditions, as well as the tendency to emphasize particular aspects of reality in line with particular theoretical and political approaches, the debates left a rich but varied legacy of studies on peasants in Africa. Since peasants still constitute a sizable proportion of the population in many African countries, the future of the continent is inextricably linked to the manner in which the concerns and interests of these rural masses are met.

See also: agrarian change; colonial Africa; pastoralism; peasant movements; plantation agriculture

References and further reading

Bernstein, H. (1981) "Notes on the State and Peasantry: The Tanzanian Case," *Review of African Political Economy* 8, 21: 44–62.

Fallers, L. (1961) "Are African Cultivators to be called 'Peasants'?," *Current Anthropology* 2, 2: 108–10.

Hill, P. (1970) *Studies in Rural Capitalism in West Africa*, Cambridge: Cambridge University Press.

Hyden, G. (1980) *Beyond Ujamaa in Tanzania: Underdevelopment and an Uncaptured Peasantry*, London: Heinemann.

Leys, C.T. (1975) *Underdevelopment in Kenya. The political economy of neo-colonialism, 1964–1971*, London: Heinemann.

Mafeje, A. (1977) "Neo-colonialism, State Capitalism, or Revolution," in P. Gutkind and P. Waterman (eds.), *African Social Studies: A Radical Reader*, London: Heinemann.

—— (1985) "Peasants in Sub-Saharan Africa," *African Development*, 10, 3: 412–22.

Post, K. (1972) "'Peasantization' and Rural

Political Movements in West Africa," *European Journal of Sociology* 13: 223–51.

FRED HENDRICKS

plantation agriculture

At the end of the nineteenth century plantation agriculture existed in all parts of Africa. In **West Africa** plantations had been an important feature of the economy of such Islamic states as Sokoto and Massina, as well as places like Dahomey and **Liberia**. The plantations mainly produced cotton and grains, and were owned either by the aristocracy or the merchant class. In **North Africa** they were established along the fertile coastal belt, either by indigenous planters (as in the case of the olive-oil plantations of **Libya**) or by European colonists (as in the case of the wheat and vine plantations of **Algeria**). In **East Africa** there were the clove and grain plantations on the Indian Ocean islands and along the coast. Plantations of rice and other crops grew rapidly in **Madagascar** following the adoption of autarkist policies by the Merina state from the 1820s. In **Southern Africa** the Portuguese had established unproductive cotton and coffee plantations in parts of colonized **Angola** and **Mozambique**, while the colonists of **South Africa** held far more successful sugar plantations in Natal.

Generally these plantations produced both cash crops for export and food crops for local consumption, unlike most twentieth-century plantations, which concentrated on export cash-crop production. Also, with the notable exception of the settler colonies, the plantations were largely owned by local ruling and commercial classes, while foreign ownership and agribusiness interests increased over the course of the twentieth century. Furthermore the nineteenth-century plantations relied on various forms of coerced labor – corvée labor levied from ordinary peasants, sharecropping, slave labor, and indentured labor – while hired wage labor became increasingly dominant in the twentieth century. The growth of the colonial plantation frontier was regionally uneven. It became dominant in parts of Southern and **Central Africa**, made considerable progress in East and North Africa, and almost failed in West Africa. With colonialism many of the locally owned plantations were dismantled and foreign capital assumed predominance. The abolition of slavery deprived the old plantation systems of West and East Africa of their main source of labor, a problem further exacerbated by colonial preferences for either peasant or settler agriculture.

From the late nineteenth century in West Africa, French, German, and British merchants and companies, such as the Royal Niger Company and Lever Brothers (the predecessor of the giant Unilever conglomerate), made vigorous efforts to establish plantations of cocoa, coffee, cotton, rubber, and palm oil. Except for southern **Côte d'Ivoire** (where a few French plantations survived and were later joined by plantations created by an indigenous planter class) and politically independent Liberia (where the Firestone Rubber Company was leased a million acres in 1926 to establish the world's largest rubber plantation), plantations made little headway in West Africa. A.G. Hopkins (1973) has attributed this to four factors:

1. the absence of a mineral revolution like that in Southern Africa weakened expatriate interests in the realm of production as a whole;
2. planters were strongly opposed by established trading interests that did not want to undermine the long-established lucrative trade in peasant produce;
3. most of the experimental plantations failed due to lack of adequate capital, of knowledge of tropical conditions, and of labor; and
4. by this time Africans had already succeeded in establishing a robust export economy by their own efforts (for example, Ghanaian cocoa production had become the world's largest by 1910).

Along the East African coast changes introduced by the British and German colonial states in **Kenya** and **Tanzania** – in land ownership and labor policies respectively – allowed the Arab–Swahili plantocracy to retain control over large tracts of land, but they ceased to be planters as their ex-slaves moved away or became squatters. In the meantime European settlers and companies were encouraged to set up plantations, which were provided with preferential infrastructural, financial, and marketing services. In Tanzania vast sisal plantations were established by German, British, Greek, and Indian capital. For much of the colonial period these plantations provided the biggest sources of employment and export earnings. Tea became the dominant plantation crop in Kenya when Brooke Bond established its first African tea plantation in the country in the 1920s, soon followed by others. Kenya's policy of actively discouraging Africans from growing profitable cash crops was not officially abandoned until the 1950s, although even before then peasants contributed a growing share of the country's exports. The plantation and peasant economies were more evenly balanced in Tanzania, while in **Uganda** peasant agriculture was the clear favorite, although a few large-scale estates were established – some by the government itself in the 1950s. Plantation agriculture also had a limited impact in **Ethiopia**, where some sugar plantations were established in the Awash Valley in the 1950s by a Dutch company fleeing newly independent Indonesia.

Plantation agriculture in North Africa also exhibited uneven patterns of development. Peasant agriculture remained dominant in **Egypt**, although there was a clear trend towards concentration of large holdings. By 1914, for example, 1.4 percent of all owners held 44.2 percent of the agricultural land, up from 15 percent in 1897. In the Maghreb settler agriculture, which included some very large estates, grew quite considerably. In Algeria settler farming was promoted at the expense of peasant production, which was marginalized through massive land dispossession. By the mid-1930s the Europeans accounted for 90 percent of wine production – the most profitable area of the agricultural sector – and Algeria had become the third largest wine producer in the world after France and Italy. As European estate agriculture developed, rural Algerian society became more proletarianized, pauperized, and stratified. By 1950, for example, 1.3 percent of landowners held 23 percent of the land in indigenous hands, while 69.5 percent held 18.7 percent. In **Tunisia** settler estates amounted to some 700,000 hectares by 1931, which (as in Algeria) were located in the best-watered and most fertile parts of the country. Following the conquest of Libya in 1911, the Italian government granted large estates to wealthy Italians to encourage colonial settlement and production. Settler-estate agriculture started later in **Morocco** – in 1918 – but grew rapidly in the 1920s. Following the **Great Depression** huge fruit orchards were established in the region as part of agricultural diversification from wine and olives. In **Sudan** in the early 1900s the Sudan Plantation Syndicate was granted a concession to develop cotton production in the fertile Gezira Plain, in a cooperative arrangement that involved the syndicate, the government, and local peasants. The scheme came on-stream in 1925, following the construction of the Sennar Dam, and transformed agricultural production and economic development in the country.

It was in Central and Southern Africa, however, that plantation and settler agriculture assumed supremacy. The colonial economies of **French Equatorial Africa** (AEF), the Belgian Congo, and Portuguese Angola and Mozambique depended extensively on concession companies, which in the early years instituted plundering economies characterized by the use of forced labor and forced cultivation through which millions of people died. By 1914 vast territories in French and German equatorial Africa were divided among forty companies. The South Cameroons Company, one of the largest, was granted 20 million acres from which it was authorized to collect rubber, without payment, forever. The system was particularly brutal in the Belgian Congo, where by 1930 the "state fields" covered more than a million hectares from which peasants produced 15,000 tonnes of rice and 30,000 tonnes of cotton that were collected by around a dozen companies that owned 111 ginning mills. At the beginning of colonial rule Portugal, an old but weak imperial power, sought to use concession companies as instruments of administrative and economic colonization, and through them to gain recognition from the other powers and attract foreign capital. The concession companies were particularly strong in Mozambique, where the Mozambique Company, the Zambesia Company, the Niassa Company, and the Boror Company were granted charters that allowed them to levy taxes, trade peasant produce, and establish plantations in their areas of jurisdiction, for which the state guaranteed forced labor. Sugar, cotton, coconuts, and sisal became the main plantation crops. Workers and peasants responded to this ruthless regime of agrarian exploitation – which changed little until **decolonization** – through flight, maroonage, migrations to neighboring countries, sabotage of farming operations and equipment, social banditry, and revolts. Although Portugal tried, with limited success, to reserve Angolan agriculture for Portuguese capital, the plantation economy that developed there based on cotton, coffee, and sugar was no less extensive and exploitative.

Elsewhere in Southern Africa plantation agriculture varied in importance. It was insignificant in the economies of **Botswana** and (initially) **Swaziland**, which depended on **migrant labor**, while it became increasingly important in the agrarian economies of **Malawi** and later of Swaziland, which were dominated respectively by tea and sugar production. On South Africa's part, agriculture was progressively dominated by European settler and corporate farming (including large plantations, such as the sugar plantations of Natal), all buttressed by draconian discriminatory legislation, including the Native Lands Act of 1913 that reserved 87 percent of the land for whites, that progressively underdeveloped and impoverished African farming. Similar measures were enacted in **Zimbabwe**, where half the land was allocated to the minuscule white population and white commercial agriculture concentrated on tobacco for export and maize for internal consumption.

After independence plantation agriculture in Africa continued to grow. The acreage devoted to traditional plantation crops like coffee, tea, tobacco, and sugar expanded as post-independence governments sought to increase their foreign exchange earnings to finance development in the 1960s and 1970s, and to service debts in the 1980s and 1990s. Falling terms of trade for agricultural commodities, combined with pressures from the **international financial institutions** and internal class interests against fundamental economic transformation, all served to sustain export production, in which plantation agriculture retained a vital role. But the plantation sector exhibited three major new tendencies.

First, the sector was increasingly Africanized, either through nationalization or through acquisition by an African agrarian bourgeoisie. The former was the case in socialist-oriented states, from Angola and Mozambique to Algeria and Tanzania, with Tanzania being the country where the famous *ujamaa* program of rural development was launched. The latter occurred in capitalist-oriented states like Kenya, Malawi, and Morocco. There were differences of course. For example, Mozambique's reforms were premised on a Leninist distrust of the rich and middle peasantry, while Tanzania's were rooted in populist notions of peasant solidarity; in Malawi plantation agriculture was maintained at the expense of the peasant sector, while in Kenya both forms of agriculture were promoted – in fact the peasant sector had become dominant by the end of the 1960s.

Second, new luxury products entered the repertoire of plantation agriculture. These included fruit, vegetables, and flowers. For example, in the late 1960s the US company Del Monte, now a subsidiary of the food and tobacco giant R.J. Reynolds, established one of the largest pineapple plantations in the world in Kenya. In the early 1970s Bud Antle, a subsidiary of another American food giant Castle and Cooke, set up huge vegetable farms in **Senegal**. And in the 1980s, amid widespread food shortages, many African countries boasted record exports of flowers to Europe, some of them produced on large estates.

Third, agribusiness adopted new strategies, partly in response to the policies of the new governments and partly as a reflection of growing centralization and concentration of agrarian capital on a global scale, by which direct control over production was increasingly supplemented or replaced by control over processing, transportation, marketing, and distribution. Agribusiness firms derived a growing share of their profits from management and service contracts and consultancies, sometimes for their now nationalized plantations. Alternatively some ceded production to outgrowers, which reduced labor costs and vulnerability to market fluctuations because they were under little obligation to buy the commodities when prices fell.

Reference and further reading

Boahen, A. (ed.) (1985) *UNESCO General History of Africa. Africa Under Colonial Domination 1880–1935*, London: Heinemann.
Dinham, B. and Hines, C. (1984) *Agribusiness in Africa*, Trenton: Africa World Press Inc.
Hopkins, A.G. (1973) *An Economic History of West Africa*, London: Longman.
Mkandawire, T. and Naceur, B. (eds.) (1987) *The State and Agriculture in Africa*, Dakar: CODESRIA.

PAUL TIYAMBE ZELEZA

population

By the end of the twentieth century Africa had an estimated population of 818 million, which continued to grow at a rapid rate of 2.4 percent per year. With a doubling time of approximately twenty-eight years, Africa's population was projected to increase to about 1.1 billion by 2025. By then the region would have four times as many people as North America, and 500 million more people than Latin America. In 2000 Africa was second in regional population only to Asia, which seemed poised to maintain its lead over all other regions of the world.

Like any other region Africa's population experienced considerable fluctuations and transformations over time, rising from approximately 1 million about 25,000 years ago to 5 million by 3000 BC, 37 million by AD 600 and about 100 million by 1650. For the next two centuries Africa's population stagnated, even declining to 95 million by 1850. This population decline can be attributed to the impact of **slavery** and the introduction of infectious diseases by Europeans. The Atlantic slave trade not only depopulated much of Africa, but also altered the age and gender structure of the continent, leaving several communities with only women and children. Another factor that had an impact on African populations during the eighteenth and nineteenth centuries was the introduction by Europeans of communicable diseases, such as smallpox, influenza, and measles. The downward spiral in Africa's population began to be reversed following the abolition of the slave trade, although colonial conquest and the **genocides** associated with some colonial regimes, such as the Germans in **Namibia** and King Leopold in the **Congo**, led to population decline in those countries. By 1900 Africa's population was estimated at 120 million, and it had reached 222 million by 1950. After 1950 Africa's population began to increase exponentially: from 642 million in 1990 to 881 million in 2001.

Explaining population growth

The demographic transition theory can be employed to illustrate the changes that have occurred over time in Africa's population. The model was utilized to describe the population history of industrializing Europe. Its hypothesis is that European countries went through four demographic stages, each associated with a different level of social and economic development. In essence the hypothesis is that population growth slows down once a country moves from a pre-industrial economy to an industrial one. The first demographic stage – the *high stationary stage* – is characterized by high birth and death rates, which is symptomatic of pre-industrial Europe, as well as of Africa between 1750 and 1900. During this period high birth rates in Africa were offset by high death rates, associated with infectious diseases imported from Europe and famines. For example, during the late 1800s and early 1900s outbreaks of smallpox, influenza, and cerebro-spinal meningitis had a devastating effect among the Kikuyu in **Kenya**. In addition, periodic droughts and locusts ravaged the regions of central Kenya, destroying several crops. By the end of the twentieth century there were no African countries in this demographic stage. Most African countries were in the second stage – a *high expanding stage* – signifying declining death rates but consistently high birth rates. At the third stage – the *late expanding stage* – birth rates began to decline, while death rates declined further. Late twentieth-century China, Taiwan, Singapore, and South Korea best typified this stage. The declining birth rates were a latent response to economic development, as people adjusted to economic growth, **urbanization**, and industrial development. In **North Africa**, **Tunisia** – with a birth rate of 19 per 1,000 people

– was virtually at this stage, while **Morocco** and **Algeria** seemed to be approaching it. South of the Sahara, **South Africa**, **Zimbabwe**, **Ghana**, and **Botswana** were gradually approaching the third stage. At the final stage – the *low stationary stage* – birth and death rates are low, indicating some degree of the economic stability associated with industrial development. Critiques of the demographic transition model question its empirical and predictive value on the basis that conditions in late twentieth-century Africa differed markedly from those that prevailed in European countries as they moved through the demographic transition. For example, the birth rates of 45 births per 1,000 people that were reported in some African countries were much higher than the rates of 35 per 1,000 experienced by European countries when they were experiencing a demographic transition in the early nineteenth century. This reflected sociocultural differences related to early and universal marriages in Africa, as opposed to late and infrequent marriages in Europe. Also it seems fairly simplistic to establish a causal link between industrial development and fertility, considering the underlying complexity and multidimensional nature of fluctuations in fertility. For example, how do we explain significant fertility declines – as in the predominantly agricultural economy of Kenya or the less-developed economy of **Mozambique** – in the late twentieth century?

Much of the concern surrounding Africa's rapid population growth was focused on the relationship between population and resources, a debate that is rooted in Malthusian theory. Thomas Malthus (1766–1834) postulated that population would always outstrip food supply, thereby placing much emphasis on population as a powerful driver of environmental degradation, poverty, and human deprivation. Accordingly population will continue to surpass the means of subsistence unless it is controlled through a series of preventive checks, including moral restraint, birth control, and delayed marriage. Neo-Malthusian proponents continue to treat population pressure as a "law of nature" that inevitably leads to a depletion of resources, large-scale famine, and mass poverty in affected regions of the world. Paul Ehrlich's *Population Bomb* (1968) provided a doomsday scenario about humanity breeding itself into oblivion. The Club of Rome's 1972 report *The Limits to Growth* (published 1986) examined the dynamic interaction among population, resource-use, food production, industrial output, and pollution, predicting that there would be a catastrophic collapse of population around the year 2025 due to a dramatic decline in mineral and land resources. Critiques of Malthus de-emphasized the role of population and offered other explanations for human deprivation and poverty that were linked to technological, political-economic, structural, societal, and institutional factors. Malthus did not foresee the impact of technological progress, innovation, and human creativity. He assumed that a limited supply of land could only sustain a finite amount of food supply; he could not anticipate the impact that technological developments in fertilizer production, genetic engineering, and high-yield varieties of seeds (the Green Revolution) would have on increased food production. The problem with declining food production in late twentieth-century African countries was not so much a problem of overpopulation or limited land, as a structural and institutional problem related to price distortions, income inequality, land-tenure issues, land distribution, a dilapidated rural infrastructure, and lack of investment in the rural farm economy.

The antithesis to Malthusian theory is economist Esther Boserup's (1965) contention that population growth can serve as a stimulus for improving the human condition. Boserupian theory argues that agricultural development is caused by population trends, instead of the other way round. In other words agricultural production and associated technological changes are unlikely unless population increases; increasing population densities, in turn, lead to more intensive cultivation. Related to Boserup's thesis is the "Cornucopian" viewpoint that throughout history population growth has been accompanied by rising living standards and increased wealth. Human ingenuity and technological advancements offset any reductions in resources caused by a growing population. Julian Simon's *Theory of Population and Economic Growth* (1986) states that more people translate into bigger markets, easier communications, greater economies of scale, and higher productivity. Marxian perspectives also downplay the significance of overpopulation, instead attributing poverty and human deprivation to a capitalist mode of production that denies the poor access to food and resources, and accentuates the gap between rich and poor countries. World systems theorists and dependency theorists have argued that this gap is perpetuated by a dominance–dependence relationship that results in an unequal exchange of resources between rich and poor, such as the exchange of raw materials for industrial products. Africa thereby ends up in a subordinate position, becoming vulnerable to the rules and regulations of an international system controlled by advanced countries. Regardless of these perspectives the rapid rate at which population was growing in African countries during the second half of the twentieth century was cause for concern. Undoubtedly the historical precedent set by industrialized countries demonstrated the advantages of having a growing population and accompanying large domestic market to support industrial products. Countries such as Botswana and **Zambia** in fact argued that they were underpopulated and used the argument to justify their stance of rejecting antenatal population policies. These may be logical arguments, but not in the context of a country experiencing rapid population growth rates and very short doubling times.

Impact of colonial policies on population in Africa

The 1884 Berlin Conference marked the beginning of the formal era of colonialism in Africa. It was perhaps the most significant turning point in Africa's history, since it shaped the social, economic, and political futures of countries, and ushered in the demographic partition and division of Africa. It also signaled the imposition of French acculturation policies in much of north, west and equatorial Africa; of British indirect rule in much of south and east Africa; of Portuguese assimilation in **Angola** and Mozambique; and of Belgian paternalism in **Congo** and Ruanda-Urundi (see **Burundi**; **Rwanda**). European policies specifically related to the institution of plantation and extractive economies, forced labor recruitment, and harsh taxation policies had an impact on survival rates during the formal colonial era. The imposition of a cash-crop economy had far-reaching ramifications on African households, as men were forced into work camps, thereby increasing the burden on women who had to support children, manage the family farm, and care for the elderly. In the former Portuguese colonies of Angola and Mozambique much of the local population (or *indígenas*) was forced into providing cheap labor for the mines, agricultural schemes, and circumscriptions or segregated work camps, which fragmented families and society, and suppressed efforts to foster nationalism and unity. In French colonial Africa large concessionary companies had complete control over local labor, and Africans were coerced into paying a poll tax to finance colonial government. In **Niger** all males over twelve years of age were mandated to provide five days of labor annually. In essence **migrant labor** created a gender division of labor, as men were extracted to work in mines, farms, military service, and on railway building projects, while women assumed new agricultural functions.

The wage economy fueled labor migration and created social-class distinctions between urban/rural elites and cash-crop/subsistence farmers. The early 1900s witnessed the growth of mining and plantation towns. It is estimated that in 1910 there were about 2.5 million people living in African cities with populations greater than 100,000 people. With more railways being constructed, an increasing number of **peasants** began to travel greater distances in search of cash to secure tax money. Forced labor migration had implications for mortality and fertility. Working under oppressive conditions lowered one's resistance to disease, and increased the incidence of ill-health and likelihood of early death. For example, tuberculosis was prevalent among mineworkers in South Africa as early as the 1920s. Long working hours, low wages, inadequate food and shelter, and unsanitary work environments in **French Equatorial Africa** resulted in death rates that exceeded 110 deaths per 1,000 workers recruited. The repressive conditions associated with French African colonies resulted in refugee migrations into British colonial territories, such as **Nigeria** and **Cameroon**, where labor and tax policies were less burdensome. Revolts were not, however, necessarily confined to French colonies. The Maji Maji uprising (1905–6) in German-controlled **Tanzania** was triggered by resentment over a cotton scheme, and resulted in more than 100,000 African deaths. Several Africans lost their lives in a 1886 revolt against the building of railways in **Senegal**. In **Zimbabwe** the Ndebele war of 1893 and the Shona–Ndebele uprising of 1896–7 revolved around land. On a completely different scale labor migration was a fertility-inhibiting factor, since the absence of men diminished the chances of women getting pregnant.

It is difficult to establish any definitive population estimates for colonial Africa due to the limited number of censuses taken at the time. Most scholars agree, however, that the late nineteenth century and early twentieth century were periods marked by high mortality rates for the reasons outlined above. Some have even called this the worst single period in African demographic and medical history. By the mid-1930s mortality rates in Africa began to decline, as medical missionaries and researchers turned their attention to tropical diseases, and colonial conditions began to improve – thanks in no small measure to the protracted struggles by the colonized African peoples themselves. Africa was now poised for a period of population growth as the urbanization process began to take effect, and as new towns and administrative centers evolved.

Population growth in late twentieth-century Africa

The main concerns about population trends in late twentieth-century Africa related to relatively rapid rates of natural increase, high infant mortality rates, declining life-expectancy rates, and a large number of young dependents. Africa's rate of natural increase – the surplus of births over deaths – was 2.4 percent, the highest of any region in the world, and almost twice as high as the world average of 1.3 percent. This high rate was driven by high birth rates (38 births per 1,000) and high fertility rates (an average of 5.2 children born to females during their reproductive years). There were regional variations in fertility rates. For example, northern and southern Africa had relatively lower fertility rates (3.6 and 3.1 respectively), while central, western, and eastern Africa had higher rates (6.6, 5.8, and 5.7 respectively). There were also variations by place of residence (urban areas had lower fertility rates than rural areas) and socioeconomic status (higher income and well-educated Africans had lower fertility rates).

Cultural factors were the strongest forces driving high fertility rates in Africa. Most females in "traditional" societies married at an early age. High rates of remarriage and polygamy negated any potential effects that divorce or widowhood might have had. Furthermore belief systems, customs, and traditions had a significant impact. The predominantly patrilineal societies placed a high premium on lineage and spiritual survival. The family lineage was seen as an extension of the past and a link to the future; any attempts at family planning were therefore strongly resisted. Fertility was equated with virtue and spiritual approval, and so barren women were treated with disdain and ostracized from society. Also, in a male-dominated society decisions about reproduction and family size were usually deferred to the husband, which explained the low rates of contraception – especially in rural Africa. Children were regarded as economic assets – a source of wealth and prestige, as well as a labor reservoir for household chores. They were also required to offer tribute to their parents. This flow of wealth to the elderly was a socially sanctioned and religiously necessary tribute. Such a high premium was placed on children that African women who aspired to elevate their status would comply with their husband's request to have more children. Fertility was further enhanced through child fosterage, where children were raised and cared for by their grandparents or foster parents. About a third of children in **West Africa** were fostered, strengthening family ties, offering companionship to widows, enhancing the children's education, and enabling them to assist with domestic chores. This practice lessened the economic burden placed on parents who would otherwise have been responsible for more children. Another fertility-enhancing factor was ethnic rivalry. In countries like Kenya, Nigeria, **Ethiopia**, and **Uganda** where ethnic tensions run high, there was intense competition for economic and political resources. Communities were reluctant to commit ethnic suicide by reducing their pace of fertility since numbers were relevant to the sharing of resources and power.

The high fertility rates explain why Africa's population was so young. By the end of the twentieth century in the majority of African countries more than 44 percent of the population was under fifteen years of age. The region's workforce faced the economic burden of supporting a large segment of its **youth**. Large subsidies were required for health care, education, and job-training programs to accommodate future employment. This momentum of younger and rapidly growing populations promised to carry over into the future and affect demands for housing, employment, and job benefits. It also seemed likely to translate into continued overall population growth as the youth of the 1990s reached their reproductive years. Even in those instances where fertility rates were beginning to decline, populations seemed likely to increase substantially before leveling off at the recommended replacement rate of 2.1 children per family. The World Bank's fertility projections indicated that the only countries that were likely to reach these levels by 2030 were Botswana, South Africa, Kenya, Morocco, Namibia, **Lesotho**, Tunisia, Zimbabwe, and the small island countries of **Cape Verde**, Reunion, the **Seychelles**, and **São Tomé and Príncipe**. These countries had higher standards of living, higher literacy rates, and had embarked on aggressive family-planning campaigns to control population growth. By 2030 the rest of Africa may have reached a fertility level of 3.0, and added at least 900 million more people to the 2000 population of 818 million.

In December 1992 African leaders, meeting at the Third Population Conference in **Dakar**, pledged to improve the quality of life for Africans. A major goal set at the conference was to reduce the regional natural growth rate to 2 percent by the year 2010. At the end of the century this seemed to be a pretty ambitious goal. Evidence suggested that fertility decline was slow, although countries such as Zimbabwe, Botswana, **Egypt**, Kenya, Ghana, Morocco, Namibia, South Africa, and Tunisia had made some headway because of comprehensive and community-based approaches to family planning. Other goals set at the Dakar conference included increasing the regional rate of contraceptive use from 10 to 40 percent by 2010, and achieving a life expectancy of fifty-five years and an infant mortality rate of 50 per 1,000 live births by 2000. To fulfill these goals African governments needed the political will to commit themselves to comprehensive family-planning strategies that were consistent with broader environmental and socioeconomic development policies. Specific policies that had to be considered included respecting individual **human rights**; creating effective delivery of modern medical methods and information systems, by integrating family planning with maternal and other health-care programs; promoting community-based, market-based, and social marketing strategies; improving the social, economic, and educational status of women; effective targeting of at-risk populations; and forging effective partnerships with **non-governmental organizations** and the private sector.

See also: colonial Africa; colonial conquest and resistance; health and disease

References and further reading

Aryeetey-Attoh, S. (ed.) (1997) *Geography of Sub-Saharan Africa*, Englewood Cliffs: Prentice-Hall.

Boahen, A. (1985) *General History of Africa. VII: Africa under Colonial Domination 1880–1935*, Paris: UNESCO.

Boserup, E. (1965) *The Conditions of Agricultural Growth*, London: Allen & Unwin.

Caldwell, J. (1994) "Fertility in Sub-Saharan Africa: Status and Prospects," *Population and Development Review* 20, 1: 179–87.

Club of Rome (1986) *The Limits to Growth*, New York: Universe Books.

Conah, G. (1987) *African Civilizations*, Cambridge: Cambridge University Press.

Cordell, D. and Gregory, J. (1987) *African Population and Capitalism*, Boulder: Westview Press.

Ehrlich, P. (1968) *Population Bomb*, New York: Ballantine.

Fyfe, C. and McMaster, D. (eds.) (1981) *African Historical Demography, Volume II: Proceedings of a Seminar Held in the Centre of African Studies*, Edinburgh: Centre of African Studies, University of Edinburgh.

Population Reference Bureau (2001) *2001 World Population Data Sheet*, Washington, D.C.: Population Reference Bureau Inc.

Simon, J. (1986) *Theory of Population and Economic Growth*, London: Basil Blackwell.

Tarver, J. (1996) *The Demography of Africa*, Westport: Praeger.

SAMUEL ARYEETEY-ATTOH

press

Africa's post-colonial mediascape is a rich and fascinating blend of traditions, influences, and technologies. The most modern forms of communications technologies coexist with indigenous media. Journalistic styles reflect exposure to both Anglo-Saxon and Hispanic press cultures, and their intermixture with African values, to produce a unique hybrid. One finds people in tune with print and online newspapers, just as one finds people who straddle indigenous and modern media, creatively drawing on both to negotiate their way over the continent's communicative hurdles and through its hierarchies. Africa's creativity refuses to be subjected to simple distinctions between old and new technologies, since its peoples are daily modernizing the indigenous and indigenizing the modern with novel outcomes. No technology seems to have been used too much to be used again, just as nothing is too new to be blended with the old for even newer results. Such creativity is informed not only by cultures amenable to conviviality, interdependence, and negotiation, but also by colonial histories of deprivation and debasement.

Colonial Africa

The first newspapers in Africa probably date back to 1798 in **Egypt**, 1800 in **South Africa**, 1801 in **Sierra Leone**, 1822 in **Ghana**, 1826 in **Liberia**, and 1859 in **Nigeria**. The first newspapers in Egypt were published in French during Napoleon's invasion. Locally owned papers in Arabic appeared soon after, during Muhammad Ali's reign (1805–49). Initially these were sponsored by the state, with the most important of them being *al-Waqa'i 'al-Misriyya* ("Egyptian Events"), established in 1828. From the 1860s the private press began its spectacular growth and assumed dominance, led by *al-Ahram* ("The Pyramids"), which was founded in 1876 and became a daily in 1881. *al-Ahram* prided itself on being a neutral conveyor of news, although it became, like other Egyptian papers, a vehicle for attacks against British imperialism and debates about Egyptian culture and identity after the British occupation in 1882. At the turn of the century the Egyptian press exploded: 250 new papers appeared between 1900 and 1914, as compared to only 23 between 1852 and 1880, although many had short lifespans because of economic constraints. In the interwar years, especially after independence in 1922, the Egyptian press entered its "golden age." In 1937 there were 250 Arabic and 65 foreign-language papers, and by the late 1940s the press enjoyed a circulation of over half a million. In the Maghreb the development of an indigenous press was relatively slow, hampered in **Algeria** (and to some extent **Tunisia**) by intolerant settler colonialism and in Libya by Italian fascism.

In **West Africa** the press also developed quite early. Anglophone West Africa's head-start has been attributed to the presence of a Western-educated elite, the growth of missionary activity, and the absence of European settlers. In 1858 Charles Bannerman launched the *Accra Herald*, later the *West Africa Herald*, while African missionaries in Abeokuta, Nigeria, produced the *Iwe Ihorin* in **Yoruba**. During the first half of the twentieth century a host of private newspapers were established by African businessmen and nationalists, from Herbert Macaulay (who founded the *Lagos Daily News* in 1925) to Nnamdi Azikiwe (who founded the *West African Pilot* in 1937). The nationalists used the press to articulate their demands for independence. By 1959 Azikiwe's National Council of Nigeria and the Cameroons controlled ten newspapers, while Obafemi Awolowo's Action Group controlled fourteen. By then there was also a sizable foreign media presence in the British colonies, spearheaded by the Mirror Group and Thompson–Amalgamated Press. By contrast in francophone West and Equatorial Africa, where the elite was supposed to be assimilated and to therefore savor the culture of the imperial metropole, the development of a local press was actively discouraged through the imposition of heavy taxes on newsprint and printing machinery. The early local press was restricted to European settlers. For example, before 1900 **Senegal** had three settler papers, one of which circulated in both France and the colonies. Nevertheless the first African-run papers had emerged by the 1920s, first in **Benin**. In 1933 in **Dakar** Charles de Breteuil, a Frenchman, established *Paris-Dakar*, precursor to what became the most powerful commercial newspaper chain in **francophone Africa**. In the rest of French West and Equatorial Africa newspapers were not established until after the **Second World War**. **Cameroon** established a relatively vibrant press. All together between 1945 and 1960 some 365 papers appeared and disappeared in francophone Africa.

In **Southern**, **Central**, and **East Africa** the press was largely created by Europeans to serve the information, education, and entertainment needs of the European settler communities, leaving the African readership in search of alternative channels of communication. At the turn of the century the most significant of the Southern African papers was the *Cape Argus*. Established in 1857, the *Cape Argus* spread its tentacles across the region when the mining magnate Sir John Cecil Rhodes, who had bought a controlling interest in it, colonized **Zimbabwe** and established the *Rhodesia Herald* in 1892. In 1931 the Argus Group set up the Bantu Press, which over the next two decades founded a series of newspapers for African readers in South Africa, **Lesotho**, **Botswana**, **Swaziland**, **Zambia**, Zimbabwe, and **Malawi**, and later for European settlers in Zambia. In East Africa the first paper was the *East African Standard*, established in 1902, which catered to settler interests, although it was founded by an Asian businessman, A. Jeevanjee, who subsequently founded the first daily papers in **Tanzania** (*Tanganyika Standard*) in 1930 and **Uganda** (*Uganda Argus*) in 1953. The Standard Group maintained close ties with the South African Press association, which were severed at independence. Some nationalists also founded their own papers: for example, Jomo Kenyatta's *Muigwithamia* ("Work and Play") and Oginga Odinga's *Nyanza Times*.

The African press under colonial rule was both a sign of hope and despair: Hope for those who saw in it an opportunity for self-expression, and despair for colonialists who perceived it as a threat to power and privilege. Literacy and the press may have been regarded as signs of modernity, but the colonizers were generally unwilling to grant the colonized freedom to determine the content of what they read, especially as the press soon became a powerful vehicle for political resistance and African self-assertion. Hence almost all colonies instituted strict laws regulating the right of Africans to set up and operate newspapers. Economic measures were also sometimes imposed to make it difficult for African newspaper proprietors to operate. Despite this the print media remained invaluable for African elites to articulate their anti-colonial struggles, especially as broadcasting (developed from the 1930s) was under much tighter state control.

When faced with repressive state policies and measures, African elites eager to communicate their liberation agenda adopted various strategies. They continued publishing openly at the risk of arrest, published underground, or used alternative channels of communication. These last included indigenous media, as well as political rumor-mongering and derision, which were known under various names in different regions: *radio trottoir* in francophone Africa; *radio boca a boca* in **lusophone Africa**; *radio one battery*, *bush telegraph*, *pavement radio*, and *radio mall* in **anglophone Africa**. These strategies were quite useful in the Algerian revolution, where Frantz Fanon – as a member of the Services de Presse du Front de Libération Nationale in **Tunis** – was able to take advantage of *El Moudjahid* (in which articles were not given bylines) to disseminate his revolutionary ideas on colonialism in Algeria and Africa.

The post-colonial period

Independence was characterized by contradictory trends. In some countries state ownership of the press increased as the one-party states bought, nationalized, or established new papers. In Zambia, for example, Kenneth Kaunda's government took control of the *Times of Zambia*, while in neighboring Malawi the *Daily Times* was bought by a private conglomerate controlled by the president. In **Kenya** the ruling party established its own paper, the *Kenya Times*, in conjunction with the British-based Robert Maxwell Group, to compete with the two leading dailies, the *East African Standard*, controlled by Lonhro, and the *Nation*, established in 1960 by the Aga Khan and soon establishing itself as the leading newspaper in East Africa. In other countries the state sought to encourage local private ownership as against foreign ownership. For example, in Nigeria the federal government established the Nigeria Press Ltd. to provide printing facilities. The Ibru Group and Moshood Abiola soon established media empires, centered around the *Guardian* and *Concord* newspapers respectively.

In general, independence maintained and enhanced attempts by governments to control the press. They drew inspiration from and added to the rich repertoire of colonial repressive laws to keep the press and **civil society** in check. They also used commercial and other mechanisms, including patronage and bribery. The assumption was that a critical press endangered development and nation-building. If the colonial press was either at the service of settler communities or victim of repressive laws, from the 1960s to the 1980s the post-colonial press was either the mouthpiece of government or subjected to draconian laws and censorship, including self-censorship. States sought to make the press partners in nation-building and development. Notions of "development communication," "development journalism," and "rural journalism" even became part of scholarly vocabulary and research. In the meantime many African countries set up national news agencies, and the richer papers subscribed to international news services, such as Reuters, AFP, UPI, and AP. By the 1970s, however, there was widespread dissatisfaction with the domination of the international agencies in reporting Africa to the rest of the world, and often to itself; African journalists and politicians, sometimes for different reasons, joined the struggle for a New World Information Order (NWIO), which echoed demands for a New International Economic Order (NIEO). It was in this context that the Pan-African News Agency was created by the **Organization of African Unity** in 1979, as a vehicle by which to decolonize Africa's media and raise the continent's global media presence.

All the talk about NWIO and NIEO could not, however, hide the fact that all was not well within Africa itself. When both development and nation-building proved increasingly elusive, the press and other arms of civil society started to clamor for a second liberation, especially from the late 1980s. The restrictive and repressive laws against the press were targeted for reform at the dawn of this second liberation struggle. Thus the struggles for democracy opened up space for, and were facilitated by, an explosion of the press. In countries that only a few years earlier had one or two newspapers, suddenly dozens appeared. For example, by the mid-1990s more than three dozen papers had sprung up in Cameroon, about two dozen in Malawi, and more than sixty in tiny **Rwanda**.

Despite the wind of change that blew through the 1990s the press continued to face difficulties and challenges related to the legal framework regulating working conditions, finance, marketing, and external competition. Journalists in each country grappled with their own specific legal legacies. For example, the Nigerian press, often counted among the continent's most vibrant and critical, had to struggle with a battery of restrictive laws imposed by generations of military regimes. In South Africa, where the first liberation was only achieved in 1994, by the end of the decade the press had yet to break free from its past record of black marginalization, although the level of black press ownership and representation had increased. In Algeria in the 1990s journalists were targeted for persecution and even assassination, together with other members of the secular intellectual elite, by radical Islamists. In **Ethiopia** the limited press freedom gained after the overthrow of Mengistu Mariam's dictatorship in 1991 was abruptly curtailed a few years later when war broke out with **Eritrea**.

In extreme cases, there were countries that bucked the democratization trend, where outmoded legislation inherited from one-party and colonial predecessors continued to be used to criminalize dissent and curtail the critical instincts of the press. This was evident, for example, in Zimbabwe, where Mugabe's beleaguered regime imposed new restrictions on the local and foreign press. Elsewhere the tendency was for new laws to grant freedom in principle while providing, often through selective application of the law and the use of extra-legal measures, the curtailment of press freedom in practice. The use of derogatable and clawback measures by the state to limit the right of expression and press freedom was particularly strong in francophone Africa. For example, in **Côte d'Ivoire** – despite legalization of political parties in 1990 – a new law was passed in 1991 that authorized suspension or seizure of publications that disparaged the head of state, gave away national secrets, or derided the nation. In Benin, a year after the new democratically elected government assumed power, attempts were made to reimpose censorship.

The persistent political and legal constraints facing the press were often aggravated by economic, technical, and professional difficulties. In the poorer countries, where local or foreign corporate investment in the press was limited or non-existent, liberalization did not immediately open the floodgates of capital into the industry. Not surprisingly, after the initial euphoria of the second liberation, many of the tabloid newspapers that had mushroomed in countries like Malawi equally quickly collapsed. Even the official press did not always escape financial difficulties, especially in an era of **structural adjustment programs**, cuts in public expenditure, and media pluralism. Consequently many newspapers operated with skeletal staff, and were unable to undertake extensive background research or specialized investigative reporting for news stories. Ironically the professional limitations of the African press, accumulated over decades of repression, became evident in many of the newspapers established in the 1990s, when greater press freedom attracted politicians and opportunists for whom the press offered a chance for self-enrichment or to pursue other ambitions. Press liberalization also reinforced competition for advertising and readers, which in many cases was a recipe for "yellow journalism." All these challenges made newspapers and the life of journalists exciting and uncertain. Lack of job security, poor salaries, and poor working conditions made the profession less attractive to highly qualified people, and rendered some press workers susceptible to compromise, bribery, and corruption. Notwithstanding these challenges, it was clear that the African press had become a formidable part of civil society, at once a mirror and a beacon, reflecting and contributing to Africa's age-old yearnings for democratization, self-determination, and development.

Further reading

Ayalon, A. (1995) *The Press in the Arab Middle East: A History*, New York: Oxford University Press.

Bourgault, L.M. (1995) *Mass Media in Sub-Saharan Africa*, Bloomington: Indiana University Press.

Kurian, G.T. (ed.) (1982) *World Press Encyclopedia*, London: Mansell Publishing.

Lush, D. (1998) "The Role of the African Media in the Promotion of Democracy and Human Rights," in S. Kayizzi-Mungerwa, A.O. Olukoshi and L. Wohlgemuth (eds.), *Towards a New Partnership with Africa: Challenges and Opportunities*, Uppsala: Nordiska Afrikainstitutet.

Oloyede, B. (1996) *Press Freedom in Nigeria: A Critical Analysis of Salient Issues*, Abeokuta: Kunle Alayande Printing & Publishing Co.

Onadipe, A. (1998) "The Media in Africa: In the Eye of the Storm," *West Africa*, 4186: 262–5.

FRANCIS B. NYAMNJOH
PAUL TIYAMBE ZELEZA

professionals

It is useful to regard professionals in Africa as those individuals who practice a vocation or occupation requiring advanced education and training, as well as significant intellectual skills. These occupations include medicine, law, theology, engineering, and teaching. While many types of skilled knowledge and practice existed in pre-colonial Africa –

including blacksmiths, storytellers, and religious leaders – many of these activities were associated with particular castes or activities that relied on forms of apprenticeship to a knowledgeable elder. While these activities largely continued to exist through the colonial and post-colonial periods, many of them were at least partially supplanted by the work of professionals trained according to European models. The coexistence of these two systems – one a system of ideally separate and universally applicable competence, the other of interrelated and socially embedded knowledges – is at least partially related to what has been viewed as either an incomplete implantation of capitalism and modern professions on the continent or, more accurately, their interdevelopment within local contexts.

Modern professionals in twentieth-century Africa mainly comprised doctors, nurses, lawyers, engineers, and clergy. In addition, due to insufficient educational infrastructure, those with valuable specialized knowledge maintained profession-type monopolies over their trades. For example, information-technology specialists utilized the relative scarcity of their knowledge to secure an economic autonomy that resembled that of other professions. At the same time a lack of economic and political infrastructure made it difficult for other modern professionals to maintain control over their respective domains. For example, professional lawyers were underutilized in countries or regions where legal institutions were either not well developed or suppressed by authoritarian regimes. Similarly the devolution of medical functions to nurses and other public-health agents, for reasons of cost and preventive effectiveness, decreased the ability of physicians to maintain control over their traditional professional domain. Moreover legal standards and licensing were a crucial, legitimizing aspect of many professions' monopoly of knowledge. The porousness of these legal boundaries in many African countries contributed to a mutual destabilization of professionals' authority.

Social and political contexts

The societal base of modern professionals in Africa arose from the early colonial activities of indigenous petty-bourgeois actors. During the nineteenth century segments of the population, particularly in areas of **West Africa** and the Maghreb, were involved in trading and negotiating between Africans, colonialists, and colonial enterprises. As colonialists began to establish direct links with producers, they pushed out or blocked the moves of indigenous merchants and nobles. As their social basis shifted, some of these privileged actors attempted to consolidate their power in order to compete with Europeans. Others avoided confrontation by investing in the European education necessary for their children's eventual incorporation into the ranks of colonial enterprises and bureaucracy. Early teaching and training was often accomplished by missionaries encouraged by colonial administrators, and many of the original professionals in Africa thus began as functionaries, secretaries, and interpreters for Europeans. Within a generation, Africans had taken the next step beyond these functionary positions to become professionals of the modern sort.

However, through the early part of the twentieth century there was little or no institutional basis for the education or practice of professionals in Africa that actually belonged to Africans. All professionals received their secondary or tertiary training either in the European metropoles or in centers of colonial power on the continent, such as **Senegal** for the French subjects. Beyond this African intellectuals of a European cast were blocked from developing an autochthonous class. Many colonialists had seen early on that the development of an elite class of Africans who saw themselves as the equal of any European could provide a potent source of unrest. Thus in the interwar period most colonial powers attempted to prevent any concentration of power or responsibility in the hands of indigenous African functionaries and professionals. Yet many of these educated functionaries were already distanced from popular society because their societal position and cultural influences drew upon both European and African sources of authority. Their resulting rapprochement with European and metropolitan forces effectively separated many indigenous professionals from more popular aspects of their own society.

It was only after the **Second World War** – amid the growing resentment of the working classes, rural classes, indigenous merchants, and traditional producers – that colonialists began to consider the European-educated African middle class as a potential force for guaranteeing stability in the colonies. This situation differed somewhat in settler colonies, where Europeans worked against development for Africans, except where it concerned their work and life in menial trades or as migrant laborers in mines and on plantations. Having inserted themselves into colonial government, many members of the African middle class had some interest in maintaining the bureaucratic infrastructure through which they gained power and status. Yet the inherent racism of the colonial bureaucracy also sowed resentment among these individuals, contributing to their desire for independence. After independence it was primarily a middle class of African professionals and intellectuals who eventually took control of the new modern states; where both a settler class and a class of indigenous professionals existed – as in **Mozambique**, **Angola**, **Guinea-Bissau**, **Zimbabwe**, and **Namibia** – armed conflict was necessary before this could happen. Because of these constraints it was only after the Second World War that the educational bases for the professions, properly speaking, were developed in Africa, and a technocratic class of indigenous professionals began to reproduce itself across the continent.

Specialized schooling became crucial to the development of professionals in Africa. Most of the professional schools that opened in Africa outside of settler regions were created during the 1950s and 1960s, though some private religious schools (in **Egypt** and **Ethiopia**, for example) were established earlier in the century. Most educational systems were based on the enlightenment model of the European academies. In the French colonial system, the early colonial Teacher Training School at Sebikotane, Senegal, was later transferred to Goree Island, and renamed after the colonial governor William Ponty. This school was then followed by an expanded system throughout **French West Africa** that included the School of Medicine and Pharmacy in **Dakar** in Senegal, the Professional Terrasson de Fougères School in **Bamako** in **Mali**, and the Rural Training School at Dabou in **Côte d'Ivoire**. Some educational institutions, such as the Islamic schools in Egypt, were modernized to include professional education in medicine, law, theology, and education. Yet these educational improvements had become a necessity for colonial powers working to establish an increasingly indirect rule over the colonies through a stratum of sympathetic indigenous actors. Indeed the improvements made by the British to educational institutions in their African colonies during the 1950s were instituted as a means of continuing to guide the development of the local population while acquiescing to their needs.

A similar motivation could be attributed to nationalists, whose own efforts at improving compulsory and professional education were aimed at training replacements for Europeans who held professional positions within the colonial bureaucracy and society in general. However, in several African countries expatriate functionaries remained until the need for them declined and popular pressure forced the Africanization of state bureaucracies. As professionals had a focal role to play in the newly independent states, many of the organizations that consisted of large numbers of professionals, like the Sierra Leone People's Party, were integrally involved in the processes of national liberation or in gradual **decolonization**. However, even though independence leaders like Julius Nyerere of **Tanzania** saw broad-based education as a crucial factor in development and social change, some were also wary of professional education and the social forces it might produce.

Post-independence strategies of modernization fostered a gradual progression from traditional to modern (professional and vocational) skill sets, postulating that such progress would also bring development. Yet this trajectory was far from given, in that professional employment was never guaranteed. Furthermore the European models of infrastructure and **civil society** that such professionals worked to dogmatically institute were not entirely relevant in African contexts. Public and private investment in professional education directly related to the level of return on that education, suggesting links between economic development and enrollment in professional education. In the countries of **francophone Africa**, enrollment in tertiary education was highest in **Morocco** and the lowest in **Rwanda**. In the countries of **anglophone Africa**, enrollment in professional education was even higher, with **Egypt** having the highest levels and Tanzania the lowest. While general relationships are identifiable, it is necessary to establish how particular modern professions fit with the ideological foundations and practical hegemony of colonialism's "civilizing mission" in the twentieth century.

The development of some professions

During the colonial period the development of health personnel, like that of other professionals, involved either colonial or expatriate professionals, all of whom were trained in the metropoles. Their first tasks were to protect Europeans, and treat or screen African laborers. This situation continued even after independence, as in **Zambia** where over a third of physicians (and all of the district health personnel) were expatriate Europeans until the early 1980s. Health services for the masses were left to European medical missions until after the Second World War, when national liberation movements pushed for the expansion of education and health facilities. The first Africans trained in medicine were part of medical corps in the **First World War**, but there were not even very many of them before independence.

It was not until the 1950s and 1960s, as the possibility of independence loomed larger on the horizon, that excellent centers for professional medical education, like the schools in Ibadan and Makerere, were established on the African continent. In **South Africa**, however, settlers' racist concerns about educating Africans were played against colonial concerns about providing services for black regions of the country. The University of Natal was therefore founded away from other white institutions and strictly to provide personnel for labor reserves. African professionals were classified as unnecessary and even dangerous in the larger South Africa. They were thus confined to the reserves and the University of Natal, which became a focus of black organization.

The development of medical professionals in Africa was fueled by government-supported health care in the post-independence period. The majority of medical professionals across Africa were employed by state health services, employment that in many places was all but guaranteed. In places like **Kenya** and **Ghana** a substantial amount of health care was privatized, while in a few other places (Tanzania, for example) medical professionals operated either in government services or in affiliation with missions and **non-governmental organizations** (NGOs). However, most of these services were structured around urban, curative, and capital-intensive (hospital-based) European models.

Given the power of government in many countries, there was little impetus for the development of professional organizations to guarantee the quality of and the rates of return for professional medical services in the private sector. Nevertheless, because of international lending arrangements, the last two decades of the twentieth century saw an increase in the proportion of professional medical services provided by NGOs across the continent. Along with these increasingly free-market arrangements, the 1970s and 1980s saw a marked increase in attempts by traditional birth-attendants and healers to establish professional credibility. By 2000 nearly every country in Africa had at least one organization working for the professional training, licensing, or recognition of traditional African medical practitioners.

Professional teachers were also valuable resources in colonial and post-colonial African society. During the colonial period the role of teaching and training was crucial to instituting European models and standards of education and societal achievement. Teaching was therefore vital for the colonial endeavor. Though much of the initial European teaching in Africa was conducted by European missionaries, teachers were also the first of the modern African professionals to follow the secretaries and functionaries of the early colonial period. Many of the early professionals first passed by way of schoolteaching.

It was only after the Second World War that educational institutions in Africa were expanded because of pressure from **nationalist move-**

ments. After independence, nationalist governments continued this expansion by initiating vast education and teacher training programs to jump-start the process of development and modernization. Economists had long drawn links between education, health, and prosperity, suggesting that it is impossible to have successful modern agriculture and modern industry without large educational investment in human resources. While the training of primary and secondary school teachers was moderately successful in providing broad education and effective pedagogy in Africa, many teachers at the university level did not acquire training in pedagogy outside of their disciplinary specializations. Furthermore the difference in training among teachers at primary, secondary, and tertiary levels perpetuated a tension in African educational institutions. Teachers and academic professionals – particularly in smaller towns and cities, rural areas, and areas troubled by poverty and war – were caught between productive and critical learning. For example, organizations such as the Teachers League of South Africa advocated improved education, expanded infrastructure, and equality of provision between black and white areas. While this critical function proved quite useful, academics in the post-colonial and post-apartheid eras had some difficulty participating in nation-state processes.

As with other professionals, teachers and academics faced the difficulty of being distanced from the larger part of their societies. Many of the languages of instruction and styles of thought in higher education were originally derived from former colonial education systems. In the 1970s and 1980s the scope for teachers to instruct or academics to research was linked to donors providing their institutions with support and their projects with parameters. This persistent external tie led many to consider such intellectuals as part and parcel of a neo-colonial condition by which, although colonial rule had disappeared, the control of former colonial powers persisted in the kinds of thought and language available in former colonies.

Beyond medical and teaching professionals, however, clergy were undoubtedly some of the first Europeans on the continent to carry out professional work. Like Muslim clerics in preceding centuries, European and African clergy were involved in much of the linguistic and philosophical development of the early colonies in Africa. Working between religious traditions, these individuals worked at understanding and adapting the cultural forms of Christianity to locations where it had been previously unknown. Again many of these clergy were originally expatriate Europeans, with the first professional African clergy also trained in colonial centers. It was not until the 1960s that seminaries and other training institutions for religious professionals were finally developed in Africa.

Though many have looked on the Christian clergy with derision because of their adherence to supposedly foreign religions, it must be remembered that – in places like South Africa – much of the hard work of cultural adaptation, survival, and resistance came through churches and the work of religious professionals. Along with these professionals, one might also include Muslim clerics and traditional religious specialists. As mentioned above, many of these have attempted and succeeded in the professionalization of their methods of care for psychological and spiritual needs. All across Africa such work at negotiating "traditional" and "modern" categories, while potentially threatening to other professionals, helped mediate changing social conditions.

The profession most crucial to the initial expansion of colonial power and resource exploitation was undoubtedly engineering. The earliest engineers in Africa were part of colonial administrations or enterprises, and worked on aspects of building and transportation. During the twentieth century, however, their efforts were turned towards establishing processes of production, such as mining, irrigation, and transportation. After independence, having already established productive capacities in raw materials, engineering began to concern the water, construction, and sanitation infrastructure necessary for changing populations. Without legal institutions in many places, there was neither any assurance of professional quality nor any incentive to establish such assurances. Thus African engineers with professional degrees were very much the exception, and many projects were carried out on a small scale.

Investment by the colonial powers was designed to ameliorate conditions for Europeans, and for European firms seeking to extract resources and labor power. The same might be said of investment by private interests. Smaller, more contingent projects were likely to be carried out by local tradesmen, working on an ad hoc basis, partly because the population and infrastructure shifts that occurred after independence happened so quickly that organized planning was not able to keep up. The most prominent period for African engineering was therefore immediately after independence, when projects for building apartments, boulevards, suburbs, monuments, and urban areas were carried out. In the last decades of the twentieth century such projects were increasingly funded by international and bilateral organizations that relied on foreign experts for planning and often execution. As grand planning at a municipal and national level, professional engineering in Africa therefore often existed as a neo-colonial endeavor. Consequently the most prominent roles for African engineers were in a range of projects in agriculture, forestry, and natural-resource development.

In addition to these professional developments, the need for professional management skills was also a colonial legacy. In places like Senegal a large number of French technocrats remained in the national government after independence and well into the 1970s. The lack of Africans and the presence of expatriates in managerial positions led to significant mismanagement of natural and human resources that might otherwise have been used in the service of the newly independent nation-states. Furthermore those professionally trained Africans that were assigned to the management of ministries, often had little training for those positions. As national budgets were trimmed in the latter part of the century to cover debt repayments and **structural adjustment programs**, the need to train managers and engage in rational resource-planning became evident. Yet, although private business and management schools did crop up, most management in Africa developed out of supplementary training for established professionals. In many African countries the appointment to managerial positions in state enterprises and bureaucracies was part of the political process, and not always based on merit. Many professionals were interested in reform – notably lawyers, activists, and religious leaders – but they tended to be professionals whose skills were geographically specific and so less easily transferable to other labor markets.

Several significant problems plagued African professionals' activities and involvement on the continent. The first, and perhaps most important, of these concerned the relationship of professionals and intellectuals with the lower classes and larger rural populations of their countries. This problem related to their involvement as both agents and critics of national governments and their development projects. The second problem involved the movement of qualified professionals out of Africa, colloquially referred to as the "brain drain." The third problem, one which suffused both of the former problems, was that of rampant gender bias in Africa, bias that affected women's presence in and access to professional development and employment.

The first problem manifested itself in several ways. Professionals in Africa perpetuated social and cultural distance from the rest of the population. This distance undermined both their cultural authority and their ability to establish and maintain popular support for professional infrastructure. Many degree-level professionals began working as middle-level managers, with no contact or sense of alignment with the primarily rural populations with whom they were concerned. This stratum-specific socialization continually reproduced professionals in Africa, while also limiting the value of their social capital. Maintaining links between trained individuals and the communities they were supposed to work for and participate in thus became a component of making professionals' work in Africa more effective.

For much of the skilled work that was available in Africa, a degree was not necessary. Professionals rarely had enough input in policy and strategy to fortify their monopolies. Professional education also suffered from budget cuts and the benign neglect of donor organizations and technical assistance agencies in the 1980s and 1990s. In many countries it was the time-honored methods of employment in politics and commercial enterprise that provided a large measure of continued success, which produced other kinds of professionals like accountants and insurers. Given some of these difficulties and the rise of internationally funded NGOs, it is not surprising that the percentage of professional work done in Africa by imported foreign "experts" rose significantly in the late twentieth century.

Professionals' relationships with NGOs intensified in the era of privatization. In the 1980s some governments contracted out basic services to NGOs and mission organizations, making them the principal employers of professionals. This migration into the private sector accelerated the defunding of the public sector, while donor projects frequently became opportunities for professional collection of rents. In some countries, where the geographic mobility of professionals was constrained, limited opportunities for professional advancement fostered competition and illegal or otherwise unsavory attempts to monopolize power in those institutions where professionals were able to find employment. Indeed a relationship was noted between the lack of sufficient numbers of professionals in certain fields, and the availability of other rent-seeking opportunities. Consequently numerous African governments were plagued by corruption, patronage, inflated public payrolls, fiscal scarcity, shortages of available inputs into infrastructure, and weak performance rewards. As a result, military professionalism, as an intensive apparatus for state control and personnel- or resource-exploitation, was paradoxically tied to weak nation-state institutions for popular participation.

Second, unemployment and international wage differences caused a "brain drain" from Africa. Political and economic instability, known to cause the flight of capital, also encouraged the emigration of qualified professionals. According to UN estimates, between 1960 and 1975 some 27,000 well-educated Africans departed for the North, between 1975 and 1984 another 40,000 left, increasing to 80,000 in 1987, and an average of 20,000 departed from Africa every year from 1990. Egypt alone has lost 45,000 scientists since 1950. In fields like medicine, the brain drain limited the number of specialists present on the continent, as many skilled professionals could find better paying employment outside their home countries, a situation made more probable by training abroad. Those who remained in their country of origin often were recruited by NGOs and other international agencies, or had neither popular nor economic standing. This lack pushed professionals into the post-colonial bureaucracy, the university system, and an increasing number of NGOs and multinational institutions. In order to stem the flow governments subsidized professionals by guaranteeing them positions. This served as a way of recuperating educational investments that would be lost if those individuals emigrated. Such investment in professional education was necessarily high because of recurrent costs, low efficiency, low quality, lack of relevance to national development needs, and an excess supply of trained personnel. In the era of privatization in the 1990s the recuperation of these costs was abandoned in favor of avoiding incurring them in the first place. Thus various mechanisms of structural adjustment were instituted to cut education budgets, reduce enrollment, and decrease the number of professionals available.

Finally, almost universally across Africa there has been a 10 to 20 percent lower enrolment in professional education for women than for men; as late as 1992 education, medicine, and law were the primary professions for women. Indeed women were disproportionately represented among the ranks of teachers and nurse/midwives. Many of the gender disparities in the ranks of professionals were related to social differences between traditional African models of gender relations and those learned in higher education. These differences were suggested by the fact that friendships and marriages for professionals were frequently among those in the same stratum of class and education. In addition professional development was correlated with weakening kinship bonds, the loss of respect for older people, and failure to follow traditional rituals.

See also: architecture; education: colonial; education: post-independence; health and disease; intellectuals: colonial; intellectuals: post-independence

Further reading

Kasongo-Ngoy, M.M. (1989) *Capital scolaire et pouvoir social en Afrique*, Paris: L'Harmattan.

Mafeje, A. (1994) "Les intellectuels africains: origine et options sociales," in M. Diouf and M. Mamdani (eds.), *Liberté académique en Afrique*, Dakar: CODESRIA.

Mamdani, M. (1994) "L'intelligentsia, l'état et les mouvements sociaux en Afrique," in M. Diouf and M. Mamdani (eds.), *Liberté académique en Afrique*, Dakar: CODESRIA.

Mukonoweshuro, E.G. (1993) *Colonialism, Class Formation and Underdevelopment in Sierra Leone*, Lanham: University Press of America.

Nyquist, T.E. (1983) *African Middle-Class Elite*, Occasional Paper No. 28, Grahamstown: Institute of Social and Economic Research, Rhodes University.

Zghal, A. *et al.* (1980) *Les classes moyennes au Maghreb*, Paris: Editions du Centre National de la Recherche Scientifique.

BJORN WESTGARD

R

Rabat, Morocco

Rabat is the capital of **Morocco**. The city was made the administrative capital after the establishment of the French protectorate in 1912. Rabat is also one of the four imperial cities of Morocco, along with Fes, Marrakesh, and Meknes. Rabati identify themselves with the Moorish population expelled from Spain between 1492 and 1497. The city is located on the Atlantic Coast, alongside the Bou Regreg River that divides it from Sale, the other Moorish city. In 1999 both sides of the river were inhabited by an estimated 1,608,000 people. Rabat houses Morocco's central administration, foreign embassies, and international organizations, as well as the national library, the archeological museum, the national theater, the conservatory of music, the national zoo, the first modern Moroccan university (Mohammed V), and many other sports facilities and tourist attractions. Rabat also possesses large green spaces and forests.

The history of the city goes back 3,000 years to the time of Phoenician expansion. Rabat was built in the tenth century BC, near the ruin of an ancient Roman harbor at the month of Bou Regreg. The city owes its flowering to Sultan Yakub el-Mansur, who made it the capital of the Almohad Empire, and the base for his conquests of Spain and **North Africa** in the twelfth century. This history is still visible in the city's architecture, especially in its walls, Jewish quarters (Mellah), casbahs, and Moorish districts. The Hassan Tower, left uncompleted by el-Mansur, is testimony to Rabat's historical prestige.

The French decision to make Rabat their capital was meant to marginalize Fes, the former capital, and thereby undermine its intellectual and symbolic supremacy. The adoption of new allies by the French necessitated the marginalization of the traditional elite, who were educated in the Qaraouine university of Fes. The French established modern centers for anthropological and Amazigh studies, and created the first local French periodicals about Morocco. *Hesperis Journal* was one of the main sources of knowledge gathered in this period about the Arabic, Jewish, and Amazigh populations of Morocco. The periodical continued after the independence of Morocco, under the name *Hesperis Tamuda*.

By the end of the twentieth century the majority of the Rabati population was composed of civil servants, students, administrators, and diplomats. This mix provided the city with its cosmopolitan character. Rabat continued to show sympathy with leftist political parties and unions during the municipal and legislative elections of the 1990s, while its progressive character was visible on the streets and beaches where fashionably dressed young men and women reflected the city's interaction with transnational agents and organizations, and demonstrated the extent of the middle classes in Rabat. But far from the center and residential areas one could see newly urbanized and poor rural populations. An emerging class of laborers followed the industrialization of the city in the 1980s and 1990s. Besides the traditional manufacturing sectors of leather handicrafts, pottery, and jewelry, industrial activities included the garment industry, fish processing, and carpet-making. Indeed Rabati women produced a special kind of carpet and embroidery, both of which were named Rabati.

The cosmopolitan and multicultural character of Rabat was one of the most distinctive features of the city from the 1980s. Along with **Casablanca**, Rabat was home to the major Moroccan **non-governmental organizations** (NGOs) for human and women's rights. NGOs in many other fields also established offices in Rabat, in close proximity to the statistical research bureaux. These organizations influenced the modern history of Rabat by organizing several peaceful, but massive, marches, culminating in 2000 with a march in favor of changes to family law.

Further reading

Abu-Lughod, J.L. (1980) *Rabat: Urban Apartheid in Morocco*, Princeton: Princeton University Press.

ZAKIA SALIME

race and ethnicity

Many think of race as a biological identity and ethnicity as a cultural identity. The debate focuses on whether one can indeed speak of "races" biologically, and whether "culture" should be understood as primordial or as historically constructed. In this entry I will shift the ground and discuss "race" and "ethnicity" as political identities, imposed through the force of colonial law, and reproduced by law and the state in the post-colonial period.

Legal and political identities

To understand how political identities may be defined through the force of law, let us use an African example that could be taken from any indirect rule colony in the first half of the twentieth century. In most African colonies the census classified the population into two broad, overall groups. One group was made up of what were called *races*, the other of what were referred to as *tribes*. This single distinction illuminates the technology of colonial rule. Five observations can help elaborate this technology.

First, why does the census divide the population into two kinds of exclusive groups, some tagged as races and others as tribes? On examination one can discern a clear pattern: *non-natives* are tagged as races, whereas *natives* are said to belong to tribes. Races comprised those not indigenous to Africa (Europeans, Asians), or those who were constructed as not indigenous (Arabs, coloreds, Tutsi). Tribes – called "ethnic groups" in the post-colonial period – were all those defined as indigenous in origin. The state thus distinguished between those not indigenous (races) and those indigenous (tribes).

Second, this distinction had direct legal significance. All races were governed under a single body of law: the civil law. True, civil law was full of discriminations: racial discrimination distinguished between *master races* (Europeans) and *subject races* (Asians, Arabs, coloreds, and so on), the point being to exclude subject races from the exercise of certain rights that were considered the prerogative only of members of the master race. But this discrimination needs to be understood as internal to civil law, which included all races. This, however, was not true of tribes and "customary law." There was never a single customary law to govern all "tribes" or natives as one racialized group. Each tribe was ruled under a separate set of laws: customary law. It was said that tradition was tribal. Natives must thus be divided into tribes, with each tribe governed by a body of law that reflected its own traditions. Yet most would agree that the cultural difference between races – such as whites, Asians, and Arabs – was greater than that between different tribes. To begin with, different races spoke different languages that were mutually unintelligible. Often they practiced different religions. They also came from different parts of the world, each with their own historical archive. Different tribes, in contrast, were neighbors and usually spoke languages that were mutually intelligible.

My point is simple: Even if races were as different culturally as whites, Asians, and Arabs, they were ruled under a single, imported European body of law, called civil law. Even if their languages were similar and mutually intelligible, tribes were governed under separate laws, called customary laws, which were in turn administered by ethnically distinct native authorities. With races the cultural difference was not translated into separate legal systems. Instead it was contained, even negotiated, within a single legal system, and was enforced by a single administrative authority. But with ethnicities the case was the opposite: Cultural difference was reinforced, exaggerated, built up into different legal systems and, indeed, separate administrative and political authorities. In a nutshell different races were meant to have a common future; different ethnicities were not.

My third observation: The two legal systems were entirely different in orientation. We can understand the difference by contrasting English common law with colonial customary law. English common law was presumed to change with circumstances. It claimed to recognize different interests and interpretations. But customary law in the colonies assumed the opposite. It assumed that law must not change with changing circumstances. Rather, any change was considered prima facie evidence of corruption. Both the laws and the enforcing authorities were called "traditional." Indeed Western colonial powers were far more concerned to establish the traditional credentials of their native allies than they were to define the content of tradition. Their preoccupation was with defining, locating, and anointing the traditional authority. Most importantly traditional authority in the colonial era was always defined in the singular. We need to remember that most African colonies did not have the political history of an absolutist state. Instead of a single state authority whose writ was considered law in all social domains, the practice was for different authorities to define separate traditions in different domains of social life. The rule-defining authority thus differed from one social domain to another; besides chiefs, the definers of tradition could include women's groups, age groups, clans, religious groups, and so on. The big change during the colonial period was that Western colonial powers exalted a single authority, called "the chief," as *the* traditional authority. Marked by two characteristics, age and gender, the authority of the chief was inevitably patriarchal. As David Laitin (1986) showed in his study of Yorubaland, the practice was to look for those local elites most in danger of being sidelined, local elites that had legitimacy but lacked authority. Their position was then sanctified, their point of view enforced as customary, and their authority in law reinforced as traditional.

My claim is that the colonial powers were the first fundamentalists of the modern period. They were the first to advance and put into practice the two propositions that (1) every colonized group has an original and pure tradition, whether religious or ethnic; and (2) every colonized group must be made to return to that original condition, and that return must be enforced by law. Put together these two propositions constitute the basic platform of every religious or ethnic fundamentalism in the post-colonial world.

Fourth, this legal project needs to be understood as part of a political project. The political project was highlighted by the central claim of the indirect-rule state that natives are by nature tribal. Even though it was first fully implemented by Britain in those African lands it colonized in the late nineteenth century in the aftermath of the Berlin Conference, this claim had already been made by Sir Henry Maine, Law Member of the Viceroy's Commission in post-1857 India. To quote Maine from *Ancient Law*:

> I repeat the definition of a primitive society given before. It has for its units, not individuals, but groups of men united by the reality or the fiction of blood-relationship.
>
> (Maine 1867: 178)

In time, this very claim that natives are by nature tribal, would be advanced as a reason why African colonies have no majority, but only tribal minorities. This claim needs to be understood as political, not because it is not true, but because this truth does not reflect an original fact. It is rather a fact created politically, and enforced legally.

It is not that ethnicity did not exist in African societies prior to colonialism; it did. I want to distinguish between ethnicity as a cultural identity – an identity based on a shared culture – from ethnicity as a political identity. Ethnicity as a cultural identity is consensual, but when ethnicity becomes a political identity the legal and administrative organs

 race and ethnicity

of the state enforce it. After making a distinction between ethnic groups, between those considered indigenous and those not, these organs proceed to discriminate between them: those considered indigenous are granted rights considered "customary," such as the right to use land, but those considered not indigenous – no matter how long they may have been resident in the land – are denied these same rights. When the political authority and the law it enforces identify subjects ethnically and discriminate between them, then ethnicity turns into a legal and political identity.

This takes me to my fifth observation. When law imposes a cultural difference, the difference becomes reified. Prevented from changing, it becomes frozen. But as the basis of legal discrimination between those who are said to belong and those said not to belong, between insiders entitled to customary rights and outsiders deprived of these rights, these culturally symbolic differences become political.

The distinction between cultural and political identities is important for this argument. As a rule, cultural identities are non-coercive, consensual, voluntary, and can be multiple. All postmodernist talk of hybridity and multiple identities belongs to the domain of culture. Once enforced by law, however, identities cease to be all of these. A legal identity is not voluntary, nor is it multiple. The law recognizes you as one and no other. Once it is enforced legally, cultural identity turns into a legal and political identity. Such an identity cannot be considered a vestige of tradition because of its ancient genealogy, nor can it be dismissed as just an invention of the colonial power because of its legal enforcement. On the one hand, even if grounded in long histories that precede colonialism, political ethnicity is no simple vestige of tradition; as a political identity, it is the outcome of an encounter with Western modernity mediated by colonial power. On the other hand, this political identity is not just invented, manufactured out of thin air; the raw material from which it is constructed is precisely the cultural history of the colonized.

Thus ethnicity as a political identity reflects both a connection with a history preceding colonialism and a remaking of that history by the colonial power. This is why we can neither simply embrace nor simply dismiss ethnicity as a political identity. We need, rather, to problematize it by a historicizing move. To make this point, I shall elaborate on the modern state and political identities.

Indirect rule and political identities

The modern state stands up to time by giving itself both a past and a future. The production of the past is the stuff of *history-writing*, just as the securing of a future is the domain of *law-making*. Between history-writing and law-making there is a strategic alliance. Law identifies agency in history. By enforcing group identities on individual subjects, the law institutionalizes group life.

The history of the modern state and the colonial project can be traced from a modest to an ambitious project, from *direct rule*, which was preoccupied with shaping elite preferences, to *indirect rule*, which aimed to shape popular preferences. Direct rule focused on native elites. It aimed to create native clones of Western modernity through a discourse of civilization and assimilation. In contrast indirect rule aimed to shape mass preferences through a discourse grounded in tradition. But indirect rule did not accept tradition benignly, as a historical given. It treated history as a raw material, putty from which to shape "genuine" tradition. Whereas direct rule was dogmatic and dismissed native tradition as backward and superstitious, indirect rule was analytical. The political project known as indirect rule aimed to unpack native tradition, to disentangle its different strands, to separate the authoritarian from the emancipatory. It was thereby able to repack tradition as authoritarian and ethnic, and to harness it to the colonial project. By repacking native passions and cultures selectively, it aimed to pit these very passions and cultures against one another.

Theoretically the experience of indirect rule should alert us to the relationship between culture and politics. When the raw material of political identity is drawn from the domain of culture, as in ethnic identity, it is the link between identity and power that allows us to understand how cultural identities are translated into political identities, and thus to distinguish between them. At the same time to historicize political identity by linking it to political power is to acknowledge that all political identities are historically transitory and all require a form of the state to be reproduced.

Let us return to the political identities created by colonialism in Africa: race and ethnicity. In the language of politics, races were identified as *settlers* and ethnic groups as *natives*. Settler (races) and native (tribes) were the core political identities created by colonialism. When natives organized against colonialism, in a movement we call nationalism, the key debates concerned the boundaries of the nation: Who was the nation? Did the political identity "settler" include only the master race (whites) or did it also include subject races (Asians, Arabs, coloreds, Tutsi)? The answer distinguished militant nationalism (by which settlers were identified only with the master race, the colonizers) and conservative nationalism (which equated settlers with all those who were non-indigenous, all those defined by colonial law as races).

What is at stake in this argument? Settlers and natives were synonymous with races and tribes (ethnic groups) as defined in colonial law. If we understand this, it then follows that settler and native go together; there can be no settler without a native, and vice versa. Either the two are reproduced together, or the two are abolished together. What produces them as political identities is a form of the state that valorizes one's origin. The colonial state, for example, valued the fact of being non-indigenous and gave rights to the non-indigenous (races), whereas it stigmatized the indigenous (tribes) and deprived them of political rights. To do away with settler (race) and native (tribe) as political identities required no less than a political project that can transform the nature of the state as constructed by colonial power.

Lenin once chided Rosa Luxemburg with being so preoccupied with Polish nationalism that she could not see beyond it, and so risked being locked in the world of the rat and the cat. For the rat there is no animal bigger in the presence of the cat: neither lion, nor tiger, nor elephant; for the cat there is none more delicious than the rat. The political world set in motion by the modern state and modern colonialism also endlessly generates paired identities. For every settler there is a native. In a world where cats are few and rats are many, one way for cats to stabilize rule is to tag rats by tapping their historicity through a discourse on origins, indigenous and non-indigenous, ethnic and racial. This is why in a world where rats have belled cats, it is entirely possible that rats may still carry on living in the world as defined by cats, fired by the very identities generated by institutions created in the era of cats. The point is simple and yet fundamental: you can turn the world upside down, but still fail to change it. To change the world, you need to break out of the worldview of not just the cat, but also the rat; not only of the settler, but also of the native.

Political power and political identity: Majority and minority in politics

Writers on minority rights often tend to assume the existence of majorities and minorities as a given. They assume that cultural identity must translate into political identity; cultural minorities (ethnic groups) would thus inevitably translate into political minorities. I have argued differently. Instead of taking group identities as a given, I have tried to historicize the process of group formation. This has allowed me to distinguish cultural from political identities, by linking political identities to the process of state formation.

The proliferation of political minorities (as ethnic groups) in the post-independence African context was not a necessary reflection of the cultural map of Africa. Rather, this proliferation was the outcome of a particular form of the state, the indirect-rule state, whose genesis lies in the colonial period. The real distinction between race and ethnicity is not that between biology and culture, with race a false biological identity and ethnicity a true and historically created cultural identity. Rather, both race and ethnicity need to be understood as political identities in relation to a particular form of the state: race as a political identity of those constructed as not indigenous (settlers), and ethnicity as an identity of those constructed as indigenous (natives). Africa's real political challenge was to reform and thus sublate the form of the state that continued to reproduce race and ethnicity as political identities.

Colonial power not only shaped the agency of popular strata. It was also stamped on the agency of the intellectual. Colonial power was etched not only on the boundaries of the public sphere, it was also imprinted on the margins of scholarly works. Just as colonial power set into motion first the settler and then the native in the public sphere – settlers as races and natives as tribes – so it preoccupied the intellectual imagination with the question of *origins*. How origin was understood depended on the language of power, specifically on how power framed agency through customary law.

In the African context customary law framed agency – and "custom" – as ethnic. It is no mere coincidence that the post-colonial African preoccupation was with who was a native and who was not, and that the native imagination in post-colonial Africa tended to absorb the immigrant into a script of invasion. The challenge, I have argued, is neither to deny separate histories, nor to build on this separation. It is, rather, to distinguish our notion of political community from that of cultural community, and as a consequence to separate the discourse on political rights from that on cultural or historical origins. The challenge is to create a single political community and citizenship from diverse cultural and historical groups and identities.

See also: law; society: colonial; society: post-independence; state: colonial; state: post-independence

References and further reading

Appiah, K.A. (1992) *In My Father's House: Africa in the Philosophy of Culture*, New York and Oxford: Oxford University Press.

Césaire, A. (1972 [1955]) *Discourse on Colonialism*, New York: Monthly Review Press.

Fanon, F. (1967) *The Wretched of the Earth*, London: Penguin.

Hegel, G.W.F. (1991) "The Geographical Basis of History," *The Philosophy of History*, Buffalo: Prometheus Books.

Laitin, D. (1986) *Hegemony and Culture: Politics and Religious Change amongst the Yoruba*, Chicago: University of Chicago Press.

Maine, H. (1867) *Ancient Law: Its Connection with the Early History of Society and Its Relations to Modern Ideas*, London: James Murray.

Mamdani, M. (1996) *Citizen and Subject: Contemporary Africa and the Legacy of Late Colonialism*, Princeton: Princeton University Press.

—— (2001) *When Victims Become Killers: Colonialism, Nativism and Genocide in Rwanda*, Princeton: Princeton University Press.

MAHMOOD MAMDANI

radio and television

Colonial period

Radio, unlike television, was introduced into most African countries during the colonial period. The first African radio broadcast took place in **South Africa** in 1924, just two years after the British Broadcasting Corporation commenced its operations. This was followed in **Kenya** (1927), Southern Rhodesia (1932), and **Mozambique** (1933).

Radio had a narrow purpose during its early days. It helped disseminate news to Europeans about their countries. The four stations named above were, for example, set up exclusively for the white settler communities. Radio was especially important during the **Second World War**. It provided the fastest means for Europeans in Africa to keep track of developments on the war front, and for Africans to follow the fate of their compatriots serving in various places. It is interesting to note that during the war Africa served as a broadcast node for some of the colonial powers that were under occupation. The Free French, for example, set up transmitters in **Douala** and **Brazzaville** as a countervailing measure in response to pro-Vichy transmissions coming out of **Dakar**. In the same vein the London-based Free Belgian administration, acting as the legitimate government of its German-occupied home country, transmitted messages to its compatriots from a base in its colonial territory of Leopoldville in the Belgian Congo.

Another function of radio was entertainment, particularly for Europeans. It was also used to discourage political agitation and involvement among Africans. This political use of radio led to the initiation of indigenous language broadcasts, so that large numbers of Africans could understand the messages. The pace-setter in indigenous language broadcasts was Northern Rhodesia, from 1941.

By 1960 over a hundred African languages were being used for radio broadcasts on the continent. These were mostly in the British colonies, where official policy promoted the use of indigenous languages on the airwaves. This was in contrast to the French colonies, where local languages were not encouraged. Furthermore the geographical contiguity of the French colonies made it easy to broadcast to the various territories in a single lingua franca from a central location, by using relay stations.

In its early days radio ownership among Africans was limited. Sets were expensive and used valves, requiring large amounts of electricity, which was unavailable to most Africans. It is noteworthy that some chiefs were provided with radio sets by the colonial authorities, and many indigenous listeners accessed the medium at chiefs' palaces or local administrative centers.

The invention of the transistor in 1948 allowed more Africans to access radio. Transistor radios required less electricity than earlier sets and could run on relatively inexpensive, low-voltage batteries. They were also less bulky than their valve counterparts. Their portability and affordability gradually made them a common feature of the African landscape. To promote the use of radio sets within Africa, a small low-cost battery – the "Saucepan Special" – was marketed.

Radio transmission during the colonial period was the monopoly of the government, a system that, by and large, still characterizes the electronic media in most African countries. State control of the airwaves was due partly to the huge expense involved in establishing such media, but also to the desire to exercise absolute discretion over a medium with far-reaching capabilities. Radio's ability to reach a wide audience with a single transmission, and to do so instantaneously, made it a potent political instrument that could not be left in private hands. Control over broadcasting in the British colonies was devolved to "autonomous" statutory corporations only in the immediate pre-independence period, while the French colonial state did not flinch in its perception of broadcasting as an extension of state power and control.

Post-colonial period

Following independence African countries sought to harness radio as a tool for socioeconomic and political development. Under the rubric of developmental journalism, the media were expected to promote the developmental objectives of their states. On a continent where illiteracy rates were very high, radio was seen as the most effective way of disseminating development-support information.

In view of limited resources, most countries initially adopted short-wave transmission in order to reach their widely dispersed populations. Transmitters could be at a single location, from which information would be broadcast to outlying areas. To address the technical difficulties associated with short-wave transmissions, such as vulnerability to the vagaries of the weather and weak signals the farther away a receiver is from the source, many countries are introducing FM stations that allow better reception. Shortage of electricity, human resources, and relevant infrastructure remain the main constraints on the use of this broadcast technology. Apart from small island states, South Africa has gone farthest in providing a nationwide network of FM stations.

The post-colonial state tried to maintain its control over radio because it conferred power. Not surprisingly broadcasting stations were the first targets of any coup. Capturing the centralized broadcast station generally made political takeover a *fait accompli*.

The 1952 coup in **Egypt** marked the beginning of independent media suppression in Africa, as President Nasser nationalized the press and channeled it, exclusively, towards serving the interest of the Arab Socialist Party. By 1975 there were only five private radio stations on the continent outside of **North Africa** and the white-ruled territories in **Southern Africa**. Until the early 1990s, therefore, the electronic media were generally state-owned and served the interests of those in power. They were characterized by self-censorship, and constrained by the ideology of developmental journalism.

Television

As noted earlier, television is a post-colonial phenomenon, and stations were exclusively state-owned until the mid-1990s. In 1959 **Nigeria** was the first country in sub-Saharan Africa to introduce a television service, while **Botswana** was the latest to do so in 2000. Television sets long preceded television transmission in many countries. Thus Tanzanians who owned sets in the early 1990s could only use them in conjunction with VCRs to watch films, since the only television transmission station in **Tanzania** was a small one in Zanzibar.

Television has not experienced the rapid expansion in private operations that radio has seen since the early 1990s. This is due to the larger investment required, as well as the slower potential for recouping that investment. However, satellite television is growing as a service for the elite. Following the launch of the first ArabSat satellite in 1985, Egypt became the first North African country to establish a national satellite television service in 1990. The South African company Multichoice provides satellite television services to several countries in sub-Saharan Africa. There is also access to Microwave Multipoint Distribution System (MMDS) services in some cities, particularly in **francophone Africa**. In **Abidjan** 13 percent of households have access to this service, while 9 percent do in **Dakar**. There are, however, criticisms that the programs broadcast on these channels do not address matters relevant to the continent, but are filled with cheap, imported foreign programs that threaten local productions and African values.

This criticism is not unique to satellite and MMDS television. African television stations generally run significant amounts of foreign programs because they are ready-made and cheap, which makes them a convenient way for under-resourced stations to fill their airtime. In **Morocco**, for example, national production of television programs is estimated at less than 25 percent of the total output – and the quality of national productions leaves a lot to be desired.

It is important to recognize efforts towards regional collaboration in broadcasting. These include the Regional African Satellite Communications System (RASCOM), the Pan African Telecommunications Network (PANAFTEL), and the Union of National Radio and Television Organizations of Africa (URTNA). URTNA, which was established in 1962, seeks to address some of the concerns about foreign dominance of the continent's broadcasting landscape by promoting collaboration and exchange in areas such as program production, personnel training, and marketing.

The post-1990 period

The last decade of the twentieth century saw the emergence of various private radio stations. In **Ghana**, for example, there was an increase in private radio and television stations from none in 1993 to over forty radio stations and three television stations in 2000. By February 2000 the Moroccan government had received twenty-three applications requesting permission to establish private radio stations. This change in ownership and proliferation of private electronic media has its roots in the significant democratization trends of the early 1990s.

Despite the trend toward media liberalization, some countries (such as **Zimbabwe** and **Algeria**) refuse to ease state control of the electronic media. Hence, although many private stations offer alternative and critical views on issues, a large proportion of them seem content to restrict themselves to non-controversial areas, such as music, in order to avoid the wrath of the state. These fears are not unfounded. The director of news programming for the Voice of Palestine radio station in **Tunisia** was arrested in May 2000, ostensibly for incitement and defaming the president. In September 2000 the government in the **Democratic Republic of Congo** banned several radio stations, allegedly for their critical coverage of events in that country.

There is growth as well in the number of international broadcasters beaming signals to Africa. CNN, Sky, the BBC, and RFI are among the networks that have spread their operations deep into Africa. They have:

> expanded their broadcast range, not only with stronger and more effective transmitters, but also, in the case of radio, through using local

independent FM stations as subsidiary outlets relaying hours of their coverage.

(Fardon and Furniss 2000: 2)

Developments in communication technologies are changing the nature of African broadcasting. The internet is enabling some African radio and television stations to disseminate their programs, live or by demand, to geographically distant audiences around the globe. Digital radio broadcasts to a number of African countries have been made possible by the launch in 1998 of a satellite over Africa by Worldspace, a US-based company.

The number of radio sets in Africa grew from 2,640,000 in 1955 to 124,560,000 in 1995, and radio receivers in sub-Saharan Africa per 1,000 inhabitants increased from 94 in 1980 to 172 in 1996 (UNESCO 1998). Despite these strides, access to the electronic media remains restricted. Part of the reason for this, especially in the case of television, is the fact that most programs are in the colonial languages. This is due to the large foreign content in programming. Economic imperatives also compel the media, most of which depend on advertising revenues, to target an elite audience that tends to have such languages in common.

There are gender differences in access as well. Illiteracy figures among African males and females were 33.5 percent and 54 percent respectively in 1995 (UNESCO 1998). A larger proportion of women than men are therefore unable to benefit from the discourses and activities of the media, because of the limitations imposed by foreign languages. Overall the plight of rural women is the most severe, because they epitomize the intersection of poverty, illiteracy, patriarchal subjugation, and rural deprivation. The limited presence of rural radio stations means that the needs and views of those communities remain marginalized within the media. The high cost of television sets puts regular access to television programming out of the reach of many people, so overall radio provides the best way of reaching the majority of Africans. It does not suffer the financial problems associated with television, nor the literacy problems that newspapers face.

See also: press

References and further reading

Alabi, N. (2001) "The Windhoek Seminar: Ten Years On: Assessment, Challenges and Prospects," background paper on behalf of the West African Journalists Association, http://www.unesco.org/webworld/com_media/wpfd/2001_docs_en.html.

Bourgault, L.M. (1995) *Mass Media in Sub-Saharan Africa*, Bloomington and Indianapolis: Indiana University Press.

Fardon, R. and Furniss, G. (eds.) (2000) *African Broadcast Cultures*, Oxford: James Currey.

Faringer, G.L. (1991) *Press Freedom in Africa*, Westport: Praeger.

McFadden, P. (1998) "Examining Myths of a Democratic Media," *Review of African Political Economy* 78: 653–7.

Mytton, G. (1983) *Mass Communication in Africa*, London: Edward Arnold.

Tettey, W.J. (2001) "The Media and Democratization in Africa: Contributions, Constraints and Concerns of the Private Press," *Media, Culture and Society* 23, 1: 5–31.

UNESCO (1998) *UNESCO Statistical Yearbook 1998*, Paris: UNESCO.

WISDOM J. TETTEY

rain forest *see* tropical rain forest

refugees

During the first part of the twentieth century the international community defined "refugees" as people who were outside their country of origin and were without the protection of their state's government. The international community only included those European states that were signatories to various international instruments. Most Africans were under colonial rule, and the problems of African refugees were not addressed until after the **decolonization** process had begun in the 1950s. It is of interest to note that some African colonies, such as **Uganda**, became a sanctuary for European refugees during the **Second World War**. On the other hand, thousands of Europeans, Jews, and people of Indian, Pakistani, and Arab descent were forced into exile from Africa.

Later in the twentieth century the **United Nations** (UN) initially defined a refugee as a person who had a well-founded fear of persecution based on race, nationality, religion, membership of a particular social group, or political opinion. A refugee's persecution had to be based on events that occurred in Europe prior to 1951. Thus African refugees were not covered by the definition. Furthermore refugees had to reside outside their country of national origin. This definition was later revised in 1967 to include people outside Europe and people who became refugees after 1951. However, the amended definition excluded many Africans who had been persecuted or displaced by violence or natural disasters. The **Organization of African Unity** (OAU) recognized these weaknesses and expanded the definition in 1969 to include people who were externally or internally displaced due to external aggression, occupation, foreign domination, or events that disturbed public order. However, neither organization addressed the consequences of gender-based persecution, even though many African women become refugees because of forms of gender-based persecution that include rape and other forms of sexual violence.

Moreover, regardless of international definitions and instruments, it was still the asylum state that granted or denied refugee status. Often the asylum state took into consideration the political, economic, social, environmental, and diplomatic consequences of hosting refugees before they granted asylum. Therefore the determination of refugee status was wrapped up in domestic politics, rather than being a matter of international law.

Although the plight of African refugees was not addressed by the international community until the 1960s, various developments forced thousands of people to flee their homelands. Colonialism and its accompanying brutalities and exploitation were the main producers of refugees in the first half of the twentieth century. During the early years of the twentieth century Europeans continued to invade all parts of Africa in an effort to impose colonial rule. Africans tried to resist these invasions, and many became refugees. The confiscation of Africans' land, and the subsequent expulsion of Africans from their homelands to make room for European settlers or European farms and plantations, also produced many refugees. The forced recruitment of African labor to mine copper, diamonds, gold, and other minerals contributed to the refugee population too, along with the use of conscripted labor for public works projects. In addition thousands of Africans were forced from their places of origin to work on European plantations to produce various cash crops, including coffee, sugar, cocoa, and rubber. Finally, the various taxes imposed by the colonial governments (such as hut, cattle, and poll taxes) led many people into exile.

The African resistance to colonial rule produced refugees both before and after the Second World War. For example, **Uganda**, which was still under British rule in 1954, became host to refugees from **Kenya** who were fleeing the aftermath of the Mau Mau rebellion. **Zambia**, which was also a British colony, was host to refugees from throughout **Southern Africa**. The most significant manifestation of anti-colonial sentiment – the wars of national liberation – produced large refugee movements. The war against the French in **Algeria** was particularly brutal, and many people became refugees. The liberation struggles against Portuguese rule in the colonies of **Mozambique**, **Angola**, and **Guinea-Bissau** pushed thousands of people across borders during the 1960s and 1970s. Liberation struggles in Southern Africa against the minority regimes in Rhodesia, **Namibia**, and **South Africa** also created large influxes of refugees.

After most African colonies became independent, the ramifications of decolonization began to become apparent. Some parts of Africa were engulfed by **human rights** violations, ethnic conflict, religious intolerance, political instability, civil war, and secessionist movements. National borders that had been created arbitrarily by the Europeans in the nineteenth century were also sometimes disputed. If these disputes were not settled peacefully and instead military operations were undertaken, people inevitably fled to neighboring countries as refugees. While these post-independence conflicts occurred between African nationals within the context of sovereign nations, the involvement of other actors should not be overlooked. For example, African nationals were not totally responsible for the civil wars and accompanying human rights violations that produced millions of refugees in the Horn of Africa during the twentieth century. The rivalry between the two superpowers – the United States and the Soviet Union – played a significant role in the conflict between **Somalia** and **Ethiopia**, and in the civil wars in both countries. The proliferation of weapons that fueled the conflict in the region was generated by the superpowers. The liberation struggles in Southern Africa were drawn out by the involvement of the United States, China, and the Soviet Union, as well as by the apartheid government of South Africa, which engaged in armed interventions in neighboring countries and supported various rebel groups in its efforts to rid the region of communism.

During the last four decades of the twentieth century many African countries were both producing and receiving refugees. The root causes of these refugee movements included border disputes, civil wars, ethnic conflicts, human rights violations, drought, and famine. They included refugee movements generated by the Nigerian civil war, by border disputes between Morocco and Algeria, by the crisis in **Congo**, by ethnic disputes in **Rwanda** and **Burundi**, by civil war in **Liberia** and **Sierra Leone**. Organizations were established throughout Africa in response to repressive governments and governments that refused to heed calls for self-determination. Often conflicts between these governments and the opposition groups destroyed the infrastructure of the countries they were fighting over. For example, the civil war in **Sudan** between the government and various factions destroyed most of the schools, health facilities, roads, and bridges in the southern part of the country. Economic activity came to a standstill as thousands of civilians were forced to flee. The same can be said for any country in Africa that has experienced a civil war that spawned a refugee crisis. The civil wars in Angola and Mozambique, as well as the military raids by the apartheid government of South Africa into other countries in the region, destroyed roads, bridges, and transportation links, thereby affecting the economic activities of neighboring countries too, including **Zimbabwe**, **Malawi**, and **Zambia**.

The countries throughout Africa that hosted these thousands of refugees experienced a number of economic and environmental problems, along with political and social problems that made life for refugees very precarious. When countries faced economic crises, refugees, illegal aliens, immigrants, and others who were considered "foreign" were often blamed when, in fact, both internal and external factors were the cause of decline in most African economies. Nevertheless, reduced budgets meant that fewer social services were available to citizens, and refugees were viewed as competitors for a shrinking pool of resources. Hostilities often developed when refugees and nationals had to compete for food relief, housing, land, police protection, medical and educational facilities.

Several host communities and governments called for the repatriation – even forced deportation – of refugees when environmental problems developed. The bulk of African refugees came from rural areas in their countries of origin. Many of them were therefore farmers and pastoralists who relied on the land and animals for their livelihood, with many of them bringing their livestock with them. This increase in the number of people and animals in areas that were experiencing drought conditions exacerbated already existing environmental problems, with scarce grazing land and water resources becoming overburdened. For example, the western regions of **Tanzania** experienced severe environmental problems in the 1990s as large influxes of refugees from Rwanda, Burundi, and the Democratic Republic of Congo sought safety from the ethnic conflicts and civil wars in their homelands. Following the 1994 **genocide** in Rwanda, thousands of refugees crossed the border in a very short period of time. Deforestation occurred after refugees cut down hundreds of trees for firewood, charcoal, and shelter.

Security issues in or around host communities became political issues in some African countries. In other words many host communities and their governments argued that refugees were the cause of increased levels of violence that threatened internal security. There were many instances of refugees who crossed into neighboring countries with weapons that they used against members of those host communities or other refugees to commit armed robbery, rape, and even murder. Many host governments therefore adopted policies that forced refugees into camps, restricted their mobility, or forcibly deported them. Host governments had the responsibility to protect refugees, but in reality they often did not have the capacity, resources, or political will to uphold either their own laws or their obligations under international law regarding refugees.

During the second part of the twentieth century Africa's refugee population disproportionately consisted of women and children. Many of the women fled because they had witnessed human rights violations, were the victims of human rights violations, feared gender-based persecution such as rape, or had been affected by natural disasters. Many of the women fled alone, leaving them vulnerable to sexual and physical violence during their flight to safety – or even after they reached a country of asylum. There were many cases of refugee women being sexually assaulted by security and military personnel, members of host communities, or other refugees in camps. There were many medical and psychological problems associated with this type of violence, including sexually transmitted diseases, unwanted pregnancies, isolation, and depression. Many women became victims of sexual assault when they were collecting firewood and water. As convenient sources of firewood were depleted, the women had to walk longer distances from the camps, putting them at greater risk of sexual assault and other forms of physical violence. Women were also at risk of rape and physical abuse in several areas of the refugee experience: sexual favors might be demanded in exchange for documentation, assistance, or offers of protection. Women's safety was also endangered when they were put in closed detention centers alongside regular prisoners. Finally, some refugee women were forced into prostitution for their economic survival, or to get food, basic necessities, and documentation.

Three permanent solutions to global refugee problems were devised in the twentieth century: resettlement in a third country, local integration, and repatriation. The first solution – resettlement – proved unacceptable, especially to Western countries. Local integration was quite successful in some countries of asylum, such as Tanzania, Kenya, and Sudan. These countries had generous asylum policies that provided land, educational and health facilities, economic opportunities, and at times even citizenship. However, by the end of the twentieth century many African governments' asylum policies had shifted from being hospitable to being hostile, with repatriation increasingly seeming the most attractive solution to many African host governments and communities. However, there were instances of refugees, forcibly repatriated to countries that were still experiencing civil unrest, who were killed or injured as a result.

Further reading

Adelman, H. and Sorenson, J. (eds.) (1994) *African Refugees: Development Aid and Repatriation*, Boulder: Westview Press.

Beyani, C. and Stringer, C. (1995) *African Exodus*, New York: Lawyers Committee for Human Rights.

Harrell-Bond, B. (1986) *Imposing Aid: Emergency Assistance to Refugees*, New York: Oxford University Press.

Kibreab, G. (1985) *African Refugees: Reflections on the African Refugee Problem*, Trenton: Africa World Press Inc.

CASSANDRA RACHEL VENEY

regional integration

The quest for regional integration on the African continent is an ongoing challenge, rooted in multiple traditions, and having different trajectories. Regionalism has both an external and an internal logic. First, a region may be a phenomenon imposed from the outside. Regions were formed, for example, during the colonial period or during the **Cold War** under the pressure of military and economic alliances. In Africa the external imposition and composition of regions was largely shaped by the colonial experience, but it was reinforced during the post-colonial period. Regional organizations such as the **Central African Federation**, the Southern African Customs Union (SACU), and the regional bodies prevalent in French West and Equatorial Africa had specific colonial heritages, and were formed for the protection and promotion of white settler and colonial interests. The **League of Arab States**, which has a number of African member-states, grew in strength against the specific backdrop of the Cold War.

Regions, in addition, generally have an internal logic and coherence, binding nations with threads of commonality. The notion of a region usually implies some form of territorial contiguity, although regions in Africa were also delineated along historic, political, or linguistic lines. The **Organization of African Unity** (OAU), in recognition of these arbitrary definitions, generally divided Africa into five regions: East, West, North, South, and Central. Often the member-states of African regional organizations were linked through a particular functional unity, derived from colonial networks of labor migration, trade, or communication. The **East African Community** (EAC), the **Common Market for Eastern and Southern Africa** (COMESA), and the **Southern African Development Community** (SADC) are good examples of regional organizations formed with this particular background. Interestingly, many regional organizations in Eastern, Central or Southern Africa were formed either in support of or in opposition to the industrial/mineral economy of **South Africa**.

Attempts at post-colonial regional integration had to deal with one particular question: the dilemma of colonial borders. Following the Berlin Conference of 1884–5 African colonies were formed as territories of European conquest and settlement. The colonial state, therefore, was very much a creation of European history in Africa – a fact not lost on many Africans throughout the wars of resistance against settler colonialism in particular. Even though all boundaries throughout the world are more or less artificial, it is significant to note what was different about the state in Africa. The African state was the product of a history of conquest, and that specific alien conquest faced a crisis of legitimacy and was directly challenged by the **nationalist movements**.

The response of African scholars and political leaders to the above-stated ironies was to embrace **Pan-Africanism**. A Pan-Africanist ethos enveloped the relations among African states as they gained independence, leading to the formation of the OAU on 25 May 1963. In order to understand Africa's international relations, it is instructive to look at the Charter of the OAU: Of the seven principles guiding the organization, the OAU's commitment to the total liberation of the African continent looms large.

The OAU, now titled the African Union (AU), was founded as a compromise organization, bringing together two divergent trends that had emerged during the struggle for **decolonization**. The first trend, promoted by the "Casablanca Group" of newly independent states, supported a Pan-Africanist vision, pushing for the abolition of borders in a movement towards a "United States of Africa." The second trend was promoted by the "Brazzaville Group" and "Monrovia Group." They argued for a looser federation of states, founded on the basis of sovereign equality.

The question of borders was one of the most sensitive for the OAU, and the member-states decided in 1964 that the frontiers inherited from colonial times would not be subject to alteration. The crisis of legitimacy that alien conquest had faced was now enshrined in the major instrument of a continental body, and subsequently of regional bodies such as the Economic Community of West African States (ECOWAS), the SADC, and the EAC, leaving a very complicated legacy for post-colonial regimes. This position taken by the OAU, with many African nations still under colonial rule, was taken for very pragmatic reasons. These included the fear of neo-colonialism – in other words, the promotion of "Great Power" interests through proxy governments – and the risk posed by secessionist or irredentist claims to the economic and political stability of newly independent states.

Taking this into cognizance, regional integration in Africa in many senses sought to bridge the two contradictory impulses – that is, promotion of a Pan-Africanist vision, on the one hand, and on the other the defense of territorial integrity and sovereignty in the face of possible militarism and economic domination. The regional approach was a gradualist movement toward broader continental integration, but at the same time it was an approach that strove to preserve the right of African peoples to negotiate and redefine sovereignty in the face of existing definitions. In other words this regionalism model allowed African nationalism both to preserve its age-old Pan-African ideals and to realize the pressing dreams of building new nation-states.

The OAU, being a continental body, had important relationships with the various regional arrangements. Existing bodies included the Inter-Governmental Authority on Drought and Development (IGADD), the Central African Customs Union (UDEAC), the Maghreb Union, EAC, SADC, SACU, and COMESA. Officially these regional bodies were supposed to constitute stepping stones towards the African Economic Community (AEC), now the African Union, as agreed at the OAU Summit in **Harare**, **Zimbabwe**, in 1997. This was a more informal understanding of the role of regional bodies on the continent. However, after SADC was formed in 1992, and especially with South Africa set to become a new member of it, its potential led to calls for such smaller bodies to constitute organizations with a *raison d'être* that was separate from the African Union. The resuscitation of the EAC in 2000, the maintenance of the CFA franc zone in former French West and Equatorial Africa, and the growing strength of Maghreb Union and ECOWAS seemed to indicate that there was a significant tension between differing conceptions of regional integration. Were regional bodies truly stepping stones toward a wider Pan-Africanist end, or were these institutions becoming ends in themselves? Would regional organizations inadvertently further balkanize Africa?

This paradox had important implications at the regional level. First, there were two competing viewpoints on regional integration in Africa. The first viewpoint was exemplified by the Lagos Plan of Action (LPA), signed in 1980 by African heads of state and government. This framework, developed by the OAU, was similar to what is referred to as a "closed" model of integration, under which industrialization (as well as infant industry protection and development) is the cornerstone of cooperation. Soon after the LPA was announced, the World Bank in 1981 produced *Accelerated Development in Sub-Saharan Africa: An Agenda for Action*, also known as the Berg Report. This report essentially advocated a model of regional integration that promoted liberal market reforms in Africa, and free trade on a non-preferential basis. This model was based on the presumption, derived from the neo-liberal paradigm, that economic liberalization and interdependence promoted security and stability, mainly by pressurizing governments towards institutionalized cooperation by creating specific material incentives and disincentives.

The record of regional mechanisms such as COMESA, SADC, and EAC, which essentially followed the model proposed by the Berg Report, presents a complicated picture. These regional bodies were largely donor-supported and dependent regional arrangements, and therefore the implications of allowing an unfettered "market mechanism" to operate in highly dependent and vulnerable economies seems highly problematic. Who were the agents of market reform, and to whom were they responsible? This particular model of regional integration led to interdependence and inequality that could undermine regional security. The EAC is a classic example of the difficulties facing such regional organizations: it collapsed in 1979 due to socioeconomic and, subsequently, political pressure. In 1963 the Central African Federation also had collapsed, in part because of disparities between member-states, especially the different levels of benefit accruing to the participants.

In the case of SACU, the custom's union was designed specifically to benefit South Africa at the expense of **Botswana**, **Swaziland**, **Lesotho**, and **Namibia**. Following the elimination of apartheid and the first democratic elections in South Africa in 1994, SACU was under pressure to renegotiate the terms of revenue-sharing. Regional integration had obvious implications for the citizens of the constituent member-states, both positively and negatively. Regional integration could lead to the freer movement of both people and goods, eliminating visa requirements for travel and lowering barriers to trade. Increasingly ECOWAS was noted as a body in which barriers to free movement had been significantly lowered. At the same time, in particular for the citizens of vulnerable economies, regional integration without careful regulation could lead to deepening inequity and poverty, and regional schemes that had unfavorable consequences for a country's citizens were invariably abandoned.

The OAU was transformed into the African Union on 2 March 2001 at the OAU's 5th Extraordinary Summit, through the Constitutive Act of the African Union that had previously been adopted at the July 2000 Lome Summit. In Article 3 of the Constitutive Act, it is noted that one of the objectives of the Africa Union is to "coordinate and harmonize the policies between the existing and future Regional Economic Communities for the gradual attainment of the objectives of the Union." This clearly recognised that the processes of economic and political integration needed to be accelerated, but the mechanisms through which this integration would take place were not outlined. This omission was probably deliberate, reflecting the tension between competing notions of the purpose of African regional organizations. The key for regional integration in Africa, therefore, lay in recognising the interaction between domestic, regional, and continental issues, and the creative management of real and imagined tensions.

Thus, after independence, African regional integration schemes were confronted by five main challenges. First, there was the problem of how to distribute benefits equally among member-states that often varied in size and level of development. Second, there were institutional and organizational difficulties related to decision-making. The heads of state in whom decision-making powers were vested were, for obvious reasons, more interested in preserving state sovereignty than ceding effective power to regional bodies. Member-states usually also belonged to multiple regional organizations that covered different parts of the same region, as was the case with COMESA and SADC, leading to conflicting loyalties. Third, there were ideological and political challenges, especially at the height of the Cold War, during which member-states would typically espouse conflicting ideologies – capitalist or socialist – and political systems – military regimes, one-party regimes, and semi-democratic regimes. Under such circumstances it became difficult to create a common sense of purpose, or to agree on programs for change. Fourth, there was the question of external dependence and interference, in which continued "special" commercial and economic relationships between African states and their former colonial powers undermined regional integration, as happened with the francophone/anglophone divide in ECOWAS that was orchestrated by France. Finally, there was lack of political will: African leaders often paid little more than lip-service to the idea of regional integration, reflecting an absence of pressure from below.

References and further reading

Bach, D.C. (ed.) (1999) *Regionalisation in Africa: Integration and Disintegration*, Oxford: James Currey.

Evans, D., Holmes, P. and Mandaza, I. (1999) *SADC: The Costs of Non-Integration*, Harare: Sapes Books.

Hettne, B. and Söderbaum, F. (1998) "The New Regionalism Approach," *Politeia* 17, 3: 6–21.

Mistry, P.S. (2000) "Africa's Record of Regional Cooperation and Integration," *African Affairs* 99, 397: 553–73.

Organization of African Unity (1992) *Resolving Conflicts in Africa: Proposals for Action*, Addis Ababa: OAU.

World Bank (1981) *Accelerated Development in Sub-Saharan Africa: An Agenda for Action*, Washington, D.C.: World Bank.

TANDEKA NKIWANE

religions, African *see* African religions

Rhodesia, Northern *see* Zambia

Rhodesia, Southern *see* Zimbabwe

Rift Valley

The Great Rift Valley is a geological fault that runs from Jordan Valley in the Middle East across the Red Sea into the vast lowlands of eastern and southern Africa. Approximately 8,700 kilometers long, it is a narrow landmass that sheers through **Ethiopia**, **Kenya**, **Tanzania**, **Malawi**, and **Mozambique**. The Rift Valley traverses various ecological zones, the most distinct physical features being chains of lakes expanding over magnificent depressions, volcanic systems, and in eastern Africa the highland areas. Some of these lakes are fresh water, fed by small and large streams, and have for centuries sustained local fishing, herding, and farming. More recently they have supported a growing industry in ecotourism.

The natural beauties of the Rift Valley are captured in ubiquitous brochures: bird-watching near Lake Nakuru or safaris in the National Parks of Kenya, the Serengeti-Mara in Tanzania, the vast tea, sugarcane, and coffee plantations in Malawi. These present a reassuring image that all is well in the Rift Valley, but the image more often exposed by **non-governmental organizations** and academics is of famine, drought, environmental degradation, and the marginalization of the valley's major ethnic groups. This "rift" in the representation of the Rift Valley is a candid reminder of the legacy of colonialism, and of synchronic changes in the historical and political objectives of post-colonial modes of resource exploitation. These objectives took shape with the increasing penetration of Europeans into the interior of Africa, in conjunction with evolving colonial and post-colonial requirements for more labor, land, or other resources.

In pre-colonial Africa, trade among the different ethnic groups was widespread, as was conflict for resources, trade routes, livestock, and land. Cattle-raiding between the Boran and Garri, the Turkana and Samburu, and other ethnic groups is well documented. Prior to the fifteenth century, the gradual settlement of Arabs in **Mogadishu**, **Mombasa**, Malindi, Lamu, and various seaports led to the expansion of agriculture and of ivory trade routes in **East Africa**. The Europeans followed with first exploration, then excavation, and later colonization, ushering in the systematic alienation of land from indigenous peoples and the gradual replacement of local production systems. This process took several forms, the most evident being the sedentarization of pastoral groups, the establishment of plantation agriculture in the Kenyan highlands, the irrigation schemes in the Awash valley on Afar territory, and the tea and coffee plantations near Lake Malawi. Similarly the British converted the rich Rift Valley delta into huge cotton plantations through Sudan's Gezira irrigation scheme along the Nile.

Ideological justification for this displacement of farmers and herders was easily found: Europeans attributed growing problems of range degradation, deforestation, and soil erosion around local settlements to the poor land-management practices of local inhabitants. However, resource management in the form of hunting wild animals for subsistence or trade was merely supplanted by the indiscriminate hunting for sport by colonists, a sport that attracted European and American aristocrats including US President Theodore Roosevelt. All this changed the appearance and meaning of both hunting and the Rift Valley landscape itself. Local hunting, deemed to be "inefficient," was increasingly marginalized, with serious implications for local ecological management. Those animals that were not hunted by European and American adventurers, now became objects of tourism. Thus began the long historical progression of tourism from hunting wild animals to protecting them in national parks. These parks were expanded and protected, without involving local people, despite rapid population growth. The result was increasing conflict between people and park administrators in Kenya, **Uganda**, and Ethiopia. Pastoral groups were increasingly forced to compete for grazing land with neighboring agro-pastoralists, state-sponsored ranch developments, and national parks. The Afar in Ethiopia lost most of their seasonal grazing areas near the Awash valley to state development ventures. Agricultural development in the Ogaden region of Ethiopia and **Somalia** along the Jubba and Shebele Rivers led to the cultivation of bananas and cotton for export. Irrigation enabled large estates to be developed in some of the arid regions of Kenya, for coffee plantations in Uganda, and for sugar plantations in Malawi. Lake Victoria, Lake Turkana, Lake Abyata, and Lake Malawi continued to support local fishing communities, however.

After independence, the environmental policies of the East African countries rarely addressed the socioeconomic needs of local inhabitants, nor the political/ecological interface informing such relationships. There is no doubt that, faced with the unabated demands of **structural adjustment programs**, as well as increasing entrenchment in the global market, most African nation-states tended to ignore the need to keep a balance between environmental conservation and development, as mediated by various degrees of local people's investment and disinvestment in resource management, use, and access. The ecological aspects of the Great Rift Valley continued to be altered, sometimes in dramatic ways, but often in ways that were imperceptible. Even as the Rift Valley continued to provide historical data on how the earliest hominid species used various resources, late twentieth-century generations looked at the Rift as a natural history museum, inhabited by rare and diverse animal species, often repackaged as a tourist sanctuary. The historical development of tourism as a rentier industry for colonial and then post-colonial states, sustained in the capitalist spirit of converting nature into private, profitable territories, had occurred at the expense of local communities. At the turn of the twenty-first century, the commodification of the Rift Valley continued in the form of ecotourism and of mineral prospecting and exploitation. This was clearly seen in the exploration for petroleum deposits in Lake Malawi, in assessments of the Rift's geothermal potential, in gold excavation in Boranaland in southern Ethiopia, and in the introduction of new commercial fish species to some of the region's lakes.

Throughout history the Great Rift Valley has been host to many different livelihoods. It has been home to the Afar, Masai, Boran, Turkana, and a number of other ethnic groups. Its terrain, rivers, and lakes have undergone constant change at the hands of human beings or through the processes of nature itself. In sum it has left – and continues to leave – an unmistakable imprint on the African continent.

See also: environmental change; environmental movements

Further reading

Lane, C. (ed.) (1998) *Custodians of the Commons: Pastoral Land Tenure in East and West Africa*, London: Earthscan.

Smith, A. (1998) *The Great Rift: Africa's Changing Valley*, London: BBC Books.

SOSINA ASFAW

Rwanda

Rwanda, with an area of 26,338 square kilometers and an estimated population of 9 million in 2000, borders **Uganda**, the **Democratic Republic of Congo** (DRC), **Tanzania**, and **Burundi**. Its history is not only tied to shortage of land, population pressure, and a legacy of institutionalized inequality, but also to genocidal feuds between the Hutu majority and the Tutsi minority.

The very concept of a Rwandese nation is contested. Two opposing views have surfaced in the aftermath of the 1994 **genocide**. One thesis holds that the Twa, the Hutu, and the Tutsi are one people with a common historical origin, language, clan structure, religion, and (in important respects) culture. The contrary view contends that these are distinct ethnic – even racial – groups that migrated as separate "races" into modern Rwanda. The two views are held by rival Tutsi and Hutu intellectuals. In reality the Hutu/Tutsi identities operated more like castes (albeit with a degree of social mobility) than ethnic groups. A wealthy Hutu could become a Tutsi through a process called *Kwihutura* and, although this was rare, a Tutsi who lost wealth could fall to Hutu status (*Gucupira*). These identities were rigidified under colonial rule, which started in the 1890s and coincided with succession disputes and Hutu uprisings that followed the death of Mwami Rwabugiri (1860–95). Colonialism was resisted, most fiercely through the Nyabingi cult, which was not defeated until 1928.

Under colonial rule Tutsi power increased. German and – after the **First World War** –

Belgian rule erased existing Hutu–Tutsi reciprocal relations: Hutu chiefs were replaced with Tutsi chiefs, and the Tutsi were given a monopoly over administrative jobs and educational opportunities. A two-tier education system, established in the 1930s, prepared the Tutsi for leadership and the Hutu for labor and the priesthood. A forced labor system (*ubureetwa*), codified in 1924, demanded that the Hutu provide labor for 142 days annually, and carry a card specifying their ethnic identity. Overtaxed, starved, and embittered the Hutu staged a short-lived rebellion in 1910.

In the 1950s Belgium capitulated to demands from the United Nations for the establishment of elected advisory structures. Suspicious of the militant nationalist and Pan-African proclivities of the Tutsi elite, the Belgians replaced Tutsi chiefs with Hutu chiefs, and began to back Hutu political aspirations, even though the Catholic Church described the Tutsi–Hutu inequalities as incompatible with Christian morality. In 1957 a small Hutu Catholic elite produced the "Hutu Manifesto," which called for an end to Tutsi domination. The Tutsi took a reactionary stance in defense of their privileges and supremacy. In July 1959, following the death without heir of Mwami Matara III, the Belgians decided to establish a republic. In defiance of the Belgian Resident-General, the Tutsi aristocracy enthroned Mwami Kigeri, Matara's half-brother, and intimidated and killed Hutu leaders. The ensuing Hutu–Tutsi fighting forced Mwami Kigeri to flee the country and made some 22,000 Tutsis into internal refugees.

Fighting between the supporters of the new Party of the Movement for Hutu Emancipation (PARMEHUTU) and the pro-Tutsi National Rwandese Union (UNRA) marred elections for local assemblies in October 1960. The Hutu gained control of the provisional government, led by Grégoire Kayibanda as prime minister. PARMEHUTU won another overwhelming majority in a second round of voting, and in July 1962 Kayibanda became president of the new republic. Tutsi supremacists in exile formed guerrilla militias known as the Inyenzi ("cockroaches"), which repeatedly infiltrated Rwanda in the early 1960s. Then in December 1963 10,000 Tutsis were massacred in retaliatory attacks. By 1964 the number of Tutsi refugees was 150,000. The killing of Hutus by Tutsi soldiers in Burundi rekindled anti-Tutsi feelings in Rwanda in 1972. In the mayhem that ensued the following year, General Juvenal Habyarimana overthrew Kayibanda in 1973.

Habyarimana banned PARMEHUTU, discouraged ethnic politics, and emphasized economic development. But he prevented the return from exile of the Tutsis, arguing that Rwanda could not support them because of an acute shortage of land and limited number of jobs. His government harassed, tortured, and detained Tutsis, caused numerous disappearances, imprisoned 8,000 without trial, and subjected more than 1,000 to summary execution. Poverty, indebtedness, and mismanagement exacerbated the political crisis. Over-reliance on coffee and tea precipitated a food crisis, and made the country vulnerable to the vagaries of global commodity markets. Sharply rising debts and the imposition of **structural adjustment programs** in 1990 increased the cost of health and education, as well as creating mass poverty. In an ethnically defined political and social order, the Tutsi minority bore the brunt of these economic woes and retrenchment policies.

The Rwanda Patriotic Front (RPF) invaded the country in 1991. This devastated the economy, undermining food and coffee production, as well as Rwanda's tourist industry. The government increased spending on the military at the expense of health provision, education, and food production. Underlying the RPF insurgency was the question of the citizenship, return, and security of over 2 million refugees. This was the dominant subject of the Arusha Accord between the RPF and the Habyarimana government in 1994, which provided for power-sharing between the Hutu and the Tutsi, offered security to refugees and returning Tutsi, and promised new elections by 1995. But before the accord could be implemented, Habyarimana was assassinated in April 1994 by suspected Hutu extremists, the Interahamwe, who opposed accommodation with the Tutsi and democratization. These extremists, led by the Hutu intelligentsia, embarked on a genocidal campaign that killed between 500,000 and 1 million Tutsis and Hutu moderates. Shamefully the international response was indifference: the United Nations even pulled out when the killings began. In July 1994 the RPF captured **Kigali**, Rwanda's capital, provoking the flight of more than 2 million Hutus into neighboring countries.

In the late 1990s Rwanda faced the severe challenges of rebuilding a battered economy and political institutions, and of bringing justice to the perpetrators of the genocide. Both the country's judicial system and the Arusha Tribunal, set up by the international community, were overwhelmed. To make matters worse, Rwanda found itself embroiled in war over the DRC.

Further reading

Newbury, C. (1988) *The Cohesion of Oppression: Clientship and Ethnicity in Rwanda, 1860–1960*, New York: Columbia University Press.

Prunier, G. (1995) *The Rwanda Crisis: History of a Genocide*, New York: Columbia University Press.

PETER KAGWANJA

S

Sahara

In the imagination the Sahara evokes huge areas of sandy wastes and unbearable heat. Such imaginings are both valid and invalid. The Sahara is not entirely uninhabitable. It is complex in terms of the different environments it contains, as well as the different peoples. The Sahara was harsh enough to have limited unrestricted overland contact between North Africa and sub-Saharan Africa for millennia. However, it was never a complete barrier, with contacts dating back to the formative era of the peopling of the continent. How did the Sahara evolve? What are its major characteristics and what challenges does it present? How have people, plants, and animals adapted to life there? What are the environmental implications of changes in the Sahara?

The Sahara covers more than 9 million square kilometers of the African continent. It is the largest of the hot deserts of the world. Except for a narrow belt along the Mediterranean coast and the extreme northwestern part of the continent, it covers much of northern Africa from the Atlantic Ocean to the Red Sea. The north–south extent of the Sahara is almost 2,000 kilometers. Its southern boundary is rather undefined, tending to include more or less of the transition zone marked by the Sudano-Sahelian belt of Africa, with relatively wetter conditions in the semi-arid southern parts of the zone. **Chad**, **Niger**, **Mali**, **Mauritania**, Western Sahara, **Morocco**, **Algeria**, **Libya**, **Egypt**, and **Sudan** carry the core regions of the true Sahara.

The Sahara desert, a subtropical desert, owes its main origin to the presence of the semi-permanent subtropical high-pressure belt centered between latitudes 20°N and 30°N. In this belt of semi-permanent high pressure, descending cold dense air is heated by compression, lowering its relative humidity and creating arid conditions at the surface. The segment of the Sahara in Mauritania and Western Sahara where the desert has extended itself right up to the Atlantic coast has been argued to be the result of a superimposition of the effects of the cool Canary currents on the semi-permanent high-pressure belt. Other analysts believe that human action has allowed the Sahara to extend that far through past land-use practices.

As a true desert the main attribute of the Sahara is aridity. Lack of rainfall and high potential evapotranspiration rates restrict biotic life. Rainfall is generally lacking, with a low average total amount of rain per year, but it is also infrequent and unpredictable. The average rainfall in most areas of the central Sahara is less than 250 millimeters per annum; some areas (such as the Atlas mountains in Morocco or the highland areas of northern Libya) can receive over 500 millimeters of rain per annum, but these are exceptions. Cloudsey-Thompson (1977) presented stark figures in describing the rainfall pattern. For example, at Tamanrasett in Algeria 160 millimeters of rain was received in one year, but in another year only 6.4 millimeters fell. In 1951 about 679 millimeters of rain was recorded at Elkowit in the Red Sea hills, while in 1952 only 40 millimeters fell in the same area. Mean daily temperatures easily climb to 40°C, and the highest temperature ever recorded in the world – 58°C – was taken in the Sahara at al-Azizia in Libya on 22 September 1922.

The low and infrequent rainfall, together with high evaporation rates, creates extreme dryness. Even though plant and animal life have adapted to these extreme conditions, they are abundant only in areas sheltered enough to preserve some soil moisture, where extreme evapo-transpiration rates are slightly controlled, or where the water-table is high enough for plant roots to gain access to moisture. Due to the extreme climatic conditions, soil quality in the desert and land bordering the desert is susceptible to degradation. Plants do not easily recover from disturbance, and growth rates are seriously affected by moisture deficiency. Without surface cover, shifting dunes can have a major effect on marginal areas of the desert, and it is on this basis that predictions are often made of the likely southward march of the Sahara.

While information from satellite images and field surveys does not confirm that the Sahara is advancing in any significant way, the productive potential of the semi-arid areas around the Sahara could indeed be degraded to a desert-like condition. Cycles of extended periods of drought in these Sahel regions also create temporary desert conditions, though these normally bounce back with the return of normal rains. It has been reported that during a drought in 1940–1 about 340,000 square kilometers of land became desert, and that between 1964 and 1974 the Sahara moved southwards by 150 kilometers (Hidore 1996). While these figures did not draw any distinction between temporary surface deterioration and perennial desert, they dramatized the vulnerability of the desert margins.

The Sahara was already in existence some 17 or 18 million years ago, but has experienced cycles of greater rainfall and more extensive vegetation since then. Evidence from fossils, ancient pollen, and various cave paintings of flora and fauna indicate the presence of woodlands and savannas as late as 6,000 years ago. Even while dry, the Sahara has been home to a variety of peoples who are dispersed among the numerous oases. The Amazighs, Hassania, Tuaregs, and the Bedouins are typical desert-dwellers. In addition there are treasures lying beneath the Sahara that offer wealth, in the form of petroleum and natural gas, to countries like Algeria and Libya. There are even huge underground aquifers in Libya that offer hope for future irrigation projects.

The Sahara is of significant interest to policymakers because of the constant threat of its expansion. Agencies including the United Nations Environment Program (UNEP) and the United Nations Sudano-Sahelian Office (UNSO) have been working tirelessly to assist in gathering information on desertification, attempting to understand its mechanisms and how to minimize its impact on the most vulnerable surrounding regions. Environmental education, land-use planning, population restrictions, and poverty alleviation are some of the measures that need to be put in place if the spread of the Sahara is to be held back, particularly in the Sahel regions.

References and further reading

Cloudsey-Thompson, J.L. (1977) *Man and Biology of Arid Zones*, Baltimore: University Park Press.

Hidore, J.J. (1996) *Global Environmental Change: Its Nature and Impacts*, Upper Saddle: Prentice-Hall

WILLIAM Y. OSEI

São Tomé and Príncipe

Due to its insularity and history of **plantation agriculture**, **slavery**, and creolization, São Tomé and Príncipe is in many aspects more akin to the Caribbean island states than to other countries of the nearby African continent. It covers a total area of 1,001 square kilometers and had a population of 145,000 in 1999. From the 1850s immigrant Portuguese planters, attracted by the introduction of coffee (1787) and cocoa (1822), gradually dispossessed the native creoles (known as *forros*) through purchase and deceit. By the turn of the century the Portuguese plantations, which employed thousands of contract workers from **Angola**, **Cape Verde**, and **Mozambique**, occupied 90 percent of the land. At that time cocoa output already exceeded that of coffee, and it has remained the dominant export product ever since. Cocoa production peaked in 1909 with

30,300 tonnes; thereafter production fell continuously, due to dropping prices and crop yields, and reached only 9,234 tonnes in 1961. Due to comparatively high production costs the large estates became inefficient and unprofitable.

In 1900 the islands had a total population of 42,130, of whom there were 21,510 indentured laborers, 19,430 native creoles, and 1,190 whites. The contract workers outnumbered the *forros* until the **Second World War**. In 1909 British chocolate producers launched a boycott of São Tomé cocoa in protest against the inhuman working conditions of the contract workers there, forcing the Portuguese government to improve the situation of the plantation workers. Nonetheless, until 1961 colonial law placed categorized African plantation workers as "indigenous," and thus inferior to the *forros* who were classified as "citizens." The *forros* themselves had always rejected manual work in the plantations, considering it unworthy of their free status.

When it became known in February 1953 that the colonial government was planning to resolve a labor shortage by obliging the *forros* to accept wage labor on the plantations, the *forros* reacted with a spontaneous uprising. On the orders of Governor Carlos Gorgulho (1945–53) police and white volunteers unleashed a wave of violence against the indigenous population, killing numerous innocent people. In 1960 a few exiled *forros* created the Comité de Libertação de São Tomé e Príncipe (CLSTP), which demanded political independence. However, the effectiveness of the CLSTP was undermined by constant personal conflicts, and it ceased to exist in 1966. It was not then until 1972, in Santa Isabel in **Equatorial Guinea**, that exiled nationalists constituted the Movimento de Libertação de São Tomé e Príncipe (MLSTP), appointing Manuel Pinto da Costa as secretary-general. The MLSTP did not engage in political action on the islands themselves, but rather operated in the diplomatic world abroad. Following the Portuguese Carnation Revolution of 25 April 1974 the Lisbon government recognized the MLSTP as the sole representative of the people of São Tomé. Due to the turmoil of the **decolonization** process in the islands, the remaining 2,000 resident Portuguese left, depriving the small country of trained personnel in all sectors.

On 12 July 1975 São Tomé and Príncipe achieved independence and adopted a constitution that instituted a one-party state modeled on the Soviet example. Manuel Pinto da Costa became head of state, and Miguel Trovoada his prime minister. In September 1975 the MLSTP regime nationalized Portuguese-owned plantations, which were then regrouped into fifteen large state-owned agricultural enterprises. The regime's foreign policy favored political relations with socialist countries, although economic relations with Western countries were also maintained. The first years after independence were characterized by constant power struggles within the MLSTP leadership, and alleged coup attempts. In August 1979 a population census provoked massive anti-government riots, since the *forro* population perceived the census as an attempt to introduce forced labor on the estates. A month later Miguel Trovoada was accused of having instigated the census revolt; he was detained for twenty-one months before being released into exile to France. After Trovoada's detention the regime became more radical, with Pinto da Costa reaching the apogee of his dictatorial power. However, due to economic mismanagement, corruption, and a lack of know-how, da Costa's regime was increasingly faced with serious economic problems. Cocoa production dropped from 10,000 tonnes in 1974 to 3,400 tonnes in 1984. At the same time attempts to diversify the economy were a complete failure and incurred high foreign debts.

Consequently the MLSTP decided to drop its socialist policies, replacing its socialist allies with Western donors. From 1984 the government gradually liberalized the economy, and entrusted foreign companies with the management of some of the state-owned plantations so as to rehabilitate cocoa production. In 1987 the government agreed to follow a **structural adjustment program** laid out by the International Monetary Fund (IMF) and the World Bank. In late 1989 the delegates of a National Conference organized by the MLSTP advocated the introduction of multi-party democracy. The democratic transition occurred without political unrest, and resulted in the emergence of new parties and transformation of the MLSTP into the neoliberal MLSTP/PSD, with the additional acronym standing for Partido Social Democrático (Social Democratic Party).

In the first democratic elections in January 1991 the opposition Partido de Convergência Democrática-Grupo de Reflexão (PCD-GR) gained an absolute majority and took over power. In March 1991 Miguel Trovoada, who had meanwhile returned from exile, was voted president in an uncontested election. The relationship between president and government was plagued by power-struggles and conflict over funding, causing considerable political instability. The conflict culminated in the dismissal of two consecutive PCD-GR prime ministers by President Trovoada in 1992 and 1994 respectively. In October 1994 the MLSTP/PSD won early elections and returned to power. In 1996 President Trovoada was reelected for a second five-year term. Two years later the MLSTP/PSD obtained an absolute majority in the legislative elections. Elections since 1991 have been relatively free and fair, but the country's institutional capacities have remained weak as corruption became rampant. Despite receiving large amounts of foreign aid in the 1990s, the rehabilitation of cocoa-growing and diversification of the economy did not show the expected results in São Tomé and Príncipe, and mass poverty increased.

Further reading

Hodges, T. and Newitt, M. (1988) *São Tomé and Príncipe. From Plantation Colony to Microstate*, Boulder and London: Westview Press.

Seibert, G. (1999) *Comrades, Clients and Cousins. Colonialism, Socialism and Democratization in São Tomé and Príncipe*, Leiden: CNWS Publications.

GERHARD SEIBERT

savanna

Wide daily and seasonal temperature ranges and extremely marked seasonal rainfall characterize the savanna tropical climate and vegetation region. Wrapped around the rain-forest belt of **Central Africa**, it is found between latitudes 5° and 20° both north and south. Vegetation varies from woodlands and tall grasses in the wetter zones immediately adjacent to the rain forest to short grasslands and occasional patches of dry scrub in the drier areas adjacent to the desert. In the northern savanna the peak rainfall occurs generally between May and October, and diminishes with increasing distance from the equator. Three months, December through February, are practically rainless. In the south the pattern is reversed. Rainfall occurs between October and May, and precipitation decreases with increasing distance toward the south.

Africa's savannas are the product of climatic influences, human activity, and periodic fires (sometimes caused by lightning). To survive the alternating seasons of very dry and very wet weather, most native vegetation enters a dormant phase during the dry season, then bursts into leaf and blooms with the coming of the rains. Due to the highly variable precipitation, trees and shrubs are usually drought-resistant. Adaptations that protect such plants include small thick leaves, rough bark, and waxy leaf surfaces. With the exception of the baobab, most trees are characteristically flat-topped or umbrella-shaped. In regions of higher rainfall, such as **East Africa**, periodic fires maintain savanna vegetation. Consuming dry grass at the end of the dry season, the fires burn back the forest vegetation, check the invasion of trees and shrubs, and stimulate new grass growth. While fires do not kill the underground parts of grass plants, only the fire-resistant tree species are able to survive them above ground.

While the role of climate in creating and sustaining Africa's savannas is undisputed, the effect of human activity has been the subject of heated debate. The widely accepted idea that in recent centuries, including the twentieth, human activity – shifting cultivation, fire-setting practices, and overgrazing – had produced widespread environmental degradation that transformed what were originally forests into savannas with forest islands, leading to increasing desertification, has been challenged as false and unfounded. Research in the 1990s suggested that intensive land-use by livestock in the southern savanna during the course of the twentieth century did not result in erosion and desertification, but rather produced more wooded vegetation. Greater grazing and trampling limited the ability of grass to regenerate, but increased cattle manure provided a favorable environment for tree growth. Thus increased grazing pressure from Fulbe pastoralists and their herds in the Katiali region of **Côte d'Ivoire**, for example, produced more wooded savanna, not less. Similarly historical evidence showed that forest islands in the savanna were not the relics of more extensive forest cover that had been lost, but instead had either been created by local populations or extended from much smaller forest patches.

The economic and biological contribution of the savanna region was, however, not in question. Staples such as yams, sorghum, millet, cassava, cowpeas, and corn were some of the more popular crops. Rice was an important crop in some places, and guinea corn, a drought-resistant variety of sorghum, was grown in drier areas. The most significant commercial crops included sesame, cotton, and groundnuts. Corn production benefited from heavier rainfall, which frequently permitted two crops a year. Irrigation schemes sought to bring more and more land under cultivation.

The savannas of Africa are the zoological gardens for large tropical animals. Such herbivores as the elephant, rhinoceros, giraffe, zebra, and antelope roam freely here, as do such carnivores as the lion, leopard, cheetah, hyena, jackal, and wild dog. Many species of poisonous snakes and crocodiles are also found here. During the dry season herbivores find grasses and water along the banks of streams, on forest margins, and in isolated water-holes, where danger of attack by carnivores increases greatly. However, during the twentieth century it was poaching, overhunting, and habitat loss that decimated the great herds of game animals in African savannas. Overgrazed national parks, such as can be found on the Serengeti plains of **Kenya**, provided home for the remaining animals. By the end of the twentieth century there were fears that without adequate and effective preservation efforts the great herds of the African savanna would soon be reduced to a few zoo specimens. Rapidly growing human populations were increasingly pressurizing management agencies to allow encroachment on game reserves so that cattle-grazing and agriculture could expand.

The savanna was also an area of explosive conflict between herders, farmers, and government environmentalists, especially after independence. Competition for water and forage for livestock was a frequent cause of fighting among the Turkana of northwest Kenya. Similar conflicts were documented between herders and farmers in northern Côte d'Ivoire. In **Mali** Fulbe pastoralists faced severe problems in sustaining their existence. The encroachment of rice cultivators, along with government-mandated tenure arrangements and management structures, drastically reduced the amount of pastureland available to them. Thus herders faced increasing insecurity as conflict proliferated between cultivators, fishermen, and government officials, each seeking to use more of the diminishing resources of the grassy savanna in the Niger Bend.

Clearly conservation policies in Africa's savannas were becoming more vigorously contested. The view of the savanna landscape as recently degraded forest had justified repressive colonial and post-colonial policies that sought to reverse what was seen as destructive land-management techniques. When research in the 1990s came to support, for example, the timely application of bushfires as a central feature of land management, it was promoting a practice that had carried the death penalty in many countries from the 1970s. Conservation policy that deemed the exclusion of people as necessary for the preservation or reestablishment of nature was similarly being questioned. The outcome of these debates promised to determine the future of Africa's savannas.

See also: environmental change; environmental movements; pastoralism

Further reading

Anderson, D. and Grove, R. (1987) *Conservation in Africa: People, Policies and Practice*, Cambridge: Cambridge University Press.

Azarya, V., Breedveld, A., de Bruijn, M. and Dijk, H.V. (eds.) *Pastorialists Under Pressure? Fulbe Societies confronting Change in West Africa*, Boston: Brill.

Fairhead, J. and Leach, M. (1996) *Misreading the*

African Landscape: Society and Ecology in the Forest–Savanna Mosaic, Cambridge: Cambridge University Press.

JOSEPH RANSFORD OPPONG

Second World War

If Africans gained little from the **First World War**, in spite of their contributions, it was a different story with the Second World War (1939–45). It became one of the principal instigators of radical nationalism, and marked the beginning of the dismantling of colonial rule across the continent. The war began in September 1939, when Nazi Germany attacked Poland, and rapidly spread to Belgium, France, the Netherlands, Britain, and the USSR. Japan and Italy allied with Germany to form the Axis Powers, together winning most of their battles up to 1942. Thereafter the Allied forces began to record successes, culminating in the defeat of both Germany and Japan in 1945.

Africa was affected by the Second World War in many ways. There was fighting in **North Africa** and the Horn. After the First World War Germany had been left with no colonies in Africa, but its ally Italy conquered **Ethiopia** in 1935 and also controlled **Somalia**. The Italians and the British clashed in **East Africa**. In the case of North Africa, the British and the Sanusiyya forces fought to dislodge the Italians in **Libya**. Germany and Italy invaded **Egypt**, and a war with British forces ensued. There were problems of loyalty in **francophone Africa**, arising from the division in France itself: Germany occupied France in 1940, and the neutral Vichy government was established; General de Gaulle fled France to establish a government-in-exile, the Free French, who later received support from the French colonies in Africa. Expeditions by the forces of Free France in the **Congo** and **Gabon** brought Equatorial Africa onto the side of the Allied powers, and Free France gained the support of **Madagascar** and **French West Africa** in 1942. When the Italians and Germans were driven out of North Africa in 1943, Free France established its capital in **Algiers**.

Africa's involvement in the Second World War took various forms. First, the continent supplied resources that enabled the war to be fought. When Britain and France lost Southeast Asia, they became more dependent on Africa for essential raw materials, notably tin, rubber, and palm products. In many colonies Africans were organized or forced to produce massively for export. In addition Africans were called upon to contribute other material and financial resources to subsidize the war through increased taxation and fund-raising drives, such as the War Relief Funds established in British colonies. Also new industries to process raw materials sprang up in many countries, beginning the first phase in the creation of a number of modern factories. Secondary industries provided goods that could not be imported or were in short supply. Before the war in most of the colonies, with the exception of the settler colonies, the colonial authorities discouraged the creation of such industries.

Second, Africans were recruited to serve in the European armies. The numbers are staggering. In British West Africa alone the four British colonies supplied 167,000 soldiers. In its East African colonies and **Zimbabwe**, **Zambia**, **Malawi**, and Somaliland, the British recruited or conscripted 280,000 men. The French also recruited thousands of Africans, many of whom died from illnesses or in combat. For instance, of 80,000 African troops who served in France, about 20,000 died when Germany invaded France in May 1940. Among the accomplishments of the African soldiers were their active role in driving the Italians out of **Somalia**, Ethiopia, and **Eritrea**, and the Nazi armies out of Libya and **Tunisia**. Africans were also used in Burma to fight the Japanese.

Third, numerous places held strategic importance for the Allied forces. West Africa was used as a staging post for troops and supplies being sent to the eastern war zone. With the movement of troops and supplies through the Mediterranean very difficult, the sea route around the Cape in **South Africa** became significant. Ports in **Freetown**, **Accra**, **Lagos**, Libreville, **Cape Town**, and **Dar es Salaam** acquired importance. During the war in North Africa, airplanes flew to **Cairo** through Takoradi, Accra, Lagos, **Kano**, **N'Djamena**, and

Khartoum, making all of them places of strategic interest to the Allies.

Impact

The Second World War profoundly affected colonial economies and politics. Economically forced production devastated many farmers and rural areas. Where export production was intense, the African economy became more dependent on external markets. Rural poverty increased, while rising inflation and widespread shortages reduced living standards in the cities. In British West Africa the war gave rise to significant economic restructuring. The British authorities introduced measures to control large commercial firms. The firms served as agents, while the government became produce buyers. The supply boards became the predecessors of the post-1945 marketing boards that determined prices of cash crops and kept surpluses in reserve. In addition the colonial authorities placed restrictions on imports – firms could trade goods from Britain freely, but needed licenses to import from other countries. This made it difficult for new companies or those distrusted by the government to become agents. Many African businesses suffered, although some traders successfully moved into the retail sector.

Africa was drawn into the war because of its strategic and economic importance. Thus it contributed to the success of the Allied powers in the war. In return many colonial officers and governments began to talk about ways to "reward" Africans for their impressive contributions. They also sought to anticipate and prevent anti-colonial opposition by initiating economic and political reforms. In the French-speaking colonies French citizenship was extended to the entire population, and the worst aspects of colonial rule, such as the use of forced labor and the *indigénat* (a law that enabled any French administrator to arrest, fine, or imprison a colonial subject without trial), were brought to an end. In 1945 the British enacted the Colonial Development and Welfare Act, which included provision for building schools, universities, hospitals, roads, and other infrastructural elements. France introduced its own development program, called the Fonds d'Investissement et de Développement Economique et Social (FIDES – Investment Fund for Social and Economic Development).

The soldiers returned to their countries with new attitudes and ideas about themselves, the continent, and the European powers. Africans had served as equals with European soldiers, and claims by white officers that they were agents of civilization could no longer hold after they had involved innocent Africans in this barbaric war. The demobilized soldiers became members of the new political movements that were now demanding total independence for their countries. Other developments contributed to the intensification of nationalism during and after the war. As the Allied powers fought to save themselves from German domination, their wartime propaganda broadcast the right to self-determination that was enshrined in the Atlantic Charter of 1941. A new generation of African politicians and elites were aggressive in seeking the application of this same right to their countries and peoples.

Some developments weakened the colonial system: increased **urbanization** enabled Africans to build larger political movements, rural poverty alienated Africans from the colonial authorities, and the war experience itself led to intense anti-colonial political consciousness and to the formation of political parties and trade unions. Ideas about colonial injustice and exploitation gained widespread currency. In Europe progressive citizens and political parties were critical of their governments' control of and activities in Africa and Asia. If, they argued, they objected to the Germans controlling the French, why should Europeans control Africans? Africans seized on this, calling the Second World War a war for the freedom of all races and peoples. Thus the slogan of the war was interpreted in anti-racist terms. Anti-colonial politicians and people in Europe similarly called on their governments to let Africans manage their own affairs. In Britain, for instance, the Labour Party and the Fabian Colonial Bureau were anti-colonial. Even the French, who had been eager to maintain tight control of their African possessions, were now using the language of equality and liberty in reference to the colonies.

Global politics and power were altered in ways that reduced the influence of Europe. In Southeast

Asia the colonial powers were humiliated by the success of Japan. France was badly split between those who supported the Vichy regime, which was pro-Germany, and the Free French, who supported the Allied powers. The German occupation of France, which lasted for four agonizing years, was another source of humiliation, with an accompanying loss of prestige and wealth. Britain fared better, but at great expense in terms of lost lives and wealth. By 1945 both France and Britain were considerably weakened, and their international prestige and power undermined. Two new superpowers emerged – the USSR and the United States – and neither had any colonies in Africa. Both were critical of European rule in Africa and called on their European allies to disband their empires in order to fulfill their own agendas: the expansion of free trade for the United States and the expansion of communism for the USSR. The **United Nations** (UN), established in 1945, not only supported self-determination in its charter, but required the colonial powers to submit annual reports on how they were managing their colonies. These reports were open to criticism from colonial subjects, thus putting the colonial powers on the defensive. Political leaders in the colonies could also send delegations to the UN to lodge protests.

African nationalism also benefited from international developments and movements bolstered by the Second World War. Asian nationalism became so strong that the British had to concede independence to India, Pakistan, Sri Lanka, and Burma in 1947 and 1948. A year later a new China was born. The examples of the successful Asian countries further encouraged the demands of the African **nationalist movements**. Support for African liberation also received a boost from the **African diaspora** through **Pan-Africanism**. The 1945 Fifth Pan-African Congress held in Manchester called for Africa's independence. The leaders in the Pan-Africanist movement and many of the African student activists in Europe and North America were able to draw on communist and socialist ideas to construct a post-colonial vision for Africa. These ideas were variously sponsored by the Council on African Affairs in New York, the Labour Party in Britain, and by the Soviet Union itself. The Soviet Union was presented as an ideal country, having no ambition to exploit other countries. Indeed, for those looking for a non-capitalist path to development, the Soviet Union provided an attractive alternative. It was believed that socialism would bring about rapid development in Africa.

During the war, and in its immediate aftermath, far-reaching political changes occurred in different parts of Africa. There was greater African participation in politics, constitutional change, the formation of political parties, and eventually the transfer of power to Africans. A year after the war was over, Africans in the French colonies were allowed to establish political parties, allowing for expressions of nationalism that had been previously prohibited. In the British colonies educated Africans were appointed to the Executive Councils, thus ending the monopoly on power held by white officers. Also for the first time Africans were appointed into the administrative service, the most important arm of the colonial government, with additional steps taken to "Africanize" other branches of the civil service. Furthermore new constitutions were introduced to enable Africans to participate in government: examples include the 1946 Richards' Constitution in **Nigeria**, and the Burn's Constitution on the Gold Coast. African nationalists criticized these constitutions as inadequate and succeeded in getting them revised, ultimately leading to their independence. In North Africa the Sanusiyya were able to push for Libya's independence in 1951. In Morocco in 1947 the French appointed Moroccans as government ministers, thus beginning a process that led to independence in 1956. Thus wartime conditions and the reforms that followed marked a watershed in the modern history of Africa.

Further reading

Kerslake, R.T. (1997) *Time and the Hour: Nigeria, East Africa, and the Second World War*, New York: Radcliffe Press.

Killingray, D. and Rathbone, R. (1986) *Africa and the Second World War*, New York: St. Martin's Press.

Mazrui, A.A. (1993) *UNESCO General History of*

Africa. VIII. Africa Since 1935, Berkeley: University of California Press.
Moorehead, A. (1997) *Desert War: The North African Campaign, 1940–1943*, New York: Penguin.

TOYIN FALOLA

Senegal

Senegal, with an area of 196,722 square kilometers, is located in **West Africa** on the Atlantic coast, bordering **Guinea-Bissau** and **Mauritania**. It had an estimated population of 9.5 million in 2000, dominated by the Wolof, Sereer, Pulaar, Mandinka, Joola, and Soninke peoples. Direct colonial conquest took place during the second half of the nineteenth century. Following the ban on **slavery** in 1848, the economic structures of the colony were progressively transformed; specifically, groundnuts emerged as a major export crop, and the financial institutions and economic structures set up that were to dominate the Senegalese economy until well after independence.

Despite many forms of resistance the French conquest of Senegal was completed during the first decades of the twentieth century. But the French were unable to restructure local societies in such a way as to organize direct domination over the local populations; they were unable to rule without the marabouts, who were heavily involved in the cash-crop economy. In their turn local politicians (such as Léopold Sédar Senghor, Mamadou Dia, and Lamine Guèye) were compelled to cooperate with the leaders of the Muslim Brotherhoods. In short the Islamo-Wolof model remained the central matrix in the process of state-formation in Senegal.

Senegal won its independence in 1960. As early as 1848, in the name of the assimilationist policy adopted by the French, the colony had been endowed with elective institutions in the *Quatre communes* (Gorée, Saint-Louis, **Dakar**, Rufisque). But only the citizens of these *communes* had the right to vote, and politics was largely determined by local considerations. When the rural population's right to vote was recognized after the **Second World War**, urban political elites relied on the marabouts and canton chiefs to exert their political influence.

Senegal was characterized by remarkable political stability; its presidents were Léopold Sédar Senghor until 1980, Abdou Diouf (1981 to March 2000), and Abdoulaye Wade (from March 2000). Full multi-party politics was established in 1981, but political life was dominated by the Union Progressiste Sénégalaise (UPS – becoming the Parti Socialiste (PS) in 1976), the Parti Démocratique Sénégalais (PDS), the Alliance des Forces de Progrès (AFP), and the Union pour le Renouveau Démocratique (URD). Under Abdou Diouf the political elites initiated a series of agreements, and some opposition leaders entered the cabinet. These procedures played a crucial part in the preservation of the country's stability. However, with the separatist demands put forward by the Mouvement des Forces Démocratiques de la Casamance, a low-intensity conflict troubled the southern region of the country from the early 1980s.

Léopold Sédar Senghor and Cheikh Anta Diop played a major role in the evolution of political ideas in Senegal. While the former became famous for his defense of Negritude, the latter – an intellectual and Senghor's political opponent – was notable for his research on the pre-colonial and ancient history of the continent. Mamadou Dia, who was Senghor's political partner until the December 1962 crisis, also strongly influenced intellectual life in Senegal. The historian Abdoulaye Ly, the linguist Pathé Diagne, the economist Amady Aly Dieng, the writers Birago Diop and Cheikh Hamidou Kane are other major figures in the Senegalese intellectual landscape. By the beginning of the 1990s, 26 percent of the state budget was spent on education, but the rate of primary schooling was only 58 percent. The country had two universities.

Senegal enjoyed a dense and varied cultural life. Music was one of its main access points into the globalized world. Senegalese musicians used a variety of styles – one simply has to compare Samba Diabaré Samb, Khar Mbaye Madiaga and Soundioulou Cissokho to Youssou N'Dour, Coumba Gawlo Seck and Baaba Maal, or to the young rappers. Senegal was also famous for its cinema – Sembène Ousmane was the outstanding Senegalese movie director – while Ousmane Sow's powerful works dominated the field of sculpture.

From colonial times the Senegalese economy was based on groundnuts. But its share of exports gradually diminished, particularly after the devaluation of the CFA franc in 1994. Senegal was among the first African countries to implement **structural adjustment programs** at the end of the 1970s. Until the early 1990s the results were rather ambiguous, because the reforms had either not been implemented or had been only partially implemented as a result of "resistance from above." The devaluation of the CFA franc marked the beginning of a new era, with major structural reforms aimed at building the basis for sustainable growth, stable public finances, and a redefinition of the state's scope for intervention. But essentially any economic improvement was required for the servicing of Senegal's foreign debt, which constituted a major constraint on the state's capability to invest. As a result poverty increased enormously.

Senegal's population remains predominantly Muslim, Senegalese **Islam** structured by the Brotherhoods. The population was concentrated in the central and western parts of the country, with 65 percent of the population living in 14 percent of the territory. Internal and international migration was intense. So was urbanization: the urbanization rate was 23 percent in 1960, but 39 percent in 1988. The population was young – 47.6 percent of Senegalese were under fifteen. Wolofization was a long-term trend – 67.2 percent of the Senegalese used Wolof as their first language, and 24.1 percent as their second language, a phenomenon that also dated back to the colonial period.

Despite limited natural resources, after independence Senegal made some progress in developing its human resources. The country benefited from a political system that made only limited use of coercion. Because of the quality of its leadership, Senegal played a role in West Africa out of all proportion to its actual economic weight. Despite attempts at political integration inside the Mali Federation (January 1959–August 1960) and the Senegambian Confederation (1982–9), the dreams of African unification that were dear to Senegalese leaders failed to materialize. Nevertheless Senegal played an active role in regional and international organizations, some of which were headed by the country's citizens, including Amadou-Mahtar M'bow at UNESCO and Pierre Sarney at Amnesty International.

Further reading

Diop, M.C. (ed.) (1994) *Senegal. Essays on Statecraft*, Dakar: CODESRIA.

Founou-Tschuigoua, B. (1981) *Fondements de l'économie de traite au Sénégal: La surexploitation d'une colonie*, Paris: Silex.

MOMAR COUMBA DIOP

sex and sexuality

The experience of sexual objectification defined the reality of the colonial situation. Hence questions of domination were thoroughly imbricated in the control of African sexuality. From the beginning of the colonial period onwards, female bodies symbolized the conquered land. The nakedness of Africa in early iconography and visual representations, thus represented the availability of both the land and the people to be overwritten by the designs of Western imperialism. From the first moment of conquest, colonial discourses represented Africa as a land of hyperfecundity and sexual profligacy – a "porno-tropics" (McClintock 1995) for the European imagination, upon which the wildest sexual fears and desires could be projected. African men were stereotyped as having larger organs of generation and African women were stereotyped as having excessive sexual appetites. Thus sub-Saharan Africa became a sort of "sexual playground" in the European imagination, and a harem of African concubines was one of the many perks enjoyed by white European colonists. The idea that Africans were people who were unable to control their sexuality, and thus should be subject to control by others, continued to inform discussions about African sexuality throughout the twentieth century. In contrast North African women, such as those from **Algeria** who wore the veil, were subjected to more "Orientalist" forms of discourse, which constructed them as sexually mysterious and sexually forbidden, due to the allegedly aggressive nature of Algerian men.

The fact that all colonial societies were racially segregated meant that sexuality was immediately implicated in all forms of colonial rule. Sexuality was a means for the simultaneous maintenance and erosion of racial difference. Fears of cultural and racial pollution prompted hysteria around the issue of sexual behavior, which exposed the instability of "race" as a social category. An obsession with racial purity found its highest expression in white settler colonies like Rhodesia, **Kenya**, and **South Africa**, which quickly developed a series of laws, such as South Africa's Prohibition on Mixed Marriages Act, that aimed at eliminating interracial sexual contact. The power dynamics that structured colonial society, however, meant that every white man felt it was his right to have sexual access to any African woman. The proximity to African women afforded by domestic social arrangements, which frequently placed African women in European households as maids and nannies, and the indifference shown by the police and social-service agencies towards the issue of the sexual abuse of African women, fostered a general climate of sexual license. As a result European men took up with African women with impunity, and a sizable "mixed-race" population emerged in South Africa, **Zimbabwe**, **Namibia**, and **Mozambique**. The existence of this "mixed-race" population was a source of strain for the ruling colonial apparatus, as governing elites struggled to incorporate them as a "buffer class" to whom were extended certain limited rights, based on the notion that their "white" racial heritage gave them a higher degree of "civilization." Most white settler colonies established government departments that were responsible for overseeing the sorting of human bodies into manageable racial categories, and administering tests to determine the degree of racial purity or admixture. Thus sexuality and human reproduction became profoundly implicated in the evolution of the colonial state, as a racially stratified colonial system would quickly have become inoperable without a systematic method of racial classification.

Because sexuality and human reproduction profoundly impact the reproduction of human labor power, the control of African sexuality was always profoundly implicated in the quest for colonial subjugation of African economies. Starting in the nineteenth century and continuing into the twentieth, missionaries and settlers embarked on a studied campaign to stamp out the practice of polygamy throughout **East**, **West**, and **Southern Africa**. They sought to eliminate the practice in **North Africa** too, but **Islam** seemed impervious to European efforts at proselytizing. Although religious propaganda railed against the practice as an affront to the Christian ideal of home and family, white farmers and mining magnates were very clear that their opposition to the practice stemmed from the fact that polygamy was the basis of the African rural subsistence economy, which allowed African communities to reproduce themselves without engaging in wage labor. Thus the process of primitive accumulation, or separating indigenous people from their means of subsistence and thus forcing them into market relations in order to reproduce themselves, was profoundly dependent upon the policing of African male and female sexuality. In short the hut and poll taxes, alongside religious prohibitions on the "sexual slavery" of African women, worked together to transform African household organization so as to produce a malleable labor force.

Once African subsistence communities had been permanently dislocated, African people in East, South, and West Africa began a pattern of steady migration into urban areas, where new sexual and social arrangements came to the fore. Prostitution emerged as one such form, as African women who were denied access to other forms of economic activity sold their bodies as commodities on the open marketplace. The process of **urbanization** also profoundly transformed the sexual lives of African men. Male prostitution, particularly among children, was not unknown. In Southern Africa men who migrated to the mines lived in single-sex dormitories where homosexual relations were not uncommon.

The increasing incidence of casual sexual liaisons and temporary sexual partnerships also led to an increase in sexually transmitted diseases. In Africa, as was the case in Europe, discussions of sexuality always encompassed both a medical and a moral dimension. In the early twentieth century, for example, a debate ensued over what colonial officials in the **Uganda** protectorate felt was a "syphilis epidemic" among the indigenous population. As would be the case in a variety of colonial contexts, the syphilis epidemic was constructed as a problem of female morality and thus the solution was seen to lie in the control of African female sexuality. The loss of colonial control over African female sexuality, in turn, symbolized for the British the loss of control over African society in general. Female sexuality was thus of concern to colonial administrators because its control and containment was an important measure of how effective the policy of indirect rule was in buttressing existing systems of social control. Colonial authorities constructed the syphilis problem as having been caused by the disintegration of patriarchal authority, which they sought to shore up, not so much to contain syphilis, but to buttress the system of indirect rule whereby colonial authorities relied upon traditional elites to be their functionaries. Thus the control of African female sexuality, and the establishment of a particular form of colonial rule, went hand in hand.

The "epidemic" that has attracted the most attention in the contemporary period is that of Acquired Immune Deficiency Syndrome, or AIDS, which is currently the leading cause of death among sexually active youth and adults in a number of African countries. As was the case in the colonial period images of Africa as a land of sexual promiscuity and disease have resurfaced in discussions of the AIDS epidemic, which was at one time rumored to have originated on the African continent. Popular stereotypes and medical discourses have also constructed the transmission of AIDS in Africa as primarily a moral problem. In this instance, however, African men, rather than African women, are constructed as sexually irresponsible. Like syphilis in the early twentieth century, the medical treatment of AIDS in the late twentieth century is overlaid and overdetermined by conflicts in the political and economic arenas. The United States conducted experiments on pregnant African women infected with AIDS, in which some women were given drugs that could prevent the transmission of the virus to their infants and others were simply given placebos – effectively condemning them to death. The fact that a research program such as this one would never exist in Europe or North America is testimony to a continuing undervaluation of African lives, which began during the colonial period. The post-apartheid South African government also embarked on an extensive suit against American pharmaceutical companies who, in order to protect their profits, sought to deny African countries the right to purchase and manufacture generic AIDS drugs. Thus AIDS cannot be seen only or even primarily as a sexual/medical problem, as the care of AIDS patients is determined more by the exigencies of the political and economic realm, than by the medical or interpersonal requirements.

In the post-colonial era African activists have become increasingly concerned with how issues of sexuality are implicated in the control of African people by their own governments. In Zimbabwe, for example, Robert Mugabe embarked on a campaign of vilification and repression directed at homosexuals, declaring that their behavior represented a perversion of traditional African values and setting forth a debate over whether homosexuality existed in pre-colonial African societies. In Kenya, South Africa, and **Sierra Leone** the incidence of rape and sexual abuse of young girls has increased precipitously. Figures released by the South African government suggest that a woman is raped every sixty seconds. In many instances young women are subject to sexual abuse at the hands of classmates and teachers, thus further reducing the access of African women to formal education. In Sierra Leone, on the other hand, women became the sexual property of soldiers and mercenaries, and rape became an integral part of the regime of terror enacted by rival gangs of mercenaries.

Activists on the continent have taken great pains, however, to preserve their autonomy from European or American activists and **non-governmental organizations**, lest these issues become the basis for once again reducing African women – and the myriad of social and economic forces that structure their lives – into a simplified politics of the vulva. From the mid-1970s onward the topic of female circumcision, or "female genital mutilation," captured the attention of Western feminists and activists, many of whom reinscribed and reaffirmed images of African women as agentless victims, African men as sexual savages, and African culture as a collection of useless and dangerous superstitious practices that needed to be stamped out by enlightened agents of Western modernity. In the post-colonial moment African activists have thus taken pains not only to assert their right to define for themselves the causes and consequences of sexual politics in African communities, but also to define for themselves the parameters that determine which issues constitute issues of "sexuality," instead of blindly adopting Western metaphysical constructs that define any issue having to do with men, women, and reproductive activity as, necessarily, sexual.

Recent work on African epistemology and language suggests that Western, body-oriented concepts of gender and sexuality have been misapplied in the African context. African scholars working in the fields of gender and sexuality have challenged the idea that, simply because men and women reside in a particular society, sexual distinctions (as defined by Western metaphysics) necessarily determine or explain the form that social stratification takes. The work of Oyeronke Oyewumi (1997), for example, has shown that the category "woman," which is foundational in Western discourses about gender and sexuality, simply did not exist in some African societies prior to sustained contact with the West. Thus the cultural logic of Western social categories, which is based on an ideology of biological determinism whereby genital physiology and sexuality provide the rationale for the organization of the social world, was not universal. Ifi Amadiume's (1987) exploration of "male" daughters and "female" husbands has also shown that the social categories of "husband" and "wife" are not physiologically determined in Africa, further pointing to the inapplicability, in the African context, of Western conceptual categories as they relate to sexuality. Amadiume shows that all Igbo females are husbands, although there are females who are wives in the family lineage. Furthermore the term "husband" is not equivalent to male. Rather, "husband" is a relational term that identifies members of the family into which a female is married. Critiques emerging from Africanist scholarship have thus exposed the fact that even when the perpetuators are progressive Western feminists, rather than retrograde European colonials, the attempt to subsume African social and sexual practices into predetermined Western categories does nothing more than create the very reality that is purportedly being described.

References and further reading

Amadiume, I. (1987) *Male Daughters, Female Husbands*, London: Zed Books.

McClintock, A. (1995) *Imperial Leather: Race, Gender, Sexuality and the Colonial Contest*, New York: Routledge.

Nnaemeka, O. (1998) *Sisterhood: Feminisms and Power from Africa to the Diaspora*, Trenton: Africa World Press Inc.

Oyewumi, O. (1997) *The Invention of Women: Making African Sense of Western Gender Discourses*, Minneapolis: University of Minnesota.

Vaughan, M. (1991) *Curing their Ills: Colonial Power and African Illness*, London: Polity Press.

ZINE MAGUBANE

Seychelles

The Seychelles, covering an area of 455 square kilometers, is located in the western Indian Ocean, about 1,600 kilometers east of the African continent. There are an estimated 115 islands and islets in the archipelago. The largest of the group are Mahé, Praslin, Silhouette, Cosmoledo, and Aldabra. The Seychelles had an estimated population of 78,846 in 1998. For most of the twentieth century the economy of the islands was dependent on the export of coconut oil and copra, produced mostly on large plantations. Until the 1950s the bulk of exports went to Europe, after which the principal markets for Seychellois copra shifted to India and Pakistan. From the 1970s tourism and the fishing became the most important industries.

The islands take their name from the Vicomte Moreau de Séchelles, Comptroller-General under King Louis XV of France. French settlers first arrived in 1770, followed by the British in 1811. From 1814 to 1903 the British administered the territory as a dependency of **Mauritius**, while from 1903 to 1976 the Seychelles was a separate British colony. The colony became home to several African leaders forced into exile by the British in the early 1900s, such as Asantehene Prempeh I (**Ghana**) and Kabaka Mwanga of Buganda (**Uganda**).

The majority of the Seychellois in the twentieth century were descendants of slaves or liberated slaves brought by the French and the British from Mauritius, **Madagascar**, and the coast of **East Africa** during the eighteenth and nineteenth centuries. There was a long history of interracial marriage and interbreeding between Africans, Europeans, Indians, and Chinese. The latter two groups began arriving in the late nineteenth century. The Seychellois developed one of the most multiracial societies in the world, although they often defined themselves and others sharply in terms of race, color, and class: *grand blancs* were whites who claimed descent from the original French land-owning elite; *petit blancs* were other whites; *rouges* were "reds" or those with brown skin who claimed to be of mixed European, African, Indian, or Chinese descent; and *noirs* were black Africans. All those at the darker end of the skin-color spectrum were called *créoles*. Land ownership, income, level of education (including literacy in French and English), and descent all played important roles in determining social status.

Until the 1940s politics in the Seychelles was defined mostly by the "white" elite's concern over: keeping local political autonomy, promoting commerce, protecting their private property, keeping taxes low, ensuring a cheap unskilled labor supply, and supporting Catholic education for "white" children. For a brief time after the **Second World War**, a struggle began to stir between the *grands blancs* and those who sought to speak for the *créoles*. In the postwar years the "white" elite became divided over efforts by British colonial administrators to introduce land-settlement schemes for landless *créoles*, establish an elected colonial legislature, and make universal educational reforms, including the teaching of English and the improvement of schools for *créole* children. These initiatives coincided with the emergence of a *créole* spokesman, Charles Evariste Collet. Collet was a *créole* barrister, the son of an Indian labor leader who had been deported from Mauritius. In 1922 Collet had left the Seychelles to pursue his Quaker religious studies abroad, having been denied higher education at home because of his color. By the late 1930s he had gained experience as a political leader, serving as general secretary of the League for the Advancement of Coloured Peoples in London. In 1946 he returned home to the Seychelles with a French barrister wife. Under Governor Percy Selwyn-Clarke, Collet served the colonial government: first as an appointed representative to the colonial Legislative Council, then as Acting Attorney-General, and finally as Chief Inland Revenue Officer. His chief enemies were leading members of the Planters' and Taxpayers' Association. By 1950 the power of the *grand blancs* had prevailed in the Legislative Council and Collet's political career was over.

Political competition did not reemerge until 1963, when two major political parties were formed: the Seychelles Democratic Party (SDP) led by James Mancham and the Seychelles People's United Party (SPUP) led by France Albert René. Both were of mixed descent. René, who appears white, would later profess to better represent the aspirations of the *créole* majority. Following the 1967 elections, the SDP and the SPUP began to share the stage, having both won seats in the Legislative Council. In the elections of 1970, under a new constitution, the SDP won a decisive advantage over the SPUP. Consequently Mancham became the first chief minister of the Seychelles, and worked to strengthen investment in tourism and economic integration with Britain. Meanwhile the SPUP sought full independence. In 1975 the two parties formed a coalition. On 29 June 1976 the independent Republic of Seychelles was declared, with Mancham as president and René as prime minister.

A year later the SPUP staged an armed coup, while Mancham was in Britain, and installed René as president. In 1979 the SPUP was renamed the Seychelles Peoples Progressive Front (SPPF) and became the sole legal party. Elections were soon held to legitimize the new political order. Thereafter René's government pursued a "socialist" economic strategy, introduced Creole as the official language (replacing French and English), and emphasized the development of agriculture and the fishing industry. In November 1981, with the help of soldiers sent from **Tanzania** by President Julius Nyerere, the SPPF government was able to thwart an attempted coup by South African mercenaries. From 1979 to 1991 René's regime was frequently characterized by bouts of violence against political opponents, both at home and abroad. During the 1990s privatization and economic liberalization policies were reintroduced, opposition political parties were allowed, the SPPF changed its name to the Seychelles National Party, and legislative and presidential elections were held twice. In 2000, while some members of the opposition controlled seats in the national legislature, France Albert René was still president.

Further reading

Franda, M. (1982) *The Seychelles: Unquiet Islands*, Boulder: Westview Press.

Scarr, D. (2000) *Seychelles Since 1770: History of a Slave and Post-slavery Society*, London: Hurst & Co.

JOSEPH S. CARUSO

Sierra Leone

Sierra Leone, with an area of 71,740 square kilometers, is bordered by **Guinea** and **Liberia**. It had an estimated population of 5.1 million in 2000. Sierra Leone is a multi-ethnic polity, but with two demographically dominant ethnic groups: the Mende in the southeast, accounting for just over 30 percent of the total population, and the Temne of the north, accounting for just under 30 percent. There are also some eighteen other ethnic groups, of which none account for more than 10 percent of the population. The largest number of believers are Muslims, though religious conflict is uncommon in Sierra Leone, perhaps due to the fact that people who subscribe to the major religions can be found among all the ethnic groups.

The establishment of Sierra Leone dates to 1787 when the Sierra Leone Company founded a settlement for freed slaves: **Freetown**. Ten years later the company was given a Royal Charter, and Freetown became a municipality. Following Britain's decision to abolish the slave trade in 1807, in 1808 the Crown took over the administration of the company, which by now had been burdened with the problems of defense and an ever-growing population.

In 1896 the informal bifurcated nature of Sierra Leone was formalized in statute, following the declaration of a protectorate, which meant that inhabitants of the protectorate were now under British protection and subject to "native laws and customs." Those from the colony of Freetown, who were categorized as British subjects, were now subject to British customary law. By the mid- to late 1800s the Creoles had emerged as a social group with the potential to challenge not just European commercial and administrative dominance, but also the protectorate's elites, though the Creoles soon met another fierce competitor: the Lebanese trader. A railway system was constructed in the late 1890s, linking the capital to Pendembu in the east and Makeni in the north. A third network was built in the 1930s, following the discovery of iron in Marampa, connecting the new mines to the port of Pepel.

Throughout the twentieth century Sierra Leone has epitomized the symptoms of a peripheral economy: highly dependent on external sources for balancing the budget; dependent on the export of primary produce and mining for foreign-exchange earnings; a monoculture economy dependent on a single export item for foreign-exchange earnings (iron ore between 1930 and 1950, and diamonds between 1950 and 1990). The country is well endowed with mineral resources: gold, diamonds, bauxite, rutile, platinum, chromite, and iron ore all have been mined at one time or another; its seas and rivers are replete with good deposits of fish. In the late colonial and early post-independence periods an attempt was made to establish an import substitution sector, but this failed. The failure was largely due heavy reliance on imports, and the absence of any forward or backward linkages with the local economy, thus the industries became a drain on the very foreign-exchange savings that they were supposed to be generating. The ensuing crisis of deficient foreign-exchange earnings has left Sierra Leone with a long history of implementation of **structural adjustment programs**.

At independence in 1961 Sierra Leone inherited all the trappings of a democratic polity: an elected parliament, an independent judiciary, a free press, and an efficient civil service. But in 1967, after the government was voted out of office, the defeated prime minister, Sir Albert Margai, instigated a military coup, which marked the first of several army interventions in politics. The junta of middle-ranking officers ruled for a year before they were removed from office by non-commissioned officers, who then invited the victorious prime minister, Siaka Stevens, to take over the reins of government. Stevens ruled Sierra Leone with an iron fist. During his time in power corruption became endemic, and he gradually dismantled the democratic constitution. As a result his term in office was marked by economic and political decline, as he fought to "informalize" state and society by ruling through the "shadow" state, which included the powerful ethnic cabal known as the "Akutay." Stevens' appointed successor was Major General Momoh, a phlegmatic character without the skill and guile of his mentor. It was not long before political, economic, and social grievances had been transformed into a serious challenge to the state: the year 1991 marked the beginning of a long and bloody civil war. In 1992 junior army officers, who complained about corruption and the failure of the state to provide the army with the necessary tools to fight the war, overthrew Momoh. The youthful Captain Valentine Strasser, who was initially welcomed as a hero by citizens of the capital, assumed power. However, it was not long before Strasser's youthful antics, and in particular his perceived procrastination over the issue of return to civilian rule, led to his overthrow by his deputy.

Before long civil war had broken out between the elected civilian government and the Revolutionary United Front (RUF), led by former army corporal Foday Sankoh, who received material, logistical, and moral support from warlords in Liberia. The war caught the attention of the international community, because of wanton acts of violence against innocent civilians, the widespread abduction of children, and the role played by the sale of diamonds in fueling the war. Despite two peace agreements in 1996 and 1999, including the Lome Peace Accord of 1999 that offered a blanket amnesty to rebel leaders, violence continued. After an attempted putsch by rebel leaders followed the departure of ECOMOG peacekeeping troops from Sierra Leone, resulting in many deaths and yet another major political emergency, in May 2000 British troops were dispatched to evacuate British and Commonwealth citizens. The intervention of British and UN troops brought a certain degree of peace and tranquillity to the country.

Further reading

Morgan, E.C. and Dixon-Fyle, M. (1999) *Sierra Leone at the End of the Twentieth Century: History, Politics and Society*, New York: Peter Lang.

Zack-Williams, A.B. (1995) *Tributors, Supporters and Merchant Capital: Mining and Underdevelopment in Sierra Leone*, Aldershot: Ashgate.

A.B. ZACK-WILLIAMS

slavery

The history of slavery in twentieth-century Africa is largely about the end of slavery, rather than about changes in slavery itself. In much of the continent where slavery had existed it came to an end in the first three decades of the twentieth century, although it reportedly persisted to the end of the century in countries like **Mauritania** and **Sudan**. But we need to understand what ended in order to understand how it ended and what came after it. The history of slavery in Africa is a complicated phenomenon for several reasons. Although forms of dependency and oppression in Africa similar to the Western concept of slavery lasted well into the twentieth century, these practices were not exactly the same as those forms of Western slavery found in the economies of the South Atlantic well into the nineteenth century. This should in no way be taken to mean that similar, but different, forms of forced dependency and oppression – African slavery if you will – were necessarily less harsh than or preferable to Western slavery; instead the distinction is made simply because the failure of Western colonial powers clearly to understand these differences is very important in explaining their failure to bring about the quick and effective end to slavery in Africa, as well as their failure to create a free market for labor, both of which they promised in their various justifications for colonial conquest.

Put simply, Africa was land-rich and people-poor. In addition, because of climatic and environmental conditions, labor yields were low, which made labor expensive relative to available surpluses. Under these conditions African markets in stolen labor (that is, slaves) gave the consumers of this labor a decided economic advantage, and so slavery had emerged in almost all areas of Africa well before the twentieth century. For many centuries these internal markets had extended well beyond Africa: first into the Red Sea and the Indian Ocean, then across the **Sahara**, and finally throughout the South Atlantic. The idea of African slavery only makes sense in terms of understanding these different contexts of forced dependency and oppression. It was these contexts more than the ways in which slaves were exploited or treated that account for the differences between African and Western slavery. In other ways the practices, statuses, and institutions associated with forced dependency and oppression that could be found in Africa were extremely varied – from slaves used in subsistence farming to slaves working in the growing, processing, manufacture, or transportation of trade goods.

Whatever its other diagnostic features, slavery in Africa (as elsewhere in the world) was about how labor was obtained – through seizure and trade in the first generation, and through oppression and segregation in subsequent generations. When slavery was formally abolished in tropical Africa, at different times in different colonies in the early part of the twentieth century, what was abolished were certain ways of obtaining labor. However, new ways of obtaining labor had already emerged by the time abolition occurred. In colonial Africa many people had their labor coerced and stolen from them, making slave labor and the many forms of colonial labor different forms of unfree labor. Seen in this light, slavery in twentieth-century Africa had strong similarities with the other forms of labor that followed it, despite the rhetoric and ideology that surrounded abolition, and even though there remained important differences in how the two types of labor were obtained. Abolition, although a source of freedom for many individual slaves, often meant little more than the replacement of certain forms of coercion for other forms. For free Africans, who were subject to colonial rather than slave masters in the early decades of the twentieth century, the denial of freedom to slaves had been much more complete and total than the denial of freedom was to them as colonial subjects, but only some Africans had been slaves at the beginning of the twentieth century, whereas almost all Africans became colonial subjects.

Europeans began to fulfill their abolitionist rhetoric by ending slave raiding and trading in Africa, one of the main ideological justifications for imperialism. However, the abolition of slavery itself was another matter; one that they felt required caution. In the nineteenth century, for example, Britain had abolished the slave trade with its Caribbean colonies, as well as with the Cape Colony in **Southern Africa**, a generation before abolishing slavery in these same colonies; however, despite this gradualism, the supply of labor in both areas was adversely affected. So in India it was slave trading rather than slavery that the British outlawed in 1843, as accommodation and relativism came to inform attitudes toward slavery itself. Because of these and similar nineteenth-century experiences, European colonial administrators in Africa were aware that the transition from unfree to free labor would be difficult to manage without economic disruption.

Across those areas of Africa conquered by European powers in the last decades of the nineteenth century and the early decades of the twentieth century, the seizure of, and trade in, people was effectively suppressed by colonial powers. However, the elimination of those forms of oppression and segregation associated with slavery were left in place for some time to come. So, for example, slavery was not officially abolished in northern Nigeria until 1936. Colonial accommodation of slavery was due in part to their lack of real power to abolish it without losing the support of those African classes and elites, many of them leaders of recently conquered African states, who profited enormously as slave owners. It was also due to the reluctance of colonial regimes to face the same problems with labor supply in some parts of the Caribbean after emancipation. Labor was fundamental to the economic viability of colonial rule in Africa. Workers were required to build the infrastructure of colonial rule, as well as to produce the various products for export that were at the heart of colonial economies. Unable to recognize that labor was both scarce and relatively expensive in Africa (that is, once again, relative to the available surpluses), and unwilling to pay attractive wages, colonial regimes assumed that – because Africans were often not eager to sell their labor voluntarily – they were lazy. The difficulties that colonial economies had in obtaining labor were blamed on African culture. Until labor was readily available, a free market in labor would not be possible. Until then those cultures would have to be changed, and this would require coercion.

In the intervening period colonial regimes had to come up with new ways of obtaining labor in order to meet the new labor needs of colonial administrations and economies. In the Cape Colony the British had learned lessons in the nineteenth century that they and other colonial governments were to use again in other parts of tropical Africa in the twentieth century. When the slave trade was ended and labor shortages became acute, the British instituted coercive labor legislation that forced the indigenous people of the region, who had previously been dispossessed but not enslaved, to work for European settlers. The terms of employment were extremely harsh. In the middle of the century, after the abolition of slavery itself in the Cape Colony, labor was supplied through the seizure of land from societies beyond the colony's frontier. Newly dispossessed people became dependent on employment opportunities in the colony. Several decades later the British extracted labor from recently conquered territories elsewhere in Southern Africa through taxation. Eventually all these techniques matured into the system of cheap, coerced labor that came to be known as apartheid, which was brought to an end in 1994. However, freedom from apartheid, as with freedom from slavery, was not necessarily economic freedom from the structures that both apartheid and slavery had been predicated upon: Many black South Africans found themselves in situations not different from those that African slaves had experienced at the end of slavery two to three generations before. In both cases people were forced to find ways of surviving without land or other alternative resources, such as social networks, to fall back on.

In the early part of the twentieth century – after slave raiding and trading had been abolished, at which point many colonial governments began to refuse to recognise slavery in their colonial courts – slaves freed themselves and developed a variety of methods of survival: some remained dependent on their former masters, for whom they continued to work, albeit under somewhat different conditions; others fled their former masters, and either sought out other patrons with whom they could negotiate better terms or found land on which they could regain some degree of autonomy. First-generation slaves often attempted to return to their natal communities. In all cases the degrees of freedom that they were able to create for themselves were dependent on their initiative in the context of local conditions; they were not given freedom, but created it for themselves as and how they were able.

After this – but before slavery itself was formally abolished – taxation, land seizure, and labor contracts were all used to coerce labor out of people and their communities. As a result of these measures, wages were almost always lower than the replacement costs of labor; it was a similar differential that had made slavery so attractive to would-be masters. The difference was to be borne by the worker's communities, and most particularly women, who were forced to meet the replacement costs of workers by making up the shortfall in production caused by the absence of migrant male workers and to go on having children who would follow in their father's footsteps to the mines or farms of the colonial economy. These communities became both formal and informal labor reserves, which were conceptualized as essential, patriarchal domains of African tradition. In such imaginary colonial worlds, women had few rights. In many parts of Africa during the nineteenth century the lines that separated married women and slave women had become somewhat blurred; the status of free women often declined in those areas where enslaved women were more readily available than in previous periods, as men could now marry women who had no rights. Colonial regimes in the twentieth century created elaborate systems of control – most notably those exercised through colonial courts – to make all marriages into institutions where men had patriarchal control over their wives. In many colonies during the first decades of the twentieth century the attitudes that informed colonial policy held that the servitude of enslaved and married women were not much different, and furthermore both were part of African "traditions" that were necessary to the reproduction of colonial labor.

At the end of the nineteenth century the link between slavery, abolition, and colonial subjection had been established in King Leopold's Congo Free State, where some of the worst (but by no means all) colonial atrocities were committed in order to force people to produce ivory and rubber for export. Because of international reaction Leopold was forced to relinquish his personal colony to the Belgian government in 1908. However, the lessons that should have been gained from the international scrutiny of these abuses were not learned. The regime of Belgian rule in the Congo, although it abolished slavery officially in 1910, remained extremely harsh even by the standards of other colonial powers in Africa at the time. And all colonial regimes continued to use forced labor for many years to come, despite several other international campaigns calling for its abolition. The French did not abolish forced labor in their colonies until 1946, and then did so after effective African rather than international protests.

Further reading

Cooper, F. (1980) *From Slaves to Squatters: Plantation Labor and Agriculture in Zanzibar and Coastal Kenya, 1890–1925*, New Haven: Yale University Press.

—— (2000) "Conditions Analogous to Slavery: Imperialism and Free Labor Ideology in Africa," in F. Cooper, T. Holt and R. Scott (eds.), *Beyond Slavery: Explorations of Race, Labor, and Citizenship in Postemancipation Societies*, Chapel Hill: University of North Carolina Press.

Lovejoy, P. (2000) *Transformations in Slavery: A History of Slavery in Africa*, 2nd edn., Cambridge: Cambridge University Press.

Lovejoy, P. and Hogendorn, J. (1993) *Slow Death for Slavery: The Course of Abolition in Northern Nigeria, 1897–1936*, Cambridge: Cambridge University Press.

Martin, K. (1998) *Slavery and Colonial Rule in French West Africa*, Cambridge: Cambridge University Press.

Roberts, R. and Miers, S. (1988) "The End of Slavery in Africa," in S. Miers and R. Roberts (eds.), *The Ending of Slavery in Africa*, Madison: University of Wisconsin Press.

SEAN HAWKINS

socialisms and socialists

Two of modernity's co-projects have been nationalism and development; socialisms in Africa have been a part of both. They had a short life of scarcely fifty years, corresponding to the early phases of national liberation, beginning with the Officers' Coup under Nasser in **Egypt** in 1952, and reaching a symbolic end with **South Africa** meeting late twentieth-century neoliberal economic realities. Since the mid-1990s twentieth-century African socialisms appear all but dead.

African socialisms have been many, but regardless of variations in ideas and practices they minimally consisted of five things:

1 a degree of commitment to state ownership, connected with notions of equity and the redistribution of wealth;
2 the imperatives of development, overcoming economic backwardness, and increasing well-being;
3 the need to create appropriate institutions to shape development and politics;
4 the quest for solidarity that went beyond class and "tribe"; and
5 the need to forge a bond between culture and the state.

African socialism would be measured by defining

itself through discernible traits that marked it as being genuinely African.

Some overlap exists between the different forms of African socialism; in essence there were three broad categories:

1 North African ("Arab") socialisms, which confronted the power and authority of traditional classes and elites, and were concerned with balancing the competing identities of secularist nationalism, socialism, and Islamism;
2 African socialisms, which claimed to draw upon and modernize an inheritance of pre-colonial, indigenous socialist/communal practices; and
3 Afro-Marxist (or Afro-Communist) socialisms, which came into and out of power between 1963 and 1995, some brought to power through coups and others through the national liberation struggles in **lusophone Africa** in the early 1970s.

The origins of socialisms in Africa go back at least to the turn of the nineteenth century. African socialism is actually discussed as early as 1913 in **Sierra Leone**, and even earlier in Egypt and **South Africa**, where the first two communist parties were born in 1921 and 1923 respectively. Generally proscribed under colonialism, socialism did not make a significant entry into African politics until after the **Second World War** and during the later phases of development of the **nationalist movements**. Individual communists were active in trade unions and in political parties, but communist parties only played a major role in two countries: South Africa, where the communist party was still numerically strong at the end of the twentieth century, and **Sudan**, where it played a role in the nationalist movement, remaining influential until Nimeiri's pogroms against communists in the early 1970s. No Marxist party born out of working-class or peasant activism ever claimed state power in Africa. However, from 1917 until the mid-1970s Marxism–Leninism would be the defining socialism throughout colonial Africa; even when communism was seen as a threat to their interests, many Africans were impressed by the rapidity of its modernizing accomplishments, achieved through centralization, planning, and single-party rule.

North African ("Arab") socialisms

The forms of North African socialism discussed in this section were established in Egypt under both Nasser and Sadat (1960–74), in Bourguiba's **Tunisia** (1954–86), in **Algeria** under Ahmed Ben Bella and Boumedienne through to the reforms of the mid-1980s, and in Qaddafi's **Libya** from 1969 into the twenty-first century.

For Africa the significance of the Officers' Coup in Egypt lay in its implementing state capitalism and the single-party state, demonstrating the effectiveness and legitimacy of achieving power through armed force, and identifying compelling figures around whom cults of personality developed and with whom the state and state initiatives could be identified. Although he was initially opposed to socialism, Nasser proclaimed "Arab" socialism to justify the expropriation of land from large landowners, nationalizing foreign capital, and eventually banning religious and political opposition, with each of these three areas identified as frustrating national progress. Through developmental planning socialism promised rapid economic and social development by modernizing and catching up, and an ethic of redistribution effected by the state rather than by class interests. As with all African socialisms, multi-party democracy was viewed by North African socialists as a divisive luxury that progress could not afford; labor, once an independent source of support, was not expected to have an independent role, other than supporting the developmental efforts of the state. A trademark of African socialisms was their invocation of the "people," when the people had little decision-making influence.

As much to challenge traditional elites and the *ulemma* as to promote Tunisian independence (which was not achieved until 1956), Habib Bourguiba's neo-Destourism invoked modernist (*ijtihadist*) nationalism and socialism. Like Nasser, he put strategic sectors under state planning, and through nationalizations embarked on state capitalist development. Bourguiba asserted the state's need to direct and redistribute wealth, rather than own and socialize property. Declaring himself president-for-life, proscribing other political parties, and maintaining firm control over Islamists, he was eventually overthrown in 1987, but not before bequeathing to his successors the most secular, modern, and developed North African state.

Central to Algeria's protracted independence struggle was the attempt to balance national identity against the post-independence modernization the economy. Ben Bella and the FLN committed Algeria to *autogestation* on abandoned *pied noir* agricultural land and in abandoned factories; they also prohibited political parties and accepted a centralized state, fearing the unleashing of latent religious, class, and ethnic interests. Houari Boumediene's coup in 1965 normalized the revolution: he promoted technocratic development through state-led industrialization based on oil and natural gas rents, while limiting political participation and attempting to control the clergy and Islamists by making Islam appear compatible with socialism. After his death in 1978 the accumulated effects of Ben Chadli's (1978–91) economic and political liberalization unfettered forces that had been repressed by one-party rule. All pretense at socialism was abandoned after the breakdown of the welfare state, the release of ethnic loyalties, and the descent into a brutal civil war as a result of the Islamist backlash against elections annulled by the military in 1993.

Muammar al-Qaddafi's Arab state socialism (*Jamahiriya* – "people's" – socialism) was introduced in 1977, eight years after the overthrow of the Libyan monarchy. Qaddafi also evoked an Islamic-based socialism. Founded on a type of voluntarism that was tied to the peculiar ideological whims of its leader, this socialism was used as a bulwark against Islamists questioning the legitimacy of secular notions of socialism. From the 1970s, benefiting from extensive oil rents, Qaddafi was able to maintain investments in large capital projects, while enacting distributive state-welfare policies to offset the mobilization of opposition to his authoritarian system of government.

The African socialists

The following section discusses the African socialisms represented by Nkrumah's rule in **Ghana** (1957–66), Ahmed Sékou Touré in **Guinea** (1958–84), Modibo Keita's **Mali** (1960–8), Julius Nyerere in **Tanzania** (1960–85), Léopold Senghor's **Senegal** (1960–81), and Kaunda's **Zambia** (1964–91).

Assorted nationalist politicians elaborated on various themes relating to the heritage of pre-colonial, kin-based systems of social reciprocity; obligations to social egalitarianism; and a consensus system of political order. It seemed irrelevant that this view was historically problematic; what mattered was marking difference. Nkrumah claimed that "African personality" could be differentiated from Marx's understanding of "man's" place in socialism because African socialism had a clear moral base within pre-colonial communities, and could serve as a foundation for African justice after independence. Keita claimed Malians would build upon their Islamic past, which had insisted on social egalitarianism and duties to the weakest and poorest in society, while Touré declared the absence of extensive private property in Africa allowed for the Africanization of Marxism. Like the others, Nkrumah's policies followed a trajectory of one-party socialism: rapid industrialization, a centrally planned economy, the extensive expansion of the public sector, and the widening of health care and education. Structural reforms were needed in all sectors of the economy to establish economic and financial **decolonization**, as well as socialist structures throughout the country. Viewing one-partyism as being the best option for development and nation-building, all of these states moved to single-party rule, in tandem with jailing opposition leaders, banning strikes, and restricting the independent role of unions.

Senghor's socialism is cultural metaphor. Concerned with identifying mores in African societies that could modify the corrosive values of Western individualism, African socialism was translated into a cultural disposition. Close economic ties between Senegal and France constrained socialization of production on a scale that would bare comparison with that in other African socialist states. Socialization was also limited because conservative members of the coalitions supporting the ruling party, especially the Islamic Brotherhoods, maintained control over groundnuts, Senegal's main export crop. Conversely African humanism was in evidence in Kaunda's eclectic amalgam of ideas drawn from Western liberalism, Fabian and

Christian socialisms, and African collectivism. Nationalization appeared to be a rationalization of state patronage and personal accumulation for political elites. For over a decade after independence many urban-based Zambians benefited from state subsidies and an expanded welfare system derived from high copper prices on world markets. A decade after that, services collapsed because of low export commodity prices and accumulated debt, unraveling the financing of overfed bureaucracies that were an inevitable target when **structural adjustment programs** came into force.

The most sustained African socialist experiment was Nyerere's attempt to modernize pre-colonial reciprocity networks, or *ujamma*. Conceived initially as forestalling the development of classes and inequality, it saw peasant production being modernized through a policy of education aimed at enabling self-reliance, by which the peasantry were persuaded to accept villagization, the cornerstone of rural development. Hardly cooperative modernization from below, by 1976 villagization had ended up as a bureaucratized state effort to replace rural households by forcing 9 million scattered peasants into "development" villages. For Nyerere villagization was about the necessity of centralizing economies and concentrating resources in block settlements; the peasantry's appreciation of socialism would come later. This appreciation never came. Dependent on foreign aid for development initiatives, Tanzania was anything but self-reliant. It foundered on a price depression for its export commodities, the costs incurred in removing Idi Amin from power, and the state's inability to empower its peasantry. After a decade of economic failure and forced by demands from aid agencies to adjust its economy, Nyerere was the last *ujamma* socialist by the time he left office in 1985.

Afro-Marxism

Also known as "rhetorical Marxists," regimes that can be considered Afro-Marxist were the **Congo** under Massemba-Debat through to Sassou Ngeusso (1963–91), **Ethiopia** under Mengistu Haile Mariam (1974–91), **Somalia** under Siad Barre (1969–90), Mathieu Kérékou's **Benin** (1972–91), and Didier Ratsiraka's **Madagascar** (1975–93). **Mozambique** under Samora Machel (1975–86), who came to power through the national liberation struggle, is included too.

Except in Congo (Brazzaville), Afro-Marxism came about during a period of **Third World** triumphalism. Successful left-wing insurgencies in Southeast Asia, Africa, and Latin America gave fresh hope to policies of non-alignment and alternative Marxisms. Afro-Marxists called themselves Marxist–Leninist, however, and claimed they ruled on behalf of peasants and workers, proclaiming the hegemony of the vanguard party. In Benin Mathieu Kérékou adopted economic planning, and nationalized the banks and primary industries. Most regimes to some degree followed suit, following ruinous economic policies, as exemplified by Madagascar whose growth rates declined below −2 percent between 1976 and 1991.

In overthrowing the old monarchy of Haile Selassie, the Ethiopian revolution was a genuine social revolution. However, it experienced some of the worst domestic bloodletting outside Sudan and prior to the Rwandan **genocide**; enacted a forced resettlement of millions of peasants; underwent the worst famine in modern African history; and endured two pointless wars, one attempting to keep **Eritrea** as part of Ethiopia and one with Somalia over the Ogaden. Commitment to socialism in these states was largely rhetorical, bearing little relationship to the realities that their societies faced, and the language and practice of Afro-Marxism appears divorced from the realities it was being forced on. With the exceptions of Agostinho Neto and Amilcar Cabral in Mozambique, Afro-Marxists gave scant attention to matters of culture. Neto and Cabral's FRELIMO had to contend with economically destructive incursions from South Africa, and with the repercussions of the **Cold War** and South Africa's sponsorship of Renamo's sadistic violence, but some of their failures must also be blamed on superficially modernistic formulations and practices. Despite policies of "people's power," FRELIMO generally displayed an inability to understand peasant life, often deemed superstitious and backward, and an unwillingness to deal seriously with the ethnic regionalism that peasants inhabited and worked within.

Mozambique also came to represent the fragility of Afro-Marxist regimes as it transformed itself and its ideology collapsed. The other Afro-Marxist regimes either collapsed (as in Ethiopia and Somalia) or changed themselves from adherents to an imported ideology into supplicants to the global administrators of adjustment policies (Ngeusso, Kérékou, Ratsiraka, Machel, and Chiluba). With the collapse of the Soviet Union, their usefulness in post-Cold War *realpolitik* depended on the degree to which they accepted the advice of the International Monetary Fund and World Bank. Like the Stalinist Marxism–Leninism they had appealed to in seizing power, their regimes were topsoil deep. Unable to change the forces and relations of production, and with few institutions through which the state could build, develop or sustain itself, they left a legacy of failure and often death.

Thus, at least in name, Africa has been home to many socialisms. Since 1952, of the fifty-four states in Africa, more than half at some point have identified themselves as socialist or social democratic, on the pages of their liberation charters and/or by retaining the terms "socialist" or "socialism" in their constitutions. If such naming has any consequence, socialism's impact on Africa has been enormous. But, by their own measures, African socialisms failed to meet people's needs.

Further reading

Benot, Y. (1970) *Idéologies des indépendances africaines*, Paris: Maspero.

Choueri, Y.M. (2000) *Arab Nationalism: A History*, Oxford: Blackwell.

Goldbourne, H. and Cohen, R. (eds.) (1992) *Democracy and Socialism in Africa*, Boulder: Westview Press.

Gyekye, K. (1997) *Tradition and Modernity: Philosophic Reflections on the African Experience*, New York: Oxford University Press.

Hughes, A. (ed.) (1992) "Marxism's Retreat from Africa," *Journal of Communist Studies* 8, 1: 4–20.

PABLO IDAHOSA

society: colonial

The main purpose of all colonies was to provide the raw materials that would supply the factories of industrial Europe. This goal could not be accomplished unless colonial societies were structured in such a way as to provide smooth and efficient administration, the maintenance and effective organization of the principle means of production, and a functioning workforce of higher level administrators and functionaries, as well as manual laborers. The basic structures of colonial societies can thus be understood as having evolved in response to meeting those basic needs. The measures that were introduced to facilitate the desired social outcome hinged upon key contextual factors: whether a colony was settler or non-settler; whether the production system was organized around trade, labor reserves, or concession companies; which religious system was dominant; demographic factors; the strength of traditional elites; the nature and extent of African resistance; and so on.

Every colonial power had, as its first priority, the separation of Africans from their independent means of subsistence, thereby forcing them to work for wages or to produce for the colonial economy. The colonial powers encountered a variety of different indigenous social formations, which demanded different techniques of subjugation. These different techniques inspired a variety of African responses. This dynamic interaction gave rise to colonial societies that, although they varied in their specifics, had a core set of features and processes in common.

All colonial societies witnessed demographic changes. From the time of colonial conquest to the mid-1930s population in much of Africa was in a state of decline, due to wars of conquest, ecological disasters, and the impact of forced labor and labor migration which sometimes took workers into new and strange environments where there were diseases against which they had no immunity. As these conditions changed from the 1930s **population** growth resumed, and colonial social structures were consolidated. Urbanization and colonial education were among the most important transmitters of colonial culture (see **education:**

colonial; **urbanization**). It was thus in the urban centers that colonial society developed its most salient features.

Colonial society witnessed the emergence of new class formations, the most important of which was the growth and expansion of the working classes. The size and shape of the working class varied, depending on whether or not the colony was organized around **migrant labor**, agricultural exports, or forced labor. Migrant labor economies tended to produce large-scale, well-organized working classes that were almost completely dependent on wage labor and had little access to independent means of production. Economies organized around crop production and export were characterized by peasantries that still maintained some independent access to the means of production, but nevertheless were dependent on the market. Economies organized around forced labor, on the other hand, were characterized by semi-proletarianized workers who relied on a range of strategies for evading forced labor.

Working-class formation also affected, and was affected by, gender relations and family forms (see **families**). Generally colonial patriarchal ideologies combined with indigenous patriarchal ideologies tended to reinforce women's subordination, exploitation, and oppression. Many elite women were progressively marginalized as they lost their political power and control over trading and manufacturing activities. But there were other women who took advantage of the expanding petty commodity markets, or who sought to retain their autonomy by migrating to the rapidly growing colonial cities, where they often engaged in trading and other activities.

The creation of new class formations necessarily led to changes in social organization and the emergence of new forms of association, many of which reflected the new forms of class and gender stratification that emerged in the wake of colonization. The proletarianization of women, for example, led to the emergence of women's associations within the larger **nationalist movement**. Women in the Transkei region of **South Africa**, for example, organized a series of boycotts against European merchants in 1921. The Aba women's rebellion of 1929 was yet another gendered revolt, this time sparked off by the imposition of direct taxation alongside new local courts. Educated elites also sought to ameliorate and reform many of the harsher and more repressive aspects of colonial society. They primarily sought to secure increased access to missionary education, as well as increased political representation on legislative and executive councils. The channels through which elites articulated their aspirations and grievances played a very important role in shaping the contours of colonial societies, and can be divided into five basic types: welfare associations, social/literary clubs, ethnic associations, religious association, and political associations.

These associations evinced varying degrees of political radicalism. The Ethiopian churches, which were particularly strong in **Southern** and **Central Africa**, emphasized personal and spiritual improvement through self-discipline. Secular elite societies, which emerged throughout the continent, advocated a similar program. In contrast the religious associations that thrived in **North Africa** were more likely to agitate for the complete overthrow of the colonial system, as the dialectic between religion and nationalism produced a more radical institutional response. **African religions** also demonstrated a high degree of variability and adaptability in the face of the transformations in the social structure brought about by colonial rule. The strength of traditional religious elites, and the degree to which they were given autonomy in the colonial regime, also profoundly shaped the trajectory of colonial societies. Cult priests and spirit mediums played a central role in many rebellions against the imposition of taxes and forced labor systems.

Colonial societies were critically informed by the emergence of print capitalism – the founding of the **press** – which, just as it had in Europe, encouraged the development of an "imagined community" that transcended regional, ethnic, and religious differences. Furthermore new identities were formed and negotiated in response to colonial rule. Colonial societies witnessed the emergence of new types of leisure activity that emerged dialogically, as a result of the fusing of diverse people in new settings. **Leisure** was often part of complex struggles over the organization of urban space, daily life, and the social imaginaries of different segments of colonial society. The mines were a particularly fecund source of new cultural forms, particularly in the areas of **music** and **dance**. The rural areas of Central and **East Africa** were also well known for the ways in which cultural symbols, embodied in song and dance (and hence unintelligible to colonial officials), became important tools of both socialization and resistance. Dance associations, which spread from East Africa into the Belgian Congo, were particularly well known for the subversive ways in which they allowed African people to critique colonial officials and the conventions of European colonial society.

Finally, colonial societies were not only shaped by internal factors and pressures, but by external ones as well. Anti-colonial and nationalist activities increased precipitously in the wake of the growth of **Pan-Africanism**, which facilitated the growth of nationalist movements. Pan-Africanism was not confined to politics; it also involved cultural traffic between the continent and the **African diasporas**, especially in the areas of popular culture.

Africanist scholarship has been plagued by theoretical and methodological battles over the interpretation of colonial society. The very notions of what constituted "colonial society," and which units of analysis should be given the most attention in its analysis, are strongly influenced by the theoretical assumptions that underwrite particular schools of thought, as well as the methods of analysis associated with them. It is possible to identify four broad categories within which most theoretical analyses of colonial society fall: pluralist, Marxist, nationalist, and post-colonial. Although each of these schools of thought seeks to understand the economic system imposed by colonial rule, the interaction between different ethnic and racial communities, the impact on gender relations, and the transformations that occurred in the cultural realm, each school differs in the emphasis or importance they place on these various social factors, as well as in what they regard to be the correct method for analyzing such factors.

Pluralist approaches

Starting from the earliest decades of the twentieth century there emerged a considerable body of literature dealing with problems of what was then called "acculturation" or "culture contact" and social change in colonial society. Social anthropology, which incorporated the earlier writings and methodologies used by missionaries and colonial administrators, centered on analyzing the ways in which the colonial situation forced various communities into contact with each other, and the changes that occurred therefrom. The Pluralist School was underwritten by the assumption that colonial societies were "plural societies" characterized by different ethnic groups and races living in close proximity, occasionally coming into conflict, and influencing one another through the diffusion of culture. The pluralists were most concerned to document changes in African attitudes, and thus the units they took as most meaningful for the analysis of colonial society were clothes, occupations, education, and leisure/cultural activities. These were taken to be reliable indices of the degree to which African people were becoming acculturated or "Westernized" as a result of living among Europeans in colonial society. Hence Clyde Mitchell's (1961) work on the Kalela dance among the African population of the Zambian Copperbelt focused on how the dancers' style of dress and deportment indicated their aspirations toward a European way of life, which he felt arose from their cultural contact and negotiations with whites.

A similar sort of analysis was extended to the understanding of family forms in colonial societies, which were taken as a reliable index of whether "tribalism" or "tribal values" were able to withstand the experience of acculturation that was the concomitant of living in colonial society. The work of Horace Miner (1953), for example, focused on family structures among the Arab, Tuareg, and Songhai in Timbuctoo. He argued that Arab people were able to maintain the integrity of their extended family forms, even in the face of immense culture contact and strong pressure towards acculturation. Miner's work catalogued helping patterns, socializing patterns, friendship networks, and support activities among the three populations, and concluded that acculturation had impacted family forms, but nevertheless extended family ties retained their traditional importance. Similar types of analysis were applied with respect to family forms in **West Africa**. Research on slum populations in **Lagos** by Aldous (1965) confirmed that the residents of central Lagos, like their rural counterparts, continued to regard the needs of kinfolk as their first obligation.

All of these studies proceeded from the assumption that:

> the Europeans are in a position of social superiority and the Africans aspire to the civilization which is the particular characteristic and perquisite of the socially superior group.
>
> (Mitchell 1961: 13)

However, their analyses did not extend to the specifics of European life, religion, and culture in Africa. Nor did they consider the fact that European cultures could undergo their own processes of "acculturation" or "Africanization." In fact the colonial situation fell completely outside their analyses. The failure of pluralist analyses to account for the ways in which colonialism, as a global system of economic relations, imposed a new urban order on the colonized societies – and further how this order fundamentally altered patterns of social organization, family structure, and culture – was the major impetus behind the critique of pluralism, structural functionalism, and empiricist approaches launched by Marxist social scientists.

Marxist approaches

Marxist critiques were launched by the South African anthropologist Bernard Magubane, who attacked the indices used by the pluralists for studying colonial society and social change. He argued that their analyses mystified the real social relations, because they failed to account for the fact that the trajectory of British colonialism in Central and Southern Africa was of the industrial–extractive type, whereby the advanced sector (mining camps and towns) was more organically connected to the metropole than to its own rural hinterland. He attacked:

> [their] general reluctance to analyze African societies in the context of the colonial situation or as extensions of capitalist societies. This results in a tendency to regard any crisis as having been generated by forces wholly independent of capitalist characteristics.
>
> (Magubane [1969] 2000: 30)

For him the social changes that were taking place among Africans in colonial societies were not simply the result of "acculturation" or "culture contact," but evolved in response to the economic exigencies of colonialism. Furthermore he stressed the importance of seeing Africans' desire to acquire material goods as being indicative not of a hapless desire to be European, but rather as an index of their desire to confront and transform the situations they faced as a result of being reduced to non-persons in the colonial society.

The framework for the idea that colonial society in Africa could only be understood by seeing Africa as part of the capitalist world system was articulated most clearly by Immanuel Wallerstein, and can be seen in the work of a number of scholars. Leroy Vail and Landeg White's (1980) work on capitalism and colonialism in **Mozambique** analyzed how the Portuguese government attempted to control the region by means of neo-mercantilist policies that forced the Quelimane district to furnish Portugal with regulated quantities of produce. They also demonstrated that the leisure activities of workers, particularly those popular protest and work songs that took up colonial themes, were not examples of "acculturation," but rather an index of the African population's resistance to alien rule. Likewise Tabitha Kanogo's work on squatters in **Kenya** analyzed the development of various institutions, such as voluntary self-help educational programs (*harambee*), that enabled African people to "turn the White Highlands into a place in which they could feel 'at home'." She demonstrated that the development and transformation of indigenous cultural forms were closely connected to the fact that "squatters had to cope with their positions as workers in a colonial situation." Thus she saw workers' efforts at the wholesale transfer of cultural and political institutions, such as elders' councils (*ciama*), circumcision (*irua*), and marriage ceremonies, as evidence neither of the persistence of "tribalism" nor of the failure of "acculturation," but rather as dynamic responses to the colonial situation –

responses that changed in order to "meet the growing challenges from the settler economy" (Kanogo 1987: 74).

Patrick Manning's work on the expansion of European and Muslim culture in **francophone Africa** also demonstrates that changes in African religious practices were closely related to the changes introduced by the spread of global capitalism. Thus he analyzed Christian conversions not as examples of "Westernization," but rather as dynamic responses to a changing world. Manning asked the question: "Why then should Africans have found any advantage in Christianity or Islam?" In answer he suggested that conversion came about because:

> [Africans] were now in a world-wide political system, that of colonies and their European mother countries, so their beliefs should extend to a world-wide frame of reference. In this sense, conversions to Islam and Christianity may not have been renunciations of the old religions, but translation of the old religions into new terms.
>
> (Manning 1988: 102)

Nationalist approaches

The refusal to see the processes of cultural change that occurred as a result of colonialism as simply "Westernization" was articulated forcefully by nationalist historians, who sought to demonstrate (to use Terence Ranger's phrase) African "activity, adaptations, choice, and initiative" (Ranger 1968: 5). In a famous essay on the invention of tradition in colonial Africa, Ranger argued that social and cultural traditions were invented and manipulated by both the Europeans and Africans to serve their own interests. This happened in four particular situations, whose processes and purposes he outlined:

1. elders tended to appeal to "tradition" in order to defend their dominance over the rural means of production against challenges from the **youth**;
2. men appealed to "tradition" to ensure that the increasing role that women played in the rural areas, especially in regions dominated by male migrant labor, did not result in any diminution of male control;
3. ruling aristocracies appealed to "tradition" in order to maintain or extend their control over their subjects; and
4. indigenous people appealed to "tradition" to ensure that migrants who settled among them did not achieve political or economic rights.

For their part, the educated Africans who realized that the way towards real power did not lie with the polities of the past, began to invent traditions of nationalism. Using this model, historians have analyzed the contexts in which various cultural and social practices developed, from music and dance to **law** and marriage.

The emphasis on exploring Africans as agentic subjects, and colonial society as a site marked by ethnic, racial, and class conflicts and cultural inventions that structured and gave meaning to large-scale concepts like "the West" and "Africa," was anticipated by the inventors of "Negritude." Negritude was both a philosophy of history and a mode of anti-colonial resistance; it sought to extend the idea of colonial society beyond a focus on individual societies, instead seeing colonized people the world over as sharing similar experiences and a similar consciousness. For Léopold Sédar Senghor, one of the founders of the movement, the experience of colonialism was a racial experience that created what he called a "collective personality" among black people. Like Marxist and world system analyses, Negritude focused on the fact that European colonialism systematically underdeveloped the colonized world. Like pluralist scholars, they concerned themselves with assessing the impact of the European cultures and values that were imposed on African societies during colonialism.

Negritude, however, completely reversed the hierarchy of values that underwrote pluralist scholarship. Aimé Césaire, for example, opened his *Discourse on Colonialism* with a damning indictment of the West: "Europe is morally, spiritually indefensible" (Césaire [1955] 1972: 9). He vigorously disputed the idea that Europe brought anything resembling civilization to its colonies, for it did not come with a single human value. Indeed he even suggested that the actions that European colonizers sanctioned in colonial societies prepared the way for Nazism and the Third

Reich: the savage exploitation and murder of colonized peoples inevitably led to oppression and mass murder in Europe itself. Thus, unlike the pluralists, Negritude scholars placed equal emphasis on exposing the changes wrought by colonialism in the societies and cultures of the colonizer and in the societies and cultures of the colonized.

Frantz Fanon, an activist scholar who opposed many of Negritude's doctrines despite the fact he was heavily influenced by them, also analyzed the categories of "blackness" and "whiteness" in ways that went beyond a focus on individual colonial societies. He articulated a powerful theoretical reversal of the processes that pluralists positively described as "Westernization," showing how the material practices of colonialism engendered feelings of both racial inferiority and cultural dislocation in African communities. Unlike the pluralists, however, he did not see this cultural dislocation as having been produced by clashing cultures, but rather as a logical response to a deformed system. Fanon also disagreed with the ways in which Negritude scholarship focused on reclaiming the glories of the pre-colonial past or on reversing racist stereotypes by assigning positive instead of negative values to them. He saw Negritude as simply reinforcing the idea that Africans were backward and simple, arguing instead that theoretical energies should be directed at showing the vitality of African resistance to colonial rule, in particular how national identities are forged as part of the fight against colonial oppression.

In his studies of French colonialism in Algeria, for example, Fanon counterposed the meanings that Algerian women's clothing had for Algerians with those they had for the French. Fanon documents how French authorities believed that Algerian women who walked the streets in modern French fashions had accepted Western values, and thus could not be sympathetic to the revolution. Resistance fighters were able to use French ignorance to their advantage, clothing female revolutionaries who proceeded to enact various forms of counter-insurgency in Western dress. Fanon demonstrated that while the colonizers saw the *haik* (veil) as a symbol of the backwardness, the impenetrability to modern reason, and the retrogressive gender ideologies of Algerian society, it was actually a mutable symbol. Thus, when the French authorities discovered that women in Western attire were frequently aligned with the resistance movement, the revolutionaries changed tactics, using veiled women as couriers for documents and weapons. Thus the veil not only came to represent Algerian resistance to colonialism, but was also a powerful weapon in colonial struggle in its own right.

Post-colonial approaches

Post-colonial scholarship, despite its misleading name, is the latest intellectual trend to take colonial society as its focus of inquiry. The "post" in post-colonial is not taken to mean "past," but rather is used to capture the idea of engaging with, moving through, and moving beyond coloniality. Post-colonial scholars borrow a number of its analytical models from Marxist scholarship, and their themes from the work done by Negritude scholars. In particular they eschew a narrow focus on individual colonial societies in favor of looking at how colonialism worked as a system of economic relations and discourses, which produced a set of ideological constructions that are currently termed "Africa." Thus they seek to understand the ways in which colonial societies were shaped by systems both of economic relations and of cultural and symbolic representations that impacted Africans and Europeans profoundly, albeit in different ways. Thus, while acknowledging the importance of class relations in structuring the relationship between the colonizer and the colonized, post-colonial scholars also seek to use other analytical methods alongside class analysis – including deconstruction, symbolic interactionism, literary criticism, discourse analysis, and psychoanalysis. In post-colonial analyses, colonial society emerges not as a space of "acculturation" or even a space of economic or racial "exploitation," but rather as a space of cultural negotiation or "hybridity" or "creolization."

Much post-colonial scholarship borrows heavily from the theoretical framework first articulated by Frantz Fanon, in which "blackness" and "whiteness" were mutually interdependent ideological constructions. Rather than focusing on races coexisting in a plural society or on the ways in which racism functions to further entrench capitalist exploitation, post-colonial scholars focus on the ways in which race is socially constructed in colonial societies. Thus Kwame Appiah has theorized the ways in which colonial and anti-colonial discourses work together to fix racial essences on bodies. Anne McClintock and Saul Dubow have done similar work on the construction of race in South Africa, McClintock showing how the idea of race emerged in concert with those of gender and sexuality.

Thus, when post-colonial scholars consider the ways in which African modes of dress or "self-fashioning" changed with the advent of colonialism, they focus on the ways in which the struggles over how African bodies were to be clothed and represented

> were a crucial site in the battle of wills and deeds, the dialectic of means and ends, that shaped the encounter between Europeans and Africans. And transformed both in the process.
>
> (Comaroff and Comaroff 1991: 222)

Similarly religion, particularly conversion to Christianity, is seen as further evidence of how Africans, although "encompassed by the European capitalist system" sought to "seize its symbols, to question their authority and integrity, and to reconstruct them in their own image" (ibid.: xii). Post-colonial scholarship on Arab nationalism in the Middle East and North Africa has also shown how

> [nationalists] invested colonially created territorial units with their own meanings of community or nation by drawing upon myths of Arab origin or the Islamic golden age of the Caliphates, even though some early Arab nationalists were Christian.
>
> (Loomba 1998: 197)

Because post-colonial scholarship was originally the province of literary critics, it is overwhelmingly concerned with questions of language and the impact of language on identity formation. Gender and sexuality, and their relationship to the production of race, together with the ways in which they were transformed by colonial rule, have also been at the forefront of post-colonial scholarship. Unlike pluralists, who sought to examine how Westernization altered sexual and family relationships, or Marxists, who sought to analyze how the migrant labor system transformed African family forms and gender relationships, post-colonial scholars instead focus on the symbolic importance of sexual and racial alterity in the representation of the colonized as "other." Their analysis reveals that the policing of the sexual and racial boundaries of sexuality in colonial society was a critical component of the project to demarcate "self" and "other," both within individual colonial societies and in the empire as a whole, with female bodies marking the "boundaries" of empire.

See also: civil society; colonial conquest and resistance; economy: colonial; education: colonial; peasants; sex and sexuality; state: colonial; women's movements; workers

References and further reading

Aldous, J. (1965) "Urbanization, the Extended Family, and Kinship Ties in West Africa," in P.L. van den Berghe (ed.), *Africa: Social Problems of Change and Conflict*, San Francisco: Chandler Publishing.

Appiah, K. (1992) *In My Father's House: Africa in the Philosophy of Culture*, London: Oxford.

Césaire, A. (1972 [1955]) *Discourse on Colonialism*, New York: Monthly Review Press.

Comaroff, J. and Comoroff, J. (1991) *Of Revelation and Revolution*, vol. 1, Chicago: University of Chicago Press.

Dubow, S. (1995) *Scientific Racism in Modern South Africa*, Cambridge: Cambridge University Press.

Fanon, F. (1967) *Black Skin, White Masks*, New York: Grove.

Kanogo, T. (1987) *Squatters and the Roots of Mau Mau*, London: James Currey.

Loomba, A. (1998) *Colonialism/Postcolonialism*, London: Routledge.

Magubane, B. (2000 [1969]) "Pluralism and Conflict Situations: A New Look," repr. in *African Sociology – Towards a Critical Perspective: The Collected Essays of Bernard M. Magubane*, Trenton: Africa World Press Inc.

Manning, P. (1988) *Francophone Sub-Saharan Africa*,

1880–1985, Cambridge: Cambridge University Press.

McClintock, A. (1995) *Imperial Leather*, London: Routledge.

Miner, H. (1953) *The Primitive City of Timbuctoo* Philadelphia: American Philosophical Society.

Mitchell, C. (1961) *Tribalism and the Plural Society*, Oxford: Oxford University Press.

Ranger, T. (1968) "Introduction," in T. Ranger (ed.), *Emerging Themes in African History*, Nairobi: Oxford University Press.

Vail, L. and White, L. (1980) *Capitalism and Colonialism in Mozambique*, Minneapolis: University of Minnesota Press.

ZINE MAGUBANE

society: post-independence

Social change in Africa is a problematic phenomenon. One problem is that the very term "social change" suggests that such change has a direction, that it is part of some wider, identifiable process, such as the growth of capitalism or economic development. Another problem is that it presupposes not only a future, but also a past – a fixed point from which change can be measured. Recent social theory has suggested that neither our views about a fixed past nor a directional future are relevant to understanding social change in Africa. Instead what has emerged in recent studies has been an awareness of the fluidity and adaptability of social relations in Africa – indeed their constant variability over hundreds and hundreds, if not thousands, of years. Given the persistence of social change in Africa, it is important to bear in mind that social change is not the opposite of social continuity, just as social continuity is not synonymous with tradition. In addition change has come to be seen less in terms of the intersection of the past with the present, but rather in terms of the intersection of local worlds with global influences.

From optimism to uncertainty and pessimism

Over the second half of the twentieth century views about Africa's future moved from extreme optimism to extreme pessimism. These moods affected the analysis and understanding of social change in Africa, particularly as they related to the continent's future. With **decolonization** in the 1950s came unprecedented economic growth, but it did not last, and nor did the hopes that independence and prosperity inspired. Instead political instability, civil strife, and economic crises contributed both to uncertainty among African intellectuals about the capacity of the continent to free itself from its past and to cynical despondency among foreign observers. One of the continent's greatest writers, the playwright and activist Wole Soyinka, commented at the end of the 1990s:

> The crimes that the African continent commits against her kind are of a dimension and, unfortunately, of a nature that appears to constantly provoke memories of historic wrongs inflicted on the continent by others.
>
> (Soyinka 1999: 19)

But as African intellectuals struggled to put the first two generations of independence into historical perspective, many Western commentators were inclined to write Africa off by removing it from the realm of hope and exiling it to a land of despair where it was cut off from time and so without a future. Robert Kaplan, an influential exponent of a perspective called "Afropessimism," wrote of the continent in the 1990s as being burdened by nature and isolated from the world. Unlike Soyinka, he did not look to the past to understand the present; on the contrary he sought to exonerate the past and blame the continent's problems on its geography: "even as Africa's geography was conducive to humanity's emergence, it may not have been conducive to its further development" (Kaplan 1996: 7). The magnitude of the AIDS crisis, and its contribution to other problems of **health and disease** in Africa, unfortunately provided a certain license for despair about the continent's future and the direction of social change. Yet conditions that might have caused serious social disintegration in other parts of the world had not yet done so in Africa; one of the most important things that Afropessimists overlooked was Africa's history of dealing with adversity. Although fear sometimes victimized its carriers, care and compassion were the dominant reaction to those afflicted with AIDS. Whether these would continue to prevail were questions for the twenty-first century, but by the end of the twentieth century the crisis had not resulted in social breakdown because of the resilience of social values and the adaptability of social networks.

Just as moods changed about Africa's future, theories regarding the nature and dynamics of social relations also changed over the second half of the century, as scholars came to realize that social relations were not the result of given structures, but the outcome of dynamic human interactions, shifting values and needs, changing emotional priorities, and varying relations between men and women. This entry deals with such parallel realities – that is, with how the thinking of scholars studying African social relations changed, and how that in turn transformed the history of social change in Africa. These two perspectives are inextricable, as the former affected and has continued to affect our understanding of the latter; our understanding of social change is as dependent on our analytical paradigms as it is on any direct evidence that we have of recent change – and such evidence is itself highly fragmentary, still very preliminary, and extremely varied.

From detribalization to modernization

In the second half of the twentieth century Africa witnessed social changes and challenges that – with the exception of the AIDS crisis – were not that much different than those that had confronted colonial society. For example, colonial practices of coercion and inducement that had brought **migrant labor** from rural areas to regions of commercial farming and industrial mining had become deeply etched into many post-colonial states and cultures – as firmly as colonial railway networks were etched onto the landscape of most of Africa. Changes in the meaning of ethnicity, in the choice of religious affiliations (such as **Christianity** and **Islam**), and the nature of gender relations all continued to challenge the control of the state over **civil society**. What was new was the intensity and speed of some of these changes, due to the weakening or liberalization of state control in the post-colonial period.

As colonial policies that had restricted the freedom of Africans to live where they wanted to, to produce what they wanted to, and to associate with whom they wanted to were gradually done away with in most parts of Africa in anticipation of political independence, colonial ideologies that had once advocated "tradition" now urged "modernization." The quest for modernity was inherited by political leaders of independence movements, many of their followers, as well as by most foreign advisers. From the perspective of departing colonial empires and newly independent nations, existing forms of social relations were seen as the enemy of social change, and social change was seen as necessary for the realization of modernity; this was because these types of relationships, ranging from kinship to "tribalism," were thought to be static and inflexible. Kinship in particular was seen as inimical to such values of modernity as individualism and capitalism. Accordingly kinship was seen as a vestige of tradition.

As Frederick Cooper (1996) has argued, this shift in colonial ideologies was mirrored in a similar shift in Western academic thinking about Africa. In the 1940s new research by rural anthropologists, particularly those working in **Southern Africa**, increasingly showed that the paternalistic colonial project of conservation had masked significant changes in rural Africa, most of which were regarded as serious and troubling disruptions to social life. This work led to fears of social disintegration and detribalization – the two were linked in so far as "tribe" was seen as the foundation of a set of primordial attachments, which included kinship, that were responsible for social stability. But fears that wage labor and **urbanization** would lead to detribalization and social decay dissolved in the 1950s, and came to be replaced by an appreciation of the adaptability of Africans to new social conditions. During this decade urban anthropologists and sociologists all posited a complex process of adaptation whereby new forms of urban association, such as working-class associations and **women's movements**, would not entirely displace older, rural forms, but would nevertheless result in new forms of social organization. For these observers the city was the primary arena of change, the site of an emerging African modernity.

From the middle of the century a major shift in population from the countryside toward towns and cities was underway throughout the continent; some of it was temporary, and had been experienced with labor migration during the colonial period, but a great deal of it was permanent. Less than 15 percent of the African population lived in cities in 1950; by the end of the century, 37.3 percent did. The ratio had risen to more than half in at least fourteen countries. But urban and rural areas remained politically, economically, and socially connected. For much of the post-colonial period governments redistributed resources from the countryside to the city, privileging cities in ways that colonial governments had once favored settlers and metropolitan interests. Rural areas continued to produce many people who moved away from the countryside in search of the new hopes and opportunities that political independence and the economic boom of the 1950s had inspired; later people left for more negative reasons, such as poverty and landlessness. In the early stages remittances from people living in the city sometimes helped relatives back in the countryside; conversely, in the later stages people in the countryside often supported those living in the city. Urbanization created new types of urban communities, households, and **families**. However, even after fifty years of unprecedented urban growth, a large majority of Africans continued to live in rural areas, and so social change in rural Africa is the focus of this entry.

Looking at rural Africa, modernization theory of the 1950s and 1960s had difficulty understanding the values of agricultural communities. Instead of the forces of modernity posing a threat to the social fabric and concomitant social values of agriculturists, as they were seen to do by those who feared detribalization, modernity was seen as threatened by traditional values. Although modernization theory conceded that urban Africans were capable of self-directed change, rural Africans were still seen to be prisoners of tradition as manifest in "subsistence" production and extensive webs of kinship, both of which prevented social reproduction, production, and consumption from being governed by market values. Instead household production and kinship relations were seen as governed by a static past, and as something primordial and incompatible with economic rationality and individualism. The idea of modernization was predicated on a faith in the power of capitalism to replace "subsistence" production with market production, collective labor with wage labor, "communal" tenure of land with private ownership, and kinship with individualism.

From the middle of the 1970s, many African countries entered a period of economic crisis that was to last for another two decades. Rural decline, as measured by a fall in per capita food production, began in the early 1960s and lasted until the middle of the 1980s. Although state policies – such as those that favored cities and discriminated against peasant producers, which created a dependency on foreign commodity markets and at the same time siphoned off profits through marketing boards, as well as encouraged labor migration – were largely responsible for this decline, one theory explained some of this decline in terms of peasant values (an "economy of affection" – that is, webs of kinship, ethnic obligations, community alliances, and religious affiliations) that were antithetical to those of capitalism. Goran Hyden (1983) argued that Tanzanian **peasants** in the 1970s remained "uncaptured" by the modern world because they were able to participate in market economies without having to abandon their traditional moral economies. His work brought needed attention to the moral economy of rural Africa, but it also inadvertently highlighted the problem of viewing kinship and other social networks in temporal terms; by privileging capitalism as uniquely modern, the "economy of affection" was treated as an anachronistic tradition, when in fact it was just as contemporary as capitalism and even more powerful.

From social structures to social capital and social networks

While Hyden was studying peasants in **Tanzania**, Pierre Bourdieu published a study that examined social practice (as opposed to social structures) at both a theoretical and a practical level. Based on his research among the Kabyle of **Algeria**, he redirected studies of African kinship away from notions of structure and tradition toward those of strategy and practice, treating "kin relations as something people *make*, and with which they *do* something" (Bourdieu 1977: 35). He articulated in a particularly influential way an important lesson that has only fully emerged in studies of African social history in the last decade of the century, which was that social relations were much more dynamic and elastic than previous theories had assumed or allowed. Two of the most important historical studies to emerge in the 1990s were written by scholars looking back on the pre-colonial past. In 1990 Peter Ekeh published a seminal article that called upon historians to historicize the strongly ahistorical studies of African kinship that had been produced around the 1930s. In particular he posited the idea that the slave trade had "strengthened and elaborated" kinship systems as forms of social protection against the violence and insecurity of that period. In the aftermath of the slave trade, the colonial state had only "heightened and enhanced" the relevance of kinship through its own regimes of violence and insecurity, as well as through its attempt to conserve traditional social relations through colonial courts and other administrative structures. All this occurred at just the same time as anthropologists first enshrined their understanding of African kinship. Similarly Jane Guyer and Samuel Eno Belinga (1995) noted that studies of social relations in Africa often asserted the primacy of kinship structures, ignoring improvisational tendencies.

At around the time that Ekeh's article appeared, Jan Vansina published an extremely important study of Equatorial Africa. Using historical linguistics to uncover the social world of ancient societies in this region, he demonstrated that houses – the basic social form for millennia – were characterized in the beginning by an "ideology of belonging" that used kinship terminology as a fiction with which to incorporate friends, clients, and dependents – as well as relatives. Membership of houses was consequently flexible, so "free men had a wide choice as to the establishment they cared to join" (Vansina 1990: 75; Schoenbrun 1998: 95, 99). Despite the continuity the colonial states pretended to maintain through their ideological commitment to tradition, colonial Africa was also full of social adaptation to changing circumstances. The passing of the colonial state, with its ideology of tradition, and the intensification of economic and political challenges in the post-colonial period, created conditions that produced similar flexibility in the building of social relations.

Therefore thinking of social relations as being buttressed by an underlying social structure or tradition was misleading, as this suggested that social relations were the product of predetermined biological (familial), emotional (psychological), and gender (patriarchal) realities. Colonial rule reinforced these assumptions through the creation of "customary law," which was applied through colonial courts. However, it was far less about maintaining continuity than about trying to manage social change. Social change remained a continuous process in post-colonial Africa, even though "customary law" continued to be an arena for contestation about what changes were or were not ideologically permissible. By the end of the twentieth century, social relations were increasingly thought of as resources that people created and drew upon, rather than as structures through which they simply lived their lives. Of particular relevance were the concepts of social capital and social networks. The first concept, although understood in different ways, pertained generally to the idea that the relationships an individual creates, which eventually result in social networks, were forms of capital that individuals could draw upon for different kinds of support.

Social capital and economic capital were interdependent rather than oppositional forms of wealth. Vansina has showed, as did Guyer and Eno Belinga, that in Equatorial Africa, where a rich array of pre-colonial currencies had facilitated the conversion of things into commodities, forms of wealth were most often converted into followers. For most rural dwellers in post-colonial Africa one of the primary values of money was its ability to be converted into social capital through the construction of social networks from which resources, such as land, labor, and agricultural capital, could later be mobilized. Sara Berry showed that in post-colonial Africa social relations – albeit that they were ambiguous, shifting, and highly negotiable –

were as important as market exchanges in organizing economic activity.

Such perspectives allowed scholars to appreciate just how crucial social networks and social capital were in the second half of the twentieth century in enabling people to survive the deteriorating economic and political conditions of the post-colonial period. They helped deflect the insecurities and stresses of everyday life in extremely important ways. As a result, it made it possible to understand that although the history of the second half of the twentieth century was largely perceived as one of economic and political failure, it was also one of tremendous social success. Given the harshness of conditions that people encountered through much of the continent – such as economic decline and retrenchment, exacerbated by **structural adjustment programs**, political oppression and conflict, and deteriorating health and environmental conditions – this success was perhaps the greatest achievement of late twentieth-century Africa. The social changes that made this success possible were about doing those same things and deploying the same strategies, albeit in different ways, that Africans had been using since time immemorial. It is in this way that social change in independent Africa was really about an abiding continuity; not with the past, but with a constantly changing present.

From the global to the local and vice versa

Although rural Africans knew money could be converted into social capital by being used to build social networks, they were also well aware of money's potential to erode social relationships in the post-colonial period. By the 1990s scholars were becoming increasingly aware of the resurgence of the values of moral economies throughout Africa in the face of these challenges. Generally this took the form of a revival of belief in what has been called "witchcraft"; however, far from such social movements being atavistic, they were quintessentially modern, reacting to the effects of **globalization** in local terms. Attempts to eradicate witchcraft, which were at the heart of such movements, were intended as social critiques of what were deemed to be antisocial forms of behavior. Belief in witchcraft was not a reaction to capitalism *per se*, but to the enormous inequalities that uneven resource accumulation and allocation were creating in local economies across Africa. The continent remained the poorest region of the world, and yet it had one of the highest levels of unequal income distribution – thereby making inequalities all the more pronounced.

In the generation after the **Second World War** many of those features associated with modernity – such as wage labor and cash cropping – succeeded without the disintegration of social relations. This certainly did not mean that social relations remained the same – the meaning of kinship changed at the same time as other forms of social relationships (especially those made necessary by the move from rural to urban settings) gained new meanings and importance. But at the same time, many of those who prospered built less inclusive social networks – ones that excluded those who were not prospering – and so shifted priorities from creating social capital to accumulating economic capital. As inequalities in income and access to resources increased – not only between households within the same communities, but also between men and women in the same household – social tensions were heightened between some individuals and communities, as well as between many men and women. By the 1990s views about modernity had changed substantially. For example, in their introduction to a collection of essays about witchcraft in Africa, Jean and John Comaroff (1993) remarked that the idea of modernity, which had helped to commoditize culture as tradition, had become an unsustainable teleology that dissolved if it was analyzed too closely. According to them, the so-called "struggle" between tradition and modernity in Africa was actually the story of the intersection of global and local worlds.

But as many scholars pointed out, although increasing accusations of witchcraft were interesting in how they articulated important debates about a moral economy that had been provoked by economic inequality and people's sense of desperation and insecurity, witchcraft was often more than just talk – and could have tragic consequences. This was brought home acutely in **South Africa** in the aftermath of the 1994 elections that brought an end to the apartheid regime. In the Northern Province, the country's poorest region, there were 300 cases of alleged witches having been killed between 1985 and 1995; in the first six months of 1996 alone, there were 676 cases. The desperation engendered by apartheid rule was the context of the former cases, whereas the heightened but frustrated hopes of liberation, which had not delivered what people who were still desperate had expected independence would bring, were the context for the latter.

However, it would be wrong to see the social values maintained by investment in social capital and realized through social networks as the cause of this violence. The aspirations of many alienated people in post-colonial Africa had more to do with the failure of economic promises that people associated with independence, modernity, and the West. This point brings us back to one made at the beginning: namely, the direction of social change in Africa. There is no denying that the logic of social capital and social networks can have negative effects; they are not just about surviving, as witchcraft killings highlight. After its near defeat in 1993, the Revolutionary United Front withdrew to the forests of **Sierra Leone**, where it used initiation ceremonies to create social networks of support among the children that it seized in its raids, turning them into soldiers or cutting off their hands if they refused. As horrible as this particular use of social network-building was, we must recall that a hundred years earlier King Leopold's Force Publique carried out the exact same atrocities in what is now the **Democratic Republic of Congo** in its effort to initiate Equatorial Africans into the economic networks of imperial Europe. This brings us neatly back to Soyinka's comment about the "burden of memory" with which I began.

To return to urban Africa, students of cultural globalization sought to investigate the traffic of cosmopolitan cultural values and practices from and into Africa, as mediated by the popular media, transnational capital, and the **African diasporas**. There was little consensus, however, on the predominant directionality of the flows and their impact on African cultures and societies. Some depicted Africa as a victim in yet another domain of globalization, while others argued that this was one domain in which Africa stood its ground, becoming as much an exporter as an importer of transnational cultural commodities and practices, especially in the realms of **music**, **dance**, and fashion, as well as (to a much smaller extent) **cinema** and cuisine.

See also: economy: post-independence; labor movements; society: colonial; workers

References and further reading

Berry, S. (1993) *No Condition is Permanent: The Social Dynamics of Agrarian Change in Sub-Saharan Africa*, Madison: University of Wisconsin Press.

Bourdieu, P. (1977) *Outline of a Theory of Practice*, Cambridge: Cambridge University Press.

Comaroff, J. and Comaroff, J.L. (eds.) (1993) *Modernity and its Malcontents: Ritual and Power in Postcolonial Africa*, Chicago: University of Chicago Press.

Cooper, F. (1996) *Decolonization and African Society: The Labor Question in French and British Africa*, Cambridge: Cambridge University Press.

Ekeh, P. (1990) "Social Anthropology and Two Contrasting Uses of Tribalism in Africa," *Comparative Studies in Society and History* 32: 660–700.

Ferguson, J. (1999) *Expectations of Modernity: Myths and Meanings of Urban Life on the Zambian Copperbelt*, Berkeley: University of California Press.

Geschiere, P. (1997) *The Modernity of Witchcraft: Politics and the Occult in Postcolonial Africa*, Charlottesville: University of Virginia Press.

Guyer, J.I. and Belinga, S.M.E. (1995) "Wealth in People as Wealth in Knowledge: Accumulation and Composition in Equatorial Africa," *Journal of African History* 36: 91–120.

Hyden, G. (1983) *Beyond Ujamaa in Tanzania: Underdevelopment and the Uncaptured Peasantry*, London: Heinemann.

Kaplan, R. (1996) *The Ends of the Earth: A Journey to the Frontiers of Anarchy*, New York: Random House.

Piot, C. (1999) *Remotely Global: Village Modernity in West Africa*, Chicago: University of Chicago Press.

Schoenbrun, D.L. (1998) *A green place, a good place: Agrarian change, gender, and social identity in the Great*

Lakes region to the 15th Century, Social History of Africa series, Portsmouth, NH: Heinemann.

Soyinka, W. (1999) *The Burden of Memory, the Muse of Forgiveness*, New York: Oxford University Press.

Vansina, J. (1990) *Paths in the Rainforest: Toward a History of Political Tradition in Equatorial Africa*, Madison: University of Wisconsin Press.

SEAN HAWKINS

Somalia

Somalia has an area of 637,657 square kilometers, and borders **Kenya**, **Ethiopia**, and **Djibouti**. It had a population of 10.8 million in 2000. During the late nineteenth century the Somali country came under the control of four imperial powers: Great Britain (Somaliland), Italy (Somalia), France (Djibouti) and Ethiopia (Haud and Ogaden). The Somali people resisted in various ways, particularly from the late 1890s to 1920. Colonial rule was disastrous for the Somalis: it ushered in an era of violence, ill health, economic decline, and state despotism. The imposition of colonial borders led to ecological degradation and the decline of rural life, which was based predominantly on **pastoralism**. Traditionally, Somali pastoralists in the northern region of the Somali country (British Somaliland) practiced transhumance, which involved periodic movement between the interior plateau (dry seasons) and the Haud (rainy seasons), thereby protecting the ecology from overgrazing and deforestation. The imposition of boundaries between Somaliland and Ethiopia under the 1897 Anglo-Ethiopian Treaty, however, undermined the system of transhumance and led to overgrazing, soil erosion and deforestation; the countryside, which had been characterized as a "park-like country" by many observers at the beginning of the twentieth century, had become a dry, dusty, windswept waste by the 1940s. As the rural economy declined, paupers migrated to the new colonial towns in the interior and the ancient, pre-colonial towns on the coast.

Between 1920 and 1941 the colonial administration in British Somaliland adopted a "care and maintenance" policy that emphasized law and order rather than development; in the late colonial period, however, the administration undertook various development policies within the framework of "mass education." In Italian Somalia, in contrast, more aggressive development policies were adopted, particularly during the Fascist era, when colonial settlement was encouraged and successfully established along the southern region of the Shabelle River, between Shalambood and **Mogadishu**. There settlers established plantations that produced cash crops (bananas) for the Italian market. The form of labor control in the plantations was compulsory labor; indeed armed guards supervised the workers. Italy, moreover, had regional ambitions: the establishment of an East African Empire that was to consist of Ethiopia and the Somali territories. Italy invaded and conquered Ethiopia in 1935, and Somaliland in 1940, but the Italian Empire was short-lived: the British invaded the region in 1941, and conquered Somaliland, Somalia, and Ethiopia. In 1942 the sovereignty of Ethiopia was restored by the British (although the Haud and the Ogaden remained under British rule until 1954). Somalia was returned to Italy in 1949 as a United Nations Trusteeship Territory for ten years, with the independence of Somalia set for 1 July 1960. Meanwhile the 1954 Anglo-Ethiopian Agreement was signed (which was based on the 1897 Anglo-Ethiopian Treaty) under which the Haud and the Ogaden were ceded to Ethiopia. The agreement stimulated anti-colonial nationalism in all the Somali territories, which was led by the Somali Youth League (formed in 1943) in Somalia and the Somali National League (established in 1947) in Somaliland. Because of the growth of radical nationalism, the British Cabinet decided to grant independence to Somaliland in 1960. On 1 July 1960 the two newly independent territories (Somaliland and Somalia) formed a union: the Somali Republic, which between 1960 and 1969 adopted an effective democratic system through which members of the national and local governments were elected.

In 1969 Mohamed Siad Barre staged a military coup that ended the democratic system, and ushered in an era of dictatorship. During his dictatorship the government adopted disastrous administrative and economic policies, including trade restrictions, heavy taxation on the commodity trade, heavy borrowing from overseas lending institutions, and the expansion of a corrupt and incompetent bureaucracy in which "bureaucrats multiplied bureaucrats." In addition the rural economy was ignored and marginalized: neither environmental protection nor the improvement of rural incomes were given a central place in Siad's development policies, leading to the 1974–5 famine that reduced the whole rural population to abject poverty, with thousands dying of hunger and malnutrition. Meanwhile Siad built an elaborate security state, which he used for internal repression and external aggression. In 1977 he invaded Ethiopia in order to recover the territories ceded to Ethiopia under 1954 Anglo-Ethiopian Agreement. When Somalia lost the war, anti-Siad sentiment increased in the army among the officer class (who attempted a coup in 1978), the elite, and the rural population whose sons were used as cannon fodder in the war. Siad responded by dividing the opposition along clan and regional lines, and using genocidal violence throughout the country, particularly in the north where he targeted the Isaaq. In 1981 the Isaaq responded by forming the Somali National Movement in London. They established a military base in Ethiopia, from which they waged guerrilla war against the government from 1982 to 1991. In 1990 the war reached the south with the formation of another opposition movement: the Somali National Congress, led by Mohammed Farah Aidid. Aidid easily disposed of Siad in 1991, as the army had already been decimated by the long civil war in the north.

When Siad fled Mogadishu in 1991, the Somali National Movement declared the northern region an independent state (Somaliland Republic). Meanwhile the Somali National Congress split into a military wing, under the leadership of Aidid, and a political wing, under the leadership of Ali Mahdi. This led to a vicious civil war that engulfed Mogadishu and the whole southern region of the country. In December 1992 the United States military intervened in Somalia, in order to help rebuild the state, but their mission was a failure and they were forced to withdraw in 1994. For the rest of the decade Somalia had no central government, despite several attempts to create one.

Further reading

Mohamed, J. (1999) "Epidemics and Public Health in Early Colonial Somaliland," *Social Science and Medicine* 48: 507–21.

Samatar, A.I. (1989) *The State and Rural Transformation in Northern Somalia, 1884–1986*, Madison: University of Wisconsin Press.

JAMA MOHAMED

South Africa

South Africa is situated in **Southern Africa** and had an estimated population of 43 million in 2000. The country is divided into nine provinces, and has three capitals: Pretoria (administrative), **Cape Town** (legislative), and Bloemfontein (judicial). Twentieth-century South African history is marked by the institutionalization of racial discrimination, **urbanization**, industrialization, and mass resistance culminating with a process of negotiations that ushered in a democratic state.

The peace brokered after the Anglo-Boer War (1899–1902) led to the unification of South Africa in 1910. The South African Party (SAP) became the governing party. A racially exclusive state was established, in which blacks were barred from direct parliamentary representation. The SAP was defeated in 1924 by a coalition of the National Party and the Labor Party. In 1934 the National Party and South African Party merged to form the United Party. At this time a faction of the old National Party broke away to form the Purified National Party.

At the beginning of the twentieth century mining was the dominant sector of the economy. Mining stimulated urbanization and industrialization, with manufacturing becoming the leading sector in the 1940s. The control of African urbanization was a central preoccupation of successive administrations. The contradictory desire for African labor in the towns but residency in the reserves – the requirements for economic growth without black political representation – compelled the enactment of a series of laws designed to uphold the fiction of a "white South Africa." The 1913 Land Act limited African landownership to the reserves, the Native Affairs Act

(1920) entrenched a dual system of governance, and the Native Urban Areas Act (1923) restricted African migration; the government also passed an Immorality Act (1927), which criminalized sexual relations between individuals of different races. The Rand Revolt of 1922, which was a protest by white mineworkers against skilled employment for Africans, destroyed any possibility of a multi-racial class-based alliance, and led instead to the development of a "white labor aristocracy" who were protected by the job color bar.

The African Political Organization (APO), formed in 1902, and the African National Congress (ANC), formed in 1912, were black political organizations that emerged in opposition to the government's segregation policies, while the Industrial and Commercial Workers Union (established in 1919) championed the rights of black workers. Until the 1940s the ANC relied on petitions and deputations in an attempt to persuade government to grant blacks the franchise, but their efforts were disregarded – indeed the state intensified its segregation policies.

By the 1930s state intervention had produced a political economy in which Africans were squeezed out of the agricultural sector and forced into a system of **migrant labor**. In urban areas African mineworkers were herded into single-sex hostels. State housing schemes were developed for Africans, but these were usually inadequate and far from the city centers. The urbanized African population nonetheless increased from 336,800 in 1904 to 1,146,000 by 1936. A large proportion of Africans settled in the slum areas bordering city centers or, for those in domestic service, in the backyards of their employers. The commercialization of the agricultural sector had also driven smaller Boer farmers and their families into the cities, where they swelled the ranks of a white underclass. These poor whites also settled in the "racially mixed" slum areas.

Intra-white capitalist tensions (the "poor white problem") and the inability to stem the tide of African urbanization, together with the intensification of black opposition, provided a fertile ground for the reemergence of Afrikaner nationalism. Afrikaner capitalists were concentrated in the declining agricultural sector, while the urban economy was dominated by the English. Afrikaners resented their increasingly impoverished position. The National Party (NP) expressed grave concern about the failure of "influx" control measures and about "racial mixing" in the slum areas, positing these conditions as a threat to white women and a phenomenon that would lead to the decay of the *volk* as a whole. Advocating racial separation, the social and economic development of the *volk*, greater repression of black opposition, and more stringent "influx" control measures – in a word: apartheid – the NP won the 1948 elections.

Apartheid was not a radically new ideology or policy framework. Rather, in the face of rapid social change, it represented an attempt to turn back the tide. It attempted to refine, intensify, and expand those practices and policies geared towards the reproduction of white rule that already existed in South Africa. The Prohibition of Mixed Marriages Act (1949), the Population Registration Act (1950), and the Group Areas Act (1950) were introduced as a means of rigidifying groups and creating separate (and unequal) spheres of development. Under the apartheid system Africans were divided into ten ethnic groups, each of which was forced into "self-determination" as a mechanism for averting any claim to political rights. The enforcement of the Group Areas Act and Bantustan system led to the forced movement of numerous people, relocated into unyielding over-populated rural land or dormitory townships that were far from downtown areas.

Although there had been many attempts to impose "influx" control on African women, they remained largely exempt until the 1950s. The ANC Women's League, launched in 1943, initiated anti-pass protests; this formed part of the wider ANC-led Defiance Campaign of the 1950s. The Federation of South African Women (FEDSAW) was formed in 1954, seeking to mobilize a wider range of women. In 1955 the ANC formed an alliance with colored, Indian, and white political organizations (the Congress Alliance), and drafted the Freedom Charter as the guiding document for the alliance. Africanists within the organization broke away to form the Pan African Congress (PAC). The Defiance Campaign climaxed with the Sharpeville Massacre of 1960, and the implementation of a state of emergency. After Sharpeville the NP banned the ANC, PAC, and South African Communist Party (which had been formed in 1921). These organizations went into exile and began an armed struggle. Internal political mobilization virtually came to a halt in the 1960s.

In 1961 South Africa withdrew from the British Commonwealth and became a republic. The 1960s were a decade of economic growth, with a simultaneous rise of diversified monopoly-based capitalism. But by the late 1970s the state was beginning to atrophy. The Black Consciousness Movement (formed in 1969) revived internal political protests. Industries were beset with strikes from a fast-growing unionized black labor force and, after the Soweto student boycotts in 1976, black student protests became the norm nationally. These events, together with increased international isolation and disinvestment campaigns, forced the NP into a series of reform measures that would ultimately lead to their relinquishing their monopoly on power. In 1983 the NP created the Tricameral Parliament, extending representation to coloreds and Indians. These reforms failed to regenerate state capacity, instead sparking off a new wave of protest.

Civil society organizations (student and youth movements, **labor movements**, **women's movements**, and civic associations), which had mushroomed since the late 1970s, came together under an umbrella organization – the United Democratic Front (UDF) – in 1983. In 1985 black trade unions formed the Congress of South African Trade Unions. Together these two organizations conducted sustained local and national campaigns that rendered the black townships essentially ungovernable. They demanded the abolition of apartheid, and the formation of a non-racial state. These organizations aligned themselves to the ANC, and popularized the Freedom Charter. Paradoxically, the emphasis on unity in the 1980s was accompanied by intra-black violence, primarily between Inkatha and UDF/ANC supporters in Natal and the Rand.

By the late 1980s South Africa was at an impasse. The NP was unable to crush the resistance, and its supporters were becoming divided between those seeking compromise and extremists who wanted more repressive measures. Although the government had been weakened, the ANC and its allies were unable to exact a military defeat. In addition international pressure was being placed on both the ANC and NP to reach a negotiated settlement. When De Klerk became president in 1989, he immediately began talks with the ANC.

The 1990s was a period of rapid transformation. Nelson Mandela and other political leaders were set free, organizations were unbanned, and the Convention of a Democratic South Africa (CODESA) set up as the forum for negotiations. By 1993 an interim constitution was agreed upon, and in April 1994 the first national democratic elections were held, with the ANC emerging victorious. A Government of National Unity (GNU), with Nelson Mandela as president and De Klerk and Thabo Mbeki as joint vice-presidents, was established. The NP pulled out of the GNU in 1996, and has been experiencing a steady decline in support.

In government the ANC commenced with a comprehensive Reconstruction and Development Program (RDP). But by 1996 it had become concerned about levels of unemployment, and the lack of foreign investment and economic growth. Government then shifted to a neoliberal reform program that emphasized "Growth, Employment, and Restructuring" (GEAR). South Africa held its second national democratic elections in 1999. The ANC increased its parliamentary majority, and the Democratic Party became the official opposition. Nelson Mandela retired, and Thabo Mbeki became president. Though much has been transformed, South Africa remains burdened by the racial iniquities of the past.

Further reading

Davenport, T.R.H. (1991) *South Africa: A Modern History*, 4th edn., Johannesburg: Macmillan.

Reynolds, A. (1999) *Election '99: South Africa from Mandela to Mbeki*, New York: St. Martin's Press.

CHERYL HENDRICKS

Southern Africa

There is no agreement about what exactly constitutes the Southern African region. Until the political transformations of the 1970s and 1980s, the term most commonly applied to **South Africa** and its political and economic offshoots, propelled by the insatiable demands for cheap labor by the mining industry. According to this version, South Africa is both the center and subject of Southern Africa, the linchpin on which everything else hangs. Other versions, developed in the 1970s and 1980s, saw Southern Africa as made up of "Frontline States" suffering from South African destabilization policies. This view was acknowledged in the formation of the **Southern African Development Community**, initially established to undermine South African regional hegemony. In this view Southern Africa included the Portuguese colonies of **Mozambique** and **Angola**, and reached as far north as **Tanzania**. For the purposes of this entry, the region designated as Southern Africa comprises South Africa, **Swaziland**, **Lesotho**, **Botswana**, **Namibia**, Mozambique, Angola, **Zimbabwe**, **Malawi**, and **Zambia**. What stands out about the twentieth century in Southern Africa is the longevity of white minority rule there. Southern Africa contains two of mainland Africa's longest colonized areas: **Luanda** in Angola and **Cape Town** in South Africa. It also contains five of the last countries in Africa to achieve independence: South Africa (1994), Namibia (1990), Zimbabwe (1980), Mozambique and Angola (both 1975).

By the late nineteenth century all of Southern Africa's peoples fell within the ambit of one or another European power. Within a set of boundaries based on the economic and security interests of the new European rulers were netted disparate African populations, turned into colonial subjects. Their lives were transformed from independent producers to squatters, wage laborers, and mostly rural-based female reproducers of these laborers, all in service of white capitalist profit. This was done through colonial policies of taxation, forced labor, repression of traditional authorities and customs, and land alienation. Speeding this process along were a series of natural disasters in the mid-1890s. Of course African subjugation did not happen everywhere at the same pace or to the same degree. Indeed the twentieth century in Southern Africa begins with a series of last stands from various African communities seeking to retain a way of life. Examples include the Bambatha rebellion of 1906–8 in South Africa and the Herero and Nama war of 1904–7 in Namibia. The Ovambo, also in Namibia, were not completely incorporated into Southwest Africa until after the German defeat in the **First World War**. Like the Ovambo, Bakongo resistance in northern Angola and Yao resistance in northern Mozambique were not quelled until the First World War.

Africans were not the only ones to resist incorporation into the colonial state. The Boers – who the British feared would build an alliance with the Germans to the west, and the mining capitalists blamed for limits to their profit on the Rand – also resisted and had to be pacified by the British through the Anglo-Boer War of 1899–1902. But like the Confederate States at the conclusion of the US Civil War, the Boers/Afrikaners lost the war but did rather well with the peace. A "Maize and Gold Alliance" brought together the interests of the Randlords and the Boer landowners, which benefited Boer farmers as much as it did the mineowners, but marginalized Africans, burdening them with taxes and a pass-law system of influx control, all designed to facilitate the **migrant labor** system. Mineowners organized themselves and set up the Witwatersrand Native Labor Association (WNLA) to recruit and distribute migrant labor from the neighboring colonies in the north, particularly from Nyasaland. The defeated Boer Republic was granted self-governing status in 1906. If Africans believed that they were better under imperial rather than settler rule, they lost this confidence in 1910 when the Union of South Africa was formed. Although Britain's protectorates – Swaziland, Lesotho, and Bechuanaland – managed to escape inclusion, they were locked into South Africa's economy as firmly as any of its provinces.

Land alienation was part and parcel of colonial domination in Southern Africa. So was male labor migration, and indeed the two often went hand in hand. While the process began during the previous century, land alienation was extended and formalized during the twentieth century. The 1913 Native Land Act in South Africa restricted Africans to 13 percent of the land. In Southern Rhodesia the 1930 Land Apportionment Act allotted 22.4 percent of the country's land to Native Reserves, 8.4 percent to Native Purchase areas, and 50.8 percent of the land (including all of the country's urban regions) to European areas. Swaziland's 3,000 whites controlled virtually two-thirds of the total land in 1915. Basutoland lost most of its fertile lands in the nineteenth century, and was a *de facto* reserve of "Egoli," or Johannesburg and the gold mines of Witwatersrand. Places where Africans had retained much of their land, such as Bechuanaland, suffered from colonial agricultural marketing policies that gave preference to whites. The experience north of the Zambezi was similar. In Northern Rhodesia the Colonial Office attempted to increase settler numbers by alienating 12 million acres of the colony's best land for white farming. In the Shire Highlands of Nyasaland a handful of settlers owned nearly 34 million acres, while about one-eighth of all land belonged to the African Lakes Company until 1930, when it reverted to African hands. Protectionist policies for white farmers were intensified during the 1930s world-wide depression, making it hard for rural Africans to resist incorporation into the capitalist wage-labor system. By the 1940s many rural areas were virtually dependent on migrant remittances.

At the beginning of the twentieth century by far the strongest demand for labor came from the gold mines of South Africa. South Africa's development as the most powerful and industrialized country in modern Africa was built on the labor of a poorly paid, mistreated, and disenfranchised workforce drawn from throughout the region. In Zimbabwe and Mozambique this labor was called *chibaro* (involuntary) labor. Recruiting agents were granted monopolies over certain zones, and were able to fix wages at low rates. Nyasaland became a pool of labor for the farms and mines of Southern Rhodesia. Northern Rhodesian Africans migrated to the Belgian Congo, Southern Rhodesia, and South Africa, although the opening of the copper mines in the 1930s shifted some migrant routes to the Copperbelt. During the interwar years Northern Rhodesia – like Nyasaland, Mozambique, Basutoland, Swaziland and Bechuanaland – was little more than a massive labor reservoir.

The Portuguese granted the WNLA a recruiting monopoly in Mozambique. In return Mozambique was granted a fixed proportion of the Transvaal's railway traffic, and WNLA members agreed to use the port facilities at Lourenco Marques (**Maputo**). Capitation fees and wage remittances were another major source of state income. A 1926 treaty between Portugal and South Africa fixed a quota of 100,000 workers who were reimbursed in part by gold remittances to the Bank of Portugal, which paid the miners in local currency on their return home from work. Southern Rhodesia, the second largest industrial economy in the region, formed the Rhodesia Native Labor Bureau (RNLB) whose reach fell over much of Northern Rhodesia and parts of Nyasaland and Mozambique. In the meantime large plantations were established in both Angola and Mozambique. On these plantations Africans had to produce fixed quotas under a brutal system of labor control.

Racially discriminatory policies were imposed in all walks of life, prompted by settler fears of African competition, black class-consciousness, or of being overtaken by a black majority. Segregationist policies were given credence and scientific legitimacy by anthropologists and other "experts" purporting to have proof of the dangers that detribalization and rapid social change brought. Both South Africa and Southern Rhodesia espoused explicit policies of segregation. In Southern Rhodesia these policies were entrenched during Prime Minister Huggins' administration, with its "Two Pyramids" policy. In South Africa they were perfected after the victory of the Nationalist Party in 1948 in its policy of apartheid. While the Portuguese espoused African assimilation, so many obstacles were placed in the way that only a statistically insignificant number of Africans had assimilated by independence. Even in the British protectorates with small European populations, the ideology of racial segregation and the promotion of white supremacy held sway.

Segregation was deeply resented, especially by the mission-educated Africans who, perhaps unexpectedly, became the face of the next phase of anti-colonial resistance. They grew resentful of the racism within the mission church. Many joined the so-called "Ethiopianist" movement of religious independency. Colonial governments loathed these manifestations of African psychological and spiritual independence and sought to repress them, but to no avail. By 1945 hundreds of independent churches had sprung up throughout Southern Africa. Demonstrations and strike action were another form of protest. While the African National Congress (ANC) would later become the face of African nationalism and protest in South Africa, in the first half of the twentieth century it was the African rank-and-file that initiated most demonstrations. In 1919 thousands of dockworkers in **Cape Town** went on strike for better wages. Inspired by this strike the Industrial and Commercial Workers Union was formed to represent the black working class. While white workers were also organizing at the time, their unions were segregated and fought for protection and benefits at the expense of African workers.

Africans had even fewer political outlets in the Portuguese colonies. Reforms made during what was known as the Republican Period (1910–26) allowed political organizations, trade unions, and the press to flourish. For a while it appeared that the Africans and settlers in Angola would strive for similar things, but Africans soon broke away to form organizations publicizing black grievances and demanding economic and educational benefits. Tagged as ungrateful, these organizations were crushed. For their part many rural Africans looked to tradition in times of trouble. Thus, in many areas, witchcraft eradication movements remained as powerful indications of social distress. A good example of this is the Mcape Movement in Nyasaland, which arose in the 1930s during the **Great Depression**, drought, and locust invasions. The movement offered its members medicine that was said to deliver them from witchcraft.

The **Second World War** had a huge impact on the region's economy, and on the development of African nationalism. With a shortage of imports from Europe, South Africa had to produce its own manufactured goods, and for the first time the contribution manufacturing made to the economy overtook those of mining and agriculture. A similar scenario occurred in Southern Rhodesia. Angola benefited with growing export earnings from cotton and coffee. The increase in urban-based manufacturing jobs, combined with the continuing problems of land alienation and rural poverty, led to a growth in African migration to the cities, and an increasing number of these migrants were women. However, the need for employment outstripped the availability of jobs, resulting in urban poverty and squalor.

Africans responded with more protests. In 1946, for instance, African mineworkers went on strike in South Africa. The brutal suppression of this strike resulted in a radicalization of the ANC, which agreed to an alliance with the South African Communist Party that same year. Worker militancy also increased in Southern Rhodesia, where there was a railway strike in October 1945 that was led by the recently established Rhodesia Railways African Employees' Association. This strike spread across the Zambezi, up to the Copperbelt in Northern Rhodesia; in 1948 general strikes were called in both Salisbury and **Bulawayo**.

In addition to labor activism the Second World War shook up the region's politics. Tens of thousands of African men returned from the war with widened horizons and heightened expectations. They found their demobilization packages to be blatantly inferior to those given to returning white soldiers, and nothing had changed on the discrimination front. Some had been exposed to the 1941 Atlantic Charter about the right to "self-determination" and were impatient for change. But, while African political consciousness grew, white resistance to change did as well. The Nationalist Party won the 1948 elections in South Africa, and instituted a barrage of destructive apartheid policies. The governments of Southern Rhodesia, Northern Rhodesia, and Nyasaland amalgamated to form the **Central African Federation** in the hope that an enlarged state would make them economically powerful enough to resist African pressure towards majority rule. With a similar goal in mind the Portuguese colonies and Southwest Africa attempted to fortify white rule by encouraging white immigration.

During this period, African political parties were organized and banned. For example, the Zambia African National Congress and Nyasaland African Congress were both banned in 1959. In Southern Rhodesia the ANC was also banned, reemerging as the Zimbabwe African People's Union in 1962. In

South Africa the ANC and the Pan African Congress (PAC) were each banned in 1960, following the police massacre of peaceful African demonstrators at Sharpeville. In the same year the South-West African People's Organization (SWAPO) formed as a guerrilla army. In Angola the Popular Liberation Movement (MPLA) was formed in 1956; it was not banned, but its leaders were imprisoned. In Mozambique the National Liberation Front (FRELIMO) was formed in 1962, and faced violent repression by the Portuguese.

By the end of the 1960s most of Africa was politically independent, including the Southern African countries that had been British Protectorates: Swaziland, Lesotho, Zambia, Malawi, and Botswana. However, the rest of the population of Southern Africa found their hopes dashed. Economic growth during the 1960s emboldened the South African government to carry out massive population removals in which hundreds of thousands of people were relocated from so-called "white areas" to the "homelands." Moreover it continued to ignore the UN Resolution 435, which mandated cessation of South Africa's illegal occupation of Namibia. Rhodesia followed South Africa's example and issued its own Unilateral Declaration of Independence, which forced the two dominant liberation parties – the Zimbabwe African People's Union (ZAPU) and the Zimbabwe African Nationalist Union (ZANU) – to wage a long guerrilla war. There was similar intransigence in Portuguese Mozambique and Angola. With Portugal under the fascist Salazar regime, and its overseas colonies playing a vital role in the economic welfare of that relatively impoverished European country, African political demands for independence were met with violent repression, launching protracted liberation wars.

The 1970s in Southern Africa were a time of escalating violence. Liberation wars scored successes, with Angola and Mozambique winning their independence in 1975. Both of them then embarked on the socialist path of development. The task of reconstruction proved daunting because of civil wars. Nevertheless the liberation of Mozambique accelerated the victory of the liberation movement in Zimbabwe, which was able to strike at Zimbabwe's eastern regions from bases in Mozambique. In 1980 Zimbabwe became an independent government, under an initially socialist ZANU government. This left only South Africa and Namibia to be liberated. The National Party of South Africa dug in its heels. In Namibia the South African Defense Force fought SWAPO and its Cuban allies. South Africa, with the support of the Reagan administration in the United States, used the Cuban presence and the pretext of staving off communism to resist a withdrawal. Meanwhile militancy increased at home, and the anti-apartheid movement grew abroad. The massacre of peaceful student protesters at Soweto in 1976 began a spiral of state violence in South Africa, and ignited international outrage.

Due to international pressure, and with an agreement that Cuban troops would be withdrawn, South Africa finally left Namibia. SWAPO won the country's first democratic elections in 1990 and formed a government. The demise of South Africa itself soon followed, thanks to international isolation and sanctions, growing internal resistance that made the country increasingly ungovernable, and growing military incursions from liberation movements in the surrounding countries. The ANC and PAC were unbanned, and apartheid legislation abolished. In 1990 Nelson Mandela was released from jail after twenty-seven years, and four years later South Africa held its first non-racial elections. They were won by the ANC.

Unfortunately liberation did not end the region's problems. The destructive impact of the civil wars fought against Renamo in Mozambique and UNITA in Angola had prevented development in the two countries and resulted in huge civilian casualties. By the end of the twentieth century the socialist experiments in Zimbabwe, Mozambique, and Angola had long since been abandoned. Southern Africa was stricken with one of the world's highest rates of HIV/AIDS infection, and the majority of its governments were under stifling debt. There were bread riots in the streets, yet strict sanctions by the International Monetary Fund prevented governments from doing anything to quell the rioters. While the economies of Botswana, South Africa, and Namibia were in reasonable shape, the rest of the region was in serious trouble. Meanwhile several governments, led by Zimbabwe, became embroiled in the civil war in the **Democratic Republic of Congo**. While some countries enjoyed a movement toward democratization and greater freedom, Zimbabwe was falling more deeply into political chaos. Indeed the end of the twentieth century in Southern Africa could be described as the best of times and the worst of times. South Africa was free and had adopted one of the most progressive constitutions in the world, championing **human rights**, including gay and lesbian rights, at the very same time as Zimbabwe was vigorously denying its people those rights. The century began with instability and crisis in Southern Africa, and it ended with them; it began with foreign institutions dominating Southern African economies, and ended with the same. But a glimmer of hope remained in the rise of **civil society** on every front.

Further reading

Denoon, D. and Nyeko, B. (1986) *Southern Africa Since 1800*, London: Longman.

Kaarsholm, P. (ed.) (1991) *Cultural Struggle and Development in Southern Africa*, London: Baobab Books.

Maasdoorp, G. (ed.) (1996) *Can South and Southern Africa Become Globally Competitive Economies?*, London: Macmillan.

Mwanza, A.M. (1992) *Structural Adjustment Programs in SADC*, Harare: Sapes Books.

Oden, B. (ed.) (1993) *Southern Africa After Apartheid*, Uppsala: Nordiska Afrikainstitutet.

Palmer, R. and Parsons, N. (1977) *The Roots of Rural Poverty in Central and Southern Africa*, London: Heinemann.

Vieira, S., Martin, W.G. and Wallerstein, I. (1992) *How Fast the Wind? Southern Africa, 1975–2000*, Trenton: Africa World Press Inc.

LYNETTE JACKSON

Southern African Development Community

The Southern African Development Community (SADC) is a regional organization, formalized in 1992. By 2000 SADC comprised fourteen member-states, with a collective population of approximately 125 million: **Angola**, **Botswana**, **Democratic Republic of Congo** (DRC), **Lesotho**, **Malawi**, **Mauritius**, **Mozambique**, **Namibia**, **Seychelles**, **South Africa**, **Swaziland**, **Tanzania**, **Zambia**, and **Zimbabwe**. The SADC's secretariat was located in **Gaborone**, Botswana.

The forerunner of SADC was the Southern African Development Co-ordination Conference (SADCC). SADCC was in essence an economic outgrowth of the "Frontline States" of **Southern Africa**, and had been formally constituted in April 1980. SADCC was formed specifically not only to exclude apartheid South Africa, but also to extend and promote cooperative relations in the political and economic spheres. A key objective of SADCC was to harmonize development among the countries of Southern Africa (excluding South Africa and Namibia), and to reduce economic dependence on apartheid South Africa.

When negotiations leading to democratic elections in South Africa began, SADCC was converted into the Southern African Development Community in recognition of the positive developments in the region, not to mention the removal of a major source of insecurity. SADC pursued the more comprehensive goal of **regional integration**, as well as political integration. Its mandate also called for the development of a common foreign policy. At its formation SADC comprised Angola, Botswana, Lesotho, Malawi, Mozambique, Namibia, Swaziland, Tanzania, Zambia, and Zimbabwe. South Africa was admitted in 1994, Mauritius in 1995, and Seychelles and DRC in 1997.

Southern Africa as a region is a conglomeration of divergent trends. The member-states of SADC ranged from the landlocked nation of Malawi, with a per capita gross domestic product (GDP) of US$182, to the small island-nation of the Seychelles, with a per capita GDP of US$7,384. Most countries had extremely low to medium level per capita GDP, with the exceptions of Botswana and South Africa, and the majority of countries had a very small manufacturing and industrial sector, with the exceptions of South Africa and Zimbabwe. South Africa alone was home to approximately one-third of the region's population, but generated about 75 percent of its GDP.

The formation of SADC heralded a new phase in regional cooperation and security in Southern Africa. In other regions of the world the early 1990s revival of discourse on integration and security was often considered a by-product of the end of the **Cold War**. In Southern Africa it was the end of apartheid in South Africa in 1994 that marked the watershed in regional politics. With South Africa as the "engine of growth," it was anticipated that Southern Africa as a region would be able to use the structures of the SADC to promote and maintain regional security, stability, and growth.

Primarily an economic body, in September 2000 SADC members signed a landmark trade protocol outlining the intention of forming a free trade area by 2008. In addition to its annual summits of heads of state and government, SADC also hosts annual "consultative conferences" with donor partners. SADC has traditionally operated on the basis of decentralized and country-led sectors of responsibility. In 2001 it had nineteen such sectors, ranging from the traditional (such as energy, water, transport and communications, and food security) to sectors designed to address newer issues (such as finance and investment).

Whereas SADC's vocation was essentially economic, it was also committed at its foundation to the formation of "a framework and mechanisms to strengthen regional solidarity and provide for mutual peace and security." This focus on political issues in addition to economic cooperation was buttressed with proposals, endorsed by Southern African **non-governmental organizations**, for the formation of a Human Rights Commission. It was further agreed that the "Frontline States" would disband, so that all operations could be integrated into this SADC sector. Similar to all SADC sectors, there would be one country responsible for coordinating its operations. Following some controversy, compromise was reached with the establishment of the SADC Organ on Politics, Defense, and Security in 1996. This continued to be a contested body within SADC.

The SADC region had experienced massive flows of refugees across borders, armed insurgencies, and many other security threats that made regional cooperation in the sphere of politics and security essential. But hopes for the creation of a single political economic space in Southern Africa were dashed in the late 1990s when SADC member-states became embroiled in regional conflicts, particularly a crisis in the DRC that involved the armies of Angola, Namibia, and Zimbabwe from 1998. These violent conflicts, in addition to the continuing war in Angola, divided SADC, with member-states – far from cooperating – pursuing competing interests. The aspirations of SADC were also undermined by the region's HIV/AIDS crisis, which was the most severe in the world: SADC member-states like Botswana, South Africa, Zimbabwe, and Swaziland had HIV infection rates of around 25 percent of their populations.

The vision of creating a vibrant regional organization to harness the resources and talents of the richest region of Africa remained a concrete SADC aspiration, however. At the 1999 **Maputo** summit a review of the SADC institutional structures and operations was recommended, with a report on the restructuring of SADC institutions presented in December 2000. The report recommended the elimination of the nineteen decentralized SADC sectors, and their replacement with four centralized directorates. These were: trade, finance, industry, and investment; infrastructure and services; food, agriculture, and natural resources; and social development, human development, and special programs.

By the end of the twentieth century SADC was faced with serious challenges, such as unresolved regional conflicts, minimal intra-regional trade, and uneven development, as well as the devastating HIV/AIDS pandemic. At the same time it remained potentially the most vibrant regional organization on the African continent. In combination its member-states were the wealthiest on the African continent – actually and potentially – and there existed an industrial base on which a regional political economy could be built that would not depend on extractive monocrop agriculture.

Further reading

Mandaza, I. and Tostensen, A. (1994) *Southern Africa: In Search of a Common Future. From the*

Conference to a Community, Gaborone: SADC Secretariat.

Simon, D. (ed.) (1998) *South Africa in Southern Africa: Reconfiguring the Region*, Athens: Ohio University Press.

TANDEKA NKIWANE

Southern African Development Co-ordination Conference *see* Southern African Development Community

Southern Rhodesia *see* Zimbabwe

sports

Football (soccer) is the most popular sport in Africa, but there are also many other forms of sport that are enjoyed by children and adults across the continent. There is a wide variety of indigenous sports that are unique to particular communities, and others that are popular across the continent and indeed across the globe. Wrestling, competitive dancing, gambling, acrobatics, hunting, running, swimming, canoeing, sailing, and horse and camel racing have been popular in different parts of the African continent for centuries. African children also grow up playing a number of games that have similar forms in many parts of the world. Some of the games played by African children that promote the development of athletic ability include running bases, hopscotch, hockey, skipping (or jump-rope), red-rover, tag, baseball, jacks, marbles, skipping rocks, and four square.

Many of the most popular international sports were introduced to Africa during the colonial era, including football, cricket, boxing, and netball. Colonial administrators, Christian missionaries, and company managers often encouraged African men to participate in sports, believing (as many nineteenth-century reformers did in Europe) that sport had the ability to instill moral values, respect for authority, and an appreciation for the value of clock-measured time. From the 1890s through to the end of the colonial era, most mission- and state-supported schools incorporated competitive team sports (and occasionally athletics) into their curriculums. By the 1920s many European sports had become popular right across the continent. In addition to teams organized through schools and work, African men in most major urban centers had begun to organize their own independent football teams and leagues by this time. Through their participation in various sports, including football, recent migrants to the towns could make friends and develop contacts that would assist them in locating better jobs or housing. In many places sports clubs doubled as mutual aid or even burial societies. In response to growing pressure from African sports enthusiasts, and in a labored attempt to shape the meaning of sport in African urban life, the colonial authorities, social workers, mine managers, and missionaries increasingly began to invest in equipment, leagues, and playing fields in the late 1920s and early 1930s.

Nonetheless it was really only after African nations gained their independence that significant financial investment was made in competitions, stadiums, training facilities, coaches, and equipment. In 1957 the first continent-wide football competition, known as the African Cup of Nations, was held. This event has been held every two years since then. In 1965 **Brazzaville**, **Congo**, hosted the first pan-African athletic competition, known as the All Africa Games, drawing more than 2,500 athletes from thirty African nations. In 1999 South Africa hosted the seventh All Africa Games. There were nineteen different events, ranging from football and netball to gymnastics, cycling, swimming, boxing, and karate.

Although many of the most popular sports played in Africa had their origins in Europe, African enthusiasts adapted them to local situations and infused them with elements of indigenous recreational and **leisure** aesthetics. In regions of the continent where drum and dance competitions were popular, football often borrowed from the organizational principles of the dance troupes, drawing the majority of their members from particular class, ethnic, clan, or neighborhood groups. Like competitive dancing, football matches that pitted key social and political rivals against each other often drew the largest and most appreciative crowds. The aesthetics of play also borrowed from dance competitions, with bold, creative, individual moves generally found more appealing in Africa than the slow, collective, passing game emphasized in Europe. From **Johannesburg** to **Zanzibar** and **Lagos**, football clubs were also often supported by particular musicians and bands, helping to make team-sponsored celebrations social events that incorporated the entire community, including women, children, and others who might have had little interest in the football itself. In both colonial and post-colonial Africa team clubhouses have often featured as important nodes of neighborhood and community social life. Clubs and individual athletes across the continent also frequently incorporate magic and charms into their game. Healers and diviners are still commonly employed by football teams to ritually prepare players and fields prior to matches, while individual athletes (including runners, swimmers, and boxers) can also be found wearing special charms to ensure their success.

Sport in Africa has also often been infused with politics. During the colonial era people on the African continent were frequently "groomed" to accept their relative "place" within the colonial hierarchy through their recruitment to participate in particular sports or clubs. In British Africa, for example, cricket was a game reserved for whites, Asians, and others who were being trained for positions of authority within the colonial political economy. The result is that, outside of **South Africa** and the other settler colonies, cricket is a game that generates little enthusiasm on the continent. Boxing, on the other hand, is extremely popular in many parts of the continent, as athletes and facilities were supported by the colonial authorities, who thought boxing "appropriate" for working-class African men. Many nationalist, labor, and youth leaders launched their political careers after being recognized and becoming popular through sport. World athletes also launched the first successful boycott of apartheid South Africa. From 1960 to 1992 South Africa was prohibited from participating in the Olympic Games, as well as many other international athletic competitions, because of its racist domestic policies. During the post-colonial era African female athletes have utilized their fame to challenge gender inequalities at home. Female Olympians from **North Africa**, including Nawal el-Moutawakil (**Morocco**) and Hassiba Boulmerka (**Algeria**) brought international attention to struggles between Muslim women and the misogynist practices of Islamic fundamentalists during the late 1980s and early 1990s. In 1984 Nawal el-Moutawakil won Olympic gold in the 400-meter hurdles, making her the first African woman to be awarded an Olympic medal. Rather than applauding her success members of the religious right in Morocco chastised, pressurized, and threatened her until finally she abandoned sport. Hassiba Boulmerka endured nearly two years of similar abuse from Islamic fundamentalists in Algeria, who claimed it was a sin for a woman to run in public; she went on to win the gold medal in the 1,500-meters at the 1992 Olympics.

Despite a long history of discrimination against female athletes and women's participation in competitive sport, African women have made major advances on the international sports scene in recent decades. During the colonial era women were often actively discouraged by school and church authorities from participating in organized sports, which were considered to be a masculine pursuit. One of the few athletic games considered "appropriate" for girls in British Africa was netball. Since independence some African nations have begun to promote women's involvement in other forms of sport, but male athletes and men's sports leagues continue to receive the bulk of funding provided by African governments and independent financiers. Africa has a long way to go before gender parity is achieved in sport. Nonetheless, the success of female athletes from all parts of the continent has provided inspiration to a new generation of young girls, while simultaneously forcing national and international sponsors to take notice of women's athletic potential. In **Nigeria**, for instance, the women's national team consistently outperformed the men's team in international competitions during the 1990s. The Nigerian women's team, the Super Falcons, won three successive titles in the African Women's Nations Cup: 1991 (the first such competition), 1995, and 1998. The Super Falcons were also the only African team to qualify for the first Women's

World Cup, held in 1991. By 1999, however, financial and fan support for women's soccer on the continent had grown to the point that twelve African nations had female teams competing for a place in the Women's World Cup. African women are also highly competitive in netball: in 2000 the South African netball team was ranked fifth in the world, while the Malawian team was ranked eleventh.

The international reputation of African men's soccer has also improved considerably. Like Africa's female football players, the men have had to struggle not only to improve their skills, but also to overcome significant forms of discrimination that hindered their ability to compete. It was only after African teams boycotted the 1966 World Cup that they were given adequate representation in one of the most prestigious international sporting events. Previously the World Cup had been dominated by Europe, with Africa and Asia competing for a single place among the qualifiers. In 1970 Morocco became the first African nation to compete in the World Cup. In 1994 three African nations – **Cameroon**, Morocco, and Nigeria – qualified. African teams have also been highly competitive in Olympic soccer. Nigeria won the Olympic gold in 1996, and were succeeded as champions by Cameroon in 2000. The success of the Cameroonian team was truly astonishing to watch, and fans across the continent – and in fact across the globe – held their breath as the Indomitable Lions advanced on the gold. They defeated the favorites, Brazil, in the quarter-finals, despite having had two players sent off. In the final against Spain, Cameroon came back from a two-goal deficit to tie the game, before winning the gold medal 5–3 on penalties.

Many African football players now play professionally for European teams. Supporters of such practices argue that playing in Europe has given African footballers more opportunities for international competition, higher salaries, and better training facilities, and that ultimately these benefits "trickle down" to the African nations these players were recruited from. However, there are also many vocal opponents of these practices, who argue that European recruitment drains African football of its best players, and that commitments to league teams in Europe often hinder the development of strong national teams in Africa because players are not available for practice and matches. Owners and managers of European clubs have also become increasingly dissatisfied with the necessity of sharing the time and talents of African players with national teams. Promising young athletes in other sports are also increasingly being recruited by scouts from universities in the United States and Europe.

Running is certainly the area of competitive sport where contestants from the African continent have made their biggest mark internationally. Runners from **Kenya** and **Ethiopia**, in particular, have dominated long-distance track events for decades. During the 2000 Olympics Gezahgne Abera of Ethiopia won the men's marathon, with Eric Wainaina of Kenya taking the silver, followed by Tesfaye Tola of Ethiopia winning the bronze. Tegla Loroupe of Kenya currently holds the world record, set in 1999, for the fastest women's marathon at 2 hours 20 minutes and 43 seconds. The men's world record for the fastest marathon is also held by an African: Khalid Khannouchi of Morocco. Africans also hold the world records in the 3,000 meters, 5,000 meters, and 10,000 meters. Overall Ethiopia came twentieth in the overall rankings at the 2000 Olympics, taking eight medals, while Kenya was ranked twenty-ninth, with seven medals.

The prospects for African athletes and sports on the continent are promising. Despite severe financial restraints, the number of African children attending schools where they are able to play competitive sports and where promising athletes can be identified has increased substantially since the 1960s. Training facilities, stadiums, and financial support for athletes are also generally better today than they were at independence. The success of female athletes internationally has also forced national governments to begin to address gender inequalities in funding and access to sporting opportunities.

Further reading

Armstrong, G. and Guilianotti, R. (eds.) (2002) *Football in Africa*, Basingstoke: Palgrave.

Baker, W. and Mangan, J.A. (eds.) (1987) *Sport in Africa: Essays in Social History*, New York: Africana Publishing.

Fair, L. (1997) "Kickin' It: Leisure, Politics and Football in Colonial Zanzibar, 1900s–1950s," *Africa* 67, 2: 224–51.

Jarvie, G. (1985) *Class, Race and Sport in South Africa's Political Economy*, London: Routledge.

Martin, P. (1995) *Leisure and Society in Colonial Brazzaville*, Cambridge: Cambridge University Press.

LAURA FAIR

state: colonial

The colonial states of Africa were largely constructed between 1890 and 1914. Study of these states as complex institutional and ideological systems began, however, only in the late 1960s as an outgrowth of broader research on the political economy of colonialism, particularly in the work of the British economist Geoffrey Kay (1972) and the Guyanese historian Walter Rodney (1972), and the gradual opening of colonial archives. Prior to then, research had focused largely on the personnel, practices, and problems of colonial administration from the perspectives of the various imperial powers. Systematic analytical and critical research was rare. In the 1970s and 1980s monograph studies of individual colonial states and their relations with and impact on indigenous African societies began to appear. In the 1990s attention increasingly focused on the legacy of colonial states for understanding the pervasive crises of governance and development in African nations, particularly in the detailed comparative analysis of the American political scientist Crawford Young (1994) and the controversial analysis of the process of indirect rule by the Ugandan political scientist Mahmood Mamdani (1996).

As the violence of the last phase of European expansion and conquest reached its climax in the 1890s, the powers found they had to convert superior force into stable, continuous control of the vast territories and large populations now under their dominion. Machine guns and artillery could create heaps of corpses and destroy villages, but they could not secure production, trade, or tax revenue. Treaties with African rulers that granted European hegemony were easily ignored without the continuous presence of political agents of the colonial power. Military power had to be converted into political authority under civilian officials, with at least a minimum of tacit consent from the African subjects, and viable economies created linking the colony to the metropole.

Colonial domination took a variety of political forms. **Algeria**, whose conquest began in 1830, was treated as a part of France and its administration replicated that of the metropolitan state, coming under the domination of the large settler population. **Tunisia** in the 1880s and **Morocco** in the early twentieth century became protectorates in which the indigenous monarchs and state structures were retained under the control of French officials. In **Egypt** a long British occupation exercised control over the indigenous state, turned briefly into a formal protectorate, and then in 1922 became an ostensibly independent monarchy that remained under British suzerainty until 1951. Protectorates in Basutoland (**Lesotho**) and **Swaziland** retained the structure of existing African states under British colonial agents, while a few states like **Rwanda** and **Burundi** became individual colonies.

In some parts of the continent the colonial powers initially attempted to exercise control without commitment of metropolitan resources through the use of chartered private companies, which were granted rights to any sources of profit they could find in return for exercising effective administrative control in a territory. These schemes were notable failures. They included the Imperial British East Africa Company in what became **Kenya**, the Deutsche Ost-Afrika Gesellschaft in Tanganyika (later part of **Tanzania**), numerous concessionaire companies in the French Congo, and – the largest company state of all – the Congo Free State of King Leopold II of Belgium. Such attempts to combine political control and the accumulation of profits proved disastrous, from both the failure of most to find sources of profit, except from the voracious collection of resources such as ivory and natural rubber, and the violence and atrocities visited upon the indigenous African population by company agents. It became increasingly clear to metropolitan governments, pressed by aroused public opinion at home, that a civil apparatus of control had to be established that was institutionally separate from European economic interests in the colonies. At the same time the small entrepôt colonies along the coast of **West Africa**, with their rudimentary administrative apparatuses often largely staffed by local African creoles, had few linkages with their vast hinterlands and provided no usable model for effectively ruling vast populations of peasants and pastoralists.

Where the colonial powers controlled such extensive territories that they contained numerous kingdoms, chiefdoms, and stateless societies, the colonists found no alternative but the establishment of subordinate states, lacking full international sovereignty and under the formal control of the metropolitan state, in each colony. Each of these states presented to its subjects a façade of omnipotent and omniscient power. The potent authoritarian agent of imperialism, its expanding apparatus intervened in ever wider areas of the colonial political economy, directing change to serve the interests of the metropole while containing and suppressing indigenous social forces. In the vivid phrase used in the Belgian Congo, it was *Bula Matari* – the "crusher of rocks." Behind this façade of unchallenged power, however, there was another reality of a far less powerful colonial state, a paternalistic mediator that struggled to retain a precarious hegemony over the contending interests of colonial society. Constantly strapped for resources and personnel, eternally searching for new sources of tax revenue, plagued by poor communications and inadequate information, and actually possessing only limited coercive force, it was sustained by a combination of exhortation and threat with the cooptation and accommodation of indigenous social forces. Rather than an unassailable ruling power, free of any ties to or constraints from the African societies subject to its control, the actual colonial state developed complex linkages with those societies that shaped not only its own development, but also the development of the colonial political economy, the distribution of wealth and power, and the patterns of social and cultural change in each African community.

Constructing the colonial state

The principal component of the metropolitan state replicated in the colonies was the authoritarian "guardian bureaucracy" of central and field administration with roots reaching back into the pre-1789 *ancien régime*. Throughout the colonial period the structural foundation of colonial states and the immediate agents of domination were the field administrators in the territorial subdivisions of a colony. This prefectural organization was the most common feature of colonial administration and the key linkage between colonial states and indigenous social forces. For France and the other continental powers it represented a well-known and practiced instrument of control. For Britain, however, it was a state form unknown in the metropole, but explicitly adopted and refined in the encounter with indigenous social forces in the non-white colonies of the Empire, particularly in the reformed Indian Civil Service, and transferred to the new colonies of Africa.

Up to the end of the **Second World War**, District Commissioners and Officers in British colonies, *chefs de circle* in French Africa, and their equivalents in Belgian and Portuguese colonies, were the principal and often the sole agents of the state at the local level. They exercised an authority over the African populations that was both diffuse and wide-ranging, and had responsibility for virtually all state activities – "law, order and good government" in the usual British formula. Although a formal bureaucratic hierarchy linked the field officers to the central administration in the colonial capital, and through that to the metropolitan authorities in London, Paris, Berlin or Brussels, in practice the field officers enjoyed substantial autonomy from their immediate superiors and exercised great discretion in the implementation of policy in their areas. Similarly the governors and central administrations of each colonial state enjoyed substantial autonomy from metropolitan control. Each British colony dealt directly with the Colonial Office as a discrete entity, and there was no machinery for enforcing a centrally agreed policy. Imperial policy was generally confined to vague principles, with the specific application left to the discretion of each colonial government and many policy areas left totally to local discretion. French administration was similarly decentralized in practice, with rapidly changing ministers in Paris exercising only limited and sporadic influence over colonial policy, and the governors-general of the regional colonial federations of French West and Equatorial Africa (AOF and AEF) having little day-to-day control over the state apparatus in each colony.

The higher authorities exercised a degree of indirect control through the metropolitan recruitment and training of colonial officials. The early officials were often haphazardly hired in the colonies. Such men, described by a governor of **Senegal** as the "lost children of the mother country" and by a governor of Kenya as "vagabonds and cowpunchers," earned evil reputations for incompetence and brutality. In the quarter of a century before 1914 metropolitan authorities in both Britain and France ended the local recruitment of officials, organized them into a formal administrative service similar to the elite cadres of the metropolitan bureaucracy, and assumed firm control over their recruitment and training to ensure their competence and reliability. By the interwar period the colonial officials of both countries were preponderantly drawn from the upper middle class of the metropole. British administrators were selected by interview from public school and Oxbridge graduates who had to demonstrate appropriate character and a "habit of authority," while French officials graduated from the Ecole Coloniale, one of the *grandes écoles* in Paris for servants of the state. In German colonies the early cadres of officials dominated by military officers had just been largely replaced by civilians recruited on the same criteria as metropolitan civil servants when Germany's colonial empire was ended by the **First World War**.

The most potent instrument of metropolitan control over colonial states was financial supervision based on the principal of fiscal self-sufficiency. In British Africa any colony unable to meet the costs of its administration from local taxes and revenue passed under the supervision of the Treasury, which pruned its budget until it could live within its means. French Africa was held on a similarly tight rein under a 1900 law that mandated the "financial autonomy" of the colonies. In addition colonies had to contribute to the costs of military, communications, and educational services provided by the metropolitan state. Metropolitan grants for infrastructure investments and development were meager and colonies had to rely on loans raised in metropolitan capital markets that added debt-servicing charges to their financial burdens. Such metropolitan meanness meant that colonial regimes, without further direction, had an acute interest in developing commodity production and trade at least sufficient to provide a tax-base to meet the costs of its own reproduction. The revenue-hunger of colonial states led to efforts to tax or impose fees on every possible commodity or transaction, as well as hut and poll taxes on the African population, but kept state activities constantly restricted and under-funded.

For field administrators the complex task of effective control required juggling the contradictory imperatives of attending to the need for accumulation and revenue demanded by their superiors, local settlers, and metropolitan economic interests, and maintaining a degree of legitimacy with local populations. The dilemma was always how far Africans could be pressed for labor, commodity production, and taxes before they would disobey and resist. Dealing with it required a real and visible degree of relative autonomy vis-à-vis external interests and pressure, and some attention to African interests. The central contradictions of colonialism were reflected in the ideology of paternalistic authoritarianism that dominated colonial states. For both the British notion of the "dual mandate" and the French concept of the "civilizing mission" envisioned bringing the "child races" of Africa to a higher level of civilization through a paternal trusteeship introducing them to the civilizing disciplines of wage labor, commodity markets, and Christianity. It embodied also elements not only of late nineteenth-century scientific racism and social Darwinism, but also the Romantic neo-traditionalism and anti-modernism that characterized the bureaucratic elites of the European powers.

Constructing the colonial economy

The colonial states, tied as they were to the level of

development of indigenous production and trade for their own fiscal survival, intervened actively in the shaping of the colonial economies. The basic structures were in place by 1914 and consolidated during the interwar decades, with little significant modification until the post-1945 period. The colonies were structured to provide low-cost agricultural and mineral raw materials for export to their respective metropoles, and a market for manufactures imported from them. Up to 1945 the level of capital investment in these economies from both public and private sources was extremely limited and comprised only a fraction of the total foreign investment and trade of Britain and France. Most of the limited public investment by the colonial state went to provide railways, harbors, roads, and communications infrastructure for the trading economy, and tended to be concentrated on coastal port cities and their links to the regions of production in the hinterlands.

In coordination with metropolitan merchant capital, colonial states moved to control the inputs, quality, quantity, and price of agricultural commodities through official marketing or trading centers, peasant cooperative societies in French colonies, and commodity marketing boards in British colonies; as well as through the growth of specialist technical departments in agriculture, veterinary services, forestry, public works, transport, and communications. The level of state intervention in the economy of the colonies significantly exceeded that of the state in the metropolitan economies throughout the colonial period.

Such activity spurred the penetration of capitalist forms of production, exchange and wage labor that began to transform indigenous societies and linked them to metropolitan capital and the wider world economy. The result, however, was only a partial restructuring of indigenous social forms, which continued to function throughout rural Africa. Instead of a transformation, the result was a contradictory and syncretic process producing a partial transformation, destruction, and preservation of African societies contained in a myriad of intermediate and hybrid forms scattered across the countryside. It was a consequence both of frequent African resistance to cash cropping and wage labor, and of the increasing reluctance of colonial states to press change beyond the point where an adequate supply of commodities and labor was forthcoming to the requirements of trade and taxation. And it was reflected in the reluctance of most colonial states to encourage permanent African commitment to wage labor and residence in cities. The result of the partial transformation/ partial preservation of African societies was a series of contradictory developments that undermined social order and threatened the control of African societies. First, new sources of income introduced new and/or accentuated existing internal class-differentiation in African societies, as well as regional differences between societies integrated into the colonial economy in different ways, which produced increasing conflict both within and between different communities. Second, development of wage labor and cash-crop production also produced growing conflicts between Africans and European settler, plantation, mining, and mercantile interests. Third, the introduction or expansion of cash cropping at the expense of traditional food production and agricultural fallowing practices, combined with growing **population** and class differentiation, produced soil depletion, erosion, declines in production, and the spread of malnutrition and rural poverty. The resulting conflicts defined the problems of political control for the colonial state.

Maintenance of political control

Colonial domination was a complex process involving far more than the threat or use of force. Instead a process of negotiation and bargaining by the colonial state achieved a *modus vivendi* in the countryside based on the active participation of a minority and the tacit acquiescence of the majority of the African population. Colonial states frequently backed off from the implementation of unpopular policies in the face of African opposition. The task of achieving the delicate balance of control fell to the local agents of the colonial state, the district administrators, who were the key linkage between the state and indigenous social forces. The substantial discretion accorded these officials and their diffuse and wide-ranging responsibilities for virtually all state activities in their areas allowed them to construct and maintain in highly personal fashion the varied local structures of control and collaboration.

The discretion of field administrators was not unlimited, however, since they could not question or ignore the commitment of the state to extract African labor, promote cash-crop production, and collect taxes. The flow of labor, commodities, and tax revenue provided the higher authorities with an index of an officer's effectiveness and they could be promoted, transferred, or sanctioned accordingly. Even the broad coercive powers at the command of field officers had to be used with restraint to generate submission and obedience rather than continuing resistance from the African population. Repeated use of force would also attract sanctions from the higher authorities. They were thus also disciplined by an ultimate dependence on local consent and that required a degree of responsiveness to indigenous interests and grievances. The ideology of authoritarian paternalism involved depiction of the state as a benevolent guide and protector of African interests rather than agent of metropolitan or settler interests. Moreover by the 1920s colonial states were increasingly concerned about the possibility of social disorder and the collapse of "tribal authority" in the face of the changes introduced in the colonial economies, and attempted to preserve and even restore "traditional" authority and institutions to preserve social stability.

Beneath the European field officers the actual agents of day-to-day control and policy implementation were the literally thousands of chiefs and headmen working in every village and administrative subdivision of colonial Africa, no less than 2,206 cantonal chiefs and 47,000 village chiefs in French West Africa alone. The supposed contrast between French "direct rule" and British "indirect rule," often discussed during the colonial period, was actually a myth. Instead both French and British colonial rule relied on local variations of indirect rule through indigenous agents from the rulers of Morocco and Tunisia to village headmen of remote rural communities. These men could be the holders of pre-colonial political offices as kings, chiefs, and heads of local communities, confirmed in their titles if they were willing to cooperate with the colonial authorities, and usually paid an official salary. In stateless societies, however, they were simply colonial appointees, with little indigenous precedent or sanction for their role.

The process of collaboration was the basis for the stabilization of colonial control and for development of an indigenous class of accumulators of wealth, within the narrow opportunities provided by the colonial economy, that overlapped with the indigenous levels of the political control-apparatus. This class included the chiefs and headmen, who were particularly encouraged to take opportunities for accumulation in production and trade, along with wealthy peasants and traders and an emerging salariat of teachers, artisans, and clerks. Promoting material rewards for those who loyally served the colonial state brought the prefects directly into the process of class formation, and the public resources at their disposal gave them sources of patronage they directed towards the chiefs and other members of the African petty-bourgeoisie. Chiefs and headmen employed the resources and wealth at their disposal to construct their own wide networks of patron–client relations. The result was that the state became for Africans the principal focus for the accumulation of wealth, and patron–client politics the principal linkage between the colonial state and African societies.

The colonial state also played a crucial role in the increasingly sharp definition of ethnic boundaries and identities under colonialism. To colonial officials all Africans were members of "tribes" and they were classified, counted, and mapped accordingly. Chiefs and headmen also played an active role in the process of ethnic development. First, they served only in their local areas and could not be promoted or transferred to other posts or parts of the colony. A chief was a chief only in a particular "tribe." Second, for colonial officials the chiefs, headmen, and elders were the principal sources for the definition of the "custom and tradition" the state increasingly sought to preserve and protect from further disruption. Third, their power, wealth, and control of patronage made chiefs a principal focus of a complex internal process through which issues of culture, communal membership, and identity; access to land, livestock, and other resources; and the reciprocal obligations of the rich and powerful and the poor and powerless were contested and revised in each ethnic community.

The incorporation of the chiefs and headmen into the state apparatus also relieved them of the diverse communal constraints on arbitrary power that generally characterized pre-colonial African political office. This permitted many chiefs to abuse their power and extort money and other resources from their subjects. Patronage and corruption became endemic problems at the lower levels of the colonial state and undermined its tenuous legitimacy. Increasingly seen by the populace as creatures of the state, the chiefs often compromised its authority as they undermined their own position.

Development, decline, and decolonization

After 1945 the colonial states both grew rapidly in scale and complexity and found their control increasingly challenged. Starting during the **Great Depression** in the 1930s and continuing during the Second World War colonial administrations increasingly intervened to expand commodity production, while both Britain and France began to tie colonial economies more directly to metropolitan needs. Through its wartime bulk-buying system and expansion of marketing boards throughout its African colonies, Britain grasped control of colonial production and marketing. After the war such efforts became increasingly focused and systematic; a massive expansion of state intervention and pressure on indigenous African societies that constituted a "second colonial occupation," intensifying the penetration of capitalist production and markets. For both Britain and France it involved an unprecedented commitment of public capital, and the establishment of new colonial development agencies. Focused initially on using colonial products and markets to aid the recovery of war-ravaged metropolitan economies, the effort turned to an emphasis on "development" in the colonies, with growing expenditure on programs of education, health, and welfare, in addition to agricultural development and the beginnings of industrial investment.

The era of colonial development brought new personnel, institutions, and policies to the colonial state to manage the development efforts. Power in the state shifted upwards to the central administration, and left local administrators increasingly focused on their primary control functions. At the same time development programs enormously enlarged the patronage resources of the state, and made it the principal source of employment and accumulation for the indigenous population. The state became the central focus of a growing competition and conflict both within and between ethnic communities, as well as between the local populace and their European rulers, for access to public goods.

New political movements, ethnic associations, trade unions, and an active vernacular **press** found a mass base among **peasant** farmers, urban **workers**, demobilized war veterans, and unemployed **youth** disgruntled by low commodity prices and wages, rapid inflation, lack of employment, and inadequate provision of social services. The initial reaction of colonial administrations was often repression, but rather than restoring order this called forth increasing mobilization and resistance. By the 1950s colonial states, rather than instruments of order and control, had become the focus of disruption and conflict. Paternalistic authoritarianism had become a problem rather than a solution for metropolitan interests. The logic of **decolonization** involved finding a new *modus vivendi* with African political leaders at the central rather than the local levels of the state. Power was transferred to a group judged capable of maintaining order and preserving the existing patterns of production and marketing. The process was complicated, however, where there were large numbers of white settlers (as in Southern Rhodesia, Kenya, and Algeria) or where the metropole lacked the capacity to retain economic hegemony (as in Portuguese **Angola** and **Mozambique**). In these territories settler-driven repression to maintain racial hegemony and violent anti-colonial struggles preceded eventual decolonization.

Aside from liberal democratic institutions hastily tacked on shortly before independence, and the rapid "Africanization" of their personnel, the bureaucratic apparatus of colonial states, including the grass-roots structures of collaboration and control, remained largely intact in the post-colonial era. Moreover the **nationalist movements** that confronted colonial states were, beneath their anti-colonial unity, often uneasy coalitions across divisions of class and ethnicity, that began to unravel in a competitive scramble for control of state patronage and resources. The enduring legacy of the colonial state in Africa remains in the combination of bureaucratic authoritarianism and pervasive ethnically focused patronage politics.

See also: colonial Africa; colonial conquest and resistance; economy: colonial; race and ethnicity; society: colonial

References and further reading

Berman, B.J. (1990) *Control and Crisis in Colonial Kenya*, London: James Currey.

Cohen, W.B. (1971) *Rulers of Empire: The French Colonial Service in Africa*, Stanford: Hoover Institution.

Gann, L. and Duignan, P. (1979) *The Rulers of Belgian Africa, 1895–1914*, Princeton: Princeton University Press.

Heussler, R.L. (1963) *Yesterday's Rulers: The Making of the British Colonial Service*, London: Oxford University Press.

Kay, G. (1972) *The Political Economy of Colonialism in Ghana*, Cambridge: Cambridge University Press.

Mamdani, M. (1996) *Citizens and Subjects: Contemporary Africa and the Legacy of Late Colonialism*, Princeton: Princeton University Press.

Rodney, W. (1972) *How Europe Underdeveloped Africa*, London: Bogle-L'Ouverture.

Suret-Canale, J. (1964) *Afrique Noire: l'ère coloniale, 1900–1945*, Paris: Editions Sociales.

Young, C. (1994) *The African Colonial State in Comparative Perspective*, New Haven: Yale University Press.

BRUCE J. BERMAN

state: post-independence

At the end of the **Second World War**, only three African countries enjoyed nominal political independence: **Liberia**, which had been founded in the nineteenth century as a home for former slaves from the United States; **Egypt**, which had been granted internal self-rule under a restored monarchy in 1922; and **Ethiopia**, which was briefly occupied from 1936–41 by the Italian fascist regime. The independence era began with the independence of **Libya** in 1951. In 1956 **Morocco**, **Sudan**, and **Tunisia** joined Libya. South of the **Sahara**, **Ghana** achieved its independence in 1957, and in 1960 alone seventeen countries in **North**, **Central**, and **West Africa** gained their independence. They were followed in the first half of the 1960s by the mainly British colonies in **East Africa**, and in the late 1970s and 1980s by the British and Portuguese white-settler colonies of **Southern Africa** and by **Guinea-Bissau** in western Africa. The formal end of apartheid in **South Africa** in 1994 marked the culmination of the **decolonization** process in the twentieth century.

"Politics" can be parsimoniously defined as the ways in which societal groups seek to reconcile their competing interests in public arenas, and "governance" as the institutional architecture and normative framework of rule. It is important to reiterate that, contrary to the inclination for unguarded generalization in commentary on African politics and governance, the dynamics and consequences of patterns of changes have varied among African societies because they are enormously diverse. Two key determinants of the dominant patterns were the nature of colonial political legacies, and the socioeconomic and cultural constitution of societies. Politics and governance after independence moved through three broad phases: Phase 1, in the 1950s and 1960s, represented a period of institutional experimentation with nation-state building; Phase 2, in the 1970s to early 1980s, was a period of elaboration of authoritarian rule; and Phase 3, in the 1980s and 1990s, was a time of economic crisis and reconfiguration of state–society relations.

Confronting the challenges of independence

Africans inherited from colonial rulers weakly institutionalized states; political systems that were marked by a lack of accountability, and in which state–society relations were premised more on paternalistic and individualistic patron–client relations than formal institutions; and highly fragmented societies in which communal identities and consciousness had been actively promoted and notions of a shared national citizenship were of limited resonance. Thus, as has often been remarked, at independence, the new ruling elite confronted the dual challenge of simultaneously promoting nation-building and economic development.

The nationalist elite celebrated the end of colonial rule as the beginnings of an "African Renaissance," and many proclaimed as imperative drawing upon Africa's maligned cultural heritage as a guide to future development. In reality, like their counterparts in other regions recently freed from colonial rule, African nationalists were committed to the modernization of their societies. Nation-building for them meant the elaboration of the structures and institutions of the modern nation-state as it had evolved in the West. This vision of nation-building as the defining project of political modernity and of political modernity as synonymous with Western-type nation-states accorded with the core assumptions of liberal modernization theory, which was the reigning conceptual framework for the comparative study of politics of newly independent societies in 1950s and 1960s. Born out of the "behavioral revolution" in the social sciences in the United States after the **Second World War**, the "first generation" of modernization theorists drew upon classical theories of democratic pluralism. They saw political modernization-cum-nation-building as a unidirectional and largely conflict-free transition from "traditional" political systems in which primordial loyalties were the primary determinant of political participation to Western-style multi-party democratic political systems that were predicated on secular cultures and the political equality of citizens. Economic modernization, which they defined as entailing a progressive shift from agrarian to urban-based industrial economies, resulted in patterns of sociocultural and behavioral changes that advanced political modernization. Economic modernization enlarged the urban-based working class and, especially, professional middle class that had been lead agents of the growth democratic pluralism in the West.

The intensification of political conflict during the run-up to independence and shortly after mocked the assumptions of nationalists and modernization theorists of easy pathways to nation-building. The sources and gravity of conflict varied across nations and in time. But, most importantly, there was the disjunction between heightened expectations for improvements in the material conditions of life (more jobs, higher commodity prices, better social services, and so on) that nationalists had promised would result from political independence, and the weak institutional capacities of the new states to fulfill these expectations. As the end of colonial rule became obvious, attention shifted from a common struggle against the colonial system to struggles among the elite for control of successor states. Nationalist coalitions began to disintegrate as the elite increasingly appealed to ethnoregional communities for support in their struggle for power. Not only did the limited class-differentiation discourage politicians from relying on the working class (or any other class) for support, but the grouping of the preponderantly rural populations into constituencies that were more or less demarcated by ethnicity and other markers of group difference encouraged appeals to communal ties. Opposition to incumbent governments, therefore, usually assumed the form of communal-based challenges.

The new governments responded to these centrifugal forces by centralizing and consolidating power around the state, and repressing political pluralism. Colonial political and administrative legacies influenced the manner in which both processes unfolded in different countries. The former French colonies inherited highly centralized presidential political systems, with governments headed by weak prime ministers appointed by and answerable to the president. The consolidation of power therefore proceeded by expansion of presidential power and authority. With Ghana as the trailblazer, the ex-British colonies jettisoned the variants of Westminister-type parliamentary systems with which they had entered independence in favor of presidential systems. As bureaucracies expanded to support the growing development and social-service functions of states, they were rapidly Africanized, and political loyalties to regimes began to compete with or replace merit as the criterion for recruitment and advancement in civil services and other public institutions. In the second half of the 1960s, disillusioned with laissez-faire approaches to economic development, Africa governments (regardless of ideological hue) turned to more interventionist, state-led approaches to economic development, which made control of political power all the more crucial for access to resources and socioeconomic mobility. The repression of political participation was accomplished through cooptation or violent elimination of the opposition, and the undermining of the capacity for political organization of nascent civil societies. By the late 1960s the effectiveness of efforts to stymie political pluralism was confirmed by the ubiquity of single-party regimes across all regions of the continent. By the early 1970s only a limited number of countries – notably **Botswana**, **Gambia**, and **Senegal** – had managed to retain multiparty political systems. The founding fathers (for they were all men) of African nations elaborated versions of African socialism and other "nativist" ideologies to rationalize autocratic rule (see **socialisms and socialists**). These ideologies turned on arguments that liberal democracy was a conflict-inducing form of governance, and demanded citizens to exchange their political freedoms for the benefits of economic development.

Elusiveness of political stability and elaboration of autocratic rule

The paradoxical results of the reversion of early independent regimes to colonial-style autocracy became more evident as the 1970s progressed. On the one hand, while a number of countries experienced acute political conflict – some even descended into civil war, such as **Nigeria** in 1967, while others experienced major regionalist challenges to the authority of the central state, including the inaptly named **Democratic Republic of Congo** – authoritarian rule had arguably contributed to the improbable survival of most states. On the other hand, it fostered political instability and the degradation of the institutions necessary for effective governance and peaceful resolution of political conflicts.

The centralization and personalization of power eroded the accountability of rulers to the ruled, and the blurring of the divide between politics and public administration fed incompetence and corruption. With the repression of political pluralism, patron–client networks grew as the institutional foundation of state–society relations. The apparently monolithic single parties were flimsy devices of patronage politics, whereby political power was maintained through the downward and unequal distribution of public resources. In mockery of the premises on which it was justified, authoritarian rule did not dampen the salience of ethnoregional-based political competition and conflict. It simply led to their internalization within state and party structures, with regimes continuing as alliances of regional elites whose power was based on patronage networks sustained by ethnic and other communal bonds. With the centralization of economic power, political control became excessively important to the acquisition of wealth – political competition among the elite assumed a "winner-takes-all" form. The dominant mode of regime-consolidation encouraged a mercenary political ethos: the perception that the main business of politics was to gain control of state institutions for personal gain and to enable the leader to reward supporters. Moreover it ensured that popular judgment of the legitimacy of regimes was premised on a sense of communal advantage and disadvantage.

The second phase of politics and governance in the independence era was thus characterized by efforts to elaborate autocratic rule. With destruction of institutions for the peaceful transfer of power, the military coup d'état became the primary mechanism of regime change. The militarization of politics intensified in the 1970s. The overthrow of the Egyptian monarchy in 1952 by the group of "Young Officers" led by Nasser inaugurated the modern era of the coup in Africa. In 1963 the government of **Togo** was felled by its military, and in 1964 the armies of **Tanzania**, Kenya and **Uganda** mutinied over poor wages and living conditions. In 1966 alone, civilian regimes in six

African countries (among them Ghana and Nigeria) were overthrown by their militaries. According to an authoritative estimate, between 1951 and 1985 African countries experienced 64 successful coups out of 126 attempts that are known about. By the end of the 1980s over half of the African states were under some form of military or quasi-military rule. Militaries typically explained their seizure of power as action to save the nation from internecine conflicts among civilian politicians, and the masterminds of coups presented themselves as "caretaker administrations" that would return states to civilian control after the restoration of order. In reality the first successful or attempted coup d'état most often presaged a cycle of coups and counter-coups.

Military autocracies differed in their effectiveness as managers of public affairs. They were also differentiated by the degree of violence they unleashed on societies: the autocratic rule of pre-1980s military regimes in Nigeria and Egypt's quasi-military regime were relatively moderate in comparison to the incredibly violent and tragicomical regime of Idi Amin in Uganda (1971–9), the self-proclaimed Emperor Bokassa's rule in the **Central African Republic** (1965–79), or Sani Abacha's period of government in Nigeria (1993–8). These differences aside, military autocracies generally aggravated institutional decay for a host of reasons. Because militaries mirrored the cleavages of their societies, military autocracies simply reproduced in different contexts extant patterns of political competition among the elite. Even the most autocratic civilian regimes needed some modicum of popular support, and under normal circumstances relied on formal and informal structures to mediate conflicting societal interests. Military regimes were less accountable than their civilian counterparts, as they ruled through close circles of military officers and senior civilian bureaucrats, and had a pronounced preference for the use of force in resolving political conflict. With their ingrained disdain for the rough-and-tumble of civilian politics – a fact which was noticeable in their inaugural measures, which would predictably include the proscription of political organizations and political participation – military leaders compounded the degradation of institutional capacity for effective governance and peaceful resolution of political conflict. It was not surprising that, although initially welcomed by populations tired of the excesses of civilian politicians, support for military regimes was always ephemeral and they frequently became victims of counter-coups.

The trajectory of political events across Africa in the 1960s and early 1970s paralleled, more or less, the experiences of developing countries in other regions. From the late 1960s these events occasioned revisions of liberal modernization theory, beginning with acknowledgment that, contrary to earlier suppositions, processes of socioeconomic change engendered intense political conflict. It was now argued that modernizing societies were prone to "political decay" because the mobilization of new social groups into politics outpaced the institutionalization of political authority. Based on such reasoning, revisionist theorists implied or asserted that the creation of political order – that is, the nurturing of institutional capabilities that would enable the ruling elite to effectively regulate political participation – was a necessary task prior to undertaking nation-building. This switch from championship of democracy to advocacy of order, especially among American social scientists like Samuel Huntington (1968), supported the foreign-policy objectives of the US government, which had became committed to viewing social conflict in developing countries through the prism of superpower rivalries, and saw pro-Western authoritarian regimes (military and civilian) as the best guarantors of political order and its interests.

This period also witnessed the growing prominence of radical frameworks for the analysis of the political economy and politics of developing countries, drawing on a range neo-Marxian theories and other critical traditions of political economy. For the study of Africa the most prominent was the dependency school. In contrast to old and revisionist modernization theorists, who regarded modernization as a primarily endogenously driven process, dependency scholars contended that the economic, political, and social structures of developing societies were shaped by their subordinate positions within the world economy and its hierarchically organized state-systems.

To Africanists and African exponents of the dependency approach – prominent among them were Nigerian political economist Claude Ake (1981), Egyptian economist Samir Amin (1974), Ugandan political scientist Mahmood Mamdani (1996), and Guyanese historian Walter Rodney (1972) – post-independence states acted as mediators of relations between transnational capitalists and dominant domestic groups. The primary interest of Africa's ruling elite was to use state power to transform themselves into capitalist classes or bureaucratic bourgeoisies. Authoritarian rule was necessary to contain the political instability caused by competition among the elite to commandeer state-controlled resources, and popular protest against the growing inequalities engendered by dependent models of capitalist development. Many liberal scholars conceded their argument that states were the primary vehicles of socioeconomic inequalities, and therefore, instigators of political conflict and instability. Despite their very important contributions, the proposals of dependency scholars of alternatives to existing forms of political organization and governance were not convincing. They claimed that change was contingent on the ascendancy to power of progressive elite groups who were dedicated to non-dependent patterns of development that would serve the interests of ill-defined masses.

Reconfiguring state–society relations and rethinking frameworks of analysis

African economies began to stagnate in the mid-1970s, and – with the exception of a small group of states including Botswana, **Lesotho**, and **Mauritius** – continued to decline through what was termed the "lost decade" of the 1980s. The deepening economic crisis further corroded the tenuous legitimacy of independence regimes. Against the backdrop of pervasive corruption, economic regression weakened their ability to maintain patronage networks, intensified elite competition over declining pools of public resources, and emboldened the disaffected among them to challenge incumbent governments. As the capacities of states to provide basic public services (including public security) declined, more and more of their citizens turned to greater reliance on kinship networks and community organizations for survival and protection against the predatory practices of the ruling elite. Symptomatic of the determination of societal groups to escape the power of states and the ruling elite was the growth of "second" or "parallel" economies on which much scholarly attention focused in the 1980s. Second economies provided some relief from dire economic conditions, and represented new domains of capital accumulation outside of states; they also threw into bold relief the breakdown of the rule of law, normalization of criminality, and collapse of the moral authority of states. Their expansion was accompanied by withdrawal of citizens from state-regulated structures of political participation. The neoliberal **structural adjustment programs** failed to arrest either economic decline or the political ramifications of such decline.

The crisis of economies and state legitimacy led to a fundamental rethinking of frameworks of analysis of relations between politics, governance, and development in Africa. This rethinking accorded with the key tenets of an emergent global discourse of development. By the 1980s the ascendancy of the neo-classical economies, the rise to power of neo-conservative governments, and the general rightward drift of political opinion in the West (along with the collapse of Eastern European Communist states) combined to establish a new global discourse on development that insisted successful development required the simultaneous promotion of free-market economies and liberal forms of governance. Africanists disagreed over the weight of external factors in the making of the crisis, but were unusually united in their insistence that authoritarian rule and economic mismanagement were leading causes, and that liberalization of economies and politics was imperative to transcending Africa's development impasse. Interestingly even Africa's radical intellectuals, with their visceral disdain of capitalism and suspicion of liberal democracy, were persuaded of the need for market-driven economies and democracy as the foundations of sustainable economic development and nation-building. But their embrace of the new development discourse remained guarded because of a discomfort with the apparent insistence of Western governments and **international financial institutions** on universally applicable institutional frameworks for the development of market economies and democracy. Prior to the 1980s liberal and radical explanatory models of politics and governance were state-centric in that they concentrated on the practices of states and ruling elites. Another significant aspect of the rethinking of frameworks of analysis was a shift from such state-centric models of explanation to models that emphasized the myriad interactions of states and societies in the production of politics and in the character of governance. There were normative implications to this shift, as it tilted concern toward the ways in which societal reactions to the crisis signaled possibilities for the reconfiguration of state–society relations along democratic lines.

The prevailing mode among Africanists through the 1980s was one of "Afropessimism" – an inability to imagine ways in which politics and governance could be restructured to provide an environment for sustainable development. This contrasted with a growing interest among intellectuals on the continent, under the auspices of continental research organizations such as the Dakar-based Council for the Development of Social Research in Africa, in exploring how new social movements could be agents of democratization. The sudden and largely unanticipated groundswell of popular movements demanding an end to authoritarian rule at the close of the 1980s and in the early 1990s gave rise to a new optimism about Africa's participation in the "Third Wave of Democracy." In contrast to the era of nationalist struggle and decolonization, when the mobilization of rural society was pivotal, these movements were urban-centered and mobilized by middle-class professional organizations and **human rights** advocacy groups, under the leadership of mainstream churches, labor unions, and so on. This led many to opine that the continent was witnessing a "resurgence" of **civil society** that could be seen as a harbinger for democratization. The growth of pro-democracy movements led to a dramatic return to multi-party politics and competitive elections across the continent in the early 1990s. In the 1980s an average of two national elections were held annually across Africa. By 1994 the spread of multi-party electoral competition had yielded fourteen new governments. By the end of the 1990s only a small number of nations had not held multi-party elections.

Two broad perspectives prevailed in explanation of this return to multi-party politics. One perspective emphasized internal factors, arguing that unrelenting economic adversity and enfeeblement of patronage networks emboldened cross-sections of the population to demand more accountable and representative forms of governance. The second claimed that external factors were paramount, especially the new international aid regime that made development assistance conditional on the willingness of recipient states to promote free-market economies and democracy. According to this perspective, the heightened dependence of African states on foreign aid compelled regimes to acquiesce to pressures from Western governments and international financial institutions to introduce multi-party electoral competition. These perspectives were not necessarily contradictory. Western governments had never been shy in their support of autocratic regimes for economic and geostrategic reasons. With the end of the **Cold War** and the growing willingness of citizens to query their governments' support of regimes that abused human rights, many governments could now afford to publicly condemn the maleficence and arbitrariness of autocratic rulers, and support opposition movements that did not threaten their core economic interests. The democracy movements posed immediate challenges to the authority of incumbent regimes, and made their survival contingent on the amplification of repression or political reform. The growth and resilience of these movements, in the face of muscular efforts by regimes to contain them, revealed the limits of repression in the reproduction of political authority.

At the close of the twentieth century analysis of politics and governance in African remained preoccupied by the prospects of democratic transition. The euphoria that greeted the rebirth of multi-party politics had waned by the second cycle of African elections in the mid-1990s. Judging from the flurry of activity (especially from the private **press**, political parties, and autonomous interest-based associations) and general resolve of citizens to defend their democratic rights, on balance African societies were considerably freer in the last years of the twentieth century than they had been in the 1980s. Apart from the most obdurate autocrats (such as Robert Mugabe of **Zimbabwe**) who increasingly seemed like historical relics, most African rulers seemed to have accepted the need to legitimize their power through electoral competition, at least in the short term. But successive cycles of electoral competition did not alter the inequalities of power, whether structured by class, gender, ethnicity, or region. These elections redefined the context of elite competition for power, but they also affirmed the resilience of patronage networks as the institutional bedrock of political power. Owing to their lack of autonomous resource-bases, and susceptibility to the divisions of class, gender, ethnicity, region, race, and so on, civil societies had scant impact on electoral competition and its outcomes. The rebirth of multi-party politics appeared to reinvigorate communal-based competition and conflict. Although encouraged by the elite in their struggle for power, communal-based political conflict in many cases expressed the determination of groups to redress or defend perceived imbalances in the distribution of political and symbolic power between communities. In cases such as Algeria and Egypt in the 1980s or Nigeria in the late 1990s, the growth of political **Islam** arguably articulated a deep discomfort with Western modernity and a longing for alternative models of political organization and governance.

In sum, it remains unwise to attempt to predict the future trajectory of governance and politics in Africa, but the concentration of scholarly attention on democratic transitions is understandable. However, as Richard Sklar, a noted theorist of "developmental democracy" observed, democracy does not emerge in a pure form: democratic values, institutions, and practices evolve discontinuously, and progress towards democracy in some spheres is not necessarily matched by progress in others. Moreover it remained the case that political liberalization was only one – and not even necessarily the most significant – aspect of the reconfiguration of African state–society relations at the end of the twentieth century. The unexceptional lesson of the political history of the independence era is, then, that future trajectories continue to be shaped by the complex and varied ways in which international and domestic forces intersect. These intersections will define the possibilities and patterns of economic development and social change, and how Africans manage the challenges of their still incipient nation-building projects.

See also: nationalist movements; state: colonial; state: post-independence; Third World

References and further reading

Ake, C. (1981) *A Political Economy of Africa*, Harlow: Longman.

Amin, S. (1974) *Accumulation on a World Scale: A Critique of the Theory of Underdevelopment*, trans. B. Pearce, New York: Monthly Review Press.

Bratton, M. and van de Walle, N. (1997) *Democratic Experiments in Africa: Regime Transformation in Comparative Perspective*, New York: Cambridge University Press.

Chazan, N. *et al.* (1999) *Politics and Society in Contemporary Africa*, 3rd edn., Boulder: Lynne Rienner.

Eyoh, D. and Sandbrook, R. (2002) "Pragmatic Neo-Liberalism and Just Development in Africa," in A. Kohli, C. Moon and G. Sorenson (eds.), *Just Development*, Tokyo: United Nations University Press.

Herbst, J. (2000) *States and Power in Africa: Comparative Lessons in Authority and Control*, Princeton: Princeton University Press.

Huntington, S. (1968) *Political Order in Changing Societies*, New Haven and London: Yale University Press.

Hutchful, E. and Bathily, A. (eds.) (1998) *The Military and Militarism in Africa*, Dakar: CODESRIA.

Mamdani, M. (1996) *Citizens and Subject: Contemporary Africa and the Legacies of Late Colonialism*, Princeton: Princeton University Press.

Rodney, W. (1972) *How Europe Underdeveloped Africa*, London: Bogle-L'Ouverture.

Sklar, R. (1987) "Developmental Democracy,"

Comparative Studies in Society and History 29, 4: 686–714.

DICKSON EYOH

structural adjustment programs

Structural adjustment programs (SAPs) comprise those policy measures that were prescribed by the donor community to the governments of African and other developing countries whose economies were experiencing crises of different dimensions and proportions following the two oil shocks of the 1970s. The programs made their grand entry into the African economic crisis-management framework in the early 1980s. They were introduced at a time of global neoliberal ascendancy, with the decline of Keynesian economic policy-making. Considerably boosted by the rise to power of conservative, "free" market-oriented governments in some of the key Western countries – especially the Group of Seven (G7) countries and their leaders, including Ronald Reagan in the United States, Margaret Thatcher in the United Kingdom, Brian Mulroney in Canada, and Helmut Kohl in Germany – neoliberalism was quickly incorporated into the thinking and policy prescriptions of the International Monetary Fund (IMF) and the World Bank, and extended to the economic reform agenda of developing countries that were experiencing difficulties with their balance-of-payments situation. African countries – the majority of which suffered problems with their external accounts in the context of the oil shocks of the 1970s, the accelerating decline of their terms of trade, and evidence of mounting internal problems of accumulation – were among the first group of developing countries to adopt the adjustment prescriptions of the IMF and World Bank.

Within the specific African context, the groundwork for the promotion of structural adjustment programs as the way out of the economic crises facing the continent was laid with the publication of the infamous Berg Report (World Bank 1981), which had been commissioned by the World Bank at the beginning of the 1980s. Published against the backdrop of the Lagos Plan of Action (LPA), which African leaders had adopted as their own autonomous framework for overcoming the economic problems in their countries, the Berg Report represented a diametrically opposed view that repudiated the diagnoses of the LPA and the solutions it proposed, including an intensification of the process of regional cooperation and integration. It was the Berg Report's view that the origins of the African economic crises were the result of interventionist state policies that distorted or stifled the market and its free functioning, and this analysis prevailed in the years ahead. It was also significant that the Berg Report located the sources of Africa's problems exclusively in internal, domestic policies, neglecting external factors that included the declining terms of trade experienced by African countries. Not surprisingly the solutions that Berg prescribed consisted of wholesale price and trade liberalization measures, attuned to the goals of achieving free-market economies and promoting the private sector.

Not a few scholars have observed that the Berg Report represented a misreading of the economic history of post-colonial Africa, and pointed to its total neglect of the achievements of the 1960s and 1970s, including the fairly significant rates of growth recorded by many countries directly after independence. The Berg Report also ignored the fact that, like much of the rest of the world, African countries had mostly followed the dominant Keynesian macro-economic management strategies that were the order of the day – and there had been no shortage of "international experts" advising them to adopt these very policies. Nonetheless it was this misreading of Africa's economic policy terrain, and the deliberate downplaying of successes recorded at all levels, that informed the political-ideological framework within which the SAPs of the IMF and World Bank were designed and pursued. The post-colonial state was to be the first and major victim of the missionary zeal with which the neoliberal free-market campaign was launched and prosecuted.

In their original formulation the SAPs were conceptualized in two phases: the stabilization phase and the structural reform phase. In practice, however, both phases tended to be collapsed together to produce the features that have become the universal symbols of adjustment across the entire developing world:

1 massive and repeated currency devaluation within the context of different types of currency flotation;
2 price liberalization;
3 interest- and exchange-rate deregulation;
4 public enterprise commercialization/privatization/liquidation;
5 trade liberalization through an across-the-board tariff reduction;
6 withdrawal of subsidies, cost recovery, and the introduction of user-charges on social services;
7 a wage and salary freeze;
8 retrenchment of the public sector, especially civil-service employees, in order to eliminate "excess capacity",
9 the introduction of broad-ranging civil service and governance reforms;
10 export promotion and support for the private sector, including private/non-governmental initiatives;
11 the quest for the creation of a minimalist state; and
12 the extension of the logic of the market to all spheres of activity.

These measures were presented as central to contemporary economic policy as the processes of **globalization** gathered pace on the basis of a neoliberal agenda for trade, finance, and capital deregulation.

From the 1980s African countries were forced to implement the adjustment prescriptions of the IMF and the World Bank through the instrumentality of donor conditionality and cross-conditionality clauses. For instance, African governments were to find that no debt rescheduling negotiations were possible with the London and Paris Clubs of creditors without a prior IMF/World Bank "clean bill of health." This was also applied to requests for fresh loans or debt cancellations. The "clean bill of health" would only be issued when the African government in question adopted an adjustment framework that was acceptable to the IMF and the Bank. Thus for some twenty years a narrow, ideologically driven orthodoxy prevailed in the search for a framework for the reform of African economies. Even the few African countries – **South Africa**, **Namibia**, and **Botswana** – that did not have formal adjustment agreements with the IMF and World Bank were compelled to adopt "shadow" programs, whose thrust was essentially orthodox. A good example of this is the South African "Growth, Employment, and Restructuring" (GEAR) program, which replaced the more comprehensive, redistributive, and developmentalist "Reconstruction and Development Program" (RDP) that had been adopted when the ANC government first came to power in 1994.

Yet despite all the effort invested in compelling African countries to adopt the reform path charted for them by the donor community, and notwithstanding the fact that virtually all of the countries in Africa toed the donor line, structural adjustment failed to achieve the goals set for it by its authors – namely, to stem the tide of decline, stabilize African economies, return them to the path of growth, and transform their structures. If anything, structural adjustment became part and parcel of the dynamic of decline in African economies. Initially the IMF and the Bank dismissed the evident difficulties as merely temporary. As problems persisted the blame was shifted to African governments, who were allegedly reluctant to reform or adopted an unhelpful "stop-start" approach. There was also a suggestion that African governments were captured by vested interests intent on obstructing reform in order to keep the privileges they had accumulated under the old interventionist model of development, which had encouraged a flowering of growth-retarding patronage and clientelist systems. An influential literature on the "political economy of adjustment" proliferated, discussing Africa's state-based/-dependent elites, and their craving for rents and rent-producing niches.

It was only in the face of persistent evidence of outright failure or lackluster performance, even in those countries described by the IMF and World Bank as "good adjusters," that questions began to be raised about the validity and appropriateness of the adjustment model Africa had been made to follow for some two decades. In the late 1990s a high-profile critique of the adjustment model came from none other than Joseph Stiglitz, who had for a short period in the 1990s been chief economist of the World Bank. In fact he was simply echoing critiques of the adjustment orthodoxy that had been made much earlier by many scholars and policy-makers in developing countries. One of the criticisms of orthodox adjustment that became commonplace in the second half of the 1990s, but had been dismissed when it was first raised in the 1980s, related to the one-size-fits-all approach to reform. All adjusting countries were made to implement the same package of measures, irrespective of the source, nature, and severity of their economic problems – an approach that led the IMF and World Bank to be described as bad doctors who prescribed the same drug to all patients irrespective of their ailments.

Other weaknesses of orthodox structural adjustment included:

1 internal contradictions resulted in one aspect of a policy that was being promoted canceling out another (for example, the impact of devaluation, trade liberalization, and massive worker retrenchment on industrial output, capacity utilization, and turnover);
2 the one-sided anti-state thrust of the programs was pursued despite the fact that the market and private sector cannot function effectively without an effective state;
3 complete neglect of the adverse social consequences and subsequent treatment of social dimensions of adjustment as a residual category, the consequence being that the basic incompatibility between orthodox economic reform and the quest for poverty reduction/ eradication remained;
4 the promotion of an ideal-type notion of the market and its functioning that was far from reality (the IMF and World Bank thus felt justified in reducing Africa to a huge experimental economic laboratory, but remained insensitive to the evidence of market failure that was staring them in the face);
5 an obsession with macro-indicators to the neglect of the basic tasks/challenges of development that ought to have been the primary purpose of economic policy; and
6 the huge cost of the implementation of structural adjustment in terms of political instability, with the repression of popular opposition to it undermining democratic economic policy-making.

Within the context of ongoing discussions about the end of the so-called "Washington Consensus" that resulted in structural adjustment, African critiques of two decades of orthodox market-based reforms were also actively taking stock of the effects of the maladjustment of the continent. The key challenge that many were defining by the end of the 1990s centered on how to bring development back in – after all, before it was transformed by the IMF and World Bank into the very essence of development, structural adjustment was (in theory at least) meant to be a temporary diversion from development. Bringing development back to center-stage of African policy-making also had implications for the rehabilitation of the state as a legitimate and central player in the economic, social, and political processes on the continent. The other challenge was how to ensure that the developmental state was disciplined into accepting the popular democracy that alone could guarantee its social legitimacy and provide the necessary safeguards against a return to the authoritarianism of the early post-colonial model of accumulation. The question of a developmental democracy for Africa has, therefore, also emerged as a central element in the discourse about how to move Africa beyond orthodox structural adjustment programs.

See also: agrarian change; debt crises; economy: post-independence; food crises; manufacturing: modern; state: post-independence

References and further reading

Engberg-Pedersen, P., Gibbon, P., Raikes, P. and Udsholt, L. (eds.) (1996) *Limits of Adjustment in Africa*, Copenhagen: Centre for Development Research.

Gibbon, P. and Olukoshi, A. (1996) *Structural Adjustment and Socio-economic Change in Sub-Saharan Africa: Some Conceptual, Research and Methodological Issues*, Uppsala: Nordiska Afrikainstitutet.

Mkandawire, T. and Olukoshi, A. (eds.) (1995) *Between Liberalisation and Repression: The Politics of Structural Adjustment in Africa*, Dakar: CODESRIA.

Mkandawire, T. and Soludo, C. (1998) *Our Continent Our Future*, Trenton: Africa World Press Inc.

World Bank (1981) *Accelerated Development in*

Sub-Saharan Africa: An Agenda for Action, Washington, D.C.: World Bank.
—— (1994) *Adjustment in Africa. Reforms, Results, and the Road Ahead*, New York: Oxford University Press.

ADEBAYO O. OLUKOSHI

Sudan

Sudan is the largest country in Africa, covering 2.5 million square kilometers. It had an estimated population of 32 million in 2000, and is bordered by **Egypt** to the north, **Eritrea** and **Ethiopia** to the east, **Kenya**, **Uganda** and the **Democratic Republic of Congo** to the south, and **Central African Republic**, **Chad** and **Libya** to the west. Sudan proclaimed its independence on 1 January 1956. The north is predominantly Muslim, while the south is principally Christian. In addition to **Islam** and Christianity, many Sudanese adhere to indigenous beliefs. Although 40 percent of the population considers itself "Arab," the meaning of the term remains undefined.

In 1898 a joint Anglo-Egyptian force under Lord Kitchener defeated the Mahdists at the Battle of Omdurman, taking control of the whole of northern Sudan apart from Darfur. Condominium rule in the Sudan began with the conclusion on 19 January 1899 of an agreement between the British government and the government of the Khedive of Egypt. The thirteen-year rule of the Mahdists (1885–98) had not only effectively destroyed the old Turkish-Egyptian administrative system but also weakened the social fabric of Sudanese society. When the British colonized the Sudan in 1898, the colonial state became preoccupied with two concerns: the problem of slavery, and the need to establish law and order in southern Sudan. Influenced by the colonial discourse on Africa, the British administrators introduced new policies for labor control and indirect rule in southern Sudan, but they had to face the reality of the social and economic foundations of society in the north. Since the nineteenth century the dominant ruling groups from the north had created an idealized Arab-Islamic community, and those who did not belong to this imagined community were considered to be enslaveable. In order to avoid a revival of Mahdism, the British administration tolerated this practice of **slavery** in the north. For the purpose of securing laborers for colonial economic projects, the British administration divided the peoples of the Sudan into three distinct racial categories: "Arab," "Sudanese" (or ex-slave), and "Fallata" (or West African).

Indirect rule was adopted in 1921 as a strategy for "tribal" administration and development. This policy, coupled with the Milner Commission's recommended policy of decentralized rule in Sudan, separated "Africans" from "Arabs," providing the means by which the Sudan could be divided into two different political entities. The first step was to cut off the south from the north through the promulgation of the Passport and Permits Ordinance in October 1922, which empowered the governor-general to declare any part of Sudan a "Closed District." Southern Sudan accordingly became a closed region into which people from other parts of the Sudan were not allowed to enter without permission. In addition British administrators in the south were no longer required to attend the meeting of the governors that was held annually in **Khartoum**. Instead they held their meetings in Kenya and Uganda. It was not until 1930 that people of southern Sudan were finally forced to accept British rule. "Chiefs" were created and legitimized to rule the people and implement government policies.

Colonial rule in the Sudan brought together different regions, with various levels of socio-economic development, under a centralized state. The centerpiece of agricultural development was the vast cotton-growing Gezira Scheme, completed in 1925 after the construction of the Sennar Dam. Profits were to be divided between the condominium government, the private Sudan Plantations Syndicate, and the tenant farmers who actually cultivated the cotton. Additional agricultural schemes were later established in Kassala and Gash. Despite the importance of these schemes, they directly affected only a small part of the population. Most peasants grew subsistence crops, principally *dura* (the staple food grain in Sudan) and cash crops other than cotton, including gum Arabic (which remained Sudan's leading export until the turn of the 1930s), sesame, and groundnuts. Animals and animal products were also important. Much of the economic investment in Sudan's transport and communications infrastructure before the **First World War** was undertaken through subventions from the Egyptian government. Education and economic development were largely concentrated in the northern parts of the country. Three categories of people benefited from this economic policy: large-scale merchants, "tribal" leaders, and religious leaders. The last group included two prominent traditional families – the Mahdi and the Mirghani – who were able to accumulate considerable wealth through dues paid to them by their supporters.

In the 1930s and 1940s the Arab-oriented nationalist leadership was able to take advantage of economic opportunities opened up for them by colonial policies. By virtue of their positions as civil servants or religious and "tribal" leaders, they gained access to credit, and were able to engage in the trade of various export commodities. From then onwards the dominant "Sudanese" discourse on nation-building began to equate membership of the state with being Arab and Muslim. Race and descent, not citizenship, became the two criteria for defining who should or should not lead the emerging nation. These ideological visions of racial stratification provided the tragic cultural and political logic that was to shape much of the violence during the post-colonial period.

Northern Sudanese nationalists, however, accused the British of either planning to divide Sudan into two states or planning to attach the south, or part of it, to Uganda. Consequently the northern Sudanese Graduate Congress in Khartoum exerted strong pressure on the government to grant self-rule and independence to the whole Sudan, including the south. In December 1946 the Civil Secretary, Sir James W. Robertson, former governor-general of **Nigeria**, decided that the future of the southern Sudan was to be bound to that of the north. Southerners and senior British officials working in the south criticized his decision, however. As a result of this criticism a conference was held at Juba in June 1947, but the conference was purely consultative: it was called to gather advice on how best to implement the decision that had already been made. Just before Sudan's independence was granted in 1956, the Equatorial Corps revolted in Torit and other major cities of the south in August 1955. This revolt inaugurated the first phase of a civil war that was to last for seventeen years.

Politics in the Sudan from 1956–69 were characterized by Muslim sectarian domination of the main northern political parties, and the existence of weak southern political parties. Southern demands for federalism, along with the weakness of the sectarian parties, forced the civilian government in 1958 to hand over political power to General 'Abboud, the commander of the army. The military ruled until 1964, when public discontent over the weak economy, political repression, and an escalating civil war in the south forced them out of government. Civilians then ruled until Colonel Jaafar Nimeiri overthrew the government on 25 May 1969. Political independence was seen by sectarian political parties, such as the Umma Party and the Democratic Unionist Party, as a means of maintaining the Sudan's territorial "integrity" and removing an "artificial" barrier to the progress of Islam and Arab culture in southern Sudan. With increasing cultural oppression and physical violence, southerners formed the Anya-Nya – the military wing of the Sudan African National Union. The Anya-Nya intensified the fight for the right to self-determination in the south, and the Nimeiri regime proposed the establishment of a secular socialist state with regional autonomy for a unified south. The Addis Ababa Agreement of 1972 duly ended this first phase of civil war in Sudan.

However, Nimeiri and Hassan al-Turabi (the leader of the Muslim Brothers) had orchestrated the redivision of the south, which formed part of a plan to weaken the south in preparation for the imposition of Islamic *shari'a* law on the entire country. The south reacted with a revolt in 1983, led by John Garang, and the formation of what later became the Sudan People's Liberation Movement (SPLM) and Sudan People's Liberation Army (SPLA). The SPLA/M provided the first fully articulated secularist discourse in the modern political history of Sudan. In 1989 a group of military officers, supported by the National Islamic Front (NIF) under the leadership of Hassan al-Turabi, conducted a military coup that deposed the civilian government of Sadiq El-Mahdi. The Islamic regime that was established in its place pursued *jihad* against the south, and this escalation of the civil war had grave social, economic, and environmental consequences. From 1989 to the end of the 1990s the NIF laid the foundations of an Islamic state in the Sudan, during which period racist policies and practices (including slavery) dramatically increased in the country. Famine became the Sudanese government's most effective tool of **genocide**. By 1993 the total number of people who had died in southern Sudan was more than 1.3 million. At least one in five southern Sudanese had died as result of famine, war, or disease.

Further reading

Deng, F.M. (1995) *War of Visions: Conflict of Identities in the Sudan*, Washington, D.C.: Brookings Institution.

Lesch, A.M. (1998) *The Sudan: Contested National Identities*, Bloomington: Indiana University Press.

AMIR H. IDRIS

Swahili

A member of the Bantu linguistic family, Swahili (also known as Kiswahili) is the most widely spread indigenous language in Africa. It is used by millions of people in **Kenya**, **Tanzania**, **Uganda**, **Comoros** islands, **Democratic Republic of Congo**, **Rwanda**, and **Burundi**, as well as in parts of **Somalia**, **Mozambique**, and **Malawi**. The language itself dates back to the tenth century or earlier. By the eighteenth century it had already developed a flourishing written tradition in Arabic script under the impetus of **Islam**. But the language remained overwhelmingly a coastal phenomenon until late in the 1700s, when the growing momentum of Arab trade carried the language into the interior as far as the Congo. As the nineteenth century unfolded, trade expanded, and the multi-lingual settlements that were established in its wake needed a lingua franca like Swahili.

In Tanganyika (now **Tanzania**) Swahili made further gains during the German colonial era. The Maji Maji war of resistance that broke out in 1905 was important for the future of the language, both because Swahili featured significantly as a trans-ethnic medium of communication among the African combatants and because German policy of political penetration included a linguistic policy that favored Swahili even more after the war than before. In their attempt to pacify the combatants the Germans were forced to centralize their administration; and that centralization also involved the promotion of Swahili for ease of communication between colonizer and colonized.

The defeat of the Germans during the **First World War** had its own impact on the fortunes of Swahili. By that time the orthographic romanization of the language was already well underway as part of the Western legacy. Kenya, Tanganyika, Uganda, and Zanzibar were now all under the same British colonial administration. In 1930 the British proceeded to form the Inter-Territorial Language Committee, which was to be paramount in the standardization of Swahili and in promoting regionally usable literature in the language.

Because Swahili developed within an Islamic culture, it carried many Islamic associations. But these associations were not held against the language by Christian missionaries in the earliest days of European colonization. On the contrary, quite a number felt that – since both Islam and Christianity were monotheistic religions drawn from the same Middle Eastern ancestry – Swahili would serve well for the conversion of indigenous Africans to Christianity. The stage was thus set for the ecumenicalization of Swahili. In time, however, most missionaries found "vernacular" languages better tools for cultivating the African soul than Swahili.

The spread of Swahili was given further impetus by the inter-ethnic and inter-territorial recruitment of Africans into the colonial armed forces. By creating conditions for rural-to-urban migration and the emergence of an urban labor force, colonialism also stimulated the use of Swahili among workers. The growth of trade unionism in

East Africa added a new and important organizational role for Swahili – a role independent of educational policy. The importance of Swahili was enhanced in a situation where the labor force was not only multi-ethnic, but also international. Increasingly the language became indispensable in labor mobilization against colonialism (especially in Tanzania and Kenya). In due course it established a solid constituency among urban workers, a status it continues to enjoy to this day.

With regard to Swahili in education, the British remained ambivalent throughout the colonial period. Their educational Swahili policies were usually ad hoc, changing from place to place and moment to moment. The British administration's enthusiasm for Swahili waned further when the growth of anti-colonialism in East Africa began to benefit from using Swahili as a trans-ethnic, grass-roots language of mobilization.

After independence, however, the language quickly acquired national status in both Tanzania and Kenya. With the Arusha Declaration of 1967 it became the medium of instruction at primary level, with plans to extend it to higher levels of education too. The Tanzanian call to education for self-reliance became a crucial foundation in the universalization and development of Swahili for scientific purposes. From 1986 the language also became a compulsory subject in all elementary and secondary schools in Kenya. Due primarily to ethno-nationalist currents of one sort or another, however, Swahili did not acquire much of an educational value in the rest of the Swahili-speaking world.

The wars in the Great Lakes region may have further consolidated the regional status of Swahili. The language played a key role in the inter-ethnic struggle of the National Resistance Army (NRA), under Yoweri Museveni, against Milton Obote. When the National Resistance Movement (the political wing of Museveni's army) finally assumed power, Swahili became the official language of its army. As an off-shoot of the NRA, the Rwanda Patriotic Front (RPF) later took Swahili with it into Rwanda, giving the language a new legitimacy in that country. Soon after, in 1996 and 1997, Laurent Kabila mobilized Swahili as the language of command in a multi-ethnic army pitted against the forces of Mobutu Sese Seko. Swahili became important not only because many of the fighters who were recruited already had a command of the language, but also because of the participation in the war of officers and troops from Rwanda. So when Joseph Kabila eventually took power in the Democratic Republic of Congo in 2001, he was essentially continuing the pro-Swahili orientation of his assassinated father.

The momentous spread of Swahili that was precipitated by the conjunction of all these forces has not, however, been without its gender imbalances. Among native speakers, women are probably the more skilled users of Swahili; among non-native speakers, however, men not only outnumber women in using Swahili, but also have a better command of the language. After all, many of the processes that favor the acquisition of Swahili, including rural-to-urban migration, employment in the urban workforce, and recruitment into the armed forces have continued to be predominantly male-oriented.

Further reading

Mazrui, A.A. and Mazrui, A.M. (1995) *Swahili, State and Society: Political Economy of an African Language*, London: James Currey.

Whiteley, W.H. (1969) *Swahili: The Rise of a National Language*, London: Methuen.

ALAMIN M. MAZRUI

Swaziland

Swaziland has an area of 17,364 square kilometers, and its population was estimated at 1.1 million in 2000. The country is bordered by **South Africa** and **Mozambique**, and its administrative and judicial capital is **Mbabane**, while Manzini is the industrial hub of the country. The modern Swazi state was crafted between the end of the eighteenth century and the beginning of the nineteenth. The history of Swaziland was shaped by its geographical location, especially by its powerful neighbor, South Africa, and by the encroachment of European settlers. From 1902 to 1968, during British colonial rule, the Swazi lost control of about

66 percent of their land, although from the 1940s Swazi rulers were able to buy back some of the land they had lost.

The discovery of gold in the Lembombo range brought European prospectors, called "concessionaires," to the kingdom, which had been embroiled in a long and bitter succession dispute following the death of Mswati II in 1865. In 1889 Britain and the Boer Republic decided to turn Swaziland into a "political dependency," effectively ending attempts by Mbadzeni, the beleaguered monarch, to retain Swazi independence. Swaziland remained a dependency of Transvaal until 1899, when the Anglo-Boer War broke out. Boer disarray enabled the kingdom to reclaim some autonomy, but this proved short-lived, with Britain taking control of Swaziland at the end of the war in 1902.

The economy of the small kingdom, like those of its neighbors, was heavily influenced by South Africa. **Migrant labor** to South African farms, mines, and factories became an important occupation of many Swazi men, and a source of revenue for their families and the state. Migrant labor disrupted the country's social structure, however, transforming family and gender relations as women were increasingly left in charge of rural production and households. Large settler farms and a plantation economy also emerged in Swaziland itself, on land acquired by the concessionaires, with cash crops such as cotton, tobacco, and sugar being produced. When not working for settler farmers and ranchers, Swazi **peasants** eked out an increasingly difficult existence in the remaining third of the country.

The political situation began to change with the installation in 1921 of Sobhuza II, who enjoyed a long reign (he stayed alive until 1982). Sobhuza began a process of buying some of the European-owned land, most of which he redistributed to Swazis, a gesture of patronage that gained him popularity and consolidated the legitimacy of his monarchy. After the **Second World War** Swaziland gradually shed its image as a colonial backwater with a picturesque monarchy, as investment poured into the country's commercial farming, forestry, and mining sectors, as well as an incipient manufacturing sector. Economic growth was accompanied by the expansion of a middle-class elite, which began agitating for independence. They were strongly opposed to the British intention of ceding the colony to South Africa. British enthusiasm for this scheme waned somewhat with the victory of the National Party and its institution of apartheid in 1948. Swazi nationalists were organized around the Ngwane National Liberatory Congress (NNLC), which organized a series of strikes in 1962 and 1963, including a general strike that was crushed by British troops supported by the king. The king's supporters formed a royalist party: the Imbokodvo National Movement.

Independence was granted in 1968, with the monarchy stronger than ever. All political parties were banned. Sobhuza maintained that Swaziland was a single nation unified by its culture, traditions, and language, and the Swazi had a right to develop a system of governance based on their history and the selective adoption of foreign practices. For him and his supporters, political parties represented a foreign practice that his people had yet to understand. The political situation began to change a little when King Mswati III succeeded his father in 1968, at the age of sixteen. The monarchy was nevertheless forced to recognise the winds of democratization blowing across the continent. In the early 1990s two commissions were appointed, both headed by princes. The first commission, on politics, reported that the Swazis did not want political parties, but recommended a secret ballot for national elections. This was implemented in the 1993 elections, replacing an open voting system in which voters filed past the candidate of their choice. The second commission, on the economy, recommended that the country should reposition itself strategically in view of the changes taking place in the Southern African regional economy, especially in South Africa and Mozambique (see **Southern Africa**).

Economic reforms were implemented after much consultation, but differed little from the **structural adjustment programs** being adopted elsewhere in the region. Economic growth rates declined from 6.5 percent between 1982 and 1991 to 2.5 percent in 2000, which was less than the population growth rate of 3.2 percent. Indeed economic reform was used to emphasize the need for national unity, a thinly veiled argument against pluralism and political reform. Economic reforms were compromised by capital flight to the newly democratic South Africa and postwar Mozambique, as well as by Swaziland's high levels of HIV/AIDS infection.

Nevertheless, it was clear the political situation was changing. New political groups emerged in the 1990s. The most active was the People's United Democratic Movement (PUDEMO). Formed in 1983 with the active support of students at the University of Swaziland, PUDEMO was instrumental in the victory of King Mswati during succession conflicts in the 1980s. It refined its political strategy in 1990 by sponsoring a **civil society** environmental organization among the **youth**. The NNLC was revived from 1998, under the leadership of Obed Dlamini, a former prime minister (1989–93). A third party was the Swaziland Democratic Alliance (SDA), created by civil society organizations. The **labor movement**, especially trade unions affiliated with the Swaziland Federation of Trade Unions (SFTU), also flexed its muscles, organizing mass boycotts between 1995 and 1997 that paralyzed several political and economic institutions. It was clear that Swaziland was entering a new era; its direction, however, was anyone's guess.

Further reading

Booth, A.R. (2000) *Historical Dictionary of Swaziland*, London: Scarecrow Press.

Matsebula, J.S.M. (1988) *A History of Swaziland*, Cape Town: Longman.

ACKSON M. KANDUZA
CASSANDRA RACHEL VENEY

T

Tanganyika *see* Tanzania

Tanzania

Tanzania, with an area of 945,087 square kilometers and an estimated population of 34 million in 2000, is located in **East Africa** and bordered by **Burundi**, **Kenya**, **Malawi**, **Mozambique**, **Rwanda**, **Uganda**, and the **Democratic Republic of Congo**. The twentieth-century history of the Republic of Tanzania is divided into three periods: German colonial rule from the 1880s ended as a consequence of defeat in the **First World War**; the British period began with the occupation of German East Africa in 1917, and ended in 1961; the third period is the independence era.

Conquest of the territory was completed with the defeat of Chief Mkwawa of the Hehe in 1898. German military government relied on coastal Muslims and the Nyamwezi of the western interior for administrative and military personnel. Economic exploitation favored white settlers, who established coffee plantations in the northeast highlands and sisal in the lowlands. Peasant agriculture was encouraged in areas not confiscated by Europeans. The colonial economy relied on voluntary and forced **migrant labor**. Colonial economic "development" also relied on railways. The northern railway (1911) served settler interests, while the central railway from **Dar es Salaam** to Kigoma (1914) passed through areas of **peasant** agriculture. Christian missions proliferated, and by 1911 over 100,000 children were in mission schools.

In the southeastern region African grievances exploded in the Maji Maji Rebellion (1905–7) over local grievances, including forced cotton cultivation and porterage, although the rebellion also contained millenarian elements and was unified through the remarkable leadership of the spirit medium Kinjikitile. After initial successes the revolt was brutally suppressed by the Germans, who laid waste to the countryside, leaving up to 250,000 dead from war and famine. German excesses led to the appointment of the first civilian governor, Count Albrecht von Rechenberg (1906–11), who attempted to reform labor practices, protect African land from further alienation, and change the economic emphasis from settler plantations to peasant agriculture, all in the teeth of settler opposition.

The First World War came as a disaster to the colony, further devastating the south. Most of the troops on both the German and British sides were African. More significant was forced recruitment for the Carrier Corps, in which over a million East Africans served as porters and about 100,000 died. African peasants suffered from forced requisition of livestock and crops, leading to starvation and disease for many. British control over the territory, renamed "Tanganyika," was confirmed by the League of Nations Mandate (1922). From 1925 indirect rule was introduced, under which existing or newly appointed chiefs became colonial civil servants with their own courts and treasuries. Law, tradition, and custom were interpreted from the perspective of the often unpopular Native Authorities, and so the interests of **youth** and women were circumscribed.

The combination of earlier conflict, disruption of the economy, famine, and ecological disasters led to a demographic crisis; the decline in population was not to be reversed until about 1930. Economic stagnation between the wars was partly a consequence of imperial priorities. For the British, until the early 1930s, Tanganyika was subservient to wider East African demands, which favored settler-dominated Kenya. By that time the economic system was characterized by racial stratification, with Europeans and Asians in control of the most productive enterprises. Africans were largely confined to small-scale peasant production and labor migration.

In the richer cash-crop areas such as Buhaya, Usukuma, and Kilimanjaro, peasant cooperatives became a seedbed for political protest. In addition ethnic associations were formed by successful peasants or urban migrants. Association members utilized their mission education and contributed to an emerging political awareness through opposition to the stacked colonial economy and job discrimination. In Tanga and Dar es Salaam the Tanganyika African Association (TAA) emerged in the late 1920s, and later formed the nucleus of the Tanganyika African National Union (TANU), which led the country to independence.

The **Second World War** stimulated the emergence of a genuine nationalist movement. Forced labor was reintroduced, the economy was squeezed, and Tanganyikan soldiers contributed to the British war effort. The new torchbearers of protest were transport workers, who played a crucial role in the export economy. Dock workers in Tanga and Dar es Salaam mounted strikes in 1937, 1939, 1943, and 1947 – the last of these a general strike that was supported as far away as Tabora.

Immediately after the war the colonial government planned for increased exports of agricultural products to meet the needs of the weakened British economy, in return for government reforms that included faster agricultural and rural development, representative local government, and "multi-racialism" in local and national politics. Alongside these initiatives was a new emphasis on education. In the west and south the expensive Groundnut Scheme was a complete failure, while in the north the Meru people strongly opposed further alienation of land to white settlers.

It was in this context that TANU, founded in 1954, emerged as the dominant political force. TANU went further than the TAA in its demands. Government harassment only had the effect of bringing more support from interest groups, such as the newly formed Tanganyikan Federation of Labor (1955), and from women. The most remarkable of the TANU elite was Julius Nyerere, who had studied at Makerere then Edinburgh universities. A teacher, he resigned to concentrate on full-time political organization and, with his colleagues, traveled the country mobilizing support. Within a short time TANU was massively popular, with branches forming in the most remote areas. The party's goal was self-government under majority rule, and they strongly opposed the government's policy of "multi-racialism." With the appointment of the moderate Governor Turnbull multi-racialism was dropped. In the 1960 election for an expanded Legislative Council TANU won all the seats except one, and Nyerere was appointed chief minister. Progress towards independence continued until Tanganyika was finally granted independence on 9 December 1961.

In 1964, a year of unusual turbulence, an army mutiny on the mainland was suppressed with the help of British troops, and there was revolution in neighboring Zanzibar. There a seemingly gerrymandered election had returned an Arab-dominated government. Revolutionary violence destroyed the Arab elite and shattered the plantation-based economy. Afterwards the Afro-Shirazi Party (ASP), representing the indigenous Shirazi and immigrants from the mainland, took power under Abeid Karume, but the political gap between the main parties seemed unbridgeable. In these circumstances Karume and Nyerere decided on formal unification between Tanganyika and Zanzibar, although Zanzibar retained its own regional government and received strong national representation.

Through the 1960s into the 1980s TANU initiated a remarkable experiment in socialist development, guided by Nyerere's ethical philosophy based on indigenous values of socialism, democracy, equality, and self-reliance. The Arusha Declaration (1967) included the controversial Leadership Code, which outlawed acquisitive behavior for TANU leaders. Nyerere chose political and social goals over productivity. This eventually resulted in unresolved tension between the goals of self-reliance, equality, and welfare for the masses, as against productivity, reliance on exports, and greater inequality.

The most problematic feature of Tanzanian socialism was *ujamaa*, in which dispersed rural homesteads were concentrated into village communities with the aim of providing better services, local input into decision-making, and communal production and income distribution. The result was falling agricultural production. Given the poor performance of exports, the country became increasingly reliant on foreign aid, while administration was overly bureaucratic. On the credit side there were advances in welfare, basic literacy, life expectancy and, for a time, industrial production, as well as the opening of the Tanzania–Zambia Railway in 1975, and constitutional reform with the merger of TANU and the ASP to form the Chama Cha Mapinduzi (CCM) in 1977.

Under Nyerere Tanzania played an important role in African affairs and in wider North–South relations, with Nyerere respected as an articulate advocate of a more just international order and as a leader in the **Non-Aligned Movement**. In **Southern Africa** Tanzania supported liberation movements struggling against colonial and apartheid rule. In the 1990s Tanzania became a haven for refugees from the conflicts of the Great Lakes region.

During the 1980s the economy almost collapsed due to a foreign-exchange crisis related to rising fuel costs and falling export prices, cuts in imports, and the failure of the villagization program. But economic crisis was also related to the high costs of the 1979 war with Uganda, which ousted the tyrant Idi Amin. A succession of **structural adjustment programs** inspired by the International Monetary Fund and progressive liberalization of the economy followed, including an increasing reliance on tourism, so that by the early 1990s Nyerere's socialist experiment was over. Nyerere retired in 1985. His pragmatic successor Ali Mwinyi Hassani managed the retreat from socialism, and himself was succeeded by Benjamin Mkapa. Nyerere died in 1999, revered as the father of the nation, a principled leader, and a great African statesman.

See also: African religions; colonial conquest and resistance; labor movements; socialisms and socialists; state: colonial

Further reading

Iliffe, J. (1979) *A Modern History of Tanganyika*, Cambridge: Cambridge University Press.

Yeager, R. (1989) *Tanzania: An African Experiment*, Boulder: Westview Press.

STEPHEN J. ROCKEL

telecommunications

Throughout the twentieth century telecommunications developed more slowly in Africa than in any other region of the world, for a number of reasons. For most of the century most of the continent was under colonial control, and the colonialists only developed internal communication in Africa as far as it satisfied their interests. Native African participation in the governing bodies of world telecommunication was also restricted by this colonial situation, and Africa (like most of the world) was not the scene of any of the major research and development in telecommunications. By the end of the twentieth century African governments, regional bodies, and international organizations – such as the World Bank and International Telecommunication Union (ITU) – were busy trying to make up for lost time in African telecommunications.

When the Afristar satellite was launched in 1998 it was the first time in the history of world telecommunications that Africa had been the focus of a significant "first." Although Africans did not develop the Afristar satellite technology, its goal was to obviate communication problems caused by high rates of illiteracy in Africa. It was the first satellite designed to broadcast directly to consumer radio receivers, and it was promoted by the company run by an entrepreneur of mixed Sudanese and Ethiopian parentage, Noah Samara. Prior to that event all major milestones in the history of world telecommunication were created by non-African companies, initially to solve the communication problems of North American and European societies. These achievements included the invention of the telegraph by Morse in 1844, Marconi's transmission of the first radio signal in 1901, the launch of the first communication satellite by the Soviet Union in 1965, and the creation of ARPANET (predecessor to the internet) by the United States government in 1969.

It was only in the latter half of the twentieth century that Africa began to play a significant role in the ITU, the body most influential in the regulation and development of world telecommunication. The ITU, established in 1865, has the distinction of being the world's oldest international organization. However, it was initially an exclusive European body. In 1914 nine African countries were members of the ITU (which was then called the International Telegraph Union): the Belgian Congo, **Egypt**, **Eritrea**, **Algeria**, **Madagascar**, **Morocco**, **Senegal**, the Union of **South Africa**, and **Tunisia**. However, all these countries were under European colonial control, and the two African states that were politically independent at the time – **Liberia** and **Ethiopia** – were not members. There was little change by the beginning of the **Second World War**, when **Egypt** was the only Africa member-state that had an independent vote in the body. **Decolonization** drastically changed Africa's presence in the decision-making forums of international telecommunication. Of the 132 countries that attended the 1979 ITU's World Administrative Radio Conference (WARC), a majority came from developing nation-states, 40 of which were independent African countries.

The diffusion of telecommunication technologies in Africa has reflected this neglect. Africa did not feature in a major way in the global system of telephony and other communication services that developed around three main spheres of interest. The first sphere was in the North Atlantic, linking the United States, Canada, the United Kingdom, the European continent, and the Middle East. The second sphere was the British **Commonwealth** system. The third sphere was that which linked the United States to its Pacific interests. Africa played a role in the Commonwealth system. The Commonwealth Telecommunications Conference drew up a plan that would link the major Commonwealth countries, and included the smaller countries by means of short overland and sea connections. The main arteries of the Commonwealth system were a link from Britain to Australia and New Zealand (via the United States and Fiji), and a link from the United Kingdom around the west coast of Africa to South Africa. The system also included shorter links from the UK to Bermuda and Tortola via the United States.

In the single year 1960, seventeen African countries gained political independence, but these new governments inherited little in terms of telecommunication infrastructure. A 1962 ITU report noted that the continent had no submarine telephone cables, no microwave radio-relay systems, and no satellite earth stations. That same year UNESCO reported that for every hundred people in Africa there was only one copy of a daily newspaper, two radio receivers, and 0.5 seats in permanent cinemas. This compared to UNESCO's minimum standard at the time of ten daily newspapers, five radio receivers, and two cinema seats for every hundred people. It was not until 1976 that even South Africa, one of the most prosperous African countries, got television service. Even when the first satellite earth stations in Africa were installed in 1969 – in Morocco and **Kenya** – they were not used for internal African communication. African countries were not even invited to participate in the establishment of the US-led International Telecommunications Satellite Organization (INTELSAT) in 1964. However, INTELSAT had an African membership before the end of the 1960s, consisting mainly of the North African countries (that is, **Libya**, Algeria, Morocco, **Sudan**, Egypt, and Tunisia) and the continent's larger states (that is, **Nigeria**, South Africa, and Ethiopia). By 1990 thirty-six African countries were members of INTELSAT. However, the pattern of telecommunication links mainly serving connections with the world outside of Africa continued. At the turn of the 1990s a majority of sub-Saharan countries still did not have direct telecommunication links with each other. That meant that calls between Sudan and Ethiopia, for example, had to be routed through London and Rome, and calls between **Gabon** and **Congo** had to go through Paris. As late as 1998 applicants for telephones in **Malawi**, **Sierra Leone**, **Swaziland**, and **Tanzania** faced the prospect of waiting ten years for installation.

Although Africa has been the continent with the worst telecommunications, its underdevelopment relative to Europe and North America was shared with other regions of what has been collectively labeled the "global south" – those poorer countries of the international system that share a heritage of colonialism, imperialism, and high levels of social inequality. In 1977, when the rate of telephones per 100 people was 70.7 in North America, the comparative rate was 5.2 in Asia, 4.5 in South America, and 0.4 in Africa. It was during the 1970s that demands were made at the **United Nations** (UN) for the creation of a New World Information and Communication Order (NWICO), a program that would rectify such inequality in telecommunication and other forms of communication, such as the mass media. The international organization that led the call for NWICO was the United Nations Educational, Scientific, and Cultural Organization (UNESCO), headed at the time by an African, Amadou-Mahtar M'Bow from Senegal. The NWICO debate led to the creation of the International Program for the Development of Communication (IPDC) at UNESCO, a fund for the financing of communication development projects as a means of correcting the imbalance in the distribution of the world's communication resources. Africa accounted for more than half of UNESCO's communication aid money by the early 1980s. The IPDC only assisted government projects in its formative years, but following the recommendation of a UNESCO-sponsored seminar of sixty African publishers and journalists in **Windhoek**, Namibia, it modified its rules in 1992 to include non-government projects too.

The controversial NWICO proposal also put pressure on the ITU to be more active in telecommunication development. It produced a report in 1985 on worldwide telecommunication development and solutions to the problem, and in subsequent years devoted special attention to the problems of Africa. By the 1990s the periodic Africa Telecom trade shows had become a popular means of focusing attention on the telecommunication concerns of the continent.

The desire to devote more attention to telecommunication development in Africa was given more urgency in the 1990s because of the revolution in the nature of the international economy and the model of economic development that had become so attractive under new global economic conditions. From the 1970s onwards services (such as banking, insurance, and data-processing) expanded to occupy more than 50 percent of the workforces of most of the world's leading economies, and the same proportion of those countries' gross national product. The foundation of this so-called "post-industrial" economy was telecommunications. By the 1980s this form of economic organization was fueled more by the convergence of telecommunication and digital-computing technologies. Telecommunication, previously thought to be a "natural monopoly" and run in most countries of the world by inefficient PTTs (Post, Telephone, and Telegraph companies), changed as an industry. The most influential economic wisdom in the leading economies said that the industry would be better run if it was privatized and deregulated, especially in light of the fact that the very meaning of telecommunications had changed to include the "telematics" industries created by the merger of telecommunications and computing. This move to privatization and expanded competition in telecommunications in the leading economies put pressure on small, dependent economies (especially in Africa) to follow suit. An ITU report, prepared in 2001 for the 2002 World Telecommunication Development Conference, noted that by the end of the 1990s three-quarters of the forty-two African countries south of the Sahara had privatized or were privatizing their PTTs. A majority of African governments were therefore viewing privatization as the best means of bringing their underdeveloped telecommunication infrastructures up to par with other regions of the world. This policy strategy was underwritten by the ITU on the grounds that if any region of the world did not have adequate telecommunications it was a danger to the "global economy," as the global economy is based on the premise that geography is now less of an impediment to trade because telecommunication provides the arteries of exchange.

African countries had to pursue a three-pronged strategy to meet this challenge: The first prong was the crafting of effective government policy; the second was the creation of regional telecommunication initiatives; and the third was taking advantage of Africa's tardiness in acquiring telecommunication technologies by employing the newest technological developments (such as cellphones and satellites). While many countries embarked on regulatory reform based on policies that had been in place for several years, in Africa the basics were still not in place in many countries as late as the 1980s. Thus the three basic tasks for government policy in Africa were:

1 drafting and enacting basic telecommunication legislation,
2 establishing regulatory bodies, and
3 capitalizing public telecommunication companies or appointing private firms to provide service.

However, the ITU has noted that seven main problems continued to plague the African telecommunication sector at the end of the twentieth century:

1 poor management,
2 lack of trained and experienced staff,
3 exorbitant tariffs and profiteering,
4 the lack of technology developed to solve African problems,
5 inadequate local financial resources,
6 poor educational standards, and
7 poverty.

The World Bank reported that, by the end of the century, 46 percent of sub-Saharan Africa's population lived on less than a dollar a day. That fact, coupled with high tariffs, meant that (in the estimation of the ITU) 80 percent of the population would not be able to afford telephone service, and 95 percent would not be able to afford access to the internet.

The main regional initiatives African countries undertook to improve telecommunication in the continent were in the realm of coordinating the regulation and provision of service. The Pan-African Telecommunications Union (PATU) was established as a body to coordinate regulation. Two continent-wide service initiatives were the creation of the Pan-African Telecommunications Network (PANAFTEL) and of the Regional African Satellite Communication System (RASCOM). PANAFTEL was created to provide direct telecommunication links between African countries, removing the need to route calls out of the continent. RASCOM aimed to create a regional satellite communication system.

Because Africa came late to telecommunication technology of all types it had the advantage of being able to leapfrog the old technologies. In many African countries the first telecommunication services used new wireless technologies, such as cellphones and satellite telephones. Consequently there was a rapid growth in cellphone usage in Africa during the early 1990s. The Pyramid Research company reported that in Africa and the Middle East subscribers to cellular phones increased 76 percent between 1990 and 1995. Many of the most efficient providers of this service were private companies. For example, in the case of **Cameroon** the ITU reported that a private company was able to connect 100,000 subscribers within one year (2000), while the government-run company had only been able to connect 5,000 subscribers during the period 1994 to 1999.

Africa did a lot to prepare for the so-called "global information infrastructure" (GII) that was expected to become the lifeline of the new post-industrial world economy. The GII was declared the foundation of a proposed "global information society" (GIS) during the ITU Development Conference in Buenos Aires in 1994. A year later the proposal was given support by the G7 Ministerial Conference on the Information Society in Brussels. The G7 also established the Global Information Infrastructure Commission (GIIC) to work with private industry on developing international communications policy. In the years that followed there was much international activity concerning plans for the development of this new telecommunications infrastructure. It is significant that early UN and ITU conferences on how such infrastructure could be created in developing nations all stressed the need for government planning. Such was the case at the 1996 Information Society and Development (ISAD) Conference in South Africa, as well as the Africa Regional Telecom Development Conference in **Abidjan** at which the African Green Paper on network and physical infrastructure development was adopted in the same year. The UN Economic Commission for Africa (ECA) also adopted its Africa Information Society Initiative, also in 1996. The UN Commission on Science and Technology for Development (UNSTD) created a panel in 1997 to study and report on the problem of providing information technologies to developing countries.

The need to be part of the GIS only added to the complicated challenges faced by Africans at the end of the twentieth century. African governments were being called on to develop telecommunication policies that would take their countries into the new century at a time when the ideas dominant in the international economy were dictating less government involvement. In addition to the glaring gap in availability of telecommunication services between cities and rural areas, there was also the gap to be bridged between relatively telecommunication-rich states (such as South Africa and **Gambia**) and those that were much less well endowed (such as **Congo** and **Somalia**). Also, at a time when the World Bank and ITU were advocating private investment as the preferred means to develop telecommunications infrastructure, Africa was still suffering from being relatively unattractive to that kind of funding. In 1998 the publication *African Business* reported that of the US$95 billion raised for telecommunication privatization over the previous four-year period, only US$1.7 billion was raised in Africa; most of that amount was in South Africa.

The essence of the telecommunications challenge facing Africa was summed up in the Yaounde Declaration issued by African ministers responsible for telecommunication and information technologies in May 2001. These ministers declared:

- that we undertake to devote more actions to the timely addressing of issues relating to telecommunications and to information and communication technologies, these being issues which we consider to be of prime concern;
- that bridging the digital divide must of necessity entail development of the telecommunication and sound and television broadcasting infrastructure, and that development partners must consider this parameter, in particular with respect to rural areas;
- that it is essential that African countries, given the importance of telecommunications and information technologies in political, economic, social and cultural development, adopt innovative strategies and policies designed to stimulate development, particularly reform of the telecommunication and information technology sector;
- that each African country should henceforth define a common, or at least coordinated, national policy and strategy for the development of telecommunications and information technologies that takes account of multimedia convergence (telecommunications, information technologies and broadcasting).

See also: press; radio and television

Further reading

Mansell, R. and When, U. (eds.) (1998) *Knowledge Societies: Information Technology for Sustainable Development*, New York: Oxford University Press.

Noam, E.M. (ed.) (1999) *Telecommunications in Africa*, New York: Oxford University Press.

Riverson, L.K. (1993) *Telecommunications Development: The Case of Africa*, Lanham: University Press of America.

Udofia, C.I. (1981) *Africa and the International Telecommunication Union*, Ph.D. thesis, Wayne State University.

MARK D. ALLEYNE

television *see* radio and television

theater

Africa's cultural diversity has created a theater that is diverse and distinctive. The various social organizations, languages, religions, and mythologies, and historical, political, and social experiences that differ from country to country, contribute to a multiplicity of narrative pools from which theater can draw. Yet the bases of this diversity are often the bases also of unifying elements. For instance, many African societies evolved similar secular performance forms to meet their needs for self-apprehension and entertainment. Also the exposure of African dramatists and theater artists to European models of theater has often been a unifying force, notably through the language and modes of presentation of a substantial literary theater. Furthermore critical activities, which mediate the reception of the theater, encourage the transcultural communication of aesthetic values. African theater, particularly popular theater, is often mobile, making it possible for different countries – especially those that are in close geographic and linguistic proximity – to share experiences. An inquiry into specific theatrical expressions in tandem with a comparative approach to historical developments, forms, and traditions across different cultures may yield the most satisfying study of African theater.

Theater is part of our vocabulary

Secular performance forms in Africa date to ancient times and include pantomimes, dance-drama, mask theater, shadow theater (a form of dramatic entertainment, performed by casting shadows on a curtain, that is found in **Egypt** from the first century AD), and a wide array of oral dramatic forms that range from court theater (heroic recitations and praise-poems for special occasions) to the more everyday market comedy of itinerant troupes. In various combinations these performance forms use role-play, dialogue, mime, movement, dance, song, puppetry, costumes, scenic spectacle, and so on. With different degrees of sophistication, the performances provide the kinds of entertainment values associated with theater. The environments in which these traditional performance modes have thrived were receptive to European forms of theater, the appropriation of which began in the nineteenth century.

Europe's contact with Africa in the nineteenth century was to have a pronounced cultural impact. Theater for Europeans had become associated with performances motivated primarily by their value as entertainment: they were based on substantive – often scripted – texts that were rehearsed; participants were separated into performers and spectators; and the performance space was clearly delineated, typically involving the use of an enclosed building. This normative and somewhat anachronistic definition of theater, temporally encoded by the specific tastes of nineteenth-century Europe, has been pervasive. But if this hegemonic and essentialist definition of theater came to Africa through contact with Europe, on the whole Africans turned this sense of theater to their benefit, using it to stimulate further diversification of their own forms of theatrical expression, (re)generating a cultural entity through which they were able to reflect their experiences and perform cultural exchange with the rest of the world.

Africans experienced European theater through different European adventurers, missionaries, traders, and imperialists. The ensuing European influence was not uniform over Africa. In **Southern Africa** European theater – particularly British, Dutch, French, and German – became a staple import from the 1790s, reflecting the ethnic identities of the European settlers. The political and economic ascendancy of Dutch and British settlers in **South Africa** and **Zimbabwe** (then Rhodesia) entrenched cultural institutions that promoted Afrikaner and/or British theatrical traditions in these countries. However, this hegemony was undermined right from the start through the persistence of indigenous forms of entertainment and the appropriation by Africans of imported theatrical styles as a site of resistance to white domination. For example, the tradition of black township music-theater in South Africa syncretized performance modes like the isiZulu's *ingoma* (song), the isiXhosa's *ntsomi* (a dramatic mode of storytelling) or the Sesotho's *lithoko* (praises) with Western choral and vaudeville forms. Loren Kruger (1999) has traced this tradition through Griffiths Motsieloa's performances in the 1930s; Todd Matshikiza's composition for the "jazz opera" *King Kong*, which premiered in Sophiatown in 1959; Gibson Kente's musicals from the 1960 into the 1980s; Mbongeni Ngema's works from the 1980s, including *Asinamali* and *Sarafina!*; and Walter Chakela's *Bloke*, which was produced in 1994.

In **North Africa** the new theater was partly introduced by Europeans, following Napoleon's invasion of **Egypt** in 1798. The invaders were accompanied by all the paraphernalia of modernity, including printing presses, scientists, and theater performers. Far more pronounced than the influence of the European conquerors was the role of the Egyptians themselves, however, including the Khedives Said and Ismail. These rulers pursued modernization in the second half of the nineteenth century through the expansion of physical infrastructure in Egypt and the active patronage of French and Italian touring theater troupes. Indeed Ismail's brother financed the education in Italy of Ya'qub Sannu (1839–1912), the founder of modern Egyptian theater. Maghreb Africa – comprising **Morocco**, **Algeria**, and **Tunisia** – experienced French cultural influence from the start of French occupation of **Algiers** in 1830.

In **West Africa** French infiltration, rather than massive settlement, began in **Senegal** in the 1850s. It spread throughout the region (with the exception of **Liberia**) over the next forty years, reaching those areas that were to become **Gambia**, **Ghana**, and **Nigeria**, as well as parts of **Cameroon**. Contact with European theater in **French West Africa** was less through the large-scale importation of commercial European performing troupes, although some did visit, than was the case in southern and northern Africa. More influential were the educational institutions and cultural centers. A famous example is the Ecole William Ponty – founded in 1903 in Senegal – where the educators exposed students to French theatrical traditions, while sowing the seeds for a francophone theater with a strong indigenous subject matter and form through the ethnographically oriented projects (called *devoirs de vacances*) that were required from students. These holiday projects concluded with student dramatizations of their findings from their own societies, including oral histories, legends, sayings, and customs. Some of these students later became pioneers of theater in **francophone Africa**. In **Central Africa** the French and Belgians made less effort to encourage indigenous cultural enrichment. A pseudo-assimilationist attitude prevailed in Portuguese-occupied areas. Whereas educators like those in William Ponty were interested in indigenous cultural expressions – albeit to get to know, and thereby assimilate, native West Africans – the Portuguese colonialists generally devalued traditional religious and artistic forms, substituting their own mission school-inspired dramatizations of didactic European and African folktales, and encouraging the formation of amateur production groups to stage modern European theater.

In anglophone West and **East Africa**, educational and missionary institutions – interacting with visiting European and, sometimes, American theater troupes, especially in the coastal towns – were a major source of the transmission of European theater forms in the early decades of the twentieth century. But the rapid emergence in places like Ghana and Nigeria of an itinerant, fully fledged indigenous-language theater on the heels of imports in the 1920s offered a counter (re)creative influence, which led to an explosion of distinctive popular and literary theaters in West Africa by the middle of the twentieth century.

Individual figures from European theater who had the widest influence in Africa at the beginning of the twentieth century were Shakespeare and Molière, followed by Brecht, Racine, John Gay, Shaw, and Sheridan. Straight performances and translations or adaptations of works by these and other Europeans were common. For instance, Egyptian Muhammad Jalal (1829–98) translated and adapted plays by Molière, Racine, and Corneille into Arabic, while Yaq'ub Sannu widely translated Molière's plays, and even embraced the French dramatist's name as a sobriquet. Perhaps the most famous translations of Shakespeare's plays were those by Julius Nyerere, the first president of **Tanzania**, who rendered *Julius Caesar* and *The Merchant of Venice* into Swahili.

By the middle of the twentieth century the influence of European authors on the African stage had waned, supplanted or rivaled by playwrights such as Tawfiq al-Hakim (1899–1987) in Egypt, Khalid Abdul Rahman Abdul Rous (1908–85) in

Sudan, Bernard Dadié (1916–) in **Côte d'Ivoire**, Kateb Yacine (1929–) in Algeria, Athol Fugard (1932–) in South Africa, and Wole Soyinka (1934–) in Nigeria – to name but a few. African troupes were now exporting their theater within Africa and outside the continent, some of the most famous troupes being those of George Abyad (1880–1952) and Fatimah Rushdie (1909–96) in Egypt, Hubert Ogunde (1916–90) in Nigeria, and Mbongeni Ngema (1955–) in South Africa. Some of the earlier European theater continued to be produced, particularly in South Africa, Egypt, and Kenya, which had a high investment in commercial theater houses. In developing a modern African theater, writers, directors, and other theater practitioners increasingly took the route of creating original work using *all* the resources at their disposal. The creation could be through individual action or the collective efforts of a group, as in the workshop tradition exemplified by the Market Theater Company founded by Barney Simon and Mannie Manim in South Africa in 1976.

Major trends in spoken theater

The three trends in African spoken theater – literary, popular, and theater for development – while suggesting distinctive forms are not watertight compartments, but overlap in some respects. For instance, the West African popular theater that was prominent from the mid-1930s to the early 1980s and is associated in Nigeria with the private theater companies, such as those led by Hubert Ogunde, Oyin Adejobi, Kola Ogunmola, and Duro Ladipo, was professional and commercially very successful, bearing in these two regards some kinship with South African entrepreneurial theater, such as that of Pieter Toerien. Also some theater originating from university centers – which was scripted and, in many other regards, literary – was often taken on the road, seeking to appeal to a mass audience through its subject-matter, chosen linguistic register, and manner of transmission, and arguably succeeding in doing so. Examples include the University of Zambia's Chikwakwa Theater, founded in 1970s, which toured towns and rural areas with translations of plays originally written in English, stimulating a generation of plays in local languages. In Kenya there was the growth of open-air theater in the mid-1970s in the rural community of Kamiriithu under the inspiration of writer Ngũgi wa Thiong'o (1938–), who previously had been identified with literary theater written in English. The Kamiriithu community's theater productions were attended by students, civil servants, and industrial and agricultural workers from the community and surrounding areas. The community's most famous and successful production, the full-length play *Ngahiika Ndenda*, was scripted in Gikuyu by Ngũgi and Ngũgi wa Mirii, drawing on the history of the people's struggle for land as an analogy to the contemporary social situation in which workers were contending with the multinational factories to which they were constrained to sell their labor. The government, made highly uncomfortable by the play and fearful that it might raise public consciousness and provoke rebellion, banned it.

Popular theater tends to be defined as theater with mass-audience appeal through its presentational form and physical/financial accessibility. The salient aspects of oral popular theater include improvisation, particularly in dialogue, which is nonetheless disciplined by the storyline, structure and pace – all suggested by a virtual script, which the directors and performers have in their heads. The dialogue and variations on it become defined over the course of rehearsals, with key ideas and phrases that are central to each segment of the play retained, while a stock of substitutable materials is kept in mental reserve, making possible a fluid performance that can adjust to variations in audience reaction. The patronage of a mass audience is underscored by the choice of venue, chosen or constructed in accordance with the audiences' lifestyles; alternatively the theater can be taken to the people as an itinerant form. Being so close to the ground, the themes of popular theater reflect the daily struggles of people within a particular social ethos: domestic comedies, human adventures, mythical stories, legends, histories, and all the vicissitudes of human existence – the tragedies, trials, and so on. Oral popular theater forms are so well defined as text-in-performance that transcriptions of performances, when published, are very coherent – they seem to only need stage directions to make them look like literary theater.

Mediated by linguistic accessibility, popular theater was the mode in which theater in indigenous African languages and different creole and pidgin languages, as well as colloquial Arabic, was very prominent. But popular theater in a place like South Africa was manifested also in English and Afrikaans, and in hybridized forms of these languages that featured large doses of indigenous and newly fabricated expressions, especially as the resistance movement against apartheid gained momentum and used the medium of theater to press for political and social change. In Ghana, where the concert party – a form of slapstick musical comedy – emerged in the 1920s, the impetus for the swift establishment of the form as popular theater was a combination of linguistic and social accessibility. Karin Barber, John Collins, and Alain Ricard point to a "process of democratization with diffusion" (Barber, Collins and Ricard 1997: 14), through which the concert party went from English-language performance by a Fanti known as Teacher Yalley, who pioneered the form and used high admission fees to target the elite, to shows featuring more and more actors and intentionally accommodating wider audiences through lower admission fees and an admixture of English, Fanti, and pidgin in the dialogue. Biodun Jeyifo (1985) and Barber suggest that the Yoruba popular traveling theater of Nigeria was a popular form partly by virtue of its affordability and mobility – the latter referring to the plays' circulation not only in the Yoruba-speaking states in Nigeria but extending to theYoruba-speaking communities that have settled in other parts of Nigeria and in neighboring countries. The classes of people who generated the plays also contributed to the plays' popularity. The performer-creators usually originated from the artisanal classes, who constituted a big intermediate population between the literate and illiterate classes, and consequently were able to appeal to a wide cross-section of audiences. Through the subject matter and a display of linguistic virtuosity by the generators and performers of the plays, the oral popular form sought to capture the spirit of the culture.

Another example of a popular theater is Hausa theater. The plays, lacking playwrights or scripts, had their own conventions of structure, character, and theme. This form of theater reached mass audiences in the country from its very beginnings, with performing troupes springing up everywhere to perform live or on radio and television. A description by Beik (1987) of a scene from a play she saw explains the fascination this theatrical form exerted. The scene featured rows of Islamic worshippers at their prayers, with **youths** playing the roles in oversized robes borrowed from their fathers. Then a group of dancing girls came on stage, led by a drummer. From their ritual bending and bowing and touching their foreheads to the ground, the first row of worshippers were soon moving to the sound of the music. The second row made up of older men resisted for a while, but gradually succumbed to the music with the motions of their prayer, then the next row did the same, and finally the leader of the prayer succumbed. All now seduced, they danced off the stage without having uttered a word in dialogue, leaving the audience in uproarious laughter. What gave this piece of theater such dynamism – a dynamism that, in Beik's words, "held the fine edge between parody and blasphemy" (Beik 1987: 2)? The play capitalized on the tension between the familiar and the surprising, thriving on its audience's appreciation of the humor and willingness to play along.

Popular theater underwent transformations of the aesthetic parameters within which it developed. At the beginning the concert parties of Ghana and **Togo**, and the Yoruba popular theater of Nigeria, presented the dialogue through songs. Gradually spoken dialogue replaced sung dialogue, the general rationale being that the shift prevented the performances from dragging on too long. Some Yoruba performance troupes saw this shift as one that accorded with modernization. In some popular theater, as in East Africa, there were recurring character types, reminiscent of the oral narrative tradition. However, in the modern Yoruba oral theater, the performers often kept the names of certain characters that they performed from one play to another, a practice that helped them sustain an image they wished to project in their acting, and enhanced their public recognition.

Scripted plays existed in the indigenous and creole languages, in classic and colloquial forms of **Arabic**, and in the former colonial European languages. Where there is the situation of diglossia in North Africa the classical form of Arabic was taken as the language of "high" culture, and the colloquial form as that of "low" culture, resulting in a conflict over the language in which a play could be performed and published. In **Mauritius**, where English was the official language but French widely spoken, the move to democratize the theater that is associated with the plays of Dev Virahsawmy, Azize Asgarally, and Henri Favory from the early 1970s led to the rise of Creole as the language of dramatic communication. Several African playwrights, desirous of communicating with audiences beyond their immediate geographical location or constrained by the limited number of speakers of their own language due to colonial policies, used former colonial languages – bending these languages to their own purpose. The most internationally renowned African playwrights, such as Soyinka, Fugard, and Dadié, used English or French. Within this group of playwrights were also bilingual writers, such as Ngũgi wa Thiong'o, who started writing in English in the 1960s and switched to Gikuyu in the late 1970s, but resumed writing in English in the 1990s, and the South African Reza de Wet, who produced and published the first versions of her plays in Afrikaans, but promptly followed them with English self-translations. The Algerian Kateb Yacine began his writing career in French, and later turned to colloquial Arabic – the language he found best suited his revolutionary vision of drama. But condescending attitudes towards the use of colloquial Arabic rather than the classical form as a language of cultural representation prevented Kateb's Arabic plays, though often performed, from being as widely published as his works in French.

In Zimbabwe and South Africa colonial policies sought to keep Africans and Europeans apart, and attempted to make Africans write in their native languages in order to promote a linguistically narrow ethnic nationalism among the black population, thereby effectively undermining unified resistance to white domination. In South Africa the apartheid government set up regional Performing Arts Councils in the early 1960s to promote the development of a national theater, but the resources of the PACs were reserved for whites only, who focused on Eurocentric theater forms. In Zimbabwe, regardless of the motivation behind the colonial linguistic policy, there emerged a strong body of Shona and Ndebele literature and dramatic writing, which generated ample material to support scholarly activity. In contrast language policies in South Africa, which was more ethnically diversified, met a more ambivalent reaction, with a number African playwrights, wary of being coopted into sustaining apartheid policy, deliberately choosing to write or produce theater in English.

By the third quarter of the century a strong corpus of literary theater in both the indigenous and the former colonial languages had developed across the whole continent. But the lack of translations from one indigenous language to another restricted the circulation of these works. For example, Ethiopia's foremost playwright – in terms of the range, breadth, and depth of his creations – Tsegaye Gabre-Medhin, published in Amharic. Only a fraction of his work has been translated into English, however, so his contribution to theater has not been fully appreciated internationally. The relative critical ignorance of creole and mestizo theaters, notably from Mauritius and **lusophone Africa**, has also curtailed knowledge of these dimensions of African theater.

The themes of African literary theater targeted at trans-local audiences generally closely reflected social and political developments on the continent. Broad designations of forms of creative productivity include "pre-/post-national," "post-independence," "protest," "disillusionment," "anti-apartheid," "post-apartheid," and "global era." These designations are not consistent: they mix criteria. Besides, they suggest a linear and deterministic teleology. Finally, they do not give any indication of stylistic achievement. Literary theater in Africa is really more diversified than this. Examples of remarkable theatrical creations include Soyinka's *A Dance of the Forests* (1963), *The Road* (1965), and *Death and the King's Horseman* (1975); Guillaume Mbia-Oyono's *Three Suitors, One Husband* (an English translation of *Trois prétendants à un mari*, 1964); Fugard's *The Blood Knot* (1961), and (with Winston Ntshona and John Kane) *The Island* (1974); Ama Ata Aidoo's *Anowa* (1970); and Reza de Wet's *Crossing* (1994). These plays capture significant moments and resonant existential situations through original tropes and symbols; they challenge reified ideologies – whether based on national, gender, or other templates of social reference; they have multiple significations; and they provide, through a dextrous use of theatrical devices, riveting entertainment.

Theater for development was stimulated by a search for equitable development in rural and urban Africa beginning in the early 1970s. It drew inspiration also from the radical pedagogies of the South American social theorists and activists Paulo Freire and Augusto Boal, and the non-illusionist theater of the German-American dramatist Bertolt Brecht. Some scholars used the term "popular theater" to describe this "people's theater," due to its democratizing impulses and its community-orientation, highlighting the porosity of form. Using the term "theater for development," however, may help distinguish this theater from the artisanally produced, widely circulated, and commercial theatrical forms. Theater for development strove to serve as a catalyst for self-generated awareness, exploring solutions to problems, and stimulating actions for change. It was facilitated by professionals, including development officers, educational institutions or playwrights motivated by a vision of theater as a mode of self-articulation and self-empowerment. Furthermore dramatizations in theater for development tended to be short, often not longer than one-act plays. From the 1980s theater for development increasingly became a part of the training programs of many university drama departments. Practitioners and theorists included Oga S. Abah, Chuck Mike and the Performance Studio Workshop based in Nigeria, Hansel Ndumbe Eyoh of Cameroon, Penina Mlama of Tanzania, and Zakes Mda of South Africa.

At the end of the twentieth century theater was continuing to respond to African societies' complex needs for self-representation and recreation. It achieved these ends through a creative synthesis of indigenous resources and foreign influences – transforming the latter to reflect the preferences, purposes, and aspirations of the African milieu. While one form out of the three overlapping forms – popular theater, literary theater, and theater for development – might be in decline in one region, a parallel form would be on the rise in another region at the same time. For instance, from the 1980s the West African popular traveling theater virtually gave way to other syncretic entertainment forms, notably video theater. In contrast, in **Mozambique** interest in popular theater was on the rise from the 1980s, as foreign films (which had been dominant in the entertainment industry in the country) became more expensive. Mozambicans packed the theater houses in **Maputo** and Sofala to see the comedies of the Mutumbela Gogo and Madze Matchetche theater troupes, or the song-and-dance theater of Companhia Nacional de Canto e Dança, which put on performances to raise social awareness but, through heightened choreography and artistry, prevented their didacticism from becoming off-putting. More translations and comparative studies will make African literary theater more accessible transculturally and minimize the isolation of lusophone and Arabic theaters from the rest of the continent. A critical interface between African theater produced in indigenous languages and that produced in European languages also has the potential to enrich the creation and enjoyment of theater across the continent.

References and further reading

Banham, M., Gibbs, J. and Osofisan, F. (eds.) (1999) *African Theatre in Development*, Oxford: James Currey and Bloomington and Indianapolis: Indiana University Press.

Barber, K., Collins, J. and Ricard, A. (1997) *West African Popular Theatre*, Oxford: James Currey and Bloomington and Indianapolis: Indiana University Press.

Beik, J. (1987) *Hausa Theatre: A Contemporary Art*, New York and London: Garland Publishing.

Conteh-Morgan, J. (1994) *Theatre and Drama in Francophone Africa*, Cambridge: Cambridge University Press.

Eyoh, H.N. (1999) "Popular Theatre Re-visited. With an Additional Bibliography on Popular

Theatre and Theatre for Development," in A. Fuchs (ed.), *New Theatre in Francophone and Anglophone Africa*, Amsterdam and Atlanta: Rodopi.

Jeyifo, B. (1985) *The Truthful Lies: Essays in a Sociology of African Drama*, London and Port of Spain: New Beacon Books.

al-Khozai, M. (1984) *The Development of Early Arabic Drama (1847–1900)*, London and New York: Longman.

Kruger, L. (1999) *The Drama of South Africa: Plays, Pageants and Publics Since 1910*, London and New York: Routledge.

MODUPE OLAOGUN

Third World

The term "Third World" was popularly used to refer to developing or underdeveloped countries in Africa, Asia, and Latin America from the 1960s until the 1980s. From the 1990s these countries were increasingly described as part of the global "South," while the developed or industrialized countries were considered as part of the "North." The notion of the Third World was both intellectual and ideological in its origins and orientations. It was intellectual in that it sought to provide frameworks of comparative economic and political analysis for a group of countries characterized (although not exclusively) by histories of colonization, relatively low levels of industrialization, weaknesses in **international trade**, and political vulnerabilities to external domination and internal authoritarianism. It was an ideological notion in so far as these countries sought, with varying degrees of collective determination, to speak with one voice in global economic, political, and security matters. Both agendas were fraught with paradigmatic and practical difficulties that increasingly and ultimately made the concept of the Third World of dubious analytical and political value, although many of the ideas, images, and struggles it spawned became part of conventional wisdom in the social sciences and international relations.

Ideas of the Third World

The term "Third World" was apparently coined in the 1950s by the French demographer and economic historian Alfred Sauvy, in reference to countries that represented a "Third Force" between the Western and Eastern blocs. The idea of the "Third World" as a constellation of "non-aligned" countries was given added force by those leaders of the newly independent countries in Asia and Africa, especially Nehru of India, Sukarno of Indonesia, Nkrumah of **Ghana**, and Nasser of **Egypt**, who sought to create the **Non-Aligned Movement** (NAM) that would stand above, and perhaps diffuse, the bitter ideological conflicts of the two superpower blocs. Thus for many political and intellectual leaders in the newly designated Third World countries, the term "Third World" was a badge of honor, offering a radical critique of the global order and the structure of international relations, rather than what it was to become later: a pejorative description of poverty and helplessness.

The idea of the Third World implied the existence of a first and second world. To some, the "First World" referred to the developed capitalist countries, while the "Second World" referred to the developed socialist countries. In another definition, associated with Chinese leader Mao Zedong's "Three Worlds Theory," the "First World" comprised the two superpowers – the United States and the Soviet Union, both of which he saw as imperialistic – while the "Second World" consisted of the European countries, Japan, and Canada. In either definition most countries of Asia, and all of Africa and Latin America, belonged to the Third World.

In its first progressive incarnation, the term "Third World" referred to, and articulated, six key objectives:

1 non-alignment in the military and diplomatic spheres;
2 solidarity – the notion that Third World countries had common interests arising out of their contemporary economic and political conditions, which could only be altered if they acted in unison;

3 anti-imperialism – the widespread conviction that underdevelopment and powerlessness were products of European imperialism, colonialism, and neo-colonialism, which had to be eradicated if the Third World countries were to develop and make progress;
4 regionalism – belief in the emancipatory and empowering potential of regional integration through pan-nationalist movements, such as Pan-Arabism and **Pan-Africanism**, which could overcome the effects of colonial balkanization;
5 commitment to the creation of a new international order, ranging from the campaigns in the 1970s for a New International Economic Order (NIEO) and New World Information and Communication Order (NWICO), to the proposals for a World Development Fund and environmentally sustainable development in the 1980s, or for debt relief and against racism in the late 1990s;
6 drawing attention to the question of poverty.

This last objective was perhaps the most important. Perceptions about the nature, causes, and solutions to poverty in Third World countries shifted, but there was no denying that poverty was a serious problem – and was even getting worse in some countries and regions. By the end of the 1980s the majority of the world's poor still lived in Asia – 800 million of them (520 million in South Asia and 280 million in East Asia), as compared to 180 million in Africa. The growing conflation of poverty, or more broadly underdevelopment, with the Third World facilitated the inclusion of Latin America increasingly into the Third World's orbit, not only because the region had millions of poor people, but also because it was there that theories of underdevelopment and dependency, which were to be so influential in conceptions of the Third World, were first developed.

But the notion of and aspirations toward Third World ideological solidarity and developmental homogeneity were often undermined by diversity, disparities, differences, and discord that in reality characterized Third World countries. There was a diversity of cultures and histories, for example, between the Latin American settler and mestizo societies that gained their independence in the nineteenth century, and the predominantly indigenous societies of Africa that gained their independence in the second half of the twentieth century. Disparities of wealth, economic systems, resources, and levels of development, which became more glaring with the rise of the oil-rich countries in the 1970s and the newly industrialized countries (NICs) of East Asia in the 1980s, were equally apparent. These disparities were not confined to widening gaps *between* countries, but also *within* countries: The national bourgeoisie in many Third World countries were often separated from their own working and peasant classes as much as they had affinities with the bourgeois classes of the North. Also common were differences of ideologies and polities. Some espoused socialism or capitalism, such as Cuba and **Côte d'Ivoire**, respectively, with democratic or authoritarian one-party or military regimes, as was the case with India, China, and Nigeria, respectively. And discord within the Third World was rampant, **regional integration** was often weak – nowhere did it approach the level of the European Economic Community (later the European Union) – and sometimes conflict degenerated into open warfare. Between 1945 and 1992 there were 149 major wars in the world, most of them fought in and between Third World countries, although many were proxy wars for the superpowers. In 1994 alone there were 164 armed conflicts, many of them ethnic conflicts in Third World countries.

Theories of Third World development

Notwithstanding these realities, the concept of the Third World remained quite popular until the 1990s. Its power was primarily derived from the challenges that the concept itself and the problems of Third World development generally posed to theories of modernization and the global order. Before the **Second World War** the question of the wealth and poverty of nations was often discussed in the language of race and environment, that Africans and Asians were poor because of climatic and racial reasons. Such explanations were discredited after a war fought against fascist racism. The search was on for more "rational" explanations, as poverty became increasingly problematized as a peculiar Third World condition, a process that was facilitated by the rise of development discourses among Third World nationalists themselves seeking justifications for their struggles for independence, and superpower ideologues trying to win support for their rival socioeconomic systems. Two broad paradigms emerged to explain and eradicate Third World underdevelopment: modernization theory and dependency theory.

Modernization theory initially reveled in postwar optimism, especially among US social scientists, that it was possible for the poor countries to develop along the path already charted by the Western countries. Modernization was seen as a process of social transformation characterized by evolutionary progress from tradition to modernity, social differentiation, structural functionalism, and the secularization and rationalization of social life and action. It required changes in cultural patterns, the adoption of what the American sociologist Talcott Parsons (1951) called the norms of "universalism," "achievement," "neutrality," and "specificity" in place of the "particularism," "ascription," "affectivity," and diffuseness characteristic of traditional societies. W.W. Rostow (1971) outlined the five stages involved in the modernization process (from traditional society to transitional society, through the "take-off" stage to the "drive to maturity," and finally to the age of high mass-consumption), while David McClelland (1961) stressed psychological preconditions, that the modern personality has a high need for achievement, autonomy, order, and understanding of natural and social systems.

Out of this body of ideas, as well as neoclassical economics, emerged development economics. Preoccupied with the marginalist analysis of market processes and the problems of resource allocation, and equipped with deductive abstract models and universal laws independent of time and place, as well as faith in perfect competition and perfect rationality, neoclassical economics acquired an aura of scientific objectivity and ideological neutrality. In reality, of course, its concepts were abstractions from, and rationalizations (if not legitimations) of the capitalist system. According to this paradigm Third World poverty was attributable to internal conditions arising out of undeveloped factors of production: land was poor because of climatic factors, the soil quality of the tropics, and backward agricultural practices; labor was also poor because it was largely uneducated and had low productivity; and capital was equally poor because of low investment. Compounding these problems was the unfavorable policy environment: the prevalence of state authoritarianism, corruption, and excessive intervention; a proclivity for protectionism in which both tariffs and taxes were too high; and failure to exploit comparative advantage by embarking on wasteful industrialization projects.

In order to develop, therefore, Third World countries needed to adopt market-favorable policies and keep their doors open to free trade; to Western investment, technology, models, and advice; and to patiently follow the preordained stages of modernization. Thus development was conceived as an economic problem amenable to value-free technical and technological solutions. This enabled the professionalization and institutionalization of development practice, and the repudiation of the broader historical, international, social, cultural, and political contexts and consequences of economic transformation. The era of development experts was born. Critics charged that neoclassical development theory ignored history, both of the developed and developing countries, that it absolved colonialism and contemporary imperialism, and mystified the operations of capitalism. Specifically, modernization theory was attacked for its simplified use of the term "tradition" (conceived as an obstacle to progress without understanding that what passed for tradition had often in fact been invented during colonialism), and for failing to clarify who benefited from "progress." Modernization theory was also attacked for its belief in a unilinear path to modernity, for its dichotomous models (traditional/modern societies, subsistence/market economies, formal/informal sectors), for its tautological arguments (listing a catalogue of internal obstacles to development often amounted to saying the poor were poor because they were poor), and for its simplistic psychologisms.

Dependency theory emerged out of the challenges to modernization theory. Its roots can be traced to three traditions:

1 Marxist theories of imperialism and colonialism,
2 African theories of neo-colonialism, and
3 Latin American theories of dependency.

The earlier Marxists, including Marx himself, believed that capitalism had a "double mission" – that it was both exploitative and progressive, destroying archaic modes of production and introducing capitalism, which was a more advanced mode. Subsequently Marxists, especially from Lenin onwards, placed more emphasis on the destructive and exploitative aspects of imperialism. In the hands of dependency writers, imperialism became a "one-armed bandit" (to use Walter Rodney's colorful phrase – Rodney 1972). In Lenin's highly influential monograph, *Imperialism. The Highest Stage of Capitalism* (1978 [1916]), in which he tried to systematize the Marxist theory of imperialism, imperialism marked an actual stage in the evolution of capitalism – a stage that would eventually give way to socialism. It had five features: the rise of monopolies, the emergence of finance capital, the export of capital, the division of the world among capitalist associations, and colonialism.

Since colonialism was only one feature of imperialism, it followed that **decolonization** did not imply the end of imperialism. The notion that the newly independent countries of Africa and Asia were subject to "neo-colonialism" was popularized by Kwame Nkrumah in his *Neo-Colonialism: The Last Stage of Imperialism* (1963), in which he argued that the achievement of political independence meant little without economic independence, for the two could not be separated. Neo-colonialism entailed continued domination by the major powers. It was perpetrated through the terms of trade, need for aid, repatriation of profits, technological dependency, and multinational corporations and multilateral financial institutions. Numerous studies sought to demonstrate that terms of trade for exports from "Third World" countries, made up mostly of primary products, either fluctuated violently or continued to fall; that instead of foreign investment, or so-called "aid," there was a net transfer of capital from the developing to the developed countries – reaching US$250 billion by 1985 – through repatriation of profits, and increasingly through debt repayments as well. Neo-colonialism operated through alliances between comprador Third World bourgeoisies and Western interests.

Many of these ideas echoed dependency theory, which emerged in Latin America, led by economists at the United Nations Economic Commission for Latin America, formed in 1948. These economists critiqued international trade, and supported import substitution as a means of reducing export dependency and dislocation. The apparent failure of the import substitution strategy by the 1960s, as well as the spread of authoritarian regimes, led to more a more thoroughgoing critique, which was joined and influenced by Latin American revolutionaries and Marxists in the North. The region's continued underdevelopment, despite a century of independence, was blamed on an unequal international trading system, and a conjunction of interest between the Latin American bourgeoisie and state and the Western states and capital, which blocked autonomous capitalist development. Dependency theory postulated that underdevelopment was a process resulting from incorporation into the world system, so that development and underdevelopment were two sides of the same coin, reproducing each other – that is, the developed countries were developed precisely because Third World countries were underdeveloped. Thus underdevelopment was characterized by:

1 a hierarchy of states and power relations between centers and peripheries;
2 repatriation or expropriation of surplus from the Third World through the mechanisms of unequal exchange or unequal rewarding of factors, especially the labor factor (that is, wages);
3 economic disarticulation marked by uneven productivities and poor linkages between sectors, and by the dominance of foreign capital and the fragmentation of indigenous capital; and
4 Third World ruling classes operating as junior partners – clientele classes – of the international capitalist system, which blocked the emergence of genuine national bourgeoisies.

Dependency theory became highly influential in the 1960s and 1970s, and provided the intellectual ammunition for those seeking non-capitalist paths of development at home and the restructuring of the international economic and political order. But it provoked determined intellectual and political assaults. Intellectually, attacks came from both die-hard neoclassical liberals and Marxists. The theory was accused of economism, because its treatment of class was insufficiently dynamic. It was also attacked for simplistic conflation of spatial and social exploitation in its emphasis on the hierarchies of exploitation among rather than within countries, which hid the rich of the poor countries and the poor of the rich countries. Moreover its tendency to freeze Third World countries in a perpetual state of underdevelopment was too static and generalized, and ignored the dynamic changes taking place. Far from being a product of a senile, decaying capitalism, Bill Warren (an old-style Marxist) argued, imperialism was the product of young, vigorous economies: it was the "pioneer of capitalism" (Warren 1980). Independence mattered, for it provided opportunities for the bourgeois classes of the Third World to alter their relations with the North, which facilitated the development of the forces of production, especially industrialization.

The emergence of the NICs was seized on by many critics as proof of the possibility of Third World development. Indeed the NICs seemed to destroy the very notion of a homogeneous Third World that was wallowing in poverty. The demise of dependency theory and its development prescriptions was accelerated by the emergence of conservative regimes among the major Western powers in the late 1970s and early 1980s, which forced the international financial institutions to abandon the "basic needs" and redistribution rhetoric they had briefly flirted with at the height of the NIEO struggles of the 1970s. Its demise was assured by the collapse of the Soviet Union. The triumph of neoliberalism led to anguish among progressive social scientists over the crisis or impasse of development theory and practice. And as **globalization** acquired analytical lustre, many claimed globalization rendered all old global divisions irrelevant. In the meantime the increasingly debt-ridden Third World countries, now increasingly called "the South," were adopting (often under duress from the Bretton Woods institutions – the World Bank, International Monetary Fund, and World Trade Organization) the **structural adjustment programs** of free-market capitalism.

Africa and the Third World

Africa was central to the emergence of the Third World as an intellectual/ideological construct and political movement. Africa's Third World significance derived from four factors:

1 all the conditions associated with the Third World, whether positive or negative, political or economic, were prevalent in Africa;
2 the founding of the Third World movement coincided with decolonization, in which Africa was a central player;
3 after decolonization African states and leaders and their concerns featured prominently in all international movements associated with the Third World, from the United Nations to the Non-Aligned Movement; and
4 the continent established important ties, with various degrees of closeness, with all the major Third World regions.

In short, post-independence African states became an integral part of the Third World, both because of their sheer numbers and because of the importance accorded to African interests in Third World politics, from development to the elimination of apartheid in **South Africa**.

It is important to note that Africa's interests in Third World affairs pre-dated the formal establishment of the movement. Pan-Africanists from W.E.B. DuBois and George Padmore to Kwame Nkrumah were keenly aware of, and sought to promote, relations between the colonized peoples of Africa and those of Asia. The need for Afro-Asian solidarity was proclaimed at the very first Pan-African Congress of 1900, and repeated even more forcefully at the 1945 Congress. Thus the Afro-Asian Bandung Conference of 1955, which called for economic, cultural, and political co-operation between Africa and Asia in their struggles for independence and development, preached to the converted. In fact it has been argued that although African countries differed, sometimes violently, on many international issues, on the question of Third World solidarity they often displayed a high degree of cooperation.

Afro-Asian dialogue and solidarity laid the foundations of the Third World movement. Their commonality of interest was promoted by three factors. First, unlike Latin America which had received its independence in the nineteenth century from Spain (with the exception of Brazil which was a Portuguese colony), the anti-colonial struggles in Africa and Asia occurred at the same time and were largely fought against the British and French. Given such similarities, it is not surprising that **nationalist movements** in both continents learned from each other, nor that developments in one affected developments in the other. For example, the independence of India and Pakistan in 1947 had an electrifying impact on and weakened colonialism in British colonial Africa, while France's defeat in Indochina in 1954 emboldened the Algerian liberation fighters. Second, the presence of a large Asian diaspora in eastern and southern Africa facilitated linkages between the two continents, especially with India. It is not surprising that India was an indefatigable opponent of apartheid South Africa, where its own nationalist hero Mahatma Gandhi had started his struggles, and the country played a key role from 1946 in isolating South Africa from the international community. Third, after independence the common challenges of development, nation-building, and maintaining sovereignty in a sharply polarized world of superpowers fostered continued cooperation. The formation of an Afro-Asian caucus at the UN, and in 1957 the Afro-Asian Peoples' Solidarity Organization (a **non-governmental organization** that complemented the efforts of state actors who would later coalesce around the NAM and the Group of 77), provided organizational forums for contacts and cooperation. From the late 1960s Afro-Asianism declined, according to some, or according to others was transformed with the growth of NAM and the NIEO.

Africa's relations with the Caribbean and Latin America were both close and distant – close in the sense that the two regions were home to the largest African diaspora populations, and distant because until independence there were hardly any state-to-state relations, notwithstanding the flow of cultural traffic and influences. Caribbean activists had of course played a major role in Pan-Africanism, and influenced the growth of such cultural movements as Negritude. In the 1960s Africa's cultural relations with the Caribbean continued, as exemplified by the Caribbean presence at the Second World Black and African Festival of Arts and Culture (FESTAC) in Nigeria in 1977. From 1975 the Caribbean and African states worked in concert in the Africa-Caribbean-Pacific Group of States in various rounds of negotiations with the European Economic Community. By then the politics of southern African liberation had also taken center-stage, and Caribbean nations provided wide-ranging support to the efforts of the **Organization of African Unity** and the liberation movements themselves to rid the region of settler colonialism. The most forthright was Cuba, which by 1980 had 19,000 combat troops in **Angola** and another 17,000 in **Ethiopia** (helping in the war against Somalia), and up to 12,000 civilian advisers and technical workers (including doctors) in several African countries. Cuba provided a bridge between the Caribbean and Latin America. Latin America had initially been ambivalent about the NAM, because it was seen as an Afro-Asian movement preoccupied with decolonization. As more prominence was given to questions of economic development, Latin America began to play an important role in the Third World movement, inspiring the formation of the United Nations Conference on Trade and Development (UNCTAD), and the activities of the Group of 77 and movement for the NIEO. From the mid-1970s Brazil, Latin America's largest country and home to the largest African diaspora population, embarked on expanding relations with the newly independent countries of lusophone Africa (Angola, **Mozambique**, and **Guinea**), with powerful African countries (such as Nigeria), and later with post-apartheid South Africa.

Closer to home, particularly intimate (if complicated) relations were established between Africa and the Arab world, helped by the fact that the majority of Arab states were in Africa. The role of facilitator was seized by Nasser's Egypt with alacrity. Nasser saw Egypt as being at the center of three circles: Arab, African, and Islamic. In the 1970s and 1980s Afro-Arab relations hinged on three issues. First, mutual support against settler domination in Palestine by Israel and in South Africa by the apartheid regime (Israel and South Africa themselves established close relations). In 1973, following the Arab-Israeli war (during which Egyptian, and therefore African, territory was occupied by Israel), twenty-one African states severed diplomatic relations with Israel. The second issue centered on economic and technical cooperation, especially following the sharp rises in oil prices in the 1970s. A number of organizations were created in response, such as the Arab Bank for Economic Development in Africa, the Special Arab Fund for Africa, and the Fund for Arab-African Technical Assistance. Third, there was the issue of cultural cooperation, which was formally addressed through the Organization of Islamic States, and less formally through the **League of Arab States**. Informally, there were also the Islamic networks, especially those inspired by the spread of **Islamic reform movements**.

See also: African diasporas; Commonwealth; economy: post-independence; international trade; non-African diasporas; Organization of the Islamic Conference

References and further reading

Edmondson, L. (1993) "Africa and the Developing Regions," in A.A. Mazrui and C. Wondji (eds.), *UNESCO General History of Africa. Africa Since 1935*, Oxford: Heinemann.

Fieldhouse, D.K. (1999) *The West and the Third World*, Oxford: Blackwell.

Harris, N. (1986) *The End of the Third World: Newly Industrializing Countries and the Decline of an Ideology*, London: Penguin.

Lenin, V.I. (1978 [1916]) *Imperialism. The Highest Stage of Capitalism*, Moscow: Progress Publishers.

McClelland, D. (1961) *The Achieving Society*, Princeton: Princeton University Press.

Nkrumah, K. (1963) *Neo-Colonialism: The Last Stage of Imperialism*, London: Panaf Books.

Packenham, R. (1992) *The Dependency Movement: Scholarship and Politics in Development Studies*, London: Harvard University Press.

Parsons, T. (1951) *The Social System*, Glencoe: Free Press.

Rodney, W. (1972) *How Europe Underdeveloped Africa*, London: Bogle l'Ouverture.

Rostow, W.W. (1971) *Stages of Economic Growth: A Non-Communist Manifesto*, Cambridge: Cambridge University Press.

Smith, B.C. (1996) *Understanding Third World Politics: Theories of Political Change and Development*, Bloomington: Indiana University Press.

Warren, B. (1980) *Imperialism: Pioneer of Capitalism*, London: Verso.

Worsley, P. (1967) *The Third World*, 2nd edn., London: Weidenfeld & Nicolson.

PAUL TIYAMBE ZELEZA

Togo

Togo has an area of 56,000 square kilometers. It is located in **West Africa**, along the Gulf of Benin, sandwiched between **Ghana**, **Benin**, and **Burkina Faso**. The country had an estimated population of 5 million in 2000, dominated by the Ewe subgroups (40 percent) and the Kabye (25 percent). At the end of the twentieth century the economy was still dominated by phosphates, cocoa, coffee, cotton, sea transportation, and a modest manufacturing sector. French was the official language, though Ewe, Mina, and other minority languages were spoken beyond their ethnic boundaries. The system of government was multi-party and quasi-democratic. Among the southern groups, especially the Ewe, Christianity was the dominant religion, while the Moba, Mossi, Kotokoli, and Tchamba were largely Muslims; traditional religions remained powerful in all communities, especially outside urban centers.

The German Reich annexed Togo as a *Schutzgebiet* (protectorate) in 1884, and by 1900 German colonial control stretched the length and breadth of Togo. The German colonial capital was moved from Zebe to **Lome**. While the extension of colonial authority was a brutal military process that was fiercely resisted by the Kotokoli, the Kabye, and Konkomba, once occupation was complete a system of roads and railroads, built by German money and forced labor, facilitated the economic exploitation of the territory. In 1914 British, French, and African troops invaded and captured German Togoland, and for the duration of the war British troops controlled much of the Ewe region, as well as reuniting the Konkomba kingdoms.

The League of Nations mandates officially began in 1922, with one-third of what became Togo under British control, and two-thirds under the administration of France. The Ewe subgroups were further divided by the border, while the Konkomba regained unity under their capital Yendi. Many smaller groups, such as the Akposso, were divided from their farmlands. During the mandate the French forced large numbers of Kabye to settle in the center and south, officially to combat overcrowding but really to provide cheap labor reserves for the plantations and industrialization. During the same period the capital grew rapidly, and all of Togo's ethnic groups and religions gained a foothold in what had historically been a Ewe region. The main administrative developments of this period included increased centralization, the enhancement and invention of "traditional" chiefly authority, and the entrenchment of political authority among the Ewe-speaking elite.

The anti-colonial movement began in earnest in the 1930s. Two popular protests – a market-women's revolt in 1933 and the suppression of a pro-German lobby group called the Bund der Deutschen Togoländer – are considered formative moments for anti-colonial sentiment. After these incidents the French enjoined elite Togolese to form a Cercle des Amitiés Françaises to counter murmurings of resistance. Sylvanus Olympio, the organization's first vice-president, ultimately turned the group into an pro-independence party called the Comité de l'Unité Togolaise (CUT), founded in 1945. The CUT sparred with a rival, conservative group that was led by the future president Nicolas Grunitzky, but the CUT ultimately prevailed. After a UN-sponsored plebiscite that resulted in British Togoland joining the newly independent Republic of **Ghana** in 1957, French Togoland followed suit. Election to the French Union in 1958 paved the way for the foundation of the independent République Togolaise in 1960.

With independence the Ewe subgroups, led by President Olympio, sought to quickly replace the French administrative cadre. Olympio's initial Pan-African and pluralist concerns gave way to authoritarianism and arbitrary rule. With greater literacy and economic resources, including a monopoly on cocoa, cotton and coffee sales, the Ewe elite were overrepresented in government and administration. Even during the French occupation, however, northern groups (such as the Kabye and Kotokoli) represented over 80 percent of the armed forces. This ethnically imbalanced distribution of political and military capital set the stage for sub-Saharan Africa's first coup d'état. Olympio was murdered as he attempted to scale the wall of the US embassy in 1961.

A second coup in 1967 ended southern dominance, and a Kabye, Colonel Eyadema, became president. The president oversaw a program of rapid economic development, buoyed by rising phosphate prices. The infrastructure was expanded with the construction of new roads, regional markets, and import substitution industries. There was redistribution of economic resources, as large numbers of northerners entered the political and administrative arena, and development projects were launched in the north. During the late 1970s, taking his lead from Mobutu's Zaire (now **Democratic Republic of Congo**), Eyadema launched a program of *authenticité* that essentialized ethnic identities, further exacerbating the north/south division. Inflated primary export prices, coupled with a tourism boom, meant that Togo briefly had a very buoyant economy. By the late 1980s, however, economic stagnation caused by an enormous international debt prefigured Togo's subsequent social and political turmoil.

North–south ethnic tensions occasionally flared into violence in the 1990s, though official and unofficial political propaganda and the stated platform of political parties greatly exaggerated existing cleavages. During 1991 and 1992 a democratic revolution, modeling itself on the 1991 constitutional convention that dethroned Matthieu Kérékou of Benin, resulted in the brief loss of the presidency by Eyadema. Hundreds of thousands of Kabye fled north to escape political violence in the south, and at the same time southerners fled to neighboring Ghana and Benin. Western embassies closed, and expatriates and donors were evacuated. Eyadema, with the aid of French military hardware and political support, soon reasserted his control in a violent bloodbath. By the end of the decade southerners were still being exposed to brutality and harassment, but rule in the north was also maintained by violence and intimidation. Eyadema succeeded in gaining some political legitimacy in Western eyes via the ballot box in 1993 and 1998, though both elections were marred by fraud and violence. In the late 1990s both Amnesty International and the UN Commission on Human Rights led investigations into alleged **human rights** abuses in Togo. In the meantime the economy seemed to be making a modest recovery, buoyed by a rise in export earnings.

Further reading

Decalo, S. (1996) *Historical Dictionary of Togo*, 3rd edn., Baltimore and London: Scarecrow Press.

Marguerat, Y. (1994) *Population, migrations, urbanisation au Togo et en Afrique noire: articles et documents (1981–1993)*, Lome: Presses de l'Université du Bénin.

BENJAMIN NICHOLAS LAWRENCE

trading diasporas

A trade diaspora is an "interrelated net of commercial communities forming a trade network" (Curtin 1984: 2). Communities of traders living among strangers and associated into networks date from the beginnings of urban life and are found throughout the world. A variety of such diasporas for the trans-Saharan trade, based on kinship and ethnicity, developed in **West Africa** from the fourteenth century. Under the pre-industrial social conditions of the time, technical problems existed that included lack of effective central institutions to ensure respect of contracts, lack of regular transportation and communication services, and the ethnic heterogeneity of communities involved. These problems were overcome when traders from one ethnic group controlled all or most stages of trade in particular commodities. Trade diasporas are not only of historical significance, however. They took on new forms and performed new functions in the modern era.

A classic case of a trade diaspora in nineteenth- and twentieth-century Africa, reinforced by the bonds of **Islam**, was that of the **Hausa** in West Africa, who lived in communities in Yoruba towns and monopolized long-distance trade in cattle and kola between the forest belt and **savanna** in **Nigeria**. Their diaspora was made up of a network of culturally distinctive communities in which Hausa customs provided the stable institutional organization for trade. Reliable information about changing conditions of supply and demand, along with speedy transactions, were essential because kola was perishable and cattle herds vulnerable to tsetse fly; both needed to be moved quickly. Although very large amounts of money were involved, as well as extensive credit, sometimes between total strangers of different ethnicity, there was little reliance on modern institutions of banking, insurance, police and courts, or on the exchange of documents. Instead the Hausa developed their own complex and extensive business organization. Their culture and their adherence to Islam did not just result in a way of life, but also incorporated a political ideology which furthered their trading interests. Their adoption of the Tijaniyya order in the 1950s, in response to the disintegrative effect of party politics, led to a more effective centralization of their organization and strengthened Hausa identity and exclusiveness.

African trading diasporas in the twentieth century were not always Islamic, nor as extensive as those of the Hausa and others in West Africa. After independence in 1960 the Nande of Kivu, the eastern region of the **Democratic Republic of Congo** in **Central Africa**, organized a trading diaspora that on a smaller scale. It was based on ties of ethnicity and kinship or friendship, and was not supported by a religious ideology. By the late 1970s the Nande had a near monopoly on the commerce of vegetables by road from Kivu to Kisangani, and on shipping less perishable vegetables (such as beans) onwards by boat down the Zaire River to **Kinshasa**. Nande living in these cities oversaw transshipment and reception of goods, transmitted information, and arranged credit, and Nande traders gave each other mutual assistance on the road. Family members and friends cooperated in owning and running these trading enterprises. The control of all stages of the trade by trusted agents enabled the Nande to cope with the problems of the post-independence state of Zaire (renamed the Democratic Republic of Congo in the late 1990s). These problems were the lack of effective state institutions, deterioration of transport and communication systems, scarcity of goods, restricted access to capital, and distrust between peoples of different regions and ethnic groups. These conditions had beset the country from the time of independence in 1960. Organization of a trade diaspora brought the Nande success in their trading enterprises, despite the long years of chronic political and economic crisis in their country.

As part of the process of the **globalization** of capitalism, trade diasporas increasingly extended from Africa to other continents, particularly in unofficial and unrecorded trade. In **Senegal**, for example, the government ceased to protect domestic manufactured goods from foreign competition in 1986. In the ensuing rush into export and import business, the Mouride Islamic Brotherhood (most of whose members were from the Wolof ethnic group) achieved dominance through their ability to create a trade diaspora of networks tying distribution points in **Dakar** to Mouride immigrant communities in international wholesaling centers in Europe or the United States. These trading networks, generally associated with a major wholesaler in Dakar, did not only send goods to Senegal but also participated in buying and selling for the local (primarily African-American) market in the United States, which brought them new items to trade at good prices back home. They were thus exploiting new opportunities that arose in the process of globalization. Individual traders specialized in particular commodities, and made use of specific networks for them. These complex networks could extend over several countries, as the traders made use of various kinds of personal ties to achieve their objectives. These ties could be looked on as investments in the social capital of personal relations. If the traders were only to operate from Dakar, they could not be as successful as they were with their overseas connections and enterprises because they would not have had access to such a varied range of ties. So strong were the religious sanctions of the Muslim communities of this diaspora that betraying trust and confidence brought grave consequences to all aspects of an individual's life. The hierarchical structure of these international networks, with their division of labor and the placing of disciples by their marabouts at strategic points of the network, contributed to their commercial success.

Other Muslim **merchants** who were not Mouride and originated in the Senegal River valley, form diasporas in the trade of diamonds and other precious stones, such as emeralds and sapphires, the semi-precious malachite of Congo-Kinshasa, and ivory. In parallel with this trade, there developed another in manufactured goods, high-quality wax-print cloth, food, and cars. All this activity contributed over the years to the development of the Senegal River valley. The traders, primarily Soninke and Haalpulaaren, moved between established communities in West and Central Africa, **Southern Africa**, and the eastern countries of the continent. From there they traveled beyond Africa to Southeast Asia and the Middle East. But these communities, unlike those of the Mourides, were not tightly structured: close ties were formed through marriage rather than through reliance on membership of a brotherhood.

Trading diasporas of the late twentieth century were of particular interest for showing us how Africans preserved their own practices and forms of knowledge as they incorporated themselves into the world economy. These diasporas illuminated African forms of modernity and the remodeling of African tradition as the traders took part in, and contributed to, the process of globalization. The intercontinental diasporas of the Mourides were one example. The founder of the brotherhood in Senegal was Amadou Bamba; Touba, the village founded by him, was their holy city, the site of his mausoleum, and the place of their annual pilgrimage. The movement of his largely peasant followers to the cities took place in three stages: between the two world wars, then again after the **Second**

World War, and finally after the drought of the 1970s. These migrants went first to Senegalese cities, taking up commerce and informal activities so as to be able to journey out of the country to seek economic success. Wealth and travel were associated for them. Import–export and service activities soon became part of the Mouride identity. They moved on to European, American, and Asian cities as traders and workers, thus participating actively in economic globalization. In cities where they were present in large numbers, they lived in special neighborhoods. They preserved their identity and exclusiveness through having their own locality, through their religious celebrations, and through participating together in meals and leisure activities. Their diasporic culture excluded foreign values through daily collective acts, and produced an intense solidarity. This social and ritual interaction is the basis for their organization of financial relationships and the unbreakable trust that obtains among them. They traveled widely, combining professional and territorial mobility to take advantage of economic opportunities, and to impose their own order on the chaos of the market. But with their dress of boubous and tasseled hats, and their photo medallions of their marabouts, they did not conform to the Westernized identity of modernity. Although they took part in the process of globalization, they refused to appropriate or assimilate to the language and habits of modernity as conceived by the West and by world Islam. They did not subvert the world economy, but they confronted it with their new ways of doing business, their new forms of accumulation, and their success. In so doing they contributed to its cosmopolitanism.

Some African transnational traders operated on the margins of, or outside, the law, evading visa and currency regulations and taxes as they moved out of oppressive circumstances to trade in the international economy. Some traders from Congo-Kinshasa and Congo-Brazzaville in west Central Africa, for example, traveled all over the world to pursue their commercial activities. They imported a wide range of commodities (including electronic goods, appliances and electronic equipment, secondhand cars, cloth and clothing, jewelry, and shoes) into their home countries. In their trade between Europe and Central Africa, in return for these manufactured goods, they imported a great variety of African foods, as well as compact discs and videos of African popular music, beauty products, and wax-print cloth to supply the immigrant African communities of Brussels and Paris.

When they arrived in strange countries, these traders relied on ties of ethnicity, kinship, friendship, locality, and nationality for help with food and lodging, for assistance in coping with strange languages, and for finding the goods they wanted. Their trading networks were not like the highly organized diasporas that operated throughout history in West Africa. Instead the personal ties of the networks through which they operated their trade were instrumentally activated as needed. This trade was extremely responsive to changing markets and to political conditions (which could determine the ease or difficulty of getting visas to particular countries). The direction and commodities of the trade could change quite rapidly. These traders were primarily young people who found themselves marginalized and constrained in their search for a better life by the oppressive practices of the wealthy and powerful in their home countries, and by the domination of corporate and Western governmental interests abroad. Some of them capitalized their trade by participation in the international drug trade or by theft, and they engaged in a variety of ways of smuggling their goods as they struggled to engage with the difficulties they confronted in their search for opportunity.

The trade diasporas of the twentieth century have thus adapted to the jet age and the communications revolution. The problems to which they provided solutions had changed in some respects, but in others were remarkably similar to those of earlier centuries.

See also: African diasporas; families; international trade; non-African diasporas

References and further reading

Bredeloup, S. (1994) "L'aventure contemporaine des diamantaires sénégalais," *Politique Africaine* 56, 5: 77–93.

Cohen, A. (1969) *Custom and Politics in Urban Africa: A Study of Hausa Migrants in Yoruba Towns*, Berkeley and Los Angeles: University of California Press.
—— (1971) "Cultural Strategies in the Organization of Trading Diasporas," in C. Meillassoux (ed.), *The Development of Indigenous Trade and Markets in West Africa*, Oxford: International African Institute.
Curtin, P. (1984) *Cross-Cultural Trade in World History*, Cambridge: Cambridge University Press.
Diouf, M. (2000) "The Senegalese Murid Trade Diaspora and the Making of a Vernacular Cosmopolitanism," *CODESRIA Bulletin* 1: 19–30.
Ebin, V. (1992) "A la recherche de nouveaux 'poissons': stratégies commerciales mourides par temps de crise," *Politique Africaine* 1, 5: 86–99.
Grégoire, E. and Labazée, P. (eds.) (1993) *Grands Commerçants d'Afrique de l'Ouest*, Paris: Karthala-ORSTOM.
MacGaffey, J. and Bazenguissa-Ganga, R. (2000) *Congo–Paris: Transnational Traders on the Margins of the Law*, Oxford: International African Institute, in association with James Currey and Indiana University Press.

JANET MACGAFFEY

traditional religions *see* African religions

transport

Prior to the arrival of Europeans in Africa, some parts of Africa had well-established trade routes for long-distance trade. For example, on the southern edge of the **Sahara**, Timbuctoo and Gao stood at the crossroads of the age-old trans-Saharan trade. However, modern transportation and communication systems were largely developed during the colonial and post-colonial eras. Throughout the colonial territories the authorities built railways directed toward resource-rich areas. The only exception to the rule was in **North Africa**, where a lateral railway line was built during the colonial era along the Mediterranean coastal zone all the way from Marrakesh in **Morocco** to Tunis in **Tunisia**. However, with the discovery of rich petroleum reserves in the interior of **Libya** and **Algeria**, these nations built additional short lines into the interior during the post-independence era, for the haulage of crude oil to coastal ports for export. In post-colonial Africa governments invested heavily in roads, airports, and seaports wherever possible. The model of transport development follows the Taaffe, Morril and Gould (1963) model, in which settlements were developed in a linear fashion, first along the coast and then along the routes that developed between coastal points and resource-rich interiors. This model of transport development was based on the transport histories of nations such as **Nigeria**, **Ghana**, **Tanzania**, and **Kenya**. Indeed one main feature of African transport routes is their lack of lateral integration.

When the Europeans began to move inland from coastal settlements during the last decade of the nineteenth century, they did so to pre-existing African towns. The inland ventures were usually for military purposes. As Griffiths (1995) notes, in 1874 in present-day Ghana the British went inland to attack **Kumasi**, capital of Asante. They soon built a military road from **Accra** to Kumasi as they went, and in 1923 built a railway along the same route. In Nigeria British penetration was also to pre-determined points: to pre-existing African cities such as **Ibadan** and Benin, and later to **Kano** and Sokoto. Throughout the continent, colonial transport routes (roads and railways) were built from the coastal ports that Europeans had established to interior areas, mostly endowed with major agricultural and mineral resources, or to important pre-colonial settlements such as Ibadan. In most instances these routes followed well-trodden pre-colonial trading paths. The same was true of harbors; in some places the ports of established centers were simply improved (as in **Dakar**, **Lagos**, and **Freetown** in **West Africa**; **Luanda** in **Central Africa**; **Mombasa** in **East Africa**; and **Cairo** and **Algiers** in North Africa), while elsewhere entirely new ones were built.

Southern Africa witnessed the most extensive transport building program during the colonial era, thanks to settler colonialism and the discovery of huge mineral resources. The discovery of diamonds at Kimberley in 1867 prompted Europeans to begin building a fairly integrated network of roads and railways, which was the exception rather than the rule of colonial transportation systems. Before 1870 there was no need to build railways or roads into the interior, and the few goods that came from the interior (such as hides and ivory) were hauled to the coast by means of ox-drawn wagons. The presence of the Cape Fold mountains and the Great Escarpment in the southwest, as well as the Drankensberg mountains to the east, only made the costs more prohibitive. In 1870 there were just 110 kilometers of railway in **South Africa**, which linked **Cape Town** with Stellenbosch, Paarl, and Wellington across the Cape Flats. The discovery of diamonds brought in a frenzy of transportation and infrastructural development. Railways were built from Cape Town, Port Elizabeth, Durban, and East London to the diamond fields in the interior, and later to the Witwatersrand goldfields. Thus the discovery of diamonds at Kimberley, centrally located in South Africa, was the main force that prompted the colonial government to invest heavily in transportation, leading to the opening up of the entire country. By 1915 South Africa had a well-integrated system of railways. The building of an equally impressive road system did not begin until the 1940s, something that was prompted by the onset of the **Second World War**. By the end of the twentieth century South Africa's relatively well-developed and well-maintained transportation system was the envy of the Southern African subregion, if not the entire continent.

Zimbabwe (then Southern Rhodesia) also attracted a large contingent of European settlers due to both the discovery of gold and attraction of fertile soil for large-scale farming. Around the early 1900s Zimbabwe saw a similar frenzy to South Africa in the development of railways. A railway was completed in 1900 from the Mozambican port of Beira to **Harare** (then Salisbury), and another from Mafikeng to **Bulawayo**. The discovery of mineral wealth in the present-day Copperbelt in **Zambia** led to the extension of the railway system from Harare to this part of Africa in 1905. Later the railway was extended to the Katanga (Shaba) province in the Congo. The Belgians who controlled the Congo also built their own line from Port Francqui (Ilebo) on the Congo River system to Elisabethville (**Lubumbashi**), which was completed in 1926, in advance of the railway line from **Angola**, which in 1928 also reached Katanga. Furthermore the onset of the **First World War** had propelled South Africa to develop the Cape network of railways, which was soon joined with the German rail system at De Aar in **Namibia**.

Due to the rich mineral resources found throughout Southern Africa, this part of Africa has the largest rail network on the continent, estimated at over 32,200 kilometers of track across twelve countries. Most of this network is concentrated in South Africa, which boasts 22,540 kilometers. The main purpose of this network was to exploit African mineral resources, but it also encouraged development along the nodes: for example, along the Durban–Johannesburg and Harare–Bulawayo corridors, as well as along the Zambian rail line. The network facilitated the exploitation of resources, and ensured British domination of the region. Later, in the 1980s, the concentration of the railways in South Africa ensured the country's apartheid regime was able to exert undue influence economically and politically on the surrounding states.

Other parts of Africa were not so fortunate as Southern Africa. Often colonial governments built a series of railway lines from a port only to a specific inland point that had some resources to exploit or that was perceived to be of strategic importance in defending the colony. This was the case in East Africa, where the British and Germans built a series of lines from coastal ports such as Mombasa and **Dar es Salaam** into the interior to exploit resources or for military purposes. West Africa also had its fair share of lines running from the coast into the interior, but without any lateral connections. Their purpose was to facilitate exploitation of minerals and cash crops, and to provide ease of access to crush any political uprisings by the colonized peoples. In some cases (such as **Liberia**, **Guinea**, and **Sierra Leone**) different gauges were used for individual lines within each country, making lateral linkages impossible.

Although the bulk of the railway system was built during the colonial era, there have been some major infrastructural developments during the post-independence era that began for most African countries in the early 1960s. Perhaps one of the most celebrated major transportation developments during the post-colonial era was the completion by the Chinese in 1975 of the 1,680-kilometer Tanzania–Zambia railway (TAZARA) from Dar es Salaam to the Copperbelt in Zambia. This railway was built not for economic profit but to moderate the political and economic influence that South Africa and white Rhodesia (now Zimbabwe) had on Zambia, as Zambia was one of the "Frontline States" fighting for the independence of Rhodesia. During the 1970s **Malawi** too built its own new railway line to the port of Nacala in **Mozambique**, so as to offer an alternative to the longer route to the sea via Beira. Other post-colonial railways include the line to Maiduguri in northeastern Nigeria, to Packwach in **Uganda**, and the trans-Gabon railway. Most of these were developed to access remote areas.

While railroads were mainly a colonial undertaking, the building of paved roads was a post-colonial venture for most African governments. At the time of independence there were very few paved roads in Africa. For example, when Malawi became independent there were only a seventy-kilometer paved road linking **Blantyre** and Zomba, and another seventy-kilometer road venturing into the tea-growing areas of Thyolo and Mulanje. Road-building gained momentum in the post-colonial period but, as Griffiths (1995) laments, many trunk roads merely duplicated routes already served by rail, often from ports into the interior. Throughout Africa post-colonial governments invested heavily in the building of paved roads. However, instead of a carefully interconnected road system between and among African countries, these roads generally came from the interior to the coast, continuing the colonial pattern in which the trade of African countries was generally oriented towards their former colonial powers, instead of promoting intra-African trade. Indeed the lack of urgency felt about the development of an interconnected road system in Africa was exemplified by the slow progress in building the trans-African highway. The council of Ministers of the Economic Commission for Africa passed a resolution in 1971 to build a trans-African highway, and in 1981 the Trans-African Highway Authority was launched to build the road. It was to run from Lagos to Mombasa, taking advantage of pre-existing roads for much of its distance. However, by 2000 the central section through **Cameroon**, **Central African Republic**, and the Congo had not yet been built.

In addition to building roads, post-colonial governments also invested heavily in air transportation. Major airports were built for intercontinental flights, and national or regional airlines set up, many of which acquired large jet planes for travel to faraway European lands and the United States. Very little was done to invest in smaller planes for internal and intracontinental connections. However, as economic conditions deteriorated in the 1980s and 1990s, many African airlines folded. Those that remained began to emphasize intra-continental flights, rather than overseas flights. Among the strongest of those that remain are Kenyan Airways, Ethiopian Airlines, Nigerian Airlines, South African Airlines, and Egypt Air.

In conclusion, it can be seen that many of the railway transportation systems in Africa were built during the first half of the twentieth century under colonial rule, with the sole purpose of exploiting African resources and controlling African peoples. As such, with the exception of Southern Africa, railways mainly ran from the coast to some interior resource-rich locality, without any lateral connections. Post-independence developments have concentrated on building roads, most of which follow the railway routes laid out during the colonial era. African transportation infrastructure is directed towards external rather than internal trade. During the era of **structural adjustment programs** from the early 1980s to the 1990s, transportation infrastructure (particularly the maintenance of roads) crumbled due to lack of resources. For example, the major highway from **Kinshasa** to the Atlantic Ocean port is impassable during the main rainy season. Many development experts, including some governments, stressed that without a well-integrated transportation system between and within African countries, Africa would not be able to unshackle itself from the chains of exploitation that were forged during the colonial era. They emphasized that, in order for the continent to lessen its dependent role in the world trading system, African countries will have to develop a continental transport infrastructure that will enable them to promote intra-African trade. Indeed organizations such as the **Southern African Development Community** (SADC) had recognized the importance of a well-maintained and well-connected transportation system, and were working towards achieving that goal.

References and further reading

Griffiths, I.L.L. (1995) *The African Inheritance*, London: Routledge.

Pedersen, P.O. (2000) *The Changing Structure of Transport Under Trade Liberalization and Globalization and Its Impact on African Development*, Copenhagen: Centre for Development Research.

Taaffe, E.J., Morril, R.L. and Gould, P. (1963) "Transport Expansion in Underdeveloped Countries: A Comparative Analysis," *Geographical Review* 53: 503–29.

EZEKIEL KALIPENI

Tripoli, Libya

Tripoli is currently the *de facto* capital of **Libya**. It is located on the Mediterranean coast in the northwest province known as Tripolitania. Tripoli's metropolitan area has been expanding rapidly: by the end of the twentieth century it measured more than seventeen kilometers east to west, and about eight kilometers north to south. The city had a population of over 1.5 million.

After the reconsolidation of Ottoman rule in Libya in 1835, Tripoli began to grow slowly. The Ottoman governors established a military college, a big marketplace, primary schools, and telephone connections between Tripoli and the second largest city, Benghazi. According to the first census in 1911 the total number of inhabitants was 30,000, with foreigners (mainly Europeans) and Libyan Jews constituting one third of the population and Libyan Muslims the rest. A typical Islamic city, Tripoli was walled for defensive purposes; as the city became overcrowded, the population gradually inhabited the desert areas outside the walls.

With the Italian invasion of Libya's coastal cities in 1911, Ottoman rule collapsed, but Italian control had also weakened by the end of the **First World War**, enabling a group of Tripolitanian notables to declare an independent republic. Negotiations between the republic and the Italian authorities resulted in "the Fundamental Law," which provided for a special form of Libyan-Italian citizenship, and the republic gradually faded.

The reconquest of Libya by the Italian fascist regime in 1923 triggered a new militant resistance movement, and the Italians did not gain complete control of Tripoli until 1932. Between 1932 to 1943 Tripoli was remodeled on a European model. The Italian rulers established new residential and commercial areas outside the walled city, a central business district, and industrial zones, building factories for olive-oil manufacture, flour milling, and soap and wine production. In addition tens of thousands of Italians emigrated to Tripoli, constituting about half the population by 1941.

After the Italian defeat in the **Second World War**, the British ruled Tripoli for a short time. When Libya was declared an independent kingdom in 1951, Tripoli remained the seat of government for the constitutional al-Sunnusi monarch. It continued to serve as the capital until 1969. During this period the city expanded as a result of the presence of a US military base (the largest outside the United States) in Tripolitania, five kilometers east of Tripoli's central business district. With the discovery of oil in the early 1960s Tripoli's social and economic development accelerated. Large groups of rural migrants arrived, and new quarters were built for the rich. Generally construction boomed, reflecting rising incomes.

When the group of young Free Officers led by Muammar al-Qaddafi overthrew the monarchy in 1969 and declared an Arabic republic, there were major consequences for Tripoli. First, the Revolutionary Command Council evacuated the American base in 1970. Second, it confiscated all the property of the Italian population, encouraging them and the large Jewish community to leave the country. Third, Arabs of other nationalities were encouraged to migrate to Libya; in less than a decade they constituted about 14 percent of Tripoli's population.

In 1986 the United States accused Libya of sponsoring terrorism, and US airplanes bombed Tripoli, destroying its airport and barracks, and causing civilian casualties. In 1987 Colonel Qaddafi declared the city of al-Jufra the official capital of Libya, moving many departments there. Tripoli, however, remained the country's main cultural and commercial center.

Further reading

Misallati, A. (1981) *Tripoli, Libya: Structure and Functions as an Arab-Islamic City*, unpublished Ph.D. thesis, University of Kentucky.

RIHAM MAHROUS KHAFAGY

tropical rain forest

Tropical rain forest (TRF) covers less than 10 percent of the earth's surface, but contains more than 50 percent of all species. Their wealth of biodiversity is exceptional and unrivaled: nearly half of all vertebrates, and 60 percent of known plant species are found in the TRF. In Africa the extensive areas of TRF are found in **West Africa**, where the TRF belt stretches from **Guinea** in the west to **Cameroon** in the east. From an ecological perspective, TRF protects and enriches soils, as well as regulating the hydrologic cycle. It also affects local and regional climate, influences watershed flows of surface and groundwater, and helps to stabilize the global climate by sequestering carbon. From an economic perspective, timber is generally considered as the commodity with greatest value from TRF environments. For example, international trade in tropical timber was valued at more than US$8 billion per year in the 1990s, with European companies the main markets for exports of African logs.

In spite of the economic benefits of TRF environment, the net domestic benefits gained by African countries for depletion of their forest resources have been surprisingly small. For example, in a 1980 sample of African countries the value-added in the forestry sector averaged 3.3 percent of gross domestic product. This low figure substantially overstated its contribution to income. It also failed to take into account the fact that in Africa TRF constitutes the primary livelihood for people who live within or around the forest margins. These indigenous inhabitants are valuable participants in the management of TRF. Studies have shown that forest-dwelling communities in Africa possess knowledge of several medicinal plants, most of which have never been investigated by Western scientists.

As elsewhere there are conflicting accounts and estimates of the extent and rate of forestry loss in Africa during the twentieth century. Some studies suggest an annual rate of loss of 0.8 percent, but country studies (based on extensive use of satellite imagery, land-use data, and vegetation mapping backed by ground surveys) strongly indicate higher annual rates of TRF loss. For example, in **Côte d'Ivoire** alone the deforestation rate in 1980 was estimated at about 300,000 hectares per year – nearly 7 percent. This is a country where forest was reported to have once covered 45 percent of the total land area.

Although there is great uncertainty attached to estimates of total area of TRF and its rate of loss in Africa, some estimates of forest loss are clearly more reliable than others. However, to date, there has been no universally agreed methodology for measuring and calculating deforestation rates, coupled with the fact that different timescales are used. Furthermore some African countries lack baseline data against which to compare recent changes. Thus much of the uncertainty in deforestation rates results from the different criteria used to define and measure deforestation, the lack of attention to remote-sensing measurements, and overconfidence in the use of expert judgment.

Two main perspectives are often used to explain the loss of TRF in Africa during the twentieth century. The first explanation focuses on population growth (that is, the human-ecological framework). Advocates of this approach suggest that **population** growth and pressure created land scarcities, which in turn led to the expansion of agriculture into TRF regions. The human-ecological argument is deficient in many ways. Although the approach can explain forest loss at the national or global scale, it provides very limited insight into the local processes (household level) and causes of the problem in Africa. It also fails to incorporate the role of political, historical, and socioeconomic factors that might influence forest loss, especially at the local level. For example, there were areas in Africa with large populations and relatively low rates of forest loss, as well as areas with very few people, a short settlement history, and rapid rates of forest loss.

The second explanation of the causes and processes of TRF loss builds on neoclassical economics and dependency theory. Its proponents argue that faulty incentive systems affect economic and demographic behavior, especially those based on the use of common-property resources like TRF. The role of the state in forest management is also seen as central to the political-economic argument on the causes of TRF loss. The contention has been that forest loss is encouraged by land-tenure rules that confer title to the forest on parties who "improve" it by clearing the land for some other use. In **Ghana** rights to use the resources of the forest, which had been governed by local communities, were taken over by central government in the early 1970s. As a result the rate of forest loss increased, because traditional leaders no longer had a strong incentive to limit and control shifting cultivation, or timber-extraction operations. Proponents of this explanation argue that rapid loss of TRF environments coincided with the incorporation of forest regions in Africa into an expanding international economy.

Over the course of the twentieth century several initiatives have been suggested, established, or adopted to check TRF loss. Some were local and national, while others were significantly international in orientation. The most significant of these initiatives included the establishment of national parks in TRF areas, including the Kakum National Park in Ghana (1992), Cross River National Park in **Nigeria** (1991), and the Korup National Park in Cameroon (1987). These were steps in the right direction. However, there were several negative implications for the rural people who depend on TRF for their livelihood. To succeed with their conservation objectives, TRF national parks in Africa must also address the development needs of these people.

Further reading

Oates, J.F. (1999) *Myth and Reality in the Rain Forest: How Conservation Strategies are Failing in West Africa*, Berkeley: University of California Press.

Sayer, J.A., Harcourt, C.S. and Collins, N.M. (1992) *The Conservation Atlas of Tropical Forest: Africa*, Cambridge: World Conservation Union, Gland/World Conservation Monitoring Centre.

UWEM E. ITE

Tunis, Tunisia

Tunis is the largest city and capital of **Tunisia**. It had an estimated population of 2.3 million in 2000. It is an ancient city, founded in the ninth century BC by the Libyans, who had surrendered the site of Carthage to the Phoenicians. As Carthage flourished, the city of Tunis was overshadowed by its dazzling neighbor. The modern city of Tunis was built under French rule, which lasted from 1881 until 1956. The French built a modern European quarter. During the French occupation the population of Tunis increased significantly. Europeans, as well as Muslims, settled in the city, attracted by the booming commercial and industrial activities.

Given this long history the city reflects a mixture of old and new. Tunis, which enjoys an elevated location, is divided into two sectors: the old, walled, Muslim city (the *medina*), and the modern European quarter. The old sector, with its narrow, winding alleys and rich legacy of monuments and antiquities, neighbors the ruins of ancient Carthage. The old city boasts several famous markets, such as Souk el-Attarine (which specializes in perfumes and other local handicrafts) and the Souq Birka (the Gold Market), as well as a vast array of buildings that played an important role in Tunisia's history. These include the National Library, built in 1813, and the Sidi Yousef Mosque, built in the seventeenth century and first mosque with an octagonal minaret. There is also the Dar Hussein mansion, with its richly artistic Islamic decorations. It was occupied by the French army during the colonial era, but made into the National Art and Archeology Institute after independence. The Bardo Museum displays a vast quantity of Carthaginian, Roman, Byzantine, and Arab treasures. The

Carthage Museum also has a priceless collection, with Prehistoric, Punic, Roman, and Byzantine artifacts. For its part, the modern sector has one vital artery: Habib Bourguiba Avenue. The architecture along this street ranges from baroque and rococo to ultra-modern.

During the **Second World War** Tunis fell to the Axis Powers for a short period from November 1942 to May 1943. When Tunisia gained its independence in 1956, Tunis became its national capital and the country's commercial and industrial center, with major plants manufacturing textiles, clothing, carpets, chemicals, and processed foods, as well as cement and metal building structures. Its port, Halq al-Wadi, became the site of thermoelectric factories. The city also became a major tourist attraction, with 4 million Europeans visiting the country each year in the 1990s. The annual Festival of Carthage, the city's various cultural centers and theaters, and the renowned age-old thermal baths, not to mention other ancient historical sights including the remains of the magnificent Roman aqueducts, all proved popular with tourists.

Tunis also played an important national and regional political role. During the colonial period it was the center of nationalist activities against French rule. As its population increased after independence – to nearly a quarter of the total population of Tunisia – the city remained at the center of the country's politics. Its regional role was enhanced when it was chosen as the headquarters of the Arab League in 1979 (the headquarters were moved to **Cairo** in 1990); the Tunisian Shazli el-Qaleibi served as the League's Secretary General over the same period.

Further reading

Woodford, J.S. (1990) *The City of Tunis: Evolution of an Urban System*, Cambridgeshire: Middle East and North African Studies Press.

HAMDI ABDULRAHMAN

Tunisia

Tunisia, with an area of 163,610 square kilometers, borders **Libya** to the south and **Algeria** to the west. It had an estimated population of 9.7 million in 2000. The most widely known city in the region, Carthage, is in the heart of Tunisia, and the country has been part of a series of empires from the Romans to the Arabs. With the gradual weakening of the Ottoman Empire, Tunisia was threatened by the French, who had conquered neighboring Algeria in 1830. Fearing Tunisian revolutionary threats to their presence in Algeria, the French duly invaded in 1881, taking advantage of a border incident. The French military occupation, initially declared to be only temporary, became permanent when Tunisia was made into a Protectorate.

The French occupation was met initially with some resistance in the south, with the help of the Ottomans in Tripolitania. Resistance elsewhere was muted because the Bey was allowed to remain as figurehead monarch, and the Muslim judicial system allowed to function normally. Also the reformist movement founded by the disciples of the minister Khair al-Din, forefather of the Tunisian Renaissance, called for a rapprochement between the Islamic world and the West, as it wished to see the modernization of various aspects of Tunisian society, including education. Led by Mohamed al-Asram, a group of reformists who called themselves "Young Tunisians" appealed to the French public, but their pro-French sentiments and zeal were not reciprocated, and they began to support the radical demands for reform that were being spearheaded by railway workers. The French response was the deportation of two leaders of the Young Tunisians, and the imposition of martial law. This lasted from 1912 until 1921.

In terms of agriculture the French administration sold lands to French settlers, unlike their policy in Algeria, rather than make free land grants. The result was that number of settlers in Tunisia lagged behind the number in Algeria, despite various efforts by the colonial administration to encourage them. Nevertheless by 1914 about a fifth of Tunisia's cultivable land was in the hands of settlers. On the whole, the French succeeded in modernizing agriculture, with tangible positive effects on Tunisia's economy.

Nationalist resistance remained at a low ebb until after the **First World War**, when the

Destour (Constitution) Party was established. They demanded constitutional government and equal rights for Tunisians. The party leader, Abdel Aziz al-Thaalibi, was immediately arrested. Two years later Mohamed al-Nasir Bey made the same demands, and threatened to abdicate if they were not met. The French then introduced minor reforms to appease the population. More than a decade later, in 1934 Habib Bourguiba, a young lawyer, abandoned the Destour Party to form his own new organization, named the Neo-Destour Party. When the Popular Front government assumed power in France in 1936, the Neo-Destour Party succeeded in consolidating its power. However, the Popular Front government collapsed, and the Neo-Destourists were again subject to repression, a policy that they met with a campaign of civil disobedience. Two years later Bourguiba was arrested, and his party was dissolved. After the outbreak of the **Second World War** Bourguiba was deported to France, but he was released by the Nazis during the Vichy regime. In 1943 he was allowed back into Tunisia, where the Bey formed a new pro-Destour government. However, after the fall of Vichy France, the Bey was deposed and Bourguiba, accused of collaboration with the Nazis, fled to **Egypt**. Amid the wave of **decolonization** that engulfed the Arab countries, the French were forced to make further concessions. In 1951 a nationalist government took office, and Bourguiba was allowed back once more, only for a new wave of repression to be unleashed and Bourguiba exiled again. This time there was violent resistance, with rebels based in the Tunisian mountains, and finally in July 1954 Tunisia was promised its independence. After a rift within the ranks of the Neo-Destour Party, the first Tunisian elections took place in April 1956. Bourguiba was elected president of the first National Assembly. In 1957 the rule of the Bey came to an end, and Tunisia was proclaimed a republic with Bourguiba its first president. The next few years witnessed a further deterioration in French–Tunisian relations. After being forced to withdraw from its naval base at Bizerte in 1963, France stopped all financial aid to Tunisia, causing serious economic hardship. In the 1960s Tunisia consolidated its ties with neighboring Arab nations.

Bourguiba, the proponent of a secularist ideology, ruled the country for thirty years, during which period he established a strong one-party system, repressed Islamic fundamentalism, and established major rights for women, the first of which was the abolition of polygamy. Despite his self-proclamation as president-for-life, Bourguiba was overthrown in a coup staged in 1987 by his own prime minister, Zein el-Abidin ben Ali. Ben Ali introduced some reforms and instituted a multi-party system, allowing some freedom for the **press**. In 1989 the first free elections were held, with a massive victory for Ben Ali's Democratic Constitutional Assembly Party. Ten years later a constitutional amendment was adopted, which allowed the first free presidential elections to take place. The opposition was able to enter parliament for the first time in 1994, securing 20 percent of the seats in the October 1999 elections. Positive steps were also made in the field of **human rights**. In the meantime Tunisia embarked on a policy of economic reform, trying to strike a balance between a free-market economy and social welfare. The government initiated a multi-sectoral reform campaign to lay the foundation for a robust and competitive economy, and there were some indications of significant improvement in the standard of living: life expectancy increased from 67 in 1984 to an average of 72.4 in 1999, and per capita income increased from 952 dinars in 1986 to 2,716 dinars in 2000.

Further reading

Abun-Nasar, J.M. (1987) *A History of the Maghrib in the Islamic Period*, Cambridge: Cambridge University Press.

Perkins, K.J. (1989) *Historical Dictionary of Tunisia*, Metuchen: Scarecrow Press.

HAMDI ABDULRAHMAN

U

Uganda

Uganda has an area of 241,139 square kilometers, and is bordered by **Kenya**, **Rwanda**, **Sudan**, **Tanzania**, and the **Democratic Republic of Congo** (DRC). The country had an estimated population of 24.6 million in 2000.

Uganda was created out of diverse sociopolitical formations by British colonialism from 1890. Kabaka Mwanga of the Buganda kingdom soon became concerned by colonial interference in his kingdom's affairs, and by the violent conflicts between Catholic and Protestant missionaries. He decided to expel the missionaries, which provoked the latter to seek support from the colonial administration to fight Mwanga's forces, and Mwanga himself was exiled to the Ssese Islands on Lake Victoria.

In 1900 the Buganda agreement was signed introducing private land-ownership, the first such agreement with any of Uganda's kingdoms. The introduction of private *mailo* lands marginalized clan leaders, and turned most of the former Buganda peasant occupants into tenants. Out of their discontent was spawned the Bataka movement in the early 1920s, which demanded restoration of the traditional rights of clan heads and reductions in rent. The colonial government responded by restricting the amount of rent peasant tenants paid, and provided them with security of tenure against eviction. Impressed by the elaborate administrative structure of Buganda, the British administrator Lord Lugard decided to promote it as the administrative model for the rest of Uganda, and the basis for the system of indirect rule that was later popularized elsewhere.

The central aim of colonial policy, however, remained the production of cash crops, especially cheap cotton, for the Lancashire textile industry, and later coffee. Cotton production was assigned to the Buganda chiefs, who in return for the private estates they had received forced the **peasants** to grow cash crops. With new needs generated by the cash economy, especially for money for taxation, peasants increasingly took to growing cotton. In the meantime the rest of the country was turned into a labor reservoir for Buganda's cash-crop economy. Other areas were not permitted to grow cash crops, so **migrant labor** flowed into Buganda. Relative prosperity continued until the **Second World War**, which disrupted growth, especially of cotton production. In the post-Second World War period, coffee overtook cotton as Uganda's major cash-crop export.

In the 1940s, nationalist activities began to pick up. The 1950s saw an acceleration of nationalist demands for self-rule and for greater participation in the economy by Africans, under the leadership of the **nationalist movement** known as the Uganda National Congress. The colonial government responded by trying to create a middle class through the establishment of import substituting industries and the promotion of rich peasants as "progressive" farmers. The Uganda Development Corporation (UDC) was set up in 1952 to spearhead industrialization by engaging in joint investment with private partners. Industry required power, and the Owen Falls Dam was constructed at Njinja to provide it. Farmers were encouraged to form cooperatives and sell their cash crops to marketing boards, while Asians who had previously worked in the cash-crop marketing sector were compelled to go into large-scale wholesaling, the service sector, or other industries, usually in partnership with the UDC.

But the nationalist tide could not be held back. In 1961 a general election was held. The Democratic Party (DP) won, and its leader Ben Kiwanuka became the first African chief minister in Uganda. In the elections that followed independence on 9 October 1962, however, the DP lost power to an alliance of the Uganda People's Congress (UPC), led by Milton Obote, and Kabaka Yeka (KY). Obote duly became prime minister. The multi-party model of government soon ran into problems when the UPC–KY alliance fell apart in 1966. Obote's government used the army to abolish the monarchies. The leader of KY, who was Kabaka of Buganda and the president of Uganda, fled into exile in Britain, where he eventually died. Obote then declared himself executive president, and in December 1969 the country was turned into a one-party state. In the same year Obote declared his intention of turning Uganda "socialist" – what was dubbed the "Move to the Left" – which was followed by the nationalization of key industries.

In January 1971 Obote was overthrown by Idi Amin, the army officer he had used to attack the Kabaka in 1966. He went to exile in neighboring Tanzania, from where he made a bid to regain power in 1972 through a futile invasion. This led the Amin dictatorship to unleash a reign of terror. The economy began to decline precipitously, thanks in part to the expulsion of Ugandan Asians who had previously dominated the country's commercial and industrial sectors. Amin's regime collapsed in April 1979, under pressure from the Tanzanian army, which was retaliating to Amin's invasion of the Kagera salient in Tanzania. The Tanzanians were supported by a small force of Ugandan exiles. A two-year transition government headed by Yusufu Lule was established. But Lule's reign lasted for only sixty-eight days. He was then replaced by Godfrey Binaisa, who was overthrown by the military commission in May 1980. These years were characterized by growing insecurity. In December 1980 the commission arranged a controversial multi-party election, which resulted in the return to power of the UPC – with Obote as a president. Obote's second reign was dogged by the problems of economic reconstruction and political instability.

In 1981 Yoweri Museveni started to wage a guerrilla war. His victorious National Resistance Army (NRA) marched into Kampala in 1986 and seized power. Political party activities were suspended. The NRA government introduced what it called a "no-party" democracy – a movement system, based on popular committees. These introduced some innovations, like representatives of women and disabled people. National elections were held under the new system in 1996 and 2001, although the second was characterized by violence and the results contested in the Supreme Court. In the meantime economic growth resumed, and – although conflict continued in the north and the country became embroiled in the war in the DRC – peace had returned to much of the country by the beginning of the twenty-first century.

Further reading

Hansen, H.B. and Twaddle, M. (eds.) (1998) *Developing Uganda*, Kampala: Fountain Publishers.

Mamdani, M. (1976) *Politics and Class Formation in Uganda*, London: Monthly Review Press.

KAFUREEKA LAWYER
JOSEPHINE AHIKIRE

United Nations

The United Nations (UN) was founded on 24 October 1945. The original fifty-one founding members had grown to 189 states by the year 2000, making the UN the most universal of all international organizations. Its key principles include sovereign equality, non-intervention, non-aggression, and respect for the political independence and territorial integrity of member-states. The main purposes of the UN are:

- to maintain international peace and security,
- to develop friendly relations among states based

on equal rights and self-determination of peoples,
- to achieve solutions to social and economic problems, and
- to advance respect for **human rights**.

The order of priorities listed is not random, but reflects the priority accorded peace and security issues at the time the UN Charter was drafted – at the conclusion of the **Second World War**. Thus issues affecting international security have historically been accorded priority over other issues, such as socioeconomic development and human rights. However, since roughly the early 1990s and the end of the **Cold War**, attempts have been made to revisit these priorities. This has been reflected in the increased prominence accorded to humanitarian and other social issues, and issues arising from **environmental change** and development.

The UN is a highly complex multi-purpose organization. It can more accurately be seen as a system that provides a framework for decision-making and coordination among a number of constituent umbrella organs and a network of affiliated agencies, rather than as a single organization. It consists of six central organs that form the core of the UN system: the General Assembly, the Security Council, the Economic and Social Council (ECOSOC), the Trusteeship Council, the International Court of Justice (ICJ), and the Secretariat. The UN system also encompasses over thirty affiliated autonomous specialized agencies, as well as functional offices and commissions. These collectively address a wide range of international issues, and provide technical assistance and expertise to help solve international problems.

The General Assembly is the main deliberative body of the UN. Each member of the UN is represented in the General Assembly, each state has one vote, and each vote is of equal weight. The Security Council has the primary role in matters of international security. It has fifteen members, five of them permanent (China, France, Russia, the United Kingdom, and the United States), and ten rotating members who sit for two-year terms. Only the permanent members have the power to block – or veto – a resolution on substantive issues. Absent a veto, resolutions require an affirmative vote from nine members, and these resolutions are binding on all members of the UN. The ECOSOC is under the overall authority of the General Assembly, and coordinates UN economic and social activities. The Trusteeship Council was formed to assist former colonies, known as "trust territories," to achieve independence. The ICJ is the main judicial organ of the UN. The Secretariat carries out the administrative and substantive work of the other organs, and is headed by a Secretary-General who serves a five-year term.

In furtherance of the goal of maintaining peace and security, the UN has developed a number of strategies. These include enforcement measures (such as those taken against Iraq during and after the Persian Gulf War in 1991), various diplomatic peacemaking strategies, and peacekeeping operations. Newer strategies, including post-conflict peacebuilding, were added to the repertoire of UN peace operations in the 1990s. The UN has also served as a forum for the negotiation of a number of treaties and agreements on arms control and disarmament. The late 1980s and 1990s witnessed a dramatic expansion in the deployment of UN forces into various parts of the world to help bring about peaceful solutions to armed conflicts and provide humanitarian assistance. Its record of achievement has been mixed. Intervention by the UN was instrumental in bringing about peaceful settlements in the conflicts in **Mozambique** and **Namibia**, for example. There were also some dramatic setbacks, however: The UN was forced to withdraw from **Somalia** in 1995, and **genocide** was carried out in **Rwanda** in 1994, even though the UN had peacekeeping troops and observers in the country.

Although subordinated to the Security Council in matters of international security, the General Assembly, as the most representative organ in the UN, wields considerable influence. It has sponsored global conferences and multilateral treaties on a range of issues, and provides a forum for the articulation of what might be termed "world public opinion." Developing countries, in particular, have looked to the General Assembly as the main forum for agenda-setting and interest articulation. Arguably certain issues that have become major international concerns, such as poverty and underdevelopment, the **debt crises**, global environmental change, and the Acquired Immunity Deficiency Syndrome (AIDS) crisis, would not have achieved such prominence without the General Assembly. The General Assembly also provides a forum for collective legitimization and delegitimization. The series of resolutions on **South Africa** that resulted in apartheid being declared an international crime is an example of this process.

The UN has played a valuable role in international affairs. While some of the criticisms leveled against the organization are justified, many critics fail to realize that the UN is not an autonomous entity. Its jurisdiction is limited by its very principles – especially those on sovereign equality and non-intervention – and it relies on member-states for its operating budget, troop contributions for peacekeeping, and so on. In essence the UN can only be as effective as its member-states allow it to be. The fiftieth anniversary of the UN in October 1995 was an occasion for celebration of its achievements, and for reflection on its shortcomings and possible future directions. As the organization looks forward, a number of challenges remain. These include institutional reform, improving representation and democratic decision-making, and finding ways of accommodating the increased demands of an emerging global **civil society**.

Further reading

Report of the Commission on Global Governance (1995) *Our Global Neighborhood*, New York: Oxford University Press.

Weiss, T.G., Forsythe, D.P. and Coate, R.A. (1994) *The United Nations and Changing World Politics*, Boulder: Westview Press.

JAMES BUSUMTWI-SAM

urbanization

The process of urbanization is nothing new to Africa. Urban settlements first appeared on the continent more than 5,000 years ago. While these settlements developed in **North** and **West Africa**, important urban settlements were also flourishing along the eastern seaboard for trading activities. However, with few exceptions urbanization in **Southern Africa** is a relatively recent phenomenon, brought about by European colonization. In spite of the pre-colonial urban developments in Africa, only 5 percent of Africa's population at the end of the nineteenth century was living in urban areas.

Studies of African urbanization suffer from the tendency to encapsulate African cities under an all-encompassing rubric – "traditional," "pre-industrial," or "peripheral" – ignoring the enormous diversity of the processes and patterns of urbanization on the continent. Specifically there is a tendency to compare African urbanization unfavorably with European and North American urbanization; instead of being examined for what they are, African cities are depicted as pale replicas of cities in the developed world, lacking the latter's industrial base, social infrastructure, and other structural characteristics. Many studies of post-colonial urban policy tend to attribute Africa's rapid urbanization rather simplistically to urban bias, without carefully analyzing Africa's exceedingly complex politics, which is often mediated as much by class as by ethnicity, as much by region as by religion, by political as by economic forces, by national as by international dynamics, just to mention some of the salient factors. It is important that African cities be examined on their own terms, as both cause and consequence of the continent's specific trajectories of economic development, political struggles, demographic processes, social rhythms and imaginaries.

Twentieth-century urbanization in Africa is a tale of slow growth at first, then rapid expansion, marked by struggles between different value systems, priorities, and mechanisms embodied in modernist conceptions and structures of the city, and in the conflicting imaginations and needs of the ruling and popular classes, each seeking to shape urban space and social life in their own image. African cities greatly increased in number and size, and from 1940 to the end of the century Africa experienced the highest urban growth rate in the world, although it remained the least urbanized continent. In 1900 an estimated 1.5 million Africans, or 1 percent of the total population, lived in cities of 100,000 people and over. This had risen to 10 million in 1950 or 5.2 percent of the population, and 20 million and 8.1 percent of the population by 1960. By 1975 104 million Africans, or 25.2 percent of the population, lived in cities of all sizes, rising to 310 million and 37.3 percent of the population in 2000 (as compared to the world average 47.5 percent).

Patterns of urbanization were uneven across the continent. In 1970, for example, the urban population as a percentage of the total population was 30 percent for North Africa, 25 percent for Southern Africa, 14 percent for West Africa, 12 percent for **Central Africa**, and 8 percent for **East Africa**. By 2000, out of Africa's fifty-six countries and islands, less than 10 percent of the total population were in urban settlements in two countries (**Rwanda** 6.7 and **Burundi** 9), 10 to less than 20 percent for five countries (**Uganda** 14.2, **Ethiopia** 14.9, **Malawi** 15.6, **Eritrea** 19, **Niger** 19.2), 20 to less than 30 percent for seven countries (**Chad** 22.8, **Guinea-Bissau** 25.2, **Lesotho** 27, **Sudan** 27.3, **Somalia** 27.9, **Tanzania** 28.2, **Gambia** 29.9), 30 to less than 40 percent for fifteen countries (**Mali** 30.4, St. Helena 30.7, **Madagascar** 30.8, **Democratic Republic of Congo** 31, **Kenya** 31.8, **Botswana** 33.3, **Guinea** 33.6, **Togo** 33.7, **Benin** 33.9, **Comoros** 34, **Zimbabwe** 36, **Swaziland** 36.1, **Angola** 36.2, **Burkina Faso** 37.5, **Ghana** 39.2), 40 to less than 50 percent for thirteen countries (**Sierra Leone** 40.2, **Mozambique** 41.1, **Central African Republic** 41.6, **Mauritius** 41.7, **Namibia** 42.9, **Nigeria** 43.3, **Zambia** 44.7, **Senegal** 44.7, **Egypt** 46.4, **Côte d'Ivoire** 47, **Liberia** 48.1, **Equatorial Guinea** 48.4, **Cameroon** 49.3), 50 to less than 60 percent for eight countries (**São Tomé and Príncipe** 50.6, **Morocco** 50.9, **South Africa** 53.1, **Gabon** 53.8, **Seychelles** 58.9, **Mauritania** 59, **Algeria** 59.7, **Tunisia** 59.9), and over 60 percent for six countries (**Cape Verde** 62.6, Western Sahara 63.1, **Congo** 63.3, Reunion 71.2, **Djibouti** 84.3, **Libya** 88.4).

Colonial urbanization

Urbanization during the colonial period involved both the establishment of new colonial cities and the transformation/expansion of old indigenous cities. The new cities were located at seaports and along railroads, and at strategic points in the interior, as centers of commerce and administration. European powers viewed the African colonies as a source of raw materials and an outlet for exports of manufactured goods. Consequently the spatial structure of most African economies became strongly focused on a small number of port cities, where the newly established **transport** systems into the interior concentrated, and where migrants began to flock from the rural hinterlands.

Each colonial power brought its distinctive urban and architectural style to the colonies. Generally in all colonies the city center contained administrative and commercial buildings, and residential areas lay out of the city center. In all colonial cities the colonial officials and resident European population lived in the better part of the city, which would be provided with the available social services – water and sanitation, schools, clinics, and shops – while Africans lived in the poorer neighborhoods. Of course residential segregation was worse in the newer cities, especially those with large settler populations, such as South Africa, Zimbabwe, Angola, Mozambique, Kenya, and Algeria. The African neighborhoods, in turn, were often differentiated according to class and occupation. Some employers, such as the railways, police, army, and other public agencies, usually provided housing, while private-sector workers and those engaged in the informal sector lived in congested shantytowns.

Colonial cities grew largely as a result of rural–urban migration. Interestingly, at first Africans were reluctant to migrate to these cities, and for three main reasons. First, living conditions in the cities were generally poor. The new migrants lived in flimsy shacks with inadequate water and sanitation services, so that diseases were rampant and death rates high. For example, in Elisabethville (**Lubumbashi**) in the Belgian Congo, 240 out of every 1,000 migrants to the city died. Second, working conditions were also poor. Wages were quite low, so that migrants could not afford to bring their families. Indeed, in many colonies workers were not only paid "individual" rather than "family" wages, but labor stabilization was limited until after the **Second World War**. Third, transport costs to and from the cities were high, reflecting the low levels of wages and transport development, which forced many urban migrants to walk for days or even weeks. These conditions began to change after the Second World War, thanks to economic transformations, especially the establishment of import substitution industrialization and the expansion of the public sector (both of which required stabilized skilled and semi-skilled labor), as well as the struggles of African workers and city-dwellers themselves.

The spatial arrangement of land-uses and infrastructure in African cities during the colonial period varied depending on the city and the colonial power. In North Africa the colonial urban pattern was superimposed on age-old cities, so that the cities became divided into two main parts: the Westernized modern part and the indigenous old African quarter (known as the *medina*). In Algeria the French erased many of the earlier indigenous urban centers and built new towns for the influx of settlers. In other cases, such as Fes and Marrakesh in Morocco, the colonial authorities built new towns at a distance from the *medina*. These towns were built on the European model of a grid-iron street layout and wide roads. In Egypt the British built European forms onto the existing *medina* with new Western-style quarters for Europeans. The modernization of **Cairo**, which had begun in the nineteenth century, accelerated following the British occupation of 1882, when new British-style buildings were constructed for colonial administrators, British troops, and commercial companies. But it was not until the 1920s, following self-government in 1922, that Cairo entered its period of fastest growth – a pattern that was to be replicated across the continent after independence.

In West Africa colonial cities were either established in new locations or incorporated existing cities. In the old cities government offices, houses for Europeans, and commercial offices were built several kilometers away from the indigenous part of the city. While this was justified in terms of health and security, the main motive was racial segregation. Just like in North Africa the new central business districts of West African cities were laid out on a rectangular grid system. Examples of old cities include **Ibadan** and **Lagos**, both of which expanded rapidly as the colonial economy grew. The growth of Lagos was accelerated when it became the capital of Nigeria in 1914, and with the coming of modern transport which facilitated the physical expansion of the city, allowing residents (both rich and poor) to live further away from the island and commute to work. The cities that grew fastest included those that were chosen as ports, railway termini, or colonial capitals. Examples of such towns in West Africa include **Dakar**, **Accra**, and **Abidjan**.

Unlike North and West Africa, the leading cities of twentieth-century Southern Africa were introduced through colonialism. Many of Southern Africa's leading cities were founded as mining centers or to service the mining industry. **Johannesburg**, the region's largest city, was founded in 1884 following the discovery of massive gold reserves. In Zimbabwe **Harare** was established by colonists financed by the British South African Company looking for mineral riches. In Zambia the towns of Kitwe and Ndola were established due to the discovery of rich copper deposits. Within a decade of its founding Johannesburg boasted over 100,000 inhabitants, and had become South Africa's commercial and industrial hub, eclipsing the much older **Cape Town**. It also earned the distinction of being the country's most segregated city, in which African workers lived in crowded hostels or dusty townships. Residential racial segregation characterized the cities of the **migrant labor** economies of the entire Southern African region. Europeans, Asians, and Africans lived in separate parts of the city, thanks to racist housing policies and massive income disparities between the different racial groups. The poorly paid, mostly male, workers could only afford to live in either the purpose-built and tightly regulated high-density residential areas or in shantytowns or unplanned housing areas on the outskirts of the cities.

The pattern in East Africa was a mixture of the West African and Southern African patterns. Old cities existed, principally **Mombasa**, where a colonial urban pattern was gradually but incompletely imposed. In contrast **Nairobi**, which started as the headquarters of the Uganda Railway, developed as the quintessential colonial settler city, whose rapid expansion was assured when it became Kenya's capital in 1908, and as a transportation and commercial center for the burgeoning settler economy and the neighboring landlocked countries of East Africa. **Dar es Salaam** combined elements of Nairobi and Mombasa, in that its founding preceded European colonial rule, but it was not as old as Mombasa. Having been founded only in the 1860s, Dar es Salaam owed its importance to its status as the colonial capital and transportation and commercial center for Tanzania and the landlocked countries in the interior.

Urbanization after independence

After independence Africa's urbanization accelerated. A number of reasons have been given to explain the extremely rapid rate of urbanization. Among the so-called "pull factors" is the fact that conditions generally improved in the immediate post-independence years. Employment opportunities increased as African governments embarked on development based on secondary industries and public-sector expansion. Urban wages rose, either in absolute terms or at least relative to rural incomes. Transportation systems also improved or became cheaper, making cities more accessible, which was further facilitated by the removal of restrictions against Africans entering and residing in cities, especially in former settler colonies that had been obsessed with influx control. There were also several "push factors." Deteriorating conditions in rural areas forced landless people or the educated **youth** to migrate to the cities to share in the fruits of *uhuru* (independence). Finally new cities were built. In Malawi, for example, Lilongwe – which at the time of independence was a small trading outpost – became the fastest growing city in the country once it was made the capital city in the 1970s. Similarly Dodoma in Tanzania, Abuja in Nigeria, and **Gaborone** in Botswana grew as new capital cities.

The spatial and social structure of African cities changed considerably as race increasingly gave way to class as a marker of residential segregation, and as the gender demographic imbalance of the colonial era disappeared: More women moved to the cities, and the cities became more welcoming to **families**. Also the architectural landscape of African cities changed noticeably, as skyscrapers mushroomed in the central business districts – housing the offices of government ministries, commercial and industrial companies (both local and transnational), hotels, conference centers, and **non-governmental organizations** – and as the symbols of nationhood and city life proliferated – stadiums, hospitals, schools, universities, and luxury suburbs for the growing middle classes. But Africa's rapid urbanization made it difficult to provide sufficient social services. In many cities housing became scarce, sanitation and utilities were inadequate, and schools were in short supply. Also health services were poor, streets were congested, and recreational facilities limited. Above all unemployment rose. In short many African cities became highly inequitable and socially and environmentally unsustainable.

From the 1980s many African economies entered a period of severe economic crisis. Attempts at economic recovery mainly took the form of reform programs fashioned by the World Bank and the International Monetary Fund. However, instead of economic rejuvenation, the result was more economic retrogression as deregulation, currency devaluations, and privatization imposed by **structural adjustment programs** (SAPs) led to massive retrenchment, thereby swelling the already bloated ranks of the unemployed. This propelled the growth of the so-called "informal sector," which soon became the main employer in many African cities. Throughout Africa informal-sector jobs are estimated to have grown by 6.7 percent per annum between 1980 and 1989, employing more than 60 percent of the workforce in African cities in 1990. In many informal-sector surveys selling goods or services was found to be the single most important survival mechanism, and a significant proportion of households in all income categories reported that for at least a portion of the year they were obliged to undertake some form of petty trading in order to make ends meet.

The implementation of SAPs affected African cities in complex and contradictory ways. When combined with declining real wages, the economic crisis worsened by the SAPs made city life quite harsh for many workers – and even for elements of the increasingly pauperized middle classes. The growth of the informal sector reflected the temporal–spatial dispersal of work and income-generation activities. To meet the challenges they faced, working people in the cities began to change their places and times of work; they diversified their range of remunerative occupations and locations in order to reproduce themselves; they were, in short, seeking to restructure the temporal geography of work, the places of production, and the production of places. The apparent disruption of the established rhythms and places of remunerative work, represented materially and visually by the increasing intermingling of previously separated urban architectural and functional spaces and forms, created the sense of disorder that fueled the inflationary discourse of informalization and the dread among the local and visiting elites that the boundaries of social and spatial modernity were dissolving. Informalization of the economy was seen in the invasion of central business districts by informal-sector traders. Parts of central Johannesburg increasingly began to look like Lagos and Cairo, with their armies of street hawkers. By 2000 those three cities were among the largest in Africa, with estimated populations of 2.2 million, 13.5 million, and 10.7 million respectively. Other large cities included **Kinshasa**, with more than 5 million; **Algiers**, with more than 4 million; and **Casablanca**, **Maputo**, Cape Town, and **Khartoum**, each with more than 3 million people. Altogether there were about three dozen cities with more than 1 million inhabitants.

The 1980s and 1990s also saw an increase in more negative aspects of the informal economy, such as smuggling, black marketeering, and prostitution. Crime and violence by unemployed youths in urban areas were also on the increase. It has been argued that the rise in prostitution and poverty, combined with deteriorating health facilities, compounded by the effects of structural adjustment, facilitated the spread of HIV/AIDS. Data from Malawian urban centers, for example, indicate that Malawian cities were among the hardest hit by the AIDS epidemic. However, in spite of the darker side of the informal economy in the African city, the contribution of informal and small-scale enterprises should not be underestimated. Informal activities provided a major coping mechanism in a world of economic turbulence for the majority of urban residents throughout Africa. The side of the informal sector that consists of talented and creative individuals who make worthwhile contributions to the urban economy – artisans, basket-weavers, tinsmiths, tailors, and vendors – seems to far outweigh the image of the informal sector as a reservoir of people who engage in social vices and criminal activity. More importantly it needs to be emphasized that the rapid growth of the informal sector, for good or for bad, was a direct result of the SAPs.

Other coping mechanisms in response to urban hardship included farming, which increased in many cities, leading to the ruralization of urban spaces and the dissolution of some of the sharp urban/rural dichotomies. All these changes and challenges facilitated the continuous remapping of urban cultural spaces, as is evident, for example, in the spatial reorganization of popular culture and leisure activities, which increasingly moved from the posh city centers to residential neighborhoods. Migration was another coping strategy. Patterns of migration became more complex than ever: rural–urban, rural–rural, urban–rural, urban–urban, and international. There are indications that in such countries as Nigeria, Ghana, Tanzania, Uganda, and Zambia, the rates of rural–urban migration declined noticeably. In the meantime some studies showed that urbanization was also becoming more diversified, as migrations to smaller towns increased as they became popular places of retirement for those fleeing the large and expensive primate cities.

Governance of African cities

The changing economic structures and infrastructures in African cities resulted in heated debates about urban governance. The pre-colonial systems of urban governance were largely discarded or replaced by colonial governments, who introduced more bureaucratized forms. For example, in the development of cities under British rule the growth of an urban settlement was usually accompanied by the introduction of a police station, prison, post office, and the resident's office. The resident was the person responsible for the day-to-day administration of the settlement. His – they were mostly men – tasks were multiple: he would serve as judge, tax collector, administrator, and so on. Later the urban settlement might be raised to that of a sanitary area, since the presence of a Sanitary Board was synonymous with a town council. The chairman of this board was the resident, and soon his title was changed to that of district commissioner. This board was responsible for public health, planning, and raising of revenue for the development of the *boma* (that is, the district headquarters). Soon the district headquarters might have a telegraph line connected to it from some other major settlement. Roads and other infrastructure might be planned and developed to suit colonial and racial planning traditions. As noted earlier, in most colonial settings physical space was invariably used to promote the separation of social space. Right at their inception, cities were divided into sectors: one part would be for the natives; another would be for the residences of the district commissioner, his fellow colonial officers, and other Europeans; yet another section might be reserved for other races, such as Asians in Southern and East Africa, or Lebanese in West Africa.

Colonial town councils or boards often consisted of nominated members or members elected on restricted franchise, mostly confined to the resident European population, although sometimes including members of the propertied and educated local elite. They had powers with regard to public health and planning, and some limited revenue-collection powers. As the colonial cities grew, city governance evolved with the introduction of mayors and city councils with broader powers. Soon after independence, city governance became more democratic as officers (councilors) in the city government were subject to periodic elections based on the city wards or councils they represented. The mayor, also elected, became the executive officer of city government. Very large cities began to see a more decentralized form of government, by which the mayor controlled the metropolitan local government, while the metropolitan area itself was sometimes divided into several local councils with their own smaller governments.

Democratic city governance generally disappeared as national politics became more authoritarian in many countries. By the same token the democratization of national politics in the 1990s affected city governance. Indeed it was from the cities that struggles for democratization, which engulfed Africa from the 1980s, emanated. One major city after another was rocked by civil disturbances as urban **civil society** began flexing its muscles to challenge the authoritarian and corrupt municipal and national governments, demanding popular participation, transparency, and accountability. There were, of course, noticeable national and regional differences in the ways in which the urban social movements and struggles manifested themselves. In the predominantly Muslim societies of North Africa, Islam provided an important institutional and ideological framework for civil associations. Islamic groups, or organizations influenced by them, began to challenge autocratic rule as the developmentalist capacities and ambitions of the state were curtailed by SAPs. The struggle between the state, Islamic movements, and secular forces turned into deadly violence in Algeria following the cancellation of the 1992 elections. In Southern Africa urban politics was driven by the need to deracialize the colonial spatial order and political economy, and realize the popular democratic and developmentalist dreams of the national liberation struggle. Particularly impressive were the South Africa urban-based social movements, which helped spearhead the transition not only to a new democratic national order, but also new structures of urban governance, which emerged out of hundreds of local negotiating forums. From these developed new urban local governments that were more integrated, inclusive, participatory, and accountable than any the country had ever known.

By the end of the 1990s the political map of Africa had changed significantly as democratization spread. In many of Africa's cities there emerged what some have called "a multiplicity of governance regimes," in which local community organizations brought about a new political culture, recognizing the plurality of actors in urban management. The growth of new forms of urban management of the city, often despite the state, reflected the renewal of the social infrastructure of civil society beneath the decaying signs of physical infrastructure. This reflected, it could be argued, a fundamental shift in the public imagination of the city and the closure of previous exit options. The city had become a place hundreds of millions of Africans called "home," a place that was worth struggling for. And so they sought to reinvent it, to reshape its signs, spaces, symbols, and social structures, to make them work for them.

See also: architecture; leisure; state: colonial; state: post-independence

Further reading

Anderson, D.M. and Rathbone, R. (eds.) (1999) *Africa's Urban Past*, Oxford: James Currey.

Baker, J. and Aina, T.A. (eds.) (1997) *The Migration Experience*, Uppsala: Nordiska Afrikainstitutet.

David, S. (1992) *Cities, Capital and Development: African Cities in the World Economy*, London: Belhaven Press.

Drakakis-Smith, D. (ed.) (1992) *Urban and Regional Change in Southern Africa*, London: Routledge.

Fay, M. and Opal, C. (2000) *Urbanization Without Growth: A Not So Uncommon Phenomenon*, Washington, D.C.: World Bank.

Grove, A.T. (1994) *The Changing Geography of Africa*, Oxford: Oxford University Press.

Kalipeni, E. and Zeleza, P.T. (eds.) (1999) *Sacred Spaces and Public Quarrels: African Cultural and Economic Landscapes*, Trenton: Africa World Press Inc.

Swilling, M. (ed.) (1997) *Governing Africa's Cities*, Johannesburg: Witwatersand University Press.

EZEKIEL KALIPENI
PAUL TIYAMBE ZELEZA

V

visual arts

This history of visual art in Africa (incorporating painting, sculpture, drawing, printmaking, ceramics, and weaving) attempts to outline the central sociopolitical aspirations of artists and creative producers, as well as the political philosophy and social realities of nations, as these changed across the decades. The key historical events and processes of the twentieth century have all played important roles in shaping the form and character of Africa's visual arts, including (but not limited to) colonization, the development of **nationalist movements**, and liberation; the two world wars; post-independence conflict; **structural adjustment programs**; and **globalization**. At the dawn of the twenty-first century Africa had maintained its rich array of age-old artistic traditions: ivory-carving, gold smithing, mural painting, wood sculpture, soap-stone sculpture, mosaics, textiles, leatherworking, bead-making, illuminated manuscripts, calligraphy, and **architecture**.

1890–1920: Resistance and colonization

From 1890 to the end of the Second World War local and regional art traditions in Africa were increasingly disrupted by the explosion of campaigns of colonial conquest and stiff African resistance, during which some of the major historic centers of African art – notably Asante and **Benin** – were destroyed and works of art looted or destroyed. In many regions art production was disrupted as locals were pressed into forced or **migrant labor**, or put under heavy taxation burdens, to build the colonial economy (see **economy: colonial**). These events resulted in, first, the disruption of the traditional apprenticeship system that was crucial for the training of sculptors, weavers, muralists, potters, and carvers; and, second, the impoverishment of the traditional class of patrons of art and crafts, which led to a drop in art commissions due to their limited financial resources.

Nevertheless art production and training continued, even in places that had been burnt to the ground. By 1901 in Osi, western **Nigeria**, Areògun had just completed his sixteen-year sculpting apprenticeship with master-sculptor Bamgbose of Osi, while in **Lagos** Aina Onabolu had just concluded a favorably received first exhibition of drawings, including still lifes, landscapes, and portraits produced in a naturalistic style. In **Cairo** the first generation of Egyptian artists graduated from the School of Fine Arts in 1911. Astute master-artists/craftspeople in other cities and towns recognized the potential of the new colonial economy, and restructured their operations to produce "antiquities" for undiscriminating foreigners or commissioned works for an emerging class of patrons (missionaries and colonial officials, educated Africans, and affluent local merchants). This restructuring resulted in two paths for the production of visual art. The first was dominated by wood- and ivory-carvers, potters, leatherworkers, and painters of illustrated manuscripts, all of whom had acquired their skills through the traditional apprenticeship system and continued to produce highly skilled indigenous art. The second path was taken by those who produced works in the styles and modes of Western art, and broke down into those who were self-taught and those who attended modern art schools.

1920–40: Traditional arts revival and realism as a political tool

By 1920 most of Africa was effectively under colonial rule. In **Morocco** and **Algeria** the French pursued a policy of segregation, by which Moroccans and Algerians were restricted to the old *medinas* (walled cities), while European communities lived in the *villes nouvelles* (or colonial settlements). This spatial division was carried over to the arts by means of an educational policy that discouraged Moroccan and Algerian students from studying modern art and restricted them to the indigenous arts of leatherwork, carpet-weaving, embroidery, pottery, metal and brass smithing, sculpting in wood and stone, ceramics, and tile-making. By contrast, in the British colonies the task of fostering and promoting traditional arts was left to local initiative. In **Kumasi**, with the incorporation of the traditional rulers into the colonial administrative system of "indirect rule," the new Asantehene had to replace all the insignias of office that had been looted after the sacking of Kumasi. This replacement and the attendant resumption of traditional rites and festivals returned the office of the Asantehene to its role as the grand patron of the arts. The same happened in Benin, following the appointment of Oba Eweka II after the death in exile of Oba Ovonramwen. Again the restoration of the Benin cultural calendar of rituals, events, and political personages became the catalytic force for the revival and expansion of traditional arts. It was these local conditions much more than the art workshop experiments of Christian missions that led to the resurgence of wood- and ivory-carving, bronze-making, textile-weaving, and coral- and beadwork in different British colonies.

Local support for art remained strong until the onset of the **Great Depression** in 1929. In 1920 Onabolu held a solo exhibition of 200 works to show the public:

> some of the pictures he had been able to paint without the aid of an Art master, and thereby prove that God is impartial in his endowment of various talents to mankind.
>
> (quoted in Agoro 1980: 9)

In the major cities, such as Lagos, **Johannesburg**, and **Accra**, workers and the educated elite were the primary audience for photographers and artists. The financial anxiety created by the ailing economy and inflation, as well as pay freezes and pay cuts, gradually caused salaried workers to spend less on art. Interestingly this period also witnessed the emergence of a new generation of artists utilizing Western artistic tools for their creative aspiration. In Nigeria there were sculptors J.D. Akeredolu, Areògun and Idia Ovia; in **Ethiopia** they included Gebre Selassie Adil, Araya Dawit, Abebe Wolde Giorgis, and Wolde Medhin Yitagesu; in **Egypt** there were Hafez El-Raay, Hassan Hishmat, Saad El-Khadem and his wife Effat Nagui, Ahmed Sabri, and Yousif Kamil; from **Tunisia** there were Yahia Turki and Aly ben Salem; and from **South Africa** the painters Gerard Bhengu, John Mohl, Ernest Mancoba, Gerard Sekoto, and George Pemba, and the sculptors Hezekiel Ntuli and Samuel Makoanyane. Initially many of these artists were self-taught, but later they received training in art schools. By contrast quite a number of Ethiopian artists received their training as apprentices to the painters of illuminated manuscripts. Because Egypt already had a fine arts school in Cairo, some of the artists received their training there before traveling to Europe for further study.

This generation of modern African artists produced their work in the context of the ongoing colonial project. They encountered and were forced to deal with the arrogance and racism of white colonial officials, so those who depended on their works for a livelihood had to be strategic. For their European audience they produced the kind of works they knew this audience wanted to see. But they also produced the kind of works that centered their sense of their own humanity and gave dignity and emotional depth to their lives and environment. Middle-class African professionals in Sophiatown and Soweto purchased such paintings by Mohl, Sekoto and Mancoba in the pre-apartheid era of the 1930s. The same was the case with Onabolu in Nigeria, and Yitagesu in Ethiopia. Even when these artists seemed to be producing only for the tourist market, one cannot simply assume that they had lost their integrity. Consider Makoanyane, who has been much denigrated for mass-producing clay images of his grandfather, a warrior under Chief Moshesh. Even he exacted revenge on his exploiters. Through his clay figure, Makoanyane had quietly and smoothly forced his white collectors, including a number of art institutions, to participate in the commemoration and preservation of the memory of his grandfather, as well as of the history of the nation that their forebears had despoiled.

Artists found ways to refocus the primitivizing lens of Europe in their paintings, drawings, sculptures, and mosaics. Some of the watercolors of Selassie Adil, Dawit, Giorgis, and Yitagesu directly challenged the narratives of European colonial officials and adventurers that represented Africans as savages. They painted everyday market scenes, potters at work, dignified portraits, and epic events like the dramatic Ethiopian defeat of the Italians at the Battle of Adwa. Although this caliber of artist engaged in the dignified portrayal of African life and customs, folklore, motifs, and landscape, they also depicted the barbarism of colonial rule. For example, in the 1930s Tunisian artist Hatem El-Mekki created a series of large, powerful paintings that indicted the French for their massacre of the inhabitants of Sakiet Sifi Youssef. Egyptian artists, Youssef Kamel and Hosni al-Banany painted figurative scenes of medieval Cairo that implicitly offered that culture as an alternative to the growing Europeanization of Egyptian culture. Another group of Egyptian artists, best represented by Ezzat Mostafa, painted themes of working-class life, while Hishmat liberated his art by molding his statutes from the clay of Egyptian soil.

Artists also responded to continental political events of the day. One event that captured people's imagination was the 1935 fascist Italian occupation of Ethiopia, a country that was then seen as the symbol of African independence, given that it had by itself successfully defeated a European colonial power. In the arts, therefore, Ethiopianism fostered a Pan-African spirit of self-empowerment and self-rule, which manifested itself locally as Negritude in **francophone Africa**, as African Personality in **anglophone Africa**, and as Arabism in **North Africa**. Dreams about Ethiopia's liberation inspired visual artists to confidently celebrate and draw inspiration from their various cultural heritages, and to let their paintings, sculptures, and drawings become a metaphor for cultural and political freedom.

1940–60: Anti-colonialism through Negritude and Arabism

To try to locate African visual art within an explanatory frame that ignores the larger political and economic conditions of history and its production misses the full significance of that history. In North Africa Arabism provided the basis of anti-colonial resistance. This vision was fundamentally secular, based as it was on national identity rather than on religion. Not necessarily looking to the Koran, Moroccan, Tunisian, and some Egyptian artists used their local visual heritages of decorative design to unleash intense creativity. The choice of abstraction as an artistic style propelled them to develop deeper organic ties to different artistic heritages and to the masses whose artistic schemes were largely non-figurative. In Morocco Ahmed Louardighi and Labiad Miloud, gardeners-turned-artists, depicted themes drawn from folk tales, from local carpets and tiles, and from the bloody events they witnessed in the 1950s as a result of the struggle for independence. In Egypt, Abd al-Hadi al-Gazzar, Ahmed El-Rashidi, and Sherifa Fathy drew critically from diverse aspects of the local tradition, focusing on the aesthetic appeal of Arabic calligraphy, sometimes endlessly reproducing the single word "Allah" in Arabic as a kind of invocation. Inji Eflatoun, a notable woman artist, strove to free modern Egyptian art from the then prevailing bonds of academicism and formalism. From the 1950s onwards Omar al-Nagdy and Saleh Reda borrowed decorative elements from the older folk-art tradition of *mashrabiyyas*, as well as from stained-glass designs, color, arabesque woodwork, inscriptions, and popular symbols, to enrich their modern visions.

Because of colonialism's continental scope the nationalist liberation struggle fostered a sense of oneness as Africans. Although they each had their own style, personality, and preferred media, artists in all the regions engaged in anti-colonial critiques through their paintings and sculptures. They were often inspired by the speeches of nationalist leaders and intellectuals. As Nigerian artist Benedict Enwonwu put it years later:

> If we painted any picture it was about this freedom. If we sang a song, if like Senghor we wrote or recited poems, we philosophized.
>
> (private conversation, July 1989)

The urge to be independent and free opened the artists' creative imagination, as demonstrated by their use of styles ranging from realism to abstraction. The Senegalese artist Papa Ibra Tall created scintillating abstract tapestries, while in Tunisia Abdelaziz Gorgi produced spectacular clay-tile murals. Senegalese painter Iba N'Diaye, Nigerian sculptors Enwonwu and Felix Idubor, and South African painters Gerard Sekoto, Mohl and Mancoba also produced powerful works; while sculptors Vincent Kofi and Kofi Antubam of **Ghana** produced pieces of art that recalled the boisterous forms of Asante carving.

Nationalist impulses intensified in the 1950s. On their return to Ethiopia and **Sudan** in the late 1950s after training abroad, Gebre Kirstos Desta, Alexander (Skunder) Boghossian, Afewerk Tekle, Lemma Guya, El-Salahi, Amir Nour, and Ahmed Shibrain sought to reconfigure their art in line with local aesthetics, without sacrificing their artistic independence. El-Salahi and Shibrain's early efforts were limited to decorative versions of Koranic verses. But as they mastered the design element of calligraphy, these transformed and evolved into spectacular forms. The Arabic letters began to sprout forms, sometimes figurative shapes that gradually took on a life of their own. Skillfully blending their political goals and creative objectives, they also ensured that their works avoided becoming mere political propaganda.

European colonial administrations tended to view art as a waste of time, and hence did very little to encourage and fund it. Consequently most of the art schools were built as the result of individual initiative and pressure. Upon his return to Nigeria in 1921 after a sojourn in London and Paris, Onabolu relentlessly pressurized the colonial government to include art class in the educational curricula of secondary schools. In **Uganda** in 1936 Margaret Trowell, a British artist and the wife of the Surgeon-General, founded a school that later became the basis of the School of Fine Arts at Makerere University College. In the 1940s and early 1950s two French artists arrived in the Congo – adventurer Pierre Roman-Defossés in **Brazzaville** in 1944 and Pierre Lods in Leopoldville in 1951 – and set up informal art workshops. Both workshops placed less emphasis on technical training than on expressiveness. Products of the school – Pili Pili, Ilunga, N'Kula, Bela, Mwenze, Paul Elenga, René Bokoko, and Raphael Movnkala – gained international attention because their "exotic" expressive paintings and sculptures were marketed as authentic "African" styles, even though there was nothing authentic or indigenously African about them.

The Polly Street Art workshop was built on similar model. David Koloane recalls that black South African artists were instructed to create in a primitive, untutored way. They were discouraged from pursuing academic training on the pretext that it would spoil their "essence." In the 1960s Ulli Beier and Suzanne Wenger repeated a similar art experiment in Oshogbo in Nigeria, while Frank McEwen did so in **Zimbabwe**. Beier and Wenger encouraged their students – Twin Seven Seven, Adebisi Fabunmi, Jacob Afolabi, Jimoh Burimoh, Asiru Olatunde, and Rufus Ogundele – to draw in an untutored manner and deliberately misspell words, as illiteracy and primitiveness were the essence of being African. Proponents of this view still constituted a formidable force as late as the 1990s; internationally they controlled the definition and representation of African art.

While some Europeans interested in Africa art were engaged in presenting a primitive view of modern African art, African intellectuals and academically trained artists did their best to combat the misrepresentation. They tried to preserve the highest standards for art, launching various initiatives to support artists in their craft. Between 1940 and 1955 Seth Cudjoe – a doctor, painter, and sculptor – founded the West African Arts Club in London for African artists studying in the city. In 1955 doctor-artist Oku Ampofo and a group of Ghanaian artists founded the Akwapim Six; in 1960 Mohl and a group of black South African artists founded the Artists' Market Association; and in 1978 another organization, the Federated Union of Black Artists (FUBA), was formed. The number of art organizations, associations, and networks increased from the late 1950s with the establishment of art schools and departments of Fine Arts in university colleges in Sudan, Ghana, Nigeria, Ethiopia, and Uganda. The objective of these national associations was not only to encourage artists to achieve their goals, but also to create a community of culturally connected artists who would be able to discuss relevant issues about art, creativity, and aesthetics.

1960–80: Independence, identity, and indigenization

Independence had an important effect on visual art in Africa. Many artists who had deployed their energy and imagination in the liberation struggle relaxed their guard, expanding the range of their vision and beginning to explore more personal questions of identity. Between the 1960s and 1970s a whole new generation of artists swiftly emerged, many the products of university fine art schools. They were well trained, technically proficient, and articulate. Contemporary and modern African art entered an exciting period of experimentation, with artists such as Ladi Kwali, Erhabor Emokpae, Okpu Eze, Afi Ekong, Demas Nwoko, Bruce Onobrakpeya, Yusuf Grillo, Uche Okeke, Lamidi Fakeye, and Twin Seven Seven (from Nigeria); El-Salahi, Shibrain, Musa Khalifa, Nour, Mohamed Bushara, Kamala Ibrahim Ishag, Mohamed Omer Khalif, Ahmed El-Rashidi, and Sherifa Fathy (from Sudan); Ali Derwish, Elias Jengo, Fatma Abdullah Abubakar, and Selby Mvusi (from **Tanzania**); Valente Malagatanga and Bertina Lopez (from **Mozambique**); Rosemary Karuga (from Uganda); Desta Boghossian, Afewerk Tekle, Desta Hages Tekele, Aynalem Gebre-Mariam Antal, and Almaz Selelene Tesfa-Yohannes (from Ethiopia); Grace Salome Kwami, E. Owusu Dartey, F.A. Gyamp, John Osei Okyere, Oku Ampofo, the Akwapim Six, Amon Kotei, and Ato Delaquis (from Ghana); and El-Hadji Sy, Souleymane Keita, and Issa Samb (from **Senegal**).

Farid Belkahia, Mohamed Melihi, Toni Maraini, and Mohamed Chabaa returned to Morocco in the early 1960s after completing their studies in Europe and the United States and formed what became known as the "Casablanca Group." They initiated a set of discourses and practices designed to draw public attention to the richness of the local visual heritage, and thereby to "decolonize" Moroccan art. What interested the group was the variety of decorative motifs found in the crafts, the surfaces of which richly combined graphic and painterly elements. They decided to investigate and employ their local artistic heritage, including media such as henna, saffron, and leather. They focused on traditional local arabesque designs as the complex elaboration of an unfolding conception of time, space, and movement.

In Sudan, partly as a reaction to the towering presence of El-Salahi and partly in protest against the pressure to conform to a non-figurative style, some young radical Muslim artists (such as Mohamed Bushara) riled conservative elements in society by choosing the representational path. Bushara freely used human figures, arguing that "a work should stand for itself" ("Bushara at the Slade" 1979: 40). However, the human figures he used were stretched out of proportion and, indeed, out of recognition. Kamala Ishag also intervened in the Sudanese art world, charting a new direction with a group known as the "Crystalist School." Ishag's ideas were drawn from the rites, rituals, and ceremonies of Zar, a spirit possession cult practiced by women. The group engaged in a spiritual investigation of the meaning of life – in the process they produced works that have a haunting mystical quality.

Senegal, under Senghor, embarked on an ambitious project to create a continental forum in which African visual artists, writers, and performers could showcase their art. In 1966 Senegal hosted the first Festival Mondial des Arts Nègres, a Pan-African celebration of art that brought together artists, critics, scholars, and patrons from throughout Africa, Europe, and the diaspora. In

1969 Algeria hosted the first Festival Culturel Panafricain; in 1973 **Kinshasa** was host to the Congrès Extraordinaire de l'Association des Internationals Critiques d'Art (AICA); and in 1977 Nigeria hosted the second Black Festival of Arts and Culture, a cultural extravaganza known as FESTAC. After that numerous other art initiatives, congresses, biennial shows, and festivals were launched in different countries in Africa. These included Panafest in Ghana, DAK'ART in Senegal, and the first and second Johannesburg Bienniales in South Africa.

In 1967–70 Nigeria's eruption in bloody civil war affected the production of art. The artists on the Biafran side, many of whom worked in the directorate of information, deployed their skills in sensitizing the world to the tragic loss of human lives in the region, curating photographic and art exhibitions that traveled to different cities across the world. Between 1971 and 1985 Uganda entered its own turbulent period, first under the dictatorial rule of Idi Amin and then, for a second time, under the leadership of Milton Obote. The incalculable loss of human life that occurred under both regimes had a negative effect on the arts. In 1974 Ethiopia also followed this tragic path, with a revolution against the monarchy installing the brutal regime of the Derge, who unleashed a range of policies and programs that resulted in an unprecedented exodus of Ethiopians from the country. Artists who remained found severe constraints placed on their civil liberties and creative independence. Sudan did not escape this instability either; its internal political paralysis and war between the north and the south created severe security problems that led to the dispersal of its artists.

The issue of women artists in Africa is a problem that many claim to be concerned about, but few are seriously interested in solving. Although each decade had its share of women artists, most male art historians and critics proved reluctant to acknowledge their presence and document their works. Rather they were quickly passed over by curators, critics, and writers who either believed that their works lacked intrinsic merit or that they did not satisfy some vague standard of (male) professionalism. Owing to the prevalent gender bias in the field, few women artists were documented or celebrated in the literature. Nevertheless the following is a short list of women artists who came to attention prior the end of the 1970s: Inji Eflatoun, Effat Nagui, Grace Kwami, Lucy Akinwale, Sherifa Fathy, Afi Ekong, Clara Ugbogada-Ngu, Ladi Kwali, Bertina Lopez, Kamala Ishag, Rosemary Karuga, Theresa Musoke, Fatma Abubakar, Desta Hages Tekele, Aynalem Gebre-Mariam Antal, Almaz Selelene Tesfa-Yohannes, Gladys Mgudlandlu, Allina Ndebele, Dinah Molefe, Elizabeth Mbatha, Helen Sebedi, and Bongiwe Dhlomo. Through their work these women collectively challenged the masculinization of African art and culture. However, the social difficulties they faced in their professional careers cannot be overemphasized. They had to balance family obligations and hold down regular jobs while pursuing their artistic careers, often with minimal support from their spouses. Three women who did a lot to give African women artist international visibility during the last decades of the twentieth century were sculptor Sokari Douglas Camp, *adiré* (batik and quilts) artist Nike Davis Okundaye, and potter Magdalene Odondo.

1980–2000: Neo-colonialism, structural adjustment programs, and globalization

The last two decades of the twentieth century produced immense changes in the visual arts landscape. With the end of settler colonialism in **Southern Africa**, South African artists could begin to freely interact with their peers in other regions of Africa. Most importantly they could participate in continent-wide art festivals and competitions. Prior to the Soweto Uprising, South African art was represented by the township art that emerged in the 1950s and 1980s, and subsequently metamorphosed into workshop schools (among which Thupelo gained international attention). The protests, funeral services, and marches found powerful visual expression in the art produced by township art workshops, a throwback to the Polly Street Art Center. Artists such as Lucas Sithole, Louis Maquebela, Ben Macala, Solomon Sedibane, Dumile Feni, Helen Sebedi, Bonigwe Dhlomo, and Dumisani Mabaso used art to document and tell the complex story of the atrocities and violence of the state, the Sharpeville Massacre, the Bantustan forced evictions, the pass laws, the infamous township police, and the South African Defence Force.

By the mid-1980s the imposition of **structural adjustment programs** had particularly chilling effect on art production. As economies collapsed, art materials became unaffordable, and artists strove to redefine their relevance to their communities. Improvisation became the basis for survival. In the early part of the 1990s in Senegal a popular art and social movement emerged known as "Set Setal" (which means "to make clean" or "to make proper"). Though the goal of the movement was to clean up **Dakar**, proponents used street art and murals to beautify the city. This anti-establishment movement attracted disenfranchised members of society who were galvanized to paint hundreds of murals on Dakar streets, some of which contained public health messages or portraits of local religious leaders, nationalist heroes (such as Lat Dior, who had fiercely resisted the French), and international figures (such as Nelson Mandela and Mohammed Ali). Under the leadership of Issa Samb and El-Hadji Sy, the movement became a forum for providing materials and technical advice to the Senegalese **youth**, while artists produced public artworks that reflected Senghor's cultural politics.

In the last decade of the twentieth century African art underwent further dramatic changes as economically depressed and war-torn regions slowly returned to normality.

Reference and further reading

Agoro, O.O. (1980) "Aina Onabolu: Pioneer of Modern Nigerian Art Tradition," B.A. thesis, University of Nigeria, Nsukka, June 1980.

Ali, W. (ed.) (1990) *Contemporary Art from the Islamic World*, Northampton: Interlink Publishing Group.

Brown, E. (1966) *Africa's Contemporary Art and Artists*, New York: Division of Social Research and Experimentation, Harmon Foundation Inc.

"Bushara at the Slade" (1979) *African Arts* 12, 3: 40.

Deliss, C. (1995) *Seven Stories about Modern Art in Africa*, London: Whitechapel Art Gallery.

Karnouk, L. (1988) *Modern Egyptian Art: The Emergence of a National Style*, Cairo: American University in Cairo Press.

Mount, M. (1973) *African Art: The Years Since 1920*, Bloomington: Indiana University Press.

Nzegwu, N. (ed.) (1998) *Issues in Contemporary African Art*, Binghamton: International Society for the Study of Africa.

NKIRU NZEGWU

West Africa

In *Contemporary West African States* (1989), O'Brien, Dunn, and Rathborne insisted on several critical issues for the understanding of West Africa, ranging from the nature of the state to its imperfections and limitations during the first decade of independence. They go on to indicate that at the end of that period the question of the decadence of West African society and of "the difficult survival of the state" arises. According to them, the new situation was provoked by a corrupted public service, bad governance, and a total incapacity among the ruling class to manage social conflicts. The consequences of these combined factors provoked institutional disintegration, and permanent economic and political destabilization. Despite this situation – and the political, economic and institutional deviations that accompanied it – they consider that the West African states "without exception" continue on their paths towards stabilization. Their greatest success during these years was to escape from the most dramatic forms of political disintegration, as were observed in countries such as **Uganda**, **Sudan**, Zaire, and **Mozambique**.

The history of West Africa since the mid-twentieth century illustrates both the promises and the failures of the entire continent. First, the promises were anchored in the figures who flowed from the independence of the Gold Coast (which became **Ghana**) under the leadership of one of the most creative thinkers of **Pan-Africanism** and African unity, Kwame Nkrumah. There was the re-imagining of African cultures and civilization conducted in different directions by the founder of the Negritude movement, Léopold Sédar Senghor, and the historian of the reconnection with Ancient Pharaonic Egyptian civilization, Cheikh Anta Diop; the pro-Western liberalism of Félix Houphouët-Boigny from **Côte d'Ivoire**; the anti-imperialist rhetoric of Sékou Touré, who resisted French neo-colonial arrangements; the very professional historical research and writing of Abdoulaye Ly (**Senegal**), Joseph Ki-Zerbo (**Burkina Faso**), Adu Boahen (Ghana), Kenneth O. Dike and J.F. Ade Ajayi (**Nigeria**), which aimed at understanding the impact of the Atlantic economy and colonization on African societies. There was also an extraordinarily diverse literature, whose main figures are the Nigerians Chinua Achebe and Wole Soyinka, the Senegalese Cheikh Hamidou Kane and Ousmane Sembène, Olympe Bely-Quénum from **Benin**, the Ivoirien Bernard Dadié, and the Cameroonian Mongo Beti.

Second, there was the multiplication of military coups d'état, and the establishment of authoritarian military regimes in **Congo** (1963); Nigeria, Burkina Faso, and Ghana (1966); **Sierra Leone** (1967); **Mali** (1968); **Niger** (1974); **Chad** (1975); **Mauritania** (1978); and **Liberia** (1980). Among the countries that had escaped the earlier round of military regimes – **Gambia**, Côte d'Ivoire, Senegal and **Cameroon** – Gambia succumbed in 1994 and Côte d'Ivoire in 1999, while a tentative military coup failed in Cameroon in 1984 after the resignation of the first president Amadou Ahidjo in 1982. The region also experienced civil wars: for example, in Nigeria in the late 1960s, and in Liberia and Sierra Leone from the late 1980s, where child-soldiers committed unimaginably barbaric acts. Thus several parts of West Africa ended the century in incredible violence.

How could a region that seemed (despite problems like the Nigerian civil war and the many military coups) to escape from the violent upheavals that characterized the African continent during the 1950s, 1960s and 1970s have emerged from the literature on Africa as an irrefutable illustration of Africa diving into anarchy and barbarism, and as the perfect symbol of the failure of **regional integration** and economic development in Africa? The sale of the airline Air Afrique to its major shareholder, the French company Air France, confirmed the failure of the dreams of regional integration.

The short history of West Africa during the last four decades of the twentieth century could be divided into a period of stability and a period of instability. Both periods owe a lot to the region's historical and geographical circumstances, which provide an indispensable framework for understanding the interactions between actors who held different resources and carried heterogeneous memories, despite the generalized nationalist pledge to imagine nations and build states.

Geography

West Africa spreads from the Atlantic Ocean in the west to Lake Chad in the east, from the fringes of the **Sahara** in the north to Mount Cameroon in the south. It consists of three ecological regions: sahel, **savanna**, and **tropical rain forest**. These three areas are inhabited by different ethnic groups that, despite their common traits, present an extraordinary diversity of cultures, ways of life, methods of production, and religious beliefs, giving particular characteristics to each different part of region. These multiple human and ecological differences justify L. Mabogunje's (1976) remark that geography has structured the history of West Africa, the main characteristic of which is the intensity of human migration. These migratory movements, dictated by the nature of the territory and available resources, have had a profound impact on political, social, cultural, and religious organizations. He points out how the incursions and displacements (forced or voluntary) and fusion or succession of peoples on the same territories have profoundly transformed the population of West Africa, thus establishing a close interaction between the people and their land, between the course of history and environmental elements. The history encouraged by this particular geography has imposed logics of conflict and cooperation that turned the region into an extraordinary laboratory for successful and failed political, economic, cultural, and ideological formulas over the twentieth century.

History

Historically West Africans were sedentary farmers or nomadic herders, Muslims, Christians or followers of **African religions**, who influenced one another but also fought vigorously at crucial moments. Such conflicts were based on autochthony, ethnic origin, and religious beliefs, and the way that these affected access to or exclusion from local and international resources. Four historical eras left their mark on twentieth-century West African history: the era of the Sudanese empires of Ghana, Mali, and Songhai; the era of Atlantic **slavery**; the era of colonization; and the era of independence. Some nationalists stressed the need for West African integration and citizenship. This idea was mainly advocated by Léopold Sédar Senghor from Senegal, who attempted in vain to save the colonial federation of **French West Africa**, and by Kwame Nkrumah, the first president of Ghana who struggled to promote African unity.

The first historical moment of importance is the period of prominence of the Great Empires that circumscribed a geography favoring the sahelian regions and trade across the Sahara with **North Africa** – in fact favoring the Mediterranean economy in general. It redefined the ethnic geography of the region, traced new borders between human groups, and provoked important migrations. One of the most significant factors in the transformations that took place was the spread of **Islam**. Its consequences were paradoxical in both the political economy of the region and the fusion or explosion of ethnic groups. Islam imposed itself as a permanent variable in the history of the region, manifesting itself later in the Holy Wars of the eighteenth and nineteenth centuries, continuing with the creation of new political configurations, and carrying on into resistance movements and/or collaboration with colonial conquest and domination, as well as with post-colonial nation-building processes. Islam fundamentally contributed to the economic and ideological reinforcement of the political architecture and the enunciation or denunciation of forms of domination and inequality.

The second important historical element was the slave trade, which progressively reoriented economic channels from the fringes of the Sahara toward the Atlantic coast, integrating West Africa into a new world economy. This new economic configuration favored certain ethnic groups, who became brokers and/or built powerful slave states like Asante and the Wolof sates of Kajoor, Bawol, and Waalo. The West African section of the Atlantic economy and politics came about violently – a violence that created ethnic identities and relocations. The population of the Atlantic coastal regions dramatically increased, while the border regions between states became empty due to conflict and raiding. The economy of war and plunder that was imposed on the region configured a geography of wealth and power that depended on politics and war. These transformations were accompanied by the emergence of a Creole society, the establishment of a new culture (due to new interactions between Europeans and Africans, and to the development of colonial factories and forts), and the incorporation of a very important servile population into hierarchical and state-organized societies. Egalitarian societies that were organized by lineage, on the contrary, retreated to areas inaccessible to warriors, or produced prophetic and messianic narratives and practices that helped to preserve memories of dissidence, revolt, and resistance.

After the abolition of the Atlantic trade, the economy and the geopolitics of the Atlantic region under European rivalries led to the creation of zones of commercial influence and later – comprising the third important historical moment – colonies. The economic and social crisis that followed the end of the economy of war and plunder, opened the way to important cultural and political changes by which a conquering Islam and revitalized local religions attempted to propose new community formulas. With respect to Creole societies, they tried to imagine an African modernity, which consisted of reinventions of Christian religious texts and the promotion of education. The colonial period, which added to the region's ethnic, social, and religious plurality, brought about political collapse and the establishment of new forms of economic exploitation. The West African Atlantic coast and its hinterland were divided between France, Great Britain, and Portugal. The territorial discontinuity and administrative forms used to govern such heterogeneity resulted in a fragmentation that threatened to destroy the historical and geographical memories of West African societies.

Post-colonial challenges

In the 1960s accession to independence in the different European colonies happened in a period marked by the **Cold War** and the reconstitution of the old French Empire. France maintained its influence in West Africa, which retained the colonial currency – the CFA (Communauté Française d'Afrique – French African Community) franc. The sole exception was **Guinea**, which voted for independence in 1958, and consequently suffered French sanctions and the hostility of Senegal, Côte d'Ivoire, Mauritania, and Mali. Under the leadership of the Partido Africano da Independência do Guinée e Cabo Verde (PAIGC – African Party for the Independence of Guinea and Cape Verde), **Guinea-Bissau** and the islands of **Cape Verde** plunged into a national war of liberation against Portugal, which launched reprisal operations against the neighboring countries of Senegal and Guinea.

The integration of countries such as Senegal, Burkina Faso, Mali (after Moussa Traoré's coup), Côte d'Ivoire, Benin, Niger, **Togo**, and Cameroon into the francophone monetary zone created economic options that favored the preservation of colonial agricultural products (coffee, cocoa, groundnuts, palm nuts) and mining (uranium, phosphates, oil), an economy of exploitation that challenged neither the prevailing world economic order, nor the increasingly decisive interventions of the Bretton Woods institutions (the World Bank and International Monetary Fund), which had succeeded in replacing France from 1994. The devaluation of the CFA franc, which occurred in this period, illustrated the establishment of a new economic architecture dominated by **structural adjustment programs** and a situation of economic crises that provoked powerful social movements. Urban **workers** (both men and women) joined farmers and "modern" urban dwellers, **youth**, and migrant workers moving between rural areas and African and Western cities. More or less economically and ideologically stable communities led by elders were shaken by increasingly ferocious competition, and by the emergence in public roles of younger people who fought not only for survival but also for a new social, ideological, economic, and political order. With the exception of Senegal, which tried by every means possible to maintain institutional and democratic procedures that would preserve civil liberties and an accountable multi-party system in what has been called a "semi-democracy," authoritarian one-party systems dominated West African states. This was true regardless of ideological orientation, as demonstrated by Marxist Benin and neoliberal Côte d'Ivoire. These political systems left the people only one recourse to justice: violent demonstrations by social movements, particularly students and teachers. Guinea-Bissau, which became independent along with the Cape Verde islands in 1975, did not escape this general trend. Following "Niño" Vieira's coup d'état, Cape Verde seceded and became independent under the leadership of the Partido Africano da Independência de Cabo Verde (PAICV) in 1980. The Marxist regimes that were established in the two countries had difficulty responding to social demands: Cape Verde relied on its migrants (more numerous than its residents) in order to survive economically, while Guinea-Bissau plunged into a general crisis that was exacerbated by the hegemony of the military segment of the ruling class. The disappearance of support following the collapse of the Soviet Union led Guinea-Bissau to abandon socialism and join the CFA zone.

In **anglophone Africa**, particularly Nigeria and Ghana, economic policies did not have the anticipated results, despite the establishment of national currencies (the naira in Nigeria and the cedi in Ghana). Its reliance on oil revenues plunged Nigeria into a rentier economy, a cycle of destruction of the agricultural sector, and the search for political stability through the constant creation of new states. With respect to Ghana, the country paradoxically adopted revolutionary rhetoric but liberal economic policies under the leadership of Jerry Rawlings and the surveillance of the World Bank. In the meantime Liberia and Sierra Leone fell into civil war, which prevented neither the US company Firestone from exploiting its huge rubber plantations nor the diamond multinationals from continuing their smuggling, despite the barbaric acts of the allies and soldiers of the Liberian president Charles Taylor and the Revolutionary United Front (RUF) soldiers of Fode Sonko. Faced with economic and social challenges, especially the difficulty of achieving national integration within the old colonial frameworks, West African countries tried to devise various mechanisms, including regional integration, to hasten economic development and respond to social demands (above all the improvement of education). But the common formula adopted to reach these goals was authoritarian government, be it military, civilian, liberal, or Marxist.

The failures of these strategies and mechanisms led to various reforms undertaken under the pressure both of internal forces and of external political pressure and economic conditionality. The reforms adopted varied from one country to another. For example, while Nigeria seems to have taken the path of creating more states under strong federalism, Senegal pursued a slow but persistent democratization process that resulted in the construction of a **civil society** capable of promoting popular participation and the liberal exercise of power. The different forms of political transformation in each country were both intended to produce stability, and aimed at the institutionalization of the political process. Senegal achieved this goal through the peaceful elections of February and March 2000, while Nigeria decided to end its series of military regimes with the election of Olusegun Obasanjo in 1999. Ghana followed a similar path with the election of John Kufor in 2001, which brought Jerry Rawlings' military-turned-civilian regime to an end.

The wave of political democratization across the region in the 1990s had been initiated in 1989 in Benin through the Sovereign National Conference, which provided a unique formula for confronting economic and political crises, negotiating reform with the involvement of all the major players from political parties and civil-society organizations. The elections organized in 1991, following the national conference, led to the defeat of President Matthieu Kérékou, who was replaced by Nicéphore Soglo. Soglo was in turn defeated by Kérékou in 1996. The Benin formula, which was soon being demanded by all opposition parties in **francophone Africa**, was also used in Niger and Mali. In the case of Niger, however, the transition to democracy was interrupted by a military coup, the tentative restoration of a civil authoritarian regime, a second bloody coup, and finally a return to peace and an elected government.

Until 1999 other countries, such as Guinea, Cameroon, Togo, Mauritania, and Côte d'Ivoire, ignored the increasing demands for democracy from their people. The ruling classes of these countries succeeded in resisting pressure for democratization through a series of institutional subterfuges. These resulted in an extraordinary fragmentation of the opposition by accentuated repression and intimidation from the state, and above all the manipulation of ethnic, cultural, and religious differences. Côte d'Ivoire's argument over "the *ivoirité*" of sectors of its population, allowing only so-called "indigenous" Ivoiriens to participate in elections, is the most perfect illustration of such subterfuges. By the end of the 1990s the political trajectory of these countries remained difficult to determine: Would they follow the transition model through reforms and elections, or the civil war model of Liberia or Sierra Leone? Guinea seemed to be heading toward the second alternative, while Burkina Faso seemed to have followed the first option.

By the 1990s pressure from internal movements and the world economy shook West Africa, leaving the region poised on the cusp of a new historical phase with an uncertain trajectory. What was clear, however, was the fact that the apparent failure of the nationalist project had led to a revitalization of the discourse on ethnicity and religious membership, with the rise of extremist movements in Senegal, and the extreme violence in Nigeria, Côte d'Ivoire, Mali, and Niger. These discourses were developing against the historical dynamic of West Africa, a region where migrations over the centuries had led to a reconstruction of ethnic relationships across borders that suggested possibilities for regional regrouping and wider citizenship.

References and further reading

Ajayi, J.F.A. and Crowder, M. (eds.) (1976) *History of West Africa*, 2 vols., London: Longman.

Hopkins, A.G. (1973) *An Economic History of West Africa*, London: Longman.

Mabogunje, L. (1976) "The Land and Peoples of West Africa," in J.F.A. Ajayi and M. Crowder (eds.), *History of West Africa*, vol. 1, London: Longman.

O'Brien, D.C., Dunn, J. and Rathborne, R. (eds.) (1989) *Contemporary West African States*, Cambridge: Cambridge University Press.

Richards, P. (1996) *Fighting for the Rain Forest. War, Youth and Resources in Sierra Leone*, London: James Currey.

MAMADOU DIOUF

Windhoek, Namibia

Windhoek, the capital of **Namibia** and the country's commercial, industrial, communications, and cultural center, is situated on an inland plateau surrounded by the Eros, Auas, and Khomas mountains. In 2000 it had an estimated population of 200,000. Nama chief Jonker Afrikaner, who was head of a settlement in the same location in the 1840s, gave the city the earliest version of its current name: *winterhoek*, which literally means "windy corner." This later became Windhoek. From 1890 the modern city evolved around a

German settlement. In June 1902 a new railway line reached Windhoek from the coast, ensuring the growth of the developing city. German colonial troops were defeated by **South Africa** during the **First World War**, and South Africa assumed control of the colony in 1915. Although South Africa retained control of the colony, German architectural and cultural influences have been retained in the city through the whole of the twentieth century. Located in the center of the Namibia, Windhoek became a key transshipment point for goods coming from the coast and other areas of the colony. By mid-century the population had reached 20,460, up from 716 in 1920, and it included "Coloureds," Afrikaners, Germans and other Europeans, and Ovambo peoples from the north of the colony, as well as the original settlers of the area: the Herero, Nama, and Damaras.

Earlier practices of segregation by white colonists were intensified in Windhoek after the Afrikaner-led Nationalist Party gained control in South Africa. They treated Namibia as a fifth province and imposed their apartheid laws there. The new laws reserved Windhoek city for whites only, and in 1959 the living quarters of all black and colored Namibians were torn down. Coloureds were moved to a township called Khomasdal that was five kilometers outside town, while blacks were forced to occupy a township the residents named Katatura (this means "we do not have a permanent dwelling place"). The protests against this forced removal soon gave birth to Namibia's nationalist movement, which was to wage a protracted war of liberation under the leadership of the South West African People's Organization (SWAPO).

Namibia gained its independence in 1990, thanks to SWAPO's struggles and regional realignments and negotiations to end the undeclared war between South Africa and **Angola**. The last decade of the twentieth century was marked by the beginnings of desegregation and new architectural construction. The legacy of apartheid remained evident in general residence patterns, with most blacks still living in Katatura, which was the most populous part of the metropolitan area. Yet there was a significant movement of blacks into the city center after independence, and open spaces between the townships began to be developed into new residential areas. The construction of new buildings, including a new Supreme Court, also enhanced the city center.

Tourism, the fastest growing sector of the Namibian economy, drew visitors into the city through Windhoek's international airport, located forty-seven kilometers from the city. In the 1990s the Post Street Mall – a square with wide pavements, shopping malls, restaurants, and cafes – was the city center's major business and shopping district. Windhoek was also the location of the University of Namibia; the Zoo Park, which was home to many mammals (including eland, gemsbok, mountain zebra, blue wildebeest, springbok, and kudu); the Namibian Craft Center, which provided a permanent showcase for local handicrafts; and the National Museum, which occupied three locations in the city, displaying the country's rich natural and cultural heritage.

Further reading

Pendleton, W.C. (1996) *Katatura, A Place Where We Stay: Life in a Post-apartheid Township in Namibia*, Athens: University of Ohio Press.

T.J. DESCH-OBI

women's movements

The myriad individual and collective acts, conscious or unconscious, that women across the world employ to combat gender oppression and its multiple intersections with other forms of social subjugation can hardly be squeezed into one universal definition. Hence no single history of or discourse on women's movements in Africa can capture the complex and often contradictory forms of resistance that women exert on the structures of power that shape their daily lives. But in operative terms women's movements may be defined as political struggles enveloping a variety of women's groups that present the necessary platforms for addressing women's concerns. Understood in these terms, analyses of women's movements in literature are often associated with the mobilization of women in Europe and North America in the 1960s, which subsequently complemented or helped to ignite similar forms of collective action in other parts of the world, including Africa. Until the late 1980s the range of discourses on women's movements in the global South were largely subsumed within the feminist development discourses that emerged in the early 1970s – the Women In Development (WID), Women And Development (WAD), and Gender And Development (GAD) debates.

The WID discourse, a set of liberal feminist analyses of Southern women's experiences, drew largely from modernization theory. Women's lack of integration into the development process, proponents argued, resulted in their marginal social status within the modern economies of the South. They proposed the use of legal and administrative interventions to expand women's social opportunities outside the domestic sphere. WAD analyses emerged in the late 1970s as an alternative theoretical blueprint, critiquing WID's homogenization of Southern women's experiences. Drawing from Marxist debates on class formation in capitalist states, it focused mainly on the female majority outside the formal sectors of Southern nations, particularly their exploitation within the international capitalist system. By the early 1980s critics of WID and WAD discourses were beginning to formulate under GAD broader analyses of women's oppression in the South, placing the issues of both class division and gender subjugation within the larger context of changes in the global economy.

But the WID-WAD-GAD debates gave way in the late 1980s to a heated controversy on the political economy of knowledge-production (the politics of who-speaks-for-whom), which introduced serious divisions between the feminist sisterhoods of the global North and South. A plurality of voices from the South critiqued the existing literature, challenging the Western assumptions that dictated, among other things, what constitutes a women's movement and the course of its development in any social space. Women's movements in Africa may therefore be understood in the light of the developments in feminist scholarship, but only in terms of the manner in which they informed the analyses of female mobilization that came with colonization, the struggle for political independence, and nation-building in late twentieth-century society. In this regard women's movements in most of Africa shared a number of characteristics with those in other regions of the South, setting them apart from similar movements in the West. For one thing they often arose in these countries along with the shift from agrarian economies to dependent capitalist economies. For another they often attained a marked visibility only after national transitions to political independence, as women began to insert their well-articulated concerns into public debates. Thus, unlike in the West, women's movements in the South had a shorter time-frame in which to find a balance between their involvement as citizens in nationalist struggles for political independence and feminist struggles to improve their social status as women.

Confronting colonization: The transformation of women's movements in Africa

Pre-colonial African history recorded an assortment of prominent women who stood out as heroes among their people although they did not necessarily defend specific female constituencies. Before Western feminism made its debut on the local scene in the early 1970s African women mobilized themselves, albeit in smaller groups, within social formations that were later demarcated into nation-states. In pre-colonial times, for instance, women in many parts of **West Africa** (for example, Fanti fish traders in **Ghana**; Women farmers in Baule, **Côte d'Ivoire**; and the nomadic Tuareg dairy women of **Niger**) enjoyed some degree of economic independence built on a rich associational history. Even in parts of Africa dominated by **Islam**, where women's commercial activities were restricted to various degrees, those in rural areas were relatively free to engage in agricultural and commercial activities. These economic bases enabled women to carve out larger social spheres for addressing their collective interests. In all of Africa there was a strong presence of female kinship ties that in many ways asserted their authority within lineages and clans, religious cults that made female participation central to their activities, and village organizations that were responsible for settling disputes. These modes of organizing often fed into networks women formed for credit pooling and assistance with farmwork. While virtually autonomous from the larger public domain dominated by men, these female collectives rarely challenged patriarchal structures that reinforced women's subordinate status in society. Moreover they tended to be community-based, with geographical distance, and ethnic and religious differences limiting the potential for extensive networking.

Colonization signaled another phase in the manner in which African women organized their affairs as individuals and groups, as they sought to resist or adjust to the social developments that were gradually changing the normal course of life. While some of their actions were general responses to the local and external forces that threatened their economic domains, others were more strategically directed at the colonial powers. With respect to the former, women in African villages and cities initiated various forms of action and protest. Examples include the women in colonial **Dar es Salaam**, **Tanzania**, who successfully mobilized the support of their communities to resist colonial attempts to invade their commercially lucrative territory of beer brewing. Similarly, female urban-dwellers in many African colonial cities (such as prostitutes in early twentieth-century **Nairobi**, **Kenya**, and female petty traders in the Copperbelt of **Zambia** during the 1920s and 1930s) persistently fought off the stigma of "bad women" in order to establish their independence as single women. As the above examples indicate, these modes of resistance were largely carried out by the female majority who were confined to the informal sector of African economies in transition.

In most of Africa women's political mobilization came with the struggle for national independence. Women's entrance into the formal sector of emerging modern economies was greatly undermined by their limited access to schooling and paid work. African women entered the elite colonial circles as housewives to civil servants and businessmen, and it took them several decades to establish any appreciable presence in the public sphere. Increasing resistance to colonial rule, however, catapulted elite women in many African countries into the public sphere. African women played a significant role in national liberation struggles between the 1940s and 1960s (the period in which many African countries fought for and gained political independence). They expressed their solid support for elite men at the forefront of the struggles, either as women wings of political parties (in Zambia and **Sierra Leone**, for instance) or as distinct women's organizations, such as the Nigerian Women's Union (NWU) and the Women's Union (WU) in **Sudan** (which was affiliated to the Sudanese Communist Party).

The patterns described above were fairly common across Africa, except in a few countries where women's political mobilization had a much longer history and reflected the unique patterns of national formation and development. The origins of the Egyptian women's movement, for instance, can be traced as far back as the 1890s, when a small group of middle-class women began to organize outside the purview of the public authorities. By the time **Egypt** attained self-rule in 1922, women had emerged as a collective from the shadow of anti-colonial struggles to question their social status, taking off the veil as the major symbol of their subordination. In the 1940s and 1950s, when most of Africa was engulfed in anti-colonial struggles, the women's movement in Egypt had expanded into a populist forum embracing many female groups outside the elite circles. Except for the few periods of political repression during the Nasser era, a national women's movement existed continuously in Egypt since those early times. **South Africa** also had a pattern of female activism that was historically distinct from many other African countries. In the 1910s and 1920s a number of white women initiated the struggle for female suffrage. The larger female majority was however drawn to the Bantu Women's League that was established within the African National Congress (ANC) in 1913. Closely affiliated to the ANC, the South African women's movement gradually began to chart a feminist path for women's liberation. Their demand to be recognised as equal citizens with men was boldly reflected in the Women's Charter of 1954, for example, as well as in the ANC's own Freedom Charter in 1955. From the 1960s, when many ANC leaders were imprisoned, died or sent into exile, the women leaders within the party helped to sustain the struggle against apartheid. By the 1970s Winnie Mandela stood out as the official symbol of the struggle.

Despite these contributions to national liberation struggles, women in most African countries earned little recognition in the post-independent era. In many cases women's organizations that fully embraced the nationalist struggles of the colonial era lost a good deal of ground, regrouping under much weaker political outfits that avoided any direct confrontation with the emergent indigenous governments. The NWU in Nigeria, for instance, did not survive the nation's political transition. In 1959 (shortly before Nigeria's independence in 1960) the National Council of Women's Societies (NCWS) was created as an umbrella for women's organizations across the country. It maintained very strong links with the incumbent regimes, whose support (financial and otherwise) it usually thrived on. It directed its efforts towards improving women's general welfare, and steered a neutral course with respect to debates about (and campaigns against) their marginalization in contemporary society. Similarly in Sudan the WU and its affiliate, the SCP, were eventually banned in 1971, along with other political groups, by the Nimeiri regime that had taken over power from the duly elected but unstable democratic government in 1969. With the installation of a one-party state, Nimeiri's Sudanese Socialist Union (SSU) created its own women's affiliate, the Sudanese Women's Union (SWU), which was to be the sole national organization responsible for advising the government on matters of women's welfare.

The transition to independent states diminished any political influence African women had, and rendered them second-class citizens beside their male counterparts. Colonization eroded women's power-bases, and left new African states with formal political structures that drew largely from its deeply entrenched legacies. The latter neither reasserted women's previous political authority in any measure, nor established new avenues for their integration into the modern structure. Colonization and the struggle for political independence also carefully nurtured and helped to maintain serious internal ethnic, religious, and political crises in post-colonial African states, with unstable governments that could hardly withstand the attendant pressures. Often women were caught in the middle of these conflicts with divided loyalties that undermined their ability to organize and present a united front. In Islamic countries such as Sudan, **Somalia**, and **Algeria**, where women solidly backed the struggle for independence (in many cases upholding the veil as a strong symbol of national identity), religion ultimately reinforced their subordination in newly independent states that grossly marginalized their political participation and confined them to the domestic sphere. With severely limited rights to family inheritance, women's relationships with men remained unquestioned as the basic means of establishing social identity and economic autonomy.

In many African countries the precarious balance of statutory, customary, and in some cases Islamic law that privileged kinship ties over conjugal ties, seriously limited women's inheritance rights. Even in non-Islamic states – such **Ghana**, Zambia, and Kenya – where statutory law clearly expanded women's inheritance rights, customary law often prevailed, especially in cases where a husband died intestate. It was also not unusual for the dictates of statutory law to be set aside and customary law applied to women's disadvantage. This general climate of dissatisfaction among women set the stage for women's mobilization in the post-colonial era.

Women's movements in the early post-colonial era

Post-independent Africa before the 1970s offered a much narrower space for women's collective action. Incoming regimes often rewarded women's efforts with varying degrees of improved access to schooling, paid work, and health care, but refused to make any substantial changes to their marginal status. Two major forms of women's organization emerged in the post-independent era: the prominent urban middle-class female organizations and those that served the female majority – rural women and their counterparts living on the fringes of urban society. The latter had a much smaller profile, and focused mostly on income-generating projects and commercial alliances to strengthen women's economic base for family subsistence. Given their more buoyant economic status the urban middle-class women's organizations had a freer space to mobilize around the broader issues of women's subordinate status in society. Such groups sought to develop effective political lobbies to expand women's representation in schooling, paid work, and government, even as they pursued charitable causes to improve the lives of less-privileged women.

In the Islamic states, such as Algeria, Somalia, and Sudan, urban women's organizations also had to confront the problematic coexistence of patriarchy, religion, and Western influence. Female organizations in these countries sought to establish a strong national identity as Muslim women, even as they refuted the stereotypical perceptions about them as willing victims at the hands of their men. These socially contentious situations often led to a divided women's movement. On the one hand were women's organizations that firmly supported religious fundamentalism. This strand of female mobilization was typified by the Muslim Sisters in Sudan, who firmly embraced the institutionalized religious beliefs of their close affiliate, the Muslim Brothers, and benefited from their close ties with the Nimeiri regime. On the other hand were women's organizations that stood in opposition to any structures of power in the contemporary society that reinforced women's subordination. A striking example of the latter group was the Arab Women's Solidarity Front (AWSF) in Egypt. The 1960s and 1970s witnessed highly charged public debates on circumcision. At the center of these debates was the internationally acclaimed physician and feminist writer Dr. Nawal El-Saadawi. Along with a number of prominent Egyptian women, Dr. Saadawi fought for the elimination of the practice, presenting strong opposition to the state and the religious establishment. This struggle led to the eventual formation of the AWSF in 1982. Given the problematic relationship between women and the state in such countries, those that aligned with the state and its religious affiliates often found themselves in a more receptive political climate. While in some cases they garnered impressive support from a less-privileged female majority, they often forfeited the opportunity to wage a stronger battle against women's low social status. Those in opposition trod a dangerous and difficult path that made every advance a well-earned victory. Even in situations where a fledgling national women's collective existed, strong cultural differences fueled persistent contestations over the issues that came to the table and the strategies fielded to achieve commonly acceptable solutions. Female circumcision was a very good example. Not only did the debates around the practice create strong dissent among African women, Muslims and Christians alike, but they also introduced serious disagreements between African and Western female scholars.

Beyond the obstacles presented by broader social forces, women's movements in post-independent Africa appeared to be plagued by two major issues. First, African women's political, social, and economic roles were seriously constricted by a set of gender ideologies (indigenous–Western hybrids) constructed around their primary roles as wives and mothers. Often women in African countries were forced to build their political platforms around their socially acceptable roles in society, cautiously framing their demands to avoid overstepping their boundaries of operation. For instance, women's primary roles as mothers and wives were often employed as the basic rationale for improving their access to formal education. In the same vein women's roles in food production, which for the most part sustained their profile in the agricultural sector and the attention of the international community, provided an acceptable platform for African women to speak as crucial contributors to, but not equal partners with, men in national development. Second, there were hardly any effective linkages between urban middle-class women and their counterparts in both the urban and the rural segments of the informal sector. Beyond the various charitable causes pursued by the former, there was very little that connected their broader and strategic goals of female emancipation to the latter's struggle for immediate economic survival.

The state of affairs in most African countries had not changed substantially by the end of the twentieth century. It is therefore in the context of the conditions stated above that the impact of Western feminism on African women's collective actions from the 1970s should be placed.

Struggles over African women's movements from the 1970s

The second wave of the women's movement in Western countries brought women's agenda into the public debate, and forced the international community to listen to their concerns as a global voice. With the rise of international feminist movements in the 1970s various forms of women's organizations emerged in many African countries. Following the course of WID analyses and the growing influence of a transnational women's movement committed to drawing attention to women's needs in the developing world, many African governments sought ways to integrate their women into the modern institutions of society, particularly the political system. But, as in previous times, women's efforts appeared to be either complemented or undermined by the actions of the state.

Some African states became adept at exploiting the growing profile of African women on various international feminist fronts. Most African governments joined the WID revolution by installing their own brands of "state feminism" – which in simple terms refers to state-directed processes aimed at advancing women's status through their integration into government machineries and political systems. After the **United Nations** (UN) Decade for Women (1975–85), with its 1985 closing conference held in **Nairobi**, Kenya, governments in developing countries voiced a greater concern about women's rights. Following the recommendations of the Convention on the Elimination of All Forms of Discrimination Against Women, most African governments created their own portfolios (agencies, ministries, or commissions) for addressing women's concerns.

The creation of women's machineries in many African states did not expand women's sphere of collective action or exert much pressure on the state. State feminism often did not boost the efforts of the independent women's movements outside its political grip. In the majority of cases the political regimes in the developing world, including authoritarian regimes, used state-directed reforms to brush up their **human rights** image (to facilitate their access to foreign aid and credit), while silencing the progressive elements within the women's movements. By the late 1970s the barriers posed by the social divisions within the African women's movements had become obvious, as groups of women within countries and across the continent recognised the need to join forces to fight for common causes, such as women's rights in marriage, access to land, and protection from violence. Although many WAD observers of Africa's development saw these divisions as largely class-based, reflecting the differing loyalties of the segregated classes, African female scholars placed their own analyses of the situation in the larger context of the complexities and contradictions of nation-building – with its imperialist undertones – that mediated the relations of gender.

The economic decline in the early 1980s, marked by the introduction of **structural adjustment programs** (SAP) in many countries, as well as by the subsequent wave of democratic transitions that swept the continent, heralded another phase for women's movements across Africa. Women's increasing burden for family subsistence across the classes, as well as the more permeable political forum democratization presented, seemed to provide fairly solid ground for alliances across women's groups and with other groups involved in the democratic struggle. But following the previous pattern of anti-colonial struggles, the alleged forces of democratization from the late 1980s (except in a few cases) neither provided a strong backing for women's movements, nor invited their active involvement on the frontline. In **Southern** and **East Africa** such transitions in some instances were paralleled by the rise of autonomous women's organizations, many of which took advantage of the fairly open political space to challenge women's absence from the formal structures of power and leadership. In Tanzania, for instance, state-directed reforms complemented the efforts of a fairly independent national women's movement. Although the latter operated outside the formal political space, it made considerable inroads into the structures of power within the state by challenging traditional client-based political patronage. State reforms in Tanzania led to the introduction of affirmative action in political representation, which by the 1990s granted women a 15 percent quota in parliament and a 25 percent quota in local government councils. Women were also appointed to a few high-profile positions. Moreover, legislative revisions in the 1990s expanded credit opportunities for women, introduced a sexual offenses bill, and removed the legal ban on school attendance placed on pregnant girls.

Similarly in **Zimbabwe** the efforts of women's organizations received some positive responses from the state. Over the last two decades of the century legislation was passed to officially recognize women's franchise from the age of eighteen, and divorce laws were reformed to expand women's rights in civil marriage. Prior to the introduction of SAPs, women also greatly benefited from government literacy campaigns and programs to improve health care. But, as in the case of Tanzania, government reforms hardly shifted the clear boundaries that separated the general concern over women's welfare and the larger question of women's subordinate social status.

For the most part, however, state feminism in Africa bred a social climate in which African women were forced to build their political platforms around their socially acceptable roles in society. In many West African countries state feminism asserted itself in bolder terms, however. Many political regimes in these countries substituted established women's machineries in the urban centers (or created new ones) for women's agencies run by the consorts of men in power. Ghana and Nigeria present good examples. Before the democratically elected government of President Agyekum Kuffour took over office in 2001, the Rawlings regime's portfolio for women's welfare was run by the First Lady Nana Konadu Agyeman Rawlings and her middle-/upper-class female associates. Mrs. Rawlings' December 31st Movement was nationally recognised as the state's adviser on women's issues, and as the official voice of Ghanaian women. In Nigeria the First Ladies of the military regimes of Babangida and Abacha (which preceded the Obasanjo civilian government elected in 1999) were responsible for developing state policies and programs for women's welfare. While these state-"inscribed" machineries gained some support from less-privileged women (with a few benefits thrown their way), they generally helped to prop up incumbent authoritative regimes and stifle the efforts of more radical female groups.

It needs to be noted, however, that state feminism did not often succeed in eliminating all opposing elements within African women's movements. In the Nigerian case, for instance, the militant Women In Nigeria (WIN) offered some degree of opposition to state feminism. WIN was founded in 1983 by female academics and professionals dissatisfied with NCWS's uncritical stance and implicit allegiance to the malestream social order. The organization's radical stance also attracted alliances with other anti-government groups. Clearly dissociating itself from the NCWS umbrella, WIN attempted to forge linkages with women's groups at the grass-roots level, attacking in strong feminist terms the subordination of women reinforced by the state in its public campaigns and meetings. Unfortunately WIN's presence was mainly felt in the urban areas within elite circles, and its radical stance attracted little support from men. Given its limited resource-base the organization did not have any considerable impact on rural women.

Outside elite circles the majority of women's organizations in Africa continued to mobilize around issues of daily survival. The economic downturn marked by the introduction of SAPs in most of Africa in the 1980s and 1990s continued to encourage their mobilization around matters of economic survival. Across the continent women battled the effects of SAPs; whether as market-traders in **Accra** in Ghana, female fish-sellers in Zairian villages, or female food farmers in the rural areas of **Malawi** and **Cameroon**, women struggled under increased burdens in their attempt to provide family subsistence as the men's economic opportunities dwindled in both informal and formal sectors. With most of them operating outside the latter, women were forced to employ both traditional and new survival strategies to feed the family or generate income, including petty trading, food farming and processing, sewing, soap-making, illegal brewing of beer and alcohol, fabric-dying, and prostitution. In this state of affairs the existence of female cooperatives that shared labor or pooled credit became even more important.

Women's political protests under these conditions tended to be limited to non-strategic outbursts against public incursions into their economic spaces. For instance, in open markets and city streets women staged protests against public price-control policies on "essential commodities," and the imposition of higher taxes on market stalls by municipal councils. Given the prevailing state of political instability, the near collapse of existing material infrastructure, and women's generally poor access to education, the expansion of multicultural cooperation into the developing world in the form of production zones that provided cheap labor made only minimal incursions into Africa – in a few countries such as **Morocco**. The Islamic legal system in Morocco clearly codified women's subordinate status to men and the ruling class, so their rightful place in the domestic sphere as wives and mothers within a patriarchal structure was unquestioned. However, women's improved access to schooling granted them relative freedom of movement before marriage. Not surprisingly the offshore production zone in Morocco only attracted young women awaiting their passage into the proper role of non-working mothers and wives. But even as significant contributors to household income these young women's bargaining power within the patriarchal family remained largely unchallenged until the massive struggle for family reform in the 1990s.

The future implications of late twentieth-century developments

By the end of the twentieth century the future progress of African women's movements did not necessarily seem to rest on the domestic state of affairs within specific countries, but on the myriad global linkages they had established in the 1990s. The growing presence of international feminist networks with strong linkages to **non-governmental organizations** (local and foreign) on the ground promised to reshape the nature of female mobilization in Africa in the future. GAD discourses heralded these developments, highlighting the impact of social, economic, and political rearrangements in the new world order that variously mediated women's well-being across the globe. Most important among these networks were the movements on violence against women, which successfully implanted themselves into international human rights struggles. With the support of these international movements many female collectives were sprouting up throughout the continent to seek and share strategies for addressing the various forms of violence women suffered in Africa. This development potentially provided an opening for women to unite over specific sets of issues around which they could build a common platform to promote gender rights and equality. Although beleaguered at various times, a good number of national movements in Africa survived the onslaught of state feminism. Moreover organizations such as the Nairobi-based African Women's Development and Communication Network (FEMNET) and the African Women's Committee on Peace and Development (AWCPD) were also developing important linkages that female organizations, local and national, could count on for support in fighting their own battles. Furthermore the debate on the political economy of feminist scholarship from the late 1980s raised serious controversies over what constituted female collective action and its various manifestations in specific social spaces. The appearance of the resounding voices of African female scholars in various international intellectual forums was seen as a major development that was bound to influence substantially the nature of new discourses on female organizing in the African context. The Association of African Women Scholars (AAWS), for example, stayed at the forefront of emerging debates on gender studies in Africa during the 1990s. However, many leaders within and observers of these movements at the close of the century were clearly aware that these developments could not replace the difficult and challenging tasks of building female collectives at the grass-roots level, establishing effective networks among women's organizations in the cities and villages (and across ethnic groups), and harnessing their efforts towards the building of united fronts.

See also: families; labor movements; nationalist movements; peasant movements; sex and sexuality; society: colonial; society: post-independence

Further reading

Brettell, B. and Sargent, C. (eds.) (2001) *Gender in Cross-Cultural Perspectives*, Englewood Cliffs: Prentice-Hall.

Coquery-Vidrovitch, C. (1997) *African Women: A History*, Boulder: Westview Press.

Imam, A., Mama, A. and Sow, F. (eds.) (1997) *Engendering African Social Sciences*, Dakar: CODESRIA.

Nnaemeka, O. (ed.) (1998) *Sisterhood, Feminisms and Power: From Africa to the Diaspora*, Trenton: Africa World Press Inc.

Rai, S. (ed.) (2000) *International Perspectives on Gender and Democratization*, Basingstoke: Macmillan.

Tripp, A.M. (2001) "Women's Movements and Challenges to Neopatrimonial Rule: Preliminary Observations from Africa," *Development and Change* 32: 33–54.

Tucker, J. (ed.) (1993) *Arab Women: New Boundaries, New Frontiers*, Indianapolis: Indiana University Press.

Wieringa, S. (ed.) (1995) *Subversive Women: Women's Movements in Africa, Asia, Latin America and the Caribbean*, London: Zed Books.

PHILOMINA OKEKE

workers

Since pre-colonial times human labor has played a pivotal role in Africa's economic, social, and political development, and it has remained at the core of the struggle over power and economic resources. In a continent constrained by a low level of technological development, production for household consumption and exchange depended heavily on human labor. But the manner in which labor was mobilized, organized, and controlled was determined by numerous factors, including the natural environment, social structures, cultural practices, and power relations. In pre-colonial African states the ruling groups used various forms of personal ownership of individuals such as captives, slaves, and clients to extract labor, to generate wealth, and to maintain hegemony. The caravan traders who operated in the coastal regions of the continent, in the **savanna**, and in the **Sahara** relied heavily on a large number of teamsters, porters, sailors, and artisans. In less centralized societies genealogical leaders and senior males controlled household production and exploited the labor of women and junior members of the family. Moreover the mobilization and organization of human labor cannot be separated from its social and cultural context. African **peasants**, pastoralists, workers, and artisans each had their own conception of work, time, and authority. They developed work habits that reflected their physical environment and cultural values.

A remarkable development in twentieth-century Africa was the growth and the expansion of wage labor under European colonial rule. Indeed the abolition of all forms of coerced labor and the generalization of wage labor were at the core of the colonial project, and became an arena of major struggle, negotiation, and adaptation throughout the colonial period. This struggle centered on the relentless efforts of colonial regimes to inculcate European work habits in African workers, and thereby transform them into a reliable, productive, and disciplined workforce.

Historiography of African workers

Despite their pivotal role in Africa's social and political development, African workers, peasants, women, slaves, and other marginalized groups have received little scholarly attention. From the 1970s, however, the history and the experience of African workers and subaltern groups began to receive considerable attention, and African labor history was transformed from a neglected field into a vibrant academic enterprise. In addition to the growing popularity of social history, interest in African workers was prompted by their vital role in the **decolonization** process and in the post-colonial era in general. The studies of Richard Sandbrook (Sandbrook and Cohen 1975), Robin Cohen (Gutkind, Cohen and Copans 1978), and others opened up the subject and put it at the center of research on African social history. This early literature naturally reflected the theoretical paradigms of the 1970s and 1980s, which were preoccupied with the process of class formation, proletarianization, trade unions, and labor movements. Influenced by orthodox Marxism these studies have portrayed the working class as a homogeneous entity whose members shared the same perceptions and aspirations by virtue of their position within the capitalist structure.

A number of studies focused on specific groups, such as miners, dockers, and railway workers. Given the intensity and length of industrial development in **Southern Africa** it is not surprising that mine workers received the lion's share of scholarly attention. But transportation workers figured prominently in the works of Ralph Grillo (1973), Richard Jeffries (1978), and Frederick Cooper (1978), pointing out the militancy of railway workers, whose strategic position in the economy posed the most serious challenge to colonial and post-colonial governments.

In subsequent years, however, the study of African labor history was dramatically reshaped by new questions and issues deemed crucial for understanding working-class culture, consciousness, and politics. The range of topics vastly expanded to include working-class **families**, **leisure**, popular culture, gender, and so forth. Beyond the initial focus on the predominantly male workers in the formal sector, the study of African labor history moved to encompass female and casual labor, peasants, petty traders, slaves, and other marginal groups. In short the new literature stressed the importance of examining workers in their broader social and political contexts, and in relation to other social groups such as peasants, nomads, urban dwellers, and the middle class.

Beyond concern with wage laborers in government departments and private firms, there was growing interest in the history of non-wage workers in the so-called "informal sector" of the economy. For instance, the works of Charles Van Onselen (1982), Claire Robertson (1984), and Luise White (1990) focused on prostitutes, taxi drivers, market women, and domestic servants, underscoring their role in the reproduction of labor. Among the most important themes these studies highlighted was the gender division of labor, which relegated women to non-waged economic activities.

The new literature also bridged the gap between labor history and urban history by stressing the interdependence of the urban space and working practices and by conceptualizing the city as the locus for reproduction of the working class. Indeed the questions of how and where workers lived and the manner in which they developed neighborhoods and communities are crucial elements for understanding their culture and experience.

Beyond early concern with the role of industrial control, time, and discipline in shaping and molding African workers, considerable attention was now given to the question of what African workers themselves brought to the workplace. The most pioneering works in this regard dealt with Southern Africa. For instance, in her study of Zulu mine workers in Natal, Keletso Atkins (1993) showed how Zulu work habits and concepts of time, authority, and discipline permeated the workplace and forced employers to make major adjustments in working conditions. Working-class culture also figured prominently in Patrick Harries' (1994) study on Mozambican migrant workers in **South Africa**. Harries criticized the dominant paradigm in African labor history for its focus on workers' resistance, militancy, and activism. He rejected the notion that working-class culture is shaped solely by the struggle against employers and capitalist strategies of social control. By focusing on the culture of drunkenness, desertion, and social deviance among Mozambican migrant workers, Harries tried to underscore the wide range of experiences and cultural resources that shaped the worldview of these workers. In short the emphasis on the cultural matrix represented a major departure from the old paradigms that conceived of working-class politics and consciousness as a mere derivation of socioeconomic structure.

Historians of African labor also began to move beyond the confines of the workplace and union halls to examine workers in their families, neighborhoods, and communities. Indeed among the most important aspects of African workers' experience are leisure and social activities. This was the subject of Phyllis Martin's (1995) book on leisure in colonial **Brazzaville**, in which she explored recreational activities such as football, **music**, **dance**, and fashion among urban residents of the city. Martin's study illustrated the manner in which these activities fostered the development of strong social networks and the emergence of particular identities among the African population of this colonial town. According to Martin leisure activities were arenas of contest and mediation within European and African subcommunities, as well as between them.

The questions of gender and the impact of wage labor on household structures and family life attracted considerable attention during the 1980s and 1990s. Lisa Lindsay (1996) has dealt with the impact of wage labor and colonial labor policies since the **Second World War** on household structure and family life among Yoruba railway workers in **Nigeria**. As several scholars have pointed out, the postwar labor reforms aimed at the creation of a more stable and differentiated working class, through the provision of family wages, decent housing, and social services. According to Lindsay these policies were premised on the European conception of the male worker as head of the household and primary bread-winner. Application of these concepts in the African context had serious implications for gender relations and domestic life. Lindsay argued that the notion of the male worker as bread-winner conflicted with a Yoruba social structure in which women engaged in various commercial activities and enjoyed a considerable degree of economic independence. In short the new literature not only showed the need for a more expansive working-class history, but it also underscored the importance of examining the history of African workers in different regional and cultural contexts. Such an approach would illuminate not only the myriad factors that shaped workers' consciousness and behavior, but also the different ways in which they constructed their identity and expressed their consciousness.

African workers in the twentieth century

An integral part of the so-called "civilizing mission" of Europeans in Africa was the generalization of a free labor market and the abolition of various forms of coercion, particularly **slavery**. Indeed the abolition of slavery was one of the most important justifications for European colonial conquest. Since the middle of the nineteenth century European missionaries, traders, explorers, and anti-slavery groups had launched a large-scale campaign in which they appealed to European governments and the general public to rescue Africa from the evil of enslavement and anarchy. This was indeed the situation on the coast of **East Africa**, where a group of immigrants from the Arabian peninsula had established large plantations on the coast and adjacent islands in the mid-nineteenth century, and used thousands of African slaves, most of whom had been captured from the interior. While slavery and the slave trade were abolished in the Atlantic world in the nineteenth century, they remained rampant in the Nile Valley, **North Africa**, the savanna, and coastal **West Africa**.

However, the efforts of European colonial governments to establish and generalize a wage labor system faced serious challenges, emanating from the colonizers' own approach, as well as from local realities. With regard to the question of slavery colonial regimes in Africa soon realized that the abolition of slavery would have far-reaching implications. They believed that slavery had always been an integral part of African life and that a sudden abolition would cause economic collapse. They also feared that the abolition of slavery would create a serious political and social backlash by alienating the slave-owning groups whose support was deemed essential, particularly during the early years of colonial rule. Moreover colonial officials were apprehensive about the social consequences of abolition, and the prospects of thousands of slaves leaving their owners and flocking into the cities, where they would upset colonial urban order. It is not surprising, therefore, that colonial governments in different parts of Africa adopted a gradualist approach to the question of slavery. In the first place they made a distinction between slavery and the slave trade. They focused on curbing the latter, but tolerated the former for at least several decades after the establishment of their rule. Colonial officials habitually discouraged the slaves from leaving their masters, and often returned those who ran away. Although many slaves made relentless efforts to gain their freedom, the majority chose to remain in bondage rather than face the economic and social uncertainty of leaving their owners. Even those who were manumitted continued to maintain close ties with their former owners.

However, the establishment of colonial rule and the extraction of African resources generated great demand for labor. The building of roads and railway lines, public works, transportation of goods and materials, mining, and military service required a large number of workers. During the early decades of colonial rule European officials had great difficulty in inducing Africans to undertake wage labor. In addition to the harsh conditions of work and low pay, the vast majority of Africans did not need to abandon their farming and pastoral activities to seek wage employment. As a result colonial officials adopted several strategies to obtain workers. In addition to taxation, they targeted runaway and liberated slaves, refugees, and other displaced persons. However, one of the most controversial methods was the use of forced labor. Indeed the most notorious example was that of King Leopold II in the Congo Free State, whose atrocities attracted large-scale condemnation. Forced labor was also rampant in French and Portuguese colonies.

The expansion of colonial enterprises such as mining and cash-crop production prompted large segments of the African population to seek wage employment. This process was much more advanced in Southern Africa, where the establishment of the mining industry in the second half of the nineteenth century and the loss of land to white settlers forced thousands of Africans to join the wage-labor market. One of the most important consequences of mining activities in Southern Africa was the creation of a **migrant labor** system. A large number of Africans from the neighboring colonies of Nyasaland, Tanganyika, **Angola**, and **Mozambique** moved back and forth between the mining camps in South Africa and their homelands. Mining activities also played an important role in the colonial economies of the Congo, Rhodesia, **Ghana**, Nigeria, and **Sierra Leone**. In addition to mining and railway work, a large number of Africans were employed as agricultural laborers. A vivid example was that of the Gezira cotton scheme in **Sudan**, which was established by the Anglo-Egyptian administration in the mid-1920s and became the largest agricultural scheme on the continent. The scheme generated a huge demand for labor that could not be met locally. Consequently, with the encouragement of British colonial authorities, thousands of immigrants from northern Nigeria, **Niger**, and **Chad** became seasonal agricultural laborers in the Gezira. Many of them eventually settled in Sudan, particularly in the Gezira region.

Although colonial regimes succeeded in attracting a large number of Africans to wage employment, they had great difficulty in controlling them and in transforming them into a disciplined, productive, and reliable workforce. In joining the colonial wage-labor market, Africans were motivated by several strategies, such as the desire to earn cash to fulfill certain social obligations or to invest in land. They worked for a limited period of time and oscillated between wage and non-wage employment. The employers themselves, who were apprehensive about the consequences of large-scale proletarianization, were unwilling to pay a family wage, preferring to hire a large mass of single men. The compound system in the mining camps of Southern Africa was a vivid illustration of this pattern. Thousands of Africans were given short-term contracts and housed in large compounds, where they were subjected to various forms of control and abuse. Moreover European employers had serious difficulty instilling in their African workers European work habits and discipline. As the case of the Zulu workers in Natal had shown, Africans brought to the workplace their own work habits and notions of time and authority.

As a result of the intensification of capitalist enterprise under colonial rule and the transformation of rural economies, many Africans flocked into the cities to make a living. While many had found wage employment in government departments and in private enterprise, the vast majority eked out a living by engaging in non-wage activities in the informal sector of the urban economy. They became petty traders, cab drivers, tailors, and barbers. This was particularly the case for women, who had few opportunities in the wage-labor market and resorted to such activities as trading, selling food and drinks, domestic service, and prostitution. By engaging in these activities and establishing their informal settlements in the cities, this "floating" population was viewed by colonial officials as a nuisance and became the target of colonial vagrancy laws, evictions, and removals. Yet these non-wage workers supplied goods and services to the poor segment of the urban population and played a crucial role in the reproduction of labor.

For obvious reasons the development of wage labor was much more advanced in South Africa than in the rest of the continent. The mineral discoveries in the second half of the nineteenth century and subsequent expansion of the industrial sector of the economy led to the emergence of an industrial workforce that included thousands of European immigrants and a large number of Africans. The workforce in the South African mines was divided along racial lines, whereby Europeans were assigned to supervisory positions while Africans were relegated to unskilled and menial tasks. Nonetheless the relentless attempts of mineowners to reduce labor costs sparked off confrontation with European workers, culminating in a large-scale strike in 1922. Although the strike was defeated, white workers were able to use their voting power and elect a new government in 1924. The Pact Government introduced a number of reforms that were intended to coopt white workers and set them apart from black workers.

Following the Land Act of 1913, which deprived the vast majority of black South Africans of land ownership, the number of black workers in the mines (as well as in other industries) increased dramatically. Despite their lack of legal rights black workers organized themselves and founded in 1919 the Industrial and Commercial Workers Union (ICU), whose membership reached about 100,000 in the 1920s. The ICU launched a series of strikes that were defeated by the mineowners, who enlisted the support of the state. As a result of internal splits and mismanagement the ICU began to decline and finally collapsed in the late 1920s. It was succeeded by the Congress of Non-European Trade Unions (CNETU), which was dissolved in 1946 following the defeat of a major strike by mine workers. Despite the repressive policies of the apartheid regime black workers continued to protest their harsh working conditions and low wages. In 1955 the South African Congress of Trade Unions (SACTU) was formed. SACTU membership included both white and black workers, and established close links with the African National Congress (ANC) and the South African Communist Party. But SACTU was crushed following the government ban on the ANC. Following the political reforms of the 1980s, which allowed the formation of non-racial trade unions, a number of unions have emerged, such as the Federation of South African Trade Unions (FOSATU). One of the most powerful unions that was established in 1985 was the Congress Of South African Trade Unions (COSATU), which represented over half a million workers. However, a number of trade unions, such as the Council of Unions of South Africa (CUSA), adopted a more nationalist posture and focused exclusively on organizing black workers. It is a commonplace that the South African trade union movement played a pivotal role in the anti-apartheid struggle, and remained a powerful force following the transition to black majority rule in 1994.

In other parts of Africa, during the first three decades of European colonial rule, officials were mainly concerned with the question of how many African workers they could obtain and control with the least possible cost. Colonial administrators were apprehensive about the consequences of full-scale proletarianization and the emergence of an African working class, with its own aspirations and agendas. Indeed the first generation of African workers were largely males who moved between the city and the countryside. However, gradually a significant segment of African workers became committed to wage labor and urban life. Despite the absence of legalized trade unions, African workers began to assert themselves and demand better working conditions. They expressed their discontent through informal forms of resistance such as work-slows, desertion, and sabotage, as well as open strikes. This process reached a peak during and immediately after the Second World War. One of the most militant groups of workers that spearheaded these strikes were transport and communications workers. In view of their large numbers and their concentration in strategic sectors of the colonial economy these workers posed the most serious threat to colonial regimes. For instance, the dock workers of the port city of **Mombasa** launched a series of large-scale strikes in 1939, 1942, 1945, and 1947–8. Labor uprisings occurred in Nigeria in 1945, in the port city of **Dakar** in 1946, and in the Sudanese railway town of Atbara in 1947. One of the most well-known strikes, which occurred in 1947–8, was that of the railway workers of **French West Africa**. Strikes took place among non-wage employees, as well as white-collar workers. In addition to wage increases, better working conditions, decent housing, and improved social services, African workers demanded the right to organize trade unions and other institutions of collective bargaining.

Large-scale strikes and growing labor militancy posed a serious threat to colonial regimes, forcing them to rethink their labor policies and adopt new strategies. These strategies aimed at the development of a stable, productive, and differentiated working class. The stabilization policy entailed the provision of family wages, decent housing, health care, and social services. The provision of a family wage was premised on the European notion of the male worker as head of household and primary bread-winner. Stabilization policy also involved the legalization of trade unions and the introduction of labor legislation that was intended to create a non-political labor movement. However, the legalization of trade unions led to further militancy, as unions began to play a broader political role that extended far beyond workplace issues. The rise of **labor movements** in many parts of Africa took place during the height of the nationalist struggle for independence. Realizing the ability of unions to mobilize large constituencies, African nationalist leaders vigorously sought the support of the labor movement. But the alliance between the nationalist leaders and the trade union movement was short-lived. Once independence was achieved and nationalist leaders had come to power, they tried either to coopt the labor movement or suppress it.

It is evident that, for the most part, the anti-colonial struggles in Africa have resulted in the establishment of politically assertive but socially conservative regimes. These regimes inherited the institutions of the colonial state and displayed great hostility towards the social movements that helped them to come to power. The post-colonial African rulers considered the existence of strong, radical, and independent trade unions as a serious threat to their authority. They stressed the primacy of economic development and nation-building over workers' demands and rights. Nkrumah, Nyerere, and Sékou Touré saw themselves as patrons of the working class and tried to coopt it in their one-party states. But the emphasis on economic development (which entailed alliances with foreign business), the maintenance of high productivity, and the reduction of wages sparked off fierce battles between the labor movement and the post-colonial regimes in Africa. In 1961 the Ghanaian railway workers launched a massive strike against the efforts of Nkrumah's government to control their union, and received widespread support (Jeffries 1978: 72). Similar action was taken by Nigerian workers, who organized a successful general strike in 1964. In the same year Sudanese trade unions and professional associations launched large-scale campaign of civil disobedience and a general strike that led to the downfall of the military regime of General 'Abboud.

During the 1970s and the 1980s African workers faced great difficulties. The wave of military coups, the rise of authoritarian regimes, and the sharp decline of African economies had deleterious effects on the living conditions of African workers. Compounding these problems were the **structural adjustment programs** of the 1980s, which had a catastrophic impact on wage and non-wage-earners alike. Rampant inflation and a sharp increase in the prices of basic commodities triggered large-scale riots in many parts of the continent that were ruthlessly suppressed. Despite these challenges African labor movements remained at the forefront of the struggle for democracy and progressive social change.

See also: economy: colonial; economy: post-independence

References and further reading

Atkins, K. (1993) *The Moon is Dead! Give Us Our Money! The Cultural Origins of an African Work Ethic, Natal, South Africa, 1843–1900*, Portsmouth: Heinemann.

Beinin, J. and Lockman, Z. (1987) *Workers on the Nile: Nationalism, Communism, Islam, and the Egyptian Working Class, 1882–1954*, Princeton: Princeton University Press.

Cooper, F. (1978) *On the African Waterfront*, New Haven: Yale University Press.

—— (ed.) (1983) *Struggle for the City: Migrant Labor, Capital, and the State in Urban Africa*, Beverly Hills: Sage.

—— (1996) *Decolonization and African Society: The Labor Question in French and British Africa*, New York: Cambridge University Press.

Freund, B. (1988) *The African Worker*, New York: Cambridge University Press.

Grillo, R. (1973) *African Railwaymen*, London: Oxford University Press.

Gutkind, P., Cohen, R. and Copans, J. (eds.) (1978) *African Labor History*, Beverly Hills: Sage.

Harries, P. (1994) *Work, Culture, and Identity: Migrant Labourers in Mozambique and South Africa c.1860–1910*, Portsmouth: Heinemann.

Jeffries, R. (1978) *Class, Power, and Ideology in Ghana: The Railway Men of Sekondi*, Cambridge: Cambridge University Press.

Lindsay, L. (1996) "Putting the Family on Track: Gender and Domestic Life on the Colonial Nigerian Railway," Ph.D. dissertation, University of Michigan.

Martin, P. (1995) *Leisure and Society in Colonial Brazzaville*, New York: Cambridge University Press.

Miers, S. and Roberts, R. (eds.) (1988) *The End of Slavery in Africa*, Madison: University of Wisconsin Press.

Robertson, C. (1984) *Sharing the Same Bowl: A Socioeconomic History of Women and Class in Accra, Ghana*, Bloomington: Indiana University Press.

Sandbrook, R. and Cohen, R. (eds.) (1975) *The Development of an African Working Class: Studies in Class Formation and Action*, London: Longman.

Van Onselen, C. (1982) *New Babylon: Studies in the Social and Economic History of the Witwatersrand*, London: Longman, 2 vols.

White, L. (1990) *The Comforts of Home: Prostitution in Colonial Nairobi*, Chicago: University of Chicago Press.

AHMAD SIKAINGA

world wars *see* First World War; Second World War

Y

Yaounde, Cameroon

Founded during the period of German colonization, Yaounde is the second largest city of **Cameroon**, and the country's political and administrative capital. It grew from a settlement established in 1888 by the German scientist and explorer Georg August Zenker in the hilly territory between the Nyong and Sanaga rivers, which was inhabited by the Ewondo people. Hans Dominik, a German soldier and colonial administrator, encouraged the development of the settlement into an outpost of the colonial administration, although Buea was the colony's administrative capital. After the **First World War**, when Germany lost its colonial possessions, France took over the section of Cameroon that included Yaounde, and adopted it as the capital of the French Cameroons. Throughout the colonial era **Douala** was the economic hub of the colony; Yaounde remained the administrative center and the economic center of a vibrant agricultural region. The city grew to incorporate the hillside villages of the Mvog-Ada, Mvolye-Mvog, Beti, and Effoulan – all sub-clans of the Ewondo people.

Yaounde was retained as the political and administrative capital after independence. It was also the location of diplomatic missions and of international and regional organizations, among them the Bank of Central African States. The country's national university, the University of Yaounde, and affiliated professional schools of medicine, journalism, higher education, engineering, civil administration, and so on (known locally as the *grandes écoles*) were located in the city. The population expanded dramatically after independence, and particularly following the abolition of the two-state federal system with which Cameroon entered independence in 1972. The imposition of a unitary structure of government led to bureaucratic centralization, the concentration of civil servants in the city, and regular pilgrimages by non-resident civil servants to follow the progress of their documents through various ministries. From 100,000 in 1960, the city's population had increased to 276,000 in 1975, 832,000 in 1985, and an estimated 1.1 million in 2000. Post-independence national and city governments invested heavily in developing the city's infrastructure and the administrative buildings that defined its center, especially after the upsurge in petroleum revenues in the 1970s.

With industrial activity limited to a sugar-refinery and factories producing cigarettes and plywood, Yaounde's economy continued to be overwhelmingly dependent on government and regional agriculture. The arrival in the city of people from other regions transformed its cultural character from a primarily Ewondo town at independence into a multi-ethnic and cosmopolitan city at the end of the twentieth century. While some of the migrants concentrated in particular neighborhoods (for example, the Fulani from the north in Briquetrie and the Bamilike from the west in Mokolo), the residential locations of both the elite and the common people were multi-ethnic. The massive influx of people and the continuous expansion of the city's boundaries surpassed the government's capacity to maintain adequate urban infrastructure and services, particularly health, housing, roads, and public security. The situation worsened in the late 1980s as Cameroon's economy went into steep decline, forcing the government to abandon often half-completed administrative buildings and to substantially curtail the provision of basic services. In the 1990s the city appeared decrepit, with its infrastructure well below the needs of its population, and even the carefully laid-out neighborhoods of the local elite and diplomatic missions in need of maintenance and the enforcement of urban-planning codes. Post-independence national governments maintained tight control over the administration of the city by directly appointing its chief administrative officer: the Government Delegate. Periodically rocked by student protests in the 1980s, the city became the site of major confrontations between the incumbent regime and the opposition in the 1990s.

Further reading

Zoa, A.-S. (1995) *Les ordures à Yaounde: urbanisations, environnement, et politique au Cameroon*, Paris: L'Harmattan.

DICKSON EYOH

Yoruba

By 2000 the Yoruba language was spoken by about 40 million people. It was the first language for people living predominantly in southwestern **Nigeria**, **Benin**, and parts of **Togo**, with many more Yoruba-speaking communities spread across different parts of **West Africa**. Yoruba is a member of the Defoid language family, which is itself a constituent member of the Benue Congo phylum. Yoruba has about fifty geographic dialects, marked by differences in pronunciation, grammatical structure, and vocabulary. Some Yoruba dialects are also used in the New World as liturgical languages: for example, the Nago dialect of Brazil and the Lucumi dialect of Cuba. There is also a remnant of Trinidadian Yoruba in the West Indies.

Aside from the various dialects of the Yoruba language, there is standard Yoruba, which is recognized as the norm for the written language in books, newspapers, magazines, and any literary texts. It is the form of Yoruba used for educational purposes, and for radio and television. Standard Yoruba is understood by speakers of all the various dialects. It is the variety represented in major dictionaries and grammars of the language that have been prepared over the past two centuries.

Early studies of Yoruba language began with the work of missionaries whose main goals were to translate scriptural texts into the language, and to train a core of evangelists to read and write in it. As a result these early studies concentrated on establishing Yoruba orthography, writing grammars that were, for the most part, sketchy adjuncts to a dictionary, translating the Bible, some catechisms, and John Bunyan's *Pilgrim's Progress*.

By the beginning of the twentieth century there were several grammars and some dictionaries, and the orthography had already been fixed, popularized, and standardized. There was also a substantial number of literary texts. By the mid-twentieth century Yoruba linguists started to attempt a systematic description of the Yoruba language. Numerous articles based on different aspects of Yoruba grammar were written around this period. The composition, collection, and publication of Yoruba oral poetry were also undertaken by many Yoruba scholars. By the 1960s reliable Yoruba texts were available for a proper and careful study of Yoruba literature. Between 1936 and 1963 Fagunwa, who was rightly regarded as the father of the Yoruba novel, wrote several books that have since become classics.

Similarly, by the mid-twentieth century, the works of dramatists like Adebayo Faleti, Odunjo, Kola Ogunmola, Hubert Ogunde, and Duro Ladipo became popular. In addition literary studies moved away from mere collection, composition, and publication of various oral traditions and into literary analysis. However, during this period the analyses were done through the medium of the English language. The domain of use of Yoruba was restricted because of competition with English, which was and continues to be the official language of Nigeria. Even in Yoruba classes, the Yoruba grammar and literary analysis were taught in English because of lack of Yoruba equivalents for many grammatical and literary terms.

However, by the late 1960s and early 1970s there was a dramatic change in the attitude of Yoruba speakers and scholars towards the use and study of Yoruba in Nigeria. This change in attitude, attributed by many to a growth in nationalist feeling, led to the spread of the language to wider domains, such as education, the media, administration, and public affairs. Yoruba people started taking pride in their language and culture. As a result the desire to study and use the language in different settings increased.

Around this same period Yoruba scholars started to ask which linguistic medium was the best for the early education of children. Many scholars came to the conclusion that children learn better in their mother tongue. This decision led to the introduction of mother-tongue education, which meant that suitable materials in Yoruba had to be made available for teaching the various courses, such as arithmetic, social studies, science, and so on. Yoruba studies blossomed under this educational policy.

Similarly provision was made for the use of Yoruba (along with the two other major Nigerian languages, Igbo and Hausa) in public affairs, in the National Assembly and the House of Assembly of the Yoruba-speaking states. Yoruba was also used in political broadcasts and campaigns, as well as in public education programs on the radio and television.

At the university level Yoruba students were required to study Yoruba language, literature, culture, history, philosophy, thought, and beliefs, with Yoruba used as the medium of instruction. Extending the domains of Yoruba usage to the above areas led to more active and serious studies of the language. Various Yoruba committees oversaw the development of Yoruba vocabulary. By the 1980s Yoruba metalanguage was developed to a stage where the language was equipped with adequate and appropriate terms for the teaching, writing, and presentation of academic works and reports in all areas of Yoruba studies.

By the end of the twentieth century Yoruba scholars had started using the language to write serious academic research papers, dissertations, and theses, with only summaries of their work provided in English. A Yoruba dictionary of legislative terms was also developed. The late twentieth century also saw Yoruba becoming viable for serious study-courses in Asia, the Caribbean, and the Americas. Various textbooks were developed to help foreigners study the language. Yoruba fonts were developed so that people could use Yoruba in emails and on the worldwide web. Many multimedia materials for studying Yoruba language and culture were also developed. The century ended with discussion about the establishment of a Yoruba World Center. The goal of this center was to internationalize the study of Yoruba language and culture, and to investigate the past, present, and future of the millions of Yoruba people who live in Nigeria, Brazil, Cuba, Trinidad, Tobago, Jamaica, Benin, Togo, the Americas, Europe, and other parts of Africa.

Further reading

Bamgbose, A. (1984) *Yoruba: A Language in Transition*, Lagos: Longman.

Olatunji, O. (forthcoming) *Yoruba Studies in the Twenty-first Century.*

ANTONIA FOLARIN-SCHLEICHER

youth

Today young people and youth in general are emerging as a central theme of African studies. Located at the heart of both analytical apparatuses and political action, they have become an obsessive preoccupation for politicians, social workers, and communities in Africa – for different reasons, of course. We have to acknowledge that the centrality of this subject is justified by the extraordinary turnaround in the way African societies see themselves over the last three decades of the twentieth century. Since the end of the **Second World War** youth has been substituted for the themes that had previously constituted the basic objects of research on, and explanation of, African societies and the condition of Africans: These had been the deepening financial crises and jolts occurring in efforts at democratization in the

1990s, or the political ruptures that began on the continent at the end of the 1980s.

Several factors seem to have been involved in this repositioning of the study of African youth. First of all the high proportion of young people in African populations contrasts strikingly with their disappearance from developed countries due to the continuing decline in birth rates. In fact young people constituted the majority of the African population by 2000. This had economic, cultural, political, and social consequences, because each of these registers influenced the procedures by which young people were integrated into society, in terms of both civic responsibilities and entitlements. At the same time it was heavily influenced by the interaction of local and global pressure that defined contemporary Africa, which was caught between the dissolution or fragmentation of national geography and memories of it, on one hand, and the return to local temporalities that allowed themselves to be borne by the impulses of global temporality, on the other, whether this return was religious, aesthetic, cultural, or political and economic – or all these at once.

There was also the failure of the nationalist political enterprise, which had set itself the double objective of economic development and the implementation of social justice. It had supervised young people and assigned them a major role that drew both on the language of universal rights and social rights and on specific African cultures, thus leading to continual redefinitions of young people and the modalities for socializing them.

Finally the violent irruption of youth into the public and domestic spheres seems to have resulted in the construction of African youth as a threat, and to have provoked a panic within society as a whole that was simultaneously moral and civic. At issue were the bodies of young people and their behavior, in so far as it escaped the constraints of social construction, and particularly with regard to their sexuality and pleasure, as well as the formulas of their action and presence *qua* social juniors. The tensions produced by the new situation had several problematic consequences, the most important of which were:

1 the redefinition of the relationships between identities and citizenship in the whirlwind of **globalization**, which combined a metamorphosis of the processes of socialization;
2 the production of new forms of inequality that were represented and imagined in various ways; and
3 the extraordinary mutation of the chronological and psychological construction of the passage from youth to adulthood.

The new trajectory could be summed up as a radical transformation of the idea of citizenship, together with the collapse of both the domestic and the public spheres, and the production of new forms of identification that appealed to multiple resources. These were accompanied by a refashioning of the indices and signs of autochthony and membership, of inclusion and exclusion, that was associated with the reconfiguration of national territory, domestic or sacred spaces, forms of organization, networks of loyalties, and so on. In most cases these elements suggested new expressions of political action that could be violent or non-violent, formal or informal, but all confronted the erosion of state and of family obligations. The latter were often accompanied by new associative formulas, political commitments, and aesthetic formulations on the margins of institutions and traditional codes of conduct.

Youth and colonialism

The colonial period offers an interesting viewpoint on questions related to African youth. In fact it is a period during which an important tension was generated between the traditional domain and the new opportunities presented by colonial domination. The former imposed socialization and incorporation devices on society that were based on initiatory cycles, the grammar of which was produced and controlled by adults, particularly elders. The passage to adulthood was reflected in the achievement of three objectives:

1 residential autonomy (the creation of a home),
2 having paid employment and marriage for men and women,
3 the creation of a kitchen and a home when joining the house of the husband and the participation in a domestic unit of production.

For both men and women the control of these domains by the elders, combined with the implementation of the law and interpretation of religious duties, resulted in a situation in which young people were very dependent on elders.

It is precisely this situation that colonial domination weakened by introducing new political, economic, social, and cultural opportunities. This offered young people opportunities to escape from traditional prescriptions and the social control of the elders. By opening up new domains distinct from traditional ones, particularly in urban and agricultural production areas, as well as in mining and commercial zones, colonization created a new geography, and sometimes gave young people resources that could ensure a certain autonomy vis-à-vis the elders, social rules, religion, and traditional morals. The financial resources from the sale of agricultural products or from salaries, conversion to Christianity or Islam in urban areas, resulted in the creation of new forms of socialization, which assured the access of young men to women and the other attributes of adults. For young people settling in cities and having a job, even prostitution, accelerated the process of individualization and the entrance into adulthood.

Colonization resulted in a desynchronization of childhood and adulthood. It achieved this through two mechanisms: the first was offering new opportunities to dependent people, and the second was the system of economic exploitation, which was founded on the involvement of young people in work and the exploitation of their labor power. During the colonial period young Africans, be they *évolué* ("modern") or not, swung between two poles: on the one hand, engaging in creative transactions between traditional prescriptions and colonial opportunities, and, on the other, domination by and resistance of colonial political, economic, and cultural policies.

Youth and the post-colonial state

African political culture in general and the struggle for independence in particular made use both of pre-colonial communitarian resources – African values – and of the indisputable signs of administrative modernity and post-colonial politics in order to redefine, in an unprecedented way, the meaning of African youth. The post-colonial project sought to go beyond a colonial ethnology/anthropology that had been preoccupied by rituals of initiation and socialization to a sociology focused on the generational and gender division of labor, and on social and economic mobilization, passing by way of a psychology that tried to understand the mental structures, the ritual and supervised modes of behavior of different age groups, and the psychosociological consequences of taking the main steps toward "adult life" and their impact on the construction of the identity in young people.

In its cultural and political versions the nationalist project sought to do two things: maintain the boundary between elders and juniors in order to legitimize its role as the foundation for a restoration of African values, and put young people at the center of its ideological apparatus of economic development and national liberation. Youth was the hope not only of African nations under construction, but of the whole world. Adhering to the central ideology of economic development, youth was constructed as the chief actor in African societies' struggle against underdevelopment, poverty, misery, and illiteracy. As both subjects and objects of training and mobilization, young people incarnated the future and represented the promise of a restored identity, both national and pan-African, in opposition to colonial alienation and post-colonial forms of domination and subordination. Bearers of the double project of modernization and return to the sources of African culture, young Africans were called on to promote and respect their political, social, and cultural responsibilities as citizens, with a view to constructing African democracies. Such approaches accentuated the cultural prestige of young people as the chief agents of transformation for African societies. The paradox was that young people achieved this status only in so far as they were channeled and supervised by adults.

The failures of nationalist economic, cultural, and political models had particularly dreadful effects on young people. They were left along the wayside by the many failures of economic development, as well as a social crisis in work or education, which required money and time that young people were not prepared to invest, preferring to take risks for the promise of immediate profit. Both constitutional and legal approaches to the supervision of young people and traditional modes of socialization through rites of initiation were considered outdated, and were substituted by surveillance, harassment, and repression, foreshadowing new forms of public and domestic violence. A new transnational youth had been produced by African **families**, communities, and nations.

The closure of the nationalist moment: The new politics of representation

The bankruptcy of the nationalist project of development was manifested in the recurrent economic crises that began in the early 1970s, along with economic and ideological adjustments that accelerated migration into the cities and to the West. In this new situation the construction of youth as "the hope of the world" was replaced by representations of youth as dangerous, criminal, and decadent, their sexuality unrestrained and threatening for the whole of society, as was dramatically shown by the extraordinary prevalence of AIDS.

Not only were young people losing the prestigious status that nationalism had given them in its ascendancy, but they were no longer a national priority. This loss of status was reflected in the physical and intellectual collapse of the institutions of supervision and education, the absence of health care, and the massive and aggressive presence of young people on the streets, public garbage dumps, and urban and rural underground. The reclassification of young people was manifested in institutionalized hostility toward them, which increasingly took violent forms that, combined with indifference or disdain on the part of the elites, rendered their present difficult and their future unpredictable.

Without power, work, education, or **leisure**, young Africans constructed places of socialization and new sociabilities whose function was to mark difference within the margins or at the heart of society, simultaneously as victims and active agents, circulating in a geography that escaped the limits of the national territory. These transformations affected both geography and history – that is, history when conceived as a chronology that defined age groups by their degree of connection with society through rights and duties. The ideological and cultural reorganization that flowed from this took place in the spaces deserted by political power and dominant cultures, increasing the significance of marginal spaces and areas from which states retreated and in which emptiness and indetermination were dominant. These were places that were ready to be filled, conquered, and named, favoring the rites and rituals intended to express new identities. The function attributed to these spaces, which escaped the geometric logics of public and administrative control, communitarian prescriptions, and state surveillance, was to serve as supports for carefully considered acts that expressed within the public sphere – in a violent, artistic, or spiritual way – a desire for recognition.

This geography – often understood by moralists and pessimists as a geography of delinquency, but by optimists and dissidents as a geography of resistance – first of all incorporated the street, the suburbs, the forests, craggy and rugged landscapes, frontier regions, and prohibited zones where drugs or mineral riches – gold and diamonds in particular – were produced. Second, it was a geography of the forms of development that were possible outside conventional images of success. It helped construct unprecedented modalities of membership. Erasing the national territory and its histories, it offered African youth opportunities for entry on the world stage, usually through pain, disorder, and violence. Migrant and clandestine workers – as well as sometimes musicians, artists, and "golden boys" – became actors in the theater of globalization, resolved to make their way into the world market's economy of desires and consumption. Finally, this geography was the expression of the impossibility of incorporating young people into obsolete and above all inefficient post-colonial cultures, and of the bankruptcy of procedures of socialization through education and work, which made the street into the cultural arena where young people could struggle against the dominant cultures.

It is not easy to give an account of the history that accompanied this new geography, because of its very diversity. In fact, each geography has its own history and the competing histories simultaneously overlap and feed on each other. The accentuation of inequalities, the globalization of desires, and the creation of a young people's consumer culture based on American-influenced international popular youth culture, combined with the emergence of African "golden boys" (who emerged from European and American universities, on the one hand, and from zones where trafficking in drugs or diamonds was common, on the other), were repositioning Africa in mercantile relationships in which revolution was yielding to negotiation and bargaining as the means of liberating Africa.

The plural history that informed these adjustments challenged nationalist history and its narrative of the stages of development from childhood to adulthood. The refusal to be embedded in the memory of the state and the nation was accompanied by a rejection of community memories – and sometimes family memories too. The latter were, at least, reconsidered and reworked, transfiguring or deflecting their moral purpose in order to confound modern or traditional elites, confronting them with the contradictions between their rhetoric and their practices.

This autonomous narrative was often fragmented because of the multiplicity of sources that had been drawn on in the process of producing it, thus there was a constant preoccupation with erasing ethnic, national, and continental borderlines. In a way it provided a territory for the imagination of young Africans, a territory that paradoxically escaped them in all the violence and supervision of borders – a situation in which migrants were imprisoned within the margins of wealthy societies, and the xenophobia in Western countries was on the rise.

Mistrust of indigenous memories and the nationalist ideology of development was organized in a systematic and sometimes violent challenge to the construction of the life of young people as being "on hold" between a glorious past, a present of sacrifices, and a radiant future. In opposition to the conception of life as only possible because it was prepared and supervised by adults, risky behavior in the street, the underground, and informal economic practices created alternative means of expression and presence in the public sphere for young people. Thus they were able to define new modalities of action and propose new forms of musical, iconographic, and military expression, using political, economic, and religious formulas. The result was to put into circulation forms of modernity that introduced different histories, local or global, into temporal or geographic contexts that, as mentioned above, resulted from the crisis of the state and the family. They not only acted on genealogy but also rearranged the construction of time and the meaning of the sequence of past, present, and future, along with the values that were attributed to young people as they passed from childhood to adulthood. The best illustration of this work on temporality was seen in the extraordinary vitality of "born-again" Christian movements and sects, in particular Pentecostalism, and in the reform-minded efforts of indigenous Muslims – or indeed the subversive forms of Islam often called "fundamentalist." Strongly rooted in ideologies of renaissance (literally meaning "born again"), both as a form of purification and as a return to origins, these movements addressed themselves to young people, were composed of young people, and/or were heavily dominated by young people. Taking for granted young Africans' despair about the disjunction between their dreams and aspirations, on the one hand, and the opportunities offered to them and their current circumstances, on the other, the religious discourse called for a complete and deliberate rupture from the past, and laid out a different future. In this way the religious movements promoted new communitarian formulas, and the constitution of a new form of individuality on the margins of the ethnic group and the state.

The rearrangement of the past favored new ways of understanding the present differently, of reconfiguring unemployment, of reversing educational failure, of preventing domestic and public violence and corruption, and of assuaging people's disappointments in a world that was no longer their own. The religious present restored people's dignity and spoke to them of a future that was already there. Religious movements were attractive not only because they offered modes of being and belonging, but also because they constructed new – and usually literary – ways of imagining the community. Not only did the new versions of the past put into circulation a mastery of the present and a legitimization of rejection of ancestors, traditions, and the state, but at the same time they structured the modalities of passage from the autochthonous to the universal or global.

The literary imagination gave the young a new weapon, new power, and texts. It is precisely this systematic reference to texts that produced cohesion and a very strong feeling of belonging. Beyond national borders, new technologies (digital and audiovisual) were appropriated in such a way as to recreate the dynamics of the oral and the spectacular. Along with the literary and iconographic imagination, these erased distance and created a ritual community, whose imagined geography was so powerful that it could challenge the geography of borders and physical distances. It delocalized memory and suggested a cosmopolitan historicity.

Not much attention was paid to these new practices. Instead observers and academic scholars focused on more spectacular manifestations of youth in Africa. The latter were increasingly seen as masking other practices and forms of socialization that were far more structuring. They were accompanied by identity-related logics, as in the case of religious formulas, whether or not they were influenced by globalization. These processes provoked the explosion of old frames of reference and subverted systems of values to the benefit of new forms of territoriality and new communitarian networks and communications, through the use and reinterpretation of elements present in former repertoires but mixed with world culture.

The enterprise of *déracinement* (in its literal sense of "uprooting") of post-colonial legitimacies was discernible in several events, from the musical and iconographic activities of young Senegalese to riots orchestrated by schoolchildren and university students in **Mali**. It would also be seen in how the administration and politicians were deprived of their hold on certain neighborhoods in Nigerian cities unless they operated through the mediation of "area boys," or in the crucial role played by disaffected youth in the armed conflicts in **Liberia** and **Sierra Leone**.

It is difficult to account for this ambivalence, except perhaps by trying to understand the territory on which both pleasure (leisure and clothing) and violence were made as visible as possible, on the bodies of young people and in the ways in which they displayed themselves (or were displayed), the ways they exhibited themselves (or were exhibited) in the public arena.

Youthful bodies

In most African societies distress as well as success adhere to the body and are read on the body, especially among young people. Their bodies – clothed, adorned with jewels, powdered, perfumed, and shaped – also bore the violent marks of the desire to be attractive (especially among women), and the scars left by the struggle for survival or "a good life" through the exercise of licit or illicit activities such as prostitution, war, or delinquency. By practices such as prostitution, violence, or living on the street, through legal professional activities or life on the margins, young people abolished the gap between adolescence and adulthood, and in some cases between childhood and adolescence. The practice of sex or the exercise of violence thus became rites of passage and initiation that inaugurated, like the new religious practices, a historicity of dissidence.

By escaping the political and moral discourses that hemmed them in, and by moving through the cracks opened up by the crisis of the state and society, African youth provoked unprecedented moral and social panic. Young people were seen and constructed as a menace, as much because of their pleasures and leisure activities as because of the violence they sometimes committed. These two aspects became inseparable, and their most evident expression was in reactions to the AIDS epidemic that ravaged the Africa from the mid-1980s. To kill, to experience violence and pleasure, to move along the obscure paths of the migrant, of witchcraft, of the urban and rural underground – all these produced new cultures and new sociabilities, new meanings of pleasure, of life, and of death. One tragic illustration of this situation was the crisis of the "penis shrinkers" (*rétrécisseurs de sexe*) that shook **West Africa** from **Senegal** to

Cameroon during the 1990s. A phenomenon that moved from one place to place and city to city, young people were accused by other youngsters of having stolen their penises. In most cases, a hysterical crowd would lynch the people thus accused.

The body was also perceived as the site where a youth culture that was supposed to be also a counterculture – the very counterculture that allowed youngsters to enter combat against the dominant culture – was expressed. Postures and bodily gestures, like music and varied iconographies, were part of this struggle to position the body in space, to give the body a presence that made it both a weapon and a text. Did that make African youth culture a counterculture? The question remained open, especially if we consider that young people were often inclined to readopt the norms of the very society whose margins they occupied.

Combining violence, madness, pleasure, sex and the temptations of a wholly religious chastity, the desire for autochthony and the desire to tear themselves out of the continent in order to erase everything that attached them to the place, young Africans symbolized the uneven trajectory of an Africa in search of its rhythm. With a plurality more often creative than murderous, it was a continent attempting to find for itself a global present that was an indigenous present too.

Further reading

Abdullah, I. and Bangura, Y. (eds.) (1997) "Lumpen Youth Culture and Political Violence: The Sierra Leone Civil War," *Africa Development*, special issue, 23: 3–20.

Cruise O'Brien, D. (1996) "A Lost Generation. Youth Identity and State Decay in West Africa," in R. Webner and T. Ranger (eds.), *Postcolonial Identities in Africa*, London: Zed Books.

De Boeck, F. (1999) "Domesticating Diamonds and Dollars: Identity, Expenditure and Sharing in Southern Zaire," in B. Meyer and P. Geschiere (eds.), *Globalization and Identity. Dialectics of Flow and Closure*, Oxford: Blackwell.

Diouf, M. (1996) "Urban Youth and Senegalese Politics: Dakar 1988–1994," *Public Culture* 19: 225–49.

Honwana, A. (1999) "Negotiating Post-War Identities: Child Soldiers in Mozambique and Angola," *CODESRIA Bulletin* 1–2: 4–13.

Richards, P. (1996), *Fighting for the Rain Forest. War, Youth and Resources in Sierra Leone*, Oxford: James Currey and Portsmouth: Heinemann.

MAMADOU DIOUF

Z

Zaire *see* Democratic Republic of Congo (known as Congo Free State from 1885 to 1908, the Belgian Congo from 1908 to 1960, Zaire from 1971 to 1997).

Zambia

Zambia, with an area of 752,610 square kilometers, is located in **Southern Africa**, bordering **Angola**, **Namibia**, **Democratic Republic of Congo**, **Malawi**, **Mozambique**, **Zimbabwe**, and **Tanzania**. In 2000 it had an estimated population of 10.8 million. The country, formerly the British colony of Northern Rhodesia, was renamed Zambia at independence in 1964. The colony was initially founded by the British South Africa Company (BSAC).

As in many parts of Africa the era of European conquest in Zambia lasted from the 1870s to the **First World War**. Explorers, adventurers, Christian missionaries, or the representatives of speculative capitalism made Zambia one of the most important theaters of European expansion and colonization in Southern Africa. From the 1890s Zambia's history evolved in close association with that of Malawi and Zimbabwe. Having secured Zambia and Zimbabwe as chartered company territories in 1890, and because of Britain's reluctance to pay for the colonial administration in Malawi, Cecil Rhodes and the BSAC moved into Malawi with the hope of turning it into their third territorial acquisition. Zambia was also affected by developments in **South Africa**. The BSAC was based there and its colonization schemes were intended to extend British imperial hegemony south and north of the Zambezi. In 1923, when white settlers in Zimbabwe rejected the political patronage of BSAC and the intention of international capital to merge Zimbabwe into South Africa, Zambia too was saved from becoming part of South Africa. When the British took control of Zambia in April 1924, they encouraged a policy of close association between Zambia, Zimbabwe, and Malawi. This policy bore fruit when the three countries formally became part of the **Central African Federation** between 1953 and 1963. African nationalism in Zambia and Malawi eventually led to the demise of the federation.

The BSAC had come in search of minerals, and mining soon became the mainstay of the Zambian economy. By the time of the First World War iron ore, zinc, lead, vanadium, copper, and gold were being mined in different parts of the country, but a truly vibrant capitalist mining industry only began between 1927 and 1934, when vast copper deposits were discovered in what became known as the Copperbelt Province. The Copperbelt played a decisive role in the subsequent economic and political history of Zambia. For the first time in 1927–8, and especially from 1933, the British colonial administration balanced its budget; in fact it was able to produce a surplus for the next three decades. Large-scale mining in Zambia was stimulated, first, by enormous demand in the industrial world for copper (especially for car manufacturing and electricity) and, second, by the end of the BSAC charter in 1923, which led to the relaxation of mineral exploration and investment laws, encouraging large companies to come and invest. The biggest mines were owned by Anglo-American Corporation (formed in 1917 in **Johannesburg** and the colossus of South African mining finance) and the Rhodesian Selection Trust, which was dominated by American capital. After the **Great Depression** the mining industry, which relied on **migrant labor** drawn mostly from within Zambia itself, entered a period of rapid expansion, boosted by rising demand and stable prices during the **Second World War** and the Korean War, until the copper slump of 1958–9.

The fortunes and misfortunes of the mining industry laid the foundations of Zambian nationalism. Job losses and raised taxes provoked the labor strikes of 1935, followed five years later by another wave of strikes. After the Second World War trade unions were formed, including a miners union in 1947. In response, and anxious for a stabilized labor force, mining companies began to provide better houses, schools, and social facilities for their workers. But this could not hide the fact that Zambia's riches were being expatriated: from 1953 to 1963 there was a massive outflow of £260 million in the form of mining dividends and royalties, and a further £97 million went to the federal government in **Harare**. The nationalist elites were outraged at this exploitation of their country's resources. In the 1950s they began agitating for independence. The formation of the mineworkers' union coincided with the amalgamation of political organizations into the Northern Rhodesia Federation of Welfare Societies in 1948. In 1951 the Northern Rhodesia Congress of Trade Unions was formed, while the nationalist movement regrouped into the Northern Rhodesia African National Congress. But labor was united and resolved to sustain its autonomy from the nationalist movement, which tirelessly sought to subordinate it. Independence was achieved in 1964 under the leadership of Kenneth Kaunda's United National Independence Party.

The nationalist government inherited an economy heavily dependent on mining, and an industry with a highly politically conscious labor force. The new government acquired dominant shares in the industry. Buoyant copper prices enabled Kaunda's government to introduce free education and medical services, and to embark on import substitution industrialization. The Kaunda regime also used the proceeds from the mining industry to support regional liberation struggles in the remaining settler colonies of Southern Africa, whose liberation movements opened offices in **Lusaka**. But the collapse of copper prices in the mid-1970s, accompanied by the oil crisis, greatly weakened the economy and curtailed the regime's economic and political ambitions. Subsidies for food, education, and health services were withdrawn in the 1980s as part of a **structural adjustment program**.

In the meantime popular discontent mounted, led by the **labor movement** and new **civil society** organizations. In 1991 multi-party elections were held, which were won by the opposition Movement for Multi-Party Democracy, led by Frederick Chiluba, a former labor leader. Chiluba subsequently became president. His government carried on with economic liberalization, and even sold the government's shares in the mines to private investors. The government was unable to stem economic decline, however, and Chiluba damaged his own reputation when he tried to change the two-term limit for president – an attempt that was thwarted by widespread protests.

Further reading

Ihonvbere, J.O. (1996) *Economic Crisis, Civil Society, and Democratization: The Case of Zambia*, Trenton: Africa World Press Inc.

Roberts, A.D. (1976) *A History of Zambia*, London: Heinemann.

ACKSON M. KANDUZA

Zanzibar, Tanzania

Zanzibar is a group of islands off the east coast of Africa, and part of the United Republic of **Tanzania**. In many respects Zanzibar's history is a riddle, for even the most basic historical question as to "Who are the Zanzibaris?" is a difficult one to answer, not only by outsiders but also by the citizens themselves. Zanzibar's population represents one of the most diverse, cosmopolitan societies in Africa. Many of its inhabitants, particularly from the second half of the nineteenth century, are descended from people who settled on the islands from elsewhere. They came from mainland **East Africa**, Arabia, Persia, and India, even China and Japan, and intermarried with the local population. At various points in time Zanzibari identity – as much as citizenship – has been bitterly contested among the various groups living on the islands, most notably in the "Revolution" of 12 January 1964.

Zanzibar comprises two major islands: Unguja and Pemba. They are separated from the mainland by a channel some forty kilometers wide. Despite being relatively small (Unguja has an area of 1,660 square kilometers, Pemba only 950 square kilometers) they are the largest islands on the East African coast. Statistics for Zanzibar are notoriously unreliable. The last population census was held in 1988, when it was estimated that 640,578 people were living in the islands, of whom just over a quarter resided in Zanzibar town (157,634), the capital of the islands. From 1988 the population grew by about 3 percent each year. The vast majority of the local population were Sunni Muslims, although there were small Christian, Hindu, and other religious communities (they accounted for less than 5 percent of the total population).

The British ruled Zanzibar for almost three-quarters of a century. In November 1890, following the signing of the Anglo-German Heligoland Agreement, the islands were declared a British Protectorate. At the time Zanzibar was the center of a commercial empire that dominated trade and politics in East Africa, at least as far as the coastal towns and certain areas in the hinterland were concerned. In colonial times the Sultan of Zanzibar was the notional figurehead of the government, but real political power lay in the hands of the British.

Zanzibar regained its independence on 10 December 1963. However, the elected government to which the British relinquished power was to last for only about a month. It was violently overthrown on 12 January 1964 by a "Revolution" that only a few people in Zanzibar had anticipated. It is believed that several thousand people died, and many more fled the islands. The newly established Revolutionary Council immediately abolished all signs of, and institutions that it believed represented, the "Arab" domination of the island, including, of course, the post-colonial constitutional monarchy. The Council also nationalized a number of clove plantations (the economic backbone of the economy since the nineteenth century), community-based schools, import and export companies, and urban property that had belonged to those who had fled the country or been killed.

Soon after the revolution the leader of the Revolutionary Council, Abeid Karume, and the first President of Tanganyika, Julius Nyerere, agreed to set up a loose union between the two countries, forming the United Republic of Tanzania. The union took effect on 26 April 1964. Zanzibar retained its internal political sovereignty, however. In the 1960s and early 1970s the Zanzibar government received considerable material and technical assistance from the People's Republic of China, the USSR, and the German Democratic Republic.

Abeid Karume was assassinated on 7 April 1972. After that Zanzibar experienced a considerable degree of political and economic liberalization, albeit at the price of ever-closer union with the mainland. An important stepping stone in this process was the merger of the two government parties – the Zanzibar-based Afro-Shirazi Party (ASP) and the Tanganyika African National Union (TANU) – in 1977 to form Chama Cha Mapunduzi (CCM – the Party of the Revolution), which remained in power for the rest of the twentieth century.

Following the trend of democratization elsewhere in Africa, multi-party politics arrived in Zanzibar in the early 1990s. The Zanzibar parliamentary elections of 1995 and 2000 were closely contested and, according to foreign observers, blatantly rigged by the government. Political protest by the main opposition movement, the Civic United Front (CUF) was violently suppressed. Following the 1995 elections the CUF and the CCM tried to resolve their disagreements on numerous occasions, but no lasting solution had been reached by the end of the decade.

Enjoying a leading position in the world spice

market for much of the twentieth century Zanzibar's economy was based primarily on the export of cloves. In the interwar years the British had made some effort to develop the islands. Considerable engineering and building works were carried out, particularly in Zanzibar town, including the construction of a deep-water harbor. Yet these investments were geared mainly towards integrating Zanzibar more firmly into the British colonial economy, with costs and benefits highly unequally distributed between the British and their Zanzibari subjects (see **economy: colonial**).

After the revolution agriculture, particularly clove production, experienced a gradual decline. The newly established small-scale import substitution (shoes, cigarettes) and export-oriented manufacturing industries (clove-oil production, fish canning) did not contribute significantly to the wealth of the islands. However, from the mid-1980s Zanzibar increasingly became a popular destination for tens of thousands of European tourists. A substantial number of holiday resorts, luxury hotels, and guesthouses were built to cater for their needs and whims. Yet, owing to the political crises, the expansion of the tourist industry occurred in fits and starts, and in 1996–7 and again in 2000–1 the industry suffered severe setbacks. Whether tourism would ultimately replace clove production as the main source of government revenue, income, and employment remained to be seen.

Further reading

Clayton, A. (1981) *The Zanzibar Revolution and its Aftermath*, London: Hurst.

Sheriff, A.M.H. and Ferguson, E. (eds.) (1991) *Zanzibar Under Colonial Rule*, London: James Currey.

JAN-GEORG DEUTSCH

Zimbabwe

Zimbabwe, which covers an area of 390,759 square kilometers and had a population of 12 million people in 1999, is a landlocked country in **Southern Africa**, bordered by **Botswana**, **Zambia**, **South Africa**, and **Mozambique**. Zimbabwe's population, 75 percent of whom live in the rural areas and the rest in urban centers, is made up of two major ethnic groups, the Shona (80 percent) and the Ndebele (19 percent), along with other minorities that include a small white population. Most Africans practice traditional religions, but the country also has sizable Christian and Muslim communities. A British colony until April 1980, Zimbabwe operates a parliamentary system of government with an executive presidency. It is a member of the **Southern African Development Community** (SADC), the **Organization of African Unity** (OAU), and various other international organizations. Like its southern neighbor South Africa, Zimbabwe has one of the most diversified economies on the continent. Its economy is based on agriculture, mining, and manufacturing, the last having developed since the **Second World War** and more rapidly in the Unilateral Declaration of Independence (UDI) years (1965–79), because of the import substitution industrialization strategies that the then internationally ostracized Rhodesia had to pursue.

Before British colonialism the Shona economy was based on the production of millet and sorghum, stock-rearing, mining, pottery-making, salt production, trade, fishing, and hunting and gathering. By the seventh century AD the Shona were part of the Indian Ocean trade network, exchanging gold, ivory, copper, and iron for pottery from Persia, porcelain from China, and glassware from India. From the twelfth century the Shona established the Mwene Mutapa and Rozvi Empires – the former reached its peak between 1450 and 1500, and the latter in the seventeenth and eighteenth centuries. The Rozvi Empire collapsed in the 1840s at the hands of Mzilikazi's Ndebele invaders, who had fled northwards from Zulu king Tshaka's rule and established their capital at **Bulawayo**. At Mzilikazi's death his son Lobengula ruled the Ndebele until 1893. The Ndebele economy rested partly on crop cultivation, but mainly on large cattle herds raided from neighboring societies.

On the basis of a fraudulently acquired document, the Rudd Concession, by which Lobengula had been tricked into signing away his territory and sovereignty, Cecil John Rhodes' British South Africa Company (BSAC) colonized Zimbabwe. The beginning of the colonial period was marked by a band of adventurers, known as the Pioneer Column (which Rhodes had funded), hoisting the Union Jack over Harare in 1890. In 1893 European settlers destroyed the Ndebele kingdom, and incorporated it into the colony. In a last-ditch effort to stave off settler rule, in 1896 both the Shona and the Ndebele rose in the first Chimurenga/Umvukela armed uprisings, which were suppressed in 1897 after much bloodshed.

Thereafter the white settler population and economy expanded rapidly, mostly at the expense of the African majority, who were increasingly politically and economically marginalized. In 1930, for instance, government passed the Land Apportionment Act, which divided land along racial lines and excluded Africans, then 95 percent of the population, from half of the best agricultural land. In 1953 Rhodesia (Zimbabwe), Nyasaland (**Malawi**), and Northern Rhodesia (Zambia) established the **Central African Federation**, which collapsed in 1963 over economic and political differences. In 1965 the Rhodesian Front Party government, under Prime Minister Ian Smith, issued their Unilateral Declaration of Independence (UDI) from Britain. In response Britain and the international community imposed economic sanctions on Rhodesia.

Meanwhile African nationalists responded to UDI by waging a guerrilla war, spearheaded by two liberation movements: Joshua Nkomo's Zimbabwe African Peoples Union (ZAPU) and Ndabaningi Sithole's Zimbabwe African National Union (ZANU), later led by Robert Mugabe. In an attempt to undermine the guerrilla war, in 1978 Smith engineered an internal-settlement arrangement through which he coopted some internally based politicians to establish a sham majority-rule government, with Bishop Abel Muzorewa as prime minister of the now re-named Zimbabwe-Rhodesia. However, this failed to either end the war or gain international recognition for the country. The liberation guerrilla war ended only when the British brokered the Lancaster House peace agreement in 1979, followed by internationally supervised general elections in 1980. ZANU won an overwhelming victory. Zimbabwe became independent under a government of national unity, with Mugabe as prime minister. In 1989 Mugabe became executive president.

In 1982 Mugabe dismissed ZAPU ministers from government and confiscated ZAPU property after caches of arms were discovered there. Some former ZAPU cadres undertook an anti-government guerrilla campaign in protest. The government responded by deploying its Korean-trained Fifth Brigade, which massacred thousands of Ndebeles before, in 1987, ZAPU and ZANU signed a Unity Accord. Under the terms of this Accord ZAPU was incorporated into the now-renamed ZANU-Patriotic Front (ZANU-PF) Party.

Meanwhile, because of apartheid South Africa's destabilization campaign and the government's massive and unsustainable social-sector spending, the economy performed poorly in the 1980s, leaving Zimbabwe little choice but to implement a **structural adjustment program** (SAP) sponsored by the International Monetary Fund and World Bank between 1990 and 1995. The SAP and its 1998 successor, the Zimbabwe Program for Economic and Social Transformation (ZIMPREST), ruined the economy and left the country facing problems of runaway inflation, massive unemployment, deepening poverty, and a crumbling health system at a time when the HIV/AIDS pandemic was rapidly worsening.

Because of these economic hardships, exacerbated by government corruption and misgovernment, and by the disastrous decision in 1998 to send the Zimbabwean army into the **Democratic Republic of Congo** to defend the Laurent Kabila regime, anti-government sentiment grew, culminating in the formation of the Movement for Democratic Change (MDC) opposition party in 2000. Led by former Zimbabwe Congress of Trade Unions (ZCTU) secretary-general Morgan Tsvangirai, MDC won over half of the seats in parliament in the general elections of June that year. ZANU-PF responded by unleashing a reign of terror, marked by the murder of and widespread physical assaults on suspected members of the opposition party, as well as government-orchestrated invasions of white-owned farms and industries by ZANU-PF supporters, all in an attempt to reassert ZANU-PF dominance in advance of presidential elections scheduled for 2001.

Further reading

Mandaza, I. (ed.) (1986) *Zimbabwe: The Political Economy of Transition, 1980–1986*, Dakar: CODESRIA.

Palmer, R. (1977) *Land and Racial Domination in Rhodesia*, London: Heinemann.

ALOIS MLAMBO

Zulu

The Zulu language, called isiZulu, is one of the eleven official languages of **South Africa**. With more than 10 million native speakers isiZulu represents the largest linguistic group in South Africa today, and is the most commonly spoken African language in urban centers. IsiZulu belongs to the Nguni group of Bantu languages that include Xhosa, isiSwati, Zimbabwean and Transvaal Ndebele, and Malawi Ngoni. On purely linguistic grounds these varieties are more like dialects of the same language, but are considered to be different languages for non-linguistic reasons, including the fact that speakers of each respective dialect consider themselves to be "different" on ethnic, social, and historical grounds.

During the Shaka Wars there was a scattering of Nguni-speaking people to **Mozambique**, **Zimbabwe**, **Zambia**, **Malawi**, and **Tanzania**, spreading the Zulu language along the way. Zulu military history has been a constant inspiration of literary imagination, and today, after years of repression and marginalization of their culture under apartheid, many Zulu people feel a sense of new pride in their history and cultural heritage. Their centuries-old traditions have remained the cornerstones of Zulu culture, as is evident from their oral performances of praise poetry. The fusion of Zulu musical culture with various modern forms, including jazz, choral music, and gospel singing, has produced a unique sound, and Zulu music styles have become global trademarks of South African culture.

The development of the Zulu language was greatly influenced by colonialism and the Christianization project. Christian missionaries introduced literacy, developed isiZulu as a written language, established printing presses, and developed Zulu literature (both religious and secular). The full translation of the Bible into isiZulu appeared in 1883, the same year that John Colenso's translation of John Bunyan's *Pilgrim's Progress* appeared. These two translations, which were soon followed by translations of well-known English classics, represented an important step in the emergence of Zulu written language and literature. Pioneer linguistic studies of the Zulu language were done by scholars of various nationalities, such as Lewis Grout, an American who published *Isizulu: A Grammar of the Zulu Language* in 1859; Hans P.S. Schreuder, a Norwegian bishop who published *Grammatik für Zulusproget* in 1850; John Colenso, the Anglican bishop of Natal who published *Elementary Grammar of the Zulu–Kafir Language* in 1855; and Jacob Ludwig Dohne, a German who published *Zulu–Kafir Dictionary* in 1857.

The colonial education policy, which stipulated that the medium of instruction in the lower grades be in the local language, was also instrumental in the development of Zulu language and literature. This trend was enhanced by the establishment of institutions such as the African independent churches, newspapers, and schools, all of which contributed greatly to the form and structure of written Zulu language. The Ohlange Institute, one of the most prominent private schools in South Africa, was founded in 1901 by John L. Dube, who also established the independent African newspaper *Ilanga lase Natal* (1903) and was founding president of the African National Congress. Dube's newspaper acted as the interface between Zulu oral and written literature, since it published the first recordings of orally composed texts in isiZulu.

John Dube also made a pioneering contribution to the development of the Zulu historical novel with the publication of his *Insila ka Tshaka* (1933). Later R.R.R. Dhlomo also drew on Zulu history in a series of historical novels, as did Benedict W. Vilakazi, who emerged in the period prior to the **Second World War** as an outstanding and gifted poet, novelist, and linguist, as well as a keen student of traditional poetry. In his two poetry collections – *Inkondlo kaZulu* (1935) and *Amal'ezulu* (1945) – Vilakazi employs the traditional Zulu oral artform to great effect in describing the plight of black miners. After the war C.L.S. Nyembezi published three exceptional novels: *Mntanami! Mntanami!* (1950), *Ubudoda abukhulelwa* (1953), and *Inkinsela yase Mgungundlovu* (1961). But the most remarkable growth in Zulu literature was in drama, starting with the publication of Nimrod Ndebele's *Ugubudele namazimuzimu* (1941), followed by *Mhla iyakwendela egodini* (1961) by Leonard I.J. Mncwango.

Zulu language and literature was also affected by the policy of apartheid. The 1953 Bantu Education Act prescribed the child's mother-tongue as the medium of instruction in schools. Although the main purpose of this was to limit the role of Africans in the South African economic structure to manual labor, it resulted in the creation of a fast-growing market for vernacular literary production. The protection of African languages afforded by the Act, plus the 1959 tribalization of the higher education system by the establishment of the University of Zululand as a so-called "homeland institution," meant that even minor writers now found an outlet for their work, which resulted in a considerable increase in the publication of poetry, fiction, and drama. The negative side of this was that the audience created by the apartheid regime was made up of school-children and semi-literate adults, a situation that stifled any possible growth of the sophisticated and ambitious literature begun by Dube, Dhlomo, and Vilakazi.

History remained an inspiration for the Zulu literary imagination, as can be seen from publications like *Bafa baphela* (1973) by Jessie Gwayi, which based on the woman warrior Mmanthathisi, and *Buzani kuMkabayi* (1982) by C.T. Msimang. D.B.Z. Ntuli, who wrote *Ubheka* (1961) and *Indandatho yasithembiso* (1970) – the first radio play by a black author in South Africa – is perhaps the most representative of writers in the Zulu language towards the end of the twentieth century. Mazisi Kunene, another prominent South African writer who composed his plays, lyrical poems, and epics in isiZulu, demonstrated a sophisticated use of traditional Zulu concepts and imagery. Unfortunately, because of apartheid, his works were only available in their English self-translations. These included epics like *Emperor Shaka the Great* (1979) and *Anthem of the Decades: A Zulu Epic* (1981).

Further reading

Gerard, A.S. (1981) *African Language Literatures*, Washington, D.C.: Three Continents.

Heine, B. and Nurse, D. (eds.) (2000) *African Languages*, Cambridge: Cambridge University Press.

Ntuli, D.B. and Swanepoel, C.F. (1993) *Southern African Literature in African Languages*, Pretoria: Acacia Books.

LUPENGA MPHANDE

Index

Index